THE GOLDEN LEGEND

Jacobus de Voragine

The Golden Legend

Readings on the Saints

TRANSLATED BY

William Granger Ryan

WITH AN INTRODUCTION BY

Eamon Duffy

Princeton University Press
PRINCETON AND OXFORD

Copyright © 1993 by Princeton University Press
Introduction to the 2012 edition
copyright © 2012 by Princeton University Press
Published by Princeton University Press, 41 William Street,
Princeton, New Jersey 08540
In the United Kingdom: Princeton University Press,
6 Oxford Street, Woodstock,
Oxfordshire OX20 1TW
press.princeton.edu

Cover illustration: Menabuoi, Giusto de (fl.1349–1390).
Ceiling frescoes in the
Baptistery of the Cathedral of the Assumption of Mary,
Padua, Italy. Photo courtesy of Scala/Art
Resource, NY.

All Rights Reserved

First printing, 1993
First paperback printing, in two volumes, 1995
First single-volume paperback edition,
with an introduction by Eamon Duffy, 2012

Library of Congress Control Number 2011939496
ISBN 978-0-691-15407-7

British Library Cataloging-in-Publication Data is available

This book has been composed in Adobe Bembo

Designed by Jan Lilly

Printed on acid-free paper. ∞

Printed in the United States of America

1 3 5 7 9 10 8 6 4 2

CONTENTS

CONTENTS

CONTENTS

CONTENTS

INTRODUCTION TO THE 2012 EDITION

Eamon Duffy

The *Legenda Aurea*, or *Golden Legend*, of Jacobus de Voragine was one of the most influential books of the later Middle Ages. It is a compendium of saints' lives and of liturgical and doctrinal instruction, culled in the 1260s from a wide range of patristic and medieval sources. Its compiler, Blessed Jacobus de Voragine (the Latin form of Jacopo or Giacomo de Varrazze, ca. 1229–1298), intended his book as an aid for busy priests and preachers in need of a handy source of vivid anecdote, instruction, and edification to bulk out their sermons and catecheses.[1] Many such compilations were produced in thirteenth-century Europe, as the Church sought both to promote more active religious engagement among parish clergy and laypeople, and to police the orthodoxy of popular belief and practice. The new orders of mendicant friars were in the forefront of this campaign to instruct and enthuse ordinary Christians, and Jacobus, an Italian Dominican friar who became Prior of the Lombard Province in 1267, was working in a tradition established earlier in the same century by members of his own relatively new order. Jean de Mailly began work on his *Abbreviatio in gestis et miraculis sanctorum* in the late 1220s, within ten years of the foundation of the Order of Preachers, and his fellow Dominican Bartholomew of Trent produced his *Epilogus in gesta sanctorum* in the mid-1240s.[2] Jacobus drew freely on both these collections, but those books, popular as they were, survive now in just a couple of dozen manuscripts apiece. Jacobus's *Legenda Aurea*, by contrast, has survived in almost a thousand manuscript copies of the Latin text alone, with another five hundred or so manuscripts containing translations of all or part of the *Legenda* into one or another of the great European vernaculars. His own order seems not at first to have considered Jacobus's *Legenda* definitive, and other Dominicans went on compiling similar hagiographical works well into the fourteenth century. But even in Jacobus's own lifetime his book, doubtless transmitted across Europe through Dominican networks initially, had moved well beyond the confines of the order, and was establishing itself as the most widely used compendium of its kind. As early as the 1280s it was already one of the shaping influences on local hagiographical projects far removed from Italy, such as the vernacular

---

[1] The only full-length study is G. Monleone, *Jacopo de Voragine e la sua Cronaca de Genoa* (Rome: Istituto storico italiano per il Medio Evo, 1941).

[2] For both, see Sherry L. Reames, *The Legenda Aurea: A Reexamination of Its Paradoxical History* (Madison: University of Wisconsin Press, 1985), pp. 164ff.

South English Legendary.[3] Within two generations, hagiographical compilers all over Europe were adopting Jacobus's framework and lifting material wholesale from his book. Its popularity earned it the nickname the *Golden Legend*, with the implication that it was worth its weight in gold: the word "legenda" then meant simply a text to be read aloud, with none of the associations with fiction or fancy that the word "legend" has since acquired. In the two centuries after its composition, Jacobus's *Legenda* was translated and retranslated into most of the major languages of Western Europe. There were seven versions in French alone, and two in English. And with the advent of printing, Jacobus's text became as big a bestseller in the new medium as it had been in the old. Between 1470 and 1500, at least eighty-seven Latin editions of the *Legenda* were printed, as well as sixty-nine editions in various vernaculars, including four editions in English, considerably more than all the known printings of the Bible in any language during the same period.[4]

At first sight modern readers may find this remarkable medieval popularity a bit of a puzzle. The *Legenda Aurea* is not an easy book to use. For convenience of reference, any modern encyclopedia of religion would be likely to present its subject matter alphabetically. Jacobus organized his book on quite different principles. A brief and rather confusing prologue claims that its contents are arranged under "four distinct periods" corresponding simultaneously to epochs in the world's history, to phases of human life, and to the representation of those phases within the cycle of the liturgy. Jacobus characterizes these four periods as the times of deviation, of renovation, of reconciliation, and of pilgrimage. In practice, however, his book actually falls into five unequal sections, corresponding to the main divisions of the liturgical year: namely, the periods from Advent to Christmas (covered in chapters 1–5); from Christmas to Septuagesima (i.e., the Sunday nominally seventy days before Easter) (chapters 6–30); from Septuagesima to Easter (chapters 31–53); from Easter Day to Pentecost (chapters 54–76); and from the octave of Pentecost to Advent again (chapters 77–180). The lives of the saints occupy just 153 of the 182 chapters in the standard modern edition of Jacobus's book, and are clustered chronologically, as their feast days fall within these larger liturgical seasons. Twenty-three nonhagiographical chapters mark off the larger divisions of the book, and these are devoted to the systematic exposition of the medieval Church's understanding of salvation, arranged according to the main liturgical seasons and feasts. The feast days covered include the Annunciation, Advent, Nativity of Christ (i.e., Christmas Day), Circumcision, Epiphany, the Sundays leading up to Lent—Septuagesima,

---

[3] Manfred Gorlach, *The Textual Tradition of the South English Legendary* (Leeds: University of Leeds, 1974), although Gorlach is inclined to minimize the influence of Jacobus.

[4] Robert Francis Seybolt, "Fifteenth Century Editions of the *Legenda Aurea*," *Speculum* 21, no. 3 (July 1946), pp. 327–338; brief discussion by Alain Boureau in André Vauchez, ed., *Encyclopaedia of the Middle Ages* (Chicago, London: Fitzroy Dearborn Publishers; Paris: Editions du Cerf; Rome: Città nuova, 2000), pp. 620–621, and sources there cited.

Sexagesima, and Quinquagesima—Quadragesima (i.e., the first Sunday of Lent), the Ember Day fasts, the Passion, Resurrection, the Rogation days, Ascension, Pentecost, and the Invention (i.e., Discovery) and Exaltation of the Holy Cross. To these, Jacobus added a cycle of Marian feasts (the Birth, Purification, and Assumption of the Virgin), which he used to set forth an elaborate and ardent theology of the Virgin Mary, the feasts of All Saints, All Souls (in the course of which he expounds the doctrine of purgatory), and the Dedication of a Church.

Most of these expository chapters differ markedly from the chapters devoted to the lives of the saints. Instead of the eventful narratives enlivened by miracle stories and other sensational happenings that characterize most of the "sanctorale" entries, in these "temporale" chapters Jacobus offers a dense doctrinal and symbolic analysis of the main features of the Christian faith as the medieval church understood it. In effect, these sections of the *Legenda* form an encyclopedic handbook of doctrine, clearly designed to provide material for instruction and preaching. Though presented in highly compressed form, these parts of the book are also self-consciously learned, and abundant citations of sources and authorities are mustered to underpin Jacobus's teaching. Although these chapters occupy less than one-sixth of the book's total bulk, they contain at least half of Jacobus's thousand-plus citations from the writings of early Christian Fathers and theologians like Saint Augustine, Saint John Chrysostom, Saint Bede, and Saint Bernard, as well as from the standard medieval theological reference books, like Peter Comestor's *Historia Scholastica* and Cassiodorus's *Historia Tripartita*. The scholastic urge to order, systematize, tabulate, and analyze is especially in evidence here, reminding the reader that Jacobus was an exact contemporary of Saint Thomas Aquinas (they entered the Dominican order in the same year, 1244). But Jacobus was essentially deploying here an intensive form of a characteristic medieval form of catechesis, which was routinely organized and structured into numbered categories—the ten commandments, seven deadly sins, four cardinal and three theological virtues, seven corporal works of mercy, and so on. In this mode, Jacobus's chapter on the Passion of Christ [53] is structured around a dense series of numerical lists, themselves divided into subclauses and lesser lists—the five pains of the Passion, the four prerogatives of Christ's nature, the four modes of mockery to which he was subjected, the three reasons for his silence before his judges, the three special fruits of his passion, and the fourfold benefits flowing from his death by crucifixion. That dense and at times dauntingly numerical framework for doctrinal and devotional exposition is especially characteristic of Jacobus's "temporale" chapters, but it spills over also into some of the lives of the saints—for example, in his account of the preaching of Saint Andrew [2], or the whole chapter on the birth of John the Baptist [86]. The complexity of this expository material reminds us that the *Legenda* was never intended as straightforward devotional reading for the ordinary layman, although it would eventually be adapted for just such use. It was essentially a handbook for preachers, a quarry from which material could be extracted, to be presented more palatably and discursively in the pulpit. Many vernacular sermon collections drew very heavily on the *Legenda*, such as the late-fourteenth-century English *Festial* compiled by the Augustinian Canon John Mirk, for whom Jacobus's text was the invariable and in many cases the sole source of sermon material. It is notable, though, that Mirk, like many other homilists normally dependent on Jacobus, often modified or set aside altogether these formidable doctrinal sections, in favor of greater simplicity and more entertaining anecdotage.[5]

But important as these "temporale" chapters are for the structure of his book, Jacobus's coverage of the greater feasts and seasons is highly selective. The whole forty days and six Sundays of Lent are dealt with in a single short and scrappy entry [34], and he provides no coverage for the major liturgical celebrations of either Palm Sunday or Maundy Thursday. By the same token, Jacobus ignores the brand-new feast of Corpus Christi (established by Pope Urban IV in 1264). Despite its recent institution, this seems a surprising omission, given Thomas Aquinas's authorship of the texts for the feast, and the wider Dominican investment in the propagation of orthodox Eucharistic teaching. Because he also omits any treatment of Maundy Thursday, there is no extended discussion of the Mass in Jacobus's book, a striking omission in an age increasingly concerned about heresy.

The omission of Corpus Christi gives Jacobus's *Legenda* an old-fashioned look, and that impression of old-fashionedness deepens into positive archaism when we come to consider the list of saints whose lives he does include. The early thirteenth century had been momentous for the development of notions of sanctity, and in the actual process of saint-making. The popes had only recently established their monopoly over the canonization of saints, formerly a general episcopal prerogative, and the Roman introduction of more rigorous (and more expensive) forms of scrutiny of the lives and miracles of candidates for sanctity would lead to a marked reduction in the numbers of canonizations.[6] But in the seventy years before Jacobus wrote the *Legenda*, successive popes had nevertheless carried out more than twenty canonizations, and these new papal saints embodied a wide spectrum of holiness and states of life—from Homobonus of Cremona, a married layman revered for his goodness to the poor, to holy queens and empresses like Margaret of Scotland, Cunegund of Bamberg, or Elisabeth of Hungary. There had been saintly bishops like Hugh of Lincoln, Richard of Chichester, and the Irishman Laurence O'Toole, clerical martyrs like Stanislas of Cracow, and the founders and early heroes and heroines of the mendicant orders, Francis and Claire of Assisi, Anthony of Padua, and,

---

[5] For Mirk's dependence on Jacobus, see Susan Powell, ed., *John Mirk's Festial, Vol. 1* (Oxford: Early English Text Society O.S. 339, 2009), pp. xxxii–xxxvii.

[6] For these developments, see André Vauchez, *Sainthood in the Later Middle Ages* (Cambridge: Cambridge University Press, 1997), pp. 33–84.

among the Dominicans, Saint Dominic and Saint Peter Martyr.[7] As a mendicant friar himself, Jacobus predictably included long chapters on the lives of the two great founders, Francis [149] and Dominic [113], as well as a similarly extended treatment of the Dominican order's great martyr, Peter of Verona [63], who had been murdered by heretics in Jacobus's native Lombardy in 1252. He also fairly unsurprisingly included a life of the English martyr-archbishop Thomas Becket [11], an icon for the authority and independence of the Church whose shrine was one of the great pilgrimage venues of Europe. But there Jacobus's interest in modern sanctity appears to have ended: he ignored not only all the other papal canonizations of the preceding hundred years, but all saints of whatever kind from the preceding five centuries. The standard text of the *Legenda* does admittedly include a life of Elisabeth of Hungary [168], canonized in 1235, but that life is so very different in tone and style from virtually every other life in the *Legenda* that it may very well be an interpolation by another hand.

Jacobus's saints, therefore, are overwhelmingly drawn from a traditional list of those who had been venerated for centuries. They include the major figures of the New Testament (the Apostles, Evangelists, Saint John the Baptist, Saint Mary Magdalene, Saint Stephen), the Fathers, Doctors, popes, monks, and hermits of the early Church (Saint Silvester, Saint Augustine, Saint Gregory the Great, Saint Anthony, Saint Benedict), and above all, the martyr saints of the first four Christian centuries. These lives of the martyr saints, filled as they are with lurid detail of gruesome sufferings, with defiance and rejection of the world, and larded with spectacular miracles, undoubtedly appeal to a medieval taste for romance, excitement, and pious entertainment. These qualities gave the *Legenda Aurea* much of its distinctive character, and its huge popularity. But they were also precisely the qualities against which sober sixteenth-century religious reformers, both Catholic and Protestant, would react, which would lead to the widespread repudiation of Jacobus's book as a tissue of unedifying tall tales, and would help to give the word "legend" its negative connotations.

The entry for the martyr Saint Agnes [24] can be taken as representative of Jacobus's handling of the lives of such saints. The historical Saint Agnes was a young girl (twelve years old, according to Saint Ambrose, whose treatise *De Virginitate* is the earliest source) executed for her Christian faith in the Diocletian persecution circa 305. She was buried outside Rome on the Via Nomentana, where in the later fourth century a basilica was erected over her grave. She became one of Rome's most important saints, and her name is one of those recited during the canon of the Mass. Celebrated by Ambrose, Jerome, Augustine, and other fourth- and fifth-century writers as an exemplar of heroic virginity, the scant details of her martyrdom were soon elaborated. According to Ambrose, she was killed by burning; according to her shrine inscription by Pope Damasus, at her execution Agnes's hair grew miraculously to cover her naked body; and according to the hymn writer Prudentius, her chastity was

---

[7] See the table of canonizations in Vauchez, *Sainthood*, pp. 252–256.

tested by exposure in a brothel. These and many other details were elaborated in the highly colored fifth-century *Acts of the Martyrdom of Saint Agnes*, which was Jacobus's main source. He also used and quoted extensively from Saint Ambrose's panegyric on Agnes in *De Virginitate*.[8]

Jacobus's account of Saint Agnes opens, as is his custom, with a fanciful etymological paragraph, offering three different explanations of Agnes's name. It may have come from *agnus*, the Latin for "lamb," reflecting her lamb-like meekness. Alternatively, it might derive from the Greek word *agnos*, "pious," because she was pious and compassionate. Or yet again, it might derive from the Latin participle *agnoscendo*, "knowing," because "she knew the way of truth." In fact, however, there is nothing remotely meek about Jacobus's portrait of Agnes. In his account, she is a defiant, even an aggressive paragon of chastity, the vowed bride of Christ, "a child in body but already aged in spirit." As she returns from school one day, the son of the prefect of Rome sees her in the street and is smitten by her beauty. She repudiates the hapless young man's tentative advances immediately and ferociously, calling him "the spark that lights the fire of sin, you fuel of wickedness, you food of death," and taunting him that "The one I love is far nobler than you. . . . His mother is a virgin, his father . . . is served by angels." Agnes then goes on to enumerate the five transcendent virtues of Christ as a heavenly lover. The lovesick youth, unable to compete, takes to his sickbed, and his worried father attempts to persuade Agnes to yield to his son, first by wheedling and then with threats. When she persists in defiant fidelity to her heavenly husband, the prefect charges her with being a Christian, has her stripped naked, and sends her to a brothel. En route, however, her hair grows to preserve her modesty. Once in the brothel, an angel surrounds her in an even more glorious garment of blinding light, and the brothel itself becomes a place of prayer and spiritual healing. The lovesick young man now shows his true colors by inciting his companions to gang-rape Agnes, and is punished by being throttled by the devil. At the bereaved father's request, Agnes raises the bad lad from the dead, but is then accused of being a witch by jealous pagan priests. The now chastened prefect seeks to release her, but out of cowardice hands the case over to his deputy, who condemns Agnes to be burned. The flames part around her and consume the hostile bystanders. The irrepressible Agnes is finally dispatched when a soldier thrusts a dagger into her throat. Jacobus adds a brief account of the martyrdom by stoning of Agnes's mythical foster sister, Emerentiana, complete with an appearance of the glorified Agnes, clad in gold and attended by angels and a snow-white lamb. He also provides two post-mortem miracle stories, both of which relate directly to Agnes's shrine church on the Via Nomentana. In the first of these, the emperor Constantine's daughter, Constance, a leper, makes a pilgrimage to Agnes's grave and sleeps

---

[8] The compact discussion by J. P. Kirsch of the elaboration of the legend in the early sources, in his article on Saint Agnes in the *Catholic Encyclopedia*, retains its value, despite its venerable age. It is available online at www.ewtn.com/library/MARY/CEAGNES.HTM.

there, in search of a cure. Agnes appears to her in a dream and heals her, and the grateful Constance builds the basilica over Agnes's grave and vows to live a virginal life there with her maidens. In the second miracle, a priest assailed by lust is cured of temptation when he betroths himself to Agnes by placing a jeweled ring on the finger of the statue of her "that stood in her church." Jacobus provides two quite different versions of this story but assures the reader that "it is said that this ring can still be seen on the finger of the statue." The entry concludes with a paragraph of extended quotation from Saint Ambrose's eulogy of Saint Agnes in his *De Virginitate*.

This is a lot of color to crowd into fewer than 1,500 words (in the Latin). Such a torrent of incident leaves no room for religious subtlety or refined psychologizing. Jacobus's Agnes is less a holy human being than a cipher for a drastically two-dimensional representation of the virtue of chastity. The saint's monotone angry defiance is in play from the very opening of the account, and the saturation of the story in the miraculous moves it closer to folk or fairy tale than to any kind of biographical study. The story exemplifies Jacobus's apparent fascination with the multiple forms of torture and execution undergone by the martyrs—one modern analysis has identified eighty-one different forms of suffering, mutilation, and death in Jacobus's narratives.[9] The medieval reader or listener, as well as being entertained, would doubtless have found plenty to relate to, not least the easily recognizable features of contemporary religious practice reflected in the miracles, which feature pilgrimages, shrine images, vows, and ex-voto gifts. He or she would have found in the stories vivid, even lurid, assurances of God's power and providence. But there would not have been much here to emulate, no template, apart from ritual matters, for ordinary Christian living. This was holiness presented not so much as a pattern to be imitated, but as a power to be harnessed, and a source of intercession to be supplicated.

The miraculous elements in such stories were eventually to earn Jacobus the contempt of humanist and protestant scholars as a peddler of fable to the gullible. But it is worth noting that in his account of the miracle of the lustful priest, Jacobus in fact offered his readers two different and incompatible versions of the episode, leaving them to choose which, if either, they accepted, just as in the etymology he offers three quite different explanations of Agnes's name. Jacobus's etymologies were in a long tradition of medieval learning derived from Isidore of Seville's vast *Etymologiae*, the most widely used encyclopedia of the Middle Ages. The first users of the *Legenda* would have recognized both the genre itself and the element of intellectual playfulness implicit in it. And however marvelous the stories he relates, Jacobus can also display both skepticism and some sophistication in his handling of the incidents and evidence that form the body of his narrative. Famously, in his account of Saint Margaret [93], he

---

[9] Alain Boureau, *La Legende doree: La systeme narratif de Jacques de Voragine* (Paris: Cerf, 1984), pp. 118–120.

repeated the story of how the saint had allegedly been swallowed alive by the devil in the form of a dragon, but burst from his stomach by making the sign of the cross. Jacobus commented, "What is said here, however, . . . is considered apocryphal, and not to be taken seriously." This is not an isolated case. In his account of Saint Andrew [2] he reports Andrew's alleged rescue of the Apostle Matthew from kidnappers, but adds, "[So] we are told; but I find the story very hard to believe." Reporting a revenge miracle in which a servant who slapped Saint Thomas was devoured by lions and dogs, Jacobus cites a long passage from Saint Augustine that casts doubt on the story [5]: "Augustine, in his book *Against Faustus*, will have none of this act of vengeance and declares that the incident is apocryphal." In the same way, in his section on the Passion of Christ [53], Jacobus compares accounts of the horrible end of Pontius Pilate from an apocryphal Gospel and from the *Historia Scholastica*, and comments, "[L]et the reader judge whether the story is worth the telling." In his life of Saint Hilary [17] he expresses disbelief about the story of Hilary's triumph over a heretical "Pope Leo." These expressions of skepticism are often underpinned by appeal to contradictions or disagreements between authorities and evidences: in his life of Saint Matthew [43] he raises a doubt about the morality of casting lots in the making of decisions, citing varying opinions from Saint Jerome, Saint Bede, and Pseudo-Dionysius.

Jacobus, then, was clearly aware that even revered patristic authorities might contradict one another, and he often leaves it to the reader to choose between conflicting accounts. But we are certainly not dealing here with the kind of critical approach to historical evidence that was ushered in by the Renaissance, and by whose standards the *Legenda* was found lamentably wanting. The contradictions and doubts that trouble Jacobus do so as inconsistencies within a doctrinal system. He doubts the story of the heretical pope defeated by Saint Hilary because a priori popes cannot be heretical, not because the source is suspect. The debate about the casting of lots interests him not because ancient authorities contradict one another about it, but because the legitimacy of lots was a theological question still unresolved in his own day, with a direct bearing on practical morality. He is concerned to guard the internal coherence of Catholicism, not the authenticity of historical evidence.[10]

The range of Jacobus's sources has been quantified by Alain Boureau, and subjected to a more detailed if essentially unsympathetic analysis by Sherry Reames.[11] The breadth of the material he drew on is impressive: the Gospels, the book of Psalms, the book of Isaiah, the Pauline epistles, and the Acts of the Apostles head the list of biblical authorities, and Jacobus also made use of apocryphal writings such as the Gospel of Nicodemus. But he also drew heavily on patristic writers, above all Saint Augustine, Saint Gregory the Great, Saint Jerome, Saint John Chrysostom, and Saint Ambrose (in that order). Among his

[10] Cf. Boureau, *Legende doree*, p. 101.
[11] Boureau, *Legende doree*, pp. 75–108; Reames, *Legenda Aurea*, passim.

medieval contemporaries or near contemporaries, Saint Bernard equals Saint Augustine in the number of citations. A cluster of lives of hermit saints grouped at the end of the book was extracted from the accounts of the desert fathers in the Latin *Vitae Patrum*, Jacobus's account of Saint Anthony was abbreviated from the life by Saint Athanasius, and the story of Barlaam and Josephat, a Christianized version of the life of the Buddha, was taken from a Latin version of a seventh-century Syrian monastic text, attributed in Jacobus's day to Saint John Chrysostom.

Given the scaling-down inevitable in a compilation, all of these materials are paraphrased and drastically reduced, even when Jacobus is following his original's narrative framework very closely. There are exceptions: more than half his long chapter on Saint Paul consists of an immense extended quotation from Chrysostom's sermon *"De laudibus Pauli"* [90]. His life of the fourth-century Roman widow Saint Paula [29] is a shortened version of Jerome's magnificent eulogy in *Epistola* 108, recognizably Jerome's in emphasis and rhetoric, despite the abbreviation. His life of "A Virgin of Antioch" [62] is lifted entire from Ambrose's *De Virginitate*. His life of Saint Augustine [126], one of the longest in the *Legenda*, abbreviates the contemporary life by Possidius but supplements it extensively from Augustine's own autobiographical writings, especially the *Confessions* and the *Soliloquies*.

Modern commentators have been uncomplimentary about Jacobus's use of his early Christian materials, seeing in his abbreviations not merely the inevitable problems of reduction, but an invariable coarsening and externalization of religious motive and feeling, which reflected a similar hardening in the religious culture of his own time.[12] On this account the *Legenda*'s focus on sanctity as heroic virtue in conflict with the world, and the typology of the saint as normally a martyr, a cleric, or a monk, deliberately turns away from some of the most vital and inclusive religious energies of his own time, in favor of an unimaginative clericalization of the concept of the holy. None of Jacobus's saints were ordinary men and women living ordinary lives. Jacobus's saints are uncomfortable people, insofar as they can be said to be people at all, often at odds with the world around them. Their virtues are those of absolute world-renunciation and denial, and they themselves are often beset by enemies—demonic forces, unbelieving parents and family, heretics, and hostile secular rulers. In his handling not merely of a contemporary figure like his confrere Peter Martyr, but of remoter exemplars like Saint Ambrose [57], Jacobus certainly reflected anxieties about some of the most pressing preoccupations of the Church of his own day—in the case of Ambrose, the struggle between papacy and Empire; and in the case of Peter Martyr, the campaign to obliterate heresy, in which the Dominican Order was so heavily involved.

Jacobus was indeed a man of his own times. A patriotic Lombard, he included under the pretext of a life of Pope Pelagius a chronicle of Christian

---

[12] This is the central argument of Reames's *Legenda Aurea*.

history that focused predominantly on the events and notables of his own region [181], and which earned his book the nickname "The Lombardic History." He was a man immersed in affairs, as administrator of a great religious order, as a papal diplomat, and finally as an outstanding and much-loved Bishop of Genoa. But Jacobus can hardly be blamed for being of his own times. If he did not transcend the limitations of institutional Christianity in the thirteenth century, he embodied some of its most distinctive energies, as well as some of its tensions and contradictions. His book quite evidently touched a contemporary nerve, and was seen and seized on for three centuries as an indispensable pastoral resource, as well as a source of entertainment and of inspiration and source material for poets, dramatists, and painters.

It was inevitable that the Protestant reformers would see in the *Golden Legend* a source and embodiment of superstition and idolatry, everything they despised and rejected in medieval Christianity. But even before and beyond the Reformation, it had come to seem old-fashioned and passé. In the mid-fifteenth century the great Catholic reformer Nicholas of Cusa forbade his clergy to teach their people the fables of the *Legenda Aurea*, and to successive generations of Catholic humanists, trained by Erasmus to look back to the pure sources of early Christianity, and to ground their religion on sound historical truth and solid moral worth, Jacobus's book, with its far-fetched miracles and martyrdoms, came to seem anathema. The lives of the saints should be sober and credible, exemplars of virtue rather than chronicles of wonders. The Spanish humanist Luis de Vives articulated this new mentality when he declared, "[H]ow unworthy of the saints, and of all Christians, is that history of the saints called the Golden Legend. I cannot imagine why they call it Golden, when it is written by a man with a mouth of iron and a heart of lead. What can be more abominable than this book? What a disgrace to us Christians that the preeminent deeds of our saints have not been more truly and accurately preserved, so that we may know or imitate such virtue, when the Greek and Roman authors have written with such care about their generals, philosophers and sages."[13]

Counter-Reformation Catholicism would reform the cult of the saints accordingly, purging the breviary lections of the more bizarre episodes culled from Jacobus, and in the hands of the seventeenth-century Jesuit scholar Jean Boland, hagiography became an exact science. In this new climate, Jacobus's book fell into eclipse. It would not emerge again from obscurity until the nineteenth century, when Romantic admiration for the Middle Ages and an interest in the sources of medieval and Renaissance art would send readers back to the *Golden Legend*, as a repository of ancient lore, and as the distillation of both the imagination and the soul of the Christian Middle Ages.

---

[13] Cited in Reames, *Legenda Aurea*, p. 52.

ACKNOWLEDGMENTS

This translation of Jacobus de Voragine's *Legenda aurea* is based on the only modern Latin edition of the work, produced by Dr. Th. Graesse in 1845. The translator acknowledges his indebtedness not only to Graesse but to two translations, one in French, *La légende dorée de Jacques de Voragine*, by the Abbé J.-B. M. Roze, 3 vols. (Paris: Edouard Rouveyre, Editeur, 1902), and the other in German, Iacobus de Voragine *Legenda aurea*, by Richard Benz, 2 vols. (Jena: Eugen Diederichs, 1917–1921). I am grateful to my colleagues at Yale Divinity School, and particularly to Professor John W. Cook, Director of the Institute of Sacred Music, Worship, and the Arts, for their encouragement as the work progressed. My sister Margot Ryan gave valued assistance by proofreading the text, and Mark Looney, of the Institute staff, helped substantially in the final preparation of the manuscript. Above all I owe thanks to the Menil Foundation, and to Dominique de Menil in person, for support and encouragement in carrying this undertaking to conclusion.

THE GOLDEN LEGEND

Prologue

Here begins the Prologue to *Readings on the Saints*, otherwise called the *History of the Lombards*, which was compiled by Brother Jacobus, Genoese, of the Order of Friars Preachers.

The whole time-span of this present life comprises four distinct periods: the time of deviation or turning from the right way, the time of renewal or of being called back, the time of reconciliation, and the time of pilgrimage. The time of deviation began with Adam, or rather with his turning away from God, and lasted until Moses. The Church represents this period from Septuagesima to Easter, and the Book of Genesis is read, since that book tells of the fall of our first parents. The time of renewal or of being called back began with Moses and ended with the birth of Christ, during which time mankind was renewed and called back to faith by the prophets. The Church observes it from the beginning of Advent until the Nativity of the Lord. Isaiah is read then, because he treats clearly of this recall. The time of reconciliation is that during which we were reconciled by Christ, and the Church marks it from Easter to Pentecost: the Book of the Apocalypse, or Revelation, in which the mystery of this reconciliation is fully treated, is read. The time of pilgrimage is that of our present life, for we are on pilgrimage and constantly engaged in warfare. The Church observes this time from the octave of Pentecost to the beginning of Advent, and the Books of Kings and of Maccabees are read because they record many wars, thus reminding us of our own spiritual struggles. Finally, the interval between the Lord's birthday and Septuagesima falls partly within the time of reconciliation, a time of rejoicing, namely, from Christmas to the octave of Epiphany, and [partly in the time of pilgrimage, namely, from the octave of Epiphany] to Septuagesima.[1] This fourfold division of historic time can be related to the seasons of the year, winter corresponding to the first period, spring to the second, summer to the third, autumn to the fourth, and the sense of this comparison is clear enough. Or it may be related to the phases of the day, the first time to night, the second to morning, the third to midday, the fourth to evening.

Although the time of turning from the right way came before renewal, the Church begins the cycle of her offices with the time of renewal rather than with that of deviation—in other words, with Advent rather than Septuagesima—and this for two reasons. She does not wish to start from error, for she puts reality

---

[1] The words in brackets, missing in Graesse, are supplied from Jacobus de Varagine, *Legenda aurea* (Ulm: Joh. Zainer, ca. 1476), in Yale's Beinecke Library, 1972/+117.

before the sequence of time, just as the Evangelists often do; and besides, the renewal of all things came with the coming of Christ, and therefore the season of Advent is designated the time of renewal and recall: "Behold, I make all things new" (Apoc. 21:5). So it is proper for the Church to renew the sequence of her offices with this season.

In order to keep the sequence of times as the Church has set it, we shall deal first with the feast days that fall within the time of renewal, which she observes from the beginning of Advent to the birth of Christ. Next we shall dwell on those that occur within the period that falls partly within the time of reconciliation and partly within that of pilgrimage—the period represented by the Church from Advent to Septuagesima. Thirdly, we shall see the feast days celebrated in the time of deviation, from Septuagesima to Easter, and fourthly those within the time of reconciliation, from Easter through the octave of Pentecost. Lastly, we shall treat of feasts occurring within the time of pilgrimage, from the octave of Pentecost to the beginning of Advent.

※

---

1. The Advent of the Lord

The Lord's advent is celebrated for four weeks to signify that his coming is fourfold: he came to us in the flesh, he comes into our hearts, he comes to us at death, and he will come to judge us. The fourth week is seldom completed, because the glory of the saints, which will be bestowed at the last coming, will never end. So it is, too, that the first responsory for the first Sunday of Advent, which includes the *Gloria Patri*, has four verses corresponding to the aforesaid four comings; let the attentive reader figure out which verse best fits each coming.

While the Lord's comings are four, the Church specially memorializes two of them, the one in the flesh and the one at the Last Judgment, as is clear from the office of the season. Therefore the Advent fast[1] is partly one of rejoicing, by reason of Christ's coming in the flesh, and partly one of anxiety at the thought of the Judgment. To bring this to our minds the Church sings some of her joyful chants because of the coming of mercy and rejoicing, and puts aside some others because the Judgment will be very strict and prompts anxiety.

---

[1] The penitential fast used to be of precept in Advent as well as in Lent.

4

With regard to the Lord's coming in the flesh three aspects are to be examined—its timeliness, its necessity, and its usefulness.

The timeliness is manifest first as regards man himself, who by the law of his nature lacked knowledge of God. Hence he fell into the worst errors of idolatry. Therefore he was compelled to cry out: "Enlighten my eyes."[2] Then came the Law with its commandments, and man became aware that he was powerless to obey. Previously he had cried: "There are those willing to fulfill the command, but not yet anyone to command." For thus far he was only instructed, not freed from sin nor helped by any grace to do good; so now he was compelled to cry out: "There is one to command but no one to fulfill the command." Therefore the coming of the Son of God was opportune and timely, since man was now convicted of ignorance and helplessness: if Christ had come earlier, man might have attributed salvation to his own merits and would not have been thankful for his cure.

Secondly, the Lord's advent was timely because he came in the fullness of time: "When the fullness of time was come, God sent his Son."[3] Augustine says: "There are many who ask why Christ did not come sooner. It was because by the will of him who made all things in time, the fullness of time had not arrived. When that fullness had come, the One came who freed us from time, and, freed from time, we are to come to that eternity in which there will be no time." Thirdly, the whole world was wounded and ailing, and since the disease was universal it was the moment for a universal medicine to be applied. Augustine: "The great physician came when throughout the world mankind lay like a great invalid."

Hence the Church, in the seven antiphons that are sung before the Lord's birthday, shows the multiplicity of our ills and for each of them begs a remedy of the physician. Before the Son of God came in the flesh, we were ignorant or blind, liable to eternal punishment, slaves of the devil, shackled with sinful habits, enveloped in darkness, exiles driven from our true country. Therefore we had need of a teacher, a redeemer, a liberator, an emancipator, an enlightener, and a savior. Because we were ignorant and needed to be taught by him, we call out in the first antiphon: "O Wisdom, you came forth from the mouth of the Most High, reaching from end to end and ordering all things mightily and sweetly. Come, and teach us the way of prudence!" Yet it would be of little profit if we were taught but not redeemed, so we ask to be redeemed by him when we cry to God in the second antiphon: "O Adonai and leader of the house of Israel, you appeared to Moses in the flames of the burning bush, and on Sinai gave him the Law. Come, stretch out your arm and redeem us." And what good would it do if we were instructed and redeemed, if after redemption we were still held captive? Therefore we pray to be set free, when we plead in the third antiphon: "O Root of Jesse, you are raised as a banner to the peoples. Before

[2] Ps. 13:4.   [3] Gal. 4:4.

you kings shall remain silent, with you all nations will plead for help. Come to set us free, do not delay!" Yet of what use would it be to captives if, being redeemed and given their freedom, their shackles were still not stricken from them so that they could be under their own control and go freely wherever they wished? So it would do us little good if he redeemed and freed us but left us in chains. Therefore in the fourth antiphon we pray to be delivered of all the bonds of sin: "O Key of David, you open and no one closes, you close and no one opens. Come, and from the prison house release man enchained and sitting in the shadow of death!" But because the eyes of those who have been in prison for a long time grow dim and they no longer see clearly, even after we are set free from prison, we still have to have our eyes opened to the light, so that we may see where we ought to go. Therefore in the fifth antiphon we pray: "O rising Dawn, splendor of light eternal and sun of justice! Come, and enlighten those who sit in darkness and the shadow of death." And if we were taught, redeemed, freed from all enemies, and enlightened, how would it benefit us unless we were to be saved? So in the next two antiphons we beg for the gift of salvation, saying: "O King of the Gentiles, for whom they long, O Headstone who make the two one! Come and save man, whom you formed out of the slime of the earth." And likewise, "O Emmanuel, our king and our lawgiver, awaited by the nations and their savior! Come and save us, O Lord our God!" So first we plead for the salvation of the pagans, saying, "O King of the Gentiles," and then pray for the salvation of the Jews, to whom God gave the Law.

THE USEFULNESS OF THE COMING OF THE LORD

As for the usefulness of Christ's coming, different saints define it differently. God himself testifies that he came and was sent to be useful in seven ways, as we see in the fourth chapter of Luke: "The Spirit of the Lord is upon me, etc."[4] There he states the reasons one after the other: to console the poor, to heal the sorrowful, to free the captives, to enlighten the ignorant, to remit sins, to redeem the whole human race, and to reward merit.

Augustine points to three ways in which Christ's coming is useful, saying: "In this evil age what is there in abundance except to be born, to labor, and to die? These are the wares in which here on earth we trade, and to trade in them our merchant came down. And because every merchant gives what he has and receives what he does not have, Christ gave and received in this market. He received what there is plenty of here, namely, birth, toil, and death, and what he gave us is to be reborn, to rise again, and to reign for all eternity. This tradesman from heaven came to us to receive shame and give honor, to undergo death and give life, to bring ignominy upon himself and give glory."

[4] Luke 4:18–19.

Gregory proposes four causes or kinds of usefulness for the Lord's advent: "All the proud of heart born of Adam's race look for the good things of life, shun adversity, flee humiliation, seek glory. The Lord incarnate came into their midst seeking adversity, spurning the world's goods, embracing opprobrium, fleeing glory. So the long-awaited Christ came and taught new things, wrought new wonders by his teaching, and, doing wonders, bore ills."

Bernard has it otherwise, saying: "Miserably we labor under a threefold sickness. We are easily misled, weak in action, and fragile in resistance. If we wish to distinguish between good and evil, we are deceived; if we attempt to do good, we lack strength; if we strive to resist evil, we are overcome. So the coming of the Savior is necessary. Dwelling in us he enlightens our blindness; remaining with us he helps our infirmity; standing for us he protects and defends our fragility." Thus Bernard.

Concerning the second advent, namely, the Last Judgment, we should consider both what will precede it and what will accompany it. Three things will precede it: fearful signs, the fallacious claims of the Antichrist, and a storm of fire. Luke's gospel sets down five signs to precede the Judgment: "There shall be signs in the sun and the moon and the stars, and upon the earth distress of nations by reason of the confusion of the roaring of the sea and the waves."[5] The book of Apocalypse describes the first three signs: "The sun became black as sackcloth, and the moon red as blood, and the stars from heaven fell upon the earth." Rev.[6] The sun is said to be darkened because its light was taken away so that it might seem to be mourning the father of a family, namely, man; or because a greater light, that of the radiance of Christ, had risen; or, to express it metaphorically, because, as Augustine says, the divine vengeance will be so severe that even the sun will not dare to look upon it. Or, according to a mystical interpretation, Christ the sun of justice will be darkened because no one will have the courage to confess him. "Heaven" here means the upper air, and "stars" means shooting stars or meteors, because by their substance they resemble stars, and in common speech stars are said to "fall from heaven" when meteors are seen. In this case Scripture adopts the common usage. The event will certainly create a powerful impression because of its fiery nature, and the Lord does this to terrify sinners. Or the stars are said to fall because they emit fiery tails, or because many men who appeared to be stars in the Church will fall headlong, or because the stars will withdraw their light and become invisible.

About the fourth sign, distress of nations, we read in Matthew 24: "There shall then be great tribulation, such as there has not been from the beginning of the world."[7] As for the fifth sign, the confusion of the roaring of the sea, some think this means that with a thundering noise the sea will cease to be what it was before, as Apocalypse says: "The sea is no more."[8] Others understand the roar-

---

[5] Luke 21:25.　　[6] Rev 6:12–13.
[7] Matt. 24:21.　　[8] Rev. 21:1.

ing as the great noise made as the sea rises forty cubits above the mountains and then crashes down. Gregory reads the text literally: "Then there was a new and unheard-of disturbance of the sea and the waves."

Jerome, in his *Annals of the Hebrews*, finds fifteen signs preceding the Judgment, but does not say whether they will be continuous or intermittent. On the first day the sea will rise forty cubits above the tops of the mountains, standing in place like a wall. Only on the second day will it come down and be almost invisible. On the third day the sea beasts will come out above the surface and will roar to the heavens, and God alone will understand their bellowing. On the fourth day the sea and the waters will burn up. On the fifth the trees and grasses will exude a bloody dew: also on this fifth day, as others assert, all the birds in the sky will gather together in the fields, each species in its place, not feeding or drinking but frightened by the imminent coming of the Judge. On the sixth day buildings will collapse. It is said that on this same sixth day fiery thunderbolts will pour out of the setting sun and run across the sky all the way to its rising. On the seventh the rocks will collide with each other and split into four parts, and each part, it is said, will crash against the other; and no man will hear the sound, only God. On the eighth will come a worldwide earthquake, which will, we are told, be so great that neither man nor beast will be able to stand, and all will fall prostrate on the ground. On the ninth the earth will be leveled and the mountains and hills reduced to dust. On the tenth, men will come out of the caves and go about as if demented, unable to speak to each other. The eleventh day will see the bones of the dead rise and stand above the tombs from the rising of the sun to its setting, so that the dead will be able to come out. On the twelfth the stars will fall: all the fixed and wandering stars will spread fiery trains, and then will again be generated from their substance. It is said that on that day, too, all the animals will come into the fields, growling and grunting, not feeding, not drinking. On the thirteenth the living will die in order to rise again with the dead. On the fourteenth heaven and earth will be burned up. On the fifteenth a new heaven and a new earth will come to be, and all the dead will rise again.

Also to precede the Last Judgment will be the false pretensions of the Antichrist. He will try to deceive all men in four ways, first by cunning argument or false exposition of the Scriptures. His aim will be to persuade people, and to prove from Scripture that he is the Messiah promised in the Law, and he will destroy the law of Christ and establish his own: "Appoint, O Lord, a lawgiver over them";[9] and the *Gloss*: "That is the Antichrist, giver of perverse law." The book of Daniel has: "They shall place [in the sanctuary] the abomination unto desolation";[10] and the *Gloss*: "The Antichrist will sit in the temple of God pretending to be God, in order to do away with the law of God."

He will also try to deceive by working miracles; 2 Thessalonians: "Whose coming is according to the working of Satan, in all words and signs and lying

---

[9] Ps. 9:21.   [10] Dan. 11:31.

wonders";[11] Apocalypse: "He did great signs, so that he made also fire to come down from heaven unto the earth";[12] and the *Gloss*: "As the Holy Spirit was given to the apostles in the form of fire, the wicked spirit will also be given in the form of fire." A third means of deception will be his conferring of gifts. Daniel: "He shall give them power over many and shall divide the land gratis";[13] and the *Gloss*: "The Antichrist will give many gifts to those he deceives, and will distribute the land to his army, for those whom he could not conquer by terror he will overcome through avarice." His fourth method will be the infliction of torments; Daniel: "He shall lay all things waste and shall prosper and do more than can be believed."[14] And, speaking of the Antichrist, Gregory comments: "He kills the strong, conquering in the body those who had remained unconquered."

The last occurrence preceding the Judgment will be the storm of fire, which will go before the face of the Judge. God will send this fire, firstly for the renewal of the world: he will purge and renew all the elements. Like the waters of the Deluge, the fire will climb fifteen cubits higher than the mountains, as the *Scholastic History* says, "higher than the works of men could reach." Secondly, the fire will be for men's purification, because the place of purgatory will be for those who are then found still living. Thirdly, the fire will increase the torments of the damned and, fourthly, will provide greater illumination of the saints. According to Saint Basil, once the purgation of the world is accomplished, God will separate the heat of the fire from its light and will send all the heat to the region of the damned to torture them, and all the light to the region of the blessed for their greater enjoyment.

Several circumstances will be attendant upon the Last Judgment itself. Firstly, the Judge's procedure in judging. He will come down into the valley of Josaphat and judge the good and the wicked, setting the good on his right and the wicked on the left. It is to be believed that he will occupy an elevated place, so that all may see him. Nor should we think that the whole gathering would be crowded into that small valley; to think so, Jerome says, would be childish. They will be both in the valley and in the surrounding areas: countless thousands of people can stand in a small space, especially if they are pressed closely together. Moreover, if need be, the elect, due to the lightness of their bodies, could hover in the air, while the damned could be held aloft by the power of God.

Then the Judge will address himself to the wicked, upbraiding them for failing to do the works of mercy. At this all will lament for themselves, as John Chrysostom, commenting on Matthew, says: "The Jews will lament, seeing the One they thought of as a dead man now living and life-giving, and at the sight of his wounded body will be unable to deny their crime and will know themselves convicted. The Gentiles also will lament because, having allowed them-

---

[11] Rev. 2:9.   [12] Rev. 13:13.
[13] Dan. 11:39.   [14] Dan. 8:24.

selves to be deceived by the philosophers' reasonings, they thought that to worship a crucified God was irrational and stupid. Christian sinners will lament on account of their sins, because they loved the world more than God and Christ. Heretics will lament because they called the Crucified a mere man and now see him, whom the Jews made to suffer, as the Judge. And all the tribes of the earth will mourn, because there no longer is any power to resist him nor possibility of escaping from his presence nor room for repentance nor time to make satisfaction. All is distress, nothing is left to them but grief."

Secondly, among those to be judged, different ranks or groups will be set apart. According to Gregory there will be four divisions, two among the reprobate, two among the elect. There are some who will be judged and will perish, such as those to whom it is said: "I was hungry and you gave me no food, etc."[15] Others are condemned without being judged, such as those of whom it is said: "He who does not believe is already judged."[16] They will not hear any word from the Judge, since they were unwilling to receive his word in faith. Then there are those who are judged and who reign. As the perfected, they will judge others—not that they will pronounce sentence, this being the prerogative of the Judge himself, but they are said to judge insofar as they will assist the one judging. This assistance is granted them to honor the saints, since to sit with him who judges is a great honor, as the Lord promised: "When the Son of man shall sit on his glorious throne, you also will sit on twelve seats, judging the twelve tribes of Israel."[17] It also confirms the sentence, as at times those who assist the judge approve his sentence and put their signatures to it as a mark of approval: "To execute on them the judgment written, this is glory for all his faithful ones."[18] Again, by so assisting the Judge, the saints condemn the wicked by the fact that they lived their lives righteously.

A third accompaniment to the Judgment will be the insignia of the Lord's passion, namely, the cross, the nails, and the marks of his wounds. First, they will give evidence of his glorious victory; therefore they will appear resplendent in glory. Hence Chrysostom, commenting on Matthew, says: "The cross and the wounds will shine more brightly than the sun's rays." Consider also the great power of the cross. The sun will be darkened and the moon will not give her light, that you may learn how much more radiant the cross is than the moon, how much more splendid than the sun. Second, the insignia will put his mercy in evidence, showing how great is the mercy by which the good are saved. Third, they will show forth his justice, making clear how justly the wicked are condemned because they had no regard for the precious blood he shed for them. He will reproach them in such words as Chrysostom, in his commentary on Matthew, has him say: "For your sake I became man, was bound and mocked and scourged and crucified; and what service did you render me in return for the

---

[15] Matt. 25:42. [16] John 3:18.
[17] Matt. 19:28. [18] Ps. 149:9.

price of my blood? I held you higher than my glory, I, who being God came as a man; and you held me lower, viler than all your possessions. The most worthless things on earth you loved more dearly than my goodness and my faith." Thus Chrysostom.

Fourthly, have in mind the sternness of the one judging. "No fear can influence him, for he is omnipotent": so Chrysostom. Nor is there any power that can resist him, nor possibility of fleeing from him. "Bribes cannot corrupt him because he is so rich," says Bernard. And Augustine: "He will come on that day, when pure hearts will be of more avail than shrewd words, and a good conscience more than full purses; he is not fooled by words nor swayed by gifts." The day of judgment is awaited, and that most impartial judge will be present. He is no respecter of powerful persons, and no bishop or abbot or count will be able to corrupt his palace with gold or silver. Being all good, he is not moved by hatred, because hate cannot fall upon the good: "Thou hatest none of the things which thou hast made."[19] Love will not dissuade him, because he is most just, so he will not let even his brothers, i.e., false Christians, go free: "No brother can redeem."[20] He will not err, because he is all wise. Pope Leo says: "Tremendous is his insight, which penetrates the impervious, to which every secret is open, the obscure is lightened, the speechless respond, silence confesses, the mind speaks even without words. And therefore, since such and so great is his wisdom, against it no arguments of lawyers, no sophisms of philosophers, no eloquent speeches by orators, no subtleties from the sharp-witted, will have the slightest weight." And Jerome comments: "'How much better off the tongue-tied and mute will be than the fluent of speech, shepherds than philosophers, rustics than orators; how the mutterings of dullards will do better than the astute arguments of Cicero!"

Fifthly, there will be the dread accuser. Indeed, three accusers will stand up against the sinner. The first to accuse will be the devil. Augustine writes: "The devil will then be there, reciting the words of our profession and throwing up to us our actions, the places and times of our sins, and what good we should have done at those moments. And then this adversary will say: 'O most just Judge, give judgment that this sinner is mine because of his sin, since he did not choose to be yours by grace. He is yours by his nature, mine by his misery, yours due to your passion, mine by my persuasion; you he disobeyed, me he obeyed; from you he received the robe of immortality, from me the rags he now is clothed with; he threw off your robe and comes here with mine. O fairest of judges, judge that he is mine and must be damned with me.' Woe to such a one! How could he open his mouth, being found deserving to be counted with the devil!" Thus far Augustine.

The second accuser will be one's own sin. Each one's own sins will accuse him; "They shall come with fear at the thought of their sins, and their iniquities

---

[19] Wisd. 11:25.   [20] Ps. 48:8 (Douay).

shall stand against them to convict them."[21] Bernard writes: "Then all his deeds will speak together: 'You did us, we are your actions; we will always be with you and will go with you to judgment.'" Many and divers crimes will be his accusers.

The third accuser will be the whole world. Hear Gregory: "If you ask who will accuse you, I say, 'The whole world. When the Creator is offended the entire creation is offended.'" Chrysostom comments on Matthew: "There will be nothing we can say in response on that day when heaven and earth, the waters, the sun and the moon, night and day and the whole world will oppose us before God, testifying to our sins; and if all were silent, our very thoughts and especially our works will stand against us before God, forcefully accusing us."

Sixthly, there will be the infallible witness. The sinner will indeed have three witnesses against him. One will be above him, namely, God, who will be judge and witness: "I am judge and witness, says the Lord."[22] Another will be within him, namely, his conscience. Augustine: "Whoever you are who fear your future judge, straighten your conscience at present; for what will speak to your case is the testimony of your conscience." A third witness will be at his side, his own angel assigned to be his guardian; and the angel, knowing everything he has done, will bring testimony against him. "The heavens (i.e., the angels) will reveal his iniquity."[23]

Seventhly, there is the sinner's self-accusation concerning all this. So Gregory says: "Oh how narrow are the ways for the condemned! Above them an angry judge, below them the horrid abyss, on the right their accusing sins, on the left hordes of demons dragging them to torment, inside of them their burning conscience, outside, the world afire. So straitened, whither shall the sinner flee? To hide will be impossible, to show himself, intolerable."

Eighthly, the irrevocable sentence; for that sentence can never be revoked, nor can there be any appeal from it. In judicial cases no appeal is acceptable, for any of three reasons. The first is the supremacy of the judge: hence no appeal can be made from a king's sentence within his kingdom, because in his kingdom he has no one above him. Likewise there is no appeal against the emperor or the pope. The clear evidence of the crime is a second reason, because when the crime is known to all, there is no appeal. The third reason is that the case may not be deferred, because some harm might follow upon such deferral. So in the present case no appeal is possible. The judge is supreme: he has no one above him, he is beyond all by his eternity, his dignity, and his power. There might be some way to appeal from an emperor or a pope to God, but none from God to anyone else, there being no one higher. Furthermore, the crime is evident: all the crimes and misdeeds of the condemned will then be known and manifest. Jerome: "That day will come when our deeds will be visible as in a painted picture." Finally the case cannot be deferred. Nothing done there is subject to delay: everything will be accomplished in a moment, in the twinkling of an eye.

---

[21] Wisd. 4:20.   [22] Jer. 29:23.   [23] Job 20:27.

2. Saint Andrew, Apostle

Andrew is interpreted beautiful, or responding, or manly, from *ander*, which means male, a man; or Andrew, Andreas, is like *anthropos*, i.e., man, from *ana*, above, and *tropos*, a turning. So Andrew was one who turned upward toward heavenly things and was lifted up to his Creator. He was beautiful in his life, responding in wise doctrine, manly in suffering, and raised up in glory. The presbyters and deacons of Achaia wrote an account of his martyrdom, which they had witnessed with their own eyes.

Andrew and several other disciples were called by our Lord three times. The first time he called them to know him. That was the day when Andrew, standing with John his teacher and another disciple, heard John say: "Behold the lamb of God who takes away the sins of the world." Immediately he and the other disciple went and saw where Jesus lived, and they stayed with him all day; and later Andrew found his brother Simon and led him to Jesus. The next day they returned to fishing, their regular occupation. Later Jesus called them a second time, this time to his friendship. Coming with a great crowd to the shore of the lake of Genesareth, which is also called the sea of Galilee, he went into the boat that belonged to Simon and Andrew, and at his bidding they made a large haul of fish. Then Andrew called James and John, who were in another boat, and they followed the Lord, after which they again returned to their work. But soon Jesus called them again, this time to be his disciples. Walking one day beside the same lake, he signaled them to throw aside their nets, and said: "Follow me, I will make you fishers of men." And they followed him and did not go back to their usual work. Still a fourth time, moreover, the Lord called Andrew, on this occasion to be his apostle, as Mark reports in his third chapter: "He called those he had chosen for himself and they came to him, and he saw to it that they were twelve in number."

After the Lord's ascension into heaven the apostles separated, and Andrew went to Scythia, while Matthew went to Murgundia, also called Ethiopia. But the Ethiopians, refusing to heed Matthew's preaching, put out his eyes, bound him with chains, and threw him into prison, intending to put him to death in a few days. Meanwhile the angel of the Lord appeared to Andrew and commanded him to go to Ethiopia to be with blessed Matthew. Andrew answered that he did not know the way there, whereupon the angel ordered him to go to the seacoast, and there to board the first ship he encountered. This Andrew promptly did, and the ship, aided by a favorable wind, swiftly carried him to the town where Matthew was. Then, the angel guiding him, he made his way into the evangelist's prison, which he found open. Seeing Matthew he wept much and prayed; and the Lord, in answer to his prayer, restored to Matthew the sight of his eyes, which the cruelty of the unbelievers had taken from him.

Matthew then departed and went to Antioch. Andrew stayed in Murgundia, where the inhabitants, furious at their prisoner's escape, seized the apostle and dragged him from place to place with his hands bound. His blood flowed freely, but he prayed to God unceasingly for his tormentors and in the end converted them. Then he set out for Achaia. This, at any rate, is what we are told; but I find the story very hard to believe, because Matthew's deliverance and cure by Andrew would imply—and this is very unlikely—that the great evangelist was unable to obtain for himself what Andrew secured for him so easily.

A young man of noble family had been converted by Saint Andrew and joined his company against the will of his parents, whereupon they set fire to the house where he lived with the apostle. When the flames were at their height, the young man sprinkled a vial of water on them and the fire died out. Then the parents said: "Our son has been turned into a sorcerer." They brought a ladder and tried to climb up and rescue their son; but God struck them blind, so that they could no longer see the rungs of the ladder. A man who was passing called up to them: "Why go to so much trouble? Do you not see that God is fighting for them? Stop now, or God's wrath may fall upon you!" Many, witnessing this, believed in the Lord. As for the youth's parents, they died after fifty days and were buried in a tomb.

A woman who had married a murderer was brought to bed but could not give birth. She said to her sister: "Go and pray to our mistress Diana for me." The sister prayed, but it was the devil, not Diana, who answered: "It is useless to invoke me, for I can do nothing for you. Go instead and find Andrew the apostle: he can help your sister." She went therefore and sought out Saint Andrew, and brought him to the bedside of her ailing sister. "You deserve your suffering," he said to her; "you married badly, conceived badly, and called upon the devil. But repent, believe in Christ, and you will be delivered." The woman made an act of faith and brought forth a stillborn child; and her pangs ceased.

An old man named Nicholas came to Andrew and told him: "Master, I am now seventy years old and have always been given to sins of lust. Yet I have read the gospel and have prayed to God to grant me the gift of continence, but I cannot resist concupiscence, and I fall back into my evil ways. Now it has happened that driven by lust and forgetting that I carried the gospel on my person, I went to a brothel; but the harlot, when she saw me, cried out: 'Get out, old man, get out! Don't touch me or try to come near me. I see marvelous things about you, and I know you are an angel of God!' Astonished by what she said, I remembered that I was carrying the gospel. Now, holy man of God, let your prayer obtain my salvation!" Hearing all this the saint began to weep and remained in prayer for hours; and then he refused to eat, saying: "I will eat nothing until I know that the Lord will take pity on this old man." After he had fasted for five days, a voice came to him: "Andrew, your prayer is granted. But just as you have mortified your body by fasting for him, so likewise he must fast in order to win salvation." The old man did so. For six months he fasted on bread and water, and then fell asleep in peace, full of good works. And again Andrew heard the voice, this time saying to him: "Your prayer has restored to me Nicholas whom I had lost."

A certain Christian youth told Saint Andrew in secret: "My mother, seeing my good figure, tried to make me do wrong with her; and when I absolutely refused, she went to the judge and accused me of that very crime. Pray for me and save me from an unjust death, because I will not defend myself. I would rather die than expose my mother to such shame." So the young man was summoned before the judge, and Andrew went with him. The mother insistently charged her son with wanting to violate her, and the son, despite being asked several times whether this was true, said not a word. Then Andrew spoke to the mother: "O cruelest of women, your own lust makes you willing to send your only son to death!" The woman said to the judge: "Sir, my son attached himself to this man after failing to have his way with me." This made the judge very angry, so he ordered the young man to be put in a sack smeared with pitch and tar and thrown into the river, and Andrew to be kept in jail until he, the judge, decided on a form of torture that would kill him. But Andrew prayed, whereupon a stupendous clap of thunder terrified them all, a huge earthquake threw them to the ground, and the woman, struck by lightning, shriveled up and crumbled to ashes. The others begged the apostle to pray that they might be spared. Andrew prayed for them, and the storm fell calm. At this the judge believed, as did his whole household.

When the apostle came to the city of Nicaea, the townspeople told him that seven devils had stationed themselves along the road outside the city gate and were killing anyone who passed that way. The saint, with all the people looking on, commanded the demons to come to him, and at once they came in the shape of dogs. The apostle ordered them to be off to some place where they could not harm anyone. The devils vanished, and those who had witnessed the miracle accepted the faith of Christ. But when Andrew arrived at the gate of another town, he came upon the body of a young man being carried out for burial. Asking what had happened to the youth, he was told that seven dogs had come and killed him in his bed. The apostle, in tears, cried out: "I know, Lord, that these were the seven demons I chased out of Nicaea!" Then he said to the father: "What will you give me if I restore your son to life?" "I have nothing dearer to me than my son," the father answered, "so I will give him to you." And when Andrew had prayed to the Lord, the young man rose and followed him.

Some men, to the number of forty, were on their way by sea to receive the word of faith from Andrew, when the devil raised a storm and all were drowned. But their bodies were cast up on the shore by the waves. The apostle quickly brought them back to life, and they all told what had befallen them. Whence it is that we read in a hymn from the saint's office:

> Quaterdenos juvenes,
> Submersos maris fluctibus,
> Vitae reddidit usibus.[1]

Then blessed Andrew settled in Achaia, filled the whole region with churches, and led a great number of people to the Christian faith. Among others, he converted the wife of the proconsul Aegeus and baptized her. As soon as the proconsul heard of this, he came to the town of Patras and commanded the Christians to sacrifice to the idols. Then Andrew came to meet him and said: "You have earned the right to judge men on earth. Now what you ought to do is to recognize your judge who is in heaven, worship him, and turn completely away from false gods." Aegeus spoke: "So you are that Andrew who preaches the superstitious sect which the princes of Rome recently ordered us to exterminate." Andrew: "That is because the Roman rulers have not yet known that the Son of God has come on earth, and has taught that your idols are demons and their teaching an offense to God. So God, being offended, turns away from those who worship them and does not hear their prayers; and they, no longer heard by God, are made captive by the devil and deluded by him until their naked souls leave their bodies, carrying nothing with them but their sins." "Yes," Aegeus retorted, "and because your Jesus was teaching this nonsense, they nailed him to a cross." Andrew replied: "It was to give us salvation, and not to expiate any misdeeds of his own, that he freely accepted the agony of the cross." Then said Aegeus: "How can you say that he freely suffered death, when we know that he was handed over by one of his disciples, imprisoned by the Jews, and crucified by the soldiers?"

Andrew thereupon set out to prove, by five arguments, that the passion of Christ was voluntary. Christ had foreseen his passion and had foretold it to his disciples, saying: "Behold, we go up to Jerusalem, and the Son of man shall be betrayed."[2] When Peter tried to dissuade him, Jesus said: "Go behind me, Satan!"[3] He made it plain that he had the power both to suffer death and to rise again, saying: "I have the power to lay it (my life) down, and I have power to take it up again."[4] He knew in advance the man who would betray him, since he dipped bread and gave it to him, and still made no attempt to avoid him. Finally, he had chosen the place where he knew the traitor would come to betray him. Andrew also declared that he himself had been present at all these moments; and he added that the cross was a great mystery. "It is not a mystery

---

[1] Forty young men, / who had been drowned in the waves of the sea, / he restored to the uses of life.

[2] Matt. 20:18.

[3] Matt. 16:23.

[4] John 10:17-18.

at all," Aegeus replied, "but a punishment. However, if you refuse to obey my command, I will give you a taste of your mystery!" "If I were afraid of the pain of the cross," Andrew answered, "I would not be preaching the glory of the cross. But first let me teach you its mystery. Maybe you will believe in it, worship it, and be saved."

He then began to explain the mystery of redemption to the proconsul, proving, by five arguments, how necessary and appropriate this mystery is. Since the first man had brought death into the world by means of wood, a tree, it was appropriate that the Son of man should banish death by dying on a cross of wood. Since the sinner had been formed out of clean earth, it was fitting that the reconciler should be born of an immaculate virgin. Since Adam had stretched out his greedy hands toward the forbidden fruit, it was fitting that the second Adam should open his guiltless hands on the cross. Since Adam had tasted the sweetness of the apple, Jesus had to taste the bitterness of gall. And since he was giving his own immortality to man, it was by a fitting exchange that he took human mortality, because if God had not become man, man could not have become immortal. To all this Aegeus's reply was: "Go teach these inanities to your own people, but now obey me and offer sacrifice to the all-powerful gods!" And Andrew: "To almighty God I offer daily a Lamb without stain, who remains alive and whole after all the people have eaten him." Aegeus asked how this could be, and Andrew answered: "Become his disciple and I will tell you." Aegeus: "Well, then, I will torture an answer out of you"; and, enraged, he had him imprisoned.

The next morning, taking his place in the judgment seat, he again called upon Andrew to sacrifice to the idols, saying: "If you refuse to obey me, I shall have you hung upon the cross you boast about!" And he threatened him with other torments. The apostle responded: "Make them the worst you can think of! The more bravely I bear suffering in his name, the more acceptable I shall be to my king." Aegeus commanded twenty-one men to seize him, flog him, and bind him hand and foot to a cross, so as to make his agony last longer.

While the saint was being led to the cross, a great crowd gathered, shouting: "An innocent man is condemned to shed his blood without cause!" The apostle, however, begged them not to try to save him from martyrdom. Then, seeing the cross in the distance, he greeted it, saying: "Hail, O cross sanctified by the body of Christ and adorned with his limbs as with precious stones! Before the Lord was lifted up on you, you were greatly feared on earth, but now you draw down love from heaven and are accepted as a blessing. I come to you assured and rejoicing, so that you may joyfully accept me, the disciple of him who hung upon you, for I have always loved you and yearned to embrace you. O good cross, honored and beautified by the limbs of the Lord, long desired, constantly loved, ceaselessly sought, and now prepared for my wishful heart! Take me away from the world of men and return me to my Master, that he, having redeemed me by means of you, may receive me from you." Having said these words, he

17

shed his garments and gave them to the executioners, who fixed him to the cross as they had been commanded. For two days Andrew hung there alive and preached to twenty thousand people. On the third day the crowd began to threaten the proconsul Aegeus with death, saying that a saintly, gentle man should not be made to suffer so; and Aegeus came to have the saint released. Seeing him, Andrew exclaimed: "Why have you come here, Aegeus? If to seek forgiveness, you will be forgiven; but if to take me down from the cross, know that I will not come down alive, for already I see my king awaiting me." When the soldiers tried to free him, they could not even touch him: their arms fell powerless at their sides. Meanwhile Andrew, knowing that the people wanted to rescue him, uttered this prayer from the cross, as Augustine quotes it in his book *On Penance*: "Lord, do not let me come down alive! It is time for you to entrust my body to the earth. You entrusted it to me, and I have borne it so long and watched over it and worked so hard, and now I wish to be discharged of this obedience and relieved of this most burdensome garment. I think of how I have labored to carry its weight, to control its unruliness, to support its weakness, to compel its slow responses. You know, O Lord, how often it has struggled to draw me away from the purity of contemplation and awaken me from the repose of that most sweet stillness, how many and how grave pains it has inflicted on me. O most kind Father, I have resisted the assaults of this body for so long, and with your help I have mastered it. Just and loving Rewarder, I beg of you not to leave it any longer in my care! I give back what you entrusted to me. Commend it to the earth so that I will not have to take care of it, and it will not curb and hamper me, thirsting as I am to come freely to you, the inexhaustible source of life and joy." Thus Augustine.

As Andrew finished his prayer, a dazzling light shone out of heaven and enveloped him for the space of a half hour, hiding him from sight; and as the light faded, he breathed his last. Maximilla, Aegeus's wife, took away the body of the holy apostle and gave it honorable burial. But Aegeus, before ever he got back to his house, was seized by a demon and died in the street, with the crowd looking on.

We are told also that a flourlike manna and sweet-smelling oil used to issue from Saint Andrew's tomb, and that by this sign the people of the region could predict the next year's crops. If the flow was meager, the crops would be poor; if abundant, the yield would be plentiful. This may have been true in the past, but now it is said that the saint's body was transferred to Constantinople.

A certain truly devout bishop venerated Saint Andrew above all other saints and began whatever he was about to do with the invocation, "To the honor of God and Saint Andrew." This aroused the devil's envy, and he turned all his cunning to the task of deceiving the bishop. So he took the form of a marvelously beautiful woman, who came to the bishop's palace and said that she wanted to confess to him. The bishop sent word that she should apply to his own confessor, to whom he gave the necessary faculties, but she refused on the ground that the bishop himself was the only one to whom she could reveal the secrets of her conscience. In the end he allowed her to be brought before him, and she said: "I pray you, my lord, have pity on me, young as I am as you can see, tenderly nurtured and of royal blood. I have come here, alone and in the garb of a pilgrim. My father, a mighty king, wanted to give me in marriage to a great prince, but I told him that I held the marriage bed in horror because I had vowed perpetual virginity to Christ, and could never consent to carnal commerce. With the choice of either yielding to his will or suffering dire punishment, I got away secretly, preferring to live in exile rather than break faith with my spouse. The fame of your sanctity had come to my ears, and I have sought refuge under the wings of your protection, hoping to find a place with you where I might enjoy the secret silence of holy contemplation, avoid the pitfalls of life, and escape from the disorders of the noisy world."

The bishop, admiring her noble origin and her physical beauty as well as her fervor and eloquence, answered her kindly: "Be reassured, my child, and have no fear. He for whose love you have given up everything, yourself, your kin, and all your possessions, will heap graces upon you in this life and the fullness of glory in the next. I, as his servant, offer you all that is mine. Please choose wherever you wish to dwell; and today I invite you to dine with me." "O my father," she replied, "do not ask this of me. It might stir up some suspicion that would damage your good name." "Not at all!" said the bishop. "There will be others present, we shall not be alone. There cannot be the slightest suspicion that there is anything amiss."

So the bishop, the woman, and the rest of the company went to the table, the woman seated facing the prelate and the others to either side. The bishop could not take his eyes from her face nor contain his admiration for her beauty; and, the eye being fixed, the inner man was wounded. The ancient enemy, aware of this, drove his dart deep into the bishop's heart, at the same time making the alluring face more and more beautiful. The bishop was on the verge of consenting to the thought of proposing a wicked act to the woman at the first opportunity, when suddenly a pilgrim came pounding on the door and loudly demanded admittance. As no one opened to the stranger and the noise from outside increased, the bishop asked the woman whether she would mind if the pilgrim was allowed to come in. She replied: "We shall propose a very difficult question to him. If he can give a satisfactory answer, let him in. If not, let him be driven away as an ignorant person, unworthy to be in the presence of a bishop!"

The plan appealed to all present, and they looked around to see who might be wise enough to propound the question. Then the bishop said to the woman: "No one of us, my lady, is so well able to do this as you are. You surpass us all in wisdom and eloquence, so you shall propose the question." So the woman said: "Ask him to name the most wonderful thing that God has made in a small form." The question was relayed to the stranger, who answered the messenger:

"It is the variety and excellence of the human face: for among so many human beings, from the beginning of the world to its end, no two could be discovered whose faces resembled each other in every respect, or ever will be; yet in each face, small as it may be, God places the seat of all the senses of the body." This solution pleased the company, and they said: "This is a true and excellent answer." Then the woman said: "Let us propose a second and harder problem, so that we may better gauge his knowledge: ask him at what point earth is higher than the heavens." The stranger replied: "It is in the empyrean heaven, for there the body of Christ resides; and the body of Christ is higher than any heaven, yet it was formed of our flesh, and our flesh was made of earth. Therefore at that point earth is higher than the heavens." Hearing this, the company applauded the stranger's wisdom, but the woman spoke again: "We shall give him one more question, this one far more difficult, more obscure, harder to solve than any other could be. This will let us plumb the depth of his knowledge. If he has the answer, he is indeed worthy to sit at the bishop's table. Ask him therefore how far it is from earth to heaven." The pilgrim's reply to the messenger was: "Go back to the one who sent you to me and put that question carefully to him. He knows the answer better than I do and can answer it better, because he traversed the distance when he fell from heaven into the abyss. I never fell from heaven and so never measured the distance. He is not a woman but the devil, who took on a woman's likeness." The messenger, frightened by what he had heard, hurried to report it to those inside. They sat stunned and bewildered by the message, but the ancient enemy vanished from their midst.

The bishop, coming to himself, bitterly reproached himself and with tears prayed for pardon for his fault. He sent the porter to bring the pilgrim into the house, but the stranger was nowhere to be found. Then he called the people together, explained to them everything that had happened, and asked them to fast and pray that God might deign to reveal the identity of the stranger who had saved him from so great a danger. That very night it was revealed to the bishop that it was Saint Andrew himself who, to save him, had come dressed as a pilgrim. Thereafter the bishop was more than ever devout in his veneration of the holy apostle.

The prefect of a certain city had taken possession of a field that belonged to a church dedicated to Saint Andrew. At the prayer of the bishop, the prefect was immediately stricken with fever as a punishment for his sin. He thereupon asked the bishop to pray for him, promising to return the field to the church if he recovered his health; but once he had been made well he took back the field. Then the bishop again resorted to prayer and extinguished all the lights in the church, saying: "There will be no more light until the Lord is avenged upon his enemy and the church recovers its loss." The prefect promptly fell ill again, this time with a higher fever, so once more he begged the bishop to pray for him, saying that he would give back the stolen field and another of equal size. The bishop's answer was: "I have already prayed, and God has answered my prayer."

The sick man then had himself carried to the bishop, whom he forced to go into the church to pray for him again; but hardly had the bishop entered the church when the prefect died, and the field was restored to the church.

✳

3. Saint Nicholas

The name Nicholas comes from *nicos*, which means victory, and *laos*, people; so Nicholas may be interpreted as meaning victory over a people, i.e., either victory over vices, which are many and mean, or as victory in the full sense, because Nicholas, by his way of life and his doctrine, taught the peoples to conquer sin and vice. Or the name is formed from *nicos*, victory, and *laus*, praise—so, victorious praise—or from *nitor*, shining whiteness, and *laos*, people, as meaning the bright cleanness of the people. Nicholas had in him that which makes for shining cleanness, since, according to Ambrose, "the word of God makes clean, as do true confession, holy thoughts, and good works."

The life of Saint Nicholas was written by learned men of Argos, called Argolics, Argos being, according to Isidore, a town in Greece, so the Greeks are also called Argolics. Elsewhere we read that his legend was written in Greek by the patriarch Methodius and translated into Latin by John the Deacon, who added much to it.

Nicholas, a citizen of Patera, was born of rich and pious parents. His father was named Epiphanes, his mother, Johanna. When, in the flower of their youth, they had brought him into the world, they adopted the celibate life thenceforth. While the infant was being bathed on the first day of his life, he stood straight up in the bath. From then on he took the breast only once on Wednesdays and Fridays. As a youth he avoided the dissolute pleasures of his peers, preferring to spend time in churches; and whatever he could understand of the Holy Scriptures he committed to memory.

After the death of his parents he began to consider how he might make use of his great wealth, not in order to win men's praise but to give glory to God. At the time a certain fellow townsman of his, a man of noble origin but very poor, was thinking of prostituting his three virgin daughters in order to make a living out of this vile transaction. When the saint learned of this, abhorring the crime he wrapped a quantity of gold in a cloth and, under cover of darkness, threw it through a window of the other man's house and withdrew unseen. Rising in the morning, the man found the gold, gave thanks to God, and celebrated the wedding of his eldest daughter. Not long thereafter the servant of God did the same thing again. This time the man, finding the gold and bursting into loud praises, determined to be on the watch so as to find out who had come to the relief of his penury. Some little time later Nicholas threw a double sum of gold into the house. The noise awakened the man and he pursued the fleeing figure, calling out, "Stop! Stop! Don't hide from me!" and ran faster and faster until he saw that it was Nicholas. Falling to the ground he wanted to kiss his benefactor's feet, but the saint drew away and exacted a promise that the secret would be kept until after his death.

Some time later the bishop of Myra died, and all the bishops of the region gathered to choose a successor. Among them was one bishop of great authority, upon whose opinion the decision of the others would depend. This prelate exhorted the others to fast and pray; and that very night he heard a voice telling him to post himself at the doors of the church in the morning, and to consecrate as bishop the first man he saw coming in, whose name would be Nicholas. In the morning he made this known to his colleagues and went outside the church to wait. Meanwhile Nicholas, miraculously guided by God, went early to the church and was the first to enter. The bishop, coming up to him, asked his name; and he, filled with the simplicity of a dove, bowed his head and answered, "Nicholas, the servant of your holiness." Then all the bishops led him in and installed him on the episcopal throne. But he, amidst his honors, always preserved his former humility and gravity of manner. He passed the night in prayer, mortified his body, and shunned the society of women. He was humble in his attitude toward others, persuasive in speech, forceful in counsel, and strict when reprimands were called for. A chronicle also states that Nicholas took part in the Council of Nicaea.

One day some seamen, threatened by a violent storm at sea, shed tears and prayed as follows: "Nicholas, servant of God, if what we have heard about you is true, let us experience your help now." At once there appeared before them a figure resembling the saint, who said to them: "You called me, here I am!" And he began to assist them with the sails and ropes and other rigging of the ship, and the storm died down immediately. The sailors eventually came to the church where Nicholas was and recognized him instantly, although they had never seen him in the flesh. They thanked him then for their deliverance, but he told them to thank God, since their rescue was due not to his merits, but only to the divine mercy and their own faith.

There came a time when Saint Nicholas's province was beset by a famine so severe that no one had anything to eat. The man of God learned that several ships laden with grain were anchored in the harbor. He hastened there promptly and begged the ships' people to come to the aid of those who were starving, if only by allowing them a hundred measures of wheat from each ship. But they replied: "Father, we dare not, because our cargo was measured at Alexandria and we must deliver it whole and entire to the emperor's granaries." The saint answered: "Do what I tell you, and I promise you in God's power that the imperial customsmen will not find your cargo short." The men did so, and when they arrived at their destination, they turned over to the imperial granaries the same quantity of grain that had been measured out at Alexandria. They spread news of the miracle and glorified God in his saint. Meanwhile the grain they had relinquished was distributed by Nicholas to each according to his needs, and so miraculously that not only did it suffice to feed the whole region for two years but supplied enough for the sowing.

In the past this region had worshiped idols; and even in Saint Nicholas's time there were rustics who practiced pagan rites under a tree dedicated to the wicked goddess Diana. To put a stop to this idolatry the saint ordered the tree cut down. This infuriated the ancient enemy, who concocted an unnatural oil that had the property of burning on water or on stone. Then, assuming the form of a nun, he came alongside a ship carrying people on their way to visit the saint and called to them: "I wanted so much to come with you to the holy man of God, but I cannot. May I ask you to offer this oil at his church and to paint the walls with it in memory of me." And forthwith he vanished. Then they saw another craft nearing them with honest people aboard, including one person who bore a striking likeness to Saint Nicholas, and this one asked them: "What did that woman say to you and what did she bring to you?" The people gave a full account of what had taken place. "That was the shameless Diana herself," he replied, "and if you want proof of it, throw that oil out over the water." They did so, and a huge fire flared up on the sea and, contrary to nature, burned for hours. When the travelers finally came to the servant of God, they said: "Truly you are the one who appeared to us at sea and delivered us from the wiles of the devil."

About that time there was a tribe that had risen in rebellion against the Roman Empire, and the emperor sent three princes, Nepotian, Ursus, and Apilion, to put them down. The three were forced by adverse winds to put in at an Adriatic port, and Nicholas, anxious to have them restrain their men from robbing his people on market days—something that happened regularly—invited them to his house. Meanwhile, during the saint's absence, the Roman consul, corrupted by a bribe, had ordered three innocent soldiers to be beheaded. As soon as the holy man heard of this, he asked his guests to accompany him, and they hurried to the spot where the execution was to take place. There he found the condemned men already on their knees, their faces veiled, and the executioner brandishing his sword over their heads. Nicholas, afire with zeal, threw himself upon the headsman, snatched his sword from his hand, unbound the innocent men, and led them away safe and sound.

The saint then hastened to the consul's headquarters and forced the door, which was locked. The consul came hurriedly to greet him, but Nicholas spurned him and said: "You enemy of God, you perverter of the law, how dare you look us in the eye with so great a crime on your conscience?" And he heaped reproaches upon him, but the princes pleaded for him, and the saint, seeing the man repentant, forgave him kindly. Thereupon the imperial emissaries, having received the bishop's blessing, continued their journey and put down the rebels without bloodshed; and when they returned to the emperor, he gave them a splendid reception.

Some other courtiers, however, envying their good fortune, bribed the imperial prefect to go to the emperor and accuse the princes of lese majesty. The emperor was beside himself with anger at the charge, and ordered the accused to be thrown into jail immediately and to be put to death without trial that very night. When the three heard this from their jailer, they tore their garments and wept bitterly. Then one of them, Nepotian, recalled that the blessed Nicholas had lately, in their presence, saved three innocent men from death, and exhorted his companions to invoke the holy man's aid. The result of their prayer was that Saint Nicholas appeared that night to Emperor Constantine and said: "Why have you had these princes arrested unjustly and condemned them to death when they are innocent? Hurry, get up and order them to be set free at once! Otherwise I shall pray God to stir up a war in which you will go down to defeat and be fed to the beasts." "Who are you," the emperor asked, "to come into my palace at night and talk to me this way?" Nicholas answered: "I am Nicholas, bishop of the city of Myra." The saint also appeared that night to the prefect, whom he terrified by saying: "Mindless and senseless man, why did you agree to the killing of innocent men? Go at once and see that they are set free. If you don't, your body will be devoured by worms and your house swiftly destroyed." The prefect retorted: "Who are you, to face us with such threats?" "Know," the holy man replied, "that I am Nicholas, bishop of the city of Myra."

The emperor and the prefect rose from sleep, told each other their dreams, and lost no time summoning the three princes. "Are you sorcerers," the emperor demanded, "to delude us with such visions?" They replied that they were not sorcerers, and that they had done nothing to deserve the sentence of death. Then said the emperor: "Do you know a man named Nicholas?" At the mention of the name they raised their hands to heaven and prayed God to save them, by the merits of Saint Nicholas, from the peril in which they found themselves. And when the emperor had heard from them about the life and miracles of the saint, he said: "Go, and thank God, who has saved you at the prayer of this Nicholas. But also bring gifts to Nicholas in my name and ask him not to threaten us anymore, but to pray the Lord for me and my reign."

Some days later the princes went to visit the servant of God. They threw themselves at his feet saying: "Truly you are a servant of God, truly you love and worship Christ." Then they told him everything that had happened; and he, raising his hands to heaven, offered heartfelt praise to God and sent the princes home after instructing them thoroughly in the truths of the faith.

When the Lord wished to call Nicholas to himself, the saint prayed that he would send his angels. And when he saw them coming, he bowed his head and recited the Psalm *In te Domine speravi*; and coming to the words *In manus tuas Domine commendo spiritum meum*, which mean "Into your hands, O Lord, I commend my spirit," he breathed forth his soul to the sound of heavenly music. This was in the year 343. He was buried in a marble tomb, and a fountain of oil began to flow from his head and a fountain of water from his feet. Even today a holy oil issues from his members and brings health to many.

One day this oil stopped flowing. This happened when the successor of Saint Nicholas, a worthy man, was driven from his see by jealous rivals. As soon as the bishop was restored, however, the oil flowed again. Long afterward, the Turks razed the city of Myra. Forty-seven soldiers from the town of Bari happened to be passing through, and four monks opened the tomb of Saint Nicholas to them: they removed his bones, which were immersed in oil, and carried them to Bari, in the year of the Lord 1087.

A man had borrowed some money from a Jew, giving him his oath on the altar of Saint Nicholas that he would repay it as soon as possible. As he was slow in paying, the Jew demanded his money, but the man declared that he had repaid it. He was summoned before the judge, who ordered him to swear that he had paid his debt. However, the man had put the money in a hollow staff, and before giving his oath he asked the Jew to hold the staff for him. He then swore that he had returned the money and more besides, and took back his staff: the Jew handed it over all unaware of the ruse. On his way home the dishonest fellow fell asleep by the roadside, and a coach, coming along at high speed, ran over him and killed him, also breaking open the staff and spilling the money. Being informed of this, the Jew hurried to the spot and saw through the trick; but, though the bystanders urged him to pick up his money, he refused unless the dead man were restored to life by the merits of Saint Nicholas, in which case he himself would become a Christian and accept baptism. At once the dead man was revived, and the Jew was baptized in the name of Jesus Christ.

Another Jew, seeing the miraculous power of Saint Nicholas, ordered a statue of the saint and placed it in his house. Whenever he had to be away for a long time, he addressed the statue in these or similar words: "Nicholas, I leave you in charge of my goods, and if you do not watch over them as I demand, I shall avenge myself by beating you." Then, one time when he was absent, thieves broke in and carried off all they found, leaving only the statue. When the Jew came home and saw that he had been robbed, he said to the statue: "Sir Nicholas, did I not put you in my house to guard my goods? Why then did you not do so and keep the thieves away? Well, then, you will pay the penalty! I shall make up for my loss and cool my anger by smashing you to bits!" And he did indeed beat the statue. But then a wondrous thing happened! The saint appeared to the robbers as they were dividing their spoils and said to them: "See how I have been beaten on your account! My body is still black and blue! Quick! Go and give back what you have taken, or the anger of God will fall upon you, your crime will become common knowledge, and you will every one of you be hanged." "And who are you," the thieves answered, "to talk this way to us?" "I am Nicholas, the servant of Jesus Christ," he replied, "and the Jew whom you robbed has beaten me in revenge!" Terrified, they ran to the Jew's house, told him of their vision, learned from him what he had done to the statue, restored all his property, and returned to the path of righteousness. The Jew, for his part, embraced the faith of the Savior.

A certain man, for love of his son who was learning his letters at school, annually celebrated the feast of Saint Nicholas in solemn fashion. On one particular occasion the boy's father laid on a sumptuous feast, to which he invited many clerks. During the meal the devil, dressed as a pilgrim, knocked at the door and asked for alms. The father ordered his son to take alms to the pilgrim, and the youth, not finding him at the door, pursued him to a crossroad, where the demon waylaid and strangled him. Hearing this, the father moaned with grief, carried the body back to the house and laid it on a bed, and cried: "O dearest son, how could this have happened to you? And, Saint Nicholas, is this my reward for the honor I have paid you all this time?" And while he was saying these things, the lad opened his eyes as if he were just waking up, and rose from the bed.

A nobleman had asked Saint Nicholas to pray the Lord to grant him a son, and promised that he would go with his son to the saint's tomb and would offer him a gold cup. His prayer was answered and he ordered the cup to be made, but he was so pleased with it that he kept it for himself and ordered another of like value. Then he took ship with the boy, to travel to the saint's tomb. On the way the father told his son to fetch him some water in the first cup. The boy tried to fill the cup with water, but fell into the sea and disappeared. Though stricken with grief, the father pursued his journey in order to fulfill his vow. He came to the church of Saint Nicholas and placed the second cup on the altar, whereupon an unseen hand thrust him back with the cup and threw him to the ground. He picked himself up, returned to the altar, and again was thrown down. And then, to the astonishment of all, the boy arrived whole and unharmed, carrying the first cup in his hands. He told how, the minute he had fallen into the water, Saint Nicholas had plucked him out and had kept him hale and hearty. At this the father rejoiced and offered both cups to the blessed Nicholas.

A rich man had obtained a son through the intercession of Saint Nicholas and called him Adeodatus. He also built a chapel in his house in honor of the saint and there solemnly celebrated his feast every year. The place was close to the territory of the Agarenes, and it happened that Adeodatus was captured by the Agarenes and carried off to serve their king as a slave. The following year, while the father was devoutly celebrating the feast of Saint Nicholas, the boy, serving the king with a precious cup in his hands, thought of his capture, his parents' grief, and the joy that used to be theirs on the feast day, and began to sigh and weep. The king demanded the reason for his tears and said: "Your Nicholas can do as he likes, but you are going to stay right here." Suddenly a mighty wind blew up, demolished the king's palace, snatched up the boy and the cup, and carried him to the threshold of the chapel where the parents were celebrating, to the great joy of all. Other sources would have it, however, that the aforesaid youth was of Norman origin and was on his way to the Holy Land when he was captured by the sultan, who had him whipped on the feast of Saint Nicholas and threw him into prison. There the boy fell asleep and woke to find himself in the chapel his father had built.

4. Saint Lucy, Virgin

Lucy comes from *lux*, which means light. Light is beautiful to look upon; for, as Ambrose says, it is the nature of light that all grace is in its appearance. Light also radiates without being soiled; no matter how unclean may be the places where its beams penetrate, it is still clean. It goes in straight lines, without curvature, and traverses the greatest distances without losing its speed. Thus we are shown that the blessed virgin Lucy possessed the beauty of virginity without trace of corruption; that she radiated charity without any impure love; her progress toward God was straight and without deviation, and went far in God's works without neglect or delay. Or the name is interpreted "way of light."

Lucy, the daughter of a noble family of Syracusa, saw how the fame of Saint Agatha was spreading throughout Sicily. She went to the tomb of this saint with her mother Euthicia, who for four years had suffered from an incurable flow of blood. The two women arrived at the church during the mass, at the moment when the passage of the Gospel was being read that tells of the Lord's cure of a woman similarly afflicted. Then Lucy said to her mother: "If you believe what you have just heard, you should also believe that Agatha is always in the presence of him for whose name she suffered martyrdom; and if in this faith you touch the saint's tomb, you will instantly recover your health."

So, when all the people had left the church, the mother and her daughter stayed to pray at the tomb. Lucy then fell asleep, and had a vision of Agatha standing surrounded by angels and adorned with precious stones, and Agatha said to her: "My sister Lucy, virgin consecrated to God, why do you ask me for something that you yourself can do for your mother? Indeed, your faith has already cured her." Lucy, awakening, said to her mother: "Mother, you are healed! But in the name of her to whose prayers you owe your cure, I beg of you to release me from my espousals, and to give to the poor whatever you have been saving for my dowry." "Why not wait until you have closed my eyes," the mother answered, "and then do whatever you wish with our wealth?" But Lucy replied: "What you give away at death you cannot take with you. Give while you live and you will be rewarded."

When they returned home, they began day after day to give away their possessions to satisfy the needs of the poor. Lucy's betrothed, hearing about this, asked the girl's nurse what was going on. She put him off by answering that Lucy had found a better property which she wished to buy in his name, and for that reason was selling some of her possessions. Being a stupid fellow he saw a future gain for himself and began to help out in the selling. But when everything had been sold and the proceeds given to the poor, he turned Lucy over to the consul Paschasius, accusing her of being a Christian and acting contrary to the laws of the emperors.

Paschasius summoned her and commanded her to offer sacrifice to the idols. Lucy's answer was: "The sacrifice that is pleasing to God is to visit the poor and help them in their need. And since I have nothing left to offer, I offer myself to the Lord." Paschasius retorted: "Tell that story to fools like yourself, but I abide by the decrees of my masters, so don't tell it to me." Lucy: "You obey your masters' laws, and I shall obey the laws of my God. You fear your masters and I fear God. You are careful not to offend them, I take pains not to offend God. You want to please them, I wish to please Christ. Do then what you think will be of benefit to you, and I shall do what I think is good for me." Paschasius: "You have squandered your patrimony with seducers, and so you talk like a whore"; but Lucy replied, "As for my patrimony, I have put it in a safe place, and never have had anything to do with any seducers of the body or of the mind." Paschasius: "Who are these seducers of the body and the mind?" Lucy: "You and those like you are seducers of the mind, because you induce souls to turn away from their Creator. As for the seducers of the body, they are those who would have us put the pleasures of the flesh ahead of eternal joys."

This moved Paschasius to say: "The sting of the whip will silence your lip!" Lucy: "The words of God cannot be stilled!" Paschasius: "So you are God?" Lucy: "I am the handmaid of God, who said to his disciples, 'You shall be brought before governors and before kings for my sake, but when they shall deliver you up, take no thought how or what to say, for it is not you that speak but the Holy Spirit that speaks in you.'" Paschasius: "So the Holy Spirit is in you?" Lucy: "Those who live chaste lives are the temples of the Holy Spirit." "Then I shall have you taken to a brothel," said Paschasius, "your body will be defiled and you will lose the Holy Spirit." "The body is not defiled," Lucy responded, "unless the mind consents. If you have me ravished against my will, my chastity will be doubled and the crown will be mine. You will never be able to force my will. As for my body, here it is, ready for every torture. What are you waiting for? Son of the devil, begin! Carry out your cruel designs!"

Then Paschasius summoned procurers and said to them: "Invite a crowd to take their pleasure with this woman, and let them abuse her until she is dead." But when they tried to carry her off, the Holy Spirit fixed her in place so firmly that they could not move her. Paschasius called in a thousand men and had her hands and feet bound, but still they could not lift her. He sent for a thousand yoke of oxen: the Lord's holy virgin could not be moved. Magicians were brought in to try to move her by their incantations: they did no better. "What is this witchery," Paschasius exclaimed, "that makes a thousand men unable to budge a lone maiden!" "There is no witchery here," said Lucy, "but the power of Christ; and even if you add ten thousand more, you will find me still unmovable." Paschasius had heard somewhere that urine would chase away magic, so he had the maiden drenched with urine: no effect. Next the consul, at the end of his wits, had a roaring fire built around her and boiling oil poured over her. And Lucy said: "I have prayed for this prolongation of my martyrdom in order to free believers from the fear of suffering, and to give unbelievers time to insult me!"

At this point the consul's friends, seeing how distressed he was, plunged a dagger into the martyr's throat; but, far from losing the power of speech, she said: "I make known to you that peace has been restored to the Church! This very day Maximian has died, and Diocletian has been driven from the throne. And just as God has given my sister Agatha to the city of Catania as protectress, so I am given to the city of Syracusa as mediatrix."

While the virgin was still speaking, envoys from Rome arrived to seize Paschasius and take him in chains to Rome, because Caesar had heard that he had pillaged the whole province. Arriving in Rome he was tried by the Senate and punished by decapitation. As for the virgin Lucy, she did not stir from the spot where she had suffered, nor did she breathe her last before priests had brought her the Body of the Lord and all those present had responded Amen to the Lord. There also she was buried and a church was raised in her honor. Her martyrdom took place about the year of the Lord 310.

5. Saint Thomas, Apostle

The name Thomas means abyss; or it means twofold, the Greek word for which is *didimus*; or it comes from *thomos*, which means a dividing or separating. Thomas is called abyss because he was granted insight into the depths of God's being when Christ, in answer to his question, said: "I am the way and the truth and the life." He is called twofold because he came to know the Lord's resurrection in two ways—not only by sight, like the others, but by seeing and touching. He is called dividing or separating because he separated his heart from the love of the world; or because he set himself apart from the other disciples by not at first believing that Christ had risen. Or again, Thomas comes from *totus means*, a total wanderer, one who is wholly outside himself in the love and contemplation of God; for there were three wondrous things about him that showed his love of God. Prosper speaks of this in the book *On the Contemplative Life:* "What is loving God other than to have in one's heart a fervent desire to see God, to hate sin, and to despise the world?" Or Thomas comes from *theos*, God, and *meus*, my, and therefore means "my God," because he said "My Lord and my God" when he was sure that Christ had risen.

Thomas the apostle was at Caesarea when the Lord appeared to him, saying: "Gundofor, king of India, has sent his provost Abbanes to find a man skilled in architecture. Come along and I will send you with him." Thomas answered: "Lord, send me anywhere you wish except India." God replied: "Go in safety, because I will be your guardian; and when you have converted the Indians, you shall come to me with the palm of martyrdom." Thomas: "You are my Lord and I am your servant: your will be done."

The provost was walking in the marketplace, and the Lord asked him: "Young man, what are you looking for?" The man's answer was: "My master sent me to bring home men learned in the architectural arts, to build a palace in the Roman style." Then the Lord introduced Thomas to him, stating that he was expert in that art.

The two took ship and put in at a city where the king was celebrating his daughter's nuptials and had issued an order bidding everyone to attend; otherwise his majesty would be offended. So Abbanes and the apostle went to the wedding feast. A Hebrew girl with a flute in her hand was going around saying complimentary things to each of the guests. She saw the apostle and recognized him as a Hebrew because he ate nothing and kept his eyes directed heavenwards, so she sang to him in the Hebrew tongue: "One is the God of the Hebrews, who created all things and established the seas in their place." The apostle troubled her to repeat those very same words. The wine steward meanwhile, noticing that the apostle was not eating or drinking but sat with his eyes turned toward heaven, struck him a blow on the cheek. The apostle addressed him: "It is better for you to receive here and now a punishment of brief duration, and to be granted forgiveness in the life to come. Know that I shall not leave this table before the hand that struck me is brought here by dogs." The servant went out to draw water, a lion killed him and drank his blood, dogs tore his body to pieces, and a black one carried his right hand into the midst of the feast. This greatly disturbed the whole company. The girl told them what the apostle had said, and then, throwing aside her flute, prostrated herself at Thomas's feet.

Augustine, in his book *Against Faustus*, will have none of this act of vengeance and declares that the incident is apocryphal, for which reason it is regarded as suspect on more than one point. It may, however, be surmised that what the apostle said to the steward was not intended as seeking revenge but as teaching a lesson: if Augustine's words are weighed carefully, they do not seem to express outright disapproval. In the book quoted he says: "The Manicheans read apocryphal books that were written under apostles' names by unknown fablemongers. At the time these books were written, they might well have been received by holy Church as authoritative, if saintly and learned men then living were able to examine them and found elements of truth in them. In any case those people read there that when the apostle Thomas was present, as a pilgrim and totally unknown, at a nuptial banquet, a servant slapped him with his open hand, and the apostle invoked upon him a cruel and immediate punishment; for when the man went to fetch water for the guests, a lion attacked and killed him and a dog carried to the apostle's table the hand that had dealt him a light blow on the head. What could be more cruel than this? Yet this may not be true, because, if I am not mistaken, the book also says that the apostle prayed for the offender to receive pardon in the world to come. So the compensation of a greater benefice was effected, so that by the fear aroused it was made known to those who had not known him how dear to God the apostle was, and the other man was assured of eternal happiness after this life, which had to end sooner or later.

"Whether this story is true or false is of no interest to me now. Certainly the Manicheans, who accept these writings as serious and true although the Church canon rejects them, are at least compelled to admit that the virtue of patience, which the Lord taught when he said: 'If someone strikes you on the right cheek, turn the other to him also,' can exist in the heart though not expressed outwardly by word or gesture. So the apostle, who had received the blow, rather than offering the other cheek to the servingman or urging him to strike again, would have prayed the Lord to spare the wrongdoer in the afterlife but not to let the wrong go unpunished here below. Certainly his inward disposition was one of love while he sought the outward correction as an example. Moreover, whether this story be fact or fiction, why are the Manicheans unwilling to believe that this was the thought and intention in which God's servant Moses struck down makers of idols with the sword? And if we compare punishments, what difference does it make whether the penalty be to die by the sword or to be torn to pieces by wild beasts? After all, judges, enforcing the public laws, condemn those who commit major crimes either to the beasts or to the headsman." Thus far Augustine.

Back, then, to Thomas . . . At the king's request the apostle blessed the bridegroom and the bride, saying: "Lord, give these young people the blessing of your right hand and sow in their hearts the seed of life." Then he left them, and the bridegroom found in his hand a palm branch laden with dates. After eating the fruit the couple fell asleep and both dreamed the same dream. They saw a king adorned with precious gems, who embraced them and said: "The apostle has blessed you in order that you may share eternal life." They awoke and told each other their dream, and the apostle came in to them and told them: "My King has just appeared to you, and he brings me here though the doors are closed, that through my blessing upon you you may preserve the purity of your bodies—that purity which is the queen of virtues and the fruit of eternal salvation. Virginity is the sister of the angels, the possession of all goods, victory over the passions, the prize and reward of faith, the overthrow of the demons, and the assurance of eternal joys. Lust begets corruption, of corruption pollution is born, guilt rises from pollution, confusion follows upon guilt." When he had said these things, two angels appeared to them and said: "We are the angels sent to be your guardians, and, if you are faithful to the apostle's counsel, we offer all your prayers to God." Thereupon the apostle baptized them and diligently instructed them in the truths of faith. After a long time the bride, whose name was Pelagia and who had taken the holy veil of consecration, suffered martyrdom. Her husband, called Dionysius, was ordained bishop of that city.

The apostle and Abbanes pursued their journey and came to the court of the king of India. Thomas drew up the plans for a magnificent palace, and the king gave him a large store of treasure so that he might get on with the building of the palace. Then the king set out for another province; and the apostle distributed to the people all the money he had received from the king.

During the two years of the king's absence the apostle was zealous in preaching and converted great multitudes to the faith. But when the king returned and learned what Thomas had done, he threw him into a dungeon, and Abbanes with him, intending to have them flayed and burned alive. Thereupon the king's brother, whose name was Gad, died, and preparations were under way to give him a splendid funeral. But on the fourth day after his death he returned to life, and all who saw him were terrified and fled. Gad said to the king: "Brother, the man whom you wish to have flayed and burned alive is a friend of God, and all the angels are his servants. These angels brought me to paradise and showed me a marvelous palace built of gold and silver and precious stones; and while I was admiring its beauty, they told me: 'This is the palace that Thomas built for your brother.' I said to them: 'I would like to be the doorkeeper here!' They answered: 'Your brother has shown himself unworthy of it. If you yourself wish to have it for your dwelling, we will pray the Lord to raise you to life, and you can buy the palace from your brother and pay him all the treasure he thinks he has lost.'" Gad then ran to the prison, begged the apostle to forgive his brother, struck off his chains, and pressed him to accept a precious mantle. Thomas's answer was: "Do you not know that those who yearn for power in heavenly things have no desire for earthly possessions?"

The apostle now emerged from his prison. The king came to meet him, threw himself at his feet, and pleaded for pardon. "God has granted both of you much," Thomas said, "in order that he might show you his secrets. Believe in

Christ and be baptized, so that you may share in the everlasting kingdom." The king's brother said: "I have seen the palace you built for my brother and have bought it for myself!" The apostle responded: "That depends on your brother's decision." The king broke in: "The palace will be mine! Let the apostle build you another; or if that is not possible, we shall live there together!" Thomas told them: "In heaven there are countless palaces, prepared from the beginning of time, and they are won by prayer and the giving of alms. As for your riches, they can precede you there but they cannot follow you."

A month later, the apostle called together all the poor people of the region, and when they were all assembled, he summoned the sick, the lame, and the feeble to come forth from the crowd. Then he prayed over them, and those among them who had received the faith responded Amen. Then a great light came from heaven and flashed over the apostle and all the rest for half an hour, and they fell to the ground as if struck dead by lightning. The apostle rose and said: "Stand up! My Lord has come like lightning and has cured them all!" So everybody stood up whole and healthy, and glorified God and his apostle.

Then Thomas began to teach the people and explained to them the twelve degrees of virtue. The first degree is to believe in a God one in essence and trine in persons. The apostle showed them by means of tangible examples how three persons can be in one essence, and said: "Man's wisdom is one, yet it is composed of understanding, memory, and reason. Reason is the power by which you discover what you have not yet learned; memory enables you to retain what you have learned; understanding allows you to comprehend what is shown or taught to you. The vine, too, is made up of three elements, wood, leaves, and fruit, and yet they form one vine. One head comprises four senses—sight, taste, hearing, and smell—they being several and the head being one." The second degree of virtue consists in receiving baptism; the third in abstaining from fornication; the fourth in controlling greed; the fifth in shunning gluttony; the sixth in doing penance; the seventh in perseverance in good works; the eighth in generous care of strangers; the ninth in seeking the will of God and doing it willingly; the tenth in seeking out what God does not want us to do and not doing it; the eleventh in love of friends and enemies; the twelfth in watchful care to observe all of this. And when the apostle had finished his preaching, he baptized nine thousand men, not to mention the women and children.

Next Thomas went to Upper India and gained fame by his many miracles. He brought the light of faith to Syntice, who was a friend of Migdomia the wife of Carisius, a cousin of the king. Migdomia asked Syntice: "Do you think I might see the apostle?" Then, taking her friend's advice, she put off her rich garments and mingled with the poor women who were hearing the apostle's preaching. Thomas began to expound upon the misery of this life and said, among other things: "This is indeed a miserable life, subject to all sorts of misfortune, and so fleeting that when one thinks one has it well in hand, it slips away and is gone." Then he exhorted his hearers to receive the word of God gladly and offered four reasons, comparing the word to four kinds of things: to an eye-salve, because it enlightens the eyes of our intellect; to a potion, for it purifies and cleanses our will of all carnal love; to a plaster, because it heals the wounds of our sins; and to food, because it delights us with the love of the things of heaven. And just as these things can do no good to the ailing person unless he uses them well, so the word of God cannot benefit the ailing soul unless it is heard devoutly. Migdomia believed the apostle's preaching and thereafter shunned her husband's bed with horror. At this Carisius complained to the king and had Thomas thrown into prison. Migdomia visited him there and implored him to pardon her for being the cause of his plight; but he consoled her kindly and said that he was happy to bear all his suffering. Then Carisius asked the king to send the queen, his wife's sister, to his wife, hoping that she might bring Migdomia back to him. But the queen, carrying out her mission, was converted by the very one she sought to lead astray; and seeing the great miracles the apostle performed, she said: "Those who refuse to believe so many signs and works are damned by God!" Meanwhile Thomas spoke briefly to all present on three points: they should love the Church, honor the priests, and come together gladly to hear the word of God.

When the queen returned home, the king asked her: "What kept you away so long?" The queen's answer was: "I thought Migdomia was stupid, but on the contrary she is very wise. She led me to the apostle of God and let me learn the way of truth. The really stupid ones are those who will not believe in Christ!" And from then on she refused to lie with her husband. The king, dumbfounded, said to his brother-in-law: "I tried to get your wife back for you, and instead I have lost my own; she treats me worse than yours treats you!"

The king then ordered the apostle to be brought before him, hands bound, and commanded him to counsel the wives to return to their husbands. The apostle proceeded to prove to the king, by three examples—a king, a tower, a spring of water—that as long as the men persisted in their error, the women must not do as commanded. "You," he said, "being a king, want no dirty servants around you, but only clean servingmen and handmaids. How much more surely should you believe that God loves chaste, clean servants? Am I wrong in preaching that God loves in his servants what you love in yours? I have raised a high tower, and you tell me, the builder, to tear it down? I have dug a deep well and brought up a flowing spring, and you tell me to shut it off?"

This was too much for the king. He sent for iron plates fired to red heat and ordered the apostle to stand barefoot on them. Instantly, at a sign from God, a spring rose from the ground and cooled the iron. Then the king, following his brother-in-law's advice, had him thrown into a fiery furnace, but it was extinguished immediately, and the apostle emerged unharmed the next morning. Carisius said to the king: "Command him to sacrifice to the god of the sun. That will bring down on him the wrath of his god, who so far has been protecting him." So they tried to force Thomas to do this, but he said to the king: "You are greater than the things you make, yet you spurn the worship of the true God and worship a handmade idol instead. You think, as Carisius does, that my God will be angered with me after I worship your god; but it is against your god that he will be angered, and he will destroy him the moment I adore him. If my God does not destroy yours when I offer him worship, I will offer sacrifice: if the contrary, promise me that you will believe my God." To this the king retorted: "How dare you speak to me as equal to equal!"

Now the apostle, speaking in Hebrew, commanded the demon who was in the idol to demolish it as soon as he bent the knee before it. Then, falling to his knees, he said: "See, I adore, but not this idol; I worship, but not this metal; I adore, but not this graven image. I adore my Lord Jesus Christ, in whose name I command you, O demon lurking inside, to destroy the idol!" And at once the image melted as if it were made of wax. At this all the priests bellowed like cattle, and the high priest of the temple, raising his sword, drove it through the apostle, crying: "Thus shall I avenge the insult done to my god!" The king and Carisius fled, seeing that the people wished to avenge the apostle and burn the high priest alive. The Christians meanwhile carried away the saint's body and gave it honorable burial.

Long afterwards, around the year of our Lord 230, Emperor Alexander, at the request of the Syrians, transferred the apostle's body to the city of Edessa, which formerly was called Rages of the Medes. In that city no heretic, no Jew, no pagan can live, no tyrant can do harm, since Abgar, king of the city, had been found worthy of receiving a letter written by the hand of the Lord. If any people stirs up an insurrection against the city, a baptized child, standing above the city gate, reads the letter; and that very day, thanks to the Savior's writing and the merits of Thomas the apostle, the enemy either goes away or makes peace.

In his book *On the Life and Death of the Saints* Isidore says of Saint Thomas: "Thomas, a disciple of Christ who bore a resemblance to the Savior, not believing what he heard, believed when he saw the Lord. He preached the Gospel to the Parthians, the Medes, the Persians, the Hircanians, and the Bactrians. Setting foot on the shores of the Orient and penetrating into the interior, he preached to the peoples there until the day of his martyrdom. He died from the thrust of a lance." So Isidore. Chrysostom also says that Thomas made his way to the land of the Magi who had come to adore the Christ, and that he baptized them and they helped to propagate the Christian faith.

✳

---

*About the feasts that occur within
the time that falls partly in the time of reconciliation and
partly in the time of pilgrimage*

We have spoken about the feasts that occur in the time of renewal, which began with Moses and the prophets and lasted until the advent of Christ in the flesh, and which the Church represents from the beginning of Advent to the Birth of Christ. We now take up the feast days that occur within the period that falls partly in the time of reconciliation and partly in the time of pilgrimage. This period the Church represents from the Birth of Christ to Septuagesima, as was noted in the Prologue.

✳

---

6. The Birth of Our Lord Jesus Christ According to the Flesh

The birth of our Lord Jesus Christ in the flesh took place, according to some sources, 5,228 years after Adam, while others say 6,000 years, or, according to Eusebius of Caesarea in his chronicle, 5,199. Methodius seems to have arrived at the figure 6,000 by mystical rather than chronological calculation.

In any case Octavian was the Roman emperor at the time. His first given name was Octavian: he was called Caesar after Julius Caesar whose nephew he was, Augustus because he augmented the state, Emperor to pay honor to his dignity by distinguishing him from the earlier kings, he being the first to bear this title. When the Son of God became incarnate, the universe enjoyed such peace that the emperor of the Romans reigned alone and peacefully over the whole world. It was the Lord's will that since he was coming to give us peace in time and in eternity, temporal peace should lend luster to the time of his birth.

In those days Caesar Augustus, being master of the world, wished to know how many provinces, cities, fortresses, villages, and men there were in the world. He therefore decreed, as we read in the *Scholastic History*, that all the men in his empire should go to the city from which they drew their origin, and pay to the governor of the province a silver denarius as a profession of their submission to the Roman Empire, since the coin bore Caesar's name and image. This payment was called both profession and enrollment, but for different reasons. The word *profession* was used because each man, when he remitted the head tax (the aforementioned denarius) to the provincial governor, placed it on his own head and declared aloud and in public that he was a subject of the empire. *Enrollment* meant that those who paid the head tax were given a number which was recorded in the rolls.

This first enrollment was carried out by Cyrinus the governor of Syria. It was designated "first" (as we are told in the *Scholastic History* regarding Cyrinus) because Judea is said to be the umbilicus of our habitable earth, and therefore the census was initiated there and later carried on throughout the surrounding regions and by other governors. Or "first" here stands for "universal," the others being local; or perhaps the first enrollment was the head count made in the city by the governor, the second counted the cities in a region and was made by Caesar's legate, and the third accounted for the regions and was made in the presence of Caesar.

Joseph, being of the house and family of David, went up from Nazareth to Bethlehem to be enrolled. The time was approaching for Mary to be delivered, and Joseph took her with him. Not knowing how long he would be away, and unwilling to leave this treasure that God had entrusted to him in the care of strangers, he preferred to guard her with his own vigilant attention. As they drew near to Bethlehem (as Brother Bartholomew, drawing upon the *Book of the Infancy of the Savior*, testifies in his compilation), the Virgin saw part of the populace rejoicing and part lamenting. An angel explained this to her, saying: "Those who rejoice are the people of the Gentiles, who in the seed of Abraham will receive eternal blessing. Those who grieve are the Jewish people, rejected by God in accordance with their deserts."

So Joseph and Mary came to Bethlehem. They were poor and could find no lodging in the inns, which already were full of people who had come for the same purpose; so they had to take shelter in a public passage. This passage, according to the *Scholastic History*, was located between two houses. It provided some overhead covering and served as a meeting place for townspeople who came there to talk or eat together in their free time, or when the weather was bad. Perhaps Joseph set up a manger for his ox and his ass, or, as some think, peasants coming in to market were used to tying up their animals there and the crib was ready to hand. In that place, at midnight, the eve of Sunday, the blessed Virgin gave birth to her Son and laid him on hay in the manger. This hay, which the ox and the ass abstained from eating, was brought to Rome by Saint Helena, as we learn from the *Scholastic History*.

The birth of Christ was miraculous as regards the mother, the child born of her, and the mode of the birth.

As regards the mother, she was a virgin both before and after giving birth, and the fact that she remained a virgin is assured by five proofs. The first is from the prophet Isaiah, who in his seventh chapter says: "Behold, a virgin shall conceive and bear a son, and his name shall be called Emmanuel." The second is by way of figure: it was prefigured both by Aaron's rod, which blossomed without any human care, and by Ezechiel's gate, which always remained closed. The third is Joseph's guardianship: he watched over her and so was a witness to her virginity. There is a fourth proof, for Bartholomew (apparently borrowing from the *Book of the Infancy of the Savior*) has it that when the hour had come for Mary to be delivered, Joseph called two midwives, the one being called Zebel and the other Salome—not that he doubted that the Virgin would bring forth the Son of God, but that he was following the custom of the country. When Zebel, probing and realizing that Mary was a virgin, cried out that a virgin had given birth, Salome did not believe it and tried to find out for herself, but her hand instantly withered; then an angel appeared and told her to touch the child, and she was cured immediately. The fifth proof is a miraculous event. As Pope Innocent III testifies, during the twelve years when Rome enjoyed peace, the Romans built a Temple of Peace and placed a statue of Romulus in it. Apollo was asked how long the temple would stand, and the answer was that it would be until a virgin bore a child. Hearing this, the people said that the temple was eternal, for they thought it impossible that such a thing could happen; and an inscription, TEMPLUM PACIS AETERNUM, was carved over the doors. But in the very night when Mary bore Christ, the temple crumbled to the ground, and on its site the church of Santa Maria Nuova stands today.

The birth of the Lord was no less miraculous as regards the Child himself. As Bernard says, in one and the same person the eternal, the ancient, and the new wondrously came together: the eternal, namely, the Godhead, the ancient, namely, the flesh descended from Adam, and the new, since a new soul was created. Moreover, as the same author says, God wrought three mixtures or three works, so marvelously singular that such things had not been done before nor would be done ever again. For God and man, a mother and a virgin, faith and the human heart, were conjoined. The first is indeed a marvel, because God and the slime of the earth, majesty and infirmity, such great degrees of baseness and sublimity were joined; for nothing is more sublime than God and nothing more base than mud. The second conjunction is just as miraculous. From the beginning of the world it was unheard-of that there was a virgin who became a mother or a mother who remained a virgin. The third wonder is inferior to the other two but great nonetheless: the marvel is that the human heart could believe that God became man and the virgin who bore him was still a virgin. So far Bernard.

The mode of the birth also was miraculous. It was above nature, by the fact that a virgin conceived; above reason in that God was begotten; above the human condition, in that the birth was painless; and above what is customary, since the conception was by the Holy Spirit, for the Virgin begot her Son not from human seed but from a mystic breath. Indeed the Holy Spirit took the most pure and most chaste blood of the Virgin and out of it formed that body. So it is that God showed a fourth wondrous way of making man. Anselm says: "God can make man in four ways, namely, without a man or a woman (as he made Adam), from a man without a woman (as he made Eve), from a man and a woman (the usual way), and from a woman without a man (as was done miraculously today)."

The birth of the Lord was made known in a multiplicity of ways. To begin with, it was made manifest through every level or class of creatures. There are the creatures which have existence only, such as things that are simply material or corporeal, like stones; others have existence and life, like plants and trees; others have existence, life, and sensation, namely, the animals; still others, in addition to the above endowments, have reason, as human beings do; and finally some creatures have understanding, or knowledge, and these are the angels.

Through all these creatures the birth of Christ is today made known. Of those that are purely corporeal there are three kinds, the opaque, the transparent or pervious, and the lucid, or luminous. Opaque creatures manifested the Nativity, for example by the destruction of the temple in Rome, as above described, and also by the collapse of other statues that fell in a great many other places. For instance, we read in the *Scholastic History* that the prophet Jeremiah, going down to Egypt after the death of Godolias, indicated to the Egyptian kings that their idols would fall to pieces when a virgin bore a son. For that reason the priests of the idols made a statue of a virgin holding a male child in her lap, set it up in a secret place in the temple, and there worshiped it. When King Ptolemy asked them the meaning of this, they told him that it was a mystery handed down by the fathers, who had received it from a holy man, a prophet, and they believed that what was foretold would really happen.

Now regarding transparent or pervious corporeal beings: in the night of the Lord's birth the darkness of night was turned into the brightness of day. In Rome it also happened (as attested by Orosius and Pope Innocent III) that a fountain of water turned to oil and burst into the Tiber, spreading very widely all that day; and the Sibyl had foretold that when a fountain of oil sprang up, a Savior would be born.

Then there are the luminous corporeal creatures, such as the supercelestial: these too revealed the Nativity. For on that very day, according to what the ancients relate and Chrysostom affirms, the Magi were praying on a mountaintop and a star appeared above them. This star had the shape of a most beautiful boy over whose head a cross shone brilliantly. He spoke to the Magi and told them to make their way to Judea, where they would find a newborn child. That same day three suns appeared in the East and gradually melded into one solar body. This signified that knowledge of the one and triune God was about to be given to the world, or that he in whom soul, flesh, and divinity were united had now been born. In the *Scholastic History*, however, it is said that the three suns appeared not on the day of the Nativity but some time earlier: Eusebius in his chronicle puts it after the death of Julius Caesar. The emperor Octavian (as Pope Innocent says) had brought the whole world under Roman rule, and the Senate was so well pleased that they wished to worship him as a god. The prudent emperor, however, knowing full well that he was mortal, refused to usurp the title of immortality. The senators insisted that he summon the sibylline prophetess and find out, through her oracles, whether someone greater than he was to be born in the world. When, therefore, on the day of Christ's birth, the council was convoked to study this matter and the Sibyl, alone in a room with the emperor, consulted her oracles, at midday a golden circle appeared around the sun, and in the middle of the circle a most beautiful virgin holding a child in her lap. The Sibyl showed this to Caesar, and while the emperor marveled at the vision, he heard a voice saying to him: "This is the altar of Heaven." The Sibyl then told him: "This child is greater than you, and it is he that you must worship." That same room was dedicated to the honor of Holy Mary and to this day is called Santa Maria Ara Coeli.

The emperor, understanding that the child he had seen was greater than he, offered incense to him and refused to be called God. With reference to this Orosius says: "In Octavian's day, about the third hour, in the limpid, pure, serene sky, a circle that looked like a rainbow surrounded the orb of the sun, as if to show that One was to come who alone had made the sun and the whole world and ruled it." So far Orosius. Eutropius gives a similar account of the event. And Timotheus the historian reports that he had learned from ancient Roman histories that in the thirty-fifth year of his reign Octavian went up the Capitoline hill and anxiously asked the gods who would succeed him as ruler of the empire. He then heard a voice telling him that an ethereal child, begotten in eternity of the living God, was presently to be born of a virgin undefiled, the God-man without stain. Having heard this, he erected an altar on which he inscribed the title: THIS IS THE ALTAR OF THE SON OF THE LIVING GOD.

Christ's birth was manifested also by creatures having existence and life, like plants and trees. Thus, on the night of the Christ's birth, the vineyards of Engedi, which produce balsam, bloomed and bore fruit from which balsam flowed.

Living and sentient creatures gave their own testimony. Setting out for Bethlehem with Mary, who was with child, Joseph took along an ox (perhaps to sell it for money to pay the head tax and buy food and the like) and an ass, no doubt for Mary to ride on. The ox and the ass, miraculously recognizing the Lord, went to their knees and worshiped him.

Humankind, the creatures possessed of reason and discernment, were represented by the shepherds. At the hour of the Nativity they were watching over their flock, as was customary twice a year on the longest and shortest nights. It was the custom among the Gentiles to observe these nocturnal vigils at each solstice, namely, the summer one around the feast of John the Baptist and the winter one close to Christmas, by way of veneration of the sun; and the Jews may have borrowed the practice from the neighboring peoples. So the angel of the Lord appeared to the shepherds, announced the birth of the Savior, and told them how they could find him, whereupon a host of angels sang: "Glory to God in the highest and peace to men of good will." The shepherds went and found everything just as the angel had told them.

We have noted that this manifestation came also through Caesar Augustus, who then decreed that no one should dare to call him God, as Orosius testified. In some chronicle we also read that as the day of the Lord's birth drew near, Octavian built public roads throughout his empire and remitted all the Romans' debts. And even the sodomites gave witness by being exterminated wherever they were in the world on that night, as Jerome says: "A light rose over them so bright that all who practiced this vice were wiped out; and Christ did this in order that no such uncleanness might be found in the nature he had assumed." For, as Augustine says, God, seeing that a vice contrary to nature was rife in human nature, hesitated to become incarnate.

Lastly, the creatures possessing existence, life, discernment, and understanding showed forth the birth of the Lord, when the angels announced it to the shepherds, as noted above.

We may also consider that the manifestation of Christ's birth was useful to us in several ways. Firstly, it served to confound the demons, for they could no longer overpower us as they had before. We read that Saint Hugh, abbot of Cluny, on the night of the Nativity had a vision of the Blessed Virgin holding her Son in her arms and saying: "The day is come when the oracles of the prophets are fulfilled. Where now is the Enemy who until now prevailed over men?" At the sound of her voice the devil came up through the floor to taunt the Virgin; but iniquity gave the lie to itself, because while he prowled around the monks' quarters, their devoutness drove him from the oratory, their pious readings from the refectory, their scant bedding from the dormitory, their patience from the chapter house. Furthermore we read in a book by Peter of Cluny that the night before the birth of the Lord the Blessed Virgin appeared to Saint Hugh, abbot of Cluny, holding her Son in her lap and playing with him, and the Child said: "You know, Mother, that the Church celebrates my birthday with great praise, feasting, and dancing. And where now is the power of the devil? What can he do now? What can he say?" Then the devil was seen to rise out of the ground, as it were, and say: "Even if I cannot enter the church where your praises are chanted, I shall get into the chapter house, the dormitory, the refectory!" But when he tried to do this, he found the chapter house door too narrow for his gross girth, the door of the dormitory too low for his height, and the door of the refectory fastened with bars and bolts, these being the charity of those who served there, their eagerness to hear the readings, and the sparseness of the food and drink consumed there. So, confounded, he vanished.

Secondly, Christ's birth is useful to us in obtaining pardon for sin. We read in a certain book of examples that a fallen woman, finally repenting of her sins, despaired of pardon. Thinking of the Last Judgment she considered herself worthy of hell; turning her mind to heaven she thought of herself as unclean; dwelling on the Lord's passion, she knew she had been ungrateful. But then she thought to herself that children are more ready to be kind, so she appealed to Christ in the name of his childhood, and a voice told her that she had won forgiveness.

Thirdly, the Nativity benefits us by curing our infirmities. Bernard says about this benefit: "The human race labored under a threefold malady, beginning, middle, and end. Man's birth was unclean, his life perverse, his death perilous. Christ came and brought a threefold remedy: his birth cleansed ours, his life put order in ours, his death destroyed ours." Thus far Bernard.

Lastly, the Lord's birth serves us by humbling our pride. So Augustine says that the humility of the Son of God, which he demonstrated in his incarnation, was for us "an example, a sacrament, and a medicine. A most fitting example it was for man's imitation, a high sacrament by which we were delivered from the bonds of sin, and a most powerful medicine, which heals the tumor of our pride." So far Augustine. For the pride of the first man was cured by the humility of Christ. Note how exactly the Savior's humility corresponds to the pride of the betrayer. The first man's pride was against God; it went as high as God and even above God. It was against God because it was contrary to the commandment by which he forbade eating from the tree of the knowledge of good and evil. It reached God's height because Adam aspired to divinity, believing what the devil had said: "You will be like gods." It was above God, as Anselm says, because it willed what God willed that man should not will. Thus Adam placed his own will above the will of God. But God's Son, according to John of Damascus, humbled himself for the sake of mankind, not against us: his humility reached man's level and above man. It was for men's sake because it was for their welfare and salvation; it reached men's level because the mode of birth was similar, and it was above them by the dissimilarity of the birth. In one way Christ's birth was like our own, namely, that he was born of a woman and came forth through the same portal, but in another way it was unlike ours, because he was conceived by the Holy Spirit and born of the Virgin Mary.

---

7. Saint Anastasia

The name Anastasia is derived from *ana*, meaning above, and *stasis*, meaning standing or stand; for the saint stood on high, raised above vice and sin to virtue.

Anastasia was born into a noble Roman family; her father, Praetaxtatus, was a pagan, but her mother Faustina was Christian. Anastasia was raised in the Christian faith by her mother and Saint Chrysogonus. Given in marriage against her will to a young man named Publius, she feigned an enfeebling sickness and kept herself apart from him. Then he found out that she was visiting the Christians in prison and ministering to their needs, dressed as a poor woman and accompanied by one of her handmaids. He therefore kept her in strict confinement, even denying her food, hoping to cause her death and to live in luxury on her great wealth. Anastasia, expecting to die, wrote piteous letters to Chrysogonus, who replied with consolatory messages. However, it was her husband who died, and she was set free.

She had three very beautiful servingmaids who were sisters, of whom one was named Agapete, the second Theonia, the third Irene. All three were Christians. A certain prefect was smitten with desire for them and, when they refused his advances, had them shut up in a room where the cooking utensils were stored.

There he went, intent upon having his way with them; but he was deprived of his senses and, thinking that he was dealing with the three virgins, caressed and kissed the stoves, kettles, pots, and other utensils. Having satisfied himself in this manner he went out blackened with soot and his clothes in tatters. His slaves, who were waiting for him outside and saw him in this condition, thought they were seeing a demon, beat him with sticks, and ran away, leaving him alone. He set out to complain to the emperor, and on the way some struck him with rods; others threw mud and dust at him, thinking he had gone mad. His eyes, however, were blinded and he could not see how he looked to others, nor could he understand why they were mocking him instead of paying him the honor to which he was accustomed. He thought, of course, that he was dressed in white clothes as everybody else was. Finally he was told of his sorry state and thought that the maidens had worked some magic upon him. He therefore commanded that they be brought before him and stripped, so that he might at least enjoy the sight of their nudity, but it turned out that their clothing clung so tightly to their bodies that no one could take it off. The prefect was surprised at this and fell into a sleep so deep that he snored and could not be awakened even by blows. Finally the virgins were crowned with martyrdom.

As for Anastasia, the emperor handed her over to another prefect, with permission to marry her if he could make her sacrifice to the gods. The prefect led her to the bridal chamber and tried to embrace her: instantly he was stricken blind. He went to the idols and asked if he might be cured. Their answer was: "Because you saddened the holy Anastasia, you have been turned over to us to be tortured forever with us in hell." And as he was being led to his house, he died in the arms of his servants.

Anastasia was then entrusted to still another prefect, with orders to hold her in the tightest security. This man knew that she was very rich and said to her secretly: "Anastasia, if you want to be a Christian, do as your Lord commanded when he said that anyone who did not renounce all his possessions could not be his disciple. Give me therefore all that is yours, then go wherever you wish and be a true Christian!" But she replied: "God commanded that I give up all that I have and give to the poor, not to the rich. But you are rich! Therefore if I gave you anything, I would go against God's command."

Then Anastasia was thrown into a dreadful prison to be starved to death, but Saint Theodora, who already had gained the crown of martyrdom, fed her for two months with food from heaven. Finally she was taken, with two hundred virgins, to the island of Palmaria, to which many Christians had been banished. Some days later the prefect summoned all of them to his presence, and had Anastasia bound to a stake and burned alive; the rest he put to death in various ways. Among them there was a man who had been despoiled of his wealth several times, and who repeated over and over: "At least you cannot take Christ away from me!" Apollonia had the body of Saint Anastasia buried in her garden, and there built a church in her honor. She suffered martyrdom in the reign of Diocletian, which began about the year of the Lord 287.

8. Saint Stephen

The name Stephen—Stephanus in Latin—comes from the Greek word for crown—*stephanos*: in Hebrew the name means norm or rule. Stephen was the crown of the martyrs in the sense that he was the first martyr under the New Testament, as Abel was under the Old. He was a norm, i.e., an example or rule, showing others how to suffer for Christ, as well as how to act and live according to the truth, or how to pray for one's enemies. Or Stephen (Stephanus) comes from *strenue fans*, speaking strenuously or with zeal, as the saint showed in his manner of speaking and his brilliant preaching of the word of God. Or Stephen may be understood as *strenue stans* or *fans anus*, laudably standing and instructing and ruling over old women, here meaning widows, because the apostles put him in charge of the widows, who were literally old women. So Stephen is a crown because he is first in martyrdom, a norm by his example in suffering and his way of life, a zealous speaker in his praiseworthy teaching of the widows.

Stephen was one of the seven deacons whom the apostles ordained for ministry. As the number of the disciples increased, the Christians of Gentile origin began to murmur against those converted from Judaism, because the widows among the former were being neglected in the daily ministry. The cause of these complaints may have been either that the widows were not allowed to do any service, or that they were given too much work to do in the daily round. Whatever the trouble was, the apostles had assigned some services to the widows, so that they could devote themselves entirely to preaching. Now, confronted with these complaints, they called all the disciples together and said to them: "It is not right that we should give up preaching the word of God to serve tables . . . (The *Gloss* adds: 'Because the food of the mind is better than feasts for the body.') . . . Therefore, brethren, pick out from among you seven men of good repute, full of the spirit and of wisdom, whom we may appoint to this duty . . . (The *Gloss*: '. . . to serve or to supervise the servers.') . . . But we will devote ourselves to prayer and to the preaching of the word." This plan pleased the assemblage and they elected seven men, of whom Stephen stood out foremost and as leader, and brought them to the apostles, who imposed hands on them.

Now Stephen, full of grace and fortitude, did great wonders and signs among the people. Then the Jews, being jealous of him and wanting to discredit him and find him guilty, joined issue with him in three ways—by argument, by suborning false witnesses, and by putting him to the torture. But he won the arguments, convicted the false witnesses, and triumphed over his torturers, and in each encounter aid was given him from heaven. In the first, the Holy Spirit aided him with divine wisdom. In the second it was his face, like the face of an angel, that terrified the false witnesses. In the third Christ himself appeared, ready to give aid and to strengthen the martyr. In each of the three conflicts, therefore, three aspects are to be noted—the battle joined, the aid given, and the triumph achieved. A brief review of the incidents will show all this clearly.

Thus, when Stephen's miracles and preaching aroused the envy of the Jews, they launched the first battle, trying to defeat him by argument. Some of them who rose belonged to the synagogue of the Libertines, so called either after the region they came from or because they were sons of people called *Liberti*, i.e., freedmen, men manumitted from slavery and given their freedom. So they were of servile stock and at first resisted the faith. There were also Cyrenians from the city of Cyrene, Alexandrians, and men from Cilicia and Asia. All of them disputed with Stephen. There we have the first battle. Then comes the triumph: they could not stand up against his wisdom. Lastly, there is the aid—the Spirit, who spoke in him.

Stephen's opponents saw that they could not overcome him by that approach and craftily turned to the second one, namely, the testimony of false witnesses. Into the council they brought two false witnesses who accused the saint of four blasphemies, namely, against God, against Moses, against the Law, and against the Tabernacle or Temple. There is the battle. All of those sitting in the council gazed upon Stephen and saw that his face was like the face of an angel. There is the aid. Then came the victory, when the false witnesses were refuted point by point. The high priest asked Stephen if their testimony was true, and the blessed one proved that he was innocent of the four charges brought against him, taking them in order. Blasphemy against God? The God, he said, who spoke to the fathers and the prophets was the God of glory, and he praised God's glory according to the three ways the term could be explained. God is the God of glory in the sense that he bestows glory: "Whosoever shall glorify me, him will I glorify."[1] He is the God of glory in the sense that he contains glory in himself: "With me are riches and glory."[2] He is the God to whom all creation owes glory: "To the King of the ages, immortal, invisible, the only God, be honor and glory forever."[3] So God glorifies, is glorified, and is worthy of glorification.

Stephen then took up the second accusation, blasphemy against Moses, by commending Moses on many grounds, but principally on three—the fervor of his zeal when he struck and killed an Egyptian; his working of miracles, which he performed in Egypt and in the desert; and his familiar friendship with God, since he spoke familiarly with God more than once. As for the charge of blasphemy against the Law, he commended the Law on three grounds: by reason of the Giver, God himself, of the administrator, mighty Moses, and of the purpose, because the Law gives life. Coming to the accusation of blasphemy against the Temple, he refuted it by commending the Temple on four grounds: that it was

[1] 3 Kings 2:30.   [2] Prov. 8:18.   [3] 1 Tim. 1:17.

ordered by God, that the way it was to be built was shown in a vision, that it was completed by Moses, and that it contained the Ark of the Covenant. The Temple, he added, succeeded the Tabernacle. By his reasoning, therefore, blessed Stephen proved himself clean of the crimes of which he was accused.

The Jews realized that the second attack was as futile as the first, so they resorted to the third, the inflicting of torture and pain, thus embarking on the third battle. Blessed Stephen saw what they were about and, wishing to observe the Lord's command regarding fraternal correction, tried to correct them and recall them from such malice by three means: first, by shaming them; second, by arousing their fear; third, by demonstrating his love for them. To shame them he reproached them for their hardness of heart and for putting saints to death. "You, stiff-necked and uncircumcised in heart and ears, you have always resisted the Holy Spirit. Like father, like son! Which of the prophets did your fathers not persecute? They even killed those who foretold the coming of the just One." Thus, as the *Gloss* says, he posited three degrees of wickedness—resisting the Holy Spirit, persecuting the prophets, some of whom, with increasing malice, they put to death. Shame on them! The forehead of a strumpet was theirs; they knew not how to blush and so be deterred from pursuing their evil designs. But, far from feeling shame, his hearers were cut to the heart and gnashed their teeth at him.

Next, therefore, he tried to correct them by fear, saying that he saw Jesus standing at God's right hand as though ready to help him and condemn his adversaries. Indeed Stephen, full of the Holy Spirit and looking up steadfastly to heaven, saw the glory of God and said: "Behold, I see the heavens opened and Jesus standing on the right hand of God!" But for all his efforts to correct them through shame and fear, they not only did not desist but were worse than before, and, crying out with a loud voice, they stopped their ears (so as not to hear blasphemy, the *Gloss* explains) and with one accord ran violently upon him, cast him outside the city, and stoned him. In doing this they judged that they were acting according to the Law, which made it mandatory to stone a blasphemer outside the camp. And the two false witnesses, who by law were to cast the first stone, took off their garments (lest these be made unclean by contact with the blasphemer, or in order to be more at ease while throwing the stones) and laid them at the feet of a young man whose name was Saul and who later was called Paul. He, by standing guard over their garments and giving them more freedom to stone the victim, shared the guilt of all of them in the stoning.

Stephen had failed to win them over through shame or fear: now he had recourse to his third weapon, love. Could he have shown greater love than by praying for himself and for them? He prayed for himself, that his passion might not be prolonged and their guilt thereby augmented, and for them, that they be not held guilty of this sin. We read that as they were stoning him, he called upon God and said: "Lord Jesus, receive my spirit." And, falling to his knees, he cried out with a loud voice, saying: "Lord, lay not this sin to their charge, because they know not what they do!" See here his wondrous love! He stood while praying for himself, but praying for those who stoned him he knelt, as though he desired that the prayer he offered for them be heard even more than the prayer he poured out for himself. He knelt for them rather than for himself, because, as the *Gloss* says at this place, their greater iniquity demanded a greater supplication to remedy it. In this the martyr also imitated Christ, who in his passion prayed for himself, saying: "Into thy hands I commend my spirit"; and for his executioners, saying: "Father, forgive them, for they know not what they do." And when Stephen had made his prayer, he fell asleep in the Lord. The *Gloss* notes: "How beautifully it is said that he fell asleep, and not that he died, because he offered a sacrifice of love and fell asleep in the hope of resurrection."

Stephen's martyrdom took place on the third day of August in the year of our Lord's ascension. Saint Gamaliel, and Nicodemus who stood up for the Christians in all the councils of the Jews, buried him in a plot of land that belonged to Gamaliel, and made great mourning over him.

A violent persecution now broke out against the Christians who were in Jerusalem: since Stephen, one of their leaders, had been killed, the rest were hotly pursued, to the point that all the Christians (except the apostles, who were braver than the others) scattered throughout the territory of the Jews. This accorded with the Lord's command to them: "If they persecute you in one town, flee to another."

The eminent doctor Augustine relates that the blessed Stephen shone because of the countless miracles attributed to him. He raised six dead persons to life, cured many who were suffering from various illnesses, and performed other miracles worth remembering. Augustine says, for instance, that flowers which had been laid on the saint's altar cured sick persons to whom they were later applied. Cloths laid on the altar likewise cured many. In the twenty-second book of *The City of God* he reports that a blind woman recovered her sight when flowers taken from the altar were applied to her eyes. In the same book he tells the story of one of the city's leading men, named Martial, who was an unbeliever and absolutely refused to be converted. This man fell gravely ill, and his son-in-law, a devout Christian, went to the church of Saint Stephen, took some flowers from the altar, and placed them secretly on the bed near his father-in-law's head. The sick man slept on them and, when he awoke at the break of dawn, called out that someone should go and bring the bishop to him. The bishop was not at home, but another priest came to Martial's bedside. Martial declared that he now believed, and asked to be baptized. Thereafter, as long as he lived, he repeated the words: "Christ, receive my spirit," not knowing that these were Saint Stephen's last words.

Augustine also tells of a lady named Petronia, who had suffered for a long time from a very serious illness and had tried many remedies without the slightest success. At one point she consulted a certain Jew, who gave her a ring with a stone in it and advised her to tie it with a string against her bare flesh, because the stone had power to cure her. She followed his advice, but it did her no good. Then she went to the church of the first martyr and prayed earnestly to Saint Stephen for help. Immediately the ring fell to the ground, although the string was unbroken and the ring and the stone undamaged; and at that instant the woman's health was completely restored.

Still another miracle from the same source. . . . At Caesarea of Cappadocia lived a noble lady who was bereft of her husband but was surrounded by a fine flock of children, including seven boys and three girls. One day they offended their mother and she laid a curse upon them. Divine punishment followed the mother's curse, and the children were stricken with a dreadful ailment. Their limbs were afflicted by a horrible trembling, and they were ashamed to be seen by the people around them; so they wandered far and wide, and wherever they went, they were stared at. Two of them, a brother and a sister named Paul and Palladia, reached Hippo and told their story to Saint Augustine, who was bishop of that city. It was then two weeks before Easter, and the brother and sister went every day to the church of Saint Stephen, beseeching the saint to obtain their health. On Easter day, when the church was filled with the faithful, Paul suddenly went through the gates of the sanctuary and prostrated himself in faith and reverence before the altar, praying; and while the assemblage waited for him to come out, suddenly he stood up cured, and the trembling of his body never returned. The lad was brought to Augustine, who showed him to the people and promised to write an account of this miracle and read it to them the next day. While he was still speaking and the sister, Palladia, was standing there shaking in every limb, she suddenly broke from the crowd, went through the gates to Saint Stephen's altar, seemed to fall asleep, and rose entirely cured. She in turn was shown to the assembly, and a great chorus of thanksgiving went up to God and Saint Stephen for the health of the two young people. We should add that Orosius, coming back to Augustine after a visit to Saint Jerome, had brought relics of Saint Stephen, and it was through these relics that the miracles just described, and many others, were effected.

It is worth noting that Saint Stephen's martyrdom occurred not on the day after the Lord's birth, but, as we have already said, on the morning of the third day of August, the day the finding of his body is celebrated. The reason for this exchange will be explained when we treat of the Finding. For the present suffice it to say that the Church had two motives in placing the three feasts which follow the Nativity as they now stand. The first was that Christ, the spouse and head, might have his companions close by him. When Christ, spouse of his spouse the Church, was born into this world, he took to himself three companions. Of these the Song of Solomon says: "My beloved is white and ruddy, chosen out of thousands." "White" refers to John the Evangelist, the beloved confessor; "ruddy" to Stephen the first martyr; "chosen out of thousands" to the virginal multitude of the Holy Innocents. The Church's second motive was to group together, in the order of their dignity, all the different classes of martyrs, associating them closely with the birth of Christ, which was the cause of their martyrdom. For there are three kinds of martydom: the first is willed and endured, the second willed but not endured, the third endured without being willed. Saint Stephen is an example of the first, Saint John of the second, the Holy Innocents of the third.

✳

9. Saint John, Apostle and Evangelist

John (Johannes) is interpreted grace of God, or one in whom is God's grace, or one to whom a gift is given, or to whom a particular grace is given by God. By this we understand four privileges which God bestowed upon Saint John. The first is the special love of Christ for him. Christ loved John above the other apostles and gave him greater signs of love and familiar friendship. Hence he is called the grace of God, because to the Lord he was graced. Christ is also seen to have loved him more than Peter. But there is the love which is in the heart and the love which is manifested outwardly, and the latter is of two kinds—one which consists in showing familiar friendship, the other in the conferring of outward benefactions. As regards the love of the heart, Christ loved the two apostles equally; as to the showing of familiar friendship, he loved John more, and as to outward benefactions he showed Peter more love.

The gift referred to in the second meaning of the name is John's freedom from fleshly corruption, because he was chosen as a virgin and so is one who had in him the grace of virginal chastity: he had thought of marrying but instead was called by the Lord. Thirdly, the name means one to whom a gift is given, and in John's case this gift was the revelation of secrets. For to him it was given to know many profound secrets, such as the divinity of the Word and the end of the world. And the particular grace or favor implied in the fourth meaning was the entrusting to John of the mother of God. For this he was called the one to whom God has given a gift; indeed the greatest possible gift was given by the Lord to John when the mother of God was entrusted to his care.

The life of the apostle was written by Miletus, bishop of Laodicea, and was summarized by Isidore in his book *On the Birth, Life, and Death of the Holy Fathers.*

When, after Pentecost, the apostles separated, John, apostle and evangelist, beloved of Christ and chosen as a virgin, went to Asia and there founded many churches. The emperor Domitian, hearing of his fame, summoned him to Rome and had him plunged into a caldron of boiling oil outside the gate called the Porta Latina; but the blessed John came out untouched, just as he had avoided corruption of the flesh. Seeing that this treatment had not deterred him from preaching, the emperor exiled him to the island of Patmos, where, living alone, he wrote the Apocalypse, the Book of Revelation. That same year the emperor was murdered because of his cruelty, and the Senate revoked all his decrees. Thus it came about that John, who had been deported unjustly, returned to Ephesus with honor, and the crowds ran out to meet him, crying: "Blessed is he who comes in the name of the Lord!"

As he entered the city, a woman named Drusiana, who had been a dear friend of his and had looked forward more than anyone to his return, was being carried out for burial. This woman's kinsmen, and the widows and orphans of Ephesus, said to Saint John: "Here we are about to bury Drusiana, who, following your directions, nourished all of us with the word of God. Yearning for your return she used to say: 'Ah, if only I could see the apostle of God once more before I die!' And now you have come back, and she was not able to see you." John thereupon ordered them to set down the bier and unbind the body, and said: "Drusiana, may my Lord Jesus Christ raise you to life! Arise, go to your house and prepare food for me!" Drusiana got up and went straight to her house as the apostle had commanded, and it seemed to her that she had awakened from sleep, not from death.

The day after the apostle arrived in Ephesus, a philosopher named Crato called the people together in the public square to show them how they should despise the world. He had ordered two young men, brothers and very rich, to sell their entire patrimony, to buy the most priceless gems with the proceeds, and to smash them to bits while everybody watched. The apostle, however, happened to be passing, and he called the philosopher and denounced this sort of contempt of the world, citing three reasons. For one thing it wins the praise of men but is condemned by divine judgment. For another, such contempt cures no vices and therefore is worthless, as any medicine that never cures a disease is said to be worthless. Thirdly, contempt of riches is meritorious only when they are given away to the poor, as the Lord said to the rich young man: "If you wish to be perfect, go and sell all you have and give to the poor."

Hearing this, Crato replied: "If your master is truly God, and if it is his will that these gems should benefit the poor, then you put them together again, thus winning glory for him as I have won the applause of men." Saint John gathered the fragments of the gems in his hand and prayed; and the stones were restored to their former shape. At this the philosopher and the two young men believed, and they sold the gems and gave the money to the poor.

Their example induced two other young highborn young men to sell everything they owned and give the proceeds to the poor, and they became the apostle's followers. But one day they saw their former slaves flaunting elegant and costly raiment while they themselves had but one cloak between them, and they began to have regrets. Saint John saw this in their gloomy expression, so he had some sticks and pebbles brought to him from the seashore, and turned them into gold and precious stones. Then he sent the youths to show their new possessions to all the goldsmiths and jewelers, and they came back a week later to tell him that those experts had never seen gold so pure or gems so fine. The apostle said to them: "Go and buy back the lands you sold! Since you have lost the treasures of heaven, flourish, but only to wither; be rich for a time, but only to be beggars for eternity!" He then went on to speak against riches, enumerating six reasons that should deter us from an inordinate desire for wealth. The first is in Scripture, and he told the story of the gluttonous rich man, whom God rejected, and the poor man Lazarus, whom God rewarded. The second comes from nature itself: man is born naked and without wealth, and he dies without wealth. The third is seen in creation: just as the sun, the moon, and the stars, the rains and the air, are common to all and their benefits shared by all, so among men everything should be held in common. The next reason is fortune itself. The rich man is the slave of his money; he does not possess it, it possesses him; and he is the slave of the devil, because the Gospel says that the lover of money is a slave of mammon. Fifth comes care and worry: the rich worry day and night about how to get more and how to keep what they have. Sixth and last, he showed that wealth involves the risk of loss. In the acquisition of riches there lies a twofold evil: it leads to swollen pride in the present life and to eternal damnation in the next; and for those doomed to damnation there is a double loss—of divine grace at present and of eternal glory in the future.

While Saint John was carrying on this discourse against riches, a young man who had been married only a month before was carried out for burial. His mother, his widow, and the rest of the mourners came and prostrated themselves at the apostle's feet, begging him to revive him in the name of God, as he had done for Drusiana. The apostle, after weeping and praying for a long time, raised the dead man to life and ordered him to tell the two disciples already mentioned how great a penalty they had incurred and how much glory they had lost. He did so, speaking at length about the glories of paradise and the pains of hell, which he had seen; and he said: "O wretched men, I saw your angels weeping and the demons gloating over you!" He further told them they had lost eternal palaces built of shining gems, filled with banquets, abounding in delights and lasting joys. He also spoke about the eight pains of hell, which are named in the following verse:

Vermes et tenebrae flagellum frigus et ignis
Daemonis adspectus scelerum confusio luctus,

i.e., worms, darkness, the lash, cold, fire, the sight of the devil, remorse for sins, grief.

The revived man and the other two then fell at the apostle's feet and implored him to obtain mercy for them. Saint John replied: "Do penance for thirty days, and during that time pray that the sticks and stones may revert to their former nature." After this was accomplished, he said to them: "Go and put those things back where you found them." They did so, and the sticks and stones became again what they had been before. Thereupon the young men received the grace of all the virtues that had been theirs.

When Saint John had preached throughout the region of Asia, the idol-worshipers stirred up a riot among the populace, and they dragged him to the temple of Diana and tried to force him to offer sacrifice to the goddess. Then the saint proposed this alternative: if by invoking Diana they overturned the church of Christ, he would offer sacrifice to the idols; but if by invoking Christ he destroyed Diana's temple, they would believe in Christ. To this proposal the greater number of the people gave their consent. When all had gone out of the building, the apostle prayed, the temple collapsed to the ground, and the statue of Diana was reduced to dust.

Thereupon the high priest Aristodemus incited a still greater commotion among the people, and two parties were at the point of coming to blows. The apostle asked the priest: "What do you want me to do to restore order?" He answered: "If you want me to believe in your God, I will give you poison to drink. If it does you no harm, it will be clear that your master is the true God." John replied: "Do as you say!" "But first," came the answer, "I want you to see it kill some others, to make you fear its power the more." So Aristodemus hied himself to the proconsul, obtained the release of two criminals condemned to decapitation, and, in the presence of the crowd, gave them the poison. They drank it and fell dead. Then the apostle took the cup, armed himself with the sign of the cross, drained the drink, and suffered no harm; and all present began to praise God.

Aristodemus, however, was not yet convinced and said: "If you can bring the two dead men back to life, I will not hesitate to believe." The apostle handed him his cloak. "Why do you give me your cloak?" the other asked. John's answer: "To make you think twice and give up your unbelief!" "No mantle of yours will ever make me believe!" the priest retorted. John said: "Go and spread this cloak over the corpses, and say, 'The apostle of Christ has sent me to you, that you may rise in the name of Christ.'" He did as he was bidden, and the dead men arose at once. Then the high priest and the proconsul believed, and the apostle baptized them and their families. At a later time they built a church in honor of Saint John.

Saint Clement relates, as we find in Book IV of the *Ecclesiastical History*, that the blessed John once converted a handsome but headstrong young man and commended him as a "deposit" to a certain bishop. Some time later, however, the young man left the bishop and became the leader of a band of robbers. Eventually the apostle came back to the bishop and asked him to return his deposit. The bishop, thinking that he was talking about money, was taken aback, but the apostle explained that he meant the young man whom he had so solicitously entrusted to his care. The bishop answered: "O my venerable father, that man is dead, spiritually at least; he lives on yonder mountain with a band of thieves and has become their chief." At that the saint tore his mantle, beat himself about the head with his fists, and cried: "A fine guardian you have been for the soul of a brother whom I left with you!"

Quickly he ordered a horse saddled, and rode fearlessly toward the mountain. The young man, seeing him coming, was overwhelmed with shame, mounted his horse, and rode off at top speed. The apostle, forgetting his age, put spurs to his mount and chased the fugitive, calling after him: "What, beloved son! Do you flee from your father, an old man, unarmed? My son, you have nothing to fear! I shall account for you to Christ, and be sure I will gladly die for you, as Christ died for all of us. Come back, my son, come back! The Lord himself has sent me after you!" Hearing this, the young man, filled with remorse, turned back and wept bitterly. The apostle knelt at his feet and, as though repentance had already cleansed it, began to kiss his hand. Then he fasted and prayed for the penitent, obtained God's pardon for him, and later ordained him a bishop.

We also learn from the *Ecclesiastical History* (and from the *Gloss* on the second canonical epistle of John) that once when John went to take a bath in Ephesus, he saw the heretic Cerinthus in the baths and immediately hurried out, saying: "Let us get out for fear the bathhouse might cave in on us, because Cerinthus, an enemy of the truth, is bathing here."

Someone gave a live partridge to the blessed John (as Cassian tells us in his *Conferences*), and he gently held and stroked the bird. Seeing this, a boy laughed and called to his companions: "Come and watch this old man playing with a little bird like a child!" The saint, knowing by the spirit what was going on, called him and asked what it was that the youngster held in his hand. The boy said that it was a bow, and John asked what he did with it. The answer was: "We shoot birds and animals!" Then the lad stretched his bow and held it taut in his hand, but when the apostle said nothing, he loosened it. John asked him why he loosened the bowstring, and he replied: "Because if you keep it stretched too long, it gets too weak to shoot the arrows." So John told him: "That's how it is with human fragility: we would have less strength for contemplation if we never relaxed and refused to give in now and then to our own weakness. So too the eagle, which flies higher than any other bird and looks straight into the sun, yet by its nature must come down again; and the human spirit, after it rests awhile from contemplation, is refreshed and returns more ardently to heavenly thoughts."

According to Jerome, Saint John stayed on in Ephesus into his extreme old age. He grew so feeble that he had to be supported by his disciples on his way to the church and was hardly able to speak. At every pause, however, he repeated the same words: "My sons, love one another!" One day the brethren, wondering at this, asked him: "Master, why are you always saying the same thing?" The saint replied: "Because it is the commandment of the Lord, and if this alone is obeyed, it is enough."

Helinandus reports that when Saint John was about to write his gospel, he first called upon the faithful to fast and to pray that his writing might be worthy of the subject. We are told also that when he retired to the remote place where he was to write the divine book, he prayed that he might not be disturbed at his work by wind or rain; and even today the elements maintain the same reverence for the spot. Thus Helinandus.

Finally, according to Isidore, when the saint was in his ninety-ninth year, the sixty-seventh from the Lord's passion, Christ appeared to him with his disciples and said: "Come to me, my beloved, the time has come for you to feast at my table with your brothers." John rose and prepared to go, but the Lord said: "You will come to me on Sunday." Early Sunday morning the whole populace gathered in the church that had been built in his name. At the first cockcrow he preached to them, exhorting them to be steadfast in the faith and fervent in observing the commandments of God. Then he had a square grave dug near the altar and saw to it that the earth was carried outside the church. He went down into the grave and, raising his hands to God, said: "Lord Jesus Christ, you have invited me to your table, and behold I come! I thank you for welcoming me there and knowing that I have longed for you with all my heart." When he had said this prayer, a light shone around him, so bright that he was hidden from sight. When the light faded away, the grave was seen to be filled with manna, which continues to be generated to this day, so that the bottom of the grave looks as if it were covered with fine sand, as would happen at the bottom of a spring.

Saint Edmund, king of England, never refused anyone who asked a favor in the name of Saint John the Evangelist. Thus it happened one day when the royal chamberlain was absent that a pilgrim importuned the king in the saint's name for an alms. The king, having nothing else at hand, gave him the precious ring from his finger. Some time later an English soldier on overseas duty received the ring from the same pilgrim, to be restored to the king with the following message: "He for whose love you gave this ring sends it back to you." Hence it was obvious that Saint John had appeared to him in the guise of a pilgrim.

In his *Life and Death of the Saints* Isidore wrote: "John changed branches from the forest trees into gold and the pebbles of the beach into precious stones; he made broken jewels whole; at his command the widow came back to life; a youth was revived and the soul returned to his body; unharmed he drank a poisonous draft and restored life to those whom the poison had killed."

10. The Holy Innocents

The Holy Innocents are so called for three reasons—by reason of their life, of the death they suffered, and of the innocence they attained. They are called innocent because their life was in-nocent, i.e., not doing injury, since they never injured anyone: not God by disobedience, nor their neighbor by injustice, nor themselves by any sin. Therefore the Psalm says: "The innocent and the upright have adhered to me"; for they were innocent in their lives and upright in faith. They suffered innocently and unjustly; hence the Psalmist: "They have poured out [innocent] blood." And by their martyrdom they attained baptismal innocence, being cleansed of original sin. Of this innocence the Psalm says: "Keep innocence and behold justice"; i.e., keep the innocence of baptism and thereafter behold the justice of good works.

The Holy Innocents were put to death by Herod of Ascalon. Holy Scripture mentions three Herods, all three notorious for their cruelty. The first is called Herod of Ascalon. During his reign the Lord was born, and by him the Innocents were killed. The second is called Herod Antipas. He ordered the beheading of Saint John the Baptist. The third is Herod Agrippa, who put Saint James to death and imprisoned Saint Peter. All this is expressed in the following verse:

> Ascalonita necat pueros, Antipa Johannem,
> Agrippa Jacobum, claudens in carcere Petrum.

Let us look briefly at the story of the first Herod. Antipater the Idumaean, as we read in the *Ecclesiastical History*, married a niece of the king of the Arabs, and by her had a son whom he called Herod and who later was surnamed Herod of Ascalon. This Herod was appointed king of Judea by Caesar Augustus, and so the scepter was for the first time taken away from Judea. Herod had six sons—Antipater, Alexander, Aristobulus, Archelaus, Herod Antipas, and Philip. Alexander and Aristobulus were born of the same mother, a Jewess, and were sent to Rome to be educated in the liberal arts: after their return home Alexander became a grammarian and Aristobulus was known for the vehemence of his oratory. The two often quarreled with their father over the succession to the throne. Herod was offended by these disputes and took steps to make Antipater his heir, so the two brothers began to plot his death. For this reason he drove them out, and they went to Caesar to make complaint about the wrong done them by their father.

It was about this time that the Magi came to Jerusalem and diligently sought information about the birth of the new king. Herod was troubled when he heard of this, fearing that someone might have been born of the true royal line and might expel him as a usurper of the throne. He asked the Magi to bring him word of the child once they had found him, pretending that he too wished to worship the newborn king, although his intention was to kill him; but the Magi went back by another way into their country. Herod, when he saw that they did not return to him, thought that they had been deceived by the star and had been ashamed to face him, so he decided to give up his search for the child. However, when he heard what the shepherds had reported and what Simeon and Anna had prophesied, all his fears returned. He thought the Magi had played a low trick on him, and he determined to massacre all the male infants in Bethlehem so that the unknown child of whom he was afraid would be sure to perish.

But Joseph was warned by an angel and took the Child and his mother into Egypt, to the city of Hermopolis, where he stayed for seven years, until the death of Herod. And when the Lord came into Egypt, all the idols in the land were destroyed, as had been foretold by the prophet Isaiah. It is also said that just as when the exodus of the children of Israel from Egypt took place the firstborn lay dead in every house in Egypt, so now there was no temple in which the idol was not shattered. And Cassiodorus tells us in his *Tripartite History* that in Hermopolis in the Thebaid there is a tree called *persidis*, which cures any sickness if one of its fruits, or a leaf, or a piece of its bark is applied to the neck of the sick person. When blessed Mary fled into Egypt with her Son, this tree bent down to the ground and devoutly adored the Christ. Thus Cassiodorus.

While Herod was planning the murder of the children in Bethlehem, he was summoned by letter to appear before Caesar Augustus to answer the accusations of his two sons. His journey toward Rome took him to Tharsis, and it occurred to him that the Magi had taken passage in ships from that city. He therefore had all their ships destroyed by fire, fulfilling the prediction: "With a vehement wind thou shalt break in pieces the ships of Tharsis."

After the father and his sons had presented their arguments before Caesar, the emperor decreed that the sons should obey their father in all things, and that the king should pass on the kingdom to whomever he wished. Herod then returned from Rome emboldened by the confirmation of his authority, and forthwith ordered the killing of all the male children in Bethlehem who were two years old and under, figuring from the time he had learned from the Magi.

But the phrase "two years old and under" can be taken two ways. If "under" is read as referring to time elapsed, the sense would be "from infants two years old down to babies one day old." Herod had gathered from the Magi that the Lord was born the day the star appeared to them; and since a year had passed with his journey to and from Rome, he concluded that the Lord was a year old plus any remaining days. So, fearing that the child might be a changeling—in other words (since even the stars were at his service), he might have changed his age or his bodily appearance—the king vented his rage on children older than this one child and up to two years of age, or *under*, i.e., down to, the age of one day. This interpretation is more in keeping with common usage and is regarded as the truer one.

Yet the phrase is differently construed according to Chrysostom, and "under" indicates the order or sequence of numbers, so the sense is "from children the age of two and on down to three, four, etc." Chrysostom says that the star appeared to the Magi for a year previous to the Savior's birth, and that after Herod had heard the Magi, he was away for another year on his trip to Rome. He thought that Jesus was born when the Magi saw the star and would now be two years old, so he killed all the males two years old and *down to* the age of five but not *under* two. There seems to be some likelihood to this interpretation, because some of the Holy Innocents' bones have been preserved and are so large that they could not have come from two-year-olds. Yet it might be thought that at that time men grew far larger than they do now.

Herod was punished immediately. Macrobius tells us, and we also read in a chronicle, that an infant son of the king had been given to a woman in Bethlehem for nursing and was slain with the other children. Then what the prophet had foretold came to pass: "the sound of weeping and wailing"—namely, the voices of the bereaved mothers—"was heard in Rama," i.e., on high. And, as we read in the *Scholastic History*, God, the most just Judge, did not allow Herod's great wickedness to go without further punishment. By divine decree it happened that the one who had deprived many fathers of their sons should be even more miserably deprived of his own. Once more, then, Herod had reason to suspect his sons Alexander and Aristobulus. One of their accomplices confessed that Alexander had promised him many gifts if he succeeded in poisoning his father. Moreover, Herod's barber told of the rewards promised him if he slashed the king's throat while shaving him, and added that Alexander had warned him not to hope for much from an old man who had his hair dyed in order to look young.

All this made the father angry. He had the two put to death and designated Antipater as the future king, but later substituted Herod Antipas to reign instead of Antipater. Moreover, he had a paternal fondness for Agrippa and for Philip's wife Herodias, the children of Aristobulus, whom he had adopted. For this double reason Antipater conceived a hatred for his father so unbearable that he tried to poison him, but Herod, foreseeing this, put him in prison. When Caesar Augustus heard that he had done away with his sons, he said: "I would rather be Herod's swine than his son, because he spares his swine but kills his sons."

Finally, when Herod was seventy years old, he fell ill with a deadly disease, being tormented by high fever, an itch all over his body, incessant pain, inflammation of the feet, worms in the testicles, a horrible smell, and shortness and irregularity of breath. His physicians placed him in a bath of oil, but he was taken out almost dead. Then, hearing that the Jews were looking forward joyfully to the moment of his death, he had young men from the noblest families in all Judea taken into custody, imprisoned them, and said to his sister Salome: "Well I know that the Jews will rejoice at my death, but I foresee many of them grieving and many stately funerals if you carry out my wish: just kill all those young Jews I hold in prison. Then all Judea will mourn over me, against their will though it be."

It was Herod's custom to eat an apple, which he peeled himself, after every meal. One day, while peeling his apple, he was seized with a violent coughing spell and turned his knife against his breast, looking around to see that no one could prevent him from killing himself; but a nephew of his grasped his hand and stopped him. However, a great cry erupted in the palace, as though the king were indeed dead. Antipater, hearing the noise, was overjoyed and promised large rewards to his jailers if they would free him. This in turn came to Herod's ear, and, taking his son's exultation more grievously than his own imminent death, he sent some of his sergeants to put an end to him, and named Archelaus to succeed to the throne.

Five days later Herod died, most fortunate of men in many ways, yet most unhappy in domestic matters. His daughter Salome freed all those whom he had ordered her to execute. But Remy, in his commentary on Saint Matthew, says that Herod did stab himself to death with his paring knife, and that Salome put the prisoners to death as her brother had commanded.

---

11. Saint Thomas of Canterbury

Thomas means depth, or twofold, or cut down. He was profound in his humility, as is shown by his hair shirt and his washing the feet of the poor; twofold in his office, teaching the people by word and example; and cut down in his martyrdom.

Thomas of Canterbury, while he was at the court of the king of England, saw things happening that were contrary to religion. He therefore left the court and took service with the archbishop of Canterbury, who made him his archdeacon. At the archbishop's request, however, he accepted the office of chancellor to the king, so that he might use the prudence with which he was endowed to put a stop to the wrongs being done to the Church by evil men. The king conceived so strong an affection for him that when the archbishop died, he nominated Thomas to the see of Canterbury. Thomas, although he strenuously resisted the offer, finally obeyed and bent his shoulders to the burden. The new dignity immediately made him a different and perfect man. He began to mortify his flesh by fasting and wearing a hair shirt and haircloth drawers that came down to the knees. He was careful to hide his holiness: mindful of the proprieties, he made his outer dress and his furnishings conformable to what those around him wore. Every day he went on his knees and washed the feet of thirteen poor men, saw to their food, and gave each one four silver pennies.

But the king made every effort to bend Thomas to his will at the expense of the Church. He wanted the archbishop to confirm certain customs that were contrary to the Church's liberties, as his predecessors had done. Thomas absolutely refused, thus drawing upon himself the wrath of the king and the barons. There came a time, however, when with the rest of the bishops he was harassed by the king, even with threats of death; and, misled by the advice of the chief men of the state, he gave oral consent to the royal demands. But when he saw the danger to souls that would ensue from his action, he imposed ever more severe penances upon himself and suspended himself from the ministry of the altar until the pope should judge him worthy to be reinstated. Then the king demanded that he confirm in writing the verbal approval he had given. He refused manfully and, holding high his cross of office, walked out, while the impious shouted after him: "Lay hold of the thief! Hang the traitor!"

Now two of the foremost barons, who were loyal to Thomas, came to him shedding tears and told him under oath that many of the barons were conspiring to murder him. Therefore the man of God, fearing for the Church more than for himself, took flight, and was welcomed in Sens by Pope Alexander. The pontiff recommended him to the monastery at Pontigny, and he settled down in France. In the interim the king had sent to Rome, asking that legates come and put an end to their differences; but the request was repulsed, and this exacerbated his anger against the archbishop. Therefore he laid hands on everything that belonged to Thomas and his kinsmen and condemned the whole family to exile, without consideration of age, sex, rank, or condition. Meanwhile Thomas was praying daily for England and the king. Then it was revealed to him that he was to return to his church, and subsequently to leave this world with the palm of martyrdom and be with Christ in heaven. So, after seven years of exile, he was allowed to go back to England and was received with full honors.

Some days before the saint's martyrdom a young man, who had died and miraculously returned to life, said that he had been led to the highest circle of the saints and amidst the apostles had seen one empty throne. He had asked whose throne that was, and an angel had answered that it was reserved for a great priest from England.

There was a priest who celebrated the mass every day in honor of the Blessed Virgin Mary. He was accused of this and summoned before the archbishop, who suspended him from his office as being simpleminded and unlearned. At the time Saint Thomas had to mend his hair shirt, which he hid under his bed until he could find time to take care of it. Then Blessed Mary appeared to the priest and said: "Go to the archbishop and tell him that she for love of whom you said those masses has mended his hair shirt, which is under his bed, and has left there the red silk she used in the sewing. Tell him also that she sent you to him, and that he is to lift the suspension he imposed on you." Hearing this, Thomas was astounded to find his shirt mended, lifted the priest's suspension, and ordered him to keep the whole matter secret.

The archbishop continued to maintain the rights of the Church as in the past, and the king was unable to move him by pleas or by force. Therefore the king's armed soldiers went to the church and loudly asked where the archbishop was. Thomas went to meet them and said: "Here I am! what do you want?" They answered: "We have come to kill you! You cannot live any longer!" He said to them: "I am ready to die for God, to defend justice, and to protect the freedom of the Church. If therefore you are looking for me, I adjure you, in the name of almighty God and under pain of anathema, to do no harm to any of those around me. As for me, I commend myself and the cause of the Church to God, the Blessed Virgin Mary, Saint Denis, and all the saints." Having said these words, he bowed his venerable head to the swords of the wicked, and they split his skull and spilled his brains over the pavement of the church. Thus the martyr was consecrated to the Lord, in the year of the Lord 1174.

It is said that at the moment when the clergy were about to intone the *Requiem aeternam*, the mass of the dead, choirs of angels came and interrupted the singers, and began to chant the mass of the martyrs, *Laetabitur justus in Domino*, with the clergy joining in. This change was certainly the work of the right hand of the Most High—a chant of sorrow turning into a canticle of praise, and what had begun as prayers for the dead becoming hymns of praise for him who died as a martyr. Indeed he is shown to have been endowed with extraordinary sanctity and to be a glorious martyr of the Lord, since angels visited such honor upon him and ushered him into the choir of the martyrs. Saint Thomas suffered for the Church, in a church, a holy place, at a sacred moment, among his priests and religious, in order to bring out both the holiness of the one who suffered and the cruelty of his persecutors.

God deigned to work many other miracles through his saint. By Thomas's merits the blind saw, the deaf heard, the lame walked, the dead were brought back to life. Indeed the water in which cloths stained by his blood were washed brought healing to many.

An English lady, who was eager to attract men's attention and therefore to be more beautiful, wanted her eyes to change color, so she made a vow and walked barefoot to the tomb of Saint Thomas. There she knelt in prayer but, when she stood up, found that she was blind. Repentant, she began to pray to the saint that her eyes, even if their color was unchanged, be restored as they had been before—a favor that was granted her, but not before she had been at great pains to obtain it.

A trickster carried a pitcher of ordinary water instead of Saint Thomas's water to his master at table. The master said: "If you have never stolen anything from me, may Saint Thomas allow you to bring water in; but if you have been guilty of theft, may it evaporate at once!" The servant agreed, knowing that he had just filled the pitcher with water. Wonder of wonders! They tipped the pitcher and found it empty, and the servant was caught in a lie and, worse still, was exposed as a thief.

A bird that had learned to speak was being chased by a hawk, and cried out a phrase it had been taught: "Saint Thomas, help me!" The hawk fell dead and the bird escaped.

A man for whom Saint Thomas had had great affection fell gravely ill. He went to the saint's tomb, prayed for health, and was made whole. But when he got home cured of his illness, he began to think that perhaps the cure was not in the best interest of his soul. So back he went to the tomb and prayed that if health was not propitious for his spiritual good, he would rather be ill; and promptly he was ill again.

As for the saint's killers, the wrath of God dealt with them severely. Some of them gnawed their fingers to bits, others became slavering idiots; some were stricken with paralysis, still others went mad and perished miserably.

12. Saint Silvester

Silvester is derived from *sile*, which means light, and *terra*, earth, as though to say the light of the earth, i.e., the Church, which, like good earth, has fertility in good works, the blackness of humiliation, and the sweetness of devotion. Good earth is recognized by these three qualities, as Palladius says. Or the name comes from *silva*, forest, and *theos*, God, because Saint Silvester drew savage, untaught, insensitive men to the faith. Or, as the *Glossary* says, the name means verdant, devoted to plowing and planting, shaded, thickly wooded; and Silvester was verdant in his contemplation of heavenly things, a farmer in his cultivation of himself, shaded in his cool withdrawal from all fleshly desires, and wooded, being planted amidst the trees of heaven. Eusebius of Caesarea compiled his legend, and Saint Blaise, in a council of seventy bishops, recommended it as worthy of being read by Catholics.

Silvester's mother, whose name was Justa, was just in name and in reality. A priest called Cyrinus taught him his lessons. He was known for his generous hospitality. Timothy, a very devout Christian, was received into his household, although other people avoided the man for fear of persecution. Timothy steadfastly preached the faith of Christ for a year and three months, after which he gained the crown of martyrdom. The prefect, Tarquin by name, thought that Timothy had been a very wealthy man and demanded his riches of Silvester, threatening him with death; but later, when he was assured that the martyr had not possessed wealth, he ordered Silvester to offer sacrifice to the idols, or to undergo various kinds of torture on the following day. Silvester's reply was: "Fool, you will die tonight and will suffer perpetual torments, and, willing or not, will recognize the God we worship as true God!"

Silvester therefore was committed to jail and Tarquin was invited to dinner. While he was eating, a fish bone stuck in his throat, and he could neither swallow it nor spit it out. So it happened that Tarquin died in the middle of the night and was carried to the tomb amid mourning, while Silvester was set free from prison amid rejoicing, because he was held in deep affection not only by Christians but even by pagans: he was angelic in appearance, polished in speech, shapely in body, holy in his actions, wise in council, Catholic in his faith, patient in hope, and unstinting in charity.

Melchiades, the bishop of the city of Rome, died, and Silvester, despite his strenuous resistance, was elected supreme pontiff by the entire populace. He had the names of all orphans, widows, and poor people collected in a register, and saw to it that their needs were provided for. He decreed that Wednesdays, Fridays, and Saturdays were to be observed as fast days, and Thursday to be solemnized like Sunday. To the Greek Christians who said that Saturday should be solemnized rather than Thursday, Silvester responded that this was not right, both because what he ordered was in conformity with the apostolic tradition and because Saturday should commemorate the Lord's lying in the tomb. The Greeks replied: "Christ was buried for only one Saturday, and his burial is observed by fasting once every year." Silvester: "Just as every Sunday celebrates the glory of the Resurrection, so every Saturday honors the Lord's burial." So the Greeks gave in regarding Saturday but continued to argue forcefully about Thursday, saying that there was no reason for Christians to solemnize that day. Silvester, however, upheld the dignity of Thursday on three counts: on that day the Lord ascended into heaven and instituted the sacrament of his body and blood, and the Church confected the holy chrism. Finally all parties gave their assent to this reasoning.

Constantine continued to persecute the Christians, and Silvester left the city and settled in the mountains with his clerics. The emperor himself, in punishment for his tyrannical persecution, fell victim to the incurable disease of leprosy. In time, upon the advice of the priests of the idols, three thousand infants were brought together to be slaughtered so that the emperor could bathe in their fresh, warm blood; but when he came out to the place where the bath was to be prepared, the children's mothers crowded forward to meet him with their hair in disarray, crying and wailing pitifully. Constantine wept and halted his chariot, stood up, and said: "Hear me, counts and fellow knights and all you people here present! The honor of the Roman people is born of the font of piety.[1] Piety gave us the law by which anyone who kills a child in war shall incur the sentence of death. What cruelty it would be, therefore, if we did to our own children what we are forbidden to do to aliens! What do we gain by conquering barbarians if we allow cruelty to conquer us? To have vanquished foreign nations by superior power is proper to warlike peoples, but vice and sin are overcome by moral strength. In warfare we consider ourselves stronger than our enemies, but in this moral contest we overcome ourselves. Whoever is bested in this latter struggle wins victory by being conquered, whereas a victor is conquered after his victory if cruelty wins out over piety. Therefore let piety win in this conjuncture. Well it is for us to be victorious over all our adversaries if we win by piety alone. He indeed proves himself to be master of all, who shows himself to be the servant of piety. It is better for me, therefore, to die, the life of these innocents being spared, than by their destruction to recover my life—an uncertain recovery at best, whereas what is certain is that the life so recovered is a cruel one."

Constantine then ordered the children to be returned to their mothers and an abundance of gifts and plenty of wagons to be provided for them. So the mothers, who had come in tears, went home rejoicing.

The emperor returned to his palace. That night Saints Peter and Paul appeared to him and said: "Because you shrank from shedding innocent blood, the Lord Jesus Christ has sent us to tell you how to regain your health. Summon Silvester the bishop, who is in hiding on Mount Sirapte. He will show you a pool into which you will immerse yourself three times and so be fully cured of the disease of leprosy. In exchange you are to do something for Christ: demolish the temples of the idols, restore the Christian churches, and become a worshiper of Christ henceforth!" Constantine awoke and immediately sent soldiers after Silvester, who, seeing them coming, thought that he was called to receive the palm of martyrdom. He commended himself to God, encouraged the men who were with him, and went fearlessly to face the emperor. Constantine saluted him with the words: "We are happy that you came!" After Silvester greeted him in return, he gave a full account of the vision he had had in a dream. He asked who

---

[1] Piety: the traditional Roman virtue of *pietas* consisted of dutifulness toward gods, parents and family, and society. It included kindness and compassion.

the two gods were who had appeared to him, and Silvester answered that they were not gods but apostles of Christ. Then, at the emperor's request, the bishop sent for images of the apostles, and Constantine, examining them, exclaimed that they looked like the two who had appeared to him. Silvester therefore made him a catechumen, imposed a week-long fast upon him, and told him to open the jails. When the emperor went down into the water of baptism, a marvelous, brilliant light shone around him: he emerged from the pool clean of his leprosy and made it known that he had seen Christ.

The first day after his baptism, Constantine proclaimed as law that in the city of Rome Christ was to be worshiped as truly God; the second day, that anyone who blasphemed Christ would be punished; the third day, that anyone doing a Christian a wrong would be shorn of half his goods; on the fourth, that just as the Roman emperor was supreme in the world, so the bishop of Rome would be the head of all the world's bishops; on the fifth, that anyone taking refuge in a church was to be held immune from all injury; the sixth, no one could build a church within the walls of any city without the permission of the local bishop; on the seventh, that the tenth part of the royal income was allotted to the building of churches. On the eighth day the emperor went to the church of Saint Peter and tearfully accused himself of his faults. Afterwards he picked up a tool and turned over the first shovelful of earth at the foundation of the basilica that was to be built there, then carried out twelve baskets of earth on his shoulders and threw it outside the building site.

When Helena, mother of Constantine Augustus, who was in Bethany at the time, heard about her son's conversion, she wrote a letter praising him for renouncing the worship of false gods, but upbraiding him roundly because he was leaving behind the God of the Jews to worship a crucified man as God. The emperor wrote back that Helena should bring with her to Rome the foremost doctors of the Jews, whom he would confront with the Christian doctors so as to bring out the true faith by mutual discussion. Saint Helena therefore brought 161 of the most learned men of the Jews, among whom there were twelve who outshone the rest by their wisdom and eloquence. When Silvester and his clergy and the aforesaid Jews came together to debate in the emperor's presence, by common consent they established as judges two Gentiles named Crato and Zenophilus, men of great learning and high reputation, whose role was to act as arbiters between the disputants. Though they were pagans, they were nonetheless fair and faithful judges. They decided between them that when one speaker stood up and was speaking, no one could interrupt.

Now the first from among the twelve, Abiathar by name, began by saying: "Since these people say that there are three Gods, the Father, the Son, and the Holy Spirit, it is obvious that they go against the Law, which says, 'See ye that I alone am God and there is no other God besides me.'[2] And if they say that

---

[2] Isa. 45:5.

Christ is God because he wrought many signs, under our Law also there have been many who worked a great number of miracles yet never dared on that account to claim for themselves the name of divinity, as does the one whom these people adore." Silvester answered him as follows: "We worship one God, but we do not think of him as being so alone as not to have the joy of having a Son. Moreover, we can show you the trinity of Persons out of your own books. We say there is the Father, of whom the prophet says, 'He shall cry out to me, Thou art my Father, my God.'[3] We say there is the Son, of whom the same says, 'The Lord said to me, Thou art my Son, this day I have begotten thee.'[4] And of the Holy Spirit the same says, 'By the word of the Lord the heavens were established, and all the power of them by the Spirit of his mouth.'[5] Also, when God said, 'Let us make man to our own image and likeness,'[6] he clearly demonstrated both the plurality of Persons and the oneness of the divine nature. Although there are three Persons, God is one, and we can show this by a visible example." He took hold of the emperor's purple mantle and made three folds in the cloth, saying: "Here you see three folds." Then he unfolded the cloth and said: "You see that the three folds are one piece of fabric, as the three Persons are one God. . . . It has also been said that Christ should not be believed to be God on account of his miracles, since many other holy men performed miracles without claiming to be God as Christ willed to assert his divinity on the ground of his works. Certainly God never allowed those who rose up in pride against him to escape dire punishment, as is obvious in the examples of Dathan and Abiron and many others. How then could Christ have lied, saying that he was God if he was not, since no punishment befell him as a result of his claim, which was accompanied by many a display of divine powers?" Then the judges spoke: "Clearly Abiathar is outdone by Silvester, because reason itself teaches that if Christ were not God and yet said he was God, he never could have brought the dead to life."

So the first Jewish doctor stepped down and the second, whose name was Jonas, took his place. "Abraham," he said, "received from God the order to be circumcised and was justified thereby, and all the sons of Abraham were justified through circumcision. Therefore anyone who is not circumcised will not be justified." Silvester answered him: "We know that before being circumcised Abraham pleased God and was called God's friend. Therefore it was not circumcision that sanctified him but his faith and righteousness that made him pleasing to God. He did not receive circumcision to sanctify him but to mark him with a difference."

Jonas thus defeated, the third master, Godolias, came forward and said: "How can your Christ be God, since you state that he was born, tempted, betrayed, stripped naked, given gall to drink, was bound, and was buried, whereas all these things are impossible in God?" Silvester: "We prove from your own books that

[3] Ps. 89:26.   [4] Ps. 2:7.
[5] Ps. 32:6.   [6] Gen. 1:26.

all these things were predicted of Christ. Of his birth Isaiah said, 'Behold a virgin shall conceive and bear a son.'[7] Zechariah said of his temptation, 'The Lord showed me Jesus the high priest standing before the angel of the Lord, and Satan stood on his right hand to be his adversary.'[8] The psalmist says of his betrayal, 'My bosom friend, in whom I trusted, who ate of my bread, has lifted his heel against me.'[9] He was stripped of his clothing, and the psalmist says, 'They parted my garments amongst them, and upon my vesture they cast lots.'[10] Of his bitter drink, the psalmist says, 'They gave me gall for my food, and in my thirst they gave me vinegar to drink.'[11] He was bound, and Ezra says, 'You have bound me not as a father who freed you from the land of Egypt, crying out before the judge's tribunal; you have humiliated me, hanging me upon the wood; you have betrayed me.' Of his burial Jeremiah says, 'In his burial the dead will live again.'" And when Godolias could make no response, judgment was given and he was dismissed.

It was now the turn of the fourth master, Annas, who said: "This Silvester affirms that the things that were said of others were predicted of his Christ. He still has to prove that these things really were foretold of his Christ." Silvester: "Give me someone other than Christ whom a virgin conceived, who was fed with gall, crowned with thorns, and crucified, who died and was buried, rose from the dead and ascended into heaven!" At this Constantine said: "If he can give us no one else, let him admit that he has lost the argument." When Annas could not name anyone, he stepped to one side and the fifth doctor, Doeth by name, came forward.

Doeth began: "If Christ was born of the seed of David and sanctified, as you say he was, then he should not have been baptized in order to be sanctified again." Silvester: "As Christ's circumcision put an end to circumcision, so in Christ's baptism our baptism was instituted for sanctification. Christ was not baptized to be sanctified but to sanctify." Doeth said nothing, and Constantine spoke: "Doeth would not remain silent if he had anything to say by way of refutation."

Then came the sixth doctor, Chusi, who said: "We would like to have this Silvester expound to us the reasons for this virginal birth." Silvester: "The earth from which Adam was formed was incorrupt and virginal, because it had neither opened itself to drink human blood nor been cursed with the curse of thorns; it had not had a dead man buried in it nor been given to the serpent to eat. Therefore it was fitting that the new Adam be born of the Virgin Mary, in order that as the serpent had conquered a man formed from the virgin earth, he might be conquered by one born of a virgin, and that he who had emerged as Adam's conqueror in paradise should become the Lord's tempter in the desert, so that having conquered Adam eating, he should be conquered by Christ fasting."

---

[7] Isa. 7:14. [8] Zech. 3:1. [9] Ps. 41:9.
[10] Ps. 22:18. [11] Ps. 69:21.

Chusi was finished, and Benjamin, the seventh master, said: "How can your Christ, who could be tempted by the devil by being challenged to make bread out of stones when he was hungry, then by being lifted up to the pinnacle of the Temple, again by being bidden to adore the devil himself . . . how could he be the Son of God?" Silvester answered: "If the devil conquered because he was listened to by Adam eating, it is certain that he was overcome by Christ fasting and spurning him. We profess that Christ was tempted not in his divinity but as man. Moreover, he was tempted in three ways in order to ward off all temptations from us and to show us how to deal with them. It often happens in human experience that a victory by continence is followed by the temptation to worldly glory, and this temptation is accompanied by a craving for power and eminence. Therefore Christ overcame these temptations to give us a lesson in withstanding them."

Now the eighth master, Aroel, spoke. "It is certain that God is the summit of perfection and that he needs no one. Of what use, then, could it be to him to be born in Christ? Secondly, how do you call Christ the Word, for this too is certain, that before he had a son, God could not be called Father; therefore if afterwards he is called Christ's Father, he has become subject to change." Silvester replied: "The Son was begotten of the Father before all time, in order to create what did not yet exist, and he was born in time to remake those that had been lost. He could have remade them by his sole word, but he could not redeem them by his passion unless he became man, because he was not capable of suffering in his divinity. Nor was it an imperfection but a perfection, that in his divinity he could not suffer. Moreover, it is clear that the Son of God is called the Word, because the prophet says, 'My heart has uttered a good word.' God also was always Father because his Son always existed, for his Son is his Word and his Wisdom and his Power. The Son was always in the Father as his Word, according to the text, 'My heart has uttered a Word.'[12] He was always the Father's Wisdom: 'I came out of the mouth of the Most High, the firstborn before all creatures.'[13] He was always the Power: 'Before the hills I was brought forth, nor had the fountains of waters as yet sprung out.'[14] Since, therefore, the Father was never without his Word, his Wisdom, and his Power, how can you think that the name Father came to him in time?"

Aroel being dismissed, Jubal, the ninth doctor, said: "We know that God did not condemn nor curse marriage. Why therefore do you refuse to have the one you worship born of a marriage—unless it is your intention to denigrate marriage? Another question: how can one who is almighty be tempted, and how does one who is power suffer, or one who is life die? And lastly, you are forced to say that there are two sons, the one whom the Father begets, the other born of the virgin. And again, how can it be that the humanity which is assumed suffers without injury to the divinity which assumed the humanity?"

[12] Ps. 44:2.   [13] Sir. 24:5.   [14] Prov. 25:24.

To all this, Silvester responded: "It is not to condemn marriage that we say Christ was born of a virgin, and we have already stated the reasons for his virginal birth. Nor is marriage discredited by that assertion; on the contrary, it is honored, because this virgin who became Christ's mother was herself the child of a marriage. Christ was tempted in order to vanquish all the devil's temptations; he suffered in order to bring all suffering under subjection; he died to thwart the reign of death. In Christ there is the one and only Son of God: as Christ is truly God's invisible Son, the Son is the visible Christ. What is invisible in him is God, what is visible is man. We may show by an example that the man assumed can suffer while the godhead assuming does not suffer. Let us use the emperor's purple mantle as an example. It was wool, and blood was applied to this wool and gave it its purple color, but when the wool was held in the fingers and twisted into thread, what was twisted? The color that signifies the royal dignity, or the wool that was wool before it was dyed purple? So then, the wool stands for the man, the purple color for God. God was present in Christ's passion when Christ suffered on the cross, but was not subjected to suffering in any way."

The tenth master, Thara, said: "I am not pleased by this example, because the color is twisted with the wool!" All present disagreed, but Silvester said: "Very well, take another example! Imagine a tree filled with the splendor of sunlight. When the tree is cut down, it feels the sharp bite of the ax, but the sunlight suffers nothing from the blow! So, when the man suffered, the divinity underwent no suffering."

Sileon, the eleventh doctor, now spoke. "If the prophets foretold these things about your Christ," he said, "we would like to know the reasons for all this mockery and suffering and death!" Silvester: "Christ suffered hunger that he might feed us; he thirsted in order to quench our dryness with a life-giving draft; he was tempted to liberate us from temptation; he was taken captive to deliver us from capture by the demons; he was mocked to free us from the demons' mockery; he was bound in order to untie for us the knot of bondage and malediction; he was humiliated in order to exalt us; he was stripped of his garments to clothe with his pardon the nakedness of our primal privation; he accepted the crown of thorns in order to give back to us the lost flowers of paradise; he was hung upon the tree to condemn the evil desires that a tree had stirred; he was given gall and vinegar to drink in order to bring man into a land flowing with milk and honey and to open for us fountains running with honey; he took mortality upon himself to confer immortality upon us; he was buried to bless the tombs of the saints; he rose to restore life to the dead; he ascended into heaven to open heaven's gates; he is seated at God's right hand to hear and grant the prayers of the faithful."

When Silvester had finished speaking, applause rang out from the whole company, including the emperor and the Jews; but Zambri, the twelfth Jewish master, was highly indignant and said: "It's a wonder to me that you, all-wise judges, are beguiled by these ambiguous word games and allow that the omnipotence of God can be comprehended by human reason! But enough of words, let us get down to deeds! Great fools they are who worship a crucified man, for I know the name of the almighty God, a name the power of which the rocks cannot withstand and which no creature can bear to hear! And so that you may have proof that I am speaking the truth, let a wild bull be led here to me, and when I murmur that name in its ear the bull will die instantly!" Silvester asked him: "How is it that you have heard that name and did not die?" "You, enemy of the Jews that you are," Zambri retorted, "cannot know this mystery!"

A bull was brought in, so ferocious that a hundred men could hardly restrain it; and when Zambri whispered a name in its ear, the animal roared, rolled its eyes, and fell dead. At this all the Jews cheered and hurled insults at Silvester, who said: "He did not utter the name of God but the name of the foulest of demons! Our God not only lets the living die but also brings the dead to life. To kill and not restore life . . . lions, serpents, wild beasts can do that! If this doctor wants me to believe that the name he pronounced was not that of a demon, let him pronounce it again and bring what he killed back to life! For it is written of God, 'I will kill and I will make to live.' If he cannot do this, there is no doubt but that he named a demon who can kill a living being but cannot bring a dead one to life."

The judges then pressed Zambri to awaken the bull, but Zambri said: "Let Silvester awaken it in the name of Jesus the Galilean, and we will all believe in Jesus, for even if Silvester can sprout wings and fly, he cannot do this!" All the Jews then promised that they would believe if Silvester brought the bull to life. He therefore prayed and, bending down to the bull's ear, said: "Bull, get up and go back nicely to your herd!" The bull got to its feet and went away gently and quietly. Thereupon the queen, the Jews, the judges, and everybody else were converted to the faith.

Some days later, the priests of the false gods came to the emperor and said: "O holy emperor, since you adopted the Christian faith, the dragon we have in the pit has killed more than three hundred people a day with its breath!" Constantine consulted Silvester about this, and the bishop answered: "I, by the power of Christ, will make the beast desist from all such mischief!" The priests promised that if he did this, they would believe. Silvester prayed and the Holy Ghost appeared to him, saying: "You will be safe. Go down to the dragon with two priests, and when you reach the beast, speak to it as follows, 'Our Lord Jesus Christ, who was born of a virgin, crucified, and buried, who rose again and is seated at the right hand of the Father, is to come to judge the living and the dead. Therefore you, Satan, wait for him here in this pit until he comes.' Then you will tie up its mouth with a thread and seal it with a ring with a cross on it. Come back to me afterwards hale and unharmed, and you all will eat the bread I shall have prepared for you."

Silvester, with his two priests carrying lanterns, went down by forty steps into the pit, and he spoke to the dragon as instructed. Then, while the animal growled and hissed, he tied up its maw and sealed it. On their way up out of the pit they met two magicians, who had followed them to see whether they actually went all the way to the dragon: the two were almost dead, overcome by the brute's foul breath. The saint brought them out with him unharmed, and the two, with a countless multitude, were converted at once. Thus the Roman people were delivered from a twofold death, namely, from the worship of the devil and the dragon's venom.

At length the blessed Silvester, nearing death, admonished his clergy on three points: they should practice charity among themselves, should rule their churches with diligence, and should protect the flock from being bitten by wolves. After that he fell asleep happily in the Lord about the year of the Lord 320.

13. The Circumcision of the Lord

The day of the Lord's circumcision is noteworthy and solemn for four reasons: it is the octave of his birth, and it commemorates the imposition of a new and saving name, the shedding of his blood, and the seal of circumcision.

First, it is the octave of the birth of Christ. If the octaves of other saints are solemn days, how much more solemn should the octave day of the Saint of saints be! Yet it does not seem that the Lord's nativity should have an octave: his birth led to death, whereas the deaths of the saints have octaves for the reason that the saints are then born with the birth which leads to eternal life and thus to their eventual rising in glorious bodies. For the same reason the birthdays of the Blessed Virgin and Saint John the Baptist should not have octaves, nor should the Lord's resurrection, which has taken place already.

But note that, as Praepositivus says, there are supplementary octaves, for instance, the octave of the birth of Christ, in which we supplement what had been inadequately celebrated on the feast itself, namely, the office of the one who bore him; for that reason it was customary in former times to sing the mass *Vultum tuum*[1] in honor of the Blessed Virgin. There are also octaves of veneration, including Easter, Pentecost, certain of Mary's feasts, and that of Saint John the Baptist; octaves of devotion, which can be instituted for any saint; and

---

[1] *Vultum tuum*, first words of a mass for feasts and commemorations of the Blessed Virgin in the old Roman missal.

octaves of figuration instituted for saints as signifying the octave of resurrection.

Secondly, this day is solemnized because of the imposition of a new and saving name. On this day indeed a new name was conferred upon the Child, the name that came from the mouth of God the Father; and there is no other by which we can be saved. This is the name that, according to Bernard, is honey in the mouth, music in the ear, and a cry of joy in the heart. He also says that the name is like oil: it gives light, it nourishes when preached, it brings calm when meditated, and anoints when invoked.

We know from the gospels that the Lord had three names—Son of God, Christ, and Jesus. He is called Son of God because he is God from God; Christ, because he is man, assumed as to his human nature by a divine Person; Jesus, because he is God united to humanity. Regarding this triple name Bernard says: "O you who are in the dust, wake up and give praise! Lo, your Lord comes with salvation, he comes with anointing, he comes with glory; for Jesus does not come without salvation, nor Christ without anointing, nor the Son of God without glory, for he himself is salvation and ointment and glory."

Previous to the Lord's passion this triple name was not perfectly known. The first was known by conjecture, as, for instance, by the demons who said that he was God's Son. The second also was known to a particular few who recognized him as the Christ. As for the third, it was known as the name by which he was called, Jesus, but not as to its meaning, which is savior.

After the Resurrection, however, the full meaning of the three names was more clearly manifested; of the first by the certain knowledge that he is the Son of God, of the second by its diffusion throughout the world, of the third as to the reason for the name. Consider the first name, Son of God. That this name rightly belonged to Jesus is brought out by Hilary in his book *On the Trinity*: "That our Lord Jesus Christ is truly the only-begotten Son of God is made known in many ways—by the Father's testimony, by his own statements about himself, by the apostles' preaching, by the faith of religious people, by the demons' admission, by the Jews' denial, by the Gentiles' recognition of him in his passion." Hilary also says: "We know our Lord Jesus Christ in these ways—by his name, his birth, his nature, his power, and what he said of himself."

The second name, Christ, means anointed, for he was anointed with the oil of gladness above his fellows. That he is called the anointed one implies that he was prophet, pugilist, priest, and king, because these four types of persons were usually anointed with oil. He was a prophet in his knowledge of doctrine, a pugilist in his bouts with the devil, a priest in reconciling all with the Father, and a king in his distribution of rewards. We ourselves are named after this second name, Christ, from which comes the title Christian. Of this name Augustine says: "Christian is the name of justice, kindness, integrity, patience, chastity, modesty, humanity, innocence, and piety. And you, how can you claim that name and defend your right to it—you, in whom so few of that great number of virtues subsist? A Christian is one who is Christian not in name only but in action." So far Augustine.

The third name is Jesus. According to Bernard, this name suggests food, a fountain, a remedy, and a light. This food has a multiple effect; it enlivens, it fattens, it strengthens, and it invigorates. Bernard says: "This name Jesus is food. Are you not strengthened every time you recall it? What else builds up the spirit of the one pondering it as this name does? What so refreshes the tired heart, strengthens the virtues, fosters chaste loves?"

The holy name is also a fountain, and the same Bernard says: "Jesus is a sealed fountain of life, which flows out into the plains in four streams. So Jesus became for us wisdom, righteousness, sanctification, and redemption—wisdom in his preaching, righteousness in absolving us of sin, sanctification in behavior or in conversion, redemption in his passion." Thus Bernard. And elsewhere he says: "Three streams flowed from Jesus—the word of sorrow, in which is confession, the sprinkled blood, in which is affliction, and the water of cleansing, in which is repentance."

Thirdly, the name Jesus is a remedy, and Bernard says: "This name Jesus is a medicine. Nothing else so inhibits outbursts of anger, calms the tumor of pride, heals the wound of envy, restrains the welling up of unchaste desire, extinguishes the flame of lust, allays thirst, soothes the itch of greed and of every sort of vice." And fourthly, the name is a light, and he says: "Where in the whole world, think you, is there so bright and sudden a light of faith as shines from Jesus preaching or from Jesus preached? This is the light that Paul carried to the Gentiles like a lamp on a lampstand."

Furthermore this name has much sweetness, whence Bernard says: "What you write has no taste for me unless I read in it the name of Jesus. If you debate or make speeches, I find no savor unless I hear his name." Likewise Richard of Saint Victor: "Jesus is a sweet name, a name of delight, a name that comforts the sinner, a name of blessed hope. Therefore, Jesus, be to me Jesus!" It is also a name of great power, as Peter of Ravenna says: "You shall call his name Jesus, i.e., the name that gave sight to the blind, hearing to the deaf, walking to the lame, speech to the mute, life to the dead; and the power of this name drove all the might of the devil from the bodies of the possessed." It is a most excellent and sublime name; so says Bernard: "It is the name of our Savior, of my brother, of my flesh and my blood, the name hidden from the ages but revealed at the end of the ages, so wonderful, so ineffable, so inestimable a name, the more inestimable that it is more wonderful, the more welcome that it is freely given!"

The name of Jesus was imposed upon him by God the eternal, by the angel, and by his putative father, Joseph. Jesus is interpreted savior, and he is called savior for three reasons, namely, on account of his power to save, his disposition to save, and his act of saving. Insofar as the name bespeaks power to save, it was fitting that it be imposed by God the eternal; signifying the disposition to save, it was imposed by the angel as belonging to him from the moment of his conception; denoting the act of saving, it was imposed by Joseph in anticipation of the Lord's passion. Therefore the *Gloss* on the text "You shall call his name Jesus" says: "You shall impose the name that was imposed by the angel or by the eternal." And here the *Gloss* touches upon the threefold naming above set forth. When it is said: "You shall impose . . . ," the naming by Joseph is referred to; ". . . that was imposed by the angel or by the eternal" refers to the other two namings. Rightly therefore on this day, which is the head of the year by decree of Rome the head of the world and is designated by the head letter (A) of the alphabet, Christ, the head of the Church, was circumcised, a name was imposed upon him, and the octave day of his birth is honored.

The third reason for solemnizing this day is the shedding of Christ's blood, because today marks the first time he shed his blood for us, as he was to do five times in all. The first was the circumcision, and this was the beginning of our redemption. The second was when he prayed in the garden, and this showed his desire for our redemption. The third, the scourging, merited our redemption, because by his bruises we are healed. The fourth was his crucifixion, and this was the price of our redemption, since he made payment for what he had not taken away. The fifth was when the soldier opened his side with a spear, and this was the sacrament of our redemption, for blood and water issued forth: this prefigured our cleansing by the water of baptism, because that sacrament has its efficacy from the blood of Christ.

Fourthly, we pointed to the circumcision as a seal that Christ deigned to receive on this day. He had many reasons for wanting to be circumcised. The first was for his own sake, to show that he had assumed a real human body, because he knew that there would be those who would say his body was not real but a phantasm. Therefore, to refute their error, he chose to be circumcised and to shed blood, because no phantasm can bleed. The second was for our sake, to show us that we should be circumcised in the spirit. According to Bernard the circumcision we should undergo is twofold—external in the flesh, internal in the spirit. The external circumcision takes three forms, namely, in our manner of living, lest it be blameworthy, in our actions, lest they merit reproach, and in our speech, lest it evoke contempt. Internal circumcision likewise has three forms, namely, in our thoughts, which must be holy, in our affections, which must be pure, and in our intention, which must be right. So far Saint Bernard.

Moreover, Christ was circumcised for our sake in order to save us. As one member might have to be cauterized to preserve the health of the whole body, so Christ chose to be cauterized in one member in order to bring health to the whole mystical body: "In whom you are circumcised not with circumcision made by hand in despoiling of the body of the flesh, but in the circumcision of Christ."[2] To this the *Gloss* adds: "from vices, as with a very sharp rock, 'for the rock was Christ.'"[3] This recalls Exodus: "Immediately Sephora took a very sharp stone and circumcised the foreskin of her son."[4] The *Gloss* explains this in

---

[2] Col. 2:11.   [3] I Cor. 10:4.   [4] Exod. 4:25.

two ways. The first way goes as follows: "You are circumcised, I say, with a circumcision not made by hand, i.e., not by the work of man but by the work of God—by a spiritual circumcision. This circumcision consists in the stripping off of the body of flesh, in other words, in putting off the carnal man, meaning the man of fleshly vices and desires, in the sense in which the word flesh is used. Thus Saint Paul: 'Flesh and blood cannot possess the kingdom of God.'[5] You are, I say, circumcised with a circumcision not made by hand but with a spiritual circumcision." The second way: "You are circumcised, I say, in Christ, and this by a circumcision not made by hand, i.e., not by circumcision according to the Law, which is done by stripping away the flesh of the body, namely, the skin of the flesh that is removed by legal circumcision. You are not, I say, circumcised with that circumcision, but by Christ's circumcision, the spiritual one which amputates all the vices. Hence we read in Romans: 'He is not a real Jew who is one outwardly, nor is true circumcision something external and physical. He is a Jew who is one inwardly, and real circumcision is a matter of the heart, spiritual and not literal. His praise is not from men but from God.'[6] So you are circumcised with a circumcision not made by hand in the despoiling of the body of flesh, but with the circumcision of Christ."

The Lord's third reason for accepting circumcision had to do with the Jews, who thus would have no excuse. For if he were not circumcised, the Jews could have excused themselves, saying: "We do not accept you because you are not like our fathers." And his fourth reason had the demons in mind, to keep them from learning the mystery of his incarnation. Since circumcision was done as a counteragent to original sin, the devil thought that this man, who was circumcised, was also a sinner who needed the remedy of circumcision. For the same reason the Lord willed that his mother, though a perpetual virgin, should be married.

The fifth reason for Christ's circumcision was that all justice might be fulfilled. Just as he wished to be baptized so that all righteousness, i.e., perfect humility (which means subjecting oneself to an inferior) would be fulfilled, so also he chose to be circumcised in order to show us the same humility, in that he, the author and master of the Law, subjected himself to the Law. And a sixth reason was to demonstrate approval of the Law of Moses, which was good and holy and was to be fulfilled. He had come not to destroy the Law but to fulfill it: "For I say that Christ Jesus was minister of the circumcision for the truth of God, to confirm the promises made to the fathers."[7]

But why was circumcision performed on the eighth day? Many reasons can be cited. The first is based on a historical or literal understanding of the term *eighth day*. Rabbi Moses,[8] an eminent philosopher and theologian though a Jew, explains this. The flesh of a boy child only seven days old was still as tender as

---

[5] 1 Cor. 15:50.   [6] Rom. 2:28–29.   [7] Rom. 15:8.

[8] Moses ben Maimon, better known as Maimonides (1135–1204), known in his own time and since not only as an eminent philosopher and theologian but as a physician and author of medical books.

it had been in the mother's womb, but by the eighth day it became stronger and more solid. Therefore God did not want babies to be circumcised before the eighth day because the softness of their flesh might lead to serious injury. He also did not want postponement beyond the eighth day for three reasons, which are stated by the same philosopher. The first was to avoid danger, since the infant might die if there was a longer delay. Secondly, to mitigate the child's suffering: circumcision is very painful, so the Lord commanded that it be done while babies still have little imagination and would not feel the pain so much. Thirdly, to be considerate of the parents' grief, because a great many infants die as a result of being circumcised, and if boys were not circumcised until they were grown up and then died as a result, the parents would grieve more than if the children had died when they were only eight days old.

The second reason for holding to the eighth day is based on an anagogical or mystical understanding. The rite was performed on the eighth day to help us understand that within the octave of resurrection we will be circumcised of all punishment and all misery. By this reasoning the eight days are eight ages—from Adam to Noe, from Noe to Abraham, from Abraham to Moses, from Moses to David, from David to Christ, from Christ to the end of the world, then the age of the dying, and finally the age of the resurrection. Or by the eight days we are to understand eight goods that will be ours in eternal life. These are enumerated by Augustine, who says: "What does 'I will be their God' mean, if not 'I will be for them the gratification of their every honorable desire? I will be to them life, health, food, plenty, glory, honor, peace, and every good.'" Or by seven days we are to understand man himself, who consists of body and soul. Four of the days are the four elements of which the body is composed, and three are the three potencies of the soul, the concupiscible, the irascible, and the rational. Therefore man, who now has seven days, will, when conjoined to the unity of eternal immutability, have eight days, and on that eighth day will be circumcised of every penalty and fault.

The third way to understand the eighth day is in the tropological or moral sense, and in this sense the eight days can yield various meanings. The first day can be the knowledge of our sins: "For I know my iniquity, and my sin is always before me."[9] The second can be the decision to shun evil and do good, which we see in the prodigal son, who said: "I will arise and will go to my father."[10] The third day, shame for sin; so the apostle: "What fruit therefore had you then in those things of which you are now ashamed?"[11] The fourth, fear of the judgment to come: "For I have always feared God as waves swelling over me";[12] and Jerome: "Whether I eat or drink or whatever else I do, it seems to me that that voice is always sounding in my ears, 'Rise, O dead, and come to judgment.'" The fifth day will be contrition: "Make mourning as for an only son, a bitter

---

[9] Ps. 50:3.   [10] Luke 15:8.   [11] Rom. 6:21.
[12] Job 31:23 (Douay).

lamentation."[13] The sixth, confession: "I have acknowledged my sin to thee."[14] The seventh, hope of pardon; for although Judas confessed his sin, he did not hope for pardon and therefore did not obtain mercy. The eighth will be the day of satisfaction, and on that day man will be spiritually circumcised not only of his faults but of all punishment. Or the first two days are for sorrow for sin committed and the desire of amendment; the next two for confession of the wrongs we have done or the good we have failed to do; the other four are for prayer, shedding of tears, mortification of the flesh, and generous almsgiving. Or the eight days can be eight things which, diligently considered, will circumcise us of all will to sin, so much so that serious thought devoted to any one of them will make a great prescription for living a good life. Bernard enumerates seven of these, saying: "Seven things are of the essence of man, and if he pondered them, he would not sin forever: they are his vile matter, shameful conduct, lamentable outcome, unstable condition, pitiable death, miserable dissolution, and abominable damnation." The eighth day can be the consideration of ineffable glory.

A fourth way of understanding the eight days and the eighth day is the allegorical or spiritual interpretation. According to this, five days will be the five books of Moses, two will be the Prophets and the Psalms, and the eighth the Gospel doctrine. In the first seven days circumcision was not perfectly done, but on the eighth there is perfect circumcision of all faults and punishment, now hoped for, at last possessed. The reasons for circumcision can therefore be summed up as six: cautery, sign, merit, remedy, figure, and example.

What about the flesh removed by the Lord's circumcision? It is said that an angel carried it to Charlemagne, and that he enshrined it at Aix-la-Chapelle in the church of the Blessed Mary and later transferred it to Charroux, but we are told that it is now in Rome in the church called Sancta Sanctorum, where there is the following inscription:

Circumcisa caro Christi sandalia clara
atque umbilici viget hic praecisio cara,

which means, "Here are the circumcised flesh of Christ and his bright sandals, here too is preserved a precious cutting of his umbilicus." For that reason a station takes place at this church on this day. But if all this is true, it is certainly to be wondered at. Since the flesh belongs to the true human nature, we believe that when Christ rose, the flesh went back to its glorified place. There are some who say that this is true according to the opinion of those who hold that only what was handed on from Adam belongs to the true human nature, and that alone rose from the dead.

It is worthy of note that in ancient times the pagans and Gentiles observed many superstitious rites on the first day of January, and that the saints were at

---

[13] Jer. 6:26.   [14] Ps. 50:5.

great pains to uproot these superstitious practices even among the Christian folk. Augustine talks about this in one of his sermons. He says they believed that their leader Janus was some kind of god, to whom they paid much veneration on this day, and that they made his image with two faces, one looking forward and the other backward, because it was the end of one year and the beginning of the next. Also on this day some of them put on monstrous masks, others wore the skins of animals, still others the heads of beasts, thus showing that they not only dressed like beasts but had bestial feelings. There were even some who clothed themselves in women's dress, shamelessly tricking out their soldierly muscles in feminine finery. Others followed the auguries so closely that if someone asked for fire from their hearth or some other favor, they would refuse it. The giving and receiving of devilish gifts was also practiced. Others laid out sumptuous tables in the night and left them there all night long, believing that they would enjoy such abundant feasting throughout the year. And Augustine adds: "Anyone who participates in these pagan customs may well fear that the name of Christian will do him no good. Whoever takes a friendly part in the games of the ungodly may be sure that he also shares in their sins. Therefore, brothers, it is not enough for you to shun this evil. Wherever you see it, denounce it, rebuke it, put it down." So says Augustine.

14. The Epiphany of the Lord

On the feast day of the Lord's epiphany four miracles are commemorated, and therefore the day has four different names. On this day the Magi adored Christ, John baptized him, he changed water into wine, and he fed five thousand men with five loaves.

When Jesus was thirteen days old, the Magi, led by the star, came to him: therefore the day is called Epiphany, from *epi*, which means above, and *phanos*, meaning an appearing, because then the star appeared from above, or the star, appearing from above, showed the Magi that Christ was the true God. On the same day, twenty-nine years later, he had entered his thirtieth year (he was then twenty-nine years and thirteen days old) and, as Luke says, was beginning his thirtieth year; or, as Bede has it and the Roman church affirms, he was already thirty years old. Then, I say, he was baptized in the Jordan, and therefore the day is called Theophany, from *theos*, meaning God, and *phanos*, apparition. The whole Trinity appeared on that day, the Father by voice, the Son in the flesh, the Spirit as a dove.

On the same day one year later, when he was thirty or thirty-one years plus thirteen days old, he changed water into wine; so the day is called Bethany, from *beth*, house, because by working the miracle in a house he appeared as true God. Still another year thereafter, when he was thirty-one or thirty-two, he fed the five thousand men with five loaves, as Bede says and as we hear in the hymn that is sung in many churches and begins *Illuminans altissimus*. So the day is called Phagiphany, from *phagos*, which means a mouthful or to eat. There is some doubt, however, whether this fourth miracle occurred on this particular date. Bede does not say this explicitly in his original, and in John 6 we read: "The Pasch was near at hand."

Four appearances, then, happened on this day, the first through the star, in the manger; the second through the Father's voice, in the Jordan; the third in the changing of water into wine at the wedding feast; the fourth in the multiplication of the loaves in the desert. But the first appearance is the principal one celebrated on this date, and so we will go on with that story.

When the Lord was born, three Magi came to Jerusalem. In Greek their names were Apellius, Amerius, and Damascus; in Hebrew, Galgalat, Malgalat, and Sarachin; in Latin, Caspar, Balthasar, and Melchior. Concerning what sort of magi they were there are three opinions based on the threefold meaning of the word *magus*. Magus means deceiver, sorcerer, or wise man. Some say that these kings were called magi, deceivers, because of what they did, namely, that they deceived Herod by not returning to him. Hence the Scripture: "Herod, perceiving that he was deluded by the wise men, etc." Or magus may mean sorcerer, as Pharaoh's sorcerers were called magi. Chrysostom says that the three kings were called magi because they had been sorcerers but were later converted, and that the Lord chose to reveal his birth to them and to lead them to himself, thereby extending to all sinners the hope of pardon. Or again, magus is the equivalent of wise man; in Hebrew the magus is called a scribe, in Greek a philosopher; the Latin is *sapiens*, wise man, and the Magi were so called because they were men of great wisdom.

These three, wise men and kings, came with a numerous company to Jerusalem. But, it may be asked, why to Jerusalem, since the Lord was not born there? Remy assigns four reasons for this. His first is that the Magi knew the time of Christ's birth but not the place. Because Jerusalem was the royal city and the high priest had his seat there, they supposed that so great a child would be born nowhere else. His second reason is that the city where the scribes and those learned in the Law resided would be the place to learn where the child was born. The third, that the Jews would be left without an excuse, since otherwise they might have said: "We knew the place of his birth but not the time, and therefore we do not believe." Thus the Magi showed the Jews the time, and the Jews showed the Magi the place. The fourth reason would be that the Jews' indifference was condemned by the Magi's zealous search. The Magi believed one prophet, the Jews refused to believe a number of them; the former searched for a foreign king, the latter did not bother to look for their own; the Magi came a great distance, the Jews lived close by. These kings were Balaam's descendants, and they came having seen the star in accordance with their father's prophecy: "A star shall rise out of Jacob, and a man shall spring up from Israel."

Still another reason for their coming is adduced by Chrysostom in his commentary on Matthew. He asserts, referring to what some others said, that certain men who probed hidden secrets chose twelve from among their number, and if one of them died, his son or a close relative took his place. Year after year the chosen twelve went up once a month to the top of the mountain of victory, stayed three days, bathed, and prayed God to show them the star that Balaam had foretold. On the day of Christ's birth, while they were there, a star came to them above the mountain: it had the shape of a most beautiful child over whose head a cross gleamed. The child addressed the wise men, saying: "Go to the land of Judah as fast as you can, and you will find there the newborn king whom you seek"; and they set out immediately. But we must speak about how in so short a time, namely, in thirteen days, they were able to travel so great a distance, from the East to Jerusalem, which is said to be at the center of the world. According to Remy, this was possible because the Child toward whom they hastened had power to lead them to him in that brief space of time. Or it may be said, following Jeremiah, that they were mounted on dromedaries, very swift animals that run as far in one day as a horse can in three. The word dromedary, by the way, comes from *dromos*, running, and *ares*, strength.

When the Magi reached Jerusalem, they inquired, saying: "Where is he that is born king of the Jews?" They did not ask *whether* he was born because they already believed that, but *where* he was born; and as if someone had asked them how they knew that this king had been born, they added: "We have seen his star in the East, and are come to adore him"—in other words, "We, being in the East, have seen the star which showed that he was born." We have seen it, I say, placed over Judea. Or, "We, being in our own region, saw his star in the east" (meaning "to the east of us"). By these words, as Remy says in his *Original*, they professed their faith in the One who is true man, true king, and true God: true man, since they said, "Where is he who is born?"—true king, since they said, "king of the Jews"—true God, because they added, "We have come to adore him." The commandment was that none should be adored save God alone.

Herod, hearing this, was troubled, and all Jerusalem with him. The king was troubled for three reasons. First, the Jews might accept the newborn king as their own, and expel Herod as a foreigner. Hence Chrysostom: "As even a light breeze sways a branch high up on the tree, so a whisper of rumor can disturb men in high station, burdened as they are with the weight of their honors." Second, he was afraid the Romans would blame him if someone whom Augustus had not appointed were called king of Jerusalem, because the Romans had decreed that no god should be worshiped nor any man called king without the emperor's permission and approval. Third, this king, supreme in his land, was troubled because, as Gregory says, with the birth of the King of heaven the height of heaven is opened, and earthly heights are brought low.

All Jerusalem also was troubled, and this for three reasons. First, the impious cannot be gladdened by the coming of the just One. Second, they thought to flatter their troubled king by showing him that they too were disturbed. Third, as conflicting winds whip up the waves of the sea, so kings who are set against each other stir up the populace, and the Jews feared that contention between the present and the coming king could breed sedition among their own people. This last reason is Chrysostom's.

Herod then assembled all the priests and scribes and inquired of them where the Christ would be born. When they told him that this would be in Bethlehem of Judah, he secretly summoned the wise men and diligently questioned them about the time of the star, so that he might know what to do in case the Magi did not return to him; and he told them to bring him word once they had found the child, pretending that he himself wanted to adore him, whereas he intended to kill him.

Note that when the Magi entered Jerusalem, the star no longer guided them, and this for three reasons. The first was to make them look for Christ's birthplace, so that they would be assured of his birth both by the appearance of the star and by the predictions of the prophets; and so it happened. The second was that when they sought human help, they deserved to lose the help from above. The third was that, as the apostle says, signs are given to infidels but prophecy to the faithful: therefore the sign that was given to the Magi while they were still infidels would not appear to them while they were still among the believing Jews. These three reasons are touched upon in the *Gloss*.

When the Magi departed from Jerusalem, the star went before them until it came and stood above where the child was. There are three opinions—Remy gives them in his *Original*—about what sort of star this was. Some say it was the Holy Spirit, who appeared to the Magi as a star as he later descended as a dove upon Christ at his baptism. Others, including Chrysostom, say that the star was an angel, the same angel who appeared to the shepherds; but since the shepherds were Jews and used reason, the angel appeared to them as a rational being, whereas, since the Magi were pagans and did not have the use of reason, the angel appeared to them as a star. Still others hold what is thought to be the truer explanation, namely, that the star was newly created and returned to the underlying matter after its mission was accomplished.

This star, according to Fulgentius, differed from others in three ways: in its location, since it was not fixed in the firmament but was suspended at a level of the air close to earth; in its brilliance, because it was brighter than other stars, so bright indeed that sunlight could not dim it and even at midday it appeared brightest of all; and in its motion, because it went before the Magi like a traveler, not going round in circles but straight ahead. Three other differences are treated in the *Gloss* on Matthew 2, the first words of which are: "This star of the Lord's birth. . . ." Here the first difference is in the star's origin, because the other stars were created at the beginning of the world, this one at a moment in time. It was different, secondly, in its purpose, because the other stars, as Genesis tells us, were set in the heavens to be for signs and seasons, but this one to show the Magi their way. The third difference was in duration: the other stars are perpetual, but this one, once its purpose was fulfilled, returned to the underlying matter.

Seeing the star, they rejoiced with exceeding great joy. Note that the star the Magi saw was a fivefold star—a material, a spiritual, an intellectual, a rational, and a supersubstantial star. The first, the material star, they saw in the East. The spiritual star, which is faith, they saw in their hearts, for if this star of faith had not shone in their hearts, they never would have come to the vision of that first star. They had faith in Christ's humanity (for they said: "Where is he who is born . . ."), in his royal dignity (for they said: ". . . king of the Jews . . ."), and in his divinity (". . . we have come to adore him"). The third, the intellectual star, is the angel they saw in sleep, when they were warned by an angel not to go back to Herod: but according to some other *Gloss* it was not an angel but the Lord himself who warned them. The fourth, the rational star, was the Blessed Virgin, whom they saw with the Child. The supersubstantial star, which was Christ himself, they saw in the manger; and of these two last stars we read: "Entering into the house they found the Child with Mary his mother." Each of these five is called "the star." Thus the first, Ps. 8:4: "the moon and the stars which thou hast founded"; the second, Ecclus. 43:10: "the glory of the stars (i.e., of the virtues) is the beauty of heaven (i.e., of the celestial man)"; the third, Bar. 3:34: "The stars have given light in their watches and rejoiced"; the fourth in the hymn *Ave maris stella*; the fifth, Apoc. 22:16: "I am the root and stock of David, the bright and morning star."

At the sight of the first and second of these stars the Magi rejoiced. Seeing the third, they rejoiced with joy. The sight of the fourth made them rejoice with great joy, and of the fifth, with exceeding great joy. Or, as the *Gloss* says: "He who rejoices with great joy rejoices about God, who is the true joy," and adds, "with great joy" because nothing is greater than God, and "with exceeding great joy" because great joy may be more or less great. Or the evangelist intended to show, by the mounting emphasis in these words, that men rejoice more over things lost and found again than over what they had always possessed.

The Magi entered the little house and found the Child with his mother. They fell to their knees and offered their gifts of gold, frankincense, and myrrh. Here Augustine exclaims: "O infancy, to whom the stars are subject! O Infant, great and glorious, over whose swaddling clothes the angels keep watch, to whom the stars do obeisance, before whom kings tremble and seekers of wisdom kneel! O blessed house! O seat of God second only to heaven, lighted not by a lamp but by a star! O heavenly palace wherein dwells not a bejeweled king but a God clothed in flesh, who lies not on soft cushions but in a hard crib, sheltered not by a golden ceiling but by a roof of thatch blackened by soot yet studded with stars! I am amazed when I see the cloths and perceive the heavens, I am shaken when in the crib I look upon a beggar Child whose glory rises above the planets!" In the same vein Bernard writes: "What are you doing, O Magi, what are you doing? You worship a baby at the breast, wrapped in poor cloths, in a shabby hut! Is this a God? What are you doing? Offering him gold? Then he is a king! But where is his royal hall, where is his throne, where his throng of courtiers? Is this stable his palace, this manger his throne, his courtiers Joseph and Mary? Here the wise men give up their wisdom in order to become wise." Hilary also speaks about this in the second book of his treatise *On the Trinity*: "A virgin gives birth, but the birth is of God. The baby whimpers and the angels sing their praises, the cloths are soiled and God is adored. So the dignity of power is not lost as the humbleness of the flesh is made manifest. Behold in the infant Christ not only lowliness and weakness but the sublimity and excellence of divinity." And Jerome, in his commentary on the Epistle to the Hebrews, says: "Look upon the cradle of Christ and see heaven! You behold the infant crying in his crib, listen at the same time to the angels' songs of praise. Herod pursues, but the Magi adore, the One whom the Pharisees know not but the star points out. He is baptized by a menial but the voice of a thundering God is heard; he is immersed in the waters but the dove descends, indeed the Holy Spirit as a dove."

Why did the Magi offer these three gifts? There are several reasons. The first, it was traditional among the ancients, as Remy says, that no one presented himself empty-handed before a god or a king, and the Persians and Chaldeans were used to offering gifts such as these. The Magi, as we read in the *Scholastic History*, came from the borderland of Persia and Chaldea where the Saba river flows (so the region is called Sabaea). Another reason is given by Bernard: they offered gold to the holy Virgin to relieve her poverty, frankincense to dispel the bad odor of the stable, and myrrh to strengthen the child's limbs and drive out harmful worms. A third reason is that the gold was offered for tribute, the incense for sacrifice, and the myrrh for burial of the dead. So these three gifts corresponded to Christ's royal power, divine majesty, and human mortality. A fourth is that gold symbolizes love, incense prayer, and myrrh the mortification of the flesh; and these three we ought to offer to Christ. Lastly, the gifts signify three attributes of Christ, namely, his most precious divinity, his most devout soul, and his intact and uncorrupted flesh.

These three attributes were also symbolized by the three articles that were in the Ark of the Covenant. Aaron's rod, which blossomed, betokened the flesh of Christ, which rose from the dead; Ps. 27:7: "And my flesh hath flourished again." The tables of stone on which the commandments were written stood for his soul, in which were all the treasures of the knowledge and wisdom of the hidden God. The manna signified his divinity, which has all savor and all sweetness. The gold, therefore, being the most precious of metals, we understand to be the precious divinity of Christ, the incense his prayerful soul because incense signifies devotion and prayer; Ps. 141:2: "Let my prayer be directed as incense in thy sight." The myrrh, which preserves from corruption, prefigured his uncorrupted flesh.

The Magi, having been warned in sleep not to return to Herod, went back to their country by another route. See now the stages of their progress! A star led them and they followed it; men—nay, prophets—taught them; an angel showed them the way home; and they rested in Christ.

The bodies of the Magi used to be at Milan, in the church of the Friars Preachers, but are now in Cologne. Helena, the mother of Constantine, first brought them to Constantinople, and later they were transferred to Milan by Saint Eustorgius, the bishop of that city. After the emperor Henry took possession of Milan, he moved the bodies to Cologne on the Rhine river, and there they are honored by the people with great veneration and devotion.

---

15. Saint Paul, Hermit

This Paul was the first hermit, as Jerome, who wrote his life, testifies. To escape the persecution of Decius he took refuge in a boundless desert, and there, unknown to men, he lived for sixty years in a cave.

The emperor Decius had two names and was also known as Gallienus. His reign began in the year 256. Paul, seeing the tortures that Decius was inflicting on Christians, fled to the desert. At that time two young Christian men were apprehended. One of them had his whole body coated with honey and was exposed under a blazing sun to be stung to death by flies, hornets, and wasps. The other was laid upon a downy bed in a pleasant place cooled by soft breezes, filled with the sound of murmuring streams and the songs of birds, redolent with the sweet odor of flowers: he was bound down with ropes entwined with flowers, so that he could not move hand or foot. Then a very beautiful but totally depraved young woman was sent to defile the body of the youth, whose only love was for God. As soon as he felt the disturbance of the flesh, having no weapon with which to defend himself, he bit out his tongue and spat it in the face of the lewd woman. Thus he drove out temptation by the pain of his wound and won the crown of martyrdom. It was the sight of such tortures as these that caused Paul, terrified, to seek safety in the desert.

Meanwhile Saint Anthony thought that he was the first monk to live the eremitic life, but it was made known to him in a dream that there was another such hermit, holier than he. Anthony set out through the forest to find this hermit. First he met a hippocentaur, a creature half man and half horse, who directed him to go to the right. Next he encountered an animal carrying some dates, the upper part of whose body was that of a man, the lower parts those of a goat. Anthony required him in the name of God to say what he was, and he answered that he was a satyr (a creature the pagans erroneously believed was a god of the forest). Finally a wolf came to meet him and led him to Saint Paul's cell. Paul, however, knowing that Anthony was approaching, had closed and locked his door. Anthony begged him to let him in, declaring that he would rather die where he was than go away. After a time Paul yielded and opened the door, and they fell into a warm embrace.

When it was time for food, a crow flew down, carrying a loaf formed of two halves. Anthony wondered at this, but Paul told him that God provided him daily with food: this day the quantity was doubled to take care of the guest. There followed a pious argument: which of them was worthy to divide the loaf? Paul deferred to Anthony as his guest, Anthony to Paul as his senior. In the end both took hold of the loaf and broke it into two equal parts.

As Anthony was on his way back to his own cell, he saw angels bearing the soul of Saint Paul heavenwards. Hurriedly retracing his steps, he found Paul's body kneeling upright in the attitude of prayer. He thought the saint was still alive, but finding that he was indeed dead he exclaimed: "O blessed spirit, what you practiced in life you now exemplify in death!" He had no means of burying the body, but two lions came up, dug a grave, and, when the saint was buried, went back to the forest. Anthony took Paul's mantle, which was woven of palm leaves, and wore it on solemn occasions. Paul died about the year 287.

16. Saint Remy

The name Remigius (Remy) comes from *remi*, to feed, and *geos*, earth, one who feeds earthlings with sound doctrine. Or the name comes from *remi*, shepherd, and *gyon*, wrestling, one who tends his flock and wrestles. Remy fed his flock with the word of his preaching, the good example of his life, and the support of his prayer. Moreover, there are three kinds of arms—for defense, such as the shield, for attack, like the sword, and for protection, like the breastplate and the helmet. Remy struggled against the devil with the shield of faith, the sword of the word of God, and the helmet of hope. His life was written by Hincmar, archbishop of Rheims.

Remy was a glorious confessor of the Lord, noted for his learning. His birth was foreseen by a hermit in the following manner. When the Vandal persecution had devastated the whole of France, a certain recluse, a holy man who had lost the sight of his eyes, prayed the Lord for the peace of the Church in France. An angel appeared to him and said: "Know that the woman named Cilina will give birth to a son, Remy by name, who will free his people from the attacks of their wicked enemies." When the hermit awoke, he went immediately to the home of Cilina and told her all he had seen in a vision. She did not believe him because she was already old, but he went on: "Know this, that when you are nursing your child, you are to anoint my eyes with your milk and so restore my sight."

All these things happened as foretold, and in due time Remy fled from the world and became a hermit. His fame spread, and when he was twenty-two years old, the entire population of Rheims elected him their archbishop. He was so gentle that the birds came to his table and ate crumbs of food from his hands. And once when he was a guest in the house of a certain matron and her supply of wine was running short, Remy went to the cellar and made the sign of the cross over the wine cask; and after he had prayed, the wine overflowed the cask and half-filled the cellar.

Clovis, king of France, was at that time a pagan, and his wife, a very devout Christian, could not win him to the faith. But when he saw a huge army of the Alemanni coming against him, he made a vow to the Lord God whom his wife worshiped that if he was granted victory over the Alemanni, he would accept the faith of Christ. His wish was fulfilled, and Clovis went to the blessed Remy and asked to be baptized. When he arrived at the baptismal font, the sacred chrism was missing, but a dove flew down with a phial of chrism in its beak, and the bishop anointed the king with it. This phial is preserved in the church at Rheims, and to this day the kings of France are anointed with this chrism.

A long time passed, and a certain Genebald, a prudent, worthy man, took in marriage one of Remy's nieces; but for religious motives they separated, and Remy ordained Genebald as bishop of Laon. Genebald, however, allowed his wife to visit him often for instruction, and as a result of their frequent meetings his passions were aroused and the two lapsed into sin. The woman conceived and bore a son, and sent word to the bishop. He was dismayed and sent back the following message: "Because the child was acquired by robbery, I want him called Latro (robber)." However, to avoid arousing suspicion, Genebald allowed his wife to visit him as before, and, despite his tears over the first sin, they sinned again. This time she gave birth to a daughter, and when the bishop was informed of this, he answered; "Name this child Vulpecula (little fox)."

Finally Genebald came to his senses and presented himself to Saint Remy, prostrated himself at the prelate's feet, and wanted to take off the stole he wore as a bishop. The saint forbade him and, when he heard what had happened, gently consoled the penitent bishop and shut him up in a cramped cell for seven years, meanwhile governing the church of Laon himself. On Holy Thursday of the seventh year, while Genebald was absorbed in prayer, an angel of the Lord stood before him, told him that his sin was forgiven, and ordered him to leave his cell. He answered: "That I cannot do, because my lord Remy locked the door and put his seal upon it." The angel said: "So that you may know that heaven is opened to you, the door of this room will be opened without damage to the seal," and the door opened at once. But Genebald threw himself in the entrance with his arms extended in the form of a cross and said: "Even if my Lord Jesus Christ were to come to me here, I shall not go out unless my lord Remy, who shut me in, comes here himself." Then Saint Remy, admonished by the angel, went to Laon and reestablished the bishop in his see. Genebald persevered in holy works for the rest of his life, and his son Latro succeeded him as bishop, and he also was a saint.

Remy, renowned for his many virtues, went to his rest in peace about the year of the Lord 500. On this same day the birthday of Saint Hilary of Poitiers is celebrated.

※

---

17. Saint Hilary

Hilary, or Hilarius, looks much like *hilaris*, hilarious, cheerful, because the saint was always cheerful in the service of God. Or the name is like *alarius*, which comes from *altus*, high, and *ares*, virtue, because he was high in knowledge and virtuous in his life. Or the name is from *hyle*, the primordial matter, which is obscure, and Hilary's words, both spoken and written, were obscure and profound.

Hilary, a native of the region of Aquitania, who eventually became bishop of the city of Poitiers, rose like the bright morning star among the other stars. At first he was married and had one daughter, but while still a layman led the life of a monk. His way of life and the depth of his learning caused him to be elected bishop of Poitiers, and he defended the true faith against the heretics, not only in his own city but throughout France. At the urging of two bishops who had fallen into heresy he, together with Saint Eusebius of Vercelli, was exiled by the emperor, who favored the heretics.

The Arian heresy was spreading in all directions, and the emperor gave permission to the bishops to convene and to debate the truths of the Christian faith. Hilary came to the meeting, but the same two bishops, who could not withstand his eloquence, had him sent back to Poitiers. He went to the island called Gallinaria, which was overrun by snakes, but the snakes fled from him. He raised a stake in the middle of the island as a boundary mark which he forbade the reptiles to pass, so that for them half the island was like the sea, not the land. And when he returned to Poitiers, he restored to life an infant who had died without baptism: the saint lay in the dust for a long time and prayed, and the two rose together, the old man from his prayer and the infant from death.

Hilary's daughter Apia wanted to marry, but the bishop persuaded her to choose holy virginity instead. Then, seeing her firm in her resolve but fearing that she might weaken, he prayed the Lord not to let her live any longer but to take her to himself. His prayer was heard: a few days later the maiden migrated to the Lord, and her father buried her with his own hands. The mother of the blessed Apia, weighing in her mind what had happened, begged the bishop to obtain the same grace for her that he had for their daughter. He did this, and by his prayers sent his wife ahead to the heavenly kingdom.

At that time Pope Leo, led astray by the perfidy of the heretics, convoked a council of all the bishops, and Hilary went to it though he was not invited. The pope, hearing that he had arrived, gave orders that no one should rise to greet him or offer him a seat. Hilary came in and Leo said to him: "Are you Hilary the cock?"[1] "I am not a cock," the saint responded, "but I was born in Gaul and I am a bishop from Gaul." Leo: "So you are Hilary from Gaul, and I am Leo, apostolic bishop and judge of the see of Rome!" Hilary: "You may be Leo, but not the Lion of Judah, and if you sit in judgment, it is not in the seat of majesty." The pope rose angrily, saying: "Wait a little while until I come back, and I'll deal with you as you deserve." Hilary: "If you don't come back, who will answer me in your place?" Leo: "I won't be long, and when I get back, I'll take your pride down a peg!"

The pope went out to take care of a need of nature, but was seized with dysentery and perished miserably. Meanwhile Hilary, seeing that no one gave him a seat, sat down on the ground, quoting the Ps. 23:1: "The earth is the Lord's." On the instant, by the will of God, the ground on which he sat rose up and put him on the same level with the other bishops. Then, when the pope's wretched end was made known, Hilary rose, confirmed all the bishops in the Catholic faith, and sent them home so confirmed.

There is, however, some doubt about this miraculous death of a Pope Leo, not only because there is nothing about it in the *Scholastic History* or the *Tripartite History*, but also because the *Chronicle* has no record of a pope by that name at that time. Furthermore, Jerome says: "The holy Roman church has always kept itself spotless and will so continue for all time, unstained by any heresy." It

---

[1] A play on words. *Gallus* means either "a Gaul" or "cock."

might, however, be thought that at that time someone named Leo was pope, not by canonical election but by tyrannical usurpation; or perhaps Pope Liberius, who was on the side of the heretical emperor Constantine, was also called Leo.[2]

At length, after performing many miracles, and being old and infirm, Hilary, knowing that his end was near, called for the priest Leontius, for whom he had deep affection. It was night, and he asked Leontius to go outside, and to report to him anything he heard. Doing as he was told to, Leontius came back and said he had heard nothing but the noise of the city crowds. The priest watched at the bedside of the dying bishop and again, around midnight, was ordered to go out and to report what he heard. This time he came back to say that he had heard nothing. Then a great light, so bright that the priest could not bear it, shone about the bishop, and as the light slowly faded, the saint departed to the Lord. He flourished about the year 340, in the reign of Constantine.[3] His feast day is on the octave of Epiphany.

Two merchants owned a block of wax, and one of them offered the wax at the altar of Saint Hilary though the other refused to do so. Promptly the wax split into two parts, one remaining with the saint, the other returning to the merchant who had refused to offer it.

※

---

18. Saint Macarius

Macarius is derived from *macha*, skillfulness, and *ares*, virtue, or from *macha*, beating, and *rio*, master. Saint Macarius was skillful in outwitting the deceits of the demons and virtuous in his life; he beat his body to tame it and was masterly in ruling his brother monks.

Macarius the abbot, making his way one day across a vast desert, paused to sleep in a tomb where the bodies of pagans were buried, and pulled out one of the bodies to use as a pillow. The demons tried to frighten him, and one of them called to him in a woman's voice: "Get up and come bathe with us!" Another

---

[2] Indeed there was no Pope Leo before Pope Leo I the Great, 440–461. Pope Liberius was exiled by Constantius II (not "Constantine") for refusing to approve Arian errors. Later he subscribed to a compromise formula drawn up by Arian bishops, and still later repudiated his own subscription. Cf. references in n. 1 to chapter 103 on Saint Felix, Pope, below.

[3] According to *Butler's Lives of the Saints* (New York: P. J. Kenedy & Sons, 1963), 1:79, Hilary became bishop of Poitiers about the year 350 and died about the year 368.

demon entered the body and, as if he were the dead man, answered: "I cannot come because some pilgrim is lying on top of me!" But the saint, not terrified at all, answered the body, saying: "Get up and go, if you can!" Hearing this the demons fled, crying out in a loud voice: "Sir, you have defeated us!"

Another day, when abbot Macarius was passing through a swamp on his way to his cell, he met the devil, who carried a scythe with which he tried to cut down the saint but could not strike him. The devil addressed him: "I suffer much violence from you, Macarius, because I cannot prevail against you. How is this? Whatever you do, I do. You fast, I eat hardly anything. You deprive yourself of sleep, I am always awake. There is only one thing by which you outdo me!" "And what is that?" asked the abbot. "Your humility," the demon replied, "and that is why I cannot prevail against you."

Being sorely tried by temptations of the flesh, Macarius filled a large sack with sand and walked in the desert for several days carrying the sack over his shoulders. Theosebius met him and asked why he was carrying so heavy a load. His answer: "I am tormenting my tormentor!"

Another time the saint saw Satan passing by dressed like a man, and wearing a linen cloak with a number of flasks protruding from its pockets. "Where are you going?" Macarius asked him. "I am taking drink to the monks," was the answer. "But why so many bottles?" "I want to satisfy their tastes," said the devil. "If one flask doesn't please one of them, I offer a second and a third, until he finds one that he likes." Macarius met him again on his way back and asked: "How did you do?" Satan responded: "They are all so holy that no one consented to drink, except one whose name is Theotistus." Macarius hurried off in search of this monk and by his exhortations converted him. Another day he met the devil equipped as before and asked him where he was going. "To the brethren." On the way back the two met again and the old abbot asked: "How did things go today?" "Badly!" "How so?" "Because now they are all holy, and, worst of all, I have lost the one I had, and he has become the holiest of the lot!" At this the saint offered thanks to God.

One day Saint Macarius found the skull of a dead man and, having prayed, asked the skull whose head it had been. The answer was that he had been a pagan. Macarius put the question: "Where is your soul?" "In hell!" The next question was whether he was very deep in hell. "As deep as the distance between heaven and earth." "Are there any deeper down than you?" "Yes, the Jews!" "And still deeper than the Jews?" "The farthest down of all are false Christians, who, having been redeemed by the blood of Christ, think little of so great a price."

At times when Macarius walked farther and farther into the desert in search of solitude, he thrust a reed into the ground every so often, so as to be able to find his way back. But once, when he had gone ahead for nine days and stopped somewhere to rest, the devil collected all the reeds and laid them beside the saint's head. This made his return journey very difficult.

One of his monks was deeply troubled by the thought that as long as he stayed in his cell, he was useless, whereas if he lived among other people, he might be of service to many. The monk told Macarius about these disturbing thoughts, and the abbot said: "My son, this is the way to answer them: 'This at least I do for Christ. I stay here within the walls of my cell.'"

Once a flea bit Macarius and he killed it with his hand, and a great deal of blood came out of it. As a punishment for having so avenged the injury done him he lived naked in the desert for six months and came out with bites and scabs all over his body. After that he fell asleep in the Lord, renowned for his many virtues.

═══════════════ ✳ ═══════════════

19. Saint Felix

This saint is called Felix *in Pincis*, either from the place where he was buried, or because he is reputed to have been killed with styluses: *pinca* is the word for stylus. The story is that Felix was a schoolmaster and was exceedingly strict with his pupils. He was also a Christian, and as he professed his faith openly, the pagans seized him and turned him over to the boys he taught; and they stabbed him to death with their styluses. The Church, however, seems to hold that he was a confessor, not a martyr.

Whenever Felix was led before an idol to force him to sacrifice to it, he blew on it and it fell to pieces. Another account tells us that Maximus, bishop of Nola, was fleeing from his persecutors and fell to the ground exhausted from hunger and cold. An angel sent Felix to assist him, and Felix, who had no food with him, saw a cluster of grapes hanging from a thornbush and squeezed the juice into the bishop's mouth. Then he took the old man on his shoulders and carried him home. When the bishop died, Felix was elected to succeed him.

One day when he was preaching and his persecutors were looking for him, he slipped through a narrow opening in the wall of a ruined house and hid there. In a trice, by God's command, spiders spun a web across the space. The pursuers, seeing the web, thought that no one could have gone through the opening, and went on their way. Then Felix took refuge in another place and a widow brought him food for three months, but she never saw his face. Finally peace was restored and he returned to his church, where he went to his final rest in the Lord. He was buried outside the city, in a place called Pincis.

Felix had a brother who was also called Felix. When the persecutors tried to make him worship the idols, he said to them: "You are the enemies of your gods, because if you take me to them, I will blow upon them as my brother did, and they will be shattered."

Saint Felix is said to have kept a garden. It happened that some men came one night to steal his vegetables, but something forced them instead to spend the night cultivating the garden. Coming upon them in the morning Saint Felix greeted them, and they confessed the wrong they had intended to do. Then they went away, forgiven.

Some pagans came to seize Felix but were stricken with intolerable pain in their hands. They howled with the pain, and Felix said to them: "Say 'Christ is God' and the pain will leave you." They said the words and were cured. A priest of the false gods came to him and said: "Sir, my god saw you coming and took flight. I asked him why he fled, and he answered: 'I cannot bear this Felix's holiness!' Therefore, if my god fears you so much, how much more should I fear you!" Felix then instructed him and he was baptized. To some who were worshiping Apollo Felix said: "If Apollo is truly God, let him tell me what I am holding in my hand." What he held was a paper on which the Lord's Prayer was written. Apollo made no answer and the pagans were converted.

When the time came for him to die, Saint Felix celebrated mass, gave the *Pax* to his people, stretched himself on the floor of the church in prayer, and departed to the Lord.[1]

20. Saint Marcellus

Marcellus comes from *arcens malum*, keeping evil away, or from *maria percellens*, striking the seas, i.e., striking and beating back the adversities of life in the world. The world is likened to the sea, because as Chrysostom says in his *Commentary on Matthew*, in the sea there is confusion of sound, constant fear, the image of death, tireless clashing of the waves, and never-ending change.

---

[1] Some elements in this brief legend appear in the life of Saint Felix of Nola as written by Saint Paulinus of Nola. *Butler's Lives of the Saints* (New York: P. J. Kenedy & Sons, 1963), 1:81, notes ". . . the invention of a 'St. Felix in Pincis.' This confusion was probably due to the existence of a church on the Pincio at Rome dedicated to St. Felix of Nola." Saint Felix of Nola was commemorated in the pre–Vatican II Roman Calendar as "Priest and Martyr" but is not included in the current liturgical calendar.

Marcellus was supreme pontiff in Rome and reproached the emperor Maximian for his relentless cruelty to Christians. He celebrated the mass in the house of a Roman lady, which was consecrated as a church. The emperor in his wrath turned the house into a stable for cattle and confined Marcellus there to care for the animals. After many years of this servitude he fell asleep in the Lord about the year 287.

21. Saint Anthony

Anthony (Antonius) comes from *ana*, above, and *tenens*, holding, meaning one who holds on to higher things and despises worldly things. Saint Anthony despised the world because it is unclean, restless, transitory, deceptive, bitter. So Augustine says: "O sordid world, why are you so clamorous? Why do you mislead us? You want to hold us though you pass away: what would you do if you stayed? Whom would you not deceive with sweetness, you who, being bitter, lure with sweet foods?"

Saint Anthony's life was written by Saint Athanasius.

When Anthony was twenty years old, he heard the following words read in church: "If thou wilt be perfect, go sell what thou hast and give to the poor." He sold all he had, gave the proceeds to the poor, and from then on lived the life of a hermit. He bore countless trials inflicted by the demons. Once when he had overcome the spirit of fornication by the virtue of faith, the devil appeared to him in the form of a black child, prostrated himself, and admitted that he was conquered. Anthony had prayed to God to let him see this demon of impurity that plagued young people; and, seeing the demon in the form just described, he said: "Now that I have seen you in all your ugliness, I will fear you no longer."

Another time, when he was living hidden away in a tomb, a crowd of demons tore at him so savagely that his servant thought he was dead and carried him out on his shoulders. Then all who had come together mourned him as dead, but he suddenly regained consciousness and had his servant carry him back to the afore-mentioned tomb. There, lying prostrated by the pain of his wounds, in the strength of his spirit he challenged the demons to renew the combat. They appeared in the forms of various wild beasts and tore at his flesh cruelly with their teeth, horns, and claws. Then of a sudden a wonderful light shone in the place and drove all the demons away, and Anthony's hurts were cured. Realizing that Christ was there, he said: "Where were you, O good Jesus, where were you? Why did you not come sooner to help me and heal my wounds?" The Lord answered: "Anthony, I was here, but I waited to see how you would fight. Now, because you fought manfully, I shall make your name known all over the earth." Indeed, so great was the saint's fervor that when the emperor Maximian was putting Christians to death, Anthony followed the martyrs, hoping to merit martyrdom, and was exceedingly sad when that grace was not granted him.

Another time he had gone into a cave and found there a silver dish. He said to himself: "How did this silver dish get here, since there is no trace of man's presence? It is so big that if it had fallen from some traveler's pack, it could not have been missed. O devil, this is your doing, but you will never be able to change my will!" No sooner were the words uttered than the dish vanished in a puff of smoke. Later he found a huge mass of real gold, but the gold went up in flames.

Now the saint sought refuge in the mountains, where he lived for twenty years and became known for his innumerable miracles. Once when he was rapt in ecstasy, he saw the whole world covered with snares connected one to the other, and exclaimed: "Oh, how can anyone escape these traps?" And he heard a voice say: "Humility!" Again he was carried aloft by angels, but demons were there to bar his way, proclaiming the sins he had committed from childhood on. To them the angels said: "You should not tell these things, because by the mercy of Christ they are wiped away. If you know how he became a monk, tell that!" The demons had nothing more to say. Anthony was borne upward in freedom and freely set down on earth.

Anthony tells us this about himself: "I once saw a very tall devil who dared to claim for himself the power and knowledge of God, and he asked me: 'What do you want me to give you, Anthony?' But I spat in his face and set upon him armed with the name of Christ, and he vanished at once." Again the devil appeared to him in a shape so high that his head seemed to touch the sky. When Anthony asked him who he was, he said he was Satan, and added: "Why do the monks attack me and the Christians curse me?" Anthony answered: "What they do is just, because you harass them at all times with your insidious schemes." Satan: "I never harass them, but they harass each other! And I am reduced to nothing because Christ reigns everywhere!"

An archer once saw Saint Anthony taking his ease with his brethren and was displeased at the sight. Anthony said to him: "Put an arrow to your bow and shoot!" The archer did so, but when he was ordered to do the same thing a second and third time, he said: "If I go on doing this, my bow will break!" Anthony: "So it is with us as we do God's work. If we stretch ourselves unduly, we are quickly broken, so it is good for us to relax from our rigors from time to time." Hearing this, the man was edified and went his way.

Someone asked Anthony what he should do to please God. The saint replied: "Wherever you go, have God always before your eyes; follow the testimony of

Holy Scripture in all you do; and whenever you settle down someplace, don't be too quick to go somewhere else. Observe these three rules and you will be saved." An abbot asked him: "What should I do?" Anthony: "Don't trust in your own righteousness; practice moderation in food and talk; and don't worry about things done in the past." Again, Anthony said: "Just as fish too long out of water die, so monks who tarry outside their cells and keep company with lay people weaken in their resolve to live a quiet life." And again: "Anyone who lives in solitude and quiet is saved from three kinds of warfare—against hearing, talking, and seeing. All he still has to fight against is his heart."

Several monks came with an old man to visit Abbot Anthony, and the saint said to them: "You are in good company with this old man." Then he asked the man: "Good father, have you found these brothers good?" "They are good enough, but their house has no door on it. Anyone who wants to walks into the stable and unties the donkey." What he meant was that whatever came into their heads came out through their mouths. Abbot Anthony also said: "It is well to know that there are three movements of the body; one is from nature, one from too much food, and one from the devil."

A monk had renounced the world but not totally, because he kept some of his belongings. Anthony told him to go and buy meat, and he did so; and on the way back he was attacked and bitten by dogs. Anthony told him: "Those who renounce the world and still want to have money will likewise be assailed by demons and torn apart."

The saint was finding life in the desert tedious and prayed: "Lord, I want to work out my salvation, but I cannot control my thoughts." He arose and walked out, and saw someone sitting at work and then rising to pray; and this was an angel of the Lord, and the angel said to him: "Do as I am doing, and you will be saved."

Some of the monks asked Anthony about the state of their souls, and the following night a voice called him and said: "Get up, go out, and see what you see." What he saw was a huge, terrifying being whose head towered to the clouds, and also figures with wings trying to fly upwards but being held back by the monster's outstretched hands; yet there were others freely flying upwards, and these he could not stop. Anthony heard sounds of great joy mixed with sounds of grief, and understood that it was the devil, holding back some guilty souls and groaning because he could not halt the heavenward flight of the holy ones.

One day when Anthony was at work with his brethren, he looked up to heaven and beheld a sad vision. He knelt and begged God to avert the coming mischief; and, when the monks questioned him, with tears and sobs he said that a crime unheard-of throughout the ages was imminent. "I saw," he said, "the altar of God surrounded by a pack of horses that tore and trampled everything around them with their hooves; for the Catholic faith is about to be torn asunder by a violent storm, and men will trample like horses upon Christ's sacraments."

Then the voice of the Lord sounded, saying: "My altar will be dishonored." In fact, two years thereafter the Arians rose up and split the unity of the Church, defiled the baptistry and the churches, and slaughtered Christians on the altars as if they were lambs of sacrifice.

A certain highly placed Egyptian named Ballachius, an Arian, attacked the Church of God, turned virgins and monks out into the streets naked, and had them whipped in public. Anthony wrote him: "I see the wrath of God coming upon you. Stop persecuting Christians unless you want to incur God's anger, because he is threatening you with death soon to come." The unhappy man read the letter, laughed at it, spat on it, threw it to the ground, had its bearers whipped, and sent them back to Anthony with the following message: "You, who discipline your monks with such care. Soon the rigor of our discipline will be visited upon you!" Five days later, as he was about to mount his gentle horse, the animal bit him, knocked him to the ground, and trampled and crushed his legs. In three days he was dead.

Some of the monks asked Anthony to tell them the word of salvation, and he said: "You have heard the Lord saying, 'If someone strikes you on the right cheek, turn to him also the other.'" They replied: "That we cannot fulfill." He said: "Then at least bear the one blow patiently." "We cannot do that either." Anthony: "Well, at least do not strike rather than be struck." "Even that is too much!" So Anthony said to his disciple: "Prepare a fortifying drink for these brothers, because they are so frail!" But, to the brothers: "All I can say to you is, 'Pray!'" All this we read in *Lives of the Fathers*.

At last, in the 105th year of his life, the blessed Anthony embraced his brethren and expired in peace during the reign of Constantine, which began about the year 340.[1]

22. Saint Fabian

Fabian (Fabianus) is like *fabricans*, building, and Fabian built heavenly bliss for himself, gaining it by a triple right—by adoption, by purchase, and by a fight well fought.

---

[1] Constantine II, who reigned 337–340.

Fabian was a citizen of the city of Rome. When the pope died and the people gathered to elect a successor, Fabian went along to see what the outcome would be. Lo and behold, a white dove came down upon his head, and the people, filled with wonder, elected him as supreme pontiff.

Pope Damasus tells us that Pope Fabian sent seven deacons to all areas of the Church and assigned seven subdeacons to them to write down the Acts of the martyrs. Haymon wrote that when the emperor Philip wished to be present at the vigil of Easter and to share in the mysteries, Fabian forbade him to do so until he had confessed his sins and taken his place with the penitents.

In the thirteenth year of his pontificate Fabian was beheaded by order of the emperor Decius and so won the crown of martyrdom. He suffered about the year of the Lord 253.

23. Saint Sebastian

Sebastian comes from *sequens*, following, *beatitudo*, beatitude, *astim*, city, and *ana*, above; therefore one who pursues the beatitude of the city on high, the city of supernal glory—in other words, one who acquires and possesses that city. Augustine says that this possession costs five payments: poverty pays for the kingdom, pain for joy, toil for rest, dishonor for glory, and death for life. Or Sebastian is derived from *bastum*, saddle; for Christ is the horseman, the Church the horse, Sebastian the saddle on which Christ rode to do battle in the Church and obtain the victory of many martyrs. Or the name means surrounded, or going about; for the saint was surrounded by arrows as a porcupine is with quills, and he went about among the martyrs and strengthened them all.

Sebastian was a most Christian man. A native of Narbonne and a citizen of Milan, he was so well thought of by the emperors Diocletian and Maximian that they made him commander of the First Cohort and attached him to their personal retinue. Sebastian sought military rank for the sole purpose of being able to visit Christians under torture, to encourage them when he saw that their spirit was weakening.

Two twin brothers of the high nobility, named Marcellian and Marcus, were about to be beheaded for the faith of Christ, and their parents came to try to get them to change their minds. Their mother came first, her hair disheveled, garments torn, and breasts bare, and she cried: "O my dearest sons, misery unheard-of and grief unbearable surround me! Woe is me, I am losing my sons who go willingly to death! Yet if the enemy were taking them away, I would follow their captors through the thick of battle! If they were condemned to prison, I would break in if it cost me my life! What new way of dying is this, that the headsman is exhorted to strike, life's only wish is to be ended, death is invited to take over? New is this mourning, new this misery, when the youth of one's offspring is lost of their own accord, and in their pitiful old age the parents are forced to live on!"

Now the father arrived, supported by his slaves, his head sprinkled with dust, and he cried out to heaven: "I come to bid farewell to my sons on their way to death! Unhappy me, that the funeral rites I had prepared for myself I will carry out for my children! O my sons, staff of my old age and twin fruit of my loins, why do you love death so much? Come hither, young men, and mourn my sons with me! Come, old men, and weep with me for my sons! Gather here, you fathers, and see to it that you do not suffer woes like mine! Let my eyes fail with weeping, that I may not see my sons fall beneath the sword!"

Then came the wives of the two, setting their children in front of them and saying with loud cries: "To whom are you leaving us? Who will guide the lives of these infants? Who will divide your great possessions? Alas, what iron hearts are yours, that you disdain your parents, spurn your friends, cast away your wives, abandon your children, and of your own will hand yourselves over to the executioners!"

All this began to soften the hearts of the two men. Then Saint Sebastian, who was present, broke into the midst of the gathering and said: "O you strong soldiers of Christ, do not let these tearful blandishments cause you to forsake the everlasting crown!" And to the parents he said: "Do not fear, they will not be separated from you but will go to heaven and prepare starry dwellings for you. Since the world began, life has betrayed those who placed their hopes in it, has deceived their expectations, has fooled those who took its goods for granted, and so it has left nothing certain and proves itself false to all. Life induces the thief to steal, the angry to rage, the liar to deceive. It commands crimes, orders wickedness, counsels injustice. But this persecution, which we suffer here on earth, flames up today and tomorrow blows away, today burns hot and cools tomorrow: it comes on in an hour and in another is gone. But the pain of eternity is ever renewed to stab more deeply, is increased to burn more fiercely, is fanned to prolong the punishment. Therefore let us stir up our desire, our love for martyrdom! The devil thinks he conquers by making martyrs, but while he catches he is caught, while he binds he is bound, while he wins he loses, while he tortures he is tortured, while he strangles he is killed, while he mocks he is laughed at!" As Saint Sebastian was saying all this, suddenly a radiance shone from heaven and shed light upon him for almost an hour, wrapping him in its splendor like a shining cloak, and seven radiant angels surrounded him. A youth also appeared at his side and gave him the kiss of peace, saying: "You will always be with me!"

Now Zoe, the wife of Nicostratus in whose house the two holy young men were kept under guard, fell at the saint's feet and begged forgiveness, nodding and gesturing because she had lost the power of speech. Sebastian said: "If I am Christ's servant, and if all that this woman has heard from my mouth and has believed is true, may he who opened the mouth of Zechariah his prophet let her speak!" Immediately the woman's speech returned and she said: "Blessed be the words of your mouth, and blessed be all who believe what you have said! For I have seen an angel holding a book before you in which everything you said was written."

Hearing this, her husband also knelt at Saint Sebastian's feet and prayed for forgiveness. Then he loosed the martyrs' bonds and told them to go free. They answered that they would not give up the victory they were about to win. The Lord had endowed the saint's words with such grace and power that not only did he confirm Marcellian and Marcus in their acceptance of martyrdom but also converted their father, whose name was Tranquillinus, their mother, and many others of their household to the faith, and the priest Polycarp baptized all of them.

Tranquillinus suffered from a painful disease, but as soon as he was baptized, his illness was cured. The prefect of the city of Rome was afflicted with the same disease and asked Tranquillinus to bring to him the person who had cured him. So Sebastian and the priest Polycarp went to the prefect, who asked them to restore his health, and Sebastian told him that he would first have to renounce the worship of false gods and empower him to demolish his idols: then only would he regain his health. The prefect said that his slaves, not Sebastian, should destroy the idols, but Sebastian answered: "They are afraid to strike their gods, and if they did it and the devil harmed them, the infidels would say that this was because they had laid hands on their gods." So Polycarp and Sebastian girded themselves and reduced more than two hundred idols to fragments.

Then they said to Chromatius, the prefect: "We have shattered the idols and you are not cured. This must be because you have not yet renounced your false beliefs, or else you are holding back some idols." The prefect admitted that he had a room in which the whole order of the stars was represented. His father, he said, had spent two hundred pounds of gold on the work, and by it he could foretell future events. Sebastian insisted: "As long as you keep that room intact, you yourself will not be made whole." The prefect then gave his consent, but his son Tiburtius, a forthright young man, spoke up: "I will not suffer so great a work to be dismantled; but rather than seem to stand in the way of my father's recovery, I will have two ovens fired, and if my father is not cured once the room is destroyed, these two will be roasted alive!" Sebastian replied: "Do as you say!" While the room in question was being taken apart, an angel appeared to the prefect and told him that the Lord Jesus had cured him of his malady. The prefect realized that he was indeed cured, and ran after the angel to kiss his feet, but the angel would not allow this because the man had not yet received baptism. So he and his son Tiburtius and fourteen hundred persons among his family and retainers were baptized.

Meanwhile Zoe was seized by the pagans, subjected to long torture, and died a martyr. Learning of this, Tranquillinus burst out: "The women are winning the crown ahead of us! Why do we go on living?" And he was stoned to death a few days later. Saint Tiburtius was ordered to burn incense to the gods or to walk barefoot over burning coals. He made the sign of the cross and walked unshod over the coals, saying: "I feel as if I am treading on rose leaves in the name of our Lord Jesus Christ." Fabian, the prefect, retorted: "Everyone knows that Christ has taught you the arts of magic!" Tiburtius: "Be still, unhappy man! You are not worthy to pronounce that sweet holy name!" The prefect, indignant, had him beheaded. Marcellian and Marcus were tied to a stake and chanted the words of the Psalm: "Behold how good and how pleasant it is for brothers to dwell together in unity!" The prefect shouted at them: "Wretches, put aside your madness and save yourselves!" "Never have we feasted so well!" they responded. "Please leave us just as we are for as long as we are clothed in our bodies!" The prefect ordered soldiers to run them through with lances, and thus they consummated their martyrdom.

After all this, the prefect denounced Sebastian to the emperor Diocletian, who summoned the saint and said to him: "I have always had you among the first in my palace, and all this time you have been acting secretly against my welfare and offending the gods." Sebastian: "I have always worshiped God who is in heaven, and prayed to Christ for your salvation and the good estate of the Roman Empire." But Diocletian gave the command to tie him to a post in the center of the camp, and ordered the soldiers to shoot him full of arrows. They shot so many arrows into his body that he looked like a porcupine, and left him for dead. Miraculously set free, he stood on the steps of the imperial palace a few days later and, as the emperors came out, firmly reproached them for their cruel treatment of Christians. "Isn't this the Sebastian whom we ordered shot to death?" the emperors exclaimed. Sebastian answered: "The Lord deigned to revive me so that I could meet you and rebuke you for the evils you inflict on the servants of Christ!" The emperors then ordered him to be beaten with cudgels until he died, and had his body thrown into the sewer to prevent the Christians from honoring him as a martyr. The following night Saint Sebastian appeared to Saint Lucina, revealed to her where his body was, and asked that it be buried near the remains of the apostles, which was done. Sebastian suffered under the emperors Diocletian and Maximian, whose reign began about the year of the Lord 287.

In the first book of his *Dialogues* Pope Gregory reports that a woman in Tuscany, recently married, was invited by friends to attend the dedication of a church to Saint Sebastian; but the night before she was to go there, she was aroused by carnal desire and could not refrain from lying with her husband. Morning came, and, fearing to be shamed in the sight of men more than before God, she went to the church. No sooner had she set foot into the place where the saint's relics were kept than the devil seized her and began to torment her as all looked on. A priest of the church snatched the altar cloth from the altar and threw it around her, whereupon the devil laid hold of the priest. The woman's friends took her to sorcerers who might, by their incantations, drive the devil from her, but as the magic formulas were pronounced, by the judgment of God a legion of demons, 6,666 in number, infested the woman and tormented her more and more severely. Then a certain man eminent for his holiness, whose name was Fortunatus, prayed for her and she was saved.

In the *Annals of the Lombards* we read that during the reign of King Gumbert all Italy was stricken by a plague so virulent that there was hardly anyone left to bury the dead, and this plague raged most of all in Rome and Pavia. At this time there appeared to some a good angel followed by a bad angel carrying a spear. When the good angel gave the command, the bad one struck and killed, and when he struck a house, all the people in it were carried out dead. Then it was divinely revealed that the plague would never cease until an altar was raised in Pavia in honor of Saint Sebastian. An altar was built in the church of Saint Peter in Chains, and at once the pestilence ceased. Relics of Saint Sebastian were brought to Pavia.

Ambrose, in his Preface for Saint Sebastian, says: "Lord, the shedding of the blood of the blessed martyr Sebastian for the confession of your name shows your wonderful works: you confer strength in weakness and success to our efforts, and at his prayer give help to the infirm."

24. Saint Agnes, Virgin

The name Agnes comes from *agna*, a lamb, because Agnes was as meek and humble as a lamb. Or her name comes from the Greek word *agnos*, pious, because she was pious and compassionate; or from *agnoscendo*, knowing, because she knew the way of truth. Truth, according to Augustine, is opposed to vanity and falseness and doubting, all of which she avoided by the virtue of truth that was hers.

Agnes was a virgin most sensible and wise, as Ambrose, who wrote the story of her martyrdom, attests. When she was thirteen years old, she lost death and found life. Childhood is computed in years, but in her immense wisdom she was old; she was a child in body but already aged in spirit. Her face was beautiful, her faith more beautiful.

One day she was on her way home from school when the prefect's son saw her and fell in love. He promised her jewels and great wealth if she consented to be his wife. Agnes answered: "Go away, you spark that lights the fire of sin, you fuel of wickedness, you food of death! I am already pledged to another lover!" She began to commend this lover and spouse for five things that the betrothed look for in the men they are to wed, namely, nobility of lineage, beauty of person, abundance of wealth, courage and the power to achieve, and love transcendent. She went on: "The one I love is far nobler than you, of more eminent descent. His mother is a virgin, his father knows no woman, he is served by angels; the sun and the moon wonder at his beauty; his wealth never lacks or lessens; his perfume brings the dead to life, his touch strengthens the feeble, his love is chastity itself, his touch holiness, union with him, virginity."

In support of these five claims, she said: "Is there anyone whose ancestry is more exalted, whose powers are more invincible, whose aspect is more beautiful, whose love more delightful, who is richer in every grace?" Then she enumerated five benefits that her spouse had conferred on her and confers on all his other spouses: he gives them a ring as an earnest of his fidelity, he clothes and adorns them with a multitude of virtues, he signs them with the blood of his passion and death, he binds them to himself with the bond of his love, and endows them with the treasures of eternal glory. "He has placed a wedding ring on my right hand," she said, "and a necklace of precious stones around my neck, gowned me with a robe woven with gold and jewels, placed a mark on my forehead to keep me from taking any lover but himself, and his blood has tinted my cheeks. Already his chaste embraces hold me close, he has united his body to mine, and he has shown me incomparable treasures, and promised to give them to me if I remain true to him."

When the young man heard all this, he was beside himself and threw himself on his bed, and his deep sighs made it clear to his physicians that lovesickness was his trouble. His father sought out the maiden and told her of his son's condition, but she assured him that she could not violate her covenant with her betrothed. The prefect pressed her to say who this betrothed was, whose power over her she talked about. Someone else told him that it was Christ whom she called her spouse, and the prefect tried to win her over with soft words at first, and then with dire threats. Agnes met this mixture of cajolery and menace with derision, and said: "Do whatever you like, but you will not obtain what you want from me." The prefect: "You have just two choices. Either you will sacrifice to the goddess Vesta with her virgins, since your virginity means so much to you, or you will be thrown in with harlots and handled as they are handled."

Because she was of the nobility, the prefect could not bring force to bear upon her, so he raised the charge of her Christianity. Agnes said: "I will not sacrifice to your gods, and no one can sully my virtue because I have with me a guardian of my body, an angel of the Lord." Then the prefect had her stripped and taken nude to a brothel, but God made her hair grow so long that it covered her better than any clothing. When she entered the house of shame, she found an angel waiting for her. His radiance filled the place with light and formed a shining mantle about her. Thus the brothel became a place of prayer, and anyone who honored the light came out cleaner than he had gone in.

The prefect's son now came with other young men, and invited them to go in and take their pleasure with her, but they were terrified by the miraculous light and hurried back to him. He scorned them as cowards and in a fury rushed in to force himself upon Agnes, but the same light engulfed him, and, since he had not honored God, the devil throttled him and he expired. When the prefect heard of this, he went to Agnes, weeping bitterly, and questioned her closely about the cause of his son's death. "The one whose will he wanted to carry out," she said, "thus got power over him and killed him, whereas his companions, frightened by the miracle they saw, retreated unharmed." The prefect persisted: "You can prove that you did not do this by some magical art, if you are able to bring him back to life by your prayer." So Agnes prayed, and the youth came to life and began to preach Christ publicly. At this the priests of the temples stirred up a tumult in the populace, shouting: "Away with the witch, away with the sorceress who turns people's heads and befuddles their wits!" On the other hand the prefect, impressed by the miracle, wished to set her free but, fearing that he would be outlawed, put a deputy in charge and went away sadly.

The deputy, Aspasius by name, had Agnes thrown into a roaring fire, but the flames divided and burned up the hostile crowd on either side, leaving the maiden unscathed. Aspasius finally had a soldier thrust a dagger into her throat, and thus her heavenly spouse consecrated her his bride and martyr. It is believed that she suffered in the reign of Constantine the Great, which began in A.D. 309. Her kinsmen and other Christians buried her joyfully and barely escaped the pagans who tried to stone them.

Saint Agnes had a foster sister named Emerentiana, a holy virgin who had not yet received baptism. She stood by the grave and continued to berate the pagans, who proceeded to stone her to death. At once God sent an earthquake with lightning and thunder, and a large number of pagans perished; and from that time on they did not harm those who came to the virgin's tomb. The saint's parents and relatives, watching beside her grave on the eighth day, saw a chorus of angels clothed in shining gold garments, and in their midst Agnes, similarly clad and with a lamb whiter than snow standing at her right hand. Agnes consoled them: "Do not mourn my death but rejoice and be glad with me, because I now have a throne of light amidst all these holy ones." In memory of this, the octave of the feast of Saint Agnes is observed.

Constance, Constantine's daughter and a virgin, was stricken with leprosy, and when she heard of the vision just described, she went to the saint's grave. While praying there she fell asleep and saw Saint Agnes, who said to her: "Be constant, Constance! If you believe in Christ, you will be freed of your disease." Awakening at the sound of the voice she found herself completely cured. She received baptism and had a basilica erected over the saint's grave. There she continued to live a virginal life and by her example gathered many virgins around her.

Paulinus, a priest serving the church of Saint Agnes, was tormented by a violent temptation of the flesh and, not wishing to offend God, sought permission of the supreme pontiff to contract marriage. The pope, knowing the priest's goodness and simplicity, gave him a ring set with an emerald and ordered him to go before a beautiful statue of Saint Agnes that stood in her church, and to command her, in the pope's name, to allow herself to become his betrothed. When the priest delivered this order, the statue immediately extended the ring finger, accepted the ring, and withdrew the hand, and the priest was delivered of his temptation. It is said that this ring can still be seen on the finger of the statue. Elsewhere, however, we read that the pope told a priest that he wanted him to commit himself to a certain spouse, to take care of her and nourish her, and that this spouse was the church of Saint Agnes, which was falling into ruins. The pope gave him a ring that would mark his espousal to the aforesaid statue, and the statue extended its finger and withdrew it. Thus the priest espoused the statue.

In his book *On Virgins*, Ambrose says of Saint Agnes: "The old, the young, the children sing of her! No one is more worthy of praise than the one who is praised by all! All men are her heralds, who by speaking of her proclaim her martyrdom. Marvel, all of you, that she stood forth as God's witness although at her age she could not yet decide about herself! So it came about that what she said regarding God was believed, although what she said about man was not yet believed, because what is beyond nature is from the author of nature. This is a new kind of martyrdom! One hardly capable of suffering is already ripe for victory, one unready to fight is yet able to win the crown, one masters virtue before reaching the age of judgment! Bride hastens not to the bridal chamber as the virgin marched to the place of torture, joyous her approach, swift her stride!" And, from Ambrose's Preface: "Saint Agnes, disdaining the advantages of noble birth, merited heavenly honors; caring nothing for what human society desires, she won the society of the eternal king; accepting a precious death for professing Christ, she at the same time was conformed to his likeness."

25. Saint Vincent

The name Vincent may be interpreted as burning up vice, or as conquering fires, or as holding on to victory. Saint Vincent did indeed burn up vices, getting rid of them by mortification of the flesh; he conquered the fires of torture by dauntless endurance of pain and held on to victory over the world by despising it. He conquered three things that were in the world, namely, false errors, impure loves, and worldly fears, which he overcame by wisdom, purity, and constancy. In this regard Augustine says: "The martyrdoms of the saints have taught and do teach us how to conquer the world, with all its fallacies, fervors, and fears."

It is said that Augustine compiled an account of Vincent's passion. Prudentius celebrated it in verse.

Vincent, noble by birth and nobler by his faith and religious devotion, was deacon to Valerius the bishop.[1] Since he was readier of speech than the bishop, Valerius entrusted his office of preaching to the deacon and devoted himself to prayer and contemplation. The two were brought to Valencia by order of Dacian the governor and held in harsh confinement. Then, when he supposed that they were almost dead from hunger, he ordered them brought into his presence. When he found them in good health and spirits, he was angry and burst out: "What do you say for yourself, Valerius, you who act contrary to the rulers' decrees in the name of religion?" Valerius was hesitant in answering, and Vincent said to him: "Venerable father, don't mutter to yourself as if you were feebleminded, but speak out loud and clearly! Or, holy father, if you so command, I will undertake to reply to this judge." "My dear son," said the bishop, "I had long since commissioned you to speak for me; and now I leave it to you to answer for the faith in which we stand." Vincent then turned to Dacian and said: "What you have said comes down to our denying our faith; but know that for right-thinking Christians it is wicked and blasphemous to repudiate the worship of God!"

Wrathful, Dacian ordered the bishop to be sent into exile. On the other hand Vincent, that contumacious and presumptuous youth, had to be made an example that would put fear into others, so by the governor's command he was stretched on the rack and torn limb from limb. When he had been thus mutilated, Dacian said to him: "Tell me, Vincent, how does your miserable body look to you now?" But the saint, smiling, replied: "Indeed, this is what I have

---

[1] Of Saragossa.

always longed for!" Angrier than ever, the governor began to threaten him with every sort of torture unless he yielded to his commands, but Vincent exclaimed: "O happy me! The harder you try to frighten me, the more you begin to do me favors! Up, then, wretch, and indulge your malicious will to the full! You will see that by God's power I am stronger in being tortured than you are in torturing me!"

At this the governor began to shout and whip his brutal servants on with words and blows, whereupon Vincent taunted him: "The way you talk, Dacian! What you're saying proves me right and my torturers wrong!" At this the governor, beside himself with rage, called out to the ruffians: "Miserable wretches, you're getting nowhere! Get on with it! You've been able to torture parricides and adulterers into admitting anything and everything, yet this Vincent all alone has withstood everything you tried!" Challenged, the torturers drove iron hooks into the saint's sides so that the blood spurted from his whole body and the entrails hung out between the dislocated ribs.

Now Dacian spoke: "Have pity on yourself, Vincent! Recover your splendid youth and be spared further torments!" "You venomous tongue of the devil," Vincent retorted, "I have no fear of your torments! The only thing I do fear is that you pretend to want to have mercy on me. Indeed the more wrathful I see you, the greater and fuller is my rejoicing! Don't forgo a single jot or tittle of your tortures . . . then you will have to admit yourself defeated in all of them!"

So he was taken down from the rack and carried to a gridiron with a fire under it. The saint reproached the torturers for being too slow and hastened ahead of them toward the suffering that awaited him. Willingly mounting the grill he was seared, singed, and roasted, and iron hooks and red-hot spikes were driven into his body. Wound was piled upon wound, and, as the flames spread, salt was thrown on the fire so that the hissing flames could make the wounds more painful. The weapons of torture tore past his joints and into his belly, so that the intestines spilled out from his body. Yet with all this he remained unmovable and, turning his eyes toward heaven, prayed to the Lord.

When his men reported this to Dacian, he said: "Too bad! You're beaten so far, but now let us keep him alive and make him suffer longer! Shut him up in the darkest of dungeons, cover the floor with sharp fragments for him to lie on, shackle him to a post, leave him without any sort of human consolation, and when he is dead, let me know." The heartless knaves carry out the wishes of their still more heartless master. But behold! The King for whom the soldier suffers commutes his suffering to glory. The darkness of the dungeon is dispelled by dazzling light, the sharpness of the potsherds is changed into the softness of flowers, the shackles fall from his feet, the saint enjoys the solace of angels; and when he walks on the flowers and joins in the angels' chant, the lovely melody and the wonderful perfume of the flowers spread abroad. The guards are terrified by what they witness through the cracks in the dungeon walls, and are converted to the faith.

Hearing what had happened, Dacian, in a fury, said: "Now what more can we do to him? See, he has bested us! Let him be transferred to a couch and laid on soft pillows. We must not make him ever more glorious by having him die in torment, but after he is refreshed, let him be punished and tortured again!" So Vincent was carried to a soft couch, but after he had rested there for a short while, suddenly he breathed his last. This was about the year A.D. 287, in the reign of Diocletian and Maximian.

When this news came to him, Dacian, seeing himself thus defeated, was thunderstruck. "I was not able to break him while he was alive," he mused, "but I can still punish him now that he is dead, and so ease the pain I feel and claim the victory after all!" He gave orders to expose the saint's body in an open field to be devoured by bird and beast, but it was quickly surrounded by a guardian band of angels and no animal could reach it. Then a crow, voracious by nature, attacked birds bigger than himself and drove them away with the beating of his wings; and when a wolf came up, the crow chased him by biting him and cawing loudly. Then the bird lighted and turned his head toward the body, staring at it fixedly as if marveling at the guard of angels.

Learning of the latest events, Dacian said: "I can see that I can't take his measure even now that he's dead!" But he ordered the corpse to be weighted down with a huge millstone and cast into the sea, so that what could not be consumed by earthbound beasts might at least be devoured by marine monsters. Sailors therefore transported the body far out to sea and threw it overboard, but the corpse returned to the shore faster than the sailors could get there. Then Vincent revealed its whereabouts to a certain lady, who, with some others, found it and gave it honorable burial.

Of this martyr Augustine says: "Blessed Vincent was victorious in words, victorious in pain, victorious in confessing his faith, victorious in tribulation, victorious burned, victorious submerged, victorious ashore, victorious in death." Augustine also says: "He was stretched and twisted to make him suppler, scourged to make him learn better, pummeled to make him more robust, burned to make him cleaner." Ambrose in his Preface says of him: "Vincent is racked, beaten, scourged and burned but still unconquered: his courageous stance for the holy Name is unshaken, the fire of zeal heats him more than the hot iron, he is more bound by the fear of God than by fear of the world, he is determined to please God rather than the judge, he longs to die to the world rather than to God." And Augustine again: "We are confronted with a wondrous play—an iniquitous judge, a bloodthirsty torturer, a martyr unconquered, a contest between cruelty and piety."

Prudentius, who shone during the reign of Theodosius the Elder which began in A.D. 387, says that Vincent replied to Dacian: "Torments, dungeons, iron claws, fiery spikes, and death, the ultimate pain—all this is play to Christians." Then Dacian said: "Bind him, bend him, twist his arms, pull him apart until the joints of his limbs snap and break and through the wounds the palpitation of his liver can be seen." This soldier of God laughed, mocking the bloody hands that could not force the iron claws still deeper into his limbs. When he lay in the dungeon, an angel said to him: "Get up, glorious martyr, stand up fearless and be counted our comrade in the angelic troop. O soldier most unconquerable, stronger than the strongest, the cruel, bitter tormentors themselves fear you, their conqueror!" Prudentius exclaims: "O renowned above all, you have won the palm of a double victory, you have gained two laurel crowns together!"

26. Saint Basil, Bishop

Basil was a venerable bishop and an eminent doctor of the Church. His life was written by Amphilochius, bishop of Iconium.

Basil's great holiness was made manifest in a vision granted to a hermit named Ephrem, who, being rapt in ecstasy, saw a column of fire the tip of which touched heaven, and heard a voice from above saying: "Basil is as great as the immense column you see before you." Ephrem therefore went into the city on the feast of the Epiphany because he wanted to look upon this great man. When he saw the bishop clothed in shining white vestments, moving solemnly in procession with his clergy, he said to himself: "I know now that I have gone to all this trouble for nothing! This man, who enjoys such honor, certainly cannot be the great saint I expected to see! We who have borne the burden of the day and the heats are not so rewarded, whereas this man, with all his honors and his throng of attendants, is a column of fire. . . . I wonder!"

Basil knew in spirit what was going through Ephrem's mind and had the hermit brought before him; and when he came into the bishop's presence, he saw a tongue of flame coming out of his mouth as he spoke. "Truly Basil is great," Ephrem exclaimed, "truly Basil is a column of fire, truly the Holy Spirit speaks through his mouth!" And to the bishop Ephrem said: "I beg of you, my lord, to obtain for me the ability to speak Greek." "You have asked for something very difficult," Basil replied. Nevertheless he prayed for the hermit, who at once began to speak in Greek.

There was another hermit who, seeing Basil somewhere in procession in his pontifical robes, looked down on him, thinking in his heart that the bishop took much pleasure in such pomp. And a voice spoke to him, saying: "You there, you have more delight in stroking your cat's tail than Basil takes in his accoutrements!"

Emperor Valens, who was partial to the Arians, confiscated a church that belonged to the Catholics and gave it to the heretics. Basil went to the emperor and said: "Your majesty, it is written that the honor of the king loves judgment and the judgment of the king loves justice. Why then has your heart ordered that the Catholics be excluded from their church and it be given to Arians?" "So here you are, Basil," the emperor retorted, "shaming me again! This is unworthy of you!" Basil replied: "What is worthy of me is to die, if I must, for justice!"

Then Demosthenes, who was in charge of the emperor's table and was also a partisan of the Arians, spoke in defense of the heretics and treated the bishop insolently. "Your business is to see that the king's meals are well prepared," Basil answered, "and not to cook up divine dogmas!" The steward, in confusion, had no more to say.

Valens now addressed the bishop: "Basil, go and give judgment in this case, but do not be swayed by immoderate love of the people." So Basil went before the Catholics and Arians and proposed that the doors of the church be closed and sealed with the seal of each party, and that the church would belong to the party at whose prayer the doors opened. This satisfied everybody. The Arians then prayed for three days and three nights, but when they came to the church the next morning, the doors were not opened. Then Basil led a procession to the church, prayed, gave the doors a light blow with his pastoral crook, and said: "Lift up your heads, O ancient doors, that the king of glory may come in!"[1] The doors flew open at once, all the people went in, thanking God, and the church was returned to the Catholics.

As we read in the *Tripartite History*, Valens promised great rewards to Basil if the latter would come around to his way of thinking, but the bishop said: "That sort of promise might beguile children, but those who are nourished with the words of God do not allow one syllable of the divine dogmas to be altered." The emperor was indignant, the same history tells us, and prepared to write a decree sentencing the bishop to exile; but first one pen, then a second, then a third broke in his hand, and the hand began to tremble violently. The emperor gave up and destroyed the decree.

A highly respected man named Heradius had an only daughter whom he intended to consecrate to the Lord, but the devil, foe of the human race, got wind of this and inflamed one of Heradius's slaves with love for the girl. The man, knowing that as a slave he could not possibly win the embraces of so noble a lady, turned to a sorcerer and promised him a lot of money if he could advance his suit. The sorcerer told him: "I can't do that, but, if you wish, I'll send you to the devil my master, and if you do as he tells you, you will get what you desire." The young man said: "I'll do it!" Therefore the soothsayer wrote a letter

[1] Ps. 24:9 (RSV).

to the devil and sent it by the hand of the slave. The letter read: "Since it behooves me, my lord, with care and dispatch to draw people away from the Christian religion and attract them to your service so that you may grow day by day, I am sending you this youth who is burning with desire for a certain young woman. I ask that he may have his wish, so that in this individual I may gain glory and may be able to win over others to you."

When he gave the letter to the slave, he said: "Go and stand on the tomb of a heathen at midnight and cry out to the demons. Hold this letter up in the air, and they will come right away!" So the youth went and summoned the demons, throwing the letter into the air. In an instant the prince of darkness, surrounded by a swarm of demons, was at hand; and when he had read the letter, he asked: "Do you believe in me, that I can bring about what you want?" "I believe, my lord!" he answered. The devil: "And do you renounce your Christ?" The slave: "I renounce him!" "You Christians are a perfidious lot," the devil retorted. "Sometimes when you need me, you come to me. Then, when your wish is gratified, you deny me and turn to your Christ; and he, out of the abundance of his clemency, takes you back! But if you want me to fulfill your desire, write me a script in your own hand, in which you profess to renounce Christ, your baptism, and the Christian faith; to be my servant; and to be condemned with me at the Last Judgment."

The slave wrote as directed, repudiating Christ and indenturing himself to the service of the devil. At once his new master called up the spirits who were in charge of fornication, and commanded them to go to the aforesaid maiden and set her heart afire with love for the slave. They carried out his orders so thoroughly that the girl threw herself sobbing on the ground and cried out to her father: "Have pity on me, father, have pity on me! I am sorely tormented by my love for one of our slaves! Show me your fatherly love, and wed me to this man whom I love and for love of whom I suffer torture! Otherwise you will shortly see me dead and will have to account for me on the Day of Judgment!"

Her father wailed aloud and said: "Oh, wretched me! What has happened to my poor child? Who has stolen my treasure? Who has put out the soft light of my eyes? I had hoped to join you to your heavenly spouse, and counted on winning my salvation through you, and here you are, maddened by a lascivious love! O my daughter, let me join you to the Lord as I had planned! Do not drive my old age to the netherworld with grief!" The girl, however, continued to cry out: "Either grant my wish quickly, father, or you will see me dead very soon!" She was weeping bitterly and almost raving; and finally her father, in the depths of desolation and being badly advised by his friends, gave in to her wish, had her married to the slave, and handed over all he owned to her, saying: "Be on your way, my poor, poor daughter!"

Now, while the couple had made their home together, the young man did not go to church or make the sign of the cross, nor did he commend himself to God in any way. Some of their acquaintances noticed this and said to his wife:

"Do you know that your husband, whom you chose for yourself, is not a Christian and never enters a church?" When she heard this, she was filled with dread, threw herself to the ground, tore her flesh with her fingernails, beat her breast, and said: "O wretched me! Why was I born, and when I was born, why did not death take me at once?" She told her husband what she had heard, and he declared that there was not a word of truth in it; what she had been told was entirely false. "If you want me to believe you," she said, "you and I will go to church together tomorrow!"

Seeing that he could no longer hide the truth, the former slave then told his wife the whole story from the beginning, and the young woman groaned aloud. Then she hurried to blessed Basil and told him all that had happened to her husband and to herself. Basil summoned the husband, heard the story from him, and asked: "My son, do you want to turn back to God?" "I want to, my lord," he answered, "but I can't! I made my profession to the devil, renounced Christ, put my renunciation in writing, and gave it to the devil."

"Don't worry, my son!" said Basil. "The Lord is kind and will accept you as a penitent." He laid his hands on the youth and made the sign of the cross on his forehead. Then he shut him in a cell for three days, after which he visited him and asked him how things were with him. "I can't stand it, my lord," he said. "They shout at me and terrorize me and attack me! They hold up my script as an excuse for their treatment, saying: 'You came to us, not we to you!'" "Don't be afraid!" Basil said. "Just believe!" He gave him a little food, again made the sign of the cross on his forehead, closed his cell, and prayed for him. A few days later he visited him and said: "How are things now, my son?" "I still hear their shouting and their threats, father," the man answered, "but I no longer see them." Basil again gave him food and blessed him, closed the door, and continued to pray for him. After a number of days he went back and asked: "How now?" The young man replied: "I'm doing well, O saint of God! Today I saw you in a vision, fighting for me and beating the devil!"

The bishop then led him out of his cell, summoned all the clergy and religious and the whole populace, and urged all to pray for the man. Then he took him by the hand and led him to the church. There the devil came on with a horde of demons and, though invisible, took hold of the slave and tried to tear him away from the bishop's grasp. The young man called out: "Saint of God, help me!" But the evil one assaulted him with such force that in dragging the one he wanted he was also pulling the saint along. Basil said to him: "Most wicked spirit, is your own damnation not enough for you, that you try to bring down God's handiwork with you?" "You wrong me, Basil!" said the devil. "I did not go after him, it was he who came to me! He denied his Christ and made his profession to me, and I have it in his own handwriting!" Basil answered: "We will not stop praying until you give up the script." And as Basil prayed and held up his hands to heaven, the script, carried down by the breeze, came and settled in Basil's hands as all looked on. He caught it and asked the youth: "Do you recognize this writing, brother?" "Yes, it is my own hand," he replied. Whereupon Basil destroyed the script, led him into the church, made him worthy to receive the sacrament, instructed him and gave him rules for right living, and restored him to his wife.

There was a woman who had many sins on her conscience and had written them down on paper; at the end of the list she added one sin more serious than the others. Then she gave the list to blessed Basil, asking him to pray for her and by his prayers to wipe out the sins. So he prayed and, when he opened the paper, found that all the sins were deleted except the most serious one. The woman said to Basil: "Take pity on me, servant of God, and beg forgiveness of that sin as you obtained it for the rest."

The bishop said to her: "Leave me, woman, because I am a sinful man and need forgiveness as much as you do!" When she insisted, however, he told her: "Go to that holy man Ephrem, and he will be able to obtain what you are asking for." So she went to the holy man Ephrem, and when she told him why she had come, he said: "Leave me, woman, because I am a sinful man, and go back to Basil, my daughter, and he, the one who obtained pardon for the rest of your sins, will be able to do the same for this one. But hurry, if you are to find him still alive!"

The woman came to the city only to find Saint Basil being carried to his tomb. She followed, however, and began to call out: "Let God look upon us and judge between you and me, because you, though you could have won God's mercy for me, sent me off to someone else!" Then she threw her paper on the bier. A moment later it fluttered down to her, and when she unfolded it, she saw that that sin had been completely deleted. So she, and all who were present, gave heartfelt thanks to God.

Before the man of God departed from his body but while he was seriously ill with the malady of which he was to die, he called for a Jew named Joseph, a man highly skilled in the art of medicine, as though he needed the physician's services. Basil loved this man dearly because he foresaw that he was to convert the Jew to the Christian faith. However, as soon as Joseph took the bishop's pulse, he knew that he was at death's door and said to those in attendance: "Get ready whatever is necessary for his burial, because his death is imminent."

Basil heard this and said to Joseph: "You don't know what you're saying!" Joseph answered him: "Believe me, my lord, as surely as the sun will set this afternoon, so surely will your light go out today!" Basil: "And if I do not die today, what will you say?" Joseph: "But that is not possible, my lord!" Basil: "And if I survive till tomorrow at the sixth hour, what will you do?" Joseph: "If you are still alive at that hour, I will be the one to die." Basil: "Yes, may you die to sin, but live to Christ!" Joseph: "I know what you mean. If you survive till that hour, I will do what you are exhorting me to do."

Then blessed Basil, although by the law of nature he should have died within minutes, besought the Lord to grant him a delay, and he lived to the ninth hour the next day. Joseph was amazed when he saw this and believed in Christ; and

Basil, overcoming the weakness of the body by the power of his spirit, rose from his bed, went to the church, and baptized the Jew with his own hands. Then he went back to his bed and joyfully yielded up his soul to God. He flourished about A.D. 370.

---

27. Saint John the Almsgiver

John the Almsgiver held the office of patriarch of Alexandria. One night while he was at prayer, he saw in a vision a very beautiful maiden standing by him, wearing a crown of olive leaves. Seeing her he was astonished and asked her who she was. "I am Pity," she said, "and it is I that brought the Son of God down from heaven. Take me for your spouse and all will be well with you." John saw that the olive crown represented pity and compassion, and from that day on he became so compassionate that he was called *Eleymon*, the compassionate, the almsgiver. He always called the poor his masters, as the Hospitalers to this day call the poor their masters. He therefore met with his serving people and said to them: "Go through the city and make me a list of my masters, down to the last one." They did not understand what he meant, so he said: "Those whom you call the poor, the beggars, they are the ones I declare are our masters and helpers, for they are able to help us to get to heaven."

To encourage people to give alms he used to tell them that once some poor men were warming themselves in the sun, and they began to talk about those who gave alms, praising the good and reviling the bad. There was a certain Peter, a tax-collector, very rich and powerful but utterly pitiless toward the poor. When they came to his door, he drove them away angrily, and not one of them could be found who had ever had an alms from him. Then one of these men said: "What will you give me if I get something from him today?" They made a wager, and he went to Peter's house and begged for an alms. Peter came home at that moment and saw the poor man standing at his door. Just then his slave was carrying some wheaten loaves into the house, and Peter, finding no stone to throw, snatched up a loaf and hurled it angrily at the beggar. The man caught it and hurried back to his companions, showing them the alms that he had received from the tax-collector's hand.

Two days later the rich man lay mortally ill and saw himself in a vision standing before the Judge. Some black men were heaping up his evil deeds on one side of the scale, while opposite stood some white-clothed persons who looked sad because they could find nothing to put on their side. Then one of them said: "True, we have nothing but one wheaten loaf, which he gave, reluctantly, to Christ two days ago." He put the loaf on the scale, and it seemed to balance all the bad deeds on the other side. The white-robed angels said to him: "Add something to this loaf, or the demons will have you!"

The tax-collector woke up and found that he was cured of his illness, and said: "If the one loaf that I threw at that man in anger could do me so much good, how much more would it do for me if I gave all I have to the needy!" Then, one day when he was walking along dressed in his finest garments, a man who had lost all he had in a shipwreck asked him for something to wear. At once he took off his expensive cloak and gave it to the man, who took it and sold it as soon as he could. When the tax-collector went home and saw his cloak hanging in its place in the house, he was so sad that he could not eat, and said: "I was not worthy to have a needy man keep something to remember me by." But then while he was asleep he saw a personage more brilliant than the sun, with a cross on his head and wearing the cloak that he, Peter, had given to the man in need. "Why are you weeping, Peter?" the apparition asked. When Peter explained the cause of his sadness, the other asked: "Do you recognize this cloak?" "Yes, Lord," he answered. "I have been wearing it," the Lord told him, "since you gave it to me, and I thank you for your kindness, because I was freezing from the cold and you covered me."

Peter came to himself, began to bless the poor, and said: "As God lives, I will not die until I have become one of them!" He therefore gave all he had to those in need, then called in his notary and said to him: "I'm going to tell you a secret, and if you breathe a word of it or if you don't heed what I say, I'll sell you to the barbarians!" Then he gave him ten pounds of gold and said: "Go to the holy city and buy goods for yourself, and sell me to some Christian stranger and give the proceeds to the poor!" The notary refused, but Peter told him: "If you don't listen to me, I'll sell you to the heathens!" So the notary took him as one of his slaves, clothed in rags, to a silversmith, sold him for thirty pieces of silver, took the money, and distributed it to the poor.

Peter, now a slave, did the most menial work, and was treated with contempt and pushed and struck by the other slaves, who even called him a fool. The Lord, however, appeared to him frequently and consoled him, showing him the clothing and other gifts given to the poor. Meanwhile the emperor and everyone else bemoaned the loss of so valuable a man. Then some of his former neighbors came from Constantinople to visit the holy places and at one point were invited by Peter's master to be his guests. While they were at dinner, they whispered to each other: "That servant looks like our friend Peter, doesn't he?" And as they stared at him curiously, one said: "It certainly is Peter, and I'll get up and hold him!" But Peter sensed what was going on and got away. The doorman was a deaf-mute who opened the door only at a signal, but Peter ordered him to open, not by signs but speaking. The man heard at once and received the power of speech, answered Peter, opened the door, and let him out. Then, going into the house, he said, to the surprise of all who heard him speak: "That slave who worked in the kitchen has gone out and run away, but wait! He must be a servant of God, because when he said to me, 'I tell you, open!' a flame came out of his mouth and touched my tongue and ears, and right away I could hear and speak!" They all jumped up and ran after Peter, but could not find him. Then everyone who belonged to that house did penance for the vile way they had treated so good a man.

A monk named Vitalis wanted to test Saint John to see whether he would listen to rumors and be easily scandalized, so he went into the city and got a list of all the prostitutes. He went to them one by one and said to each one: "Give me this night, and don't do any other business." Then he went to the woman's house, knelt in a corner, and stayed there praying for the woman. In the morning he left, forbidding everyone to reveal what he was doing. One of the women, however, did make his way of life known, and at once, in answer to the old man's prayer, she began to be tormented by a demon. All the others said to her: "You're getting what you deserve from God because you told a lie! That scoundrel went in to you to commit fornication and for nothing else!"

That evening Vitalis said to all who were listening: "I've got to go, because there's a certain lady who's expecting me!" To many who blamed him for doing wrong he replied: "Have I not a body like everyone else? Or is God angry only with monks? Monks are men just like the rest!" But some said to him: "Go ahead and take one wife, father, but stop wearing that habit and giving scandal to others!" Vitalis, pretending to be angry, said: "I won't listen to you, leave me alone! Anyone who wants to be scandalized, let him be scandalized and let him beat his head against the wall! Did God appoint you to judge me? Go and mind your own business! You won't have to account for me!" He said these things at the top of his voice, and complaints reached blessed John, but God hardened John's heart so that he did not credit what he heard. Vitalis pleaded with God to reveal to someone after his death what he had been doing, so that it should not be imputed as sin to those who were scandalized by his actions. And in fact, Vitalis brought many of those women to conversion and found places in a monastery for a number of them.

One morning, however, as he was leaving the house of one of the prostitutes, a man on his way in to commit sin met him and slapped his face, saying: "Isn't it time, you wretch, for you to mend your ways and quit your filthy conduct?" Vitalis answered: "Believe me, you'll get from me such a slap that all Alexandria will come running!" And so it happened . . . Some time later the devil in the guise of a Moor gave the man a blow, saying: "This is the slap that Father Vitalis sends you!" And at once a demon began to torment him, so that all came running at the sound of his cries; but he repented, and was set free by the prayer of Vitalis. And when the man of God felt his death approaching, he left a written admonition: "Judge not before the time!" The women confessed what he had done, and all glorified God, blessed John first of all, who said: "Would that I had received the slap that he received!"

A poor man in pilgrim's dress came to John and begged an alms. John called his steward and said: "Give him six gold pieces!" The man took the money, went away and changed his clothes, came back, and again begged alms of the patriarch, who called his steward and said: "Give him six gold pieces!" After the beggar had left, the steward told the patriarch: "That's the second time today. All he did was change his clothes, but because you asked, I gave." Blessed John pretended not to know this. The mendicant, however, changed clothes again and begged alms of John a third time. The steward touched the patriarch's arm and nodded that this was the same man. Blessed John responded: "Go and give him twelve gold pieces! It may be my Lord Jesus Christ, testing me to see whether this man can go on asking more than I can go on giving!"

One time a certain high official wanted to invest some of the church's money in trade, but the patriarch firmly refused to give his consent because he intended to dispense the money to the poor. The two argued the point acrimoniously and parted in anger. But as the day waned, the patriarch sent word by his archpriest to the gentleman, saying: "My lord, the sun is setting." Hearing this, the official burst into tears and came to John, begging his pardon.

A nephew of John had been grossly insulted by a shopkeeper. He complained tearfully to the patriarch and refused to be comforted, and the patriarch responded: "How could anyone dare to contradict you or say a word against you? Trust my insignificant self, my child! This very day I will do something to that man that will make all Alexandria wonder!" The boy took comfort at what he heard, thinking that his relative would have the shopkeeper soundly whipped. The patriarch, seeing that the youngster was calmer, clasped him to his bosom, kissed him, and said: "My son, if you are really the nephew of my humble self, prepare to be insulted and beaten by everybody! True kinship is not determined by flesh and blood but by strength of mind." Quickly therefore he sent for the shopkeeper and dispensed him from all rents and payments. All who heard about this marveled at it and understood what John had meant when he said he would do something to the man that would make all Alexandria wonder.

The blessed John learned of the custom that as soon as an emperor was crowned, tomb-builders should take four or five small samples of marble of different colors, call upon the emperor, and say: "Out of what marble or metal does your majesty desire that your tomb be built?" John followed the custom and gave orders for the construction of his sepulcher, but prescribed that the monument was to remain unfinished until his death, and further ordered that at any celebration or festivity, some of those present with him and his clergy should come and say to him: "My lord, your tomb is unfinished. Give the orders for its completion, because you know not at what hour the thief may come."

A certain rich man saw that blessed John's couch was covered with cheap, thin bedclothes because he gave away better ones to the poor, so he bought a very costly quilt and gave it to the patriarch. John, finding it over him, could not sleep all night, thinking that three hundred of his masters could be covered for the price of this one bedcover; and he lamented all night long, saying: "How many lay down tonight without supper, how many lie in the public square soaked with rain, how many are there whose teeth chatter with the cold? And here you are, fed with fine fat fish and resting in your big bed with all your sins on top of you, warming yourself with a bedcover worth thirty pieces of silver! Humble John will not be so covered another time!" So the next morning he had the article sold and the price distributed to the poor. His wealthy friend learned of this, bought the quilt back, and gave it to blessed John, asking him not to sell it this time but to cover himself with it. John accepted it but ordered it to be sold and the proceeds to be passed on to his masters. The rich man again went and bought back the coverlet, took it to John, and said to him with a laugh: "Let's see who will give up first, you with your selling or I with my buying back!" In this way the saint gently plucked the rich man, so to speak, and told him that one might thus rob the rich with the intention of benefiting the poor without committing a sin, because each party gained thereby—the one because he was saving souls, the others because they received so great a reward.

In his effort to motivate people to give alms generously, blessed John often told the story of Saint Serapion. Serapion had just given away his coat to a poor man when he met another one who was suffering from the cold. To him he gave his shirt and sat nearly naked with his gospel book in his hand. A passerby asked him: "Father, who robbed you?" Serapion showed him the gospel book and said: "This did." But later, seeing another poor man, he sold the book and gave him the price. Somebody asked him where his gospel book was, and he replied: "The Gospel commands us, 'Sell all you have and give to the poor,' and I had the Gospel here and sold it as it commanded."

Another time when someone asked blessed John for an alms and he ordered five pence to be given to him, the man was indignant that more had not been given, and burst out with obscenities and cursed the patriarch to his face. His attendants wanted to rush at the beggar and give him a thrashing, but John would have none of it and said: "Let him be, brothers, let him curse me. Here I am, sixty years old, insulting Christ with my misdeeds, and shall I not bear with one curse from this man?" And he had his purse placed open in front of the fellow so that he could take from it as much as he wanted.

People were going out of the church after the reading of the Gospel and standing around at the doors, exchanging idle talk. Once, after the reading, the patriarch went out with them and sat down in their midst. They all seemed surprised at this, but he said to them: "My children, where the sheep are, there should the shepherd be! Therefore either you go in and I will go in with you, or you stay out here and I will do the same." He did this just once and so taught the people to stay in church.

A young man had run off with a nun, and the clergy denounced him to Saint John, saying that he ought to be excommunicated on the ground that he had lost two souls, his and the nun's. John restrained them, saying: "Not so, my sons, not so! I will show you that you yourselves are committing two sins. The first is that you go against the Lord's commandment, which says, 'Judge not, that you may not be judged.' The second, because you do not know for certain that they are still living in sin today and have not repented."

It frequently happened that when blessed John was at prayer and was rapt in ecstasy of spirit, he was heard arguing with God in words like these: "So, good Jesus, let us see which of us outdoes the other—I in giving your gifts away, or you in providing them."

The time came when he was stricken with a high fever and realized that his end was near, and he said: "I thank you, O God, because you have listened to my indigence begging your bounty that when I die I should be found to possess no more than a single penny; and I now order that that penny be given to the poor." His venerable body was laid in a tomb in which the bodies of two other bishops had been buried, and in a wonderful way those bodies made room for Saint John and left him a place between them.

Shortly before he died, a woman had committed a sin so heinous that she dared not confess it to anyone ever, but John told her at least to write the sin down (since she knew how to write), seal the paper, and bring it to him, and he would pray for her. She agreed to this, wrote out the sin, carefully put her seal on the paper, and handed it over to the saint, but a few days later he sickened and fell asleep in the Lord. When the woman heard that he was dead, she feared that she would now be shamed and disgraced, thinking that he would have entrusted her paper to someone and that it would fall into the hands of some stranger. She approached Saint John's tomb and there, with floods of tears, cried out, saying: "Alas, I thought I would avoid dishonor, and now I am disgraced in the eyes of all!" She wept bitterly and asked Saint John to show her where he had put her writing; and behold, Saint John came forth from the tomb in full pontifical regalia and borne up on either side by the two bishops who lay at rest with him. He said to the woman: "Why do you come and disturb us? Why do you not leave me and these saints who are with me . . . why do you not leave us in peace? Look! Our stoles are wet with your tears!" Then he held out her writing, sealed as it had been before, and said: "There is your seal! Open the paper and read it!" She opened the paper and saw that her sin had been completely erased, and that in its place was written, "Because of John, my servant, your sin is wiped out." So the woman poured out her thanks to God, and blessed John returned to the tomb with the other bishops. He flourished about the year of the Lord 605, in the reign of Emperor Phocas.

28. The Conversion of Saint Paul, Apostle

Saint Paul's conversion took place in the same year during which Christ suffered and Stephen was stoned, counting the year not in the normal way from January to December, but simply as a space of twelve months; for Christ suffered on the 25th day of March and Stephen was stoned in the same year on the 3d day of August, while Paul was converted on the 25th day of January.

Why is Paul's conversion celebrated, while that of other saints is not? Three reasons are usually given for this. The first is the example that Paul set: no sinner, no matter how grievous his sin, can despair of pardon when he sees that Paul, whose fault was so great, afterwards became so much greater in grace. The second is the joy of the Church, which had been greatly saddened through his persecution and received so much greater happiness through his conversion. The third is the miracle by which the Lord turned this cruel persecutor into so faithful a preacher.

Paul's conversion was miraculous by reason of the one who brought it about, by reason of the means used to dispose Paul for conversion, and by reason of the subject, Paul himself. Miraculous, first, because the one who converted him was Christ, who showed his marvelous power in what he said: "It is hard for you to kick against the goad,"[1] and in changing Paul so suddenly that, once changed, he replied: "Lord, what do you want me to do?"[2] Augustine comments: "The Lamb that was slain by wolves turns a wolf into a lamb: he who previously spent his fury in persecuting is now ready to obey." Christ also showed his wondrous wisdom, in that he cured Paul of the tumor of pride, offering him the depths of humility, not the heights of majesty. "I who speak to you," he said, "am Jesus of Nazareth, whom you are persecuting." The *Gloss* adds: "He does not call himself God or the Son of God, but says, 'Take upon yourself the depths of my humility and rid your eyes of the scales of pride.'" Moreover, he showed his wondrous forbearance, since he converted Paul at the very moment when Paul, in act and in intention, was persecuting the Christians. Paul's mind was set on evil, since he breathed forth threats and the will to slaughter Christians; what he attempted was perverse, since he went to the high priest, forcing himself, as it were, upon him; and his action was malicious since he was on his way to Damascus to put the Christians in chains and take them bound to Jerusalem. Therefore his journey was utterly wrongful, yet the divine mercy converted him.

[1] Acts 9:5.   [2] Acts 9:6.

Second, the conversion was miraculous because of the means used to dispose the one to be converted, namely, the light that made Paul ready for conversion. That light is said to have been sudden, immense, and heaven-sent: "And suddenly a light from heaven shone around him."[3] Paul had three vices, the first being wanton boldness, which he demonstrated by going to the high priests: "He was not summoned," says the *Gloss*, "but went on an impulse, driven by his zeal." His second vice was insolent pride, because he is said to have breathed out threats of violence against the disciples of the Lord. The third was that he understood the Law according to the flesh; so the *Gloss*, commenting on the words "I am Jesus whom you are persecuting," says: "It is I, God of heaven, speaking, whom you, with your Jewish way of judging things, think of as being dead." Therefore the divine light was sudden, in order to frighten the bold one, and immense, to bring the haughty, overbearing one down to lowly humility, and heavenly, to change his fleshly understanding and make it heavenly. Or it could be said that the disposing means was triple—the voice that called out, the shining light, and the display of divine power.

Finally, Paul's conversion was miraculous by reason of the subject in whom it was effected—Paul himself. Three things happened to Paul, outwardly and miraculously: he fell to the ground, he was blinded, and he had neither food nor drink for three days. He was thrown to the ground in order to be straightened up in his perverse intentions. Augustine: "Paul was prostrated in order to be blinded, blinded in order to be changed, changed in order to be sent, and sent in order that he might suffer for the truth." Augustine again: "He was enraged and was crushed in order to become a believer; the wolf was crushed and became a lamb; the persecutor was crushed and became the preacher; the son of perdition was crushed to be brought erect as the vessel of election." He was blinded to be enlightened in his darkened intelligence. Hence it is said that in the three days during which he remained blind, he was taught the Gospel, for he himself testifies that he did not receive it from man nor through a man, but through a revelation of Jesus Christ. Augustine: "I say that Paul was Christ's true fighter, taught by him, anointed by him, crucified with him, and glorious in him. He mortified his body so that the flesh would be ready for the doing of good. His body was thenceforth well disposed to every good work. He knew how to be full and to be hungry, to thirst and to abound; he was at home everywhere and could cope with every situation." Chrysostom: "Tyrants and peoples breathing fury he regarded as so many gnats, death and crucifixions and a thousand tortures were to him child's play and he embraced them willingly. He felt more adorned when bound with chains than if he were crowned with a royal diadem, and he accepted wounds more gladly than others would receive rich gifts." And three things are said to have been in him in contrast to three that

---

[3] Acts 9:3. The whole story of Paul's conversion, and much of the language used here, is found in this chapter.

were in our first parent. Adam stood up against God and Paul prostrated himself on the earth; Adam's eyes were opened and Paul's were blinded; Adam ate forbidden food and Paul abstained from permitted food.

29. Saint Paula

Paula belonged to the high Roman nobility. Saint Jerome wrote her life as follows.[1]

If all the members of my body were turned into tongues and all the skills of the human voice were applied to the task, I still could say nothing worthy of the virtues of the holy and venerable Paula. She was noble by birth but far more noble by her sanctity, powerful earlier by reason of her wealth but later more renowned for her poverty; and I call to witness Jesus and the holy angels, and particularly her own angel, the companion and guardian of this admirable woman, that I say nothing by way of flattery or blandishment, and that what I am about to say in testimony to her virtue falls far short of her deserts. Does my reader want to know Paula's virtues in brief? She left poor all those who belonged to her, she being poorer than any of them. As a jewel of inestimable price shines out among many gems, and as the radiance of the sun dims and darkens the tiny fires of the stars, so she surpassed all others by her humility and made herself least among all in order to be greater than all. The more she lowered herself, the higher she was lifted up by Christ. She hid but was not hidden: by fleeing vain glory she merited the glory that follows virtue like a shadow and evades those who seek it while seeking those who despise it.

Paula was the mother of five children—Blaesilla, over whose death I consoled her in Rome; Paulina, who made Pammachius, her saintly and admirable husband, heir to all her property and projects, for whom I wrote a small book about her death; Eustochium, the daughter who still lives in the Holy Land and is a precious adornment of the Church; Rufina, whose early demise sorely distressed

---

[1] This chapter is excerpted from Jerome's letter on the life of Saint Paula (cf. Migne, *PL* 22:878–906). All but a dozen or so words are taken from Jerome: Jacobus extracted paragraphs and snippets sufficient to establish Paula's sanctity by dwelling on the usual virtues—humility, charity, poverty, *contemptus mundi*, chastity. The "snippets" are often taken out of context, which at times obscures the train of thought. Jerome's "letter" is five or six times as long as Jacobus's chapter, and its rhetorical, eulogistic style is totally foreign to our author.

her mother's loving spirit; and a son, Toxocius. After Toxocius she bore no more children; from this you might understand that she did not wish to engage in conjugal union any longer. After her husband's death she mourned him so much that she almost died of grief, but then turned so ardently to the service of God that she might seem to have desired her spouse's death. And what is there to say about her giving to the poor all the abundant riches and treasures of her grand, noble house?

Paulinus, bishop of Antioch, and another bishop, Epiphanius, came to Rome, and Paula was so impressed by their virtues that she thought of leaving home and country. What more shall I say? She went down to the port, and her brother and close relatives and friends, and, more important than these, her children, followed her and tried to dissuade their most loving mother. Rufina, who was about to be married, held back her tears and begged her mother to wait for her wedding. While the sails were hoisted and the ship, propelled by the rowers, was heading toward the deep, little Toxocius stood on the shore with outstretched, pleading hands. Yet Paula, dry-eyed, looked toward heaven, putting her love of God above her love for her children. She knew not herself as mother in order to prove herself Christ's handmaid. As she fought her grief, her entrails were twisted in pain as if being torn from her body. Her full faith made her able to bear this suffering: more than that, her heart clung to it joyfully, and for love of God she put aside love of sons and daughters. Her only comfort was in Eustochium, who shared her plans and accompanied her on the voyage. The ship put to sea, and while all her fellow passengers were looking back to the shore, Paula looked away so as not to see what she could not see without pain.

The vessel reached port in the Holy Land, and the proconsul of Palestine, who knew her family very well, sent servants ahead to prepare rooms for her in his palace, but she chose a humble cell instead. She visited all the sites where Christ had left traces, with such ardor and zeal that she could hardly leave the first places she saw except that she wanted to hurry on to the others. She prostrated herself in adoration before the cross as if she could see the Lord hanging on it. On her way into the cave of the Resurrection she kissed the stone that the angel had removed from the entrance and, as if thirsting for the yearned-for waters of faith, licked with her tongue the place where the Lord's body had lain. What floods of tears, what storms of sighs, what torrents of grief she poured out there all Jerusalem, indeed the Lord himself whom she besought, can testify.

Next she went to Bethlehem and, entering the Savior's cave, saw the Virgin's sacred refuge; and in my hearing she swore that with the eyes of faith she saw the Infant wrapped in swaddling clothes, whimpering in the manger, the Magi adoring the Lord, the star shining overhead, the virgin mother, the watchful guardian, the shepherds coming in the night to see the word that had come to pass, as though to affirm again the words of John the Evangelist: "In the beginning was the Word, and the Word was with God, and the Word was made flesh." She saw the innocent children slain, Herod raging, Joseph and Mary fleeing to Egypt. Then she spoke with joy mixed with tears: "Hail, Bethlehem, house of bread, where that bread was born which came down from heaven! Hail, Ephrata, most fertile land whose fertility is God! David spoke confidently, saying, 'We will go into his tabernacle; we will adore in the place where his feet stood.' And I, a miserable sinner, am deemed worthy to kiss the crib in which the infant Lord cried, to pray in the cave where the virgin mother brought forth God. Here is my place of rest, because it is my Lord's native place. Here I shall dwell, because my Savior chose it."

Paula abased herself with such humility that someone who wanted to see her because of the renown of her name, seeing her, could not believe this was the woman he sought, but must be the lowest of the maidservants. She was surrounded by crowding choirs of virgins, yet in the way she dressed or spoke or walked, she seemed the least of all. Never, from the time her husband died until the day of her own passing, did she sit at table with any man, though she knew the man was saintly or was in high pontifical station. She did not use the baths unless illness demanded it. Except when beset with high fevers she had no bed craped with soft quilts but took her rest on the hard ground covered with sackcloth—if indeed one can speak of rest when her days and nights were joined together by almost continuous prayer. She wept so bitterly for slight faults that one would have thought her guilty of the grossest crimes; and when we admonished her, as we[2] frequently did, to spare her eyes and save them for reading the gospels, she said: "This face, which against God's command I used to paint with rouges and whiteners and mascaras, deserves to be made ugly! The body that enjoyed so many pleasures ought to be made to suffer! Long laughter must be atoned for by steady weeping, soft linens and costly silks call for the rough feel of the hair shirt as reparation. In the past I did everything to please my husband and our world. Now I want to please Christ."

If, among so many and such great virtues, I should wish to emphasize her chastity, such praise would seem superfluous. While she was still living a worldly life, she set an example for all the matrons of Rome and so conducted herself that even the meanest gossip would not dare to spread a false rumor about her. I admit the error I committed when I rebuked her for her prodigal almsgiving, quoting the words of the apostle: generosity yes, but "I do not mean that others should be eased and you burdened, but that as a matter of equality your abundance at the present time should supply their want, so that their abundance may supply your want."[3] I urged her to use foresight or she might not have anything left to give away, and other similar arguments. Her response was modest, brief, and wisely put: she called the Lord to witness that everything she did was done for his name, and her one wish and vow was that she might die a beggar, unable to leave as much as a penny to her daughter, and that for her burial she might be wrapped in a shroud that was not her own. In conclusion she said: "If I beg I

<hr />

[2] Jerome.   [3] 2 Cor. 8:13–14.

shall find many who will give to me; but if one poor beggar should die because he does not receive from me what I can give him even if I have to use what belongs to someone else, who will be held accountable for his life?"

Paula was unwilling to pour out money for stones that will pass away with the earth and the world, but chose rather to spend it on the living stones that roll around on the earth, out of which, as John says in the Apocalypse, the city of God is built. Except on feast days she used little or no oil in her food, and that gives an idea of her attitude toward drink and fish and milk and honey and eggs and everything else that appeals to the sense of taste—things that some think they are very abstemious in using, and are sure of their virtuousness even while they gorge themselves. I know one scandalmonger (that vilest breed of man) who, as if he were doing a kindness, told Paula that she seemed to some people to be carried away by the ardor of her virtues, and to be out of her mind, and that she should take better care of her brain. To this she replied: "We have become a spectacle to the world, to angels, and to men; we are fools for Christ's sake, but the foolishness of God is wiser than men."[4]

She had founded a monastery for men and handed it over to be ruled by men. She had also gathered together a large number of young women coming from various regions and from the noble, middle, and lowest strata of society. For these women she established three groups and three monasteries, so that they worked and had their meals separately, coming together only for chanting the Psalms and praying. If disputes arose among them, she brought agreement about by the gentleness of her way of speaking. She curbed the fleshly urges of the very young ones by imposing frequent double fasts, preferring to have them suffer in body rather than in spirit. She said that cleanliness of body and dress was uncleanness of the soul, and that the same fault which men of the world regarded as light or of no consequence was, in the monasteries, a very serious matter. When others were ailing, she gave them whatever they wanted, even allowing them to eat meat, whereas if she was ill, she granted herself no such indulgence. In this her treatment was obviously unequal, since she compensated for her clemency to others by her hardness to herself.

What I am about to tell you I saw for myself. One year in the month of July Paula fell into a violent fever. After we had despaired of her life, she began, by God's mercy, to breathe more easily. The physicians determined that to recover her strength she should take a little thin wine, and should not drink water for fear of bringing on dropsy. I secretly asked the holy bishop Epiphanius to admonish or even compel her to drink wine. But she, quick and insightful as she was, saw through the ruse at once and smiled, knowing that what the bishop said came from me. What more is there to tell? When the holy pontiff, after delivering many exhortations, came outside, I asked him how he had fared, and he answered: "I succeeded so well that she almost persuaded me, an old man, not to drink wine!"

---

[4] 1 Cor. 4:9–10; 1:25.

She bore grief patiently but was stricken by the deaths of those dear to her, particularly of her children; the loss of her spouse and her daughters brought her close to death. She made the sign of the cross on her lips and her breast, hoping by that sign to ease the sorrow she felt as wife and mother, but she was overcome by her emotion, and the mother's inner pain disturbed her believing soul. Conquering by strength of spirit, she was conquered by the fragility of the body.

She had the Holy Scriptures by heart, and while she loved the story they told and called it the foundation of truth, she preferred the spiritual interpretation and made of it the summit of her soul's edification. And I shall say something else, though it may seem unbelievable to the envious. I studied the Hebrew language from adolescence with much toil and sweat, got to know it fairly well, and have kept at it constantly so as not to lose it. Paula wanted to learn Hebrew and did learn it so well that she sang the Psalms in Hebrew and spoke the language without any Latin peculiarities. Even today we see her sainted daughter Eustochium doing the same thing.

Thus far we have sailed with favorable winds, and our lithe ship has glided through the curling waves of the sea, but now rocks and shoals lie ahead for my story. Who indeed could speak without weeping about Paula's last days on earth? She was prostrated by a very serious illness—or better, she was finding what she most longed for, which was to leave us and be united more fully to the Lord. Why do I delay and by delaying make others endure my grief any longer? This most prudent of women felt the approach of death. Parts of her body and limbs were cold, and only the warmth of her soul kept life in her sacred, holy breast. Yet, as though she was on her way to her own and cared no longer about strangers, she kept whispering these verses: "I have loved, O Lord, the beauty of thy house and the place where thy glory dwells," and "How lovely are thy tabernacles, O Lord of hosts! I have chosen to be abject in the house of my God."[5] And when I asked her why she would not speak and did not answer when asked whether she had pain, she replied in Greek that she felt no trouble and saw everything as quiet and tranquil. After that she fell silent and lay with her eyes closed as if to shut out human things. Until she breathed forth her soul, she repeated the same verses, in so low a voice that even bending over to listen we could hardly hear what she was saying.

A great crowd of people from the cities of Palestine came to her funeral. No monk of those living hidden in the desert could bear to stay in his hovel, no virgin could be detained in the secrecy of her cell: all thought it would be a sacrilege not to pay their final duty to so wonderful a woman until she was laid to rest under the church and next to the cave where the Lord was born. Her venerable daughter the virgin Eustochium, like a child being weaned, could hardly be lifted from her mother's body, whose eyes she kissed, to whose cheeks she clung, whose whole body she embraced, with whom she herself wished to be buried. Jesus is witness that to her daughter the mother left not a penny but

---

[5] Ps. 25(26):8; 83(84):1, 11.

only the care of the poor, the immense multitude of brothers and sisters whom it is hard simply to feed, and impious to turn away.

Farewell, O Paula, and assist with your prayers your worshiper in his extreme old age!

※

30. Saint Julian

Julian, Julianus, begins like *jubilus*, jubilant, and *ana* means upward; so Julian is close to *Jubilans*, one who strives upward toward heaven with jubilation. Or the name comes from *Julius*, one who begins, and *anus*, old man, because in God's service Julian was old in his long-suffering, but one who began by knowing himself.

Julian was bishop of Le Mans. It is said that he was Simon the Leper, whom Christ cured of leprosy and who invited the Lord to a festal meal. After Christ's ascension the apostles ordained Julian as bishop of Le Mans. He was renowned for his many virtues. He raised three dead persons to life and in time went to his rest in peace. He is also said to be the Julian who is invoked by travelers in search of good lodging, for the reason that he welcomed Christ as a guest in his house. But it seems more likely that this was another Julian, namely, the one who killed both his parents unwittingly. The story of this Julian will be told further on.

There was another Julian, this one from Auvergne, noble by birth but more noble by his faith, who out of his desire for martyrdom went so far as to offer himself to the persecutors. Finally the consular official Crispinus sent one of his men to put Julian to death. When Julian got word of it, he jumped up at once, ran out, fearlessly set himself in front of the man who was looking for him, and welcomed the blow that beheaded him. The attackers picked up the sacred head and carried it to Saint Ferreolus, a friend of Julian, threatening him with the same death unless he sacrificed to the gods. He refused. They put him to death and buried Julian's head in one tomb with the body of Ferreolus. Many years later Saint Mamertus, bishop of Vienne, found Saint Julian's head held in Ferreolus's hands: the head was undamaged and free of wounds, as if it had been buried that very day.

Among this saint's many miracles, here is one that is often told. A certain deacon was about to make off with some sheep belonging to Saint Julian's church, and the shepherds tried to stop him in the name of the saint. "Julian doesn't eat sheep!" he retorted. Not long thereafter he was seized with a violent, debilitating fever and admitted that it was the martyr who was burning him. Then he had water splashed over him to cool the heat, but instantly a cloud of smoke and a horrible stench arose from his body. All those who were present fled, and the deacon died shortly afterwards.

Gregory of Tours tells us that there was a peasant who started out to plow his field on a Sunday, but at once the fingers of his right hand stiffened and stuck fast to the handle of the hatchet he used to clean the plowshare. Two years later, however, he prayed in Saint Julian's church and was cured.

There was still another Julian, the brother of Saint Julius. These two brothers went to the most Christian emperor Theodosius, asking his permission to tear down the temples of the idols wherever they found them, and to build churches of Christ. The emperor was pleased to grant their request and wrote a command that everyone should obey them and give them help, under pain of death. So the saintly brothers Julian and Julius were building a church at a place called Gaudianum, and, in obedience to the emperor's command, all who passed that way helped in the work.

It happened that some men were going by with a wagon, and they said to each other: "What excuse can we give these people so as to be able to go on freely and not have to give some work here?" And they concluded: "Let's put one of us into the wagon flat on his back and cover him up with sheets. We'll tell them we have a dead man in the cart, and they'll let us be on our way." So they picked one of their number and put him in the wagon, telling him: "Keep quiet and close your eyes and lie there like a dead man until we are in the clear!" So they covered him over and came to Julian and Julius, servants of God, who said to them: "Good fellows, stop for a bit and give us a hand here!" The men answered: "We can't stop here because we have a dead man in the wagon." Blessed Julian said to them: "What good does it do to tell us such lies?" "We are not lying, sir," they said, "and it's just as we told you!" Saint Julian replied: "So be it! Let things be as you have said."

The men goaded their oxen and moved on, and when they had gone far enough, they stood by the wagon and began to call their companion by name, saying: "Up with you now and drive the oxen, and we'll move along faster!" Getting no answer they nudged him and said: "Stop playing games! Come out and do your job!" When there still was no answer, they pulled off the covers and found him dead. Thereupon such fear penetrated one and all that no one dared to lie to the servant of God from then on.

There was another Julian, who unwittingly killed both his parents. When this Julian, noble by birth, was young, he went out one day to hunt and began to chase a stag whose trail he had picked up. Suddenly, by the will of God, the stag turned to face him and said: "Are you tracking me to kill me, you who are going to kill your father and mother?" Filled with dread at hearing this, and fearing that what he had heard from the stag might indeed happen to him, he left everything and went away secretly. Having reached a very remote region he took service with a prince, and carried on so manfully in wartime and peacetime that the prince dubbed him a knight and gave him a widow, a noblewoman, in marriage, with a castle as dowry.

Meanwhile Julian's parents, deeply saddened by the loss of their son, wandered everywhere in search of him and in time reached the castle where Julian made his home. As it happened, Julian was away, but his wife met them and asked who they were. They told her all about their son, and she realized that they were her husband's father and mother—I think because she had often heard the same story from her spouse. She therefore welcomed them cordially and, for love of them, left her husband's bed to them and slept in another room. In the morning she went to church. Julian, arriving home, went to his bedroom to awaken his wife. Finding a couple asleep in his bed and supposing that they were his wife and her lover, he silently drew his sword and killed them both. Then he went out of the castle and saw his wife on her way home from church. Surprised, he asked her who the couple were whom he had found in his bed, and she said: "They are your parents, they have been looking for you for the longest time, and I settled them in your bed."

At this news Julian almost fainted and, weeping bitterly, said: "Woe is me, wretch that I am, what shall I do now? I have slain my dear, dear parents! See . . . I have tried so hard to escape the stag's prediction, and now I have fulfilled it in this horrible way! But now, sweet sister, farewell! I shall not rest until I know that God will accept my penance!" But his wife responded: "Far be it from me, dearest brother, to desert you and let you go away without me! I have shared your joy, now I shall be with you to share your sorrow!"

They set out together and came to a broad river where many people were in danger of their lives. There they established a very large hospice in which they might work out their penance. They never failed to give transport to any who wished to cross the river, and received all poor folk kindly in their hospice. A long time passed, and one freezing night, when Julian, tired out, was getting some rest, he heard a plaintive voice calling his name and begging in the most doleful tones for transport. Quickly rising and going out, he found the man almost perishing from the cold, carried him into the house, lit a fire, and tried to warm him. But the stranger did not respond, and Julian, fearing that he might die, put him in his own bed and carefully covered him up. In a short while the stranger, who had looked so infirm and almost leprous, rose splendid in midair and said to his host: "Julian, the Lord sent me to tell you that he has accepted your penance, and that both of you will, in a little time, find rest in the Lord." The messenger disappeared, and not long thereafter Julian and his wife, full of good works and almsgiving, went to their eternal rest.

Finally there was another Julian, no saint but a most wicked wrongdoer, namely, Julian the Apostate. This Julian had been a monk and made a great show of religion and piety. A certain woman (as Master John Beleth tells us in his *Summa de officio ecclesiae*), had three jars filled with gold, but she filled the tops of the jars with ashes so as to conceal the gold. Then she entrusted the jars for safekeeping to Julian, whom she regarded as a very holy man, in the presence of several monks, without indicating in any way that there was gold in them. Julian accepted the jars and, finding this large supply of gold in them, stole the treasure and filled the jars with ashes. After a while, when the woman came to reclaim her deposit, he returned to her the jars filled with ashes: but when she looked for the gold, she could not convict him of stealing it, because there was no witness to say that there had been gold; the monks who had been present at the original transfer had seen nothing but ashes. So Julian got the gold, fled to Rome with it, and, by means of it, in time procured the consulship and eventually became emperor.

From childhood Julian had been instructed in the arts of magic, which delighted him, and he had many masters to teach him. We learn from the *Tripartite History* that one day, when he was still a child and his teacher had left him alone, he began to read the incantations of the demons, and a whole horde of demons appeared before him looking like black Ethiopians. Julian, seeing this, made the sign of the cross at once, and the whole crowd of demons vanished. When the master returned and Julian told him what had happened, his teacher explained that the evil spirits particularly hate and fear that sign.

When he acceded to the empire, he remembered this, and, since he intended to use magic to attain his ends, he renounced the Christian faith, destroyed crosses wherever he found them, and persecuted Christians to the full extent of his power, thinking that otherwise the demons would be less likely to obey him. We read in *Lives of the Fathers* that when Julian invaded Persia, he sent a demon to the West to bring back news from there. The demon arrived at a certain place but was immobilized there for ten days because a monk was praying day and night at that same spot. The demon went back having achieved nothing, and Julian asked him: "What took you so long?" The evil spirit answered: "For ten days I was held up by a monk praying out in the open, and, since I could not get past him, I came back empty-handed." This angered the emperor, who declared that when he reached that place, he would have his revenge on the monk. Since the demons had promised Julian a victory over Persia, his soothsayer asked some Christian: "What do you think the son of the carpenter is doing today?" The Christian answered: "Making a coffin for Julian!"

When the emperor had advanced as far as Caesarea of Cappadocia (as we read in a history of Saint Basil and as Fulbert, bishop of Chartres, confirms), Saint Basil met him and sent him four barley loaves as a gift. Julian was offended, disdained to accept the loaves, and in return sent Basil a bundle of hay, with the message: "You have offered us the fodder of irrational animals. Take back what you sent." Basil replied: "We indeed sent you what we ourselves eat, but you have given us what you feed your beasts with." To this, Julian responded angrily: "When I have subjugated Persia, I will raze this city and plow up the land, and it will be called not 'man-bearing' but 'grain-bearing.'"

The following night Basil had a vision in the church of Saint Mary in which he saw a multitude of angels, and in their midst a woman seated on a throne. The woman said to her attendants: "Quickly summon Mercury to me! He shall put to death the apostate Julian, who in his insolent pride blasphemes me and my Son!" This Mercury was a soldier who had been killed by Julian himself for the faith of Christ and was buried in this church. Instantly Saint Mercury, whose arms were preserved nearby, stood at attention and received her orders to prepare to fight. Basil woke up, went to the place where Saint Mercury lay at peace near his arms, opened the tomb, and found neither the body nor the weapons. He questioned the watchman as to whether he had removed anything from the tomb, and the man swore that he had seen the arms the evening before in the place where they had always been kept. Basil then went back to his house, but in the morning came again, and in the usual place found the saint's body and his weapons, including the lance, which was now covered with blood.

Then someone came from Julian's army and reported as follows: "While Emperor Julian was still with the army, an unknown soldier came up with his arms and his lance, put spurs to his horse and rushed with impetuous bravery upon Julian, drove his lance through his body, vanished, and was not seen again." Julian, while he was still breathing, filled his hand with his blood (as we are told in the *Tripartite History*) and tossed it into the air, saying: "Galilean, you have conquered!" With these words he expired miserably. His men left him unburied, and the Persians stripped off his skin and with it covered a cushion for the king's throne.

About the feasts that occur within
the time of deviation

Having spoken about the feasts that occur within the time that falls
partly in the time of reconciliation and partly in the time of pilgrimage, which time the Church represents from the Birth of Christ to
Septuagesima, we shall now take up the feasts that occur within the
time of deviation, which the Church represents from Septuagesima
to Easter.

31. Septuagesima

Septuagesima designates the time of deviation or turning away from God, Sexagesima the time of widowhood, Quinquagesima the time of pardon, Quadragesima, or Lent, the time for spiritual penance. Septuagesima begins on the Sunday on which the introit *Circumdederunt me gemitus mortis*[1] is sung, and ends on the Saturday after Easter.

Septuagesima was established for three reasons, as we learn from Master John Beleth's *Summa de officiis*. The first reason was to make compensation. The holy fathers had decreed that in order to pay due reverence to the day of the Lord's ascension, on which day our human nature rose to heaven and was lifted above the choirs of angels, Thursday should always be treated as a solemn holy day, and no fast should be observed on that day. Indeed, in the primitive Church, Thursday was celebrated equally with Sunday, and a solemn procession was held to represent the procession of the disciples or of the angels themselves. There was a popular proverb which said that "Thursday is Sunday's cousin," because in times past it was just as dedicated a day. But then the feasts of the saints intervened and it was burdensome to celebrate so many feasts, so the solemnizing of Thursday fell into disuse. By way of compensation the holy fathers added a week of abstinence before Lent and called it Septuagesima.

The second reason for the institution of Septuagesima is that this season signifies the time of deviation, of the fall away from God, of exile and tribulation for the whole human race from Adam to the end of the world. Now this exile extends through the period of seventy days and is included in the passage of seven thousand years: we understand seventy days as representing seventy hundreds of years. We count six thousand years from the world's beginning to the Lord's ascension, and we understand the remaining time to the end of the world as the seventh millennium: only God knows when it will end.

It was in the sixth age of the world that Christ snatched us, by baptism, out of this exile, restoring to us the robe of innocence and the hope of eternal reward, but it is when our time of exile is over that we shall be perfectly graced with both robes. That is why in this time of deviation and exile we put aside the chants of joy. In the office of the eve of Easter, however, we sing one Alleluia, expressing our thanks for the hope of an eternal homeland and the recovery, through Christ, of the robe of innocence in the sixth age of the world. This Alleluia is followed by a tract,[2] signifying the labor by which we still have to fulfill God's

---

[1] The sorrows of death surrounded me.

[2] The tract consisted of verses from the Psalms chanted or recited in the mass, replacing the Alleluia, on certain penitential days in the liturgical year.

commands. On the Saturday after Easter, which, as has been said, brings an end to Septuagesima, we sing two Alleluias, because when this world's term is completed, we will obtain the double robe of glory.

A third reason for the observance of Septuagesima is that it represents the seventy years the children of Israel spent in captivity in Babylon, when they hung up their lyres and said: "How shall we sing the Lord's song in a foreign land?" So we also, in Septuagesima, put aside our songs of praise. But then, when in the sixtieth year Cyrus gave them leave to return home, they began to rejoice, and we too, on Holy Saturday, as it were in the sixtieth year, sing Alleluia to recall their joy. They, however, had to work hard getting ready for the return journey and putting their baggage together, and we add to the Alleluia the tract which recalls that labor. Then on Easter Saturday, the last day of Septuagesima, we sing two Alleluias, symbolizing the fullness of joy with which they arrived in their own land.

The time of captivity and exile of the children of Israel also represents the time of our own pilgrimage, because as they were set free in the sixtieth year, we are liberated in the sixth age of the world. And as they worked hard to get their bundles ready, so we also, freed as we are, must labor to fulfill the commandments. But when we shall have come into our true homeland, all labor will cease, our glory will be complete, and we shall sing a double Alleluia in body and soul.

In this time of exile, therefore, the Church, weighed down with many troubles and almost driven to despair, with deep sighs cries out in her liturgy, saying: "The sorrows of death have surrounded me." Thus the Church describes the manifold tribulations she bears on account of the misery she has brought upon herself, the double punishment inflicted upon her, and the wrong done by some. Yet to save her from despair a triple healing remedy and a triple reward are offered both in the Gospel and in the Epistle.[3] The remedy, if she wishes to be completely delivered from her tribulations, is this: she must labor in the vineyard of the soul, pruning away vices and sins; in the race of the present life she must run by doing the works of penance; and then she must fight staunchly in the struggle against all the devil's trials. If she follows this prescription, she will receive a threefold reward, because to the laborer the day's wages will be given, to the runner the prize, and to the fighter the crown.

Then again, since Septuagesima signifies the time of our own captivity, we are offered a remedy by which we can be freed from captivity: by running, to escape from it, by fighting, to win over it, and with the day's wages, to buy our freedom.

---

[3] Readings in the mass of Septuagesima Sunday in the pre–Vatican II missal (1 Cor. 9:24–27 and 10:1–5; Matt. 20:1–16).

32. Sexagesima

Sexagesima begins on the Sunday when the introit *Exsurge, quare obdormis Domine*[1] is sung, and ends on the Wednesday after Easter. It was instituted as a compensation, a sign, and a representation.

First, as a compensation: Pope Melchiades and Saint Silvester decreed that two meals should be eaten every Saturday, for fear that due to abstinence from food on Friday, which is a fast day throughout the year, man's constitution would be weakened. To compensate for the Saturdays of this season, therefore, the popes added a week before Lent and called it Sexagesima.

Second, as a sign: Sexagesima (sixtieth day) signifies the time of the Church's widowhood and her grief at the absence of her Spouse, because a sixtieth part of the crop is owed to widows.[2] To console the widowed Church for the absence of her Spouse, who has been carried off to heaven, two wings are given to her, namely, the practice of the six works of mercy and the fulfillment of the Ten Commandments. Now *sexagesima* means 60—6 times 10—the 6 standing for the six works of mercy and the 10 for the Decalogue.

Third, as a representation: Sexagesima signifies not only the time of widowhood, but also the mystery of our redemption. The number 10 stands for man, who is the tenth drachma,[3] because man was created to make up for the ruin of the nine angelic orders. Or 10 means man because his body is composed of four humors and in his soul he has three powers—memory, intellect, and will—which were made to serve the most blessed Trinity, enabling us to believe in the three Persons faithfully, to love them fervently, and to keep them always in memory. The number 6 represents the six mysteries through which man, 10, is redeemed: they are Christ's incarnation, birth, passion, descent into hell, resurrection, and ascension into heaven.

Sexagesima is prolonged to the Wednesday after Easter, that day's introit being *Venite benedicti Patris mei*,[4] because those who have practiced the works of mercy will hear these words (as Christ himself testifies) when the door is opened to the Church-bride and she enjoys the embrace of her Spouse.

---

[1] Arise, why sleepest thou, O Lord?

[2] Commentators on Matt. 13:23, the parable of the sower, attribute the hundredfold yield to virgins, the sixtyfold to widows, and the thirtyfold to wives, according to their different degrees of merit.

[3] In chapter 37, "The Purification of the Blessed Virgin Mary," Jacobus notes that tithing (here called decimation) identified the redeemed," because the tenth drachma signified man."

[4] Come, ye blessed of my Father.

In the epistle of the mass for Sexagesima Sunday the Church is admonished to imitate Paul's example by bearing patiently the tribulation that is hers due to the absence of her Spouse. In the gospel she is encouraged to persevere in sowing the seed of good works. The Church, which almost in despair had cried out: "The sorrows of death have surrounded me," now, in control of herself again, prays for help in tribulation and to be freed of her troubles, saying: "Arise, why sleepest thou, O Lord? Arise, and cast us not off to the end. Why turnest thou thy face away and forgettest thou our want and our trouble? For our soul is humbled down to the dust: our belly cleaveth to the earth. Arise, O Lord: help us and redeem us for thy name's sake!" In this introit she repeats her "Arise" three times. There are those in the Church who are oppressed by adversity but not discouraged; others are oppressed and discouraged; still others are neither oppressed nor discouraged, but are in danger because they have no adversity to put up with and so may be broken by prosperity. Therefore the Church calls upon the Lord to arise from sleep, and to strengthen the first group, since by not rescuing them from their adversity he seems to be sleeping; to convert the second group, because he seems to have turned his face from them and somehow to have cast them off; to help the third group and set them free.

33. Quinquagesima

Quinquagesima lasts from the Sunday on which the introit *Esto mihi in Deum protectorem*[1] is sung until Easter Sunday. It was instituted as a completion, a sign, and a representation.

As a completion: we ought to fast for forty days as Christ did, but in Lent there are only thirty-six fast days because there is no fasting on Sundays. Sundays are exempted both to mark our joy and reverence for the Lord's resurrection, and to follow the example of Christ, who on the day of his rising from the dead took food twice—once when he came in to the disciples, the doors being closed, and they offered him a piece of a broiled fish and a honeycomb, and again, as some say, with the two disciples going to Emmaus. Therefore, to supply for the Sundays, four days of fast were added before Lent. Then the clergy, seeing that as they were ahead of the people by their ordination, they should also

---

[1] Be unto me a protecting God.

be ahead of them by their holiness, began to fast and abstain for two more days in addition to the added four. Thus a whole week was added before Lent and was called Quinquagesima, and Pope Telesphorus confirmed this, as Ambrose tells us.

Secondly, Quinquagesima signifies the time of remission, i.e., a season of penance in which everything is forgiven. Every fiftieth year was a jubilee year, a year of remission, because all debts were remitted, slaves were freed, and every man recovered his own property. This signified that by penance the debts of sins were wiped out, and everyone was freed from slavery to the devil and returned to the possession of heavenly dwellings.

Thirdly, as representation: Quinquagesima represents not only the time of remission, but the state of beatitude. In the fiftieth year slaves were set free; on the fiftieth day after the lamb was sacrificed, the Law was given; the fiftieth day after Easter the Holy Spirit was sent. Therefore the number 50 represents beatitude—the receiving of freedom, knowledge of the truth, and perfection of charity.

In the epistle and gospel of Quinquagesima Sunday three things necessary to make works of penance perfect are brought to our attention, namely, charity, which is proposed in the epistle, the reminder of the Passion, and faith, which is understood in the restoration of sight to the blind man. These are set forth in the Gospel: faith itself makes the works acceptable and appeasing to God, because without faith it is impossible to please God; and the memory of the passion of our Lord makes penance easy. Hence Gregory says: "If Christ's passion is kept in memory, there is nothing that will not be borne in tranquillity of spirit." Charity prompts continous works of penance, because, as Gregory says, the love of God cannot be idle: if there is love, it produces great works, and if no works are forthcoming, there is no love.

So, as at the beginning the Church, almost in despair, had cried out: "The sorrows of death have surrounded me," and later recovered herself and begged to be helped, now, her confidence renewed and her hope of pardon revived through penance, she prays, saying: "Be unto me a God, a protector, and a house of refuge, to save me. For thou art my strength and my refuge; and for thy name's sake thou wilt lead me and nourish me." Here she asks for four favors—protection, strength, refuge, and guidance. All her children are in the state of grace or the state of sin, in adversity or in prosperity. The Church prays for strength for those in grace, that they may be confirmed in grace; for those in sin she prays God to be their refuge; for those in adversity she asks protection in their troubles; and for the prosperous she prays that God may lead them to make innocent use of their goods.

Quinquagesima, as we have said, ends on Easter Sunday, because penance makes us rise to newness of life. During Quinquagesima the Fiftieth Psalm, the *Miserere*, is very frequently recited.

34. Quadragesima

For Quadragesima, the first Sunday of Lent, the introit *Invocavit me*[1] is sung. The Church, weighed down with so many tribulations, had cried out: "The sorrows of death surrounded me," and afterwards, having caught her breath, had called for help, saying: "Arise, O Lord" and "Be unto me a God, a protector." Now she shows that she has been heard, saying: "He has cried to me and I have heard him." Note, however, that Lent has 42 days, including the Sundays, but when six Sundays are taken out, only 36 days of fast are left. This number of days amounts to one-tenth of the year, because the year has 365 days, of which 36 days are one tenth. But four days are added preceding the first Sunday in order to fill out the sacred number of 40 days, which number the Savior consecrated by his fast in the desert.

Three reasons can be assigned to explain why we observe the fast for this number of days. The first, given by Augustine, is that Matthew has forty generations leading to the coming of Christ: "To this purpose the Lord came down to us through forty generations, that we should ascend to him through forty days of fasting." Augustine adds another explanation: "In order that we may reach the fiftieth, a tenth must be added to the fortieth, because in order to attain our blessed rest we must labor throughout the whole time of this present life. Hence the Lord stayed with his disciples for 40 days, and the tenth day thereafter sent the Holy Spirit, the Paraclete."

Master Praepositivus, in his *Summa de officiis*, gives a third reason, saying: "The world is divided into four parts and the year into four seasons; man is constituted of four elements and four complexions; and we have transgressed the New Law, which comprises the four gospels, and the Old Law in its Ten Commandments. It is proper, then, that the 4 be multiplied by the 10, making 40, and that we fulfill the commandments of the Old and New Laws throughout the time of this life. Our body, as we have said, consists of four elements, and these have, as it were, four 'seats' in us: fire is predominantly in the eyes, air on the tongue and in the ears, water in the genitals, and earth in the hands and the other members. So curiosity lodges in the eyes, scurrility in the tongue and ears, sensual pleasure in the sexual organs, cruelty in the hands and other members. The publican in the gospel confesses all four of these: he stood afar off to confess his sensuality, which smells bad, as if to say: 'I dare not come nearer, Lord, lest my

---

[1] He has cried to me.

stench reach your nostrils.' He did not lift his eyes to heaven, thus confessing his curiosity. He beat his breast with his hand, confessing cruelty. When he said: 'God, be merciful to me, a sinner,' he accused himself of scurrilous conduct, because sinners are often called buffoons, scurrilous fellows, or better, lechers." Thus far Praepositivus.

Gregory also, in one of his homilies, proposes three reasons: "Why is the number 40 retained for the fast, unless it is that the power of the Decalogue reaches its fullness through the four books of the holy Gospel? Moreover, we subsist by the four elements in this mortal body, and we contravene the Lord's commandments by indulging the body. Therefore, since we have violated the precepts of the Decalogue in yielding to the desires of the flesh, it is right that we should castigate the flesh 4 × 10 times over. Again, from Quadragesima Sunday to Easter day there are six weeks or 42 days, from which the six Sundays are subtracted from the fast, leaving 36 days of fasting. Now there are 365 days in the year, so we are, so to speak, giving a tenth of our year to God." This from Gregory.

Why is it that we do not observe our fast at the same time when Christ fasted? He began his fast immediately after he was baptized, but we connect ours rather with Easter. Master John Beleth, in his *Summa de officiis*, assigns four reasons for this. The first is that Christ suffered for us, and if we wish to rise with him, we ought to suffer with him. The second is that we imitate the children of Israel. Once when they made their exodus from Egypt, and again, from Babylonia, they celebrated the Pasch, thus proving that we are imitating them. And so, following their example, we fast at this time, in order to merit our escape from Egypt and Babylonia, i.e., from this world, and our passage into the land of our eternal heritage. A third reason is that the fires of lust usually burn more hotly in the spring, and to calm the body's cravings we have our longest fast in this season. And fourthly, immediately after the end of our fast we are to receive the Body of the Lord. As the Israelites, before they ate the paschal lamb, chastised themselves by eating wild bitter lettuces, so we ought to chastise ourselves by doing penance, in order to be worthy to eat the Lamb of life.

35. The Ember Day Fasts

The ember day, or four-season, fasts were instituted by Pope Callistus and are observed four times a year, following the four seasons of the year.

There are many reasons for this practice. The first is that spring is warm and humid, summer hot and dry, autumn cool and dry, winter cold and wet. Therefore we fast in the spring to control the harmful fluid of voluptuousness in us; in summer, to allay the noxious heat of avarice; in autumn, to temper the aridity of pride; in winter, to overcome the coldness of malice and lack of faith.

The second reason for these four periods of fast is that the first one falls in March, i.e., in the first week of Lent, so that the vices that are in us may wither—they cannot be completely extinguished—and the seeds of the virtues may sprout. The second fast falls in summer, in Pentecost week, because the Holy Spirit comes at that time and we ought to be fervent in the Spirit. In September we fast before Saint Michael's feast, because then the fruits of the earth are harvested and we should offer to God the fruits of good works. The fourth fast comes in December because then the grasses die, and we should die to the world.

The third reason is that we fast in order to imitate the Jews. They fasted four times a year—before Passover, before their Pentecost, before the feast of Tabernacles in September, and before the feast of Dedication in December.

The fourth reason is that man consists of the four elements, as regards the body and three powers, the rational, the concupiscible, and the irascible, as regards the soul. In order to control these elements and powers in us, we fast for three days four times a year, the number 4 referring to the body, the number 3 to the soul. These reasons are proffered by Master John Beleth.

The fifth reason, as stated by John of Damascus, is that in the spring there occurs an increase of blood, in the summer, of choler, in the autumn, of melancholia, and in winter, of phlegm. Therefore we fast in spring to weaken the blood of concupiscence and senseless gaiety in us; the sanguine person being libidinous and volatile. In summer we fast to weaken the bile of wrathfulness and falsity, because the choleric person is naturally inclined to bad temper and deception. In the autumn we fast to counteract the melancholia of cupidity and despondency, because the melancholic is naturally greedy and gloomy. In the winter our fasting reduces the phlegm of sluggishness and laziness, the phlegmatic being by nature dull and slothful.

The sixth reason is that spring is compared to air, summer to fire, autumn to earth, and winter to water. So in spring we fast to tame our high spirits and our pride, in summer to damp the fire of greed and covetousness, in autumn to overcome the earth of spiritual frigidity and murky ignorance, in winter to harness the water of our lightheadedness and inconstancy.

A seventh reason is that spring is related to childhood, summer to adolescence, autumn to adulthood or the prime of life, and winter to old age. Therefore we fast in spring in order to preserve the innocence of the child, in summer to develop strength by living chaste lives, in autumn to grow young by constancy and mature by righteousness. In winter we strive by fasting to grow in prudence and virtuous living like the old, or rather, to make satisfaction for any offense we have given to God in earlier years.

William of Auxerre has given us an eighth reason: we fast four times in the year to atone for our failures in the same four seasons. Furthermore, we fast for three days in order to atone in a day for the faults committed in each month; we fast on Wednesday because Judas betrayed the Lord on that day, on Friday because that is the day Christ was crucified, on Saturday because that day he lay in the tomb and the apostles grieved over the violent death of their Master.

36. Saint Ignatius

The name Ignatius comes from *ignem patiens*, which means being afire with love of God.

Ignatius was a disciple of Saint John and bishop of Antioch. We read that he wrote a letter to the Blessed Virgin in these terms: "To Mary the Christ-bearer, her Ignatius. You ought to strengthen and console me, a neophyte and disciple of your John, from whom I have learned many things about your Jesus, things wondrous to tell, and I am dumbfounded at hearing them. My heart's desire is to be assured about these things that I have heard, by you who were always so intimately close to Jesus and shared his secrets. Fare you well, and let the neophytes who are with me be strengthened in the faith, by you, through you, and in you." The Blessed Virgin Mary, mother of God, answered him as follows: "To my beloved fellow disciple Ignatius, this humble handmaid of Christ Jesus. The things you have heard and learned from John are true. Believe them, hold on to them, be steadfast in carrying out your Christian commitment and shape your life and conduct on it. I will come to you with John to visit you and those who are with you. Stand firm and do manfully in the faith. Do not let the hardships of persecution shake you, and may your spirit be strong and joyful in God your salvation. Amen."

So respected was blessed Ignatius's authority that even Dionysius, the apostle Paul's disciple who was eminent in philosophy and supreme in divine knowledge, adduced Ignatius's work as authoritative in confirmation of what he himself taught. In his book *On the Divine Names*, Dionysius states that there are some who reject the use of the name *amor* in relation to the things of God, saying that in these things *dilectio* (*agape*, love) is more divine than *amor* (*eros*, love). Dionysius, wishing to show that the noun and name *amor* can be used in everything relating to God, says: "The divine Ignatius writes, 'My Love *(amor meus)* has been crucified.'"[1]

We read in the *Tripartite History* that Ignatius heard angels standing on a mountain and singing the antiphons. He thereupon made it a rule that the antiphons were to be sung in the Church, and the Psalms to be intoned in accordance with the antiphons.

Blessed Ignatius had for a long time prayed for the peace of the Church, fearing the danger of persecution not for himself but for weak Christians. Therefore when the emperor Trajan, who came to power in the year of the Lord 100, was returning from a victorious campaign in the East and was threatening all Christians with death, Ignatius went out to meet him and declared openly that he was a Christian. Trajan responded by having him loaded with chains and turning him over to ten soldiers with orders to take him to Rome; he also warned Ignatius that in Rome he would be given to the wild beasts and eaten alive. On the journey to Rome Ignatius wrote letters to all the churches, strengthening them in the faith of Christ. We read in the *Ecclesiastical History* that in one of these letters, addressed to Rome, he asked the faithful there not to interfere with his martyrdom. In this letter he says: "From Syria to Rome, by land and by sea, already I fight day and night with the beasts, being linked and chained to ten soldiers as savage as leopards, whose assignment is to guard me and get me to Rome. Kind treatment simply makes them more ferocious, but I learn more and more from their wickedness. . . . O salutary beasts that are being readied for me! When will they come? When will they be turned loose? When will they be allowed to feast on my flesh? I shall invite them to devour me! I shall beg them to begin, lest they be afraid to touch my body as they have been with some others. I shall use force, I shall throw myself upon them! Pardon me, Romans, I beg of you! I know what is best for me—fire, crosses, wild beasts, my bones scattered about, limb being torn from limb and flesh from bone, all the devil's tortures piled upon me, if only I may gain Christ!"

[1] The Greek distinction between *agape* and *eros*, and the Latin between *dilectio* or *caritas* and *amor*, does not come out in English, which translates all these terms as "love." In the passage referred to (*DN* 4.12, 708 B-C) Dionysius notes that the sacred writers used *diligo-dilectio* and *amo-amor* with the same meaning (cf. Pseudo-Dionysius, *The Complete Works* [New York: Paulist Press, 1987], p. 81).

When he arrived in Rome and was brought before Trajan, the emperor asked him: "Ignatius, why do you stir up rebellion in Antioch? Why do you try to convert my people to Christianity?" Ignatius answered: "Would I might convert you, too, so that you might possess the highest principate of all!" Trajan: "Offer sacrifice to my gods and you will be the chief of all the priests!" Ignatius: "Neither will I sacrifice to your gods nor do I aspire to your high rank. Whatever you wish to do to me, do it! You will not change me at all!" Trajan then issued orders: "Beat him about the shoulders with leaded scourges! Tear at his sides with nails and rub his wounds with sharp stones!" When all these things had been done to him and he remained unmoved, Trajan said: "Bring live coals and make him walk barefoot over them!" Ignatius: "Neither fiery flames nor boiling water can quench the love of Christ Jesus in me!" Trajan's answer: "It's the devil's magic at work, that you can suffer so much and still not give in!" Ignatius: "We Christians have nothing to do with sorcery, and our law condemns sorcerers to death, but you who worship idols, you are the sorcerers!" Trajan said: "Tear his back open with hooks and pour salt in his wounds!" Ignatius: "The sufferings of this time are not worthy to be compared with the glory to come!" Trajan ordered: "Now take him away chained as he is, and bind him to a stake! Keep him in the bottom of the dungeon, let him go without food or drink for three days, and then throw him to the beasts to be devoured!"

Three days later the emperor, the Senate, and the whole city gathered to see the bishop of Antioch in combat with the wild beasts, and Trajan said: "Since Ignatius is so haughty and hardheaded, bind him and loose two lions at him, so that there won't be any relics left of him!" Then Ignatius spoke to the people crowded around and said: "Men of Rome, know that my labors will not go unrewarded, and that it is not for loose morals that I suffer these pains but for loyalty to my duty." Then, as we read in the *Ecclesiastical History*, he continued: "I am the wheat of Christ! May I be ground fine by the teeth of the beasts, that I may be made a clean bread!" When the emperor heard these words, he said: "Great is the patience of the Christians! Where is the Greek who would bear so much for his God?" But Ignatius responded: "It is not by my own strength that I endure all this, but by the help of Christ!" Then he began to provoke the lions, egging them on to attack him and eat him. Two savage lions therefore leapt upon him, but they only smothered him, not breaching his flesh in any way. Seeing this, Trajan's wonder knew no bounds, and he left the scene with orders that anyone who wanted to remove the body should be allowed to do so. Christians then came and took the saint's body and gave it honorable burial.

When Trajan received letters in which Pliny the Younger expressed high esteem for the Christians whom the emperor had ordered put to death, he regretted his treatment of Ignatius and gave orders that Christians were no longer to be sought out, but that if a Christian fell into the hands of the law he should be punished. We also read that in the midst of all sorts of tortures blessed Ignatius never ceased calling upon the name of Jesus Christ. When the executioners asked him why he repeated this name so often, he replied: "I have this name written on my heart and therefore cannot stop invoking it!" After his death those who had heard him say this were driven by curiosity to find out if it was true, so they took the heart out of his body, split it down the middle, and found there the name *Jesus Christ* inscribed in gold letters. This brought many of them to accept the faith.

In his commentary on the Psalm *Qui habitat*,[2] Saint Bernard wrote of our saint: "That great Ignatius, who had listened to the disciple whom Jesus loved and was himself a martyr, whose precious relics enrich our poverty, in letters that he wrote to Mary saluted her as 'Christ-bearer'—a title of the highest dignity and a mark of immeasurable honor."

37. The Purification of the Blessed Virgin Mary

The purification of the Virgin Mary took place forty days after the birth of Jesus. This feast has traditionally been known by three names—Purification, Hypopanti, and Candlemas.

The feast is called Purification because on the fortieth day after her Son's birth the blessed Virgin came to the Temple in order to be purified according to the custom prescribed by the Law, although she was not bound by that Law. The twelfth chapter of Leviticus prescribed that a woman who had received seed and borne a male child would be unclean for seven days and must abstain from association with men and from entering the Temple. When the seven days were complete, she was clean as regards association with men, but as regards entering the Temple she was unclean for thirty-three days more. Thus, forty days having passed, on the fortieth day she should go to the Temple and offer her son with gifts. If, however, she had borne a daughter, the number of days was doubled as regards both association with men and entrance into the Temple.

To explain why God commanded that a male child should be offered in the Temple on the fortieth day, three reasons may be adduced. One is that the child is brought into the Temple building on the fortieth day, just as the soul most frequently enters the body, as into its temple, on the fortieth day: this we learn

[2] Psalm 90 (91).

from the *Scholastic History*. (The physicians, however, say that the male body is completely formed in forty-six days.) A second reason is that since the soul is stained by its infusion into the body on the fortieth day, it is fully cleansed of the stain on the fortieth day after birth when the child is brought into the Temple and gifts are offered for him. The third reason: we are given to understand that those who resolve by faith to observe the Ten Commandments proclaimed by the four evangelists will merit entrance into the temple of heaven.

In the case of a woman who gives birth to a female child the number of days is doubled as regards entering the Temple, just as the formation of the female body takes twice as many days. The organization of the male body takes forty days and the soul is infused most often in forty days, but the formation of the female body and the infusion of the soul take twice as long. There are three reasons (omitting the natural ones) for this doubling of the time. First, since Christ was to take flesh in the male sex, he willed to honor this sex and to endow it with more grace, so that the child would be formed and the mother cleansed sooner. Secondly, since the woman sinned more than the man, so her troubles are doubled above those of the man in the outer world and should be doubled inside the womb. Thirdly, this makes it clear that the woman has somehow wearied God more than man has, since she has sinned more. God is wearied somehow by our wicked doings, as he himself says (Isa. 43:24): "You have burdened me with your sins, you have wearied me with your iniquities"; and in Jeremiah he says (Jer. 6:11): "I am full of the wrath of the Lord, I am weary of holding it in."

The Blessed Virgin was not bound by this law of purification, because it was not by receiving seed that she conceived, but by a mystical inbreathing. That is why Moses added, "having received seed." He did not need to add this with regard to other women, all of whom conceive in the normal way; and Bernard notes that the words were added by Moses for fear that blasphemy might be visited upon the mother of the Lord.

Mary, however, wished to submit to this law for four reasons. Her first was that she might give an example of humility, wherefore Bernard says: "O blessed Virgin! You have neither cause nor need for purification, but did your Son need circumcision? Be among women as one of them, for so your Son is among boys." This humility was not only on the mother's side but on the Son's. He likewise willed to submit to the Law in this matter: by his birth he held himself as a poor man, by his circumcision as a poor and sinful man, but on this day as a poor and sinful man and a slave; as poor, in that he chose the offering of the poor, as sinner in that along with his mother he willed to be purified, as slave in that he willed to be redeemed. At a later time he willed also to be baptized, not that there was guilt to be purged, but that he might show the depth of his humility. Thus Christ chose to accept for himself all the remedies established against original sin, not because he had any need of them, but to manifest his humility and to show that these remedies were effective in their time.

Five remedies against original sin were instituted in the course of time. According to what Hugh of Saint Victor says, three of these, namely, offerings, tithing, and the killing of a sacrificial victim (which most fully expressed the work of our redemption), were established by the Old Law. The method of accomplishing redemption was expressed by the offering; the price of redemption by a sacrifice in which blood was shed, and the identity of the redeemed by tithing, because the tenth drachma signified man.

The first remedy, therefore, was offering: thus Cain offered gifts out of the fruits of the earth, and Abel out of his flocks. The second remedy, tithing: thus Abraham offered tenths to the priest Melchizedek, because, as Augustine says, tithes are given out of what the giver really cares about. In the case of the third remedy, the killing of a victim, the sacrifices themselves, according to Gregory, were directed against original sin because of the requirement that at least one of the parents be a believer, and sometimes both parents could be unbelievers. So a fourth remedy, circumcision, was instituted, because this was valid whether or not the parents were believers. But this remedy was effective and could open the gate of paradise only for males, so baptism, which was common to both sexes and opens paradise to all, succeeded circumcision.

We see that Christ took all five remedies upon himself in one way or another. As to the first, the Lord was offered by his parents in the Temple. As to the second, he fasted for forty days and nights, because, having no goods out of which to pay a tithe, he at least offered four times ten days to God. He made the third remedy his own both when his mother offered two turtledoves or young pigeons so that they could be sacrificed for him, and when he offered himself as a sacrifice on the cross. He accepted the fourth remedy when he allowed himself to be circumcised, and the fifth when he was baptized by John.

Christ's second reason for submitting to the Law was that he might fulfill the Law. The Lord had not come to abolish the Law but to fulfill it. If he had not abided by the Law, the Jews could have excused themselves and said: "We do not accept your teaching because you are not like our fathers and you do not observe the traditions of the Law." On this day, indeed, Christ and his mother submitted to a threefold law: first to the law of purification, as an example of virtue, so that we, after we have done all things well, may say that we are unworthy servants; second to the law of redemption, as an example of humility; third to the law of offering, as an example of poverty.

The Lord's third reason was that the law of purification was to be terminated; for as the coming of daylight dispels the darkness and at the sun's rising the night shadows vanish, so the coming of true purification put an end to symbolic purification. For then came our true purification, i.e., Christ, who is called purification in the active sense, since he purifies us through faith, as it is said: "cleansing their hearts by faith" (Acts 15:9). That is why fathers are no longer held to payment, nor mothers to going into the Temple and being purified, nor sons to being bought back.

The fourth reason was to teach us how we should be purified. There are five ways by which, beginning in infancy, we are to purify ourselves. They are the vow, which signifies renunciation of sin; water, which signifies washing by baptism; fire, which indicates infusion of spiritual grace; witnesses, signifying a multitude of good works; and war, which signifies temptation. So the blessed Virgin came to the Temple, offered her Son, and redeemed him with five shekels. Note that some firstborn were redeemed, like the firstborn of the twelve tribes, who were redeemed with five shekels: some were not redeemed, like the firstborn of the Levites, who were never redeemed but, when they grew to adulthood, always served the Lord in the Temple. There were also the firstborn of clean animals, which again were not redeemed but were offered to the Lord. Some firstborn animals were substituted for, as a lamb was offered in place of the firstborn of an ass, and some were killed, like the firstborn of dogs. So, since Christ was of the tribe of Judah, one of the twelve tribes, he should be redeemed, and they offered for him to God a pair of turtledoves or two young pigeons, these being the offering of poor people: rich people offered a lamb. Scripture does not say "young turtledoves" but "young pigeons," because young pigeons are always available while young turtledoves are scarce, though the mature doves can always be found. Nor are two pigeons called for, but two turtledoves, because the pigeon is a lascivious bird and therefore God did not want it offered to him in sacrifice: the dove, on the other hand, is a virtuous bird.

But have we not seen that the Blessed Virgin Mary had received a large amount of gold from the Magi only a short while earlier? It would seem, therefore, that she could have afforded to buy one lamb. It must be said, as Bernard asserts, that the Magi did indeed bestow a great weight of gold, because it is unlikely that such great kings would have offered a trifling amount to such a child. Yet there are those who think that the Blessed Virgin did not keep the gold but immediately disbursed it to the poor, or perhaps had the foresight to save for the impending seven-year sojourn in Egypt. Or it may be that they did not offer so large a quantity of gold, since the gift had a mystical significance. A commentator has it that three offerings were made for Christ: thus the first came *from* him by his parents, the second, namely, the birds, was made *for* him, and the third *by* him on the cross for all men. The first offering showed his humility, because he submitted to the Law, the second his poverty, because he chose the offering of the poor, the third his love, because he gave himself up for sinners. The characteristics of the turtledove are set down in the following verses:

> Alta petit turtur, cantando gemit, veniens ver
> Nuntiat et caste vivit solusque moratur,
> Pullos nocte fovet morticinumque fugit.[1]

---

[1] It soars to the heights, its song has a mournful note, / it announces the coming of spring, lives chastely and stays alone, / warms its young in the night, and shuns carrion flesh.

The pigeon's characteristics are likewise noted in verse:

> Grana legit, volitat sociata, cadavera vitat,
> Felle caret, plangit sociam, per oscula tangit,
> Petra dat huic nidum, fugit hostem in flumine visum,
> Rostro non laedit, geminos pullos bene nutrit.[2]

The second name for today's feast is *Hypopanti*, which is equivalent to Representation, because Christ was presented in the Temple. Or *hypopanti* signifies a meeting, because Symeon and Anna met the Lord when he was offered in the Temple. The word comes from *hypa*, which means to go, and *anti*, which means against, toward. So then, Symeon took the Child in his arms. Note that here Christ was overshadowed or made little of in three ways. Firstly, his truth was set at naught, for he, who is the truth and through himself as truth leads every man, and is the way that leads to himself as the life, on this day allowed himself to be led by others, when they carried the Child Jesus to Jerusalem, as the gospel tells us. Secondly, his goodness was hidden, since he, who alone is holy and good, chose to be purified with his mother as though he were unclean. Thirdly, his majesty was made little of, in that he, who upholds all things by the word of his power, on this day allowed himself to be held and carried in an old man's arms, although he upheld the one who carried him, as it is said: "The old man carried the child, the child governed the old man."

Then Symeon blessed him, saying:

> Now thou dost dismiss thy servant, O Lord, according to thy word,
>   in peace;
> Because my eyes have seen thy salvation,
> Which thou hast prepared in the face of all peoples,
> A light to the revelation of the Gentiles and the glory of thy people Israel.[3]

Symeon calls him by three names—salvation, light, and glory of thy people Israel. The meaning of this triple naming can be taken four ways. First, as related to our being made righteous, "salvation" means the remission of guilt, and the name Jesus is interpreted "savior" because he will save his people from their sins. "Light" indicates the giving of grace, "glory of the people" the giving of glory. Second, as related to our regeneration: the first name, salvation, is implied because the child is exorcised and baptized, and so, as it were, cleansed of sin; recalling the second name, light, a lighted candle is given to him; as to the third name, he is offered at the altar. Third, as related to the day's procession: candles are blessed and exorcised, then lighted and given into the hands of the faithful,

---

[2] It collects grains, flies in groups, avoids cadavers, / has no spleen, mourns a companion, touches with kisses; / nests in the rocks; it flies from the enemy seen in the river, / inflicts no wound with its beak, and carefully feeds its two young.

[3] Luke 2:29–32.

and the people go into the church singing hymns. Fourth, as related to the threefold naming of this feast: it is called Purification in relation to the cleansing from sin, and so is called "salvation." It is called Candlemas in relation to illumination by grace, whence the name "light." It is called Hypopanti in relation to the granting of glory, indicated by the words "the glory of thy people Israel"—for then we shall meet Christ in the air (1 Thess. 4:16). Again, it might be said that in this canticle Christ is praised as peace, salvation, light, and glory; peace, as our mediator; salvation, as our redeemer; light, as our teacher; glory, as our rewarder.

The third name for today's feast is Candlemas, because on this day candles are carried in the hand. The Church established this usage for four reasons. The first is to do away with an erroneous custom. On the calends of February the Romans honored Februa, mother of Mars the god of war, by lighting the city with candles and torches throughout the night of that day. This they did every fifth year (that span of years being called a *lustrum*) in order to obtain victory over their enemies from the son whose mother they so solemnly celebrated. Also in February the Romans sacrificed to Februus, i.e., to Pluto and the other gods of the underworld, that the gods might be propitious to the souls of their ancestors: they made solemn offerings to them and sang their praises throughout the night by the light of candles and torches. Pope Innocent says that the Roman wives observed a feast of lights that had its origin in some poets' fables, according to which Proserpina was so beautiful that the god Pluto, smitten with desire, abducted her and made her a goddess. Her kinsmen sought her for a long time through the forests and woodlands with torches and lanterns, and the Roman wives imitated this, going about with torches and candles. Since it is hard to relinquish such customs and the Christians, converted from paganism, had difficulty giving them up, Pope Sergius transmuted them, decreeing that the faithful should honor the holy mother of the Lord on this day by lighting up the whole world with lamps and candles. Thus the Roman celebration survived but with an altered meaning.

Another reason for solemnizing the feast of Candlemas was to show the purity of the Virgin Mary. Some people, hearing that she had accepted purification, might think that she had needed to be purified. Therefore, to show that she was totally pure and radiant, the Church ordered that we should carry luminous candles, as if the Church were in effect saying: "O blessed Virgin, you need no purification! You are wholly shining, wholly resplendent!" Mary needed no purification. She had not conceived by receiving seed and had been made perfectly clean and holy in her mother's womb. Indeed she was made so completely glorious and holy in the maternal womb, and in the coming of the Holy Spirit upon her, that no slightest inclination to sin remained in her. Moreover, the power of her holiness reached out to others and was poured into them, so that in them, too, every movement of concupiscence was extinguished. That is why the Jews say that despite Mary's exceeding beauty no man could ever desire her, for the reason that the power of her chastity penetrated all who looked upon her, and all lustful desires were quenched in them. So Mary is compared to the cedar tree, because as the cedar kills snakes with its odor, so her holiness shed its rays upon others and killed the snaky movements of the flesh in them. She is also compared to myrrh, because as myrrh kills worms, so her sanctity kills lust. Moreover, this prerogative was hers alone and was not granted to others who were sanctified in the womb nor to virgins: their holiness and chastity were not transfused into others and did not extinguish their fleshly desires, whereas the power of the Virgin's chastity penetrated the hearts of the libidinous so deeply that it immediately rendered them chaste.

The third reason for celebrating the feast of Candlemas is to recall the procession that occurred on this day, when Mary and Joseph and Symeon and Anna formed a solemn procession and presented the child Jesus in the Temple. On the feast day we too make a procession, carrying in our hands a lighted candle, which signifies Jesus, and bearing it into the churches. In the candle there are three things—the wick, the wax, and the fire. These three signify three things about Christ: the wax is a sign of his body, which was born of the Virgin Mary without corruption of the flesh, as bees make honey without mingling with each other; the wick signifies his most pure soul, hidden in his body; the fire or the light stands for his divinity, because our God is a consuming fire. So someone has written:

> Hanc in honore pio
> Candelam porto Mariae.
> Accipe per ceram
> Carnem de Virgine veram,
> Per lumen numen
> Majestatis que cacumen.
> Lychnus est anima
> Carne latens praeopima.[4]

The fourth reason for celebrating this feast is to instruct us. We learn that if we wish to be purified and clean before God, we must have three things in us, namely, true faith, good works, and a right intention. The lighted candle in the hand is faith with good works; for as a candle without a light is said to be dead, and as a light does not illumine without a candle and seems to be dead, so works without faith and faith without good works can be called dead. The wick hidden within the wax is the right intention, and Gregory says: "Let the work be visible to the public in such a way that the intention remains in hiding."

---

[4] This candle I carry in honor of holy Mary. / Take the wax for the true body born of the Virgin. / Take the light for God and his supreme majesty. / Take the wick for the soul concealed in the fat flesh.

A certain noble lady was deeply devoted to the Blessed Virgin. She had a chapel built next to her house and employed her own chaplain, and her wish was to hear mass in honor of Blessed Mary every day. As the feast of the Purification approached, the priest went off on some business of his own and the lady could not have mass on that day. Or, as we read elsewhere, for love of the Virgin she had given away everything she owned, even to her clothes; and so, having nothing to wear, she could not go to church and would be without mass on the feast day. She was grieved at this and went into her own chapel or her room and prostrated herself before the Blessed Virgin's altar. Then suddenly she was rapt in spirit, and it seemed to her that she was in a beautiful church. She looked and saw a large number of virgins coming into the church, led by a most radiant virgin who was crowned with a sparkling diadem. When they were all seated in the proper order, another group, this time of young men, came in and were seated in order. Then came a man carrying a large bundle of candles. He gave a candle to the virgin who had led the procession, then distributed them to the other virgins and the young men, and finally came to the lady and offered her a candle, which she gratefully accepted. Then she looked toward the choir of the church and saw two candle-bearers, a subdeacon, a deacon, and a priest wearing the sacred vestments, moving in procession to the altar to celebrate a solemn mass. The matron sensed that the two acolytes were Saint Vincent and Saint Laurence, the deacon and subdeacon were angels, and the priest was Christ himself.

After the recitation of the *Confiteor* two handsome young men went to the middle of the choir and with high, clear voices and fervent devotion began the office of the mass; and all those in the choir took up the chant. When it was time for the offertory, the Queen of the virgins and the other virgins, together with all those in the choir, genuflected and offered their candles to the priest, as is customary. The priest waited for the lady to offer her candle to him but she would not come forward, and the Queen of the virgins sent a messenger to tell her that it was rude of her to keep the priest waiting. She, however, answered that the celebrant should go on with the mass because she was not going to offer her candle. The Queen then sent another messenger, to whom the lady made the same response, namely, that she would give to no one the candle that had been given to her, but would keep it out of devotion. This time the Queen gave the following order to the messenger: "Go and ask her again to give up her candle, and if she refuses, take it away from her by force!" When the messenger went and heard the lady repeat her refusal, he said that his orders were to wrench the candle away from her. Then he tried with all his strength to take the candle away, but she clung to it even more strongly. A long struggle ensued, each of them pulling on the candle with might and main, until suddenly it broke, and one half remained in the messenger's hands, the other in the lady's. At that very moment she came to herself and found that she was still prostrated before her altar with the broken candle in her hand. Wondering at this, she offered devout thanks to the Virgin Mary for not letting her go without mass on the feast day and providing a way for her to participate in the ceremony. She put the candle carefully away and kept it among her most precious relics; and it is said that all who touched it were freed at once from whatever infirmity befell them.

There was another matron who was pregnant and one night, in a dream, saw herself holding a banner tinted the color of blood. Awakening, she was promptly bereft of her senses, and the devil deluded her, so that she thought she was holding the faith of Christ, to which she had always adhered, between her breasts, but that it was escaping from her grasp. She found no cure for this delusion until she passed the whole night of this day's feast in a church of the Virgin Mary, and there was fully restored to health.

---

38. Saint Blaise

Blaise (Blasius) is like *blandus*, bland, or is formed from *bela*, meaning habit or disposition, and *syor*, small; for the saint was bland through the sweetness of his discourse, virtuous by habit, and small by the humility of his way of life.

Blaise set a powerful example of gentleness and holiness, and the Christians in Sebaste, a city in Cappadocia, elected him to be their bishop; but because Diocletian's persecution was raging, Blaise, though now a bishop, retired to a cave and there led the life of a hermit. Birds brought him food, and wild animals flocked to him and would not leave until he had laid hands on them in blessing. Moreover, if any of them were ailing, they came straight to him and went away cured.

The prefect of that region once sent his soldiers out to hunt, and they, after sighting no game elsewhere, came by chance upon Saint Blaise's cave, where they discovered a great herd of wild beasts standing in front of it. The hunters could not possibly take them all and, astonished at what they saw, reported it to their commander. The prefect at once dispatched more soldiers with orders to bring in the bishop and any Christians they found.

That same night Christ appeared three times to Blaise, saying: "Rise and offer sacrifice to me!" Then the soldiers arrived and said: "Come out, the prefect summons you!" Saint Blaise answered them: "You are welcome, my sons! Now I see that God has not forgotten me!" As he went along with them, he never stopped preaching and worked many wonders before their eyes. For instance, a woman, whose son was dying because a fish bone had stuck in his throat, laid the boy at the bishop's feet and tearfully begged him to cure her child. Saint Blaise laid his hands on him and prayed that this child, and anyone else who sought help from God in his name, should obtain the benefit of health. The boy was cured instantly. Another poor woman, a widow, possessed nothing but a single pig, and a wolf had violently made off with the pig. The woman implored Saint Blaise to get the pig back, and the saint smiled and said: "Good woman, don't be sad, your pig will be returned to you." Within minutes the wolf came up and gave the pig back to the widow.

Blaise now entered the city and, by the prefect's order, was locked up in jail. The next day, however, the prefect had him brought before him and, when he saw him, welcomed him with cozening words, such as: "Greetings, Blaise, friend of the gods!" "Greetings likewise to Your Excellency!" Blaise responded, "But do not call them gods but demons, because they are given over to eternal fire along with all who honor them!" This made the prefect angry, and he ordered Blaise to be beaten with cudgels and put back in jail. Blaise said to him: "Foolish man, do you hope that your punishments will take my love of God away from me, when I have my God in me to give me strength?"

The poor widow who had recovered her pig heard what had happened, killed the pig, and delivered its head, with the feet, a candle, and a loaf, to Saint Blaise. He thanked her, ate, and told her: "Every year offer a candle in the church named for me, and all will be well with you and with all who do the same." The widow year after year did as he told her and enjoyed great prosperity.

The prefect now had the bishop brought out of prison but could not induce him to bow to the gods, so he ordered the torturers to hang him from a rafter and tear his flesh with iron spikes, then to put him back in jail. Seven women, however, followed and collected the drops of his blood, so they were arrested and ordered to sacrifice to the gods. They said: "If you want us to adore your gods, place them reverently at the edge of the lake, so that we can wash their faces and worship them more cleanly!" This made the prefect happy, and what they had asked was quickly done. But the women snatched up the idols and threw them into the middle of the lake, saying: "Now we shall see if they are really gods!" When the prefect heard of this, he was beside himself with rage, beat himself with his fists, and shouted at his men: "Why didn't you hold on to our gods and keep them from being plunged into the bottom of the lake?" "The women fooled you with their talk," the men retorted, "And so the gods got immersed!" The women also had their say: "The true God can't be fooled, and if these idols were gods, they would have known ahead of time what we intended to do!"

Furious, the prefect called for the preparation of molten lead, iron combs, and seven breastplates fired red-hot and arranged to one side, seven linen shirts to the other. Then he ordered the women to choose which of these they wanted to put on. One of the women, who had two small children with her, boldly ran forward, picked up the linen shirts, and threw them into the fire. The children said to their mother: "Dearest mother, don't leave us behind! You have filled us with the sweetness of your milk, so fill us with the sweetness of the kingdom of heaven!" The prefect ordered the women to be hung up and their flesh to be slashed with iron rakes; and their flesh was seen to be white as driven snow, and from their torn bodies milk flowed instead of blood. They bore these tortures without flinching, and an angel of the Lord came to them and encouraged them stoutly, saying: "Have no fear! The good workman, who has started his work well and brings it to a good end, merits a blessing from the one for whom he works and receives a wage for his work; and joy is the wage he possesses!"

Then the prefect had them taken down and thrown into the furnace, but the fire was extinguished by God's power and the women emerged unharmed. The prefect admonished them: "Have done with your magical arts and adore our gods!" They answered: "Finish what you've started! We are called now to the heavenly kingdom!" So he sentenced them to be beheaded. They knelt in readiness for the blow of the sword and worshiped God, saying: "O God, you have brought us out of darkness and into your marvelous light, you have made us your sacrifice! Now receive our souls and let us enter into eternal life!" Their heads fell and they migrated to the Lord.

The prefect had Blaise brought before him and said to him: "Either adore the gods or don't!" "Impious man," Blaise retorted, "I do not fear your threats! Do as you will! I turn my body over to you completely!" The prefect ordered him to be thrown into the lake, but he made the sign of the cross over the water and instantly it became like dry, firm land under him. "If your gods are true gods," he said to the bystanders, "show their power by walking on the water!" Sixty-five men walked in and promptly drowned. Then an angel of the Lord descended and said to him: "Come out, Blaise, and receive the crown God has prepared for you!" He came out, and the prefect said: "Well, have you absolutely decided not to worship the gods?" Blaise answered: "Know, wretch, that I am a servant of Christ and do not adore demons!" The order was given to behead him, and he prayed to the Lord that anyone who besought his intercession when suffering from throat trouble or any other illness should be heard and healed immediately. And behold, a voice came to him from heaven, saying that what he prayed for would be done. And so the saint was beheaded with the aforementioned two children, about the year of the Lord 283.

39. Saint Agatha, Virgin

Agatha comes from *agios*, which means holy, and *theos*, God—hence saint of God. According to Chrysostom, there are three requirements for sainthood, and Agatha was perfect in all three—namely, cleanness of heart, the presence of the Holy Spirit, and abundance of good works. Or the name comes from *a*, which means without, *geos*, earth, and *theos*, God—therefore a goddess, as it were, without earth, i.e., without love of earthly things. Or it comes from *aga*, speaking, and *thau*, completion, and Agatha spoke completely and perfectly, as is clear from her answers. Or again from *agath*, servitude, and *thaas*, higher, because one of her answers was: "To be a slave of Christ is proof of the highest nobility." Or from *aga*, solemn, and *thau*, consummation, because she was solemnly consummated, i.e., buried, which refers to the angels who buried her.

The virgin Agatha was highborn and a great beauty, living in the city of Catania, where she worshiped God at all times and in all holiness. Quintianus, the consular official in Sicily, who was baseborn, libidinous, greedy, and a worshiper of idols, was determined to get her in his grasp. Being of low degree he would gain respect by lording it over a noble, her beauty would satisfy his libido, he would steal her riches to feed his avarice, and, being a pagan, he would force her to sacrifice to the gods.

So he had her brought before him and quickly perceived the firmness of her resolution. He therefore turned her over to a procuress whose name was Aphrodisia and her nine daughters who were as lascivious as their mother. He gave them thirty days to overcome her resistance. They tried to change her mind, at times by promising her pleasure, at others by threatening her with pain. They hoped to win her over from her good resolve, but blessed Agatha said to them: "My determination is built on rock and founded in Christ! Your promises are raindrops, your threats are rivers, and however hard they beat upon the foundation of my house, it cannot fall." Having said this, she prayed and wept day after day, thirsting to attain the palm of martyrdom. Aphrodisia saw that her will could not be shaken, and told Quintianus: "It would be easier to split rocks or reduce iron to the softness of lead than to move or recall that girl's mind from its Christian intention."

Then Quintianus summoned her again. "What is your social standing?" he asked. She answered: "I am freeborn and of illustrious lineage, as my ancestry attests." Quintianus: "If you are so highborn, why does the way you live make you seem to be of servile status?" Her answer: "I am the slave of Christ, therefore I show myself as a person in service." Quintianus: "If you are of noble birth, why do you call yourself a slave?" Agatha: "Because to be a slave of Christ is proof of the highest nobility." "Make your choice!" Quintianus said. "Either sacrifice to the gods or submit to torture!" Agatha retorted: "May your wife be like your goddess Venus, and may you be like your god Jupiter!" Quintianus ordered her to be slapped in the face, and said: "Don't let your loose tongue insult your judge!" Agatha answered: "I marvel that a sensible man like you can fall into such stupidity as to call gods those whose lives neither you nor your wife would want to imitate! Indeed you consider it an insult if you are said to follow their example. If your gods are good, I've made a good wish for you: if you repudiate any association with them, then you agree with me!" "What's the use of all this idle talk?" Quintianus exclaimed; "sacrifice to the gods or prepare to suffer!" Agatha: "If you promise me the wild beasts, the sound of Christ's name will gentle them! If you try fire, angels will serve me with a healing dew from heaven! If you resort to wounds and torments, I have the Holy Spirit, through whom I make naught of all that!" Then, because what she said was making him look foolish in the public eye, Quintianus had her put in jail; and to jail she went happy and triumphant, as if invited to a banquet, and commended her trial to the Lord.

The next day Quintianus said to her: "Forswear Christ and adore the gods!" When she refused, he ordered her stretched on the rack and tortured, and Agatha said: "These pains are my delight! It's as if I were hearing some good news, or seeing someone I had long wished to see, or had found a great treasure. The wheat cannot be stored in the barn unless it has been thoroughly threshed and separated from the chaff: so my soul cannot enter paradise unless you make the headsmen give my body harsh treatment." This made Quintianus so angry that he ordered the executioners to twist her breast for a long time and then cut it off. Said Agatha: "Impious, cruel, brutal tyrant, are you not ashamed to cut off from a woman that which your mother suckled you with? In my soul I have breasts untouched and unharmed, with which I nourish all my senses, having consecrated them to the Lord from infancy."

The tyrant ordered her back to prison, and forbade the jailers to allow any physician to care for her or anyone to bring her food or water. But toward the middle of the night an aged man, preceded by a boy carrying a light, came to her. He brought various medicaments and said to Agatha: "Though this mad consul has inflicted torments on you, the way you have answered him has tormented him even more, and though he has caused your breasts to be injured, his exuberance will turn to bitterness. I was there when all this was done to you, and I saw that your breast could be healed." Agatha: "I have never applied any material remedy to my body, and it would be shameful to lose now what I have preserved for so long." The aged man said to her: "I am a Christian, so you need not be ashamed." Agatha: "How could I be ashamed, since you are so old and a grandfather, and I am so cruelly mangled that no one could possibly desire me?

But I thank you, kind sir and father, for deigning to have such solicitude in my regard." "But why," the old man asked, "why do you not allow me to heal you?" "Because I have my Lord Jesus Christ," Agatha replied, "and he by a single word can cure everything and by his word restores all things. If he so wills, he can cure me instantly." The aged man smiled. "I am his apostle," he said, "and he sent me to you. Know that in his name you are healed." And Peter the apostle vanished. Agatha knelt in thanksgiving, and found that all her hurts were healed and her breast restored to her bosom. The jailers, terrified by the dazzling light, had fled and left the jail open, but some who were left asked her to go away. "Far be it from me," she said, "to run away and lose the crown of patience, and also to expose my guards to trouble!"

After four days passed, Quintianus again told her to worship the gods, or still worse punishments would be hers. Agatha answered: "Your words are silly and useless, they are wicked and pollute the air! You mindless wretch, how can you want me to adore stones and abandon the God of heaven who has healed me?" "Who healed you?" Quintianus asked. Agatha: "Christ the Son of God!" Quintianus: " You dare to pronounce the name of Christ again, when I do not want to hear it?" Agatha: "As long as I live I shall invoke Christ with heart and lips!" Quintianus: "Now we'll see if Christ will cure you!" He ordered Agatha to be rolled naked over potsherds and live coals strewn on the ground. While this was going on, a tremendous earthquake shook the city and caused the palace to collapse, crushing two of Quintianus's counselors. At this the whole populace came running and shouting that such things were being visited on them because of the unjust treatment meted out to Agatha. So Quintianus, caught between the earthquake and the popular uprising, ordered Agatha back to prison. There she prayed, saying: "Lord Jesus Christ, you created me, you have watched over me from infancy, kept my body from defilement, preserved me from love of the world, made me able to withstand torture, and granted me the virtue of patience in the midst of torments. Now receive my spirit and command me to come to your mercy." And, having finished her prayer, she called out in a loud voice and gave up her spirit, about the year of the Lord 253, in the reign of the emperor Dacian.[1]

Faithful Christians came, anointed her body with spices, and laid it in a sarcophagus. Then a young man clothed in silken garments and accompanied by over a hundred handsome youths wearing rich white vestments, none of whom had ever been seen in that region, approached the saint's body and placed at the head a marble tablet, after which he and his companions vanished from the sight of all. On the tablet was inscribed: MENTEM SANCTAM, SPONTANEAM, HONOREM DEO ET PATRIAE LIBERATIONEM, which may be understood as meaning: "She had a holy and generous soul, gave honor to God, and accomplished the liberation of her country." When this miracle was noised abroad, even pagans and Jews began to venerate the tomb in great numbers.

---

[1] Graesse notes that "recent editions add 'otherwise called Decius.'"

As for Quintianus, he was on his way to look for and make off with Agatha's riches when his two horses began to gnash their teeth and kick out with their hooves, and one of them bit him and the other kicked him into the river, and his body was never found.

One year from the day of Agatha's birth into the new life of heaven, the mountain that looms over Catania erupted and spewed a river of fire and molten rock down toward the city. Then crowds of pagans fled from the mountain to the saint's tomb, snatched up the pall that covered it, and hung it up in the path of the fire; and, on the very day of the virgin's birth, the stream of lava halted and did not advance a foot farther.

About this virgin saint, Ambrose says in his Preface: "O holy and glorious virgin, who faithfully shed her blood as a martyr in praise of the Lord! O illustrious, renowned virgin, upon whom shone a twofold glory: since amidst harsh torments she wrought all sorts of miracles and, strengthened by support from above, merited to be cured by the apostle's visitation! So the airs bore his bride heavenward to Christ, and glorious obsequies shine about her mortal frame as the angel choir acclaims the holiness of her soul and the liberation of her native land."

---

40. Saint Vaast

Vedastus, the Latin form of Vaast, comes from *vere*, truly, *dans*, giving, and *aestus*, heat, and the saint truly gave himself the heat of affliction and penance. Or the name may come from *veh*, woe, and *distans*, distant, because eternal woe was distant from him. The damned will say "woe!" continually—woe! because I have offended God, woe! because I did the devil's will, woe! that I was born, woe! that I cannot die, woe! because I am so sorely tormented, woe! because I shall never be set free.

Vaast was ordained bishop of Arras by Saint Remy. When he came to the city gate, he found two beggars there, the one blind, the other lame. They asked for an alms and he said to them: "I have neither silver nor gold, but what I have I give you"; whereupon he prayed, and both of them were made whole. Then there was an abandoned church, covered with thorns and brambles, in which a wolf had made its lair. Saint Vaast ordered the wolf to go away and not to dare come back, and the wolf obeyed.

After he had labored as bishop for forty years and by word and work had converted many to the faith, he saw a column of fire descending from heaven upon his house. He realized that his end was at hand, and a short while later he fell asleep in the Lord, about A.D. 550.

As the corpse was being transferred for burial, Audomatus, an old man who was blind, lamented that he could not see the bishop's body, and instantly his sight was restored. Later, however, at his prayer, he became blind again.

---

41. Saint Amand

The name Amand means lovable, and the name fitted the man, for he had three qualities that make a person lovable. First, he was friendly toward others; Prov. 18:24: "A man amiable in society will be more friendly than a brother." Second, he was honorable in his conduct, as it is said of Esther (Esther 2:15): "She was agreeable and amiable in the sight of all." Third, he was upright and virtuous; 2 Sam. 1:23: "Saul and Jonathan were lovely, and comely in their life."

Amand, the son of noble parents, entered a monastery. While he was walking in the monastery garden, he came upon a huge serpent and, by praying and making the sign of the cross, made it go back to its pit never to come out again. Then he went to the tomb of Saint Martin, where he stayed for fifteen years, wearing a hair shirt and living on barley bread and water.

Then he went to Rome and was spending the night in prayer in the church of Saint Peter, when the watchman irreverently put him out of the building. Saint Peter appeared to him as he slept at the church door, and directed him to go to Gaul and to rebuke King Dagobert for his crimes. The king resented this and ordered Amand out of his kingdom. Later the king, who had no son, prayed the Lord to grant him a son, and his prayer was answered. He began to think about whom he should have to baptize his son, and it came to him that Amand might be the one to ask. Amand was sought for and brought to the king, who knelt at his feet and begged the saint to forgive him and to baptize the son whom the Lord had granted him. Amand graciously consented to the first request but, fearing to become involved in worldly affairs, declined the second and left the court. In the end, however, he yielded to the king's prayer; and at the baptism, while all were silent, the infant pronounced the response: "Amen."

Dagobert then had Amand installed as bishop in the see of Maastricht, but the people there disdained his preaching, and he withdrew to Gascony.[1] There a jester who ridiculed him with scornful words was seized by a demon, and, tearing at his own flesh with his teeth, he confessed that he had wronged the man of God, and died a miserable death. Then there was a time when Amand was washing his hands and another bishop saved the water, with which he afterwards cured a blind man.

On another occasion Amand, at the king's bidding, wished to establish a monastery in a certain location, but the bishop of a nearby city took offense at this and sent his men either to kill Amand or force him to leave the place. They went to him and tried to deceive him: he was to come with them, they said, and they would show him a very good site for his monastery. Amand had foreknowledge of their evil intentions but, because he longed for martyrdom, went with them to the peak of the mountain where they planned to murder him. But suddenly the mountain was enveloped in rainstorms so dense that the murderers could not even see each other. Thinking that they were about to die, they fell to their knees and implored his pardon, also begging him to let them get away alive. He prayed fervently and the weather turned serene. The repentant fellows went home, and Amand, having escaped their plot, performed many other miracles and eventually died in peace. He flourished about A.D. 653, in the time of the emperor Heraclius.

42. Saint Valentine

The name Valentine, in Latin *Valentinus*, is made up of *valorem*, value, and *tenens*, holding; and Saint Valentine held on to—persevered in—holiness. Or the name is like *valens tiro*, valiant soldier of Christ. A valiant soldier is one who has never fallen, who strikes hard, defends himself bravely, and conquers decisively. Thus Valentine never failed by shunning martyrdom, he struck hard by putting down idolatry, he defended his faith by confessing it, he conquered by suffering.

---

[1] *Vasconia* in the text. Historically, Amand's activity as a missionary bishop was carried on in the area that is now Belgium. There is no evidence that he was ever in southern France. Cf. *Butler's Lives of the Saints* (New York: P. J. Kenedy & Sons, 1963), 1:263.

Valentine was a venerable priest, whom the emperor Claudius summoned before him. "What is this, Valentine?" he asked. "Why do you not win our friendship by adoring our gods and abandoning your vain superstitions?" Valentine answered: "If you but knew the grace of God, you would not say such things! You would turn your mind away from your idols and adore the God who is in heaven." One of the people standing by Claudius said: "Valentine, what have you to say about the holiness of our gods?" "All I have to say about them," Valentine replied, "is that they were wretched human beings full of every uncleanness!" Claudius spoke: "If Christ is true God, why do you not tell me the truth?" Valentine: "Truly Christ alone is God! If you believe in him, your soul will be saved, the empire will prosper, and you will be granted victory over all your enemies!" Claudius responded, saying to those around him: "Men of Rome, heed how wisely and rightly this man speaks!" Then the prefect said: "The emperor is being led astray! How shall we give up what we have believed from infancy?"

At this the heart of Claudius was hardened, and he turned Valentine over to the prefect to be held in custody. When Valentine came into this man's house, he said: "Lord Jesus Christ, true light, enlighten this house and let all here know you as true God!" The prefect said: "I wonder at hearing you say that Christ is light. Indeed, if he gives light to my daughter who has been blind for a long time, I will do whatever you tell me to do!" Valentine prayed over the daughter, her sight was restored, and the whole household was converted to the faith. Then the emperor ordered Valentine to be beheaded, about A.D. 280.

43. Saint Juliana

Juliana was betrothed to Eulogius, the prefect of Nicomedia, but refused to become his wife unless he accepted the faith of Christ. Her father therefore commanded that she be stripped and soundly beaten, then handed her over to the prefect. Eulogius said to her: "My dear Juliana, why have you played false with me, rejecting me this way?" She answered: "If you will adore my God, I will consent, otherwise I will never be yours!" "I can't do that, dear lady," the prefect replied, "because the emperor would have me beheaded." Juliana: "If you are so afraid of a mortal emperor, how can you expect me not to fear an immortal one? Do whatever you please, because you will not be able to win me over!"

So the prefect had her severely beaten, and ordered her hung up by the hair of her head for half a day, and molten lead to be poured on her head. None of this, however, did her the slightest harm, so he had her bound in chains and shut up in prison. There the devil came to her in the guise of an angel and said: "Juliana, I am an angel of the Lord, who has sent me to you to warn you to sacrifice to the gods, if you do not want to be subjected to long torture and die a dreadful death!"

Juliana wept and prayed, saying: "O Lord my God, do not let me perish, but show me who this is that's giving me such advice!" Then a voice spoke to her, telling her to lay hold of her visitor and force him to admit who he was. She grasped him firmly and questioned him, and he told her that he was a demon and that his father had sent him to deceive her. "And who is your father?" she asked. He answered: "Beelzebul, who sends us out to do all sorts of mischief and has us whipped unmercifully whenever we are outdone by Christians. So I know it will go hard with me because I have not been able to get the better of you!" He admitted, among other things, that he was kept farthest away from Christians when they were celebrating the mystery of the Lord's Body and when they were engaged in prayer and preaching. Juliana tied his hands behind his back, threw him to the ground, and gave him a thorough thrashing with the chain that had bound her, while the devil cried aloud, pleading with her and saying: "My lady Juliana, have pity on me!"

Now the prefect gave orders to bring Juliana out of jail, and she came out dragging the demon, still in bonds, after her. The demon continued to plead with her, saying: "Lady Juliana, stop making a fool of me or I'll never again be able to mislead anyone! Christians are supposed to be merciful, but you haven't shown me any mercy at all!" But she dragged him from one end of the market-place to the other and finally tossed him into a sewer.

When news of this reached the prefect, he had Juliana stretched on a wheel until all her bones were broken and the marrow spurted out, but an angel of the Lord shattered the wheel and healed her instantly. Seeing this happen, the people around believed, and 500 men and 130 women were beheaded forthwith. Then Juliana was put into a tub filled with molten lead, but the lead became like a cool bath. At this the prefect cursed his gods, who were unable to punish a mere girl for heaping such insults upon them. Then he ordered her beheaded, and while she was being led to the place of execution, the demon whom she had whipped appeared in the guise of a young man, shouting and saying: "Don't spare her! She slandered your gods and gave me a terrible beating last night! Give her what she deserves!" When Juliana opened her eyes a little and saw who was shouting, the demon ran away exclaiming: "Woe is me! I think she still wants to catch me and tie me up!"

When blessed Juliana had been beheaded, the prefect went to sea with thirty-four men, and a storm came up and they were all drowned; and when the sea cast the bodies on the shore, they were devoured by the birds and the beasts.

44. The Chair of Saint Peter

There are three kinds of "chair"—the royal chair, or throne, 2 Sam. 23:8: "David sitting in the chair, etc."; the priestly chair, 1 Kings 1:9: "Now Eli the priest was sitting on a stool before the door of the temple of the Lord"; and the magisterial or professorial chair, Matt. 23:1: "The scribes and the Pharisees have sat on the chair of Moses." Peter sat on the royal chair because he was first among all kings; on the priestly chair because he was the shepherd of all clerics; and on the magisterial chair because he was the teacher of all Christians.[1]

The Church commemorates the Chair of Saint Peter with a feast day because blessed Peter is said to have been raised on this day to the seat of honor in Antioch. There appear to be four reasons for the institution of this solemnity. The first is that when blessed Peter was preaching in Antioch, Theophilus, governor of the city, said to him: "Peter, why are you corrupting my people?" Peter then preached the faith of Christ to Theophilus, who immediately had him imprisoned and deprived of food and drink. The apostle was almost exhausted but regained some strength, turned his eyes to heaven, and said: "Christ Jesus, helper of the helpless, come to my aid! These trials have almost destroyed me!" The Lord answered him: "Peter, did you think I had deserted you? You impugn my kindness when you are not afraid to say such things against me! The one who will relieve your misery is at hand!"

Meanwhile Saint Paul heard of Peter's imprisonment. He presented himself to Theophilus, asserted that he was highly skilled in many arts and crafts, and said that he knew how to sculpt in wood and stone and could do many other kinds of work as well. Theophilus pressed him to stay on as a member of his household. A few days later Paul went secretly to Peter in his cell and found him very weak and almost dead. Paul wept bitterly and took Peter in his arms, weeping profusely, and burst out: "O my brother Peter, my glory, my joy, the half of my soul, now that I am here you must recover your strength!" Peter opened his eyes, recognized Paul, and began to cry but could not speak. Paul quickly opened the other's mouth, forced food into him, and thus got some warmth into his body. The food strengthened Peter, who threw himself into Paul's embrace and both of them shed a flood of tears.

---

[1] The term "chair" is derived from the Greek/Latin word *cathedra*, seat, and, as used here, usually indicates a seat of special dignity, a throne. In Church language the *cathedral* is the church in which the bishop's chair, *cathedra*, is located—the center, so to speak, of his "see," a word derived from the Latin *sedes*, which also means "seat."

Paul left the jail cautiously and went back to Theophilus, to whom he said: "O good Theophilus, great is your fame, and your courtliness is the friend of honor. But a small evil counteracts great good! Think about what you have done to that worshiper of God who is called Peter, as if he were someone of importance! He is in rags, misshapen, reduced to skin and bones, a nobody, notable only for what he says. Do you think it is right to put such a man in jail? If he were enjoying the freedom to which he is accustomed, he might be able to do you some useful service. For instance, some say that he restores the sick to health and the dead to life!" Theophilus: "Idle tales, Paul, idle tales! If he could raise the dead, he would free himself from prison!" Paul: "Just as his Christ rose from the dead (or so they say) yet would not come down from the cross, so Peter, following Christ's example (it is said), does not set himself free and is not afraid to suffer for Christ!" Theophilus: "Tell him, then, to bring my son, who has been dead for fourteen years, back to life, and I will release him unharmed and free!" Paul therefore went to Peter's cell and told him he had solemnly promised Theophilus that his son would be brought back to life. "That's a hard promise to keep, Paul," said Peter, "but God's power will make it easy!" Peter was taken out of prison and led to the tomb. He prayed, and the governor's son came to life immediately.

There are some things here, however, that sound improbable, for instance, that Paul would pretend that he had the natural skills needed to do and make a variety of things, or that the son's sentence of death was suspended for fourteen years. But however that may be, Theophilus and the whole population of Antioch, together with a great many other people, believed in Christ. They built a magnificent church and erected an elevated throne in the center, to which they lifted Peter up so that he could be seen and heard by everybody. He occupied that chair for seven years, but afterwards went to Rome and ruled the see of Rome for twenty-five years. The Church, however, celebrates this first honor because it was the beginning of the custom by which bishops are distinguished by place, power, and name. Thus what we read in Ps. 106:32 is fulfilled: "Let them exalt him in the church of the people, and praise him in the chair of the ancients."

Note that the church in which blessed Peter was exalted is threefold, namely, the church of the militant, the church of the malignant, and the church of the triumphant. He was exalted in this threefold church by the three feasts that are celebrated in his honor. In the church of the militant he was exalted by presiding over it and ruling it laudably in spirit, in faith, and in his virtuous life; and this refers to today's feast, which is named for the pontifical Chair, because Peter then assumed the pontificate in the church of Antioch and ruled it in a praiseworthy manner for seven years. Secondly, Peter is exalted in the church of the malignant, in that he dispersed it and converted it to the true faith; and this refers to the second feast honoring him, which is named after his chains, because he dispersed this church and brought many back to the faith. Thirdly, he is exalted in the church of the triumphant; and this refers to the third solemnization, which is that of his passion, because by his passion he entered the church triumphant.

Furthermore, the Church during the year celebrates three feasts in Peter's honor for many other reasons besides the above, among them his office, his benefits, our debt to him, and the example he set for us.

First, he is honored because he was privileged. Blessed Peter enjoyed three privileges that raised him above the other apostles, and because of these three privileges the Church honors him three times in the year. He enjoyed a higher dignity than the others by his authority, since he stood forth as prince of the apostles and received the keys of the kingdom of heaven. He was more fervent than the others in his love, for he loved Christ with greater fervor, as is manifest from many passages in the gospels. His power was more efficacious, since, as we read in the Acts of the Apostles, the infirm were cured when his shadow passed over them.

Second, he is honored because of his office in the Church. He was supreme pontiff over the universal Church, and, since he was prince and prelate of the whole Church that is spread over the three parts of the world, namely, Asia, Africa, and Europe, the Church celebrates his feast three times in the year. Third, he is honored for the benefits he provides. Having received the power of binding and loosing, he frees us from three kinds of sins, namely, sins of thought, of word, and of action, or our sins against God, our neighbors, and ourselves. And there is still another triple benefit that the sinner obtains through the power of the keys, namely, absolution from guilt, commutation of punishment from perpetual to temporal, and remission of part of the temporal punishment. And on account of this threefold benefit, Saint Peter is triply honored. Fourth, he is honored on account of our debt to him. Since he has fed and feeds us in three ways, namely, by word, by example, and by temporal aid or the suffrage of his prayers, we are triply indebted to him and therefore honor him with three feasts. A fifth reason is the example he gives us, because no sinner should despair even if he, like Peter, has denied God three times, provided that, like Peter, he confesses God in his heart, by his speech, and through his actions.

A second reason for the institution of today's feast is one that is taken from the *Itinerarium* of Saint Clement. There we read that Peter was going about, preaching the Gospel, and when he approached Antioch, all the people of that city came barefoot, clothed in sackcloth, and sprinkling ashes on their heads, to meet him. They did this by way of penance, because they had taken sides against him with Simon the Magician. Seeing their repentance, Peter thanked God. Then they brought to him all the people who were sickly or were possessed by demons. Peter had them laid out in front of him and called down God's blessing upon them, and an immense light appeared and all were cured, whereupon they ran after Peter and kissed his footprints. Within a week over ten thousand men were baptized. Theophilus, governor of the city, had his house consecrated as a basilica, in which he erected an elevated chair for Peter so that he might be seen and heard by all. Nor does this account contradict what has been said above. It is quite possible that after Peter, due to Paul's intervention, was magnificently welcomed by Theophilus and the townspeople, he may have left the city. Then Simon Magus may have perverted the people and stirred them up against the apostle, but later they would have done penance and again given Peter an honorable reception.

The feast of the Chair of Saint Peter used to be called the feast of Saint Peter's Banquet, and this brings us to the third reason for its institution. It was an ancient custom of the pagans (as Master John Beleth tells us) to offer a banquet on the tombs of their ancestors every year on a certain day in the month of February. Then, during the night, demons consumed the food, but the pagans thought it was the souls of the dead, which they called shades, that wandered among the tombs and did away with the viands. According to the same author the ancients said that when the souls are in the human body, they are called souls, when they are in the underworld, they are *manes*, ghosts, when they ascend to heaven, they are called spirits, and, when they are recently buried or wander around the tombs, shades. The holy fathers of the Church wanted to eradicate this custom of the banquets but saw that it would be difficult to do so, and in its stead instituted the feast of the Chair or Enthronement of Saint Peter. This combined the Roman and the Antiochene feasts on the same day when the old banquets were held, and so there are some even now who call this feast the Feast of Saint Peter's Banquet.[2]

The fourth reason for the institution of today's feast is reverence for the clerical tonsure. It is noteworthy that, according to a tradition held by some, the clerical tonsure had its origin here. When Peter began to preach the Gospel at Antioch, the pagans shaved the top of his head as a sign of contempt for the name of Christian; and in time the tonsure, which had been imposed on the prince of the apostles as a badge of shame, was passed on to all clerics as a mark of honor. There are three things worthy of note regarding this clerical "crown," namely, the shaving of the head, the cutting off of hair, and the circular shape of the tonsure. The top of the head is shaved for three reasons, of which two are given by Dionysius in the *Ecclesiastical Hierarchy*.[3] He says that the shaving of the head signifies a clean, plain, artless way of life; for three things follow upon the cutting off of hair or the shaving of the head, namely, preservation of cleanness, lack of ornament, and denudation. Preservation of cleanness follows, because hair collects dirt; lack of ornament, because hair is worn as an ornament. Thus the tonsure signifies a clean, unpretentious life. This means that clerics should have interior cleanness of mind and a lack of concern for external fashion. The

[2] The traditional date of this feast in the Roman calendar is 22 February, which almost exactly coincided with the final day of the Roman feasts of the dead, the 21st.

[3] Graesse mistakenly has *in Coelesti Hierarchia*. The correct reference is *The Ecclesiastical Hierarchy*, chap. 6, sec. 2, in Pseudo-Dionysius, *The Complete Works* (New York: Paulist Press, 1987), 246–247.

denuding of the scalp signifies that there should be nothing between the cleric and God: clerics should be immediately united to God and should behold the glory of the Lord with face unveiled. The cutting off of hair gives us to understand that clerics should cut away all superfluous thoughts from their minds and should have their hearing prepared and ready for the word of God, thus completely removing from themselves everything temporal except the strictly necessary.

There are many reasons for the circular shape of the tonsure. First, the circle has neither end nor beginning, and by this it is understood that clerics are ministers of God, who has neither beginning nor end. Second, the round shape has no angles, and this means that clerics should have no soiled areas in their lives, since (as Bernard says) where there are angles there are dirty spots. They should also have truth in their teaching, because truth (as Jerome says) does not like angles. Third, the circle is of all shapes the most beautiful; hence God made his heavenly creatures in this shape. This means that clerics should have beauty inwardly in their thoughts and outwardly in their conduct. Fourth, the circle is the simplest of all shapes, for no figure (as Augustine says) consists of only one line; the circle is the only one that is closed by a single line. This signifies that clerics should have the simplicity of doves, according to the word of the Lord: "Be simple as doves."

===== ✳ =====

45. Saint Matthias, Apostle

The Hebrew name Matthias means given by God, or gift of God, or it can mean humble or small. Saint Matthias was given by God when God chose him out of the world and gave him a place among the seventy-two disciples. He was a gift of God when, being elected by lot, he won the name of apostle. He was small in that he always preserved true humility. Humility (as Ambrose says) is threefold. There is first the humility that is imposed from without on a person, who is then said to be humiliated; second, the humility of reflection, which comes out of one's self-knowledge; third, the humility of devotion, which proceeds from knowledge of the Creator. Matthias had the first humility by suffering martyrdom, the second by having a low estimate of himself, and the third by bowing before the majesty of God. Or his name may come from *manus*, which means good, and *thesis*, which means position. Matthias, the good, was positioned in the place of the evil one, Judas.

Bede is believed to be the author of the life of Matthias which is read in the churches.

Matthias the apostle was given the place of Judas; but first let us briefly see something of Judas's birth and origins. We read in a certain admittedly apocryphal history that there was in Jerusalem a man, Ruben by name, who was also called Simon, of the tribe of Dan, or, as Jerome has it, of the tribe of Issachar, and who had a wife named Cyborea. One night, after they had paid each other the marital debt, Cyborea fell asleep and had a dream that she related, terrified, sobbing and groaning, to her husband. She said: "I dreamed that I was going to bear a son so wicked that he would bring ruin upon our whole people." Ruben answered: "That's a very bad thing you are saying, a thing that should not be repeated, and I think a divining spirit had hold of you!" "If I find that I have conceived and if I bear a son," she said, "there can be no doubt that it was not a divining spirit but a revelation of the truth."

In due time the son was born, and the parents, filled with fear, began to wonder what to do with him. They abhorred the thought of killing him but were unwilling to nurture the destroyer of their people, so they put the infant in a basket, which they set afloat in the sea, and the waves carried it to an island called Scariot. Judas therefore took the surname of Iscariot from the island. The queen of this island, who was childless, was walking on the beach. She saw the basket floating in the surf and had it brought ashore. In it she found this beautifully formed infant and sighed: "Oh, if only I might have such a child, how relieved I would be, because my kingdom would not be left without a successor by my death!" She therefore had the infant nursed secretly while she pretended to be pregnant. When the time came, she lied by announcing that she had borne a son, and the word spread throughout the kingdom. The king was overjoyed at having a son, and the whole nation shared his joy. The child, of course, was brought up in royal style.

Not long afterward, however, the queen conceived of the king and gave birth to a son. As the two boys grew up, they often played together, and Judas frequently maltreated the royal child and made him cry. The queen resented this and, knowing that Judas was not her son, often chastised him for his misdeeds, but Judas continued as bad as ever. Finally the truth came out and it was known that he was not the queen's child but a foundling. When Judas himself learned this, he was bitterly ashamed and secretly killed the king's son, who had been thought to be his own brother. Then, fearing that he would be put to death for this crime, he fled to Jerusalem with other youths who were part of a tribute payment, and took service (like finding like) in the household of Pilate, who was then governor of Judea. Pilate noticed that Judas was a man after his own heart and began to treat him as a favorite, finally putting him in charge of his whole domain; and Judas's word was law.

One day Pilate was looking out from his palace at a nearby orchard and was seized with such a desire for some of the fruit that he almost fainted. The orchard belonged to Ruben, Judas's father, but Judas did not recognize his father nor did Ruben know his son, because Ruben thought that his child had perished in the sea, and Judas had no idea who his father was or where he came from. Pilate called for Judas and told him: "I crave that fruit so much that if I don't get some of it, I'll die!" Thus prompted, Judas jumped over into the orchard and speedily picked some apples. At that moment Ruben came along and found Judas picking his apples, whereupon a violent argument started, words led to insults, and insults to blows and injuries on both sides. Finally Judas struck Ruben at the back of the neck with a stone and killed him. He then delivered the apples to Pilate and told him what had happened.

As daylight faded and night came on, Ruben's body was found and it was thought that he had been overtaken by sudden death. Pilate awarded all Ruben's belongings, including his wife Cyborea, to Judas. Then one day Judas, finding Cyborea heavyhearted and tearful, urged her to tell him what was troubling her. "Alas, I am the unhappiest of women," she answered. "I drowned my baby son in the sea, I found my husband stricken with sudden death, and to all my sorrows Pilate has added a new one, handing me over, saddened as I am and totally unwilling, to be your wife!" She went on to tell him all about her baby, and Judas told her all that had happened to him. So they discovered that he had taken his mother to wife and had killed his father. Cyborea then persuaded him to repent, and he turned to our Lord Jesus Christ and begged forgiveness for all his crimes. So far, however, what we have set down comes from the aforesaid apocryphal history, and whether it should be retold is left to the reader's judgment, though probably it is better left aside than repeated.

Be that as it may, the Lord made Judas his disciple and then chose him to be an apostle. Indeed he loved him so dearly that he made him the keeper of the purse and finally bore with him as his betrayer. So Judas carried the purse and stole the alms that were given to Christ. At the time of the Lord's passion he protested because the ointment that was worth three hundred pence had not been sold so he could steal that money too. Then he went out and betrayed his Lord for thirty pieces of silver, each coin being worth ten pence, and so he made up the three hundred pence lost over the ointment—or, as some say, he regularly stole one-tenth of all that was given to Christ, and therefore sold the Lord for the tenth part of the lost sale price of the ointment, i.e., three hundred pence. However, he was sorry for what he had done, threw back the money, and hanged himself with a halter, and, as the gospel tells us, "burst asunder in the middle and all his bowels gushed out." Thus his mouth was spared defilement since nothing came out through it, for it would have been incongruous that a mouth which had touched the glorious lips of Christ should be so foully soiled.

It also was fitting that the bowels which had conceived the betrayal should burst and spill out, and that the throat from which had emerged the voice of the traitor should be strangled by a rope. Moreover, Judas perished in the air, so that the one who had offended the angels in heaven and men on earth was kept out of the regions belonging to angels and to men, and was left in the air in the company of demons.

Between the Lord's ascension and Pentecost the apostles were together in the upper room, and Peter remarked that the number twelve—the number of apostles chosen by the Lord to preach the faith of the Trinity to the four quarters of the world—was diminished. Rising in the midst of his brothers, he said: "Men and brothers, it behooves us to replace Judas with someone who will testify with us to Christ's resurrection, because the Lord told us, 'You will be witnesses to me in Jerusalem and in all of Judea and Samaria and to the uttermost part of the earth.' Now a witness should testify only to things he has seen, so we should choose one from among the men who have been with us all the time, and have seen the Lord's miracles and heard his teaching." They therefore put forward two disciples, namely, Joseph, who was called the Just on account of his holiness and was the brother of James of Alpheus, and Matthias, of whom nothing more is said in praise because his being chosen as an apostle is praise enough. They prayed, saying: "O Lord, you know the hearts of all! Show us which of these two brothers you have elected to take the place in this ministry and apostleship that Judas lost!"[1] They cast lots and the choice fell on Matthias, who therefore was numbered with the eleven apostles.

Note that this one example does not, as Jerome says, mean that the use of lots is approved as common practice: privileges allowed to a few do not make general law. Or again, as Bede says, before the truth came it was licit to make use of figures. The true host was immolated in the passion but consummated at Pentecost, and therefore in the election of Matthias lots were used so as not to depart from the Law which prescribed that the high priest be selected by lot. After Pentecost, when the truth had been made public, the seven deacons were ordained not by lot but through election by the disciples, the prayer of the apostles, and the laying on of hands. Regarding the kind of lots the above were, we have two opinions from the holy fathers. Jerome and Bede agree that they were the same kind of lots as those whose use we find very frequently in the Old Testament. On the other hand Dionysius, who was a disciple of Paul, considers it irreligious to hold this opinion and declares that as he sees it, this lot was nothing other than a brilliant ray of light sent down from God upon Matthias to show that he was to be received as an apostle. So, in *The Celestial History*,[2]

---

[1] Acts 1:23–26.

[2] Cf. *The Ecclesiastical Hierarchy* (again, not *The Celestial*), chap. 5, sec. 3, in Pseudo-Dionysius, *The Complete Works* (New York: Paulist Press, 1987), p. 241. Note that in this English version the translator has rendered the words *sors divina* as "divine *choice*," whereas I have translated them "divine *lot*."

Dionysius says: "Of the divine lot that by God's will fell upon Matthias, others have said different things, which, in my opinion, are not in accord with religion. I shall now state my own understanding: the Scriptures used the term 'lot' to describe a certain divine gift which showed the apostolic group that Matthias was accepted by divine election."

Judea was assigned to Matthias the apostle by lot, and he preached there assiduously, wrought many miracles, and went to his eternal rest in peace. In some codices, however, we read that he was crucified and ascended into heaven with the martyr's crown. It is said that his body is buried under a porphyry slab in the church of Saint Mary Major in Rome, and that his head is shown to the people there.

In another legend, found in Trier, we read among other things that Matthias, of the tribe of Judah, was born in Bethlehem of illustrious parentage. At his studies he quickly acquired much knowledge of the law and the prophets, shunned everything lascivious, and overcame the temptations of adolescence by the maturity of his conduct. He schooled himself in virtue and was quick in understanding, ready in compassion, not puffed up by prosperity, steady and intrepid in adversity. He made every effort to carry out in action what he prescribed by command, and to demonstrate his oral teaching by putting it in practice. While he was preaching throughout Judea, he cleansed the lepers, drove out demons, made the lame walk, the blind see, and the deaf hear, and raised the dead to life. He was brought before the high priest and to many accusations responded: "I do not need to say much about the things you charge me with, things you call crimes, because to be a Christian is not a matter of crime but of glory!" The pontiff asked him: "If you were given time to reflect, would you recant?" Matthias: "Far be it from me to apostatize and repudiate the truth, having once found it!"

Matthias was very learned in the law, clean of heart, prudent in judgment, keen in solving problems concerning the sacred Scripture, cautious in counseling, and frank in his speech. During his preaching in Judea he converted many to the faith by signs and miracles. This made the Jews envious and they haled him before the council. Two false witnesses, who had brought charges against him, were the first to hurl stones at him, and he demanded that these stones be buried with him in testimony against the witnesses. While he was being stoned, he was beheaded with an ax in the Roman manner, raised his hands to heaven, and breathed his last. His body was translated from Judea to Rome and from there to Trier.

In another legend we read that Matthias went to Macedonia and preached there. He was given a poisoned potion that had blinded all who drank it, but he drank it in Christ's name and it did him no harm. More than 250 people had been blinded by the drink, and Matthias restored their sight by laying his hand on each of them. But the devil appeared to them in the likeness of a child and persuaded them to kill him, on the ground that he was undermining their religion. He was there in their midst, but they looked for him for three days and could not see him. On the third day, however, he made himself known to them and said: "Here I am!" They tied his hands behind his back and put a rope around his neck, tortured him cruelly, then shut him up in prison. There the demons gnashed their teeth at him but could not get near him. The Lord came in a great light, lifted him from the ground, loosed his bonds, comforted him gently, and opened the door of the prison for him. He went out and resumed his preaching of the word of God. There were some who still obstinately resisted his preaching, and to them he said: "I give you notice that you will go to hell alive!" and the earth opened and swallowed them. The rest, however, were converted to the faith.

✳

46. Saint Gregory

The name Gregory (Gregorius) is formed from *grex*, flock, and *gore*, which means to preach or to say, and Saint Gregory was preacher to his flock. Or the name resembles *egregarius*, from *egregius*, outstanding, and *gore;* and Gregory was an outstanding preacher and doctor. Or Gregorius, in our language, suggests vigilance, watchfulness; and the saint watched over himself, over God, and over his flock—over himself by virtuous living, over God by inward contemplation, over the flock by assiduous preaching—and in these three ways he merited the vision of God. So Augustine says in his book *De Ordine:* "He who lives well, studies well, and prays well sees God."

Gregory's life was written by Paul, historian of the Lombards, and at a later time was more carefully compiled by John the Deacon.[1]

Gregory was born into a senatorial family. His father's name was Gordianus, and his mother's, Silvia. While still an adolescent he reached a high level of learning. He was also exceedingly wealthy, yet he considered leaving all behind him and committing himself to a religious way of life. For a long time, however, he put off this conversion. He thought that he might more safely put himself in the service of Christ by appearing to remain in the world as an urban magistrate; but the demands of secular affairs soon weighed on him so heavily that he was snared in them not only in appearance but in his mind.

---

[1] Tradition has awarded Pope Saint Gregory I (590–604) the title "the Great." Only one other pope, Saint Leo (440–461), is so called.

After his father died, Gregory built six monasteries in Sicily and established a seventh in his own house within the city walls, dedicating this one in honor of Saint Andrew the Apostle. He lived there, laying aside his silken robes with their adornment of gold and gems for the rough tunic of a monk. In a short time he attained such holiness that in the very beginning of his new life he could already be counted among the perfect. Indeed the measure of his perfection may be gauged from words he later wrote in the prologue to his *Dialogues*: "My unhappy spirit, stricken with the wounds of its present cares, recalls how different life was in the monastery—how the spirit let everything go by beneath it, and rose above the transitory to think upon nothing but the things of heaven. Even while still retained in the body it escaped the confinement of the flesh by contemplation and loved death itself (the thought of which is so painful to most people) because death is the entrance to life and the reward of labor." Furthermore he chastised his body so severely that his stomach was weakened and he barely stayed alive. He frequently suffered the kind of fainting spell called *syncope* by the Greeks, at which times he seemed close to death.

One day when he was busy writing in one of his monasteries, over which he presided as abbot, an angel of the Lord came to him in the guise of a shipwrecked seaman and pleaded for help, shedding floods of tears. Gregory had some silver coins given to him, but he came back the same day, complaining that he had lost much and had been given little, and again he received money. Yet a third time he came, making a nuisance of himself with his loud demands for help. The monk in charge of the monastery's property informed Gregory that there was nothing left to give the beggar but a silver dish in which Gregory's mother in times past had sent vegetables for his meal. The saint immediately said to give the dish to the mendicant, who accepted it joyfully and went his way. But the beggar was really an angel of God, as he afterwards made himself known.

Another day, when Gregory was walking through the marketplace in Rome, he noticed a group of young men, handsome in form and features, whose blond hair attracted admiring attention. They were slaves and were being sold. Gregory asked the trader where they came from, and he answered: "From Britain, where all the inhabitants have the same fair skin and blond hair as these do." Gregory asked if they were Christians, and the merchant replied: "No, they are benighted pagans." Gregory groaned sadly and said: "What a pity, that the prince of darkness should possess these radiant faces!" He then asked the name of that people and was told that they were called Angles. "And well named!" he said "The name sounds like Angels, and their faces are angelic." He asked what their province was called and was told that their provincial name was *Deiri*. "Again well named," said Gregory, "because they are to be rescued *de ira*, from wrath." He inquired about the name of their king, and the trader said that he was called Aelle. "Aelle is right," said Gregory, "because *Alleluia* must be sung in that land."

Shortly thereafter Gregory called upon the pope, and the pontiff, yielding to his insistent pleading, agreed to send him to convert the English. He was well on his way when the Romans, distressed at his absence, went to the pope and addressed him as follows: "You have offended Saint Peter and destroyed Rome by sending Gregory away!" This alarmed the pope, who hastened to send messengers after the saintly abbot, calling him back. Gregory had been on the road for three days and had stopped to give his traveling companions a chance to rest. He himself was reading when a locust lighted on his book, forcing him to desist from his reading and making him realize, by the very meaning of the insect's name, that he should stay in that same locus: it was the spirit of prophecy that enabled him to understand this. He therefore exhorted his companions to resume their journey as fast as possible, while he waited for the papal messengers and was compelled to turn back to Rome, sad though he was to do so. Then the pope took him out of his monastery and ordained him to be his cardinal deacon.

The Tiber once overflowed its banks so far that it came over the city walls and demolished a large number of houses. The river carried a great many serpents and a huge dragon down to the sea, but the waves smothered the beasts and tossed them onto the shore. The stench of their rotting bodies bred a deadly pestilence called the bubonic plague, and people seemed to see arrows coming from heaven and striking this one and that one. The first to be stricken was Pope Pelagius, who died within hours, and the plague swept through the population so fatally that many houses stood empty in the city.

The Church of God, however, could not be without a head, and the people unanimously elected Gregory to be their bishop, although he made every effort to dissuade them. He had to be consecrated bishop of Rome, but the plague was causing havoc in the city, so he preached to the people, organized a procession, and had litanies recited, exhorting everyone to pray zealously to the Lord. Even while the entire population pleaded with God, however, in any one hour ninety men died; but Gregory continued to urge all to pray until the divine mercy should banish the plague.

When the procession was finished, Gregory tried to flee from Rome but could not, because they watched for him day and night at the city gates. At length he changed his clothes and persuaded some tradesmen to hide him in a wine cask and get him out of the city in a wagon. When they reached a forest, he made for a hiding place in the caves and hid there for three days. A relentless search for him was under way, and a bright column of light beamed down from the heavens and appeared over the place where he had concealed himself: a certain hermit saw angels descending and ascending in this beam. Of course this led the pursuers to Gregory, and they carried him back to Rome and consecrated him as supreme pontiff.

That he accepted this highest honor against his will is clear to anyone who reads his writings. In a letter to the patrician Narsus he wrote: "When you describe the heights of contemplation, you renew my grief at my own ruin, because I hear what I had lost inwardly when I unworthily mounted outwardly to this summit of power. I want you to know that I am oppressed with such grief that I can hardly speak. Therefore do not call me Noemi, i.e., beautiful, but call me Mara, because I am filled with bitterness." And elsewhere he wrote: "If, knowing that I have been raised to the order of bishop, you love me, weep, because I myself ceaselessly shed tears; and I beg you to pray God for me." In the prologue to his *Dialogues* he says: "Due to my pastoral responsibilities, my spirit suffers from engagement in the affairs of men of the world, and after having enjoyed the beauty of spiritual quiet it is soiled with the dust of earthly business. I ponder therefore what I have to put up with, I ponder what I have lost. As I fix my attention on what I have lost, my present burden grows heavier. See, I am tossed about as if by the waves of the sea, the mighty storm winds beat upon the ship of my mind; and when I recall my former life, my eyes look back, I see the shore, and I sigh."

The plague was still ravaging Rome, and Gregory ordered the procession to continue to make the circuit of the city, the marchers chanting the litanies. An image of Blessed Mary ever Virgin was carried in the procession. It is said that this image is still in the church of Saint Mary Major in Rome, that it was painted by Saint Luke, who was not only a physician but a distinguished painter, and that it was a perfect likeness of the Virgin. And lo and behold! The poisonous uncleanness of the air yielded to the image as if fleeing from it and being unable to withstand its presence: the passage of the picture brought about a wonderful serenity and purity in the air. We are also told that the voices of angels were heard around the image, singing

> Regina coeli laetare, alleluia,
> Quia quem meruisti portare, alleluia,
> Resurrexit sicut dixit, alleluia!

to which Gregory promptly added:

> Ora pro nobis, Deum rogamus, alleluia![2]

Then the pope saw an angel of the Lord standing atop the castle of Crescentius, wiping a bloody sword and sheathing it. Gregory understood that that put an end to the plague, as, indeed, happened. Thereafter the castle was called the Castle of the Holy Angel.

In time, moreover, the pope sent Augustine, Mellitus, John, and some other missionaries to England, as he had long wished to do; and by his prayers and merits he brought about the conversion of the English to the faith.

Gregory was so humble that he would not allow anyone to praise him. To Stephen, a bishop who had written him laudatory letters, he wrote: "In your

---

[2] Queen of heaven, rejoice, alleluia, / Because he whom thou didst bear, alleluia, / Hath risen as he said, alleluia! / Pray for us, we beg God, alleluia!

letters you show me much favor (far more than I, unworthy as I am, ought to hear), although Scripture tells us, 'Praise not any man as long as he lives.' Nevertheless, although I was unworthy to hear such things, I beg you to pray that I may become worthy of them, in order that, if you said that these good things are in me because they are not, they may be in me because you said they are." Likewise in a letter to the patrician Narsus: "When in writing to me you match the name to the thing and put forth resounding statements and rhetorical touches in my regard, surely, dearest brother, you are calling the monkey a lion, which we are seen to do when we call mangy kittens leopards or tigers." And in a letter to Anastasius the patriarch of Antioch: "When you speak of me as the mouth of the Lord, when you call me a lamp, when you say that by my speaking I can benefit many and enlighten many, you cause me to question seriously my own self-estimate, for I consider who and what I am and discern no such good in myself, and I also consider who you are and am sure you are incapable of lying. Therefore when I wish to believe what you say, my infirmity contradicts me, and when I wish to argue against what you say in praise of me, your holiness contradicts me. But, Your Holiness, I ask that some good come of this our disagreement, so that if what you say of me be not so, it be so because you say it."

He wanted no pompous or high-sounding titles. To Eulogius, the patriarch of Alexandria, who had called him the universal pope, he wrote: "In the fore-word of the epistle that you addressed to me you made a point of imposing a word of prideful significance by calling me the universal pope. I beg your most kind holiness not to do this again, because what is attributed to another beyond what reason calls for is taken away from yourself. I do not seek to move ahead by means of words but by good conduct, and I do not regard as an honor something that I know causes my brother to lose honor. Therefore let words that inflate vanity and wound charity be banished." Again, when John, bishop of Constantinople, usurped this vainglorious title for himself and by fraud obtained from the synod the privilege of being called the universal pope, Gregory wrote this, among other things, about him: "Who is this man, who, contrary to evangelical statutes and canonical decrees, presumes to usurp a new name for himself, so that without lessening [the status of other bishops] he may be number one and yearns to be universal?" Nor did Gregory allow his fellow bishops to speak of him as "commanding." For this reason he wrote to Eulogius, bishop of Alexandria: "Your Charity speaks to me, saying, 'as you have commanded.' Please do not let me hear that word again, because I know who I am and who you (others) are. In terms of place you are my brothers, in terms of virtue you are my fathers."

It was also due to his profound humility that Gregory did not want women to call themselves his handmaids. Thus he wrote to the patrician lady Rusticana: "One thing I did not like in your letter was something that, while it may be said once, was said there several times—namely, again and again, 'your maidservant.'

By my office as bishop I became the servant of all: why do you speak of yourself as my servant, since even before I assumed the episcopate I was your servant? Therefore I beg of you by almighty God that I may never again find this word applied to me in your letters."

Out of humility he did not want his books to be made public during his lifetime: in his judgment they were worthless in comparison with the works of other authors. To Innocent, governor of the province of Africa, he wrote: "That you have expressed the wish to have my tract on the book of Job sent to you makes me rejoice at your interest; but if you wish to fatten on delicious food for the mind, read the treatises of your compatriot the blessed Augustine, and do not compare our bran with his wheat flour. Moreover, I do not want anything I may happen to have said to become readily available to people while I am in this body." We also read in a book translated from Greek into Latin that when a holy father, Abba John, came to Rome to visit the threshold of the apostles, he saw blessed Gregory walking in the middle of the city. He wished to meet him and do him reverence, as was proper; but blessed Gregory, seeing that the other was about to prostrate himself on the ground, anticipated John by dropping to his knees in front of him and would not rise before the father did. Here again his great humility was confirmed.

He was so generous in almsgiving that he saw to the needs not only of people close by but of others far away; thus he provided for the monks on Mount Sinai. He kept a register of those in need and took care of them liberally. He established a monastery in Jerusalem and made provision for the servants of God who lived there, and he reserved eighty pounds of gold annually for the daily expenses of three thousand handmaids of God. He invited pilgrims to his table every day. One day he was about to humble himself by pouring water on the hands of one such pilgrim and turned around to pick up a jug of water, but, when he turned back, the one whose hands he meant to wash had disappeared. He wondered at this, and that very night the Lord appeared to him and said: "On other days you have waited on me in my members, but yesterday it was I myself whom you welcomed."

Another time he ordered his steward to invite twelve pilgrims to dine with him, and the steward carried out his orders. When all were seated, however, the pope looked around and counted thirteen. He summoned the steward and asked why he had presumed, against his orders, to invite thirteen guests. The steward counted, and, finding only twelve, said: "Believe me, father, there are only twelve here." Then Gregory noticed that the countenance of one pilgrim, who was seated close to him, changed again and again: now it was the face of a young man, then was like that of a venerable ancient. When the meal was finished, the pope brought this man into a side room and insisted that he be good enough to make himself and his name known. The pilgrim answered: "Why do you ask me my name, which is marvelous? Nevertheless know that I am that shipwrecked seaman to whom you gave the silver dish in which your mother had sent you vegetables. Know for certain also that from the very day on which you gave me the dish, the Lord destined you to become the head of his Church and the successor of Peter the apostle." Gregory asked him: "How did you know that the Lord had destined me to rule over his Church?" The answer was: "I knew it because I am his angel, and the Lord sent me back so that I might always protect you, and through me you might obtain from him whatever you ask." And in the twinkling of an eye he disappeared.

At that time there was a certain hermit, a man of great virtue, who had given up all for God and possessed nothing but a cat, which he petted and fondled in his lap almost as if it were a woman who lived with him. The hermit prayed to God to deign to show him with whom he, who for love of him possessed no earthly wealth, might hope to dwell in the future by way of remuneration. One night it was revealed to him that he might hope to share a dwelling with Gregory the Roman pontiff. But the hermit groaned with disappointment, thinking that his voluntary poverty was of little benefit to him if he was to receive his reward with one who enjoyed such an abundance of worldly goods. As he went on day after day grieving at the thought of his poverty and Gregory's wealth, there came another night when he heard the Lord saying to him: "It is not the possession of wealth but the love of it that makes a man rich. How dare you compare your poverty with Gregory's riches—you, who prove every day that you love that cat, your treasure, by the way you stroke it, while he does not love the wealth that surrounds him, but despises it and gives it away openhandedly to all who need it?" The solitary therefore gave thanks to God and began to pray that he, who had thought his merit was belittled by being compared with the pope's, might in time be found worthy of dwelling with Gregory.

Upon being falsely accused before Emperor Maurice and his sons of having had something to do with the death of a certain bishop, Gregory wrote a letter to the emperor's deputy, in which he said: "One thing you might mention to my lords is that if I, their servant, had wished to have a hand in causing death or harm to Lombards, today the Lombard nation would have no king, no dukes, no counts, and would be in chaos: but because I fear God, I would be afraid to become involved in the death of any man." You see how humble he was, calling himself the emperor's servant and the emperor his lord and master, although he was the supreme pontiff. See his humility, when he refused to agree to the death of his enemies. And when Emperor Maurice persecuted Gregory and the Church of God, Gregory wrote this, among other things, to him: "Because I am a sinner, I believe that the more you inflict distress upon me, who serve him so badly, the more you placate almighty God."

One day a figure dressed in a monkish habit stood fearlessly before the emperor, brandished a drawn sword at him, and predicted that Maurice would die by the sword. The emperor, terrified, put an end to his persecution of the pope and earnestly begged him to pray that God would deign to punish him in this life for his wrongdoing, rather than reserving his punishment to the final judgment.

Then Maurice had a vision. He saw himself standing outside the judge's tribunal, and the judge calling out: "Bring Maurice here!" Thereupon the attendants seized him and set him down before the judge. The judge asked him: "Where do you want me to pay you back for the wrongs you perpetrated in this world?" The emperor answered: "Pay me my just deserts here, Lord, rather than in the life to come!" At once the voice of God gave orders that Maurice, his wife, and his sons and daughters be turned over to the soldier Phocas and be killed by him. And that is what happened: not long afterwards Phocas, one of his soldiers, put him and his whole family to death by the sword and succeeded him in the empire.

One Easter Sunday, when Gregory was celebrating the mass in the church of Saint Mary Major and pronounced the *Pax Domini*, an angel responded in a loud voice: *Et cum spiritu tuo!* From then on the popes made that basilica a station, and in testimony to this miracle no response is made when the *Pax Domini* is sung there.

Once when the Roman emperor Trajan was hurrying off to war with all possible speed, a widow ran up to him in tears and said: "Be good enough, I beg you, to avenge the blood of my son, who was put to death though he was innocent!" Trajan answered that if he came back from the war safe and sound, he would take care of her case. "And if you die in battle," the widow objected, "who then will see that justice is done?" "Whoever rules after me," Trajan replied. "And what good will it do you," the widow argued, "if someone else rights my loss?" "None at all!" the emperor retorted. "Then wouldn't it be better for you," the woman persisted, "to do me justice yourself and receive the reward, than to pass it on to someone else?" Trajan, moved with compassion, got down from his horse and saw to it that the blood of the innocent was avenged.

We also read that one of Trajan's sons was galloping his horse recklessly through the city and ran down the son of a widow, killing him. When the grief-stricken mother related this incident to Trajan, he handed over his own son—the one who had done the deed—to the widow, to replace the son she had lost, and endowed her liberally besides.

One day many years after that emperor's death, as Gregory was crossing through Trajan's forum, the emperor's kindness came to his mind, and he went to Saint Peter's basilica and lamented the ruler's errors with bitter tears. The voice of God responded from above: "I have granted your petition and spared Trajan eternal punishment; but from now on be extremely careful not to pray for a damned soul!" Furthermore, John of Damascus, in one of his sermons, relates that as Gregory was pouring forth prayers for Trajan, he heard a divine voice coming to him, which said: "I have heard your voice and I grant pardon to Trajan." Of this (as John says in the same sermon) both East and West are witness.

On this subject some have said that Trajan was restored to life, and in this life obtained grace and merited pardon: thus he attained glory and was not finally committed to hell nor definitively sentenced to eternal punishment. There are others who have said that Trajan's soul was not simply freed from being sentenced to eternal punishment, but that his sentence was suspended for a time, namely, until the day of the Last Judgment. Others have held that Trajan's punishment was assessed to him *sub conditione* as to place and mode of torment, the condition being that sooner or later Gregory would pray that through the grace of Christ there would be some change of place or mode. Still others, among them John the Deacon who compiled this legend, say that Gregory did not pray, but wept, and often the Lord in his mercy grants what a man, however desirous he might be, would not presume to ask for, and that Trajan's soul was not delivered from hell and given a place in heaven, but was simply freed from the tortures of hell. A soul (he says) can be in hell and yet, through God's mercy, not feel its pains. Then there are those who explain that eternal punishment is twofold, consisting first in the pain of sense and second in the pain of loss, i.e., being deprived of the vision of God. Thus Trajan's punishment would have been remitted as to the first pain but retained as to the second.

We are told, moreover, that the angel also said: "Because you pleaded for a damned person you are given a dual option: either you will endure two days of torment in purgatory, or you will certainly be harassed your whole life long by infirmities and pains and aches." Gregory chose to be stricken throughout his life by pains rather than to endure two days in purgatory, and so he was constantly struggling with fevers or coping with gout or shaking with severe pains or racked with excruciating stomach cramps. Indeed, he wrote as follows in one of his letters: "I am beset with so much gout and so many kinds of pain that my life is to me a most grievous punishment; daily I grow weak with suffering and sigh expectantly for the remedy of death." In the same vein, in another letter: "The pain I bear is mild at times and very severe at others, but never so mild as to go away and never so severe as to kill me. So it happens that though I am dying daily, I am held at bay by death. I am so thoroughly penetrated by noxious humors that living is an ordeal and I look forward eagerly to death, which I think is the only remedy for my sufferings."

A certain woman used to bring altar breads to Gregory every Sunday morning, and one Sunday, when the time came for receiving communion and he held out the Body of the Lord to her, saying: "May the Body of our Lord Jesus Christ benefit you unto life everlasting," she laughed as if at a joke. He immediately drew back his hand from her mouth and laid the consecrated Host on the altar, and then, before the whole assembly, asked her why she had dared to laugh. Her answer: "Because you called this bread, which I made with my own hands, the Body of the Lord." Then Gregory, faced with the woman's lack of belief, prostrated himself in prayer, and when he rose, he found the particle of bread changed into flesh in the shape of a finger. Seeing this, the woman recovered her faith. Then he prayed again, saw the flesh return to the form of bread, and gave communion to the woman.

Certain princes asked Gregory for some precious relics, and he gave them a swatch from the dalmatic of Saint John the Evangelist, but they regarded this as worthless and unworthy of their rank, and indignantly returned it to him. Then Saint Gregory, having prayed over it, asked for a knife and slashed the patch of cloth. Blood gushed at once from the cut, thus miraculously demonstrating the preciousness of relics.

One of Rome's rich men left his wife and for that was denied communion by the pope. The man took this as a personal affront but, since he could not openly resist the authority of the supreme pontiff, sought help from sorcerers. They promised to use their incantations to send a demon into the pope's horse, to madden it and endanger both horse and rider. So, when Gregory happened to be riding by on his palfrey, the magicians sent in their demon and upset the horse so much that no one could hold it. Gregory, however, knew by the Spirit that a demon was at work, and by making the sign of the cross over the animal delivered it from the spell, which fell upon the sorcerers in the form of perpetual blindness. They then admitted their guilt and later attained the grace of baptism. The pope, however, would not have their eyesight restored, for fear they might take up their magical arts again; but he gave orders that their living was to be provided from church funds.

We also read, in a book which the Greeks call *Lymon*, that the abbot who presided over Saint Gregory's monastery informed the pope that one of his monks had laid away three pieces of money for himself. Gregory, to put the fear of punishment in the other monks, excommunicated the guilty brother. Some time later the offender died, Gregory being unaware of his death; and he, aggrieved that the monk had died without absolution, wrote a prayer as an epitaph, absolving the defunct from the bond of excommunication. He gave this script to a deacon with orders to read it over the dead monk's grave. The order was carried out, and the following night the deceased appeared to the abbot and told him that he had been held in custody, but had been set free the previous day.

Gregory remodeled the Church's offices and chant, and founded a school for the chanters, for which he built two houses, one next to Saint Peter's basilica, the other near the Lateran church. There the couch on which he reclined while he attended to the singing and the rod with which he used to threaten the choir boys, together with an antiphonary from his own hand, are preserved with due veneration. To the canon of the mass he added the words *diesque nostros in tua pace disponas atque ab aeterna damnatione nos eripi et in electorum tuorum jubeas grege numerari*.[3]

---

[3] And [we pray thee] order our days in thy peace, and command that we be saved from eternal damnation and numbered in the flock of thy chosen.

At length blessed Gregory, having reigned for thirteen years, six months, and ten days,[4] departed this life full of good works. On his tomb these verses are inscribed:

> Suscipe terra tuo de corpore sumptum,
> Reddere quod valeas vivificante Deo,
> Spiritus astra petit, leti nil vira nocebunt,
> Cui vitae alterius mors magis ipsa via est.
> Pontificis summi hoc clauduntur membra sepulchro,
> Qui innumeris semper vixit ubique bonis.[5]

His death occurred in the year 604 from the incarnation of the Lord, under the emperor Phocas.

After blessed Gregory's death a great famine scourged the whole region, and the poor people, for whom Gregory always provided food, went to his successor and said: "Holy father, may Your Holiness not allow us to die of hunger, since our father Gregory used to feed us." These words angered the new pope, who answered: "Gregory, to win fame and praise, may have taken it upon himself to provide for all peoples, but we ourselves can do nothing for you," and he always sent them away empty-handed. Saint Gregory appeared to him three times and chided him gently for being so frugal and for speaking unkindly of him, but the pope made no move to change his conduct. So Gregory, now stern and fearsome, appeared a fourth time and struck him a lethal blow on the head, which caused him great pain and brought him to an early death.

The famine persisted, and some of Gregory's envious associates began to defame him, declaring that he was a spendthrift who had squandered the Church's wealth. They wanted to avenge this alleged prodigality by inducing others to burn the saint's books. Some were indeed burned and his critics were of a mind to burn all of them, but Peter, Gregory's deacon, who had been very close to him and is his interlocutor in the four books of his *Dialogues*, put up a vigorous resistance. He pointed out that their action would in no way detract from the late pope's memory since copies of his books were already in circulation in various regions of the world, and added that it would be a monstrous sacrilege to destroy so many great works of so great a father, over whose head he himself had often seen the Holy Spirit in the likeness of a dove. In the end he got them to agree that if he, Peter, merited immediate death by confirming by oath the truth of what he had told them, they would desist from burning the books, but if he was not to die but survived after giving his sworn testimony, he himself would lend a hand to the book burners. In fact we read that Gregory had told

---

[4] September 590–12 March 604.

[5] Receive, O earth, what was taken from thy body, / which thou canst give back when God vivifies it. / The spirit soars to the stars; no ills can harm the happy one / for whom death itself is the way to that other life. / In this tomb are enclosed the remains of that supreme pontiff / who ever and everywhere lived in good works.

Peter that if he publicized the miracle of the vision of the dove, he would die on the spot. Therefore the venerable Peter, dressed in deacon's robes and carrying the book of the Gospels, gave witness to Gregory's holiness and, in the very act of pronouncing the words of this true confession, gave up the ghost without suffering the last agony.

There was a monk in Saint Gregory's monastery who had put aside a sum of money. Blessed Gregory appeared to another monk and told him to direct the first one to get rid of his money and do penance, because he was to die in three days. Hearing this the guilty monk was shaken with fear, did penance, and gave up his money; but he was soon stricken with such a fever that from dawn to the third hour of the third day the burning was so intense that his tongue stuck out of his mouth and he seemed to be breathing his last. His brother monks stood around him chanting the Psalms, but after some time they interrupted their psalmody and began to talk about his faults. He then revived enough to smile and blink his eyes at them, saying: "May the Lord forgive you, brothers, for wanting to bring up my failings. You put me in a difficult dilemma, because I was being accused both by you and by the devil at the same time, and did not know which accusation to answer first. But if ever you see someone at the point of death, don't denigrate him but treat him with compassion as one who, with his accuser at his side, is going to be judged by a very strict judge. I stood for judgment with the devil accusing me, but with Saint Gregory's help I gave good answers to all his charges except one only, about which I was ashamed. For that one. as you have seen, I have been sorely punished and have not yet been able to get free of it." The brothers pressed him to tell them what he had been accused of, but he replied: "I dare not say, because when blessed Gregory commanded me to come back to you, the devil protested vehemently, thinking that God himself was sending me back to do penance for that one thing. Therefore I gave blessed Gregory my warrant that I would not reveal to anyone the calumny in question." Then he shouted: "O Andrew, Andrew, may you perish this year, because by your wicked counsel you brought me to this peril!" And then and there, rolling his eyes frightfully, he expired.

Now there was in the city a man named Andrew. At the very moment when the dying monk cursed him, this Andrew was seized by a malady so lethal that he was wasting away with the flesh falling from his bones yet could not die. He called the monks of Saint Gregory's monastery together and confessed to them that with the help of the aforementioned monk he had stolen certain papers belonging to the monastery and had sold them to outsiders for money; and this man, who had been unable to die, breathed his last as he was making his confession.

In this period, as we read in the life of Saint Eugene, the Ambrosian office rather than the Gregorian was still observed by the churches, and the Roman pontiff, whose name was Hadrian, convened a council at which it was decreed that the Gregorian office was to be followed universally. Emperor Charlemagne, acting as executor of this decree, traveled round the various provinces and, by threats and penalties, compelled all clerics to obey it. He also burned the books of the Ambrosian office wherever found and imprisoned many rebellious clergy.[6]

The blessed bishop Eugene set out for the council but found that it had disbanded three days before his arrival. It was his prudent decision to persuade the pope to recall all the prelates who had taken part in the council, though they were already three days on the road. At the newly convoked council it was the unanimous decision of the fathers that the Ambrosian and Gregorian missals should be placed on the altar of Saint Peter, the doors of the church should be closed tight and carefully sealed with the seals of a large number of bishops, and the bishops themselves should spend the night praying the Lord to indicate by some sign which of the two offices he wanted observed by the churches. Everything was done as ordered. When they opened the church doors in the morning, they found both missals lying open on the altar; or, as others state, they discovered the Gregorian missal broken up and its pages scattered here and there, whereas the Ambrosian volume was simply opened and lay where it had been placed on the altar. The bishops saw this as a sign from God, indicating that the Gregorian office should be spread throughout the world, while the Ambrosian was to be observed only in the church of Saint Ambrose. The holy fathers so decreed, and their decree is followed to this day.

John the Deacon, who compiled the life of Saint Gregory, relates that while he was gathering material and writing the life, a man dressed in priestly garments appeared to him in a dream and stood beside him (as he saw it) while he was writing by the light of a lantern. The man's outer garment was white and so thin that the blackness of the robe underneath it could be seen. The man came closer and puffed out his cheeks with boisterous laughter. When John asked him how a holder of such dignified office could laugh so rudely, he answered: "Because you're writing about dead people whom you never saw alive." John: "Although I never saw this man face to face, what I write about him I learned from reading him." "I see," said the other, "that you have done as you wished, and I shall go on doing what I can!" With that he blew out John's lamp and terrified him to the point that he screamed as though he thought the other had slashed his throat. At that moment Gregory appeared, having with him Saint Nicholas at his right and Peter the Deacon at his left, and he said to John: "Why did you doubt, O you of little faith?" The adversary was then trying to hide behind the bed-curtain, and Gregory snatched a large torch from the hand of Peter the Deacon who was holding it. With the flaming torch he burned the adversary's mouth and face, blackening him until he looked like an Ethiopian. A small spark fell on

---

[6] Hadrian I (772–795) had important and generally amicable dealings with Charlemagne, sole ruler of the Frankish realm from 771 to 814. This whole episode as related here, while historically improbable at best, is indicative of Jacobus's interest in liturgical developments and of his zeal for Roman authority.

his white garment and set it afire, and he was seen to be totally black. "We have blackened him enough," Peter said to Saint Gregory, who replied: "*We* haven't blackened him. We showed that he really *is* black!" And so they departed, leaving much light behind them.

47. Saint Longinus

Longinus was the centurion who with other soldiers stood by the Lord's cross, and who by Pilate's order pierced Christ's side with a spear. Seeing the signs that accompanied his death, the darkness and the earthquake, Longinus believed in Christ. Yet according to some accounts, what did most to convince him was that, age and infirmity having left him almost blind, the blood that ran down the shaft of the spear touched his eyes and at once he saw clearly.

Longinus then quit the military career and received instruction from the apostles at Caesarea of Cappadocia. He devoted the next twenty-eight years to living the monastic life, and by word and example made many converts to the faith. When the governor ordered him to worship the idols and Longinus refused, the governor commanded that all his teeth be pulled out and his tongue be cut off, but Longinus did not lose the power of speech. Moreover, he took an ax and with it smashed all the idols, saying: "We shall see whether they are gods!" The demons came out of the idols and infested the bodies of the governor and his attendants, and all of them began to rage and rant and bark like dogs, then collapsed at the feet of Longinus. He asked the demons: "Why do you live in idols?" They answered: "We can live anyplace where Christ's name is not heard and the sign of his cross is absent!"

The governor was still in a rage and had lost his sight, and Longinus told him: "Know that you cannot be cured unless you have me put to death. As soon as I am dead, I will pray for you and ask God to restore you to health of body and soul." So the governor ordered the beheading of Longinus, after which he went to the martyr's body, prostrated himself, and with tears did penance, whereupon his sight and health came back and he spent the rest of his life in good works.

48. Saint Sophia and Her Three Daughters

This is the legend of the holy martyrs Sophia and her three daughters, Faith, Hope, and Charity.[1] Note that the principal temple in Constantinople is named after Saint Sophia, whose name means Wisdom.

Saint Sophia wisely brought up her three daughters in the fear of God. The first daughter was eleven years old, the second ten, and the third eight when she came to Rome, where every Sunday she visited the churches and won over many women to Christ. For this reason she and her daughters were charged before Emperor Hadrian. The beauty of the three girls so charmed him that he wanted to adopt them as his own daughters, but they scorned him as dirt.

Faith was punished, first, by being beaten by thirty-six soldiers, secondly, by having her breasts torn off, and all saw milk flowing from the wounds and blood from the severed breasts. The witnesses cried out against the emperor's injustice, but the young girl rejoiced and hurled insults at him. Thirdly, she was thrown on a red-hot gridiron but was unharmed, then, fourthly, was put in a frying pan full of oil and wax, and, fifthly, was beheaded.

Her sister, Hope, was then summoned but could not be persuaded to sacrifice to the idols. Therefore she was first put into a caldron full of pitch, wax, and resin, drops from which fell on some unbelievers and cremated them: finally she was killed with a sword.

Charity, the third daughter, young child though she was, was encouraged by her mother and would not yield to Hadrian's blandishments, so the impious emperor firstly ordered her to be stretched on the rack until her limbs broke and her joints parted; secondly, to be beaten with clubs; thirdly, she was scourged with lashes. Fourthly, she was thrown into a fiery furnace, out of which the flames leapt over sixty yards and killed six thousand idolaters while the child walked unscathed in the midst of the fire and shone like gold. Fifthly, she was stabbed with white-hot nails and thus, with a martyr's dancing step, passed gladly by the sword to the crown.

Now, with many persons looking on, this most virtuous mother buried the remains of her incomparable daughters and, lying down on the grave, said: "Dearest daughters, my desire is to be with you." So she breathed her last in

---

[1] Graesse notes that this legend is lacking in more recent editions.

peace, and those present buried Saint Sophia with her beloved children. She had borne the sufferings of each of them and therefore was more than a martyr.

As for Hadrian, his whole body rotted and he wasted away to death, admitting the while that he had unjustly done injury to the saints of God.

---

49. Saint Benedict

Benedict, whose name means blessed, was so called because he blessed many, or because he had many blessings, or again because all spoke well (*bene dicere*) of him, or because he merited eternal blessings. His life was written by Saint Gregory.

Benedict was a native of the province of Nursia. He was sent to Rome as a child for his liberal studies, but while still young he abandoned schooling and decided to retire to the desert. His nurse, who loved him dearly, followed him to a place called Effide. Once she borrowed a sieve from a neighbor to sift some wheat but let it fall off a table, and it broke into two pieces. Seeing her weep over this mishap, Benedict took the pieces, prayed, and found the sieve repaired.

Later on he secretly took leave of his nurse and lived for three years in a place where he was unknown to anyone except a monk named Romanus, who solicitously saw to his needs. There was no path, however, from Romanus's monastery to Benedict's cave, so the monk tied a loaf of bread to a long rope and lowered it to the saint. A little bell was attached to the rope, and when it rang, the man of God knew that Romanus had sent him food and came out and took it. But the ancient Enemy, envying the charity of the one and begrudging the other his nourishment, threw a stone and broke the bell; but Romanus found other ways to supply the saint's needs.

Some time later the Lord appeared to a priest who was readying his Easter dinner and said to him: "Here you are preparing delicacies for yourself, while yonder my servant is racked with hunger." The priest set out promptly and with much difficulty found Benedict, to whom he said: "Arise and let us take food together, because today is the Lord's Pasch." "I know it must be the Pasch," Benedict replied, "because I have the joy of seeing you." Indeed he lived so far away from anyone else that he had not known that this was Easter Sunday. The priest said: "Truly today is the day of the Lord's resurrection, and you should not be fasting, and that is why I have been sent to you." And so, blessing God, they took their meal.

One day a small black bird came to annoy Benedict, fluttering so close to his face that the saint could have caught it with his hand, but instead he made the sign of the cross and the bird flew away. Soon the devil brought to the holy man's mind the image of a woman whom he had once seen, and he was so aroused by the memory of her that he was almost overcome with desire, and began to think of quitting his solitary way of life. But suddenly, touched by the grace of God, he came to himself, shed his garment, and rolled in the thorns and brambles which abounded thereabouts; and he emerged so scratched and torn over his whole body that the pain in his flesh cured the wound of his spirit. Thus he conquered sin by putting out the fire of lust, and from that time on he no longer felt the temptations of the flesh.

Benedict's fame increased and spread abroad, and when the abbot of a nearby monastery died, the monks came to him in a body and begged him to preside over them. He refused and put them off for a long time, foreseeing that he would not be able to agree with their mode of life; but eventually he gave in and yielded to their entreaties. When he insisted that they observe the rule more strictly, however, they blamed each other for having pressed him to become their abbot, since their waywardness ran counter to his norm of right living. So, when they saw that he would not allow them to go on doing what was forbidden, and found it too hard to relinquish their bad habits, they mixed poison into his wine and served it to him at table. Benedict made the sign of the cross over it, and the wineglass shattered as if struck by a stone. Thus made aware that since it could not withstand the sign of life, it had been a drink of death, he rose at once, faced them calmly, and said: "May almighty God have mercy on you, brothers! Did I not tell you that I would not be able to fit my ways to yours?"

The saint then returned to the place of solitude that he had left. The wonders he performed multiplied, and so many disciples were drawn to him that he built twelve monasteries. In one of them there was a monk who could not stay very long at his prayers, but went out while the rest prayed and busied himself with worldly, transitory things. When the abbot of that monastery told Saint Benedict about this, the latter went there and saw a small black boy tugging at the fringe of the delinquent monk's habit and pulling him outside. He asked the abbot and a monk named Maurus: "Don't you see who it is that is pulling him away?" They answered no, and he said: "Let us pray that you also may see." They prayed, and Maurus saw but the abbot could not. The next day, when prayers were finished, the man of God found the monk outside the church and struck him with his staff to punish him for his blindness. Thereafter the monk stayed motionless at prayer, and the ancient Enemy, as if he himself had received the blow, dared not disturb his meditations.

Three of the twelve monasteries were built at the top of a steep mountain. It was a hard task to draw water at the bottom of the cliff and carry it to the top, so the brothers often besought the man of God to relocate their monasteries. Then one night he climbed the mountain with a young lad and, after praying for a long time, arranged three stones at the summit as a marker. In the morning, when he had returned to his abode and the monks came with the same request as usual, he said: "Go to the top of the cliff and you will find three stones set there. Dig at the place marked, for God can make water flow there for you." They went and found the spot, with water already oozing from the rock. They dug a hole and soon saw it filled with water; and even now it flows abundantly enough to pour down the cliff from top to bottom.

Once a man was clearing out brambles around Benedict's monastery with a scythe, and the blade came loose and fell into a deep part of the lake. The man was sorely disturbed about this, but the saint thrust the shaft into the water, and the blade came up and fastened itself to the shaft.

Placidus, a very young monk, went to draw water and fell into the river, and the current caught him and pulled him the distance of an arrow-shot from the bank, submerging him. Saint Benedict, sitting in his cell, immediately knew this by an inner vision. He called Maurus, told him what had happened, and ordered him to go and rescue Placidus. After receiving the abbot's blessing Maurus hurried on his errand, strode over the water thinking he was still on solid earth, reached the youth, and pulled him out by the hair. Maurus then went and described the incident to the man of God, but Benedict attributed the rescue not to his own merits but to Maurus's obedience.

There was a priest named Florentius whose ill will toward Benedict stirred such malice in him that he sent the saint a poisoned loaf as if it were blessed. Benedict accepted it with thanks, tossed it to a crow that regularly received bread from his hands, and said: "In the name of Jesus Christ take this bread away and drop it someplace where no one can find and eat it." The crow opened its beak, spread its wings, and began to fly around the loaf, cawing as if to say that it wanted to obey but could not do what was ordered. The saint nonetheless repeated his command over and over, saying: "Pick it up, pick it up, it won't hurt you, and get rid of it as I said to." Finally the bird carried the loaf away and came back three days later to receive the accustomed ration from the saint's hand.

Florentius, seeing that he could not kill the body of the master, burned with the desire to bring death to the souls of his disciples. To this end he ranged seven young women in the monastery garden to dance and sing in order to arouse the monks' passions. The holy man watched this from his cell and feared that his disciples might fall into sin, so he surrendered to his adversary's hostility and set out to find another place to live, taking several monks with him. Florentius, standing on a balcony, saw him depart and began to gloat; but suddenly the balcony collapsed and put an end to Florentius. Then Maurus ran after the man of God and said: "Come back, come back! The one who caused you such grief is no more!" But Benedict groaned with regret, both because his enemy had died and because his disciple was delighted over the enemy's death, and he imposed a penance on Maurus for presuming to rejoice over the death of a foe.

By going off to another area, however, he changed his location but not his real enemy. He came to Monte Cassino, where there had been a temple of Apollo. There he built an oratory in honor of Saint John the Baptist and converted the surrounding populace from idolatry to the true faith. The ancient Enemy, resenting what he had done, appeared to his bodily eyes in a horrible vision, raging at him visibly with flames shooting out of his eyes and mouth, and said: "Benedict, Benedict!" The saint did not answer, and the devil cried: "Maledict, Maledict, not Benedict, accursed, not blessed! Why do you persecute me?"

One day the brothers were trying to lift a stone that was lying on the ground to put it in the wall they were building, but they were unable to raise it: a great number of men were there but could not hoist the stone. Then the man of God came and gave a blessing, and the block was raised in no time at all. When they thought about this, they realized that the devil had been sitting on the stone and holding it down. Then, when the monks were building the wall a little higher, the evil spirit appeared to the saint and let him know that he was going after the brothers at work. Benedict immediately sent a message to them: "Brothers, be on your guard! The devil is coming after you!" The messenger had barely finished speaking when the devil overturned the wall and a young monk was crushed under the fallen stone. But the man of God had the dead body, mangled and lacerated as it was, brought to him in a sack, and by his prayer restored the youth to life and sent him back to his work.

A layman known for his virtuous life used to come once a year to visit the saint, fasting on the way. Once, while he was making this journey, another traveler, who carried provisions for the road, joined him and after some time said to him: "Come, brother, let us take some food to keep up our strength. We still have a long way to go." The pious man replied that he always fasted while making this journey, and the other said no more for a while, then renewed his invitation, meeting the same refusal. When another hour had passed and the long road had wearied them, they came to a meadow where there was a spring and whatever else might give refreshment and pleasure to the body. The fellow traveler pointed this out and urged the pilgrim to eat a little and take some rest. The proposal charmed his ears and the scene his eyes, and he consented. When he came to Saint Benedict, the saint said to him: "So, brother, the evil Enemy could not entice you the first time nor the second, but the third time he had the best of you." Thereupon the visitor threw himself at the saint's feet and bemoaned his fault.

Totila, king of the Goths, wanted to find out whether the man of God really had the spirit of prophecy, so he dressed his swordbearer in kingly garments and dispatched him to the monastery with all regal pomp. When Benedict saw him coming, he called to him: "Put off those clothes, they are not yours!" The man fell to the ground and expired, because he had dared to deceive so great a man.

A clerk who was possessed by the devil was brought to the man of God to be cured, and the saint drove the evil spirit out of him and said to him: "Go home, and from now on eat no meat, and do not take sacred orders: the day you do so you will be sold back into the power of the devil." The clerk obeyed this warning for some time, but then, seeing men younger than he being put above him by being ordained, he went against the saint's words as if he had long forgotten them, and had himself ordained to the priesthood. The devil who had left him soon took hold of him and did not stop tormenting him until he breathed his last.

A certain man sent a boy to the saint with two flasks of wine, but the boy hid one of them by the wayside and delivered the other. Benedict accepted it politely and, as the boy was leaving, warned him, saying: "Be careful not to drink from the flask you hid, but tip it cautiously and see what's inside." Abashed, the lad left him and on his way back decided to put what he had heard to the test; and when he tipped the flask, a snake wriggled out of it. And once, when the saint was at his supper, a monk, the son of a high official, was serving him and holding a light for him. This monk, stung by pride, began to think to himself: "Who is this man, whom I wait on while he has his supper, for whom I hold a light, to whom I pay service? And who am I, that I should be his servant?" Quickly the man of God said to him: "Cross your heart, brother, cross your heart! What are you saying to yourself?" Then he called the monks, had them take the lamp from the bearer's hands, and ordered him to go back to his cell and stay there quietly.

In the days of Totila a Goth named Galla, an Arian heretic, resorted to the most monstrous cruelties against the Catholic church's religious men. No cleric or monk who came face to face with him could escape death at his hands. One day, afire with the heat of greed and looking eagerly for plunder, he was inflicting various kinds of torture on a certain peasant, and the victim, unable to endure the pain, blurted out that he had put himself and his property under the protection of Benedict the servant of God. His tormentor believed this and allowed the suffering man a spell of relief, but, while desisting from his savage treatment of the peasant, had his arms bound with stout thongs and marched him ahead of his horse to find this Benedict who had taken over the man's goods. The peasant, his arms tied behind him, led his oppressor to the holy man's monastery and found him sitting at the door of his cell reading a book. The rustic said to Galla, who was following him fuming with rage: "This is Father Benedict, the one I spoke about."

Galla looked at the saint and, carried away by his perverse wrath, thought he would terrorize this monk as he was used to terrorizing others. He shouted at him: "Get up, get up, and return this fellow's property to him!" Hearing this voice, the man of God looked up from his book and stared at Galla and the man who was held in bonds. When the saint glanced at the peasant's arms, the thongs that held them miraculously fell off, more quickly than any man could have untied them. Galla, seeing the man who had been bound now standing free, was shaken at the sight of such power. He dismounted, fell to the ground, and bent his cruel, stiff neck at Benedict's feet, commending himself to the holy man's prayers. The saint hardly interrupted his reading, but called the monks and ordered them to take Galla inside, where he would receive a blessing and some food. When the Goth was brought back to him, Benedict admonished him to give up his insane cruelty. Galla took his leave and no longer dared to demand anything of the peasant whose bonds the saint had loosed, not with his hands but by a glance from his eyes.

There was a time when famine struck the region of Campania, and all the people suffered from a grievous lack of food. In Benedict's monastery the supply of wheat was already exhausted and almost all the bread had been consumed, until at mealtime the monks could find no more than five loaves. The venerable father, seeing them all in such distress, took care to correct their faintheartedness with a mild reprimand and to lift their spirits with a promise, saying: "Why are you so troubled by a shortage of bread? Today's dearth will be followed by tomorrow's plenty." The next day sacks containing two hundred measures of flour were found at the door of the saint's cell: almighty God had sent them, but by whose hands is not known to this day. When the brothers saw this, they gave thanks to God and learned not to doubt, whether in abundance or in need.

We also read that there was a man whose son was so badly afflicted with elephantiasis that his hair was falling out, his scalp was swollen, and the pus exuding from it could not be concealed. The father sent the boy to the man of God, who speedily restored him to health, for which favor they offered boundless thanks to God. Thereafter the boy persevered in good works until he fell asleep happily in the Lord.

On one occasion Benedict sent several monks to a certain place where they were to build a monastery, and set a day on which he would come and tell them how it was to be built. The night before the promised day dawned, however, he appeared in dream to the monk he had appointed as abbot and to his assistant, and designated in detail the places where the various buildings were to be constructed. But they put no faith in the vision and continued to await his arrival, until finally they went back to him and said: "Father, we waited for you to come as you had promised, but you did not come." "Why do you say this, brothers?" he answered. "Did I not appear to you and give you the ground plan? Go now and carry out the design as you saw it in the vision."

Not far from Benedict's monastery there were two nuns of noble birth who could not hold their tongues and often angered their superior with their indiscreet talk. The superior reported this to the man of God, who sent them the following order: "Curb your tongues or I will excommunicate you," not imposing the sentence of excommunication but threatening it. The nuns did not change their ways in the least, and in a few days they died and were buried in the church. When masses were celebrated there and the deacon pronounced the usual formula: "Let anyone who is not in communion go outside," the woman who had been their nurse and always made an offering on their behalf saw them come out of their tombs and leave the church. When she related this to Saint Benedict, he gave her an offering with his own hand and said: "Go and make this offering for them and they will no longer be excommunicated." This was done, and from then on, when the deacon made the customary announcement, the nuns were not seen leaving the church.

A monk who had left the monastery to visit his parents without obtaining the abbot's blessing died the very day he reached his home. He was buried, but once and again the earth threw him up. The parents came to Benedict and begged him to impart his blessing to the dead man. The saint gave them a consecrated Host and said: "Go and place this on his breast and return him to the grave." They did so, and the earth retained the corpse and did not reject it again.

Another monk, who was unhappy in the monastery and wanted to leave, importuned the man of God so much that finally, having had enough of this, he gave the needed permission. Hardly had the monk got outside the gate when he met with a dragon, which opened its maw and wanted to devour him. The monk cried out to some of the brothers who were nearby: "Hurry, hurry, this dragon wants to eat me!" They ran up but saw no dragon, and led the trembling, terrified brother back to the monastery, where he was quick to promise that he would never leave again.

A severe famine struck the whole province another time, and Saint Benedict gave away all he could find to the needy, so that there was nothing left in the monastery except a small quantity of oil in a glass jar. The saint ordered the cellarer to give this oil to someone who was asking for it. The cellarer heard the order but did not obey it, since no oil would be left for the brothers. When the man of God found out about this, he threw the jar of oil out the window, not wanting anything to be left in the monastery owing to disobedience. The glass jar landed on a huge rock, but it did not break nor was the oil spilled, and the abbot commanded that it be given to the one who had asked for it. Having sharply reprimanded the monk for his disobedience and lack of faith, the saint gave himself to prayer, and immediately a large cask that stood close by was so full of oil that it was seen to flow out over the stone floor.

Once the saint went down from the monastery to meet with his sister who had come to visit him, and while they sat at table in the evening, she asked him to stay on with her that night. He absolutely refused to do so. She then lowered her head in her hands to pray to the Lord, and when she raised her head, there came such flashes of lightning, such crashes of thunder, such torrents of rain, that no one could take as much as a step outside the house, although minutes before the sky had been marvelously clear. Her floods of tears had altered the serenity of the air and drawn down the rain. The man of God was aggrieved at this and said: "May God forgive you, sister! What have you done?" "I begged you," she answered, "and you would not listen to me. So I prayed to the Lord and he listened. Now go on your way if you can!" So it came about that they passed the whole night in holy conversation and mutual edification. And behold! Three days after he returned to his monastery, raising his eyes he saw his sister's soul in the form of a dove, penetrating the secret spaces of heaven. He then had her body brought to the monastery and laid to rest in the tomb he had prepared for himself.

One night when Saint Benedict was watching at his window and praying to the Lord, he saw spreading over the sky a light so bright that it dispelled all the darkness of the night, and the whole world was gathered as though beneath a single ray of the sun and brought before his eyes. There he saw the soul of Germanus, bishop of Capua, being carried up to heaven; and he learned later that at that same hour the bishop's soul had gone forth from his body.

During the year in which the saint was to leave this life, he predicted the day of his death to his monks. Six days before his departure he ordered his tomb to be opened. He suffered attacks of fever that grew worse day by day. On the sixth day he had himself carried to the church, and there received the Lord's Body and Blood in preparation for his end. Then, still standing and supported by his brother monks, he raised his hands to heaven and breathed his last in the midst of a prayer.

The day Saint Benedict departed this life and went to Christ, the same revelation came to two monks, one of whom was in his cell, the other some distance away. They saw a shining road strewn with rugs and lighted by countless lamps, rising toward the East from the blessed Benedict's cell to heaven. A man of venerable mien and shining aspect was standing above this road, and he asked them if they knew what the road was that they saw before them. They answered that they did not know, and he said: "This is the road by which Benedict, the beloved of God, is ascending to heaven."

The saint was buried in the oratory of Saint John the Baptist, which he had built over the ruined altar of Apollo. He flourished about the year of the Lord 518, in the time of Justin the Elder.

50. Saint Patrick

Patrick lived about A.D. 280. Once he was preaching to the king of the Scots about Christ's passion, standing before him and leaning on the staff that he held in his hand. By accident he put the sharp point of the staff on the king's foot and so pierced the foot. The king thought that the holy bishop had done this deliberately and that he himself could not receive the faith of Christ otherwise than by suffering like this for Christ, so he bore the pain patiently. Marveling at this, the saint prayed and healed the king's foot. He also obtained from God that no poisonous reptile could live in the whole province; and it is said that in answer to his prayer even the woods and bark from the trees in that region effectively counteract poison.

Then there was a man who stole a sheep from his neighbor and ate the sheep. Saint Patrick called upon the thief, whoever he might be, to make restitution for the theft, but no one came forward; so one day, when all the people were gathered together, he commanded in the name of Christ that the sheep should bleat in the belly of the one who had eaten it. The sheep bleated, the guilty man did penance, and from then on all were careful to avoid the sin of theft.

It was Patrick's custom devoutly to venerate every cross that he saw, but once he passed by a large, beautiful one without seeing it. Those who were with him wanted to know why he had not seen the cross and bowed before it. When Patrick prayed and asked the Lord whose cross this one was, he heard a voice coming out of the earth and saying: "Did you not see that I, who am a pagan, am buried there, and am unworthy of the sign of the cross?" So Patrick had the cross removed.

He preached throughout Ireland but with very meager results, so he besought the Lord to show some sign that would terrify the people and move them to repentance. He then did as the Lord commanded him, and in a certain place drew a large circle with a stick; and behold, the earth opened within the circle and a very deep, wide pit appeared. Then it was revealed to blessed Patrick that this was the place of Purgatory; that anyone who wished to go down into it would have no other penance to do and would endure no other purgatory for his sins; but that most would not come back from there, and that those who did come back would have had to stay below from one morning to the next. There were indeed many who went down into the pit and did not come out.

Long after Patrick died, a man named Nicholas, who had committed many sins, repented of his crimes and wanted to undergo the purgatory of Saint Patrick. He mortified himself by fasting for two weeks, as everyone did, then opened the gate with the key, which was kept in an abbey. He went down into the pit and discovered a door to one side, by which he went in, and saw a chapel there. Some monks in white habits were going into the chapel and reciting the office, and they told Nicholas to have courage, because he would have to endure many trials from the devil. When he asked them what help he might have against these trials, they said: "When you feel pain being inflicted upon you, cry out at once and say, 'Jesus Christ, Son of the living God, have mercy on me, a sinner!'"

The aforesaid monks then withdrew and demons appeared, urging Nicholas to change his mind and obey them. They started with bland promises, saying that they would take care of him and see that he returned unharmed to his own.

But when he refused to obey them, promptly he heard the roaring of wild beasts and a rumbling that sounded as if all the elements were in tumult. He shook with horrible fear at this and cried out: "Jesus Christ, Son of the living God, have mercy on me, a sinner!" And immediately the pandemonium was stilled.

Then Nicholas was led to another place where there was a crowd of demons who said to him: "Do you think you can escape from our hands? Never! Now, on the contrary, you will learn what it is to be mangled and tortured!" A towering, frightful fire appeared, and the demons said: "Unless you yield to us, we will throw you into the fire to be burned to ashes!" When he spurned them, they seized him and cast him into the terrible fire, and when he felt its pain, he cried out the prayer to Jesus, and the fire was extinguished.

He was led to still another place, where he saw some men being burned alive and having hot iron blades thrust deep into their bodies by the demons. Others lay prone on the ground and gnawed the earth for pain, screaming: "Spare us! Spare us!" while the devils set upon them still more grievously. He saw others being bitten by serpents, while demons dragged out their entrails with incandescent iron hooks. When Nicholas continued to resist them, they threw him into the same fire and made him feel the same blades, the same pains. But again he called upon Jesus Christ and was freed of the pain forthwith. Then he was taken to a place where men were being fried in great frying pans, and where there was a very large wheel full of flaming iron hooks upon which men were hanging by various parts of their bodies; and the wheel spun so rapidly that it threw off a globe of fire.

Next he saw a large building where there were trenches filled with molten metal, into which some men had one foot, some had two, and others were in up to the knees, others to the waist, to the chest, to the neck, to the eyes; but Nicholas called upon Christ and passed safely through all this. He proceeded farther and came in sight of a very wide hole out of which rose a horrible smoke and an intolerable stench, and men glowing like sparkling hot iron were trying to get out but were pushed back by the demons. These told Nicholas: "The place you are looking at is hell, in which our master Beelzebul dwells. We will throw you in there if you still refuse to do our will, and once you are thrown in there, you will never get help or be able to escape!" Nicholas disdained to listen to them, so they snatched him and cast him into the pit, and he was enveloped in such pain that he almost forgot to invoke the name of the Lord; but then he gathered his wits and cried out in his heart (he was unable to speak a word): "Jesus Christ, Son of the living God, have mercy on me, a sinner!" He emerged from the pit unhurt, and the horde of demons, acknowledging defeat, disappeared.

Now he was led to a place where he saw a bridge that it behooved him to cross. The bridge, however, was very narrow and as smooth and slippery as ice, and beneath it flowed a broad, deep river of sulfur and fire. He had no hope of being able to cross the bridge but remembered the words that had saved him so many times, so he confidently went toward the bridge and put one foot on it, reciting the prayer to Jesus Christ. A clamor of shouts broke out from below and frightened him so much that he barely kept his footing, but he went on with his prayer and came to no harm. Then he placed the other foot and repeated the same words, and continued to do so step by step until he was safely across.

When he reached the other side, he was in a pleasant meadow redolent of the perfume of all sorts of flowers. Now two handsome youths appeared to him and guided him toward a splendid city that gleamed marvelously with gold and precious stones. From the city gate a wonderful aroma drifted around him and refreshed him so much that he no longer seemed to sense any pain or bad odor. His guides told him that the city was Paradise. He wanted to go in, but they said that he must first return to his own, going back exactly the way he had come without any interference from the demons, who would take flight at the sight of him. After thirty days, they said, he would die a peaceful death and would come into the city as a perpetual citizen.

Nicholas went up out of the pit and found himself back in the place from which he had started. He told everyone about all the things that had happened to him, and after thirty days fell happily asleep in the Lord.

51. The Annunciation of the Lord

The feast is so named because on this day the coming of the Son of God was announced by an angel. It was fitting that the Annunciation should precede the Incarnation, and this for three reasons. The first is that the order of reparation should correspond to the order of transgression or deviation. Therefore since the devil tempted the woman to lead her to doubt, through doubt to consent, and through consent to sinning, so the angel brought the message to the Virgin by the announcement to prompt her to believing, through believing to consent, and through consent to the conceiving of the Son of God. The second reason has to do with the angel's ministry. The angel is God's minister and servant, and the Blessed Virgin was chosen to be God's mother; and as it is right for the minister to be at the service of his mistress, so it was fitting that the Annunciation be made to the Blessed Virgin by an angel. The third reason is that reparation was to be made for the fall of the angels. The Incarnation made reparation not only for human sin but for the ruin of the fallen angels. Therefore the angels were not to be excluded; and as womankind was not excluded from knowledge of the mysteries of the Incarnation and the Resurrection, neither was the angelic messenger excluded. God made both of these mysteries known through angels, the Incarnation to the Virgin Mary and the Resurrection to Mary Magdalene.

The Virgin Mary lived in the Temple from her third to her fourteenth year and made a vow to live in chastity unless God otherwise disposed. Then she was espoused to Joseph, God revealing his will by the flowering of Joseph's staff, as is more fully set forth in our account of the birth of Blessed Mary. Joseph went to Bethlehem, the city of his origins, to make the necessary preparation for the nuptials, while Mary returned to her parents' home in Nazareth. Nazareth means "flower"; hence Bernard says that the Flower willed to be born of a flower, in "Flower," in the season of flowers.

At Nazareth, then, the angel appeared to Mary and greeted her, saying: *Hail, full of grace, the Lord is with thee! Blessed art thou among women*. Bernard says: "We are invited to salute Mary by Gabriel's example, by John's joyous leaping in his mother's womb, and by the reward of being greeted in return."

Now we must first see why the Lord wanted his mother to be married. On this point Bernard gives three reasons, saying: "It was necessary that Mary be espoused to Joseph, because thereby the mystery was hidden from the demons; Mary's virginity was confirmed by her spouse; and her modesty and good name were protected." A fourth reason was that Mary's espousal took away dishonor from every rank and condition of womankind, namely, the married, virgins, and widows, since she herself was married, virginal, and widowed. A fifth: she was served and cared for by her spouse; a sixth, the genealogical line was established through the husband.

The angel said: *Hail, full of grace!* Bernard: "In her womb was the grace of the presence of God, in her heart the grace of charity, on her lips the grace of benignity, in her hands the grace of mercy and generosity." Bernard also says: "Truly *full of grace*, because from her fullness all captives receive redemption, the sick receive healing, the sorrowful consolation, sinners forgiveness, the righteous grace, the angels joy, and finally the whole Trinity receives glory and the Son of man the substance of human flesh."

The Lord is with thee. Bernard: "With you are the Lord God the Father, of whom the One you are conceiving is begotten, the Lord the Holy Spirit, of whom you conceive, and the Lord the Son, whom you clothe with your flesh." *Blessed art thou among women.* Bernard goes on: "You are blessed among women, blessed indeed above all women, because you will be a virgin mother and the mother of God."

Women had come under a threefold curse, namely, the curse of reproach when they were unable to conceive, wherefore Rachel, when she conceived and bore a son, said: "God has taken away my reproach";[1] the curse of sin when

---

[1] Gen. 30:23.

they conceived, whence the Psalm says: "Behold I was conceived in iniquities, and in sins did my mother conceive me";[2] and the curse of pain when they gave birth; so Genesis: "In pain you shall bring forth children."[3] The Virgin Mary alone was blessed among women, because to her virginity was added fruitfulness, to her fruitfulness in conceiving, holiness, and to her holiness in giving birth, happiness.

Mary is called *full of grace*, as Bernard says, because four kinds of grace shone in her spirit: the devotion of her humility, the reverence of her modesty, the greatness of her faith, and the martyrdom of her heart. She is told, *The Lord is with thee*, because four things, as the same Bernard says, shone upon her from heaven, these being Mary's sanctification, the angel's salutation, the overshadowing of the Holy Spirit, and the incarnation of the Son of God. Moreover she is told, *Blessed art thou among women*, because, according to the same author, four things also shone in her body: she was the Virgin of virgins, fruitful without corruption, pregnant without heaviness, and delivered without pain.

When Mary heard the angel's words, she was troubled and thought to herself what this greeting might mean. Here we see that the Virgin was worthy of praise in her hearing the words and her reception of them, and in her pausing to think about them. She was praiseworthy for her modesty when she heard the words and remained silent, for her hesitancy at receiving the words, and for her prudence in her thoughtfulness, because she thought about the sense of the greeting. Note that she was troubled by the angel's words, not at the sight of him: she had often seen angels but had never heard one speak as this one did. Peter of Ravenna says: "The angel had come kindly in manner but fearsome in his words," so that while the sight of him gave her joy, hearing what he said distressed her. Hence Bernard comments: "She was troubled, as befitted her virginal modesty, but not overly distressed, due to her fortitude; she was silent and thoughtful, evidence of her prudence and discretion."

To reassure her, the angel said: *Fear not, Mary, for thou hast found grace with God*;[4] and Bernard exclaims: "What grace indeed! Peace between God and men, death destroyed, life made whole!" *Behold, thou shalt conceive and bear a son and shalt call his name Jesus, which means savior, because he will save his people from their sins. He will be great and will be called the Son of the Most High.* Bernard: "This means that he, who is great God, will be great—a great man, a great teacher, a great prophet."

Mary asked the angel: *How shall this be done, because I know not man?*—i.e., I have no intention of knowing man. So she was virginal in her mind, in her body, and in her intentions. Here we see Mary questioning, and whoever questions, doubts. Why then was Zachary alone punished by being struck dumb? To this point Peter of Ravenna assigns four reasons, saying: "The One who knows

---

[2] Ps. 50:7.   [3] Gen. 3:16.   [4] Luke 1:28ff.

sinners attended not to their words but to their hearts, and judged not what they said but what they meant. Their reasons for questioning were not the same, their hopes were different. She believed, contrary to nature; he doubted, in defense of nature. She simply asked how such a thing could happen; he decided that what God wanted could not be done. He, though pressed by examples, failed to rise to faith; she, with no example to go by, hurried to faith. She wondered how a virgin could give birth; he was dubious about a conjugal conception. It was not the fact that she questioned, but how it could come about, the process of it, because there are three ways of conceiving—the natural, the spiritual, and the miraculous—and she was asking which of these would be the mode of her conception."

The angel answered: *The Holy Spirit will come upon thee, and it is he who will cause thee to conceive.* Hence the child to be born of her is said to be conceived of the Holy Spirit, and this for four reasons. The first is the manifestation of boundless love, in other words, to show that the Word of God took flesh out of God's ineffable love; John 3:16: "God so loved the world that he gave his only Son." That reason is given by the Master of the Sentences. The second was to make it clear that the conception proceeded from grace alone, not from merit: the angel's words showed that since the conception was of the Holy Spirit, it came about by grace alone, being preceded by no merit of any man. This reason is Augustine's. The third is the operative power of the Holy Spirit: the conception came about by the power and working of the Spirit: this from Ambrose. Hugh of Saint Victor adds a fourth reason, namely, the motive involved. He says that the motive leading to natural conception is the love of a man for a woman and the woman's love for the man. So, he says, because in the Virgin's heart there burned so great a love of the Holy Spirit, in her body the same love worked miracles.

And the power of the Most High will overshadow thee. This, according to the *Gloss*, is explained as follows: "A shadow ordinarily is formed by light falling on a solid body, and neither the Virgin nor any pure human being could contain the fullness of the deity: but '*the power of the Most High will overshadow thee,*' and in her the incorporeal light of the godhead took on the body of mankind, in order that she might bear God." Bernard seems to come close to this explanation when he says: "Because God is a spirit and we are the shadow of his body, he lowered himself to us so that through the solidity of his life-giving flesh we might see the Word in the flesh, the sun in the cloud, the light in the lamp, the candle in the lantern." Bernard also says that the angel's words can be read as if he said: "Christ, the power of God, will conceal in the shadow of his most secret counsel the mode by which you will conceive of the Holy Spirit, so that it will be known only to him and to you. And if the angel says, 'Why do you ask me? when you will soon experience what I am telling you!' You will know in yourself, you will know, you will happily know, but the One who works in you will be your teacher. I have been sent to announce the virginal conception, not to create it." Or, "*will overshadow thee*" means that she would be kept cool and shaded from all heat of vice.

And behold, thy kinswoman Elizabeth hath also conceived a son. According to Bernard, Elizabeth's conceiving was announced to Mary for four reasons: that she might be filled with joy, perfected in knowledge, perfected also in doctrine, and moved to a work of mercy. Jerome, indeed, says: "That her kinswoman, who was barren, had conceived was announced to Mary in order that as miracle was added to miracle, so more joy might be heaped upon her joy. Or the Virgin received the word immediately through an angel so that she might know it before it became common knowledge and not just hear it from someone else, and this lest it appear that the mother of God was kept apart from the counsels of her Son and unaware of what was happening close by on earth; or rather, so that by being fully informed of the coming, now of the forerunner and afterward of the Savior, and thus knowing the time and sequence of these events, she might later make the truth known to writers and preachers. Moreover, hearing of the older woman's pregnancy, the younger woman would think of going to her side, and thus the unborn prophet would be given the opportunity to do homage to his Lord, and the one miracle might furnish occasion for a more wondrous one."

Now Bernard: "Quick, Virgin, give your answer! O Lady, say the word and accept the Word, offer yours and accept God's, pronounce the transitory and embrace the everlasting, rise up, run, open yourself! Arise by faith, run by devotion, open by giving your consent!" Then Mary, raising her hands and her eyes to heaven, said: *Behold the handmaid of the Lord, be it done unto me according to thy word.* Bernard: "It is said that some have received the word of God in the mouth, others in the ear, still others in the hand. Mary received that word in her ear by the angel's greeting, in her heart by faith, in her mouth by her confessing it, in her hand when she touched it, in her womb when it took flesh in her, in her bosom when she nursed it, in her arms when she offered it."

Be it done unto me according to thy word. Bernard interprets this: "I will not have it *done unto me* as preached by some demagogue, or signified in a figure of speech, or imagined in a dream, but as silently breathed into me, in person incarnate, bodily living in my body." And in an instant the Son of God was conceived in her womb, perfect God and perfect man, and from the very first day of his conception he had as much wisdom and as much power as he had in his thirtieth year.

Then Mary arose and went into the hill country to Elizabeth, and John leapt in his mother's womb as a way of greeting the Virgin. The *Gloss* notes: "Because he could not give greeting with his tongue, he leapt for joy of spirit and so began to fulfill his office as Christ's forerunner." Mary attended Elizabeth for three months until John was born, and lifted him from the earth with her own hands, as we read in the *Book of the Just*. It is said that God wrought many works on this day as it came round in the course of the years, and a poet tells them in memorable verses:

> Salve justa dies quae vulnera nostra coerces!
> Angelus est missus, est passus in cruce Christus,
> Est Adam factus et eodem tempore lapsus,
> Ob meritum decimae cadit Abel fratris ab ense,
> Offert Melchisedech, Ysaac supponitur aris,
> Est decollatus Christi baptista beatus,
> Est Petrus ereptus, Jacobus sub Herode peremptus.
> Corpora sanctorum cum Christo multa resurgunt,
> Latro dulce tamen per Christum suscipit Amen.[5]

A rich and noble knight renounced the world and entered the Cistercian order. He was unlettered, and the monks, not wishing to number so noble a person among the lay brothers, gave him a teacher to see if he might acquire enough learning to be received as a choir monk. He spent a long time with his teacher but could learn no more than the two words *Ave Maria*, which he cherished and repeated incessantly wherever he went and whatever he was doing. At length he died and was buried among the brothers, and behold! a beautiful lily grew up above his grave, and one leaf had the words *Ave Maria* inscribed on it in letters of gold. Running to see this great spectacle, the monks dug down into the grave and discovered that the root of the lily sprang from the dead man's mouth. They then understood the depth of devotion with which he, whom God glorified with so prodigious an honor, had recited these two words.

A knight had a stronghold beside the road, and pitilessly robbed every passing traveler. Every day, however, he greeted the Virgin mother of God with the *Ave Maria*, never letting anything prevent him from so doing. It happened that a holy monk was making his way along the road and the aforesaid knight gave orders to waylay him, but the holy man begged the robbers to take him to their chief because he had a secret message to deliver to him. When he came before the knight, he asked him to summon his household and all the people in the castle, because he wished to preach the word of God to them. When they had come together, he said: "You are not all here! Someone is missing!" They told him that all were present, but he said: "Look around carefully and you will find that someone is absent!" Then one of them exclaimed that indeed the chamberlain had not come. "That's the one who's missing," said the monk. Quickly they went after him and brought him out in front of everybody; but when he saw the man of God, he rolled his eyes in fright, shook his head like a madman, and

---

[5] The verse begins, "Hail, good day that heals our wounds," and commemorates the sending of the angel, Christ's suffering and death, Adam's creation and fall, Abel's murder, Melchizedek's offering, the sacrifice of Isaac, the beheading of the Baptist, Peter's deliverance from prison, James's martyrdom under Herod, the rising of many bodies of the saints with Christ, and the happy end granted by Christ to the good thief.

dared come no closer. The holy man said to him: "I adjure you in the name of Jesus Christ our Lord to tell us who you are and to say openly why you are here!" The answer was: "Woe is me, the adjuration forces me against my will to admit that I am not a man but a demon who took human form and have stayed with the knight these fourteen years. Our prince sent me here to watch diligently for the day this knight would fail to recite his *Ave Maria*, thus falling into my power. I was to throttle him at once, and he, ending his life while engaged in wrongdoing, would be ours. Any day he recited his prayer I had no power over him; but, watch as I might, he never let a single day pass without praying to the Virgin."

When the knight heard this, his astonishment knew no bounds. He prostrated himself at the feet of the man of God, begged forgiveness for his sins, and thereafter mended his ways. The holy man then said to the evil spirit: "I command you, demon, in the name of our Lord Jesus Christ, to leave here and infest some place where you may not presume to harm anyone who invokes the glorious mother of God!" The demon vanished, and the knight reverently and gratefully allowed the holy man to resume his journey.

52. Saint Timothy

The feast of Saint Timothy is celebrated at Rome, to which city Timothy came from Antioch in the pontificate of Pope Melchiades and was appointed by the priest Silvester, who later became the bishop of the city, to perform functions which at that time the popes themselves were afraid to carry out. Silvester not only welcomed him to his house but, putting fear aside, praised his way of life and his teaching. Timothy preached the truth of Christ for a year and three months and made many converts, and then, being worthy of martyrdom, was captured by the pagan populace and turned over to Tarquin, the urban prefect. Weakened by torture and cast into prison for refusing to sacrifice to the idols, as a good athlete of God he was struck down on the third day and beheaded with several murderers.

Saint Silvester took the body to his house by night and invited Pope Saint Melchiades, who with all the priests and deacons spent the night praising and confirming his martyrdom. A most devoted woman named Theone asked the pope to allow her to raise a monument in her garden, at her own expense, in which Saint Timothy's body might be laid to rest near the tomb of Saint Paul. This was done, and the Christians were pleased because a martyr by the name of Timothy lay close to Paul the apostle, who had had a disciple of that name.[1]

※

---

53. The Passion of the Lord

The passion of Christ was bitter in its pains, scornful in the mockery it laid upon him, and fruitful in its manifold benefits.

The pain of the passion was of five kinds. The first was its shamefulness. It was shameful because it happened in a place of shame, namely, on Calvary, where malefactors were punished. The mode was shameful, because he was condemned to a most ignominious death, the cross being the instrument of punishment for thieves. Yet, shameful as it then was, the cross is now a sign of unbounded glory, as Augustine says: "The cross, which was the shame and torture of criminals, now adorns the forehead of emperors. If God has conferred such great honor on an instrument of punishment, how greatly will he honor his servant?"

The Lord's passion was shameful because of the company in which he suffered. He was reckoned with thieves and robbers who were criminals to begin with; but later one of them, Dismas, who was crucified at Christ's right side, was converted, as we read in the *Gospel of Nicodemus*, and the other, Gesmas, on the left side, was condemned. Thus to one the kingdom was given, to the other, torment. Ambrose says: "The author of mercy, hanging on the cross, divided the gifts and obligations of mercy among different recipients. He left persecution to the apostles, peace to the disciples, his body to the Jews, his garments to those who crucified him, his spirit to his Father, a guardian to his mother the blessed Virgin, paradise to the good thief, hell to sinners, the cross to penitent Christians. That is the testament which Christ made as he hung on the cross."

The passion was painful, secondly, because it was unjust. Christ had done no wrong, and there was no deceit in his mouth. Therefore what was done to him was done unjustly and caused him grievous pain. The principal charges unjustly brought against him were three: that he forbade the payment of tribute,

---

[1] Graesse notes that this legend is lacking "in recent (or more recent) books," and that it differs markedly from the legend with the same title, numbered 121 both here and in Graesse's edition.

that he called himself a king, and that he claimed to be the Son of God. In answer to these three acccusations we, speaking for the Savior, make three responses on Good Friday when we sing: "O my people, what have I done to you, etc.?" in which verse Christ brings up three benefits he conferred on them—delivering them from Egypt, guiding them in the desert, planting them as his fairest vine in a very good land—as if to say: "You accuse me regarding the payment of tribute; rather you ought to thank me for freeing you of tribute. You accuse me because I called myself a king; you ought to thank me for the royal fare I provided for you in the desert. You accuse me of calling myself God's Son; you should rather thank me for choosing you as my vine and planting you in a very good place."

Thirdly, Christ's passion was painful because it was his friends who brought it upon him. The pain would have been more bearable if it had been caused by people who had some reason to be his enemies, or by strangers or foreigners, or by people to whom he had been in some way troublesome. On the contrary he suffered at the hands of friends—i.e., of men who should have been his friends—and of his kinsmen—i.e., people of the same stock from which he was born. Of both of these Psalm 37:12 says: "My friends and companions stand aloof from my plague, and my kinsmen stand afar off," and Job says (19:13): "My acquaintances like strangers have departed from me, my kinsmen have forsaken me." Then there were those upon whom he had conferred many good things, as we read in John 10:32: "Many good works I have showed you from my Father. For which of these works do you stone me?" Bernard: "O good Jesus, how kindly you have dealt with men, what great and superabundant gifts you have lavished upon them, what keen, bitter sufferings you have borne for them—harsh words, harsher blows, most harsh torments!"

The fourth pain resulted from the tenderness of his body, as David says (2 Kings 23:23) in a figure of speech: "He was like the most tender little worm of the wood." Bernard: "O Jews, you are stones! You strike a softer stone, out of which the chime of mercy resounds and the oil of love gushes." Similarly Jerome: "Jesus was handed over to the soldiers to be scourged, and the scourges tore that most sacred body and the breast in which God dwelt."

The fifth pain sprang from the overall effect: it penetrated every part of his body, it smote all his senses. This pain was first of all in his eyes, because he wept, as Heb. 5:7 says, "with a strong cry and tears." Bernard: "He was lifted on high so that he might be heard over a greater distance, he spoke more loudly so that no one could have an excuse for not hearing, to his outcry he joined tears to stir men's compassion." He also wept at other times and places—at the resurrection of Lazarus and over Jerusalem. In the first instance he shed tears of love, so that some who saw him weeping said: "See how he loved him!" (John 11:35–36). In the second instance they were tears of compassion, but the third time they were tears of pain.

He suffered in his hearing, when insults and blasphemies were leveled at him. These were aimed at four particular prerogatives of Christ. He possessed preeminent nobility because in his divine nature he was the Son of the eternal King, and in his human nature he was of royal descent, so that as a man he was King of kings and Lord of lords. He possessed ineffable truth, because he is the way, the truth, and the life, and he also said of himself: "Your word is truth" (John 17:17), the Son being the Father's speech or word. He had insuperable power, because all things were made by him and without him nothing was made. And his was a unique goodness, because no one is good but God alone.

Christ heard insults and blasphemies aimed at each of these prerogatives. Against his nobility they asked: "Is not this the carpenter's son? Is not his mother called Mary?" (Matt. 13:55). His power was derided: "It is only by Beelzebul, the prince of demons, that this man casts out demons" (Matt. 12:24); and: "He saved others, he cannot save himself" (Matt. 27:42). They said he was powerless though he showed power enough to strike down his persecutors solely by the sound of his voice. When he asked: "Whom do you seek?" and they said: "Jesus of Nazareth," Jesus answered: "I told you that I am he," and they fell to the ground at once. Augustine: "He struck at this hate-ridden, fearfully armed mob with no weapon but a word; he repulsed them, laid them low by the power of his hidden divinity. What will he, who did this when about to be judged, do when he comes to judge? What will he who was about to die be able to do when he assumes his reign?"

His truth was denied: "You are bearing witness to yourself; your testimony is not true" (John 8:13). So they called him a liar, whereas he was the way, the truth, and the life. Pilate did not deserve to know or hear this truth, because he was not judging Christ according to the truth. He did begin his judging on the basis of truth, but he did not abide by the truth; therefore he was worthy to raise the question about truth, but not to hear the solution. Augustine gives another reason to explain why Pilate heard no solution to his question: it suddenly came to him that by Jewish custom one prisoner was released at the Passover, so he went out abruptly, not waiting for a solution. And Chrysostom offers a third reason, namely, that Pilate knew his question was so difficult that much time and discussion would be called for, whereas he was in haste to set Christ free and so hurried out. We read in the *Gospel of Nicodemus*, however, that when Pilate asked Jesus: "What is truth?" (John 18:38) Jesus answered: "Truth is from heaven." "Is there no truth on earth?" Pilate retorted. "How could there be truth on earth," Jesus replied, "when truth is judged by those who hold power on earth?"

As regards Christ's goodness, his accusers said that he was a sinner at heart: "We know that this man is a sinner" (John 9:24); also that he led people astray with his words: "He stirs up the people, teaching throughout all Judea, from Galilee even to this place" (Luke 23:5); and more, he violated the Law by his actions: "This man is not from God, for he does not keep the Sabbath" (John 9:16).

He suffered throughout his body, thirdly, in the sense of smell. A strong smell of decay pervaded the place of Calvary, where dead bodies were left to rot. The *Scholastic History* says that *calvaries* properly means the bare human skull: hence, because criminals were beheaded there and many skulls were strewn about, it was called the place of skulls or Calvary. Fourthly, he suffered in the sense of taste. When he cried out: "I thirst!" they gave him vinegar mixed with myrrh and gall, so that the vinegar would make him die more quickly and the guards would sooner be relieved of their watch; for it is said that the crucified died more quickly if they drank vinegar. The myrrh would also offend his sense of smell, and the gall his sense of taste. So Augustine says: "Purity is given vinegar to drink instead of wine, sweetness is drenched with gall, innocence stands in for the guilty, life dies for the dead."

Fifthly, he suffered pain through the sense of touch. In every part of his body, from the soles of his feet to the top of his head there was no soundness. Bernard says that he suffered in all his senses: "The head that angels trembled to look upon is stabbed with clustered thorns; the face, more beautiful than the faces of the children of men, is befouled by the spittle of the Jews; the eyes that outshine the sun are clouded over in death; the ears that hear the angels sing hear the taunts of sinners; the mouth that teaches angels is given gall and vinegar to drink; the feet whose footstool is adored because it is holy are fixed to the cross with a nail; the hands that shaped the heavens are spread open and nailed to the cross; the body is scourged, the side is pierced with a lance, and what more is there? Nothing is left in him except the tongue, so that he could pray for sinners and commend his mother to a disciple."

Christ's passion was painful, but it was also scornful in the mockery it visited upon him. He was mocked four times. The first was in the house of Annas, where he was blindfolded, slapped, and spat upon. Bernard: "Your lovely face, O good Jesus, that face the angels desire to look upon, they defiled with spittle, struck with their hands, covered with a veil in derision, nor did they spare it bitter wounds." The second time was in the palace of Herod, who deemed Jesus a simpleton and of unsound mind because he refused to answer him, and draped him in a white robe to make a fool of him. Bernard: "You, O man, are man and you are crowned with flowers, and I, who am God, have a crown of thorns. You have gloves on your hands and my hands have nails driven through them. You dance in white garments, and I, for your sake, was mocked when Herod clothed me in a white garment. You dance with your feet, and I have endured pain in my feet. You, in the dance, extend your arms like a cross in a gesture of joy, and I have had my arms stretched on the cross as a mark of opprobrium. I have borne pain on the cross and you take pleasure in shaping a cross with your arms. You uncover your chest and side as a sign of vainglory, and my side was pierced for you. But return to me and I will welcome you!"

But why did the Lord, in the course of his passion, remain silent before Herod, Pilate, and the Jews? We see three reasons for this. First, they were not worthy of hearing an answer; second, Eve had sinned by saying too much and Christ willed to make satisfaction by saying nothing; and third, no matter what he said, they would have distorted and perverted it.

Christ was mocked a third time in the house of Pilate, where the soldiers wrapped a scarlet cloak around him, put a reed in his hands and a crown of thorns on his head, and bending the knee, said: "Hail, king of the Jews!" We are told that the crown of thorns was plaited of furze, the thorns of which are very hard and penetrate deeply, whence it is thought that this crown drew blood from his head. About this Bernard says: "That divine head had clusters of thorns driven into the brain." There are three opinions about the principal seat of the soul in the body. It may be in the heart, since, according to Matthew (15:19): "From the heart come forth evil thoughts," or in the blood, according to Lev. 17:11 "The life of all flesh is in the blood," or in the head, since, according to John (19:30): "He bowed his head and gave up his spirit." It would seem that these three opinions were known to the Jews, at least to judge by what they did. In order to tear his soul from his body they sought it in his head by driving thorns all the way into the brain, looked for it in his blood by opening the veins in his hands and feet, and tried to reach it in his heart by piercing his side. In response to these scornful actions, on Good Friday we kneel three times before unveiling the cross, singing: "*Hagios ho theos*, Holy God, etc.," thrice honoring him who thrice was mocked for our sake.

On the cross Christ was mocked a fourth time, as we read in Matthew (27:41): "The chief priests, with the scribes and elders, mocked him, saying, 'If he is the king of Israel, let him come down now from the cross, and we will believe in him.'" On this Bernard says: "At this time he exhibits patience more than ever, commends humility, fulfills obedience, shows perfect love. These are the four jewels with which the four parts of the cross are adorned—charity at the top, obedience on the right, patience on the left, and humility, the root of all the virtues, below."

Bernard briefly sums up all that Christ suffered: "As long as I live, I will remember the labors he put forth in his preaching, his fatigues in explaining, his vigils in prayer, his temptations while he fasted, his compassionate weeping, the snares set for him in arguments with his opponents, and, lastly, in the insults, the spittings, the slappings, the derisive gestures, the nails, the reproaches."

Now we come to the manifold fruits of the Lord's passion, which can be described as threefold, namely, the remission of sins, the granting of grace, and the manifestation of glory. These three are indicated in the title placed over him on the cross: "Jesus" referring to the first, "of Nazareth" to the second, "king of the Jews" to the third, because in heavenly glory we will all be kings. Augustine says of the fruits of the passion: "Christ blotted out all guilt, present, past, and future—past sins by remitting them, present sins by holding us back from them, future sins by giving us grace to avoid them." On the same subject Augustine also says: "Let us wonder and rejoice, love and praise and adore, because through our redeemer's death we have been called from darkness to light, from death to life, from corruption to incorruption, from exile to the fatherland, from grief to joy."

How beneficial to us the mode of our redemption was is clear for four reasons: it was most acceptable to God as a peace offering, most suitable for curing humanity's illness, most efficacious to attract humankind, and best adapted to accomplish the defeat of man's Enemy.

First, the mode of our redemption was most acceptable to God as a way of placating him and reconciling us to him, for, as Anselm puts it in his book titled *Why God Became Man*, "There is nothing more painful or difficult that a man can do for God's honor than to suffer death voluntarily and not for debt but of his own free will, and no man can give himself more fully than by surrendering himself to death for God's honor." So we read in Eph. 5:2: "Christ delivered himself, an oblation and a sacrifice to God for an odor of sweetness." Augustine, in his book *On the Trinity*, tells us how this sacrifice placated God and reconciled us with God: "What could be so readily accepted as the flesh of our sacrifice being made the body of our Priest?" Thus, since four things are to be considered in every sacrifice—to whom it is offered, what is offered, for whom it is offered, and who offers it—in this sacrifice he who himself is the one mediator between the parties, reconciling us with God by the sacrifice of peace, could remain with him to whom he made the offering, could make those for whom he made the offering one in himself, and could himself be the one who made the offering and the offering he made.

Speaking about how we were reconciled through Christ, the same Augustine says that Christ is the priest through whom we are reconciled, the sacrifice by which we are reconciled, God, with whom we are reconciled, and the temple in which we are reconciled. Therefore, speaking in the person of Christ, he reproaches some who belittle this reconciliation: "When you were an enemy to my Father, he reconciled you through me; when you were far from him, I came to redeem you; when you were astray in the mountains and the forests, I came in search of you, found you amidst the rocks and the woods, and gathered you up lest you be torn to pieces by the swift teeth of wolves and savage beasts. I carried you on my shoulders, gave you back to my Father, labored, sweated, pressed thorns upon my head, exposed my hands to the nails, opened my side with a spear, was torn—I will not say by insults but by so many torments. I shed my blood, I gave my soul to unite you closely to myself . . . and you separate yourself from me."

Second, the mode of our redemption was most apt for curing humanity's sickness—apt from the point of view of the time, the place, and the way the cure was effected. It was fitting from the point of view of the time, because Adam was created and fell into sin in the month of March, on Friday the sixth day of the week and at the sixth hour of the day, and Christ chose to suffer on the day in March on which his coming was announced and on which he was put to death—the sixth day, Friday, at the sixth hour.

The place was also appropriate, whether it be considered as common, particular, or unique. The common place was the land of promise, the particular, Calvary, and the unique, the cross. In the common place the first man was formed, because it is said that he was formed in the region around Damascus, on that city's territory. Adam was buried in the particular place, or at least it is said that he was buried where Christ suffered. This, however, is not authentic, since according to Jerome Adam was buried on Mount Hebron, as is expressly stated in Josh. 14:15. Adam was deceived at the unique place—not that he was deceived on that wood on which Christ suffered, but in the sense that as Adam was deceived in the wood of the tree, so Christ suffered on the wood of the cross. A Greek history says, however, that it was the same wood.[1]

Third, the way the cure was effected was apt, because it operated through similarities and through opposites. Through similarities: thus Augustine, in his book *On Christian Doctrine*, says that as man was deceived by a woman, so men were liberated by a man born of a woman, mortals by a mortal, the dead by his death. Ambrose: "Adam was formed from the virgin earth, Christ was born of a virgin. Adam was made to God's image, Christ is the image of God. Folly came through a woman, through a woman wisdom. Adam was naked, Christ was naked. Death came by a tree, life by the cross. Adam was in the desert, Christ was in the desert."

The cure also came by way of opposites. According to Gregory, the first man had sinned by pride, disobedience, and gluttony: he wanted to be like God in the sublimity of his knowledge, to overstep the limit set by God, and to taste the sweetness of the apple. And since cures have to be worked by opposites, the way satisfaction was made for us was most fitting, because it was through humiliation, the fulfilling of God's will, and physical pain. These three are reflected in Phil. 2:8: [Christ Jesus] "humbled himself," referring to the first, "became obedient," to the second, "unto death," to the third.

Third, the mode of our redemption was the most efficacious way to attract humankind. In no other way could men have been more strongly drawn to love God and trust in him, without impairment of their freedom of choice. Bernard speaks about how we are drawn to love: "More than anything else, O good Jesus, the cup that you drank—the work of our redemption—makes you lovable. That work fully justifies your claim to our total devotion: it sweetly entices, justly demands, swiftly clasps, and strongly constrains our love. For when you emptied yourself and put off your natural splendor, then your compassion shone more brightly, your love gleamed more brilliantly, your grace cast its rays more

---

[1] For more of this kind of information about the wood of the cross, see the chapters on the Finding of the Cross (68) and on the Resurrection (54), below.

widely." And regarding our trust in God, Romans 8: "He who did not spare his own Son but gave him up for us all, has he not also given us all things with him?" On this point Bernard says: "Who is there who would not be caught up by the hope of obtaining confidence when we attend to the way his body is disposed—the head bowed to kiss, the arms outstretched to embrace, the hands pierced to pour out gifts, the side opened for love, the feet held fast to keep him with us, his body stretched to give himself wholly to us?"

Fourth, our redemption was best adapted to accomplish the defeat of man's Enemy; Job 26:12: "His wisdom has struck the proud one," and, further on, Job 40:20 (Douay): "Can you draw out Leviathan with a hook?" Christ had hidden the hook of his godhead under the bait of his humanity, and the devil, wanting to swallow the bait of his flesh, was caught by the hook of his divinity. About this artful trap Augustine says: "The redeemer came and the deceiver was vanquished; and what did the redeemer do to the one who had caught us? He held out a mousetrap, his cross, and baited it with his blood." He willed to shed his own blood, not the blood of a debtor, for which reason he withdrew from debtors. This sort of debt the apostle calls a chirograph, a handwritten bill, which Christ took and nailed to the cross. Augustine says of this bill: "Eve borrowed sin from the devil and wrote a bill and provided a surety, and the interest on the debt was heaped upon posterity. She borrowed sin from the devil when, going against God's command, she consented to his wicked order or suggestion. She wrote the bill when she reached out her hand to the forbidden apple. She gave a surety when she made Adam consent to the sin. And so the interest on the debt of sin became posterity's burden."

Bernard, speaking for Christ, reproaches those who belittle this redemption, by which he led us out from the power of the Enemy: "My people, says the Lord, what could I have done for you that I have not done? What reason is there for you to prefer to serve the Enemy rather than me? He did not create you or feed you. If this seems trivial to you, ingrates that you are, not he, but I redeemed you. What was the price? Not, indeed, corruptible gold or silver, not the sun or the moon, not one of the angels: I redeemed you with my own blood. For the rest, if such a manifold right does not elicit from you a sense of obligation to become my servants, at least, putting all else aside, agree with me for a penny a day."

Now because Christ was betrayed and brought to his death by Judas due to greed, by the Jews due to envy, and by Pilate due to fear, we might consider the punishments that God inflicted on them for this sin. But you will find an account of Judas's origin and punishment in the legend of Saint Matthias,[2] and the story of the Jews' punishment and downfall in that of Saint James the Less.[3]

---

[2] Chapter 45, above.
[3] Chapter 67, below.

What follows is what we read in a history, admittedly apocryphal, concerning the origin and punishment of Pilate.

There was a king, Tyrus by name, who seduced a girl named Pyla, daughter of a miller called Atus, and had of her a son. When her son was born, Pyla gave him a name composed of her own and her father's, and called him Pylatus, or Pilate. When Pilate was three years old, his mother sent him to the king, his father. The king already had a son born of the queen his wife, and this son was almost the same age as Pilate. As they grew older the two often competed with each other at wrestling, boxing, and shooting with a sling, but the king's legitimate son, just as he was of nobler birth, showed himself more vigorous and skillful in every sort of contest, and Pilate, consumed with jealousy and suffering from liver trouble, killed his brother in secret. When King Tyrus learned what had happened, he was grief-stricken and called his council together to decide what should be done with this criminal, murderous son of his. All were agreed that he was worthy of death; but the king, upon reflection, was unwilling to pile one wrong upon another and sent Pilate to Rome as a hostage for the tribute that he owed annually to the Romans. He hoped by this means to purge himself of the murder of his son and to be freed of the Roman tribute.

At that time there was in Rome a son of the king of France, who likewise had been sent there in lieu of tribute. He and Pilate became comrades, but Pilate, seeing himself surpassed by the other both in character and in action, and goaded by the stings of envy, took his companion's life. Now the Romans, wondering what to do with him, said: "If this fellow, who slew his brother and strangled a hostage, is allowed to live, he can be mighty useful to the Republic; and, being a brute himself, he will know how to handle our brutish enemies." They therefore decided: "He must be judged worthy of death, but let him be posted as a judge to the island of Pontus, where the people have never tolerated a judge. If his wickedness can tame their perversity, all the better; if not, let him get what he deserves." So Pilate was sent to Pontus and its hardheaded people. He knew that they were destroyers of judges and that his life hung in the balance, so he quietly worked out ways to save his skin, and by threats and promises, torture and bribery, completely subjugated this rebellious crowd. His victory won for him the title of Pilate of Pontus, or Pontius Pilate.

Herod heard about this man's way of doing things and, being a crafty schemer himself, was delighted with the other's stratagems and sent envoys with gifts and an invitation to visit. Then he made Pilate his deputy and gave him power over Judea and Jerusalem. Pilate proceeded to amass great wealth and went to Rome without informing Herod. In Rome he offered the emperor Tiberius a huge sum of money and pressed the ruler to vest him outright with the powers he held from Herod. This gave rise to enmity between the two until the time of the Lord's passion, when Pilate, to conciliate Herod, sent Christ to him. The *Scholastic History* tells us that there was another reason for their hostility. There was an individual who claimed to be the son of God and beguiled a great many people in Galilee. He led his followers to Garizim, where he said he was going to ascend into heaven. Pilate came upon them and killed them all, because he feared that the people of Judea might likewise be misled. This caused enmity between him and Herod, because Galilee was in Herod's jurisdiction. Both of these reasons may well be true.

When Pilate had handed Jesus over to the Jews to be crucified, he was afraid that his condemnation of innocent blood might offend Tiberius Caesar, and dispatched one of his familiars to make a case for him to the emperor. Meanwhile, it was announced to Tiberius, who was seriously ill, that in Jerusalem there was a physician who cured all diseases by his word alone. Therefore the emperor, not knowing that Pilate and the Jews had put this physician to death, said to one of his intimates, whose name was Volusian: "Cross the sea as fast as you can, and tell Pilate to send this healer to me so that he may restore me to health." Volusian came to Pilate and delivered the emperor's command, but Pilate, terror-stricken, asked for a fortnight's grace.

During this time Volusian made the acquaintance of a woman named Veronica, who had been in Jesus' company, and asked her where he might find Jesus Christ. She answered: "Alas, he was my Lord and my God, and Pilate, to whom he was handed over through envy, condemned him and commanded that he be crucified." Volusian was grieved at this and said: "I am deeply sorry that I cannot carry out the orders my master gave me." Veronica answered: "When the Teacher was going about preaching and I, to my regret, could not be with him, I wanted to have his picture painted so that when I was deprived of his presence, I could at least have the solace of his image. So one day I was carrying a piece of linen to the painter when I met Jesus, and he asked me where I was going. I told him what my errand was. He asked for the cloth I had in my hand, pressed it to his venerable face, and left his image on it. If your master looks devoutly upon this image, he will at once be rewarded by being cured." "Can this image be bought for gold or silver?" Volusian asked. "No," Veronica replied, "only true piety can make it effective. Therefore I will go with you and let Caesar look upon the image, after which I will return home." So Volusian came to Rome with Veronica and told Tiberius: "The Jesus you have long desired to see was unjustly given over to death by Pilate and the Jews, and, by reason of their envy, nailed to the gibbet of the cross. However, a lady came to me with a picture of Jesus, and if you look at it devoutly, you will obtain the benefit of your health." Caesar therefore had the road carpeted with silk cloths and ordered the image brought to him, and the moment he looked at it, he won back his pristine health.

Pontius Pilate was then taken prisoner at Caesar's command and shipped to Rome; and when the emperor heard that he had arrived, he was filled with fury and had him brought into his presence. Pilate, however, had taken with him the

Lord's seamless tunic and came before the emperor wearing it. As soon as Tiberius saw him clothed in the tunic, his anger vanished. He rose to meet Pilate and could not address a harsh word to him. So the emperor, who, when Pilate was absent, seemed so terrible and furious, now, in his presence, was somehow calmed. As soon as he had given him leave to go, on the other hand, he was again afire with rage and called himself a wretch for not having showed the culprit the anger that was in his heart. Swearing and protesting that Pilate was a son of death and that it was not right to let him live on the earth, he at once had him called back. But when he saw him, the emperor greeted him and his wrath subsided. All wondered, and he himself wondered, that he could be so wrought up against Pilate absent and could not so much as speak to him harshly when he was present. At length, at a sign from God, or perhaps a hint from some Christian, he had the man stripped of that tunic, and instantly his previous rage was rekindled. The emperor's astonishment mounted until he was told that the tunic had belonged to the Lord Jesus. He had Pilate remanded to prison until he could consult with a council of wise men about what should be done with the criminal. Pilate was forthwith sentenced to a shameful death, but when he heard of this, he killed himself with his own knife and so ended his life. When Caesar was informed of this, he said: "Truly he died a most shameful death, and his own hand did not spare him."

The corpse was weighted with a huge stone and thrown into the Tiber, but wicked, foul spirits made sport of the wicked, foul body, plunging it into the water and snatching it up into the air. This caused awesome floods in the water and lightning, tempests, and hailstorms in the air, and a widespread panic broke out among the people. The Romans therefore pulled the body out of the Tiber and, as a gesture of contempt, carried it off to Vienne and dumped it into the Rhone. The name of the city comes from *Via Gehennae*, the road to hell, because at that time it was a place of malediction. Or, more likely, the city was called Vienne or Bienna because it was said to have been built in a biennium. But there again the wicked spirits rallied and stirred up the same disturbances, and the people, refusing to put up with so great a plague of demons, removed that vessel of malediction from their midst and consigned it to burial in the territory of the city of Lausanne. There the populace, harried to excess by the aforesaid upheavals, took the body away and sank it in a pit surrounded by mountains, where, according to some accounts, diabolical machinations still make themselves felt. . . . Thus far we have quoted the aforementioned apocryphal history: let the reader judge whether the story is worth the telling.

It should be noted, however, that the *Scholastic History* tells us that the Jews accused Pilate to Tiberius of the savage massacre of the Innocents, of placing pagan images in the Temple despite the protests of the Jews, and of appropriating money taken from the corbona, or poor-chest, for his own uses such as building a water conduit into his house. For all these misdeeds he was deported into exile at Lyons, his city of origin, and there he died, despised by his own people. It could be, if there is any truth to this story, that Tiberius had decreed his exile and had had him deported to Lyons before Volusian came back to Rome from Jerusalem and reported to the emperor, but then, learning how he had put Christ to death, had the miscreant brought out of exile and returned to Rome. Neither Eusebius nor Bede says in his chronicle that Pilate was exiled, but only that he suffered many calamities and died by his own hand.

<hr />

About the feasts that occur within the time
of reconciliation

We have considered the feast days that occur in the time of deviation, which began with Adam and ended with Moses, and which the Church represents from Septuagesima to Easter. We now take up the feasts that occur within the time of reconciliation, which the Church represents from Easter to the octave of Pentecost.

<hr />

54. The Resurrection of the Lord

Christ's resurrection took place on the third day after his passion. Concerning the resurrection there are seven questions that must be considered. First, how is it true to say that the Lord lay in the tomb for three days and three nights and rose on the third day? Second, why did he not come to life immediately after dying instead of waiting until the third day? Third, how he rose. Fourth, why he hurried his rising rather than wait for the general resurrection. Fifth, why he rose. Sixth, how many times he appeared after the resurrection. Seventh, how he brought out the holy fathers who were in limbo and what he did there.

Regarding the first question, note that according to Augustine, to say that Christ was in the tomb for three days and three nights is a figure of speech, synecdoche, the last part of the first day being taken for the whole, the second day being counted in its entirety, and of the third day the first part standing for the whole. Thus there were three days and each day had its night preceding it. According to Bede this reversed the usual order of day and night, because previously day came first and night followed, but after Christ's passion this order was changed so that the nights came first and the days followed. This agreed with the order of the mystery, since first man fell from the daylight of grace into the night of sin and then, through Christ's passion and resurrection, came back from the night of sin to the daylight of grace.

As to the second question, let it be known that it was right that Christ should not rise immediately after dying but should wait until the third day, and this for five reasons. The first is what this delay signified, namely, that the light of his death cured our double death: therefore he lay in the tomb for one whole day and two nights, so that the day could be understood as signifying the light of his death and the two nights as our twofold death. The *Gloss* gives this reason to explain Christ's words in Luke 24:46: "It is written that the Christ should suffer and on the third day rise from the dead." The second reason was to prove that he had really died, because just as in the mouth of two or three witnesses every word may stand, so after three days one realizes what has happened to him, and therefore Christ, in order to give proof of his death and to show that he had experienced death, chose to lie buried for three days.

The third reason was to show his power, because if he had risen immediately it might not be clear that he had the power to lay down his life and to rise again from death. This reason seems to be suggested in 1 Cor. 15:3: ". . . that Christ died . . . and that he was buried . . . and that he rose again on the third day." His death is mentioned first so that as the death is shown to be a fact, so also the truth of the resurrection is demonstrated. The fourth reason is that all that was to be restored was prefigured. Peter of Ravenna proposes this reason, saying: "He willed to be buried for three days to show that he was to restore what was in heaven, to repair what was on earth, and to redeem what was in the under-world." The fifth reason was to represent the three states of the just. Gregory gives this reason in his commentary on Ezechiel: "Christ suffered on Friday, rested in the tomb on Saturday, and rose from death on Sunday. For us the present life is Friday, the time when we suffer distress and pain, but on Saturday we are, as it were, at rest in the grave because after death we find rest for our soul, and on Sunday, the eighth day, we rise from that condition with the body and rejoice in the glory of soul and body. So pain is ours on the sixth day, rest on the seventh, and glory on the eighth."[1] Thus Gregory.

Regarding the third question, namely, how Christ rose, note first that he rose powerfully, i.e., by his own power; John 10:18: "I have power to lay down [my life] and I have power to take it up again"; and John 2:19: "Destroy this temple, and in three days I will raise it up." Second, he rose happily, all misery left behind; Matt. 26:32: "After I am raised up, I will go before you to Galilee." "Galilee" is interpreted "transmigration," and Christ, when he rose, went ahead into Galilee because he crossed over from suffering to glory, from corruption to incorruption. Pope Leo: "After Christ's passion the chains of death were bro-ken; weakness passed into strength, mortality into eternity, shame into glory." Third, he rose usefully, because he seized prey; Jer. 4:7: "The lion is come up out of his den and the robber of nations has roused himself"; John 12:32: "And I, if I be lifted up from the earth, will draw all things to myself," i.e., when I am taken up from the earth, raising my soul out of limbo and my body from the tomb, I will draw all things, etc. Fourth, he rose miraculously, because the tomb remained closed. Just as he came forth at birth though his mother's womb re-mained closed, and as he came in to his disciples though the doors were shut, so also he was able to come out of the closed tomb. Hence we read in the *Scholastic History* that in the year 1111 from the Lord's incarnation a monk of Saint-Law-rence-outside-the-Walls marveled to see the cord that he wore as a cincture inexplicably thrown down in front of him, still knotted, while a voice sounded in the air: "Thus was Christ able to come out of the tomb." Fifth, he rose truly, i.e., with his own true body. Indeed, he gave six proofs that he had truly risen from the dead. First, the angel, who does not lie, said so, and second, by his frequent apparitions: in these two ways he showed that he had truly risen. Third, by eating he proved that he was not using any magical arts. Fourth, he let himself be touched, so it had to be his real body. Fifth, by showing his wounds, he proved that this was the same body in which he had died. Sixth, by coming in

---

[1] The "eighth day" is the day "after time," i.e., eternity.

through the closed doors of the house, he showed that he rose glorified.. Therefore it is evident that on all these points the disciples had had doubts about his resurrection.

Seventh, he rose immortally, since he was never to die again; Rom. 6:9: "Christ, rising again from the dead, dies now no more." Yet Dionysius, in his letter to Demophilus, said that Christ, after his ascension, told a man named Carpus: "I am ready to suffer again for man's salvation." Thus it is clear that if such a thing were possible, he was prepared to die again for mankind. The aforementioned Carpus, a man of admirable holiness, told the blessed Dionysius, as we learn from the same letter, that when a certain infidel had led one of the faithful astray, he, Carpus, took this so badly that he fell ill. Furthermore, though his sanctity was so great that he always experienced a heavenly vision before he celebrated the sacred mysteries, now, when he should have been praying for the conversion of the two men, on the contrary, he prayed daily that God would have no mercy and would put an end to their lives by burning them up. And once, when he awoke at midnight and began to say this prayer, the house he was in suddenly split in two and a huge furnace appeared in the middle. Then he looked upward and saw heaven open and Jesus there, surrounded by a multitude of angels. Next he saw the aforesaid two men standing terror-stricken near the furnace. Serpents came out of it and coiled themselves around the men, bit them, and tried strenuously to drag them into the furnace, while some other men pushed them toward it. Carpus took such pleasure at the sight of the suffering of the two that, paying no heed to the vision above, he fixed his attention on their trials and was sorry they did not fall into the furnace right away. In time, however, he looked up reluctantly and saw the heavenly vision as before; and now Jesus, taking pity on those men, rose from his supercelestial throne, came down with a company of angels, reached out, and lifted the two out of danger. Then Jesus said to Carpus, whose hand was raised: "If you wish to strike, strike me! I am ready to suffer for men's salvation. That is my pleasure, and not that other men sin."—It is to preserve these words of Christ that we have set down this account of the vision as Dionysius related it.[2]

As to the fourth question, namely, why the Lord did not wait to rise again with the rest at the general resurrection, there are three reasons for this choice. First, there is the dignity of his body. This body was of the highest dignity because it was deified, i.e., united to his divinity. Therefore, it would have been unseemly were the body to lie so long beneath the dust. Hence Ps. 15(16):10: "Nor wilt thou give thy holy one [i.e., the sanctified, deified body] to see corruption"; and Ps. 131(132):8: "Arise, O Lord, into thy resting place, thou and the ark, which thou hast sanctified." The body that contained divinity is here called the ark. A second reason would be the strengthening of faith, because if Christ had not risen at that time, faith would have perished and no one would

[2] Cf. Pseudo-Dionysius, *The Complete Works*, 278–280.

have believed that he was true God. This is obvious from the fact that all except the Blessed Virgin lost their faith at the crucifixion but recovered it once the resurrection was known; thus 1 Cor. 15:17: "If Christ be not risen again, then is our preaching vain, and your faith is also vain." A third reason is that Christ's resurrection was the exemplar of our own. Rarely would anyone be found who would hope for resurrection in the future unless it could be seen to have happened in the past. For this reason the apostle says that if Christ arose from the dead, we too shall rise, because his rising is the exemplary cause of our resurrection. Gregory: "The Lord showed by this example what he promised as a reward, so that as all the faithful knew that he had risen, so they would hope for the reward of resurrection at the end of the world." And Gregory also says: "He wanted his death to last no longer than three days, lest, if resurrection were delayed in him, in us it might be utterly despaired of. Therefore, knowing about the glory of our Head, we have hope of our own resurrection."

The fifth question asked for what purpose Christ rose. Let it be known that his resurrection procured four great benefits for us: it effected justification for sinners, taught a new way of life, stirred up hope for rewards to be received, and caused the resurrection of all. The first, justification: Rom. 4:25: "He was delivered up for our sins and rose again for our justification." The second, new way of living: Rom. 6:4: "As Christ is risen from the dead by the glory of the Father, so we also may walk in newness of life." The third, hope: 1 Pet. 1:3: "By his great mercy we have been born anew to a living hope through the resurrection of Jesus Christ from the dead." The fourth, resurrection for all: 1 Cor. 15:20: "Christ the Lord has been raised from the dead, the firstfruits of those who have fallen asleep. For as by a man came death, by a man has come also the resurrection of the dead."

Note also that, as is clear from what has been said, Christ's resurrection had four distinguishing marks. The first is that while our resurrection is deferred to the end, his was celebrated on the third day. The second is that we rise through him, whereas he rose through himself, through his own power, whence Ambrose says: "How could he, who brought others to life, look for help in restoring life to his own body?" Thirdly, we shall return to dust, but Christ's body could not be reduced to dust. Fourthly, his resurrection is the efficient, exemplary, and sacramental cause of our resurrection. Regarding the first of these causes, the *Gloss* on the verse of Ps. 29(30):6 ("In the evening weeping shall have place, and in the morning, gladness") says: "Christ's resurrection is the efficient cause of the soul's resurrection in present time and of the body's in the future." Regarding the exemplary cause, 1 Cor. 15:20: "Christ is risen from the dead, the first fruits of them that sleep." Regarding the sacramental cause, Rom. 6:4: "As Christ is risen from the dead, so we also may walk in newness of life."

We come to the sixth question: how many times did the risen Christ appear? Let it be known that he appeared five times on the day of his resurrection, and five more times on subsequent days. The first of his apparitions was to Mary

Magdalene, as in John 20:1–18 and in Mark 16:9: "[Jesus] rising early the first day of the week, appeared first to Mary Magdalene, etc." Here Mary represents all repentant sinners. Indeed, he willed to appear first to her for five reasons. The first, that she loved him more ardently; Luke 7:47: "Many sins are forgiven her because she loved much." The second, in order to show that he had died for sinners; Matt. 9:13: "I came not to call the just but sinners." The third, because harlots go ahead of the wise in the kingdom of heaven; Matt. 21:31: "The harlots will go into the kingdom of God before you." The fourth, that as a woman had been the messenger of death, so a woman should be the one to announce life: this according to the *Gloss*. The fifth, that where sin abounded, grace would superabound, as we read in Rom. 5:20.

The Lord's second apparition on Easter Day was to the women as they came back from the tomb, when he said to them: "All hail!" and they approached and took hold of his feet, as we read in the last chapter of Matthew. The women here stand for the humble, to whom the Lord shows himself because of their sex and because of their affection, for they held his feet.

His third apparition was to Simon Peter, but where and when we do not know, unless perhaps it was when Peter was returning from the sepulcher with John. It might be that Peter at some point took a different way from John's, and that then the Lord appeared to him (Luke, last chapter). Or it may have happened when Peter went into the sepulcher alone, as the *Scholastic History* says, or in a cave or underground cavern. The same history says that after he denied Christ, he fled to a cavern which is now called Gallicantus,[3] where, it is said, he wept for three days for having denied Christ, and that there Christ appeared to him and comforted him. The name "Peter" is interpreted as meaning "obedient," and Peter here represents the obedient, to whom the Lord appears.

His fourth apparition was to the disciples at Emmaus. The name is interpreted "desire for counsel" and signifies Christ's poor, who wish to fulfill this counsel: "Go, sell what you have and give to the poor." The fifth was to the disciples gathered together (John 20:19), where they represent the religious, the doors of whose senses are closed.

These five apparitions occurred on Easter Day, and the priest represents them in the mass when he turns to the people five times—the third time in silence because this turning stands for the apparition to Peter, the place and time of which are not known.

The sixth time Jesus appeared was on the octave day of the resurrection, when the disciples were together and Thomas, who had said he would not believe unless he saw and touched, was present. Here he represents those who hesitate in believing, John 20:26–29. The seventh apparition was to the disciples when they were fishing, John 21:4; they represent preachers, who are fishers of men. The eighth time was to the disciples on Mount Tabor, as in the last chapter

---

[3] *galli cantus*, i.e., cockcrow.

of Matthew: here the contemplatives are signified, because Christ was transfigured on that mountain. The ninth was when the eleven disciples were at table and Jesus upbraided them for their incredulity and hardness of heart, as we read in Mark 16:14; here we understand sinners placed in the number of transgression, which is eleven,[4] whom the Lord sometimes visits mercifully. The tenth and last apparition was to the disciples as they stood on Mount Olivet, as in the last chapter of Luke. From there he ascended into heaven, because "godliness is of value in every way, as it holds promise for the present life and also for the life to come," I Tim. 4:8.

Three other apparitions are referred to as having happened on the day of the resurrection, but the text has nothing about them. There is the one to James the Just, otherwise James of Alpheus, an account of which we shall find in the legend of James the Less.[5] It is said that Jesus was also seen on the same day by Joseph, as we read in the *Gospel of Nicodemus*. When the Jews heard that Joseph had asked Pilate for the body and had placed it in his own tomb, they were indignant, and took him and shut him up in a small room that they carefully locked and sealed. They intended to kill him after the Sabbath, but the very night of the resurrection the house was lifted up by the four corners and Jesus came in to him, dried his tears, embraced him, and, leaving the seals intact, led him out and brought him to his house in Arimathea.

The third apparition was to the Virgin Mary and is believed to have taken place before all the others, although the evangelists say nothing about it. The church at Rome seems to approve this belief, since it celebrates a station[6] at the church of Saint Mary on Easter Sunday. Indeed, if this is not to be believed, on the ground that no evangelist testifies to it, we would have to conclude that Jesus never appeared to Mary after his resurrection because no gospel tells us where or when this happened. But perish the thought that such a son would fail to honor such a mother by being so negligent! Still it may be that in this case the evangelists kept silence because their charge was only to present witnesses to the resurrection, and it would not be proper to have a mother testifying for her son. If indeed the words of the other women had been taken for ravings, how much more surely would a mother be thought to be making up stories for love of her son! So the evangelists judged it better not to write about this apparition, and left it to be taken for granted. Christ must first of all have made his mother happy over his resurrection, since she certainly grieved over his death more than the others. He would not have neglected his mother while he hastened to console others. Ambrose also testifies to this in the third book of his *De Virginibus*, say-

---

[4] Augustine, in Sermo 51, explains that since the number of commandments is 10, the number of sin is 11, because sin "transgresses"—oversteps—the number 10 (Augustinus, *Opera*, 5, col. 430 B–C; cf. Sermo 83, ibid., col. 645 A).

[5] Chapter 67, below.

[6] A "station" brought the people of the city together in one of the principal churches (in this instance, Saint Mary Major), where the pope led the solemn celebration of a major feast.

ing: "His mother saw the risen Lord, and saw him first and believed first." Mary Magdalene saw him although up to that moment she had hesitated to believe. And Sedulius,[7] treating of Christ's apparition, says:

> Semper virgo manet, hujus se visibus astans
> Luce palam Dominus prius obtulit, ut bona mater,
> Grandia divulgans miracula, quae fuit olim
> Advenientis iter, haec sit redeuntis et index.[8]

Regarding the seventh and last question, namely, how Christ led out the holy fathers who were in Limbo and what he did there, the Gospel tells us nothing openly. Yet Augustine, in one of his sermons, and Nicodemus in his *Gospel*, give us some information. Saint Augustine writes as follows: "As soon as Christ yielded up his spirit, his soul, united to his deity, went down to the depths of hell. When he came to the edge of darkness like some splendid, terrible raider, the impious infernal legions, terrified as they gazed on him, began to ask: 'Whence is he, so strong, so terrible, so splendid, so noble? That world which was subject to us never sent us a dead man like this, never destined such gifts to hell! Who then is this, who comes to our gates so boldly, and not only has no fear of our torments but also frees others from our chains? See how these, who used to moan under our blows, now, with salvation in sight, not only fear nothing but even threaten us! Never have the dead here below been so confident, nor was there a time when they could be so joyous in captivity! O our prince, wherefore have you willed to bring this one here? Your gladness has perished, your joys turned to lamentation! While you hang Christ upon the tree, you know not what losses you sustain in hell!'

"After these cries of the cruel infernal spirits, at the Lord's command all the iron bars were shattered and innumerable peoples of the saints, throwing themselves at his feet, called out with tearful voice: 'You have come, Redeemer of the world, you have come, you whom we longed for and waited for day by day! You have come down to hell for us! Leave us not when you ascend again to the upper world! Go up, Lord Jesus, leave hell stripped of its prey and the author of death bound again in his chains! Restore joy to the world, help us, put an end now to our fierce pains and in mercy set the captives free! While you are here, absolve the guilty! While you ascend, defend your own!'" Thus far Augustine.

In the *Gospel of Nicodemus* we read that Carinus and Leucius, sons of the aged Simeon, were raised to life with Christ and appeared to Annas and Caiaphas and Nicodemus and Joseph and Gamaliel, and at their urging told what Christ had done in hell. This is their story:

---

[7] Caelius Sedulius, a Christian poet of the second half of the fifth century.

[8] She remains ever virgin, to whose sight the Lord first offered himself at dawn, so that she, good mother, who in the past was the path for his coming, might, by making known the grand miracles, become also the signpost for his returning.

"While we were in thick darkness with all our fathers the patriarchs, a gold and royal purple sunlight suddenly burst upon us. At once Adam, father of the human race, rejoiced, saying, 'This is the Light of the Author of the everlasting light, who promised to send us his coeternal Light. And Isaiah exclaimed, This is the Light of the Father, the Son of God, as I, when I was alive on earth, predicted, saying, The people that walked in darkness have seen a great light.'

"Then our father Simeon came up and, rejoicing, said, 'Glorify the Lord, because I held the newborn infant Christ in my arms in the Temple and, moved by the Holy Spirit, proclaimed, Now my eyes have seen thy salvation, which thou hast prepared before the face of all peoples; a light to the revelation of the Gentiles and the glory of thy people Israel (Luke 2:25–32).' Next came one who dwelt in the desert and, when we asked who he was, said, 'I am John, who baptized the Christ and went before him to prepare his way, and I pointed him out with my finger, saying, Behold the Lamb of God! And I have come down to announce to you that Christ will soon visit us.'

"Then Seth said, 'I had gone to the gates of paradise and prayed the Lord to send his angel to give me some of the oil of mercy; I wanted to anoint the body of my father Adam who was infirm. The angel Michael appeared and told me, Do not weary yourself weeping as you pray for oil from the tree of mercy. That you cannot possibly receive until five thousand five hundred years have passed.'

"Hearing all this, the patriarchs and prophets rejoiced with great joy. Then Satan, prince and captain of death, said to Hell, 'Get ready to receive Jesus, who boasts that he is the Son of God, but is a mere man who fears death and says, My soul is sorrowful even unto death. Yet he has cured many whom I had made deaf, and has made those I lamed able to walk straight.' Hell answered, 'If you are so mighty, what sort of man is this Jesus, who fears death and yet defies your power? He says he is afraid of death because he wants to fool you, and woe to you forever and ever!' Satan answered: 'I have tempted him and stirred up the populace against him. I sharpened the spear, I mixed the gall and vinegar, I readied the wood of the cross. His death is at hand and I will bring him to you!' Hell: 'Is he the one who restored Lazarus, who was mine, to life?' Satan: 'The very one!' Hell: 'I adjure you by your power and mine, don't bring him to me! When I heard the command of his word, I shuddered with fear and couldn't even hold on to Lazarus, who shook free of his bonds and took off like an eagle, springing up with unbounded agility and getting away from us!'

"Now a voice like thunder was heard, saying, 'Lift up your gates, O princes, and be lifted up, eternal gates, and the King of glory will come in!' At the sound of the voice the demons ran and shut the bronze gates and put up the iron bars. Then David said, 'Did I not prophesy and say, Let them thank the Lord for his steadfast love, for he shatters the doors of bronze and cuts in two the bars of iron?'[9] Then again the voice rang out loudly, 'Lift up your gates, etc.' Hell,

[9] Ps. 106(107):15–16.

seeing that the voice had called out twice and feigning ignorance, asked, 'Who is this king of glory?' David replied, 'The Lord who is strong and mighty, the Lord mighty in battle, he is the King of glory!'[10]

"Then the King of glory came and poured light into the eternal darkness; and the Lord reached out and took Adam's right hand, saying, 'Peace be to you and all your sons, my just ones!' Whereupon the Lord ascended out of hell and all the saints followed him. The Lord, holding Adam's hand, entrusted him to the archangel Michael, who led him into paradise. Two men of great age came forward and the saints asked them, 'Who are you? You were not yet dead with us in hell and here you are in the body in paradise!' One of the two answered, 'I am Enoch, I was taken up here; and this is Elijah, who was carried up here in a fiery chariot. We have not yet tasted death but are being kept until the coming of the Antichrist. We will fight with him and be killed by him, and after three and one-half days will be assumed into the clouds.'

"As he spoke, another man came forward carrying the sign of the cross on his shoulders. Being asked who he was, he said, 'I was a robber and was crucified with Jesus. I believed that he was the Creator and I prayed to him and said, Lord, remember me when you come into your kingdom. Then he said to me, Truly, I say to you, today you will be with me in paradise;[11] and he gave me this sign of the cross, saying, Carry this, walk into paradise. If the angel on guard doesn't let you go in, show him this sign of the cross and say to him, Christ, who is now dying on the cross, sent me over. And when I did this and told the angel, he opened at once and led me in, placing me on the right side of paradise.'"

When Carinus and Leucius had said all this, suddenly they were transfigured and were seen no more.

Gregory of Nyssa, or, according to some books, Augustine, says about the above: "All at once, when Christ came down, the eternal night of hell was filled with light, and the dark gatekeepers, beset with fear, broke the shadowy silences between them and whispered: 'Who indeed is this terrible one who gleams with such splendor? Our hell never received such a one, never did the world disgorge the like into our cavern! He is an invader, not a debtor, a demolisher and destroyer, no sinner but a predator. We see a judge, not a suppliant, one who comes to fight, not to succumb, not to stay but to take from us what is ours.'"

---

[10] Ps. 23(24):7–10.
[11] Luke 23:42–43.

55. Saint Secundus

Secundus resembles *se condens*, which means establishing oneself, i.e., composing oneself by integrity of morals. Or the name is like *secundans*, i.e., *obsecundans*, complying with; so, complying with the commands of the Lord. Or the name is formed from *secum dux*, commander of oneself. Saint Secundus was his own commander, because he controlled sensuality by reason and directed his senses to the performance of all good works. Or *secundus*, the second, refers to *primus*, the first, for there are two roads that lead to eternal life, the first by lamenting in penance, the second by martyrdom. The precious martyr Secundus took not only the first road but also the second.

Secundus was a valiant soldier, a stout fighter for Christ, and a glorious martyr for the Lord. He won the martyr's crown in the city of Asti, and Asti is honored by his glorious presence and rejoices in having him as its special patron saint. He was instructed in the Christian faith by blessed Calocerus, who was held in prison in Asti by Sapritius the prefect. Blessed Marcianus was also imprisoned, in the city of Tortona, and Sapritius wanted to go there in order to compel him to offer sacrifice. Secundus went with him, his pretext being to have a holiday, his real purpose being to see Marcianus.

As they were riding along outside Asti, a dove came down and lighted on Secundus's head. Sapritius said to him: "You see, Secundus, our gods love you so much that they send birds from heaven to visit you!" When they came to the river Tanaro, Secundus saw an angel of the Lord walking over the water and saying to him: "Secundus, have faith, and you will walk like this over the worshipers of idols." Sapritius said: "Brother Secundus, I hear the gods talking to you!" Secundus replied: "Let us walk toward the fulfillment of our heart's desire!" When they came to the river Bormida, an angel appeared to him as before and asked: "Secundus, do you firmly believe in God, or do you perhaps have doubts?" Secundus answered: "I believe in the truth of his passion!" Sapritius exclaimed: "What *is* that that I'm hearing?" When they arrived in Tortona, Marcianus, following the angel's directions, came out of the jail and appeared before Secundus, saying: "Secundus, enter upon the way of truth and continue until you receive the palm of faith!" Sapritius said: "Who is that, speaking to us like someone in a dream?" Secundus: "A dream to you, to me an admonition and an encouragement!"

After that, Secundus went to Milan, and an angel led Faustinus and Jovita, who were being held in prison, to meet him outside the city; and he was baptized by them, a cloud providing the water. Then suddenly a dove came from heaven carrying the Body and Blood of the Lord, which it entrusted to Faustinus and Jovita. Faustinus in turn gave the sacred species to Secundus to be brought to Marcianus. By that time it was night, and when Secundus reached the bank of the river Po, the angel took hold of the horse's bridle and led him across the river and to Tortona, to Marcianus's prison. Secundus entered the prison and gave Faustinus's precious gift to Marcianus, who took it and said: "May the Lord's Body and Blood be with me unto eternal life!" Then, at the angel's command, Secundus left the prison and went to his lodging.

Soon Marcianus was condemned to die and was beheaded, and Secundus retrieved his body and buried it. Sapritius heard of this and summoned Secundus. "So far as I can see," he said, "you profess to be a Christian." Secundus: "Indeed I do profess to be a Christian!" Sapritius: "You desire a bad death!" Secundus: "Rather, that is what's coming to you!" Secundus refused to sacrifice to the gods and Sapritius ordered him to be stripped naked, but immediately an angel of the Lord was at his side and prepared covering for him. Then Sapritius had Secundus bound on a rack and stretched until his arms were drawn out of their sockets, but when an angel repaired the injury, the prefect remanded him to prison. There the angel came to him and said: "Stand up, Secundus, follow me and I shall lead you to your Creator!" Then the angel conducted him into the city of Asti and left him in the prison where Calocerus was, and the Savior with him. Seeing the Savior, Secundus prostrated himself at his feet. The Savior said to him: "Fear not, Secundus, for I am the Lord your God, and I will rescue you from all evils!" And he blessed them and ascended to heaven.

Morning came, and Sapritius sent men to the prison, but, though the doors were locked and sealed, they did not find Secundus. Sapritius therefore came from Tortona to Asti to punish Calocerus at least. He ordered Calocerus to be brought before him, and they came back and told him that Secundus was with Calocerus. So he had the two of them brought to him and said to them: "Since our gods know that you have no respect for them, they want you to die to-gether." They refused to sacrifice, so he had pitch heated with resin and poured over their heads and into their throats. They swallowed the potion with relish, as if it were the sweetest of waters, and said loudly and clearly: "How sweet to my mouth are your words, O Lord!" Sapritius then sentenced Secundus to be beheaded in Asti, and Calocerus to be sent to Albenga and put to death there. When blessed Secundus had been decapitated, angels of the Lord took his body and with praises and chants gave it burial. He suffered on the thirtieth day of March.

56. Saint Mary of Egypt

Mary the Egyptian, who is called the Sinner, led a most austere life in the desert for forty-seven years, beginning about the year of the Lord 270 in the time of Claudius. A priest named Zozimus crossed the Jordan and began to wander through the broad forest, hoping to find some holy father there, and saw a figure walking about naked, the body blackened and burned by the fiery sun. It was Mary the Egyptian. She immediately took flight, and Zozimus ran after her as fast as he could. She said to him: "Father Zozimus, why are you pursuing me? Forgive me, I cannot face you because I am a woman and naked, but lend me your mantle so that I may see you without being ashamed." Astonished at being called by name, he gave her his mantle and prostrated himself on the ground, asking her to bless him. "It behooves you, father," she said, "to give the blessing, since you are adorned with the dignity of priesthood." When he heard that she knew both his name and his office, he marveled still more and urgently besought her to bless him. Then she said: "Blessed be God, the redeemer of our souls!" She extended her hands in prayer, and he saw her lifted some feet above the earth. The old man began to suspect that this might be a spirit pretending to pray. "May God forgive you," she said, "for thinking that I, a sinful woman, might be an unclean spirit."

Now Zozimus adjured her in God's name to tell him about herself. Her answer was: "Excuse me, father, because if I tell you who and what I am, you will flee as if frightened by a serpent, your ears will be contaminated by my words, the air will be polluted with filth."

The old man forcefully insisted nonetheless, so she began: "I was born in Egypt, brother, and went to Alexandria when I was twelve years old. There, for seventeen years, I plied my trade as a public woman and never refused my body to anyone. But there came a time when some people of that region were going up to Jerusalem to pay homage to the holy cross, and I asked the sailors to allow me to go with them. When they asked me for my fare, I said: 'Brothers, I have no other fare, but take my body in payment for the passage.' So they took me aboard and I paid my fare with my body.

"I arrived at Jerusalem and went to the church with the others to worship the holy cross, but suddenly, by an invisible force, I was pushed back from the door and not allowed to enter. Again and again I got to the threshold of the entrance and suffered the pain of being repulsed, while the others went in freely and encountered no obstacle. Then I came to myself and realized that this was happening to me because of my dreadful crimes. I began to beat my breast, I shed bitter tears and sighed from the bottom of my heart. Then, looking up, I saw there an image of the Blessed Virgin Mary. I began to pray tearfully to her, asking her to obtain pardon for my sins and to let me go in and worship the holy cross, promising that I would renounce the world and thenceforth live chastely. Having offered this prayer and putting my trust in the name of the Blessed Virgin, I went again to the door of the church and entered without difficulty.

"When I had worshiped the cross with the utmost devotion, someone gave me three coins with which I bought three loaves of bread, and I heard a voice saying to me: 'If you go across the Jordan, you will be saved.' I therefore crossed the Jordan and came into this desert, where I have stayed for forty-seven years without seeing a single human being. The loaves I had brought with me turned hard as stone, but they have sufficed me for food all these years. My clothes fell to pieces in time. For seventeen years I was troubled by temptations of the flesh, but now by the grace of God I have conquered them all. There now, I have told you my whole story, and I beseech you to pray God for me."

The priest knelt and blessed the Lord in his handmaid. She said: "I beg you to come back to the Jordan on the day of the Lord's Supper and to bring with you the Body of the Lord, and I will meet you there and receive the sacred Body from your hand, because since the day I came here I have not received the communion of the Lord." The old man returned to his monastery, and the following year, when Holy Thursday was drawing near, he took the sacred Host and went to the bank of the Jordan. He saw the woman standing on the other bank, and she made the sign of the cross over the river and walked across the water. Marveling at this, the priest prostrated himself at her feet. She said: "Do not do that! You have the sacrament of the Lord on your person and you shine with the dignity of priesthood. But I pray you, father, that you may deign to come again to me next year." Then, once again making the sign of the cross over Jordan waters, she went over and returned to the solitude of the desert.

The father went back to his monastery and a year later sought the place where he had first spoken to the woman. He came to the place and found her lying there dead. He began to weep and did not dare to touch her, saying to himself: "I wish I could bury the saint's body, but I fear this might displease her." As he was thinking about this, he noticed something written in the sand beside her head, and read: "Zozimus, bury Mary's little body, return her dust to the earth, and pray for me to the Lord, at whose command I left this world on the second day of April." Thus the old man knew for certain that she had reached the end of her days immediately after receiving the Lord's sacrament and returning to the desert, and that she had crossed this expanse of desert in one hour and migrated to God, whereas it took him thirty days to cover the same distance.

Zozimus tried to dig a grave but could not. Then he saw a lion meekly coming toward him and said to the lion: "This holy woman commanded me to bury her body here, but I am old and cannot dig, and anyway I have no shovel. Therefore you do the digging and we will be able to bury this holy body." The lion began to dig and prepared a suitable grave, and when that was finished went away like a gentle lamb, while the old man made his way back to his monastery, glorifying God.

✳

57. Saint Ambrose

The name Ambrose comes from *ambra*, amber, which is a fragrant, precious substance. Ambrose was precious to the Church and spread a pleasing fragrance both in his speech and in his actions. Or Ambrose is derived from *ambra* and *syos*, which means God, he being, as it were, the amber of God, because through him God diffused fragrance everywhere, as amber does; for Ambrose was and is the good odor of Christ in every place. Or the name comes from *ambor*, which means father of light, and *sior*, small, because he was a father in begetting many spiritual children; he was luminous in his expounding of Holy Scripture; and he was small in the humble way he dealt with others. Moreover, in the *Glossary* we find *ambrosia*, the food of angels, and *ambrosium*, the heavenly honeycomb; for Ambrose was a heavenly perfume by the fragrance of his renown, a supernal flavor due to his contemplative prayer, a celestial honeycomb by the sweetness of his exposition of the Scriptures, a food for angels in his glorious fruitfulness.

Paulinus, bishop of Nola, wrote the saint's life and gave it to Saint Augustine.

Ambrose, son of Ambrose the prefect of Rome, lay asleep in his cradle in the atrium of the palace when all of a sudden a swarm of bees flew in and covered his face and mouth so completely that the bees seemed to be moving in and out of their hive. Then they soared upward to such a height that the human eye could barely follow them. Witnessing this, the infant's father was astonished, and said: "If this child lives, something great will come of him." Later on, when Ambrose, now an adolescent, saw his mother and his sister, a professed virgin, kissing the hands of priests, he playfully offered his right hand to his sister, saying that she might well do the same for him.[1] She regarded this as coming from one too young to know what he was talking about, and refused.

Ambrose made his studies in Rome and pleaded cases in the courts with such eloquence that the emperor Valentinian appointed him to govern the province

---

[1] Jacobus omits Paulinus's explanatory clause, ". . . if she kept in mind that he was to be a bishop."

of Liguria-Emilia. After his arrival in Milan, the capital of the province, the bishop of the city died and the populace gathered in the cathedral to choose a new bishop. A noisy disturbance broke out, however, between the Arians and the Catholics over the election, and Ambrose went to the church to quell the commotion. As he entered, a child's voice was heard, crying "Ambrose for bishop!" All present took up the cry and unanimously acclaimed Ambrose as their bishop.

Ambrose thereupon tried to frighten the people into changing their minds. He left the church, went straight to his tribunal, and there, contrary to his usual moderate practice, sentenced several persons to be tortured. The populace, undeterred, shouted: "Your sin be upon us!" Deeply troubled, Ambrose went home and tried to pose as a mere teacher of philosophy, but the public would have none of it and called him out again. Then he publicly had women of the street brought to his house, hoping that the people, seeing this, would revoke their decision; but this, too, failed, and the crowds continued to take his sin upon themselves. Then he determined to flee the city by night, but in the morning, when he thought he had reached Pavia, he found himself at the gate of Milan called the Porta Romana. There the people found him and would not let him out of their hands.

All this was reported to the most clement emperor Valentinian, who was delighted that judges appointed by him should be considered for the priesthood, and the worthy ruler was particularly pleased that his word to Ambrose had been fulfilled. When he had dispatched him to Milan with his new commission, he had said to him: "Go, and act not like a judge but like a bishop." Meanwhile, in the interval before the answer to the report came back, Ambrose managed to hide again, but the people found him. Then it was realized that he was only a catechumen. He was baptized immediately and within a week was elevated to the episcopal throne. Four years later, when he was visiting Rome, his sister the consecrated virgin kissed his right hand. He smiled and said: "See, I told you back then that you would kiss this bishop's hand!"

On one occasion he went to another city to ordain the newly designated bishop, to whose election the empress Justina and other heretics objected, hoping that someone from their own party would be appointed instead. One of the young Arian women, more impudent than the rest, went up to the pulpit and grasped Saint Ambrose by the sleeve of his vestment, attempting to drag him over to the women's area, where they might beat him and drive him contumeliously out of the church. Ambrose said to her: "I may be unworthy of this high priestly rank, but you have no right to lay hands on any priest, and you should have feared God's judgment and the punishment that might befall you." The sequel confirmed what he had said: the very next day he conducted her body to the grave, thus repaying insult with blessing. This put the fear of God in everyone.

After his return to Milan, Ambrose had to contend with all sorts of plots instigated by the empress Justina, who offered bribes and honors to people to win them to her cause; so there were many who tried to force him into exile. One such, more unlucky than others, was stirred to such fury that he rented a house next to the cathedral and kept a fully equipped wagon with a team of four horses there. Thus he was ready to carry the bishop into exile the moment he succeeded, with Justina's connivance, in laying hold of Ambrose. But God's judgment dictated otherwise. The very day the abduction was planned for, the plotter was taken from his house and carried into exile in his own quadriga. Ambrose, however, returning good for evil, saw to it that the man's needs were provided for.

The saint made the rules for the chant and the liturgy to be followed in the church of Milan.

In his time there were in Milan many who were possessed by demons, who cried out that they were being tortured by Ambrose. Justina, and many Arians who were in her entourage, declared that the bishop paid people to say, falsely, that they were troubled by unclean spirits and that Ambrose was tormenting them. Then, all of a sudden, one of the heretics present was seized by a demon and leapt into the midst of the crowd, shouting: "May those who do not believe Ambrose be tortured as I am tortured!" The heretics, thrown into confusion, plunged the man into a pool and drowned him.

Another heretic, particularly sharp in debate, hardheaded and totally resistant to conversion, one day heard Ambrose preach and saw an angel whispering in his ear the words the bishop was speaking to his people. Having seen this, the erstwhile heretic began to defend the faith he had previously persecuted.

There was a soothsayer who summoned demons and sent them to wreak harm on Ambrose, but they came back and told him that they not only could not reach the bishop but were unable to come near the doors of his house, because an unquenchable fire protected the whole building and scorched them even though they stood far off. And when this same soothsayer was delivered by the judge to the torturers to be punished for his evil deeds, he cried out that Ambrose tortured him even more sorely than they did.

When a certain possessed man entered Milan, the demon left him but came back into him when he quit the city. Asked about this, the demon explained that he was afraid of Ambrose.

Another man, aided and abetted by Justina, made his way into the bishop's bedroom by night in order to kill him with a sword, but when he lifted the sword to strike, his arm withered instantly.

The citizens of Thessalonica had aroused the emperor's wrath, but at Ambrose's request he had pardoned them. Later the ruler, secretly influenced by some malicious courtiers, ordered the execution of a huge number of those he had pardoned. Ambrose knew nothing of this at the time, but when he learned what had happened, he refused to allow the emperor to enter the church. Theodosius pointed out that David had committed adultery and homicide, and Ambrose responded: "You followed David in wrongdoing, follow him in repentance." The most clement emperor accepted the order gratefully and did not refuse to do public penance.[2]

A man possessed of the devil began to shout that he was being tortured by Ambrose. Ambrose ordered him to be quiet and said: "O devil, it is not Ambrose that tortures you, but your envy, because you see those who are going up to the place from which you fell so ignominiously. Ambrose knows no pride!" Instantly the possessed man was quiet. And once when the bishop was walking in the city, it happened that a man accidentally fell and lay prostrate on the ground. Seeing this, a passerby began to laugh at him. To this man Ambrose said: "You're standing now, but be careful that you don't fall!" The words were hardly spoken when down the man went and lamented his own fall as he had laughed at the other's.

Another time Ambrose went to the palace of Macedonius, master of the offices, to intercede for someone in trouble, but he found the doors closed and could not gain entrance, so he said: "Very well! One of these days you yourself will come to the church and won't be able to get in—not that the doors will be closed, because they will be wide open." Some time later Macedonius, fearful of his enemies and seeking refuge, fled to the church but could not find a way in although all the doors stood open.

The saint's abstinence was so strict that he fasted every day but Saturdays, Sundays, and major feast days. His generosity was such that he gave away everything he had to the churches and the poor, keeping nothing for himself. He was so compassionate that when someone confessed his sin to him, he wept so bitterly that the sinner himself was compelled to weep. He was humble and hardworking, and wrote out his books with his own hand except when bodily weakness forbade it. So loving and kindhearted was he that when the death of a holy priest or bishop was announced to him, he wept so copiously that he could hardly be consoled. When he was asked why he grieved so bitterly for holy men who had gone to glory, he said: "Don't think I'm weeping because they are gone, but because they have gone ahead of me, and it will be hard to find anyone worthy to replace them." His constancy and courage were so great that far from indulging the vices of emperor or prince, he was loud and persistent in reproving them.

When a certain man had perpetrated a heinous crime and was brought before him, Ambrose said: "He must be handed over to Satan to die in the flesh, lest he dare to commit any more such crimes." And no sooner had these words been

---

[2] Graesse (252n) remarks that the "little story" (*historiola*) told in this paragraph "is lacking in the editio princeps." The story is repeated below in greater detail.

pronounced than the unclean spirit, as is his wont, began to tear at the guilty man.[3]

The story is told that once when blessed Ambrose was on his way to Rome, he found hospitality in a Tuscan villa, the home of an exceedingly wealthy man. Ambrose asked him solicitously how things were with him, and he answered: "Everything has always gone well, even famously, with me. As you see, I have riches galore. I have more slaves and servants than I need. I have always had everything to my liking, nothing untoward has ever happened to me, nor anything to be sad about." Ambrose, taken aback at hearing this, said to his traveling companions: "On your feet and away from here as fast as we can go, because the Lord is not in this place. Quick, my sons, hurry! We must lose no time getting away, or the divine vengeance may catch us here and involve us also in the sins of these people." So he and his company fled, and when they had gone some distance, the earth suddenly opened behind them and swallowed that man and all that belonged to him so completely that not a trace remained. Observing this, Ambrose said: "See, brothers, how mercifully God spares those to whom he sends adversity, and how severe his anger can be against those who always enjoy prosperity." It is said that in that same place there is a very deep ravine, which stands as a reminder of what happened there.

Ambrose was aware that greed, the root of all evil, was increasing more and more among men, especially among those who wielded power and would sell anything for a price, and among those in high church office. He was deeply grieved at this and prayed God instantly to deliver him from the ills of this world. When he knew that his wish was about to be granted, he rejoiced and revealed to his brethren that he would be with them only until Easter. Then, a few days before he had to take to his bed, he was dictating a commentary on the Forty-third Psalm to his secretary, who suddenly saw a small fire in the shape of a shield covering the saint's head and then going slowly into his mouth, like a householder entering his house. His face turned white as snow but afterwards resumed its normal look. That day put an end to his writing and dictating. He was not able to complete his explanation of the Psalm, and some days later his bodily condition worsened. Then the count of Italy, who was in Milan, convoked the ranking men of the province. He told them that the death of so great a man could be a threat to the welfare of Italy, and asked them to wait upon the man of God and beg him to obtain from God the space of one more year of life. When Ambrose heard their plea, he answered: "I have not lived among you in such a way that I should be ashamed to live on, nor am I afraid to die, since we all have the good Lord."

---

[3] Graesse notes (253n) that the Ed. Pr. omits this anecdote. "Ed. Pr." might mean "first edition," or "principal edition." Neither designation could have a precise meaning.

At that time four of the bishop's deacons met and talked about who might be the right man to succeed him. They were meeting at a distance from the place where Ambrose the man of God was dying; but when they had silently nominated Simplicianus and hardly had time to pronounce his name, the saint, far from them as he was, three times exclaimed: "Old he is, but he is the right man!" When the deacons heard this, they scattered in fear and after Ambrose's death chose none but Simplicianus.

In the place where the saint lay on his deathbed, he saw Jesus coming toward him smiling joyfully. And Honorius, the bishop of Vercelli, who was expecting Ambrose's death, was asleep when he heard a voice call out three times: "Get up, because the time of his passing is near." He rose and hurried to Milan, arriving in time to give the dying bishop the sacrament of the Lord's Body. Moments later Ambrose extended his arms in the form of a cross and breathed his last with a prayer on his lips. He flourished about the year of the Lord 379. When his body was transported to the cathedral on the night of Easter, a number of baptized children saw the saint. Some of them saw him seated on the episcopal throne, some pointed him out to their parents as he went up to it; still others told how they had seen a star above his body.

A certain priest was at dinner with several others and began to speak ill of Saint Ambrose. At once he was stricken with a mortal illness, was carried to his bed, and died. In the city of Carthage three bishops were dining convivially, and one of them spoke disparagingly of Ambrose. He was told what had happened to that priest, but scoffed at the story. Immediately he received a lethal wound and ended his days then and there.

Saint Ambrose set an example by his many virtues. Firstly, he was remarkably generous: all he possessed belonged to the poor. In this regard he tells about himself that when the emperor demanded that he surrender his basilica, he responded (as recorded in the decree *Convenior*, XXIII, qu. 8): "If he had asked me for what was mine—my property, my money, and the like—I would not have opposed him, since all that is mine belongs to the poor." Secondly, he was spotlessly pure; indeed, he was a virgin. Hence Jerome tells us that Ambrose said: "We not only praise virginity, we practice it." Thirdly, he was firm in his faith. When the emperor demanded the basilica, Ambrose said (as this is recorded in the chapter quoted above): "He will take away my life before he gets my see from me." Fourthly, he invited martyrdom eagerly. In his letter *De basilica non tradenda* we read that the deputy of the emperor Valentinian sent his orders to Ambrose, saying: "Fail to respect Valentinian and I will have your head." Ambrose's answer: "May God allow you to carry out your threat, and may God turn her enemies away from the Church! Let them aim all their spears at me and slake their thirst in my blood."

Fifthly, he is a model of perseverance in prayer. Thus we read in the eleventh book of the *Ecclesiastical History* that Ambrose defended himself against the queen's fury not with his hand but with fasting and continuous vigils; with his prayers at the foot of the altar he gained God as defender for himself and for the Church. Sixthly, there was the abundance of his tears. He had three kinds of tears—tears of compassion for the sins of others, as Paulinus tells us in his *vita* that when someone confessed his sin, Ambrose wept so abundantly that he compelled the sinner to weep likewise; tears of devout yearning for the joys of eternity, as Paulinus, already quoted, says that when the saint was asked why he wept so much for holy men when they died, he answered: "Because they have gone ahead of me to glory"; tears shed for wrongs done by others, as he said of himself and we read in the decree cited above: "Against the Gothic troops my weapons are my tears, for they are enough defense for a priest. I ought not and cannot offer any other resistance."

Seventhly, consider his unyielding courage, which manifested itself through three of his guiding principles. The first of these was the defense of Catholic truth. We read in the eleventh book of the *Ecclesiastical History* that Justina, mother of the emperor Valentinian, who supported the Arian heresy, began to disturb the good order of the Church, and threatened bishops with expulsion and exile unless they revoked the decrees of the Council of Rimini. With warfare like this she beat upon that wall and tower of the Church, the most valiant Ambrose. In the preface of the mass of his feast the following is sung of him: "Thou didst strengthen Ambrose with such virtue and adorn him with so great a gift of constancy that by him demons were driven out and tortured, the Arian apostasy was crushed and withered away, and the necks of secular princes were bent to thy yoke and made humble."

The second principle that shaped his actions was the protection of the Church's freedom. Thus when the emperor wanted to take possession of a certain basilica, Ambrose opposed the monarch, as he himself attests and as it is set down in Decree XXIII, qu. 6: "I myself met with the counts, who delivered the emperor's command to yield the basilica forthwith, saying that it was his right to demand it. I responded: 'If he wants my patrimony, let him take it; if he wants my body, I am ready, and if in fetters, put them on. Do you want me dead, your will is mine. I will not use the crowd as my shield, I will not cling to the altar begging for my life but will gladly be immolated for the altars. You bring me the emperor's order to give up the basilica: we are under pressure from the royal commands: but our resolve is strengthened by the words of Scripture. Emperor, you talk like one of the foolish virgins. Do not burden yourself with the thought that you have any right to the things that are God's. Palaces belong to the emperor, churches to the priests. Saint Naboth defended his vineyard with his own blood. He did not surrender his vineyard: shall we hand over the church of Christ? Tribute is due to Caesar, let it not be denied him. The church belongs to God, let it not be donated to Caesar. If something is demanded of me or taken forcibly—my property or my house or my gold or my silver, whatever belongs to me by right—I will offer it willingly, but from the temple I can give away nothing, not one chip, since I have received it in trust, not to be picked apart.'"

His third principle was the denunciation of vice and all iniquity. Thus we read in the *Tripartite History* and in another chronicle that at one time rioting had broken out in the city of Thessalonica and the rioters had stoned several judges. Theodosius, enraged, ordered all to be put to death, making no effort to separate the innocent from the guilty, with the result that almost five thousand men were killed. So, when the emperor came to Milan and was about to enter the church, Ambrose met him at the door and forbade him entrance, saying: "Why, O emperor, do you not recognize the enormity of your presumption after doing such wrong in anger? Or can it be that imperial power precludes the admission of sin? It behooves you to let reason control power. O emperor, you are the prince, but your subjects are servants of God just as you are. With what eyes do you look upon the temple of our common Lord? How dare you set foot upon this holy pavement? How can you stretch out the hands that are still dripping with blood unjustly spilled? How could you presume to take into your mouth a taste of the Blood of the Lord, when by the fury of your words so much blood has been shed unjustly? Stand back! Go away! Do not try to add a second sin to your already great guilt! Accept the bond with which the Lord has now bound you, for it is the best medicine, the surest way to health."

In obedience to these words the emperor, groaning and weeping, withdrew to his palace. When he continued to mourn for a long while, Rufinus, commander of the army, asked him what caused such sadness. "You cannot know how sad I feel," he answered. "The churches are open to slaves and beggars, but I cannot enter them." And his speech was broken by sobs. "If you wish," said Rufinus, "I'll go straight to Ambrose and have him loose the bond he has put upon you." "You can't change Ambrose's mind," said the emperor, "because no fear of the imperial power will make him deviate from divine law." But when Rufinus assured him that he would bring the bishop around, the emperor told him to go, and he himself followed closely after him. However, the minute Ambrose saw Rufinus, he said: "You act like an impudent dog, Rufinus! You, the perpetrator of such a slaughter, you don't wipe the shame from your face, you don't blush while you bark at the divine majesty!" Rufinus nevertheless continued to plead for the emperor and said that the latter was coming after him. Afire with heavenly zeal, Ambrose said: "I declare to you that I forbid him to cross the sacred threshold, and if he goes from power to tyranny I willingly accept being put to death."

When Rufinus reported this to Theodosius, the emperor replied: "I will go to him and let him shame me to my face as I deserve!" So he went to Ambrose and implored him to remove his bonds, but Ambrose met him and refused to let him come into the church, asking: "What penance have you done for such crimes?" He answered: "It is for you to impose, for me to obey." And when the emperor pointed out that David had committed adultery and homicide, Ambrose replied: "You have followed him in sin, follow him in repentance." Willingly agreeing to this, Theodosius did not refuse to do public penance; and being thus reconciled, he went into the church and stood inside the gates of the chancel. Ambrose asked him why he was waiting there. He said that he was waiting to take part in the sacred mysteries, to which Ambrose replied: "O emperor, the space inside the chancel is reserved for priests. Go outside therefore, and participate with the rest of the people. The purple makes emperors, not priests." The emperor promptly obeyed.

Upon his return to Constantinople, Theodosius took his place outside the chancel when he went to church, but the bishop sent word to him to come inside. "It was hard for me to learn the distinction between emperor and priest," the emperor said, "and it took time to find someone to teach me the truth. Now Ambrose is the only one I would call a bishop."

Eighthly, Ambrose was outstanding for the purity of his doctrine, which had many qualities. It was profound, as Jerome says in his book *De XII Doctoribus*: "Ambrose was lifted above the depths and, a bird of the air though he went into the deep, he is seen to have gathered his fruit from on high." His doctrine was firm and solid, as Jerome says in the same book: "All his sentences are firm pillars of the faith, of the Church, and of every virtue." His work had beauty and elegance, as Augustine says in his book *On Marriage and Contracts*: "Pelagius the heresiarch praises Ambrose, saying, 'The blessed bishop Ambrose, in whose books the Roman faith shines, emerges like a flower among Latin writers.'" And Augustine adds: "No enemy has dared to question his faith nor his very correct understanding of the Scriptures." His doctrine had great authority, because the ancient authors, Augustine among them, considered his words authoritative. Hence Augustine writes to Januarius that when his mother Monica wondered that there was no fasting on Saturday in Milan, and Augustine asked Ambrose about it, Ambrose answered: "When I go to Rome I fast on the Sabbath. So you also, observe the usage of any church you happen to visit, and you will not scandalize anyone nor have anyone scandalize you." Augustine adds: "I have thought about this sentence many times, and have always held it to be and have accepted it as an oracle from heaven."

The life and martyrdom of Tiburtius and Valerian is contained in the passion of Saint Cecilia.[4]

---

[4] See chapter 169, below.

58. Saint George

The name George is derived from *geos*, meaning earth, and *orge*, meaning to work; hence one who works the earth, namely, his own flesh. Now Augustine writes in his book *On the Holy Trinity* that good earth is found high on the mountains, in the temperate climate of the hills, and in level ground: the first bears good grass, the second, grapes, and the third, the fruits of the fields. Thus blessed George was on the heights because he disdained base things and so had the fresh green of purity; he was temperate by his prudence and so shared the wine of heavenly joy; he was lowly in his humility and therefore bore the fruits of good works. Or George is derived from *gerar*, holy, and *gyon*, sand, therefore, holy sand; for he was like sand, heavy with the weight of his virtues, small by humility, and dry of the lusts of the flesh. Or again, the name comes from *gerar*, holy, and *gyon*, struggle; so a holy fighter, because he fought against the dragon and the executioner. Or George comes from *gero*, pilgrim, *gir*, cut off, and *ys*, counselor, for he was a pilgrim in his contempt for the world, cut off by gaining the crown of martyrdom, and a counselor in his preaching of the Kingdom. At the council of Nicaea his legend was included among the apocryphal writings because there is no sure record of his martyrdom. In Bede's *Calendar* we read that he was martyred in the Persian city of Dyaspolis, which formerly was called Lidda and is near Joppe. Elsewhere we read that he suffered under the emperors Diocletian and Maximian, or under the Persian emperor Dacian in the presence of seventy kings of his empire. Or we are told that he was put to death by the prefect Dacian during the reign of Diocletian and Maximian.

George, a native of Cappadocia, held the military rank of tribune. It happened that he once traveled to the city of Silena in the province of Lybia. Near this town there was a pond as large as a lake where a plague-bearing dragon lurked; and many times the dragon had put the populace to flight when they came out armed against him, for he used to come up to the city walls and poison everyone who came within reach of his breath. To appease the fury of this monster the townspeople fed him two sheep every day; otherwise he would invade their city and a great many would perish. But in time they were running out of sheep and could not get any more, so, having held a council, they paid him tribute of one sheep and one man or woman. The name of a youth or a maiden was drawn by lot, and no one was exempt from the draft; but soon almost all the young people had been eaten up. Then one day the lot fell upon the only daughter of the king, and she was seized and set aside for the dragon. The king, beside himself with grief, said: "Take my gold and my silver and the half of my kingdom, but release my daughter and spare her such a death." But the people were furious and shouted: "You yourself issued this decree, O king, and now that all our children are dead, you want to save your own daughter! Carry out for your daughter what you ordained for the rest, or we will burn you alive with your whole household!" Hearing this, the king began to weep and said to his daughter: "My dearest child, what have I done to you? Or what shall I say? Am I never to see your wedding?" And turning to the people he said: "I pray you, leave me my daughter for one week, so that we may weep together." This was granted, but at the end of the week back they came in a rage, crying: "Why are you letting your people perish to save your daughter? Don't you see that we are all dying from the breath of the dragon?" So the king, seeing that he could not set his daughter free, arrayed her in regal garments, embraced her tearfully, and said: "Woe is me, my darling child, I thought I would see sons nursing at your royal breast, and now you must be devoured by the dragon! Alas, my sweetest child, I hoped to invite princes to your wedding, to adorn the palace with pearls, to hear the music of timbrel and harp, and now you must go and be swallowed up by the beast." He kissed her and sent her off, saying: "O, my daughter, would that I had died before you, rather than lose you this way!" Then she threw herself at his feet and begged his blessing; and when, weeping, he had blessed her, she started toward the lake.

At this moment blessed George happened to be passing by and, seeing the maiden in tears, asked her why she wept. She answered: "Good youth, mount your horse quickly and flee, or you will die as I am to die." George responded: "Lady, fear not; but tell me, what are all these people waiting to see?" The damsel: "I see, good youth, that you have a great heart, but do you want to die with me? Get away speedily!" George: "I will not leave here until you tell me the reason for this." When she had told him all, he said: "Don't be afraid, child! I am going to help you in the name of Christ!" She spoke: "Brave knight, make haste to save yourself; if not, you will die with me. It is enough that I die alone, for you cannot set me free and you would perish with me."

While they were talking, the dragon reared his head out of the lake. Trembling, the maiden cried: "Away, sweet lord, away with all speed!" But George, mounting his horse and arming himself with the sign of the cross, set bravely upon the approaching dragon and, commending himself to God, brandished his lance, dealt the beast a grievous wound, and forced him to the ground. Then he called to the maiden: "Have no fear, child! Throw your girdle around the dragon's neck! Don't hesitate!" When she had done this, the dragon rose and followed her like a little dog on a leash. She led him toward the city; but the people, seeing this, ran for the mountains and the hills, crying out: "Now we will all be eaten alive!" But blessed George waved them back and said to them: "You have nothing to fear! The Lord has sent me to deliver you from the trouble this dragon has caused you. Believe in Christ and be baptized, every one of you, and I shall slay the dragon!" Then the king and all the people were baptized, and George, drawing his sword, put an end to the beast and ordered him to be moved out of the city, whereupon four yoke of oxen hauled him away into a broad field outside the walls. On that day twenty thousand were baptized, not counting the women and children. The king built a magnificent church there in honor of Blessed Mary and Saint George, and from the altar flowed a spring whose waters cure all diseases. He also offered a huge sum of money to blessed George, who refused to accept it and ordered it to be distributed to the poor. Then he gave the king four brief instructions: to have good care for the church of God, to honor the priests, to assist with devotion at the divine office, and to have the poor always in mind. Finally, he embraced the king and took his leave. Some books, however, tell us that at the very moment when the dragon was about to swallow the girl alive, George, making the sign of the cross, rode upon him and killed him.

At this time, in the reign of Diocletian and Maximian, the prefect Dacian launched against the Christians a persecution so violent that in one month seventeen thousand won the crown of martyrdom, while many others, being threatened with torture, gave in and offered sacrifice to the idols. Seeing this, Saint George, overcome with grief, gave away all his possessions, laid aside his military trappings, and put on the garb of the Christians. He then pushed into the middle of the crowd and cried out: "All your gods are demons, and our God alone is the Creator of the heavens!" This angered the prefect, who retorted: "By what rashness do you dare to call our gods demons? Where do you come from and what is your name?" George answered him: "My name is George, I come of noble forebears in Cappadocia. With the help of Christ I have conquered Palestine; but now I have left all that to serve the God of heaven more freely." The prefect, seeing that he could not win him over, commanded that he be stretched on the rack and had him torn limb from limb with hooks. His body was burned with flaming torches, and salt was rubbed into his gaping wounds. That very night the Lord appeared to him in the midst of a great light and so sweetly comforted him with his presence and his words that the saint thought nothing of his torments.

Dacian, now convinced that the infliction of pain was of no avail, summoned a certain magician and said to him: "It must be by their magical arts that the Christians make light of our tortures, and they hold sacrifice to our gods to be worthless." The magician replied: "If I cannot overcome his spells, let my head be forfeit." Thereupon, relying on his magic and invoking the names of his gods, he mixed poison into some wine and gave it to blessed George to drink; but the saint made the sign of the cross over the wine, drank it, and suffered no harm. The magician then put a stronger dose of poison into the wine, but the saint, again making the sign of the cross over the cup, drank with no ill effect. At this the magician prostrated himself at George's feet, begged his pardon with loud lamentation, and asked that he be made a Christian: for this he was beheaded in due time. The following day the prefect ordered George to be bound upon a wheel that was fitted with sharp knives, but the wheel fell apart at once and the saint remained unharmed. Dacian then had him plunged into a caldron of molten lead, but George made the sign of the cross and, by God's power, settled down as though he were in a refreshing bath.

Now, realizing that he was getting nowhere with threats and torments, Dacian thought he might bring the saint around with soft speech. "George, my son," he said, "you see how long-suffering our gods are; they put up with your blasphemies so patiently yet are ready to forgive you if you consent to be converted. Follow my advice, then, dearest son. Give up your superstition, sacrifice to our gods, and win great honors from them and from ourselves." George smiled and replied: "Why did you not say kind things to me before, instead of trying to overcome me by torture? So be it: I am ready to do as you say." Dacian, deluded, was glad to hear this and ordered the herald to call the whole populace together to see George, who had resisted so long, finally yield and worship the gods. The city was strung with garlands and filled with rejoicing, and all stood by as George came into the temple to offer sacrifice. He fell to his knees and prayed the Lord to destroy the temple with its idols so completely that, for the glory of God and the conversion of the people, nothing would be left of it. Immediately fire came down from heaven and consumed the temple, the idols, and the priests, and the earth opened and swallowed up anything that was left. Saint Ambrose says in his Preface for Saint George: "While Christianity was professed only under cover of silence, George, most loyal soldier of Christ, alone and intrepid among Christians openly professed his faith in the Son of God; and the grace of God, in return, gave him such fortitude that he could scorn the commands of tyrants and face the pain of innumerable torments. O blessed and noble fighter for the Lord! Not only was he not won over by the flattering promise of earthly power, but he fooled his persecutor and cast the images of his false gods into the abyss." Thus Ambrose.

When Dacian heard what had happened, he had George brought before him and said: "How evil can you be, you wickedest of men, that you could commit so great a crime!" George retorted: "You do me wrong, O king! Come along with me and watch me offer sacrifice again!" "You trickster!" Dacian exclaimed. "What you want to do is to get me swallowed up as you made the earth swallow the temple and my gods." "Miserable man!" George answered, "how can your gods, who could not help themselves, help you?" Enraged, the king said to Alexandria, his wife: "I shall faint, I shall die, because I see that this man has got the best of me." Her response was: "Cruel, bloodthirsty tyrant! Did I not tell you not to go on mistreating the Christians, because their God would fight for them? And now let me tell you that I want to become a Christian." Stupefied, the king cried: "Oh, worse and worse! So you too have been led astray!" Thereupon he had her hung up by the hair of her head and beaten with scourges. While she was being beaten, she said to George: "O George, light of truth, what do you think will become of me since I have not been reborn in the waters of baptism?" "You have nothing to fear, lady!" he answered. "The shedding of your blood will be both your baptism and your crown." With that she prayed to the Lord and breathed her last. Ambrose testifies to this, saying in his Preface: "For this reason the queen of the pagan Persians, though she had not yet been baptized, was shown mercy and received the palm of martyrdom when her cruel spouse had condemned her to death. Hence we may not doubt that she, crimson with the dew of her blood, gained entrance through the celestial portal and merited the kingdom of heaven." Thus Ambrose.

The following day George was sentenced to be dragged through the whole city and then beheaded. He prayed the Lord that all who implored his help might have their requests granted, and a heavenly voice came to him saying that it would be so. His prayer finished, his head was cut off and his martyrdom accomplished in the reign of the emperors Diocletian and Maximian, which began about the year of our Lord 287. As for Dacian, while he was on his way back to his palace from the place of execution, fire fell from above and consumed him and his attendants.

Gregory of Tours relates that some men were carrying away relics of Saint George and were given hospitality at a certain chapel overnight; and in the morning they were absolutely unable to move the casket containing the relics until they had shared them with the oratory. And in the *History of Antioch* we read that during the Crusades, when the Christians were on their way to besiege Jerusalem, a very beautiful young man appeared to a certain priest. He told the priest that he was Saint George, the captain of the Christian host, and that if the Crusaders carried his relics to Jerusalem, he would be with them. Then, when they had laid siege to the city, they did not dare mount the scaling ladders in the face of the Saracens' resistance; but Saint George appeared to them wearing white armor marked with the red cross, and made them understand that they could follow him up the walls in safety and the city would be theirs. Thus reassured, the army took the city and slaughtered the Saracens.

59. Saint Mark, Evangelist

Marcus, the Latin form of Mark, is interpreted: sublime by mandate, or certain, or bent over, or bitter. Mark the evangelist was sublime by mandate by reason of the perfection of his life: he observed not only the common commands but the sublime ones, such as the counsels. He was certain because he was sure about the doctrine of his gospel: he handed down the doctrine of his gospel as certain doctrine inasmuch as he had learned it from Saint Peter, his master. He was bent over in his profound humility, for it was due to his humility that he cut off his thumb, as we are told, in order to be judged unfit for the priesthood. He was bitter by the bitterness of the punishment he suffered, being dragged through the streets of the city and dying in the midst of these torments. Or Marcus may simply be *marcus*, a heavy hammer that breaks down the iron, rings out a musical note, and strengthens the anvil. Thus Mark, by the sole doctrine of his gospel, strikes down the perfidy of the heretics, rings out the praise of God, and strengthens the Church.

Mark the evangelist belonged by birth to the priestly tribe of Levi. He was a son of the apostle Peter by his baptism, and his disciple in the word of God. Mark went to Rome with Peter, and when the apostle preached the Gospel there, the faithful in Rome asked blessed Mark to put it in writing, so that it could be remembered in perpetuity. He did indeed write down the Gospel just as he had heard it from the lips of his master blessed Peter; and Peter, after examining the written text and finding it fully correct, approved it for acceptance by all Christians.

Peter saw Mark's constancy in the faith and sent him to Aquileia, where he preached the word of God and converted an innumerable multitude of pagans to the faith of Christ. He is said to have written a copy of his gospel there, and to this day the manuscript is shown in the church at Aquileia and is preserved with due devotion. Mark converted a citizen of Aquileia whose name was Hermagoras, and brought him to Peter in Rome to be consecrated as bishop of Aquileia. Hermagoras assumed the office of bishop and ruled the church in Aquileia perfectly until he was taken by the infidels and crowned with martyrdom.

Peter then sent Mark to Alexandria, and he was the first to preach the word of God there. Philo, that most learned of Jews, tells us that from the time of Mark's arrival in Alexandria a great multitude was brought together in faith and devotion and the practice of continence. Papias, the bishop of Hierapolis, also expounds his praises in exquisite language. Peter Damian has this to say about him: "[God] granted him so much grace in Alexandria that all those who flocked together to receive the rudiments of faith, quickly, by continence and persever-ance in a totally holy way of living, winged their way upwards to a peak of perfection that was really monastic. To this Mark urged them on not only by performing prodigious miracles nor by the eloquence of his preaching, but also by his illustrious example." Further on, Peter Damian continues: "It also came about that after he died, he was returned to Italy, so that the land where it had been given him to write his gospel won the privilege of possessing his sacred remains. Blessed are you, O Alexandria, purpled by that triumphal blood! Happy are you, O Italy, enriched by the treasure of that body!"

It is said that Mark was so humble that he amputated his thumb so that he could not by any human judgment be promoted to the order of priesthood. Nevertheless, Saint Peter's decision and authority prevailed, and he made Mark bishop of Alexandria. Just as he arrived in that city, his shoe fell apart, and in this Mark saw a spiritual meaning: "Truly God has cleared the road for me and has not allowed Satan to put obstacles in my way, since my dead works were already forgiven by the Lord." Mark saw a cobbler mending some old boots and gave him his shoe to be repaired, but in the course of the work the man wounded his left hand gravely and he exclaimed aloud: "One is God!" The bishop heard this and said: "Truly the Lord has prospered my journey!" He made clay with his spittle and spread it on the cobbler's hand, which was healed in an instant. Seeing this display of power, the man took Mark into his house and questioned him closely about who he was and where he came from. Mark told him forthrightly that he was a servant of the Lord Jesus. The man said: "I would like to see him!" Mark replied: "I will show him to you!" He began to instruct him about Christ, and the man was baptized with his whole household.

Now the men of that city heard that some Galilean had come there and was denouncing the cult of the gods, and they began to plot against him. Mark knew this, so he ordained the man he had healed, whose name was Anianus, to be bishop of Alexandria, and he himself went to Pentapolis. After preaching there for two years he returned to Alexandria and built a church on the rocks near the sea, at a place called Bucculi, where he found that the number of the faithful had grown substantially. The priests of the temple tried to lay hold of him, and while blessed Mark was celebrating mass on Easter Sunday, they all met there, put a rope around his neck, and dragged him through the city, shouting: "Let's haul the wild ox to the slaughterhouse!" Scraps of his flesh were strewn on the road and the stones were drenched with his blood. Then he was shut up in a jail, where he was comforted by an angel, and the Lord Jesus Christ came to give him courage, saying: "Mark, evangelist mine, fear not! I am with you to deliver you!"

When morning came, they again put a rope around his neck and dragged him hither and yon, calling out: "Haul the wild ox to the shambles!" As Mark was dragged along, he gave thanks, saying: "Into your hands, O Lord, I commend my spirit," and with these words he expired, in the reign of Nero, which began about the year of the Lord 57. The pagans wanted to burn the martyr's body, but suddenly the air was turbulent, hail drummed down, lightning flashed, and everyone's thought was to find shelter, so they left the holy body untouched, and Christians took it away and buried it with all reverence in the church.

Saint Mark was a well-built man of middle age, with a long nose, fine eyes, and a heavy beard, balding and graying at the temples. He was reserved in his relations and full of the grace of God. Saint Ambrose says of him: "Blessed Mark shone as a worker of countless miracles. It happened that a cobbler who was repairing a shoe for him wounded his left hand badly and cried out: 'One is God!' The servant of God rejoiced at hearing this. He made clay with his spittle, spread the clay on the man's hand, and cured the wound, and the cobbler was able to finish his work. Thus the saint imitated a miracle wrought by him whose Gospel he preached, who opened the eyes of the man born blind." Thus Ambrose.

In the year 468 after the incarnation of the Lord, in the reign of Emperor Leo, Venetians transferred the body of Saint Mark from Alexandria to Venice and built a wondrously beautiful church in his honor. The way this happened was that some Venetian merchants, who had business in Alexandria, by presents and promises induced the two priests who had charge of Saint Mark's body to let them secretly remove it and transport it to Venice. When the body was lifted from the tomb, an odor spread over the whole city of Alexandria—an odor so sweet that all the people wondered where it came from. As the sea journey progressed, the sailors let the crews of other ships know that they had the saint's body aboard. One of those informed said: "Maybe they gave you the corpse of some Egyptian, and you think it's the body of a saint!" Right away the ship that carried the saint's body turned itself around with astonishing speed, rammed the doubter's vessel, and could not be pulled loose until all aboard made it clear that they believed it was really Saint Mark's body.

Then one night when the ships were scudding before a high wind and the seamen, shaken by the violence of the storm and bewildered by the darkness, had no idea where they were headed, Saint Mark appeared to a monk who was guarding his body, and said: "Tell them to lower the sails quickly, because they are not far from land!" The sails came down, and at dawn all saw that they were lying close to an island. Wherever they went ashore, keeping the holy treasure hidden from everyone, the natives nonetheless came and called out: "Oh, how lucky you are to be carrying the body of Saint Mark! Do let us worship and pray to him!" Moreover, there was one incredulous seaman who was grabbed by a demon and sorely harassed until he was brought to the holy relic and declared that he believed. Being freed of the demon, he gave glory to God and thereafter held Saint Mark in high devotion.

The saint's body had been enclosed within a column formed of marble stones, and the location of the column in the church was known to very few persons, for reasons of security. What happened was that once these persons had departed this life, there was no one who knew where the sacred treasure was or could give any clue as to its whereabouts. This caused much lamentation in the church. A feeling of desolation spread among the faithful, and a cloud of grief hung over all; the devout folk, indeed, feared that their renowned patron had been taken away by stealth. Therefore a solemn fast was decreed; and lo and behold, in full sight and to the wonderment of all, the stones bounced out of the column and the casket that hid the saint's body was visible. Prayers of praise went up to the

Creator, who had deigned to show their patron to the people, and the day that had been glorified by such a prodigious event was observed as a feast in later years.

A young man whose chest was being eaten away by cancer began to implore Saint Mark's help with heartfelt devotion. Then, while he slept, someone in the garb of a pilgrim, who seemed to be hurrying to reach some destination, appeared to him. The young man asked the pilgrim who he was and where he was going in such haste. He answered that he was Saint Mark, and that he was hurrying to reach a ship in danger, whose crew was calling upon him for help. Mark extended his hand and touched the sick man, who woke up in the morning to find himself cured. In a short time that ship came to a Venetian port, and the seamen reported the danger they had been in and how Saint Mark had saved them.

In Alexandria some Venetian merchants had taken passage in a Saracen ship and, when they were at sea, saw that the ship was in imminent danger. They therefore got into the skiff that was towed by the vessel and cut the rope, whereupon the ship sank and a voracious wave swept all the Saracens under. One of them, however, invoked Saint Mark as he was able to do, and bound himself by a vow to be baptized if the saint came to his rescue, and to visit his church. Instantly a shining man appeared to him, plucked him out of the sea, and deposited him in the skiff with the Venetians. This man finally got back to Alexandria and, showing no thankfulness for his rescue, neither made a visit to Saint Mark's church nor received the sacraments of our faith. Mark appeared to him again and reproached him for his ingratitude. So, realizing the wrong he had done, he went to Venice, was reborn at the sacred font of baptism, took the name of Mark, professed faith in Christ, and lived out his life in good works.

A man was working at the top of the bell tower of Saint Mark's in Venice, and suddenly and unexpectedly fell from the tower, injured in every limb; but even as he fell, he was not forgetful of Saint Mark. He besought the saint's aid and landed on an unhoped-for plank that jutted out from the structure. A rope was passed to him, and, with all his hurts mended, he devoutly went up to finish the work he had started.

A man who was temporarily in service to a certain provincial noble had made a vow to visit the body of Saint Mark but could not obtain his master's permission to do so. In time, however, he put the fear of the Lord ahead of the fear of his master in the flesh and, without a word of farewell, devoutly went off to visit the saint. The master felt resentment at this and, when the servant came back, ordered his eyes put out. The ruffians who waited on him, more cruel than their master and ever ready to do his bidding, threw the servant of God to the ground as he invoked Saint Mark, and set about poking his eyes out with sharp-pointed sticks; but try as they might, they got nowhere with the sticks, which simply went to pieces. Their master then ordered them to break the man's legs and cut off his feet with hatchets, but the hard iron of the tools melted into lead. "Well, then, smash in his mouth and knock out his teeth with iron hammers!" But the iron forgot its strength and by God's power was blunted. The master, seeing all this, was taken aback, begged God's pardon, and with his servant visited the tomb of Saint Mark with earnest devotion.

A knight in battle had his arm so grievously wounded that the hand hung loose from the wrist. The doctors and his friends advised him to have the hand amputated, but the knight, thinking of the embarrassment of being maimed, instead had the hand tied in place with bandages and medicaments. He then invoked Saint Mark's aid, and the injury was immediately righted. All that was left of the wound was the scar, as evidence of the miracle and a monument to the great blessing granted to the knight.

A man in the city of Mantua was falsely accused by slanderers and put in prison. After forty days he could not stand confinement any longer. He disciplined himself by fasting for three days, then prayed to Saint Mark for help. The saint appeared to him and ordered him to leave the prison without hindrance. Half asleep with boredom, he thought he was suffering illusions and did not obey the saint's order, but Mark repeated the visit and the order a second and third time. Now the prisoner paid attention, and, seeing the door wide open, broke his shackles as if they were flaxen thread and walked out at midday unmolested, passing by the jailers and everyone else, seeing them all but invisible to them. He went to Saint Mark's tomb and devoutly paid his debt of thanks.

There was a time when the earth lay sterile throughout Apulia, and no rain fell to bless it with fertility. Then by a revelation it was known that this plague had befallen the land because the feast of Saint Mark was not observed there. The people therefore invoked the saint and promised that they would celebrate his feast, so Mark banished the sterility and, by sending salubrious air and the needed rain, provided the people with plenty.

About the year of the Lord 1212, in the city of Pavia and the convent of the Order of Friars Preachers, there was a friar named Julian, a native of Faenza who was known for his religious and holy life. He was young in body but aged in wisdom, and he lay mortally ill. Julian talked with the prior of the house and asked about his condition, and the prior told him that he was close to death. At once his face shone with happiness. He applauded with his hands and his whole body, and loudly exclaimed: "Make room, brothers, because for the great abundance of its gladness my soul is about to leap out of my body, and I have already heard happy rumors about it!" He raised his hands to heaven and said: "Bring my soul out of prison, that I may praise thy name! Unhappy man that I am, who shall deliver me from the body of this death?"

With this he fell into a deep sleep and saw Saint Mark coming to him and lying down beside him. Then he heard a voice saying: "What are you doing here, Mark?" Mark answered: "I have come close to this dying friar because his ministry is accepted by God!" Again the voice: "Why have you come especially to this man among so many other saints?" And Mark: "Because he had special devotion for me and with constant piety visited the place where my body rests. Therefore I came to visit him in the hour of his extremity." Then others, clad in white garments, filled the whole house. "Why have you come?" Mark asked them. "To bring the soul of this friar into the presence of the Lord," they answered.

The friar awakened and immediately sent for the prior of the house (from whom I myself heard all this), told him all that he had seen, and with much joy fell happily asleep in the Lord.

======= ✳ =======

60. Saint Marcellinus, Pope

Marcellinus ruled the Church of Rome for nine years and four months. By order of Emperors Diocletian and Maximian he was taken prisoner and brought forward to offer sacrifice. At first he refused and was threatened with various kinds of torture, and for fear of the threatened suffering he put down two grains of incense in sacrifice to the gods. This gave great joy to the infidels but caused the faithful immense sadness. However, under a weak head strong members rise up and make little of the threats of princes; so the faithful came to the pope and reproached him severely. He realized the gravity of his error and offered himself to be judged by a council of bishops. The bishops responded: "It is not possible for the supreme pontiff to be judged by anyone; but you yourself weigh your case in your own mind and pronounce your own judgment." The pope, repentant, lamented his fault and deposed himself, but the whole gathering immediately reelected him. When the emperors heard of this, they had him arrested again. He absolutely refused to offer sacrifice, so they sentenced him to beheading. Then the persecution was renewed with such fury that in one month seventeen thousand Christians were put to death.

When Marcellinus was about to be beheaded, he declared himself unworthy of Christian burial and excommunicated all who might presume to bury him. Thus his body lay above ground for thirty-five days. At the end of that time the apostle Peter appeared to Marcellus, who had succeeded as pope, and said: "Brother Marcellus, why do you not bury me?" Marcellus replied: "Have you not yet been buried, my lord?" Peter: "I consider myself unburied as long as I see Marcellinus unburied!" "But don't you know, my lord," Marcellus asked, "that he laid a curse on anyone who buried him?" Peter: "Is it not written that he who humbles himself shall be exalted? You should have kept this in mind! Now go and bury him at my feet!" Marcellus went straightaway and carried out the orders laudably.

※

---

61. Saint Vitalis

Vitalis could be from *vivens talis*, living such or living the same as, because Saint Vitalis lived outwardly in his works such as he was inwardly in his heart. Or the name comes from *vita*, life, or the word is formed from *vivens alis*, i.e., shielding oneself with the wings of the virtues. The saint was like one of the animals of God that Ezechiel saw, having four wings—the wing of hope, by which he flew to heaven, the wing of love, by which he flew to God, the wing of fear, by which he flew to hell, and the wing of knowledge, by which he flew into himself.

The account of his martyrdom is thought to have been found in the book of Saints Gervasius and Protasius.

Vitalis, a consular knight, fathered Gervasius and Protasius by his wife, Valeria. He once went to Ravenna with Paulinus, a judge, and there observed the trial of a physician named Ursicinus. Having undergone many tortures and been condemned to be beheaded, Ursicinus was shaking with fear, and Vitalis called out to him: "O doctor and brother Ursicinus, you have made a practice of curing others, do not now kill yourself with an eternal death! You have come to the palm by caring for the sufferings of many. Do not lose the crown prepared for you by God!" Ursicinus was strengthened by these words, repented of his fears, and freely accepted martyrdom; and Saint Vitalis saw to it that he received honorable burial.

After this experience Vitalis could not bring himself to rejoin his superior, Paulinus. The judge took this very badly, not simply because Vitalis would not come back to him, but also because he had dissuaded a willing Ursicinus from sacrificing to the idols, and because he had publicly declared himself a Christian. He therefore ordered him to be stretched on the rack. "Stupid man," Vitalis said, "do you think you can fool me, when I have been so zealous about liberating others?" "Take him to the palm tree," Paulinus ordered, "and if he will not sacrifice, dig a ditch there so deep that you reach water, and bury him alive and lying on his back!" His men did as ordered and buried Vitalis alive, in the reign of Nero, which began about A.D. 52.

The pagan priest who had recommended this form of punishment was seized at once by a demon, and raged and raved for seven days at the site of the burial, crying out: "You are setting me on fire, Vitalis!" On the seventh day he was pitched into the river by the demon and perished miserably.

Valeria, the wife of Saint Vitalis, was on her way to Milan when she saw some men sacrificing to the idols. They urged her to join them and to eat some of the immolated foods, but she responded: "I am a Christian, and it is not licit for me to eat food from your sacrifices!" Hearing this, they beat her so brutally that the men who accompanied her brought her half dead into Milan, and three days later she migrated happily to the Lord.

✳

62. A Virgin of Antioch

There was a certain virgin in Antioch whose story Ambrose set forth in the second book of his *De Virginibus*, as follows.

In recent times there was a virgin in Antioch who shrank from being seen in public. But the more she avoided the eyes of the lustful, the more she enkindled their desire. Beauty that is heard about but not seen is the more desired, due to two stimuli, erotic love and knowledge, since nothing displeasing meets the eye, and beauty known about is imagined as all the more pleasing. The eye is not exploring in order to judge, but the lustful heart craves.

This holy virgin was determined to safeguard her virtue and shut herself off from the eyes of the libidinous so as to discourage their hopes; but she did this so thoroughly that they stopped longing for her and sought to betray her. Hence persecution. The girl had no means of fleeing and, being young, feared that she might fall into traps set by the impure, so she prepared herself to be strong. She was so religious that she did not fear death, so chaste that she looked forward to it. The day of her crowning was at hand, and great was the expectation of all: a young girl is brought forward who professes herself ready to wage a twofold war, for her virginity and her religion. But when they recognized the constancy of her profession and her fear for her virtue, when they saw her blushing when looked at but prepared to suffer torture, they began to consider how to take away her religion and leave her the hope of saving her chastity, so that when she had been deprived of what mattered the most, they might then snatch away what was left. So the order is given: either the virgin sacrifices to the gods or she is prostituted in a brothel.

How can they think they are worshiping their gods when they vindicate them by such means? How do they live, those who judge this way? This girl has no doubts about her religion but fears for her purity and says to herself: "What do we do today—martyrdom or virginity? Either crown is denied us. But the very name of virgin is unknown to whoever denies the author of virginity. How can you be a virgin and worship a harlot? How can you be a virgin and love an adulterer? How can you be a virgin if you seek carnal love? It is more meritorious to keep the mind virginal than the flesh. Both are good if possible, but if not possible, let us at least be chaste in God's sight if not in men's. Rahab was a harlot, but after she believed in the Lord, she found salvation. Judith decked herself in silks and jewels in order to charm an adulterer, but, because she did this for religion's sake and not for love, no one thought of her as an adulteress. The example is well found, because if Judith, who committed herself to religion, saved both her chastity and her country, perhaps we too, by keeping our religion, will preserve our chastity. But if Judith had thought more of her chastity than of her religion, having lost her country she would likewise have lost her purity."

Strengthened by the thought of these examples, the virgin silently pondered in her mind the words of the Lord: "He that shall lose his life for me shall find it."[1] She wept, saying no words lest an adulterer should even hear her speak; nor did she choose injury to her chastity but recoiled from doing injury to Christ. Judge whether she, who would not commit adultery even by the sound of her voice, could commit it with her body.

This long time what I have been saying has made me feel shame, and now I shudder to bring up a series of ignominious deeds and dwell upon them. Virgins of God, shut your ears! The maiden of God is led to the bawdy house. But open your ears, virgins of God! A virgin may be exposed to prostitution, she cannot be made an adulteress. Wherever a virgin of God is, there is Christ's temple. Brothels do not defile chastity, but chastity abolishes the shame even of such places.

Now comes a rush of the wanton to the house of ill fame. Holy virgins, learn here the miracles of the young martyr, learn the language of these places! The dove is caught within, the birds of prey clamor without, all fight to see who will be the first to pounce on the prey. But she raises her hands to heaven as if she had come to a house of prayer and not to an abode of lust, and says: "O Christ, for a virgin you made wild lions tame, you can also tame the fierce hearts of men. Fire rained down on the Chaldeans. By your mercy and not by its nature the sea divided to make way for the Jews. Susanna went to her knees on the way to

[1] Matt. 10:39.

execution and triumphed over the lecherous old men. The right hand that was desecrating the gifts of your temple shriveled. Now vile hands are reaching for the body that is your temple. Do not allow this incestuous sacrilege, you who would not allow the thief to steal. And blessed be your name, because I came here to be ravished of my virginity, I will leave here still a virgin."

Hardly had she finished her prayer when a knight, formidable of aspect, broke through the crowd around her. How must the maiden have trembled, when the people made way for fear of him! But she did not forget what she had read. "Daniel," she said to herself, "had come merely to see judgment done on Susanna, but he, single-handed, won freedom for her whom the crowd condemned. It may be that a sheep is hiding here under wolf's clothing. Christ too has his soldiers, indeed his legions. Or it may be the headsman who has come, but fear not, my soul! Headsmen make martyrs!"

O virgin, your faith has saved you! The knight says to her: "Do not be afraid, my sister! I came here to save your soul, not to lose it. Save me, so that I may save you! I came in like an adulterer, but if you will it, I shall go out a martyr. Let us exchange our clothing. Mine will suit you and yours me, and both will suit Christ. Your garb will make me a true soldier and mine will keep you a virgin. You will be well clothed, and I will be better off unclothed, so that the executioner may recognize me. Take my clothing, which will hide the fact that you are a woman, and give me yours, which will consecrate me for martyrdom. Wrap this cloak around you to conceal your maidenly form and protect your chastity. Put on this bonnet, to cover your hair and hide your face: those who have been in a brothel usually hide their blushes. Be careful not to look back when you go out of here. Remember Lot's wife, who lost her natural life because she looked at unchaste men, even though with chaste eyes. Have no fear, nothing will be missing in the sacrifice. In your place I will make myself an offering to my God, and in my place you will be a soldier of Christ, fighting the good fight of chastity, waged for eternal wages—the breastplate of righteousness to clothe the body with spiritual protection, the shield of faith to ward off wounds, and the helmet of salvation. Where Christ is, there is the stronghold of our salvation. As the husband is the head of the wife, so Christ is the head of virgins."

As he said these words he took off the cloak that made him seem both a persecutor and an adulterer. The virgin offered her head to the executioner, the knight his mantle to the virgin. What a spectacle! What grace, when in a house of sin the actors, a knight and a virgin, vie with each other for martyrdom! By nature they are unlike, yet are similar by God's mercy; and the oracle "The wolf and the lamb shall feed together"[2] is fulfilled. Indeed they do not merely feed together, they are immolated together.

What more can I tell you? The cloak is exchanged, the girl flies out of the trap, yet not on her own wings, since she is borne up on spiritual wings; and—

[2] Isa. 65:25.

what had never before been seen down through the ages—a virgin of Christ walks out of a brothel. But those who saw with their eyes and did not see with their heart—wolves they were!—roared at their prey like wolves in pursuit of a lamb. One of them, more shameless than the rest, went in, but when his eyes took in the situation, he exclaimed: "What's this? A girl came in here, but I see a man! This is no fabulous doe in place of a maiden. This is real! A maiden is changed into a knight! I had heard and had not believed that Christ had changed water into wine, but here is a change of sex. Let us get out of here while we still are what we were! Could it be that I myself am changed—I who think I see one thing and see something different? I came to the brothel: what I see is a switch of persons. The change is made. I will leave, I will go out pure, I who came in an adulterer!" So the knight is judged guilty and the crown belongs to this great winner. He is condemned in place of the virgin because he was apprehended in place of the virgin. So not only virgins but martyrs came out of that house.

The story goes on that the girl ran to the place of torture, and that the two contended for the right to die. The knight said: "I'm the one who's condemned to death. That sentence sets you free. I'm the one they arrested!" The maiden cried out: "I didn't choose you to stand in for me! I wanted you as a protector of my virtue. If they're after my chastity, I'm still a woman, but if blood is what they want, I don't want anyone to bail me out. I have what I need to pay what I owe, and I'm the one for whom the sentence was intended. Certainly if I had given you as surety for a sum I owed, and when I stayed away and the judge made you pay my debt to the lender, you could get a court order compelling me to reimburse you out of my inheritance. If I refused, who would not deem me worthy of death? And how much more so when a capital sentence is involved! I will die innocent so as not to die guilty! There is no middle ground now; either I will be guilty of your blood or I will shed my own as a martyr! I came here in such haste: who will dare to shut me out? If I had stayed away, who would dare to absolve me? I would owe more to the laws as guilty not only of being a fugitive but of causing the death of another. My body is strong enough to bear death, but I could not bear to do such an injustice. There is room in this virgin for wounds, but none for dishonor. I have shrunk from shame, not from martyrdom. I changed my clothing, I have not changed what I professed to be. If you snatch my death away from me, you will not have redeemed me: you will have cheated me! So please don't argue with me, don't dare to contradict me. Don't take away the good you have done me. When you deny this latest sentence against me, you revive the earlier one. The earlier sentence voids the later one; if the second does not hold me, the first one does. We can satisfy both sentences if you allow me to suffer first. They can inflict other punishments on you, but in a virgin the price will be her chastity; so you will win greater glory if you make a martyr out of a virgin than if you turn a martyr into an adulteress."

What outcome do you expect? the two compete and the two win: the crown is not divided, a second crown is added. So the two holy martyrs did well for each other—she by giving him the opportunity for martyrdom, he by allowing her to profit by it.

The schools of the philosophers make much of two Pythagoreans named Damon and Pythias, one of whom, having been sentenced to death, asked for some time to settle his private affairs. The wily tyrant who had condemned him, figuring that he would be unable to find a bondsman, demanded that he designate someone who would suffer in his place if he failed to appear. Which of the two was the more renowned I do not know: both were famous. The one found a surety for his death, the other offered himself. So when the condemned man did not appear at the appointed time, the guarantor, unperturbed, did not refuse to die in his place. As he was being led to the place of execution, the guilty man came back, pushed his friend aside, and put his head on the block. The tyrant, admiring the conduct of the philosophers who held friendship dearer than life, begged the two whom he had condemned to admit him to their friendship: such was the grace of virtue that it won the tyrant over. . . . Praiseworthy, yes, but less so than our pair. For one thing, the others were both men, whereas one of ours was a young woman who had first to overcome the weakness of her sex; the other two were friends while our two were unknown to each other; the friends offered themselves to one tyrant, but ours to several even crueler ones; and the one tyrant granted pardon while the cruel ones dealt death. Of the two men one was bound by a compelling need, in our two there was complete freedom of choice on both sides. The two men were more calculating, having more at stake, namely, their friendship: for the virgin and the knight the goal was martyrdom. The friends contended for men, the martyrs for God. Thus Ambrose.

63. Saint Peter Martyr

The name Petrus, Peter, is interpreted as knowing or recognizing, or as taking off one's shoes; or Peter comes from *petros*, firm. Hence three privileges possessed by Saint Peter are indicated. He was an outstanding preacher and therefore is called knowing, because he had perfect knowledge of the Scriptures and, in preaching, recognized what met the needs of each hearer. He was a most pure virgin and so is called one who takes off his shoes, because he removed and put off all earthly love from the feet of his affections and inclinations: in that way he was virgin not only in his body but in his mind. Third, he was a glorious martyr of the Lord and so was firm, because he bore martyrdom with constancy in defense of the faith.

Peter the New, called Peter Martyr, of the Order of Preachers,[1] a renowned fighter for the faith, was a native of the city of Verona. He emerged like a radiant light in a cloud of smoke, or a white lily among briars, or a red rose among thorns. This brilliant preacher was the son of parents who were blinded by error; his virginal honor rose from among people corrupt in body and soul; this celebrated martyr stood out from among thorns, meaning those destined for eternal fire.

Peter did indeed have unbelieving, heretical parents, but he kept himself unsullied by their error. Once when he was seven years old and was home from school, his uncle, who reeked of heresy, asked him what he was learning. He answered that he had learned: "I believe in God the Father almighty, creator of heaven and earth." His uncle retorted: "Don't say 'creator of heaven and earth,' because God was not the creator of visible things. The devil created all that is visible."[2] The boy answered that he would rather say what he had learned and read, and would rather believe what Scripture says. Then the uncle tried to change the boy's mind by quoting his authorities, but Peter, being filled with the Holy Spirit, turned them against the uncle and slew the man with his own sword, so to speak, leaving him disarmed and unable to parry. The uncle was indignant at being outdone by a mere child and reported the whole incident to the father, using every argument he could think of to induce the father to take little Peter out of school. "I am afraid," he said, "that when young Peter has finished his studies, he will rally to the harlot church of Rome and thus confuse and destroy our faith." He did not know how truly he spoke when, like Caiaphas, he prophesied that Peter would destroy the false doctrines of the heretics. But because God was in control, the father did not agree with his brother, hoping that as Peter progressed in the grammatical arts, some master heretic would draw him into their sect.

The holy youngster saw that it was not safe to dwell with scorpions, so he left the world and his family behind and joined the Order of Friars Preachers. Pope Innocent in his letter stresses the praiseworthy life that Peter lived in that Order. "Peter in his adolescent years," he wrote, "prudently turned away from the world's deceits and entered the Order of Friars Preachers. For thirty years, upheld by a troop of virtues with faith in the lead, hope standing by, and charity accompanying, he prevailed and progressed in the defense of the faith, for which he burned with zeal. Against its fierce enemies he waged continuous warfare with intrepidity of mind and fervor of spirit, and happily brought his long struggle to a close with the victory of martyrdom. Thus Peter, firm upon the rock of

---

[1] The Order of Saint Dominic, or Dominicans.

[2] The Catharist heresy, like the Albigensian, against which Peter of Verona fought as an inquisitor, condemned all matter as evil.

faith and hurled against the rock of suffering, rose, worthy of the martyr's crown, to the rock of Christ."

Peter always guarded his virginity of mind and body, and never felt the touch of mortal sin, as is proved by the faithful testimony of his confessors. Because a slave too delicately nourished may turn against his master, Peter subdued his body by the sparse use of food and drink. For fear that through idleness and sloth he might fall victim to the wiles of the enemy, he constantly subjected himself to the just ordinances of the Lord. Since he was totally occupied with what was commanded, there was no room in his life for what was forbidden, and he was safe from spiritual failings. During the silent hours of night that are given to man for his repose, Peter, after a brief sleep, applied himself to the study of the readings[3] and spent the time for sleep in prayerful watching. It would soon be day with its tasks—the needs of souls to be cared for, sermons to be prepared and preached, confessions to be heard, and the heretics' pestiferous doctrine to be refuted with valid reasonings, for which he was blessed with a gift of special grace. Pleasing to God in his devoutness, mild in his humility, calm in obedience, tender in kindness, compassionate in his feeling for others, constant in patience, preeminent in charity, and well founded in the maturity of his conduct in all circumstances, he attracted people by the spreading aroma of his virtues. He was also a fervent lover of the true faith and zealous in practicing it, and he fought strenuously in its defense. The faith was so deeply imprinted upon his spirit, and he bound himself so totally to its service, that every one of his words and works reflected the virtue of faith. He also longed to suffer death for the faith and is known to have begged the Lord, with frequent, earnest appeals, not to let him leave this life until he had drunk for him from the chalice of his passion. Nor was he disappointed of his hopes.

Blessed Peter was renowned for the many miracles he performed in his lifetime. For instance, in Milan he was examining a heretical bishop whom the faithful had taken prisoner, and many bishops and religious and the greater part of the city population had gathered to witness the trial. Moreover, with his preaching and his questioning of the bishop the hours were getting longer and the extreme summer heat was bothering all those present, when the heresiarch said for all to hear: "O wrongheaded Peter, if you are as holy as these stupid people say you are, why are you letting them die of the heat? Why don't you ask the Lord to put a cloud in front of the sun to keep the people from death by overheating?" To this Peter responded: "If you are willing to promise to renounce your heresy and return to the Catholic faith, I will ask the Lord and he will do as you said." The backers of the heretics called out to the heresiarch, saying: "Promise! Promise!" They thought, of course, that what Peter had pledged himself to do before all the people could not be done, especially since

---

[3] No doubt the lessons from Scripture, the martyrology, and elsewhere, which were read in the liturgical hours and at other assemblies.

there was not so much as a wisp of cloud in the sky. On the other hand, the Catholics began to worry about Peter's promise, fearing that by it the Catholic faith might be discredited.

The heretical bishop refused to commit himself, but blessed Peter, with sure confidence, said: "To the end that the true God be shown to be the creator of all that is visible and invisible, and for the reassurance of the faithful and the confusion of heretics, I ask God to make some small bit of cloud form and place itself between the sun and the people." He made the sign of the cross, and for a whole hour a cloud spread across the sky like a tent, protecting the people from the sun.

A man named Asserbus, who had been paralyzed for five years and had to be pulled from place to place on a kind of sled, was brought to blessed Peter in Milan. When Peter made the sign of the cross over him, he was cured forthwith and stood up.

Pope Innocent, in the letter already referred to, relates some more miracles that God wrought through Peter in the saint's lifetime. He says: "The son of a certain nobleman had such a large growth in his throat that it was very hard for him to speak or even to breathe. Blessed Peter raised his hands over him and put his mantle around him, and the sick man was cured instantly. The same nobleman was stricken later on with violent convulsions. Thinking and fearing that he was in imminent danger of death, he had the saint's mantle, which he had kept, brought to him. He placed it on his chest and quickly vomited a worm that had two heads and was covered with thick hairs. This achieved his complete cure. The saint put his finger into the mouth of a mute young man, broke the string that tied his tongue, and obtained for him the blessing of speech. God deigned to do these and many other miracles through Peter during his lifetime." Thus far Innocent.

The plague of heresy was spreading in Lombardy and already infecting many cities with its pestiferous contagion. To wipe out this diabolical pestilence, the supreme pontiff dispatched a number of inquisitors, all members of the Order of Friars Preachers, to various areas of the province. In Milan the heretics were very numerous, occupied places of secular power, and made effective use of their fraudulent eloquence and devilish knowledge. The pope knew that blessed Peter was a man of great courage and was not to be intimidated by great numbers of enemies. He also was aware of the unshakable virtue that would keep Peter from making the slightest concession to his adversaries' power. Furthermore he knew that Peter's eloquence could easily lay bare the heretics' deceptions and that he was deeply learned in divine wisdom and could by reasoning refute the frivolous arguments of the heretics. Therefore the pope appointed this stout fighter for the faith to the city and county of Milan, and made him his chief inquisitor with plenary authority.

Peter applied himself diligently to his work as inquisitor and sought out the heretics wherever they were, giving them neither rest nor quarter. He ably confounded and powerfully repulsed them, wisely and subtly arguing with them so that they could not resist the wisdom and the Spirit that spoke through him. The heretics saw this and were pained by it, so they began to take counsel with their henchmen about killing him. They thought they would be able to live in peace if this mighty persecutor was removed from their midst. So, one day when the intrepid preacher, soon to be a martyr, was traveling from Como to Milan to search for heretics, he won the palm of martyrdom on the way.

Innocent describes the event as follows: "He was on the road from the city of Como, where he was prior of the house of the friars of his Order, to Milan, to carry on the inquisition against the heretics that had been entrusted to him by the Holy See. Then, as he had predicted in his public preaching, one of the heretics' men, won over by their pleas and payments, fell upon him furiously as he pursued his salutary purpose. It was the wolf against the lamb, the savage against the meek, the impious against the pious, the enraged against the gentle, the furious against the calm, the profane against the saint. He undertakes the assault, carries out his attempt with murderous intent, cruelly strikes the sacred head, and inflicts frightful wounds until his sword is glutted with the blood of the just. Meanwhile the venerable victim does not turn away from his assailant but presents himself as a willing sacrifice, patiently submitting to his attacker's savage blows. So he sent his spirit soaring heavenward at the very spot where he suffered, while the sacrilegious murderer still rained blows upon the minister of Christ. He uttered no word of complaint, no groan or moan, but suffered all patiently and commended his soul to the Lord, saying: 'Into thy hands, O Lord, I commend my spirit.' He also began to recite the Creed, of which even at the moment of death he was still the herald. This was reported by the assassin himself, who was captured by the faithful, and by a Dominican friar who had accompanied Peter, and was mortally wounded by the same assailant and died a few days later. But even while the Lord's martyr was breathing his last, the cruel killer snatched up a dagger and drove it into his side."

Thus, on the day of his martyrdom, Saint Peter somehow merited to be confessor, martyr, prophet, and doctor. He was confessor in that amidst torments he, with utmost constancy, confessed the faith of Christ, and on that same day, having made his confession in the usual way, he offered the sacrifice of praise to God. He was martyr in that he shed his blood in defense of the faith, prophet in that on the morning of that day he made a prediction. He had come down with the quartan fever, and his companions told him that they would not be able to reach Milan from Como. He answered: "If we cannot get as far as the friars' house, we can lodge for the night at Saint Simplicianus." And that is what happened. The brothers carried the sacred body to Milan, but the crowds were so dense that they could not get to the priory. So they deposited the holy remains for the night in the church of Saint Simplicianus. He was doctor in that even as he suffered he taught the true faith, reciting the Creed in a loud, clear voice.

Peter's venerable passion is seen to be similar in many ways to the passion of Christ. Christ suffered for the truth that he preached, Peter for the truth of the faith that he defended; Christ was made to suffer by the unbelieving Jewish people, Peter by the unbelieving crowd of the heretics; Christ was crucified at the time of Passover, Peter suffered martyrdom in the same season; when Christ suffered he said: "Into thy hands, O Lord, I commend my spirit"; Peter loudly pronounced the same prayer in his last moments. Christ, moreover, was betrayed and crucified for thirty pieces of silver, Peter was betrayed and murdered for forty pounds Pavian. By his passion Christ brought many to the faith, Peter by his martyrdom converted many heretics; for although this eminent doctor and fighter for the faith had done much in his lifetime to eradicate the pestiferous dogma of the heretics, after his death, due to his merits and sparkling miracles, the heresy was uprooted so far that great numbers relinquished their error and hurried back to the bosom of holy Church. The city and county of Milan, where many clusters of heretics had existed, were so thoroughly purged of heresy that, with many heretics exiled and many more converted to the faith, none dared to show themselves there any longer. Moreover, many of the greatest and most famous preachers of the time entered the Order, and until now[4] they are pursuing heretics and their partisans with admirable zeal. So our Samson has killed more Philistines by dying than he killed while alive. Thus the grain of wheat, falling into the ground and caught and killed by the hands of unbelievers, brings forth abundant fruit; thus the bunch of grapes, crushed in the winepress, gives out juice in plenty; thus spices, ground in the mortar, pour forth a richer perfume; thus mustard seed is all the stronger once it is pulverized.

After the holy man's glorious triumph the Lord honored him with many miracles, some of which the supreme pontiff has related, saying: "After Peter's death the lamps that hang around his tomb have several times lighted up by divine action, without any human assistance; it was indeed appropriate that for one who had shone brilliantly with the fire and light of faith, so singular a miracle of fire and light should occur. A man who, while he was at table with some others, spoke disparagingly of Peter's holiness, to prove his point took a morsel of food, saying that if what he said about Peter was unfair, he would be unable to swallow the morsel. Quickly he felt the food stick in his throat so that he could neither swallow it nor cough it up, and, as his face changed color, he realized that he could choke to death. He repented of his malicious talk and inwardly made a vow that he would never again say such things, and at once he was able to bring up the morsel and his life was saved. A woman who suffered

---

[4] Peter was martyred in 1252, and Jacobus compiled the *Legenda* in the late 1250s. "Until now" (*usque nunc*) suggests a period of time later than the composition of the *Legenda*. Graesse, 284 n. 2 and 288 n. 1, notes that most of the anecdotes in the second half of this chapter, beginning with the one that opens "In Florence a young man, a heretic . . . ," are not in the Ed. Pr. and therefore are later additions.

from dropsy came, with the help of her husband, to the place where Saint Peter had been killed. There she prayed to him and quickly recovered her health.

"The martyr himself helped women possessed by demons, forcing the evil spirits to come out of the women's bodies with much vomiting of blood; and he cured fevers and many other and diverse afflictions. A man had a skin disease that punctured a finger on his left hand in many places. Peter cured him and gave him wonderful comfort. A child had suffered a fall and was so badly injured that he had neither feeling nor movement and was mourned as dead, but some of the earth that had been spattered by the martyr's sacred blood was placed on the boy's chest and he stood up unhurt. Another woman whose flesh was being eaten away by a cancer had some of this same earth applied to her wound and was cured. And there were others who had various diseases and were brought to the saint's tomb in wagons or other vehicles. There their ills were fully cured and they were able to go home without further help."

When Pope Innocent iv inscribed blessed Peter's name in the catalog of the saints, the friars met in chapter at Milan and resolved to transfer the martyr's body to a higher place, since it had lain below ground for over a year. They found the body sound and uncorrupted, without the slightest odor of decay, as if it had been buried that very day. The friars with great reverence placed the body on a large catafalque beside the road where he had been murdered, and then displayed it whole and entire for all the people to see and venerate.

Besides the miracles above described as related in the pope's letter, a great many more are remembered. Many religious men and women and numbers of other people have seen lights descending from heaven over the site of the martyrdom, and have testified that they saw two friars in Dominican habits surrounded by these lights.

A young man named Geoffrey or Godfrey, who lived in the city of Como, had a piece of cloth that was cut from Saint Peter's mantle. A certain heretic laughed at him and said that he would believe Peter was a saint if the youth threw the cloth into the fire and the cloth did not burn. This would prove beyond any doubt that Peter was a saint, and the heretic would adhere to his faith. So the young man threw the cloth on burning coals, but the cloth bounced high out of the fire, and then on its own power jumped back upon the coals and extinguished them completely. The unbeliever said: "So! My own cloak would do the same thing!" They lighted another fire and a piece of the heretic's cloak was laid on one side, and the cloth from Saint Peter's on the other. The minute the heretic's cloth felt the heat of the fire, it went up in flames, whereas Peter's patch prevailed over the fire and put it out, and not a thread of the cloth was as much as scorched. The heretic observed this, returned to the way of faith, and told everyone about the miracle.

In Florence a young man, a heretic and a profligate, was in the friars' church with some companions, looking at a painting that depicted the martyrdom of Saint Peter; and, seeing the assassin striking him with his unsheathed sword, the young man exclaimed: "If I had been there, I'd have hit him harder!" No sooner had he uttered these words than he was stricken dumb. When his companions asked him what was the matter with him, he could not answer, so they took him home. But on the way he saw the church of Saint Michael, slipped away from his friends, and went into the church. He knelt and prayed from the heart to Saint Peter, asking the saint to spare him, binding himself by a vow to confess his sins and renounce all heresy if he was cured. Suddenly he recovered the power of speech, went to the friars' house, abjured his heresy, and confessed his sins, giving his confessor permission to preach about this to the people. Then, in the middle of the sermon, the young man stood up and, in the presence of a great multitude, told the whole story himself.

A ship was in distress far out at sea, enveloped in the blackness of night and almost swamped by the fury of the waves. The people aboard called for help from various saints but, seeing no sign of rescue, were overcome with fear of imminent doom. Then one of them, a Genoese, called for silence and addressed them as follows: "Men and brothers, have you not heard how a friar of the Order of Preachers, Friar Peter by name, was recently killed by heretics because of his defense of the faith, and how God has marked him out by many signs? Now therefore let us devoutly implore his protection, because I have good hope that we shall not have prayed in vain!" All agreed and invoked blessed Peter, asking for his help with devout prayers. As they prayed, the yardarm from which the sail hung was seen to be studded with lighted candles. The darkness was dissipated by the marvelous gleam of the candles, and in no time the blackness of the night was changed into the brightness of daylight. Looking up they saw a man, who wore the habit of the Friars Preachers, standing atop the sail, and no one doubted that it was Saint Peter. When the crew, unharmed, reached Genoa, they went to the house of the Friars Preachers, gave thanks to God and blessed Peter, and told the friars the whole story of the miracle.

A woman in Flanders had had three miscarriages, which made her husband hate her. She asked Saint Peter to come to her aid. In time she give birth to a fourth child, this one dead like the others. The mother took the child with her and committed herself totally to praying to Saint Peter, begging him devoutly to make her son live. The child came to life, and when he was to be baptized, it was decided that he would be called John; but the priest did not know what name he was to be given, and called him Peter, which name the new Christian made his own out of devotion to Saint Peter.

At Utrecht in the Teutonic province, some women sat at streetside, spinning and watching a great concourse of people going to the church of the Friars Preachers to honor Saint Peter Martyr. "You see?" they said to people standing around, "Those friars know all about raising money! Now they want to pile up a lot of money to build big palaces, so they've invented a new martyr!" While they were saying things like this, suddenly all the thread they were spinning was soaked in blood and their fingers were covered with blood. They were astonished at the sight of this and wiped their hands carefully to see if perhaps they had cut themselves. But when they found that their fingers showed no cuts, and that it was the thread itself that was running with blood, trembling and repentant they said: "Truly it's because we said bad things about the blood of the precious martyr that this stupendous miracle of blood has happened to us." They ran therefore to the house of the friars and told the story to the prior, presenting the bloody thread to him. After much urging the prior convoked a solemn preaching service, at which he related what had happened to the women, and showed all present the bloodstained thread.

Now a very opinionated master of arts heard this and began to make fun of the whole story, saying to those around him: "Just look at the way these friars beguile the hearts of simple people! Here they've got together some nice little neighbor women and had them dip thread into some blood and then pretend that a miracle had happened!" While he was still speaking, the wrath of God was visited upon him. As many looked on, he was stricken with a fever so intense that his friends had to hold him by the hand, take him away from the service, and lead him home. But the fever continued to affect him so violently that he feared he was dying, so he sent for the prior and confessed his sin to God, and made a vow to Saint Peter in the presence of the said prior, promising that if by the saint's merits he recovered his health, he would always have special devotion to him and would never again say such scandalous things. Wonder of wonders! No sooner had he pronounced his vow than he was well again.

The subprior of the aforesaid priory was bringing some very large and beautiful stones for the construction of the church already mentioned, and the boat that was carrying the stone unexpectedly ran aground and was so firmly locked in the sand that it could not be budged. The crew got down from the vessel and tried to push it free, but to no avail. They thought they had lost their ship until the subprior, ordering the others to stand aside, put his hand on the hull and, pressing lightly, said: "In the name of Saint Peter Martyr, in whose honor we are carrying these stones, back off!" Immediately the vessel was afloat, undamaged, and the seamen, climbing aboard safe and sound, sailed joyfully home.

At Sens in the province of France, a girl fell into a swift-flowing stream and was in the water for a long time, finally being pulled out dead. Her death was proven by four facts: the length of time in the water and the rigidity, coldness, and blackness of the corpse. Still, some people carried her to the church of the friars, and when they had commended her to Saint Peter, she was restored to life and health.

In Bologna, Friar John of Poland was ill with the quartan fever but was due to preach to the community on the feast of Saint Peter Martyr. In the natural course of the fever he expected an attack the night before the sermon and was afraid he might be unable to preach. He turned to Saint Peter's altar and prayed that by the saint's merits he might preach his glory, and so it happened: that very night the fever left him and he never suffered it again.

A woman by the name of Girolda, the wife of James of Vallesana, who for thirteen years was possessed by unclean spirits, went to a certain priest and told him: "I am possessed, and the evil spirit harasses me!" The priest was frightened and repaired to the sacristy, where he found a book containing the formulas for exorcism. He put on a stole under his cape and, with some other people, returned to the woman. As soon as she saw him, she said: "Where did you go, you wicked thief? And what are you wearing hidden under your cape?" The priest got nowhere with his exorcisms and could effect no cure. Then the woman went to blessed Peter while he was still alive and besought his help. Speaking like a prophet he answered her: "Have confidence, my daughter, do not despair! If I cannot at present do what you ask, the time will come when you will obtain in full whatever you ask of me." This came true: after his passion the aforesaid woman went to his tomb and was completely delivered of vexation by demons.

A woman named Euphemia, from a place called Corriongo in the diocese of Milan, was tormented by demons for seven years. When she was brought to Saint Peter's tomb, the demons began to disturb her more than usual and through her mouth to cry out: "Mary, Mary! Peter, Peter!" Then the spirits went out of her, leaving her for dead, but in a short time she arose completely cured. She declared that the demons harassed her most on Sundays and feast days, especially when the mass was being celebrated.

A woman of Beregno, Verbona by name, was plagued by demons for six years, and when she was brought to Saint Peter's tomb, a dozen men could not hold her. One of these men was a certain Conrad of Ladriano, a heretic who had come there to mock Saint Peter's miracles. He was restraining the woman with the others when the demons, speaking through the woman, said to him: "You belong to us! Why are you holding us? Did we not carry you to a certain place and did you not commit a murder? Haven't we conducted you to such and such places and haven't you committed such and such crimes?" And when they had told his many sins, which no one but he alone knew about, he was frightened beyond words. The demons tore the skin from the woman's neck and breast and went out of her leaving her half dead, but after a while she arose hale and hearty. Conrad, the aforesaid heretic, saw all this and was converted to the Catholic faith.

Once during the saint's lifetime, when a particularly acute and singularly eloquent heretic was debating with Peter, he expounded his errors with such subtlety and force that Peter, try as he might to respond effectively, did not have much success. He asked for time to think, went into a nearby chapel, wept and prayed God to defend the cause of his faith, and either to bring this prideful speaker back to the true faith or to punish him by silencing his tongue. Then he confronted the heretic and openly, before the whole audience, called upon him to state his arguments again. The man, however, was stricken mute and could not proffer so much as a word. This confounded the heretics, who took their departure, while the Catholics gave thanks to God.

A man named Opiso, a convinced heretic, had come to the friars' church to meet a female relative of his, also a heretic, and, passing by Saint Peter's tomb, saw two coins lying on it. "Fine!" he said. "We'll drink these!" Then of a sudden he began to shake all over and could not move an inch from where he stood. Frightened, he put back the coins and so was able to leave. This experience showed him Saint Peter's power, and he abandoned his heresy and converted to the Catholic faith.

In Germany, at the monastery of the Order of Saint Sixtus at Ottenbach in the diocese of Constance, there was a nun who for a year or more had suffered from painful gout in her knee, and no remedy had been found to cure it. She was unable to visit Saint Peter's tomb bodily both because she lived under a religious rule and because her serious physical condition forbade such a journey; so she thought of traveling to the tomb in her mind at least, and to visit it with sincere devotion. She learned that it would take thirteen days to go from Ottenbach to Milan, so for each of the next thirteen days she recited one hundred Our Fathers in honor of Saint Peter. Wonderful to relate, as she continued this journey in her mind, day by day and little by little she felt better, and when the last day was done and her mental stride carried her to the tomb, she knelt as if she were there in the body and with wholehearted devotion read the entire Psalter. When she had finished that, she felt freed of her infirmity to the degree that only a little pain was left. She then made the return trip just as she had made the outward one, and before she had completed thirteen days, she was entirely cured.

A man named Rufinus, from Canapicio of the Villa Mazzati, fell seriously ill. A vein had ruptured in the lower part of his body and blood flowed out continually; and no doctor was able to find a remedy. When this had gone on for six days and nights, Rufinus devoutly invoked the aid of Saint Peter and was cured so suddenly that between the offering of the prayer and the cessation of the hemorrhage there was no interval of time. When Rufinus fell asleep, he saw a friar dressed in the Dominican habit, stout and dark complexioned, whom he took to be a companion of Saint Peter Martyr, as indeed there had been one who looked like that. The friar held out his hands full of blood and sweet-smelling ointment to Rufinus, saying: "This blood is still fresh; come then to the fresh blood of Saint Peter." When he woke up, he decided to visit Saint Peter's tomb.

Several noblewomen of the castle of Masino in the diocese of Ivrea had special devotion to Saint Peter, fasted on his vigil, and went to his church to hear vespers. One of them, to honor Saint Peter Martyr, lighted a candle and placed it in front of the altar of Saint Peter the apostle. After the ladies went home, a greedy priest blew out the candle, but a flame quickly appeared and relighted it. He tried two or three times to extinguish the candle, but each time the light came back. He got tired of doing this and went to the choir, where he saw another candle before the high altar. A cleric who also fasted for the saint's vigil had lighted it in honor of Saint Peter. The priest tried twice to put this candle out and failed. The clerk watched this and called out angrily: "You devil, don't you see that this is a miracle? Don't you see that Saint Peter doesn't want you to extinguish his candle?" Both of them were astonished and terrified, and priest and clerk went up to the castle and told everybody about the miracle.

A man of Meda whose name was Roba had lost everything he owned, except the clothes he wore, at the gaming table. He went home late in the night, lighted a lamp, and went to his bed; but when he saw the tattered sheets and thought about his losses, he felt so despondent that he began to invoke the demons and to commend himself to them with impious words. At once three demons came and threw the lamp on the terrace, then seized Roba by the neck and throttled him until he could not speak a word. They made so much noise that the people in the lower part of the house came up and said: "What are you doing, Roba?" The demons answered them: "Go in peace and get back to bed!" They thought they were hearing Roba's voice and went their way. When they were gone, the demons tormented him more and more viciously. The people below realized what was happening and called in a priest, who adjured the demons in Saint Peter's name to be gone. Two of them departed. The next day Roba was taken to Saint Peter's tomb. Friar William of Vercelli came to him and began to rebuke the demon, who called him by name though he had never seen him. "Brother William," the demon said, "I will not go out of this man for you, because he is ours and does our works!" When William asked the spirit his name, he said: "I am called Balcephas." However, when he was ordered in Saint Peter's name to leave the man, he threw his victim to the ground and went out of him. Roba was well again and accepted a salutary penance.

One Palm Sunday when Saint Peter preached in Milan and a very large number of men and women had come to hear him, he said publicly and clearly: "I know for certain that the heretics are dealing for my death and that for this purpose money has already changed hands. But let them do whatever they can, I will persecute them more when I am dead than I have in this life!" It is obvious that what he said came true.

In a monastery in Florence a sister was at prayer the day blessed Peter was done to death, and in a vision saw the Blessed Virgin enthroned in glory on a high throne, and two friars of the Order of Preachers ascending to heaven and taking their places at either side of her. The nun asked who these were, and heard a voice telling her: "This is Friar Peter, who in the sight of the Lord ascends glorious like the smoke of incense." It has been corroborated that Peter's death occurred the day this religious had the vision. She suffered a long and serious illness, but devoted herself wholly to prayer to Saint Peter and soon was restored completely to health.

A schoolboy on his way from Maguelone to Montpellier jumped and fell, suffering a rupture in the groin so painful that he could not take a step. The lad had heard a preacher tell about a woman who had been cured by placing earth on which Saint Peter's blood had fallen on the cancer that was consuming her flesh. Picking up a handful of dirt, he said: "Lord God, I don't have any of that earth, but you gave that earth so much power by the merits of Saint Peter, you can give the same power to this earth!" He made the sign of the cross over it, invoked the martyr, spread the earth on the injured part, and was healed at once.

In the year of the Lord 1259, in the city of Apostella, there was a man named Benedict whose legs were swollen like wineskins, whose belly bulged like a pregnant woman's, whose face was hideous with sores, and whose whole body was so bloated that he seemed a monster. Barely holding himself erect with a staff, he begged an alms of a woman, who answered: "You are in need of a grave more than of anything else, but follow my advice! Go to the house of the Friars Preachers, confess your sins, and invoke the aid of Saint Peter!" Early the next morning he went to the house of the friars, but the door of the church was locked and he set himself down outside the door and went to sleep. And lo! a venerable man in the habit of the Preachers appeared to him, covered him with his own cloak, and led him into the church. Benedict awoke and found himself inside the church, completely cured. Many people were moved to admiration and surprise at the sight of the man who had been as good as dead and now, suddenly, was freed of his grave infirmity.

64. Saint Fabian

Saint Fabian ruled the Church of Rome for many years and finally suffered martyrdom in the reign of Decius. At his election as bishop of the city of Rome the Spirit, appearing in the form of a dove, was seen by many. Fabian ordered accounts of the passions of the martyrs, which are not carefully preserved by notaries, to be collected, and put in writing. He also had many basilicas built at the martyrs' tombs, and dedicated them himself. He established the practice of burning the old chrism and consecrating fresh chrism every year on Holy Thursday. Look for more about him at the feast of blessed Fabian and Sebastian, martyrs.[1]

---

[1] This chapter obviously duplicates the legend of Saint Fabian, pope and martyr, the subject of chapter 22. There is no reference to a Pope Fabian in the legend of Saint Sebastian. Graesse notes (291 n. 1) that the present chapter does not appear "in more recent editions."

65. Saint Philip, Apostle

Philippus, the Latin form of Philip, can be interpreted as *os lampadis*, mouth of a lamp, or as *os manuum*, mouth of hands; or it is composed of *philos*, which means love, and *yper*, above. The apostle is called mouth of a lamp because of his luminous preaching, mouth of hands because of his tireless work, and lover of the things above because of his heavenly contemplation.

After Philip the apostle had preached throughout Scythia for twenty years, the pagans laid hold of him and thrust him before a statue of Mars to make him sacrifice. Then suddenly a huge dragon emerged from the base of the statue, killed the pagan priest's son, who was tending the fire for the sacrifice, slew two tribunes whose men were holding Philip in chains, and infected the rest with the stench of its breath so that all were made ill. Philip then said: "Believe what I tell you! Smash that statue and in its place worship the cross of the Lord, and your sick will be cured and your dead restored to life." But those who were suffering called out: "Just let us be cured and we will quickly smash this Mars!" Philip commanded the dragon to hie himself to a desert place where he could do no harm to anyone, and the beast went away and was seen no more. Then he cured the sick and obtained the gift of life for the three who had died. All the people accepted the faith, and he preached to them for a whole year and ordained priests and deacons for them. The apostle went to the city of Hierapolis in Asia and there put down the heresy of the Ebionites, who taught that the body assumed by Christ was only a phantom. There with him were his two daughters, dedicated virgins both of them, through whom the Lord converted many to the faith.

Seven days before his death Philip convoked the bishops and priests and said to them: "The Lord has granted me these seven days so that I might give you good counsel." He was then eighty-seven years old. The infidels seized him, and, like his Master whom he had preached, he was nailed to a cross, and so migrated to the Lord and happily finished his life.

Isidore, in his book *On the Life, Birth, and Death of the Saints*, writes of Philip as follows: "Philip the Galilean preached Christ and led the barbarian peoples, who lived in darkness on the shores of the wild Ocean, to the light of knowledge and the haven of the faith. At the end he was crucified and stoned at Hierapolis, a town in the province of Phrygia. He died and reposes there together with his daughters." This from Isidore.

Jerome, in his *Martyrology*, says of the Philip who was one of the seven deacons, that he died at Caesarea on the sixth day of July, distinguished for the signs
and wonders he worked. Three of his daughters were buried with him there; the
fourth was laid to rest at Ephesus. The above Philip is not the same as this Philip,
because the former was an apostle and the latter a deacon; the former reposes at
Hierapolis, the latter at Caesarea; the former had two daughters who had the gift
of prophecy, the latter had four daughters. The *Ecclesiastical History*, however,
seems to say that Philip the apostle had four daughters who were prophetesses;
but in this instance Jerome is more credible.

66. Saint Apollonia

During the reign of the emperor Decius a savage persecution broke out in Alexandria against the servants of God; but a man named Divinus, a wretch of the
demons, anticipated the ruler's edict and stirred up the superstitious rabble
against the servants of the same Christ, and the mob, thoroughly aroused,
thirsted for nothing less than the blood of the pious. Their first captives were
dedicated religious, both men and women. Some of them they tore limb from
limb, hacking them to pieces. They mutilated the faces of others and put their
eyes out with pointed sticks, and threw them out of the city. Still others they led
to the idols, pressing them to worship, and when these refused and cursed the
idols, they had their feet chained together and were dragged through the city
streets, until this brutal, horrid torture reduced their bodies to shreds and tatters.

At this time there lived in Alexandria an admirable virgin, well along in years,
named Apollonia. She was wreathed with the flowers of chastity, sobriety, and
purity, and stood like a sturdy column strengthened by the Spirit of the Lord,
perceived by the Lord for the merit and virtue of her faith, admired by the
angels, and offering a spectacle and example to men. When the furious mob was
surging through the houses of the servants of God, breaking up everything with
hostile cruelty, blessed Apollonia was carried off to the tribunal of the impious,
innocent in her simplicity, dauntless in her virtue, bringing with her nothing
more than the constancy of her intrepid spirit and the purity of her untroubled
conscience. Thus she offered her devout soul to God and handed over her most
chaste body to the persecutors to be tortured. The executioners, cruelly wreak-
ing their wrath upon her, first beat out all her teeth. Then they piled up wood

and built a huge pyre, telling her they would burn her alive unless she took part in their impieties. But she, seeing the pyre already burning and after a brief moment of recollection, suddenly broke free from the hands of the wicked and of her own will threw herself into the fire with which they had threatened her. Her merciless tormentors were shocked beyond measure at finding a woman even more eager to undergo death than they to inflict it. This fearless martyr, already tried by so many kinds of torture, would not be conquered by the torments visited upon her nor by the heat of the flames, because her spirit was on fire with the far more ardent rays of truth. So it was that the material fire, ignited by the hands of mortals, could not overcome the heat infused by God in that indefatigable breast.

Oh, great and wondrous struggle of this virgin, who, by the grace of a compassionate God, went to the fire so as not to be burned and was burned so as not to be consumed, as if neither fire nor torture could touch her! There would have been safety in freedom, but no glory for one who avoided the fight. Apollonia, the stalwart virgin martyr of Christ, contemns the world's pleasures, tramples on worldly prosperity by her contemptuous appraisal, yearns only to please her spouse Jesus Christ. By a happy perseverance in her resolution to stay a virgin she remains unshaken in the midst of excruciating torments. The merit of this virgin, so gloriously and blessedly triumphant, excels and shines out among martyrs. Indeed this woman's virile spirit did not give way under the great weight of her struggle. By her love of heaven she expelled every earthly fear and grasped the trophy of the cross of Christ. Armed against fleshly lusts and all tortures by her faith rather than by the sword, she fought and she won. And this may he deign to grant us, who lives and reigns with the Father and the Holy Spirit forever and ever.[1]

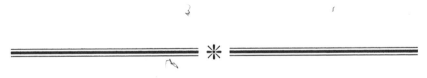

67. Saint James, Apostle

Jacobus, the Latin form of James, is interpreted as one who causes to fall, or trips someone who is in a hurry, or as one who prepares. Or Jacobus comes from *Ja*, a name of God, and *cobar*, which means burden or weight. Or again, as if the name were Jacopus, it might come from *jaculum*, lance, and *cope*, a cutting, so

---

[1] Graesse (293 n. 1), notes that this chapter is absent from "more recent editions."

one cut down with lances. James therefore was one who brought the world to a fall by his contempt for it, he tripped up the devil who is always in a hurry, and he prepared his body for every good work. Evil passions are in us due to three causes, as Gregory of Nyssa says—namely, bad bringing up or bad associations, bad bodily condition, and the vice of ignorance. And he says that those bad passions are cured by good habits, good exercise, and the study of good doctrine. Blessed James took good care of himself and so had his body prepared for every good work. He is also called a divine weight due to the gravity of his conduct, and he was cut down with lances in his martyrdom.

This apostle James is called James of Alpheus, meaning the son of Alpheus; the brother of the Lord; James the Less; and James the Just. He is called James son of Alpheus not only according to the flesh but according to the meaning of that name. Alpheus is interpreted as learned, or document, or fugitive, or thousandth, because James was learned through inspired knowledge, a document by instructing others, a fugitive from the world because he despised it, and thousandth because of his reputation for humility.

He is called the brother of the Lord because he is said to have borne a very strong resemblance to Jesus, so that very often they were mistaken one for the other. Hence when the Jews set out to capture Christ, they had to avoid taking James because he looked like Christ; so they engaged Judas, who could distinguish the Lord from James due to long familiarity with them, to point Christ out by giving him a kiss. Ignatius confirms this likeness in his letter to John the Evangelist when he says: "If I have your permission, I want to come up to Jerusalem to see the venerable James, surnamed the Just, who they say resembled Jesus Christ so closely in his features, his life, and his way with others that he might have been born his twin brother; so that, as they say, if I see James I see Christ Jesus so far as all bodily features are concerned."

Again, James is called the brother of the Lord since Christ and James, being descended from two sisters, were thought of as being descended from two brothers, Joseph and Cleophas. He is not called the brother of the Lord on the ground that he was the son of Joseph, the spouse of Mary, by another wife, as some would have it, but because he was the son of Mary the daughter of Cleophas, and this Cleophas was the brother of Joseph, Mary's spouse—although Master John Beleth says that Alpheus, James's father, was brother to Joseph, Mary's spouse. But this is not thought to be true: the Jews called "brothers" those who were related on both sides. It may also be that James was called the brother of the Lord on account of the excellence of his sanctity, which gave him right of preference, so that of all the apostles he was the one ordained to be bishop of Jerusalem.

He is called James the Less to distinguish him from James, the son of Zebedee, for James of Zebedee was born earlier than James of Alpheus, and James of Alpheus was called to be an apostle later. In many religious communities it is customary that the one who enters earlier (*prior*) is called the greater (*major*), and the one who comes later (*posterior*) is called the less (*minor*), though "the less" may be either older in years or more worthy in holiness.

James is called the Just because of the merit of his most excellent holiness. According to Jerome his holiness was so revered by the people that they strove eagerly to touch the hem of his garment. Hegesippus, who lived close to the time of the apostles, wrote as follows about James's sanctity, as we read in the *Ecclesiastical History*: "James, the brother of the Lord, assumed the rule of the Church. He has universally been called the Just from the time of the Lord down to our own. From his mother's womb he was holy. He drank no wine or strong drink, never ate meat, no razor ever came near his head, no oil anointed him, he never bathed. His clothing consisted of a linen garment. He knelt so often in prayer that his knees were calloused like the soles of his feet. For this ceaseless and surpassing righteousness he was called the Just and Abba, which is interpreted to mean the stronghold of the people and righteousness. Because of his eminent sanctity he alone of the apostles was allowed to enter the Holy of Holies." So far Hegesippus.

It is also said that he was first among the apostles to celebrate the mass. In recognition of his superior holiness the apostles awarded him the honor of being the first among them to offer mass in Jerusalem after the Lord's ascension. This was before he was ordained bishop, since we read in the Acts of the Apostles that even before his ordination the disciples were persevering in the doctrine of the apostles and in the communication of the breaking of bread, which is understood to be the celebration of mass. Or perhaps he is said to have been the first to celebrate because we are told that he was the first to say mass in pontifical vestments, just as Peter later on did in Antioch and Mark in Alexandria. James was a virgin all his life, as Jerome attests in his book *Contra Jovinianum*.

Josephus, and Jerome in the book *De viris illustribus*, tell us that after the Lord died on the day before the Sabbath, James made a vow that he would not eat until he saw Christ risen from the dead. On the day of the resurrection, when James had not tasted food until then, the Lord appeared to him and said to those who were with him: "Lay the table and prepare the bread!" Then he took the bread, blessed it, and gave it to James the Just, saying: "Rise, my brother, and eat, because the Son of man has risen!"

In the seventh year of his episcopate, when on Easter Sunday the apostles had gathered in Jerusalem, James asked each of them how much the Lord had done among the people through them, and they gave their accounts. Then for seven days James and the other apostles preached in the Temple before Caiaphas and a number of Jews, and the time was at hand when they would have wished to be baptized. Suddenly a man came into the Temple and shouted: "O men of Israel, what are you doing? Why do you let these sorcerers delude us?" He stirred up the people so much that they wanted to stone the apostles. The man climbed up to the platform from which James was preaching and threw him to the floor below, and as a result James limped badly for the rest of his life. This happened to him in the seventh year after the Lord's ascension.

In the thirtieth year of his episcopate, the Jews, seeing that they could not kill Paul, who had appealed to Caesar and been sent to Rome, turned their tyrannical persecution on James. Hegesippus reports, as we find in the *Ecclesiastical History*, that the Jews came together to him and said: "We pray you, call the people back, because they are wrong about Jesus, thinking that he is the Christ! We beg you therefore to speak to all these people who are coming for the day of the Pasch, and to disabuse them about Jesus. We all will comply with what you say, and we, together with the people, will testify that you are a righteous man and that you are no respecter of persons." They stood him therefore on the pinnacle of the Temple and shouted: "Most righteous of men, to whom we all owe deference, the people are wrong in following Jesus who was crucified! Tell us plainly what you think about him!" James responded: "Why do you question me about the Son of man? Behold, he is seated in the heavens at the right of the sovereign Power, and he will come to judge the living and the dead!"

The Christians rejoiced at hearing this and listened to him gladly. The Pharisees and the Scribes said to each other: "We made a mistake in allowing him to give such testimony to Jesus! Now let us go up and throw him down! That will frighten this crowd and they won't dare believe what he said!" Then all together, and as loudly as they could, they shouted: "Oh! Oh! The just man has erred!"

Then they went up and threw him down, and came down again and began to stone him, saying: "Let us stone James the Just!" But James, though beaten to the ground, not only could not die but even turned over, raised himself to his knees, and said: "I pray you, Lord, forgive them, for they know not what they do!" At this, one of the priests, of the sons of Rahab, exclaimed: "Stop! What are you doing? This just man whom you're stoning is praying for you!" But one of the others snatched up a fuller's club, aimed a heavy blow at James's head, and split his skull. That is how Hegesippus describes the martyrdom. James migrated to the Lord under Nero, who began to reign in the year of the Lord 57. He was buried there beside the Temple. The people were determined to avenge his death and capture and punish the malefactors, but these quickly got away.

Josephus says that the destruction of Jerusalem and the dispersion of the Jews were a punishment for the sin of killing James the Just. Jerusalem, however, was destroyed not only on account of James's death but especially on account of the death of the Lord, according to what Christ himself said: "They will not leave one stone upon another in you, because you did not know the time of your visitation."

But because the Lord does not wish the death of a sinner, and so that the Jews would have no excuse for their sin, he gave them forty years to do penance, and called upon them to do so through the apostles and especially through James the brother of the Lord, who continuously preached repentance among them.

When no amount of admonition availed, God willed to terrify them with wonders. During the forty years he had granted them for penance, many prodigies and portents occurred, as Josephus tells us. An extraordinarily brilliant star, similar in shape to a sword, hung over the city for a whole year, shooting out deadly flames. On a certain feast of Unleavened Bread, at the ninth hour of the night a light shone around the altar of the Temple, so brilliant that all thought a marvelously bright day had dawned. On the same feast day a heifer that was already in the hands of the ministers to be sacrificed brought forth a lamb. Some days later, at the hour of sunset, cars and chariots were seen racing across every quarter of the sky, and battalions of armed men clashing in the clouds and surrounding the city with unlooked-for troops. On another feast day, which is called Pentecost, the priests went at night to the Temple to conduct the usual ministries, and heard movements and crashing noises and voices saying: "Let us get away from this place!" And four years before the war, at the feast of Tabernacles, a man by the name of Jesus, son of Ananias, suddenly began to shout: "A voice from the East, a voice from the West, a voice from the four winds, a voice over Jerusalem and over the Temple, a voice over husbands and wives, a voice over the whole people!" The man was caught, beaten, whipped, but could say nothing else, and the more he was whipped, the louder he shouted. He was brought before the judge, tortured, mangled until his bones showed through the torn flesh, but he neither begged nor wept, only howling at each blow and repeating the same words, adding: "Woe, woe to Jerusalem!" All this from Josephus.

The Jews were neither converted by admonitions nor frightened by marvels, so after forty years the Lord brought Vespasian and Titus to Jerusalem, and they razed the city to its foundations. The reason for their coming to Jerusalem is explained in a certain admittedly apocryphal history. There we read that Pilate, realizing that in Jesus he had condemned an innocent man and fearing the displeasure of Tiberius Caesar, sent an envoy named Albanus to present his excuses to the emperor. Pilate's envoy was driven ashore in Galatia by contrary winds and taken to Vespasian, who at that time held the governorship of Galatia from Tiberius. The prevailing custom in that country was that anyone who had been shipwrecked had to give his goods and his service to the ruler. So Vespasian asked Albanus who he was, where he came from, and where he was going. Albanus answered: "I live in Jerusalem, that is where I came from, and I was on my way to Rome." Vespasian: "You come from the land of the wise men, you know the art of medicine, you are a physician! You must cure me!" In fact since childhood he had had some kind of worms in his nose, whence his name Vespasian. Albanus: "My lord, I know nothing of medicine and therefore am unable to cure you." Vespasian: "Cure me or die!" Albanus: "He who gave sight to the blind, drove out demons, and raised the dead, he knows that I have no knowledge of the art of healing." Vespasian: "Who is this that you say such great things about?" Albanus: "Jesus of Nazareth, whom the Jews, in their envy, put to death! If you believe in him you will obtain the grace of health." Vespasian:

"I believe, because he who raised the dead will be able to free me of this ailment."

As he said this, the worms fell out of his nose and he received his health then and there. Filled with joy, he said: "I am sure that he who was able to cure me is the Son of God. I will seek permission of the emperor and go with an armed band to Jerusalem, and I will overthrow all those who betrayed and killed this man!" And Vespasian said to Albanus, Pilate's envoy: "Your life and goods are safe and unharmed, and you have my permission to return home."

Vespasian then went to Rome and obtained Tiberius Caesar's permission to destroy Jerusalem and Judea. For years during the reign of Nero, when the Jews were rebelling against the empire, he built up several armies: hence (according to the chronicles) he was acting not out of zeal for Christ but because the Jews were renouncing Roman rule. Vespasian then marched upon Jerusalem with a huge force, and on the day of the Pasch laid siege to the city and trapped the innumerable multitude gathered there for the festal day. Some time before Vespasian's arrival the Christian faithful who were in Jerusalem had been warned by the Holy Spirit to leave the city and to take refuge in a town called Pella, across the Jordan. Thus, with all her holy men withdrawn, Jerusalem became the place where the vengeance of heaven fell, upon the sacrilegious city and its criminal people.

The Romans' first assault, however, was against a town of Judea called Jonapata, in which Josephus was both leader and ruler, and he and his people put up a brave resistance; but at length Josephus, seeing that the city's fall was inevitable, took eleven Jews with him and sought safety in an underground room. After four days without food his associates, though Josephus disagreed, preferred to die there rather than submit to servitude under Vespasian. They wanted to kill each other and offer their blood in sacrifice to God; and, since Josephus held first rank among them, they thought he should be the first to die, so that by the shedding of his blood God would be the sooner placated. Or (as another chronicle has it) they wanted to kill each other so as not to fall into the hands of the Romans.

Now Josephus, being a prudent man and not wanting to die, appointed himself arbiter of death and sacrifice, and ordered the others to cast lots, two by two, to determine which of each pair would put the other to death. The lots were cast and one man after the other was consigned to death, until the last one was left to draw lots with Josephus. Then Josephus, who was a strong, agile men, took the other man's sword away from him, asked him which he preferred, life or death, and ordered him not to waste time choosing. The man, afraid, answered promptly: "I do not refuse to live, if by your favor I am able to save my life."

Josephus now had a talk in hiding with an intimate of Vespasian with whom he himself was on friendly terms: he requested that his life be spared by Vespasian, and what he requested he obtained. He was taken before Vespasian, who said to him: "You would have deserved death, if this man's petition had not secured your freedom!" Josephus: "If anything wrong has been done, it can be set right!" Vespasian: "What can a conquered man do?" Josephus: "I will be able to do something, if what I say wins me a favorable hearing." Vespasian: "It is granted that you may say what you have to say, and if there is any good in it, it will be listened to quietly." Josephus: "The Roman emperor has died, and the Senate has made you emperor!" Vespasian: "If you are a prophet, why did you not prophesy to this city that it was about to fall under my sway?" Josephus: "I foretold it publicly for forty days!"

Shortly thereafter legates arrived from Rome, affirmed that Vespasian had indeed been elevated to the imperial throne, and took him off to Rome. Eusebius, too, states in his chronicle that Josephus prophesied to Vespasian both about the emperor's death and about his own elevation.

Vespasian left his son Titus in charge of the siege of Jerusalem. We read in the same apocryphal history that Titus, hearing of his father's accession to the empire, was so filled with joy and exultation that he caught a chill and suffered a contraction of nerves and muscles that left him painfully paralyzed in one leg. Josephus heard that Titus was paralyzed, and diligently sought information regarding the cause of the disease and the time it had struck. The cause was unknown, the nature of the illness also unknown, but the time was known: it happened to Titus when he learned of his father's election. Josephus, quick and foresighted as he was, put two and two together, and, knowing the time, surmised both the nature of the ailment and its cure. He knew that Titus had been debilitated by an excess of joy and gladness, and, keeping in mind that opposites are cured by opposites, knowing also that what is brought on by love is often dispelled by dislike, he began to ask whether there was anyone who was particularly obnoxious to the prince. There was indeed a slave who annoyed Titus so much that the very sight of him, and even the sound of his name, upset him completely. So Josephus said to Titus: "If you want to be cured, guarantee the safety of any who come in my company." Titus: "Whoever comes in your company will be kept secure and safe!"

Josephus quickly arranged a festive dinner, set his own table facing that of Titus, and seated the slave at his right side. When Titus saw the fellow, he growled with displeasure; and as he had been chilled by joy, he now was heated by his fit of fury: his sinews were loosened, and he was cured. Thereafter Titus granted his favor to the slave and took Josephus into his friendship. Whether this story is worth telling is left to the reader's judgment.

Titus maintained the blockade of Jerusalem for two years. Among the other ills that weighed heavily on the people in the besieged city, there was a famine so severe that parents snatched food from their children and children from parents, husbands from wives and wives from husbands—snatched it not only from their hands but out of their mouths. Young people, though stronger by their age, wandered about the streets like phantoms and fell down exhausted by hunger. Those who were burying the dead often fell dead on top of those they were burying. The stench from the cadavers was so unbearable that they were being buried out of public funds, and when the funds ran out, the unburied corpses were so numerous that they were thrown over the city walls. Titus, making a tour around the walls and seeing the moats filled with cadavers and the whole area infected with the smell of death, raised his hands to heaven, wept, and said: "God, you see that not I am doing this!"

The hunger was so acute that people chewed their shoes and their shoelaces. The *Ecclesiastical History* tells the story of a woman noble by birth and by riches, whose house was broken into by robbers who stole all she had, including the last bit of food. She held her suckling infant in her hands and said: "Unhappy son of an unhappier mother, for whom should I keep you alive amid war and famine and pillaging? Come now therefore, my firstborn, be food to your mother, a scandal to the robbers, a testament to the ages!" She strangled her child, cooked the body, ate half, and hid the other half. The robbers, smelling cooked meat, rushed back into the house and threatened the woman with death unless she gave up the food. She uncovered what was left of the infant. "Look here," she said, "you see I saved you the best part!" But they were filled with such horror that they could not even speak. "This is my son," she said. "The sin is mine! Don't be afraid to eat, because I who begot him ate first. Don't be either more religious than the mother or more softhearted than women! But if piety overcomes you and you dread to eat, I will eat the rest, since I've already eaten half!" Trembling and terrified, the robbers slunk away.

Finally, in the second year of Vespasian's reign, Titus took Jerusalem, reduced the city to ruins, and leveled the Temple; and as the Jews had bought Jesus Christ for thirty pieces of silver, Titus had Jews sold at the rate of thirty for one silver coin. Josephus tells us that 97,000 were sold and 110,000 perished of hunger or by the sword. We also read that when Titus entered the city, he noticed one particularly thick wall and gave orders to break into it. Inside the wall they found an old man, venerable in age and appearance. When asked who he was, he replied that he was Joseph, from Arimathea, a city of Judea, and that the Jews had had him shut in and immured because he had buried Christ. He added that from that time to the present he had been fed with food from heaven and comforted by divine light. In the *Gospel of Nicodemus*, however, it is said that though the Jews had walled him in, the risen Christ broke him out and brought him to Arimathea. It could be said that once released he would not desist from preaching Christ and therefore was walled in a second time.

Vespasian died and his son Titus succeeded him as emperor. He was a clement and generous man. His goodness was so great that, as Eusebius of Caesarea in his chronicle and Jerome both affirm, when one evening he remembered that on that day he had done nothing good nor given anything to anyone, he said: "Oh, my friends, I have lost the day!"

Long afterwards some Jews set out to rebuild Jerusalem, and when they went out the first morning, they found crosses of dew on the ground. Frightened, they fled. The second morning they came back, and, as Miletus says in his chronicle, each of them found a bloody cross sketched on his clothing. Again they fled in terror. When they returned on the third day, a fiery vapor came out of the ground and consumed them utterly.

======= ✳ =======

68. The Finding of the Holy Cross

This feast is named for the finding of the holy cross because, it is said, the cross was found on this day. It had been found earlier by Adam's son Seth in the earthly paradise, as we shall see below, by Solomon in Lebanon, by the queen of Sheba in Solomon's temple, by the Jews in the water of the pond; and on this day it was found by Helena on Mount Calvary.

The finding of the holy cross occurred more than 200 years after the Lord's resurrection. We read in the *Gospel of Nicodemus* that when Adam became infirm, his son Seth went to the gates of paradise and begged for some oil from the tree of mercy, with which he might anoint his father's body and restore his health. The archangel Michael appeared to him and said: "Waste no toil or tears trying to obtain oil from the wood of mercy, because there is no way you can acquire it before 5,500 years have gone by!" . . . this although it is believed that only 5,199 years elapsed from Adam's day to Christ's passion. Elsewhere we read that the angel offered Seth a shoot from the tree and ordered him to plant it on the mount of Lebanon. In a certain admittedly apocryphal history of the Greeks we read that the angel gave him a branch from the tree under which Adam committed his sin, informing him that when that branch bore fruit, his father would be made whole. When Seth went back and found his father dead, he planted the branch over Adam's grave, where it grew to be a great tree and was still standing in Solomon's time. Whether any of this is true we leave to the reader's judgment, because none of it is found in any authentic chronicle or history.

Solomon admired the beauty of this tree and had it cut down and used in the building of his forest house.[1] John Beleth says, however, that it was not possible to find a place where the trunk of the tree could be fitted in: it was always too

[1] I owe to the Abbé Roze (*La légende dorée* [Paris: Ed. Rouveyre, 1902], 2:53–54) a note to the effect that this house is referred to in 1 Kings 7. It was called "forest house" because so many cedar trees had been used in its construction.

long or too short. If it did not fit into a place too narrow for it and it was carefully shortened, it was immediately seen to be so short as to be completely useless. Therefore the workmen would have nothing more to do with it, and it was thrown over a certain pond to serve as a bridge for those wishing to cross.

When the queen of Sheba came to hear Solomon's words of wisdom and was about to cross this bridge, she saw in spirit that the Savior of the world would one day hang upon this very same wood. She therefore would not walk on it but immediately knelt and worshiped it. In the *Scholastic History*, however, we read that the queen of Sheba saw the wood in Solomon's forest house, and when she returned home, she sent word to Solomon that a certain man was to hang upon that wood, and that by this man's death the kingdom of the Jews would be destroyed. Solomon therefore had the wood taken out and buried in the deepest bowels of the earth. Later on the pond called Probatica[2] welled up at that spot, and the Nathineans[3] bathed the sacrificial animals there. So it was not only the occasional descent of an angel of the Lord, but also the power of the wood, that caused the motion of the water and the healing of the sick.

When Christ's time to suffer was drawing near, the aforesaid wood floated up to the surface of the pond, and the Jews, seeing it, used it in making the Lord's cross. It is said that the cross was made out of four kinds of wood, namely, palmwood, cedar, cypress, and olivewood. Hence the verse:

Ligna crucis palma, cedrus, cypressus, oliva.

There were four wooden parts to the cross—the upright shaft, the crossbeam, the tablet above, and the block into which the cross was fixed, or, as Gregory of Tours says, the crosspiece that supported Christ's feet. Hence each of these parts might be made of any of the kinds of wood enumerated above. The apostle seems to have this variety of woods in mind when he says: "You may be able to comprehend, with all the saints, what is the breadth and length and height and depth." The eminent doctor,[4] at the place referred to, explains these words as follows: "The breadth of the Lord's cross is the crossbeam upon which his hands were extended; the length means the shaft from the ground to the crossbeam, where the whole body hung from the hands; the height means from the cross-beam to the top, where the head touched; the depth is the part hidden by the earth in which the cross stood. By this sign of the cross all human and Christian action is described: to do good works in Christ and to cling to him persever-ingly, to hope for heaven, and to avoid profaning the sacraments."

This precious wood of the cross lay hidden underground for over two hun-dred years and was rediscovered by Helena, mother of Constantine. At that time

---

[2] John 5:2.

[3] *Natmei* (in Graesse) is no doubt a scribe's error (or Graesse's) for the *Nathinaei* of 1 Chron. 9:2, which the New English Bible translates "temple-servitors."

[4] Most likely Augustine, whom Jacobus, elsewhere in the *Legenda aurea*, calls *doctor egregius*, the term he uses here.

an innumerable horde of barbarians gathered on the bank of the Danube: their aim was to cross the river and to subjugate all the lands as far as the western limit. When Emperor Constantine learned of this, he moved his camp and took his stand with his army along the opposite bank of the Danube; but more and more barbarians were arriving and were beginning to cross the river, and Constantine, seeing that they were bent on drawing him into battle the next day, was stricken with terror. That night an angel awakened him and urged him to look upwards. The emperor looked toward heaven and saw the sign of the cross formed in flaming light, with the legend *In hoc signo vinces* written in golden letters. Heartened by the celestial vision he had a facsimile of the cross made, and ordered it to be carried at the head of the army. Then his troops rushed upon the enemy and put them to flight, killing a great many of them. Soon thereafter Constantine called the heads of all the temples and questioned them closely, seeking to find out what god had the cross as his sign. They said they did not know, but then some Christians came along and told him about the mystery of the cross and the faith in the Trinity. Constantine believed perfectly in Christ and received the sacrament of baptism from Pope Eusebius, or, as some books have it, from the bishop of Caesarea. Many of the things stated in this account, however, are contradicted by the *Tripartite History* and the *Ecclesiastical History*, as well as by the life of Saint Silvester[5] and the *Acts* of the Roman pontiffs. There are those who hold that it was not Constantine the great emperor who was converted and baptized by Pope Saint Eusebius, as some historians seem to imply, but Constantine's father, also named Constantine, as we find in some other histories; for this latter Constantine came to the faith a different way, as we read in the legend of Saint Silvester, and he was baptized not by Eusebius but by Silvester.

When the elder Constantine died, the younger, remembering the victory his father had won by virtue of the holy cross, sent his mother Helena to Jerusalem to find the cross, as is related below. The *Ecclesiastical History* gives a different account of this victory: it says that when Maxentius invaded the Roman empire, Emperor Constantine arrived at the Albine[6] bridge to do battle with him. Constantine was exceedingly anxious about this battle and often raised his eyes to heaven in search of help from above. Then in a dream he saw, in the eastern part of the sky, the sign of the cross blazing with fiery brilliance, and angels standing by and saying to him: "Constantine, in this sign you will conquer." And, as we read in the *Tripartite History*, while Constantine puzzled about the meaning of this, the following night Christ appeared to him with the sign he had seen in the sky, and ordered him to have a standard made with this sign on it, because this would be of help to him in combat. So Constantine, again happy and confident of victory, drew on his forehead the sign of the cross that he had seen in the sky, had the military standards changed to the shape of the cross, and carried a gold

---

[5] See above, chapter 12.

[6] Why the text has this term for what is commonly called the Milvian bridge is not clear.

cross in his right hand. After that he prayed the Lord not to allow his right hand, which he had armed with the salutary sign of the cross, to be bloodied or stained by spilled Roman blood, but to grant him victory over the tyrant without bloodshed.

Maxentius meanwhile gave orders to arrange his boats as a trap, stringing floats across the river to look like a level bridge. Now, when Constantine drew up to the river, Maxentius rushed upon him with a small band of troops, commanding the rest to come after him; but he forgot his own stratagem and started across the false bridge, thus being caught by the ruse with which he had hoped to deceive Constantine, and was drowned in the depths of the stream. Thereupon Constantine was unanimously acclaimed emperor by all present.

We read in a fairly reliable chronicle that at that time Constantine's faith was not yet perfect and that he had not yet been baptized, but that after an interval he had a vision of Saints Peter and Paul[7] and was reborn by holy baptism at Pope Silvester's hands. Then, cured of his leprosy, he believed perfectly in Christ and so sent his mother Helena to Jerusalem to search for the Lord's cross. Ambrose, however, in his letter about the death of Theodosius, and the *Tripartite History* both say that he received baptism only in his last hours, having put it off in order that he might be able to be baptized in the river Jordan. Jerome says that he became a Christian under Pope Silvester. There is doubt about whether or not he delayed baptism, so that Saint Silvester's legend is likewise questionable on more than one point. This account of the finding of the cross, which we read in the *Ecclesiastical History*, seems more authentic than the story usually read in the churches. In the latter many things are stated which clearly are not in accord with the truth, unless perhaps one would choose to say, as was said above, that not Constantine but his father, also called Constantine, was the one concerned; but this does not seem very likely, although that is what we read in certain histories from overseas.[8]

When Helena arrived in Jerusalem, she gave orders that all the Jewish wise men located throughout the entire area should come together in her presence. This Helena had previously been an innkeeper or inn-servant,[9] but because of her beauty Constantine [the elder] had attached her to himself. Ambrose has this to say about her: "They assert that this woman had been an innkeeper or servant, but was joined to Constantine the elder, who later became emperor. She was a good innkeeper, who diligently sought a crib for the Lord, a good hostess who knew about the innkeeper who healed the wounds of the man who fell among

---

[7] See the legend of Saint Silvester, chapter 12 above.

[8] The confusion about Constantine's part in the finding of the cross (or his father's, whose name was not Constantine but Constantius) no doubt goes back to the manuscript sources available to Jacobus, including not only Eusebius and the *Tripartite History* but the more or less "authentic," or frankly apocryphal, documents to which Jacobus refers. The uncertainty about the time of his baptism persists among present-day scholars.

[9] The word *stabularia* can mean either innkeeper or servant in an inn.

robbers, a good servant, who preferred to spurn all things as dung in order to gain Christ: therefore Christ lifted her up from the dunghill to the throne." Thus Ambrose. Others, however, assert, and we read in a reasonably authentic chronicle, that this Helena was the only daughter of Clohel, king of the Britons. When Constantine came to Britain, he took Helena to wife, and so the island devolved to him after Clohel's death. Even British sources attest this; yet elsewhere we read that Helena was a native of Trier.

Be that as it may, the Jewish scholars, somewhat alarmed, asked each other: "Why do you think the queen has summoned us?" One of their number, Judas by name, said: "I know why! She wants to learn from us the whereabouts of the wood of the cross on which Christ was crucified. Be cautious, therefore, and let no one of us presume to tell her! Otherwise you can be absolutely sure that our Law will be annulled and the traditions of the fathers completely wiped out. My grandfather Zacheus foretold this to my father Simon, and on his deathbed my father said to me: 'Look, my son! When they come searching for Christ's cross, show them where it is or you will be tortured; for from then on the Jewish nation will never reign, but those who adore the Crucified will rule, because Christ was indeed the Son of God.' I asked him: 'Father mine, if our forefathers truly knew that Jesus Christ was the Son of God, why did they nail him to the gibbet of the cross?' 'God knows,' he replied, 'that I was never in their counsels and often spoke against them. But because Christ denounced the vices of the Pharisees, they had him put to death on the cross. He rose again on the third day and ascended to heaven as his disciples looked on. My brother Stephen believed in him and the Jews in their madness stoned him to death. Be careful therefore, my son, and do not rashly blaspheme him or his disciples.'" It does not seem very probable, however, that this Jew's father could have lived at the time of Christ's passion, because from that time to Helena's, when this Judas is supposed to have told his story, more than 270 years had elapsed—unless, perhaps, it could be said that men lived longer then than they do now.

However that may be, the Jewish scholars now said to Judas: "We have never heard anything like that; but if the queen questions you, see to it that you tell her nothing!" When they all stood before her, she asked them about the place where the Lord had been crucified. They refused absolutely to say where it was, and she condemned them all to die by fire. This frightened them and they handed Judas over to her, saying: "This man is the son of a just man and a prophet. He is learned in the Law and will give you the answers to all your questions." So she dismissed them all except Judas, to whom she said: "You have the choice of death or life: choose which one you prefer! Show me the place called Golgotha, where the Lord was crucified, so that I may find his cross." "How could I know the place?" he responded; "More than two hundred years have gone by since then!" "I swear by the Crucified," the queen said, "that I will starve you to death unless you tell me the truth!" She therefore had him thrown into a dry well and left him to suffer the pangs of hunger. After he had been without food for six days, he asked to be pulled out of the well on the seventh, and promised to show where the cross was. He was lifted out, and when he came to the place and prayed there, the earth suddenly quaked and a mist of sweet-smelling perfumes greeted their senses. Judas, filled with wonder, clapped his hands and said: "In truth, O Christ, you are the Savior of the world!"

The *Ecclesiastical History* tells us that at that place there was a temple of Venus, which Hadrian had built so that any Christians who came to pray there would seem to be adoring Venus. For this reason few came and the place was almost consigned to oblivion; but Helena had the temple razed and the site plowed up. After that, Judas girded himself and started manfully to dig, and when he had dug down twenty yards, he found three crosses buried and took them forthwith to the queen. Since they had no way of distinguishing Christ's cross from those of the thieves, they placed them in the center of the city and waited for the Lord to manifest his glory; and behold! At about the ninth hour the body of a young man was being carried past, and Judas halted the cortege. He held the first cross and the second over the body, but nothing happened. Then he extended the third cross, and the dead man immediately came back to life. In the histories of the Church we also read that when one of the leading women in the city lay close to death, Macarius, the bishop of Jerusalem, brought in first one and then another of the crosses, to no effect; but when he placed the third beside the lady, she opened her eyes at once and rose up cured.

Ambrose says that Judas determined which was the Lord's cross by finding and reading the title that Pilate had placed on the cross. At that moment the devil was up in the air screaming and shouting: "O Judas, why have you done this? My Judas did just the opposite: I pressed him and he betrayed his master, but you, despite my interdict, have found the cross of Jesus! Through the other Judas I gained the souls of many; through you I seem to be losing those I gained. Through him I reigned among the people, through you I will be expelled from my realm. But I will pay you back in turn: I will raise up another king against you, a king who will abandon the faith of the Crucified and by torture will make you deny the Crucified!" It would seem that he said this referring to Julian the Apostate, who, when Judas had become bishop of Jerusalem, inflicted many torments on him and made him a martyr of Christ. Judas heard the devil shouting and screaming but was not frightened in the least. Unshaken, he cursed the evil spirit, saying: "May Christ damn you to eternal fire!"

Judas was later baptized and given the name Quiriacus. When the bishop of Jerusalem died, Quiriacus was ordained bishop. Now the blessed Helena did not have the nails from Christ's cross and asked the new bishop to go to the place and try to find them. He went there and prayed profusely, and at once the nails appeared on the surface, gleaming like gold, and he collected them and delivered them to the queen, who fell to her knees and bowed her head, worshiping them with much reverence. Helena brought a piece of the cross to her son and left other pieces, encased in silver, in the place where the cross had been found.

She also brought to Constantine the nails that had held the Lord's body on the cross. Eusebius of Caesarea reports that the emperor had one of them fashioned into a bit for his war bridle, and had the others welded into his helmet. Some assert, however, as does Gregory of Tours, that four nails had pierced Christ's flesh, and that Helena put two of them in the emperor's bridle, fixed the third into the statue of Constantine that dominates the city of Rome, and cast the fourth into the Adriatic sea, which until then had been a whirlpool perilous to mariners. She also commanded that this feast be solemnly celebrated annually in honor of the finding of the holy cross.

Ambrose has more to say on this subject: "Helena sought the Lord's nails and found them, and had one of them made into a bit and the other worked into the royal crown: it was right that the nail be on the head, the crown at the top, the bridle in the hand, so that the mind should be preeminent, the faith should shine forth, and the royal power should rule."

At a later time Julian the Apostate put Bishop Saint Quiriacus to death because he had found the holy cross while the emperor was trying to destroy the sign of the cross everywhere. When Julian was on his way to attack the Persians, he invited Quiriacus to sacrifice to the idols, and when the bishop refused, Julian ordered his right hand to be cut off, saying: "With that hand you wrote many letters recalling many people from the cult of the gods." Quiriacus answered him: "You are doing me a favor, you rabid dog, because before I believed in Christ, I often wrote letters to the Jewish synagogues to dissuade everyone from believing in Christ, and now you have cut this scandal from my body." Then Julian had lead melted and poured into the saint's mouth, and an iron bed prepared on which Quiriacus was laid while hot coals and fat were sprinkled over him. When the saint lay there motionless, Julian said to him: "If you will not sacrifice to the gods, at least say that you are not a Christian!" Quiriacus cursed him and refused, so he ordered a deep trench to be dug and venomous snakes to be put in it, and Quiriacus to be thrown in on top of them; but the snakes died instantly. The emperor commanded that the bishop be thrown into a caldron full of boiling oil, and the saint, making the sign of the cross, was about to step into it of his own volition, and prayed the Lord to baptize him again with the bath of martyrdom. This angered Julian, who ordered the soldiers to plunge a sword into Quiriacus's chest, and so the saint merited to finish his life in the Lord.

The great power of the cross is evident in the experience of a young notary, a Christian. A sorcerer had deluded him and promised him great wealth, then led him to a place to which the sorcerer had summoned the demons. There the notary saw a huge Ethiopian[10] seated on a high throne, around which stood other Ethiopians armed with spears and cudgels. The large Ethiopian asked the

[10] *Aethiops*, in Jacobus's time, meant a black man, the color black standing for evil as white for virtue. This followed patristic exegesis of passages in the Old and New Testaments. There was no racial implication, because black people were rarely if ever known in Jacobus's time and place.

sorcerer: "Who is this boy?" The sorcerer: "My lord, he is our slave." The demon to the notary: "If you will adore me and be my servant, and deny your Christ, I will have you seated at my right hand." The notary quickly made the sign of the cross and declared that he was in all freedom the servant of Christ his Savior; and the minute he made the sign of the cross, the horde of demons vanished. There came a time when this notary went into the church of Saint Sophia with his master, and they both stood before an image of Christ the Savior. The master noticed that the image had its eyes fixed on the notary, looking at him attentively. The master wondered at this and directed the young man to move to the right, and he saw that the image's eyes turned and were again fixed on the notary. He had the youth go to the left, with the same result. The master begged him to say how he had merited of God that the sacred image should so keep its eyes on him. The young man answered that he was not aware of having done anything meritorious, unless it was that he had refused, before the devil, to deny his Lord.

69. Saint John before the Latin Gate

While John the apostle and evangelist was preaching at Ephesus, he was taken prisoner by the proconsul and invited to sacrifice to the gods. He refused and was remanded to prison, and a letter was sent to Emperor Domitian that described John as guilty of great sacrileges, namely, of despising the gods and of worshiping a crucified man. By Domitian's order he was brought to Rome, and all his hair was cut off in mockery. Then at the city portal called the Latin Gate he was plunged into a caldron of hot oil over a blazing fire, but felt no pain and came out unscathed. (Therefore the Christians built a church at the spot and solemnized that day as the day of the apostle's martyrdom.) When even the caldron did not deter John from preaching Christ, by order of Domitian he was relegated to the island of Patmos.

The reason the Roman emperors persecuted the apostles was not that they preached Christ, since the emperors themselves did not exclude any god, but that without the authorization of the Senate they had declared Christ divine— something the Senate forbade anyone to do. Indeed we read in the *Ecclesiastical History* that Pilate once wrote to Tiberius concerning Christ, and on the strength of that letter Tiberius would have allowed the Christian faith to be preached to the Romans, but the Senate rejected the idea on the ground that Christ could not be called a god by authority of the emperor.

Another reason given in a chronicle for the persecutions was that Christ had not appeared to the Romans first. Still another was that he banned the cult of all the gods, which the Romans practiced. Another was that he preached contempt of worldly goods, and the Romans were avaricious and ambitious. Moreover, Christ himself did not want the Senate to confirm his divinity, lest that be attributed to human power. According to Master John Beleth, another reason the emperors and the Senate persecuted the apostles was that he seemed to them too proud and grudging a god, in that he did not condescend to have any other god sharing his divinity. Orosius assigns another reason, namely, that the Senate was offended because Pilate had addressed letters about Christ's miracles to Tiberius and not to themselves, wherefore the Senate would not allow Christ to be consecrated among the gods. This stung Tiberius, and he proceeded to have many of the senators put to death and condemned others to exile.

When John's mother learned that he was a prisoner in Rome, she was moved by maternal compassion and went to Rome to visit him. Upon arrival there she found that he had been sent into exile, so she set out on the homeward journey and got as far as the city of Nerulana in Campania, where she died. Her body lay for a long time in a cave, until the location was revealed by her son to Saint James. The body, giving off a pervading perfume, was transferred with much honor to the aforementioned city and occasioned many miracles.

70. *The Greater and Lesser Litanies*

The litanies occur twice in the year. The first time is on the feast of Saint Mark, and this is called the Greater Litany. The second, or Lesser Litany, falls on the three days before the feast of the Lord's ascension into heaven. The word "litany" means prayer, supplication, rogation.

The first litany has three names: Greater Litany, Septiform Procession, and Black Crosses. It is called the Greater Litany for three reasons: the first, the one who instituted it, namely, Pope Gregory the Great; the second, the place where it was instituted, namely, Rome, mistress and head of the world due to the presence there of the body of the chief of the apostles and of the apostolic see; the third, the occasion for its institution, which was a widespread and deadly pestilence. The Romans, having lived a continent and abstemious life throughout Lent and having received the Body of the Lord at Easter, afterwards threw off all restraints in feasting, in games, and in voluptuous living. Therefore God, offended by these excesses, sent a devastating plague upon them—a malady called *inguinaria* because it caused a swelling or abscess in the groin. The plague was so virulent that people died suddenly while walking in the street or at table or at play or just talking to each other. It frequently happened that someone sneezed, as they say, and expired in the very act of sneezing; so, if one heard a person sneeze, one quickly said, "God bless you!" This is said to be the origin of the custom that still prevails, of saying "God bless you" when we hear anyone sneeze. Moreover, it is said, when anyone yawned, it was often that person's last breath; so if one felt a yawn coming on, one quickly made the sign of the cross—another custom still common among us. A full account of this plague is included in the life of Saint Gregory.

Secondly, the Greater Litany is called the Septiform Procession because Saint Gregory arranged the processions associated with the litany according to seven orders or classes: first, the clergy; second, all the monks and religious men; third, the women religious; fourth, all the children; fifth, all the laymen; sixth, all widows and unmarried women; and seventh, married women.[1] In our day we cannot count on that many people, so we supply by providing seven litanies to be recited before the insignia are lowered.

Thirdly, the Greater Litany is called the Black Crosses because, as a sign of their grief over the death toll of the plague, people put on black clothing, and, probably for the same reason, crosses and altars were shrouded in sackcloth. In these days of penance likewise, penitential clothing should be worn.

The other litany, which occurs on the three days before Ascension Thursday, was instituted by Saint Mamertus, bishop of Vienne, in the time of the emperor Leo, who began to reign in 458. It began earlier, therefore, than the institution of the Greater Litany and has three names: Lesser Litany, Rogations, and Procession. It is called Lesser to differentiate it from the Greater, because it was inaugurated by a lesser bishop, in a less distinguished place, and on account of a less grave situation than the above-described plague.

The reason for the institution of this litany was the following. At that time Vienne suffered frequent earthquakes, so violent that they leveled many houses and churches, and rumblings and crashes were often heard at night. Then something more terrible happened: on Easter Sunday fire fell from heaven and reduced the king's palace to ashes. And, yet more dreadful: as in the past God had allowed demons to enter into swine, now, the Lord permitting because of the

---

[1] Graesse has the seventh category as *omnes conjugati*, presumably therefore married men and women. He notes that the Ed. Pr. has *conjugatae*, married women—"falsely," he says. But it would seem from the preceding enumeration that there was no class left *except* married women.

sins of men, evil spirits entered wolves and other wild beasts, and these, fearing no man, came running openly over the roads and into the city itself, and at times devoured children and old men and women. The bishop, faced daily with such woeful calamities, proclaimed a three-day fast and instituted litanies, and so brought these tribulations to an end. At a later time the Church established and confirmed this litany for universal observance.

The Lesser Litany is called Rogations because in these three days we implore the help of the saints. This practice should certainly be maintained, and the prayers to the saints and the fasts insisted upon, for several reasons. First, we ask God to end the wars that so often erupt in springtime. Second, we ask him to preserve and multiply the still-tender young fruits of the earth. Third, we seek his help so that everyone may be able to control the impulses of the flesh, which at this season are stronger than usual; for in the spring the blood is hotter and temptations to wrongdoing abound. Fourth, we pray for help in preparing to receive the Holy Spirit: fasting is an excellent preparation and our supplications increase our worthiness.

Master William of Auxerre offers two further reasons for observing the Rogations. The first is that as Christ, ascending, says: "Ask and you shall receive," the Church may petition him more confidently. The second is that the Church fasts and prays in order to have less flesh by mortification, and by prayer to acquire wings, because prayer is the soul's wing by which it flies to heaven. So the soul will be able freely to follow Christ in his ascent: he ascended, opening the road before us, and he flew on the wings of the winds. For a bird that has much flesh and little plumage cannot fly very well: consider, for instance, the ostrich.

The Lesser Litany is called the Procession, because on this occasion the Church holds a great procession at which the cross is borne aloft, the bells are rung, the standard is carried. In some churches men carry a dragon with a huge tail. All the saints are besought one by one for their protection. In this procession we carry the cross and ring the bells to make the devils flee in terror; for just as a king in the midst of his army has the royal insignias, namely, trumpets and standards or banners, so Christ the eternal King in the midst of his Church militant has bells for trumpets and crosses for standards. Any tyrant would be terrified if he heard in his land the trumpets and saw the banners of some powerful king, his enemy; and so the demons who are in that murky air are sore afraid when they hear Christ's trumpets—the bells—and catch sight of his standards—the crosses. It is said that this was the reason for ringing the church bells when storms were brewing, namely, that the demons who stir up the storms should hear the trumpets of the eternal King and flee aghast, letting the storms die down. Of course, there was another reason, which was that the bells would warn the faithful and incite them to pray hard in view of the impending danger.

The cross itself is the banner of the eternal King, as a hymn for Passiontide has it:

Vexilla Regis prodeunt;
Fulget crucis mysterium;
Qua vita mortem pertulit
Et morte vitam protulit.[2]

The demons are afraid of this standard, according to what Chrysostom says: "Wherever the demons see the Lord's sign, they take flight, fearing the rod that scourged them." Moreover, this is why, in certain churches, when storms come up, the cross is brought out of the church and held up against the tempest, precisely so that the evil spirits may see the standard of the King and flee in terror. There, to sum up, is why the cross is held aloft in the procession and the bells are rung—that the demons who are in the air may flee in fright and desist from harassing us.

Another reason for carrying the standard in the procession is to represent the victory of Christ's resurrection and the victory of his ascension. He ascended to heaven with much booty: thus the banner advancing through the air is Christ ascending to heaven, and as a multitude of the faithful follows the standard carried in the procession, so a great assemblage of saints accompanies Christ ascending.

The chants sung in the procession stand for the chants and praises of the angels who met the ascending Christ and led him with his company into the heavens with choruses of praise. In some churches and especially in France, the custom obtains of carrying a dragon with a long tail stuffed with straw or some such material: the first two days it is carried in front of the cross, and the third day, with the tail empty, behind the cross. The significance of this is that on the first day, before the Law, and on the second, under the Law, the devil reigned in this world, but on the third, the day of grace, he was expelled from his realm by the passion of Christ.

Again, in that procession we ask for the protection of all the saints. Several reasons for this have already been noted, but there are other general reasons for which God has commanded us to pray to the saints: our neediness, the saints' glory, and the reverence due to God. The saints can know about the prayers of their supplicants, because in that eternal mirror they perceive whatever pertains to their joy or to our aid. Therefore, the first reason is our neediness, which may be due to a lack of merit, in which case, our merits not sufficing, we pray that others may supply for us. Or we may be deficient in contemplation, and since we cannot look upon the supreme light in itself, we pray to be able at least to see it in the saints. Or our shortcomings may be in our loving, because it is not uncommon for imperfect man to feel himself more drawn to one particular saint than even to God. The second reason is the glory of the saints, for God wills that we invoke the saints in order that, obtaining what we ask for through their

---

[2] The standards of the King advance; / The mystery of the cross shines out; / the cross on which life suffered death / and by death brought forth life.

intercession, we may enhance their greatness and by glorifying them join in praising them. The third reason is the reverence due to God, in that we sinners, because we offend God, do not dare, so to speak, to approach him in his own person, but can implore the support of his friends.

In these litanies the angelic canticle *Sancte Deus, sancte fortis, sancte et immortalis, miserere nobis*[3] would frequently be sung. John of Damascus tells us in Book III that on one occasion, when, on account of some public tribulation, the litanies were being celebrated, a boy was caught up from the midst of the people and carried to heaven. There he learned this canticle, then returned to the congregation and, in full view of the people, sang the canticle and the tribulation was ended. At the Council of Chalcedon the canticle was approved. Damascenus concludes as follows: "We say also that through this canticle the demons go away." The praiseworthiness and authority of the canticle are assured in four ways: first, from the fact that an angel taught it; second, because when it was sung publicly the said tribulation ceased; third, that the Council of Chalcedon approved it; fourth, that the demons fear it.

---

71. Saint Boniface, Martyr

Saint Boniface[1] suffered martyrdom under Emperors Diocletian and Maximian in the city of Tarsus but was buried at Rome on the road called the Via Latina.

Boniface was the chief steward in charge of the properties of a noble lady named Aglaë. The two lived in illicit union, but in time, touched by divine grace, they took counsel and decided that Boniface should go in search of the bodies of some martyrs. Their hope was that if they served and paid honor to the holy martyrs by venerating their relics, they might obtain salvation through the prayers of these saints.

After traveling for some days Boniface arrived at the city of Tarsus and said to those who were with him: "Men, go and find lodging for us! I am going to look for those I want so much to see, the martyrs in their trials!" He hurried to a place where he saw the blessed martyrs—one hanging by his feet with a fire burning below him, another stretched on a rack and tormented as he had been for a long

---

[3] O holy God, holy and strong, holy and immortal, have mercy on us.
[1] Graesse notes (316) that this legend is missing in more recent books.

time, another being torn with hooks, another with his hands cut off, another raised from the ground by a stake driven through his neck. Looking from a distance at these various kinds of torture and martyrdom devised by an impious executioner, and himself aflame with love of Christ, he began to call upon the great God of the holy martyrs, and ran up and sat at their feet, kissing their chains and saying: "O struggling martyrs of Christ, trample on the devil! Persevere for a short while! The labor is slight, and much rest and ineffable satiety will follow! The torments you are suffering for the love of God are temporary and will be over in a moment, and after the briefest interval of time you will pass over to the joys of perpetual happiness! Then, clothed in the glory of immortality and enjoying the vision of your King, you will render him praises of heavenly song amidst the choirs of angels and will see these wicked men, who are torturing you now, themselves being tortured in the abyss of eternal calamity!"

Simplicius the judge saw all this and had Boniface brought before his tribunal. "Who are you?" he asked him. Saint Boniface replied: "I am a Christian and am called Boniface!" The judge angrily ordered him to be hung up and his body to be slashed with hooks until the bones showed; then splinters of wood were driven under his fingernails. The martyr of God looked up to heaven and eagerly bore his pains, and the impious judge, seeing this, ordered molten lead to be poured into his mouth. The holy martyr said: "I give you thanks, Lord Jesus Christ, Son of the living God!" Then the judge ordered a tub to be brought and filled with boiling pitch, into which the holy martyr was plunged head first, but again he remained unharmed, so at the judge's command his head was cut off with a sword. The moment this was done, a tremendous earthquake shook the ground, and many of the infidels, perceiving the power of Christ in and through the martyr, became believers.

Meanwhile the fellow servants of Boniface the martyr looked for him all night everywhere in the city and, not finding him, said to each other: "He's with some whore, or else he's dead drunk in some tavern!" As they talked, it happened that they met one of the town's prison-keepers and asked him: "Have you seen a stranger anywhere, a Roman?" He answered: "Yesterday a foreigner was beheaded in the stadium!" They asked again: "What did he look like? Our man is a sturdy fellow, heavy build, thick head of hair, and was wearing a red cloak." The jailer said: "The man you're looking for died a martyr here yesterday!" They objected: "The man we're looking for is a woman-chaser and a drunkard!" The other said: "Come and see him!" When he showed them the holy martyr's corpse and precious head, they said to him: "He's the man! Please, give him to us!" "I can't give you his body without payment," said the jailer. They gave him five hundred sols and received the holy martyr's body, anointed it with sweet spices, and wrapped it in fine linen. Then they placed it in a litter and so carried it back to Rome, rejoicing and glorifying God.

An angel of the Lord now appeared to the lady for whom Boniface had worked, and informed her about what had happened to the blessed martyr. She hurried to meet the holy body with all veneration, built a monument worthy of it about a half-mile outside the city of Rome, and laid it to rest there.

Boniface was martyred on the fourteenth day of May in Tarsus, the metropolis of Cilicia, and was buried near Rome on the ninth day of June. Blessed Aglaë renounced the world and its pomps and distributed everything she owned to the poor and to monasteries, also freeing her slaves. She devoted her life to constant prayer and fasting, and merited such great graces from the Lord Jesus Christ that she became illustrious by the miracles she wrought in his name. She lived in the habit of a religious for twelve years, died worn out by her pious works, and was buried close to the holy martyr.

72. The Ascension of the Lord

The Lord's ascension occurred forty days after his resurrection. Concerning this event seven questions are to be considered—where he ascended from; why he did not ascend immediately after the resurrection but waited forty days; in what manner he ascended; with whom he ascended; by what merit he ascended; where he ascended to; and why he ascended.

On the first point, note that he rose to heaven from the Mount of Olives, out toward Bethany. This mountain, following another translation, was also called the Mount of Three Lights, because from the west the light from the Temple fell upon it by night, for a fire burned continually on the altar; in the morning it caught the sun's rays from the east before they reached the city; and the hill's olive trees produced a plentiful supply of oil, which feeds light.

Christ appeared twice to his disciples on the day of his ascension and ordered them to go to this mountain. The first time, he appeared to the eleven apostles as they were eating in the cenacle. (All the apostles and other disciples, as well as the women, were living in the section of Jerusalem called Mello, or else on Mount Sion where David had built his palace. There was a large furnished upper room where the Lord had ordered the two disciples to prepare the paschal meal for him, and the eleven apostles were staying in this room while the rest of the disciples and the women were lodged nearby.) They were at table in the cenacle when the Lord appeared to them and rebuked them for their lack of faith; and after he had eaten with them, he ordered them to go to the Mount of Olives, on the road to Bethany, as aforesaid. There he appeared to them again and responded to their untimely questioning, then raised his hands and blessed them. After that, as they looked on, he ascended into heaven.

Regarding the place from which Christ ascended, Sulpicius, bishop of Jerusalem, says, and the *Gloss* also says, that when a church was built there later on, the spot where Christ had stood could never be covered with pavement; and more than that, the marble slabs placed there burst upwards into the faces of those who were laying them. He also says that footmarks in the dust there prove that the Lord had stood on that spot: the footprints are discernible and the ground still retains the depressions his feet had left.

On the second point, namely, why Christ waited forty days to ascend to heaven, let it be known that he did this for three reasons. The first was to provide sure evidence of his resurrection from the dead. It was harder to prove the fact of the resurrection than that of the passion, because from the first day to the third the passion could be proved, but more days were required to establish the truth of the resurrection; therefore a longer time was necessary between the resurrection and the ascension than between the passion and the resurrection. Pope Leo, in his sermon on the Lord's ascension, says: "Today the period of forty days is rounded out, a period fixed by the most sacred planning and lengthened to serve our instruction, so that while the Lord extended his bodily sojourn among us over these days, faith in the resurrection might be supported by necessary evidence. We are grateful for the divine ordering and for the holy fathers' need of delay. They doubted in order that we might not doubt." The second reason was the consolation of the apostles, because the divine consolations are more abundant than our trials, and the time of the Lord's passion was a time of tribulation for the apostles, so the days of consolation had to outnumber the days of tribulation. Thirdly, there was a mystical meaning involved: we were given to understand that the divine consolations are to be compared with our tribulations as a year is compared with a day, a day with an hour, an hour with a moment. The comparison of year to day we find in Isa. 61:2: "To proclaim the acceptable year of the Lord and the day of vengeance of our God." Thus one day of trial yields a year of consolation. The ratio of day to hour is manifest from the fact that the Lord lay dead for forty hours, a time of tribulation, and, rising from the dead, appeared to the disciples over forty days for their consolation. Hence the *Gloss* says: "He had been dead for forty hours, so for forty days he demonstrated that he was alive." The ratio of hour to moment is suggested in Isa. 54:8: "In a moment of indignation have I hid my face a little while from thee, but with everlasting kindness have I had mercy on thee."

The third question concerned the manner of his ascension. First of all, he ascended powerfully, because he did so by his own power, as we read in Isa. 63:1: "Who is this that cometh from Edom . . . walking in the greatness of his strength?" and John 3:13: "No one has ascended into heaven but he who descended from heaven." Admittedly he ascended in a globe of cloud, but he did not do this because he needed the help of a cloud, but to show that every creature was ready to serve its creator. He rose by the power of his godhead, and this indicates a difference, according to the *Scholastic History*: whereas Enoch was translated into paradise and Elijah went up by a whirlwind into heaven, Jesus ascended by his own power. Enoch, according to Gregory, was engendered by coitus and in turn engendered, Elijah was engendered but did not engender, and Jesus was not engendered nor did he engender.

Secondly, he ascended openly, because the disciples were there to observe it, according to Acts 1:9: "While they looked on, he was raised up." John 16:5: "Now I am going to him who sent me, yet no one of you asks me, 'Where are you going?'" The *Gloss*: "Therefore openly, so that no one needs to ask about what he sees happening with the eyes of his body." He willed to have them see him ascending so that they would be on hand as witnesses of his ascension, would rejoice that a human being was carried up into heaven, and would desire to follow him there.

Thirdly, he went up joyfully, because the angels were jubilant, whence Ps. 46:6 (47:5) says: "God ascended with jubilee." Augustine: "As Christ ascends, the whole heaven quakes, the stars marvel, the heavenly hosts applaud, trumpets sound and blend their dulcet harmonies with the joyous choirs."

Fourthly, he went up swiftly, as Ps. 18:6 b (Douai) says: "He has rejoiced as a giant to run the way." He must have ascended with great speed, since he traversed such a distance, as it were in a moment. Rabbi Moses,[1] the great philosopher, tells us that each orbit or heaven of any of the planets is 500 years across, i.e., the distance from one side to the other is as far as someone could travel on a level road in 500 years, and the distance between one heaven and the next is also, he says, a journey of 500 years. Therefore, since there are seven heavens, from the center of the earth to the vault of the heaven of Saturn, the seventh heaven, there will be, according to Rabbi Moses, a journey that would take 7,000 years, and to the dome of the empyrean, 7,700—i.e., as far as one would go on a level road in 7,700 years if he lived that long, each year comprising 365 days and a day's march 40 kilometers, each kilometer being 2,000 paces or cubits long. This is what Rabbi Moses says: whether it be true or not only God knows, for he, who made all things in number, weight, and measure, knows this measurement. So it was a great leap that Christ made from earth to heaven; and about this leap and some others that Christ made, Ambrose says as follows: "By a leap Christ came into this world: he was with the Father and came into the Virgin and leapt from the Virgin to the manger, went down into the Jordan, went up to the cross, went down into the tomb, rose out of the tomb, and is seated at the Father's right hand."

As to the fourth point, namely, with whom Christ ascended, let it be known that he ascended with a great catch of people and a great multitude of angels. That he took a catch of men with him is obvious from what Ps. 68:18 (RSV)

[1] Moses Maimonides, Jewish philosopher (1135–1204).

says: "Thou didst ascend the high mount, leading captives in thy train." That he ascended with a multitude of angels is clear from the question which the lesser angels, seeing Christ ascending, asked of the greater ones, as we read in Isa. 63:1: "Who is this that comes from Edom, in dyed garments from Bosra?" The *Gloss* explains that there were some angels who were not fully cognizant of the mystery of the Lord's incarnation, passion, and resurrection, and, seeing him ascending to heaven by his own power with a multitude of angels and holy men, they wondered at this mystery and said to the angels who accompanied the Lord: "Who is this king of glory?" Dionysius, in the seventh chapter of his book *On the Celestial Hierarchy*, seems to insinuate that, while Christ was ascending, three questions were asked by the angels. The superior angels exchanged the first question among themselves, the same superior angels posed the second to Christ as he ascended, and the inferior angels asked the third of the superior ones.

The superior angels, therefore, ask each other: "Who is this who comes from Edom in dyed garments from Bosra?" Edom is interpreted as meaning "bloody" and Bosra as "armed," as if they said: "Who is this who comes from a world bloodied by sin and armed with malice toward God?" or, "Who comes from a bloody world and a fortified hell?" The Lord responds (Isa. 63:1 b): "It is I, that speak justice, and am a defender, to save." Dionysius puts it this way: "For I," he says, "speak of justice and of the judgment of salvation." In the redemption of the human race there was justice, insofar as the Creator brought back his estranged creature from his master; and there was judgment, insofar as by his power he cast the devil, who had no right to invade men, out of the man he had possessed. But in this connection Dionysius raises the following question: "Since these superior angels are close to God and are enlightened immediately by God, why do they question each other as if desiring to learn from each other?" But, as he himself resolves the question and as the commentator expounds it, by the very fact that the angels ask, they show that they seek knowledge. In the fact that they first confer among themselves, they show that they dare not anticipate God's communication to them. They therefore think it best to ask questions among themselves first, lest by too hasty interrogation they forestall the illumination that comes to them from God.

The same superior angels directed the second question to Christ, saying: "Why then is thy apparel red, and thy garments like those of the one who treads in the winepress?" (Isa. 63:2). Here the Lord is said to have had a garment, namely, his body, that was red because it was running with blood, since even then, while he was ascending, he still bore open scars in his body. Here is what Bede says: "The Lord kept his wounds and will keep them until the Judgment, so that he may build up the faith in his resurrection, that he may present his wounds to his Father as he pleads for humankind, that the good may see how mercifully they were redeemed and the bad may recognize how justly they are damned, and that he may carry with him forever the trophies of his victory." Therefore the Lord answers this question as follows: "I have trodden the winepress alone, and not a man of the Gentiles was with me" (Isa. 63:3). The cross may be called a winepress, because on it he was crushed as in a press and his blood gushed forth. Or he may be calling the devil a winepress, because the evil spirit has so bound and entangled the human race with the cords of sin that whatever was spiritual in them is squeezed out and nothing but the sour pulp is left. But our warrior trampled the winepress, broke the sinners' bonds, and, ascending into heaven, opened the heavenly inn and poured the wine of the Spirit.

The third question is the one the minor angels directed to their superiors, saying: "Who is this king of glory?" (Ps. 24:8, 10). The superior angels answered them: "The Lord of hosts is the king of glory!" With regard to this question and this answer Augustine says: "The vastnesses of the air are sanctified by the divine retinue, and the whole crowd of demons flying about in the air flee away from Christ ascending. Angels, hurrying up, ask, Who is this king of glory? The others answer, There he is, the one who is shining white and rose-colored! He is the one who has neither form nor beauty, who was weak on the cross and strong in plunder, worthless in his poor body, armed in battle, foul in death, comely in resurrection, white from the Virgin, rosy from the cross, dark in shame, and bright in heaven!"

On the fifth point—by what merit Christ ascended—be it known that it was by a threefold merit, about which Jerome says this: "Because of truth, since you fulfilled what you had promised; because of meekness, since you are sacrificed like a sheep for the life of the people; because of justice, since you delivered man not by power but by justice; and your right hand, in other words, power and virtue, will lead you wondrously—i.e., up to heaven." (Cf. Ps. 44:5 Douai.)

The answer to the sixth question, namely, where Christ ascended to, is that he rose above all the heavens, according to what we read in Eph. 4:8–10: "He that descended is the same also that ascended above all the heavens that he might fulfill all things." The text says "above all the heavens" because there are several heavens—the material, the rational, the intellectual, and the supersubstantial—beyond which he ascended. The material heaven is multiple and includes the aerial, the ethereal, the Olympian, the fiery, the starry, the crystalline, and the empyrean heavens. The rational heaven is the just man, who is called a heaven by reason of the divine indwelling, because as heaven is God's seat and dwelling place according to Isa. 66:1—"Heaven is my throne"—so also the righteous soul is the seat of wisdom, according to the Book of Wisdom. He is called heaven also by reason of holy conversation, because by their conversation and desire the saints are always dwelling in heaven, as the apostle says: "Our conversation is in heaven." Or again, by reason of continuous operation, because just as heaven is moved continuously, so the saints are continuously in motion by their good works.

The intellectual heaven is the angel. Angels are called heaven because they are like heaven by reason of their dignity and excellence. Of this dignity and excellence Dionysius, in the fourth chapter of his book *On the Divine Names*, says: "The divine minds *are* above all other existent beings, they live above all other living beings, they understand above all sense and reason, and, more than all other existences, they desire the beautiful and the good and participate therein." Secondly, they are most beautiful by reason of their nature and glory. Of this beauty Dionysius in the same book says: "The angel is a manifestation of the hidden light, a mirror pure, brilliant, uncontaminated, undefiled, unspotted, receiving, if it be allowable so to speak, the beauty of the boniform deiformity of God." Thirdly, they are very strong by reason of their virtue and their power. Speaking about the strength of the angels John of Damascus, in Book II, chapter 3, says: "They are strong and ready to carry out God's will, and they are to be found promptly wherever the divine nod commands." For heaven has height, beauty, strength. Of the first two we read in Ecclus. 43:1: "The firmament on high is his beauty, the beauty of heaven"; and of the third, Job 37:18: "Thou [Job] perhaps hast made the heavens with him, which are most strong."

The supersubstantial heaven is equality with the divine excellence, from which Christ came and to which he later ascended. Of this Ps. 18:7 says: "His going out is from the end of heaven, and his circuit even to the end thereof." Therefore Christ went up above all these heavens to the supersubstantial heaven itself. That he ascended through all the material heavens is assured by what is said in Ps. 8:2: "Thy magnificence is elevated above the heavens." He went through all the material heavens to reach the empyrean heaven, but his ascension was not like that of Elijah, who went up in a fiery chariot to the sublunar region but did not go beyond it. Elijah was transferred into the terrestrial paradise, which is as high as the sublunar region but does not transcend it. Christ therefore resides in the empyrean heaven, and this is the special and proper dwelling for him and for the angels and other saints: the habitation befits the inhabitants. This heaven surpasses the other heavens in dignity, priority, location, and extent, and therefore is a fitting habitation for Christ, who transcends all the rational and intellectual heavens in dignity, eternity, immutability, and the range of his power. Likewise, it is a suitable dwelling for the saints, for that heaven is uniform and immobile and has perfect luminosity and limitless capacity, and so is suitable for the angels and the saints, who were uniform in their works, immobile in love, luminous in faith and in knowledge, and capacious in their reception of the Holy Spirit.

That Christ ascended above all the rational heavens, i.e., above all the saints, is clear from what we read in the Song of Sol. 2:8: "Behold, he comes, leaping upon the mountains, bounding over the hills." Here the mountains stand for angels and the hills for saintly men. That he ascended higher than all the intellectual heavens, i.e., the angels, is evident from what Ps. 103:2 says: "Who makest the clouds thy ascent, who walkest upon the wings of the winds," and from what we read in Ps. 17:11: "He ascended upon the cherubim, and he flew; he flew upon the wings of the winds."

Christ ascended all the way to the supersubstantial heaven, which means that he ascended to equality with God, and this is clear from the last chapter of Mark (16:19): "The Lord Jesus, after he had spoken to them, was taken up into heaven and sits at the right hand of God." The right hand of God is coequality with God. Bernard: "To my Lord, and to him alone, the Lord promised and gave a seat at the right hand of his own glory, as being equal in glory, consubstantial in essence, alike in generation, not unequal in majesty nor later in time because eternal." Or it can be said that Christ in his ascension was sublime in four distinct ways—in terms of place and of the reward received, and in his knowledge and his virtue. Of the first, Eph. 4:10: "He that descended is the same also that ascended above all the heavens"; of the second, Phil. 2:8–9: "He humbled himself, becoming obedient unto death, etc." To this, Augustine says: "Humility merits glory, glory is the reward of humility." Of the third, Ps. 17:11 (Douai) says: "He sits enthroned upon the cherubim," i.e., above all the fullness of knowledge. The fourth sublimity is evident because he also ascended above the seraphim; Eph. 3:19: "To know also the charity of Christ, which surpasses all knowledge."

Regarding the seventh question, namely, why Christ ascended, it is to be noted that his ascension was fruitful or beneficial in nine ways. The first is that it brought down the love of God upon us; John 16:7: "If I go not, the Paraclete will not come to you; but if I go, I will send him to you." The second fruit is our greater knowledge of God; John 14:28: "If you loved me, you would indeed be glad because I go to the Father, for the Father is greater than I." To this Augustine says: "Therefore I take away this servile form, in which the Father is greater than I, so that you may be able the better to see God otherwise, as spirit." The third benefit is the merit of faith. Of this Pope Leo says in his sermon on the Lord's ascension: "Then a more instructed faith began to advance, with the stride of the mind, toward the Son as equal to the Father, contact with the corporeal substance in Christ, by which he is less than the Father, no longer being needed. For this is the strength of great minds—to believe without hesitating things that the eye of the body cannot see, and to fix desire on what you cannot reach by sight." Augustine, in the *Confessions*: "He has rejoiced as a giant to run the way: he did not tarry but ran, crying out by words, by deeds, by death, by life, by descent and ascension, crying out to us to return to him, and he departed from our sight that we might come back into our hearts and find him there."

The fourth fruit is our security. Christ ascended in order to be our advocate with the Father. We can be secure indeed when we realize that we have such an advocate to plead our cause; 1 John 2:1: "We have an advocate with the Father, Jesus Christ the just; and he is the propitiation for our sins." About this security

Bernard says: "O man, you have sure access to God, when the mother stands before the Son and the Son stands before the Father, the mother shows her Son her bosom and her breasts, the Son shows his Father his side and his wounds. Surely then, where there are so many marks of love, there can be no refusal."

The fifth benefit is our dignity. Very great indeed is our dignity, when our nature is exalted to the right hand of God! The angels, having in mind this dignity of mankind, forbade men to worship them, as we read in Apoc. 19:10: "I fell down at his feet to adore him. And he said to me, You must not do that. I am a fellow servant with you and your brethren." To this the *Gloss* adds: "[The angel] allowed himself to be adored, but after the Lord's ascension, seeing a man exalted above himself, he was afraid to receive adoration." Pope Leo, in a sermon on the Lord's ascension, says: "On this day the nature of our humanity was raised up beyond the height of every power to be seated with God the Father, in order that God's grace should become more wondrous, since what men had thought to have a just claim to their veneration had been removed from their sight, yet faith did not falter nor hope waver nor charity grow cool."

The sixth fruit of the Lord's ascension is the strengthening of our hope; Heb. 4:14: "Having therefore a great high priest who has passed into the heavens, Jesus the Son of God, let us hold fast the confession of our hope"; and Heb. 6:18–19 (RSV): "That we who fled for refuge might have strong encouragement to seize the hope set before us. We have this as a sure and steadfast anchor of the soul, a hope that enters into the inner shrine behind the curtain, where Jesus has gone as a forerunner in our behalf." On this, Leo again: "Christ's ascension is our elevation, and where the glory of the head has gone before, there the hope of the body tends also."

The seventh benefit is that the way is marked out for us; Mic. 2:13: "He shall go up that shall open the way before them." Augustine: "The Savior himself has become your way: arise and walk, you have the way, don't be sluggish!" The eighth fruit is the opening of the gate of heaven; for as the first Adam opened the gates of hell, so the second the gates of paradise. So the Church sings: "You overcame the pain of death and opened the kingdom of heaven to those who believe." The ninth is the preparation of the place; John 14:2: "I go to prepare a place for you." Augustine: "O Lord, do prepare what you are preparing: for you are preparing us for yourself and you are preparing yourself for us when you prepare a place both for yourself in us and for us in yourself."

73. The Holy Spirit

On this day of Pentecost, as sacred history testifies in the Acts of the Apostles, the Holy Spirit was sent upon the apostles in tongues of fire. About this sending or coming eight points are to be considered: first, by whom the Spirit was sent; second, in how many ways he is or was sent; third, the time at which he was sent; fourth, how many times he was sent; fifth, how he was sent; sixth, upon whom he was sent; seventh, for what reasons he was sent; eighth, what led to his being sent.

On the first point, let it be noted that the Father sent the Spirit, the Son sent him, and the Holy Spirit gave and sent himself. The Father sent him; John 14:25: "The Counselor, whom the Father will send in my name. . . ." The Son sent him; John 16:7: "If I do go away, I will send him to you." In worldly affairs one can discern a triple comparison to illustrate the relationship of the sender to the person or thing sent. The sender gives being to what is sent, as the sun sends its rays; the sender gives power to what is sent, as the lancer sends the lance; the sender gives jurisdiction and authority, as the ruler sends the ambassador. This triple relationship can be seen in the sending of the Holy Spirit: he is sent by the Father and the Son as having from them being, power, and authority to act. Nevertheless, the Holy Spirit gave and sent himself, as seems to be indicated in John 16:13, where we read: "But when the Spirit of truth comes, he will guide you into all the truth." Pope Saint Leo says in a sermon for Pentecost: "The Blessed Trinity, the immutable Godhead, is one in substance, undivided in operation, unanimous in willing, equal in omnipotence, equal also in glory. The mercy of the Trinity apportioned the work of our redemption within Itself, so that the Father is propitiated, the Son propitiates, the Holy Spirit lights the fire of love."

The Holy Spirit is God, and therefore it is rightly said that he gives himself. Ambrose, in his book *On the Holy Spirit*, shows that the Spirit is God, saying: "Four things prove the manifest glory of his divinity. He is known to be God either because he is without sin, or because he forgives sins, or because he is not a creature but the Creator, or because he does not adore but is adored." And how the Blessed Trinity has given Itself to us totally is shown in this: the Father has offered us all he had, because, as Augustine says, he sent his Son as the price of our redemption and the Holy Spirit as the privilege of our adoption, and himself he holds in reserve as the inheritance due to us as adopted sons and daughters. Likewise the Son has offered himself to us totally, because, as Bernard says, he is himself shepherd, himself pasture, himself redemption, for he gave us his soul as ransom, his blood as drink, his flesh as food, and his divinity as reward. The Holy Spirit, too, offered and offers all his gifts totally to us, as we read in 1 Cor. 12:8–10: "To one indeed, by the Spirit, is given the word of wisdom; and to another the word of knowledge, according to the same Spirit; to another, faith by the same Spirit," and so on. Pope Leo says: "The Holy Spirit is the inspirer of faith, the teacher of knowledge, the font of love, the seal of chastity, and the cause of the whole of salvation."

On the second question, namely, the number of ways the Spirit is or was sent, note that he is sent in two ways, visibly and invisibly—invisibly when he penetrates into holy souls, visibly when his presence is shown by some visible sign. Of the invisible sending John 3:8 says: "The Spirit breathes where he wills, and you hear his voice but you do not know whence he comes or whither he goes." No wonder, because, as Bernard says regarding the invisible Word: "It does not come in through the eyes, because it has no color; nor through the nostrils, because it does not mingle with the air but with the mind, nor does it taint the air but makes it; nor through the jaws, because it cannot be chewed or gulped; nor through corporeal touch, because it is not palpable. So you ask: if the ways of the Word are so untraceable, how do you know he is present? The answer: I have known his presence when my heart was touched with fear; when I fled from vice, I knew the strength of his power; from what my eyes tell me and make me see, I marvel at the depth of the Word's wisdom; from the slightest amendment of my manner of life, I have come to experience his kindness and gentleness, and from the reformation and renewal of the spirit of my mind, I have somehow perceived the splendor of his beauty; and seeing all this at once, I stand in awe of the multiplicity of his greatness." Thus far Bernard.

The sending is visible when it is marked by some visible sign. It is to be noted that the sending of the Holy Spirit was shown by five kinds of visible signs. Firstly, he appeared in the form of a dove over Christ at his baptism; so Luke 3:22: "The Holy Spirit descended upon him in bodily form as a dove." Secondly, he came in a shining cloud around Christ transfigured; Matt. 17:5: "He was still speaking when lo, a bright cloud overshadowed them." As at the Lord's baptism so also at his glorification, the Holy Spirit manifested the mystery of the Blessed Trinity, in the former as a dove, in the latter as a bright cloud. Thirdly, he came as a breath; John 20:22: "He breathed upon them and said to them, 'Receive the Holy Spirit, etc.'" Fourthly, as fire, and fifthly, in the shape of a tongue; and in this double form he appeared on this day.

The Spirit showed himself in the forms of five different things to let it be known that he produces the properties of these things in the hearts in which he makes his dwelling. First, he was seen in the form of a dove. The dove's call is a moaning sound, it has no bile or bitterness, it nests in the clefts of the rock. So the Holy Spirit makes those whom he fills moan over their sins; Isa. 59:11: "We shall all roar like bears and shall lament as mournful doves"; Rom. 8:26: "The Spirit himself intercedes for us with sighs too deep for words"—i.e., he makes us plead and groan. The Spirit also frees us of the bile of bitterness; Wisd. 12:1: "O how good and sweet is thy Spirit, O Lord, in all of us"; and in the seventh chapter of the same book he is called gentle, loving, and beneficent because he makes us gentle in speech, loving in heart, and beneficent in action. He lives in "the clefts of the rock," by which we understand the wounds of Christ. In the Song of Sol. 2:10 we read: "Arise, make haste, my love, my bride, and come, my dove in the clefts of the rock," and the *Gloss* explains: "Keep my nestlings warm for me by the inpouring of the Holy Spirit"; and the *Gloss* on the clefts of the rock: "in Christ's wounds." In Lam. 4:20 Jeremiah says: "The breath (*spiritus*) of our mouth, Christ the Lord, is taken in our sins, to whom we said, Under thy shadow we shall live among the Gentiles"—as if he said: "The Holy Spirit (who is the breath of our mouth, since our mouth is Christ the Lord because he is our mouth and our flesh) makes us say to Christ, 'We shall live in your shadow, that is, in your passion (in which Christ was in darkness and despised), by remembering it continually.'"

The second visible sign was the cloud. A cloud is lifted above the earth, it cools the earth and generates rain. So the Spirit lifts those whom he fills by making them look down on the things of earth; Ezek. 8:3: "The spirit lifted me up between earth and heaven, etc."; also the same, 1:19–21: "When the living creatures rose from the earth, the wheels rose. Wherever the spirit would go, they went, and the wheels rose along with them; for the spirit of life was in the wheels." Similarly Gregory: "Once the spirit has been tasted, all flesh loses its savor."

The Spirit provides cooling against the incitements of vice; so Mary was told: "The Holy Spirit will come upon you and the power of the Most High will overshadow you"—i.e., will give you coolness from all heat of vices. Hence also the Holy Spirit is called water, which has regenerative power; John 7:38–39: "Scripture says, 'Out of his belly shall flow rivers of living water.' Now this he said of the Spirit which those who believed in him were to receive." Thirdly, the Spirit generates a rain of tears; Ps. 147:18: "His wind shall blow and the waters shall run"—i.e., the waters of tears.

Third, he was shown in the visible form of breath. Breath is mobile, hot, smooth, and necessary for breathing. So the Holy Spirit is mobile, i.e., quick at diffusing himself; indeed he is more mobile than all else that moves. On the text, "Suddenly a sound came from heaven like the rush of a mighty wind," the *Gloss* says: "No obstacles can slow the grace of the Holy Spirit." Second, he is hot in order to start a fire; Luke 12:49: "I came to cast fire upon the earth and would that it were already kindled." Hence the Spirit is compared to the hot south wind; Song of Sol. 4:16: "Awake, O north wind, and come, O south wind. Blow upon my garden, let its fragrance be wafted abroad." Third, the Spirit is smooth in order to smooth and soften. To convey this he is called by the name of ointment, as is clear from the first letter of John, 2:27: "His anointing teaches you about everything." Also by the name of dew, so the Church sings: "May he make you fruitful by the inward shower of dew." Or he is called a gentle breeze; 1 Kings 19:12: "And after the fire a whistling of a gentle air," and there was the Lord. Moreover, breath is necessary for breathing—so necessary, indeed, that if it was taken away even for a short time, a man would die very quickly. This is also to be understood of the Holy Spirit. So Ps. 104:30: "Thou shalt take away their breath and they shall fail and shall return to their dust; thou shalt send forth thy Spirit and they shall be created, and thou shalt renew the face of the earth." So also John 6:63: "It is the Spirit that gives life."

Fourth, the Holy Spirit was shown in the appearance of fire, and fifthly, in the shape of tongues, as we read: "There appeared to them parted tongues, as it were of fire: and it sat upon every one of them." Why the Spirit appeared on this day in the double form of fire and tongues will be explained further on.

About the third question, namely, at what time the sending of the Spirit occurred, note that he was sent on the fiftieth day after Easter. This day was chosen to make it clear that from the Holy Spirit come the perfection of the law, eternal reward, and remission of sins. The perfection of the law is his work, because, according to the *Gloss*, on the fiftieth day, after the preliminary immolation of the lamb, the law was given in fire, and in the New Testament, on the fiftieth day from Christ's Pasch the Spirit descended in fire; the law on Mount Sinai and the Spirit on Mount Sion, the law at the top of a high mountain and the Spirit in the upper room. By this it is implied that the Holy Spirit himself is the perfection of the whole law because the fullness of the law is love.

The fiftieth day signifies eternal reward. The *Gloss* says: "Just as the period of forty days after his resurrection, during which Christ was with his disciples, stands for the present Church, so the fiftieth day on which the Spirit is given signifies the wage of eternal reward." And the remission of sins is indicated, as the *Gloss* points out: "Therefore in the fiftieth year the jubilee indulgence was granted and sins were remitted by the Holy Spirit . . ." and the *Gloss* continues: "In the spiritual jubilee the guilty are absolved, debts are forgiven, exiles are called back to their homeland, the lost heritage is restored, slaves—i.e., men sold into sin—are freed from the yoke of servitude." Thus far the *Gloss*. Those under sentence of death are pardoned and set free, hence Rom. 8:2: "The law of the Spirit of life in Christ Jesus has set me free from the law of sin and death." The debts of sin are remitted, because love covers a multitude of sins. Exiles are called back to their homeland, so Ps. 142:10: "Thy good spirit shall lead me into the right land." The lost heritage is regained; Rom. 8:16–17: "It is the Spirit himself bearing witness with our spirit that we are children of God, and if children, then heirs." Slaves are liberated; 2 Cor. 3:17: "Where the Spirit of the Lord is, there is freedom."

Now for the fourth question, namely, how many times the Spirit was sent to the apostles. According to the *Gloss* he was given to them three times—before Christ's passion, after his resurrection, and after his ascension. The first time he came to empower them to perform miracles, the second time to forgive sins; the third time he gave them strength of heart.

First, then, because the Lord was sending the apostles to preach and drive out demons and cure sickness, he gave them the power to do miracles, and these miracles are the work of the Holy Spirit, as we read in Matt. 12:28: "If it is by the Spirit of God that I cast out demons, then the kingdom of God has come upon you." It does not follow, however, that everyone who has the Holy Spirit can perform miracles. Miracles, as Gregory says, do not make a man a saint; they show that he is a saint. Nor does it follow that everyone who does miracles has the Holy Spirit, because the wicked declare that they have performed them, saying: "Lord, Lord, have we not prophesied in thy name and cast out devils in thy name and done many miracles in thy name?" God does miracles by his own authority, angels because they are superior to matter, demons through natural forces inherent in things, magicians through secret contracts with demons, good Christians by justice publicly recognized, bad Christians by such justice simulated.

The second time Christ gave the Spirit to the apostles was when he breathed upon them and said: "Receive the Holy Spirit. Whose sins you shall forgive they are forgiven them, whose sins you shall retain they are retained." Yet no one can remit sin as to the stain which it produces in the soul, nor as to the guilt, i.e., the eternal punishment that it calls for, nor as to the offense to God: all these are remitted only by the infusion of grace and by virtue of contrition. The priest is said to absolve because he declares that the fault has been remitted, because he commutes the penalty of purgatory to a temporal one, and because he dispenses a part of the temporal punishment.

The third time the Spirit was given was on this day, when the disciples' hearts were so strengthened that they had no fear of torments; Ps. 32:6: ". . . all the power of them by the spirit of his mouth." Augustine says: "Such is the grace of the Holy Spirit that if he finds sadness he dispels it, if an evil desire he quells it, if fear he drives it out." Pope Leo says: "The apostles hoped for the Holy Spirit, not that he would then come to dwell in holy souls for the first time but that he would inflame hearts that were already sanctified with still greater fervor, and would inundate them more copiously, piling up his gifts, not starting them or working something new, but rather lavishing greater riches."

Our fifth point is the manner of the Spirit's sending, and we note that he was sent with sound and in fiery tongues, and that these tongues of fire appeared sitting upon the apostles. The sound was sudden, heavenly, vehement, and filling: sudden because no obstacle can slow the Spirit's action; heavenly because he produces heavenly effects; vehement because he induces filial fear, or because he repels eternal woe (*vehemens* = *veh adimens*, taking away woe) or because he moves the mind away from all carnal love (*vehens mentem*, moving the mind). The sound was filling because the Holy Spirit filled all the apostles, as we read:

"They were all filled with the Holy Spirit." There was in the apostles a threefold sign of this fullness. The first sign consists in not resounding, as a full wine cask does not resound, and as in Job 6:5: "Will the ox low when he stands before a full manger?"—as if to say that when the manger of the heart contains the fullness of grace, there should be no lowing of impatience. The apostles had this sign because in tribulation they uttered no complaint but rather went from the presence of the council rejoicing that they were accounted worthy to suffer reproach for the name of Jesus (Acts 5:41).

The second sign of fullness is that no more can be taken in—in other words, that's enough. When a vessel is filled with a fluid, it cannot take any more; similarly, when a man has eaten his fill, he has no more appetite. So the saints, who have the fullness of grace, can no longer receive another fluid, namely, that of earthly love; Isa. 1:11: "I am full, I desire not holocausts." In the same way those who have tasted the sweetness of heaven do not thirst for earthly pleasure. Augustine: "When anyone has drunk from the river of Paradise, one drop of which is greater than the ocean, in him the thirst for this world is quenched." This sign was in the apostles: they wanted to have nothing of their own and to share everything in common.

The third sign of fullness is overflow, as is seen in a river in flood; Ecclus. 24:23: "It overflows, like the Pishon, with wisdom." Literally, that river regularly overflows its banks and inundates the adjacent land. The apostles began to overflow, because they started to speak in various languages. The *Gloss* says: "Behold a sign of fullness; the full vase bursts, fire cannot be hidden in a man's bosom"; and so they began to irrigate what lay around them, Peter started to speak, and three thousand were converted.

The Spirit was sent in tongues of fire, and about this we shall see three things: why he came in tongues conjoined with fire, why in fire rather than in some other element, and why in tongues rather than in some other member.

First, note that there are three motives for his appearing in fiery tongues. The first was to enable the apostles to proclaim words of fire: the second, that they might preach a law of fire, namely, the law of love. Of these two Bernard says: "The Holy Spirit came in fiery tongues in order that they might speak words of fire in the languages of all the peoples, and that fiery tongues might preach a law of fire." The third reason is that they should know it was the Holy Spirit, who is fire, that spoke through them; they were not to have any doubt about this, nor to claim the conversion of others as their own doing. Thus all who heard their words heard them as the words of God.

On the second point, let it be known that there are several reasons for the sending of the Spirit in the form of fire. The first is related to his sevenfold grace, for the Spirit, like fire, lowers the lofty by the gift of fear, softens the hard by the gift of piety, enlightens the obscure through knowledge, restrains the unsure by the gift of counsel, reinforces the weak through fortitude, refines the metals by removing dross through the gift of understanding, and mounts upward by the gift of wisdom.

The Spirit came as fire also by reason of his dignity and excellence. Fire surpasses the other elements by its appearance, its rank, and its power: by its appearance because of the beauty of its light, in rank by the sublimity of its position, in power by its vigor in action. So too the Spirit excels in all these respects—in the first, because he is called the Holy Spirit without stain, in the second because he penetrates all intelligent spirits, in the third because he possesses all power, as we read in Wisd. 7:22–23.

The third reason for the Spirit's coming in fire is its manifold efficacy. This reason is explained by Rabanus as follows: "Fire has four natures; it burns, it purges, it heats, and it gives light. So likewise the Spirit burns away sins, purges hearts, dispels tepidity, enlightens ignorance." Thus Rabanus. The Spirit burns away sins; Zech. 13:9: "I will bring them through the fire and will refine them as silver is refined." The prophets prayed to be burned with this fire, saying (Ps. 25:2 Vulgate): "Prove me, O Lord; burn my reins and my heart." He purges hearts; Isa. 4:4: "When the Lord shall wash away the blood of Jerusalem from its midst by the spirit of judgment and by the spirit of burning." He dispels tepidity, and Rom. 12:11 describes those whom the Holy Spirit fills as "aglow with the Spirit." Gregory says: "The Holy Spirit appeared in fire, because he drives the torpor of coldness out of every heart he fills, and sets that heart afire with desire for his eternity." He enlightens ignorance; Wisd. 9:17: "Who shall know thy thought, except thou give wisdom, and send thy Holy Spirit from above?" And 1 Cor. 2:10 says: "God has revealed to us through the Spirit."

The fourth reason is the nature of love itself. Fire expresses the significance of love in three ways. First, fire is always in motion, and love keeps those whom the Holy Spirit fills always moving in good works. So Gregory says: "The love of God is never idle. If it is love, it accomplishes great things, and if it accomplishes nothing, it is not love." Second, of all the elements fire is the most formal: it has little matter and much form. In the same way the love of the Holy Spirit makes those whom he fills have little love for earthly things and much love for celestial and spiritual things, so that it is not carnal things loved carnally but rather spiritual things loved spiritually. Bernard distinguishes four ways of loving: to love the flesh for the flesh, the spirit for the flesh, the flesh for the spirit, and the spirit for itself. Third, fire has the power to bend high things downwards, to tend upwards, to bring fluids together and coagulate them; and by that we are to understand the triple force of love, as we learn from Dionysius's words in the book *On the Divine Names*: "Love has three kinds of force, namely, the inclinative, the elevative, and the coordinative: it inclines the higher toward the lower, elevates the lower toward the higher, and coordinates equals with equals." Thus Dionysius. The Holy Spirit produces this triple power of love in those whom he fills, because he lowers them by humility and contempt of self, elevates them toward desire for the things that are above, and coordinates them by uniformity of moral values.

Now why did the Spirit appear in the shape of a tongue rather than in that of another member? For three reasons. The tongue is the member ignited by the fire of Gehenna, is hard to control, and is useful when well controlled. Therefore, because the tongue was inflamed by hellfire, it needed the fire of the Holy Spirit; James 3:6: "Our tongue is a fire, a world of iniquity." Because it is hard to control the tongue, it needs the grace of the Spirit more than the other members do; James 3:7: "Every nature of beasts and of birds and of the rest is tamed by the nature of man, but the tongue no man can tame." Because the tongue is very useful if well controlled, it needed to have the Holy Spirit as its controller.

By appearing in the shape of a tongue, the Spirit also indicated how necessary he is to preachers. Preachers need him because he makes them speak fervently, without hesitation, and therefore he was sent in the appearance of fire. Bernard: "The Holy Spirit came upon the apostles in tongues of fire so that they might speak fiery words and that fiery tongues might preach a law of fire." They could speak confidently, not faintheartedly; Acts 2:4, 4:29: "They were all filled with the Holy Spirit and began to speak the word with all confidence." They could speak differently according to the different capacities of their hearers, and Acts says that they spoke in various tongues. They spoke usefully, for edification and benefit; Isa. 61:1: "The Spirit of the Lord is upon me, because the Lord has anointed me" . . . to bring good tidings to the afflicted.

The tongues of fire appeared sitting upon the apostles, to signify that he was needed by those who preside; and indeed the Spirit is needed by presiders and judges because he confers authority to remit sin; John 20:23: "Receive the Holy Spirit. Whose sins you shall forgive, etc." They need wisdom in order to judge; Isa. 42:1: "I have put my spirit upon him; he will bring forth justice to the nations." They need kind hearts in order to give support; Num. 11:17: "I will give them some of the spirit that is upon you; and they shall bear the burden of the people with you." The spirit of Moses was the spirit of kindness, as is clear from Num. 12:3: "now the man Moses was very meek." And they should be adorned with holiness so as to communicate holiness; Job 26:13: "His spirit has adorned the heavens."

Our sixth question concerns those upon whom the Spirit was sent, and we note that he was sent upon the disciples, who were clean receptacles, apt to receive the Holy Spirit due to seven qualities that were in them. First, they were quiet, restful people, as is indicated in the Scripture: "When the day of Pentecost had come . . . ," i.e., the day of rest. The feast of Pentecost was appointed for rest; Isa. 66:1c–2: "What is this place of my rest? . . . To whom shall I look, but to him that is humble and of a contrite spirit?" Second, they were united in love, as we read: "They were all together"—meaning of one heart and one soul. For just as a man's spirit does not give life to the members of his body unless they are united, neither does the Holy Spirit vivify spiritual members [unless they are united]. And as a fire is extinguished when the burning wood is scattered, so discord among men puts out the Holy Spirit, whence we sing about the apostles: "The God of gods found them united in charity and flooded them with his light." Third, they were in a secret place, as the text notes, "in one place," namely, in the cenacle; hence Hos. 2:14: "I will bring her into the wilderness and speak tenderly to her." Fourth, they were zealous in prayer, whence the text: "All these with one accord devoted themselves to prayer." So we sing

> Apostolis orantibus
> Repente de coelo sonus
> Deum venisse nuntiat.[1]

Prayer is necessary for the reception of the Holy Spirit, as we know from Wisd. 7:7: "I called upon God, and the spirit of wisdom came upon me." We also read in John 14:16: "I will pray the Father and he will give you another counselor."

Fifth, they were graced with humility, which is indicated when they are described as "sitting." So Ps. 104:10: "Thou makest springs to gush forth in the valleys," i.e., you give the grace of the Holy Spirit to the humble; and "What is this place of my rest? . . . him that is humble, etc." Sixth, they were joined together in peace, as we see from the fact that they were in Jerusalem, which name means "vision of peace." The Lord shows that peace is necessary for the receiving of the Holy Spirit; John 20:19f.: he first offered peace, saying "peace be with you," then breathed upon them and said: "Receive the Holy Spirit." Seventh, they were lifted up in contemplation, which is indicated by the fact that they received the Spirit in the upper room. To this the *Gloss* says: "Whoever desires the Holy Spirit rises above his fleshly dwelling and tramples it by spiritual contemplation."

The seventh point, for what reasons the Spirit was sent: note that he was sent for six reasons, which are noted in Christ's promises at the Last Supper: "The Paraclete, the Holy Spirit, etc."; John 14:26ff. Firstly, he is sent to console the sorrowful, because he is called the Paraclete, which also means consoler; Isa. 61:1–2: "The Spirit of the Lord is upon me . . . to bring good tidings to the afflicted . . . to those who mourn in Sion." Gregory: "The Spirit is called the Consoler because while he prepares the hope of pardon in those who grieve for having committed sin, he lifts their spirit out of the affliction of sadness." Secondly, he is sent to give life to the dead, and so is called Spirit, because it is the spirit that gives life; Ezek. 37:4: "O dry bones, hear the word of the Lord. Behold I will cause breath to enter you and you shall live." Thirdly, to sanctify the unclean, and so he is called *sanctus*, holy; for as he is called the Spirit, which gives life, so he is also called *sanctus*, because he sanctifies, makes holy and cleanses. Hence "holy" and "clean" are equivalent. Ps. 45(46):5: "The stream of the river makes the city of God joyful," i.e., the cleansing and overflowing grace

---

[1] While the apostles are at prayer / suddenly a sound from heaven / announces that God has come.

of the Holy Spirit gives joy to the city of God, meaning the Church of God, and by that river he has sanctified his most high tabernacle.

Fourthly, to establish love among those divided by discord and hatred: this is indicated by the title "Father." He is called Father because by his nature he loves us; John 16:27: "The Father himself loves you." Thus the Father, and we his children, and brothers toward each other and among brothers, persevere in perfect friendship. Fifthly, to save the just; this is shown by the words "in my name," the name Jesus meaning salvation. Therefore the Father sent the Spirit in the name of Jesus, in the name of salvation, to show that he came to save the nations. Sixthly, to teach the ignorant, so: "He will teach you all things."

On the eighth point, be it noted that the Spirit is given or was sent in the primitive Church, first in response to prayer: the apostles were praying, and (Luke 3:21) Jesus was praying and the Holy Spirit descended upon him. Second, through devout and attentive hearing of the word of God; Acts 10:44: "While Peter was still saying this, the Holy Spirit fell on all who heard the word." Third, through assiduous doing of works, as is indicated in the laying on of hands; Acts 8:17: "Then they laid their hands upon them, and they received the Holy Spirit." Or the laying on of hands signifies absolution, as is done in confession.

74. Saints Gordianus and Epimachus

Gordianus comes from *geos*, which means dogma or house, and *dyan*, which means bright; hence a bright house in which God dwelt. Thus Augustine says in the book *The City of God*: "A good house is one in which the parts fit well together, and which is spacious and full of light." So Saint Gordianus was well disposed by maintaining harmony, spacious through charity, and filled with the light of truth. Epimachus comes from *epi*, above, and *machin*, king, so a high king; or from *epi*, above, and *machos*, fight, so a fighter for the things above.

Gordianus was a commissioner of Emperor Julian. Once he was trying to compel a Christian named Januarius to sacrifice to the gods, but listened to his preaching and, with his wife Mariria and fifty-three others, was converted to the faith. When Julian learned of this, he sent Januarius into exile and condemned Gordianus to be beheaded if he refused to offer sacrifice. So blessed Gordianus was beheaded and his body thrown to the dogs, but when it lay untouched for a week, his retainers took it away and buried it with the body of Saint Epimachus, whom the aforesaid Julian had had put to death a short time earlier. They were buried about a mile from the city about A.D. 360.

✳

75. Saints Nereus and Achilleus

Nereus is interpreted counsel of light, or it is derived from *nereth*, i.e., never guilty. Saint Nereus was a counsel of light by his preaching of virginity; he was a lamp in his virtuous everyday life; he was hasty in his fervor for heaven, and *ne reus*, i.e., never guilty, in the purity of his conscience. Achilleus comes from *achi*, which means my brother, and *lesa*, salvation, as the saint was the salvation of his brothers. The passions of these two saints were written by Euthices, Victorinus, and Macro, servants of Christ.

Nereus and Achilleus were the eunuchs in charge of the private chambers of Domitilla, the niece of the emperor Domitian. When this lady was about to be married to Aurelian, the son of a consul, and was arrayed in jewels and purple garments, Nereus and Achilleus preached the Christian faith to her and commended virginity to her for many reasons. They showed her that virginity was dear to God, related to the angels, and innate in human beings. On the other hand, a wife was subject to her husband and exposed to kicks and punches. She might give birth to one or more deformed children. Furthermore, they said, she found it hard to accept correction from her loving mother, but she would have to put up with her spouse's high-handed reprimands.

Domitilla said many things in reply, among them this: "I know my father was a jealous man and my mother had to take much abuse from him. Is my husband bound to be like that?" They answered: "As long as men are simply betrothed, they are all sweetness and light, but once they are married, they are cruel and domineering, and sometimes they prefer the chambermaid to her mistress! Moreover, every virtue, if lost, can be recovered by doing penance: virginity alone cannot be recalled to its pristine state. The guilt can be expunged by penance, but virginity cannot be regained." Having heard them out, Flavia Domitilla accepted the faith, made a vow of virginity, and took the veil from Pope Saint Clement.

When her husband-to-be was apprised of all this, he obtained the emperor's permission and sent the virgin with Saints Nereus and Achilleus into exile on the island of Pontus, hoping that this would change her decision. Some time later he himself went to the island and offered many gifts to the saints to induce them to persuade the virgin to change, but they wanted none of it and, to the contrary, strengthened her in her faith in the Lord. When they were under pressure to offer sacrifice, they said that they had been baptized by the apostle Saint Peter and that nothing would make them offer sacrifice to the idols, so they were beheaded about A.D. 80, and their bodies were buried near the tomb of Saint Petronilla.

There were others, namely Victorinus, Euthices, and Marco, to whom Domitilla was attached, and these men Aurelian compelled to work all day as slaves on his estates, giving them dog's food to eat at nightfall. In the end he had Euthices beaten until he expired, and had Victorinus suffocated in fetid waters. Marco he ordered to be crushed to death under an enormous rock. When this monstrous rock, which seventy men could hardly budge, was thrown on Marco, he caught it on his shoulders and carried it for two miles, as if it were as light as chaff. This brought many to embrace the faith, and the consul's son had Marco put to death.

After that, Aurelian took Domitilla back from exile and sent two young women named Euphrosina and Theodora, who were foster-sisters of hers, to induce her to change her mind, but instead, she converted them to the faith. Then Aurelian came to Domitilla with three minstrels and the pledged spouses of the two maidens, to proceed with the celebration of her wedding, after which he would take her to bed, by force if necessary. But Domitilla had already con- verted the two young men, so Aurelian brought Domitilla into the bedchamber and there ordered the minstrels to sing and the others to dance with him, intend- ing to ravish the virgin thereafter. But the mimes fainted with exhaustion due to their singing, and the others likewise due to their dancing, except Aurelian himself, who danced without stopping for two days, until he collapsed and ex- pired. His brother Luxurius, with the emperor's permission, had all the believers killed. He had a fire set in the room where the three virgins were lodged, and as they prayed together, they breathed their last. The next morning Saint Cae- sarius recovered their bodies, still unmarked, and buried them.

76. Saint Pancratius

Pancratius[1] comes from *pan*, meaning all or the whole, *gratus*, pleasing, and *citius*, faster, so the whole more quickly pleasing, because Saint Pancratius was pleasing to God quickly, in his childhood. Or, as the *Glossary* says, *pancras* means booty, a *pancranarius* is one who is beaten with scourges, *pancras* is a varicolored precious stone. So Saint Pancratius robbed a booty of captives, was subjected to the scourges of torture, and was varicolored by the variety of his virtues.

Pancratius was born of parents belonging to the high nobility. He was bereaved of father and mother while in Phrygia, and was left to the care of his uncle Dionysius. They went to Rome, where they had a large patrimony. In a village that was on their estates Pope Cornelius was in hiding with a number of the faithful, and Dionysius and Pancratius were converted to the faith of Christ by this Cornelius. In time Dionysius died a peaceful death, and Pancratius was taken prisoner and presented to the emperor Diocletian. He was then about fourteen years old.

Diocletian said to him: "My dear boy, take my advice and save yourself from a bad death! Because you are still a child, you are easily misled, and because you are certainly noble and the son of a man whom I esteemed very highly, I beg of you, give up this madness, and I will treat you as if you were my own son." Pancratius answered: "I may be a child in body but my mind is older, and, by the power of my Lord Jesus Christ in me, your terror means no more to me than that idol we are looking at. As for the gods you bid me worship, they were deceivers and corrupters of their own women, who did not spare even their kin. If you today knew that your slaves were like those gods, you would promptly have them put to death! I marvel that you can worship such gods without being ashamed!" The emperor, conscious of having been outdone by a child, ordered him beheaded on the Via Aureliana, about A.D. 287. Cocavilla, the wife of a senator, took care to have him buried.

Gregory of Tours says that anyone who dared to swear falsely near the tomb of Pancratius would either be driven mad by a demon or would fall on the flagstones and die before he reached the grille of the choir. There was the case of two men who were engaged in a serious legal controversy. The judge knew perfectly well which one was the guilty party, but his zeal for justice made him lead the two to the altar of Saint Peter. There he compelled the guilty man to

[1] Pancras in England.

311

swear to his pretended innocence, and prayed to the apostle to show the truth by some sign. The man swore, but nothing happened to him. The judge, aware of his guilt and still eager to see justice done, exclaimed: "Either old Saint Peter is too forgiving, or he is deferring to one younger than himself! Let us go to young Pancratius and put the question to him!" They went, and the guilty man dared to pronounce his false oath with his hand upon the saint's tomb; but then he could not pull his hand free and eventually died there. So it is that even now it is the custom to settle difficult cases by oath, over the relics of Saint Pancratius.

*About the feasts that occur within the
time of pilgrimage*

Having dealt with the feasts that occur within the time of reconciliation, which the Church represents from Easter to the octave of Pentecost, we now turn to the feasts that fall within the time of pilgrimage, which the Church represents from the octave of Pentecost to Advent. This period does not always begin at this point in the sequence of feast days, because it varies according to the date of Easter.

---

77. Saint Urban

Urban comes from *urbanitas*, and Saint Urban was an urbane man. Or the name comes from *ur*, which means light or fire, and *banal*, which means response; and Urban was a light in his honorable conduct, a fire through his ardent love, and a response through his teaching. He was a beacon or a light because light is agreeable to look at, immaterial in its essence, heavenly in its source, and useful and helpful in its action. So this saint was agreeable in his relations with people, immaterial in his contempt for the world, heavenly in his contemplation, and useful and helpful in his preaching.

Urban succeeded Pope Callistus, during whose pontificate there was much persecution of Christians. Then Alexander, whose mother Ammaea had been converted to the Christian faith by Origen, assumed the throne of empire. His mother pleaded with him to put an end to the persecution, but the urban prefect Almachius, who had had blessed Cecilia beheaded, continued his cruel pursuit of the faithful. With the help of an adjutant named Carpasius he instituted a thorough search for Saint Urban. The pope was finally found hiding in a cave with three priests and three deacons, and was imprisoned. Then Almachius had Urban brought before him and accused him of misleading five thousand persons, among them the blasphemer Cecilia and two illustrious men, Tiburtius and Valerian. He also demanded the surrender of Cecilia's treasure. Urban answered him: "I see that greed, rather than piety toward the gods, is what motivates your cruel treatment of the saints. Cecilia's wealth had gone up to heaven by the hands of the poor!"

Saint Urban and his companions were then lashed with whips laden with lead. Urban invoked the Lord by his name Elyon, and the prefect, sneering, said: "The old man wants to look wise and therefore speaks an unknown language!" The captives could not be won over and so were remanded to prison, and Urban baptized three tribunes who came to him there with Anolinus, the jailer. When Almachius heard that Anolinus had become a Christian, he summoned him and, upon his refusal to sacrifice, had him beheaded. Saint Urban with his companions was led before an idol and ordered to sprinkle incense on the fire, but Urban prayed, and the idol fell from its pedestal and killed twenty-two priests, ministers of the fire. Again the prisoners were cruelly beaten and then led to the altar of sacrifice, but they spat on the idol, made the sign of the cross on their foreheads, gave one another the kiss of peace, and were beheaded under Alexander, whose reign began about A.D. 220.

Immediately Carpasius was seized by a demon, blasphemed his gods and praised the Christians despite himself, and was strangled by the demon. Having witnessed this, his wife and her daughter and her whole household were baptized by the priest Fortunatus, after which they buried the bodies of the saints with honor.

78. Saint Petronilla

Petronilla, whose life was written by Marcellus, was the daughter of Saint Peter the apostle. She was very beautiful, and therefore by her father's will she suffered continually from fever. The disciples were at table one day with Peter, and Titus said to him: "You have cured all sorts of illnesses, why do you leave Petronilla so sick?" "Because it's for her own good," Peter replied. "But lest it be thought that I said that because it was impossible for me to cure her," he turned and said to her, "Get up right away, Petronilla, and wait on us!" When all had been served, however, Peter said: "Now, Petronilla, back to bed!" She promptly returned to bed and the fever came back as before, but when she began to be perfect in the love of God, he cured her perfectly.

A count named Flaccus, much taken with Petronilla's beauty, came to ask her to be his wife. She responded: "If you want me for your wife, command maidens to come to me, and theirs it will be to accompany me to your house." While the count prepared the maidens for their task, Petronilla began a regimen of fasting, prayer, and the reception of the Body of the Lord, took to her bed, and after three days migrated to the Lord.

Flaccus, seeing that he had been deceived, turned to Felicula, one of Petronilla's companions, and ordered her either to marry him or to sacrifice to the idols. She refused to do either, and the prefect kept her in jail for seven days without food or drink and then tortured her on the rack, put her to death, and threw her body into the sewer. Saint Nicodemus recovered the body and buried it. For this, Flaccus had Nicodemus summoned before the judge, and when he refused to sacrifice, he was beaten with leaden rods and killed. His body was thrown into the Tiber, but was lifted out and honorably buried by a cleric named Justus.

79. Saint Peter the Exorcist

Peter the Exorcist was held in prison by the jailer Archemius. The daughter of Archemius was possessed of a demon and he often complained about this to Peter, who told him that if he believed in Christ, his daughter would be freed of the demon at once. Archemius said: "I wonder how it is that your Lord will be able to free my daughter but cannot free you from suffering for him as you are doing!" Peter answered: "My God has the power to set me free, but his will is that by way of a transitory passion we arrive at eternal glory." Archemius: "If I clamp double chains on you and your God frees you and cures my daughter, I will believe in Christ immediately!" All he had asked for happened, and Saint Peter appeared to him clad in white garments and holding a cross in his hand. Archemius prostrated himself at the saint's feet, and, since his daughter was cured, he and his whole house received baptism. He also permitted the other prisoners to go free, and any who wished to become Christians to do so; and many believed and were baptized by blessed Marcellinus, a priest.[1]

The prefect heard of this and ordered all the prisoners to be brought before him. Archemius called them together, kissed their hands, and said: "If any one of you desires to come to martyrdom, let him come fearlessly; but anyone who does not so desire may go from here unhurt." The judge learned that Marcellinus and Peter had baptized them, so he summoned them and jailed them separated from one another. Marcellinus was laid out naked on broken glass and deprived of light and water, and Peter was bound to a stake in a narrow cell high up in a tower, but an angel looked upon him, cut him loose, and put him and Marcellinus back in the house of Archemius, telling them to comfort those in the house for seven days and then to present themselves again to the judge.

When the said judge did not find his prisoners in prison, he called for Archemius, and when Archemius refused to offer sacrifice, the judge ordered him and his wife to be strangled in an underground crypt. Saints Marcellinus and Peter got wind of this and came to the place, and there, with Christians standing guard, Marcellinus celebrated the mass for seven days. The Christians said to the unbelievers: "See, we could have set Archemius free and then gone into hiding, but we would not do either the one thing or the other!" The pagans were angry at this, slew Archemius with the sword, and stoned the mother and the daughter. Marcellinus and Peter they beheaded at a black forest that is now called

---

[1] Graesse notes (343) that recent editions add "Marcellinus" to the title of this chapter.

"white" in memory of their martyrdom. This took place in the reign of Diocletian, which began in A.D. 287. An executioner named Dorotheus saw their souls, gowned in splendid, jeweled vesture, taken up to heaven by angels. This caused him to become a Christian, and eventually he died a happy death.

---

80. Saints Primus and Felicianus

Primus means highest and great. Felicianus is derived from *felix* and *anus*, meaning a happy old man. Saint Primus was called highest and great because of the dignity he gained by suffering martyrdom, of the power he displayed by performing miracles, of the holiness of his perfect life, and of the happiness he has in the glorious fulfillment of his life. Saint Felicianus was called an old man not only because he lived to a great age but on account of his venerable dignity, his mature wisdom, and the sobriety of his way of life.

Primus and Felicianus were denounced to Diocletian and Maximian by the priests of the temples, who told the emperors that if they did not make the two Christians offer sacrifice to the gods, they would not be able to obtain any benefits from the gods. By command of the emperors, therefore, the two were clapped into prison but were set free by an angel. Later they were again presented before the emperors, but clung firmly to their faith and were cruelly beaten. Then they were separated, and the prefect told Felicianus that he ought to have some regard for his age and therefore ought to sacrifice to the gods. Felicianus replied: "Look, I am eighty years old, and it is thirty years since I recognized the truth and chose to live for God, who can deliver me from your hands!" The prefect had him bound and nailed down by the hands and feet, and said to him: "You will stay there till you yield to us!" As the saint did not change the joyous expression on his face, the prefect gave orders that he was to be tortured, and nothing helpful was to be done for him.

Next the prefect had Saint Primus brought before him and said to him: "See here! Your brother has bowed to the emperors' decrees and therefore is respected as a great man in the palace! Now you do likewise!" Primus: "Though you are a son of the devil, what you said is true in part: my brother has bowed to the decree of the emperor of heaven!" This angered the prefect, and he ordered flaming torches to be held to the saint's sides and molten lead to be poured into his mouth, while Felicianus, whom they hoped to frighten, looked on; but Primus drank the lead with pleasure, as if it were cool water. This was too much for the prefect, who had two lions loosed upon the martyrs, but the beasts stretched themselves at their feet like gentle lambs. Then savage she-bears were let loose but became as gentle as the lions. Over twelve thousand men witnessed this spectacle, and five hundred of them believed in the Lord. The prefect, however, had the saints beheaded and their bodies thrown to the dogs and the birds, but the bodies remained untouched and were buried with honor by the Christians. They suffered about A.D. 287.

✳

81. Saint Barnabas, Apostle

Barnabas is interpreted as son of one arriving, or son of consolation, or son of a prophet, or son who encloses. Saint Barnabas is called "son" four times because of his fourfold sonship: the Scriptures call him son by reason of his birth, his instruction, his imitation, and his adoption. He was reborn in Christ through baptism and instructed by the Gospel; he imitated Christ by his martyrdom and was by him adopted through being rewarded in heaven. This fourfold sonship applied to Barnabas himself. With regard to others he was one who arrived, consoled, prophesied, and enclosed. He arrived by going from place to place and preaching everywhere, which we know because he was companion to Saint Paul. He consoled the poor and the afflicted—the poor by bringing alms to them and the afflicted by addressing letters to them at the behest of the apostles. He prophesied because he was gifted with the spirit of prophecy. He enclosed and united a great multitude in the faith, as is clear from his being sent to Antioch. We find these four notes in the Acts of the Apostles (11:24): "For he was a good man and full of the Holy Spirit and of faith, and a great multitude was added to the Lord." As to the first, he was a man, i.e., manly, virile; as to the second, he was good; as to the third, he was full of the Holy Spirit, and as to the fourth, he was a man of faith. His passion was compiled by his cousin John, also called Mark, and covered especially the time from this John's vision almost to the end of the saint's life. It is believed that Bede translated this life from Greek into Latin.[1]

Barnabas, a Levite and a native of Cyprus, was one of the Lord's seventy-two disciples. He is extolled and praised on many grounds in the Acts of the Apostles, for he was very well disposed and in good order as regarded himself, his God, and his neighbor.

First, he maintained good order within himself in relation to the three powers—the rational, the concupiscible, and the irascible.[2] His rational power was illumined by the light of knowledge, whence we read in Acts (13:1): "There were in the church which was at Antioch prophets and doctors, among whom was Barnabas." He had his concupiscible power in good order in that it was cleansed of the dust of worldly affections; thus we read in Acts (4:36–37) that Joseph, who by the apostles was surnamed Barnabas, had a field, but sold it and brought the price and laid it at the feet of the apostles. The *Gloss* on this text says: "He proves that one should rid oneself of what one avoids touching, and teaches that the gold which he had laid at the apostles' feet should indeed be trodden under foot." His irascible power was strengthened by his indomitable uprightness, so that he manfully undertook arduous tasks, persevered in doing what called for strength, and showed constancy in adversity. That he undertook the arduous courageously is shown by the fact that he accepted the task of converting the great city of Antioch, and also by what we read in Acts (9:26f.), namely, that when Paul, after his conversion, went to Jerusalem and wanted to join the apostles, all of whom shunned him like lambs fleeing a wolf, Barnabas boldly took him and led him to meet them. He persevered in doing what called for strength, because he chastised his body and disciplined it by fasting, whence Acts (13:1–3) says of Barnabas and several others: "They were ministering to the Lord and fasting." He bore adversity with constancy, as the apostles gave testimony about him, saying: ". . . with our well-beloved Barnabas and Paul, men who have given their lives for the name of our Lord Jesus Christ. . . ."

Second, he was in good order in his relations with God, deferring to God's authority, majesty, and goodness. He deferred to God's authority, as we see from the fact that he did not simply take upon himself the office of preaching but wanted to receive it by God's authority. We read in Acts (13:2): "The Holy Spirit said to them, 'Set apart for me Barnabas and Paul for the work to which I have called them.'" He deferred to God's majesty. As Acts (14:10f.) has it, some men wished to attribute divine majesty to him and to offer sacrifice to him

---

[1] J.-B. M. Roze (*La légende dorée* [Paris: Ed. Rouveyre, 1903], 2:132) notes that no such translation is found among the Venerable Bede's works.

[2] The concupiscible appetite, according to Thomas Aquinas, has as its object good or evil as agreeable or repellent in itself. The irascible appetite has as its object the good perceived as subject to some condition of difficulty or danger.

as to a god, calling him Jove as being the older, and Paul Mercury as being a man of foresight and eloquence. But Barnabas and Paul, rending their clothes, shouted: "Men, what are you doing? We are mortals just like yourselves, preaching to you to be converted away from these useless gods and toward the living God!" And he deferred to God's goodness. We read in Acts (15:5) that some Jewish converts wanted to restrict and diminish the goodness of God's grace (by which we are saved freely and not by the Law), asserting that this was by no means sufficient without circumcision. Paul and Barnabas bravely resisted them and proved that the goodness of God's grace alone, without the Law, sufficed. Furthermore, they referred the question to the apostles and persuaded them to write a letter refuting the error of the dissidents.

Third, he maintained good order in his relations with his neighbor, because he nurtured his flock by word, by example, and by works of mercy. He fed them with the word because he preached the Gospel with care, whence it is said in Acts (15:35): "Paul and Barnabas continued at Antioch, teaching and preaching, with many others, the word of the Lord." We see his care also in the great multitude he converted in Antioch, where for the first time the disciples were called Christians. He nurtured his flock by example, because his life was to all a mirror of holiness and an example of true religion. In every work of his he was virile, religious, and strong, conspicuous in the goodness of his way of doing things, full of every grace of the Holy Spirit, outstanding in all virtue and faith. Of these four qualities we read in Acts (11:22f.): "They sent Barnabas to Antioch," and "he exhorted them all to remain faithful to the Lord with steadfast purpose, for he was a good man, full of the Holy Spirit and of faith." He nurtured the flock with works of mercy. There are two kinds of alms or works of mercy, namely, the temporal, which consists of providing for temporal needs, and the spiritual, which consists of forgiving offenses. Barnabas had the first kind when he brought alms to the brethren who were in Jerusalem. We read in Acts (11:27f.) that when there was a great famine during the reign of Claudius, as Agabus had prophesied, "the disciples determined, every one according to his ability, to send relief to the brethren who lived in Judea; and they did so, sending it to the elders by the hand of Barnabas and Paul." And he did the spiritual work when he forgave the offense committed by John whose surname was Mark; for when this disciple left Barnabas and Paul but then came back repentant, Barnabas forgave him and again received him as a disciple, whereas Paul refused to receive him again. This caused a division between Paul and Barnabas, each of them acting for a pious reason and intention. Barnabas took John back out of the kindness of mercy, Paul refused out of strict concern for uprightness. So the *Gloss* on Acts 15 says: "Because [John Mark] had confronted him to the face but showed himself too timid, Paul rightly turned him away, lest by the contagion of his example the strengths of others might be contaminated." This division therefore did not grow out of unworthy hard feelings: it was their response to the Holy Spirit's inspiration, namely, that they should separate so that they might preach to more people.

That is what happened. When Barnabas was in the city of Icona, his cousin, the aforementioned John, had a vision in which a man splendid to look upon appeared to him and said: "Be steadfast, John, because shortly you will be called not John but Elevated!" John related this to Barnabas, who counseled him: "Take care to tell no one about the vision you have had, because last night the Lord appeared to me in the same way and said: 'Be steadfast, Barnabas! You will gain an eternal reward because you left your own people and gave your life for my name!' " And, when Paul and Barnabas had preached for a long time in Antioch, an angel of the Lord appeared to Paul and said: "Make haste and go to Jerusalem, because there a certain brother awaits you!"

Barnabas wished to go to Cyprus to visit his parents, and Paul wanted to hasten to Jerusalem, so, the Holy Spirit guiding them, they decided to separate. When Paul told Barnabas what the angel had made known to him, Barnabas responded: "The will of the Lord be done! Now I am going to Cyprus and will end my days there, and I shall see you no more!" He wept and fell humbly at Paul's feet, and Paul said with compassion: "Do not weep, because that is the will of the Lord; for the Lord also appeared to me in the night and said, 'Do not stop Barnabas from going to Cyprus, because there he will give light to many and will die a martyr's death!' "

Barnabas then departed for Cyprus with John, taking with him the book of the gospel of Saint Matthew: he held the book over sick people and thus, by the power of God, cured many. As they were leaving Cyprus, they found Elymas, the sorcerer whom Paul had deprived of his sight for a time. Elymas opposed them and forbade them to go to Paphos. And one day Barnabas saw nude men and women running to celebrate their feast. Indignant at the sight he cursed their temple, and a section of it fell in and crushed many people. Finally he arrived at Salamina, and there the sorcerer stirred up a riot against him. The Jews laid hold of him and, after inflicting many injuries upon him, haled him before the judge of the city and demanded that he be punished. Then it was learned that Eusebius, a prominent and powerful man who was related to Nero, had arrived in Salamina, and the Jews were afraid he would take Barnabas away from them and let him go free; so they put a rope around his neck, dragged him out of the city, and burned him alive. Even then the impious Jews were not satisfied. They stowed his bones in a leaden urn, intending to cast it into the sea; but John, his disciple, rose in the night with two companions, got hold of the relics, and buried them secretly in a crypt. There they remained hidden, as Sigebert says, until the year of the Lord 500, in the time of Emperor Zeno and Pope Gelasius, when the place was revealed by Barnabas and the relics were recovered.

Blessed Dorotheus says: "Barnabas first preached in Rome and became bishop of Milan."

82. Saints Vitus and Modestus

The name Vitus comes from *vita*, life. Augustine distinguishes three kinds of life: the active; the leisurely, which pertains to spiritual leisure or quiet; and the contemplative, which combines the other two. These three kinds of life were in Saint Vitus. Again, Vitus is close to *virtus*, and Vitus was a virtuous man.

The name Modestus has the sense of standing in the middle, the middle being virtue, for virtue, as a middle, stands between two extremes, which are vices. The extremes of prudence are craftiness and foolishness; of temperance, overindulgence of carnal desires and excessive self-mortification; of fortitude, cowardice and rashness; of justice, vindictiveness and excessive leniency.

Vitus, a remarkable child and a Christian, suffered martyrdom in Sicily when he was only twelve years old. His father often whipped him because he despised the idols and refused to worship them. The prefect Valerian heard of this and summoned the boy, and, when he would not offer sacrifice, ordered him beaten with rods; but the arms of the men beating him and the hand of the prefect withered at once, and the prefect cried out: "Alas, alas! I've lost a hand!" Vitus said to him: "Call on your gods and let them heal you if they can!" Valerian to Vitus: "Can you do it?" Vitus: "In the name of my Lord, I can!" He prayed and obtained instant cure for the prefect, who then said to the father: "Take your boy in hand, or he'll come to a bad end!"

The father brought him home and tried to change the son's mind by surrounding him with music and sporting girls and other kinds of pleasure. Then he shut the boy up in his bedroom, and a wonderful fragrance came out of it, steeping the house and the people in it with its odor. The father looked in through the door and saw seven angels surrounding his son, and exclaimed: "The gods have come into my house," and immediately was stricken with blindness. His cries were so loud that the whole city of Lucania was disturbed, and Valerian came on the run and demanded to know what had happened to him. He answered: "I saw fiery gods and I could not bear to look at their faces!"

They conducted the father to the temple of Jove and promised a bull with gilded horns for the recovery of his sight, but to no avail. Then he begged his son to obtain his healing, and at the son's prayer the father saw the light again. When even then he did not believe, but rather thought to kill the child, an angel appeared to Vitus's tutor, Modestus, and commanded him to take the boy in a boat and go to another land. While they were at sea, an eagle brought them their food, and they wrought many wonders when they landed.

Meanwhile the son of the emperor Diocletian was seized by a demon, who declared that unless Vitus of Lucania came, he, the demon, would never come out of the son. Vitus was sought and found and brought to the emperor, who asked him: "Boy, can you heal my son?" Vitus answered: "Not I but the Lord can!" He placed his hand on the son and the demon fled instantly. Diocletian: "Boy, take thought to yourself and sacrifice to the gods, or die a dreadful death!" Vitus refused and was put in jail with Modestus, but the chains with which they were shackled softened and fell off, and the jail was flooded with brilliant light. When this was reported to the emperor, Vitus was put into a fiery furnace but came out unscathed. Then a fierce lion was brought in to devour him, but the beast was tamed by the power of his faith. Finally Vitus, Modestus, and Crescentia, his nurse who had followed him everywhere, were stretched on the rack; but suddenly the air became turbulent, the earth shook, thunder rolled, and the temples of the idols fell in and killed many worshipers.

The emperor was frightened and hurried away, beating his breast and saying: "Woe is me, I've been worsted by one mere child!" The martyrs were quickly freed by an angel and found themselves beside a river, where they paused and prayed and gave themselves up to the Lord. Eagles guarded their bodies, which were found and given honorable burial by an illustrious lady named Florentia, to whom Saint Vitus had revealed their whereabouts.[1] They suffered under Diocletian, whose reign began in A.D. 287.

83. Saint Quiricus and His Mother Saint Julitta

The name Quiricus comes from *quaerens arcum*, seeking a bow, or from *chisil*, which means fortitude, and *cus*, black; hence strong in virtue and black by humility. Or the name comes from *quiris*, javelin, or from *quiriles*, seat. Saint Quiricus[1] was a bow, i.e., curved in his humility and in the torments of his passion. He was black in his low estimate of himself, a javelin in his conquest of the

---

[1] Graesse notes (351n) that all the details regarding the finding and burial, except the name of the lady, are more recent additions. But the account as given here is certainly in the style of Jacobus.

[1] Perhaps better known as Cyr or Cyricus.

enemy, a seat because God dwelt in him. All this, which his age denied him, was supplied in him by the grace of God.

Julitta is like *juvans vita*, aiding by life, because the saint lived a spiritual life and thereby aided many.

Quiricus was the son of Julitta, a most illustrious lady of Iconium. Wishing to evade the persecution raging there, she went to Tarsus with her three-year-old son and two servingmaids. There she was brought before Alexander, the governor, carrying her child in her arms. The maids, seeing this, ran away leaving their mistress. The governor took the child in his arms, and when the mother refused to sacrifice to the gods, had her scourged with raw thongs. When the child saw his mother being scourged, he wept bitterly and uttered loud cries. The governor, holding him on his lap, tried to calm him with kisses and other endearments, but the child, looking back toward his mother, shrugged away from the ruler's embraces, turned his head indignantly, and scratched the man's face with his fingernails, crying out, in harmony with his mother's voice: "I too am a Christian!" He struggled for a long time and finally bit the governor on the shoulder, and Alexander, enraged and in pain from the wound, threw him from the height of the tribunal, his tender brains spilling down the steps. Julitta saw this happen and joyfully gave thanks to God that her son had gone before her to the kingdom of heaven. Then Alexander ordered her to be flayed alive, plunged into boiling pitch, and finally beheaded.

The governor had the bodies of mother and son cut up so that the Christians would not be able to bury them, but the pieces were collected by an angel and buried at night by Christians. In the time of Constantine the Great, when peace was restored to the Church, one of the two maids, who had survived, showed where the martyrs' bodies were, and the relics are held in great devotion by the whole populace. They suffered about the year of the Lord 230, under Emperor Alexander.

84. Saint Marina, Virgin

The virgin Marina was her father's only child. When he was widowed and entered a monastery, he changed his daughter's attire and dressed her as a male. He then asked the abbot and the monks to admit his only son, and, when they agreed, Marina was received as a monk and was called Brother Marinus by all.

"Marinus" then began to live the religious life and to observe strict obedience. When he was twenty-seven years old and the father felt the approach of death, he called his daughter, encouraged her to remain firm in her resolution, and ordered her never to reveal to anyone that she was a woman.

Marinus often went out with an oxcart to bring back wood to the monastery, and now and then stopped at the house of a man whose daughter conceived a child by a soldier. She was questioned and declared that the monk Marinus had ravished her. When Marinus was asked why he had committed such a shameful crime, he admitted that he had sinned and was banished from the monastery. He stayed outside the gate for three years, living on scraps of bread. When the woman's son was weaned, he was sent to the abbot and entrusted to Marinus to be brought up, and he stayed with Marinus for two years. Marinus accepted all this with the utmost patience and in all things rendered thanks to God. Finally the monks, moved by his humility and patience, took him back into the monastery and assigned some of the meanest labors to him. He accepted everything cheerfully and did his work with patience and devotion.

At length, having led a life filled with good works, he migrated to the Lord. When it came time to bathe the corpse before burying it in some grubby corner, the monks saw that it was the body of a woman. They were stupefied and frightened, and admitted that they had grossly maltreated this handmaid of God. They therefore gave her honorable burial in the church. As for the woman who had defamed the servant of God, she was seized by a demon, confessed her crime, came to the virgin's tomb, and was freed of the demon. People came from everywhere to visit the tomb, and many miracles took place there. Saint Marina died on the eighteenth day of June.[1]

---

[1] "*xiv kalendas Julii.*" The usual date is 20 July.

According to *Butler's Lives of the Saints* (New York: P. J. Kenedy & Sons, 1963), 1:314, "the story of this Marina is simply one of those popular romances of women masquerading as men." *The Golden Legend* includes, besides the Marina story, those of "Saints" Eugenia (mentioned several times in the legend of Saints Protus and Hyacinthus), Theodora (who used to be celebrated on 11 September), Margaret (also called Pelagia), and Pelagia (also called Margaret). The last two had the same feast day, 8 October.

85. Saints Gervasius and Protasius

Gervasius comes from *gerar*, sacred, and *vas*, vase; or from *gena*, a stranger, one not a dweller, and *syor*, small. So, Gervasius was sacred by his meritorious life, a vase as a receptacle of virtues, a stranger by contempt for the world, small by his humble estimate of himself.

Protasius comes from *protos*, first, and *syos*, God or godly, or from *procul*, at a distance, and *stasis*, position. This Protasius was first by his dignity, godly through his love, distant from any attachment to the world.

Ambrose found their passion written in a small book placed at their head.

Gervasius and Protasius were twin brothers, the sons of Saint Vitalis and the blessed Valeria. They had distributed all their goods to the poor and were living with Saint Nazarius, who was building an oratory near Embrun. A boy named Celsus was carrying stones for him. (But what is said about Nazarius having Celsus with him at that early date may be by way of anticipation, since we gather from the legend of Nazarius[1] that Celsus was entrusted to him at a much later time.) The three men were brought before the emperor Nero, and the boy Celsus followed them wailing and complaining. One of the soldiers slapped the lad and Nazarius rebuked him for doing so, whereupon the soldiers kicked and trampled the saint, jailed him with others, and later cast him into the sea. Gervasius and Protasius were taken to Milan, and Nazarius, miraculously saved from the sea, came to the same city.

At that time Count Astasius arrived in Milan on his way to make war on the Marcomanni. The worshipers of the gods came to meet him, asserting that the gods would not respond to them unless Gervasius and Protasius first offered sacrifice. The two were promptly apprehended and urged to sacrifice. But Gervasius said that all the idols were deaf and dumb, and that Astasius would have victory from the almighty God alone. The count, angered, had him beaten with leaded whips until he died. Then he summoned Protasius and said to him: "Wretch, take thought and live, and don't die a miserable death the way your brother did!" Protasius: "Who is the wretch—I, who do not fear you, or you, who are proving that you fear me?" Astasius: "How can you, miserable man, say that I fear you?" Protasius: "You prove that you are afraid of me and afraid I will do you harm if I do not sacrifice to your gods. If you were not afraid I would do you harm by not sacrificing, you would not force me to worship the idols!" The

---

[1] See below, chapter 102.

count then ordered him to be hung on the rack. Protasius: "I am not angry with you, Count, because I expect the eyes of your heart to be blind; but I pity you, because you do not know what you are doing! Finish what you have begun, then, so that the loving-kindness of our Savior may embrace me with my brother!" Then the count ordered him to be beheaded. Philip, a servant of Christ, and his son took away the saints' bodies and buried them secretly in their house in a stone coffin, and placed at their head a small book containing the martyrs' birth, life, and death. They suffered under Nero, whose reign began in A.D. 57.

The bodies of these two martyrs remained hidden for centuries but were found in Ambrose's time in the following way. Ambrose was at prayer in the church of Saints Nabor and Felix, and was neither wide awake nor sound asleep when two handsome youths, dressed in white tunics and mantles and shod with short boots, appeared to him and prayed with him. Ambrose prayed that if this apparition was an illusion it would not occur again, but if it was a true one it would be repeated. At cockcrow the two youths again appeared in the same way, praying with him; but on the third night, fully awake though his body was worn out with vigils, he was astonished when they appeared to him with a third person, who looked like Paul the apostle in a painting Ambrose had seen. The two young men were silent, but the apostle said to him: "Here are two who desired nothing the earth could give them, but followed my counsels. You will discover their bodies at the place where you are standing. At a depth of twelve feet you will find a coffin covered with earth, which contains their bodies and a small book telling their origin and their death."

Ambrose convoked the neighboring bishops, was the first to dig down into the earth, came to the coffin, and found all just as Paul had said. Although more than three hundred years had passed, the bodies were found to be in the same condition as if they had been laid to rest that very day. Moreover, a most sweet, noble odor rose from them. A blind man touched the coffin and received his sight. Many others were cured by the merits of these saints.

It was on their feast day that peace was concluded between the Lombards and the Roman Empire. In memory of that event Pope Gregory established the custom of chanting *Loquetur Dominus pacem in plebem suam*[2] at the introit of the mass of the feast. So it is that the office of that day refers partly to the saints and partly to events that occurred at the same date.

In the twentieth[3] book of his work *On the City of God*, Augustine relates that he himself was present, as were the emperor and a great throng, when, at the tomb of Saints Gervasius and Protasius in Milan, a blind man recovered his sight. (It is not known whether this was the same blind man as the one previously mentioned.) Augustine also relates in the same place that at a villa called Victori-

---

[2] The Lord will speak peace unto his people (Ps. 84:9 [85:8]).

[3] Correctly, bk. 22, chap. 8.

ana, some thirty miles from Hippo, a young man was bathing his horse in the river when suddenly a demon seized him, tormented him, and threw him into the river as if he were dead. In the evening vespers were sung in the nearby church of Saints Gervasius and Protasius, and the young man, as if struck by the voices, came into the church screaming and clung to the altar as though he were tied to it, and could not be moved away. The demon was conjured to go out of the man and threatened to tear him limb from limb if he went out. When the demon finally did go out, one of the young man's eyes hung down his cheek by a thin vein, but they put the eye back in its place as well as they could, and in a few days, by the merits of Saints Gervasius and Protasius, the youth was completely cured.

Ambrose, in his Preface for the saints, says: "These are the ones who, signed with the celestial banner, took up the victorious weapons of the apostle, were loosed from worldly bonds, broke through the lines of the wicked enemy's vices, and, free and unhampered, followed Christ the Lord! Oh, how happy the twins who, living by the word of God, could not be soiled by any earthly stain! Oh, how glorious the cause for which they fought and won the same crown just as they issued from the same maternal womb!"

※

86. The Birth of Saint John the Baptist

John the Baptist has many titles. He is called prophet, friend of the bridegroom, lamp, angel, voice, Elijah, baptizer of the Savior, herald of the judge, and forerunner of the King. Each of these titles denotes a particular prerogative of John: the title of prophet, his prerogative of foreknowledge; the title of friend of the bridegroom, his prerogative of loving and being loved; burning light, his prerogative of sanctity; angel, his prerogative of virginity; voice, his prerogative of humility; Elijah, his prerogative of fervor; baptizer, the wonderful honor of baptizing the Lord; herald, the prerogative of preaching; and forerunner, the prerogative of preparation.

The birth of John the Baptist was announced by the archangel in the following manner. The *Ecclesiastical History* tells us that in order to broaden divine worship, King David established twenty-four high priests, of whom one was superior and was called prince of priests. He designated fifteen men from the lineage of

Eleazar and eight from that of Ithamar, and gave each a week to serve by lot. The eighth week fell to Abijah, of whom Zechariah was a descendant. Zechariah and his wife Elizabeth were old and childless.

One day when Zechariah went into the Temple of the Lord to offer incense, and a multitude of people waited outside, the archangel Gabriel appeared to him. The vision startled him, but the angel said "Fear not, Zechariah, your prayer is heard!" It is the way of the good angels, according to the *Gloss*, to reassure by kindly words those who are alarmed at seeing them, whereas the bad angels transform themselves to look like angels of light, and, if they sense that anyone is terrified by the vision of them, they terrorize him still more.

Be that as it may, Gabriel announced to Zechariah that he was to have a son whose name would be John, who would drink no wine or strong drink and would go before the Lord in the spirit and power of Elijah. John is called Elijah by reason of place, because both lived in the desert; by reason of what they ate, because both ate little; by reason of their external appearance, because both cared little about what they wore; by reason of their office, since they were both forerunners, though Elijah was forerunner to the Judge and John to the Savior; and by reason of zeal, because their words burned like torches.

Zechariah, thinking about his old age and his wife's sterility, began to doubt and, as the Jews used to do, asked the angel for a sign. Because Zechariah had not believed the message, the angel gave him a sign by striking him dumb. Note, however, that at times one may doubt and be excused for doubting. This may be because so much is promised, as, for instance, in Abraham's case. When the Lord had promised him that his seed would possess the land of Canaan, Abraham said to him: "Lord God, how can I know that I am to possess it?" God, responding, said: "Bring me a heifer three years old, etc." (Gen. 15:9f.). Sometimes it may be in consideration of one's own frailty, as in the case of Gideon, who said: "I beseech thee, my Lord, how can I deliver Israel? Behold, my clan is the weakest in Manasseh, and I am the least in my father's house!" (Judg. 6:15). So he asked for a sign and received one. Sometimes what is promised seems naturally impossible, as in the case of Sara. The Lord had said: "I will return to you and Sara will have a son," and Sara laughed behind the door of the tent. saying: "After I have grown old and my husband is an old man, shall I give myself to pleasure?" (Gen. 18:12).

Why, then, is it that Zechariah is the only one punished for doubting? In his case there was the magnitude of the promise and the awareness of his own frailty, since he considered himself unworthy to have such a son, and there was the natural impossibility. It is thought that there are several reasons for this. The first, according to Bede, is that he voiced his disbelief, and was stricken dumb so that by keeping silent he might learn to believe. The second is that he was made mute so that the miracle of his son's birth might be more obvious, since the father's speech was restored at the son's birth and one miracle was piled on top of the other. Third, it was appropriate that he should lose his voice, when a voice was being born, and silence being imposed on the Law. Fourth, Zechariah had asked for a sign from God and muteness was the sign he received. When he went out to the people and they saw that he was unable to speak, they knew, as he nodded agreement, that he had seen a vision in the Temple.

He completed his week of service and went home, and Elizabeth conceived. She then hid herself for five months, because, as Ambrose says about this, she felt some shame at having a child at her age, fearing that she might seem to have indulged in lustful pleasure despite her years. Yet she also rejoiced at being rid of the reproach of sterility. It is a source of shame for women not to have the reward that belongs to marriage, since it is in view of that reward that marriage is a happy event and that carnal union is justified.

In Elizabeth's sixth month Mary, who had already conceived, came to her, the fruitful virgin to the woman relieved of sterility, feeling sympathy for her in her old age. When she greeted her cousin, blessed John, already filled with the Holy Spirit, sensed the Son of God coming to him and leapt for joy in his mother's womb, and danced, saluting by his movements the one he could not greet with his voice. He leapt as one wishing to greet his Lord and to stand up in his presence. The Blessed Virgin stayed with her cousin for three months, helping her, and when the child was born, as we read in the *Scholastic History*, she lifted it from the earth with her holy hands, kindly acting as a nursemaid would.

This holy forerunner of the Lord enjoyed nine special and singular privileges, namely:

the same angel who announced the coming of the Lord announced the
   coming of John;
he leapt in his mother's womb;
the mother of the Lord lifted him from the earth;
he unlocked his father's tongue;
he was the first to confer baptism;
he pointed out Christ with his finger;
he baptized Christ;
Christ praised him above all others;
he foretold Christ's coming to the souls in Limbo.

On account of these nine privileges, the Lord himself called John a prophet and more than a prophet. Chrysostom asks why Christ called him more than a prophet, and answers: "It befits a prophet to receive a gift from God, but does it belong to a prophet to give God the gift of baptism? It befits a prophet to prophesy about God, but is it for God to prophesy about the prophet? All the prophets prophesied about Christ, but no one prophesied about them. Yet not only did John prophesy about Christ, but other prophets also prophesied about John. All were bearers of the word, John was the voice itself; and by as much as the voice is closer to the word (yet is not the word), by so much was John closer to Christ yet was not Christ."

According to Ambrose, John's praiseworthiness derives from five causes, namely, his parentage, his moral conduct, his miracles, his office, and his preaching.

The praise based upon his parentage, again according to Ambrose, is manifested in five ways: "Perfect praise," he says, "is for him whose good lineage shows in his moral conduct, his conduct in fairness, his office in priesthood, his deeds in conformity to the law, his righteousness in righteous decisions."

John's praiseworthiness derives, secondly, from his miracles. Some of these took place before he was conceived in the womb, namely, the announcement of his birth by an angel, the imposition of his name, and his father's loss of voice. Some were related to his conception in the womb, namely, the supernatural conception itself, and his sanctification and the fulfillment of the gift of prophecy in the womb. Some were connected with his birth from the womb, namely, the attainment of the spirit of prophecy by each of his parents, because his mother knew what his name was to be and his father gave forth the canticle. The father recovered the power of speech and was filled with the Holy Spirit, whence we read: "Zechariah his father was filled with the Holy Spirit and he prophesied" (Luke 1:67). Ambrose says: "Look at John and see how much power there was in the sound of his name, which, being pronounced, gave his voice to a mute, a son to his father, piety and a priest to the people. Before, Zechariah was speechless of tongue, sterile of offspring, bereft of his office: John is born, suddenly his father becomes a prophet, recovers his speech, receives offspring from the Holy Spirit, and again assumes his function as a priest."

Thirdly, John is praised for his conduct, because his life was one of perfect holiness. Chrysostom speaks of this holiness: "John's way of life made everyone else's look blameworthy. For instance, if you see a white garment, you say, 'That is pure white,' but if you hold it against snow, it begins to look soiled even though it is not soiled. Thus everyone seemed unclean by comparison with John."

His holiness had three kinds of testimony. The first was the supercelestial, coming from the Trinity itself: from the Father, who called John an angel; Malachy (3:1): "Behold, I send my angel, and he shall prepare the way before my face." "Angel" is the name of an office or function, not of a nature, and therefore an angel is so called by reason of his office or function; and John is called an angel because he is seen to have fulfilled the offices of all the angels. He had the office of the Seraphim. That name is interpreted as meaning ardent, because the Seraphim make us ardent and in the love of God they are more ardent, more afire. Of John it is said in Ecclus. (48:1): "The prophet Elijah arose like a fire," and John came in the spirit and power of Elijah. Second, he had the office of the Cherubim. That name is interpreted as meaning the fullness of knowledge, and John is called *lucifer*, the light-bearer, the morning star,[1] because he was the end

---

[1] Cf. Job 38:32.

point of our ignorance and the starting point of the light of grace. Third, he had the office of the Thrones, whose function it is to judge, and of John it is said that he reproved Herod, saying: "It is not lawful for you to have your brother's wife." Fourth, he had the office of the Dominations, who teach us how to rule over subjects, and John was loved by those under him and was feared by kings. Fifth, the office of the Principalities, who teach us to have proper respect for those above us, and John said of himself: "He who is of the earth belongs to the earth and of the earth he speaks," but of Christ he says: "He who comes from heaven is above all."[2] He also says, speaking of Christ: ". . . the latchet of whose shoes I am not worthy to loose."[3] Sixth, the office of the Powers, by whom the harmful powers of the air are kept in check. They could not harm John because he was already sanctified, and he kept them away from us by disposing us to the baptism of penance. Seventh, the office of the Virtues, by whom miracles are performed, and blessed John showed many miracles in himself: it is a great miracle to live on wild honey and locusts, to wear camel's hair, and the like. Eighth, the office of the Archangels, when he made revelations of greater importance, such as those that pertain to our redemption, when he said: "Behold the lamb of God, behold him who takes away the sin of the world!" Ninth, the office of the Angels, when he announced lesser truths, such as those that pertain to morals, when he said: "Do penance," and: "Do violence to no man; neither calumniate any man."[4]

Second, John had the testimony of God the Son, as is clear from the eleventh chapter of Matthew, where Christ commends him wonderfully and in many ways, saying, among other things: "Among those born of women there has risen no one greater than John the Baptist." Peter Damian says: "From that word all praises of John derive, as by that word the earth was founded, the stars are moved, and the elements have their being." And third, John had the testimony of the Holy Spirit, who, speaking through Zechariah, said: "You, child, will be called the prophet of the Most High."

Secondly, he had the testimony of the angels and heavenly powers, as we see in the first chapter of Luke, where the angel commended him in many ways. He showed how great John's dignity was in relation to God when he said: "He shall be great before the Lord"; showed how holy he was in his treatment of himself, saying: "He shall drink no wine or strong drink, and shall be filled with the Holy Spirit even from his mother's womb"; and showed how usefully he served his neighbor, when he said: "And he shall convert many of the children of Israel to the Lord their God." And thirdly, he had the testimony of subcelestial beings, namely, men and women, his father and their neighbors, who said: "What then will this child be? For the hand of the Lord was with him."[5]

---

[2] John 3:31.　　　[3] Luke 3:16.
[4] Luke 3:14.　　　[5] Luke 1:66.

Fourthly, John's praiseworthiness is founded on the gifts God gave him in his office. He was gifted while he was still in the womb, when he emerged from the womb, in his life in the world, and in his departure from the world.

In his mother's womb he had the wondrous gift of a threefold grace. First came the grace by which he was made holy in the womb, so that he was sanctified before he was born; Jeremiah (1:4f.): "Before I formed you in the womb I knew you, and before you were born I sanctified you." Second was the grace by which he was made worthy to prophesy, as when by leaping in his mother's womb he recognized the presence of God. Chrysostom, in order to show in what ways John was more than a prophet, says: "It befits a prophet to receive the gift of prophecy for the merit of his way of life and his faith. Did it befit a prophet to be a prophet before he was a man?" Moreover, the custom was to anoint prophets, and when the Blessed Virgin greeted Elizabeth, Christ anointed John as prophet in the womb, according to what Chrysostom says: "Therefore Christ made Mary salute Elizabeth, so that the words, proceeding from the womb of his mother where Christ dwelt, would enter through Elizabeth's ears and go down to John in order to anoint him there as prophet."

Third was the grace that enabled him by his merits to pass on to his mother the spirit of prophecy. Chrysostom, continuing to show how John was more than a prophet, says: "Which of the prophets, by being a prophet, could make someone else a prophet? Elijah, indeed, anointed Elisha as a prophet but did not confer on him the grace of prophesying. John, on the other hand, while still in his mother's womb, bestowed knowledge of the coming of God into her house upon his mother, and opened her mouth to the word of confession of faith, so that she recognized the dignity of the one whom she did not see in person, saying, 'Why is this granted me, that the mother of my Lord should come to me?'"

At his emergence from the womb he had a threefold gift of grace, in that his birth was miraculous, holy, and joyful. Because it was miraculous, he was not born powerless; because it was holy, he was without guilt; because it was joyful, there was no lamenting, no sorrow. According to Master William of Auxerre, John's birth or nativity is celebrated for three reasons. The first is his sanctification in the womb. The second is the dignity of the office to which he was born, for he came as a bearer of light and was the first to announce eternal joy to us. The third is the joy surrounding his birth, for the angel had said: "Many will rejoice at his birth," and therefore it is right that we too should rejoice at his birth.

In his life in the world John had many gifts. The excellence of the divers gifts of grace that were his appears in this, that he had the perfection of all the saints. He was a prophet when he said: "There shall come one mightier than I." He was more than a prophet when he pointed his finger to identify Christ. He was an apostle, for an apostle is one who is sent, and he was "a man sent from God, whose name was John."[6] He was a martyr, because he endured death for justice's sake. He was a confessor, because he confessed and did not deny. He was a virgin, and because of his virginity he was called an angel, as we have read in Malachy: "Behold, I send my angel, etc."

In his departure from the world John had a triple gift. He was made an unconquered martyr, for he then acquired the palm of martyrdom. He was sent as a precious messenger, because he then brought to those in limbo the precious announcement of the coming there of Christ and of their redemption. And his glorious death is honored because, of all those who went down into limbo, his exodus therefrom is specially solemnized and gloriously celebrated by the Church.

Fifthly, John's praiseworthiness is based upon his preaching. The angel brought out four things about his preaching when he said: "He shall convert many of the children of Israel to the Lord their God. And he shall go before him in the spirit and power of Elijah; that he may turn the hearts of the fathers unto the children and the incredulous to the wisdom of the just, to prepare unto the Lord a perfect people." There four points are touched upon, namely, the fruit of the preaching, its order, its power, and its purpose, as is clear from the letter of the text.

Note also that John's preaching was commendable for three reasons: he preached fervently, efficaciously, and judiciously. He spoke with fervor when he said to the Pharisees: "You serpents, generation of vipers, how will you flee the judgment of hell?" Yet his fervor was inflamed with charity, because he was a burning light; whence he himself, speaking in the person of Isaiah, says: "[The Lord] made my mouth like a sharp sword." His fervor was informed by truth, because he was a shining light; John 5:53: "You sent to John and he gave testimony to the truth." It was directed by discernment or knowledge, so he interpreted the law to the people at large, or to tax-collectors and soldiers, according to the needs of each. It was firm in its constancy: he preached with such constancy that it cost him his life. His zeal had to have those four qualities, according to what Bernard says: "Let charity inflame your zeal, truth inform it, knowledge rule it, and constancy sustain it."

He also preached efficaciously, since so many were converted by his preaching. He preached by word through his assiduous teaching; by example through the holiness of his life; and, preaching by his meritorious life and his devout prayer, he converted many. And he preached judiciously. The prudent good judgment he brought to his preaching came out in three ways. First, he used threats to put fear in the perverse, saying: "Now the ax is laid to the root of the trees; every tree therefore that does not bear good fruit is cut down and thrown into the fire." Second, he used promises to entice the good, saying: "Repent, for the kingdom of heaven is at hand." Third, he used moderation, attracting the

---

[6] John 1:6.

mediocre toward perfection little by little, imposing light obligations on people in general, and on tax-gatherers and soldiers in particular, in order later to carry them forward to greater things—the people at large to do works of mercy, the publicans to abstain from hungering for what belonged to others, the soldiers not to rob anyone or accuse anyone falsely, and to be satisfied with their wages.

It is to be noted that Saint John the Evangelist went to heaven on the same day the birth of John the Baptist is celebrated. The Church, however, instituted the celebration of the Evangelist's feast on the third day following the nativity of Christ because his church was dedicated on that day, and the solemnization of the birthday of John the Baptist kept its date because the angel had certified it as the day for rejoicing over the birth of the Forerunner. There is no need to dogmatize about whether the Evangelist had to yield his day to the Baptist as the lesser to the greater. It is not appropriate to argue about which of them was the greater, as is clear from a heaven-sent example. We read that there were two doctors of theology, one of whom favored John the Baptist, the other John the Evangelist. They finally agreed on a formal disputation, and each one put great care into his search for authorities and convincing arguments with which to back his particular John. On the day of the disputation, however, each of the saints appeared to his champion and said to him: "We get along very well together in heaven! Don't start disputes about us on earth!" They made the visions known to each other and to the public, and gave thanks to the Lord.

Paul, historian of the Lombards, was a deacon of the Roman church and a monk of Monte Cassino. One day he was to bless a candle, but his throat became hoarse though previously he had been in good voice. In order to obtain the restoration of his voice he composed the hymn *Ut queant laxis resonare fibris / Mira gestorum famuli tuorum*[7] for the feast of Saint John the Baptist. In the first verse he prays that his voice be restored . . . as Zechariah's was.

There are people who on this day burn the bones of dead animals, collected wherever they are found. There are two reasons for this, as John Beleth says. One is an observance that goes back to antiquity: there are animals called dragons, which fly in the air, swim in water, walk on land; and sometimes when they travel through the air they are lustfully aroused and drop their sperm into wells and flowing waters. This causes a year of plague. A preventive against this danger was invented that consisted of making a bonfire of the bones of animals, the smoke from which drove the dragons away. Since this was usually done around the time of Saint John's feast day, some people continue to observe the custom. The other reason is to represent the burning of Saint John's bones by the infidels in the city of Sebaste.

---

[7] The third and fourth lines of the first verse are *Solve polluti labii reatum / Sancte Joannes*. Loosely, the English of it would be: In order that your servants may sing the wonders of your deeds with relaxed vocal cords, absolve the guilt of polluted lips, O Saint John! The whole charming hymn may be seen in *Hymni Ecclesiae* (London: Macmillan, 1865), 282.

Lighted torches are also carried around this bonfire, because John was a burning and a shining torch, and a wheel is spun because the sun then begins to be lower in its cycle. This signifies the decline of Saint John's fame, by which he was thought to be Christ, as he himself testified when he said: "I must decrease, but he must increase." According to Saint Augustine, this is also signified in their births and deaths. About the time of John's birth the days begin to be shorter, and about the time of Christ's birth they grow longer, as the maxim has it: *Solstitium decimo Christum praeit atque Joannem.*[8] So it was also in their deaths: Christ's body was heightened on the cross, John's was lessened by a head.

Paul the Deacon tells us in the *History of the Lombards* that Rothari, king of the Lombards, was buried, with a wealth of precious ornaments, beside the church of Saint John the Baptist. Then a man, seduced by greed, broke into the tomb and stole all the treasure. Saint John appeared to this man and said: "How dared you touch what was committed to my care? From now on you cannot enter my church!" And that is exactly how things went: whenever the man tried to enter this church, he was repelled by a mighty blow to the throat, and fell back at once.

87. Saints John and Paul

John and Paul were high officials in the household of Constantia, the daughter of Emperor Constantine. At the time the Scythians were invading Dacia and Thrace, and Gallicanus, commander of the Roman army, was about to lead his troops against them. Gallicanus demanded that Constantia be given to him in marriage in return for his leadership in the war, and the chief men of Rome urged the emperor to agree. The father, however, was saddened, because he knew that his daughter, after she was cured by Saint Agnes, had made a vow of virginity and would rather die than consent to marriage; but the virgin, trusting in God, advised her father to promise her to the general when and if he came back a victor. Moreover, he had two daughters of his now-deceased wife, and he would be asked to leave them with Constantia, so that she might learn their father's ways and wishes from them. In return for this Constantia offered him the services of John and Paul, hoping for greater security; and she prayed that God would convert both the father and the daughters. These arrangements pleased all parties.

---

[8] The solstice comes ten days before Christ and before John.

Gallicanus, with John and Paul and a large army, marched off to war, but the Scythians smashed the Roman force and besieged the remnants in a town in Thrace. At this point John and Paul went to the general and said to him: "Make a vow to the God of heaven, and you will win a victory greater than any you have won before!" Gallicanus made his vow, and a youth carrying a cross immediately appeared to him and said: "Gird on your sword and follow me!" He assented and followed the youth. They sped through the enemy's camp, reached their king and slew him, and by fear alone subjugated the army and made it tributary to the Romans. Two knights in armor appeared to him in the fight and supported him on either side.

Gallicanus, now a Christian, returned to Rome and was welcomed with much honor. He asked the emperor to pardon him that he no longer wished to wed his daughter, because he had made a vow of continence to Christ. Meanwhile Constantia had converted his two daughters, and Constantine was very pleased to grant his request regarding the marriage. The general now resigned his command, distributed his wealth to the poor, and served God in poverty with other servants of the Lord. He wrought many miracles, and at the mere sight of him the demons fled out of the bodies of the possessed. The fame of his holiness spread throughout the world, and people came from the east and the west to see this Roman patrician washing the feet of the poor, serving them at table, pouring water over their hands, ministering kindly to the sick, and engaging in other forms of holy servitude.

Emperor Constantine the Great died and was succeeded by his son Constantius, who was tainted with the Arian heresy. Another Constantine, this one the brother of Constantine the emperor, had left two sons, Gallus and Julian. Emperor Constantius appointed the said Gallus a caesar and sent him to put down rebellious Judea, but later put him to death. Julian, fearing that Constantius would do away with him as he had with his brother, entered a monastery and made so great a show of religiosity that he was ordained to the office of lector. He also consulted the devil through a sorcerer and received the answer that he would become emperor.

Some time later, due to the pressure of events in the empire, Constantius appointed Julian a caesar and sent him to Gaul, where he carried out his mission effectively. When Constantius died, Julian, by then an apostate, was raised to the empire as Constantius had ordered. Julian gave orders that Gallicanus should either sacrifice to the gods or go into exile: he did not dare kill so widely admired a man. Gallicanus went to Alexandria, where the infidels stabbed him to the heart and he won the crown of martyrdom.

Julian, consumed by sacrilegious greed, covered his avarice by quoting the Gospel. When he robbed Christians of their possessions, he said: "Your Christ says in the Gospel that unless you renounce all you possess, you cannot be his disciple." Then he heard that John and Paul were supplying the needs of poor Christians out of the riches the virgin Constantia had left, and he informed them that as they had served Constantine, it was their duty to be at his service. They said: "Emperors Constantine and Constantius were proud to be servants of Christ, and we gladly served them; but since you have abandoned the religion of all the virtues, we have absolutely renounced your service and would despise ourselves if we obeyed you!" Julian replied: "I was an ordained cleric in your church, and if I had wanted to, I could have been pope. But I thought it was a waste to do nothing and live in idleness. So I made my choice for the military life, offered sacrifice to the gods, and with their help rose to the empire. You therefore, since you were raised in the imperial court, should not leave my side. I should have you with me as the first men in my palace. But if you persist in despising me, I shall have to take action, because I must not be despised!" They answered: "Since we put God before you, we certainly do not fear your threats! If we did, we might incur the enmity of the eternal God!" "If within ten days you have not changed your attitude toward me," said Julian, "you will be forced to do what you do not care to do of your own volition!" "Act as if the ten days were past, and do what you have been threatening to do!" said the saints. The emperor replied: "You think the Christians will make martyrs of you, but I will punish you not as martyrs but as public enemies!"

John and Paul spent the next ten days distributing all their wealth to the poor. On the tenth day Terentianus was sent to them and he said: "Our master Julian has sent a small gold statue of Jove to you. You are to burn incense to it, otherwise you die, both of you!" The two responded: "If Julian is your master, keep peace with him! We have no master except our Lord Jesus Christ!" He then ordered them to be beheaded secretly, and their bodies to be buried in a grave inside the house; and he circulated the rumor that they had been sent into exile. Shortly thereafter, Terentianus's son was seized by a demon and began to cry out through the house that a demon was tormenting him. Seeing this, Terentianus confessed his crime, became a Christian, and wrote an account of the passion of the martyrs. They suffered about the year A.D. 460.

Pope Gregory, in a homily on the Gospel text "If any man will come after me, let him deny himself and take up his cross," tells the story of a lady who regularly visited the church of the martyrs. One day when she went in, she found two monks in pilgrim attire standing in the church. Thinking that they were pilgrims, she ordered her attendant to give them an alms. While the attendant went about doing so, the pilgrims stood close to the lady and said: "You visit us now. On the day of judgment we shall seek you out and do whatever we can for you!" And they vanished out of her sight.

Ambrose, in his Preface for these martyrs, says: "The blessed martyrs John and Paul truly fulfilled what the voice of David said, 'Behold how good and how pleasant it is for brothers to dwell together in unity' (Ps. 133:1). These were brothers by the law of their birth, bound together in their common faith, equal to each other in their martyrdom, and forever glorious in the one Lord!"

88. Saint Leo, Pope

We read in the book of the *Miracles of the Blessed Virgin* that one day when Pope Leo was offering mass in the church of Saint Mary Major and was distributing communion to the faithful, a woman kissed his hand, and he experienced a violent temptation of the flesh. The man of God, taking cruel vengeance on himself that same day, secretly cut off the hand that had scandalized him, and threw it away. In time the people began to murmur at the pope for not celebrating the divine mysteries as usual. Then Leo turned to the Blessed Virgin and committed himself totally to her care. She quickly appeared at his side and with her holy hands put back his hand and made it firm, ordering him to proceed as before and offer sacrifice to her Son. Leo therefore proclaimed to all the people what had happened to him, and showed the restored hand to everyone.

This pope called the Council of Chalcedon and decreed that from then on virgins alone could take the veil. This council also decreed that Mary should be called "Mother of God."

At that time Attila was devastating Italy. Saint Leo spent three days and nights in prayer in the church of the apostles and then said to his associates: "If any of you wish to follow me, come along!" He went out of the city and moved toward Attila and his band. The Hun, seeing the blessed Leo, dismounted, knelt at the pope's feet, and begged him to ask for anything he wanted. Leo asked him to withdraw from Italy and to set his prisoners free. Attila's people protested: was the conqueror of the world to be conquered by a priest? Attila answered them: "I acted for my own good and yours! I saw standing at his right side a mighty warrior with his sword drawn, who said to me, 'Unless you obey this man, you and your people will perish!'"

At another time Leo prayed and fasted for forty days at Saint Peter's tomb, asking the apostle to obtain for him the remission of his sins. Saint Peter appeared to him and said: "I have prayed the Lord for you and he has forgiven all your sins. You will be held responsible only for the laying on of hands; that is to say that you will be asked whether you ordained anyone whether he was worthy or not."

Saint Leo died about A.D. 460.

---

89. Saint Peter, Apostle

Peter had three names. First, he was called *Simon Bar-Jona*. *Simon* is interpreted as obedient, or as accepting sadness; *Bar-Jona* as son of the dove, since *Bar* means son in Syriac, and *Jona* means dove in Hebrew. Peter indeed was obedient when Christ called him: at a single word of command he obeyed the Lord. He accepted sadness when, having denied Christ, he went outside and wept bitterly. He was a son of the dove because his whole intention was to serve God in simplicity. Secondly, he was called *Cephas*, which is interpreted head, or rock, or speaking forcefully: head, because he was the chief among the Church's prelates; rock, because of his endurance in his passion; speaking forcefully, by reason of his constant preaching. Thirdly, he was called *Petrus*, Peter, which is interpreted as recognizing, or taking off one's shoes, or unbinding. Peter recognized Christ's divinity when he said: "You are the Christ, the Son of the living God." He stripped the feet of his attachments to any dead and earthly works when he said: "Behold we have left all things and have followed you." He unbound us by removing the bonds of sin, which he did with the keys he received from the Lord.

Peter also had three surnames. He was called Simon *Johanna*, which means beauty of the Lord; Simon *Johannis*, meaning to whom it is given; and Simon *Bar-Jona*, son of the dove. By these surnames we are given to understand that Peter had beauty of conduct, gifts of virtue, and abundance of tears, the last because the dove's song is mournful. As to the name Peter, first Jesus *promised* that that would be his name; John 1:42: "You shall be called Cephas, which means Peter." Second, Jesus *gave* him the name; Mark 3:16: "And to Simon he gave the name Peter." Third, he *confirmed* the name; Matt. 16:18: "And I tell you, you are Peter, and on this rock I will build my Church."

Marcellus, Pope Linus, Hegesippus, and Pope Leo wrote accounts of Peter's passion.

Peter the apostle stood out among and above the other apostles. He wanted to know who the Lord's betrayer was, because, as Augustine says, if he had known, he would have torn the individual apart with his teeth. Therefore Christ would not name the traitor, because, as Chrysostom says, Peter would have risen up and killed him immediately. He walked over the water to the Lord, who chose him to be present at his transfiguration and at the raising to life of the ruler's daughter, found the coin of the tribute in the fish's mouth, received the keys of the kingdom of heaven from the Lord, accepted the charge of feeding Christ's sheep, converted three thousand men by his preaching on the day of Pentecost, foretold the deaths of Ananias and Saphira, cured Aeneas the paralytic, baptized Cornelius, brought Tabitha back to life. The shadow of his body cured the sick, and he was jailed by Herod and set free by an angel.

What food he ate and what clothes he wore he himself, as quoted in Saint Clement's book, tells us: "All I eat is bread with olives and sometimes vegetables. What I wear is what you see—a tunic and a cloak. I don't need anything else." It is also said that inside his tunic he always carried a towel with which to wipe away his frequent tears, because, when the dear memory of the Lord's presence and speech came to his mind, the surge of love made him unable to contain his weeping. When he remembered how he had denied his Lord, his sense of guilt made him shed tears again. Indeed, weeping became so habitual with him that, as Clement says, his whole face seemed to be burned with tears. Clement also tells us that when Peter heard the cock crow at dawn, he rose to pray and as usual burst into tears. He tells us—and we find this also in the *Ecclesiastical History*—that when Peter's wife was led to her martyrdom, he was overjoyed and called to her by her name, saying: "Dear wife, remember the Lord!"

Once when Peter sent two of his disciples away to preach and they had been traveling for twenty days, one of them died, and the other returned to Peter and told him what had happened. It is said that the one who died was Martial, though some say it was Maternus. Elsewhere we read that the first disciple was blessed Fronto, and his companion, who died, was a priest named George. However that may be, Peter handed his staff to the surviving disciple and ordered him to go back to his dead friend and to lay the staff upon him. He did this, and the man who had been dead for forty days promptly stood up alive.

At the time there was in Jerusalem a conjurer named Simon, who claimed to be the source of all truth. He declared that he would make those who believed him immortal, and that nothing was impossible to him. We read also in Clement's book that Simon said: "I will be publicly worshiped as God, and I will be given divine honors. Whatever I may wish to do I will be able to do. When my mother Rachel told me to go out to the wheatfield and reap the grain, I saw a scythe lying on the ground and I commanded the scythe to do the reaping by itself, and it reaped ten times as much as the other reapers did." Jerome says that Simon added: "I am the word of God, I am the beautiful one, I am the Paraclete. All that God is, I am!" At his command bronze serpents moved, bronze and stone statues laughed, and dogs sang.

According to Pope Linus, this Simon wanted to debate with Peter and to prove that he was God. On the appointed day Peter came to the meeting place and said to those gathered there: "Peace be with you, brothers who love the truth!" Simon said to him: "We have no use for your peace! If there is peace and harmony, we will make no progress in our search for the truth. Thieves keep peace among themselves! Therefore do not invoke peace but war! When two fight, there will be peace when one or the other is defeated!" Peter: "Why are you afraid to hear of peace? Wars are born of sin, but where there is no sin, there is peace. Truth comes out in discussion, righteousness is found in deeds." Simon: "Idle talk! I will show you the power of my divinity so that you may adore me at once! I am the first power! I can fly through the air, make new trees, change stones into bread, stand in fire without injury. I can do anything I choose to do!" But Peter refuted him point by point and exposed all his magical hoaxes. Then Simon, seeing that he could not prevail over the apostle and for fear of being exposed as a sorcerer, threw all his books of magic into the sea and went to Rome, where he might be accepted as a god. But Peter learned of this and followed him, and this brought him to Rome.

It was in the fourth year of the reign of Emperor Claudius that Peter came to Rome. He held his see in Rome for twenty-five years and, as John Beleth says, ordained two bishops, Linus and Cletus, to assist him, one within the city of Rome and the other outside the walls. He preached assiduously and made many converts to the faith, and cured a great many sick people of their illnesses. In his preaching he always praised and stressed chastity. This so changed the lives of four of the prefect Agrippa's concubines that they refused to have anything more to do with him. This made him angry, and he watched for an opportunity to get the better of the apostle. Then the Lord appeared to Peter and said: "Simon and Nero are plotting against you, but have no fear, because I am with you and will shield you! I will also give you my servant Paul as a solace. He will arrive in Rome tomorrow!" Peter, knowing now, as Linus says, that the time to put off his mortal tent was at hand, presided over a meeting of his brethren at which he took Clement by the hand, ordained him a bishop, and installed him in his own prelatial chair. Then Paul arrived in Rome as the Lord had foretold, and with Peter began to preach Christ.

Meanwhile Simon Magus was in high favor with Nero, and people thought without a doubt that he was the guardian of the emperor's life and welfare and that of the whole city. One day, as Pope Leo tells it, Simon was standing in Nero's presence and his visage suddenly changed so that at one moment he looked older and the next moment younger. Nero saw this and was sure that Simon was the son of God. The sorcerer, as the same Leo reports, then said to Nero: "You know perfectly well, Emperor, that I am the son of God, so order me to be beheaded, and on the third day I will rise again!" Nero therefore ordered the executioner to cut off Simon's head. The executioner proceeded to cut the head off a ram but thought he had indeed beheaded a man, Simon having created this illusion by his magical arts. Thus Simon escaped. He gathered up the animal's remains and hid them, leaving the blood to congeal on the pavement, and remained in seclusion for three days. Then he made his appearance before Nero and said: "Have my blood, which I shed, wiped up, because, though I was beheaded, here I am, risen on the third day as I promised!" The emperor was dumbfounded and was more sure than ever that Simon was God's son. This from Leo. Another time, when Simon was inside with the emperor, a demon assumed his appearance and harangued the populace outside the palace. In the end the Romans held him in such veneration that they made a statue of him and inscribed this title on it: SIMONI DEO SANCTO.[1]

Pope Leo affirms that Peter and Paul went to Nero and exposed all the mischief Simon was doing; and Peter added that as there are two substances in Christ, the divine and the human, so there were two substances in this magician, the human and the diabolical. Then, as Saint Marcellus and Pope Leo aver, Simon said: "I will not tolerate this enemy any longer! I will command my angels and they will avenge me!" Peter said to him: "I am not afraid of your angels, but they are afraid of me!" "What!" said Nero, "Are you not afraid of Simon, who proves his divinity by his acts?" Peter: "If there is any divinity in him, let him tell me what I am thinking or what I am doing; but first I shall whisper in your ear what I am thinking, so that he won't dare to lie!" Nero: "Come close and tell me what you are thinking!" Peter came close to him and said: "Have a loaf of bread brought and given to me in such a way that he can't see what is happening!" The loaf was brought and Peter blessed it and hid it in his sleeve, and said: "Let Simon, who has made himself God, say what I have thought, said, and done!" Simon answered: "Rather let Peter say what I am thinking!" "I will show what Simon is thinking," Peter responded, "by doing what he's thinking!" Then Simon shouted angrily: "Let big dogs come in and devour him!" Suddenly huge dogs appeared and rushed upon Peter, but he brought out the blessed bread and the dogs turned and fled. Then Peter said to Nero: "See, I have shown, not by words but by action, that I knew what Simon had in mind. He had promised that he would bring his angels against me, but what he brought was dogs, showing that his angels are not godlike but canine!" Simon retorted: "Listen, Peter and Paul, if I cannot do anything to you here, we will go to a place where it suits me to judge you. For the time being I spare you!" This from Leo.

Then, as Hegesippus and Linus tell us, Simon, carried away by pride, dared to boast that he could raise the dead, and it happened that a young man had just died. So Peter and Simon were summoned, and all agreed with a proposal by Simon that the one who was unable to raise the dead man should be killed. Simon then began his incantations over the corpse, and those standing around saw the dead man move his head. The witnesses shouted and wanted to stone Peter, but the apostle, having barely succeeded in quieting them, said: "If the man is alive, let him rise, walk, and talk! Otherwise be aware that it was a demon that moved his head! Let Simon be moved away from the bier so that the devil's features may be fully unmasked!" Simon was moved away and the youth lay

---

[1] TO SIMON THE HOLY GOD.

motionless until Peter, standing at a distance, prayed and then said loudly: "Young man, in the name of Jesus Christ the Nazarene, arise and walk!" And the youth instantly arose and walked about.

Now the people wanted to stone Simon, but Peter said: "He is punished enough, since he has to admit that he and his witchcraft are defeated. Our master has taught us to return good for evil!" Then Simon spoke. "Peter and Paul, know that what you desire, namely, that I would deign to award you the crown of martyrdom, will not happen to you!" Peter: "May what we desire come for us, but may no good ever come to you, because every time you speak, you lie!"

Then, as Saint Marcellus says, Simon went to the house of Marcellus, a disciple of his, and tied an enormous dog at the door of the house, saying: "Now we'll see whether Peter, who usually comes to you, will be able to get in!" In a little while Peter arrived, made the sign of the cross over the dog, and turned it loose. The animal was gentle with all the others, but chased Simon, caught him and pulled him to the ground, leapt upon him and was about to take him by the throat; but Peter ran up and called to the dog not to hurt Simon. The dog therefore did not injure his body but tore his clothes to shreds and left him naked. Then the crowd, and especially the children and the dog, ran after him until they chased him out of the city as they would chase a wolf.

Unable to bear the shame of this episode, Simon kept out of sight for a whole year. Marcellus, however, witnessed these miracles and became a follower of Saint Peter. Later, Simon came out and was welcomed back into Nero's friendship. Furthermore, as Leo tells it, he called the people together and declared that he had been gravely offended by the Galileans and therefore had decided to leave the city, which he had protected until then. He also set a day upon which he was to ascend to heaven, because he did not deign to dwell on earth any longer. The day arrived and he climbed a high tower—or, according to Linus, he went up to the top of the Capitol—wearing a crown of laurel. He jumped off and began to fly. Paul said to Peter: "I'm the one to pray now; you're the one to command!" To Nero he said: "This man Peter is truthful, you and yours are seducers!" Peter said to Paul: "Paul, raise your head and look up!" When Paul looked up, he saw Simon flying and said to Peter: "Peter, what are you waiting for? Finish what you've started, because the Lord is already calling us!" Then Peter said: "I adjure you, angels of Satan, you who are holding Simon up in the air, I adjure you in the name of Jesus Christ our Lord! Stop holding him up and let him fall!" They released him at once and he crashed to the ground, his skull was fractured, and he expired. Nero grieved at the loss of such a man and said to the apostles: "You have aroused my suspicions, and therefore I shall lose you, too, and make you a horrible example!" This from Leo.

So the emperor gave Peter and Paul into the hands of Paulinus, a man of high station, and Paulinus turned them over to the custody of Mamertinus to be guarded by two soldiers, Processus and Martinianus; but Peter converted the soldiers, and they opened the prison doors and set the apostles free. (After the martyrdom of Peter and Paul, Paulinus had Processus and Martinianus brought before him for having done this, and, when he learned that they were Christians, had them beheaded by order of Nero.) The brethren urged Peter to leave the city. He was unwilling to do so, but finally, overcome by their insistence, he started out. When he got outside the city gates, as Leo and Linus have it, and reached the place that is now called Saint Mary at the Footprints, he saw Christ coming toward him and said: "Lord, where are you going?" Christ answered: "I am going to Rome to be crucified again!" Peter: "You will be crucified again?" Christ: "Yes!" And Peter said: "In that case, Lord, I'm going back to be crucified with you!" When these words had been spoken, the Lord ascended to heaven, while Peter watched and wept. And when he realized that what had been said concerned his own passion, he returned to the city and told the brethren what had happened.

Now he was taken prisoner by Nero's men and brought to the prefect Agrippa; and, as Linus says, his face shone like the sun. Agrippa said to him: "So you are the one who glories among the common people and the little women whom you wean from their husbands' beds!" But the apostle broke in to say that he gloried only in the cross of Jesus Christ. Then Peter, being an alien, was condemned to be crucified, while Paul, because he was a Roman citizen, was sentenced to beheading. Dionysius wrote about this judgment scene in his letter to Timothy on the death of Saint Paul: "O my brother Timothy, if you had seen the way they were treated in their last hours, you would have fainted with sadness and grief. Who would not weep in that hour when the sentence came down that Peter was to be crucified and Paul to be beheaded! Then you would have seen the mob of pagans and Jews striking them and spitting in their faces! And when came the awful moment of their consummation, they were separated from each other, and these pillars of the world were put in chains as the brethren groaned and wept. Then Paul said to Peter: 'Peace be with you, foundation stone of the churches and shepherd of the sheep and lambs of Christ!' Peter said to Paul: 'Go in peace, preacher of virtuous living, mediator and leader of the salvation of the righteous!' When the two were taken away in different directions because they were not put to death in the same place, I followed my master." So Dionysius.

Pope Leo and Marcellus assert that when Peter came to the cross, he said: "Because my Lord came down from heaven to earth, his cross was raised straight up; but he deigns to call me from earth to heaven, and my cross should have my head toward the earth and should point my feet toward heaven. Therefore, since I am not worthy to be on the cross the way my Lord was, turn my cross and crucify me head down!" So they turned the cross and nailed him to it with his feet upwards and his hands downwards. At the sight of this the people were enraged, and wanted to kill Nero and the prefect and free the apostle, but he pleaded with them not to hinder his martyrdom. Hegesippus and Linus say that the Lord opened the eyes of those who were weeping there, and they saw angels standing with crowns of roses and lilies, and Peter standing with them at the cross, receiving a book from Christ and reading from the book the words that he spoke. According to the same Hegesippus, Peter began to speak from the cross. "I chose to imitate you, Lord, but I had no right to be crucified upright. You are always upright, exalted, and high. We are children of the first man, who lowered his head to the earth, whose fall is signified by the manner of man's birth, for we are born in such a way that we seem to be dropped prone upon the earth. Conditions are changed, and the world thinks that right is left and left is right. You, Lord, are all things to me. All that you are, and nothing else but you alone, is all there is to me. I give you thanks with the whole spirit by which I live, understand, and call upon you!" (In these words two other reasons for his not wishing to be crucified in an upright position are touched upon.) Finally, Peter, knowing that the faithful had seen his glory, gave thanks, commended the faithful to God, and breathed forth his spirit. Marcellus and his brother Apuleius, Peter's disciples, took his body down from the cross and buried it embalmed with sweet spices.

Isidore, in his book *On the Birth and Death of the Saints*, says: "After Peter founded the church in Antioch, he went to Rome under Emperor Claudius to oppose Simon Magus, preached there, and for twenty-five years was bishop of that city. He was crucified head down, as he had wished, in the thirtieth year after the Lord's passion." Thus Isidore.

On the day of their death Peter and Paul appeared to Dionysius, according to what he says in the aforementioned letter: "My brother Timothy, hear the miracle, see the marvel, of the day of their martyrdom! For I was present at the moment when they were separated: after their death I saw them coming in hand in hand at the gate of the city, clothed in luminous garments and crowned with crowns of brilliance and light." Thus Dionysius.

Nero did not go unpunished for this crime and others he committed, for he put an end to his life with his own hand. Here we may add a brief notice of some of these crimes.

We read in a certain history, admittedly apocryphal, that when Seneca, Nero's tutor, was looking forward to a reward worthy of his labors, Nero ordered him to choose which branch of a given tree he would prefer to be hanged from, saying that this was the reward he was going to receive. When Seneca asked why he was being condemned to death, Nero brandished a sharp sword over his head, and Seneca bowed his head and backed away from the sword, stricken with fear at the threat of death. Nero asked him: "Master, why do you bow your head and dodge the sword?" Seneca answered: "Because I am a man and therefore I fear death and am unwilling to die." Nero: "And I fear you even now, as I feared you as a child! That is why I cannot live in peace and quiet as long as you are alive!" "If I must die," said Seneca, "at least allow me to choose the mode of death that I would prefer!" Nero: "Choose quickly! Don't delay your death!" Then Seneca lay in a bathtub filled with water and opened the veins in both arms; and as the blood flowed out, his life ended. So his very name, *Seneca*, was a presage. *Se necans* means killing oneself, and though he was forced to do so, he died by his own hand.

We also read that Seneca had two brothers. One was Julianus Gallio, the famous orator who committed suicide, and the other was Mela, father of the poet Lucan—the Lucan who, we read, died by opening his veins by order of Nero.

The same apocryphal history tells us that Nero, obsessed by an evil madness, ordered his mother killed and cut open so that he could see how it had been for him in her womb. The physicians, calling him to task over his mother's death, said: "Our laws prohibit it, and divine law forbids a son to kill his mother, who gave birth to him with such pain and nurtured him with so much toil and trouble." Nero said to them: "Make me pregnant with a child and then make me give birth, so that I may know how much pain it cost my mother!" He had conceived the notion of bearing a child because on his way through the city he had heard the cries of a woman in labor. They said to him: "That is not possible because it is contrary to nature, nor is it thinkable because it is contrary to reason." At this Nero said to them: "Make me pregnant and make me give birth, or I will have every one of you die a cruel death!"

So the doctors made up a potion in which they put a frog and gave it to the emperor to drink. Then they used their skills to make the frog grow in his belly, and his belly, rebelling against this unnatural invasion, swelled up so that Nero thought he was carrying a child. They also put him on a diet of foods they knew would be suitable for the frog, and told him that, having conceived, he had to follow the diet. At length, unable to stand the pain, he told the doctors: "Hasten the delivery, because I am so exhausted with this childbearing that I can hardly get my breath!" So they gave him a drink that made him vomit, and out came a frog horrible to see, full of vile humors and covered with blood. Nero, looking at what he had brought forth, shrank from it and wondered why it was such a monster, but the physicians told him that he had produced a deformed fetus because he had not been willing to wait the full term. He said: "Is this what I was like when I came out from my mother's womb?" "Yes!" they answered. So he commanded that the fetus be fed and kept in a domed chamber with stones in it. All this, however, is not contained in the chronicles and is apocryphal.

Then Nero began to wonder about the manner and extent of the burning of Troy, and made Rome burn for seven days and seven nights. He watched the fire from the highest available tower, being delighted with the beauty of the flames and reciting verses from the *Iliad* in a grandiose, bombastic style.

The chronicles tell us that Nero fished with gold nets, and that he worked hard at music and singing so as to surpass all harpists and actors. He took a man as his wife and was accepted as wife by a man, Orosius says. Finally the Romans could tolerate his insanity no longer, so they rose up against him and drove him out of the city. Seeing that no escape was possible, he sharpened a stick to a point with his teeth and drove it through his middle, thus putting an end to his life. Elsewhere we read that he was devoured by wolves.

When the Romans came back into the city, they found the frog hiding in its nest, hurried it out beyond the walls, and set it afire. Some say that the section of the city where the frog hid is called the Lateran for that reason.[2]

In the time of Pope Saint Cornelius some Greek Christians stole the bodies of the two apostles and were carrying them off, but demons living in the idols were forced by the power of God to cry out: "Men of Rome, help! Your gods are being carried away!" The faithful took this to mean the apostles, and the pagans to mean their gods, so believers and unbelievers came together and pursued the Greeks. These were fearful, and threw the apostles' bodies into a well near the catacombs, where the faithful recovered them at a later time. Gregory, however, says in his *Register* that a violent storm of thunder and lightning frightened and dispersed them so that they left the relics in or near the catacombs.

Then there was uncertainty about which bones were Saint Peter's and which Saint Paul's. The faithful prayed and fasted persistently and obtained a response from heaven: "The larger bones belong to the preacher, the smaller ones to the fisherman." So the bones were separated and each apostle's lot was placed in the church that had been raised in his honor. Others say that Pope Silvester, when he was about to consecrate the churches, put both the large and the small bones on a scale, weighed them with much reverence, and allocated equal halves to the two churches.

Gregory, in his *Dialogue*, tells of one Agontius, a man of great humility and sanctity, who lived in the church where Saint Peter's body reposes. There was also a girl living in the church, a paralytic who crawled on her hands and knees, dragging her body along the pavement because her lower limbs were crippled. For a long time she had been imploring Saint Peter to cure her, and finally he appeared to her and said: "Go to Agontius, who lives here, and he will restore you to health." So she began to drag herself here and there in the great church, looking in every nook and cranny and trying to find out who this Agontius was. Then suddenly the man she sought was in front of her, and she said to him: "Our shepherd and foster father Saint Peter has sent me to you to have you free me from my infirmities." "If you have been sent by him," Agontius answered, "stand up!" He gave her his hand and helped her to her feet, and she was completely cured, not a trace of her debility remaining.

In the same book Gregory tells us about Galla, a young girl of the highest Roman nobility, daughter of Symmachus, a consul and patrician. Galla was given in marriage, but in the space of one year her husband died and she was left a widow. Both her age and her fortune pointed to a second marriage, but she chose to be united to God in spiritual nuptials, which begin in grief but lead to eternal joys, rather than subject herself to marriage in the flesh, which always

[2] *Lateranus* from *latente rana*, hiding frog.

begins happily but tends toward a sad end. Galla, however, was a very hot-blooded woman, and her doctors told her that unless she gave herself again to the embraces of a husband, the excessive internal heat would cause her to grow a beard, unnatural as that would be. This actually happened, but she felt no concern about the external deformity because she loved inner beauty more, nor did she fear that if the beard made her ugly her heavenly spouse would not love her. She therefore put off her secular attire and entered the monastery attached to the church of Saint Peter, where she served God for many years in simplicity, prayer, and almsgiving. Then she was stricken with a cancer of the breast. Beside her bed there were always two candlesticks with lighted candles, because, being a lover of light, she hated not only spiritual but also material darkness. At a given moment she saw Saint Peter the apostle standing at the foot of her bed between the two candles. Thrilled with joy and drawing boldness from her love, she said: "What is it, my lord? Are all my sins forgiven me?" Peter, his face beaming with kindness, nodded and said: "All forgiven! Come!" She said: "I ask that Sister Benedicta may come with me." "No," said Saint Peter, "but that other sister may come with you." Galla told all this to the abbess, and three days later she died with the other sister.

In the same book Gregory says that there was a priest, known for his holiness, who, when he was dying, cried out joyously: "Welcome, my lords! Welcome, my lords, that you have deigned to come to me, poor little servant man that I am! I come, I come! Thank you! Thank you!" When those attending him asked him to whom he was talking, he was surprised and answered: "Don't you see the holy apostles Peter and Paul, who have come here together?" And when he had repeated those same words over and over, his holy soul was released from his body.

There are some who question whether Peter and Paul suffered martyrdom on the same day. Some say it was on the same day, but that one suffered a year later than the other. But Jerome and almost all the holy fathers who have dealt with this question agree that they suffered on the same day and in the same year. This is clear also from the letter of Dionysius; and Pope Leo (or Maximus, as some think) says in a sermon: "We have good reasons to think it happened that on one day and in one place they were sentenced to death by the one tyrant.. They suffered on one and the same day so that they could go to Christ at the same time; in one and the same place so that Rome might possess both of them; under one persecutor, that equal cruelty should befall them both. The day therefore was decreed to show their merit, the place to show their glory, and the persecutor to show their bravery." So Leo.

Granted, however, that they suffered on the same day and at the same hour, they did not suffer at the same spot but at different locations. When Leo says that they suffered in the same place, he means that they were both martyred in Rome. Someone put this in verse:

Ense coronatur Paulus, cruce Petrus, eodem
Sub duce, luce, loco, dux Nero, Roma locus.[3]

Another put it this way:

Ense sacrat Paulum, par lux, dux, urbs, cruce Petrum.[4]

Although they died on the same day, however, Gregory decreed that on that day the offices should celebrate Peter more specially, and that commemoration of Paul be made the following day. This is because the church of Saint Peter was dedicated on that day, because Peter was higher in dignity and was converted earlier, and because he was the primate of Rome.

---

90. Saint Paul, Apostle

The name Paul, or Paulus, is interpreted to mean mouth of a trumpet, or their mouth, or wonderfully chosen, or miracle of election. Or Paulus comes from *pausa*, which in Hebrew means quiet or repose, and in Latin means a moderate man. These meanings denote six privileges that Paul possessed more than others do. The first is the privilege of fruitful speech, because he preached the Gospel from Illyria to Jerusalem and therefore is said to be the mouth of a trumpet. Secondly, his love of others was visceral and made him say: "Who is weak, and I am not weak? Who is scandalized, and I am not on fire?" Therefore he is called the mouth of them, i.e., the mouth of the heart, of which he himself says: "Our mouth is open to you, O Corinthians, our heart is wide." The third privilege is his miraculous conversion, and so he is called wonderfully chosen because he was chosen and converted miraculously. Fourthly, he had the hands of a workman, for which reason he is said to be a miracle of election, because it was a great wonder that he chose to earn his living with his own hands and to preach tirelessly. His fifth privilege was that of blissful contemplation. He was caught up to the third heaven and there became the quiet of the Lord, because contemplation

---

[3] Paul was martyred with a sword, Peter on a cross, the same / Ruler, day, place, the ruler Nero, the place Rome.

[4] Paul is sainted by the sword, same day, ruler, city, Peter by the cross.

requires quiet in the mind. Sixthly, he had the virtue of humility and so could be called moderate.

There are three opinions concerning Paul's name. Origen held that he always had two names and was called either Saul or Paul. Rabanus Maurus believed that originally he was called Saul after Saul the proud king but after his conversion was called Paul, which means small, because of his moderate and humble spirit. Thus he was interpreting his own name when he said: "I am the least of the apostles, not worthy to be called an apostle." Bede, however, thought that he took the name Paul from the proconsul Sergius Paulus, whom he converted to the faith. Pope Linus wrote Paul's passion.

After his conversion the apostle Paul suffered many forms of persecution, which Saint Hilary sums up as follows: "At Philippi Paul the apostle was beaten with rods and imprisoned, and had his feet bound to a log of wood; he was stoned in Lystra, pursued by evil men in Iconium and Thessalonica, thrown to the wild beasts in Ephesus. At Damascus he was let down over the city wall in a basket, in Jerusalem he was haled to court, whipped, bound, and conspired against, in Caesarea he was put in jail and charged with crimes, on the way to Italy by sea he was put in danger of shipwreck, and arriving in Rome he was tried and put to death under Nero." This from Hilary.

Paul was awarded the apostolate to the Gentiles. At Lystra he made a crippled man walk straight up, restored to life a youth who had fallen from a window, and performed many other miracles. At Mitylene a viper bit him on the hand but did him no harm; instead he shook off the beast into the fire. It is also said that those who are descended from the man whose guest Paul was are never harmed in any way by venomous snakes: for this reason, when a child is born to a man of that lineage, the father puts a serpent into the cradle, so as to be assured that the infant really is his child.

We find also that at different times Paul is portrayed as Peter's inferior, as greater than Peter, or as Peter's equal, but the fact is that he was inferior in dignity, greater in preaching, and equal in holiness. Haymon tells us that from cockcrow until late morning Paul plied a manual trade, then proceeded to preach, and that sometimes his sermons went on till nightfall. The remaining time sufficed for taking food and for rest and prayer.

When Paul arrived in Rome, Nero was not yet confirmed as emperor, and when he heard that Paul was engaged in arguing with the Jews about Jewish law and the Christian faith, he paid little attention. The apostle therefore was at liberty to go where he pleased and to preach freely. Jerome, in his book *On Illustrious Men*, says that in the twenty-fifth year from the Lord's passion, i.e., the second year of Nero's reign, Paul was sent to Rome in chains and was held in loose custody for two years during which he debated with the Jews, and then was set free by Nero and preached the Gospel in lands to the west. In Nero's fourteenth year, however, he was beheaded, in the same year and on the same day on which Peter was crucified. So Jerome.

Paul became widely known and was admired for his wisdom and the depth of his religious devotion. He became friendly with a number of people in Nero's immediate company and converted them to the faith of Christ. Some of his writings were read before the emperor and were applauded by all who heard them. Even the Senate thought highly of him. One day toward evening, however, he was preaching in a crowded upper room. A young man named Patroclus, who was Nero's cupbearer and dear to the emperor, climbed up and sat on a windowsill in order to hear him better, but after a while dozed off, fell to the ground, and was killed. Nero took the news of his favorite's death very hard and promptly appointed another to take his place. Paul knew about this by the Spirit and told some of the people present to bring him the body of Patroclus. He then restored the youth to life and sent him and his companions to the emperor.

So Nero, lamenting the death of his cupbearer, all of a sudden was told that Patroclus, very much alive, was at the door. Hearing that the youth, whom a moment ago he mourned as dead, was alive, he was frightened and refused to let him in, until finally his attendants persuaded him to admit the young man to his presence. Nero said to him: "Patroclus, you are alive?" The answer: "Caesar, I am alive." Nero: "Who brought you to life?" Patroclus: "Jesus Christ, the King of all the ages." Nero, angrily: "So he will reign forever and will do away with all the world's kingdoms?" Patroclus: "Yes, Caesar!" Nero slapped him, saying: "So now you are that king's soldier?" Patroclus: "Yes, I am his soldier because he brought me back from the dead." Then five of the emperor's ministers, who were always at his side, said to him: "Why, Emperor, do you strike this estimable youth, who is giving you truthful answers? For we too are soldiers of that unconquered king!"

At this, Nero shut them up in prison, intending to torture them as much as he had loved them previously. Then he gave orders to round up all Christians and punish and torture them without a hearing. Paul, along with the rest, was brought before him in chains. Nero said to him: "Well, sir, you serve a great king, but here you are, conquered by me! Why do you lure my soldiers away from me and attach them to yourself?" "I don't draw soldiers only from your corner of the earth," Paul answered, "but from the whole wide world, and our King will lavish upon them such gifts as will never be lacking and will exceed every need. If you consent to be a subject of this King, you will be saved. His power is so great that he will come to judge all men and will dissolve the figure of this world by fire."

Nero was enraged at what he heard; and because Paul had said that the figure of the world would be dissolved by fire, he ordered all the soldiers of Christ to be burned to death, and Paul to be beheaded for the crime of lese majesty. So massive was the ensuing slaughter of Christians that the Roman people besieged the palace and were stirring up a general sedition, shouting: "Caesar! Put a stop to this massacre, countermand your order! You are killing our fellow citizens, the guardians of the Roman Empire!"

This made Nero fearful, and he changed his edict to the effect that no Christians were to be touched until the emperor came to a considered judgment about them. So Paul was brought back and set before the emperor, and when he saw him, Nero shouted at the top of his voice: "Rid me of this malefactor! Off with this impostor's head! Away with this seducer of reason! Rid the earth of this perverter of minds!" "Nero," Paul replied, "I will suffer for a short time and will live forever unto the Lord Jesus Christ!" Nero called out: "Off with his head! Let him know that I am stronger than his king, that I have beaten him! Then we shall see whether he can live forever!" Paul: "So that you may know that I live eternally after the death of the body, when my head has been cut off, I will appear to you alive. Then you will be able to realize that Christ is the God of life, not of death."

When he had said this, Paul was led to the place of execution. On the way there the three soldiers who were guarding him asked: "Tell us, Paul, who is this king of yours whom you love so well that you would rather die for him than stay alive? What sort of reward do you expect for this?" Paul then preached to them about the kingdom of God and the pains of hell, so effectively that he converted them to the faith. They begged him to go away freely wherever he wanted to, but he said: "I am no deserter but an enrolled soldier of Christ, and I know that I shall pass out of this transitory life into eternal life. As soon as I have been decapitated, men of my faith will come and take away my body. You yourselves must note the spot and come back to it tomorrow morning. Beside my grave you will find two men praying. They will be Titus and Luke. You must tell them my reason for sending you to them. They will baptize you and make you fellow citizens and coheirs of the kingdom of heaven."

While Paul was speaking, Nero sent two soldiers to see whether he had been put to death. He wanted to convert them, but they said: "When you're dead and come back to life, then we'll believe what you say. Now come on and take what's coming to you!" When they arrived at the Ostia gate, near which he was to suffer, he came face to face with a lady who was a disciple of his. Her name was Plantilla, although according to Dionysius she was known by another name, Lemobia, perhaps because she had two names. She was weeping and began to commend herself to his prayers. "Don't be upset, Plantilla, daughter of eternal salvation," said Paul. "Lend me the veil you are wearing over your head. I will cover my eyes with it and return it to you afterwards." She handed him her veil, and the executioners laughed, saying: "Why do you let this impostor, this charlatan, have your costly veil? Now you've lost it!"

When Paul reached the place of execution, he faced the East, raised his hands to heaven, prayed for a long time in his mother tongue, and gave thanks to God. Then he bade his brethren farewell, tied Plantilla's veil over his eyes, knelt on the ground on both knees, bent his neck, and so was beheaded. As soon as his head bounded from his body, it intoned, in Hebrew and in a clear voice, "Jesus Christ," the name that had been so sweet to him in life, and that he had pronounced so often. It is said that in his letters he used the name Jesus or Christ, or both, five hundred times. From his wound a stream of milk spurted upon the soldiers' clothing, followed by a flow of blood. A vast light shone in the air, and a very sweet odor emanated from the saint's body.

Dionysius, in a letter[1] to Timothy about Paul's death, says: "In that grief-filled hour, my beloved brother, the executioner said to Paul, Bend your neck! Then the blessed apostle looked up to heaven, marked his forehead and breast with the sign of the cross, and said: My Lord Jesus Christ, into your hands I commend my spirit! Then, without hesitation or compulsion, he extended his neck and so received the martyr's crown as the executioner made his stroke and cut off Paul's head. As the blow fell, blessed Paul took off the veil, caught his own blood in it, rolled it up and folded it, and gave it to the woman.

"When the executioner returned, Lemobia asked him: 'Where have you laid my master Paul?' The soldier answered: 'He lies with his companion in the Valley of the Boxers outside the city, and his face is covered with your veil.' But she replied: 'Look! Peter and Paul have come here clothed in shining garments and wearing crowns gleaming with light on their heads.' Then she held out the veil dripping with blood and showed it to them, and because of this, many believed in the Lord and became Christians." So Dionysius.

Hearing how things had gone, Nero was frightened out of his wits, and called in friends and philosophers to discuss what had happened. While they were talking, Paul came in, though the doors were closed. He stood before the emperor and said: "Caesar, here I am, Paul the soldier of the eternal and unconquered king. Now believe, because I am not dead but alive, and you, poor wretch, will die the eternal death for having unjustly killed the saints of God." That said, he disappeared. By this time Nero was beside himself with fear and did not know what to do next, but his friends calmed him, and advised him to release Patroclus and Barnabas with the others and let them go wherever they wished.

The next morning the two soldiers, Longinus the commander and Accestus, went to Paul's grave and there saw two men, Titus and Luke, praying, and Paul standing between them. Titus and Luke were alarmed at the sight of the soldiers and started to run away, and Paul disappeared. The soldiers shouted after the two fugitives, saying: "We're not pursuing you as you think! We want you to baptize us, as Paul, whom we just saw praying with you, told us to do." The other two, hearing this, came back and baptized them joyfully.

Paul's head was thrown into a trench and could not be found because so many other people had been put to death and their heads and bodies piled into the same trench. However, we read in that same letter of Dionysius that at a later

---

[1] This "letter" is unknown.

time the trench was cleaned out, and Paul's head was tossed up along with other detritus. A shepherd stuck the head on his staff and stood the staff up in his sheepfold. Then for three consecutive nights the sheepherder and his master saw an ineffable light shining above the head. They made this known to the bishop and the faithful, who said: "That must be Paul's head!" So the bishop and a huge crowd of the faithful went out and took possession of the head, which they placed on a gold table. They wanted to put the head in its place with the body, but the patriarch responded: "We know that a great many Christians were killed and that their heads were scattered here and there, and I hesitate to put this head with Paul's body. Let us instead place the head at the feet of the body, and we will pray almighty God that if this be indeed the right head, the body may turn around and be joined to it." This suggestion appealed to everyone, and they placed the head at the feet of the saint's body. Then they prayed, and lo! to the wonderment of all, the body turned around and joined itself to the head where it belonged. So all blessed God and were sure that this was truly Paul's head. Thus Dionysius.

Gregory of Tours, who flourished in the reign of Justin II, tells us that a certain man who had lost all hope was preparing a noose to hang himself yet kept calling upon the name of Paul, saying: "Saint Paul, help me!" Then a sordid shade stood by him and urged him on, saying: "Go ahead, good fellow! Get it over with, don't waste time!" The man went on preparing his noose but continued to say: "Most blessed Paul, help me!" When the noose was ready, another shade appeared—this one in the form of a man—and said to the one that was coaxing the poor fellow: "Begone, wretch! Saint Paul has been called and is coming!" The foul shade vanished, and the man came to his senses, threw the noose away, and did suitable penance.

Gregory also says in his *Register:* "Numerous miracles come from Saint Paul's chains. Many people ask for some filings. A priest is at hand with a file, and for some of those who ask he strikes off a few filings easily and with no delay. For others who ask he files away long and hard at the chains, but nothing comes off."

In the letter we have already quoted, Dionysius piously deplores the death of his teacher Saint Paul, saying: "Who will give water to our eyes and a fountain of tears to our pupils, to enable us to mourn day and night the light of all the churches that is extinguished? Who will not weep and groan, who will not put on the weeds of mourning, will not be stunned in mind and overcome with grief? Behold! Peter, the foundation of the churches and glory of the holy apostles, has departed and left us orphans, and Paul, the friend of the Gentiles and consoler of the poor, has gone from us and is nowhere to be found! He was the father of fathers, the teacher of teachers, the shepherd of shepherds—Paul, I say, the abyss of wisdom, the high-sounding shepherd's pipe, the tireless preacher of the truth, the noblest of the apostles! This angel of earth and man of heaven, image and likeness of deity and deiform spirit, has left us—us, I say, the needy and unworthy—in this contemptible, evil world. He has gone to God, his lord and friend. Alas, my brother Timothy, beloved of my soul, where is your father, your master who loved you? Where now will he greet you from? See, you have been orphaned and left alone. No longer will he write to you with his most holy hand and say to you: Dearest son, come! My brother Timothy, what has befallen here of sadness and darkness and loss, that we have been made orphans? No longer do his letters come to you, letters that started: Paul, modest servant of Jesus Christ. No longer will he write to various cities on your behalf: Welcome my beloved son . . . Close the books of the prophets, brother, and seal them closed, because we have no one to interpret their parables and paradigms and speeches. The prophet David bewailed his son and said, Woe is me, my son, woe is me! And I say, Woe is me, my master, truly woe is me! No longer will your disciples flock to Rome and ask for us. No longer will anyone say: Let us go and see our teachers and ask them how we may best rule the churches entrusted to us, and they will interpret for us the sayings of our lord Jesus Christ and the sayings of the prophets. Yes, woe to these sons, my brother, because they are bereft of their spiritual fathers; the flock is bereft of them. And woe to us also, brother, who are bereft of our spiritual masters, who had gleaned understanding and knowledge of the Old and New Law and brought all this together in their letters. Where now is Paul's course, and the labor of his holy feet? Where now the eloquent mouth, the counseling tongue, the spirit ever pleasing to his God? Who may not wail and mourn, for those who merited glory and honor before God have been handed over to death like evildoers. Woe is me, the hour that I have looked upon that holy body, bloodied with innocent blood! Alas, my father, my master and teacher, for no guilt of yours did you die such a death! Now where shall I go to look for you, O glory of Christians and praise of the faithful! Who has silenced your voice, O high-noted reed pipe of the churches, precious pick to pluck the ten-stringed psaltery? Behold, you have gone in to the Lord your God, whom you desired, for whom you longed with your whole heart! Jerusalem and Rome, in a crooked friendship, have become equal in evil. Jerusalem crucified our Lord Jesus Christ and Rome did his apostles to death: Jerusalem now serves him whom she crucified, Rome glorifies those she slew by celebrating their memory. And now, my brother Timothy, those whom you loved and yearned for wholeheartedly, Saul I say and Jonathan, were not separated in life or in death, and I am not separated from my lord and master except insofar as base and wicked men have separated us. And this separation is only for a time, and his soul knows whom he loves, even without their speaking to him, they who are now at a distance from him. But on the day of resurrection it were a great loss to be separated from them." Thus Dionysius.

Chrysostom, in his *De laudibus Pauli*, commends this glorious apostle in many ways. He says: "He who called Paul's soul a preeminent meadow of virtues and a spiritual paradise was in no way at fault. What tongue could be found equal to praising him, since his soul possessed all the goods that are in all men, and held together not only all that is good in men but also—and this is much greater—all that is good in the angels? We will not be silent about this; indeed we really have to talk about it. For this is the highest kind of praise (the virtues and greatness of the one praised exceeding the powers of rhetoric), and so for us it is more glorious often to be bettered than always to be best. Where then can we more fittingly open the exordium of his praises than at this very point—namely, first, that we show him as possessing the good that is in all others. Abel offered sacrifice and is praised for so doing, but if we turn our attention to Paul's sacrifice, it will appear as far superior as heaven is to earth. He immolated himself day after day in and by a double sacrifice, offering the mortification both of his heart and of his body. It was not sheep or oxen that he offered, but himself doubly immolated. Nor was he satisfied even with this but strove to offer the whole world. He traveled by land and by sea, winging his way, as it were, over Greece and the lands of the heathen and every region under the sun, making angels of men— nay, more, turning these very men from demons into angels.

"What can possibly be found to equal this host, which Paul offered by the sword of the Holy Spirit on that altar which is located above the heavens? But Abel died at the hand of his envious brother, while Paul was killed by those whom he wished to rescue from innumerable evils. Do you want me to show you his countless deaths, deaths as numerous as the days of his life? We read that Noe saved only himself and his children in the ark. Paul, however, freed the whole world endangered by the waves of a far wilder flood, not by building an ark out of planks, but by writing epistles instead of shaping planks. This ark sails not just to one place but to the ends of the earth. It is not caulked with bitumen or pitch; its planks are held together by the Holy Spirit. This ark takes aboard men more witless than irrational animals and makes them imitators of the angels. Noe's ark took on a crow but sent it off again still a crow, and shipped a wolf but could not tame its savageness, but this ark did better, taking aboard hawks and vultures and making doves of them, subduing all savagery and inducing mildness of spirit.

"Abraham is admired by all because at God's command he left fatherland and kinsmen, but how could he be compared with Paul, who not only left home and kin but set no value on the whole world and indeed on heaven and the heaven of heavens, accepting Christ, clinging to this sole good, namely, the love of Christ, in place of all the rest? Neither things present, he says, nor things to come, nor might, nor height, nor depth, nor any other creature, shall be able to separate us from the love of God that is in Christ Jesus our Lord. Yes, Abraham put himself in danger when he rescued his brother's son from his enemies, but Paul snatched the whole world out of the grip of the devil, endured dangers without number, and by his own daily deaths won complete safety for others. Abraham was willing to sacrifice his son: Paul sacrificed himself a thousand times.

"There are those who admire Isaac for his patience when his enemies stopped up the wells he had dug; but Paul, seeing his wells, namely, his own body, stopped up with stones, not only accepted this, as Isaac had done, but strove to carry off to heaven those at whose hands he suffered. However much that font was stopped up, it burst forth all the more and, overflowing, fed many rivers that rose out of it. Scripture wonders at Jacob's patience and forbearance, but is there anywhere a soul staunch enough to imitate Paul's patience? It was not seven years but a lifetime of servitude that he bore for the spouse of Christ, enduring a thousand trials, burned by the sun's heat by day and chilled by the night cold, now cut by whips and bruised by stones and wrung by struggles, always jumping up to seize the captive sheep from the jaws of the devil. Then there was Joseph, who was adorned with the virtue of purity, but I am afraid it may seem ridiculous to praise Paul on this ground. He crucified himself, and not only the beauties of the human body, but also all that seems brilliant and comely in material things, looked to him as dust and ashes look to us. He was like a dead man motionless beside a corpse.

"Job, too, is admired, and he was a marvelous contender; but Paul held out not for months but for many years of struggle and emerged with honor, not scraping his ulcerous flesh with a fragment of a broken pot, but frequently plunging into the monstrous maw of the lion and fighting against innumerable trials, bearing them imperturbable as a stone. He sustained shameful treatment not from three or four friends but from all the infidels and even from his brethren, being spat upon and cursed by all. Job practiced openhanded hospitality and cared for the poor, but the care that Job gave to those weak in body Paul dispensed to sick souls. Job threw open his house to every comer; Paul's soul stood open to the whole world. Job possessed great herds of sheep and cattle and gave freely to the poor; Paul, owning nothing more than his body, ministered bodily to those in need, as he reminds us somewhere, saying: Such things as were needful for me and them that are with me, these hands have furnished (Acts 20:34). Worms and wounds inflicted sharp pains on holy Job; but if you consider the scourgings, the hunger, the chains, and the perils inflicted upon Paul by those of his own household, by strangers, and by the rest of the world, his solicitude for all the churches, his being burned by scandal given to anyone, you will see that his soul was harder than any rock, and surpassed iron and steel in strength. The pains that Job suffered in his body, Paul suffered in his spirit: a sadness more poignant than any sorrow consumed him when anyone fell into sin, so that torrents of tears flowed ceaselessly from his eyes not only by day but by night. He was afflicted more sorely than a woman in labor and said: My little children, of whom I am in labor again until Christ be formed in you.

"To save the Jews, Moses chose to be wiped out of the book of the living, and therefore offered himself to perish with the rest, but Paul offered himself *for* the rest. He wished to perish, not with those perishing; but in order that the others might be saved, he would give up eternal glory. And Moses resisted Pharaoh, but Paul resisted the devil daily. Moses resisted for the sake of one people, Paul fought for the whole world, not by sweat but by blood. John had locusts and wild honey for food, but Paul was caught up amidst the crash and clatter of the world, not settled, like John, in the quiet and peace of the desert; and for nourishment he had no locusts or honey, but satisfied his needs with much coarser food and with his zeal for preaching. John's attitude regarding Herodias was indeed very courageous, but Paul rebuked not one or two or three but many persons in similar positions of power, and tyrants far fiercer than any of them.

"It remains for us to compare Paul to the angels, and again we declare that he is magnificent, because he obeyed God with the utmost care, which is what David, admiring, said about the angels: O you his angels, you mighty ones who do his word, hearkening to the voice of his word! And what else does the prophet admire in the angels? He says: [Lord] who makest the winds thy messengers, fire and flame thy ministers! But we can find this in Paul, who purged the whole world as fire and wind do. But he had not yet won heaven, and this is above all to be wondered at, because he was busy on earth and was still encased in his mortal body. How worthy we are of condemnation, we who do not even try to imitate at least to a small degree this man who brings together in himself such a sheaf of virtues! No other nature was allotted to him than to us, he gained no soul different from ours, he lived in no other world but on the same earth and in the same area as we do. He grew up under the same laws and customs, yet in virtue of spirit he transcends all men who now are or ever were. Nor indeed is he to be admired only because in the abundance of his devotion he somehow did not feel the pains he accepted for the sake of virtue: he even thought of virtue as its own reward. We ourselves strive for virtue in view of the recompense held out to us, but he embraced and loved it even without any thought of reward. All the difficulties that seem to us to interfere with virtue he bore with perfect equanimity. He got up every day more ardent than the day before and faced the dangers that threatened him with ever-increasing bravery. When he saw that his death was imminent, he invited others to share his delight and his joy, saying: Rejoice and congratulate with me! Therefore he hurried toward the confusions and hurts that he sustained because of his zeal for preaching, rather than toward the enjoyment of the good things of life. He looked forward to dying rather than living, desired poverty rather than riches, sought toil much more than others seek rest after toil, chose grief more than others seek pleasure, prayed more earnestly and fruitfully for his enemies than others pray against theirs. To him there was one thing to be dreaded and feared, and that was to offend God, just as there was nothing desirable except to please the Lord always. I do not say just that he had no desire for present goods: he looked for nothing for the future. Do not talk to me about prizes and peoples, armies and wealth, provinces, powers: these he valued as little as if they were cobwebs. Talk to me about the goods that are promised us in heaven, and then you will see his burning love for Christ. There was nothing he craved in place of the love of Christ—not the high state of angels or archangels or anything of the kind. He enjoyed what was greater than all that, namely, Christ's love. Having that, he deemed himself blessed above all: without that love he wanted no association with lords and princes. With that love he would have preferred to be the last, the least, even one of the damned, rather than without it to live with the highest, most sublime honors. To be separated from Christ's love was to him the greatest, the only torment, to him it was hell, the only punishment, infinite, intolerable torture; but to enjoy that love was life, the world, the kingdom, it was the promise, it was blessings uncountable.

"So the things we are afraid of seemed no more important to Paul than withered grass. To him tyrants and enemies breathing wrath were so many gnats, death and torture and a thousand punishments mere child's play as long as he could suffer something for Christ. The chain he wore as a prisoner was to him more precious than the diadem with which he might be crowned. Confined in a dungeon he dwelt in heaven; he took lashes and wounds more gladly than others win laurels. He loved pains no less than prizes, and when pains came his way instead of prizes, he called them a favor, since the things that cause us sadness pleased him greatly. Moreover, he was burned with deep grief, as he said: Who is scandalized and I am not on fire?—although some say that there is a kind of pleasure in grief, for many who are wounded by the deaths of their children get some consolation out of their weeping, and grieve more when they are forbidden to grieve. Thus Paul, too, by night and by day found consolation in tears, and no one was more affected by his own ills than Paul by the ills of others. Indeed you may well judge how affected he was when he wept for the loss of sinners, since he yearned to be excluded from the glory of heaven if only they might be saved. He considered it a more painful thing that they were not to be saved than that he himself should perish.

"Therefore to whom or to what can anyone compare this man? To iron? To steel? One might well call that soul golden or steely, for it was stronger than any steel, more precious than gold or jewels, and surpassed the one metal in hardness and the other in price. And what is there to which this man's soul might be compared? To none of the things that exist . . . not one! But if the strength of steel were given to gold and the glitter of gold to steel, then perhaps such a comparison would fit Paul's soul. But suppose I suggest a likeness betweeen steel and gold and Paul, and you put the whole world on the other side of the scale: you will see that Paul obviously outweighs the world. Therefore we say that Paul is worth more or is more worthy than the world and all that is in it. Well, then, if the world is not worthier or worth more than Paul, how about heaven? But we find heaven, too, less worthy. And if he put not only heaven but whatever is in the heavens second to the love of God, how would the Lord, who is as much more generous than Paul as kindness is better than malice, not judge him more worthy than unnumbered heavens? Not only does God love us as much as he is loved by us, but so much more generously that no words can express it. God snatched Paul up into paradise and raised him to the third heaven, and not without good reason, since Paul, striding over the earth, conducted himself in all things as though he already enjoyed the company of angels. Still bound to a visible body he shared their perfection: still subject to so many bodily weaknesses he strove to appear as in no way inferior to their supernal virtues. As one having wings he flew over the whole earth by his teaching; being in the body he made little of labors and dangers; as though already possessing heaven he despised everything earthly, and he watched with unremitting concentration of his mind as though already living with the incorporeal powers.

"It has often happened that this or that people has been placed under the care of angels, but no angel ever had such authority over a nation that was committed to him as Paul has had over the whole world. Just as a long-suffering father is disposed toward a deranged son, whom he pities and weeps for the more the son abuses him, so Paul showed the greatest effusions of fatherly affection to those who plagued him the most. He often wept and grieved for those who had scourged him five times and thirsted for his blood, and prayed for them: Brethren, he said, my heart's desire and prayer to God for them [the Jews] is that they may be saved. Seeing them on the way to perdition he was sorely troubled and torn. As iron put in the fire quickly itself becomes fire, so Paul, suspended in love, became wholly love. As though he were the common father of the whole world, in love and actions he imitated the fathers of men, and went beyond not only fleshly but also spiritual fathers in solicitude and devotion. He wanted to hold up every last human being in God's sight as if he had begotten the whole world and yearned to lead all into the kingdom of God, and he spent himself soul and body for those he loved. This un-noble man, who went from place to place and made his living working on animal pelts, grew so powerful that in the space of barely thirty years he brought Romans and Persians, Parthians and Medes, Indians and Scythians, Ethiopians and Sarmatians and Saracens and every race of men under the yoke of truth; and, like a live coal thrown into a pile of hay, his fire burned up the works of the demons. His voice swept in more ardent than any fire, and everything—devil worship and tyrants' threats and traps set by false followers—gave way. More, just as before the rays of the rising sun darkness vanishes, adulterers and thieves hide in pits, bandits and murderers flee into caves, and everything is made shining and bright by the sunbeams, so, as Paul spread the Gospel abroad, error was driven out and truth came in, adultery and other abominations were chased and consumed like straw by the heat of that fire. At the same time the clear renown of truth rose like flame resplendent and mounted to the heights of heaven, raised up by those who rather seemed to be holding it down, and neither peril nor attack could stop it.

"The nature of error is such that if it meets no resistance, it goes out of fashion and fades away. On the other hand, it is of the nature of truth that under attack it comes to life and grows. God has so ennobled our race that we aspire to bear his image and likeness. We do not think that that is impossible: after all, Paul had the same body and the same soul as we have and ate the same food. God formed him as he formed you, and Paul's God is your God. Do you want to know God's gifts to Paul? Paul's very garments struck terror to the demons. More admirable than that, when Paul plunged into danger, he could not be accused of rashness, nor when dangers rose around him could he be called timid. He loved his present life because it allowed him the benefit of teaching, but at the same time disdained it because of the philosophical attitude to which contempt for the world had brought him. Finally, if you find Paul running away from danger, admire him no less than when he rejoices to confront danger; the latter is the part of courage as the former is the part of wisdom. Similarly if you find Paul boasting a little about himself, admire him as you would if you saw him despising himself, because this is the part of humility while the other is the part of greatness of soul. It was more meritorious of him to speak in praise of himself than to say nothing; indeed, if he said nothing, he would be more blameworthy than those who learned from this to praise themselves for no reason at all. If he had not been glorified, he would have caused loss to all those who had been entrusted to him, because while he humbled himself, he would have built up their pride. So Paul did better by boasting than another man would do by hiding the praises due him: the latter would gain less merit by concealing his merits than Paul gained by putting his on display. It is a serious fault to say something great and admirable about oneself, and to want to draw praise to oneself in the absence of some urgent necessity is sheer folly. It would not indicate that one was speaking according to God; rather, it is a sign of mindlessness. Such vainglory forfeits any reward that toil and sweat may have earned, for to talk boastfully about oneself is the act of a pompous, insolent person, whereas to say what is strictly necessary to the case at issue is the way of one who loves and has the good and welfare of many in mind. This was what Paul did. When he was slandered and lied about, he was forced to praise his accomplishments, particularly such as would show his worthiness, while he kept silent about other and still greater ones. I will come now, he says, to visions and revelations of the Lord . . . but I refrain (2 Cor. 12:1, 6). He had longer and more frequent converse with the Lord than any of the prophets and apostles, and was made the humbler thereby. He seems to have feared blows, but this was so that you might learn that by nature he was simply one of many: by his will he was not only above all men but was one of the angels. Not that fearing blows calls for reproach; what does deserve it is doing something unworthy of true piety out of fear of blows. The very fact that one who fears blows and wounds does not give up in a fight makes him more worthy of admiration than one who has no fear. So also, grieving is not blameworthy, but to say or do out of grief something that displeases God . . . that is blameworthy.

"What sort of man Paul was is shown by the fact that though he shared our human nature, he was somehow able to live above nature, so that even fearing death he did not refuse to die. There is nothing wrong about having a nature that is beset with weaknesses. What is wrong is to be a slave to those weaknesses. It is meritorious and admirable to overcome the weakness of nature by strength of will, as Paul did in dismissing John, also called Mark. He was perfectly right in doing this: it was called for by his commission to preach. Anyone who assumes that office must be not soft or lax but strong and firm in all circumstances. No one ought to aspire to the duties of that high office unless he is ready to expose his soul to a thousand deaths and dangers. If he is not of this stripe, he will doom many others by his example: it would be more helpful on his part to keep quiet and look out for himself. No one who yearns to govern, no one destined to fight the wild beasts or to perform as a gladiator in the arena, no one at all needs a soul and spirit so prepared to face danger and death as does the one who undertakes the office of preaching. Nowhere are the perils greater or the adversaries more cruel, nowhere are the stakes of the contest the like of those faced by the preacher: he is offered heaven as reward, hell as punishment.

"If, however, there is a display of anger among some preachers, do not regard this as evil. To be stirred to anger is not wrong, but to be angry unreasonably and with no just cause is sinful. Our provident Creator planted this emotion in us to spur somnolent and weakling souls out of their inertia and apathy. Just as the sword has an edge, so God has endowed our mind with an edge of ire for us to use if needed. Mildness of spirit is always good when it suits the moment, but when the circumstances do not call for it, even mildness is a vice. Thus Paul often put this emotion to use and was better angry than those who used impudent language.

"What was wonderful in Paul was that shackled, whipped, and wounded he was far more splendid than those adorned with jewels and purple robes, and that when he was taken in chains over the vast sea, he rejoiced as if he were on his way to a high throne of empire. He reached Rome but was not content to stay there and went running off to Spain, and there allowed no day to go by in idleness and rest, but, more ardent in preaching than fire itself, he feared no dangers and felt no shame when he was mocked. And what is still more worthy of admiration is this, that audacious as he was, always girded as for battle and breathing the fire of war, he could still show himself responsive and flexible. When the brethren ordered him, furious or rather fervent as he was, to go to Tarsus, he did not refuse. When they said he might best be lowered over the wall in a basket, he allowed it. And he did all this for the sake of one thing, namely, to have more time to preach, and so to go to Christ with many who believed through his preaching. He was fearful that he might leave this life poor, not having done enough for the salvation of many. And then . . . when those who are fighting under a commander and see the commander himself wounded and shedding his blood yet not yielding an inch to the enemy but standing firm, wielding his spear, laying his adversaries low with repeated blows, and sparing no pain, of course they follow so great a leader with all the more alacrity.

"So it was with Paul. They saw him chained and shackled in prison and preaching nonetheless. They saw him wounded yet capturing his tormentors themselves with his speech, and it built up their trust in him. This is what he meant when he said that most of the brethren had been made confident in the Lord because of his imprisonment and were much more bold to speak the word of God without fear. This in turn stimulated Paul's zeal, and he went after his opponents more relentlessly. As when fire, falling into a pile of material, spreads and burns all around it, so Paul's preaching drew in whoever heard him. His assailants became spiritual food for the fire, because through them the flame of the Gospel spread." Thus Chrysostom.

91. The Seven Brothers, Sons of Saint Felicity

Saint Felicity had seven sons, whose names were Januarius, Felix, Philip, Silvanus, Alexander, Vitalis, and Martial. By order of Emperor Antoninus, Publius the prefect summoned all of them, together with their mother, to appear before him, and tried to persuade the mother to spare herself and her sons. Her answer was: "I can neither be seduced by your blandishments nor frightened by your threats, for my security is from the Holy Spirit who is with me; and alive I will withstand you, and will vanquish you completely when you kill me!" Then, turning to her sons, she said: "My sons, look to heaven and fix your gaze above, because Christ awaits us there, so fight bravely for Christ and show yourselves faithful in the love of Christ!" Hearing this, the prefect commanded his men to slap her. Since mother and sons were obviously firm in the faith, all the sons were tortured and put to death while their mother looked on and encouraged them.

Gregory calls this blessed Felicity "more than martyr," because she suffered seven times in her seven sons and an eighth time in her own body. In his homilies Gregory says: "Saint Felicity, who by her believing stood out as a servant of Christ, by preaching became also a martyr of Christ. She feared to leave her sons after her, alive in the flesh, as other parents usually fear that their children may die before they themselves do. She brought forth her sons in the Spirit as she had borne them in the flesh, in order to give them to God by her preaching as she had given them to the world in the body. Knowing that they were the children she had borne in the flesh, she could not see them die without grieving for them, but the love that was in her was so strong that it overcame the grief she felt in her body. Rightly therefore I have said that this woman was more than martyr—this woman who died in each one of her sons and with as much desire as they had. While gaining this sevenfold martyrdom she also went beyond the palm of martyrdom, because her love of Christ was far from satisfied by her dying only once for him."

The martyrs suffered about the year of the Lord 110.

---

92. Saint Theodora

Theodora, a woman of noble rank, married to a wealthy, God-fearing man, lived in Alexandria in the time of Emperor Zeno. The devil, envious of Theodora's holiness, stirred up lust for her in another rich man, who sent her many messages and gifts in order to induce her to assent to him; but she rebuffed the messengers and spurned the gifts. He bothered her so much, however, that she had no peace of mind and her health began to suffer. Finally he sent a certain sorceress to her, who urged her forcefully to have pity on this man and to yield to his desire. Theodora answered that she would never commit so great a sin before the eyes of God who sees all, but the witch added: "Yes, God knows and sees everything that is done by day, but anything committed at dusk and sundown God does not see." The young woman asked the witch: "Is what you say true?" "It certainly is true!" the witch replied. The young woman was deceived and told the witch to have the man come to her as daylight waned, and she would do his will. When the man received this news, he was delighted, went to the lady at the appointed hour, lay with her, and left.

Theodora now came to her senses and wept bitterly, beating herself on the face and saying: "Alas, woe is me! I have lost my soul, I have destroyed the beauty of my virtue!" When her husband came home, he found her desolate and grieving, and, not knowing the reason, did his best to console her, but she would accept no comfort. The next morning she went to a monastery of nuns and asked the abbess whether God could know about a grave sin that she had committed at eventide. The abbess answered: "Nothing can be hidden from God, who knows all and sees all that is done, no matter the time it is done." Theodora wept profusely and said: "Give me the book of the gospels, that I may draw my own lot!" She opened the book and came upon the passage: "What I have written, I have written." She went home and, one day when her husband was away, cut her hair, put on men's clothing, and hurried to a monastery. She asked to be taken in with the monks and her request was granted. Asked what her name was, she said she was called Theodore. Then, as Brother Theodore, she humbly performed all the tasks assigned to her, and her service was welcomed by all.

Some years later the abbot called Brother Theodore and ordered him to yoke a team of oxen and haul a tun of oil out from the city. Her husband had wept much, fearing that she had gone off with another man; but now an angel of the Lord said to him: "Get up tomorrow and stand in the street called the Martyrdom of Peter the Apostle, and the first person you meet will be your wife." Theodora came along with her camels, saw her husband, recognized him, and said within herself; "Alas, my good husband, how hard I work to be delivered of the wrong I did you!" When she came near him, she greeted him, saying: "Joy to you, sir!" But he did not recognize her at all, and waited all day long and into the night before crying out that he had been deceived. In the morning a voice came to him, saying: "The one who greeted you yesterday was your wife."

Theodora's holiness was so great that she performed many miracles. Thus she took hold of a man who had been fatally mauled by a wild beast, and by her prayers brought him back to life, then tracked down the beast and cursed it, whereupon the animal dropped dead. And one time the devil, unable to bear her sanctity, appeared to her and said: "You whore of whores, you adulteress, you left your husband to come here and put me to shame! I shall use my fearsome powers to stir up a battle against you, and if I can't make you deny the Crucified, you can say that I don't exist!" But she made the sign of the cross and the demon vanished.

Another time, when she was on her way back with the camels and stopped someplace overnight, a girl came to her and said: "Sleep with me!" When Theodora spurned her, she went and lay with a man who was resting in the same place. When her belly grew big, she was asked who had got her pregnant, and she said: "That monk Theodore slept with me!" When the child was born, they turned it over to the abbot of the monastery. The abbot upbraided Theodore, who begged for forgiveness, and the abbot laid the baby boy on his shoulders and expelled him from the monastery.

Theodore—Theodora, after her expulsion, stayed outside the monastery for seven years, nourishing the child with milk from the herd. The devil, envious of such patience, transfigured himself, assuming the likeness of her husband, and said to her: "What are you doing here, my lady? Behold, I have pined for you all this time and have found no consolation. Come then, light of my life, because I forgive you even if you have lain with another man!" But Theodora, thinking that this was indeed her husband, told him: "I shall never again live with you, because the son of John the knight slept with me, and I wish to do penance for the sin I committed against you!" And when she prayed, he vanished and she knew it had been the devil.

At another time the devil, wishing to terrorize her, sent demons against her in the likeness of fierce beasts, and a man goaded them on and said: "Devour this whore!" But she prayed and they disappeared. Again a large troop of soldiers came, led by a prince to whom the others offered worship, and the soldiers said to Theodora: "Rise and adore our prince!" She answered: "I adore the Lord God!" When this response was reported to the prince, he ordered her to be brought and beaten until she was thought to be dead, after which the horde vanished. Still another time she saw before her a large quantity of gold, but she crossed herself and fled from the gold, recommending herself to God. Then one day she saw a man carrying a basket filled with all sorts of delicious foods, and the man said to her: "The prince who had you beaten says to accept this food and eat it, because he did that unknowingly." But she crossed herself and the man disappeared instantly.

When seven years had passed, the abbot, impressed by Theodora's patience, reconciled her and took her and her boy back into the monastery. After she had lived a praiseworthy life there for two years, she took the lad into her cell and closed the door. This was made known to the abbot, who sent some monks to listen attentively to what she might say to the boy. She embraced him and kissed him, and said: "My sweetest son, the term of my life is nearing its end. I leave you to God: you are to have him for father and helper. Sweetest son, persevere in fasting and prayer, and serve your brothers with devotion!" With these words she breathed her last and fell asleep happily in the Lord about A.D. 470, and the child, seeing her dead, wept floods of tears.

That very night a vision was shown to the abbot. He saw preparations being made for a great wedding, to which came the orders of angels and prophets and martyrs and all the saints; and behold, in their midst walked a woman alone, enveloped in ineffable glory. She came to the wedding site and sat on the bridal bed, and all stood around her and called upon her. Then a voice was heard saying: "This is Brother Theodore, who was falsely accused of fathering a child! Seven years have elapsed since then, and she has been punished for sullying her husband's bed." The abbot woke up, hurried with the monks to her cell, and found her already dead. They went in and uncovered her, and saw that she was a woman. The abbot sent for the father of the girl who had defamed her, and said to him: "Your daughter's husband has died!" The father put aside the clothing and saw that the husband was a woman. A great fear came upon all who heard this.

An angel of the Lord now spoke to the abbot, saying: "Get up quickly, mount your horse, and ride into the city. If anyone comes to meet you, take him up and bring him here!" As the abbot rode along, a man ran to meet him. The abbot asked him where he was going, and he answered: "My wife has died, and I am on my way to see her." The abbot took him up on his horse, and when they came to Theodora's body, they both wept abundantly. Then they buried her with many praises.

Her husband then occupied Theodora's cell and lived in it until he fell asleep in the Lord. Her son followed his foster-mother's example and lived her virtuous life, and when the abbot of the monastery died, the monks unanimously elected him to be their abbot.

---

93. Saint Margaret

The name Margaret is also the name of a precious jewel called *margarita*, pearl, which is shining white, small, and powerful. So Saint Margaret was shining white by her virginity, small by humility, and powerful in the performance of miracles. The power of the pearl is said to work against effusion of blood and against the passions of the heart, and to effect the strengthening of the spirit. Thus blessed Margaret had power over the effusion of her blood by her constancy, since she was most constant in her martyrdom. She had power over the heart's passions, i.e., in conquering the demon's temptations, since she overcame the devil. She strengthened the spirit by her doctrine, since her doctrine strengthened the spirits of many and converted them to the faith of Christ.

Her legend was written by Theotimus, a learned man.

Margaret, a native of Antioch, was the daughter of Theodosius, a patriarch among the pagans. She was entrusted to the care of a nurse and, when she reached the age of reason, was baptized, for which reason her father hated her. One day, when she had grown to the age of fifteen and was guarding her nurse's sheep with other young girls, the prefect Olybrius was passing by and caught sight of this very beautiful girl. He burned with desire for her immediately and sent his men after her, saying: "Go and seize her! If she's freeborn, I'll make her my wife: if she's a slave, she'll be my concubine!"

Margaret was therefore presented for his inspection, and he questioned her about her parentage, her name, and her religion. She answered that she was noble by birth, that her name was Margaret, and that she was a Christian. Said the prefect: "The first two titles fit you perfectly, because you are known to be noble and you are as lovely as a pearl; but the third does not suit you at all! No beautiful and noble girl like you should have a crucified God!" "How do you know," Margaret asked, "that Christ was crucified?" "From the Christians' books," he replied. Margaret: "Since you read in them both of Christ's suffering and of his glory, you should be ashamed to believe the one and yet deny the other!" She went on to declare that Christ had of his own will been crucified for our redemption but now lived immortal in eternity. This angered the prefect, and he ordered her to jail.

The next day he had her haled before him and said: "Vain girl, pity your beauty and adore our gods, and all will go well for you!" Margaret: "I adore the God before whom the earth trembles, the sea storms, and all creatures are fearful!" The prefect: "Unless you yield to me, I'll have your body torn to shreds!" Margaret: "Christ gave himself up to death for me, and therefore I want to die for Christ!"

By the prefect's order she now was hung upon a rack and was beaten with rods and then lacerated with iron rakes, so cruelly that her bones were laid bare and the blood poured from her body as from a pure spring. The people standing by wept and said: "O Margaret, truly we grieve for you, because we see how cruelly your body is torn! Oh, what beauty you have lost by not believing in the gods! Now, then, believe, so as at least to remain alive!" Margaret: "O bad counselors, go away! Begone! This torture of the flesh is the salvation of the soul!" To the prefect she said: "Shameless dog! Ravenous lion! You have power over the flesh, but Christ keeps the soul to himself!" Meanwhile, the prefect, unable to bear the sight of such bloodletting, drew his hood over his eyes.

Margaret was taken down and put back in jail, where a marvelous light shone around her. There she prayed the Lord to let her see the enemy who was fighting her, and a hideous dragon appeared, but when the beast came at her to devour her, she made the sign of the cross and it vanished. Or, as we read elsewhere, the dragon opened its maw over her head, put out its tongue under her feet, and swallowed her in one gulp. But when it was trying to digest her, she shielded herself with the sign of the cross, and by the power of the cross the dragon burst open and the virgin emerged unscathed. What is said here, however, about the beast swallowing the maiden and bursting asunder is considered apocryphal and not to be taken seriously.

Again the devil, still trying to deceive Margaret, changed himself to look like a man. She saw him and resorted to prayer, and when she rose, the devil approached, took her hand, and said: "Let all you've done be enough for you, and just let me be!" But she grabbed him by the head, pushed him to the ground, planted her right foot on his head, and said: "Lie still at last, proud demon, under the foot of a woman!" The demon cried out: "O blessed Margaret, I'm beaten! If I'd been beaten by a young man I wouldn't mind, but by a tender girl . . . ! And I feel even worse because your father and mother were friends of mine!"

Margaret then forced him to tell her why he had come. He said it was to press her to obey the prefect's orders. She also made him say why he tempted Christians in so many ways. He answered that it was his nature to hate virtuous people, and that though he was often repulsed by them, he was plagued by desire to mislead them. He begrudged men the happiness that he had lost and could not retrieve for himself, so he strove to take it away from others. He added that Solomon had confined an infinite multitude of demons in a vase, and after his death the demons had caused fire to issue from the vase. This made men think that it contained a huge treasure. They therefore smashed the vase, and the demons escaped and filled the air. Then, after all this had been said, the virgin lifted her foot and said: "Begone, wretch!" and the demon promptly vanished.

Margaret therefore was reassured: she had defeated the chief, she would certainly outdo his hireling. The following day she was presented to the judge before a large gathering of people. Refusing again to sacrifice to the gods, she was stripped of her clothes and her body was burned with torches; and all wondered how so delicate a girl could withstand such torture. Then the judge had her bound and put in a tub full of water, in order to increase the suffering by varying the pain; but suddenly the earth shook and the virgin came out unharmed. At that five thousand men accepted the faith and were sentenced to death for the name of Christ. The prefect, fearing that still others would be converted, quickly gave orders to behead blessed Margaret. She asked for time to pray, and prayed devoutly for herself and her persecutors and for all who would honor her memory and invoke her, adding a prayer that any woman who invoked her aid when faced with a difficult labor would give birth to a healthy child. A voice from heaven announced that her petitions had been heard, and she rose from her prayer and said to the headsman: "Brother, take your sword and strike me!" He did so and took off her head with a single stroke, and so she received the crown of martyrdom. Margaret suffered on the twentieth day of July, or, as we read elsewhere, on the twelfth of that month.

A certain saint says of this holy virgin: "Blessed Margaret was filled with the fear of God, endowed with righteousness, clothed with religion, imbued with compunction, praiseworthy for her integrity, beyond compare in her patience. Nothing contrary to the Christian religion could be found in her. She was hated by her father and beloved of Jesus Christ."

94. Saint Alexis

The name Alexis is composed of *a*, which means much or very, and *lexis*, which means word. Alexis therefore was very powerful in the word of God.

Alexis was the son of Euphemianus, a member of the highest Roman nobility who was in the first rank at the emperor's court. Three thousand slaves wearing golden girdles and silk clothing waited on him. As a high officer in the city Euphemianus was temperate in the exercise of his authority. Moreover, every day he had three tables set up in his house for the poor and for orphans, widows, and strangers in need. He himself served at these tables and did not until late in the evening take food in the fear of the Lord with other religious men. His wife, Aglaë, shared both his religious fervor and his attitude toward others. They were childless until in answer to their prayers the Lord granted them a son, after whose birth they agreed to live in chastity.

Their son was instructed in the liberal disciplines and made rapid strides in all the philosophic arts. When he was still a youth, a girl of the imperial household was chosen for him and the wedding was celebrated. On their wedding night, as he and his bride met in the silence and secret of their chamber, the saintly youth began to instruct his spouse in the fear of God and urged her to remain in the pure state of virginity. Then he gave her his gold ring and the cincture he wore around his waist, and said: "Take this and keep it as long as God pleases, and may the Lord be always between us!" Then he took some of his wealth and went to the coast, where he secretly boarded a ship and sailed to Laodicea, going from there to Edessa, a city in Syria, where an image of our Lord Jesus Christ on a fine cloth, an image no human hand had made, was preserved. Once in Edessa he distributed everything he had brought with him to the poor, put on ragged clothes, and began to sit with the other mendicants in the porch of the church of Mary the mother of God. Of the alms he received he kept the bare minimum he needed to live on and gave the rest to the other poor people.

All this time his father, sorrowful and mourning over his son's departure, sent his slaves into every corner of the world to look for him. Some of them came to Edessa and were recognized by the son, but did not recognize him and gave alms to him as they did to the other beggars. He accepted the alms and gave thanks to God, saying: "I thank you, O Lord, that you have allowed me to receive an alms from my own slaves." The servants went home and reported to the father that they had not found his son anywhere. His mother, from the day of his departure, spread a sack on the floor of her bedchamber and lay awake at night, murmuring dolefully: "Here shall I stay always in sorrow until I recover my son." The young bride, too, said to her mother-in-law: "Until I hear from my sweet spouse, I shall stay with you, like a lonely turtledove."

When Alexis had spent seventeen years in God's service in the porch of the aforesaid church, the image of the Blessed Virgin that was in the church spoke to the watchman, saying: "Bring in the man of God, because he is worthy of the kingdom of heaven. The Spirit of God rests upon him, and his prayer rises like incense in the sight of God." But the watchman did not know who this man was, so the image spoke again: "The man who sits outside at the door, that's the one." The watchman hurried out and led Alexis into the church. When other people noticed this, they began to pay him reverence, so he left the place in order to escape human glory, went back to Laodicea, and took ship to go to Tarsus in Cilicia.

By God's dispensation the ship was driven by the wind into the port of Rome. When he became aware of this, Alexis said to himself: "I will go and stay unknown in my father's house and so will not be a burden to anyone else." Therefore he waited in the street as his father was on his way back from the palace surrounded by a number of suppliants, and called after him: "Servant of God, give orders that I, a pilgrim, be taken into your house, and that the crumbs from your table be given to me as food. And may the Lord deign to be merciful to you, too, who also are a pilgrim." When Euphemianus heard this, he thought lovingly of his son, gave orders that the stranger be welcomed, and designated a cubbyhole for him in the house. He also provided that the visistor should have food from the master's table, and appointed one slave to look after him. Alexis persevered in prayer and disciplined his body with fasting and vigils. The house servants made fun of him, spilled dirty water on his head, and plied him with insults, but he bore all this with unshaken patience.

For seventeen years Alexis lived unrecognized in his father's house. Then, knowing by the Spirit that the end of his days was near, he asked for paper and ink and wrote out a full account of his life. On a Sunday, after the celebration of mass, a voice rang out in the church: "Come to me all you who labor and are burdened, and I will refresh you." All present were frightened and fell to their knees while the voice came again, saying: "Seek out the man of God, that he may pray for Rome!" They looked around but found no one, and a third time the voice sounded: "Look in the house of Euphemianus!" Euphemianus was questioned but said he did not know what this was all about. Then the emperors Arcadius and Honorius, in company with Pope Innocent, came to the house. The slave who took care of Alexis came to his master and said: "Could our stranger be the man you are looking for? He is a man of good life and great patience."

Euphemianus ran to the stranger's cubbyhole and found him dead, his face shining like the face of an angel. He tried to take the paper from the dead man's hand but could not. He went out therefore and came back with the emperors and the pope. They went in to the dead man and the emperors said: "Sinners though we are, we two rule the state, and with us is the pontiff who has pastoral care of the whole world. Therefore give us the paper you are holding, and let us see what is written on it." The pope then went up and took the script, which was relinquished readily, and had it read before Euphemianus and a great crowd of people. The father, hearing what was read, was overwhelmed with grief; his strength deserted him and he fell down in a faint. When after a while he came to himself, he tore his garments and began to pull out his gray hair and beard, threw himself on his son's body, and cried out: "Woe is me, my son! Why have you saddened me this way? Why have you stricken me all these years with grief and lamentation? Woe, woe is me, I see you now, the staff of my old age, lying on a litter and not speaking to me! Alas, alas, what consolation will I ever find?"

The mother, hearing all this, came like a lioness breaking out of a net. Tearing her robes, her hair in wild disarray, she raised her eyes to heaven, then rushed to where her son lay; but such a crowd had gathered that she could not reach the holy body. She cried out: "Make way for me, you men, let me see my son, let me see my soul's consolation, the one who suckled at my breast!" And when she finally got to the body, she lay upon it and lamented: "Alas, my son, light of my eyes, why did you do this? Why have you treated us so cruelly? You saw your father and miserable me shedding tears, and did not make yourself known to us! Your servants hurt you and made sport of you, and you allowed it!" Again and again she prostrated herself upon the body, now spreading her arms over it, now feeling the angelic face with her hands and kissing it. "Weep with me, all of you here present," she cried, "because for seventeen years I had him here in my house and did not recognize him! Because he was my only son! Because even the slaves heaped contempt on him and dealt him blows! Woe is me! Who will give my eyes a fountain of tears, so that night and day I may pour out the sorrow that is in my soul?" The bereaved spouse also ran up weeping and saying: "Ah, woe, woe! Today I am left alone, have become a widow, have no one to gaze upon or lift my eyes to. Now my mirror is broken and my hope gone. Now begins the grieving that has no end!" And the people standing around heard all this and wept loud and long.

Now the pope and the emperors placed the body on a princely litter and went before it into the heart of the city. Announcement was made to the populace that the man of God whom the whole city had been seeking had been found. The people all ran to be near the saint. Any among them who were sick and touched the holy body were cured instantly, the blind received their sight, the possessed were delivered of the demons. Seeing these wonders, the emperors and the pope undertook to carry the bier themselves, in order that they too might be sanctified by the holy corpse. The crowds were so dense that the emperors gave orders to scatter gold and silver coins in the streets and squares, hoping that the common people would be drawn away by their love of money and would let the funeral procession get through to the church. The people, however, checked their greed and in ever greater numbers rushed to touch the saint's most sacred body; but the cortege finally succeeded in getting to the church of Saint Benedict Martyr. There they worked continuously for seven days, praising God as they raised a monument adorned with gold, gems, and precious stones, and reverently laid the holy body to rest in it. From this monument emanated a fragrance so powerful that everybody thought the tomb was filled with perfumes.

Alexis died the seventeenth day of July about the year A.D. 398.

95. Saint Praxedes

Praxedes was sister to blessed Pudentiana, and they were sisters of Saints Donatus and Timothy, who were instructed in the faith by the apostles. At a time when persecution was raging, they buried the bodies of many Christians. They also distributed all their goods to the poor. Finally they fell asleep in the Lord about the year of the Lord 165, in the reign of Emperors Marcus and Antoninus II.

96. Saint Mary Magdalene

The name Mary, or Maria, is interpreted as *amarum mare*, bitter sea, or as illuminator or illuminated. These three meanings are accepted as standing for three shares or parts, of which Mary made the best choices, namely, the part of penance, the part of inward contemplation, and the part of heavenly glory. This threefold share is what the Lord meant when he said: "Mary has chosen the best part, which shall not be taken away from her." The first part will not be taken away because of its end or purpose, which is the attainment of holiness. The second part will not be taken because of its continuity: contemplation during the earthly journey will continue in heavenly contemplation. And the third part will remain because it is eternal. Therefore, since Mary chose the best part, namely, penance, she is called bitter sea because in her penances she endured much bitterness. We see this from the fact that she shed enough tears to bathe the Lord's feet with them. Since she chose the best part of inward contemplation, she is called enlightener, because in contemplation she drew draughts of light so deep that in turn she poured out light in abundance: in contemplation she received the light with which she afterwards enlightened others. As she chose the best part of heavenly glory, she is called illuminated, because she now is enlightened by the light of perfect knowledge in her mind and will be illumined by the light of glory in her body.

Mary is called Magdalene, which is understood to mean "remaining guilty," or it means armed, or unconquered, or magnificent. These meanings point to the sort of woman she was before, at the time of, and after her conversion. Before her conversion she remained in guilt, burdened with the debt of eternal punishment. In her conversion she was armed and rendered unconquerable by the armor of penance: she armed herself the best possible way—with all the weapons of penance—because for every pleasure she had enjoyed she found a way of immolating herself. After her conversion she was magnificent in the superabundance of grace, because where trespass abounded, grace was superabundant.

Mary's cognomen "Magdalene" comes from Magdalum, the name of one of her ancestral properties. She was wellborn, descended of royal stock. Her father's name was Syrus, her mother was called Eucharia. With her brother Lazarus and her sister Martha she owned Magdalum, a walled town two miles from Genezareth, along with Bethany, not far from Jerusalem, and a considerable part of Jerusalem itself. They had, however, divided their holdings among themselves in such a way that Magdalum belonged to Mary (whence the name Magdalene), Lazarus kept the property in Jerusalem, and Bethany was Martha's. Magdalene gave herself totally to the pleasures of the flesh and Lazarus was devoted to the military, while prudent Martha kept close watch over her brother's and sister's estates and took care of the needs of her armed men, her servants, and the poor. After Christ's ascension, however, they all sold their possessions and laid the proceeds at the feet of the apostles.

Magdalene, then, was very rich, and sensuous pleasure keeps company with great wealth. Renowned as she was for her beauty and her riches, she was no less known for the way she gave her body to pleasure—so much so that her proper name was forgotten and she was commonly called "the sinner." Meanwhile, Christ was preaching here and there, and she, guided by the divine will, hastened to the house of Simon the leper, where, she had learned, he was at table. Being a sinner she did not dare mingle with the righteous, but stayed back and washed the Lord's feet with her tears, dried them with her hair, and anointed them with precious ointment. Because of the extreme heat of the sun the people of that region bathed and anointed themselves regularly.

Now Simon the Pharisee thought to himself that if this man were a prophet, he would never allow a sinful woman to touch him; but the Lord rebuked him for his proud righteousness and told the woman that all her sins were forgiven. This is the Magdalene[1] upon whom Jesus conferred such great graces and to whom he showed so many marks of love. He cast seven devils out of her, set her totally afire with love of him, counted her among his closest familiars, was her guest, had her do the housekeeping on his travels, and kindly took her side at all times. He defended her when the Pharisee said she was unclean, when her sister implied that she was lazy, when Judas called her wasteful. Seeing her weep he could not contain his tears. For love of her he raised her brother, four days dead, to life, for love of her he freed her sister Martha from the issue of blood she had suffered for seven years, and in view of her merits he gave Martilla, her sister's handmaid, the privilege of calling out those memorable words: "Blessed is the womb that bore you!" Indeed, according to Ambrose, Martha was the woman with the issue of blood, and the woman who called out was Martha's servant. "She [Mary] it was, I say, who washed the Lord's feet with her tears, dried them with her hair and anointed them with ointment, who in the time of grace did solemn penance, who chose the best part, who sat at the Lord's feet and listened to his word, who anointed his head, who stood beside the cross at his passion, who prepared the sweet spices with which to anoint his body, who, when the disciples left the tomb, did not go away, to whom the risen Christ first appeared, making her an apostle to the apostles."

Some fourteen years after the Lord's passion and ascension into heaven, when the Jews had long since killed Stephen and expelled the other disciples from the confines of Judea, the disciples went off into the lands of the various nations and there sowed the word of the Lord. With the apostles at the time was one of Christ's seventy-two disciples, blessed Maximin, to whose care blessed Peter had entrusted Mary Magdalene. In the dispersion Maximin, Mary Magdalene, her brother Lazarus, her sister Martha, Martha's maid Martilla, blessed Cedonius, who was born blind and had been cured by the Lord, and many other Christians, were herded by the unbelievers into a ship without pilot or rudder and sent out to sea so that they might all be drowned, but by God's will they eventually landed at Marseilles. There they found no one willing to give them shelter, so they took refuge under the portico of a shrine belonging to the people of that area. When blessed Mary Magdalene saw the people gathering at the shrine to offer sacrifice to the idols, she came forward, her manner calm and her face serene, and with well-chosen words called them away from the cult of idols and preached Christ fervidly to them. All who heard her were in admiration at

---

[1] The question of the identity of several Marys named in the gospels, including Mary Magdalene, will not be discussed here.

her beauty, her eloquence, and the sweetness of her message . . . and no wonder, that the mouth which had pressed such pious and beautiful kisses on the Savior's feet should breathe forth the perfume of the word of God more profusely than others could.

Then the governor of that province came with his wife to offer sacrifice and pray the gods for offspring. Magdalene preached Christ to him and dissuaded him from sacrificing. Some days later she appeared in a vision to the wife, saying: "Why, when you are so rich, do you allow the saints of God to die of hunger and cold?" She added the threat that if the lady did not persuade her husband to relieve the saints' needs, she might incur the wrath of God; but the woman was afraid to tell her spouse about the vision. The following night she saw the same vision and heard the same words, but again hesitated to tell her husband. The third time, in the silence of the dead of night, Mary Magdalene appeared to each of them, shaking with anger, her face afire as if the whole house were burning, and said: "So you sleep, tyrant, limb of your father Satan, with your viper of a wife who refused to tell you what I had said? You take your rest, you enemy of the cross of Christ, your gluttony sated with a bellyful of all sorts of food while you let the saints of God perish from hunger and thirst? You lie here wrapped in silken sheets, after seeing those others homeless and desolate, and passing them by? Wicked man, you will not escape! You will not go unpunished for your long delay in giving them some help!" And, having said her say, she disappeared.

The lady awoke gasping and trembling, and spoke to her husband, who was in like distress: "My lord, have you had the dream that I just had?" "I saw it," he answered, "and I can't stop wondering and shaking with fear! What are we to do?" His wife said: "It will be better for us to give in to her than to face the wrath of her God whom she preaches." They therefore provided shelter for the Christians and supplied their needs.

Then one day when Mary Magdalene was preaching, the aforesaid governor asked her: "Do you think you can defend the faith you preach?" "I am ready indeed to defend it," she replied, "because my faith is strengthened by the daily miracles and preaching of my teacher Peter, who presides in Rome!" The governor and his wife then said to her: "See here, we are prepared to do whatever you tell us to if you can obtain a son for us from the God whom you preach." "In this he will not fail you," said Magdalene. Then the blessed Mary prayed the Lord to deign to grant them a son. The Lord heard her prayers and the woman conceived.

Now the husband began to want to go to Peter and find out whether what Magdalene preached about Christ was the truth. "What's this?" snapped his wife. "Are you thinking of going without me? Not a bit of it! You leave, I leave. You come back, I come back. You stay here, I stay here!" The man replied: "My dear, it can't be that way! You're pregnant and the perils of the sea are infinite. It's too risky. You will stay home and take care of what we have here!"

But she insisted, doing as women do. She threw herself at his feet, weeping the while, and in the end won him over. Mary therefore put the sign of the cross on their shoulders as a protection against the ancient Enemy's interference on their journey. They stocked a ship with all the necessaries, leaving the rest of their possessions in the care of Mary Magdalene, and set sail.

A day and a night had not passed, however, when the wind rose and the sea became tumultuous. All aboard, and especially the expectant mother, were shaken and fearful as the waves battered the ship. Abruptly she went into labor, and, exhausted by her pangs and the buffeting of the storm, she expired as she brought forth her son. The newborn groped about seeking the comfort of his mother's breasts, and cried and whimpered piteously. Ah, what a pity! The infant is born, he lives, and has become his mother's killer! He may as well die, since there is no one to give him nourishment to keep him alive! What will the Pilgrim[2] do, seeing his wife dead and the child whining plaintively as he seeks the maternal breast? His lamentations knew no bounds, and he said to himself: "Alas, what will you do? You yearned for a son, and you have lost the mother and the son too!"

The seamen meanwhile were shouting: "Throw that corpse overboard before we all perish! As long as it is with us, this storm will not let up!" They seized the body and were about to cast it into the sea, but the Pilgrim intervened. "Hold on a little!" he cried. "Even if you don't want to spare me or the mother, at least pity the poor weeping little one! Wait just a bit! Maybe the woman has only fainted with pain and may begin to breathe again!"

Now suddenly they saw a hilly coast not far off the bow, and the Pilgrim thought it would be better to put the dead body and the infant ashore there than to throw them as food to the sea monsters. His pleas and his bribes barely persuaded the crew to drop anchor there. Then he found the ground so hard that he could not dig a grave, so he spread his cloak in a fold of the hill, laid his wife's body on it, and placed the child with its head between the mother's breasts. Then he wept and said: "O Mary Magdalene, you brought ruin upon me when you landed at Marseilles! Unhappy me, that on your advice I set out on this journey! Did you not pray to God that my wife might conceive? Conceive she did, and suffered death giving birth, and the child she conceived was born only to die because there is no one to nurse him. Behold, this is what your prayer obtained for me. I commended my all to you and do commend me to your God. If it be in your power, be mindful of the mother's soul, and by your prayer take pity on the child and spare its life." Then he enfolded the body and the child in his cloak and went back aboard the ship.

When the Pilgrim arrived in Rome, Peter came to meet him and, seeing the sign of the cross on his shoulder, asked him who he was and where he came

---

[2] The noun is capitalized in Graesse and presumably in the original, apparently to make it serve as a proper name.

from. He told Peter all that had happened to him, and Peter responded: "Peace be with you! You have done well to trust the good advice you received. Do not take it amiss that your wife sleeps and the infant rests with her. It is in the Lord's power to give gifts to whom he will, to take away what was given, to restore what was taken away, and to turn your grief into joy."

Peter then took him to Jerusalem and showed him all the places where Christ had preached and performed miracles, as well as the place where he had suffered and the other from which he had ascended into heaven. Peter then gave him thorough instruction in the faith, and after two years had gone by, he boarded ship, being eager to get back to his homeland. By God's will, in the course of the voyage they came close to the hilly coast where he had left the body of his wife and his son, and with pleas and money he induced the crew to put him ashore. The little boy, whom Mary Magdalene had preserved unharmed, used to come down to the beach and play with the stones and pebbles, as children love to do. As the Pilgrim's skiff drew near to the land, he saw the child playing on the beach. He was dumbstruck at seeing his son alive and leapt ashore from the skiff. The child, who had never seen a man, was terrified at the sight and ran to his mother's bosom, taking cover under the familiar cloak. The Pilgrim, anxious to see what was happening, followed, and found the handsome child feeding at his mother's breast. He lifted the boy and said: "O Mary Magdalene, how happy I would be, how well everything would have turned out for me, if my wife were alive and able to return home with me! Indeed I know, I know and believe beyond a doubt, that having given us this child and kept him alive for two years on this rock, you could now, by your prayers, restore his mother to life and health."

As these words were spoken, the woman breathed and, as if waking from sleep, said: "Great is your merit, O blessed Mary Magdalene, and you are glorious! As I struggled to give birth, you did me a midwife's service and waited upon my every need like a faithful handmaid." Hearing this, the Pilgrim said: "My dear wife, are you alive?" "Indeed I am," she answered, "and am just coming from the pilgrimage from which you yourself are returning. And as blessed Peter conducted you to Jerusalem and showed you all the places where Christ suffered, died, and was buried, and many other places, I, with blessed Mary Magdalene as my guide and companion, was with you and committed all you saw to memory." Whereupon she recited all the places where Christ had suffered, and fully explained the miracles and all she had seen, not missing a single thing.

Now the Pilgrim, having got back his wife and child, joyfully took ship and in a short time made port at Marseilles. Going into the city they found blessed Mary Magdalene with her disciples, preaching. Weeping with joy, they threw themselves at her feet and related all that had happened to them, then received holy baptism from blessed Maximin. Afterwards they destroyed the temples of all the idols in the city of Marseilles and built churches to Christ. They also elected blessed Lazarus as bishop of the city. Later by the will of God they went to the city of Aix, and, by many miracles, led the people there to accept the Christian faith. Blessed Maximin was ordained bishop of Aix.

At this time blessed Mary Magdalene, wishing to devote herself to heavenly contemplation, retired to an empty wilderness, and lived unknown for thirty years in a place made ready by the hands of angels. There were no streams of water there, nor the comfort of grass or trees: thus it was made clear that our Redeemer had determined to fill her not with earthly viands but only with the good things of heaven. Every day at the seven canonical hours she was carried aloft by angels and with her bodily ears heard the glorious chants of the celestial hosts. So it was that day by day she was gratified with these supernal delights and, being conveyed back to her own place by the same angels, needed no material nourishment.

There was a priest who wanted to live a solitary life and built himself a cell a few miles from the Magdalene's habitat. One day the Lord opened this priest's eyes, and with his own eyes he saw how the angels descended to the already-mentioned place where blessed Mary Magdalene dwelt, and how they lifted her into the upper air and an hour later brought her back to her place with divine praises. Wanting to learn the truth about this wondrous vision and commending himself prayerfully to his Creator, he hurried with daring and devotion toward the aforesaid place; but when he was a stone's throw from the spot, his knees began to wobble, and he was so frightened that he could hardly breathe. When he started to go away, his legs and feet responded, but every time he turned around and tried to reach the desired spot, his body went limp and his mind went blank, and he could not move forward.

So the man of God realized that there was a heavenly secret here to which human experience alone could have no access. He therefore invoked his Savior's name and called out: "I adjure you by the Lord, that if you are a human being or any rational creature living in that cave, you answer me and tell me the truth about yourself!" When he had repeated this three times, blessed Mary Magdalene answered him: "Come closer, and you can learn the truth about whatever your soul desires." Trembling, he had gone halfway across the intervening space when she said to him: "Do you remember what the Gospel says about Mary the notorious sinner, who washed the Savior's feet with her tears and dried them with her hair, and earned forgiveness for all her misdeeds?" "I do remember," the priest replied, "and more than thirty years have gone by since then. Holy Church also believes and confesses what you have said about her." "I am that woman," she said. "For the space of thirty years I have lived here unknown to everyone; and as you were allowed to see yesterday, every day I am borne aloft seven times by angelic hands, and have been found worthy to hear with the ears of my body the joyful jubilation of the heavenly hosts. Now, because it has been revealed to me by the Lord that I am soon to depart from this world, please go to blessed Maximin and take care to inform him that next year, on the day of the Lord's resurrection, at the time when he regularly rises for matins, he is to go alone to his church, and there he will find me present and waited upon by angels." To the priest the voice sounded like the voice of an angel, but he saw no one.

The good man hurried to blessed Maximin and carried out his errand. Saint Maximin, overjoyed, gave fulsome thanks to the Savior, and on the appointed day, at the appointed hour, went alone into the church and saw blessed Mary Magdalene amidst the choir of angels who had brought her there. She was raised up a distance of two cubits above the floor, standing among the angels and lifting her hands in prayer to God. When blessed Maximin hesitated about approaching her, she turned to him and said: "Come closer, father, and do not back away from your daughter." When he drew near to her, as we read in blessed Maximin's own books, the lady's countenance was so radiant, due to her continuous and daily vision of the angels, that one would more easily look straight into the sun than gaze upon her face.

All the clergy, including the priest already mentioned, were now called together, and blessed Mary Magdalene, shedding tears of joy, received the Lord's Body and Blood from the bishop. Then she lay down full length before the steps of the altar, and her most holy soul migrated to the Lord. After she expired, so powerful an odor of sweetness pervaded the church that for seven days all those who entered there noticed it. Blessed Maximin embalmed her holy body with aromatic lotions and gave it honorable burial, giving orders that after his death he was to be buried close to her.

Hegesippus (or, as some books have it, Josephus) agrees in the main with the story just told. He says in one of his treatises that after Christ's ascension Mary Magdalene, weary of the world and moved by her ardent love of the Lord, never wanted to see anyone. After she came to Aix, she went off into the desert, lived there unknown for thirty years, and every day at the seven canonical hours was carried up to heaven by an angel. He added, however, that the priest who went to her found her closed up in a cell. At her request he reached out a garment to her, and when she had put it on, she went with him to the church, received communion there, and, raising her hands in prayer beside the altar, died in peace.

In Charlemagne's time, namely, in the year of the Lord 769, Gerard, duke of Burgundy, being unable to have a son of his wife, openhandedly gave away his wealth to the poor and built many churches and monasteries. When he had built the monastery at Vézelay, he and the abbot sent a monk, with a suitable company, to the city of Aix in order to bring back the relics of Saint Mary Magdalene, if possible. When the monk arrived at the aforesaid city, however, he found that it had been razed to the ground by the pagans. Yet by chance he discovered a marble sarcophagus with an inscription which indicated that the body of blessed Mary Magdalene was contained inside, and her whole story was beautifully carved on the outside. The monk therefore broke into the sarcophagus by night, gathered the relics, and carried them to his inn. That same night blessed Mary appeared to him and told him not to be afraid but to go on with the work he had begun. On their way back to Vézelay the company, when they were half a league from their monastery, could not move the relics another step until the abbot and his monks came in solemn procession to receive them.

A certain knight, whose practice it was to visit the relics of Saint Mary Magdalene every year, was killed in battle. As he lay dead on his bier, his parents, mourning him, made pious complaint to the Magdalene because she had allowed her devotee to die without making confession and doing penance. Then suddenly, to the amazement of all present, the dead man rose up and called for a priest. He made his confession devoutly and received viaticum, then returned to rest in peace.

A ship crowded with men and women was sinking, and one woman, who was pregnant and saw herself in danger of drowning, called upon Magdalene as loudly as she could, and vowed that if by Mary's merits she escaped death and bore a son, she would give him up to the saint's monastery. At once a woman of venerable visage and bearing appeared to her, held her up by the chin, and, while the rest drowned, brought her unharmed to land. The woman in due time gave birth to a son and faithfully fulfilled her vow.

There are some who say that Mary Magdalene was espoused to John the Evangelist, who was about to take her as his wife when Christ called him away from his nuptials, whereupon she, indignant at having been deprived of her spouse, gave herself up to every sort of voluptuousness. But, since it would not do to have John's vocation the occasion of Mary's damnation, the Lord mercifully brought her around to conversion and penance; and, because she had had to forgo the heights of carnal enjoyment, he filled her more than others with the most intense spiritual delight, which consists in the love of God. And there are those who allege that Christ honored John with special evidences of his affection because he had taken him away from the aforesaid pleasures. These tales are to be considered false and frivolous. Brother Albert,[3] in his introduction to the gospel of John, says firmly that the lady from whose nuptials the same John was called away persevered in virginity, was seen later in the company of the Blessed Virgin Mary, mother of Christ, and came at last to a holy end.

A man who had lost his eyesight was on his way to the monastery at Vézelay to visit Mary Magdalene's body when his guide told him that he, the guide, could already see the church in the distance. The blind man exclaimed in a loud voice: "O holy Mary Magdalene, if only I could sometime be worthy to see your church!" At once his eyes were opened.

There was a man who wrote a list of his sins on a sheet of paper and put it under the rug on the Magdalene's altar, asking her to pray that he might be pardoned. Later he recovered the paper and found that his sins had been wiped out.

---

[3] No doubt Saint Albert the Great, O.P., an older contemporary of Jacobus.

A man who lay in chains for having committed the crime of extortion called upon Mary Magdalene to come to his aid, and one night a beautiful woman appeared to him, broke his fetters, and ordered him to be off. Seeing himself unshackled, he got away as fast as possible.

A clerk from Flanders, Stephen by name, had fallen into such a welter of sinfulness that, having committed every sort of evil, he could do no works of salvation nor even bear to hear of them. Yet he had deep devotion to blessed Mary Magdalene, observed her vigils by fasting, and celebrated her feast day. Once when he was on a visit to her tomb and was half asleep and half awake, Mary Magdalene appeared to him as a lovely, sad-eyed woman supported by two angels, one on either side, and she said to him: "Stephen, I ask you, why do you repay me with deeds unworthy of my deserts? Why are you not moved with compunction by what my own lips insistently say? From the time when you began to be devoted to me I have always prayed the Lord urgently for you. Get up, then! Repent! I will never leave you until you are reconciled with God!" The clerk soon felt so great an inpouring of grace in himself that he renounced the world, entered the religious life, and lived a very holy life thereafter. At his death Mary Magdalene was seen standing with angels beside the bier, and she carried his soul, like a pure-white dove, with songs of praise into heaven.

97. Saint Apollinaris

The saint's name is formed of the words *pollens*, which means powerful, and *ares*, meaning virtue; and Apollinaris was powerful in virtue. Or the name comes from *pollo*, admirable, and *naris*, by which discretion is understood; and it indicates a man of admirable discretion. Or the name is formed from *a*, meaning without, *polluo*, pollute, and *ares*, virtue, and Apollinaris was a man virtuous and unpolluted by vices.

Apollinaris was a disciple of the apostle Peter and by him was sent from Rome to Ravenna, where he cured the wife of a tribune and baptized her, along with her husband and the whole family. This was reported to the judge, who summoned Apollinaris first to appear before him. The saint was then led to the temple of Jupiter to offer sacrifice there, but he told the priests that the gold and silver which was hung around the idols would better be given to the poor than dangled before demons. He was made prisoner and beaten with rods until he was left half dead, but his disciples carried him away and brought him to the house of a widow, where he stayed for seven months and recovered his health.

He then went to the city of Classe to cure a nobleman who was mute. When he entered the house, a girl who was possessed of an unclean spirit shouted at him, saying: "Leave this place, servant of God, or I'll have you bound hand and foot and dragged out of the city!" Apollinaris rebuked the girl and drove the demon out of her. Then he invoked the name of the Lord over the mute and cured him instantly, whereupon more than five hundred men accepted the faith. The pagans, however, had him beaten with clubs and forbade him to pronounce the name of Jesus; but he, lying on the ground, cried out that Jesus was true God. They made him stand barefoot on live coals, and when he continued to preach Christ with undiminished zeal, they cast him out of the city.

At that same time, however, Rufus, a patrician of Ravenna, had a daughter who was in failing health. He called Apollinaris to come and cure her, but just as the saint entered the house, the daughter died. Rufus said to him: "Would that you had not come into my house, because the great gods are angry with me and have not willed to cure my daughter! But what can you do for her?" Apollinaris replied: "Have no fear! Only swear to me that if the girl is restored to life, you will not keep her from following God her creator!" Rufus gave his word. Apollinaris prayed and the girl arose and confessed the name of Christ, was baptized with her mother and many others, and from then on remained a virgin.

The emperor heard of this and wrote to the praetorian prefect, ordering him to make Apollinaris sacrifice to the gods, or, if he refused, to send him into exile. The prefect, failing to make him offer sacrifice, first had him scourged and then ordered him to be stretched on the rack. When the saint persisted in preaching Christ, the prefect had boiling water poured into his wounds, weighed him down with chains, and was about to send him into exile, but the Christians, witnessing such inhumanity, attacked the pagans and killed over two hundred of their men. The prefect saw what was happening and went into hiding, meanwhile shutting Apollinaris up in a narrow cell. Then he put him in chains aboard a ship, with three clerics who followed him into exile and two soldiers. With two of the clerics and the two soldiers the saint survived the perils of a storm at sea, and baptized the soldiers.

Apollinaris went back to Ravenna, and was captured by the pagans and taken to the temple of Apollo. He cursed the statue of the god and it crumbled to the ground. The priests of the temple saw this and presented Apollinaris to the judge, whose name was Taurus; but the man of God restored the sight of the judge's blind son, and Taurus was converted to the faith and kept the saint on his estate for four years. After that the pagan priests accused him before Vespasian, who issued a decree that anyone who insulted the gods must either sacrifice or be excluded from the city: for it is not right, he said, that we men should avenge the gods; they themselves, if they are angered, are able to punish their enemies.

Then the patrician Demosthenes handed Apollinaris, who still refused to sacrifice, over to a certain centurion, who already was a Christian. This man asked him to go and live in a settlement of lepers in order to escape the wrath of the pagans, but these latter pursued him and beat him until he was near death. He lived, however, for seven days, and then, after giving good counsel to his disciples, breathed his last and was given honorable burial by the Christians, under Vespasian, whose reign began about the year A.D. 70.

Ambrose, in his Preface, says of this martyr: "Apollinaris, that most worthy prelate, was sent by Peter, the prince of the apostles, to Ravenna, to preach the name of Jesus to the unbelievers. There he worked many miracles in Christ on behalf of those who believed in him. He was often beaten with rods, and his already aged body was mangled with horrible tortures by the impious. But, lest the faithful might be troubled at the sight of his sufferings, by the power of the Lord Jesus Christ he worked many signs, as the apostles had done. After he had been tortured, he restored a young girl to life, gave sight to the blind and speech to a mute, freed a woman possessed of the devil, cleansed a leper of his disease, strengthened the limbs of a victim of the plague, brought down an idolatrous image and the temple that sheltered it. O pontiff most worthy of admiration and commendation, pontiff who merited the power of the apostles along with the episcopal dignity! O bravest athlete of Christ, who still, even in advanced age and constantly in pain, preached Jesus Christ the redeemer of the world!"

98. Saint Christina

Saint Christina's name suggests *chrismate uncta*, anointed with chrism. She had the balm of good odor in her relationships with others, and the oil of devotion in her mind and benediction in her speech.[1]

Christina was born of parents of the highest rank, at Tyro in Italy. Her father shut her up with twelve waiting women in a tower, where she had silver and gold idols with her. She was very beautiful and many sought her in marriage, but her parents would give her to none of her suitors because they wanted her to remain in the service of the gods. She, however, was taught by the Holy Spirit and shrank from sacrificing to the idols, hiding in a window the incense she was supposed to burn to them.

Her father came to see her and the servingwomen told him: "Your daughter, our lady mistress, abhors the worship of our gods and declares that she is a Christian!" The father spoke softly to her, seeking to win her to the cult of the gods, but she said: "Do not call me your daughter, but the child of him to whom the sacrifice of praise is due, for I offer sacrifice not to mortal gods but to the God of heaven!" "Daughter mine," the father responded, "don't offer sacrifice to one god only, or the others will be angry with you!" Christina: "Though you don't know it, you speak the truth, because I offer sacrifice to the Father, the Son, and the Holy Spirit!" The father: "If you adore three gods, why not adore the others too?" Christina: "The three I adore are one godhead!"

After this, Christina smashed her father's idols and distributed the gold and silver to the poor. The father came back to worship his gods and could not find them, but the women told him what Christina had done with them. He was angry and ordered her to be stripped and beaten by twelve men, and they beat her until they themselves dropped, exhausted. Then Christina said to her father: "O man without honor, shameless man, abominable before God, pray your gods to give the men who are worn out with beating me the strength to continue, if you can!" But he had her bound in chains and thrown into prison.

---

[1] The reader will sense how completely the following story disagrees with the "etymology" with which the chapter opens. According to *Butler's Lives of the Saints* ([New York: P. J. Kenedy & Sons, 1963], 3:173–174), this legend grew out of confusion between the story of an Eastern Saint Christina of Tyre, which contained the implausible "popular" episodes related above, and the memory of another Saint Christina, otherwise unknown, who was thought to have been martyred near Bolsena.

Her mother, hearing about all this, tore her garments, went to the jail, and prostrated herself at her daughter's feet, saying: "Christina, daughter mine, have pity on me!" She answered: "Why do you call me your daughter? Don't you know that I bear the name of my God?" The mother could not win her over, and went and told her husband how Christina had answered her. He then had her brought before his tribunal and said to her: "Sacrifice to the gods! Otherwise you will suffer all sorts of torments and will no longer be called my daughter!" Christina: "You do me a great favor by not calling me a daughter of the devil! What is born of the devil is a demon, and you are the father of Satan himself!"

The father then ordered her flesh to be torn off with hooks and her tender limbs to be broken; and Christina picked up pieces of her flesh and threw them in her father's face, saying: "Take that, tyrant, and eat the flesh that you begot!" Then the father stretched her on a wheel and lighted a fire with oil under her, but the flames leapt out and killed fifteen hundred men. The father attributed all this to magic and remanded her to prison. When it was night, he ordered his henchmen to tie a large stone around her neck and throw her into the sea. They did this, but immediately angels bore her up, whereupon Christ came down to her and baptized her in the sea, saying: "I baptize thee in God my Father, in myself, Jesus Christ his Son, and in the Holy Spirit." He then committed her to the care of the archangel Michael, who led her ashore. When the father learned of this, he beat his forehead and exclaimed: "By what witchcraft do you do this, that you work your magic in the sea?" Christina answered: "Foolish, unhappy man! I had this favor from Christ!" He sent her back to prison to be beheaded in the morning, but he, her father, whose name was Urbanus, was found dead that very night.

A wicked judge named Elius succeeded him. Elius had an iron cradle prepared and fired with oil, pitch, and resin. Christina was then thrown into this cradle and four men were ordered to rock it back and forth so as to burn her to death more quickly. Then Christina praised God, who willed that she, so recently reborn by baptism, should be rocked in a cradle like a newborn babe. The judge, angrier than ever, had her head shaved and ordered her to be led naked through the city to the temple of Apollo. There she directed a command to the idol, which collapsed into a heap of dust. At this the judge was stricken with fear and expired.

He was succeeded by another judge, named Julianus, who had a furnace stoked and fired, and ordered Christina to be thrown into it. There for five days she walked about, singing with angels, and was unharmed. Being informed of this, Julianus ascribed it to magical arts, and had two asps, two vipers, and two cobras put in with her; but the vipers licked her feet, the asps clung to her breasts without hurting her, and the cobras wrapped themselves around her neck and licked her sweat. Julian called to the court conjurer: "You're a magician too, aren't you? Stir those beasts up!" The conjurer did as ordered, and the serpents came at him and killed him in a trice. Then Christina commanded the reptiles to hie themselves to a place in the desert, and brought the dead man back to life.

Next, Julianus had Christina's breasts cut off, and milk flowed from them instead of blood. Lastly, he had her tongue cut out, but she, never losing the power of speech, took the severed tongue and threw it in Julianus's face, hitting him in the eye and blinding him. Goaded to wrath, Julianus shot two arrows into her heart and one into her side, and she, pierced through and through, breathed forth her spirit to God about the year 287, under Diocletian. Her body rests near a fortified place called Bolsena, between Orvieto and Viterbo. The tower[2] which once was near that town has been completely demolished.

[2] Graesse notes (421 n. 2) that the Ed. Pr., instead of *turris*, has *Tyrus*, which might be the Tyro mentioned earlier.

99. Saint James the Greater

The apostle James was called James of Zebedee, James brother of John, *Boanerges*, i.e., son of thunder, and James the Greater. He is called James of Zebedee, namely, the son of Zebedee, not only because he was his son in the flesh but also by the interpretation of the name. *Zebedaeus* is interpreted as giving or given, and blessed James gave himself to Christ through the martyrdom of death and was given to us by God as a spiritual patron. He is called James the brother of John because he was his brother not only in the flesh but in the similarity of their character and virtues, for both had the same zeal, the same desire to learn, and the same ambition. They had the same zeal, namely, the same eagerness to avenge the Lord. When the Samaritans refused to welcome Christ, James and John said: "Lord, do you want us to bid fire to come down from heaven and consume them?" They had the same desire to learn: hence they were ahead of the others in questioning Christ about the Day of Judgment and other things to come. They had the same ambition, because they both wanted to be seated one on the right and the other on the left of Christ. James is called son of thunder by reason of the thunderous sound of his preaching, which terrified the wicked, roused up the sluggish, and by its depth attracted the admiration of all. So Bede says of John:[1] "He spoke so loudly that if he thundered but a little more loudly, the whole world would not have been able to contain him." James is called the Greater, as the other James is called the Less, first, because he was the first of the two to be called by Christ, secondly, because of his intimacy with Christ, who seems to have had a closer relationship with this James than with the other, admitting him to his secrets, as at the raising of the daughter of Jairus and at the Lord's glorious transfiguration. He is called the Greater, thirdly, by reason of his martyrdom, because he suffered first among the apostles. Therefore as he is designated greater than the other James because he was called earlier to the grace of apostleship, so he can be called greater because summoned earlier to the glory of eternity.

James the apostle, son of Zebedee, preached throughout Judea and Samaria after the Lord's ascension, then went to Spain to sow the word of God there. But he felt that he was making no headway there and had gained only nine disciples, so he left two of them to preach in Spain and returned to Judea, taking the other seven with him. Master John Beleth says, however, that James converted only

---

[1] Also called *Boanerges* (Mark 3:17).

one disciple in Spain. While he was preaching the word of God in Judea, a certain magician named Hermogenes, who was allied with the Pharisees, sent one of his followers, whose name was Philetus, to James. Philetus was to confront the apostle and convince him, in the presence of the Jews, that his preaching was false. But James, by well-reasoned argument, showed Philetus that he preached the truth, and wrought many miracles for everyone to see. Philetus returned to Hermogenes, saying that he agreed with James's doctrine and relating his miracles. He further declared that he intended to become a disciple of James, and urged his master to do likewise.

Hermogenes was furious. By his magical skills he made Philetus so immobile that he could not make the slightest movement, and said: "Now we shall see whether your James can release you!" Philetus sent word of this to James by his servant, and James sent him his kerchief, saying: "Have him hold this cloth and say, 'The Lord upholds all who are falling; he sets the prisoners free.'" As soon as Philetus touched the kerchief, he was freed of his invisible bonds, mocked Hermogenes' magic arts, and hastened to join James.

Hermogenes' anger knew no bounds. He summoned the demons and commanded them to bring James himself in chains, together with Philetus, to him, in order that he might avenge himself upon them and also to be sure that his other disciples would not dare to visit such insults on him. The demons swarmed in the air around James and began to howl, saying: "Apostle James, have mercy on us, because we are already on fire before our time has come!" James asked them: "For what purpose have you come to me?" They answered: "Hermogenes sent us to bring you and Philetus to him, but as soon as we reached you, an angel of God bound us with fiery chains and tormented us sorely!" James: "Let the angel of God release you, and go back to him and bring him to me, bound but unharmed!" Off they went and seized Hermogenes, tied his hands behind his back, and brought him thus shackled to James, saying to their captive: "You sent us, and where we went we were burned and sorely tormented!" To James the demons said: "Give us power over him, so that we can get revenge for the wrongs he has done you and for our own fiery torments!" James said to them: "Here is Philetus standing before you! Why don't you lay hold of him?" They answered: "We cannot lay a finger on as much as an ant, as long as it is in your house!"

James said to Philetus: "Let us return good for evil, as Christ taught us to do. Hermogenes put you in bonds, now you unbind him!" Hermogenes, released, stood there not knowing what to do, and James said to him: "You are free, go wherever you want to! It is not in our religion to convert anyone against his will!" The magician replied: "I know the anger of the demons! They will kill me unless you give me something I can have with me to keep me safe!" James gave him his staff, and he went and brought all his books on magic to the apostle to be burned. But James, fearful that the smoke from the fire might do some harm to those unaware of the danger, ordered him to throw them into the sea. He did so and, coming back to the apostle, prostrated himself and clung to James's feet, saying: "Liberator of men's souls! You have borne with me while I envied you and sought to do you harm! Receive me now as a penitent!" Thereafter he began to live perfectly in the fear of God, so much so that many miracles took place through him.

Now the Jews, indignant at seeing Hermogenes a convert to the faith, went to James and inveighed against him for preaching Christ crucified. James, however, quoted the Scriptures to prove conclusively to them the coming of Christ and his passion, and many of them believed. Abiathar, who was the high priest of that year, incited an uprising among the people, then put a rope around the apostle's neck and had him brought before Herod Agrippa. At Herod's command he was led away to be beheaded. Along the road there lay a paralyzed man who called out to James, begging him to cure him. James said to him: "In the name of Jesus Christ, for whose faith I am led to execution, stand up cured and bless your Creator!" The man stood up and blessed the Lord.

The scribe who had put the rope around James's neck, and whose name was Josiah, saw this, knelt at the apostle's feet, asked for his pardon, and requested that he be made a Christian. Observing this, Abiathar had him held and said to him: "Unless you curse the name of Christ, you will be beheaded with James!" Josiah answered: "Cursed be you and all your days, and blessed be the name of the Lord Jesus Christ forever!" Abiathar had him punched in the mouth, and sent a messenger to Herod to obtain an order for his beheading. While the two were waiting to be executed, James asked the headsman for a jug of water. He then baptized Josiah, and both of them had their heads struck off and thus achieved martyrdom.

James was beheaded on 25 March, the feast of the Lord's annunciation, and was transferred to Compostella on 25 July. He was buried on 30 December, because the construction of his tomb took from August to the end of December.

According to John Beleth, who wrote a thorough account of this transferral, after John was beheaded, his disciples went at night, for fear of the Jews, got his body, and put it aboard a rudderless boat. Commending the burial to divine providence they set sail, an angel of the Lord being their pilot, and made port in Galicia, Spain. They landed in the realm of Queen Lupa, whose name, which means she-wolf, fitted her well. They carried the saint's body off the boat and laid it on a large rock, and the rock promptly softened, miraculously shaping itself into a sarcophagus for the body.

The disciples then presented themselves to Queen Lupa and said to her: "The Lord Jesus Christ sends you the body of his apostle, in order that you may welcome dead him whom you would not welcome alive!" They told her about the miracle, namely, how they had reached her territory in a rudderless ship, and asked her to grant them a suitable place for his burial. John Beleth continues that the queen, having heard all this, treacherously sent them to a man known for his cruelty—who, according to other sources, was the king of Spain—in order to gain his consent to the burial; but he took them prisoners and put them in jail. While he slept, however, an angel of the Lord opened the prison and allowed them to go free. When the cruel despot learned of this, he sent soldiers after them to bring them back, but as the soldiers were crossing a bridge, the bridge collapsed and all were drowned in the river. Word of this reached the tyrant, and he, repentant and fearful for himself and his people, sent messengers to ask James's people to come back to him, with the promise that he would grant them whatever request they made. They went back and converted all the people of that city to the Lord.

Lupa heard of this and took the news badly, and when the disciples came to tell her that the king had given his consent, she answered: "Go and take the oxen that I have in a place in the mountains, put together a wagon to carry your master's body, and build a tomb for him wherever you choose!" This was wolfish thinking, because she knew the oxen were really wild, untamed bulls, and thought they could be neither yoked nor harnessed, and if they were harnessed, would run off in different directions, demolishing the wagon, losing the body, and killing the disciples themselves.

But no wisdom can prevail against God. The disciples, not suspecting the queen's ruse, went up into the mountain. A fire-breathing dragon came charging upon them, but they met him with the sign of the cross and split him up the middle. They then made the sign of the cross over the bulls, which suddenly became gentle and submitted to the yoke. Next they put Saint James's body, with the rock upon which they had laid it, on the wagon. The oxen, with no one guiding them, hauled the body into the middle of Lupa's palace. This was enough for the queen. Recovering from her astonishment, she believed and became a Christian, granted everything the disciples asked for, gave her palace to be a church dedicated to Saint James, endowed it magnificently, and spent the rest of her life doing good works.

Pope Callistus tells us that a man named Bernard, of the diocese of Modena, was captured and chained in the bottom of a tower. There he prayed continually to Saint James, who appeared to him and said: "Come, follow me to Galicia!" The apostle broke the man's chains and then disappeared. Bernard, with the chains still hanging around his neck, climbed to the top of the tower and jumped to the ground, sustaining no injury though the tower was sixty cubits high.

Bede writes that a certain man had committed a truly enormous sin, a sin so grave that his bishop feared to absolve him and sent him to Saint James with a paper on which that sin was written. On the saint's feast day the man laid the paper on the altar and prayed to Saint James to erase the sin by his merits. He unfolded the paper afterwards and found that the sin was completely erased, so he thanked God and Saint James, and spread the word about what had happened.

We learn from Hubert of Besançon that about the year 1070 thirty men from Lorraine went on pilgrimage to Compostella, to the tomb of Saint James. All of them except one had sworn to help each other. One of the thirty fell ill, and the rest waited for him for a fortnight, after which they all left him except the one who had not made the promise. This man stayed with him at the foot of the mountain of Saint Michael, where, as evening drew on, the sick man died. The other was frightened by the loneliness of the place, the presence of the dead man, the darkness of the night, and the fierceness of the local population; but of a sudden Saint James appeared to him in knightly array, comforted him, and said: "Lift the corpse up to me, and you come up behind me on my horse!" They rode on and before dawn had traveled a fifteen days' journey, arriving at Mount Joy, a short distance from Compostella and the apostle's tomb. The saint set both the living and the dead down there, ordering the survivor to call upon the canons of Saint James to bury the dead pilgrim, and to tell those who had traveled with him that their pilgrimage was worthless because they had broken their oath. The man carried out his orders and told his astonished companions what Saint James had said.

Pope Callistus says that a certain German and his son set out, around the year 1020, on a pilgrimage to the tomb of Saint James, and stopped overnight in the city of Toulouse, where the innkeeper got the older man drunk and hid a silver drinking cup in their baggage. The two left in the morning, but the host pursued them as if they were thieves, accusing them of stealing his silver cup. They said he could have them punished if he found the cup on them, and when the article was found in their baggage, they were haled before the magistrate. They were sentenced to surrender everything they had to the innkeeper, and one of them to be hanged. The father wanted to die in place of his son and the son in the father's place, but in the end the son was hanged and the father, grief-stricken, went on to Saint James. Thirty-six days later, going back through Toulouse, he turned aside to where his son's body hung and broke out in loud lamentations. And behold, the son, still hanging, began to console his father, saying: "Dearest father, don't cry! I have never been so well off, because Saint James has borne me up and has refreshed me with heavenly sweets!" Hearing this, the father ran into the city, and the people came, took his son down from the gallows unhurt, and hanged the innkeeper.

Hugh of Saint Victor tells the story of a pilgrim on the way to Saint James, to whom the devil appeared in the guise of the saint, and, bemoaning the misery of this present life, said he would be happy if the pilgrim was willing to kill himself in his honor. The pilgrim grasped a sword and killed himself forthwith. But now the man in whose house he had been a guest was suspected of murdering him and feared for his own life. However, the man who had died came back to life and declared that while the devil who had persuaded him to kill himself was leading him to the torments of hell, Saint James met them, snatched the man away, brought him before the heavenly judge, and, despite the demon's accusations, obtained his restoration to life.

Abbot Hugh of Cluny tells us that a young man from the Lyons district, who used to go to the tomb of Saint James regularly and with great devotion, was on his way there when one night he lapsed into the sin of fornication. As he continued his journey, the devil, having assumed the appearance of Saint James, appeared to him and said to the young man: "Do you know who I am?" The youth asked who he was, and the devil said: "I am James the apostle, whom you have been visiting yearly, and I want you to know that your devotion gave me much joy; but recently you left your house and fell into fornication, yet, not having confessed your sin, you presume to come to me, as if your pilgrimage could possibly please God and me. That will do you no good. Anyone who desires to come to me as a pilgrim must first reveal his sins in confession and then do penance for them by making the pilgrimage!" After having said this, the devil vanished.

The young man was troubled in spirit and decided that he would go home, confess his sin, and then start out again on his pilgrimage. But again the devil appeared to him in the guise of Saint James and advised against this plan, asserting that his sin would not be remitted unless he cut off his male member, or made up his mind, in order to be still more blessed, to kill himself and become a martyr in his, James's, honor. Therefore one night, while his companions slept, the young man took a knife and castrated himself, then drove the knife through his belly. When his companions woke up and saw what had happened, they made ready to decamp, fearing that they might be suspected of murder. Meanwhile, a grave was being dug for the dead man, but he came to life and spoke to those who were about to get away, and who were astounded at seeing him alive. He told them what had happened to him, and said: "When I took the devil's advice and killed myself, demons laid hold of me and carried me off toward Rome; but lo and behold, Saint James came riding after us and roundly upbraided the evil spirits for lying to me. When the demons kept arguing, Saint James herded all of us to a nearby meadow where the Blessed Virgin sat in conversation with a large number of saints. Saint James appealed to her on my behalf, and she rebuked the demons severely and commanded that I be restored to life." Three days later, with nothing left of his wounds except the scars, the youth took to the road with his companions and told them the whole story in full detail.

Pope Callistus tells us that about the year 1100, a certain Frenchman set out with his wife and children to go to the tomb of Saint James, partly to escape the plague that was raging in France, but also out of a pious wish to visit the saint. When they reached the city of Pamplona, his wife died, and the innkeeper stole all his money and even the ass his children rode on. Grieving for his lost wife he continued his journey, carrying some of his children on his shoulders and leading the others by the hand. A man came along leading an ass, was moved to compassion by the pilgrim's plight, and lent him the beast to carry the children. When he came to the shrine of Saint James and was watching and praying beside the apostle's tomb, the saint appeared to him and asked whether he recognized him. The man said no, and the saint said: "I am the apostle James, who lent you my beast on your way here, and now I lend it to you for the return journey; but you should know in advance that that innkeeper will fall off the roof and die, and all he stole from you will be returned to you!" Everything happened as the saint had foretold. The man got home safe and happy, and when he lifted his children from the ass's back, the animal vanished.

A certain tyrant had unjustly despoiled a tradesman of his goods and kept him in confinement, and this man devoutly besought Saint James's aid. The saint appeared while the guards looked on, and led the man to the top of the tower. The tower then bent over until the top was level with the ground, and the prisoner stepped off without jumping and went his way. The guards went after him, but, though they passed close to him, they could not see him.

Hubert of Besançon tells us that three soldiers from the diocese of Lyons were on the pilgrimage road to Saint James, and an old woman asked one of them, for the love of Saint James, to load the sack she was carrying onto his horse, which he did. Then he came upon a sick man lying beside the road. The soldier put him on his horse and followed the horse on foot, carrying the old woman's sack and the sick man's staff. But the sun's heat and the toil of the journey were too much for him, and when he reached Galicia he fell gravely ill. His companions asked him about the state of his soul with regard to eternal salvation, but he did not utter a single word for three days. On the fourth day, when his friends were expecting him to die at any moment, he sighed heavily and said: "Thanks be to God and Saint James, because of whose merits I am set free. When you warned me about my salvation, I wanted to do what you suggested, but demons came and held me by the throat so tightly that I could not say a word for the good of my soul. I heard you but I simply could not answer. Then Saint James came in, carrying the old woman's sack in his left hand and the poor man's staff in his right—the two I helped on the road. He wielded the staff like a spear and held the sack as a shield, and set upon the demons as if in anger, threatening them with his raised staff and putting them to rout. Now you see that I am freed and can speak again. Call a priest for me, because I have not long to live." Then he turned to one of the two soldiers and said: "Don't stay in your master's service any longer, because truly he is damned and will shortly come to a bad end." After his companion was buried, this soldier told his master what the dying man had said. The master scoffed and made no effort to amend his ways, and not long afterwards was pierced with a lance in battle and perished.

According to Pope Callistus, a man from Vézelay was on a pilgrimage to Saint James when his money ran out, and he was ashamed to beg. He lay down under a tree to rest, and fell asleep and dreamed that Saint James was providing him with food. Upon awaking he discovered a cinder-baked loaf beside his head. The loaf sustained him for two weeks, until he reached home. Twice each day he ate as much of the bread as he needed, but the following day he found the loaf whole and intact in his sack.

Pope Callistus reports that about the year 1100 a citizen of Barcelona went on pilgrimage to Saint James and prayed for just one favor, namely, that thenceforth he might never be taken captive by an enemy. He was returning home via Sicily when he was captured by Saracens at sea and was sold several times as a slave, but the chains with which he was fettered always fell apart. When he had already been sold thirteen times and was bound with double chains, he called upon Saint James for help, and the saint appeared to him and said: "When you were in my church, with no thought for your soul's salvation you asked only for your body's liberation, and that is why all these misfortunes have beset you. But because the Lord is merciful, he has sent me to redeem you." At once his chains were broken, and he passed through the lands and strongholds of the Saracens carrying a part of the chain as proof of this miracle. So he returned home, where his own saw him and marveled. When anyone tried to take him captive, the sight of the chain sent him flying; and when lions and other wild beasts were about to attack him as he went about in desert places, they saw the chain, were stricken with stark terror, and turned and ran at once.

In the year 1238, in the town of Prato, which is situated between Florence and Pistoia, on the vigil of the feast of Saint James, a feebleminded youth, misled by his own simplicity, set fire to the crops of his guardian, who intended to deprive him of his inheritance. The youth was apprehended and admitted his crime, and was sentenced to be tied to a horse's tail and dragged through the streets, then burned at the stake. He confessed his sin and prayed devoutly to Saint James. Then, clad only in a shirt, he was dragged over stony ground, but neither his body nor his shirt sustained any damage. Then he was bound to the stake and wood was piled all around him. The fire was lit, the bonds were burned away, but he continued to invoke Saint James and both his body and his shirt remained unscathed. They wanted to light a new fire around him, but the people got him away and God was magnificently praised in his apostle.

100. Saint Christopher

Before Christopher was baptized, he was called Reprobus, meaning outcast, but afterwards he was called Christophoros, the Christ-bearer. He bore Christ in four ways, namely, on his shoulders when he carried him across the river, in his body by mortification, in his mind by devotion, and in his mouth by confessing Christ and preaching him.

Christopher was a Canaanite by birth, a man of prodigious size—he was twelve feet tall—and fearsome of visage. According to some accounts of his life it happened one day, when he was in the presence of a certain Canaanite king, that the idea came to him of going in quest of the greatest prince in the world and staying with him. He came to a mighty king who was regarded generally as the world's greatest ruler. When this king saw Christopher, he received him gladly and made him a member of his court.

Then one day the court jester sang some ditty before the king, in which frequent mention was made of the devil. The king was a Christian and made the sign of the cross on his forehead when he heard the devil spoken of. Christopher noticed this, and wondered why the king did it and what the sign meant. He asked the king about it and, when the ruler did not answer, said to him: "Unless you answer my question I will not stay with you any longer!" The king, thus pressed, told him: "Whenever I hear the devil mentioned, I defend myself with this sign, for fear the devil might get some power over me and do me harm!" Christopher: "If you're afraid of being harmed by the devil, this proves that he is greater and more powerful than you are, or you wouldn't be afraid of him. Therefore I am frustrated in my hope that I had found the greatest and most powerful lord in the world. So now farewell! I'll go and look for the devil, accept him as my master, and become his servant!"

Christopher left that king and went in search of the devil. He was going through a desert when he saw a great host of soldiers, and one of them, fiercer and more terrible than the rest, came to him and asked where he was going. Christopher answered: "I'm looking for the lord devil! I want to take him as my master." The other said to him: "I'm the one you're looking for!" Christopher was happy to hear this and pledged himself to serve him forever, acknowledging him as his lord and master.

They marched along the highway until they came to a cross erected at roadside. When the devil saw it, he was terror-stricken, left the road, and led Christopher over a wild and desolate tract before returning to the road. Christopher was surprised at this, and asked the devil what made him so afraid that he left the highroad and took another way through a rough wilderness. The devil refused to state his reason, and Christopher said: "Unless you tell me what this is about, I shall leave you immediately!" The demon, no longer able to evade the question, said: "There was a man named Christ who was nailed to a cross, and when I see the sign of his cross, I am filled with terror and run away!" Christopher: "Well, then, this Christ, whose sign you dread so much, is greater and more powerful than you are! Therefore I have labored in vain and have not yet found the greatest prince in the world! So good-bye to you! I'm leaving you and going in search of Christ!"

He looked long and far for someone who could give him word of Christ. Finally he came upon a hermit who preached Christ to him and instructed him diligently in the Christian faith. He said to Christopher: "This king whom you wish to serve requires that you do his will in many ways. For instance, you will have to fast frequently." Christopher: "Let him require some other form of obedience! That one I just can't do!" Again the hermit: "You will also have to offer him many prayers." Christopher: "I don't even know what that means, so I can't perform that kind of service!" The hermit than asked him: "Do you know the famous river, where many people, trying to get across, go under and perish?" "Yes I do!" said Christopher. The hermit: "You're big enough and strong enough! Go dwell by the river, and if you help those who wish to cross it, that will greatly please Christ the king whom you wish to serve, and I hope he might show himself to you there!" Christopher: "Good! That kind of service I can give, and I promise to serve him that way!"

He went to the river and built himself a shelter to live in. Instead of a staff he used a long pole to steady himself in the water, and carried across all those who wished to go. Many days later he was resting in his shelter when he heard a child's voice calling him: "Christopher, come out and carry me across!" He jumped to his feet and went out, but found no one. He went indoors and again heard the same voice calling him, but ran out and again saw no one. The third time he responded to the same call and found a child standing on the riverbank. The child begged him to carry him across the river, and Christopher lifted him to his shoulders, grasped his great staff, and strode into the water. But little by little the water grew rougher and the child became as heavy as lead: the farther he went, the higher rose the waves, and the weight of the child pressed down upon his shoulders so crushingly that he was in dire distress. He feared that he was about to founder, but at last he reached the other bank.

Setting the child down he said to him: "My boy, you put me in great danger, and you weighed so much that if I had had the whole world on my back I could not have felt it a heavier burden!" The child answered him: "Don't be surprised, Christopher! You were not only carrying the whole world, you had him who created the world upon your shoulders! I am Christ your king, to whom you render service by doing the work you do here. And if you want proof that what I am saying is true, when you get back to your little house, plant your staff in the earth, and tomorrow you will find it in leaf and bearing fruit!" With that the child vanished. Christopher crossed over and thrust his staff into the earth near his shelter. The next morning he rose and found the staff bearing leaves and fruit like a palm tree.

After that, Christopher went to Samos, a city in Lycia. He did not understand the language spoken there, and prayed the Lord to make him able to understand it. As he prayed, the judges thought he was insane and left him alone; but when the favor he had prayed for was granted, he covered his face and went to the place where Christians were being tortured and executed, to speak to them and give them courage in the Lord. One of the judges struck him in the face, and Christopher, uncovering his face, said: "If I were not a Christian, I would quickly have revenge for this insult!" Then he planted his staff in the earth and prayed the Lord that it might burst into leaf and thus help to convert the people. Leaves sprouted instantly, and eight thousand men believed and became Christians.

The king now sent two hundred soldiers to bring Christopher to him, but they found him at prayer and were afraid to tell him why they had come. The king sent as many more, but they, when they found him praying, prayed with him. Christopher rose and said to them: "For whom are you looking?" Seeing his face, they said: "The king sent us to bring you to him in bonds!" Christopher: "If I did not wish to go, you could not take me, bound or not!" They said: "Well, then, if you don't want to come, take your leave and go wherever you wish, and we'll tell the king that we could not find you anywhere." "Not so!" he replied, "I will go with you!"

So Christopher converted the soldiers to the faith, and had them tie his hands behind his back and present him, thus bound, to the king. The sight of him terrified the king, who fell from his seat. His servitors raised him, and he asked Christopher his name and country of origin. Christopher replied: "Before baptism I was called Reprobus but now am called Christopher." The king: "You have taken a foolish name, calling yourself after Christ, who was crucified and could do nothing to save himself, and now can do nothing for you! Now, then, you trouble-making Canaanite, why do you not sacrifice to our gods?" Christopher: "You are rightly called Dagnus, because you are the death of the world and the devil's partner, and your gods are the work of men's hands!" The king: "You were brought up among wild beasts, and you can do only the works of savages and talk only of things unknown to men! Now, however, if you are ready to sacrifice, I will bestow great honors upon you. If not, you will be tortured to death!" Christopher refused to sacrifice, and the king put him in jail. As for the soldiers whom he had sent after Christopher, he had them beheaded for the name of Christ.

Now the king had two shapely young women, one named Nicaea and the other Aquilina, put into the cell with Christopher, promising them large rewards if they succeeded in seducing him. Christopher quickly saw through the stratagem and knelt to pray. When the women tried to arouse him by stroking him and putting their arms around him, he stood up and said to them: "What are you trying to do and for what reason were you sent in here?" The two were frightened by the radiance of his face and said: "Saint of God, pity us! Make us able to believe in the God whom you preach!"

Word of this reached the king, who had the women brought to him, and said: "So you too have been seduced! I swear by the gods that unless you sacrifice to the gods, you will die an awful death!" They answered: "If your will is that we offer sacrifice, have the streets cleared and order all the people into the temple!" This done, they went into the temple, loosened their girdles, and threw them around the necks of the idols, pulling them to the ground and reducing them to dust. Then they said to the assistants: "Call your doctors and let them heal your gods!"

By order of the king, Aquilina was then hung up by the wrists and a huge stone was tied to her feet, thus breaking all her limbs. When she had breathed her last in the Lord, her sister Nicaea was thrown into the fire, but when she emerged unscathed, she was beheaded at once.

Christopher was then brought before the king, who ordered him to be beaten with iron rods, and to have an iron helmet, heated in the fire, placed on his head. Then he had an iron chair made. The saint was bound into it, then a fire was lighted underneath and pitch thrown on the flames. But the chair crumbled like wax, and Christopher came away from it unharmed. Then the king had him lashed to a pillar and ordered four hundred bowmen to shoot arrows at him, but the arrows hung in midair and not a single one of them could touch him. But when the king, thinking that he had been mortally wounded, came to mock him, suddenly one of the arrows came through the air, turned back, and struck the tyrant in the eye, blinding him. Christopher said to him: "Tyrant, I will be dead by tomorrow. Then make a paste with my blood and rub it on your eyes, and you will recover your sight!"

By the king's order the saint was led away to the place of execution, where after praying he was beheaded. The king took a little of his blood and rubbed it on his eyes, saying: "In the name of God and Saint Christopher," and his sight was restored immediately. Then he was baptized and issued a decree that whoever blasphemed against God or Saint Christopher was to be beheaded at once.

Ambrose in his Preface says of this martyr: "O Lord, you granted such a wealth of virtue and such grace of teaching to Christopher that by his gleaming miracles he recalled forty-eight thousand men from the error of paganism to the cult of Christian dogma. Nicaea and Aquilina had been engaged in prostitution in a public brothel, but he won them over to the practice of chastity and schooled them to receive the crown of martyrdom. For this he was strapped into an iron chair in the middle of a blazing fire but feared no harm from the heat. For a whole day the storm of arrows shot by the soldiers could not pierce him; yet one arrow struck the executioner in the eye, and the blessed martyr's blood mixed with earth restored his sight and by removing the body's blindness also illumined his mind; for the saint besought your forgiveness and by his supplications obtained the cure of diseases and infirmities."

101. The Seven Sleepers

The Seven Sleepers were natives of the city of Ephesus. The emperor Decius, who decreed the persecution of Christians, came to Ephesus and gave orders to build temples in the center of the city, so that all the people might join him in worshiping the false gods. He further ordered that all Christians were to be rounded up and put in chains, either to sacrifice to the gods or to die; and the Christians in Ephesus were so afraid of the threatened punishments that friends betrayed friends, fathers their sons, and sons their fathers.

In the city there were seven young Christian men named Maximianus, Malchus, Marcianus, Dionysius, Johannes, Serapion, and Constantinus, who were sorely distressed about what was happening among the Christian faithful. The seven held high rank in the palace but refused to sacrifice to the idols. Instead they hid in their houses and devoted themselves to fasting and prayer. For this they were denounced and brought before Decius. They affirmed their Christian faith, but the emperor gave them time to come to their senses before he came back to the city. On the contrary, they distributed their wealth to the poor, and by common consent withdrew to Mount Celion and kept out of sight there. They lived that way for a long time, while Malchus, one of their number, took it upon himself to provide for their needs. Whenever he had to go into the city for supplies, he put on the dress and appearance of a beggar.

Decius in time returned to Ephesus and commanded that the seven be sought out and forced to sacrifice. Malchus was alarmed when he heard this in the city and reported the emperor's will to his friends. This aroused their fears, but Malchus set before them the food he had brought, to give them strength to face the coming trials. After they had eaten and were talking together with sighs and tears, they suddenly, by the will of God, fell asleep. The next morning the search was on but they could not be found, and Decius was disturbed at the loss of such fine young men. Then they were denounced for concealing themselves on Mount Celion, and, moreover, for giving their property to the Christian poor and persisting in the adherence to the faith. Decius therefore ordered their parents to appear before him and threatened them with death unless they told all they knew regarding their sons' whereabouts. The parents, instead, repeated the same charges against the youths and complained that their wealth had been given away to the poor. The emperor thought about what he ought to do to the seven, and decided, by the will of God, to have the cave in which they were hiding walled up with stones, so that, thus immured, they would die of hunger and need. This was done, but two Christians, Theodorus and Rufinus, wrote an account of the martyrdom and left it concealed among the stones that closed the cave.

Three hundred and seventy-two years later, long after Decius and his whole generation had passed away, in the thirtieth year of the reign of the emperor Theodosius, there was an outbreak of heresy and widespread denial of the resurrection of the dead. This deeply aggrieved the most Christian emperor, who, seeing how the true faith was so impiously distorted, sat day after day in an inside room of his palace, wearing a hair shirt and weeping inconsolably. God in his mercy saw this and, wishing to assuage the grief of those who mourned and to confirm their faith in the resurrection of the dead, opened the treasury of his loving-kindness and awakened the aforesaid martyrs. He inspired a certain citizen of Ephesus to build a shelter for his sheepherders on Mount Celion, and to do this the masons took away the stones from the mouth of the cave and thus awakened the saints. They greeted each other, thinking that they had simply slept through the night. Then they remembered their sadness of the day before and questioned Malchus about Decius's decision concerning them. He answered as he had on the previous evening: "They're looking for us to make us sacrifice to the idols. That's what the emperor has in mind for us!" "And God knows," Maximianus responded, "we will not offer sacrifice!" Having encouraged his companions, he asked Malchus to go down to the city and buy more loaves than he had the day before, and to find out what the emperor had ordered and report what he learned.

Taking five coins with him, Malchus left the cave. He wondered for a moment about the stones lying around but, having other things on his mind, thought no more about it. He approached the city cautiously and marveled at seeing a cross over the gate. Going to another gate and another, he was dumbfounded at the sight of a cross over each of them and at the different appearance of the city itself. He crossed himself and returned to the first gate, thinking that he must be dreaming; but gathering his wits and covering his face he went in. When he came to the bread sellers, he heard people talking about Christ, and was more and more bewildered. "What's going on?" he thought. "Yesterday no one dared to utter the name of Christ, and today everybody confesses him! I don't think I'm in Ephesus at all, because the city looks different, but I don't know any other city like this!" He asked someone and was assured that he was in Ephesus, but kept thinking that there was some mistake and that he had better go back to his companions.

First, however, he went to buy bread, but when he offered his money, the sellers, surprised, told each other that this youth had found some ancient treasure. Seeing them talking about him, Malchus thought they were getting ready to turn him over to the emperor, and, more frightened than ever, asked them to let him go and told them to keep the bread and the money. But they laid hold of him and said: "Where are you from? Tell us where you found these coins of the old emperors, and we'll share with you and hide you. There's no other way you can be hidden." Malchus was so frightened that he could find nothing to say to them, and the men, seeing that he would not answer, put a rope around his neck and led him through the streets to the middle of town. Meanwhile the rumor spread that this young man had discovered a treasure. Crowds gathered round and gaped at him. He wanted to convince them that he had not found anything, and looked all around him, hoping that someone would recognize him or he would see some of his relatives, who, he thought, must be alive. But no such thing happened, and he stood there like one demented, in the middle of the crowd.

Word of this reached Saint Martin, the bishop, and Antipater, the proconsul, a recent arrival in the city. They ordered the citizens to be careful and to bring the youth and his money to them. When he was hauled along to the church, he thought that he was being brought to the emperor. The bishop and the proconsul, amazed when they saw the coins, asked him where he had found this unknown treasure. He answered that he had not found anything at all but had taken the money out of his parents' purse. They asked him what city he came from, and he replied: "I am sure I belong to this city, if indeed this is the city of the Ephesians." "Get your parents here to vouch for you!" the consul said; but when Malchus gave their names, they said he was pretending to be someone else in order to escape. "How can we believe you," the proconsul asked, "when you say the money belonged to your parents? The inscription on the coins is more than 370 years old. They go back to the first days of the emperor Decius and are not at all like our coinage. And how can your parents be that old and you so young? You are just trying to fool the wise men and elders of Ephesus. Therefore I order you to be held until you confess what you found."

Malchus then threw himself at their feet and said: "In God's name, my lords, tell me what I ask you, and I will tell you all I have in my heart. The emperor Decius who was here in this city . . . where is he now?" The bishop answered: "My son, today there is nobody on earth who is called Decius, but there was an emperor Decius long, long ago!" "My lord," Malchus replied, "what you say leaves me confused, and no one believes what I say. But come with me and I will show you my friends who are with me on Mount Celion, and believe them! For I know this, that we fled from the face of the emperor Decius, and yesterday evening I saw the emperor come into this city, if this is the city of Ephesus!"

The bishop thought this over, then told the proconsul that God was trying to make them see something through this youth. So they set out with him and a great crowd followed them. Malchus went ahead to alert his friends, and the bishop came after him and found among the stones the letter sealed with two silver seals. He called the people together and read the letter to them. They marveled at what they heard, and, seeing the seven saints of God, their faces like roses in bloom, sitting in the cave, all fell to their knees and gave glory to God.

Now the bishop and the proconsul sent word to the emperor Theodosius, bidding him come quickly to see this new miracle. He rose at once, laid aside the sackcloth in which he had been grieving, and, glorifying God, hurried from Constantinople to Ephesus. All the people went out to meet him, and together they went up to the cave. The minute the saints saw the emperor, their faces shone like the sun. The emperor prostrated himself before them and gave praise to God, then rose and embraced each one and wept over them, saying: "Seeing you thus, it is as if I saw the Lord raising Lazarus from the dead!" Saint Maximianus said to him: "Believe us, it is for your sake that God has raised us before the day of the great resurrection, so that you may believe without the shadow of a doubt in the resurrection of the dead. We have truly risen and are alive, and as an infant is in his mother's womb and lives feeling no pain, so were we, living, lying here asleep, feeling nothing!"

Then, while all looked on, the seven saints bowed their heads to the ground, fell asleep, and yielded up their spirits as God willed that they should do. The emperor rose and bent over them, weeping and kissing them, and ordered golden coffins to be made for them. That very night, however, they appeared to Theodosius and said that as hitherto they had lain in the earth and had risen from the earth, so he should return them to the earth until the Lord raised them up again. Therefore the emperor ordered the cave to be embellished with gilded stones, and also decreed that all the bishops who now professed faith in the resurrection should be absolved.

There is reason to doubt that these saints slept for 372 years, because they arose in the year of the Lord 448. Decius reigned in 252 and his reign lasted only fifteen months, so the saints must have slept only 195 years.

102. Saints Nazarius and Celsus

Nazarius is interpreted to mean consecrated, or clean, or separated, or flowering, or guarding. In man five things are required, namely, thought, affection, intention, action, and speech. A man should be holy in his thought, clean in affection, straight in intention, just in action, and moderate in speech. All these virtues were in Saint Nazarius. He was holy in his thought and therefore is called consecrated, clean in his affections and is called clean. He was straight in intention and is called separated, for it is the intention that separates works: if the eye is sound, the whole body will be full of light, but if the eye is not sound, the whole body will be full of darkness. He was just in action and therefore is called flowering, because the just shall blossom as the lily. He was moderate in speech and therefore is called guarding, because he guarded his ways and sinned not with his tongue.

Celsus, like *excelsus*, means exalted, and Saint Celsus lifted himself above himself, rising above his childhood age by the strength of his spirit.

It is said that Ambrose found an account of the life and passion of these saints in the book of Gervasius and Protasius; but in other books we read that a certain philosopher who was devoted to Nazarius wrote his passion, and that Ceratius, who buried the saints' bodies, placed the writing at their head.

Nazarius was the son of a man of high distinction, but a Jew, whose name was Africanus, and of blessed Perpetua, a most Christian woman of the highest Roman nobility, who had been baptized by Saint Peter the apostle. When Nazarius was nine years old, he began to wonder about how differently his father and mother practiced their religion, since his mother followed the law of baptism and his father the law of the Sabbath. He hesitated for a long time over which of the two he should follow, his father trying to draw him to his faith and his mother to hers. Finally, by God's will, he went his mother's way and received holy baptism from Pope Linus. His father, understanding what he had done, nevertheless tried to turn him away from his holy resolution, describing to him in detail the kinds of tortures that Christians were forced to undergo. We should note that while it is said that he was baptized by Pope Linus, this should perhaps be understood to mean not that Linus was pope when he baptized Nazarius, but that he was destined to be pope later on. As we shall see below, Nazarius lived many years following his baptism and was martyred by Nero, who in the last year of his reign had Saint Peter crucified. Linus succeeded Peter as pope.

Nazarius did not accede to his father's wish. On the contrary, he was committed to preaching Christ, and his parents feared that he would be put to death. Therefore at their urging he left the city of Rome with seven mules laden with his possessions, and, as he passed through the cities of Italy, he gave away all his wealth to the poor. In the tenth year of his wandering he arrived in Piacenza and later in Milan, where he learned that Saints Gervasius and Protasius were detained in prison. It became known that he was visiting these martyrs and exhorting them to perseverance, and he was denounced to the prefect. Persisting as he did in confessing Christ, he was beaten with cudgels and driven out of the city. As he moved about from place to place, his mother, who had died, appeared to him and comforted her son, advising him to go as quickly as possible into Gaul. He came to a city of Gaul called Gemellus,[1] where he made a great many converts. There a lady brought her son, a charming adolescent named Celsus, and

[1] Possibly Geneva.

405

asked Nazarius to baptize the boy and to take him along with him. When this came to the ears of the prefect of Gaul, he had both Nazarius and Celsus arrested and jailed with their hands tied behind their backs, intending to subject them to torture the next day. His wife, however, sent word to him that it was unjust to sentence innocent men to death and to presume to avenge the almighty gods in this way. Her words made the prefect change his mind and he released the two saints, but warned them and strictly forbade them to preach there any longer.

Nazarius then went to the city of Trier. He was the first to preach the faith there and converted many to Christ. He also built a church dedicated to Christ. When Cornelius the governor heard of this he reported it to Emperor Nero, who sent a hundred soldiers to take Nazarius prisoner. When they found him at the oratory he had built for himself, they bound his hands and told him: "The great Nero calls for you!" Nazarius answered them: "Why didn't you come to me like honest men and say, 'Nero is calling for you,' and I would have come!"

The soldiers took him to Nero in bonds. The boy Celsus cried, and they slapped him and made him follow them. When Nero saw them, he ordered them to be shut up in prison until he devised ways of torturing them to death. Meanwhile, the emperor had sent hunters to capture wild animals, and suddenly a great pack of beasts burst into his gardens and injured and killed many people. The emperor himself was wounded in the foot and had difficulty getting away to his palace. The pain of the wound kept him immobile for many days, until he remembered Nazarius and Celsus and thought the gods were angry with him for allowing them to live so long. So, by the emperor's orders, the soldiers took the two out of prison, kicking and whipping them along, and set them down in Nero's presence. Nero saw the face of Nazarius shining like the sun and thought that this was some magic trick, so he told Nazarius to have done with his wizardries and to sacrifice to the gods. Nazarius was brought to the temple and asked all present to go outside while he stayed behind and prayed; and the idols crumbled to dust. Nero, learning of this, ordered him to be thrown into the sea, and, if by chance he escaped, to be burned alive and his ashes to be scattered over the waters.

Nazarius and Celsus were therefore put into a ship, carried out to sea, and thrown overboard. At once a violent storm broke out around the ship, while a perfect calm surrounded the two saints. The ship's crew feared for their lives and repented the wrongs they had done the saints; and behold, Nazarius and Celsus came walking over the water and boarded the ship. The crew professed the Christian faith, Nazarius prayed, the sea fell calm, and the whole company landed at a place not far from the city of Genoa.

Nazarius preached for a considerable time in Genoa, then proceeded to Milan, where he had left Gervasius and Protasius. When Anolinus, the prefect, heard of this, he ordered Nazarius into exile, while Celsus stayed in the custody of a Milanese matron. Nazarius got to Rome and found his father, now far advanced in age and a Christian. He asked his father how he had come to accept the Christian faith, and the old man replied that Saint Peter had appeared to him and counseled him to follow his wife and son.

The temple priests forced Nazarius to go back to Milan, whence he had been sent to Rome. In Milan he and Celsus were brought before the judge. Then they were led outside the Porta Romana to a place called Tres Muri, and there beheaded. Christians carried the bodies away and buried them in their gardens, but that night the saints appeared to a man named Ceratius and told him to bury their bodies deep down under his house, for fear of Nero. Ceratius said to them: "My lords, please cure my daughter first; she is paralyzed!" The girl was cured immediately, and he took the bodies and buried them as the martyrs had commanded. Long afterwards, the Lord revealed the whereabouts of the bodies to Saint Ambrose, who left Celsus's remains where they were, but found the body of Nazarius looking as if it had been buried that same day, incorrupt, giving forth a wonderful perfume, the blood fresh, the hair and beard growing. Ambrose transferred the sacred relic to the church of the Apostles and there buried it with honors. The martyrs, however, suffered under Nero, whose reign began about A.D. 57.

About this martyr Ambrose says in his Preface: "The holy martyr Nazarius by his merits ascended to the celestial realm, cleansed by his rosy blood. While he was being cruelly subjected to countless forms of torture, he withstood the tyrant's fury with unshaken constancy and could not flinch before the persecutor's threats since the real agent of victory, Christ himself, fought for him. He is led to the temple to offer a libation to the profane idols, but, strengthened by divine help, he reduced their images to dust as soon as he entered. For doing this he was projected into the flowing waters of the sea far from land, but by the help of angelic support he fashioned solid footing amidst the billows. O happy, renowned battler for the Lord, who, attacking the prince of this world, made an innumerable multitude of people participants of eternal life! O great and glorious mystery, that it is rather the Church rejoicing over their salvation than the world exalting over their damnation! O beloved mother, glorified by her children's torments—the children whom she does not consign to hell with loud grieving and groaning, but follows with perpetual laud as they pass over into the eternities of heaven! O most fragrant witness, glowing with heavenly brilliance, whose precious aroma overpowers the perfumes of Saba! Ambrose found thee and made thee his perpetual patron and physician, defender of the faith, warrior in the sacred strife":

> Tu dudum multo latitantem pulvere dragma
> Invenis accensa verbi virtute superna,
> Ut pateant cunctis tua, Christe, munera sedis,
> Angelicos cernant humanaque lumina vultus.[2]

---

[2] This coin, long hid in depth of dust / Lit by the heavenly power of the word, you lately found / That all may know, O Christ, the rewards of your abode / And human eyes may look upon angel faces.

103. Saint Felix, Pope

Felix was elected and ordained pope to fill the place of Pope Liberius, who had refused to approve the Arian heresy and had been exiled by Constantius, son of Constantine, and remained in exile for three years. For this reason the clergy of Rome, with the approval and consent of Liberius, ordained Felix to fill the latter's place. Felix then convoked a council of forty-eight bishops, before whom he condemned Emperor Constantius, and two priests who sided with him, as Arian heretics. This angered Constantius, who deposed Felix from his episcopacy, and reinstated Liberius on condition that the latter be in communion only with the emperor and those whom Felix had condemned. Liberius, weary of exile, subscribed to the perverse errors of the heretics. There ensued a persecution so savage that a great many priests and clerics within the Church were killed. Liberius did nothing to prevent this. Felix was deposed from his office and retired to his private estate, and was seized there and merited martyrdom by decapitation, about A.D. 340.[1]

104. Saints Simplicius and Faustinus

Simplicius and Faustinus were brothers. In Rome, under Emperor Diocletian, they refused to offer sacrifice and endured many kinds of torture. Finally they were sentenced and beheaded, and their bodies were thrown into the Tiber. Their sister, whose name was Beatrice, recovered their bodies from the river and gave them honorable burial. The prefect Lucretius and his vicar, who coveted

---

[1] This brief chapter is almost totally at variance with now known historical facts that were not known to Jacobus. For instance, Felix is now listed in the *Annuario pontificio* as an antipope, and he did not die a martyr in 340, but died, of unknown but presumably natural causes, in 365. For a useful brief summary of the known facts concerning Popes Liberius and Felix, see *The Oxford Dictionary of the Popes* (New York: Oxford University Press, 1989), 30–32. L. Duchesne, in his edition of the *Liber pontificalis*, pars. 59–66, discusses the situation in more detail.

their estate, had Beatrice arrested and ordered her to sacrifice to the idols. This she refused to do, and Lucretius commanded her slaves to suffocate her by night. The virgin Lucia got possession of her body and buried her beside her brothers.

Lucretius the prefect moved into the coveted property and gave a great banquet for his friends, at which he spoke disdainfully of the martyrs. Then a newborn infant, wrapped in swaddling clothes and resting in his mother's lap, exclaimed for all to hear: "Lucretius, you have killed and you have usurped, and now you are given into the possession of the enemy!" Straightaway Lucretius, fearful and trembling, was seized by the demon and for three hours was so grievously tortured that there, in the midst of the feast, he died. Seeing this, those present were converted to the faith and told everyone how the martyrdom of the virgin Beatrice had been avenged at the banquet. These martyrs suffered about the year of the Lord 287.

105. Saint Martha

Martha, who was Christ's hostess, was of royal lineage. Her father was named Syrus, and her mother, Eucharia. Her father was governor of Syria and many maritime lands. By inheritance through her mother she possessed three towns, namely Magdalum, and the two Bethanys, as well as parts of Jerusalem. Nowhere do we read that she had a husband or ever lived intimately with men. This noble hostess waited on the Lord and wanted her sister to do likewise, because, as she saw it, the whole world would not be enough to serve so great a guest.

After the Lord's ascension, when the dispersion of the disciples occurred, Martha, with her brother Lazarus, her sister Mary Magdalene, blessed Maximinus, who had baptized the sisters and to whom the Holy Spirit had entrusted them, and many others, were put on rafts by the infidels without oars, sails, rudders, or food; but with the Lord as pilot they made port at Marseilles. Then they went to the region around Aix and converted the local populace to the faith. Martha spoke eloquently and was gracious to all.

At that time, in the forest along the Rhone between Arles and Avignon, there was a dragon that was half animal and half fish, larger than an ox, longer than a horse, with teeth as sharp as horns and a pair of bucklers on either side of his body. This beast lurked in the river, killing all those who tried to sail by and sinking their vessels. The dragon had come from Galatia in Asia, begotten of Leviathan, an extremely ferocious water-serpent, and Onachus, an animal bred in the region of Galatia, which shoots its dung like darts at pursuers within the space of an acre: whatever this touches is burned up as by fire. The people asked Martha for help, and she went after the dragon. She found him in the forest in the act of devouring a man, sprinkled him with blessed water, and had a cross held up in front of him. The brute was subdued at once and stood still like a sheep while Martha tied him up with her girdle, and the people killed him then and there with stones and lances. The inhabitants called the dragon *Tarasconus*, and in memory of this event the place is still called Tarascon, though previously it had been called Nerluc, i.e., black place, because the forest thereabouts was dark and shadowy.

With the permission of Saint Maximinus and her sister, Martha stayed there and devoted herself continually to prayer and fasting. Eventually a large congregation of sisters formed around her, and a great basilica dedicated to Blessed Mary ever Virgin was built. The sisters avoided meat, fats, eggs, cheese, and wine, took food only once a day, and genuflected a hundred times a day and the same number of times at night.

It happened one day when Martha was preaching between Avignon town and the Rhone river that a youth who was standing on the other side of the river wanted to hear what she was saying; but he had no boat, so he jumped in nude and started to swim across. But the swift current caught him and he drowned. It took two days to find his body, which was brought to Martha and laid at her feet. She then lay prone on the ground, her arms extended in the form of a cross, and prayed: "Adonai, Lord Jesus Christ, you once raised my brother Lazarus, your friend, to life! My dear guest, look upon the faith of these people gathered here, and give life to this boy!" She took the lad's hand, and he stood up and received holy baptism shortly thereafter.

Eusebius reports in the fifth book of his *Ecclesiastical History* that a woman who had been miraculously cured of an issue of blood erected in her garden a statue of Christ dressed in the same garment as she had seen him in, and prayed before it devoutly. The grass that grew around the statue had never had any curative power, but now any grass that touched the hem of the garment was so filled with power that it cured many of their illnesses. Ambrose says that the woman whom the Lord cured of the issue of blood was Martha herself.

Jerome has a story, also reported in the *Tripartite History*, about the emperor Julian the Apostate. The emperor, so this story goes, took away the statue of Christ above referred to and substituted one of himself, which was struck by lightning and destroyed.

During the year before her death, the Lord revealed to Martha the time of her passing. Throughout that year she suffered continually from fevers. Then, a week before she died, she heard the angelic choirs bearing her sister's soul to heaven. She called all her brothers and sisters in religion together and said: "My companions and dear friends, rejoice with me, I beg of you, because I rejoice at the sight of the choirs of angels bearing my sister's soul to the promised mansions! O my beautiful and beloved sister, may you live in the blessed abode with him who was your master and my guest!"

At that very moment Saint Martha sensed the nearness of her own death, and cautioned her companions to keep the lamps lighted and to watch with her until she died. At midnight before the day of her passing, however, when those watching with her had fallen asleep, a strong wind swept through and blew out all the lamps. She perceived a swarm of evil spirits surrounding her and began to pray: "My father Eloi, my dear Guest! My seducers, holding lists of all the wrongs I have done, are gathered to devour me! Eloi, do not abandon me, hasten to help me!" Then she saw her sister coming to her, carrying a torch with which she lighted all the candles and lamps, and while they called to each other by name, behold, Christ came, saying: "Come, beloved hostess, and where I am, there you will be with me! You welcomed me into your house, I shall welcome you into my heaven, and for love of you I shall listen favorably to those who invoke you!"

As the hour of her death drew near, she had herself carried out of doors so that she might see the heavens, and asked that she be laid down upon ashes and a cross be held before her eyes. Then she prayed in the following words: "My dear Guest, take care of your poor little servant, and, as you deigned to accept my hospitality, receive me now into your heavenly dwelling!" Then she asked to have the passion according to Luke read to her, and at the words: "Father, into thy hands I commend my spirit," she breathed her last in the Lord.

The following day, which was a Sunday, the office of lauds was being chanted around the body of the saint, while in Perigueux, at the third hour, blessed Fronto was celebrating a solemn mass. At the reading of the epistle he fell asleep, and the Lord appeared to him and said: "My beloved Fronto, if you want to fulfill the promise you once made to our hostess, rise quickly and follow me!" In an instant they were in Tarascon and led the singing of the whole office around Martha's body while those assisting sang the responses; then, with their own hands, they laid her body in the tomb. Meanwhile, in Perigueux, the deacon, who was about to chant the gospel, woke Bishop Fronto to ask his blessing, and Fronto, barely awake, answered: "My brothers, why did you awaken me? The Lord Jesus Christ brought me to the body of Martha his hostess and we carried her to her burial! Quick, send messengers there to bring back our gold ring and silver gloves. I entrusted them to the sacristan as I prepared to bury her, and forgot to retrieve them, you woke me up so suddenly!" The messengers went and found things as the bishop had said, and brought back the ring but only one glove: the sacristan kept the other in memory of the event. Saint Fronto added a detail, saying: "As we were leaving the church after the burial, a brother from that place, who was learned in letters, followed us and asked the Lord what his name was. The Lord said nothing but showed the man an open book he was carrying in his hand, on which nothing was written except this verse: 'In perpetual memory: my hostess will be just, she will not be afraid of hearing evil on the last day'; and when the book was closed, he found that the same verse was written on each page."

Many miracles took place at the saint's tomb. Clovis, king of the Franks, had become a Christian and been baptized by Saint Remy. Suffering from a grave malady of the kidneys, he went to Martha's burial place and there recovered his health. In return for that favor he endowed the place and all the land, including villas and strongholds, for three miles around on both banks of the Rhone, declaring the area free of taxes and services.

Martilla, a servingmaid to Martha, wrote her life. Later she went to Slavonia and preached the Gospel of God there, and, ten years after Martha's death, fell asleep in the Lord.

---

106. Saints Abdon and Sennen

Abdon and Sennen suffered martyrdom under the emperor Decius. When Decius had conquered Babylonia and other provinces, he found some Christians in these regions, brought them to the town of Cordoba, and put them to death with various tortures. Two officials of that area, whose names were Abdon and Sennen, took the martyrs' bodies and buried them. When the two were denounced and brought before Decius, he had them bound with chains and brought to Rome with him. There, in the presence of the emperor and the Senate, they were ordered either to sacrifice and receive their freedom and goods, or to be devoured by wild beasts. They scoffed at the idea of sacrificing and spat upon the idols, so they were dragged to the circus, and two lions and four bears were loosed upon them. The beasts, however, would not touch the saints but rather stood guard around them, so they were put to death by the sword. Then their feet were tied together and their bodies dragged into a temple and thrown in front of an idol representing the sun god. When the bodies had lain there for three days, a subdeacon named Quirinus took them away and buried them in his house. They suffered about A.D. 253.

Later, in the reign of Constantine, the martyrs themselves revealed the whereabouts of their bodies, and Christians transferred them to the cemetery of Pontianus, where the Lord granted many benefits to the people through them.

107. Saint Germain, Bishop

The name Germanus, or Germain, is formed of *germen*, seed, and *ana*, above, hence a seed from above. Three things are found in the sprouting seed, namely, a natural warmth, a nourishing fluid, and a generative power. Saint Germain is called, as it were, a germinating seed, because in him there was warmth in the fervor of his love, fluid in the richness of his devotion, and generative power in the power of his preaching, by which he begot many in faith and morals.

His life was written by the priest Constantine and addressed to Saint Censurius, bishop of Auxerre.

Germain, noble by descent, was born in the city of Auxerre and was well instructed in the liberal studies. Then he went to Rome to study law and achieved such success that the Senate sent him to Gaul, where he attained high office in the duchy of Burgundy and took special interest in governing the city of Auxerre. In the center of that city he had a pine tree, from the branches of which he used to hang the heads of the wild beasts he had killed, as trophies of his skill as a huntsman. Saint Amator, bishop of the city, often protested against this display of vanity, warning that he would have the tree itself cut down lest some bad outcome overtake the Christians on that account, but Germain turned a deaf ear. The time came, however, when in Germain's absence the bishop ordered the tree cut down and burned, and Germain, forgetting his Christian principles, deployed soldiers to besiege the city and threatened the bishop with death. Amator, however, knew by a revelation from God that Germain was to be his successor, so he yielded to the angry governor and retired to Autun. Later he returned to Auxerre, managed to close Germain up in his church, tonsured him,[1] and predicted that he would be the next bishop. That is what happened. A short time later the bishop died a happy death, and the whole populace chose Germain to succeed him.

Germain thereupon distributed his wealth to the poor, lived with his wife as brother and sister, and for thirty years subjected his body to the strictest austerity. He never ate wheaten bread or vegetables, drank no wine, did not flavor his food with salt. He took wine only twice a year, at Easter and Christmas, but even then did away with the taste by adding too much water. He began a meal by swallowing some ashes, following this with a barley loaf; and he fasted always, never eating before evening. Winter and summer he wore only a hair shirt, a

---

[1] The tonsure, a shaved area of the scalp, was the mark of clerical status.

tunic, and a hood, and unless he gave a garment away, he kept it until it was worn to shreds. He spread ashes on his bed: its only covering was a hair shirt and a sack, and there was no pillow to rest his head on. He wept a great deal, carried relics of the saints in a pouch around his neck, never took his clothes off, and seldom loosed his belt or the fastening of his shoes. Everything he did was super-human. Indeed, such was his life that if there had not been miracles, it would have been unbelievable; and there were in fact so many miracles that, had they not been preceded by his merits, they would have seemed figments of the imag-ination.

Once when he was a guest in a certain house, after the evening meal he noticed that preparations were made for another meal. Germain wondered about this and asked for whom the preparations were made. He was told that some nice women came at night, and Saint Germain decided to stay awake that night. He did and saw a troop of demons coming to the table in the guise of men and women. Germain ordered them to stay where they were, then awakened the family and asked them whether they recognized the visitors. They answered yes, that they were all neighbors. Then, after again telling the demons not to go away, he sent to the neighbors' houses and they were all found at home and in their beds. Finally, at his command, the visitors admitted that they were demons, and that this was the way they fooled humans.

At that time blessed Lupus flourished as the bishop of Troyes. When King Attila laid siege to his city, Lupus mounted above the city gate and called out to the aggressor, asking who he was who presumed to besiege them. "I am Attila, the scourge of God!" was the answer. Weeping, God's humble prelate said: "And I am Lupus, the ravager of God's flock, alas, and I deserve the scourge of God!" Then he ordered the city gates flung open. The attackers were blinded by divine power, and rushed in by one gate and out by another, seeing no one and harming no one.

Blessed Germain took Bishop Lupus with him to Britain, where heretics swarmed. While they were at sea, a wild storm came up, but Germain prayed and a serene calm settled on the waters. The people gave honorable welcome to the two bishops, whose arrival had been foretold by the demons whom Saint Germain had driven out of the possessed. The bishops convinced the heretics of their errors, brought them back to the true faith, and returned to their own sees.

Germain lay ill in a certain place when it happened that a sudden fire swept through the whole area. The people asked him to let them carry him away so as to escape the flames, but the saint stood up and faced the fire, which consumed everything around but spared the house where he lay.

He was journeying back to Britain to refute the heretics, and one of his disci-ples, who had hastily followed him, fell ill in the town of Tonnerre. On his way home Blessed Germain had the disciple's tomb opened, called the dead man by name, and asked him whether he wanted to come back and continue to do battle at his side. The dead man sat up and answered that he was happy as he was and had no wish to be recalled to life. The saint agreed that he should resume his rest, and he again laid his head down and fell asleep in the Lord.

On one occasion while he was preaching in Britain, the king of Britain refused to give shelter to him and his companions. One of the king's swineherds, after feeding his charges and receiving his wage at the palace, was on the way home and saw Germain and his fellows in sorry straits due to hunger and the cold. He kindly took them to his cottage and had his one and only calf killed for their supper. When the meal was finished, the bishop had all the calf's bones laid upon the hide, and as he prayed over them, the calf stood up whole and entire. The next day Germain accosted the king and asked him bluntly why he had refused him hospitality. The king, overcome with astonishment, could think of nothing to say in response. Germain said: "Begone then, and leave the kingdom to a better man!" Then, by God's command, he had the swineherd and his wife summoned, and, to the amazement of all, proclaimed him king. Hence the monarchs who have ruled the British people since then are descendants of that swineherd.

Once when the Saxons were making war on the Britons and found that they were undermanned, they called to the two saints, who were passing that way. The saints preached the faith of Christ to them, and all hastened eagerly to receive the grace of baptism. On Easter Sunday their fervor was so great that they threw away their weapons and proposed to fight without them. The Britons heard this and moved swiftly against the disarmed foe, but Germain, who was in among the Saxons, told them that when he shouted *Alleluia!* they should shout *Alleluia!* all together. They did this, and their enemies were so terrified by what they took to be not only the mountains but heaven itself falling upon them that they threw down their arms and retreated on the run.

One time when Germain was passing through Autun, he visited the tomb of Bishop Saint Cassian and asked the deceased bishop how it was with him. At once Cassian responded from the tomb for all to hear, saying: "I taste my sweet repose to the full and await the coming of my redeemer!" Germain: "Rest for a long time in Christ, and intercede earnestly for us, that we may merit the joy of the sacred resurrection!"

He had occasion to go to Ravenna, and Queen Placidia and her son Valentinian welcomed him with honor. At the dinner hour the queen sent him a large silver platter packed with the most exquisite viands. He accepted this gladly, gave the food to his servants, and kept the silver platter to give to the poor. By way of a return gift he sent the queen a small wooden dish containing a barley loaf. The queen was delighted with the present and later had the dish covered with silver.

Another time the aforesaid queen had invited him to dine and he graciously accepted, but he was so weakened with praying and fasting that he had to ride an ass to the palace. Then, while the banquet was in progress, the beast of burden died. The queen learned of this and had a marvelously gentle horse caparisoned and presented to the bishop, who looked at the horse and said: "Let me have my little ass back! He brought me here, he will carry me home!" He went to the cadaver and said: "Up with you, ass, and let us get back to our inn!" The animal got to its feet, shook itself as if nothing had gone amiss, and carried Germain to his lodgings.

Before he left Ravenna, the bishop predicted that he did not have long to linger in this world. Shortly thereafter, he was stricken with fever and died in the Lord seven days later. His body was transported into Gaul, as he had requested of the queen. He died about A.D. 430.

Saint Germain had promised blessed Eusebius, bishop of Vercelli, that he would assist him in dedicating a church which Eusebius had just built. When this bishop understood that blessed Germain had died, he ordered the candles to be lighted for the dedication of the church; but as often as they were lighted, they were immediately blown out. Eusebius saw this as a sign indicating either that the dedication should take place at another time or that it should be reserved for another bishop. Then Saint Germain's body was carried into Vercelli and brought into the aforesaid church, and instantly all the candles were lighted by divine power. Then Saint Eusebius remembered Saint Germain's promise and realized that what he had promised to do while living he was doing after death. This, however, should not be understood as relating to the great Eusebius of Vercelli, or that this had happened in his time, because that Eusebius died under the emperor Valens, and more than fifty years elapsed between his death and that of Saint Germain. What we have narrated took place, therefore, under another Eusebius.

108. Saint Eusebius

The name Eusebius is composed of *eu*, which means good, and *sebe*, which means eloquent or standing. Or *eusebius* can mean good worship. The saint had goodness in his constant effort to sanctify himself, and eloquence in his defense of the faith; he stood firm when he faced martyrdom, and offered good worship in his reverence for God.

Eusebius lived a virginal life even when he was still a catechumen, and received both baptism and his name from Pope Eusebius. At his baptism the hands of angels were seen lifting him from the sacred font. A certain lady, captivated by his good looks, wanted to make her way into his bedroom, but his guardian angels forestalled her entering, and when morning came, she prostrated herself at his feet and begged his forgiveness. He was ordained to the priesthood and shone with such holiness that when he celebrated mass the hands of angels were seen serving him.

Later, when the Arian pestilence was infesting all Italy and Emperor Constantius himself abetted the heresy, Pope Julian consecrated Eusebius to be bishop of Vercelli, which at that time stood first among the cities of Italy. When the heretics heard of this, they had the doors of the principal church, which was dedicated to Blessed Mary, closed and locked; but when Eusebius entered the city, he knelt before the main portal of this church, and in answer to his prayer all the doors flew open.

Eusebius deposd Auxentius, the bishop of Milan, who was corrupted by the Arian heresy, from his see, and ordained Dionysius, a true Catholic, in his place. Thus Eusebius purged the whole Western Church of the Arian plague, as Athanasius did for the Eastern Church. Arius was a priest of Alexandria, who said that Christ was purely a creature, and declared that there had been a time when Christ did not exist and that he was made for our sake: thus God created us through Christ, using him as his instrument. Therefore Constantine the Great caused the Council of Nicaea to be convened, and there the Arian heresy was condemned. Arius himself died a miserable death in a privy.

Emperor Constantius, son of Constantine, was infected by this heresy. He was extremely angry at Eusebius, and called a large number of bishops to a council to which he summoned Dionysius. He also wrote several times to Eusebius, urging him to attend the council; but Eusebius knew that malice throve in multitude, and refused to attend, pleading his advanced age as an excuse. In response to this excuse the emperor decreed that the council would be held in the city of Milan, which was not far from Vercelli. When he saw that Eusebius was still absent, he commanded the Arians to write out a statement of their faith, and ordered Dionysius, bishop of Milan, and thirty-three other bishops, to subscribe to that statement. When word of this reached Eusebius, he left his own city and set out for Milan, predicting that he would soon suffer many hardships. He came to a river that he had to cross in order to reach Milan. There was a boat far off on the other side of the river, and at his command the boat came to him with neither rudder nor pilot, and carried him and his companions across. Then the aforesaid Dionysius came to meet him, fell to his knees, and asked for his pardon.

Eusebius continued to be unmoved by either the threats or the blandishments of the emperor, and said for all to hear: "You say that the Son is inferior to the Father. Why then do you put Dionysius, my son and disciple, ahead of me? The disciple is not above the teacher nor the slave above the master nor the son above the father." Taken aback by this reasoning, the Arians brought out the profession of faith that they had written and Dionysius had signed, and put it before Eusebius. But he said: "Never will I put my signature below that of my son, to whom I am superior in authority! So burn this document and write a new one, to which I may subscribe if you wish!" So the written statement that Dionysius and the other thirty-three bishops had signed was by God's will destroyed. The Arians immediately wrote a new copy of their profession and submitted it to Eusebius and the other bishops for their signature, but these, encouraged by Eusebius, refused to sign and rejoiced together when they saw the earlier statement, to which they had subscribed, consumed by fire.

This turn of events angered Emperor Constantius, and he handed Eusebius over to the Arians to do with as they pleased. Immediately they snatched him away from the other bishops, beat him savagely, and dragged him from the top to the bottom of the palace steps and back to the top. He lost much blood from wounds in his head but still refused to give in to them, so they bound his hands behind his back and dragged him by a rope tied around his neck. The bishop, however, gave thanks and said that he was ready to die for professing the Catholic faith.

Constantius now sent into exile Pope Liberius, Dionysius, Paulinus, and all the other bishops who had acted following Eusebius's example. The Arians brought Eusebius to Scythopolis, a town in Palestine, and confined him in a cell so low-ceilinged that he could not stand erect and so narrow that he could neither stretch out his legs nor turn from one side to the other, but crouched with bent head, able to move only his shoulders and his elbows.

Constantius died and was succeeded by Julian, who wanted to please all parties and ordered the exiled bishops to be recalled, the temples to be reopened, and everyone to live in peace under whichever law he preferred. Eusebius, now free, went to Athanasius in Alexandria and told him all that he had suffered. When Julian died and Jovinian reigned, the Arians were quiet and Eusebius returned to Vercelli, where the people welcomed him with great rejoicing. But then, in the reign of Valens, the Arians, who had increased in numbers, surrounded the bishop's house, dragged him outside on his back, and stoned him. Thus he died in the Lord and was buried in the church that he himself had built. It is said that Eusebius prayed God that a grace be granted to his city, namely, that no Arian could ever live in it. According to the chronicle he lived at least eighty-eight years. He flourished about the year A.D. 350.

109. The Holy Maccabees

The Maccabees were seven brothers who, with their venerable mother and the priest Eleazar, refused to eat pork flesh and were subjected to unheard-of tortures, as is told in full detail in the second Book of Maccabees.

It is worthy of note that the Eastern Church celebrates the feasts of saints of both the Old and the New Testaments. The Western Church, on the other hand, does not celebrate feasts of saints of the Old Testament, on the ground that they descended into hell—exceptions being made for the Holy Innocents, in each of whom Christ was put to death, and for the Maccabees.

There are four reasons for the Church's solemnizing the feast of these Maccabees despite the fact that they descended into hell. The first is that they had the privilege of martyrdom. Because among all the Old Testament saints these suffered unheard-of tortures, they are accorded the privilege of having their passion celebrated. This reason is proposed in the *Scholastic History*.

The second reason is the mystical significance of their number. The number 7 is the number of universality. In these seven saints are represented all the Old Testament fathers who deserve to be celebrated. While the Church observes no feasts for them—both because they descended into limbo and because the great multitude of new saints has slipped into their places—nevertheless in these seven she pays reverence to all, because, as has been said, seven is the number by which a universality is designated.

The third reason is the example of patience under suffering. These martyrs are set before the faithful as examples, in order that their constancy may encourage the faithful to be zealous for the faith, and to be ready to suffer for the law of the Gospel as the Maccabees girded themselves steadfastly to live by the law of Moses.

The fourth reason is the cause for which they suffered. They bore tortures for the defense of their Law, just as Christians suffer in defense of the law of the Gospel.

These last three reasons are offered by Master John Beleth in his *Summa of the Divine Offices*, chapter 5.

110. Saint Peter in Chains

The feast called (in English)[1] "Saint Peter in Chains" is thought to have been established for four reasons: to commemorate Peter's liberation, in memory of Alexander's liberation, to commemorate the destruction of a pagan rite, and to obtain release from spiritual bondage.

Firstly, the feast commemorates Saint Peter's liberation. We read in the *Scholastic History* that Herod Agrippa went to Rome and became the close friend of Caius, grandson of the emperor Tiberius.[2] One day when Herod was riding in a chariot with Caius, he raised his hands to heaven and said to his friend: "Would that I might see the death of the old man, and you the master of the whole world!" The charioteer heard this and hastened to report it to Tiberius, who resented what he heard and shut Herod up in prison. Then one day when Herod was resting against a tree in whose branches an owl was perched, a fellow prisoner who was skilled in divination told him: "Have no fear, you will be set free, and you will rise to such heights that your friends will envy you; and in the midst of this prosperity you will die. As soon as you see a bird like this one hovering over you, you will know that you have not more than five days to live!"

Not long thereafter, Tiberius died and Caius succeeded him. He freed Herod, showered him with favors, and sent him to Judea to rule as king. When Herod arrived in Judea, he set his hand to afflict members of the Church. Before the days of unleavened bread he had James, the brother of John, put to death by the sword, and then, seeing how this pleased the Jews, he arrested Peter also. That was during the days of unleavened bread, and his intention was to bring him out to the people after the Passover. An angel, however, came to Peter's assistance in the night, miraculously freed him of his chains, and ordered him to go and resume his ministry of preaching. But there could be no delay in avenging a

[1] In Latin it is called *festum sancti Petri ad vincula*, feast of Saint Peter *at the chains*, or *where the chains are*. Despite the somewhat confused account set forth in this chapter, the only fairly probable historical reason for the title of the feast is that it commemorated the rededication of an ancient church in Rome, which originally was dedicated to Saints Peter and Paul. This church is said to have become the repository of the miraculous chains of the apostle in the fifth century, and began to be referred to in the sixth century as the church of Saint Peter *ad vincula*; cf. the paragraph that begins "Saint Alexander subsequently . . ." below, and the paragraph that begins "Eudoxia, daughter of Theodosius . . ." and the following paragraph. The feast was eliminated from the Roman calendar by decision of Pope John XXIII in 1960. I borrow these details from the informative account in *Butler's Lives of the Saints* (New York: P. J. Kenedy & Sons, 1963), 3:236–237.

[2] More exactly, Gaius Caesar, third son of Tiberius, also known as Caligula.

crime against the king, and the next day Herod had the prison guards brought before him so that he could punish them as painfully as possible for letting Peter get away; but he was prevented from doing so, lest Peter's escape bring harm to anyone. Instead Herod hurried down to Caesarea, and there was struck by an angel and died.

Of this last event Josephus, in Book 19 of the *Antiquities*, gives the following account. When Herod came to Caesarea and the populace of the entire province gathered to greet him, he put on a resplendent costume wondrously woven of gold and silver, and came into the theater early in the day. When the rays of the sun struck the silvery garment, the gleam of the shimmering metal and the reflected brilliance cast a redoubled light upon the spectators. The king's formidable appearance blinded the eyes of those who gazed upon him, and his artful arrogance deceived them into thinking that there was something more than human about him. Then the voices of the flattering crowd rolled and rattled around him: "Until now we thought of you," they intoned, "as being just a man, but now we avow that you are above the nature of man!" The king took pleasure in the thought that these eulogies were no more than his due, and made no effort to disown the divine honors offered to him. Then, looking up, he spied, perched on a rope over his head, an angel—that is, an owl. He realized that this was a harbinger of approaching death, and, looking out over the assembled throng, he said: "Behold, I your god am about to die!" He knew by the soothsayer's prediction that death would claim him shortly: he was stricken immediately, for five days worms fed upon him, and he died. Thus Josephus.

To commemorate the miraculous liberation of the prince of the apostles from his chains, and the dreadful vengeance that so soon fell upon the tyrant, the Church solemnly celebrates the feast of Saint Peter *ad vincula*. The epistle sung in the mass of the feast tells how this liberation came about, and it would seem from this that the feast should be called Saint Peter *out of* chains.

Secondly, the feast commemorates the liberation of Pope Alexander, who, sixth after Saint Peter, ruled the Church. Alexander and Hermes, the prefect of the city of Rome whom the pope had converted to the faith, were held in custody in different places by Quirinus the tribune. The tribune said to Hermes: "I marvel that you, a sensible, prudent man, would put aside the honor of being prefect and dream of another life!" Hermes answered him: "Years ago I too scoffed at all those dreams and thought that this present life was the only life!" Quirinus: "Show me how you know there is another life than this one, and you will have me for a disciple of your faith!" Hermes: "Holy Alexander, whom you hold in chains, can teach you better than I can!" At this Quirinus cursed Hermes and said: "I told you to give me proof of this, and now you're sending me to Alexander, whom I hold enchained for his crimes! Anyhow I'm going to double the guards on both you and Alexander, and if by any chance I see you with him and him with you, I'll pay attention to what each of you has to say and teach!"

Quirinus doubled the guards, and Hermes got word to Alexander. Then, while the pope was at prayer, an angel came to him and brought him to Hermes' cell. Quirinus was startled to find them together. Hermes proceeded to tell Quirinus how Alexander had raised his dead son to life, and Quirinus said to Alexander: "I have a daughter—her name is Balbina—and she has a goiter. I promise you that if you can obtain a cure for her, I will accept your faith!" Alexander: "Hurry and bring her to my cell!" Quirinus: "You're here, so how will I find you in your cell?" Alexander: "Go quickly! The one who brought me here will take me back there this minute!"

Quirinus fetched his daughter and went with her to Alexander's prison, where he found the pope and knelt at his feet. Meanwhile the girl began to kiss Saint Alexander's chains devoutly, in the hope of regaining her health. Alexander said to her: "My child, do not kiss my chains, but try to find Saint Peter's bonds, kiss them reverently, and you will be cured." Quirinus therefore had the prison where Peter had been held searched for the chain with which the apostle had been bound, and when it was found, he gave it to his daughter to kiss. No sooner had she done so than she was blessed with perfect health. Quirinus thereupon besought Alexander's pardon and released him from jail, and then was baptized with his household and many other persons.

Saint Alexander subsequently instituted this feast, to be celebrated on the first day of August. He also built a church in honor of Saint Peter the apostle, enshrined the saint's chains there, and called it the church of Saint Peter *ad vincula*. This feast day brings a great concourse of people to the church, where they venerate the chains.

According to Bede, the third reason for the establishment of the feast was this. Emperor Octavian and Antony, who was his relative by marriage, divided the whole empire between them in such a way that Octavian kept Italy, Gaul, and Spain in the West, and, in the East, Asia, Pontus, and Africa belonged to Antony. Antony, however, was a debauched, lascivious man. He was married to Octavian's sister, but repudiated her and took Cleopatra, queen of Egypt, as his wife. Octavian, indignant at this outrage, marched with an army into Asia and routed Antony completely. Antony and Cleopatra fled in defeat and, overwhelmed by misfortune, took their own lives.

Octavian then destroyed the Egyptian kingdom and made Egypt a Roman province. He went to Alexandria and stripped the city of its wealth, transferring the booty to Rome, and enriched the republic so much that now one denarius bought what previously had cost four. Furthermore, since the city of Rome had been devastated by the civil wars, he rebuilt it and was able to say: "I found a city of brick, I left it a city of marble." Because he had done so much to enhance the republic, he was the first to be called Augustus, and his successors were also given that title, just as they were called Caesar after Julius Caesar, Octavian's uncle. And the month that previously had been named Sextilis (because it was the sixth counting from March) was renamed August. So it was to commemorate and honor the victory which Octavian had won on the first day of August that the Romans adopted the custom of celebrating this day until the time of Emperor Theodosius, whose reign began in the year of the Lord 426.

Eudoxia, daughter of Theodosius and wife of Emperor Valentinian, made a pilgrimage to Jerusalem in fulfillment of a vow, and there a Jew offered her, for a very high price, the two chains with which Peter the apostle had been bound in the reign of Herod. She returned to Rome on the first day of August and saw the pagan Romans celebrating the day in honor of a pagan emperor. She grieved to see so much honor paid to a man who was damned, but realized that it would not be easy to turn people away from established culture and custom. Eudoxia therefore managed the affair in such a way that the observance went on, but thenceforth in honor of Saint Peter, and that all the people would name the day *ad vincula*. She consulted with blessed Pelagius, the pope, and together they persuasively exhorted the people to allow the memory of a prince of the pagans to lapse into oblivion, and to celebrate instead the memory of the prince of the apostles.

This train of thought pleased all parties, and Eudoxia produced the chains that she had brought from Jerusalem and showed them to the people. The pope, for his part, brought out the chain with which the same apostle had been bound under Nero. When the two chains were put down side by side, they miraculously joined together, as if there had always been the one chain. The pope and the queen thereupon decided that the worship which men had wrongly given to a pagan who was damned would better be altered and given to Peter the prince of the apostles. They therefore placed the newly joined chains in the church of Saint Peter *ad vincula*, and endowed the church with many gifts and privileges, and decreed that this particular day should be celebrated everywhere. So runs Bede's account, and Sigebert's agrees with it.

The power that was in this chain became apparent in the year 964. The devil had seized upon one of the emperor Otto's counts so cruelly that in sight of everyone the man tore his own flesh with his teeth. By the emperor's order the count was brought to Pope John in order to have Saint Peter's chain placed around his neck; but when another chain was laid on the raving man, nothing good happened—and no wonder, since this chain had no power. Then, however, the true chain of Saint Peter was produced and put about the afflicted man's neck. The devil could not bear the weight of so much power, cried out, and departed while all looked on. Then Theodoric, bishop of Metz, laid hold of the chain and declared that he would not give it up unless they cut off his hand. This started a serious controversy between the bishop on one side and the pope and other clerics on the other, until the emperor put an end to the quarrel by obtaining from the pope one link of the chain for the bishop.

Miletus tells us in his *Chronicle*—and we find the same story in the *Tripartite History*—that in those days a huge dragon appeared in Epirus. Bishop Donatus, who was renowned for his virtue, first made the sign of the cross with his fingers so that the dragon could see it, then spat in the beast's maw and killed it. Eight yoke of oxen were needed to haul the carcass to the place where it was to be burned: this was necessary to avoid polluting the air with the stench of its rotting.

We read in the same two sources that the devil appeared in Crete in the guise of Moses, called together Jews from all over, and led them to the top of a precipitous mountain by the sea. He promised to go ahead of them and lead them dry-shod over the water to the Promised Land. Many followed him and were killed. It is believed that he was angry because, due to the action of the Jew who had given the chain to the queen, the honor paid to Octavian had ceased, and the devil took this means of getting his revenge. Not all those Jews, however, perished on this occasion, and many who escaped hastened to receive the grace of baptism. The mountain sloped steeply toward the sea, and when people began to roll down its face, some were torn apart by sharp rocks, others fell into the water. All died. Those who were still on the summit of the mountain, and did not know what had befallen the others, wanted to go in their turn, but some fishermen, who had seen what had happened, warned them, and so they were converted. That is what we read in the *Tripartite History*.

The fourth reason for the institution of this feast may be set forth here. The Lord miraculously loosed Peter's bonds and gave him the power to bind and to loose. We, on the other hand, are held and bound by the bonds of sin, and need to have those bonds loosed. Therefore we honor Peter on the feast called *ad vincula*, in order that as he merited to be freed of his bonds and received from the Lord the power of loosing, he may absolve us of the bonds of sin. That this really constituted a reason for the establishment of the feast is clear from the liturgical readings in the day's mass. The epistle commemorates the apostle's liberation from his chains, and the gospel narrates the conferring upon him of the power of absolution, while the prayer of the mass asks that absolution be given to us through him.

Moreover, that at times he may, by the keys he received, absolve those who are liable to damnation, is clearly demonstrated by a miracle about which we read in the *Book of the Miracles of the Blessed Virgin*. In the monastery of Saint Peter in the city of Cologne there was a monk who was light-headed, lustful, and lascivious. When he was suddenly overtaken by death, the demons accused him and loudly brought charges of all sorts of sins against him. One said: "I am your greed, which often made you covetous, contrary to God's commandments." Another called out: "I am your vain pride, which made you exalt yourself boastfully before others!" Another: "I am mendacity, in which you sinned by lying." And from others, more in the same vein. To the contrary, some good works that he had done spoke up for him in defense, saying: "I am obedience, which you paid to your spiritual elders!" . . . "I am the sacred chant, and you often chanted the Psalms to God!"

Now Saint Peter, to whose monastery the monk belonged, came before God to intercede for him. To Peter the Lord replied: "Did not the prophet, inspired by me, say, 'Lord, who shall abide in thy tabernacle? Who shall dwell on thy holy hill? He who walks blamelessly, and does what is right.'[3] How can this monk be saved, since he neither walked blamelessly nor did what is right?" But the Virgin Mother joined Peter in his pleading, and the Lord gave his judgment, namely, that the monk should return to his body and do penance. Then suddenly Peter threatened the devil with the key he held in his hand, and the demon turned and fled. Peter entrusted the monk's soul to the hands of one who had been a monk in the aforesaid monastery, ordering him to replace it in the body. The second monk demanded, as a reward for transporting the soul, that his brother monk daily recite the Psalm *Miserere mei Deus*,[4] and that he sweep out his tomb from time to time. So the monk came back from death and related all the things that had happened to him.

111. Saint Stephen, Pope

Pope Stephen converted a great many pagans by his work and example, and buried the bodies of many holy martyrs. For this double reason Emperors Valerianus and Gallienus, in A.D. 260, launched a relentless search for him and his clerics, either to compel them to sacrifice to the idols or to punish them with torture and death. The emperors also issued an edict to the effect that anyone who exposed their whereabouts could take over all their property. Ten of Stephen's clerics were apprehended and beheaded without a hearing. The following day Pope Stephen was captured and led to the temple of Mars, there to worship the god or to be sentenced to death. But as he entered the temple, he prayed God to destroy it, and at once a large section of the building collapsed and all those present fled in terror. Stephen, however, went to the cemetery of Saint Lucy.

Valerianus heard of the pope's escape and sent more soldiers than before to arrest him. They found him celebrating mass in his house. When he had finished the mass, he faced the soldiers fearlessly, and they beheaded him at his throne.

[3] Ps. 14(15):1.
[4] Have mercy on me, O God; Ps. 50(51).

112. The Finding of Saint Stephen, the First Martyr

We are told that the body of Stephen the Protomartyr was found in the year A.D. 417, in the reign of the emperor Honorius. The whole story of the finding of his body includes its transfer and its being united with the body of Saint Laurence.

The finding came about as follows. In the territory of Jerusalem there was a priest named Lucian, whom Gennadius numbered among illustrious men and who wrote the present account. One Friday evening he went to bed and was half-asleep when there appeared to him an aged man, tall, comely of feature, richly bearded, wearing a white mantle adorned with crosses and small gems, shod in gilded boots. He held in his hand a gold rod with which he touched Lucian and said: "Open our tomb with great care, because we were laid away in a very unsuitable place. Go therefore and tell Bishop John of Jerusalem that we are to be reburied in an honorable setting, because, now that the world is stricken with drought and tribulation, God has decreed that he will have mercy if our help is prayed for." The priest Lucian asked: "Sir, who are you?" "I am Gamaliel," came the answer. "I nurtured Paul and taught him the Law. And the one who lies buried beside me is Stephen, who was stoned by the Jews and cast outside the city to be eaten by birds and wild beasts; but this was prevented by him for whom the martyr kept his faith intact. I therefore took up his body with all reverence and buried it in my own new tomb.

"Also buried with me is my nephew Nicodemus, who came to Jesus by night and who received sacred baptism from Peter and John. The chief priests were angry about that and would have killed him, but were deterred by their respect for our relationship. They did, however, take away all his possessions, deposed him from his high office, beat him long and hard, and left him half dead. I carried him into my house, he lived for some days, and when he died, I had him buried at Saint Stephen's feet.

"The third body in my tomb is that of my son Abibas, who at the age of twenty was baptized with me, remained a virgin, and studied the Law with my disciple Paul. My wife Aethea and my son Selemias, who refused to accept the faith of Christ, were not worthy to be buried with us. You will find them buried elsewhere, and their places in my tomb will be found empty and bare." Having said as much, Gamaliel disappeared.

Lucian woke and prayed the Lord that if this had been a true vision, it might occur a second and third time. On the following Friday Gamaliel appeared to him as before and asked him why he had neglected to do as he had directed. "It was not that I was negligent, Sir," he answered. "I had asked the Lord to let the vision be repeated a second and third time if it was truly from God." Gamaliel said: "You have thought about how, if you found us, you would be able to distinguish the relics of each of us. I now give you clues by which you will recognize the coffin and relics of each one!" He showed Lucian three gold baskets and a fourth one of silver. One of the first three was filled with red roses, the other two with white roses; the fourth was filled with saffron. "These baskets are our coffins," Gamaliel said, "and the roses are our relics. The one with the red roses is Saint Stephen's, since he was the only one of us who merited the crown of martyrdom. The baskets filled with white roses are my coffin and Nicodemus's, because we persevered with sincere hearts in confessing Christ. The silver basket filled with saffron belongs to my son Abibas, who shone by his virginity and departed this life pure." With these words Gamaliel again disappeared.

On Friday of the following week he appeared again, angry, and sternly rebuked Lucian for his hesitancy and negligence. Lucian therefore set out immediately for Jerusalem and told Bishop John all that had happened. They called some other bishops and all went together to the place that had been made known to Lucian. As soon as they began to dig, the earth shook and a sweet odor spread, and its fragrance, by the merits of the saints, freed seventy sick people of their infirmities. The relics of the saints were transferred with great rejoicing to the church of Sion in Jerusalem, where Saint Stephen had functioned as archdeacon, and were given honorable burial there. At that very hour a great rainstorm relieved the drought.

Bede, in his chronicle, mentions this vision and the finding of the relics. Stephen's body was found on the same day of the year on which his martyrdom is commemorated and is said to have occurred.[1] The Church, however, changed the dates of the feast days for two reasons. The first was that Christ was born on earth in order that man could be born in heaven. It was appropriate, therefore, that the feast of Stephen's birth in heaven should fall close after Christ's birthday, since he was the first to suffer martyrdom for Christ, and martyrdom is the martyr's heavenly birth and follows as a consequence upon Christ's birth. Therefore the Church sings: "Yesterday Christ was born on earth, in order that today Stephen might be born in heaven."

The second reason was that earlier the finding of Stephen's body was more solemnly celebrated than was his martyrdom, so as not to diminish the reverence due to the Lord's nativity and also on account of the many miracles by which God marked the finding of the relics. But since Stephen's martyrdom was more worthy of veneration than the finding, and therefore ought to be more solemnly

---

[1] 26 December. In the old Roman calendar the Finding was celebrated on 3 August.

observed, the Church transferred the feast of his passion to Christmas week, a time when it would be held in fuller reverence.

Augustine tells us about the translation of the saint's body. He says that Alexander, a senator of Constantinople, went to Jerusalem with his wife and built a beautiful oratory in honor of Stephen the Protomartyr, stipulating that when he died, he was to be buried beside the saint. Seven years after his death Juliana, his wife, decided to return to her own homeland because some prominent men had treated her badly. She wanted to take her husband's remains with her and sought the bishop's permission. The bishop placed two silver coffins in front of her and said: "I do not know which of these is your husband's!" "I know!" she exclaimed, and, hurrying forward, took the body of Saint Stephen in her arms. So it happened that she received the first martyr's body, thinking that it was her spouse's.

When she boarded the ship for her homeward journey, having the sacred relic with her, angels' hymns were heard and a fragrant odor spread abroad. Then demons stirred up a wild storm and cried out: "Woe to us, Stephen the Protomartyr is passing by and is tormenting us with dreadful fire!" The crews were afraid the ship would be sunk, and they invoked the saint, who instantly appeared and said: "Do not be afraid, I am here!" At once a great calm stilled the tempest. Then the demons' voices were heard as they shouted: "Wicked prince, burn the ship, because Stephen our adversary is aboard!" Their prince sent five demons to set fire to the ship, but an angel of the Lord thrust them into the deep. When the vessel put in at Chalcedon, the evil spirits called out: "The servant of God whom the Jews stoned is coming!" Finally the company reached Constantinople safely and installed the body of Saint Stephen in a selected church with all due reverence. This from Augustine.[2]

The bringing together of the bodies of Saint Stephen and Saint Laurence came about in the following manner. It happened that Eudoxia, daughter of the emperor Theodosius, was sorely tormented by a demon. When news of this came to her father, who was in Constantinople, he gave orders to bring the young woman to the city and have her touch the relics of Saint Stephen; but the demon who was in her cried: "I will not go out of her unless Stephen comes to Rome, because this is the will of the apostle!" When the emperor heard this, he persuaded the clergy and people of Constantinople to agree to give Saint Stephen's body to the Romans and to accept Saint Laurence's body in exchange. The emperor wrote a letter to Pope Pelagius about this, and the pope, after consulting the cardinals, acceded to the emperor's petition. Cardinals were

---

[2] The above descriptions, here attributed to Augustine, are composed for the most part of excerpts—words, phrases, sentences, passages—taken piecemeal from several documents, none of them by Augustine, including an *Epistola Luciani ad omnem ecclesiam*, an *Epistola Anastasii ad Landuleum de scriptura translationis protomartyris*, and a *Scriptura de translatione sancti Stephani*, which are published as appendixes in vol. 7 of Augustine's *Opera omnia*, St. Maur edition (Paris, 1838).

sent to Constantinople and took Saint Stephen's body to Rome, and Greeks went there to receive Saint Laurence's remains.

The protomartyr's body was welcomed at Capua, and in response to the Capuans' pious request his right arm was left to them, and the metropolitan church was built in his honor. Then the cortege arrived in Rome. The intention was to enshrine the holy relic in the church of Saint Peter in Chains, but the bearers stopped at the door and could not move a step farther. The emperor's daughter was there, and the demon in her called out: "You labor in vain, because Stephen has chosen his resting place not here but with his brother Laurence!" They carried the body to its new destination, and when Eudoxia touched it, she was freed of the demon. Saint Laurence, as if he were congratulating himself and smiling at the arrival of his brother Stephen, moved to one side of his tomb and left the middle vacant for his brother.

When the Greeks raised their hands to carry Laurence's body away, they sank to the ground as if in a faint, but the pope, with the clergy and the people, prayed for them, and toward evening they revived; yet within ten days they were all dead. As for the Latins who had sided with the Greeks in this matter, they were seized with a frenzy and could not be cured until the bodies of the two saints were entombed together. Then a voice was heard in the heavens: "O happy Rome! You now hold within yourself the bodies of Laurence of Spain and Stephen of Jerusalem, those glorious pledges!" This joining was carried out on 20 April about the year A.D. 425.

In Book XXII of *The City of God*, Augustine tells about six dead persons who were brought to life by invoking Saint Stephen. Item: one man had been dead long enough that his thumbs were tied together, but Saint Stephen's name was invoked over him and he immediately came to life. Item: a boy had been crushed to death by a wagon, but his mother carried him to Saint Stephen's church and he was restored to her alive and well. Item: a nun who was in her last agony had been carried to Saint Stephen's church and had expired there, and then, in the sight and to the astonishment of all, rose up in good health. Item: a girl in Hippo had died. Her father took her tunic to Saint Stephen's church and later threw it over the dead girl: she rose immediately. Item: a youth whose dead body was anointed with Saint Stephen's oil came to life forthwith. Item: a boy was carried dead into Saint Stephen's church and was restored to life at once.

About this martyr Augustine says: "Gamaliel, clothed in a richly adorned garment, revealed the location of the martyr's body; Saul, stripped, stoned him; Christ, wrapped in swaddling clothes, enriched him and crowned him with precious stones." Augustine again: "In Stephen shone beauty of body, the flower of age, the eloquence of the preacher, the wisdom of a most holy mind, and the operation of divinity." Again: "This strong column of God, when he was held between the hands of stoners as by a giant vise, was enkindled by his white-hot faith, was struck down yet stood up, was strangled, throttled, beaten, yet could not be conquered." Augustine on the text *You stiff-necked people. . . :*[3] "He does not flatter, he attacks with words; does not pamper, he provokes; does not tremble, he incites." And still Augustine: "Consider Stephen, your fellow servant! He was a man, as you are, came from the mass of sin, as you did, was redeemed at the same price as you were; when he was a deacon, he read the Gospel that you read or hear, and there he found written, 'Love your enemies.' He learned this by reading, he accomplished it by obeying."

113. Saint Dominic

Dominic, or Dominicus, is like *Domini custos*, the guardian of the Lord, or *a Domino custoditus*, guarded by the Lord; or the name may be interpreted according to the etymology of the word *dominus*. Dominic is therefore called the guardian of the Lord in three ways. With regard to God, he guarded the Lord's honor. With regard to his neighbor, he guarded the Lord's vineyard or his flock. With regard to himself, he minded the Lord's will and kept his commandments. He is called Dominic as being guarded by the Lord because God guarded him in each of his states of life, as a layman, a canon regular, and an apostle. The Lord guarded him in his first state by having him start out in a praiseworthy manner, in his second by making him go forward with fervor, and in the third by enabling him to achieve perfection. And lastly, he is called Dominic according to the etymology of the word *dominus*, which is equivalent to *donans minas*, condoning threats, of *donans minus*, giving less, or *donans munus*, giving a gift. For Saint Dominic was *donans minas* because he forgave injuries, *donans minus* by mortifying his body, to which he always gave less than it desired, and *donans munus* because he not only gave what was his to the poor but also sought several times to sell himself for them.

Dominic, the illustrious leader and father of the Order of Preachers, was born in Spain, in the village of Calaroga, diocese of Osma. His father's name was Felix and his mother's Joanna; from them he took his bodily origin. Before he was born, his mother dreamed that she carried in her womb a little dog which held a lighted torch in his mouth, and when the dog came forth from her womb, he

---

[3] Acts 7:51.

set fire to the whole fabric of the world. And when Dominic's godmother lifted him from the sacred font, it seemed to her that he had on his forehead a brilliant star which shed its light over the whole world. While he was still a child in the care of his nurse, he often got out of bed at night and lay on the bare ground.

For his studies he was sent to Palentia. He was so eager for knowledge that for ten years he never drank wine. When a great famine befell the city, he sold his books and furniture and gave the proceeds to the poor. His fame spread, and the bishop of Osma made him a canon regular;[1] and later on, because his life was a mirror of virtue for all, the canons appointed him to be their subprior. He devoted himself day and night to reading and prayer, ceaselessly beseeching God to deign to give him the grace to spend himself totally for the salvation of his neighbor. He also studiously read the book of the *Conferences of the Fathers* and advanced to a high degree of perfection.

With his bishop he went to Toulouse and perceived that his host there had become tainted with heretical perversity. Dominic converted him to the faith of Christ and presented him to the Lord as a sheaf of the first fruits of the harvest to come.

We read in the *Acts of Count de Montfort* that on one occasion when Dominic had preached against the heretics, he wrote out the arguments and proofs he had used in his discourse, and gave the paper to one of the heretics so that he could give thought to his objections. That night the man showed the paper he had received to his fellow heretics as they sat around a fire. They told him to throw the document into the fire: if it burned, they said, their faith (or rather their false faith) would be proven true, but if it could not be burned up, they would preach the true faith of the Roman church. The paper was tossed into the flames, but after some minutes it sprang out of the fire intact. They were all astonished, but one, more hardheaded than the rest, said: "Throw it in again, repeat the test, and we will be surer of the truth." The writing was thrown in again and again came out unscathed. But the stubborn one said: "Try it a third time and then we will have no doubt about the outcome." Back went the paper, and again it bounced out unscorched and unharmed. The heretics, however, persisting in their willfulness, bound themselves with the strictest of oaths not to make this known. But there was a soldier present who felt drawn to our faith, and he later made the miracle public. This took place near Montréal, and it is said that a similar thing happened about that time at Fanjeaux, where a formal debate with the heretics was held.

The bishop of Osma died and most of his entourage went back home, but Saint Dominic, with a few companions, stayed on and continued to preach the word of God against the heretics. The enemies of the truth made fun of him, spat at him, threw mud and ordure at him, and in derision tied a tail of straw

---

[1] Member of a body of priests not belonging to a religious order but attached to a cathedral or other church and living in community under a rule, usually the Rule of Saint Augustine.

behind him. When they threatened to kill him, he fearlessly responded: "I am not worthy of the glory of martyrdom, I have not yet merited the death you threaten me with." So, passing through a place where they were waiting to waylay him, he went ahead not only without fear, but jauntily, singing a song. They marveled at him and said: "Are you not stricken with horror at the thought of death? What would you have done if we had laid hold of you?" He answered: "I would have asked you to put me to death not with swift, sudden blows, but slowly, cutting me to pieces, bit by bit, holding up before my eyes the pieces you had cut off, then putting my eyes out and leaving my half-dead body to welter in its own blood—or else to kill me any way you please."

Once, when he found a man who, suffering from dire poverty, had yielded to the heretics' persuasion, Dominic decided to sell himself, so that with the price he got for his own person he might put an end to the man's indigence and free him from the error into which his need had driven him. And the saint would have done it, had not God's mercy provided otherwise for the poor man.

Another time a woman, loud in her lamentations, told him that her brother was held in captivity by the Saracens, and declared that she could no longer find any means of obtaining his freedom. Dominic, moved to compassion, offered to sell himself and thus redeem the captive, but God did not allow this, foreseeing that the saint would be needed for the spiritual redemption of many captives.

In the Toulouse area Dominic was the guest of some ladies who had been led into error by the heretics' ostentatious show of religiousness. Fighting fire with fire, the saint and his companion fasted all during Lent on bread and cold water and watched throughout the night, resting their weary limbs only when necessity compelled them. Thus the ladies were led to recognize the true religion.

Now Dominic began to think about establishing a religious order whose mission it would be to go from place to place, preaching and strengthening the faith against the heretics. After he had spent ten years in and around Toulouse, from the death of the bishop of Osma to the calling of the council of the Lateran, he went to Rome with Fulk, the bishop of Toulouse, to assist at the general council. In Rome he sought permission of Pope Innocent, for himself and his successors, to found an order that would be called, and would be in fact, the Order of Preachers. The pope withheld his assent for some time. Then one night in a dream he saw the Lateran basilica about to fall in ruins; but, while he watched fearfully, Dominic, the man of God, came running from the opposite side, placed his shoulders against the tottering building, and held up the whole structure. When the pope awoke, he understood the meaning of the vision and happily entertained the petition of the man of God, advising him to return to his brethren and to choose some one of the approved rules, and then to come back to him and receive his approval. Dominic therefore returned to his brothers and informed them of the pontiff's word; whereupon they, sixteen in number, invoked the Holy Spirit, and with one mind chose the rule of Saint Augustine, the renowned doctor and preacher, and decided that they would be preachers in name and in action. To the rule of Augustine they added certain stricter practices that would be observed as constitutions. As Innocent had died in the meantime and Honorius had been elevated to the supreme pontificate, Dominic obtained confirmation of the Order from Honorius in the year of the Lord 1216.

One day while he was praying in the church of Saint Peter for the expansion of his Order, Peter and Paul, the glorious princes of the apostles, appeared to him. Peter gave him a staff, and Paul a book, and they said: "Go forth and preach, for God has chosen you for this ministry." In a moment it seemed to him that he saw his sons setting out two by two and dispersed throughout the world. He therefore returned to Toulouse and sent his brethren forth, some to Spain, others to Paris, still others to Bologna; and he himself went back to Rome.

One day, before the institution of the Order of Preachers, a certain monk was rapt in ecstasy and saw the Blessed Virgin kneeling with clasped hands, praying to her Son for the human race. Several times he seemed to resist his loving mother, but she insisted, and he said: "Dear mother, what more can I do or ought I do for them? I have sent them patriarchs and prophets, and little have they amended their ways. I came to them myself and then sent my apostles, and they put me and them to death. I sent them martyrs, doctors, and confessors, and they paid no attention to them. But it would not be right for me to refuse you anything. Therefore I shall send them my preachers, through whom they can be enlightened and cleansed. If they are not, I shall come against them."

Another monk had a similar vision about that time, when twelve abbots of the Cistercian Order had been sent to Toulouse to combat the heretics. In this vision, when the Son had given the above-mentioned answer to his mother, the Virgin said to him: "Dear Son, you must not deal with them in accordance with their evil deeds, but as your mercy dictates!" Conquered by her prayers, he replied: "At your appeal I shall grant them this mercy, that I send them my preachers to instruct and admonish them. If then they do not change their ways, I shall spare them no longer."

A Friar Minor, who had long been a companion to Saint Francis, told the following story to several friars of the Order of Preachers. While Dominic was in Rome, waiting upon the pope for approval of his Order, one night in a vision he saw Christ, aloft in the air, holding three spears that he brandished over the world. His mother ran to him and asked what he was about to do. He said: "The whole world is full of three vices, pride, concupiscence, and avarice: therefore I will destroy it with these three lances." The Virgin fell to her knees and said: "Dearest Son, have pity, and temper your justice with mercy!" Christ replied: "But do you not see the wrongs they wreak upon me?" Mary answered: "My Son, curb your wrath and wait a little, for I have a faithful servant and valiant warrior, who will go all over the world and conquer it and subjugate it to your rule! And I will give him another servant to help him, who will fight loyally at his side." Jesus said: "My anger is appeased and I yield to your plea, but I would be pleased to see these men whom you wish to commit to so high a destiny." At this she presented Saint Dominic to Christ, who said: "This is a good, strong battler, and he will be zealous in doing all that you have said." Then she brought Saint Francis to him, and Christ commended him as he had the first. Saint Dominic studied this ally whom he had not known before, and the next day, finding him in the church and recognizing him without any clue other than what he had seen the night before, hurried to him and embraced and kissed him affectionately, saying: "You are my partner, you will run with me stride for stride. Let us stand together and no adversary will prevail against us." He then told Francis about the aforesaid vision in detail. Thenceforward they were of one heart and soul in the Lord, and they made it a rule that those who would follow them should live in the same harmony for all time.

Dominic had received as a novice in his Order a certain youth from Apulia, but some of the young man's former cronies demoralized him to such an extent that he decided to return to the world and insisted on resuming his ordinary clothes. When Saint Dominic heard of this, he resorted at once to prayer; and when they had stripped the youth of his religious habit and had put on his shirt, he began to cry out with loud shouts: "Help! I am burning, I am on fire, I am totally consumed! Quick, take off this accursed shirt! It's burning me alive!" He could not be quieted until the shirt was taken off, and he was clothed again in his religious garb and led back to the cloister.

One night when Saint Dominic was in Bologna and the brothers had already gone to bed, one lay brother began to be tormented by the devil. His master, Friar Rainier of Lausanne, heard this and was careful to report it to Dominic, who ordered the brother to be carried into the church and set down before the altar. When ten of the brothers had brought him in and barely managed to hold him down, Dominic addressed the devil: "I adjure you, you wretch, to tell me why you are tormenting this creature of God, and why and how you got into him!" The evil spirit answered: "I torture him because he deserves it. Yesterday in town he drank without the prior's permission and without making the sign of the cross over the wine. So I entered him in the shape of a gnat, or rather he drank me in with the wine"; and it was ascertained that the brother had been guilty of this fault. While all this was going on, however, the first bell for matins rang, and at the sound the devil, who was speaking from inside the brother, said: "Now I cannot stay here any longer, because those cowl-heads are getting up!" Thus, at Saint Dominic's prayer, the demon was forced to come out of the man.

The saint was crossing a river in the vicinity of Toulouse, and his books, which had no wrapping around them, fell into the water. Three days later a fisherman cast his line into the river and, thinking he had hooked a big fish, hauled in the books as unharmed as if they had been carefully stowed in a cupboard.

One night Dominic arrived at the door of a monastery after the brothers had gone to bed. The saint did not want to disturb their rest, so he prayed, and he and his companion went in through the locked doors. It is also related that once when, with a Cistercian lay brother, he was engaged in combating the heretics, they reached a certain church in the evening and found it closed; but the saint prayed, and they suddenly found themselves inside the church, where they spent the whole night in prayer.

After the fatigues of a journey and before he accepted hospitality, it was his custom to quench his thirst at a spring, so that once he was in the house, his host would not think that he drank more than was usual.

A scholar who suffered temptations of the flesh came, on a certain feast day, to a house of the Order to hear mass. It happened that on that day Dominic was the celebrant of the holy sacrifice. When the time came for the offering, the scholar went forward and kissed the saint's hand with deep devotion. When he had kissed it, he sensed a perfume coming from the hand, an odor sweeter than any he had ever experienced in his life; and thereafter the heat of carnal passion was marvelously cooled in him, to the point that the young man, who had been vain and lubricious, became continent and chaste. Oh, how great was the purity and cleanness that strengthened the body of him whose odor so wondrously purged away all dirt from a soul!

A certain priest, seeing the zeal with which Dominic and his friars preached, considered joining them, if only he could obtain a New Testament that he needed for his preaching. As he thought about this, a young man came along with a Testament under his coat and offered to sell it to the priest, who bought it immediately and joyfully. But as he still hesitated a little, he offered a prayer to God, made the sign of the cross on the cover of the book, and opened it. What first met his eye was the tenth chapter of the Acts of the Apostles, and he read the words that the Holy Spirit spoke to Peter: "Rise and go down, and accompany them without hesitation; for I have sent them." He rose at once and joined the friars.

At that time there was in Toulouse a master of theology, renowned for his knowledge and good name. One morning before dawn he was preparing his lectures for the day, but felt sleepy and drowsed a little in his chair; and in a vision he saw seven stars being offered to him. Marveling at the novelty of such a present, he then saw the stars grow in size and number until they lighted up the whole world. He woke up still wondering what this meant. Behold! when he had entered the school and began his lesson, Saint Dominic and six of his friars, all wearing the same habit, humbly approached the master and, submitting their proposal to him, said that they wanted to attend his lectures. He recalled his vision and had no doubt that these were the seven stars he had seen.

While Dominic, the man of God, was in Rome, a certain Master Reginald, who was dean of Saint Amianus in Orleans and had taught canon law in Paris for five years, came to Rome with the bishop of Orleans on his way to cross the sea. The master had it in mind to leave everything else and devote himself to preaching, but did not yet see how he might go about realizing this wish. He made his desire known to a certain cardinal, who told him about the establishment of the

Order of Preachers. Summoning Dominic, Reginald informed him of his intention, and decided then and there to enter the Order. But then he was stricken with a fever so grave that his life was despaired of. Saint Dominic, however, persevered in prayer and implored the Blessed Virgin, to whom he had entrusted the care of the Order as its special patroness, to deign to grant the master to him at least for a short time.

Then Reginald, awake and awaiting death, saw the Queen of mercy coming to him accompanied by two beautiful maidens. The Queen turned her smiling face to him and said: "Ask whatever you will and I will give it to you." As he pondered what to ask for, one of the maidens counseled him to make no request, but to commend himself wholly to the Queen of mercy. He did this. The Queen extended her virginal hand and anointed his ears and nostrils, his hands and feet, with a health-giving ointment she had brought, pronouncing the proper formula at each anointing. Thus at the loins she said: "May your loins be girt with the cincture of chastity"; at the feet: "Anoint the feet in preparation of the gospel of peace." She added: "Three days from now I shall send you a phial of ointment that will restore you to full health." Then she showed him a religious habit. "Look," she said, "this is the habit of your Order." This same vision came to blessed Dominic while he was at prayer.

The next day Dominic visited Reginald and found him in health. He heard all about the master's vision and adopted the habit the Virgin had shown: the friars had been using surplices. On the third day the mother of God came and anointed Reginald's body, with the result that not only the heat of the fevers but also the fires of concupiscence were extinguished in him, so that, as he later confessed, he no longer felt the slightest movement of lust. A religious of the order of the Hospitalers also saw this second vision with his own eyes, in Dominic's presence, and was astonished. After Reginald's death the saint told many of the brothers about the vision. Meanwhile Reginald was sent to Bologna, where he devoted himself to ardent preaching, and the number of friars increased markedly. Afterwards he was sent to Paris and fell asleep in the Lord some days later.

A young man, the nephew of Cardinal Stephen of Fossa Nova, fell headlong with his horse into a ditch and was lifted out dead, but was taken to Dominic, and at the saint's prayer was brought back to life. And a master builder was conducted by the brothers into the crypt of the church of Saint Sixtus, and was crushed by the fall of a ruined ceiling and died under the debris; but Dominic, the man of God, had the body brought up from the vault and by his prayers restored the man to life and health.

One day the friars who lived at this same church, about forty in number, found that they had very little bread. Saint Dominic ordered them to put the little they had on the table and divide it into small pieces. While each friar was breaking his morsel with joy, two young men, alike in form and vesture, entered the refectory with the pockets of the cloaks that hung from their necks filled with loaves. They silently laid the loaves at the head of the table where sat Dominic, the man of God, and suddenly disappeared: no one ever found out where they came from or where they went. Dominic waved his hand all around to the friars and said: "Now, my brothers, eat!"

One day when the saint was on a journey and the rain was falling in torrents, he made the sign of the cross, and it held the rain off from him and his companion as if the cross were a sort of canopy. Though the ground was flooded by the heavy downpour, not a drop fell within three or four feet around them.

Another time he was crossing a river near Toulouse in a boat, and the boatman demanded payment of his fare. The saint promised him the kingdom of heaven for the service he was providing, and added that he himself was a disciple of Christ and carried neither gold nor money. The man, however, tugged at Dominic's cape and said: "Pay the fare or hand over your cape!" The man of God raised his eyes to heaven and prayed inwardly for a few moments, then looked down and saw a coin at his feet, put there, no doubt, by the will of God. "There is what you are demanding, brother," he said. "Take it and let me go freely and in peace."

Again in his travels it happened that he was joined by another religious who was congenial in the holiness of his life but completely foreign in speech and language. Dominic was aggrieved that he could not be warmed by a mutual exchange of holy thoughts, and prayed the Lord to grant that when they conversed, each of them might speak the language of the other; and so they understood each other during the three days they traveled together.

Once a man who was possessed by many demons was brought to Dominic. He took a blessed stole and wrapped one end around his own neck and the other around the neck of the possessed man, and commanded the demons to stop molesting the man and not to bother him any longer. But the spirits began to be tortured in the man's body and cried out: "Let us go free! Why do you force us to stay here and be tortured?" The saint answered: "I will not let you go until you give me a surety that you will not enter him again." "Who would stand surety for us?" they asked. He answered: "The holy martyrs, whose bodies rest in this church!" The demons said: "We cannot give them as surety because our deserts are against it." "You had better give them," he said, "because otherwise I will by no means release you from torment." To this they responded that they would try, and after a while they said: "Despite our unworthiness we have obtained the help of the holy martyrs, and they will be our surety." He required a sign to confirm this, and they said: "Go to the casket in which the martyrs' heads are preserved, and you will find it turned around." And it was found that what they said was true.

Once when he was preaching, some women who had been led into error by the heretics threw themselves at his feet and said: "Servant of God, help us! If what you preached today is true, our minds have long been blinded by the spirit of error." He replied: "Be of good heart and wait a moment, and you will see what sort of god you have followed." At once they saw a hideous cat leap out from their midst: he was as big as a large dog, had huge, flaming eyes, a long, wide, bloody tongue that reached to his navel, and a short tail that stood up and exposed the filth of his hind parts whichever way he turned, and emitted an intolerable stench. After the beast had stalked to and fro around the women for some time, he climbed up the bell rope and disappeared into the belfry, leaving foul traces behind him. The women therefore gave thanks and were converted to the Catholic faith.

At Toulouse, Saint Dominic once convicted a number of heretics, and they were condemned to be burned alive. Looking over them, he saw a certain man, whose name was Raymond, and said to the executioners: "Save that man, do not let him be burned with the rest." Then he turned to Raymond and said to him kindly: "I know, my son, I know that one day, even though it may be years away, you will be a good man and a saint!" Raymond was freed, therefore, and persisted in heresy for twenty years. Then he was converted and entered the Order of Preachers, led an admirable life, and died a happy death.

When Dominic was in Spain with some of the friars as companions, he saw in a vision a monstrous dragon trying to draw the brothers into its open jaws. He understood the meaning of the vision and exhorted the friars to be firm in the faith, but later all of them, except Friar Adam and two lay brothers, left him. When he asked one of those who remained if he too wished to depart as the others had done, he answered: "God forbid, father, that I should leave the head to follow the feet!" The saint prayed and prayed, and within a short time, through his prayer, he converted almost all of those who had defected.

He was with the friars at Saint Sixtus in Rome when suddenly the Holy Spirit came over him. He brought the brothers together in chapter and publicly announced to all of them that four of their number would soon die, two the death of the body and two the death of the soul. Shortly thereafter, two friars migrated to the Lord and two others left the Order.

Dominic was in Bologna, where there was a certain Master Conrad the Teuton, whose entrance into the Order the friars very much desired. On the vigil of the feast of the assumption of the Blessed Mary the saint was exchanging confidences with the prior of the Cistercian monastery of Casa Mariae, and among other things he said to him: "Prior, I am going to tell you something I have never revealed to anyone, and that you must not tell anyone else as long as I live; and that is that I have never in this life asked God for anything which I did not obtain according to my wish." The prior remarked that he himself might come to the end of his life before the saint, but Dominic, moved by the spirit of prophecy, told him that, on the contrary, he would long survive him; and that is the way it turned out. Then the prior said: "Father, ask God to give Master Conrad to the Order, since the brothers so earnestly want him to enter." Dominic answered: "Good brother, you are asking for a very hard thing!" But after the hour of compline, when all had gone to rest, Dominic remained in the church and, as he usually did, prayed throughout the night.

In the morning, when the community came together for prime and the cantor intoned the hymn *Jam lucis orto sidere* (The star of light being already risen), Master Conrad, who was to be the new star of a new light, suddenly came up, prostrated himself at Saint Dominic's feet, and begged to receive the habit of the Order, which he received forthwith. Thereafter there was no more devout religious than he in the Order, nor any master whose lessons were received with more favor. And when at last he lay dying and had closed his eyes, so that the friars thought he had expired, he opened his eyes and looked around at the brothers, and said: "*Dominus vobiscum!*" They responded: "*Et cum spiritu tuo!*" Conrad added: "*Fidelium animae per misericordiam Dei requiescant in pace*" and fell asleep in the Lord.

In Dominic, the servant of God, there was a firm evenness of spirit, except when he was moved by compassion or pity; and since a joyous heart makes for a glad countenance, he manifested his inward composure by his outward gentleness. By day, when he was with his brothers and associates, there was none more affable, though with due modesty and discretion; in the night hours none was more constant in watchings and prayers. Thus he gave the day to his neighbor and the night to God. From his eyes there flowed what seemed to be a fountain of tears. Oftentimes, when the Body of the Lord was lifted up in the mass, he was rapt in such an ecstasy of spirit that he might have been looking upon Christ present in the flesh. For this reason he did not usually hear mass with the others. It was his frequent custom to pass the night in the church, so that he scarcely ever seemed to have a fixed place to rest; and when weariness overcame him and he yielded to the need for sleep, he lay down for a little while either before the altar or resting his head on a stone. Three times in the night he took the discipline with his own hand, using an iron chain—once for himself, once for sinners still in this life, and once for those who were suffering in purgatory.

He was once elected bishop of Conserano but refused absolutely to accept, declaring that he would rather quit the earth than consent to any such preferment. And sometimes, when he was in the diocese of Carcassonne, he was asked why he would not more willingly stay in his own diocese of Toulouse, and his answer was: "Because in Toulouse I find many who honor me, whereas in Carcassonne, on the contrary, everyone attacks me!" And when someone asked him in what book he had studied the most, he replied: "In the book of love."

One night while Dominic, the man of God, was praying in his church in Bologna, the devil appeared to him in the guise of a friar. The saint, thinking that he was one of his brethren, nodded to him to go to his rest with the others; but the devil mocked him by making the same sign. Then the saint, wishing to learn who it was that treated his orders so lightly, lit a candle at one of the lamps and, looking into the other's face, recognized him as the evil spirit. He reproached him vehemently, and the devil in turn upbraided him for breaking the rule of silence by speaking to him. But the saint declared that as master of the brethren he was permitted to speak, and then commanded him to say how he tempted the friars in choir. The demon answered: "I make them come too late and leave too soon!" Dominic led him to the dormitory, asking how he tempted the brothers there. The reply: "I make them sleep too long and rise late so that they miss the office, and I give them impure thoughts." Next to the refectory, Dominic asking the same question: the devil hopped about among the tables, saying over and over: "More and less, more and less!" Dominic inquired what that meant, and the devil replied: "I tempt some of the brothers to eat too much, and so they sin by gluttony, and others I tempt to eat too little and so they become weak in the service of God and the observance of the rule." Dominic led him to the parlor and again asked how he tempted the brothers there. In reply he rolled his tongue rapidly, producing a weird confusion of sounds; and being asked what this meant, he said: "This place belongs entirely to me! When the friars come here to talk, I studiously tempt them to prattle all at the same time, to confuse each other with idle words, and never to wait to hear what the other is saying." Finally, the saint led his adversary to the chapter room, but when he stood before the door, the devil would not enter and said: "Never will I go in there! For me it is a place of malediction, a hell! All that I gain elsewhere I lose there! For when I have caused a brother to sin by some negligence, quickly he comes to this accursed place and purges himself of his fault, admitting it before all. Here they are admonished, here they confess, here they are accused, here they are whipped, here they are absolved! And so, to my chagrin, I lose all I had been so happy to win elsewhere!" and with that he vanished.

When at last the term of his earthly pilgrimage drew near, Saint Dominic, being at the time in Bologna fell seriously ill. The imminent dissolution of his body was shown to him in a vision in which he saw a youth of surpassing beauty, who said to him: "Come, my beloved, come to joy, come!" He therefore called together the twelve friars of the priory at Bologna, and, so as not to leave them orphaned and without a heritage, gave them his testament. He said: "These are the things I bequeath to you in rightful possession, as my sons and heirs: have charity, keep humility, possess poverty!" He sternly forbade that anyone should bring temporal possessions into his Order, laying almighty God's terrible curse and his own on whoever might dare to besmirch the Order of Preachers with the dust of earthly riches. And as the friars were mourning inconsolably at being abandoned by him, he comforted them gently, saying: "Do not let my departure in the flesh trouble you, my sons, and be sure that I shall serve you better dead than alive!" Thereupon, being brought to his last hour, he fell asleep in the Lord in the year 1221.

His death was revealed to Gualis, the prior of the Friars Preachers at Brescia and later bishop of that city. Gualis had fallen into a light slumber, leaning against a wall in the belfry of the convent, when he saw the heavens opened and two white ladders let down to the earth, the one being held by Christ and the other by the Blessed Virgin; and angels joyously mounted and descended. Between the ladders, at the bottom, was a seat upon which a friar, his head covered, was seated. Jesus and his mother drew up the ladders until the friar was lifted into heaven, and the opening closed behind him. Gualis set out at once for Bologna and there learned that Dominic had died the very day and hour of his vision.

A friar named Rao went to the altar, in Tibur, to celebrate mass, at the very hour of the father's death. He had heard that the saint was ill in Bologna, and, when he came to the commemoration of the living in the canon of the mass, wished to pray for his recovery; but at that moment he was rapt in ecstasy, and saw Dominic, the man of God, crowned with a gold crown and shining with wondrous brightness, setting out from Bologna on the royal road, accompanied by two venerable men. Rao noted the day and the hour, and found that Dominic had departed this life at the time of the vision.

When his body had already lain underground for a long time, and his sanctity could no longer be hidden because of his miracles, which increased daily in number, the devotion of the faithful led them to transfer the saint's relics to a more honorable place. When with great effort and the use of iron tools the mortar had been broken, the stone removed, and the sarcophagus opened, an odor of such sweetness came forth that it might have come from a storeroom of perfumes rather than from a tomb. This odor was more powerful than any aromatic, and unlike the odor of any natural thing; and it penetrated not only the bones and dust of the sacred body and the coffin in which it was buried, but also the earth that was heaped around it, so that when later the earth was carried to distant places, it still retained the aroma for a long time. The fragrance also clung to the hands of the brothers who had touched the relics, so that no matter how often they were washed or rubbed together, the evidence of the perfume lingered.

In the province of Hungary a certain nobleman came with his wife and little son to visit the relics of Saint Dominic, which were preserved in Silon. But the child fell ill and died, and his father carried his body before the saint's altar and began to lament, saying: "Saint Dominic, merry I came to you and mournful I go away, for I came with my son and I go home having lost him. I beg of you, give back the joy of my heart!" And at midnight the boy returned to life and walked around in the church.

Another time a young man, the slave of a noble lady in Hungary, was fishing when he fell into the river and drowned, and his body was recovered only after a long time. The lady prayed Saint Dominic to restore him to life, and promised in return to go barefoot to venerate his relics and to give the slave his freedom. The youth was promptly brought back to life and leapt up in the sight of all, and the lady fulfilled her vow.

In the same province of Hungary a man was weeping bitterly over the death of his son and called upon Saint Dominic to bring him to life. At cockcrow the boy who had died opened his eyes and said to his father: "How is it, father, that my face is wet?" The man replied: " Your father's tears have fallen upon it, my son, because you were dead and I was left alone, bereft of all joy." The boy said: "You have shed many tears, father, but Saint Dominic took pity on your grief and by his merits obtained my return to life."

A man who had lain sick and blind for eighteen years wanted to visit the relics of Saint Dominic, and rose from his bed as if to go and do so. Suddenly he felt a surge of strength and set out at a rapid pace, and the farther he went day after day, the more both his bodily condition and his eyesight improved, until at last, when he reached his destination, he was fully cured of both infirmities.

Again in Hungary, a matron wished to have a mass celebrated in honor of Saint Dominic, but when the time for mass came there was no priest available; so she took the three candles she had prepared, wrapped them in a clean towel, and put them in a vase. She left for a short time and, coming back, saw the candles burning brightly. Many ran to see this great sight, and stood trembling and praying until the candles had burned out without damaging the towel in the least.

In Bologna a scholar whose name was Nicholas suffered such pain in the loins and the knees that he could not get out of bed, and his left thigh was so withered that he had lost all hope of cure. He therefore dedicated himself to God and Saint Dominic. Then, measuring his own full length with thread used for candles, he wound the thread around his body, neck, and chest. When he bound his knee with it, calling at each turn upon the names of Jesus and Dominic, he suddenly felt relief from his pain and cried out: "I am freed!" Then, weeping for joy and needing no crutch, he went to the church where Saint Dominic's body reposed.—In that city God, through his servant Dominic, worked miracles almost beyond counting.

At Augusta in Sicily there was a girl who suffered from the stone and was about to have it cut out; and her mother, in this dangerous situation, commended her to God and Saint Dominic. The following night the saint appeared to the girl, placed in her hand the stone that had causd her so much pain, and departed. When she awoke and found herself cured, she gave the stone to her mother and told her all about the vision. The mother took the stone to the friars' house and, to commemorate this great miracle, hung it in front of an image of Saint Dominic.

In the city of Augusta some women, after attending the solemn mass for the feast of the Translation of Saint Dominic in the friars' church, were on the way home when they saw a woman spinning wool on her doorstep. They chided her charitably for not abstaining from servile work on the great saint's feast, but she was indignant and retorted: "Observe your saint's feast yourselves, you friars' pets!" Instantly her eyes were infected with an itching tumor and worms began to wriggle out, until a neighbor woman pulled off eighteen of them. Stricken with remorse, the afflicted woman went to the friars' church, confessed her sins, and made a vow never again to speak ill of Dominic the servant of God and to observe his feast devoutly. At once she was restored to the health that had been hers.

In Tripoli, in a monastery named for the Magdalene, there was a nun called Maria, who was gravely ill and for five months had suffered from an infected leg so painful that her death was expected hour by hour. She gathered her thoughts and prayed as follows: "Dear Lord, I am not worthy to pray to you or to be heard by you, but I ask my lord the blessed Dominic to be my mediator with you and to obtain for me the blessing of recovery." When she had prayed, weeping, for a long time, she was rapt in ecstasy and saw Saint Dominic with two friars. He drew back the curtain that hung around her bed and said to her: "Why are you so eager to be healed?" She answered: "My lord, so that I may be able to serve God more devoutly." The saint then took out a marvelously fragrant ointment from under his cape and anointed her leg, and it was cured instantly. Then Dominic said: "This ointment is very precious, very sweet, and very hard to preserve." The nun asked him his reason for saying this, and he replied: "This ointment is a sign of love, and love is precious because it cannot be bought at any price, and because of all God's gifts none is better than love. It is sweet because nothing is sweeter than love, and hard to preserve because it is quickly lost if not kept with great care."

That night the saint also appeared to the nun's sister, who was asleep in the dormitory, and said: "I have cured your sister." She ran to her sister and found her in good health. Meanwhile Maria, knowing that her leg had been anointed, dried it reverently with a silk cloth. When she had told her abbess, her confessor, and her sister all that had happened, she produced the silk cloth with the ointment still on it; they were so struck with the strength and strangeness of its fragrance that they could think of no perfume with which to compare it, and put away the cloth to be preserved with reverence.

How pleasing to God the place is where the sacred body of Saint Dominic rests one miracle will suffice to show, though many miracles have made it famous. Master Alexander, bishop of Vendôme, in his notes on the text (Ps. 85:11) *Mercy and truth have met each other: justice and peace have kissed*, tells us that a certain student, who lived in Bologna and was given to worldly pleasures, saw a vision. It seemed to him that he was standing in a wide field, and a huge storm cloud hung over him. He ran to escape the tempest and came to a house, which he found closed. He knocked at the door and asked for shelter, but a woman's voice answered from within: "I am Justice, I live here and this is my house, and you cannot come in because you are not a just man!" Grieved by these words he went along and spied another house farther on. He knocked and asked admittance, but a lady inside answered: "I am Truth, I live here and this is my house, and I will not admit you because truth sets no one free who does not love truth."

Going farther he came to a third house and again begged for shelter from the storm. The lady of the house replied: "I am Peace, I live here, and there is no peace for the impious but only for men of good will. But because I think thoughts of peace and not affliction, I shall give you a word of good advice. My sister lives close by and she always offers help to those in need. Go to her and do as she tells you." When he got to the house, a voice answered: "I am Mercy, and I live here. If you want to be saved from the coming storm, go to the house where the Friars Preachers live. There you will find the stable of penance and the manger of continence and the pap of doctrine, the ass of simplicity with the ox of discretion; and Mary will enlighten you, Joseph will perfect you, and the Child Jesus will save you." When the scholar awoke, he therefore went to the friars' house, recited his vision, asked for admission to the Order, and received the habit.

114. Saint Sixtus

Sixtus comes from *Sios*, meaning God, and *status*, state or condition; hence, divine state. Or it comes from *sisto, sistis*, the verb that means to stand; hence Sixtus was one who stood fixed and firm in faith, or suffering, or doing good.

Pope Sixtus, an Athenian by birth, began as a philosopher, but later became a disciple of Christ and was elected supreme pontiff. With two of his deacons, Felicissimus and Agapitus, he was brought before the emperor Decius. The emperor, failing to persuade him to change his mind, had him led to the temple of Mars to offer sacrifice there, or, if he refused, to be imprisoned. Blessed Laurence followed him, calling out: "Where are you going, father, without your son? Whither are you hurrying, holy priest, without a minister?" Sixtus answered: "I am not deserting you, my son, nor abandoning you, but greater trials for the faith of Christ await you! Three days from now you, the levite,[1] will follow me, the priest! Meanwhile take the church's treasure and distribute it as you see fit." When Laurence had distributed the treasure among the Christian poor, the prefect Valerianus decreed that Sixtus was to be brought to the temple

---

[1] Under Jewish law the term *levite* was eventually reserved for sanctuary ministers who were not priests (descendants of Aaron) but were considered to be of the family of the patriarch Levi. In the Middle Ages deacons were called levites.

of Mars to offer sacrifice, or, if he refused, to be beheaded there. As he was led to the temple, blessed Laurence began to call after him: "Do not forsake me, holy father, because I have already given away your treasures, which you handed over to me!" The soldiers, hearing money mentioned, took Laurence prisoner, but beheaded Sixtus, Felicissimus, and Agapitus then and there.

This day is also the feast of the Lord's transfiguration. In some churches, on this day, the Blood of Christ is consecrated from new wine—when new wine can be made and is available—or at least a ripe grape is squeezed into the chalice. Also on this day clusters of grapes are blessed, and the people consume them as a form of communion. The reason for this is that the Lord, at the Last Supper, said to his disciples: "I shall not drink again of this fruit of the vine until that day when I drink it new with you in my Father's kingdom."[2] His transfiguration, and the new wine of which he spoke, represent Christ's glorious renewal after his resurrection; and therefore it is on this feast of the transfiguration, which represents the resurrection, that new wine is called for—not because the transfiguration happened on this day, as some say, but because the apostles made it known on this day. It is said, indeed, that the Lord's transfiguration took place early in the spring of the year, but that the disciples, having been forbidden to tell anyone of the vision until Christ was raised from the dead,[3] kept it a secret until they made it known on this day. This is what we read in the book called *On the Mitral Office*.

115. Saint Donatus

Donatus comes from *a Deo natus*, born of God, and this birth is threefold—by rebirth, by infusion of grace, and by glorification, hence a threefold generation by the Spirit or by God. For when saints die, it is then that they are said to be born, so the demise of a saint is not called death but birthday. A child strives to be born, so as to have more room to live in, more food to feed on, a freer air to breathe, and light to see by. And because saints issue from the womb of Mother Church through death, they gain these four things according to the mode of each and therefore are said to be born. . . . Or the name Donatus is equivalent to *dono Dei datus*, given by the gift of God.

[2] Matt. 26:29.   [3] Matt. 17:9.

Donatus was reared and nurtured with the emperor Julian up to the time when the said Julian was ordained subdeacon; but when he was elevated to the empire, he put the saint's father and mother to death, and Donatus took flight to Arezzo, lived with the monk Hilary, and wrought many miracles. When, for instance, the prefect brought his son, who was possessed of a demon, to Donatus, the unclean spirit began to cry out, saying: "In the name of the Lord Jesus Christ, do not make trouble for me or drive me out of my house, O Donatus! Why do you torment me and expel me?" And when Donatus prayed for the boy, he was soon liberated.

Then there was a man named Eustochius, a tax-collector in Tuscany, who left the public monies in the care of his wife, Euphrosina. But when the province was overrun by enemies, the woman hid the funds, and shortly afterwards illness carried her off. When the husband returned, he could not find the money and was due to be put to the torture with his sons, but he resorted to Donatus for help. Donatus went with him to his wife's tomb, prayed there, and then said in a loud voice: "Euphrosina, I adjure you by the Holy Spirit, tell us where you put that money!" And a voice came from the tomb, saying: "I buried it near the door of my house!" They went there and found the money as she had said.

Some days later Bishop Satyrus fell asleep in the Lord, and the clergy unanimously elected Donatus to succeed him. Gregory tells us in his *Dialogues* that once, when the mass was being celebrated and at communion time the deacon was ministering the Blood of Christ to the people, some pagans pushed the deacon and he fell, and the holy chalice was broken. The deacon and all the people were saddened by this accident, but Donatus gathered up the fragments, prayed over them, and restored the chalice to its former condition. The devil, however, hid one fragment and it was lacking in the repaired chalice, but its absence proves the reality of the miracle. The pagans saw the miracle, and eighty of them were converted and received baptism.

A certain spring was so polluted that anyone who drank from it died immediately. Saint Donatus, mounted on his ass, was passing that way and purified the water by his prayer, whereupon a frightful dragon burst out of the spring, coiled its tail around the ass's legs, and reared itself up against Donatus. The saint struck the beast with his whip, or, as we read elsewhere, spat in its mouth, and killed it. He also prayed to the Lord, and all the poison was gone from the spring. Another time, when he and his companions were suffering from thirst, he prayed and a spring gushed from the earth at their feet.

A daughter of the emperor Theodosius was possessed of the devil and was brought to Saint Donatus, who said: "Foul spirit, go out of her, and dwell no longer in this handiwork of God!" The demon: "Give me a way out and some place to go!" Donatus: "Where did you come from?" The demon: "From the desert!" Donatus: "Go back there!" The demon: "I see the sign of the cross on you, and fire comes out of it and burns me! I'm so afraid that I don't know where to go, but give me a clear way out and I'll go!" Donatus: "There's your clear way! Go back where you belong!" The demon left, shaking the whole house as he left.

A dead man was being carried to his grave, when another man appeared with a written bill in his hand and declared that the deceased owed him two hundred sols, and that he could not be buried until the money was paid. The widow, in tears, told blessed Donatus about this, adding that the man had already been paid in full. Donatus came to the bier, touched the dead man with his hand, and said: "Listen to me!" The deceased responded: "I'm listening!" Saint Donatus said to him: "Get up and settle your accounts with this man who won't let you be buried!" The dead man sat up, proved to everybody that he had paid his debt, took the bill, and tore it to pieces. Then he said to Saint Donatus: "Father, command me to go back to sleep!" Donatus: "Go now, my son, and take your rest!"

At that time no rain had fallen for almost three years, and the land was utterly barren. The infidels flocked to Emperor Theodosius, asking him to turn Donatus over to them, on the ground that he had brought on the drought by his magical art. At the emperor's request, therefore, Donatus came out and prayed the Lord, bringing down great floods of rain. Then, while all the others were drenched by the downpour, he went back to his house as dry as before.

The Goths were ravaging Italy at the time, and many Christians had abandoned the faith of Christ. Saint Donatus and Saint Hilarian went to the prefect Evadracianus and took him to task for his apostasy, but he arrested the two saints and tried to make them sacrifice to Jupiter. When they refused, he had Hilarian stripped and beaten until he breathed his last. Donatus he shut up in prison, and later had him beheaded, about the year A.D. 380.

116. Saint Cyriacus and His Companions

Cyriacus, who was ordained a deacon by Pope Marcellus, was apprehended with his companions and brought before Maximian, who ordered them to dig and carry the earth on their shoulders at a place where a public bath was under construction. There they found the aged Saint Saturninus, and Cyriacus and Sisinnius helped him with the carrying. Finally Cyriacus was put in prison, and the prefect called for his presence. Apronianus was leading him in when suddenly a voice coming with light from heaven said: "Come, O blessed of my

Father, inherit the kingdom prepared for you!" Apronianus believed, had himself baptized, and came before the prefect confessing Christ. The prefect: "What! Have you too become a Christian?" Apronianus: "Woe is me, that I lost so many days before I believed!" "Right you are!" the prefect retorted. "You'll lose all your days now!" And he dispatched him to be beheaded. When Saturninus and Sisinnius refused to offer sacrifice, they suffered various tortures and were beheaded.

Diocletian's daughter Arthemia was tormented by a demon, and the demon in her cried out: "I will not go out of her unless Cyriacus the deacon comes here!" So Cyriacus was brought, and when he commanded the demon to go away, the spirit answered: "If you want me to come out, give me some container to go into!" "Here's my body," Cyriacus replied. "If you can, come in!" The demon: "I can't come into your body, because it is sealed and closed on all sides. But if you force me out, know that I will make you go to Babylonia!" The demon was compelled to leave her, and Arthemia declared that she saw the God whom Cyriacus preached. The saint baptized her and went to live in security in a house graciously granted him by Diocletian and his wife Serena.

Shortly thereafter a messenger came from the king of the Persians, with the request that Diocletian send Cyriacus to him, because his daughter was possessed of a devil. The emperor asked Cyriacus to go, and the saint, taking Largus and Smaragdus with him, embarked in a well-provisioned ship and happily went off to Babylonia. When he came to the young woman, the demon called out through her mouth, saying: "Are you tired, Cyriacus?" "No, I'm not tired," said Cyriacus, "but wherever I go, I am governed by God's help!" "Yet I made you come where I wanted you to come!" said the demon.

Now Cyriacus said to the evil spirit: "Jesus commands you to come out!" And the demon, coming out at once, said: "Oh, that dread name! It forces me to go!" So the girl was cured, and the saint baptized her with her father and mother and a number of others. Many gifts were offered him, but he refused to accept them. Then he fasted on bread and water for forty-five days, after which he returned to Rome.

Two months later Diocletian died and Maximian succeeded him. Maximian was angry about his sister Arthemia and had Cyriacus arrested, then ordered him to be dragged, naked and loaded with chains, in front of the emperor's chariot. This Maximian could be called Diocletian's son in that he was his successor and was married to his daughter Valeriana. He next commanded his deputy, Carpasius, to compel Cyriacus and his companions to offer sacrifice, or else to put him to death with torture. So Carpasius had boiling pitch poured over the saint's head, hung him on the rack, and had him beheaded with all his companions.

Carpasius then got possession of Saint Cyriacus's house. In mockery of the Christians he bathed in the place where Cyriacus had usually baptized, and gave a banquet for nineteen of his cronies, at which, at the same moment, all of them died. After that the bath was closed and the pagans began to fear and respect the Christians.

117. Saint Laurence, Martyr

Laurence, or Laurentius, comes from *lauream tenens*, holder of a laurel wreath, because in the past victors or winners were crowned with laurel wreaths. The laurel tree is symbolic of victory, being delightful for its continuous greenness, and having a pleasant odor and powerful efficacy. So blessed Laurence is named for the laurel because he won victory in his martyrdom, which moved the emperor Decius, astonished, to say: "I really think we are already defeated." He had greenness in the cleanness and purity of his heart, whence he said: "My night has no darkness." He had a lasting odor of sweetness because the memory of him is perpetual, as the Psalm says: "He has distributed freely, he has given to the poor; his righteousness endures for ever."[1] Blessed Maximus says: "How would the righteousness of such a man not live on eternally—righteousness brought to perfection in his work and consecrated in his glorious martyrdom?" His efficacy showed in his powerful preaching, by which he convinced Lucillus, Hippolytus, and Romanus. The efficacy of the laurel tree consists in that it breaks up the stone, remedies deafness, and wards off lightning. Thus Laurence broke down hardness of heart, restored spiritual hearing, and provided protection against the lightning of a sentence of damnation.

Laurence, martyr and levite,[2] a native of Spain, was brought to Rome by Pope Saint Sixtus. Master John Beleth has it that this Saint Sixtus went to Spain and there came across two young men, Laurence and Vincent his cousin, both distinguished for their honorable lives and actions. He took both of them to Rome, and one of them, Laurence, stayed with him in Rome, while Vincent went back to Spain and finished his life by a glorious martyrdom. However, the dates of the martyrdoms of both Vincent and Laurence make Master Beleth's opinion questionable. Laurence suffered under Decius, and Vincent, still young in age, under Diocletian and Dacian. But between Decius and Diocletian there was an interval of forty years, during which seven emperors reigned, so that Vincent could not still have been a young man.

Blessed Sixtus ordained Laurence his archdeacon. At that time the emperor Philip and his son Philip accepted the faith of Christ and, having become Christians, did their best to exalt the Church. This Philip was the first emperor to accept the Christian faith. It is said that it was Origen who converted him,

---

[1] Ps. 111(112):9.

[2] Deacons were called levites, and Laurence was one of the seven deacons of Rome in the pontificate of Sixtus II (257–258).

although elsewhere we read that it was Saint Pontius. Philip reigned in the thousandth year from the foundation of the city of Rome, so that Rome's thousandth year might be dedicated to Christ rather than to the false gods. The millennium was celebrated by the Romans with a huge display of games and spectacles.

Emperor Philip had a certain general named Decius, skilled in the arts of war and famous. Gaul was rebelling at the time, and the emperor sent Decius to bring the rebellious province securely under the yoke of the Roman Empire. Decius carried out his mission successfully and, having achieved the victory he desired, started back to Rome. The emperor learned that he was on his way and, wishing to pay him honor, went from Rome to Verona to meet him. But when bad men feel themselves honored, they become elated with pride, and Decius began to covet the empire and to ponder how he might get rid of his master. So, one day when the emperor was resting on his bed, Decius stole into the tent and strangled his sleeping lord. Now he had to win over the army that had come north with the emperor. He did this with pleas and bribes, gifts and promises, and then led them by forced marches to the royal city.

When the younger Philip heard this, he was afraid and, as Sicardus says in his *Chronicle*, placed all his father's wealth and his own in the care of Saint Sixtus and Saint Laurence, so that, in case Decius killed him also, they could distribute the treasure to the churches and the poor. Do not let it bother you that the treasure which blessed Laurence dispensed is not called the emperor's but the Church's, because it might well be that he did dispense some of the Church's wealth along with that of Emperor Philip; or perhaps the distributed wealth is called the Church's in view of the fact that Philip had left it to the Church to be given to the poor. Moreover, there is serious doubt, as will be noted further on, that Sixtus was alive at that time.

However that may be, Philip got away and hid from Decius, and the Senate proceeded to confirm the latter as emperor. Decius wanted the killing of his lord to appear not as treason but as zeal for the gods of Rome. He therefore began a savage persecution of the Christians, ordering that they were to be slaughtered without mercy. Many thousands of martyrs fell in this persecution, and the younger Philip himself won the crown of martyrdom.

Decius now inaugurated a search for the emperor Philip's wealth, and blessed Sixtus was pointed out to him as one who worshiped Christ and had possession of the emperor's treasure. Decius ordered him to be jailed and tortured until he denied Christ and gave up the treasure. As he was led away, blessed Laurence followed him and called out: "Where are you going, father, without your son? Whither are you hurrying, holy priest, without a deacon? You never used to offer the holy sacrifice without a minister! What is it about me that has displeased your paternity? Have you tested me and found me unworthy to be your son? Try me, surely, to see whether you have chosen a minister suitable to have the dispensing of the Lord's Blood entrusted to him!" Saint Sixtus answered: "I am not deserting you, my son, nor abandoning you, but greater trials await you for the faith of Christ! We old men reach the goal by an easier race. The more glorious triumph over the tyrant is left to you as a young man. Three days from now you, the levite, will follow me, the priest!" And he gave all the treasures into Laurence's care to be dispensed to the poor.

Blessed Laurence then sought out Christians by day and by night, and ministered to all according to their needs. He came to the house of a certain widow who had hidden many Christians in her house. She had long suffered from pains in her head, and Saint Laurence, by laying on his hands, freed her of that pain. He also washed the feet of the poor and gave alms to all. The same night he came to the house of another Christian and found a blind man there, over whom he made the sign of the cross, restoring his sight.

Meanwhile blessed Sixtus refused to yield to Decius or to sacrifice to the idols, and the emperor commanded that he be led to execution. Blessed Laurence ran after him and called out: "Do not abandon me, holy father, because I have already given away the treasures that you entrusted to me!" The soldiers, hearing of money, took Laurence and passed him on to the tribune Parthenius. He in turn presented him to Decius, and Decius Caesar said to him: "Where is the Church's money, which we know is hidden with you?" When Laurence did not answer, Decius handed him over to the prefect Valerian, with orders to make him give up the treasure and sacrifice to the idols, or to die under torture. Valerian put another prefect, named Hippolytus, in charge of him, and he shut Laurence up in jail with a number of other prisoners. Among them was a pagan named Lucillus, who had wept so much that he had lost his sight. Laurence promised that he would make him see again if he believed in Christ and received baptism, and Lucillus begged to be baptized as soon as possible. Laurence got some water and said to him: "Confession of faith washes all clean!" He then questioned Lucillus closely about the articles of faith, and Lucillus confessed that he believed all of them, whereupon Laurence poured the water over his head and baptized him in the name of Christ. For this reason many who were blind came to him and went away with their sight restored.

Now Hippolytus, having observed all this, said to Laurence: "Show me the treasure!" Laurence: "O Hippolytus, if you believed in the Lord Jesus Christ I would show you the treasure and also promise you eternal life!" Hippolytus: "If you do what you say, I will do what you are urging me to do!" That same hour Hippolytus believed and received baptism with his family; and after being baptized he said: "I have seen the souls of the innocents rejoicing!"

After that, Valerian ordered Hippolytus to bring Laurence before him. Laurence said to Hippolytus: "Let us walk side by side, because glory is prepared for me and for you!" They came to the tribunal and again were asked about the treasure, and Laurence requested a delay of three days, which Valerian granted, leaving the saint with Hippolytus. During the three days Laurence brought together the poor, the lame, and the blind, and then presented them before Decius in the Sallustian palace, saying: "See here the eternal treasure, which never diminishes but increases. It is divided among these people and is found in all of them, for their hands have carried the treasure off to heaven!" Valerian: "You talk too much! Stop talking, sacrifice now, and leave your magic aside!" Laurence: "Who ought to be adored, the one who is made or the Maker?" This aroused Decius's anger, and he ordered Laurence to be whipped with scorpions and punished before him with all sorts of tortures. The saint was told to sacrifice in order to escape this treatment but answered: "Unhappy man, this is the banquet I have always desired!" Decius: "If this is a banquet, name some others as impious as yourself, and they can come and feast with you!" Laurence: "They have already given their names in heaven, and therefore you are not worthy to look upon them!"

Decius ordered the headsmen to strip Laurence and beat him with clubs, and to press hot blades to his sides. Laurence said: "Lord Jesus Christ, God from God, have mercy on me your servant, because, being accused, I have not denied your holy name, and being put to the question I have confessed you as my Lord!" Decius said to him: "I know you have eluded these torments by means of your magic, but you're not going to elude me any longer! I swear by the gods and goddesses that unless you offer sacrifice, you will die a slow and painful death!" He then commanded that Laurence be beaten long and hard with lead-laden whips. Laurence prayed: "Lord, receive my spirit!" But a voice, which Decius heard, sounded from heaven, saying: "You have still to endure many trials!" Decius, filled with rage, said: "Men of Rome, you have heard the demons consoling this blasphemer, who does not worship our gods, does not fear torments, does not quail before angry princes!" He ordered him beaten again with scorpions. Laurence smiled, gave thanks, and prayed for those who stood by.

At this time a soldier named Romanus received the faith and said to blessed Laurence: "I see a beautiful young man standing in front of you and wiping your limbs with a towel! I adjure you by God, do not abandon me, baptize me quickly!" And Decius said to Valerian: "I really think we are defeated by this man's magic art!" At his command, Laurence was taken from the stake and again confined in care of Hippolytus. Romanus brought a jar of water, knelt at Laurence's feet, and was baptized by him. Decius learned of this and had Romanus beaten with cudgels; and when Romanus freely professed that he was a Christian, Decius had him beheaded.

That same night the saint was haled before Decius. When Hippolytus wept and cried out that he was a Christian, Laurence said to him: "Hide Christ in the inner man, listen, and when I call, come!" Decius said to Laurence: "Either you will sacrifice to the gods, or you will spend the night being tortured!" Laurence: "My night has no darkness, and all things gleam in the light!" Decius gave his orders: "Let an iron bed be brought, and let this stubborn Laurence rest on it!" The executioners therefore stripped him, laid him out on the iron grill, piled burning coals under it, and pressed heated iron pitchforks upon his body. Laurence said to Valerian: "Learn, wretched man, that your coals are refreshing to me but will be an eternal punishment to you, because the Lord himself knows that being accused I have not denied him, being put to the question I have confessed Christ, and being roasted I give thanks!" And with a cheerful countenance he said to Decius: "Look, wretch, you have me well done on one side, turn me over and eat!" And giving thanks, he said: "I thank you, O Lord, because I have been worthy to pass through your portals!" And so he breathed his last. Confounded, Decius went off with Valerian to the palace of Tiberius, leaving the body on the fire, and Hippolytus took it away in the morning, anointed it with spices, and, with the priest Justin, buried it in the Veranus field. Christians kept vigil, fasting, for three days, lamenting and weeping.

There are many who question whether it is true that Laurence suffered martyrdom under this Emperor Decius, since we read in the chronicles that Sixtus came long after[3] Decius. Eutropius, however, makes this assertion: "When Decius moved to persecute the Christians, among others he slew the blessed levite and martyr Laurence." In another fairly authentic chronicle it is said that it was not under Emperor Decius, who succeeded Philip, that Laurence suffered martyrdom, but under a younger Decius, who was caesar but not emperor; for between the emperor Decius and this younger Decius, under whom Laurence is said to have suffered, a number of emperors and popes intervened. This chronicle also says that Emperor Decius was succeeded by Gallus and his son Volusianus, and they in turn by Valerian and Gallienus. The said Valerian and Gallienus set up the younger Decius as caesar but did not make him emperor. Sometimes, in antiquity, some emperors were made *Caesares* but not *Augusti*, or emperors in the full sense. Thus we read in the chronicles that Diocletian made Maximian a caesar, and later raised him to Augustus. At the time of the emperors Valerian and Gallienus, Sixtus occupied the see of Rome. Therefore this Decius Caesar, so called, who subjected blessed Laurence to martyrdom, was not made an emperor and is never called *Decius imperator*, but only *Decius Caesar*, in the legend of Saint Laurence.

The emperor Decius reigned only two years,[4] and he put Pope Fabian to death. Cornelius succeeded Fabian and suffered martyrdom under Volusian and Gallus. Cornelius was succeeded by Lucius and Lucius by Stephen. Pope Stephen suffered under Valerian and Gallienus, who ruled fifteen years, and Sixtus succeeded Stephen. This is what we read in the chronicle mentioned above. All the chronicles, including those by Eusebius, Bede, and Isidore, agree that Pope Sixtus did not reign in the time of Emperor Decius but in that of Gallienus. In another chronicle, however, we read that the said Gallienus went

---

[3] Graesse notes (493) that the Ed. Pr. has *ante* (before), while "others" have *post* (after). What follows in the text shows that *post* is correct.

[4] 249–251.

by two names, for he was called Gallienus and Decius, and under him Sixtus and Laurence suffered about A.D. 257.[5] Godfrey, in his book called *Pantheon*, says the same thing, namely, that Gallienus was called by another name, Decius, and that Sixtus and Laurence suffered under him. And if this is true, then Master John Beleth's position can also be true.

In his *Dialogues* Gregory says that there was a nun in Sabina who practiced continence in the flesh but made no effort to control her tongue. She had been buried in the church of Saint Laurence before the martyr's altar, but demons cut her body in half, and one half remained unscathed but the other was burned, so that in the morning the scorching was apparent to the eye.

Gregory of Tours says that a certain priest was repairing the church of Saint Laurence and found that one of his timbers was too short. He prayed to the saint, reminding him that he always helped the poor and asking him to supply this particular need. Suddenly the timber grew not only to the desired length but beyond it, so the priest sawed off the extra piece and cut it into small bits, with which many infirmities were cured subsequently. Blessed Fortunatus also testifies to this miracle, which occurred in the place in Italy called Brione.

Pope Gregory, in his *Dialogues*, has the story of another priest, Sanctulus by name, who was rebuilding a church of Saint Laurence that had been burned down by the Lombards, and hired a number of craftsmen to do the work. Then one day he had no food to give them. He prayed, then looked into his oven and found a fine loaf of white bread. It did not look big enough to make one meal for three people, but Laurence, unwilling to let the workmen go hungry, multiplied the loaf in such a way that it fed them all for ten days.

Vincent, in his chronicle, reports that the church of Saint Laurence in Milan possessed a crystal chalice of extraordinary beauty. The deacon was carrying this chalice to the altar in the course of some solemn ceremony, when the chalice slipped out of his hands, fell to the floor, and was shattered. The deacon, grief-stricken, collected the fragments, put them on the altar, and prayed to Saint Laurence; and the chalice came together whole and undamaged.

We also read in the *Book of the Miracles of the Blessed Virgin* that in Rome there was a judge named Stephen, who gladly accepted bribes and in return rendered crooked decisions in many cases. Thus, for instance, he alienated three houses belonging to the church of Saint Laurence and a garden belonging to the church of Saint Agnes, and held them unjustly in his possession. Then he died and went before the judgment seat of God. Laurence came up wrathful and twisted the man's arm three times, so hard that the pain was excruciating. Saint Agnes and other virgins could not bear to look at the miscreant and turned their faces away. Then the Judge pronounced sentence upon him, saying: "Since this Stephen

---

[5] The year usually given is 258, but history knows the emperor as Publius Licinius Egnatius Gallienus (not Decius), who reigned with his father Valerian from 253 to 260, and alone, after Valerian's death, from 260 to 268.

appropriated what did not belong to him, and by taking bribes sold the truth, let him be held in the same place with Judas the traitor." But now Saint Projectus, to whom the said Stephen had been very devoted in his lifetime, went to Saint Laurence and Saint Agnes and pleaded for their pardon. The two saints and the Blessed Virgin prayed for the culprit, and it was granted that his soul should return to his body and he should do penance for thirty days. From the Blessed Virgin he received the added command to recite the Psalm *Beati immaculati in via*[6] every day. When he came back to life in his body, his arm was black and burned, as if he had suffered this in the flesh, and that mark was on him as long as he lived. He made restitution of all his ill-gotten goods, did penance, and on the thirtieth day migrated to the Lord.

We read in the life of the emperor Saint Henry[7] that, though he and his wife Saint Cunegund lived as virgins, the emperor, at the devil's instigation, once suspected her of infidelity with a certain knight. He therefore made her walk barefoot a distance of fifteen feet over plowshares reddened in the fire, and as she stepped forward to do so, she said: "O Christ, as you know that I have never been touched by Henry or any other man, help me now!" But Henry was ashamed of her and struck her in the face, whereupon a voice said to her: "The virgin Mary has delivered you, a virgin!" So she strode over the glowing mass unharmed. When the emperor died, a huge crowd of demons passed by the cell of a hermit, who opened his window and asked the last demon in line who they were. "We are a legion of demons," he answered, "hurrying to be in at the death of the caesar, if by chance we can discover anything in him that belongs to us!" The hermit adjured him to stop on the way back; and on his return the demon told him: "We gained nothing, because when his false suspicion and other misdeeds were put on our side of the scale, that roasted Laurence came up with a very heavy gold bowl, and, just as we seemed to have won, he tossed the bowl on the other side and it far outweighed ours. I was so angry that I broke off a piece of the gold bowl!" What the demon called a bowl was a chalice, which the said emperor had ordered for the church at Eichstätt in honor of Saint Laurence, whom he held in special veneration. The chalice was so large that it had two handles, and it was discovered that at the moment of the emperor's death one of the handles had broken off.

Pope Gregory reports in his *Register* that when his predecessor wanted to obtain a cure for someone at Saint Laurence's body but did not know where the body was, suddenly the saint's body came to light where they had not known it to be, and all, monks and those who were attached to the church, who were present and saw the body, died within ten days.[8]

---

[6] Ps. 118(119):1, "Blessed are those whose way is blameless."

[7] Henry II, emperor of the Holy Roman Empire 1002–1024.

[8] Graesse notes (495) that the Ed. Pr. "omits" this episode. He does not say where he found it, nor why he saw fit to include this incongruous tale.

It may be noted that the passion of Saint Laurence is seen to stand out above the passions of the other martyrs, and this for four aspects of it, as we gather from the writings of Saint Maximus and Saint Augustine. The first aspect is the bitterness of his sufferings, the second, their effectiveness or usefulness, the third, his constancy or fortitude, the fourth, his wonderful fight and the mode of his victory.

First, then, his martyrdom stands out by the bitterness of his sufferings, as the holy bishop Maximus—or, according to some books, Ambrose—says: "Blessed Laurence did not undergo some brief or simple suffering. Anyone who dies by the sword dies once: one who is thrust into a furnace is liberated by one push: but Laurence was smitten with long and multiple tortures, so that he was dying all through his suffering yet did not die to end it. We read that the holy youths walked in the flames to which they were sentenced and trod upon glowing balls of fire, but Saint Laurence earned more glory than they. If they walked amid the flames, he lay stretched over the fire of his torture; and if they could trample down the fires with the soles of their feet, he contained the fire by the way his body was spread over it." They stood in pain with their hands uplifted, praying to the Lord; he, prostrate in his pain, prayed the Lord with his whole body.

Remark also that blessed Laurence is said to stand with Saint Stephen in first place among the martyrs, not because he bore greater pain than they, since we read that many of them bore as much pain and some even more. What is said above is said for six concurrent reasons. Firstly, due to the place where the saint suffered, which was Rome, the capital of the world and the apostolic see. Secondly, because of his ministry of preaching, since he fulfilled that ministry diligently. Thirdly, there is his praiseworthy distribution of the treasures, all of which he judiciously handed out to the poor. Those three reasons are put forth by Master William of Auxerre. Fourthly, his martyrdom is authenticated and approved, because, while greater torments are attributed to some others, their authenticity is uncertain and is sometimes held to be doubtful. In the Church, on the other hand, Laurence's passion is very solemnly celebrated and approved, and many saints certify and confirm it in their sermons. Fifthly, his high rank, because he was the archdeacon of the apostolic see, and after him, it is said, there was no longer an archdeacon in the see of Rome. Sixthly, there was the severity of his torments, because he endured the most painful tortures, being roasted on an iron grid. About this martyr Saint Augustine says: "[The prefect] ordered that his limbs, cut and torn by the blows of the scourges, be placed over a fire and alternately turned from one side to the other, so that, by means of the iron grill, which, because of its continual firing, had power in itself to burn, the pain would be made more violent and would last longer."

The second aspect that confirms the high eminence of his passion among martyrs is its effectiveness or usefulness. The bitterness of his suffering, according to Augustine and Maximus, made him sublime in glorification, celebrated in esteem and fame, praiseworthy by the devotion in which he was held, and distinguished for the imitation he attracted.

Firstly, he was sublime in glorification, whence Augustine says: "You raged, O persecutor, against the martyr, you planted his palm and made it grow as you heaped up his pains." Again Maximus, or, according to some, Ambrose: "Although you reduced his members to ashes, the fortitude of his faith was not reduced: he endured the loss of his body but won the prize of salvation." And again Augustine: "O truly blessed body, which torment could not turn from the faith of Christ, but holy religion crowned unto eternal rest in heaven!"

Secondly, he was celebrated in esteem and fame. Maximus, or, according to some books, Ambrose: "We may compare the blessed martyr Laurence to the mustard seed, because, rubbed and crushed by many sufferings, he merited to spread throughout the whole earth the fragrance of his mystery. Previously he was unimpressive in body, unknown and unrecognized, a nobody: after he was tortured, torn apart, roasted, he infused all the churches throughout the world with the aroma of his nobility." Again Augustine: "It is a holy thing and pleasing to God that we venerate the birthday of Saint Laurence with special devotion, because the Church of Christ, victorious by his radiant flames, on this day beams her light over the world." And again: "This noble martyr has gained so much glory in his passion that he has illuminated the entire world."

Thirdly, he was praiseworthy for the devotion in which he was held. Augustine explains why he should be praised and held in such devotion, giving three reasons. He says: "We should look to the blessed man with wholehearted devotion, first because he shed his precious blood for God, next because it won for him the high privilege before our God of showing what the Christian faith should be since the martyrs were worthy to come from its society, and thirdly, that his way of living was so holy that he found the crown of martyrdom in the time of peace."

Fourthly, his passion made him a model inviting imitation. Augustine: "The motive behind his whole passion, the motive by which the holy man was bound and committed to die, was to exhort others to be like him." He showed us three ways in which we could imitate him. The first is the strength with which he endured adversity. Augustine: "Eloquence is an easy means of exhortation and an effective means of persuasion; but examples are stronger than words, and deeds teach more powerfully than speech." His persecutors themselves could sense how glorious and worthy the blessed martyr Laurence was in this most excellent kind of teaching: his marvelous fortitude of spirit not only did not weaken, but by the example of his tolerance gave strength to others. The second way is the greatness and fervor of his faith. Maximus or Ambrose: "In his faith he conquered the persecutor's flames, and showed us that the fire of faith can overcome the fires of hell and the love of Christ can banish fear of the Day of Judgment." The third way is the ardor of his devotion. Maximus or Ambrose:

"Laurence shed light on the whole world in the light by which he was burned, and warmed the hearts of all Christians by the flames he endured." Regarding these three ways of imitating him, Maximus—or, as some books have it, Ambrose—says: "By blessed Laurence's example we are called to martyrdom, enkindled to faith, and warmed to devotion."

The third aspect by which Saint Laurence's passion stands out above the passions of other martyrs is his excellent constancy or fortitude in suffering. Saint Augustine says about his constancy and fortitude: "Blessed Laurence stayed firm in Christ throughout the tyrant's interrogation and fierce threatening, all the way to death itself. And because he had well eaten and drunk of that long-drawn-out death, being fattened by that food and drunk with that chalice he felt no torment, yielded no whit, but rose to the kingdom." So constant was he that he not only did not succumb to torture, but through the torture, as Saint Maximus says, he became more powerful in fear of the Lord, more fervent in love, more joyous in ardor. About the first of these he says: "He was stretched out over the flaming coals and often turned from side to side, but the more pain he suffered, the more patient he became in the fear of Christ the Lord." As to the second, Maximus, or, according to some books, Ambrose, says: "The mustard seed grows hot when rubbed: Laurence, when he suffers, is inflamed." Again: "A new kind of wonder! One persecutor tortured him and others, enraged, tried to improve their ways of tormenting him, but all that these keener sufferings did was to make Laurence more devoted to his Savior." Regarding the third way the same author says: "His heart was so strengthened by his faith in the greatheartedness of Christ that, paying no attention to the pain his body was suffering, he joyfully and triumphantly taunted his insane tormentor and his fires."

The fourth aspect under which Laurence's passion stands out in excellence is his wonderful fight and the mode of his victory. Blessed Laurence, as we gather from Maximus and Augustine, fought in some way against five external fires, which he bravely overcame and extinguished. The first was Gehenna, the fire of hell; the second, the fire of material flame; the third, the fire of carnal concupiscence; the fourth, that of grasping greed; the fifth, that of raging madness.

As to the extinguishing of the first of these fires, namely, the fire of hell, Maximus says: "Could one whose faith extinguished the eternal fire of Gehenna flinch from a momentary burning of the body?" The same: "He passed through a brief earthly fire but avoided the flame of the eternal fire of hell." Regarding the extinction of the second fire, namely, that of material flame, Maximus, or Ambrose according to some books: "He suffers a bodily fire, but divine love cools the material heat." Again: "A wicked king may throw wood on and build up a fiercer fire, but blessed Laurence does not feel those flames, due to the heat of his faith." Augustine: "The love of Christ could not be conquered by any flame, and the fire that burned on the outside was less ardent than the fire within."

About the extinguishing of the third fire, namely, carnal concupiscence, Maximus says: "Behold, Laurence passed through that fire, which, though it did not burn him, made him cringe but also gave him light by its light; it burned lest it burn, and he burned lest he be burned." As for the fire of avarice, and how the greed of those who coveted the Church's wealth failed and was frustrated, Augustine says: "The man who is greedy for money and an enemy of truth is armed with two torches—avarice, which seizes gold, and impiety, which takes away Christ. Cruel man, you gain nothing, you make no profit! The mortal material you looked for is taken from you, Laurence is gone away to heaven, and you perish in your flames."

As for the fifth fire, namely, the madness of the furious persecutor, Maximus tells how it was frustrated and brought to nothing: "Having conquered those who kept the fires burning, he extinguished the fire of madness that was spreading on all sides. Thus far the devil's effort had produced just one result, namely, that the faithful man ascended in glory to his Lord; and the cruelty of his persecutors sputtered and went out with their fires." He shows that the rage of the persecutors was a fire when he says: "The fury of the pagans, being enkindled, prepares a fired grill, in order to avenge by fire the flames of their indignation."

It should cause no surprise that Saint Laurence mastered these five external fires, since, as the aforementioned Maximus says, he carried three refrigerants within himself as well as three fires in his heart, by which he moderated all external fire by cooling it, and surpassed it with the greater heat of his ardor. The first refrigerant was the longing for the kingdom of heaven; the second, meditation on the divine law; and the third, purity of conscience. Through this triple refrigeration he cooled and put out all external fires. Of the first refrigerant, the desire of heaven, Maximus, or, according to some books, Ambrose, says: "Blessed Laurence, who in his senses possessed the coolness of paradise, could not feel the torment of fire." The same: "At the tyrant's feet lies Laurence's burned flesh, his lifeless body; but he whose soul already dwells in heaven suffers no harm on earth." Of the second refrigerant, meditation on the divine law, Maximus, or Ambrose, says: "While his thoughts are of Christ's precepts, anything he suffers is cool." Of the third, purity of conscience, the same author says: "This bravest of martyrs is hot and burned in every fiber of his body, but his mind is fixed on the kingdom of heaven, and by the coolness of his conscience he emerges an exultant victor."

As the same Maximus shows, Laurence also had three internal fires, by the greater heat of which he conquered all external fires. The first of the three was the greatness of his faith; the second, his ardent love; the third, his true knowledge of God, which irradiated him like fire. Of the first, the same author or Ambrose says: "As much as the ardor of his faith burned, by so much the flame of torture was cooled." That the ardor of faith is the Savior's fire we read in the Gospel: "I came to cast fire on the earth."[9] With that fire in him, Laurence did not feel the heat of flames. Of the second inner fire, the same or Ambrose says: "Laurence the martyr was burned externally by the raging tyrant's fires, but the greater flame of the love of Christ heated him inwardly." Of the third fire he says: "The persecutor's fiercest fire could not defeat this mighty martyr, because his mind was heated far more warmly by the rays of truth. Being afire with hatred of perfidy and with love of truth, he either did not feel or overcame the flames that burned him outwardly."

The office of Saint Laurence has three privileges that do not apply to the offices of other martyrs. The first is that alone among the feasts of martyrs, his feast has a vigil. The vigils of feasts of the saints have now been replaced by fasts because of many disorders. In the past, as Master John Beleth reports, the custom was that on the feasts of the saints the men, with their wives and daughters, went to the church and there spent the night by torchlight; but because many adulteries occurred during these vigils, it was decreed that the vigils be converted into fasts. The old name persisted, however, and the fasts are still called vigils. The second privilege is that Laurence's feast has an octave, as no other martyr's does except Saint Stephen, and no confessor's except Saint Martin. The third consists of the repetition of antiphons, which only Saint Laurence and Saint Paul have—Paul on account of the excellence of his preaching, Laurence for the excellence of his passion.

118. Saint Hippolytus and His Companions

The name Hippolytus comes from *hyper*, above, and *litos*, stone or rock; hence one who is founded on rock, the rock being Christ. Or the name comes from *in* and *polis*, city, and the word is equivalent to *politus*, polished, refined. Saint Hippolytus was indeed well founded on Christ the rock by his constancy and firmness, was in the city on high by desire and eagerness, and was polished and made smooth by the bitterness of the torments he endured.

---

[9] Luke 12:49.

After he buried Saint Laurence's body, Hippolytus went back to his house, gave the peace to his servants, men and women, and gave them all communion with the Sacrament of the Altar that the priest Justin had consecrated. The table was then set, but before he took food, soldiers came, arrested him, and led him to the emperor. When Decius Caesar saw him, he sneered and said: "So you too have become a sorcerer, and you took away Laurence's body!" Hippolytus: "I did not do that as a sorcerer but as a Christian!" Decius, beside himself with fury, ordered him to be stripped of the garment he wore as a Christian, and to be beaten about the face with stones. Hippolytus said to him: "You haven't stripped me, rather you've clothed me!" Decius: "How can you be so stupid, not even blushing at your nakedness? Now offer sacrifice and you will live, or else perish with your Laurence!" Hippolytus: "May I be made worthy to follow the example of Laurence, whose name you dare to pronounce with your filthy mouth!"

Decius had him beaten with rods and torn with iron rakes, but Hippolytus continued to proclaim loudly that he was a Christian. When he scorned the torments, the emperor made him put on the military apparel he had previously worn, reminding him of his military status and friendships. Hippolytus retorted that he soldiered for Christ, and Decius, his anger rising, turned him over to the prefect Valerian with orders to take possession of everything he owned and to put him to death. When it was learned that his whole household was Christian, they were all brought before the prefect and ordered to sacrifice to the idols. Concordia, his nurse, answered for all: "We wish to die chastely with our master, rather than to live dishonorably." Valerian: "Slaves can be corrected only by severe punishment!" While Hippolytus watched and rejoiced at the sight, the prefect had Concordia beaten with leaded whips until she breathed her last. Hippolytus exclaimed: "I give you thanks, O Lord, because you have sent my nurse ahead to enjoy the vision of your saints!"

Valerian now had Hippolytus and all his people led out beyond the Porta Tiburtina, and Hippolytus, to strengthen their resolve, said: "My brothers and sisters, don't be afraid! You and I have one and the same God!" Valerian commanded that all of them be beheaded while Hippolytus looked on, and that Hippolytus be tied by the feet to the necks of untamed horses and dragged over thistles and thorns until he expired. This happened about A.D. 256.

The priest Justin retrieved their bodies and buried them beside the body of Saint Laurence, but he could not find Saint Concordia's body because it had been thrown into the sewer. One of the soldiers, whose name was Porphyrius, thought Concordia might have been carrying gold or gems in her clothing, and he sought out one Ireneus, who secretly was a Christian, and said to him: "Keep this secret and get Concordia out of the sewer! I hope she had money and jewels in her clothes!" Ireneus said: "Show me the place! I'll keep the secret, and I'll let you know what I find!" But when he had pulled the body out of the sewer and found nothing, the soldier made his escape at once, and Ireneus, after calling in a Christian named Abundus, took the body to Saint Justin, who accepted it piously and buried it beside those of Saint Hippolytus and the others. When Valerian found out about this, he arrested Ireneus and Abundus and threw them alive into the sewer, and Justin rescued their bodies and buried them with the rest.

After that, Decius and Valerian mounted a golden chariot and rode into the circus to watch the Christians being tortured. But Decius was seized by a demon, and he cried out: "O Hippolytus, you are holding me bound in rough chains!" Valerian likewise cried: "O Laurence, you are dragging me with fiery chains!" Valerian died then and there, but Decius got back to his house. He was tormented for three days by the demon and pleaded: "I adjure you, Laurence, don't torture me this way!" But he died a miserable death nonetheless.

Now Triphonia, the wife of Decius, seeing what had happened, received the faith. She dismissed her people and went to Saint Justin with her daughter Cyrilla, and had the priest baptize them and many others with them. A few days later Triphonia expired while at prayer, and Justin buried her body beside that of Hippolytus. Forty-seven soldiers heard that the queen and her daughter had become Christians, so they went with their wives to Justin the priest, asking to be baptized; and Dionysius, who had succeeded Sixtus as pope, baptized them all. Claudius, now the emperor, had Cyrilla strangled when she refused to sacrifice, and ordered the soldiers beheaded. The bodies of all of them were buried with the rest in the Veranus field.

Note that here it is explicitly stated that Claudius succeeded the Decius who martyred Laurence and Hippolytus. This Decius was succeeded, according to the chronicles, by Volusianus, Volusianus by Gallienus, and Gallienus by Claudius. Therefore we should say (or so it seems) that previously Gallienus had two names and was called both Gallienus and Decius, as Vincent says in his chronicle and Godfrey in his book. Or it may be that Gallienus, to provide himself with an assistant, made someone named Decius a caesar but not the emperor: this is what Richard says in his chronicle.

Ambrose, in his Preface, says of this martyr: "The blessed martyr Hippolytus considered Christ to be his commander and preferred to be a soldier of Christ rather than to be commissioned a commander of troops. When Saint Laurence was entrusted to him to be held under guard, he did not persecute the saint but became his follower. When the treasures of the Church were distributed, he found one treasure that no tyrant could snatch from him, a treasure from which true riches could be hoped for. He spurned the tyrant's favor in order to be confirmed by the grace of the eternal King. He did not resist having his limbs torn asunder, lest he be mangled with eternal hooks."

There was an ox-driver named Peter, who, on the feast of Saint Mary Magdalene, had hitched up his team to the plow and was driving the oxen with goads and curses, when suddenly a bolt of lightning consumed both oxen and plow. Peter himself, who had been doing the cursing, was now afflicted with atrocious pain: the flesh and sinews of his leg were burned away, the bones were left bare, and the shinbone came clear out of its joint. The man went to a church of the Blessed Virgin, hid the bone in a hole in the wall, and tearfully prayed the Blessed Virgin for his healing. Then in the night the Virgin appeared to him with blessed Hippolytus, and the Virgin asked the saint to restore Peter to his former health. At once Hippolytus took the shinbone from its hiding place and inserted it in its place in the leg as a shoot is grafted into a tree. Peter suffered such pain as the insertion was done that his screams awoke the whole household, and all came with a lamp and found Peter asleep with two whole legs and two shins. The family could not believe their eyes and felt his legs again and again until they were sure the limbs were real and sound. They woke him and asked how this had happened to him. He thought they were making fun of him until, seeing that what they said was true, he was convinced and astonished. The new leg, however, was weaker than the old one and could not support his weight with good balance. Hence he walked with a limp for a whole year as testimony to the miracle, after which he again sought the Blessed Virgin's help. She appeared to him with Saint Hippolytus and told the saint that he ought to supply what was lacking in the cure. Peter awoke and saw that he was completely mended.

Peter now withdrew to a hermitage. There the devil frequently appeared to him in the form of a nude woman and forced herself upon him. The more stoutly he resisted her, the more shamelessly she threw herself upon him, tormenting him so much that finally he got hold of a priest's stole and wound it around her neck. This drove the devil away. What was left was a rotting body, and the stench was so foul that no one who saw the corpse could doubt that this was the body of a dead woman, which the devil had assumed as a disguise.

119. The Assumption of the Blessed Virgin Mary

The manner of the assumption of the Blessed Virgin Mary is related in a small apocryphal book attributed to John the Evangelist. In this book we read that after the apostles had gone off to various regions of the world to preach the Gospel, the Blessed Virgin dwelt in a house close by Mount Sion. As long as she lived, she diligently and devoutly visited all the places sacred to the memory of her Son—where he had been baptized, had fasted, had prayed, had suffered, died, and been buried, had risen and ascended into heaven. According to what Epiphanius says, she lived for twenty-four years after her Son's ascension. Epiphanius calculated that she was fourteen years old when she conceived Christ and fifteen when she gave birth; she lived with him for thirty-three years and survived him by twenty-four, so she died at the age of seventy-two. It seems probable, however, as we read elsewhere, that she lived only twelve years after her Son's death and resurrection, and so was assumed into heaven at the age of sixty, since, as the *Ecclesiastical History* has it, the apostles preached for twelve years in Judea and the surrounding country.

One day the Virgin's heart was aflame with desire to be with her Son; she was so deeply stirred in spirit that her tears flowed abundantly. She could not with serenity of soul bear his being taken away for a time and the loss of his consoling presence. Then behold, an angel stood before her amid a great light and greeted her reverently as the mother of his Lord. "Hail, blessed Mary!" he said, "receive the blessing of him who bestowed salvation on Jacob. See, Lady, I have brought you a palm branch from paradise, and you are to have it carried before your bier. Three days from now you will be assumed from the body, because your Son is waiting for you, his venerable mother."

Mary replied: "If I have found favor in your eyes, I beg you to deign to tell me your name. Even more urgently I ask that my sons and brothers the apostles be brought together here with me, so that before I die, I may see them again with my bodily eyes, and may be buried by them and render my spirit to God in their presence. And I also plead and pray that when my soul leaves this body, it may see no foul spirit, and that no power of Satan may confront me."

The angel said: "Why, Lady, do you want to know my name, which is great and admirable? Know, however, that all the apostles will gather and come to you today. They will give you noble burial, and you will breathe forth your spirit in the sight of all of them. Indeed, there is no doubt that he who long ago picked up the prophet by the hairs of his head and carried him from Judea to Babylon will be able to bring the apostles to you in an instant. And why are you afraid of seeing the wicked spirit, since you crushed his head and stripped him of his imperial power? But as you wish: you will see no demons." Having said all this, the angel ascended to heaven surrounded by much light. Moreover, the palm branch shone very brightly: the stem was green like any other branch, but the leaves gleamed like the morning star.

Now it happened that John was preaching in Ephesus when suddenly there was a clap of thunder, and a shining cloud picked him up and whisked him to Mary's door. He knocked and went in, and the virgin reverently greeted the Virgin. Seeing him, Mary was so astonished and happy that she could not contain her tears for joy, and said: "My son John, remember your master's words, by which he commended me to you as your mother and you to me to be my

son. I must tell you that I have been summoned by the Lord. I am about to pay
the debt of the human condition, and I commend my body to your heedful care,
for I have heard that some Jews have conspired together, saying, 'Men and
brothers, let us wait until the woman who bore Jesus dies. Then we will seize
her body, throw it into the fire, and burn it up!' Therefore you, John, must have
someone carry this palm branch in front of the litter when you convey my body
to the sepulcher."

"Oh!" said John, "if only all my brother apostles were here to prepare proper
obsequies for you and pay you the honors you deserve!" Even as he was speaking, all the apostles were snatched up into the clouds from wherever they were
preaching, and deposited at Mary's door. They marveled to find themselves
brought together, and said: "What can be the Lord's reason for assembling us in
this place?" John then came out to them, told them that Mary was soon to leave
the body, and added: "Take care, brothers, no one is to weep for her when she
dies. Otherwise people might be troubled and say: 'See how these men fear
death, for all their preaching to others about the resurrection!'"

Dionysius, the apostle Paul's disciple, gives a like account in his book *On the
Divine Names*. He says that the apostles came together at the dormition of the
Virgin, that he himself was there, and that each one spoke in praise of Christ and
the Virgin. He writes to Timothy[1] as follows: "As you know, we and he [Hi-
erotheus] himself and many of our holy brothers came together to view that
life-giving body which had received God. James the brother of God was there
also, and Peter, the highest and most perfect summit among those who speak
about God [*theologoi*, theologians].[2] Afterwards it seemed good that all the hier-
archs present, each according to his capacity, should praise the infinitely powerful goodness of that God-bearing frailty." So far Dionysius.

When blessed Mary saw all the apostles assembled, she thanked the Lord and
sat in their midst, surrounded by lighted torches and lanterns. About the third
hour of the night Jesus came with companies of angels, troops of prophets, hosts
of martyrs, a legion of confessors and choirs of virgins, and all took their places
before the Virgin's throne and sang dulcet canticles.

The book ascribed to John, already mentioned, tells us how the obsequies
were celebrated. First, Jesus himself began and said: "Come, my chosen one,
and I will set you upon my throne, because I have desired your beauty." The
Virgin responded: "My heart is ready, O Lord, my heart is ready."[3] Then all
those who had come with Jesus softly sang: "This is she who knew no bed in sin;

---

[1] Graesse notes that the Ed. Pr. has "Timothy" here, whereas Jacobus has "Hierotheus." In fact
the whole book *De divinis nominibus* is addressed to Timothy the fellow Elder. "Hierotheus" is
someone whom Pseudo-Dionysius praises as his famous, even divine, teacher, and who may be
fictitious.

[2] The text adds "Paul" here; Graesse notes that the Ed. Pr. omits him. A helpful English translation
of the present passage by Colm Luibheid is in Pseudo-Dionysius, *The Complete Works* (New York:
Paulist Press, 1987), 70.

[3] Ps. 108:1.

she shall have fruit in the visitation of holy souls."[4] Mary then sang about herself, saying: "All generations shall call me blessed, because he that is mighty has done great things for me, and holy is his name."[5] The cantor, taking a higher pitch, intoned: "Come from Lebanon, my spouse, come from Lebanon; thou shalt be crowned."[6] And Mary: "Behold I come! In the head of the book it is written of me that I should do thy will, O God, because my spirit has rejoiced in thee, God my Savior."[7]

Then Mary's soul went forth from her body and flew to the arms of her Son, and was spared all bodily pain, just as it had been innocent of all corruption. Christ said to the apostles: "Carry the body of the Virgin my mother to the valley of Josaphat and place it in a new monument that you will find there. Then wait for me there until I come back to you three days from now." At once the Virgin was surrounded with red roses, signifying the army of the martyrs, and with lilies of the valley, signifying the hosts of angels, confessors, and virgins. The apostles called after her, saying: "Where are you going, most prudent of virgins? Be mindful of us, O Lady!"

The spirits who had stayed in heaven, wondering at the singing of the ascending throngs, set forth in haste to meet them. They saw their King carrying the soul of a woman in his arms and observed her leaning upon him. This surprised them and they began to cry out, saying: "Who is this who comes up from the wilderness, flowing with delights, leaning upon her beloved?"[8] To them her attendants replied: "She is beautiful among the daughters of Jerusalem, as you have seen her full of charity and love." And so, rejoicing, she was taken into heaven and seated upon a throne of glory to the right of her Son; and the apostles saw that her soul was of a whiteness so bright that no mortal tongue could describe it.

There were three virgins at hand, and they removed Mary's robe in order to wash the body, which immediately shone with such effulgence that, while it could be touched and bathed, it could not be seen; and the light shone for as long as it took the virgins to perform their task. Then the apostles reverently lifted the body and placed it on a bier. John said to Peter: "Peter, you will carry this palm branch before the litter, because the Lord set you over us and ordained you as the shepherd and leader of his flock." Peter answered: "You should be the one to carry it, since you, a virgin, were chosen by the Lord, and it is fitting that a virgin should carry the Virgin's palm. You were worthy to lean on the Lord's bosom, and from there received a greater stream of wisdom and grace than the others; so it seems right that the one who received the greater gift from the Son should pay the greater honor to the Virgin. Therefore you must carry this palm of light at the funeral of her sanctity, as you have drunk from the cup of light and the source of perpetual clarity. I will carry the holy body on the bier,

---

[4] Wisd. 3:13. [5] Luke 1:48–49. [6] Song of Sol. 4:8.
[7] Ps. 40:8; Luke 1:47. [8] Song of Sol. 8:5.

and the rest of our brothers will surround it and raise songs of praise to God." Paul then said to him: "And I, who am the least of all of you, will carry it with you."

Peter and Paul then lifted the bier, and Peter began to sing with the words: *Exiit Israel de Aegypto, alleluia.*[9] The other apostles sweetly took up the chant. The Lord covered the litter and the apostles with a cloud in such a way that they could not be seen and only their voices were heard. Angels were present, too, singing with the apostles and filling the whole earth with the sound of their sweet song.

The populace was excited by such dulcet sound and melody, and came rushing out of the city to see what was going on. Then someone said: "The disciples of Jesus are carrying Mary away dead, and singing around her the melody you hear." At once they hurried to take arms and exhorted each other, saying: "Come on, let us kill all those disciples and burn the body that bore the seducer." The chief priest, seeing what was happening, was astounded and filled with rage, and said: "Look at the tabernacle of that man who disturbed us and our people so much! Look at the glory that is now paid to that woman!" After saying this he put his hands on the litter, intending to overturn it and throw the corpse to the ground. But suddenly his hands withered and stuck to the bier, so that he was hanging by his hands; and he moaned and cried in great pain, while the rest of the people were stricken with blindness by angels who were in the cloud.

The chief priest cried out: "Holy Peter, do not scorn me in this extremity! Pray the Lord for me, I beg of you! You must remember how I stood by you and defended you when the portress accused you." Peter answered: "We're busy seeing to our Lady's burial and can't do anything about curing you. However, if you believe in our Lord Jesus Christ and in this woman who conceived and bore him, I hope you will quickly receive the benefit of health." The chief priest: "I believe that the Lord Jesus is the true Son of God, and that this woman was his most holy mother." At once his hands were loosed from the bier, but his arms were still withered and the pain was as severe as before. Peter told him: "Kiss the bier and say, 'I believe in Jesus Christ God, whom this woman carried in her womb and remained a virgin after she delivered her child.'" He did as he was told and was cured instantly. Peter then told him: "Take the palm from the hand of our brother John and hold it up over the people who have been blinded. Those who are willing to believe will receive their sight, those who refuse will never see again."

The apostles now took Mary's body and laid it in the tomb. Then, as the Lord had commanded, they sat around the sepulcher. On the third day Jesus came with a multitude of angels and greeted them, saying: "Peace be with you!" They answered: "Glory to you, O God, who alone do great wonders!" The Lord then

---

[9] Cf. Ps. 114:1; Israel went forth from Egypt. . . .

asked the apostles: "What grace and honor do you think I should now confer on my mother?" They answered: "To your servants it seems just that as you have conquered death and now reign forever, you, Jesus, should bring your mother's body to life and enthrone her at your right hand for eternity."

Christ nodded his consent and immediately Michael the archangel came forward and presented Mary's soul before the Lord. Then the Savior spoke and said: "Arise, my dear one, my dove, tabernacle of glory, vessel of life, heavenly temple! As you never knew the stain of sin through carnal intercourse, so you shall never suffer dissolution of the flesh in the tomb." Thereupon Mary's soul entered her body, and she came forth glorious from the monument and was assumed into the heavenly bridal chamber, a great multitude of angels keeping her company. Thomas, however, was absent, and when he came back refused to believe. Then suddenly the girdle that had encircled her body fell intact into his hands, and he realized that the Blessed Virgin had really been assumed body and soul.

All that has been said so far, however, is apocryphal. Jerome, in his letter to Paula and Eustochium, says: "That little book must be judged to be apocryphal, except regarding some things in it that are credible because they seem to be approved by the saints. There are nine of these: every sort of consolation being promised and granted to the Virgin; the gathering of all the apostles; Mary's painless death; the preparation of a burial place in the valley of Josaphat; Christ's devout attendance; the assistance of the whole heavenly court; persecution by the Jews; the flash of miracles in every deserving case; the assumption in soul and body. But there are a lot of things narrated in the book that are pure invention rather than fact, for instance, that Thomas was not present and doubted when he came, and other like things that obviously are to be repudiated rather than maintained."

It is said that the Virgin's garments were left behind in the tomb for the consolation of the faithful, and that the following miracle was brought about by an article of her clothing. The duke of Normandy was besieging the city of Chartres. The Virgin's tunic was preserved there, and the bishop of the city attached it to a spear, thus making a sort of banner. With this for protection he went out to confront the hostile troops, with the townspeople following him. At the sight of this display the attackers were bereft of their senses, blinded, shaken to the core, thrown into disarray. The townsfolk thereupon went far beyond the divine judgment, fell upon the opposing troops, and slaughtered them unmercifully. This greatly displeased Mary, as was proved by the sudden disappearance of her tunic and the fact that the enemy militia promptly recovered their sight.

In Saint Elizabeth's *Revelations* we read that once when the saint was rapt in ecstasy, she had a vision. She saw, at a great distance, a sepulcher upon which a brilliant light fell. In the sepulcher lay a form that looked like a woman, surrounded by a multitude of angels. Shortly the woman was taken out of the tomb and lifted on high together with her many attendants; and a splendid, glorious man, carrying the banner of the cross in his right hand and accompanied by countless thousands of angels, came from heaven to meet her. Quickly taking her they led her off to heaven amidst a great chorus of song. Not long afterwards Elizabeth asked the angel with whom she frequently talked what the vision had meant. The angel answered: "You were shown how our Lady was assumed into heaven in the flesh as well as in the spirit."

In the same *Revelations* Elizabeth says it was revealed to her that Mary's assumption in the body took place forty days after her death. Blessed Mary herself, talking with Elizabeth, said: "I lived on after the Lord's ascension for a year and as many days as there are between the feast of the Ascension and the feast of my Assumption. All the apostles were with me when I fell asleep, and they reverently gave burial to my body, but I rose again after forty days." Elizabeth asked the Blessed Virgin whether she should make this known or keep it secret, and Mary replied: "It is neither to be revealed to carnal, unbelieving people, nor hidden from the devout and the faithful."

It is noteworthy that the glorious Virgin Mary was assumed and exalted integrally, honorably, joyfully, and splendidly.

She was assumed integrally in soul and body, as the Church piously believes, and as many saints not only assert but make it their business to prove, offering a number of reasons. Bernard's reasoning is as follows: the bodies of the saints are precious in the sight of God, and he makes the places where their bodies are preserved—for instance, the shrines of Saint Peter and Saint James—worthy of such reverence that the whole world comes hurrying to venerate them. Therefore if Mary's body is supposed to be on earth and yet is not visited and venerated by the faithful, it would seem (and this surely is not true) that Christ cares little about the honor due his mother's body, whereas he gives so much honor to the bodies of other saints on earth.

Jerome also says that on the fifteenth day of August Mary ascended to heaven: he says this, meaning that the Virgin was assumed bodily. On this point the Church prefers to hesitate reverently rather than define something hastily. Jerome goes on to prove that what he says should be believed. There are some, he declares, who say that for those who have risen with Christ, the final, perpetual resurrection is complete, and there are those who hold that Saint John, the guardian of Mary, also rejoices in his glorified body with Christ. Why, therefore, is this not all the more credible regarding the mother of the Savior? He who said: "Honor your father and your mother," and "I have not come to destroy the Law but to fulfill the Law," surely has honored his mother above all others: nor do we ourselves doubt that he has so honored his mother.

Augustine also affirms this belief, giving three reasons for holding it. The first is the oneness of Christ's flesh and the Virgin's. He says: "Putrescence and the worm are the shame of the human condition. Since Jesus has no part in that shame, Mary's nature, which Jesus, as we know, took from her, is exempt from it." His second reason is the dignity of her body, so he says: "The throne of God, the bridal chamber of the Lord, the tabernacle of Christ is worthy to be kept in heaven rather than on earth." Thirdly, he proposes the perfect integrity of her virginal flesh, saying: "Rejoice, Mary, with unutterable joy, body and soul, in Christ your own Son, with your own Son and through your own Son. The bane of corruption ought not to overtake her who suffered no corruption of her integrity when she gave birth to so great a Son. So she, upon whom so much grace was poured, should always be incorrupt; she who begot the integral and perfect life of all should be fully and wholly living; she should be with him whom she had borne in her womb, be beside him whom she had engendered and fed and kept warm—Mary, the mother of God, God's minister and hand-maid. Since I dare not think otherwise about her, I do not presume to speak otherwise."

Here we may quote the eminent poet:

> Scandit ad aethera
> Virgo puerpera,
> virgula Jesse.
> Non sine corpore
> sed sine tempore
> tendit adesse.[10]

Mary was assumed amidst rejoicing. Saint Gerard, bishop and martyr, says about this in his homilies: "Today the heavens welcomed the Blessed Virgin joyfully, Angels rejoicing, Archangels jubilating, Thrones exalting, Domina-tions psalming, Principalities harmonizing, Powers lyring, Cherubim and Sera-phim hymning and leading her to the supernal tribunal of the divine majesty."

High honors attended her assumption. Jesus and the whole host of the celes-tial army went forth to meet her. Hence Jerome says: "Who might be able even to think how gloriously the queen of the world advanced, with what stirring of devotion the multitude of the heavenly legions came forth to meet her, with what chants she was conducted to her throne, with what placid mien and serene visage and what divine embraces her Son received her and exalted her above every creature!"

Jerome also says: "We must believe that on this day the celestial militia came to meet the mother of God with festive celebration and shone round about her with dazzling light, leading her up to the throne of God with lauds and spiritual canticles, and that the army of the heavenly Jerusalem exulted with indescribable joy, and welcomed her with ineffable devotion and boundless rejoicing. We celebrate this feast as it comes round once a year, but it is celebrated unceasingly in heaven. We also believe that the Savior himself went to meet his mother joyfully and gladly placed her on a throne at his side. Otherwise he would not

---

[10] She mounts to the skies / the virgin mother / the shoot of Jesse. / Not without her body / but outside of time / she goes to be present.

have fulfilled what he himself had commanded in the Law: 'Honor your father and your mother.'" So far Jerome.

Finally, it was a splendid reception. Jerome: "This is the day the inviolate mother and virgin ascended the heights to her throne, and, being raised in rank next to Christ's in the kingdom, took her place in glory." Indeed, Gerard in his homilies tells to what height of heavenly glory and honor she was elevated: "The Lord Jesus Christ alone can give such greatness as he gave to his mother—greatness such that she continuously receives praise and honor from the divine majesty itself, is attended by choirs of Angels, compassed about by troops of Archangels, accompanied on all sides by the jubilation of Thrones, encircled by the dances of Dominations, by the plaudits of Powers, by the honors of Virtues, the hymns of the Cherubim and the chants of the Seraphim. The ineffable Trinity also applauds her with unceasing dance, and the grace with which the three Persons totally infuse her draws the attention of all to her. The illustrious order of the apostles extols her with praise beyond expression, the throng of the martyrs offers every kind of worship to so great a queen, the innumerable army of confessors sounds a continuous chant to her, the shining assembly of virgins sings a ceaseless chorus in honor of her glory, unwilling Hell howls to her and the impudent demons add their shrieking."

A certain clerk who had great devotion to the Virgin Mary tried every day to console her, so to speak, for the pain of the five wounds of Christ by repeating these words: "Rejoice, mother of God, Virgin immaculate, rejoice! You received joy from the angel, rejoice! You begot the brightness of eternal light, rejoice, O mother, rejoice, holy virgin mother of God! You alone are mother without spouse, all that is created and made praises you! Mother of light, be for us, we pray you, our perpetual mediatrix!" In time this clerk was stricken with an illness so grave that his end was near, and he began to be very much afraid. The Virgin appeared to him and said: "My son, you often bade me rejoice. Why do you now tremble with fear? You too rejoice, and rejoice eternally! Come with me!"

A very rich and valiant knight had squandered all his wealth with careless liberality and was reduced to such poverty that he, accustomed as he was to giving his money away, began to want for the barest necessities. His wife was a most virtuous woman and very devoted to blessed Mary. Now a solemn feast day was approaching, a day on which the knight had always made many large donations, but now he had nothing to give. Driven by embarrassment and shame, he went out to a desert place to let the feast day go by, hoping also to find some companion in misery with whom he could bemoan his bad luck and escape his feeling of humiliation.

Suddenly a fearful horse, with a still more fearful rider in the saddle, galloped up to the knight. The rider addressed him and asked the reason for his woebegone look. The knight told him everything that had happened to him, and the rider said: "If you are willing to do me a small favor, you will enjoy greater fame and more riches than ever." The knight answered the prince of darkness that he would gladly do whatever he was asked to, provided the other would fulfill his promises. The demon said: "Go home and look in a certain cupboard in your house, and you will find large amounts of gold, silver, and precious stones. And here is what you will do for me: bring your wife to me on the day I tell you."

After that exchange of promises the knight went home, found the treasures as directed, and proceeded to buy palaces, make lavish gifts, redeem his lands, and purchase slaves. Then, as the appointed day drew near, he called to his wife and said: "Get up behind me, we have a long ride ahead of us." She shook with fear but dared not refuse, so she devoutly commended herself to the Blessed Virgin and set out with her husband. They had ridden a long distance when they came to a church beside the road, and the lady dismounted and went in while her spouse waited outside. Then, as she prayed earnestly to blessed Mary, she fell asleep. Next, the glorious Virgin, dressed as the matron was and looking exactly like her, came down from the altar, went out of the church while the woman slept on inside, and mounted behind the knight. He, thinking it was his wife, continued the journey.

When they reached the place agreed upon, the prince of darkness hurried up to meet them, but when he saw who was there, he dared come no closer and said to the knight: "You treacherous fellow, why have you tricked me this way after all I did for you? I told you to bring your wife to me, and instead you have brought me the mother of the Lord. I wanted your spouse and you come here with Mary! Your wife has done me great harm and I wanted to take my revenge, and now you bring this woman to torment me and send me to hell!" The knight was stupefied at what he heard and could not say a word for fear and wonderment. Mary, however, spoke: "Wicked spirit, what rashness led you to presume to harm my devoted follower? You will not go unpunished for this, and I now impose this sentence upon you. Go down to hell, and never again dare to do injury to anyone who invokes me with devotion!"

The devil vanished, loudly lamenting his frustration. The knight got down from his horse and prostrated himself at the Virgin's feet. She rebuked him and ordered him to go to his wife, who was still asleep in the church, and to throw away all the demon's riches. He went into the church, awakened his sleeping spouse, and told her all that had occurred. They then returned home, threw out all the ill-gotten treasures, and lived thereafter praising the Virgin most devoutly. In time they acquired much wealth, blessed Mary herself bestowing it.

A certain man, whose sins weighed heavily upon him, had a vision in which he came before God's judgment seat. Satan was present and said: "You have no rights in this man's soul. He belongs entirely to me, and I have a warrant to prove it." "Where is your warrant?" the Lord asked. Satan: "I have it because you yourself dictated it and confirmed it in perpetuity, for you said: 'At whatever hour you eat of this, you shall die the death.'[11] Since this man is of the

[11] Cf. Gen. 2:17.

progeny of those who ate the forbidden food, by this public warrant I have title to him and he should be sentenced to die with me." The Lord said: "O man, you have permission to speak for yourself," but the man said nothing. The demon spoke again: "He is mine also by right of prescription, because I owned him for thirty years and he obeyed me as a slave should." But the man still remained silent. Again the demon spoke: "His soul is mine also because though he did some good, the evil he did far outweighs the good."

God, however, did not wish to pronounce sentence against him so quickly and granted him a week's reprieve, at the end of which he would again appear to refute all the devil's allegations. As he left the Lord's presence frightened and grief-stricken, he met someone who asked the reason for his sadness. The man told him the situation he was in, and the other answered: "Don't be afraid, you have nothing to fear. I will help you manfully in answering the first charge." The man asked the other's name, and the reply was: "My name is Truth." Then he came upon a second person, who promised to defend him staunchly against the second charge, and, being asked his name, said: "I am called Justice."

On the eighth day, therefore, the man again came before the judgment seat and the demon repeated his first claim, to which Truth responded: "We know that there are two deaths, the death of the body and the death of the soul in hell. The warrant you quote in your favor, O demon, does not speak of the death of hell, but only of that of the body. It is obvious that all fall under the first sentence, namely, that all must die the death of the body, but all do not die the death of hell. Your instrument, therefore, applies in perpetuity regarding bodily death, but with regard to the death of the soul it has been revoked by the blood of Christ!" So, seeing that he had lost his first point, the devil started to restate the second one, but Justice was there and answered him as follows: "Granted that you owned him as a slave for many years, his reason always opposed you, because reason always murmured against serving so cruel a master."

The man had no one to take his part against the third charge, and God said: "Let the scales be brought and all his good and bad deeds be weighed." Truth and Justice said to the sinner: "You see there the mother of mercy, seated beside the Lord. Call upon her with your whole heart and try to win her help." He did this, and blessed Mary came to his aid. She put her hand on the side of the scale where the few good deeds were, while the devil tried to pull the other side down; but the mother of mercy prevailed and the sinner was freed. He thereupon came to himself and led a better life from then on.

In the city of Bourges, about the year of the Lord 527, the Christians were receiving holy communion on Easter Sunday, and a Jewish boy went to the altar and received the Lord's Body with the others. When he went home, his father asked him where he had been, and he answered that he had gone to church with his schoolmates and had taken communion with them. The father, furious, picked the lad up and threw him into a white-hot furnace. At once, however, the mother of God, looking like a painting that the boy had seen on the altar, came to his side and kept him unharmed by the fire. The boy's mother's outcries brought together a number of Christians and Jews, and seeing the lad unscathed in the furnace they pulled him out and asked him how he had been able to escape the flames. "That venerable lady who stood above the altar," he answered, "helped me and held the fire away from me." The Christians present, understanding that he referred to the image of the Blessed Virgin, seized the boy's father and cast him into the furnace, where he was immediately burned up and reduced to ashes.

Several monks were standing on a riverbank before dawn, gossiping and exchanging idle banter, when they heard oarsmen rowing down the river at top speed. The monks asked them who they were. "We are devils," they replied, "and we are taking to hell the soul of Ebroïn, mayor of the palace to the king of the Franks and a renegade from the monastery of Saint Gall." Hearing this the monks were terror-stricken and cried out at the top of their voices: "Holy Mary, pray for us!" "You do well to call on Mary!" said the demons. "We intended to tear you to pieces and drown you, because we found you chattering away at a time forbidden by the rule." The monks went back to the cloister and the demons sped off to hell.

There was a monk much given to lechery but very devoted to blessed Mary. One night, on his way to commit the usual mischief, he passed before the altar and greeted the Blessed Virgin, then left the church. He had to cross a river, but fell in and drowned. When devils came to take away his soul, angels were there to keep it free. The devils said to them: "What are you doing here? you have no claim to this soul!" Instantly blessed Mary was present and reproached the evil spirits for presuming to lay hands on the monk's soul; but they said that they had found him about to die and bent on wrongdoing. Mary retorted: "Your accusations are false! I know that whenever he was going somewhere he first greeted me, and did the same on his way back. But if you say that you are being treated unjustly, we will submit the case to the judgment of the King of kings." When the question was argued before God, it pleased him to have the soul return to the sinner's body and there do penance for his actions. Meanwhile his brother monks noticed that matins had not been rung, so they looked for the sacristan and found him drowned in the river. They pulled the body out and wondered what had happened, when he suddenly came to life and told the whole story. Thereafter he lived out his life in good works.

There was a certain woman to whom the devil appeared in the form of a man, harassing her continually. She resorted to many remedies, sometimes sprinkling blessed water, at other times trying this and that, but nothing made the demon desist. Finally a holy man advised her to raise her hands when the evil spirit appeared and to say aloud: "Holy Mary, help me!" She did this, and the demon, as if hit by a stone, stood terrified and said: "May a bad devil enter the mouth of the one who taught you that!" And straightway he vanished and came back no more.

HOW MARY WAS ASSUMED INTO HEAVEN

The manner and circumstances of the blessed Virgin Mary's assumption are related in a sermon that was compiled from various sayings of saints and is solemnly read in many churches. In it we read: "I have kept a careful record of all that I could find in the writings of the holy fathers throughout the world concerning the venerable migration of the mother of God." Saint Cosmas Vestitor says that he had accurately preserved what he learned from persons who came after those who had been present at the sacred event, and that this must not be omitted. He says that when Christ decided to bring to himself the mother who had given him life, he sent the usual angel to announce to her the manner of her falling asleep, for fear that death, coming unexpectedly, should cause her any disturbance. His mother had implored him face to face, when her Son was still living on earth, not to let her see any malignant spirit. He therefore sent the angel ahead to deliver this message to her: "The time has come for me to take you, my mother, to myself. As you have filled the earth with joy, now make my Father's mansions joyful; console the spirits of my saints. And now that you are about to dwell in the palace of heaven, do not be disturbed at leaving the corruptible world with its vain desires. Do not, O my mother, let separation from the body frighten you, because you are called to perpetual life, to a joy that never fails, to peaceful rest, to untroubled ease, to unending refreshment, to inaccessible light, to the day that has no evening, to indescribable glory, to myself, your Son, the maker of all that is. For I am life eternal, love without compare, the ineffable dwelling, light that knows no darkness, bounty immeasurable. Give to the earth what is the earth's, without anxiety. No one will snatch you from my hand, because in my hand are all the bounds of the earth. Commit your body to me, because I deposited my divinity in your womb. Death will have no boast over you, because you begot life. No shadow of darkness will come upon you, because you gave birth to light. No damage or breakage will touch you, because you were worthy to become the vessel that held me. Come now to him who was born of you: you are about to receive the reward of motherhood, the guerdon for raising your child, the return for nursing him and keeping him warm. Dwell with your only-begotten, hasten to cling to your Son; for I know that you will not be torn by love for another son. I have shown you to be a virgin mother: now I show that you are the sustaining wall of the whole world, the ark of those who are to be saved, the raft of those tossed about by the sea, the staff of the feeble, the ladder of those mounting to heaven, the mediatrix of sinners. I will bring the apostles to you, and they will bury you as if their hands were my own. For it is fitting that these sons of my spiritual light, to whom I have given the Holy Spirit, should bury your body and take my part in your honorable obsequies."

Having said all this, the angel gave the Virgin a palm branch sent from heaven as assurance of victory over the corruption of death, and the clothing for her burial, and then repaired to heaven whence he had come. Blessed Mary called her friends and relatives together and said: "I must tell you that today I am to pass out of this life of time. Therefore we must be watchful, because when someone is dying, both the godly power of angels, and wicked spirits, come to the death-bed." At these words all began to weep and said: "You were worthy to become the mother of the author of all things, you bore him who harrowed hell, you have merited a throne above the Cherubim and Seraphim, and are you now afraid of the presence of spirits? Then what shall we do? How can we escape?" And the crowd of women wept and begged Mary not to leave them orphans. The Blessed Virgin comforted them, saying: "If you, mothers of corruptible sons, cannot bear to be separated from them even for a short while, how should I, virgin mother as I am, not wish to go to my Son, the only-begotten of God the Father? If any one of you is bereaved of a son, she will be consoled by a surviving son or one still to be born, but I have only one Son and remain a virgin; how could I not be eager to hurry to him who is the life of all?"

While these things were going on, Saint John arrived and asked how matters stood. When the Virgin told him that she was about to migrate to heaven, he prostrated himself and cried out: "What are we, O Lord, that you afflict us with such tribulations? Why did you not take me out of the body and have me buried by the mother of my Lord, rather than have me present at her funeral?" The Blessed Virgin led him still weeping into her chamber and showed him the palm branch and the clothes, and then lay down on the bed that had been prepared for the burial.

Now a tremendous clap of thunder was heard, a whirlwind descended like a white cloud, and the apostles came down like a rain shower before the door of the Virgin's house. They did not know what to make of this until John came out and revealed to them what the angel had announced to Mary. They all wept, but John consoled them. Then, wiping away their tears, they went in, reverently greeted the Virgin, and knelt to her. She welcomed them, saying: "Hail to you, sons of my only-begotten Son!" And while she heard from them the manner of their getting there, she told them all that had happened. To her the apostles said: "Looking at you in the past, O most renowned Virgin, it was as though we were seeing our Lord and master, and we were consoled. Now our only comfort is that we hope to have you as our mediatrix with God." Mary called upon Paul by name, and he said: "Hail, queen of my solace! True, I never saw Christ in the flesh, yet, seeing you in the flesh, I am consoled as if I saw him. To this day I have preached to the Gentiles that you begot God; now I shall teach them that you have been taken up to him."

After that the Virgin showed them the things the angel had brought. She also gave orders that the lamps should not be extinguished until after her death. A hundred and twenty virgins were present to attend to her burial. She put on the funeral clothes, and, bidding all farewell, composed herself on the bed, ready to die. Peter stood at the head of the bed, John at the foot, the other apostles ranged themselves at the sides, all praising the mother of God as Peter began: "Rejoice, spouse of the heavenly bridal chamber, three-branched candelabrum of the light from on high, through whom the eternal clarity is made manifest!"

This gathering of the apostles at the dormition of the most holy Virgin is attested by Saint Germanus, archbishop of Constantinople, who says: "O mother of God, you accepted the death that is inevitable to human nature, yet your eye, which watches over us, will neither slumber nor sleep. For your transmigration was not without witnesses nor was your falling asleep a lie: heaven narrates the glory of those who sang over you, the earth exhibits the truth of them, the clouds proclaim the honor that by them was paid you, the angels tell the obsequies performed for you when the apostles together came to you in Jerusalem." The great Dionysius the Areopagite gives the same testimony, saying: "As you know, we and he and many from among our brothers came together to see the body that received the Lord. James the brother of God was there, and Peter the renowned, highest summit of theologians. It was agreed that after the viewing, all these high priests, so far as each one was of immense virtue, should sing the praises of this life-giving goodness and weakness."

Cosmas again takes up the story, saying: "After this great thunderclap the whole house shook and a fragrant breeze filled the house with so much sweetness that a deep sleep overcame all present except the apostles and three virgins who carried lamps. Then the Lord descended with a multitude of angels and took up the soul of his mother. Her soul shone with such effulgence that none of the apostles could look at it. Christ said to Peter: 'Bury my mother's body with all reverence and guard it diligently for three days. Then I will come and transfer it out of reach of corruption. I will wrap it in brightness like my own in order to put union and harmony between that which was received and that which received.'" The same Saint Cosmas goes on to record a fearful, marvelous mystery, which does not lend itself to natural discussion or curious investigation, since everything that is said about the mother of God is supernatural and wondrous and awesome rather than subject to curious scrutiny. "When the soul had gone out of her body," he says, "the body pronounced these words: 'O Lord, I, who am worthy of your glory, thank you. Remember me, because I am the work of your hands and have cared for that which you entrusted to me.'

"When the others woke and saw the lifeless body of the Virgin," Cosmas continues, "they began to grieve and mourn. Then the apostles took up the body and carried it to the tomb, Peter leading off with the Psalm *In exitu Israel de Aegypto*. Choirs of angels, too, sang the Virgin's praises, so that all Jerusalem was amazed at such glorification. Then the chief priests sent a crowd armed with swords and clubs. One of them rushed at the bier, hoping to drag the body of God's mother to the earth; but because he had impiously tried to touch the corpse, his hands lost the power of touch. Both hands tore away at the elbows and clung to the litter, and the attacker was stricken with horrible pain. He begged for pardon and promised amendment. Peter said to him: 'You will never obtain pardon unless you kiss the body of the ever Virgin and confess that Christ, born of her, is the Son of God.' The culprit obeyed, and his hands were rejoined to the elbows. Peter then plucked a date from the palm branch and gave it to him, saying: 'Go into the city and touch the sick with this date. Those who believe will be cured.'"

When the apostles reached the field of Gethsemane, they found there a tomb like Christ's life-restoring sepulcher. In it they deposited the body with much reverence. They did not dare to touch this sublime vessel of God but set it down by holding the corners of the shroud. Then they closed the tomb securely and the apostles and disciples of the Lord, following his orders, stood guard around it. On the third day a shining cloud enveloped them, angelic voices sounded, an ineffable perfume spread abroad, and all were wonderstruck when they saw that the Lord had come down and was carrying away the Virgin's body in glory.

The apostles therefore kissed the sepulcher and went back to the house of John the evangelist and theologian, praising him for having been the guardian of so great a virgin. But one of the apostles had missed the ceremonies and, marveling at what he heard about them, insisted that the tomb be opened so that he could ascertain the truth of what he had been told. The apostles refused, declaring, first, that the testimony of so many witnesses ought to be enough, and second, that if the infidels got wind of this, they might spread a rumor that the body had been stolen. But the doubter sadly asked: "Why do you defraud me, your equal, of the treasure that is ours in common?" In the end they opened the tomb and found not the body but the garments and the shroud.

In the *Historia Euthimiata*, Book III, chapter XL, Saint Germanus, archbishop of Constantinople, says he had discovered—and the great John of Damascus also attests to this—that the empress Pulcheria of blessed memory built many churches in and around Constantinople during the reign of Emperor Marcianus, among them a very beautiful one at Balcherna dedicated to the Virgin Mary. She then summoned Juvenal, archbishop of Jerusalem, and other bishops from Palestine who were in the royal capital because of the council in progress at Chalcedon, and said to them: "We have heard that the body of the all-holy Virgin was buried in the Garden of Gethsemane, and it is our wish that for the protection of this city the body be transferred here with all due reverence." Juvenal stated that Mary's body, as he had learned from ancient records, had been taken up to glory, only the clothing and the burial shroud being left in the tomb. Juvenal later sent the garments to Constantinople, and they are preserved with honor in the aforementioned church. Let no one judge that I have made up this story out of my own imagination. I have put down the things I learned by studious reading of the writings of those who in turn had received their knowledge from their predecessors through a true and certain tradition. So far I have reported the words found in the sermon to which I referred.

John of Damascus, who also was a Greek, adds still other wondrous details concerning the sacred assumption of the Virgin. In his sermons he says: "Today the most holy Virgin is borne aloft to the celestial bridal chamber. Today the sacred, living ark, which carried within itself the One who fashioned it, is given its place in a temple not made with hands. Today that most sacred dove, innocent and simple, flying out of the ark—that is, out of the body that received God—has found rest for its feet. Today the immaculate Virgin, who knew no earthly passion—nay, more was instructed by heavenly intelligences—has not gone down into the earth, but, being rightly called a living heaven, dwells in celestial mansions.

"Yes, your holy, blessed soul was naturally separated from your glorious body and your body was buried in the tomb; but it does not remain in death nor is it dissolved in corruption. Your virginity remained inviolate through childbirth; now, at your migration, your body rises above all and is transferred to a better and holier life, not corrupted by death but to be the same for eternal ages. For as the radiant, luciferous sun, hidden behind a sublunar body, seems for a brief hour somehow to fail, though it is not deprived of its light since in itself it has a perennial fount of light, so you, font of the true light, inexhaustible treasure of life, though for a brief moment of time you were allowed to die bodily, you still abundantly pour into us the brightness of inextinguishable light. This your sacred dormition ought not to be called death but transmigration, or a withdrawal, or, still better, an arrival. For leaving the body you come to heaven, angels and archangels meet you, the unclean spirits quake at your ascension. You, blessed Virgin, have not simply gone to heaven like Elijah, nor mounted like Paul to the third heaven: you have risen all the way to the royal throne of your Son.

"The death of other saints is blessed because it shows that they are blessed, but this is not so for you. It is not your death nor your blessedness, nor your transmigration nor your setting out, nor yet your withdrawal, that has bestowed upon you the surety of your blessedness, because you are the beginning, the middle, and the end of all the goods that transcend the thought of man. Your protection, your perfection, your conceiving without seed, all this is God dwelling in you! So you said truly that you will be and will be called blessed, not beginning with your death but from the moment you were conceived. It is not that death beatified you but that you glorified death, banishing its sadness and converting death to joy. For if God said: 'Lest the first man put out his hand and pluck the fruit and live forever,' how could the one who carried life itself, the life with no beginning, the life that has no ending—how could such a one not live forever and ever?

"Of old, God expelled and exiled from paradise the first parents of the human race, asleep in the death of sin, already buried under a mountain of disobedience, already rotting in the drunkenness of sin: now, conversely, this woman, who brought life to the whole human race, who manifested obedience to God the Father, who rooted out all passion . . . how could paradise not welcome her? Eve lent her ear to the serpent, drank the poisonous draft, was entrapped by pleasures, subjected to the pangs of childbirth, and condemned with Adam. But this truly blessed woman, who bent her ear to God, whom the Holy Spirit filled, who bore the Father's mercy in her womb, who conceived without contact with a husband and gave birth without pain, how shall death swallow her, how shall corruption dare to do anything to the body that bore life itself?"

The same Damascenus adds in his sermons: "Of a truth, the apostles were scattered worldwide to labor at fishing for men, drawing them by the net of the word out of the depths of darkness to the table of the heavenly court or to the Father's marriage feast, when God's command, like a fishing net or a cloud, brought them to Jerusalem, gathering and collecting them from beyond the seas. Then Adam and Eve, our first parents, called out: 'Come to us, O sacred, salutary vessel, you have made our joy complete!' On the other hand a throng of saints who were corporeally present said: 'Stay here with us, you our consolation! Do not leave us orphans, you whom we have as our solace in struggle, our refreshment in toil! For how can our life be life if we are deprived of your presence?' I think that the apostles and the rest who filled the church uttered these and similar pleas while sobs often interrupted their protestations.

"Mary then turned to her Son and said: 'Be the consoler of these beloved sons whom it has pleased you to call brothers. Comfort their grief at my departure, and as I lay my hands on them, heap blessing upon blessing on them.' Then she stretched out her hands, blessed the gathering of believers, and said: 'Into your hands, O Lord, I commend my spirit. Receive my soul, which you love, which you have kept free of any guilt. Not to the earth but to you I commit my body. Keep whole this body in which it pleased you to dwell. Take me to yourself, so that where you are, you the fruit of my loins, there I may live with you!' Thereupon words like these were heard: 'Arise, come then, my beloved, O beautiful among women! You are beautiful, my dear, and in you there is no stain.'

"Hearing this summons, the most holy Virgin commended her spirit into the hands of her Son, as the apostles, weeping, kissed the tabernacle of the Lord and were filled with blessing and holiness by their contact with the sacred body. Then diseases and demons fled, air and sky were purified by the soul's ascension and the body's commitment to the earth, and water by the washing of the body; for the body was washed with exceedingly clean water—not that the body was cleansed by the water but that the body sanctified the water. Then the sacred body was wrapped in a clean shroud and placed upon a bed, lamps gleamed, ointments sweetened the air, angel hymns resounded. As the disciples and other saints who were present intoned heavenly hymns, the ark of the Lord was set upon the sacred shoulders of the apostles and carried from Mount Sion to the holy ground of Gethsemane. Angels led the way and followed after, others kept the holy body covered, and the whole community of the church accompanied the cortege.

"Some Jews, hardened in their old malevolence, also showed themselves. It is said that as the sacred body of the mother of God was carried down from Mount Sion, a Hebrew, a true limb of Satan, ran up to the body which angels feared to approach, and in a spasm of fury laid both hands on the litter and dragged it to the ground. It is further said that one hand fell off as dry as a stick, and it was a sight to see the man standing there with his useless stump, until faith changed his mind and he repented, bemoaning his crime. The bearers of the litter stood still, however, until the poor man put his hand on the most holy body, and at the touch it was restored to its pristine condition.

"So the procession reached Gethsemane, and there were kisses and embraces, sacred hymns, tears, drops of sweat, as the holy body was placed in the venerable tomb: but your soul was not abandoned in hell, nor did your body see corruption. It was fitting that the shrine of God, the spring undug, the field unplowed, the vineyard unwatered, the fruit-bearing olive, should not be detained in the bosom of the earth. It was proper that the mother be raised up by the Son, so that she might ascend to him as he had descended to her; that the body of the woman who had kept her virginity in childbirth should never see corruption; that she who had borne her Creator in her womb should abide in heavenly dwellings; that she whom the Father had made his bride should reside in celestial bridal chambers; and that what belonged to the Son should be possessed also by his mother." Thus far John of Damascus.

Saint Augustine, in one of his sermons, discusses this sacred assumption from several points of view, saying: "As we undertake to speak of the most holy body of Mary ever virgin and of the assumption of her sacred soul, we say first that in the Scriptures, after the Lord on the cross commended her to the disciple, nothing is found about her except what Luke commemorates in the Acts: 'All these were persevering with one mind in prayer with Mary the mother of Jesus.' What, therefore, should we say about her death or about her assumption? Since Scripture tells us nothing, we must seek by reason what accords with truth. Thus truth itself becomes our authority, and without truth there is no valid authority.

"So then, having in mind the human condition, we have not been afraid to say that Mary underwent temporal death; but if we say that she was subjected to the common putrefaction, to the worm and the dust, we must stop to ponder whether all this is compatible with such great sanctity, with the prerogatives of this woman in whom God dwelt. We know what was said to our first parents: 'You are dust and to dust you shall return.'[12] The body of Christ was spared this condition, since it was not subjected to corruption. Thus the nature taken from the Virgin was exempt from the general sentence. To the woman God said: 'I will greatly multiply your pain in childbirth.'[13] Mary bore pain; her soul was pierced with a sword; but she gave birth without pain. Therefore, although she shared pain with Eve, she did not share the pain of childbirth; so great a prerogative of dignity raised her up that she was exempted from some general laws. Therefore, if she is said to have undergone death but was not held fast in its bonds, is there anything impious about that? If God has willed to preserve incor-

[12] Gen. 3:19.   [13] Gen. 3:16.

rupt the modesty of his mother's virginity, why would he not wish to save his mother from the foulness of putrefaction? Does it not befit the Lord's loving-kindness to preserve his mother's honor, since he came not to abolish the Law but to fulfill it?

"It is true piety, therefore, to believe that he who honored her in her lifetime before all women with the grace of his conception, honored her in death with a salvation all her own and with special grace. To rot away and feed the worm is the shame of the human condition. Since Jesus is immune to this shame, Mary's nature is exempt from it—the nature that Jesus is proved to have assumed from her. For the flesh of Jesus is Mary's flesh, which he raised above the stars, honoring all human nature but above all his mother's. If a mother's nature be the son, it is fitting that the son's be the mother, not in the sense of a unity of person but of a unity of bodily nature. For if grace can effect a unity without the property of a special nature, how much the more so when there is unity of grace and a special bodily birth. The unity of the disciples in Christ is an example of union in grace; of them he says: 'That they may be one as we also are';[14] and again, 'Father, I will that where I am, they also may be with me.'[15] If, therefore, he wills to have with him those who are judged to be joined in union with him here by their faith, what is to be thought of his mother? Where is she worthy to be if not in the presence of her Son?

"As far as I am able to understand, therefore, this is what I believe: Mary's soul is honored by her Son with a more excellent privilege, possessing in Christ his body, which she engendered, glorified. And why not therefore her own body, through which she engendered? If no recognized authority stands in the way, I truly believe that the body through which she engendered Christ is with him in heaven, because such sanctification is more worthy of heaven than of earth. The throne of God, the bridal chamber of the Spouse, the house of the Lord, the tabernacle of Christ, is worthy to be where Christ is: heaven is more worthy than earth to guard so precious a treasure. Such integrity deserves to be succeeded only by incorruptibility, certainly not by disintegration or decay. That most holy body left as food for worms? I would be afraid to say so because I cannot even think it. That incomparable gift of grace drives such thoughts from my mind, and reflection upon many texts of Scripture invites me to say so. The Truth once said to his servants: 'Where I am, there shall my servant be also.'[16] If this is the general rule for all who serve Christ through faith and works, how much more specially does it apply to Mary! Surely she served him and ministered to him in every way, carrying him in her womb and bringing him forth to the world, feeding and warming him, putting him to rest in the manger, hiding him on the flight to Egypt, following him from childhood to the cross, never being far from where he was. She could not doubt his divinity, knowing that she had conceived him not by man's seed but by the breath of God. She was unhes-

[14] John 17:21.   [15] John 17:24.   [16] John 12:26.

itatingly confident of her Son's power as of the power of God when, as the wine ran short at the wedding, she said to him: 'They have no wine.'[17] She knew what he could do—what he did immediately by working a miracle.

"Behold Mary the servant of Christ in faith and works! If she is not where Christ wants his servants to be, where will she be? And if she is there, will it be by an equal grace? And if it is by an equal grace, is this fair of God, who renders to each according to merit? If in her lifetime Mary deserved so much greater grace than all others, will her grace be the less when she is dead? Of course not! If the death of all the saints is precious, Mary's is certainly beyond all price. In my judgment, therefore, it must be confessed that Mary was assumed into the joy of eternity by the loving will of Christ, and received with more honor than the rest since by grace he honored her more than others; and that after death she was not brought down to the common human lot—rot, the worm, the dust—because she had begotten her Savior and the Savior of all. If God's will chose to preserve unscathed the garments of the three young men in the fiery furnace, why would he deny to his own mother what he chose for someone else's clothing? For pity's sake alone he willed that Jonah should be uncorrupted in the belly of the whale; why will he not by grace preserve Mary uncorrupted? Daniel was saved from the ravenously hungry lions; is not Mary to be saved, having been endowed with such great merits and dignities?

"We know that all the benefits we have named could not have been saved by nature, but we do not doubt that for the sake of Mary's integrity grace could do more than nature could. Christ therefore made Mary rejoice soul and body in himself, her own Son, nor did he allow the ill of corruption to touch her whose integrity had suffered no corruption in bearing so great a Son. Thus she upon whom so great graces had been showered should have life in its fullness, since she gave life to her Son, who is the Life of all. If then I have spoken as I should, approve, O Christ, you and yours! If not, forgive me, I beg, you and yours!"

[17] John 2:3.

120. Saint Bernard

Bernard, Bernardus, comes from *ber*, a well or spring, and *nardus*, nard, which, as the *Gloss* on the Canticle of Canticles[1] says, is an herb humble, warm in nature, and sweet-smelling. Saint Bernard was warm in his fervent love, humble in his dealings with others, a spring in the outflow of his doctrine, a well in the depth of his knowledge, and sweet-smelling in the fragrance of his good renown.

His life was written by William, abbot of Saint Thierry, an associate of Saint Bernard, and by Arnold, abbot of Bonneval.

Bernard was born in Burgundy at the castle of Fontaines, the child of noble and very religious parents. His father, Celestin, was a knight valorous in worldly affairs and equally devout in his relations with God. His mother was called Aleth. She bore seven children, six sons and a daughter, all her sons future monks, her daughter promised to the religious life. As soon as she had brought forth a child, she offered him or her to God with her own hands. She did not allow her babies to be nursed by other women: it was as though she wished, with her milk, somehow to infuse them with her own goodness. As her children grew up and as long as they were under her care, she trained them for the desert, and fed them with coarse, common food as if to send them out to the wilderness as soon as possible.

While she was still carrying her third son, Bernard, she had a dream that was a presage of things to come: she saw in her womb a little dog, white except for its red back, and the puppy was barking. She told a certain man of God about this dream, and he responded prophetically: "You will be the mother of a very good dog, who will be the watchman of the house of God and will bark against its foes, for he will be a renowned preacher and will cure many by grace of the medicine of his tongue."

When Bernard was still a small boy, he fell seriously ill with pains in his head. A woman came to assuage his pain with her incantations, but he indignantly shouted at her and drove her away. God's mercy did not fail the child's zeal, and he rose at once and realized that he was completely relieved of his illness.

In the holy night of the Lord's nativity the boy Bernard was in the church, waiting for the morning office, and asked those with him at what hour of the

---

[1] The book called the Song of Solomon in the King James and Revised Versions is called Solomon's Canticle of Canticles in the Douay.

night Christ was born. Then and there the Infant Jesus appeared to him as though being born again from his mother's womb. Remembering that experience, Bernard, as long as he lived, was always convinced that this was the hour at which the Lord was born. From that time on he was graced both with a deeper sense of all that pertained to the Lord's birth and a more abundant eloquence in treating it; and later on, among the earliest of his written works, he produced a remarkable little book in praise of the Blessed Mother and her Child, in which he explained the Gospel lesson that begins: "The angel Gabriel was sent from God. . . ."[2]

The ancient Enemy, seeing the boy's salutary resolution, attacked his determination to live a chaste life and set many tempting traps in his path. Once, for instance, Bernard was gazing rather fixedly at a woman until suddenly, blushing at what he was doing, he rose as a stern avenger against himself and jumped into a pool of ice-cold water. There he lay until he was almost frozen, but by God's grace the heat of fleshly lust was wholly cooled in him. About that same time a girl, egged on by the devil, jumped into the bed where he was sleeping. When he became aware of her presence, he moved over calmly and silently, leaving to her the side of the bed he had been occupying, and, turning to the other side, went back to sleep. The woman put up with this expectantly for some time, then began touching and teasing him, but he remained motionless. Finally, impudent though she was, she blushed with shame, felt a flood of horror mixed with admiration, got out of bed, and hurried away.

On another occasion he was a guest in the house of a certain matron, and she was so impressed by the young man's good looks that she burned with desire for him. She had his bed made up in a separate room, but then, in the night, went to him without a sound or a qualm. The minute he felt her presence, however, he shouted: "Thieves! Robbers!" This made the woman flee and awakened the whole household. Lamps were lighted, the thief was sought but not found, and everybody went back to bed and to rest—all, that is, except the unhappy woman, who could not sleep. She rose again and sought Bernard's bed, but again he called out: "Thieves! Robbers!" Again the thief was hunted, but was not identified by the only one who knew who the real thief was. The woman tried a third time but was repulsed, and, overcome by fear and despair, finally gave up. The next day, as he renewed his journey with his companions, they made fun of him a little, asking what made him dream of thieves so often. He told them: "I really faced a thief's designs on me last night, because my hostess tried to rob me of my chastity, a treasure that, once lost, can never be recovered!"

It was already clear to Bernard that there was no safety in living with the Serpent. He began to think about fleeing the world and decided to enter the Cistercian Order. His brothers learned of this and used every means of dissuad-

---

[2] Luke 1:26.

ing him, but the Lord conferred such grace upon him that not only did he hold fast to his purpose of conversion, but won all his brothers and many others to serve the Lord in the religious life. Only his brother Gerard, a stalwart knight, considered his words idle and turned a deaf ear to his warnings. Bernard, however, already afire with faith and wondrously spurred by his zealous love for his brother, said to Gerard: "I know, brother, that misfortune alone can make you able to understand what I am saying to you!" He pressed his finger to his brother's side and said: "The day will come soon when a lance will pierce your side and will make a way to your heart for the counsel that you now reject!" A few days later Gerard was caught by enemies, received a lance-thrust at the point in his side where his brother's finger had rested, and was held, shackled, in captivity. Bernard went to him and was not allowed to get close to him, but called out: "Brother Gerard, I know that very soon you and I are going to enter the monastery!" That very night the shackes fell from his feet, the door opened of itself, and Gerard walked out happily and told his brother that he had changed his mind and wanted to become a monk.

In the year of the Lord 1112, the fifteenth from the founding of the Cistercian Order, Bernard, the servant of the Lord, who was then twenty-two years old, entered the Order with more than thirty companions. When Bernard was leaving his father's house with his brothers, Guy, the eldest, saw his youngest brother, Nivard, still a child, playing in the square with other boys. "Hello there, brother Nivard!" he called. "From now on our land and all we own is yours to take care of!" The lad gave an answer that was not at all childish, saying: "So all of you will have heaven and you leave me nothing but earth? That's certainly not a fair division!" Nivard continued to live with his father for a while, then followed his brothers.

Once he had entered the Order, Bernard, the servant of God, was so completely absorbed in the life of the spirit that he hardly used his bodily senses. He lived a whole year in the novices' cell and yet did not know that it had a vaulted ceiling. He passed very often in and out of the monastery church, which had three windows in the apse, yet he thought there was only one.

The abbot of the Cistercians sent some of his monks to build a house at Clairvaux and appointed Bernard to be their abbot. He lived there for a long time in extreme poverty, often making food out of the leaves of beech trees. The servant of God denied himself sleep to an extent beyond human endurance. He used to complain that the time spent sleeping was time lost, and considered sleep to be rightly compared to death: as sleepers looked dead to the eyes of men, so the dead looked like sleepers to God. If Bernard heard a monk snoring more loudly or lying more restlessly than normal, he could hardly bear it with patience, and claimed that such a monk slept in a carnal or worldly manner.

He took no pleasure in eating, and only fear of fainting made him take food, which he did as if it were a form of torture. It was his custom after eating to think about how much he had eaten, and if he felt that he had taken even a little more than usual, he did not allow the fault to go unpunished. He had so mastered the cravings of gluttony that he had largely lost even the ability to distinguish different tastes. If, for example, oil was mistakenly put before him and he drank it, he was not aware of it until he wondered why his lips felt oily. Raw blood was served to him by mistake, and he is known to have used it day after day in place of butter. He used to say that the only thing he tasted was water, and that was because it cooled his cheeks and throat.

He confessed that whatever he knew about the Scriptures he had learned while meditating and praying in the woods and the fields, and he sometimes said that among his friends he had no teachers except the oaks and the beeches. Finally he admitted that at times, as he meditated and prayed, the whole of Scripture appeared to him as though spread open and explained. He himself relates, in his sermons on the Canticle of Canticles, that once while he was in the very act of preaching, he tried to fix in his memory some thought suggested to him by the Holy Spirit, so that he might use it at another time—not that he did not trust the Holy Spirit's inspiration, but that he feared to trust himself too much. But a voice came to him and said: "As long as you cling to that one thought, you will not receive another."

In the matter of dress, poverty always pleased him, slovenliness never. The latter he took to be a sign of a careless mind or inordinate self-esteem or a will to attract other people's attention. He often repeated a proverb that he always had at heart: "Anyone who does what no one else does, all men will wonder at him." He wore a hair shirt for many years, as long as he could keep it a secret, but when he felt that it was known, he put the shirt off and dressed like everybody else. He never laughed but that it seemed he was forcing himself to laugh rather than to suppress laughter, and had to spur his laughter rather than to curb it.

He used to say that three kinds of patience were needed—one to bear insults, one to put up with damage to one's goods, and one to submit to bodily injury; and he proved that he had these three kinds by three examples. For instance, he had written a letter to a certain bishop by way of friendly admonition, and the bishop, extremely resentful, wrote back a very sharp letter that began: "I bid you good health and not the spirit of blasphemy," as if Bernard had written out of a spirit of blasphemy. Bernard replied: "I do not believe that I have the spirit of blasphemy, and I know that I have not wished to speak irreverently, especially to a prince of my people." Then a certain abbot had sent Bernard six hundred silver marks for the construction of a monastery, but on the way the whole sum was stolen by brigands. When Bernard heard of this, all he said was: "Blessed be God, who has spared us this burden! As for those who made off with the money, may they not be blamed too severely, both because human greed drove them to the deed, and because the size of the sum imposed a very strong temptation on them."

For a third example: a canon regular came to Bernard and asked him insistently to receive him as a monk. The saint did not consent and urged him to return to his church. "Well, then," said the canon, "why do you so strongly recommend the pursuit of perfection in your books, if you do not grant it to one who yearns for it? If I had your books in my hands, I would tear them to pieces!" Bernard: "In none of my books have you read that you cannot be perfect in your cloister. What I have commended in my books is reform of morals, not changes of place." The canon, furious, rushed at him and struck him in the face so hard that redness followed the blow and swelling followed the redness. The people who were present quickly set upon the sacrilegious assailant, but the servant of God stopped them, calling out and adjuring them in Christ's name not to touch him or do him any injury.

To those who wanted to enter the novitiate he regularly said: "If what you are eager to lay hold of are the things that are within you, leave outside here the bodies you have brought from the world! Only spirits are allowed inside, the flesh is of no avail."

His father, who had stayed alone in his house, came to the monastery and there, advanced in years and having lived a good life, died a peaceful death. His sister, who was married, worldly, and in spiritual danger amidst riches and pleasures, once came to the monastery to visit her brothers, having with her a proud retinue and splendid trappings. Bernard shrank from her as from a net spread by the devil to catch souls and would not consent to go out to her. When she saw that none of her brothers came to meet her—except one of them who was the porter at the door, who called her a dressed-up dunghill—she broke into tears. "Though I am a sinner," she said, "Christ died for such as I; and because I know that I am a sinner, I seek the counsel and conversation of those who are good. If my brother despises my flesh, let the servant of God not despise my soul! Let him come out, let him command, and whatever he commands I will do!"

With this promise in hand, Bernard and his brothers went out to her, and, because he could not separate her from her spouse, he forbade her all worldly show and reminded her of their mother as a model for her imitation. Then he let her depart. She went home and changed so quickly that in the midst of the world she led the life of an anchoress, alienating herself from everything worldly. Finally, by dint of much prayer, she obtained her husband's consent and, being dispensed by the bishop, entered a monastery.

There was a time when the man of God fell so seriously ill that he seemed about to breathe his last. He was rapt in ecstasy and saw himself being presented before God's judgment seat, while Satan stood opposite him and peppered him with malicious charges. When Satan had exhausted his list and it was the man of God's turn to speak for himself, fearless and unperturbed he said: "I admit I am unworthy, and unable by merits of my own, to gain entrance to the kingdom of heaven. On the other hand, my Lord has won the kingdom by a twofold right, namely, by inheritance from his Father and by the merits of his passion. The first he has reserved for himself but the second he gives to me; and by that gift I assert my right and shall not be confounded!" These words threw the Enemy into confusion, the meeting was closed, and the man of God came to himself.

Bernard mortified his body by so much abstinence, toil, and watching in the night that he continually suffered poor health and even very serious illness, and could follow the conventual routine only with great difficulty. One time when he was laid low with illness, his brother monks prayed for him so persistently that he felt restored to some extent, but he called them all together and said: "Why do you cling so to me, miserable man that I am? You are stronger than I and you have prevailed, but spare me, I beg of you, spare me and let me go!"

Several cities elected the man of God to be their bishop, chief among them Genoa and Milan. Neither acceding to their pleas nor making false excuses, he said that he was not his own man but was destined to the service of others. His brother monks, moreover, acting on the saint's advice, had anticipated such situations and had armed themselves with the sovereign pontiff's authority, so that no one could deprive them of the one who was their joy.

Once when he had gone to visit his brothers the Carthusians and they had been greatly edified by him in every respect, just one thing had raised a small doubt in the mind of the prior of the place: it struck him that the saddle on which Bernard rode was of fine workmanship and showed no evidence of poverty. The said prior mentioned this to one of the visiting monks and he to Bernard himself. He was taken aback and asked what saddle they were talking about: he had ridden from Clairvaux all the way to the Grande Chartreuse and had never noticed the saddle. He rode along the Lake of Lausanne for a whole day without even seeing the lake, or not seeing that he saw it. Then in the evening his companions were talking about the lake, and he asked them where this lake was—a question that made them wonder.

The lowliness of his heart surpassed the sublimity of his renown, and the whole world could not exalt him so much as he lowered himself. He was considered the highest by all, and the lowest by himself; and whereas all ranked him above themselves, he considered himself above no one. He often said that when the highest honors and the favors of the peoples were showered upon him, he felt that some other man had been put in his place and he himself was absent, or that this was a dream. When he was with the simple brothers, on the other hand, he was happy to enjoy and share their friendly humility and to be himself again. Indeed he was always to be found either praying or reading or writing or meditating, or edifying his brothers by talking to them.

Once when he was preaching to the people and they were paying devout attention to his every word, a tempting thought crept into his mind: "Now you're preaching at your best and people are listening to you willingly, and they all esteem you as a wise man." But the man of God, feeling himself beset by this idea, paused for a moment and thought whether he should go on with his sermon or end it. At once, strengthened by God's help, he silently answered the

Tempter: "You had nothing to do with my beginning to preach, and nothing you can do will make me stop," and calmly continued to the end of his sermon.

One of the monks, who in his earlier life had been a rake and a gambler, was goaded by a malignant spirit and wanted to return to the world. When Saint Bernard could not dissuade him, he asked him what he would do for a living. "I know how to play at dice," the monk answered, "and I'll make a living that way!" Bernard: "If I give you some capital, will you come back now and then and divide the profit with me?" The monk agreed gladly and promised to do as requested. Bernard ordered that he be given twenty sols, and off he went. The saint did this to be able to bring him back, and that is what happened. The man lost all he had and came crestfallen to the door of the monastery. His coming was announced to the man of God, who joyfully went out to him and held out his scapular spread wide to receive his share of the winnings. "I didn't win anything, father," he said, "and was stripped even of our capital. But take me back, if you will, in place of the money." Bernard kindly responded: "If that's the way things are, it's better that I get you back than that I lose both you and the capital!"

Once when blessed Bernard was riding along a road, he met a countryman, to whom he spoke sadly about a matter that was on his mind, namely, the instability of the human heart at prayer. The peasant, hearing this, immediately formed a low opinion of him and said that in his own prayer he always kept his heart firm and stable. Bernard wished to change the man's mind and temper his bold overconfidence, so he said to him: "Go aside a little way and, with all the attention you can bring to it, begin to pray the Lord's Prayer; and if you are able to finish it without any distraction or wandering of the heart, the beast I'm riding will be yours without doubt or question. But you must give me your word that if any other thought comes to you, you won't hide it from me." Happy with the offer, and feeling that he already owned the animal, the man withdrew, recollected himself, and began to recite the Our Father. He was not halfway through the prayer when a distracting thought stole into his heart: "The saddle . . . will I get the saddle with the mount, or not?" Becoming aware of the distraction, he hurried back to Bernard, told him the selfish thought that had come to him as he prayed, and from then on was not so rashly sure of himself.

Being young and listening to bad advice, Brother Robert, one of his monks and a close relative, left Clairvaux and took himself off to Cluny. The venerable father hid his feelings about this for some time, then decided to recall the young monk by letter. He was dictating the letter in the open air and another monk was putting it down in writing, when a sudden rainstorm came over and the writer started to fold up the paper. Bernard: "This is the work of God! Go right ahead with your writing!" The monk therefore wrote the letter in the midst of the shower as if there were no shower: it was raining all around, but at that spot the power of charity warded off the annoyance of the rain. Then an unbelievable cloud of flies invaded a monastery built by the man of God, making life unbearable for the monks. Bernard said: "I excommunicate the flies!" The next morning not a single fly was found alive.

The pope sent Bernard to Milan to reconcile the Milanese to the Church. When the saint reached Pavia on the return journey, a man brought his wife, who was possessed of a devil, to him. The devil, speaking through the poor woman's mouth, began to insult the man of God, saying: "This eater of leeks and devourer of cabbages won't get me out of my little old woman!" Bernard sent the woman to the church of Saint Syrus, but Saint Syrus wished to defer to his guest and so wrought no cure, so the woman was brought back to blessed Bernard. Then the devil began to babble through the woman's mouth, saying: "Little old Syrus will not expel me and neither will little old Bernard throw me out!" But as soon as Bernard began to pray, the wicked spirit said: "How glad I would be to get out of this old woman, tormented as I am inside her! How gladly I would leave her, but I cannot, because my great master will not let me!" Bernard: "And who is this great master?" The devil: "Jesus of Nazareth!" The man of God: "Have you ever seen him?" The answer: "Yes!" The saint: "Where did you see him?" The devil: "In glory!" The saint: "And you were in glory?" The devil: "Indeed I was!" The saint: "How is it that you left?" The devil: "Many of us fell with Lucifer!" All this talk came in a lugubrious tone from the old woman's mouth for all to hear. Then the man of God asked the devil: "Would you like to go back to that glory?" But the spirit, with a harsh laugh, said: "It's too late now!"

Bernard prayed, and the demon went out of the woman; but when the man of God left the place, the devil again took possession of her. Her husband ran after Bernard and told him what had happened. He ordered the man to tie a paper around his wife's neck, with these words written on the paper: "In the name of our Lord Jesus Christ I forbid you, demon, to presume to come near this woman from now on!" This was done, and the spirit no longer dared to molest the woman.

In Aquitaine there was a pitiable woman possessed of a wanton demon, an incubus, who for six years abused her and treated her with incredible lust. The man of God was passing through the region, and the demon sternly forbade the woman to go to him, adding the threat that the saint could do her no good, and that after he left, the demon, who had been her lover, would persecute her most cruelly. Nevertheless she went confidently to the man of God and told him, with tears and groans, what she was suffering. Bernard: "Take this staff of mine and put it in your bed, and if he can do anything then, let him try it!" She did as ordered, and when she lay in bed, the demon came in promptly but did not dare to undertake the usual activity, nor even to approach her bed; but he threatened her sharply, saying that when the saint was no longer there, he, the demon, would exact a fearful revenge. When she reported this to Bernard, he called the whole populace together and ordered them to come with lighted candles in their hands. Then, with the assembly joining in, he excommunicated the demon and forbade him thenceforth to come near this or any other woman. So the woman was completely freed of her trouble.

The man of God was in the same province as a delegate with a specific task to perform, namely, to reconcile the duke of Aquitaine to the Church, but the duke absolutely refused to be reconciled. The saint went to the altar to celebrate the mass, while the duke, still under excommunication, stood outside expectantly. When the man of God had said the *Pax Domini*,[3] he placed the Body of the Lord[4] on the paten and, taking it with him, went outside. There, his face ablaze and fire in his eye, he marched up to the duke and spoke fearsome words. "We have pleaded with you," he said, "and you have spurned us! Look here, the Son of the Virgin has come to you, he who is the Lord of the Church you are persecuting! Here is your judge, in whose name every knee must bend! Here is your judge, into whose hands that soul of yours will fall! Will you despise him as you despise his servants? Resist him if you can!" Hearing this, the duke was bathed with sweat. His limbs gave way under him, and he threw himself at the saint's feet. Bernard nudged him with his foot and ordered him to stand up and hear God's sentence. He rose all atremble and thereafter fulfilled all that the holy man prescribed.

The servant of God went into the kingdom of Germany to calm some civil strife, and the archbishop of Mainz sent a venerable cleric to accompany him. When the cleric told him that his master had sent him, the man of God replied: "Another master sent you!" The cleric wondered what that meant and affirmed that his master the archbishop of Mainz had sent him. To the contrary, the servant of Christ said: "You are mistaken, my son, you are mistaken! A greater master, Christ himself, sent you!" The cleric understood and said: "Do you think I want to become a monk? Not at all! No such thing has entered my mind!" But what followed? In the course of that journey the cleric bade farewell to the world and received the habit from the man of God.

Bernard had received a knight of the noble class into the Order, and this new monk followed the man of God for some time but then began to be bothered by a very grave temptation. Seeing how depressed he was, one of his brother monks asked him the reason for his sadness. "I know," he answered, "I know I will never be happy again!" This monk told the servant of God what the other had said, and the saint prayed for him with special fervor, whereupon the one who had been so sorely tempted and so disheartened looked as much happier and jollier than the rest as before he had been sadder. When the concerned brother reminded him in a friendly way of what he had said about being sad, he answered: "Although I said then that I never again would be happy, now I say that I shall never again be sad!"

---

[3] The peace of the Lord (be with you).
[4] The consecrated wafer.

Saint Malachy, the bishop of Ireland, whose virtuous life was written by Saint Bernard, died a happy death in Bernard's monastery, and the man of God celebrated his funeral mass. By divine revelation he knew that Malachy was already in glory. So, inspired by God, he changed the form of the post-communion prayer and, in a joyous voice, said: "O God, thou hast made blessed Malachy the equal of thy saints in merit. Grant, we beseech thee, that we, who celebrate the feast of his precious death, may imitate the examples of his life." When the cantor suggested that Bernard had made a mistake, he said: "No mistake! I know what I'm saying!" Then he went and kissed the sacred remains.

At the approach of Lent a large number of young students came to visit Bernard, and he urged them to give up their vanities and licentiousness at least during the holy season. They would not listen to a word of this, so he ordered them to drink a toast that went: "Here's to souls!" They drank the toast, and a sudden change came over them. They ended their visit and, though they had refused to mend their ways even for a short season, thereafter gave their whole lives to God.

At last blessed Bernard, happily looking forward to his death, said to his brother monks: "I bequeath to you three things to be observed, three things that I, in the course of my life, have kept in mind and have done my best to observe. I have wished to give scandal to no one, and if scandal occurred, I have kept it secret as best I could: I have always trusted the opinion of others more than my own: I have never sought to avenge an injury. Charity, humility, patience—these are the three things I leave you." Finally, after he had wrought many miracles, had built 160 monasteries, and had compiled many books and treatises, in the sixty-third year of his life, with his spiritual sons around him, he went to his eternal rest in the year of the Lord 1153.

After his death he manifested his glory to many. Thus he appeared to the abbot of a certain monastery and admonished him to follow him. The abbot followed him, and the man of God said to him: "See, we have come to Mount Lebanon. You stay here, and I am going to climb the mountain!" The abbot asked him why he intended to climb, and he said: "I want to learn!" Wondering, the abbot asked: "What do you want to learn, father? We believe that you are second to none in knowledge today!" Bernard: "Here below there is no knowledge, no grasp of what the truth is: above there is fullness of knowledge . . . above, a true conception of the truth." With these words he disappeared. The abbot noted the date and found that the man of God had migrated from the body on that day.

God wrought many other, indeed almost innumerable miracles, through his servant.

121. Saint Timothy

Timothy (Timotheus) might come from *timorem tenens*, holding fear, or from *timor* and *theos*, God, hence fear of God. That fear is aroused in every holy man, as Gregory says, when he considers where he has been, where he will be, where he is, and where he is not: where he was, because in sin; where he will be, in judgment; where he is, in misery; where he is not, in glory.

Timothy was severely tortured by the prefect of the city of Rome under Nero. His open wounds were sprinkled with quicklime, but amid these tortures he gave thanks to God. Two angels stood by him and said: "Raise your head toward heaven and see!" He looked and saw the heavens opened, and Jesus holding a jeweled crown and saying to him: "You will receive this crown from my hand." A man named Apollinaris witnessed this and had himself baptized, whereupon the prefect, seeing that both of them persevered in confessing Christ, had them beheaded, about A.D. 57.

122. Saint Symphorian

The name Symphorian is formed from *symphonia*, symphony. The saint indeed, was like a musical instrument, emitting a harmony of virtues. In this instrument, however, there were three qualities. A musical instrument, as Averrhoës says, should be of hard material in order to resonate, mellow in order to hold the note, and wide to give breadth of sound. Thus Symphorian was hard to himself in his austerity, mellow toward others in his gentleness, and wide in the broad reach of his charity.

Symphorian was a native of Autun. When he was still an adolescent, he was so serious in his conduct that he seemed to anticipate the mien and manners of older men. The pagans had a custom of celebrating the feast of Venus and parading her statue before the prefect Heraclius. Symphorian was present, and, for refusing to worship the goddess, he was given a prolonged flogging and thrown into prison. When he was brought out and ordered to sacrifice, being promised a wealth of gifts if he did so, he said: "Our God knows how to reward merit and also how to punish sins. The life we are to pay to Christ as a debt, let us pay it out of piety! Repentance is late when it consists of trembling with fear under the baleful glare of a judge. Your gifts, laced with the sweetness of honey, turn to poison in the minds of the erroneously credulous. Your greed grasps at everything and possesses nothing, because, by the arts of the devil, it is caught in the snare of a sorry profit. Your joys are like glass: they begin to shine and are shattered."

The irate judge then pronounced sentence and ordered Symphorian to be put to death. As he was being led to the place of execution, his mother called down from the wall, saying: "My child, my child, remember eternal life! Look up and see the Lord reigning in heaven, where this life is not taken away but exchanged for a better." He was beheaded, and Christians took his body away and buried it with honors.

So many miracles occurred at his tomb that he was held in high honor even by the pagans. Gregory of Tours tells us that a Christian carried away three bloodstained pebbles from the place where the martyr had shed his blood. These three pebbles he placed in a silver box and put the box in a wooden casket. This was kept in a castle, and later the castle was totally destroyed by fire, but the aforementioned casket was brought out of the ruins undamaged and unmarked.

The saint suffered about A.D. 270.

123. Saint Bartholomew

Bartholomew (Bartholomeus) is interpreted as son of one who suspends the waters, or son of one who suspends himself. The name comes from *bar*, which means son, *tholos*, height, and *moys*, water. So Bartholomew is the son of one who holds the waters on high, i.e., a son of God, who lifts up the minds of the doctors so that they may pour down the waters of their teaching. The name is not Hebrew but Syriac. The first interpretation indicates three kinds of suspension found in Bartholomew. He was suspended in the sense that he was lifted above love of the world, or in that he was sustained by the love of heavenly things, or in that he was totally supported by grace and the help of God. The second interpretation indicates the depth of his wisdom. Regarding the depth of his wisdom, Dionysius, in his *Mystical Theology*, says: "The divine Bartholomew says that there is much in theology, the science of God, and yet there is very little, and that the Gospel is broad and abundant, and yet concise." Dionysius means that Bartholomew wants to show that from one perspective everything can be affirmed of God, while from another, everything is more properly negated.

Bartholomew the apostle went to India, which is at the end of the earth, entered a temple where there was an idol named Astaroth, and began to stay there like a pilgrim. In this idol there dwelt a demon who said that he cured the sick, though he did not really cure them but merely stopped hurting them. Now, however, when the temple was filled with sick people and daily sacrifices were offered for the infirm who were brought even from distant regions, they could obtain no response from the idol. They therefore went to another city where an idol named Berith was worshiped, and asked this idol why Astaroth would give them no response. Berith answered: "Our god is bound with fiery chains and does not dare to breathe or speak since the moment when the apostle Bartholomew came in." They said: "Who is this Bartholomew?" The demon: "He is a friend of almighty God, and he came into this province to rid India of all its gods!" And they: "Give us a sign by which we can pick him out!" The demon told them: "His hair is dark and curly, his complexion fair, his eyes wide, his nose even and straight, his beard thick, with a few gray hairs. He is clad in a white, short-sleeved garment with purple tassels, and a white cloak decorated with purple gems at the corners. He has worn the same clothes and sandals for twenty years, and they show no signs of wear or dirt. He kneels a hundred times a day to pray, and as many times at night. Angels walk with him and never allow him to get tired or hungry. He is always cheerful and joyous in countenance and spirit. He foresees all and knows all, speaks and understands the language of every people. At this moment he knows what we are talking about. When you look for him, he will let you see him if he so wishes, but if he does not so wish, you will not be able to find him. Moreover I beg you, when you do find him, ask him not to come here and have his angels do to me what they have done to my comrade!"

These people spent two days looking for the apostle but never caught sight of him. Then a man who was possessed of the devil cried out: "Bartholomew, apostle of God, your prayers are burning me!" The apostle: "Be still, and get out of that man!" And the man was freed at once. Polemius, the king of that region, heard of this. He had a daughter who was given to violent fits, so he sent to the apostle and asked him to come and cure her. Bartholomew went and found the girl tied down with chains because she tried to bite anyone who came near her. He ordered her released, and when the attendants were afraid to approach her, he said: "I already hold in bonds the demon that was in her! What are you afraid of?" So they took off her chains and set her free. The king then loaded camels with gold and silver and precious stones, and sent people in search of Bartholomew, but he was nowhere to be found. The next morning, however, he appeared to the king, who was alone in his chamber, and said to him: "Why were you looking for me all day with gold and silver and precious stones? Such things are a necessity to those who seek earthly goods, but I desire nothing that is of the earth or of the flesh."

Then Saint Bartholomew began to teach the king much about the way our redemption was accomplished. He showed him, among other things, that Christ conquered the devil in a way that was appropriate and demonstrated his power, his justice, and his wisdom. It was appropriate in that the devil, who had conquered the son of a virgin, namely, Adam, who was formed out of the virgin earth, should be conquered by the Son of the Virgin. The victory demonstrated Christ's superior power, since he ejected the devil from the lordship that belonged to Christ, which the devil had usurped by bringing down the first man. And as the conqueror of a tyrant sends his adjutants to erect monuments in his honor and to do away with those of the tyrant, so Christ the victor sends his messengers everywhere to eliminate worship of the devil and to spread the religion of Christ. There was justice, in that the one who had laid hold of man by inducing him to eat the forbidden fruit should lose his hold on mankind through being conquered by a man who fasted. Wisdom was demonstrated, since the devil's tricks were bested by the arts of Christ. The devil's trick consisted in snatching Christ up the way a falcon snatches a bird, and leaving him in the desert. If he fasted there but did not get hungry, then undoubtedly he would be God: if he did grow hungry the devil would conquer him with food, as he had conquered the first man. But as things turned out, Christ, because he did get hungry, could not be recognized as God, nor could he be conquered, because he did not yield to the devil's temptation and eat bread.

When he had preached the mysteries of faith to the king, Bartholomew told him that if he chose to be baptized, he would show him his god bound in chains. The following day, therefore, when the pagan priests were offering sacrifice to the idol close by the king's palace, the demon began to cry out, saying: "Stop, you poor fools, stop sacrificing to me, or you may suffer worse torments than those I am suffering. I am wrapped about with fiery chains by an angel of Jesus Christ, whom the Jews crucified thinking they could put an end to him by death. But he took death, our queen, captive, and vanquished our prince, the author of death, with fiery chains!" All then took ropes with which to pull down the idol, but they could not. The apostle, however, commanded the demon to come out of the idol and demolish it. Out he came, and by himself destroyed all the idols in the temple. The apostle prayed and cured all the sick, then dedicated the temple to God, and ordered the demon to depart and go to the desert.

Now an angel of the Lord appeared and flew around the temple, inscribing the sign of the cross with his finger at the four corners and saying: "Thus says the Lord: 'As I have cleansed all of you of your infirmities, so this temple will now be rid of all foulness and of its inhabitant, whom my apostle has bidden to go off to a desert place.' First I will show him to you. Do not be afraid when you see him, but make the sign of the cross on your foreheads as I have inscribed it on these stones!" Then he showed them an Ethiopian blacker than soot, with a sharp face, a thick beard, hair reaching down to his feet, blazing eyes that flashed sparks like a fire-reddened iron, shooting sulphurous flames from his mouth and eyes. His hands were clamped in red-hot gyves behind his back. The angel said to him: "Because you heeded the vision of the apostle and shattered all the idols as you left the temple, I shall release you to go to some place where no man dwells, and there you may stay until the Judgment Day!" So the demon, freed of his bonds, disappeared with much clatter and howling, and the angel of the Lord flew up to heaven as all watched.

After that the king was baptized with his wife and children and all his people, resigned his kingship, and became a disciple of the apostle. At this all the priests of the temples gathered together and went to King Astyages, brother of King Polemius, and charged Bartholomew with the loss of their gods, the leveling of the temple, and the deception of the king by tricks of magic. King Astyages, indignant, dispatched a thousand men to take the apostle prisoner. When Bartholomew was brought before him, the king said: "So you are the one who subverted my brother!" The apostle: "I did not subvert him, I converted him!" The king: "As you made my brother abandon his gods and believe in your God, so I shall make you abandon your God and sacrifice to my god!" Bartholomew: "I bound the god your brother worshiped—bound him in chains—showed him thus bound, and forced him to demolish the idol. If you can do the same to my God, you will be able to make me bow before your idol. Otherwise I shall reduce your gods to splinters! And, as for you, believe my God!"

He had not finished saying this when word came to the king that his god Baldach had fallen and was lying in fragments. Hearing this, the king tore the purple robe he was wearing, and ordered the apostle to be beaten with clubs and flayed alive. Christians then took his body and gave it honorable burial. King Astyages and the temple priests were seized by demons and died. King Polemius was ordained bishop, fulfilled the episcopal office laudably for twenty years, and then, full of virtues, died a peaceful death.

There are various opinions about the kind of death Bartholomew suffered. Saint Dorotheus says that he was crucified. These are his words: "Bartholomew preached to the people of India. He also gave them the Gospel according to Matthew written in their own language. He died in Albana, a city of Greater Armenia, being crucified head downward." Saint Theodore says that he was flayed. In many books, however, we read that he was beheaded. This disagreement can be resolved by saying that he was crucified, then, before he died, taken down and, to intensify his suffering, flayed alive, and finally had his head cut off.

In A.D. 831 the Saracens invaded Sicily and devastated the island of Lipari. The body of Saint Bartholomew was enshrined there, and they broke into his tomb and scattered his bones. His remains, by the way, came to the island in the following manner. The pagans in Armenia saw that due to the frequent occurrence of miracles his body was greatly venerated, and this displeased them profoundly. They therefore put the body into a leaden coffin and tossed it into the sea, and by God's will it reached the aforesaid island. The Saracens dispersed the saint's bones, but after they left Lipari, the apostle appeared to a monk and said: "Get up and collect my bones, which have been scattered!" The monk answered him: "For what reason should we collect your bones or pay you any honor, since you allowed us to be overrun and did nothing to help us?" Bartholomew: "For a long time, due to my merits, the Lord spared this people, but their sins grew so grievous that they cried to heaven, and I could no longer obtain pardon for them." The monk asked him how he could find his bones among so many others, and the saint said: "Go and look for them at night, and when you see any that shine like fire, gather them up right away!" Everything happened just as the apostle had said. The monk found the bones, collected them, and put them on a ship bound for Benevento, the principal city of Apulia, whither the ship carried them. Some say the relics are now in Rome, but the Beneventani still insist that they have that body.

A woman brought a jug of oil to have it put in a lamp at Saint Bartholomew's shrine, but, tilt the jug as they might, nothing came out of it. The sacristans put their fingers into the jug and felt that there was oily liquid in it, and someone exclaimed: "I think the apostle does not want this oil used in his lamp!" So they went and poured it into another lamp and it flowed out freely.

The emperor Frederick razed Benevento and gave orders to destroy all the churches in the city, intending to transfer the whole city to another location. Then a certain man came upon a group of men dressed in white robes and shining brightly; they were talking among themselves and seemed to be having a serious discussion. Astonished at what he saw, the man asked who they were, and one of them answered: "That is Bartholomew the apostle, with the other saints whose churches stood in the city. They came together to confer, and to agree upon the punishment to be visited on the one who had driven them from their abodes. They have arrived at an unalterable sentence: that man must go before God's judgment seat without delay, to answer to God the Judge for all those deeds!" A short time later the emperor came to a miserable end.

We read in a book of the miracles of the saints that there was a certain master who was accustomed to celebrate solemnly the feast of Saint Bartholomew. Once, as he was preaching on the feast day, the devil appeared to him in the form of a very alluring young woman. When the master's eyes fell on her, he invited her to dinner, and while they were at table, the girl used all her wiles to make him desire her. Now blessed Bartholomew came to the door of the house in the guise of a pilgrim and begged insistently to be admitted for the love of Saint Bartholomew. The girl objected to this, so a loaf was carried out to the pilgrim by a messenger, but he refused to accept it. Instead he asked the master, via the messenger, to tell him what property or quality, in his opinion, was unique in man. The master said it was the power to laugh, but the young woman said: "No, it is sin! Man is conceived in sin, born in sin, and lives in sin!" The pilgrim approved the master's reply but noted that the woman's was more profound. He sent a second request, this time to tell him where on earth was the place, measuring not more than one foot, where God manifested the greatest miracles. The master replied: "The place where the cross stood. There God worked his wonders." "No," said the girl, "it is the human head, in which the world exists, as it were, in miniature." The apostle approved both answers, but sent in a third question: "What is the distance between the peak of heaven and the bottom of hell?" The master said that he did not know, but the woman broke in: "I'm caught! I know how far it is, because I fell the whole distance, and it is fitting that I show it to you!" Then the devil cast himself into hell with a dreadful shriek. When they looked for the pilgrim, he was not to be found.

A very similar story is told about Saint Andrew.

Blessed Ambrose, in the Preface he wrote for this apostle, sums up his legend as follows.

"O Christ, you have deigned wondrously to show your majesty to your disciples who preach to the world your trinity in the one divinity! Among those preachers your benign foresight directed blessed Bartholomew, whom you honored with a special gift of virtues, to a far distant people, and that people, remote from you as they had been in their human affairs, he merited, by his increased preaching, to bring close to you. Oh, with what praises this wonderful apostle should be celebrated! To him it was not enough to sow the faith in the hearts of nearby peoples. As if with winged feet he penetrated to the farthest borders of the lands of the Indies! He came with an innumerable throng of sick people into a devil's temple and there prevented the demon from curing anyone. Oh, how wonderful the evidence of this man's virtues! By a simple command he silenced an adversary whose long speeches exhausted his hearers! He freed a king's daughter from demonic possession and gave her back to her father loosed from her bonds and cured of her ills. Oh, how sublime the miracle of his sanctity, when he compelled the ancient enemy of the human race to shatter his own image! How worthy to be counted among the heavenly host is he for whom an angel descended from heaven to give full confirmation to his miracles! The angel showed the enchained demon in his ugly deformity to all and inscribed the Lord's saving cross on the stone. King and queen are baptized together with the people of twelve neighboring towns and follow you, our Father God, body and soul! And in the end, when the apostle is denounced by the priests of the temples, the tyrant brother of the neophyte Polemius has him, steadfast as always in the faith, beaten, flayed, and subjected to a bitter death. And the apostle, manfully facing the perils of death, carries the triumph of that glorious contest into the joys of heaven." So Ambrose.

Saint Theodore, abbot and eminent doctor, says, among other things, about this apostle: "Bartholomew, the blessed apostle of God, first preached in Lycaonia, later in India, and lastly in Albana, a city of Greater Armenia, where he was flayed alive and beheaded, then buried there. When he was being sent to preach, he heard this, I think, from the Lord: 'Go, my disciple, go and preach, go out and fight, you are fit to face dangers! I accomplished my Father's works. I was the first witness. Now you fill up what is still needed, imitate your Master, emulate your Lord, put your blood with his blood, give flesh for flesh! What I have suffered and borne for you, suffer! Your weapons are good will in toil, gentleness toward those who wrong you, patience amidst the things that pass.' The apostle did not refuse. As a faithful srvant consenting to his master's command he went forward rejoicing, as the light of the world to dispel the darkness, as the salt of the earth to preserve the insipid pagans, as a tiller of the earth to bring to fruition a spiritual crop. The apostle Peter does great progidies: Bartholomew performs mighty miracles. Peter is crucified head downward: Bartholomew, after being flayed alive, has his head cut off. As clearly as Peter grasps the meaning of mysteries, so deeply is Bartholomew able to penetrate them. They both make the Church fruitful, they weigh equally on the scale of divine graces. Bartholomew, at the center of the sacred number twelve, is in accord by his sermonizing with those preceding him and those following, as the strings of the harp make harmony. All the apostles, dividing the world among themselves, were constituted shepherds of the King of kings. Armenia, from Eiulath to Gabaoth, was Bartholomew's lot and portion. See him using his tongue as a plow to cultivate the spiritual soil, hiding the word of faith in the depths of hearts, planting the gardens and vineyards of the Lord, grafting on healing remedies for the sufferings of men, weeding out harmful thorns. He cuts down the forests of impiety, he builds fences of sound doctrine.

"But what payment do they make to him for all these services? For honor, dishonor; for blessing, malediction; for gifts, pain; for a reposeful life, a most bitter death! After he underwent unbearable tortures, his skin was pulled off as if to make a bag. After he had departed this world, he still cared for his killers, inviting the lost by miracles and beckoning them in with marvels. But nothing would check their bestial mind or draw them back from evil. What do they do next? they vent their rage upon his sacred body! The sick despise their healer, the lame the one who led them by the hand, the blind their guide, the shipwrecked their pilot, the dead their reviver. How? By throwing his holy body into the sea! Then his coffin, along with the coffins of four other martyrs, which had been treated the same way and cast into the sea, was driven from the coasts of Armenia. So, over great distances, with these four leading the way for the apostle and being at his service, so to speak, they came to the island called Lipari, close to Sicily: this was revealed to the bishop of Ostia, who was there at the time. Thus the great treasure came to one very poor, this priceless pearl to one without nobility, this most brilliant light to one lost in gloom.[1] The other four coffins went to other places, leaving the holy apostle on the said island. Of the four martyrs already referred to, the apostle sent one, namely, Papinus, to the city of Mylae in Sicily, another, Lucianus, to Messina, and the remaining two to Calabria—Gregory to the city of Colonna, Achatius to the city called Cales, and these cities enjoy their protection to this day. Saint Bartholomew's body was welcomed with hymns and praises and candles, and a magnificent temple was built to house it. A volcanic mountain contiguous to the island, which did harm to those who lived nearby because it erupted with fire, stretched itself invisibly a distance of a mile or more and hovered around the sea, so that even today it looks to those who see it like a figuration of fleeing fire.

"Hail, O blessed of the blessed, thrice blessed Bartholomew! You are the splendor of Divine light, the fisherman of holy Church, expert catcher of fish endowed with reason, sweet fruit of the blooming palm tree! You wound the devil who wounds the world by his crimes! May you rejoice, O sun illumining the whole earth, mouth of God, tongue of fire that speaks wisdom, fountain ever flowing with health! You have sanctified the sea by your passage over it, you have purpled the earth with your gore, you have mounted to heaven, where you shine in the midst of the heavenly host, resplendent in the splendor of undimmable glory! Rejoice in the enjoyment of inexhaustible happiness!" Thus Theodore.[2]

124. Saint Augustine

Augustine received his name either on account of his high dignity or because of the fervor of his love, or again due to the etymology of the name. He was *augustinus* by his high rank, because, as Augustus the emperor had excelled above all kings, so Augustine, as Remy says, surpasses all doctors. Other doctors

---

[1] The meaning here is obscure.

[2] Saint Theodore the Studite, d. A.D. 826.

are compared to the stars: "They that instruct many to justice [shall shine] as stars for all eternity."[1] But Augustine is compared to the sun, as is clear from the epistle that is sung in his honor, since "as the sun when it shines, so did he shine in the temple of God."[2] Secondly, his name befitted the fervor of his love, because, as the month of August is fervent with the heat of the weather, so Augustine is fervent with the fire of the love of God. In his *Confessions* he says of himself: "You have pierced my heart with the arrow of your love"; and in the same book: "Sometimes you put into my innermost being a very unaccustomed affection—I know not what sweetness—which, if it be made perfect in me, I know not what it will be unless it will be eternal life."

Thirdly, there is the etymology of the name. *Augustinus* comes from *augeo*, I increase, *astin*, city, and *ana*, above. Hence Augustine is one who increases the city on high, wherefore we sing of him: "*qui praevaluit amplificare civitatem*"—he who is powerful enough to enlarge the city. About this city he himself says in the eleventh book of the *City of God*: "The city of God has origin, knowledge, happiness. If one asks whence the city comes, God founded it; if whence its wisdom comes, it is enlightened by God; if whence its happiness, it has God to enjoy. From him it has subsistence and measure, contemplating him it has its light, inhering in him, its pleasure. It sees and loves, it flourishes in God's eternity, it shines in God's truth, it has enjoyment in God's goodness." Or, as the *Glossary* says, the name Augustine means magnificent, happy, excellent. The saint was magnificent in his life and excellent in his teaching, and is happy in eternal glory.

His life was compiled by Possidius,[3] bishop of Calama, as Cassiodorus says in his *Book of Illustrious Men*.

The eminent doctor Augustine was born in Carthage,[4] a city in the province of Africa, the son of very honorable parents. His father was Patricius, his mother, Monica. He was so learned in the liberal arts as to be considered a philosopher of the highest order, and a brilliant rhetorician. By himself he studied and understood the books of Aristotle and all the books on the liberal arts that he could read, as he testifies in his *Confessions*, saying: "Wicked slave of evil desires as I then was, on my own and unaided I read all the books they call liberal—all, at any rate, that I could read.[5] In the same book he says: "Whatever concerns the art of speaking and debating, or the dimensions of figures, or music and num-

---

[1] Dan. 12:3.

[2] Ecclus. 50:7 (Douay): probably from the first reading (hence "epistle") in an ancient mass for the feast of Saint Augustine.

[3] Not Possidonius, as in the text.

[4] He was born in Tagaste, in the Roman province of Africa, of which Carthage was the principal city.

[5] *quoscumque legere potui*—meaning, no doubt, all that were available to him.

bers, I understood without great difficulty and with no help from anyone. You know, O Lord my God, that all quickness in understanding and sharpness in learning are your gifts, but that did not lead me to worship you, because knowledge without love does not edify, but puffs up one's pride." He fell into the error of the Manicheans, who hold that Christ was a phantasm and deny the resurrection, and persisted in that error for nine years, while he was still an adolescent. His attachment to trifles was such that he said that a fig tree wept when a leaf or a fig was plucked.

When he reached the age of nineteen, he read a book by a certain philosopher[6] in which it was said that the world's vanity should be shunned and philosophy pursued. He liked the book very much but regretted that the name of Jesus Christ, which he had learned from his mother, did not appear in it. All this time his mother wept for him and tried to bring him around to the truth of faith. Once, as we read in the third book of the *Confessions*, she had a vision in which she saw herself standing on a wooden rule, grief-stricken, and a young man stood beside her and asked the cause of her sadness. "I mourn for the loss of my son," she told him. "Be reassured," he replied, "because where you are, there he is." And she looked and saw her son at her side. When she told Augustine about this vision, he said: "You're mistaken, mother, you're mistaken! He did not say what you quote him as saying; he said that where I am, there you are." "No, my son," she said, "what he said to me was, 'Where he is, you will be,' not, 'Where you are, there he will be.'"[7] His mother continued her efforts and, as Augustine testifies in the same book of the *Confessions*, importuned a certain bishop to deign to intercede for her son. Won over by such insistence, the bishop answered, and his words were prophetic: "Go confidently! It is impossible that the son of so many tears should perish!"

After Augustine had taught rhetoric for a number of years in Carthage, he left secretly for Rome without letting his mother know and in Rome attracted many pupils. Monica had followed him to the Carthage city gate, intending either to dissuade him or to go with him to Rome, but he managed to divert her attention and got away by night. When she discovered this in the morning, she filled the ears of God with her cries. Every day, morning and evening, she went to the church and prayed for her son. At that time the Milanese[8] appealed to Symmachus, the prefect of Rome, to send them a teacher of rhetoric. The man of God Ambrose was bishop of that city. In response to the people's request Augustine was sent to Milan. His mother, however, could not rest and, overcoming all sorts of difficulties, came to join him. She found him neither a convinced Manichean nor truly a Catholic. Augustine had begun to follow Ambrose and frequently heard him preach. He paid the closest attention to the

---

[6] According to Graesse (550n) "Others add 'Cicero.'"

[7] Monica's answer is here translated exactly as Graesse's text has it, including the obvious contradiction: cf. *Confessions* 3.11.

[8] Graesse has *Athenienses*, which cannot be right.

bishop's sermons, waiting to hear what he might say either against the heresy of the Manicheans or in its favor. The time came when Ambrose spoke at length against that error, refuting it with clear reasons and sound authorities, and the error was driven from Augustine's heart once and for all. What happened to him after this, he himself tells us in the *Confessions*: "When I first came to know you, [Christ] you assailed my weak sight, turning your brightness blindingly upon me. I shuddered with love and horror, and found myself to be far from you, in a region of unlikeness, and seeming to hear your voice as from on high, saying: 'I am the food of the full-grown! Grow and you will eat me, and you will not change me into yourself like the food of your body, but you will be changed into me.'"

The way of Christ pleased him then, but he still hung back from entering by those narrow paths, until the Lord put it into his mind to go to Simplicianus, in whom the light, namely, divine grace, shone. To him he could confide his anxieties regarding the proper mode of living in order to walk in God's ways, on which some went one way and some another. What he had to do in the world now gave him no pleasure in comparison with the sweetness of God and the beauty of his house, which he loved. Simplicianus began to exhort him, saying: "How many mere boys and girls serve God within the Lord's church, and you are not able to do what this one and that one do! Or, in truth, do they do this in and of themselves and not in their God? Why do you insist on standing all by yourself when you do not succeed in standing at all? Cast yourself upon him and he will welcome you and save you!"

In the course of their conversations the memory of Victorinus came up. Simplicianus was delighted and told how Victorinus, still a pagan, came to Rome— the fame of his wisdom earned him the very great honor of having a statue of himself in the forum—and how he repeatedly claimed that he was a Christian. When Simplicianus said to him: "I will not believe you unless I see you in church!" he jokingly replied: "So! Is it walls that make a man a Christian?" But at length he came into the Church, and a book was given to him privately so as not to embarrass him. It was the custom to give such a book, which contained the Credo or symbol of faith, so that he could read and proclaim it. He mounted a platform and recited his faith at the top of his voice, while all Rome marveled and the Church rejoiced, and the throng cried out: "Victorinus! Victorinus!" They shouted suddenly and as suddenly fell silent.

At this time Pontitianus, a friend of Augustine's, came over from Africa and told about the life and miracles of the great Anthony, who had died not long before under Emperor Constantine.[9] Augustine was so stirred by these men's examples that, troubled both in his looks and in his mind, he ran to Alypius and loudly exclaimed: "Now we've heard this! What are we waiting for? These are people without education and they rise up and seize heaven, while we, with all

---

[9] Constantius II, 351–363. Anthony died in 356.

our learning, are sinking into hell! Is it that we are ashamed to follow because they have gone ahead of us? Should we not be ashamed if we do not at least follow them?"

He ran out into the garden and, as he recalls in the same book, threw himself down under a fig tree and, weeping inconsolably, lamented aloud: "How long, how long will it be 'Tomorrow, tomorrow! Not right now, hold on a little while?'" His "now" had no end, and the "little while" went on and on. He reproached himself for procrastinating, as he wrote further on in the same book: "Woe is me! You are high in the heights and deep in the depths and you never draw back from us, and we barely succeed in returning to you! Act, Lord, do, and awaken us and call us back! Come for us and seize us and draw us with your perfume and your sweetness! I feared to be relieved of all the impediments that stood in my way, as I should have feared to be impeded by them. Late have I loved, you, O Beauty so ancient and so new! Late have I loved you! You were within me and I was outside, and I looked for you outside, and, unbeautiful as I am, I rushed after those beauties, which you have created! You were with me and I was not with you! You called and clamored and broke into my deafness, you sparkled and shone and chased away my blindness! You have let me breathe in your fragrance and I pant after you! You have touched me and I burn to enjoy your peace!" As he wept so sorrowfully, he heard a voice saying to him: "Take and read, take and read!" Quickly he opened the book of the apostle, and his eye first fell on the chapter where it is said: "Put ye on the Lord Jesus Christ, and make not provision for the flesh, to fulfill the lusts thereof."[10] And immediately every shadow of doubt was blown away.

Meanwhile he suffered a toothache so severe, as he himself says, that he was almost ready to agree with the opinion of the philosopher Cornelius, that the highest good of the soul is in wisdom, and the body's highest good is in feeling no pain. The toothache was so bad that he could not speak, wherefore, as he notes in his *Confessions*, he wrote on wax tablets, asking all to pray for him that the Lord might mitigate his suffering. So everyone knelt in prayer, and the pain subsided at once.

He wrote a letter to Saint Ambrose, conveying his wish to become a Christian and asking him to tell him which books of the Bible he should read in order to better prepare himself. Ambrose recommended the prophet Isaiah as most suitable, since that prophet had predicted the Gospel and the calling of the Gentiles. Augustine read the first chapters of the book, but did not understand it and put it aside to be read later, when he would have learned more about the sacred writings. When the Easter season came, his mother's merits and Ambrose's preaching bore fruit, and Augustine, then thirty years old,[11] with his friend Alypius and his son Adeodatus, a bright boy whom he had fathered in his youth

[10] Rom. 13:14.
[11] Thirty-three, actually.

when he was still a Gentile and a philosopher, received holy baptism. Then Ambrose, we are told, sang *Te Deum laudamus*, and Augustine responded *Te Dominum confitemur*,[12] and so, alternately, they composed the hymn and chanted it to the end, as Honorius also testifies in his book which is called *Speculum Ecclesiae*.[13] In some books, however, *Canticle Composed by Ambrose and Augustine* is given as its ancient title.

Now that he was so wondrously confirmed in the Catholic faith, Augustine relinquished all his worldly hopes and left behind the schools that he had governed. In his *Confessions* he tells how sweet was the love of God that he enjoyed thereafter. He says: "You have pierced my heart with the arrow of your love, and I carried your words transfixed in my loins. The examples of your servants, whom you brought from darkness to light and from death to life, crowded into the heart of my thought, burned there, and took away all heaviness and languor. To me as I came up out of the vale of tears and sang the gradual canticle,[14] you gave sharp arrows and devastating coals. In those days I could not have enough of the wonderful sweetness of considering your high design for the salvation of the human race. How much I cried, hearing your hymns and canticles suavely resounding in the church. I was poignantly moved by the voices, and those voices flowed into my ears and your truth flowed smoothly into my heart, and the tears ran down, and they did me much good. That was the time when those chants were composed in the church of Milan. And I called out from the depth of my heart: 'In peace in the selfsame I will sleep and I will rest.'[15] For you are the selfsame, you do not change, and in you there is rest and the forgetting of all labors. I read that whole Psalm[16] and I burned—I, who had been a bitter, blind opponent, ranting against these words that are honeyed with the honey of heaven and luminous with your light. Now I pined for such words of Scripture. Christ Jesus, my helper, how sweet it suddenly was for me to be without the sweetness of my treasured trifles! I had been afraid of losing them, and now it was a joy to be without them! You threw them out from me, you, the true and highest sweetness! You threw them out and came in in their stead, you, sweeter than all pleasures, but not to flesh and blood, brighter than all lights, yet more inward than any secret, more exalted than all honors, but not to those who exalt themselves!"

After this he set out for Africa, taking with him Nebrodius, Evodius, and his loving mother, but while they were in Ostia on the Tiber, his mother died. After her death Augustine went home to his estates in Africa, where, with those

---

[12] "We praise thee as God, we acknowledge thee as the Lord"—the opening verses of the *Te Deum.*

[13] Mirror of the Church.

[14] One of the Gradual Psalms or Canticles (Psalms 120–134), also called Songs of Degrees, or of Steps.

[15] Ps. 4:9 (Douay).

[16] Psalm 120, the one referred to above as the Gradual Canticle.

who stayed with him, he devoted himself to fasting and praying to God, wrote books, and taught the unlearned. His fame spread abroad, and he was admired both for his books and for his way of life. He was careful not to visit any city that was without a bishop, for fear he might be forced to assume that office. At this time there was in Hippo a very wealthy man, who sent word to Augustine that if he came and preached the Word to him, he might renounce the world. When Augustine heard this, he hurried to Hippo. Valerius, the bishop of that city, knew Augustine's reputation and, despite his resistance, ordained him a priest in his church. There were those who took his reluctance and his tears as a sign of pride, and told him, by way of consolation, that although the position of a priest was beneath his deserts, it was nonetheless a step toward the episcopate. Augustine immediately established a monastery for clergy and began to live according to a rule drawn up by the holy apostles. About ten bishops were elected from this monastery. Bishop Valerius, being a Greek and not very familiar with the Latin language and letters, commissioned Augustine to preach before him in his church, contrary to the usage of the Eastern Church. Many bishops protested at this, but Valerius paid no attention so long as through Augustine he was getting done what he himself was not able to do.

About this time he spoke against and refuted Fortunatus, a Manichean priest, and other heretics, expecially the Donatists, who insisted on rebaptism of lapsed Catholics, and the Manicheans. Thus he completely nullified their influence. Valerius began to fear that some other city would carry Augustine off and make him bishop, so he persuaded the archbishop of Carthage to let him resign from his office, and to promote Augustine to be the bishop of the church of Hippo. Augustine refused time after time to agree to this, but finally yielded to pressure and pleas and assumed the episcopal office. That this should not have been done to him while his bishop was alive he later both said and wrote, having learned after his ordination that the procedure was forbidden by decree of a council. He deplored what had been done and did not want it to happen to anyone else. He also did his best to persuade the bishops in council to make a law requiring that the statutes of the fathers be fully made known to those about to be ordained. We read that at a later time he said of himself: "I feel that the Lord was never so angry with me as when, though I was unworthy even to be put at an oar, he placed me at the helm to govern the Church."

His clothing, footwear, and vestments were neither too elegant nor too poor, but modest and suitable. We read that he said about himself: "I admit that I am ashamed of a costly garment, and so, if one is given to me, I sell it, so that since the garment can't belong to everybody, its price may be shared by all." His table was frugal and sparse, but along with the herbs and vegetables there was meat for the sick and other guests. At the table he preferred reading or good talk to feasting, and against the plague of malicious gossip he had inscribed the following verse on the table:

Quisquis amat dictis absentum rodere vitam
Hanc mensam indignam noverit esse sibi.[17]

Indeed, one time some of his fellow bishops, close friends of his, set their tongues to making derogatory remarks, and he had harsh words for them, saying that unless they desisted, he would either erase the inscription or leave the table. Another time he had invited some of this friends to a meal, and one of them, more curious than the rest, went into the kitchen and found nothing but cold food. He came back to Augustine and asked what dishes the master of the house had ordered for dinner. Augustine, who had no curiosity about such things as food, answered: "I don't know any more than you do!"

He said that he had learned three things from Saint Ambrose. The first was never to court a woman for someone else; the second, never to encourage someone who wanted to be a soldier; the third, to accept no invitations to dinner parties. The reason for the first is that the two might not be suited to each other and might come to quarreling; for the second, that soldiers might be given to calumny and others might put the blame on him; for the third, that he might perhaps overstep the limits of temperance.

Such was his purity, such his humility, that in his book of *Confessions* he confesses and humbly accuses himself to God of sins so slight that we would think little or nothing of them. Thus, for instance, he accuses himself of playing ball as a boy when he should have been at school; or of being unwilling to read or study unless held to it by his parents or his tutors; or of enjoying, when he was still young, the reading of poets' fables, such as the story of Aeneas, and of weeping for Dido when she died of love; or of having stolen something from his parents' pantry or table to give to his playmates; or of cheating to win in their games. He accuses himself of stealing a pear from a tree near his own vineyard, when he was sixteen years old. In the same book he confesses the slight pleasure he sometimes felt in eating, and says: "You, Lord, taught me that I should go to take food as though it were some kind of medicine. But when I pass over from the annoyance of needing to eat to the restfulness of satiety, in that very passage the trap of concupiscence is set for me, for that passage itself is a pleasure, and there is no other passage than this one, which need forces me to take. I have to eat and drink for my health, and this dangerous enjoyment adds itself as an accompaniment and often tries to go beyond, so that it is for this pleasure that I do what I say I do and want to do only for my health's sake. Excess in drinking is far from me: have pity on me lest it come near me. Intoxication sometimes overtakes your servant: have pity, that it may be far from me. And who is there, Lord, who is never carried a little beyond the bounds of need? Whoever he is,

---

[17] Whoever likes to gnaw at the lives of those absent / Will know that at this table there is no place for him.

he is certainly great, may he glorify your name! But I am not great, because I am a sinful man!"

He suspected that he might be too fond of odors, and says: "I am not too much drawn by the allurement of aromas: when they are absent I do not miss them, when they are present I do not repulse them, being ready to do without them forever. That is how I see myself, and I may be mistaken, for no one should be so sure of himself in this life, which is rightly called a total temptation. Let him who has been able to go from bad to good not go from good to bad." About the sense of hearing he confesses: "The pleasures of the ear involved me and captivated me very tenaciously, but you released and freed me. When it happens that I am moved by the singing more than by the content of the song, I confess my sin and would prefer not to hear the singer." He also accuses himself with regard to the sense of sight, for instance, of taking too much pleasure in watching a dog run, or of enjoying, as he walked through the fields, the sight of hunters hunting, or of spending too much time at home watching spiders trap flies in their webs. He confesses these faults before the Lord, and says in the same place that they distracted him from good meditations and interrupted his prayers.

He accuses himself of an appetite for praise, and of being lured by vainglory. He says: "Anyone who wishes to be praised by men while you, Lord, reproach him, will not be defended by men when you judge him, nor rescued by them when you condemn him. A man is praised because of some gift that you have given him, yet he rejoices that he, rather than the gift, is praised. Daily, without respite, we are attracted by these temptations. The human tongue is a furnace for every day. Nevertheless I would not want approval voiced by someone else to increase my enjoyment of any good that is in me; but, I admit, not only does praise increase the enjoyment, but blame diminishes it. I am sometimes saddened, however, by being praised, when what is praised in me is something that displeases me, or when minor or slight good things are given more praise than they deserve."

The holy man put down the heretics so relentlessly that they publicly declared it would be no sin to kill Augustine, any more than it would be to kill a wolf, and they added that all the killers' sins would be forgiven by God. He put up with many plots against him, for instance, when they set up an ambush on a road he was expected to travel, but by God's providence they were wrong about the road and could not find him.

He always had his fellow poor in mind and liberally shared with them any goods he might have. Sometimes, for the sake of the poor and the captives, he had vessels used in divine service broken and melted down for distribution to those in need. He never wanted to buy a house or a field or a villa for himself. He refused to accept many legacies left to him, and said that they belonged to the children and kinfolk of the deceased rather than to him. He felt no love or concern for property that he held in the name of his church, and kept his thoughts day and night on the Scriptures and the things of God. He was not interested in new buildings, firmly refusing to burden his mind with them, in order to keep it free from material cares and to devote it to continuous meditation and assiduous reading. He did not, however, deter others who wished to do building, unless he thought their plans were too ambitious.

Augustine had high praise for those who longed for death, and in this regard often cited the examples of three bishops. Ambrose, when he was near death and was asked to pray for an extension of his life, answered: "I have not lived in such a way as to be ashamed to live among you, nor do I fear death, because the Lord is good." He spoke of another bishop, who, when he was told that the Church had great need of him and therefore the Lord should let him stay with it, said: "If I am never to die, very well, but if I am to die sometime, why not now?" He also said that Saint Cyprian told this about another bishop, that when he was suffering with a grave malady, he prayed that his health might be restored. A handsome young man appeared to him trembling with indignation, and said: "You are afraid to suffer, you are unwilling to die! What shall I do with you?"

The saint would have no woman, not even his own sister or his brother's daughters, living in his house, though they all served God as he did. His reasoning was that, though there could be no suspicion concerning his sister or his nieces, such persons could not be without other women whom they needed, and men might come to visit them, which could cause the weaker ones among them to be disturbed by human temptations, or certainly to be put to shame by men's wicked suspicions. He never was willing to talk with a woman alone, unless some secret was involved.

He did well by his relatives, not to make them rich but to supply or lighten their needs. Rarely was he willing to intercede for someone in writing or by word of mouth, keeping in mind a certain philosopher who, in consideration of his own reputation, seldom did many favors for his friends and often said: "Heavy weighs the power that's called upon." When he did intervene for someone, he modulated his style so as not to impose a burden but to merit the favor sought by the courtesy of his request. He preferred to settle differences between people he did not know rather than between friends of his, because in passing judgment for strangers he would be free to point to the guilty party and so make a friend of the one for whom, justice being done, he gave a favorable judgment, but between friends he was sure to lose one of them, namely, the one against whom he had to decide.

He was invited by many churches and preached in them, converting many people from error. From time to time he used to digress from the theme of his sermon, and he said that God ordered him to do this to promote the salvation of some particular person. This happened in the case of a businessman among the Manicheans, who was listening to Augustine preaching. The man of God digressed to speak against that heresy, and the merchant was converted.

It was at this time that the Goths sacked Rome, and Christians suffered much at the hands of these idolators and infidels. This prompted Augustine to write the book *The City of God*. In it he showed that the just are bound to be oppressed in this life while the impious flourish. The book treats of the two cities, Jerusalem and Babylon, and their kings, the king of Jerusalem being Christ, the king of Babylon, the devil. Two loves, he says, build the two cities: the city of the devil is built by love of self growing into contempt of God, and the city of God by love of God growing into contempt of self.

In those days, namely, in A.D. 440, the Vandals occupied the province of Africa, ravaging all without respect for sex, rank, or age. They reached Hippo and laid siege to the city with a strong force. Amid these tribulations Augustine, more than others since he was now in old age, lived a most bitter and mournful life. His tears were his bread, flowing day and night, as he saw some killed, others in flight, churches widowed of their priests, cities demolished and their inhabitants scattered. In the midst of these misfortunes he consoled himself with a sentence from a certain wise man: "The man who thinks it a great thing that sticks and stones fall and that mortals die is not a great man." He called his brothers together and said to them: "I have asked the Lord either to rescue us from these perils or to grant patience to bear them, or to receive me out of this life, lest I be compelled to witness so many calamities."

As it happened, he obtained the third petition. In the third month of the siege he fell ill with fever and took to his bed. Realizing that the dissolution of his body was imminent, he had the seven Penitential Psalms written out and hung on the wall opposite his bed, and lying there he read them and wept constantly and copiously. In order that he might devote himself more freely to God, and that no one should distract his attention, ten days before his death he ordered that no one be admitted to his presence, unless the doctor came in or food was brought to him. But one sick man did get in and begged him to cure him of his infirmity. Augustine answered: "What are you talking about, my son? Do you think that if I could do what you ask, I would not do the same for myself?" The sick man insisted nonetheless, declaring that in a vision he had been ordered to come to the saint and receive his health. Seeing the man's faith, Augustine prayed for him and he was made well.

He cured many persons who were possessed of the devil, and performed a great many other miracles. In the twenty-second book of *The City of God* he mentions two of his miracles as if they were someone else's, saying: "I know of a certain young woman in Hippo, who anointed herself with oil into which a priest who was praying for her had let his tears drop, and in an instant she was delivered of the devil." In the same book he says: "I also know a bishop who prayed for a youth without seeing him, and at once the youth was freed of the devil." There seems to be no doubt that he was talking about himself but for humility's sake would not use his name. In the same book of *The City of God* he says that there was a man who was due to undergo surgery and was in great fear that he would die under the knife. The sick man prayed to God with much weeping, and Augustine prayed with him and for him. The man recovered his health completely without an incision.

At last, when his end was near, he taught this memorable rule, namely, that no man, no matter how high his merit might be, should die without confession and the Eucharist. The last hour came, and Augustine, sound in all his members, sight and hearing unimpaired, in the seventy-seventh year of his life and the fortieth of his episcopate, with his brothers around him and praying, migrated to the Lord. He made no last will and testament, since, as the poor man of Christ, he had nothing to bequeath. He flourished in the years around A.D. 400.[18]

Thus Augustine, that shining light of wisdom, that bulwark of the truth and rampart of the faith, incomparably surpassed all the doctors of the Church, both in native gifts and in acquired knowledge, excelling by the example of his virtues and the abundance of his teaching. Hence Saint Remy, commemorating Jerome and several other doctors, concludes as follows: "Augustine outdid them all in genius and knowledge, for, although Jerome admitted that he had read six thousand volumes of Origen, Augustine wrote so many that no one, working day and night, could write his books, nor even succeed in reading them." Volusianus, to whom Augustine wrote a letter, says of him: "Anything that Augustine happened not to know is not in the law of God."

Jerome wrote in a letter to Augustine: "I am not able to respond to your two short works, most learned and brilliant with every splendor of eloquence as they are. All that genius can say or assume or draw from the fountains of the Scriptures has there been said and treated. But I beg Your Reverence to allow me to say something in praise of your genius." In his book *Of the Twelve Doctors*, Jerome writes as follows about Augustine: "Augustine the bishop, flying like an eagle over the mountain peaks and not attending to what is at their foot, discoursed in clear language about the broad spaces of the heavens, the length and breadth of the lands, and the circle of the seas." And Jerome's reverence and affection for Augustine appear from the letters he wrote to him, in one of which he says: "To the holy lord and most blessed father Augustine, Jerome sends greetings. At all times I have venerated Your Beatitude with the honor due you, and have loved the Lord our Savior dwelling in you, but now, if I may, I add to the sum and bring my veneration to its fullness, lest we let one hour pass without a mention of your name." In another letter to the same: "Far be it from me to dare to question anything in Your Beatitude's books. I have enough to do to correct my own without criticizing anyone else's."

Gregory also, in a letter to Innocent, the prefect of Africa, writes as follows about Augustine's works: "I am gratified by your interest and your request that I send you my commentary on holy Job; but if you wish to gorge yourself on delicious fare, read the treatises of blessed Augustine, your compatriot, and by

---

[18] Augustine was born in 354, was ordained bishop in 395, and died in 430.

comparison with his fine flour you will not ask for my bran." In his *Register* he says: "We read that blessed Augustine would not live in the same house with his sister, saying: 'The women who are with my sister are not my sisters.' The caution of that learned man should teach us an important lesson."

In Ambrose's Preface we read: "In Augustine's dying we adore your magnificence, O Lord! Your power works in all, so that this man, fired by your Spirit, was not led astray by flattering promises, because you had imbued him with every kind of piety, and to you he was altar, sacrifice, priest, and temple." Blessed Prosper, in the third book of *The Contemplative Life*, speaks about him as follows: "Saint Augustine the bishop was keen of mind, suave in his eloquence, thoroughly familiar with secular literature, industrious in his labors for the Church, clear in everyday discussions, well organized in all his activities, acute in solving problems, careful in arguing with heretics, catholic in expounding our faith, cautious in explaining the canonical Scriptures." Bernard writes: "Augustine was the mighty hammer of heretics."

After his death, when the barbarians overran that region and profaned the churches, the faithful took Augustine's body and transported it to Sardinia. About A.D. 718, 280 years after the saint's death, Liutprand, the deeply religious king of the Lombards, heard that the Saracens were depopulating Sardinia, and sent a formal delegation there to take the holy doctor's relics to Pavia. Having paid a high price, they obtained the saint's body and brought it as far as Genoa. When the devout king learned of this, he went with great joy to that city and reverently met and accepted the body. However, when they wanted to carry it farther, they could not move it from the place until the king had made a vow that if Augustine allowed him to go on from there, he would build a church at that place in his honor. Once the vow was made, the body was carried away without difficulty, and Liutprand fulfilled his vow and had a church constructed as promised. The same miracle occurred a day later in a country villa called Cassella in the diocese of Tortona, and the king built a church there in honor of Saint Augustine. In addition he granted the villa itself and all its appendages to be owned in perpetuity by those who would serve that church. By this time the king saw that it pleased the saint to have a church built in his name wherever his body had rested. Liutprand feared that Augustine might choose for his final resting place a location other than the one the king wanted, so he arranged for the erection of a church everyplace where he and the relic were given hospitality overnight. So the sacred body was finally brought into Pavia, welcomed with much jubilation, and enshrined with honors in the church of Saint Peter, which is called Golden Heaven.

A miller who had a special devotion to Saint Augustine was suffering from an abscess in the leg and prayed earnestly to the saint for help. Augustine appeared to him in a vision and rubbed the leg with his hand, completely healing it. The miller awoke to find himself cured, and gave thanks to God and Saint Augustine.

A boy was sick with the stone and the physician recommended that the stone be cut out, but the boy's mother, fearing that her son would die, invoked Augustine's aid. No sooner had she finished her prayer than the boy passed the stone with his urine and was completely cured.

In the monastery called Elemosina, on the vigil of Saint Augustine's feast day, a monk was rapt in spirit and saw a shining cloud coming down from heaven. On the cloud was seated Saint Augustine, arrayed in pontifical vestments. His eyes were like two rays of the sun, lighting up the whole church, and a marvelous aroma filled the building.

Saint Bernard was once assisting at matins and fell asleep for a moment during the reading of a treatise of Saint Augustine. He saw a beautiful young man standing there, out of whose mouth gushed such a torrent of water that it seemed to be filling the whole church. Bernard had no doubt that this was Augustine, who watered the Church with the fountain of his teaching.

A man who loved Augustine deeply paid the monk who was guardian of the saint's body a large sum of money, for which the monk was to give him a finger from the body. The monk took the money but gave the man a finger, wrapped in silk, from another dead body, pretending that it was Augustine's finger. The man accepted the relic piously and worshiped it with devotion, frequently touching it to his mouth and eyes and clasping it to his bosom. Seeing his faith, God mercifully and miraculously gave him one of Saint Augustine's fingers, throwing away the supposititious one. When the man returned to his home country, many miracles occurred there, and the fame of the relic spread to Pavia. When the aforesaid monk declared that the finger belonged to some other dead man, the saint's tomb was opened and it was found that a finger was indeed missing. The abbot learned of this, took the monk's charge away from him, and punished him severely.

In the monastery of Fontaines in Burgundy there was a monk who was particularly devoted to Saint Augustine, read his writings zealously, and derived spiritual nourishment from them. For a long time he had petitioned the saint not to let him leave this life except on the day when his sacred feast was celebrated. Then, two weeks before the saint's feast day, the monk was stricken with a high fever and on the vigil of the feast was laid out on the ground to await death. And behold, a number of men, decorous and splendid in appearance and wearing white garments, entered the church in procession, followed by a venerable man clothed in pontifical vestments. A monk who was in the church was astounded at the sight of the procession, and asked the marchers who they were and where they were going. One of them said that Saint Augustine, with his canons, was on his way to his dying devotee to take his soul to the kingdom of glory. Then the solemn procession entered the infirmary, and after some time the monk's soul was released from his body, and his dear friend, shielding it from the grasp of the enemy, led it into the joys of heaven.

We also read that once, while Augustine was still alive in the flesh and was reading, he saw a demon going past him carrying a book on his shoulders. He immediately adjured the spirit to show him what writings were hidden in the book. The demon asserted that the sins of men were written there, and that he collected them from all over and kept a record of them. Augustine ordered him to let him read anything about his own sins that might be written in the book. The demon pointed to a page, but Augustine saw nothing there except that he had once forgotten to recite compline, the last hour of the divine office. So the saint required the demon to wait for him there, and he went into the church and devoutly said compline and completed the usual prayers, then went back and told the evil one to show him that page again. The devil quickly opened the book, found the page blank, and said angrily: "You have duped me shamefully, and I am sorry I showed you my book, because you wiped out your sin by the power of your prayers." Having said this, he vanished in confusion.

Some malicious persons had wronged a woman, and she went to blessed Augustine to seek his advice about the matter. She found him studying and addressed him reverently, but he neither looked at her or gave her a word of response. Thinking that perhaps due to his holiness he did not want to look a woman in the face, she came close and carefully explained her errand, but he did not turn to her or answer a word. So she left, sorely disappointed. The next day, while Augustine was celebrating mass and the woman was present, she was rapt in ecstasy at the elevation of the Lord's Body and saw herself placed before the tribunal of the most holy Trinity. Augustine also was there, standing with bowed head and discoursing most attentively and sublimely about the glory of the Trinity. Then a voice spoke to her, saying: "When you went to Augustine, he was absorbed in thinking about the glory of the Trinity and thus was completely unaware of your presence. But go back to him confidently! You will find him kindhearted, and he will give you helpful advice." The woman did as directed, and Augustine heard her kindly and gave her wise counsel.

It is also told that a certain holy man was rapt in spirit and looked upon the saints in glory, but did not see Augustine. He asked one of the saints where Augustine was, and the saint answered: "Augustine resides in the highest heaven, and there expatiates on the glory of the most excellent Trinity."

Some men of Pavia were held in confinement by the marquis of Malespina, who would allow them no water, his purpose being to extort a large ransom from them. Some of the men were almost at the point of death, some were drinking urine, but there was one, a youth, who was very devoted to Saint Augustine, and called upon him for help. Augustine appeared to the youth, took him by the right hand, and led him out to the Gravelone River. There, dipping a vine leaf in the water, he cooled the youth's tongue with it, and the young man, who had almost been ready to drink urine, now would have thought little of a draft of nectar.

The provost of a certain church, who was devoted to Saint Augustine, had been suffering from an illness so serious that he had to keep to his bed. When the saint's feast day was at hand and the bell rang for the vespers of the vigil, the priest prayed assiduously to Saint Augustine, whereupon the saint appeared to him in white vestments, addressed him three times by name, and said: "You have called on me so often, and here I am! Get up quickly and celebrate the evening office in my honor!" The provost astonished everyone by rising hale and hearty, going into the church, and devoutly conducting the service.

A shepherd had a malignant ulcer between the shoulders and was so ill with it that all his strength was gone. He prayed to Saint Augustine, who appeared to him in a vision, laid his hand on the afflicted spot, and healed it perfectly. At a later time the same man lost his eyesight. He besought Augustine's help, and one day about noon the saint appeared, rubbed the man's eyes, and restored his sight.

About the year A.D. 912, a band of more than forty men from Germany and France, all suffering from various infirmities, set out for Rome to visit the tombs of the apostles. Some of them were so bent over that they had to push themselves along on small sleds, some supported themselves with crutches. Blind men were guided by others, and there were some with crooked hands and feet. They crossed the mountains and reached a place called Carbonaria, and went on to a place called Cana, three miles from Pavia. There Saint Augustine, vested in pontificals, came out of a church built in honor of Saints Cosmas and Damian, met and greeted the men, and asked where they were going. When they told him, he said: "Go into Pavia and ask your way to the monastery of Saint Peter, called Golden Heaven, and there you will obtain the mercy you desire." The pilgrims asked him his name, and he answered: "I am Augustine, once bishop of the city of Hippo," and vanished from their sight. They went into Pavia and, arriving at the monastery, learned that Augustine's body rested there, and raised their voices in a unanimous appeal: "Saint Augustine, help us!" Aroused by this clamor, townspeople and monks flocked together to see this great spectacle. The sick men's arteries became distended and burst, and their blood flowed in such quantities that from the monastery entrance to the saint's tomb the floor was awash. When the infirm came to the tomb, all were restored to health, as if there had never been any defect in their bodies.

From that time on the fame of Saint Augustine grew, and multitudes of sick people came to his tomb, recovered their health, and left pledges of their gratitude, with the result that in time these pledges filled Saint Augustine's chapel and the portico of the church, making it difficult to get in and out, and the monks perforce stored them elsewhere.

Note that there are three things that worldly people yearn for, namely, riches, pleasures, and honors. Such was the perfection of that holy man that he despised riches, rejected honors, and shrank from pleasures. He himself affirms that he despised riches, in his book of *Soliloquies*, where Reason asks him: "Do you not covet any wealth?" and he answers: "Not now, anyway! I am thirty years old and for the last fourteen years I have ceased to desire it, and am concerned only to have enough to live on. One book of Cicero easily convinced me that riches are not at all to be desired." That he rejected honors he testifies in the same book. Reason asks him: "What about honors?" Augustine answers: "I admit that it is only lately, indeed in these last days, that I have ceased to desire them." Pleasures and riches he despised, notably the pleasures of the bed and the table. Reason asks about the first in the same book: "What about a wife? Would you not be delighted with a beautiful, virtuous, compliant, wealthy wife, especially if you were sure she would be no trouble to you?" Augustine answers: "Much as you depict her and heap her with every good quality, I have decided that there is nothing I should flee from as much as I should from a bedfellow!" Reason: "I was not asking about what you have decided, but whether you are attracted in that direction." Augustine: "I want absolutely nothing of the sort, desire nothing, even recall such things with horror and disgust!" As to the second, Reason asks: "What about food?" Augustine: "Don't bother asking about food and drink or baths or other pleasures of the body! All I want of them is what can give me hope of good health."

125. The Beheading of Saint John the Baptist

The feast of the Beheading of John the Baptist, as we find in the book *De mitrali officio*, was instituted in celebration of four events. The first is the beheading itself, the second, the collection and cremation of the saint's bones,[1] the third the finding of his head, the fourth, the translation of one of his fingers and the dedication of a church in his honor.

First, then, the feast celebrates John's beheading, which came about in the following way. We have from the *Scholastic History* that Herod Antipas, son of Herod the Great, was on his way to Rome and stopped to visit his brother Philip. He made a secret agreement with Herodias, Philip's wife, who, according to Josephus, was the sister of Herod Agrippa, that on his return journey he would repudiate his own wife and wed Herodias. This, however, was no secret

---

[1] The Graesse text has *capitis* (of the head) here, surely an error.

to the wife of this Herod Antipas, the daughter of Aretas, king of Damascus. She did not wait for her husband's return but went as fast as she could to her own homeland. Herod meanwhile came back and took Herodias away from Philip, thus making enemies of King Aretas, Herod Agrippa, and Philip.

John the Baptist took Herod to task for this, on the ground that according to the law he had no right to marry his brother's wife while his brother was alive. Because of the severity of John's rebuke and because John, by his preaching and baptizing, attracted a large following, Herod chained him and put him in prison. He also wished to please his wife but feared to lose the allegiance of John's followers. What he really wanted to do was to kill John, but was afraid of the people. Indeed, both Herodias and Herod longed to find an opportunity to get rid of John, and they seem to have arranged secretly between themselves that Herod would invite the leading men of Galilee to a banquet in honor of his birthday, and would have Herodias's daughter dance for them, after which Herod would swear to give her anything she asked for, and she would ask for the head of John. On account of his oath he would have to grant her request but would pretend to be saddened because he had sworn. That there had been this conspiracy and false pretense seems to be suggested by what the *Scholastic History* says: "It is entirely credible that Herod and his wife had secretly plotted John's death on this occasion. Likewise Jerome in the *Gloss*: "He therefore swore to find an occasion to put John to death, because if the girl had asked for the death of her father or mother, Herod would not have yielded."

So the banquet is held, the girl is present, she dances for the company, everyone is pleased, the king swears that he will give her whatever she asks, she follows her mother's instructions and demands the head of John. Two-faced Herod feigns sadness because of his oath—because, as Rabanus says, he had to do what he had sworn to do. But the sadness was only on his face. In his heart he was delighted. He excused his crime by citing his oath, thus doing an impious deed under cover of a show of piety. So the headsman is dispatched, John loses his head, the head is given to the daughter and presented by the daughter to her adulterous mother.

Augustine, in a sermon he preached on the beheading of John the Baptist, uses Herod's oath as the occasion for a story with a moral. He says: "I heard this story from an innocent and trustworthy man. When someone refused to return something he had lent him or something that was owed to him, he was distressed and provoked the borrower to swear. The borrower swore and the lender lost. That night the lender had a vision in which he was brought before the Judge, who asked him: 'Why did you provoke the man to swear an oath when you knew he would swear falsely?' The lender answered: 'He refused to give me what was mine!' The Judge: 'It would have been better to lose what was yours rather than to make him lose his soul by swearing falsely!' He was then punished by being laid on the ground and beaten so severely that when he awoke the traces of the whipping were visible." Thus Augustine.

It was not, however, on this day that John was beheaded, but during the Days of Unleavened Bread in the year preceding the passion of Christ. It was right, therefore, that on account of the mysteries of the Lord which mark that season, the lesser event should yield to the greater and be celebrated at another time.

In connection with the beheading, John Chrysostom exclaims: "John is the school of virtues, the guide of life, the model of holiness, the norm of justice, the mirror of virginity, the stamp of modesty, the exemplar of chastity, the road of repentance, the pardon of sinners, the discipline of faith—John, greater than man, equal of angels, sum of the Law, sanction of the Gospel, voice of the apostles, silence of the prophets, lantern of the world, forerunner of the Judge, center of the whole Trinity! And so great a one as this is given to an incestuous woman, betrayed to an adulteress, awarded to a dancing girl!"

Herod did not escape punishment: he was condemned to exile. The *Scholastic History* has it that the other Herod, namely, Agrippa, was a man of valor but impoverished—so poor, indeed, that in desperation he went into a tower intending to starve himself to death. When his sister Herodias heard of this, she begged her husband, Herod Antipas, to get his brother out of the tower and to provide for his needs. He did this, but while the two were celebrating together, Herod the tetrarch became overheated with wine and began to scoff at the other over the favors he had done him. Agrippa deeply resented this insult, so he went to Rome and won the favor of Caius Caesar, which led the emperor to grant him two tetrarchies, Lisania and Abilene, and to send him back, wearing the royal diadem, to be king of Judea.

Herodias, seeing that her brother now had the title of king, importuned her husband with demands that he go to Rome and procure a similar title for himself. But he was a very rich man and felt no need of promotion, preferring his life of leisure to honors that involved work. But his wife won in the end, and he went to Rome, taking her with him. Agrippa, getting word of this, wrote to the emperor, telling him that Herod had cultivated a friendship with the king of the Parthians and was determined to rebel against the Roman Empire. In proof of this charge he submitted that Herod had in his cities weapons enough to equip seventy thousand armed men. Having read the letter Caius questioned Herod, as if he had information from a different source, about the state of his affairs, and asked, among other things, whether it was true, as the emperor had heard, that Herod had such a large store of arms in his cities. Herod made no effort to deny this. Thereupon Caius took to be true what Herod Agrippa had written, and sent Antipas into exile, but granted permission to his wife to return to her own country, since Herodias was Herod Agrippa's sister and Agrippa was very dear to Caius. Herodias, however, chose to accompany her husband into exile, saying that she had shared his good fortune and would not abandon him in adversity. They were therefore deported to Lyons and ended their days there in misery. This we learn from the *Scholastic History*.

The second event commemorated by this feast is the burning and gathering, or collection, of Saint John's bones. According to some sources, his bones were burned on the very day of his martyrdom and were partly recovered by the faithful. Hence he suffered, as it were, a second martyrdom, since he was burned in his bones. Therefore the Church celebrates this second martyrdom on this day. In the twelfth book of the *Scholastic* or *Ecclesiastical History*, we read that John's disciples had buried his body at Sebaste, a city in Palestine between Elisaeus and Abdias, and that many miracles had occurred at his tomb. For this reason the pagans, by order of Julian the Apostate, scattered his bones, but the miracles did not cease, and the bones were collected, burned, and pulverized, and the ashes thrown to the winds to be blown over the fields, as both the above-mentioned histories report.

Bede, however, says that the collected bones were scattered still more widely, and so a second martyrdom seemed somehow to be suffered. Some people represent this, not knowing that they are doing so, when on the feast of the Baptist's birth they gather bones from here and there and burn them. In any case, the bones were collected to be burned, as both the *Scholastic History* and Bede have it, and some monks came from Jerusalem secretly, mingled with the pagans, and managed to carry off many of the relics. These they delivered to Philip, bishop of Jerusalem, who afterwards sent them to Anastasius,[2] bishop of Alexandria. Still later, Theophilus, bishop of the same city, enshrined the bones in a temple of Serapis, which he had purged and consecrated as a basilica in honor of Saint John. This from Bede and the *Scholastic History.* Now, however, the relics are devoutly worshiped in Genoa, and Popes Alexander III and Innocent IV, after verifying the facts, have signified their approval by granting privileges.

As Herod, who ordered the beheading of John, suffered the penalty for his crimes, so the divine vengeance was visited upon Julian the Apostate, who ordered the burning of the martyr's bones. How Julian was punished is told in the story of Saint Julian, which follows the chapter on the Conversion of Saint Paul.[3] A full account of the origins, the reign, the cruelty, and the death of this Julian the Apostate is contained in the *Tripartite History.*

Constantius, brother to Constantine the Great by the same father, had two sons, Gallus and Julian. When Constantine died, his son Constantius raised Gallus to the rank of caesar but later put him to death. This made Julian fearful, and he became a monk but also began to consult soothsayers to learn whether he might eventually be emperor. Afterwards Constantius made Julian a caesar and sent him to Gaul, where he scored many victories. One day he was passing between two columns, between which a laurel crown was suspended by a cord. The cord broke and the crown fell on Julian's head, fitting him neatly. The

---

[2] Graesse notes that the Ed. Pr. has "Athanasius."

[3] It follows the chapter on Saint Paula.

troops cheered, this being a sign that he would be emperor. The soldiers began to call him Augustus, and since there was no crown available with which to crown him, a soldier took off a necklace he was wearing and placed it on Julian's head. Thus the army made him emperor.

From then on, Julian abandoned his pretense of being a Christian, opened the temples of the idols, offered sacrifice to them, and appointed himself high priest of the pagan cult. He also had all crosses thrown down and destroyed; yet once it happened that dew fell on his clothing and on that of the others with him, and each drop of dew took the shape of a cross. After Constantius died, Julian, wanting to please everyone, allowed all to practice whatever religion they chose. He also dismissed all the eunuchs, barbers, and cooks from his household—the eunuchs because his wife had died and he had not taken another, the cooks because he preferred simpler fare, the barbers because, he said, one barber could serve many people. He wrote a number of books in which he defamed the emperors who had ruled before him. When he dismissed cooks and barbers, he acted like a philosopher, not an emperor; when he slandered or praised, he acted as no philosopher or emperor would.

Once, when Julian was sacrificing to the idols, the mark of a cross encircled by a crown was seen in the entrails of a slaughtered sheep. This sight stirred fear in the ministers, who interpreted it as foretelling the future unity, victory, and perpetuity of the cross. Julian reassured them, saying that this was a sign that Christianity should be kept down and not allowed to expand outside the circle. Another time, when he was offering sacrifice in Constantinople to the goddess Fortuna, Maris, the bishop of Chalcedon, who in his old age had lost his sight, approached him and called him a blasphemer and apostate. Julian answered him: "Well, your Galilean hasn't been able to cure you!" Maris: "I thank God for that, because he deprived me of my sight so that I would not have to look upon you, stripped of all religion as you are!" Julian had nothing to say to that and moved away.

In Antioch he had the sacred vessels and cloths brought together, threw them on the ground, sat on them, and soiled them. Very soon he was stricken in those parts of his body, with worms crawling out and gnawing at his flesh, and he suffered that condition for the rest of his life. And a prefect, also named Julian, having robbed the churches of their sacred vessels at the emperor's command, made water on them, saying: "Look there at the vessels in which Mary's Son is served!" Instantly his mouth became an anus and functioned as such thereafter.

Julian the Apostate was entering the temple of Fortuna, and the ministers of the temple were sprinkling water as a ritual cleansing upon those entering. Valentinian saw a drop fall on his mantle and angrily struck the minister, saying that the water did not purge but stained him. Julian saw this happen, and ordered Valentinian to be taken into custody and banished to the desert. Valentinian was a Christian, and as a reward he merited to be elevated to the empire.

As a mark of his hatred of Christians, Julian ordered the temple of the Jews to be restored, and allotted large sums of money for the building. But when a large supply of stones had been brought to the site, a wild wind blew and scattered the stones, a violent tremor shook the earth, and fire burst out from the foundations and consumed a great many people. Another day the sign of the cross appeared in the sky, and the Jews' clothing was covered with black crosses.

Julian invaded Persia, came to Ctesiphon, and laid siege to the city. The king offered to relinquish a part of his kingdom to the emperor if the latter would withdraw his troops, but Julian would not hear of it. Following the ideas of Pythagoras and Plato about the transmigration of souls, he thought that he possessed the soul of Alexander, or rather that he was another Alexander in another body. But suddenly a spear flew through the air and buried itself in his side, and of that wound he died. To this day no one knows who hurled the spear. Some say it was thrown by an invisible hand, others by an Ishmaelite shepherd. Still others think the assailant was a soldier who was worn out with the long marches and with hunger; but whether by man or by angel, obviously it was the command of God that was carried out. Calixtus, who was close to Julian, said that the emperor was struck by a demon. So much we learn from the *Tripartite History*.

The third event commemorated by today's feast is the finding of the head of John the Baptist, because, it is said, his head was indeed found on this day. We read in the eleventh book of the *Ecclesiastical History* that John was chained and beheaded in a castle in Arabia called Macheronta. Herodias, however, had John's head taken to Jerusalem and, as a precaution, buried close to Herod's palace, because she feared that the prophet would return to life if his head was buried with his body. In the time of Emperor Marcian, who, according to the *Scholastic History*, began to reign in A.D. 453, Saint John revealed the whereabouts of his head to two monks who had come to Jerusalem. They hurried to the palace that had been Herod's, and found the head rolled up in haircloth sacks—the cloth, I suppose, that he wore in the desert. When they were on their way back to their homeland with the head, a potter from the city of Emissa, who was running away from poverty, joined them on the road. The potter carried the pouch containing the sacred head, which the monks had entrusted to him, but he was admonished by Saint John to get away from them, and he went back to Emissa with the head. As long as he lived, he kept the relic in a cave and venerated it there, and he prospered not a little. When he was dying, he committed the relic to his sister's care, enjoining secrecy upon her, and she passed it on to her successors.

A long time passed, and Saint John revealed the presence of his head to the monk Saint Marcellus, who was living in the aforementioned cave. Here is how the revelation came about. While Marcellus was asleep, he seemed to see great crowds singing Psalms as they filed by, and saying: "Behold, Saint John the

Baptist is coming!" Then he saw blessed John, who was accompanied by an attendant at his right and another at his left, and the saint blessed all who approached him. Marcellus went to him and prostrated himself at his feet, and the saint raised him, held him by the chin, and gave him the kiss of peace. Marcellus asked him where he had come from, and John answered: "I have come from Sebaste!"

When Marcellus awoke, he wondered much about this vision. Then, another night when he was asleep, someone came and awakened him, and, once awake, he saw a star shining in the entrance to his cell. He got up and tried to touch the star, but it quickly moved to another part of the cave, and he followed it until it came to rest over the spot where John the Baptist's head was buried. Marcellus dug down and found the urn containing the holy treasure. Now a bystander refused to believe what he heard and presumed to touch the urn, but his hand immediately shriveled and stuck to the urn. His companions prayed for him and his hand came free but was still misshapen. John then appeared to him and said: "When my head has been deposited in the church, you shall touch the urn and be restored to health." The man did this and was whole again.

When Marcellus told the bishop of that city—the bishop's name was Julian— all that had happened, they took up the relic and brought it into the city. From that time on, the Beheading of Saint John was solemnly celebrated annually there, on the day of the year when the head was found and dug up, or so we gather from what the *Scholastic History* says. Later on, however, it was transferred to Constantinople. We read in the *Tripartite History* that when Valens was emperor, he ordered the sacred head to be put in a wagon and translated to Constantinople. When the vehicle came close to Chalcedon, it could not be moved a foot farther, no matter how hard the oxen were goaded, so the cortege had to halt and deposit the relic at that point. At a later time, Emperor Theodosius wished to move it again. He found a virgin lady who had been appointed its custodian, and asked her to allow him to take the sacred head away. She consented, thinking that as in the time of Valens the relic would not allow itself to be moved, but the pious emperor wrapped it in purple, took it to Constantinople, and built a beautiful church for it. Thus the *Tripartite History*. Still later, in Pepin's reign, the head was transferred to Poitiers in France, where by John's merits many dead were restored to life.

Just as Herod was punished for beheading John, and Julian for burning his bones, so also Herodias was punished for instructing her daughter to ask for the head, and the girl for doing so. There are some, indeed, who say that Herodias was not sentenced to exile and did not die in exile, but that when she had the head in her hands and taunted it gleefully, by God's will the head breathed in her face and she expired. This is the popular tale, but what was said above, namely, that she was exiled with Herod and died in misery, is what the saints hand on in their chronicles, and therefore is to be believed. As for her daughter, she was walking over an icy pond when the ice gave way under her and she was drowned, though one chronicle says that the earth swallowed her alive. This is understandable, since it is said of the Egyptians who were drowned in the Red Sea: "The earth swallowed them."[4]

The fourth event commemorated by today's feast is the translation of one of Saint John's fingers and the dedication of a church. The finger with which he pointed to the Lord[5] could not, we are told, be burned. This finger was recovered by the aforesaid monks, and later, as the *Scholastic History* has it, Saint Thecla took it into the Alps and deposited it in the church of Saint Maximus. John Beleth adds his testimony, saying that the aforementioned Saint Thecla brought the finger overseas to Normandy and there built a church in honor of Saint John. According to this author, the church was dedicated on this day, for which reason the lord pope decreed that this day should be solemnized throughout the world.

In a city of France called Marienna,[6] a lady who was very devoted to John the Baptist prayed earnestly to God that at some time a relic of Saint John might be given to her. Her prayers were not being answered, so she took confidence in God and bound herself by an oath not to eat until she received what she was asking for. After she had fasted for some days, she saw a wonderfully shining thumb lying on the altar, and joyfully accepted it as a gift from God. In no time three bishops were present, each wanting a part of the thumb, whereupon they were astonished to see three drops of blood fall on the cloth on which the relic lay, and each bishop rejoiced at having merited one drop.

Theodelinda, queen of the Lombards, built and endowed a noble church at Monza, near Milan, in honor of Saint John the Baptist. Some time later, as Paul states in his *History of the Lombards*, the emperor Constantine, also called Constans, wanted to take Italy from the Lombards and consulted a holy man, who had the spirit of prophecy, about the outcome of the war. The holy man prayed during the night and gave his answer in the morning: "The queen built the church in honor of John, and John intercedes continually for the Lombards. Therefore they cannot be conquered. There will come a time, however, when that place will no longer be honored, and then they will be conquered." And so it happened in Charlemagne's time.

Gregory, in his *Dialogues*, tells us that a man of great virtue named Sanctulus had assumed the custody of a deacon whom the Lombards had captured, on condition that if the deacon escaped, he, Sanctulus, would accept capital punishment in his stead. Then Sanctulus forced the deacon to flee and be free. For this, Sanctulus was sentenced to death and led to the place of execution, and the strongest headsman, of whom there was no doubt that with one stroke he could sever the head, was chosen to carry out the sentence. Sanctulus extended his

---

[4] Exod. 15:12.

[5] In art, John the Baptist is frequently portrayed pointing one finger at Christ.

[6] Graesse notes that the Ed. Pr. has Mamerena, while "others read Maurienna or Marienna." Such uncertainty about place names and proper names is not infrequent in the text.

neck, and the executioner, mustering all his strength, raised his arm, holding the sword aloft. At that moment Sanctulus said: "Saint John, get hold of him!" Instantly the striker's arm became stiff and inflexible, and held the sword heavenward until he swore an oath never again to strike a Christian. The man of God then prayed for him, and at once he was able to lower his arm.

※

126. Saints Felix and Adauctus

Felix, a priest, and his brother, also named Felix and also a priest, were brought before Diocletian and Maximian. The older of the two was led to the temple of Serapis to offer sacrifice there, but he blew into the face of the statue, which fell to pieces immediately. He was taken to a statue of Mercury and blew on it with the same result. For a third trial he faced a statue of Diana, and down it came. He was tortured on the rack and then, for a fourth time, led to a sacrilegious tree, there to offer sacrifice. Instead he knelt and prayed, then blew on the tree, which promptly was torn up by the roots and demolished the altar and the temple as it fell.

Word of this came to the prefect, and he ordered Felix to be beheaded at that place and his body to be thrown to the wolves and dogs. Then a man sprang forth from the crowd and freely avowed himself to be a Christian. They embraced each other and were executed together then and there.

The Christians did not know the name of the second man and called him *Adauctus*, which means added on or joined to, because he was joined to Saint Felix in winning the crown of martyrdom. The Christians buried the two in the hole left by the falling tree. The pagans tried to dig them up but were seized by the devil. The martyrs suffered about A.D. 287.[1]

---

[1] The second Felix is forgotten. Such duplication of names may result from actual multiplicity of homonyms, or from similar stories coming from different quarters. It may also be that there were two Felixes, about one of whom nothing was known.

127. Saints Savinian and Savina

Savinian and Savina[1] were the children of Savinus, a member of the high nobility but a pagan, who fathered Savinian by his first wife and Savina by his second, and derived their names from his own.

Somewhere Savinian read the verse: "Thou shalt sprinkle me, Lord, and I shall be cleansed; thou shalt wash me and I shall be made whiter than snow,"[2] and wondered what it meant but could not understand it. He went into his bedroom and sat in sackcloth and ashes, saying that he would prefer to die rather than to live and not understand the meaning of those words. An angel appeared to him and said: "Do not fret yourself to death, because you have found favor with God, and when you have been baptized you will be whiter than snow, and then you will understand what now puzzles you."

The angel left him and he was happy, and thereafter spurned the veneration of idols. His father rebuked him severely for this and often said to him: "It would be better for you to be the only one to die for not adoring the gods than to have all of us involved in your death!" Savinian therefore left home secretly and went to the city of Troyes. When he arrived at the Seine and prayed the Lord that he might be baptized in the river, he was baptized there, and the Lord said to him: "Now you have found what you have labored so long to find!" Savinian then drove his staff into the ground, and, after he had prayed, the staff produced a profusion of leaves and flowers, while a crowd of people looked on. Thereupon 1,108 men believed in the Lord.

Emperor Aurelian heard about this and sent a squadron of soldiers to take Savinian prisoner, but when they found him praying, they were afraid to come near him. The emperor dispatched a troop larger than the first, but they, finding him at prayer, knelt and prayed with him, then rose and said: "The emperor desires to see you!" When he was brought in and refused to sacrifice, at Aurelian's command he was bound hand and foot and beaten with iron bars. "Increase the torments if you can," said Savinian. The emperor ordered him to be taken to the center of the city and seated, bound, on a bench, under which wood should be stacked and drenched with oil, then ignited, and that would be the end of Savinian. But then the monarch saw him standing in the middle of the flames and praying. Stupefied, he fell on his face, then stood up and said to the

---

[1] The preferred spelling is Sabinian, Sabina, but Jacobus's spelling is retained here. At the end of this chapter Jacobus recognizes another Saint Sabina, who was revered as a Roman martyr.

[2] Ps. 50(51):9.

saint: "You foul beast, are you not satisfied with the souls you have deceived? Must you strive to deceive even us by your magical tricks?" Savinian: "Many more souls, and you yourself, are to believe in the Lord through me!"

The emperor now blasphemed the name of God, and gave orders that on the next day Savinian was to be bound to a stake and shot through with arrows; but when the orders were carried out, the arrows hung in the air to either side of him, and not one of them touched him. So the emperor came to him and asked: "Where is your God? Let him come now and rescue you from these arrows!" But instantly one of the arrows jumped out and struck the emperor in one eye, blinding it completely. This angered him, and he ordered the saint back to prison, to be beheaded the following day. Savinian, however, prayed to God that he might be transferred to the place where he had been baptized. His chains fell off, the door of the prison opened, and he walked through the soldiers and set out for the bank of the Seine. This was reported to Aurelian, who commanded that he be pursued and beheaded. Seeing the soldiers coming, Savinian walked over the water as if it were stone, and came to the spot where he had been baptized. The soldiers made their way across, but then feared to strike him, and he said to them: "Don't be afraid to strike me, and take some of my blood to the emperor, so that he may receive his sight and acknowledge the power of God." They cut off his head, but he picked it up and carried it for forty-five paces.

When the emperor touched the wounded eye with the blood, he was cured immediately and said: "The God of the Christians is truly good and great!" A woman who had been blind for forty years heard about this, so she had herself carried to that place and prayed there. Her sight was restored at once. Savinian was martyred about A.D. 279, on the first day of February. Savinian's story, however, is given here simply as an adjunct to the story of his sister Savina, since the feast is celebrated principally in her honor.

Savina, then, wept every day for her lost brother and prayed to the idols for him. At length an angel appeared to her in her sleep and said: "Don't cry, Savina! Give away all your possessions, and you will find your brother raised to the highest honors!" When she awoke, she asked her foster sister: "My friend, did you hear or see anything?" "Yes, ma'am," was the response, "I saw a man talking to you, but I don't know what he said." Savina: "You won't tell anyone?" The other: "Of course not! Do anything you like, but don't kill yourself!"

The two women started out the next morning. After the father had made every effort to find Savina and had failed, he raised his hands to heaven and said: "If you are a God powerful in heaven, destroy my idols! They have not been able to save my children!" Then the Lord thundered, and broke and crushed all the idols, and many people, seeing this, believed.

Savina went to Rome and was baptized by Pope Eusebius. She cured two blind men and two paralytics, and lived in Rome for five years. Then an angel appeared to her in her sleep and said: "What are you doing, Savina? You gave up all your riches, yet here you are, living in luxury! Get up and go to the city of Troyes, where you will find your brother!" Savina said to her maidservant: "We must not live here any longer." The servant: "Madam, where do you want to go? Everybody here loves you, and you want to die a wanderer?" Savina: "God will provide for us!"

Taking a barley loaf with her, she set out and reached Ravenna. She went to the house of a certain rich man, whose daughter was being mourned as if she were already dead. Savina asked a servingwoman to allow her to stay in the house. The woman answered: "My lady, how could you be a guest in this house, when my mistress's daughter is dying and everyone is grief-stricken?" "She will not die because of me," said Savina. She entered the house, took the girl's hand, and brought her to her feet completely cured. The family pressed her to stay with them, but she would have none of it.

When she came within a mile of Troyes, she said to her maid: "Let's rest here for a while." Then from the city came a noblemen named Licerius, who asked her: "Where are you from?" She answered: "I'm from here, from this city." Licerius: "Why do you lie to me, since your accent shows that you're a stranger here!" Savina: "Sir, it's true that I am a stranger, and that I'm looking for my long-lost brother Savinian!" "The man you're looking for," he answered, "was beheaded for Christ, and I know where he's buried." Savina prostrated herself in prayer, saying: "O Lord, you have always preserved me in chastity. Do not allow me to weary myself any longer with journeying! Do not let me move my body beyond this place! I commend to you my servant, who has borne so much on my behalf. I could not see my brother here, but grant that I may be found worthy to see him in your heavenly kingdom!" And, having finished her prayer, she migrated to the Lord.

Her maidservant, seeing her dead, began to weep because she had no means of burying her. The aforementioned man sent a herald through the city, calling for men to come and bury a woman from another land. Men came and gave her honorable burial.

On this day the feast of a Saint Sabina is celebrated. She was the wife of a soldier named Valentine, and was executed under Hadrian because she refused to sacrifice.

128. Saint Lupus

Lupus, a native of Orléans, came of royal stock and shone with all the virtues. He was elected archbishop of Sens and distributed almost all he had to the poor. One day he had invited more people than usual to his table, and the wine ran short. Lupus said to the steward: "I believe that God, who feeds the ravens, will fill up our charity." At that moment a messenger came and announced that a hundred casks of wine stood outside the door.

All the members of his official family censured him severely, claiming that he was much too fond of the daughter of his predecessor, a virgin and devout servant of God. Lupus, in the presence of his detractors, held the young woman and kissed her, saying: "What other people say does no harm to one whose conscience is clear," for he knew that she loved God ardently, and he loved her with a perfectly pure affection.

When Clothar, king of the Franks, invaded Burgundy and sent his marshal against the people of Sens to besiege the city, Saint Lupus went into the church of Saint Stephen and began to ring the bell. When the enemy troops heard it, such terror seized them that they thought they would not escape death unless they fled.

In the end the king won the realm of Burgundy and sent another high officer to Sens, but blessed Lupus did not come out to meet him with gifts. The envoy was offended and denounced him to the king, and the king sent Lupus into exile, where the saint enhanced his renown by his teaching and his miracles. Meanwhile the people of Sens put to death another bishop who had usurped Saint Lupus's place, and petitioned the king to have Lupus return from exile. When the king saw this rightful bishop, weakened and worn out by exile, God changed his heart. He threw himself at Lupus's feet and begged his pardon, and sent him back to his city with many gifts. When Lupus went to Paris, the doors of the prisons opened and the prisoners' chains fell off, allowing them to meet the saint in crowds. One Sunday, while he was celebrating mass, a jewel fell from heaven into his sacred chalice. The king kept the jewel among the saint's relics.

King Clothar heard that the bell of Saint Stephen's church had wonderful sweetness of sound, and sent to have it brought to Paris so that he might hear it more often. But this displeased Saint Lupus, and as soon as the bell was out of the city of Sens, it lost the sweetness of its tone. When word of this reached the king, he immediately ordered the bell returned, and at the seventh milestone from the city it rang with its usual dulcet sound. Therefore Saint Lupus went out to meet it, and what he had grieved at losing he welcomed back with honor.

One day he had made the rounds of the city's churches as was his custom, and when he got home, his clerics were haranguing each other because they were bent on committing sin with women. He went to the church and prayed for them, and in no time all sting of temptation left them, and they came before him and begged for his pardon.

At last, renowned for his virtues, Lupus fell asleep in peace. He flourished in the years around A.D. 610, in the time of Heraclius.

---

129. Saint Mamertinus

While still a pagan, Mamertinus once was worshiping the idols when he lost one of his eyes and one of his hands became paralyzed. He thought he had offended his gods, and went to the temple to placate them. On the way he met a monk named Savinus, who asked him the cause of his affliction. He answered: "I have offended my gods and am on my way to pray to them, that what they have taken away in anger they may restore to me in kindness." Savinus: "You are mistaken, brother, if you think the demons are gods. Go to Saint Germain, bishop of Auxerre, follow his counsel, and you will be healed at once."

Mamertinus set out again in haste, and came to the sepulcher of bishop Saint Amator and a number of other saintly bishops. It started to rain, and he took shelter for the night in a small cell built above the tomb of Saint Concordian. There he fell asleep and had a wonderful vision, in which he saw a man come to the opening of his cell and invite Saint Concordian to come to the feast that Saint Peregrinus, Saint Amator, and other bishops were holding. Saint Concordian answered from his tomb: "I can't come now, because I must stay and protect a guest from the serpents that live here." The man went and reported what he had heard, then came back and said: "Rise, Concordian, and come, taking with you Vivian the subdeacon and Julian the acolyte to perform their functions. Alexander will take care of your guest." Mamertinus then saw Saint Concordian take him by the hand and lead him to the company of the other bishops. Saint Amator asked Concordian: "Who is this man who came in with you?" Concordian: "He is my guest." Amator: "Put him out! He's unclean, and cannot be with us!" Mamertinus was about to be expelled, but prostrated himself before Saint Amator and besought his mercy, whereupon Amator ordered him to go quickly to Saint Germain. When he awoke, he hurried off to Saint Germain and knelt before him, asking forgiveness. When he told the bishop all that had happened to him, they went together to blessed Concordian's tomb, removed the stone, and found a tangle of snakes that were over ten feet long. These fled in different directions, Germain commanding them to go to places where they would not dare to harm anyone.

At last Mamertinus received baptism and was cured of his ills. He then became a monk in the monastery of Saint Germain and succeeded Saint Allodius as abbot. In his time there was in the monastery a holy monk named Marinus, whose obedience Mamertinus wished to test. He therefore assigned Marinus to the meanest work in the monastery, which was to care for the cattle. While the holy man watched over his steers and cows in a woodland, he radiated such holiness that the birds of the forest came to him and pecked food out of his hand. A boar pursued by dogs once took refuge in his cell; he snatched the boar away from the pursuers and then set it free. Another time thieves robbed him, taking away with them even his clothes and leaving him only one poor tunic, but he ran after them, calling out: "Come back, my masters, come back! I found a coin in the hem of my tunic, and you may perhaps have need of it." Back they came and took the tunic and the coin, leaving him completely naked. The robbers set out in haste for their hiding place, but after marching all night they found themselves back at Marinus's cell. He greeted them and welcomed them kindly to his dwelling, washed their feet, and provided for their needs as well as he could. They were dumbstruck at the thought of the way they had treated him, and every one of them was converted to the faith.

One time some younger monks who lived with him set a trap for a she-bear that was preying on the sheep, and in the night the animal was caught in the trap. Saint Mamertinus sensed what had happened, so he rose from his bed and went out to the bear. "What are you doing, poor beast!" he said. "Hurry away from here or you will be caught!" He loosed the trap and the bear ran off.

When Mamertinus died, his body was being transported to Auxerre, but the cortege reached a certain villa and could not move a step farther until a man lying in prison found his chains suddenly broken, jumped up free, came to the corpse, and helped the others to carry it into the city. There the body was given honorable burial in the church of Saint Germain.

130. Saint Giles

Aegidius is the Latin form of the name Giles. *Aegidius* is formed from *a*, meaning without, *geos*, earth, and *dyan*, brilliant or godlike. Saint Giles was without the earth by his disdain for earthly things, brilliant by the light of his knowledge, and godlike by the love that causes the lover to be like the beloved.

Giles, or Aegidius, was born in Athens of royal stock and was instructed in the sacred writings from childhood. One day as he was on his way to church, he came upon a sick man lying beside the road and asking for an alms. He gave the sick man his coat, and as soon as the man put it, on he was cured of his illness. Another time, as he was returning home from church, he met a man who had been bitten by a snake, but Giles prayed for him and drove out the poison. Then a man possessed of the devil was in church with the rest of the people, disturbing the faithful with his clamor, but Giles drove the devil out and cured the man. Later, when his parents had fallen asleep in the Lord, he made Christ the heir of his patrimony.

Fearing the perils of being praised by men, Giles left the city and secretly made his way to the seacoast. From the shore he saw sailors who were in danger of shipwreck, and calmed the storm by his prayer. The sailors came ashore and, learning that he wanted to go to Rome and out of gratitude for what he had done for them, promised that they would take him aboard without payment. He got as far as Arles and stayed there for two years with Saint Caesarius, the bishop of that city. There he cured a man who had been stricken with fevers for three years. Then, seeking solitude, he left Arles surreptitiously and stayed for a long time with Veredonius, a hermit known for his holiness. There, by his merits, he put an end to the barrenness of the soil. The fame of his miracles spread widely, and, always aware of the danger of human adulation, he left Veredonius and penetrated farther into the desert, where he found a cave and a small spring. There was also a doe ready to hand, and she came at certain hours and nourished him with her milk.

The king's men came hunting in that area and saw the doe. Caring nothing for other game, they pursued her with their dogs, and the doe, hard pressed, took refuge at her foster son's feet. Giles wondered why the animal was whining and whimpering, which was not at all like her, so he went out, and, hearing the hunt, prayed the Lord to save the nurse he had provided. No dog dared come closer than a stone's throw, and the pack returned to the huntsmen barking and howling vehemently. Night drew on and the hunt turned for home. They came back the next day, but their labors were thwarted again, and they returned home as before.

Word of this reached the king, and, suspecting how matters stood, he came out with the bishop and a throng of huntsmen. When the dogs did not dare to come close to the doe but turned tail howling, the huntsmen surrounded the place, which was so thickly overgrown with thorn bushes as to be impenetrable. One of them incautiously shot an arrow, hoping to drive out the quarry, but instead inflicted a serious wound on the man of God as he prayed for his doe. The soldiers then cut a way through the brambles and came to the hermit's cave. There they found the old man wearing a monk's habit, white-haired, venerable with age, and the doe stretched out at his feet. Only the bishop and the king, having ordered the rest to stay back, came to him on foot. They asked him who he was and where he came from, and why he had chosen so dense a wilderness, and who had dared to wound him. When he had answered all their questions and they had humbly begged his pardon, they promised to send a physician to care for the wound and offered him many presents. But he refused medical care and spurned the gifts, which he did not even look at. Rather, knowing that power is made perfect in weakness, he prayed the Lord not to restore his health as long as he lived.

The king came often to visit the man of God and to receive from him the food of salvation. He offered Giles great wealth, but Giles refused to accept it and proposed instead that he use the treasure to build a monastery where the monastic way of life could be followed to the letter. The king did this, and Giles, finally yielding to the royal tears and entreaties, undertook the rule of the monastery.

Now King Charles heard of Giles's renown, invited the saint to visit him, and welcomed him reverently. In the course of their conversations about the soul and salvation, the king asked his visitor to pray for him, because he had committed an enormous crime, which he dared not confess even to the saint himself. The following Sunday, while Giles was celebrating mass and praying for the king, an angel of the Lord appeared to him and deposited on the altar a scroll on which it was written that the king's sin was forgiven due to Giles's prayer, provided that the king was truly repentant, confessed his sin, and abstained from committing it thereafter. Furthermore, anyone who had committed a sin and prayed to Saint Giles to obtain pardon should have no doubt that by the saint's merits the sin was forgiven. Giles gave the scroll to the king, and Charles acknowledged his sin and humbly prayed for pardon.

The saint, now more honored than ever, set out on his return journey. At Nîmes he restored to life the son of the chief man of that city, who had just died. A short time later he foretold the destruction of his monastery by enemies and went to Rome, where he obtained from the pope not only a privilege for his church, but two cypress-wood doors on which the images of the apostles were carved. These he lowered into the Tiber, commending them to God's guidance.

When he was back at his monastery he cured a paralytic at Tiberone. In the port he found the two doors described above, and, thanking God for having preserved them from the perils of the sea, placed them at the entrance to his church, both as an ornament to the church and as a memorial of its union with the see of Rome.

In due time the Lord revealed to him through the Spirit that the day of his death was imminent. He made this known to his brothers and asked them to pray for him, then happily fell asleep in the Lord. Many testified that at the moment of his death they had heard the angels singing as they bore his soul to heaven. Giles flourished around A.D. 700.

131. The Birth of the Blessed Virgin Mary

The glorious Virgin Mary took her origin from the tribe of Judah and the royal stock of David. Matthew and Luke do not set forth the lineage of Mary but that of Joseph—who had nothing to do with the conception of Christ—because the usage of the sacred writers is said to have been to weave the series of generations of males, not of females. It is perfectly true, nevertheless, that the Blessed Virgin descended from the lineage of David: this is obvious because, as Scripture often testifies, Christ was born of the seed of David. Since, therefore, Christ was born of the Virgin alone, it is plain that the Virgin herself was born of David, through the line of Nathan.

Among David's sons there were two, Nathan and Solomon. Of the line of Nathan, son of David, as John of Damascus testifies, Levi begot Melchi and Panthar, Panthar begot Barpanthar, Barpanthar begot Joachim, and Joachim was the father of the Virgin Mary. Nathan took a wife from the line of Solomon, and of her begot Jacob. When Nathan died, Melchi of the tribe of Nathan, son of Levi and brother of Panthar, married the deceased Nathan's wife, the mother of Jacob, and of her begot Heli. Thus Jacob and Heli were brothers born of the same mother, Jacob being of the tribe of Solomon and Heli of the tribe of Nathan. Heli of the tribe of Nathan died without issues, and Jacob his brother, who was of the tribe of Solomon, took Heli's wife and raised up seed to his brother,[1] begetting Joseph. Joseph therefore was by birth the son of Jacob of the

---

[1] Cf. Mark 12:19.

line of Solomon, and by law the son of Heli of the line of Nathan: in other words, the son born according to nature was the son of the father who begot him, but, according to the law, the son of the deceased.[2] Thus John Damascenus.

We also find, in the *Ecclesiastical History* and in Bede's *Chronicle*, that all the genealogies of Hebrews and aliens were kept in the Temple's secret archives. Herod ordered the burning of these records, thinking that he might be able to pass himself off for a noble if, in the absence of proof to the contrary, he was thought to be Israelite by race. There were also some who were called *dominici* ("men of the Lord") because they were closely related to Christ and were from Nazareth. These *dominici* worked out, as well as they could, the order of Christ's human ancestry, partly from what they had learned from their forefathers and partly from some books that they had at home.

Joachim took a wife named Anna, who had a sister named Hismeria. This Hismeria was the mother of Elizabeth and Eliud, and Elizabeth was the mother of John the Baptist. Eliud was the father of Eminen, and Eminen the father of Saint Servatius, whose body is in the town of Maastricht on the Meuse, in the diocese of Liège. Anna is said to have had three husbands, Joachim, Cleophas, and Salome. Of Joachim, her first husband, she gave birth to one daughter, Mary, the mother of the Lord, whom she gave in marriage to Joseph, and who bore and brought forth Christ the Lord. Joachim died and Anna married Cleophas, Joseph's brother, and of him had another daughter, whom she likewise called Mary and who was married to Alpheus. This Mary bore her husband four sons, namely, James the Less, Joseph the Just also called Barsabas, Simon, and Jude. After the death of her second husband Anna took a third, namely, Salome, of whom she had another daughter, whom she also called Mary and whom she gave as wife to Zebedee. This Mary had two sons by her husband, namely, James the Greater and John the Evangelist. All this is summed up in the following verses:

> Anna solet dici tres concepisse Marias,
> Quas genuere viri Joachim, Cleophas, Salomeque.
> Has duxere viri Joseph, Alpheus, Zebedaeus.
> Prima parit Christum, Jacobum secunda minorem,
> Et Joseph justum peperit cum Simone Judam,
> Tertia majorem Jacobum volucremque Joannem.[3]

---

[2] I.e., the deceased first husband of the mother. Part of the confusion in this genealogy is due to its failure to include Mathan or Matthan, described in Matt. 1:15 as the father of Jacob. Our author identifies this Mathan with one of the Nathans he cites. This point does not entirely dispel the confusion, though it helps to achieve the purpose of the genealogy, which is to confirm the Davidic ancestry of Mary and Jesus.

[3] Anna is usually said to have conceived three Marys, / Whom [her] husbands, Joachim, Cleophas, and Salome, begot. / The Marys were taken in marriage by Joseph, Alpheus, Zebedee. / The first Mary bore Christ, the second, James the Less, / Joseph the Just with Simon and Jude, / the third, James the Greater and John the Wingèd.

But now a question arises: how could Mary be a cousin of Elizabeth, as has been said elsewhere? It is clear that Elizabeth was the wife of Zachary, who was of the tribe of Levi, and according to the Law a man had to choose a wife from his own tribe and family, but Luke testifies that Elizabeth was of the daughters of Aaron.[4] According to Jerome, Anna was from Bethlehem, which belonged to the tribe of Judah, but keep in mind that both Aaron and Joiada the high priest took wives of the tribe of Judah, which proves that the priestly and kingly tribes were always joined to each other by ties of blood. It may be, as Bede says, that this sort of relationship, by which women were given in marriage from one tribe to another, developed in later times, so that it would be manifest that Mary, who descended from the royal tribe, had a bond of kinship with the priestly tribe. Therefore blessed Mary was of both tribes. God willed that these privileged tribes should be mingled with each other by reason of the mystery, because the Lord Christ was to be born of them, and Christ, king and priest, would offer himself for us, would rule his followers as they struggled amid the evils of this life, and would crown them after they had won the fight. This is also suggested by the name of Christ, which means anointed, because in the Old Law only priests, kings, and prophets were anointed. Hence we are called Christians after Christ, and are also called a chosen generation and a kingly priesthood.[5] And when it was said that women should be wedded only to men of their own tribe, it is clear that this was ordered so as not to upset the distribution of the land by lot. Since the tribe of Levi had no share in this distribution among the other tribes, the women of that tribe could marry whomever they wished.

Blessed Jerome says in the Prologue to his *History of the Birth of the Virgin* that in his early youth he had read the story in some book, and many years later was asked to put it in writing, so he wrote it down as he remembered it from his early reading. Joachim, a Galilean from the town of Nazareth, took Saint Anna, a native of Bethlehem, as his wife. They were both righteous and walked without reproach in all the commandments of the Lord. They divided all their goods into three parts, one part being reserved for the Temple and its ministers, one for transient strangers and the poor, and the third for their own needs and those of their household. They lived for twenty years without offspring and made a vow to the Lord that if he granted them a child, they would dedicate it to the service of God. With this in mind they went up to Jerusalem for the three principal feasts. Once, when Joachim and his kinsmen traveled to Jerusalem for the feast of the Dedication, he went with the others to the altar to make his offering. When the priest saw him, he angrily ordered him away and upbraided him for presuming to approach the altar of God, declaring that it was not proper for one who was subject to the Law's curse to offer sacrifice to the Lord of the Law, nor for a sterile man, who made no increase to the people of God, to stand among men who begot sons.

---

[4] Luke 1:5.
[5] 1 Peter 2:9.

Joachim, seeing himself thus rejected, was ashamed to go home and face the contempt of his kinsmen, who had heard the priest's denunciation. Instead he went and lived with his shepherds. Then one day an angel appeared with great brilliance to him when he was alone. He was disturbed by the apparition, but the angel told him not to be afraid and said: "I am an angel of the Lord, sent to announce to you that your prayers have been heard and your alms have ascended in the sight of the Lord. I have seen how you were put to shame, and heard the reproach of childlessness wrongly put upon you. God punishes not nature but sin, and therefore, when he closes a woman's womb, he does this in order to open it miraculously later on, and to make it known that what is born is not the fruit of carnal desire but of the divine generosity. Did not the first mother of your race suffer the shame of childlessness until she was ninety years old, and yet bore Isaac, to whom was promised the blessing of all nations? Was not Rachel barren for a long time and yet bore Joseph, who had power over all Egypt? Who was stronger than Samson or holier than Samuel? Yet they both had sterile mothers. Believe these reasons and examples, which show that delayed conceptions and infertile childbearing are usually all the more wonderful! So then, your wife will bear you a daughter and you will call her Mary. As you have vowed, she will be consecrated to the Lord from infancy and filled with the Holy Spirit from her mother's womb. She will not live outside among the common people but will abide in the Temple at all times, lest any sinister suspicion be aroused about her. And, as she will be born of an unfruitful mother, so, miraculously, the Son of the Most High will be born of her. His name will be Jesus, and through him all nations will be saved. And let this be a sign to you: when you arrive at the Golden Gate of Jerusalem, Anna your wife will be there waiting for you. She has been worried because you were so late and will be glad at the sight of you." With these words the angel left him.

Meanwhile Anna was weeping bitterly, not knowing where her husband had gone, when the same angel appeared to her, revealed to her the same things he had told Joachim, and added that, for a sign, she should go to Jerusalem's Golden Gate, where she would meet her husband as he returned. So they met as the angel had predicted, and were happy to see each other and to be sure they were to have a child. They adored God and went to their home, joyfully awaiting the fulfillment of the divine promise. Anna conceived and brought forth a daughter, and they called her name Mary. When she was weaned at the age of three, the parents brought her to the Lord's Temple with offerings. Around the Temple there were fifteen steps, corresponding to the fifteen Gradual Psalms, and because the Temple was built on a hill, there was no way to go to the altar of holocaust, which stood in the open, except by climbing the steps. The virgin child was set down at the lowest step and mounted to the top without help from anyone, as if she were already fully grown up.

Having made their offering, Joachim and Anna left their daughter in the Temple with the other virgins and went home. Mary advanced steadily in all holiness. Angels visited her every day, and she enjoyed the vision of God daily.

In a letter to Chromatius and Heliodorus, Jerome says that the Blessed Virgin had made a rule for herself: the time from dawn to the third hour she devoted to prayer, from the third to the ninth hour she worked at weaving, and from the ninth hour on she prayed without stopping until an angel appeared and brought her food.

When Mary was in her fourteenth year, the high priest publicly announced that the maidens who were reared in the Temple and had come of age should return to their homes and be legally joined with their husbands. The other girls obeyed this edict. Only the Blessed Virgin Mary answered that she could not do so, both because her parents had dedicated her to the service of the Lord and because she herself had vowed her virginity to God. The high priest was perplexed: he did not intend, by impeding the fulfillment of a vow, to go against the Scripture that says: "Make your vows to the Lord your God and perform them,"[6] nor did he dare to introduce a custom not usual in the nation. A feast of the Jews was imminent, and he called the elders together to consult them. They were unanimous in their decision that in so doubtful a matter the counsel of the Lord should be sought. They prayed earnestly, and the high priest went inside to consult the Lord. Presently a voice sounded from the Holies for all to hear. It said: "Each unmarried but marriageable man of the house of David is to bring a branch to the altar. One of these branches will bloom and the Holy Spirit in the form of a dove will perch upon its tip, according to the prophecy of Isaiah. The man to whom this branch belongs is, beyond all doubt, the one who is to be the virgin's spouse."

Joseph, of the house of David, was among the other men, but it seemed incongruous to him that a man of his advanced age should take so tender a young woman to wife, and he alone withheld his branch when the others placed theirs on the altar. So it was that nothing happened as the divine voice had predicted, and the high priest thought to consult the Lord a second time. The voice responded that the only man who had not brought his branch was the one to whom the virgin was to be espoused. Therefore Joseph brought his branch forward, it flowered at once, and a dove came from heaven and perched upon it. So it was clear to all that Joseph was to be Mary's husband.

Once the espousals were accomplished, Joseph went back to his home city of Bethlehem to get his house ready and to make the necessary arrangements for the wedding. Mary, on the other hand, returned to her parents' home in Nazareth, together with seven virgins of her own age and breeding, whom the high priest had assigned to her because of what the miracle had shown. And in those days the angel Gabriel appeared to her as she prayed, and announced to her that she was to be the mother of the Son of God.

The day of the Blessed Virgin's birth was unknown to the faithful for a long time. Then, as John Beleth tells it, there was a holy man, diligent in the practice of contemplation, who, every year on the eighth day of September, heard, as he

---

[6] Ps. 75:12 (76:11).

prayed, the joyous choirs of angels chanting solemn paeans. He devoutly prayed to know why he heard this annually on this day and on no other. He received a response from God, that on this day the glorious Virgin Mary had been born to the world, and that he should make this known to the children of Holy Church so that they might join the court of heaven in celebrating her birthday. He passed this knowledge on to the supreme pontiff and others, and they, fasting and praying and searching the Scriptures and ancient documents to ascertain the truth, decreed that this day should be celebrated throughout the world in honor of holy Mary's birth.

There was a time when the octave of Mary's birth was not solemnized, but Pope Innocent, a native of Genoa, instituted its celebration, for the following reason. After the death of Pope Gregory, the Romans locked all the cardinals in a conclave so that they would elect a successor more quickly. But when they had not reached an agreement after several weeks, and had to endure many abuses inflicted by the Romans, they made a vow to the Queen of heaven that if by her intercession they agreed on a choice and would be free to go home, they would decree that the long-neglected octave of her birthday should be celebrated from then on. So they elected the lord Celestin and were set free. Celestin, however, died in less than a month, and their vow was translated into law by the lord Innocent.

Note that the Church solemnizes only three birthdays, namely, those of Christ, of holy Mary, and of John the Baptist. These three birthdays mark three spiritual births, for we are reborn in water with John, in penance with Mary, and in glory with Christ. Since the rebirth of baptism in adults must be preceded by contrition, as must the rebirth in glory, these two birthdays rightly have vigils, but penance is itself a vigil, and therefore our rebirth in penance does not call for a vigil. All three, however, have octaves, because they all look forward to the octave of the resurrection.

There was a knight who was dauntless in combat and also fervently devoted to the Blessed Virgin. On his way to a tournament he came to a monastery built in honor of the Virgin and went in to hear mass; but one mass succeeded another, and for the Virgin's honor he did not want to miss any of them. Finally he left the monastery and rode as fast as he could toward the field of the tourney. And behold, he was met by knights coming back from the field, and they congratulated him for jousting so well. All who had been there said the same, and all applauded his mastery in the lists. There were also some who said he had captured them, and they surrendered to him forthwith. The knight, a man of discernment, saw that the courtly Queen had honored him in a courtly way. He explained what had happened, returned to the monastery, and thereafter soldiered for the Son of the Virgin.

A certain bishop, who held Blessed Mary in the highest reverence and piety, was on his way in the middle of the night to a church of the Virgin, to make a visit of devotion. And lo! the Virgin of virgins, accompanied by a great chorus of virgins, came to meet the bishop, received him with high honor, and began to lead him toward the church to which he was going. Two of the maidens from the choir led the chant, and sang:

> Cantemus Domino, sociae, cantemus honorem,
> Dulcis amor Christi resonet ore pio.[7]

The whole chorus of virgins took up the chant, repeating the verses, while the two leaders sang the next two in time:

> Primus ad ima ruit magna de luce superbus,
> Sic homo cum tumuit, primus ad ima ruit.[8]

Thus they led the man of God in procession to the church, the two leaders always intoning the verse and the rest responding.

A woman who had lost her husband had her only son, whom she loved tenderly, for consolation. It happened, however, that the son was captured by enemies and imprisoned in chains. When she heard this, she wept inconsolably, and prayed incessantly to the Blessed Virgin, to whom she was much devoted, to obtain her son's liberation. Then, seeing that her prayers were not answered, she went alone into a church where there was a sculptured image of Blessed Mary, and, standing in front of the image, she addressed it in these terms: "O Virgin blessed, I have often asked you for the liberation of my son, and so far you have not come to the aid of this pitiable mother. I have sought your patronage for my son and see no return for my prayers. Therefore, as my son has been taken away from me, I will take your Son away from you and hold him in custody as a hostage for mine." She then went up and took the image of the Child from the Virgin's lap, went home with it, wrapped it in spotless cloths, and hid it in a cupboard, which she locked carefully. Thus she could rejoice at having a good hostage for her son and guarded it closely.

The following night the Blessed Virgin appeared to the young man and opened the door of the prison. She told him to get up and leave, and said: "Son, you will tell your mother to give my Son back to me as I have given hers back to her." The youth walked out, went to his mother, and told her how the Virgin had set him free. Overjoyed, she took the image of the Child, went to the church, and returned her Son to Mary, saying: "I thank you, my lady, for restoring my only son to me, and now I return your Son to you, because I acknowledge that I have received my own."

There was a thief who committed many robberies, but had deep devotion to Blessed Mary and often greeted her with prayers. Once, however, he was caught in a robbery and sentenced to be hanged. When he was hanged, the Virgin was

---

[7] Let us sing to the Lord, dear companions, let us carol his honor; / Let the sweet love of Christ resound in pious song.

[8] As [Lucifer] the proud one fell first from the great light into the depths, / so the first man, when he was swollen with pride, fell into the abyss.

immediately at his side, and for three days, as it seemed to him, she held him up as he hung, so that he sustained no injury. But then the men who had hanged him, passing by and finding him alive and cheery of mien, thought that they had not adjusted the noose properly and prepared to finish him off with the sword, but the Blessed Virgin held back the swordsman's weapon and they could do the criminal no harm. They learned from him how Blessed Mary had come to his aid. Wondering, they took him down and, for love of the Virgin, let him go free. He went off and entered a monastery, where he spent his remaining years in the service of the mother of God.

There was a cleric who loved the Blessed Virgin devotedly and recited her hours faithfully. When his parents died, having no other offspring they left their whole estate to him. His friends then pressed him to take a wife and manage his heritage. On the appointed day he was on the way to his wedding and was passing a church, when he remembered his service to Mary, went into the church, and began to say her hours. The Blessed Virgin appeared to him and, as if angry, said: "O foolish, unfaithful man! Why are you leaving me, your friend and spouse, for another woman?" The cleric was filled with remorse at this, but he returned to his companions, hiding his distress, and went through with the wedding. At midnight, however, he left everything behind and fled from his house, entered a monastery, and devoted himself to Mary's service.

The priest of a certain parish, a man of virtuous life, knew no other mass than the mass of the Blessed Virgin Mary, which he celebrated day after day in her honor. This was brought to the bishop's attention, and he called the priest in immediately. The priest told him that he did not know any other mass. The bishop scolded him harshly, called him an impostor, suspended him from his parish duties, and forbade him to celebrate Mary's mass. The following night Blessed Mary appeared to the bishop, rebuked him severely, and asked why he had treated her servant so badly. She added that he would die within thirty days unless he reinstated the priest in his parish. The bishop, shaken, summoned the priest, begged his pardon, and ordered him to celebrate no other mass than the one he knew, the mass of the Virgin Mary.

There was a cleric who was vain and dissolute, yet loved the mother of God devotedly and recited her office piously and promptly. One night, in a vision, he saw himself standing before God's judgment seat and heard the Lord saying to those present: "It is yours to decide what judgment the man who is looking at you deserves. I have tolerated his conduct for a long time and to this day have seen no sign of amendment in him." Then the Lord, with unanimous approval, pronounced a sentence of damnation upon the cleric. But now he saw the Blessed Virgin rise and say to her Son: "Loving Son, I ask your clemency for this man. Mitigate his sentence of damnation, and, as a favor to me, let him live, although what he really deserves is death." "I grant your petition," the Lord answered, "on condition that from now on I see him amend his ways." The Virgin turned to the man and said: "Go and sin no more, that nothing worse befall you!" The man awoke, changed his way of living, became a religious, and spent the rest of his life in good works.

In Sicily, in the year A.D. 537, as we have the story from Fulbert of Chartres, there was a man named Theophilus, who served a bishop as his administrator. Theophilus managed the Church's affairs so ably that when the bishop died, the whole populace acclaimed him as worthy of the episcopate. He was content to remain as administrator, however, and preferred to have someone else ordained as bishop. But in time this new bishop deprived Theophilus, all unwilling, of his office, and Theophilus fell into such despair that, in order to regain his honorable post, he sought the advice of a Jewish sorcerer. The sorcerer summoned the devil, who came immediately. Thereupon Theophilus, at the demon's command, renounced Christ and his mother, repudiated the Christian faith, wrote a statement of his renunciation and repudiation in his own blood, signed and sealed the script, and gave it to the demon, thus pledging himself to his service. The next day, by the devil's manipulation, Theophilus was taken back into the bishop's good graces and reinstated in his dignities of office.

In time, however, the good man came to his senses and regretted what he had done, and, with all the devotion of his heart, had recourse to the glorious Virgin. At a certain moment Blessed Mary appeared to him, upbraided him for his impiety, ordered him to renounce the devil, and made him confess his faith in her and in Christ, the Son of God, and in the whole Christian doctrine. So she brought him back into her favor and her Son's, and, in token of the forgiveness granted him, appeared to him again and returned the scroll he had given to the devil, placing it on his breast as a sign that he need not fear he might still be in the demon's service, and that through her intervention he was a free man. Theophilus, having received this gift, was overcome with joy. He went before the bishop and the whole populace, and gave a full account of the above events. All were filled with admiration and gave praise to the glorious Virgin, and Theophilus, three days later, fell asleep in the peace of the Lord.

A man and his wife had an only daughter whom they gave in marriage to a young man, and, for love of their daughter, brought the son-in-law into their house along with his wife. The girl's mother, for love of her daughter, cared for the young man so kindly that the bride's love for her husband was no greater than the mother-in-law's for her son-in-law. That being the situation, evil-minded people began to say that the woman was not doing this for her daughter's sake but was trying to take her daughter's place in the young man's affections. This false rumor unsettled the woman's mind, and, fearing it would turn into a public scandal, she parleyed with two countrymen, promising to pay each of them twenty sols if they would secretly strangle the son-in-law.

One day, therefore, she hid the two in the cellar of her house, sent her husband out on some business or other, and dispatched her daughter on some other errand. Then she asked the young man to go to the cellar and bring up some wine, and he was strangled by the two malefactors. The mother-in-law laid him out in her daughter's bed and covered him up as if he were sleeping. The husband and the daughter came home and were seated at the dinner table, and the mother told her daughter to awaken her husband and call him to dinner. When the young wife found the dead body, she raised an outcry, the whole family fell to lamenting, and the murderess feigned to lament with the others. But in time she grieved over the crime she had committed and confessed the whole story to a priest. Sometime later a dispute arose between the woman and the priest, and he accused her of the murder of her son-in-law. When the young man's parents learned of this, they had her brought to justice, and the judge condemned her to die by fire. The woman, considering the fact that her end was near, had recourse to the mother of Christ, went to the Virgin's church, and prostrated herself in tears and prayer. In a short time she was forced to come out and was thrown into a blazing fire, and all saw her standing in the middle of the flames unhurt and unharmed. The dead man's kinsmen thought the fire was not big enough and fetched wood to throw on it, but, seeing that the woman was still unscathed, attacked her with lances and spears. The judge was stupefied at what was going on and checked their assaults, but, examining her carefully, he found no sign of the fire on the woman, or other mark except the wounds from the lances. Her own people then carried her back to her house and revived her with salves and baths. But it was not God's will that she should suffer suspicion and disgrace any longer, and after she had persevered for three days in praising the Virgin, God called her forth from this life.

132. Saints Cornelius and Cyprian

Cornelius is interpreted as one who understands circumcision. Pope Cornelius understood circumcision and, understanding it, lived cut off from all superfluous, though permitted, goods, and even from necessary ones. Or the name comes from *cornu*, horn, and *leos*, people, hence the horn, or fortitude, of the people. Cyprian comes from *cyprus*, which means mixture, and *ana*, above; or it comes from *cyprus*, meaning sadness or inheritance. Saint Cyprian had a supernal mixture of grace and virtue, sadness for sins, and an inheritance of heavenly joys.

Pope Cornelius, successor to Saint Fabian, was sent into exile with his clergy by Decius Caesar, and while in exile received letters of support and comfort from

Saint Cyprian, bishop of Carthage. In time he was brought back from exile and set before Decius. When he continued unshaken in the faith, the emperor had him beaten with leaded whips, and ordered him to be brought to the temple of Mars to offer sacrifice there, or to submit to the sentence of death. A soldier asked the pope, on his way to execution, to turn aside to the soldier's house and pray for his wife, who had lain paralyzed for five years. He prayed and the woman was cured, whereupon twenty soldiers, together with the woman and her husband, believed in the Lord. By command of Decius they were taken to the temple of Mars, but they spat upon the idol and were martyred with Saint Cornelius.

Cyprian, bishop of Carthage, was brought before the proconsul Patronus in that city. When nothing could make him abjure his faith, he was sent into exile, then recalled by Angliricus, the proconsul who had succeeded Patronus, and by him sentenced to death. When the sentence was pronounced, Cyprian gave thanks to God. He came to the place of execution and ordered his ministers to pay the headsman fifteen gold pieces. Then he was given a blindfold and with his own hands covered his eyes with the cloth, and so received the crown of martyrdom, about A.D. 256.

133. Saint Lambert

Lambert was noble by birth and more noble by the holiness of his life. From his earliest years he was instructed in letters. He was so beloved for his sanctity that he was considered worthy to succeed Theodard, who had been his teacher, as bishop of Maastricht. King Childeric had great affection for him and always treated him as the dearest of all the bishops. There were those who envied him, and their malice increased, though without reason, until they drove him out of his see and deprived him of the honors due him. In his place they installed Feramund as bishop. Lambert entered a monastery and lived a most meritorious life there for five years.

One night as he rose from prayer, he unwittingly made some noise on the pavement, and the abbot, hearing it, said: "Let whoever made that noise go immediately to the cross." Lambert, clad in a hair shirt, ran barefoot to the cross and stood motionless in the snow and ice. Then in the morning, when the monks were warming themselves after matins, the abbot noticed Lambert's absence. One of the brothers told him that the bishop was the one who had gone to the cross, so the abbot had him brought inside, and with all the monks begged his forgiveness. Not only did the man of God pardon them kindly; he preached sublimely to them on the virtue of patience.

Seven years later Feramund was expelled, and by order of Pepin Saint Lambert was brought back to his see, where he displayed his power by word and example, as before. Then two miscreants began to heap troubles on him, and friends of the pontiff killed them, as they deserved. At the same time Lambert took Pepin to task concerning a lewd woman he was keeping. A man named Dodo, brother of the woman and a blood relative of the two who were killed, was also a domestic in the king's palace. He gathered a corps of armed men and surrounded the bishop's house, meaning to avenge the death of his kinsmen on the saint himself. Lambert was at prayer when a servant came to tell him what was going on, and the bishop, trusting in God, snatched up a sword to drive the attackers away. But on second thought, judging that it was better to conquer by standing firm and dying than to stain his sacred hands with the blood of the impious, he threw the weapon aside, and admonished his attendants to confess their sins and suffer death patiently. The malefactors rushed upon Saint Lambert as he knelt in prayer, and killed him, about A.D. 620. When the murderers left, some of the bishop's people, who had escaped, secretly brought his body to the cathedral church by ship, and gave it burial while the whole city mourned.

134. Saint Adrian and His Companions

Adrian suffered martyrdom in the reign of the emperor Maximian. When Maximian was offering sacrifice to the idols in the city of Nicomedia, he issued an order that all the citizens should hunt out the Christians; whereupon, either for love of the promised money or for fear of punishment, neighbors informed on neighbors and relatives delivered their own kinsmen to the torture. Thus thirty-three Christians, captured by the pursuers, were brought before the king,[1] who said to them: "Have you not heard of the punishments we have decreed against Christians?" They answered: "Yes, we've heard, and we've laughed at the stupidity of your decree!" The king was angry at this, and ordered them to be whipped with raw thongs and to have their mouths beaten in with stones, after

---

[1] In this chapter and elsewhere, Jacobus sometimes wrote "king" for "emperor."

which each one's confession of faith was to be recorded, and all were to be imprisoned in chains.

Adrian, the commander of the guard, was impressed by their constancy and said to them: "I adjure you by your God, tell me what reward you expect for enduring these torments." The saints told him: "No eye has seen, nor ear heard, nor the heart of man conceived, what God has prepared for those who love him perfectly."[2] At this, Adrian jumped in among them and said: "Record me with these, because I too am a Christian!" The emperor heard this and, since Adrian refused to offer sacrifice, ordered him to be chained and imprisoned.

When Natalia, Adrian's wife, heard that her husband was in prison, she tore her garments, weeping and sobbing loudly. But when she learned that he was jailed for confessing the faith of Christ, she was filled with joy, ran to the prison, and began to kiss her husband's bonds and those of his companions. She too was a Christian, but on account of the persecution had made no public show of the fact. She said to her spouse: "Blessed are you, my lord Adrian, because you have found riches that were not left to you by your parents, riches which those who have much will not have at that time when there will no longer be borrowing and lending, when no one will liberate another—not a father his son nor a mother her daughter, nor a servant his master nor a friend his friend, nor riches their owner." She exhorted him to spurn all earthly glory, to pay no heed to friends or relatives, and always to fix his heart on the things of heaven. Adrian said to her: "Go home, my sister, and when the time for our passion comes, I will call for you, so that you may witness our end." So she commended her husband to the other saints, bidding them encourage him, and returned home.

A short time later Adrian, learning that the day of his passion was at hand, gave money to the guards and left the saints who were with him as pledges, then started for home to call his wife as he had promised, so that she might witness their martyrdom. Someone, however, saw Adrian outside the prison, and hurried ahead to break the news to Natalia, saying: "Adrian has been set free and is on his way here." Natalia did not believe what she heard, and said: "But who could have freed him of his chains? May it not happen to me that he be freed and separated from those saints!" Even as she spoke, one of her servants came and said: "See, my master has been released."

Natalia thought that Adrian had fled from martyrdom and wept most bitterly; and when she saw him, she rose quickly and shut the door against him, saying: "May he who has run away from God keep away from me! Let it not be my lot to speak to the man who with his own mouth has renounced his Lord!" And through the door she said: "O godless wretch, who forced you to undertake what you could not finish? Who separated you from the saints? Who misled you and made you give up the covenant of peace? Tell me, why did you run away before the fight began, even before you saw the opponent? How have you been wounded, when no arrow has yet been shot? And I . . . I was wondering that

---

[2] Cf. 1 Cor. 2:9.

someone from the godless people, the race of the impious, would be offered to God! Alas, alas! Unhappy, miserable woman that I am! What shall I do, I who am joined to this man from a heathen race? It has not been granted me that for the space of an hour I should be thought of as the wife of a martyr, but rather that I should be called the wife of a renegade. How brief was my exaltation! And now my shame will last forever!"

As Adrian listened to this, his joy was boundless. He was amazed that this young woman, a beauty and a noble, to whom he had been married for fourteen months, could speak as she was speaking. He heard her all the more gladly as her words made him desire martyrdom more ardently. But when he saw that her distress was getting out of control, he said: "My lady Natalia, open the door for me! I have not run away from martyrdom as you think. I came to call you, as I promised I would!" But she did not believe him and said: "See how this deceiver beguiles me, how this other Judas lies! Away from me, wretch! Or shall I kill myself? Will that satisfy you?"

She still did not open the door, and Adrian said: "Open to me quickly, because I must go, and you will see me no more, and you will grieve that you did not see me alive. I gave the holy martyrs as pledges for my return, and if the guards don't find me when they come for me, the saints will bear their own torments and mine too!" Natalia opened the door and they fell into each other's arms, then went together to the prison, where for seven days Natalia cleansed the saints' sores with fine linens.

On the appointed day the emperor ordered the prisoners to be brought before him. Because they were weakened by the punishments they had endured, they were carried in like animals. Adrian followed them with his hands manacled. Then he alone, now carrying his own rack, was presented to the caesar. Natalia stayed close to him and said: "See to it, my lord, that you don't stumble when you see the torments! You will suffer for a moment now, but immediately you will exult with the angels."

Adrian refused to offer sacrifice and was cruelly beaten, and Natalia ran joyfully to the saints who were in prison, saying: "See, my lord and master has begun his martyrdom!" When the emperor warned him not to revile his gods, Adrian answered: "If I am tortured because I revile beings who are not gods, how will you, who revile the true God, be tortured!" The emperor: "Seducers taught you to say these things!" Adrian: "Why do you call them seducers? They are teachers of the truth." Natalia ran to the others and reported her husband's answers to them.

Now the king had Adrian beaten by the four strongest men available, and Natalia speedily carried back all his tortures, questionings, and responses to the other martyrs who were still in confinement. Adrian was so severely scourged that his entrails spilled out, and he was again put in chains and remanded to jail. He was a young man twenty-eight years of age, delicate, handsome. When Natalia saw her husband lying there, wounded from head to foot, she put her hand under his head and said: "You are blessed, my lord, you who have been made worthy to be counted among the saints. You are blessed, light of my life, you who suffer for him who suffered for you. Go forth now, my sweet, to see his glory!"

The emperor learned that many women were ministering to the saints in prison, and gave orders that they could no longer get in to do so. Natalia cut off her hair and dressed as a man, and continued to be helpful to the imprisoned saints. Her example induced other women to do the same. She asked her husband to pray for her when he was in glory, that the Lord would keep her untouched and would soon call her out of this world. The emperor found out what the women were doing, and issued orders that an anvil be brought and that the martyrs have their legs broken on it and so die. Natalia feared that Adrian would be terrified by the others' suffering, and asked the executioners to begin with him. He therefore had his feet cut off and his legs broken, and Natalia asked him to allow a hand to be cut off as well, so that he would be on a par with the other saints, who had suffered more than he had. When this was done, Adrian breathed his last, and the others stretched out their feet, died, and migrated to the Lord.

The emperor ordered that the bodies of the martyrs be burned, but Natalia hid Adrian's hand in her bosom. When the saints' bodies were cast into the fire, Natalia wanted to throw herself in with them, but a very heavy rainstorm broke out and extinguished the flames, leaving the holy bodies unscathed. The Christians, after taking counsel among themselves, had the bodies transferred to Constantinople, until, when peace was restored to the Church, they were brought back with honor. The martyrs suffered about A.D. 280.

Natalia continued to dwell in her house and kept Adrian's hand with her, having it always at the head of her bed for her life's consolation. Some while later the tribune, seeing Natalia so beautiful, so rich, and so noble, obtained the emperor's permission and sent ladies to her to seek her consent to marry him. "Who could possibly outdo me in honor," she said, "when I become the wife of so great a man? But I beg that I may be given a delay of three days to prepare myself." She said this in order to flee from the city, since she had prayed God to keep her untouched. Then suddenly she fell asleep, and one of the martyrs appeared to her, comforted her kindly, and bade her go to the place where the bodies of the martyrs had been kept.

She woke up and, taking with her nothing but Adrian's hand, boarded ship with many Christians. The tribune was informed of this and, with a company of soldiers, pursued her by ship, until a contrary wind rose and forced them to turn about, many of them being washed overboard. Then at midnight the devil, in the guise of a pilot in a phantom vessel, appeared to those who were with Natalia. Imitating a pilot's manner, he asked them: "Where do you come from and where are you headed?" They replied: "We come from Nicomedia and are headed for Constantinople." The answer came: "You are on the wrong bearing.

Bear left and correct your heading!" He was trying to make them run aground and perish; but as they were about to trim sail, Adrian, sitting in a small skiff, suddenly appeared to them and told them to stay on course, adding that it was the evil spirit who had spoken to them. He then set out ahead of them to show them the right course. When Natalia saw Adrian leading the way, her joy knew no bounds.

So they sailed into Constantinople before dawn. Natalia entered the house where the martyrs' bodies were preserved and placed Adrian's hand beside his body. Then, having said a prayer, she went to sleep. Adrian appeared to her and bade her come with him into eternal rest. She wakened and told her attendants about the dream, then bade them farewell and breathed her last. The faithful took her body and placed it with the remains of the martyrs.

<hr>

135. Saints Gorgonius and Dorotheus

Gorgonius and Dorotheus held high office in Diocletian's palace at Nicomedia, but gave up their rank in order to follow their King more freely and made it clear to all that they were Christians. The emperor was very displeased by this news. He found it hard to accept the loss of men of their quality, raised in the palace as they had been, and distinguished for their nobility of blood and of behavior. But neither threats nor blandishments could change their commitment to the faith, so they were stretched on the rack, their flesh was torn with whips and iron hooks, and vinegar and salt were poured on their open wounds. They bore all this without flinching. Next they were roasted on grates but seemed to lie there as if on a bed of flowers, feeling no hurt. Finally, at the emperor's command, they were hanged by the neck, and their bodies exposed to wolves and dogs; but they remained untouched and were buried by the faithful. They suffered about A.D. 280.

Many years later the body of Saint Gorgonius was translated to Rome. In the year A.D. 766, the bishop of Metz, a nephew of King Pepin, transferred the body to France and entombed it in the monastery at Gorze.

136. Saints Protus and Hyacinthus

Protus and Hyacinthus were personal slaves to Eugenia and were her companions in the study of philosophy. She was the daughter of Philip, who belonged to the highest Roman nobility. He was appointed by the Senate to be prefect of Alexandria, and took with him his wife Claudia, his sons Avitus and Sergius, and his daughter Eugenia. In time Eugenia knew all there was to know in the liberal arts and letters, and Protus and Hyancinthus, who had studied with her, were proficient in all branches of knowledge.

When Eugenia was fifteen years old, Aquilinus, the son of the consul Aquilinus, asked for her hand in marriage. Her answer was: "A husband is to be chosen not for his ancestry but for his morals." Then Saint Paul's writings came into her hands, and she gradually became Christian at heart. At that time Christians were allowed to live on the outskirts of Alexandria. One day Eugenia was on her way to the family villa for a spell of recreation, when, in passing, she heard Christians chanting:

> Omnes Dii gentium daemonia,
> Dominus autem caelos fecit.[1]

She said to her servants Protus and Hyacinthus, who had studied with her: "We worked our way with meticulous attention through the philosophers' syllogisms, Aristotle's arguments and Plato's ideas, the precepts of Socrates, and, to be brief, whatever the poets sang, whatever the orators or the philosophers thought; but all that is wiped out by this one sentence. A usurped authority has used words to make me your mistress, but the truth makes me your sister. Let us then be brothers, and follow Christ!"

The proposal was deemed acceptable, and Eugenia put on men's clothing and went to a monastery. Helenus, a man of God, was the head of this monastery, and Helenus would not allow a woman to come near him. Once when he was arguing with a heretic and the argument grew too heated for his liking, he had a huge fire built and lighted, the purpose being to prove that the one of them who passed through the fire without being burned had the true faith. Helenus went first into the fire and emerged unharmed, but the heretic refused to run the risk and was driven out by all. When Eugenia approached Helenus and said she was a man, he replied: "Rightly do you call yourself a man, because you act like a man though you are a woman." Her true sex was revealed to him by God.

---

[1] All the gods of the Gentiles are demons, / but the Lord made the heavens.

Eugenia therefore, together with Protus and Hyacinthus, received the monastic habit from Helenus, and thenceforth was called Brother Eugene.

When Eugenia's father and mother saw that her carriage had come home empty, they were grief-stricken and had a search made for their daughter, but she could not be found. They asked soothsayers what had happened to her, and their answer was that the gods had taken her up among the stars. The father therefore had a statue made of her and ordered everyone to worship it. Meanwhile she and her two companions persevered in the fear of God, and when Helenus died, Brother Eugene was elected to replace him.

At this time there was in Alexandria a rich and noble woman named Melancia. Brother Eugene had cured her of the quartan fever by anointing her with oil in the name of Jesus Christ. In return for this favor Melancia sent many gifts, which were not accepted. The lady took for granted that Brother Eugene was a man and visited him often, and, seeing how elegantly youthful and personally attractive he was, fell heatedly in love with him. Losing no time, she devised a plan whereby she could get him to lie with her. She pretended to be ill and sent word to him, asking that he deign to come and pay her a visit. He went, and she let him know how ardently she loved him and wanted him, begged him to come to her, then grasped him and kissed him, urging him to join her in bed. Brother Eugene was horrified and said: "You are well called Melancia, for the name says that you are filled with black perfidy and are the dark daughter of darkness, friend of the devil, leader of pollution, fuel of lust, sister of perpetual torment, and daughter of eternal death!"

Melancia, thwarted and afraid that word of her crime might get abroad, decided to be the first to accuse and cried out that Eugene was trying to violate her. Then she went to Philip the prefect and issued a complaint, saying: "A certain treacherous young man, a Christian, came in under pretext of remedying my illness, but set upon me shamelessly and was about to ravish me, and would have satisfied his lust upon me had not one maid, who was in the room, come to my rescue." The prefect, incensed at what he heard, sent a troop to bring in Eugene and the other servants of Christ bound in chains, and set a date on which all of them were to be thrown to the wild beasts in the arena. He summoned them before him and said to Eugene: "Tell us, you basest of criminals, is that what your Christ taught you—to do the works of corruption, and madly and shamelessly to assault our women?" Eugenia, lowering her head so as not to be recognized, answered: "Our Lord taught chastity, and to those who guarded their integrity he promised eternal life. We can show that this Melancia is a false witness, but it is better that we suffer than that she, once convicted, be punished and we lose the reward of our patience. In any case, have the maid who, she says, witnessed the crime, come in and testify, so that from her mouth her mistress's lies may be refuted."

The maid was brought in, but, being instructed by Melancia, she stoutly maintained that the man had tried to take his pleasure with her mistress; and all the other servants, likewise corrupted, told the same story. At this, Eugenia said: "The time for silence is past, it is now time to speak. I will not allow this wanton woman to impute crime to the servants of Christ and boast of her deception. To make sure that truth shall prevail over mendacity and wisdom conquer malice, I will show the truth, not out of personal pride but for the glory of God!" So saying, she opened her robe from the top to the waist, and was seen to be a woman. She said to the prefect: "You are my father, Claudia my mother, the two who are sitting with you, Avitus and Sergius, are my brothers, I am your daughter Eugenia, and these two are Protus and Hyacinthus."

When her father heard this and gradually recognized his daughter, he and her mother rushed to embrace her, and many tears were shed. They clothed Eugenia in cloth of gold and raised her on high, and fire came down from heaven and consumed Melancia and her coconspirators. Thus Eugenia converted her father, mother, brothers, and the whole household to the faith of Christ. Her father was dismissed from the prefecture but was ordained bishop by the Christians, and, persevering in faith and prayer, was put to death by the pagans.

Claudia returned to Rome with her sons and Eugenia, and they converted many to Christ. By order of the emperor, Eugenia was bound to a great stone and cast into the Tiber, but the stone broke loose and she walked unharmed over the waves. Then she was thrown into a roaring furnace, but the fire went out and she came forth refreshed. She was shut up in a dark jail, but a splendid light shone around her. After she had been there for ten days without food, the Savior appeared to her, held out a shining white loaf, and said: "Take food from my hand! I am your Savior, whom you have loved with your whole heart. On the day when I came down upon earth, I myself will take you up." On the day of the Lord's birth, therefore, a headsman was sent and cut off her head. Later she appeared to her mother and foretold that Claudia would follow her on the Sunday. Sunday came, and Claudia, rapt in prayer breathed her last. Protus and Hyacinthus, when they were dragged to the temple, shattered the idol with a prayer and, when they refused to sacrifice, achieved their martyrdom by being beheaded. They suffered under Valerian and Gallus, about A.D. 256.

137. The Exaltation of the Holy Cross

This feast is called the Exaltation of the Holy Cross because on this day the faith and the holy cross were raised to the heights.

It should be noted that before Christ's passion the wood of the cross was a cheap wood, because crosses used for crucifixions were made of cheap wood. It was an unfruitful wood, because no matter how many such trees were planted on the mount of Calvary, the wood gave no fruit. It was an ignoble wood, because it was used for the execution of criminals; a wood of darkness, because it was dark and without any beauty; a wood of death, because on it men were put to death; a malodorous wood, because it was planted among cadavers.

After Christ's passion, however, this wood was exalted in many ways. Its cheapness passed into preciousness, so Saint Andrew the apostle exlaimed: "Hail, precious cross!" Its unfruitfulness gave way to fertility, as in the Song of Solomon (7:8): "I will go up into the palm tree, and will take hold of the fruit thereof." What had been ignoble became sublime, as Augustine says: "The cross, which was the gibbet of criminals, has made its way to the foreheads of emperors." Its darkness turned to light, as Chrysostom says: "Christ's cross and his scars will, on the Day of Judgment, shine more brightly than the sun's rays." Its death passed into eternal life, and we sing:

Ut unde mors oriebatur, inde vita resurgeret.[1]

Its stench became an odor of sweetness: "While the king was on his couch, my nard, i.e., the holy cross, gave forth its fragrance."[2]

The feast of the Exaltation of the Holy Cross is solemnly celebrated by the Church because on that day the Christian faith itself was exalted to the heights. In the year A.D. 615, the Lord allowing his people to be scourged by the savagery of the pagans, Chosroës, king of the Persians, subjected all the earth's kingdoms to his rule. When he came to Jerusalem, however, he withdrew in fear from the sepulcher of the Lord but took away a piece of the holy cross that Saint Helena had left there. Chosroës wanted to be worshiped as God. He built a gold-and-silver tower studded with jewels, and placed in it images of the sun, the moon, and the stars. Bringing water to the top of the tower through hidden pipes, he poured down water as God pours rain, and in an underground cave he had horses pulling chariots around in a circle to shake the tower and produce a noise

---

[1] In order that whence death arose, life might rise again (from the preface for the mass of the holy cross).

[2] Song of Sol. 1:12 (RSV).

like thunder. Then he abdicated his kingdom in favor of his son and, profane as he was, settled himself in the tower as in a fane, put the Lord's cross at his side, and decreed that all should call him God. Indeed, we read in the book *On the Mitral Office* that he sat on a throne in the shrine as the Father, put the wood of the cross on his right in place of the Son, and a cock on his left in place of the Holy Spirit. He commanded that he be called the Father.

Emperor Heraclius now marshaled a large army and marched against the son of Chosroës to confront him at the Danube River. Finally the two princes agreed to meet in single combat on the bridge that crossed the river, the victor to take over the empire, both armies being spared any damage. It was also decreed that anyone who came to the assistance of his prince would have his legs and arms cut off and be thrown into the river.

Heraclius offered himself totally to God and commended himself to the holy cross with all the devotion of which he was capable. The two princes fought for a long time, and the Lord granted victory to Heraclius, who thus made the opposing army subject to his command, with the result that all Chosroës's people acknowledged the Christian faith and received holy baptism. Chosroës himself knew nothing of the outcome of the war, because he was hated by all and no one told him about it.

Heraclius journeyed to Chosroës and found him seated on his golden throne. He said to him: "Because you have honored the wood of the holy cross in your own way, you will be spared your life and your reign on condition that you accept the Christian faith and receive baptism, a few hostages being taken as guarantee. If, on the other hand, you consider this beneath you, I will kill you with my sword and cut off your head." Chosroës refused the offer and Heraclius promptly decapitated him; but, since he had been a king, he was given suitable burial. Heraclius found the king's son, a child ten years of age, with him. He had the boy baptized and with his own hands lifted him from the font, then left his father's kingdom to him. But he demolished the tower and allotted the silver to his army as spoils of war, reserving the gold and the jewels for the rebuilding of the churches the tyrant had destroyed.

Now Heraclius carried the sacred cross back to Jerusalem. He rode down the Mount of Olives, mounted on his royal palfrey and arrayed in imperial regalia, intending to enter the city by the gate through which Christ had passed on his way to crucifixion. But suddenly the stones of the gateway fell down and locked together, forming an unbroken wall. To the amazement of everyone, an angel of the Lord, carrying a cross in his hands, appeared above the wall and said: "When the King of heaven passed through this gate to suffer death, there was no royal pomp. He rode a lowly ass, to leave an example of humility to his worshipers." With those words the angel vanished.

The emperor shed tears, took off his boots and stripped down to his shirt, received the cross of the Lord into his hands, and humbly carried it toward the gate. The hardness of the stones felt the force of a command from heaven, and the gateway raised itself from the ground and opened wide to allow passage to those entering. And a most sweet odor, which, from the day and moment when the sacred cross was taken out of Chosroës's tower, had glided across the far reaches of land from Persia to Jerusalem, now made itself felt, and refreshed with the wonder of its perfume all who sensed it. Then the truly devout emperor burst forth in praise of the cross: "O cross, more splendid than all the heavenly bodies, renowned throughout the world, deserving of all men's love, holier than all things else! O cross, you were worthy to carry the ransom of the world! O sweet wood, sweet nails, sweet sword, sweet lance, you were the bearer of sweet burdens! Save the host gathered today in praise of you and signed with your banner!"

Thus it was that the precious cross was brought back to its place, and the miracles of old began again: dead men were raised to life, four paralytics were cured, ten lepers were made clean, fifteen blind people received their sight, demons were driven out, and great numbers were delivered of various infirmities. Heraclius also repaired the churches and endowed them richly. Then he went back to his own land.

Some chronicles, however, give a different version of these events. We read that when Chosroës had occupied all the neighboring kingdoms and had taken Jerusalem together with the patriarch Zachary and the wood of the cross, Heraclius wanted to make a treaty of peace with him, but he swore that he would not make peace with the Romans until they renounced the cross and adored the sun. Then Heraclius, fired with zeal, moved against him with an army, overran the Persians in a series of battles, and forced Chosroës to retreat as far as Ctesiphon. Later Chosroës fell ill with dysentery and wanted to confer the crown on his son Medasas. When his eldest son, Syrois, learned of this, he made a pact with Heraclius, then pursued his father with nobles and put him in chains. He fed the old man with the bread of afflictions and the water of distress, and in the end had him put to death with arrows. Later he dispatched all the prisoners, together with the patriarch and the wood of the cross, to Heraclius, and Heraclius took the precious wood to Jerusalem and eventually to Constantinople. So we read in many chronicles.

The pagan Sybil, as we learn from the *Tripartite History*, had this to say about this same wood of the cross: "O thrice blessed wood, upon which God was stretched!" Perhaps this was said because of the life of nature, grace, and glory that comes from the cross.

In Constantinople a Jew went into the church of Saint Sophia and there looked at an image of Christ. Seeing that there was no one about, the Jew drew his sword and struck the image in the throat. Blood poured out instantly and spattered the Jew's face and head. Terrified, he seized the image, threw it down a well, and fled. A Christian met him and asked: "Where are you coming from, Jew? You've killed a man!" "Not true!" said the Jew. But the man said again: "Of course you've committed a murder and that's why you're spattered with blood!" The Jew: "Truly the God of the Christians is great, and everything confirms faith in him. I have not stabbed a man but an image of Christ, and straightaway the blood gushed out from his throat!" The Jew then led the man to the well and they retrieved the sacred image, and it is said that the wound in Christ's throat can be seen to this day. The Jew became a Christian without delay.

In the city of Berith in Syria, a Christian who occupied a house on an annual rent had hung a picture of the crucified Christ on the wall facing his bed and there regularly said his prayers. At the end of the year, however, he moved to a different house and forgot to take the picture with him. A Jew rented the first house and invited one of his fellow tribesmen to dinner on a certain day. In the course of the festivities the guest looked around the house and came upon the picture hanging on the bedroom wall. Trembling with anger he threatened his host, demanding to know why he dared to keep an image of Jesus Christ the Nazarene. The host, who had not even noticed the picture, declared with all the oaths he could muster that he knew absolutely nothing about the image the guest was talking about. The guest, pretending to be satisfied with the answer, took his leave and went to the head man of his tribe, to make charges against the other Jew regarding what he had seen.

The Jews now gathered and went to the house, saw the picture and belabored the householder with insults, manhandled him and expelled him half dead from the synagogue. Then they trampled the picture and renewed upon it all the indignities of the Lord's passion. When they thrust a lance into the image of his body, a copious flow of blood and water issued from it and filled a vase that they held under it. They were amazed and took the blood to their synagogues, and all the sick who were anointed with it were cured immediately. Then the Jews gave the bishop of the city a full account of all that had happened, and every one of them accepted the faith of Christ and holy baptism.

The bishop kept the blood in phials of crystal and glass. He also sent for the Christian to whom the picture belonged, and asked him who had painted so beautiful an image. He said: "Nicodemus painted it and at his death bequeathed it to Gamaliel; Gamaliel left it to Zacheus, Zacheus to James, and James to Simon. So it remained in Jerusalem till the fall of the city. Then the faithful took it into Agrippa's kingdom. From there it was brought into my country by my ancestors and came to me by right of inheritance." This happened in A.D. 750. Then all the Jews consecrated their synagogues, turning them into churches. This is the origin of the custom of consecrating churches: previously only the altars were consecrated.

On account of the above miracle the Church ordained that a commemoration of the Lord's passion be made on 27 November, or, as we read elsewhere, on 9 November. For the same reason a church was consecrated in Rome in honor of the Savior, and there a phial of that blood is preserved and a solemn feast observed.

There have been many evidences of the great power of the cross, even among those not of the faith. Gregory, in the third book of his *Dialogues*, records the experience of Andrew, bishop of the city of Fondi. He had permitted a nun to live in his house, and the ancient enemy began to impress the nun's image so vividly on the bishop's mind that it was as if he were seeing her in person. So, lying in bed, he thought of doing things that should not even be spoken of. Then one day a Jew came to Rome, and when, toward nightfall, he had not found a place to stay, he took shelter in the temple of Apollo. He feared the sacrilegious nature of the place and, though he had no faith in the cross, took care to protect himself with the sign of the cross. In the middle of the night he woke up and saw a horde of evil spirits going forward to do obeisance to a potentate, who walked in front of the rest and sat down in their midst. This potentate then began to hear the case of each of the spirits and to discuss their actions, in order to find out how much evil each one had done.

For the sake of brevity Gregory does not describe the way the discussion was conducted, but it can be deduced from a moral tale that we read in the *Lives of the Fathers*. A man had gone into a temple of the idols, and saw Satan seated and his troops standing around him. Then one of the wicked spirits came forward and adored him. "Where have you come from?" Satan asked. "I was in a certain province," the spirit replied, "and there stirred up many wars, caused much disturbance and shedding of blood; and I have come to report to you." Satan: "How much time did this take you?" The spirit: "Thirty days." Satan: "Why so long?" And he ordered his assistants to beat him with scourges as hard as they could. A second demon came up, adored Satan, and said: "My lord, I have been at sea, rousing up violent storms, sinking many ships, killing a lot of people." Satan: "How long did this take you?" The answer: "Twenty days." Satan: "So much time to do so little?" And he ordered a like beating. A third came and said: "I was in a city and incited fights at some wedding feasts, and much blood was spilled, and once I killed the bridegroom himself; and I came to report to you." Satan: "How long did it take you to do that?" "Ten days!" Satan: "Couldn't you wreak more havoc than that in ten days?" And whipping was ordered. Now the fourth came forward and said: "I stayed in the desert for forty years, devoted all my efforts to one monk, and at long last I have got him to commit one sin of the flesh!" Satan rose from his throne, kissed the spirit, took his crown off his own head and placed it on the other's, had him sit beside him, and said: "You have shown skill and courage, and have accomplished more than the others!" That, or something like it, is how the aforesaid discussion went, though Gregory passed over the details.

To return to Bishop Andrew . . . When each of the spirits in the temple of Apollo had reported what he had done, one more leapt into the middle and described the sort of carnal temptation he had aroused in Andrew's mind regarding that nun, adding that the day before, at the hour of vespers, he had got the bishop to go so far as to give the woman a friendly pat on the back. The head spirit exhorted him to finish what he had started, and so to win the palm among all the others, for bringing about the ruin of a bishop.

Satan also ordered his minions to find out who the man was who had had the presumption to sleep in Apollo's temple. By this time the Jew was all atremble, but when the spirits who were sent to seek him out saw that he was signed with the mystery of the cross, they cried out in terror: "He is an empty vessel, indeed, but it's sealed!" At this outcry the horde of malign spirits disappeared. The Jew went in haste to the bishop and recounted the incident in full detail. The bishop groaned with remorse, put all the women out of his house, and baptized the Jew.

Gregory also tells us in the *Dialogues* that a certain nun went into the garden, saw a fine lettuce, and was so hungry for it that, forgetting to bless it with the sign of the cross, she bit into it avidly. She was immediately seized by the devil and fell down. However, when blessed Equitius came to her, the devil cried out: "What have I done? I was sitting on the lettuce and she came and bit me!" Equitius ordered him out, and the spirit made his exit forthwith.

In the eleventh book of the *Ecclesiastical History* we read that the pagans had painted the arms of Serapis on house walls in Alexandria. Emperor Theodosius ordered the emblems to be obliterated and signs of the cross to be painted instead. When they saw this, the Gentiles and the priests of the idols asked for baptism, saying: "A tradition handed down by the ancients says that the gods they worshiped would stand until appeared the sign in which is life." And among the characters of their writing, one, which they called sacred and which, they said, stood for eternal life, had the form of a cross.

138. Saint John Chrysostom

John, surnamed Chrysostom, the Golden-mouthed, a native of Antioch, was the son of Secundus and Anthusa, both of whom were of noble descent. The *Tripartite History* gives a full account of his life, his ancestry, his character, and the persecutions he suffered.

John early engaged in the study of philosophy but later gave that up to devote himself entirely to the sacred writings. He was ordained a priest and was considered too severe because of his zeal for chastity. He was blunt rather than gentle, and, because of his concern for doing the right thing at the moment, was incapable of looking forward prudently to the consequences of his actions. Those who did not know him well found him arrogant in conversation, but he was an excellent teacher, remarkable in his ability to expound and clarify, and peerless as an upholder of strict morality.

In the reign of Arcadius and Honorius, caesars, and the pontificate of Damasus in the see of Rome, John was ordained bishop of Constantinople. By his determination to reform the life of the clergy all at once, he aroused their hatred: they shunned him as a madman and maligned him for all to hear. He never invited guests to dine with him, nor did he wish to be invited by others, so the word was that he acted this way because his table manners were atrocious. Or, said others, he invited no one to share his meals because he permitted himself only the most exquisite and expensive foods. The truth was that his strict abstinence often caused him severe pains in head and stomach, and so he avoided festive banquets.

The people loved him for the sermons he gave in church, and they paid no attention to the things his rivals said about him. Hostility toward him grew, however, when he began to direct his criticism to persons in high places, and one episode brought matters to a head. Eutropius, the emperor's provost, who held the rank of consul, wanted to avenge himself on some persons who had fled to churches for sanctuary. He therefore had the emperor make a law abolishing such refuge and providing that those who had already availed themselves of it could be taken out of the churches. But not long afterwards Eutropius himself fell into disfavor with the emperor and fled to a church for sanctuary. Bishop John, hearing of this, came and found him hiding under an altar, whereupon he made a speech denouncing Eutropius and addressed his harsh reproaches to Eutropius himself. John's failure to take pity on the unfortunate man, and the fact that he continued to upbraid him, turned many against the bishop, while the emperor seized Eutropius and had him beheaded. For a variety of reasons John criticized and reprehended many men immoderately, and the number of his enemies increased.

Theophilus, bishop of Alexandria, was anxious to depose John and wanted to put a priest named Isidore into his place, so he was looking for grounds to justify the bishop's deposition. The people, however, defended John and eagerly received the nourishment of his teaching. John continued to compel the priests to fashion their lives on Church laws, saying that those who disdained to live by priestly standards should not enjoy the honor of priesthood. He not only governed the city of Constantinople with a strong hand, but strove to put order in several adjacent provinces by imposing appropriate laws backed by imperial authority. When he learned that in Phoenicia sacrifices were still being offered to demons, he sent clerics and monks there and saw to it that all the heathen temples were destroyed.

At that time there was a certain Gaimas, by race a Celt, by character a barbarian. He was carried away by his tyrannical ambition and perverted by the Arian heresy, yet was made the commandant of the army. Gaimas asked the emperor to give him and his followers one church inside the city. The emperor was willing and, in order to put a rein on the man's tyranny, asked John to grant him one church. But John, strong in virtue and aflame with zeal, said: "O Emperor, do not allow this, or give what is holy to dogs, and do not be afraid of this barbarian! Order both of us to be called, and in private hear what we say to each other. I will put a bit on his tongue that will stop him from making such presumptuous demands!"

The emperor was happy to hear this and summoned the two for the next day. When Gaimas requested one church for himself, John said: "The house of God is open to you everywhere, and no one is keeping you from praying!" Gaimas: "I belong to another sect, and I have the right to demand a temple for myself and my people. I have taken on many labors for the Roman state, therefore my petition should not be spurned!" John: "You have received many rewards—rewards that exceeded your deserts. You have been made commandant of the army, and more than that you wear the toga of a consul. You ought to keep in mind what you were before and how you are now regarded, how poor you were in the past and how rich you are now, what clothes you used to wear and how splendidly you are now attired. Therefore, since minimal labors have brought you maximum return, do not be ungrateful to the emperor who honors you!" That was enough to close Gaimas's mouth and force him to keep silent.

John continued to govern the city of Constantinople with a firm hand, but Gaimas, now coveted the empire itself; and since he could accomplish nothing by day, he sent his barbarians by night to burn down the emperor's palace. Then John's way of protecting the city became apparent. A great crowd of armed angels in bodily shapes appeared confronting the barbarians, who promptly took to their heels. When they reported this to Gaimas, he could not understand it, since he knew that his regular troops were garrisoned in other cities. He sent the barbarians out the following night, and they were again put to flight by the vision of angels. Finally Gaimas himself went out, saw the miracle, and fled, thinking that these troops hid by day and guarded the city by night. He went to Thrace, assembled a large army, and pillaged the land; the people were terrified by the ferocity of the barbarians. The emperor therefore imposed upon Saint John the burden of going as his ambassador to Gaimas, and John, putting old grudges out of his mind, set out with alacrity. Gaimas was touched by the saint's trustfulness and, forgetting his resentments, went out a great distance to meet him. He took John's hand and held it over his own eyes in a gesture of humility, and bade his sons embrace the bishop's sacred knees. Such indeed was the power of John's virtue: he could reduce even the most terrible men to humility and fear.

At that time a dispute arose about whether or not God had a body. Many were the disagreements and wordy battles over this question, some holding this view, others, that. Mostly it was the crowds of simple monks who were deceived and said that God was set apart by a bodily form. Theophilus, bishop of

Alexandria, preferred the contrary view. He argued against those in the church who asserted that God had a human form, and preached that God is incorporeal. The Egyptian monks learned of this, left their abodes, and came to Alexandria, where they stirred up sedition against Theophilus, even attempting to put him to death. Their actions frightened Theophilus, and he said to them: "I look at you and see the face of God!" They said: "If you really mean that God's face is like ours, anathematize the books of Origen, which contradict our belief. If you do not do this, you will be in rebellion against the emperors and God himself, and we will see to it that you are disgraced." "Don't do anything violent," said Theophilus, "and I will do what pleases you." Thus he diverted the monks' attack. Note again that the better-trained and perfect monks were not deceived, but the simple monks, excited by the ardor of their faith, rose against their brothers who held the opposite opinion, and killed many of them.

While that was going on in Egypt, John, in Constantinople, flourished in his teaching and was universally admired. Nevertheless the Arians multiplied in numbers and had a church outside the city. On Saturdays and Sundays they came in and sang hymns and antiphons all night in the streets, and at dawn, still singing, they marched through the middle of the city and out through the gates to their own church. They continued to do this in mockery of the orthodox, frequently singing: "Where are those who say that three are one in power?"

John feared that simple folk might be drawn into heresy by these songs, and gave orders that the true believers should gather and sing hymns at night, in order to drown out the singing of the others and to strengthen the faithful in their faith. He also had silvered crosses made and carried with silvered candles. The Arians, fired with zeal and envy, went so far as to commit murder. One night Brison, one of the empress's eunuchs, whom John had assigned to lead the hymn singing, was struck with a stone, but, more than that, a number of people of either party lost their lives. The emperor, disturbed by this disorder, prohibited the Arians from singing hymns in public.

At that time Severian, bishop of Gabala, a man honored by his peers and a favorite of the emperor and the empress, came to Constantinople and was warmly welcomed by John; and when John traveled to Asia, he left his church in Severian's care. But Severian was unfaithful to his trust and curried favor with the people. Serapion, one of John's clergy, took care to notify John about this. Then, once when Severian was passing in front of him, Serapion did not rise, and Severian, indignant, shouted: "If this fellow Serapion does not die, Christ was not born in human nature!" When John heard of this, he came back to Constantinople and ejected Severian from the city as a blasphemer. The empress was gravely displeased. She had John summoned and asked him to make peace with Severian. He refused to do so until she brought her infant son Theodosius and laid him on the bishop's knees, begging him and solemnly appealing to him to pardon Severian.

About that same time Theophilus, bishop of Alexandria, unjustly banished Dioscorus, a saintly man, and Isidore, who previously had been his friend. The two came to Constantinople and recited the facts to the emperor and to John. John held the men in high regard but was unwilling to take their side until he knew more about the case. A false rumor reached Theophilus, however, to the effect that John was in league with Dioscorus and Isidore and was supporting their cause. This aroused Theophilus's anger, and he marshaled all his forces, not only to avenge himself on the two men but to depose John from his see. Concealing his real intention, he sent word to the bishop of each city, saying that he wished to condemn the works of Origen. Making a pretense of friendship, he cozened Epiphanius, the holy and esteemed bishop of Cyprus, and asked him to condemn Origen's books as he himself was doing. Epiphanius, whose sanctity kept him from suspecting the other's craftiness, summoned his bishops to Cyprus and forbade the reading of Origen. Then he wrote to John, urging him to stop reading those books and to confirm what had been ordered. John, however, paid little attention to this. He went on teaching the doctrine of the Church, at which he excelled, and felt no concern about the plots that were being woven around him.

Finally Theophilus let his long-concealed hatred of John be known, and made it clear that he wanted John deposed. The bishop's enemies, and many clergymen and palace officials, thought the time opportune and did their best to have a council convoked at Constantinople against John. Then Epiphanius came to Constantinople, bringing with him the condemnation of Origen's works. Out of regard for Theophilus he declined John's offer of hospitality. Some bishops, owing to their reverence for Epiphanius, subscribed to the condemnation of Origen, but many more refused to do so. Among the latter was Theotinus, bishop of Sichia, a man renowned for the rectitude of his life, who responded to Epiphanius as follows: "Neither will I do injury to him who long since went to his rest, nor do I presume to risk being guilty of blasphemy by condemning works that our predecessors did not see fit to reject, and in which I also find no wrong doctrine. Those who heap insults on these works do not know themselves. Athanasius, defender of the Council of Nicaea against the Arians, appealed to this man as a witness of his own faith. He put Origen's books on a level with his own, and said: 'Origen, that admirable, tireless man, gives us this testimony to the Son of God, asserting that he is coeternal with the Father.'"

John had not taken it amiss when Epiphanius, acting outside the rules, performed an ordination[1] in his church, but asked him nevertheless to stay with him among the bishops. Epiphanius answered that he would neither stay with him nor pray with him unless he, John, dismissed Dioscorus and subscribed to the

---

[1] Or "issued an ordinance"; *facere ordinationem* could mean either one, both here and below. It is also not clear whether *in sua ecclesia* refers to Epiphanius's church or to John's.

condemnation of Origen's books. John refused to comply, and Epiphanius was turned against him by the saint's enemies. Epiphanius condemned Origen's works and pronounced a judgment against Dioscorus, and began to defame John as their defender. John sent the following message to him: "You have done many things contrary to the rules, O Epiphanius! First you performed an ordination in a church that belongs under my jurisdiction; second, on your own authority you have celebrated the sacred mysteries; again, when I invited you, you made excuses; and finally, you trust overmuch in yourself. Therefore take care lest there be an uprising among the people and the danger of it fall upon you!"

Having received this message, Epiphanius left the city, but before he set out for Cyprus, he sent word to John: "I hope you will not die a bishop." To this John responded: "I hope you never reach your homeland." Both hopes were realized: Epiphanius died on his way home, and John in time was deposed from his see and finished his life in exile.

At the tomb of this very holy man Epiphanius, demons were driven out of the possessed. He was a man of wondrous liberality toward the poor. Once he gave away all the church's money and nothing was left for himself. Then a stranger came along, offered the saint a bag full of money and went his way, and no one knew where he came from nor where he went. Another time a couple of poor men decided to trick Epiphanius into giving them some money. One of them lay stretched out on the ground, and the other stood over him and wept, as if he were dead, and complained that he had no money to pay for his friend's burial. Epiphanius came by, prayed that the dead man might rest in peace, and supplied the other with funds for the burial. Then he consoled the mourner and went his way. The man shook his companion and said: "Get up, get up! Today let us feast on the fruit of our labors!" He shook him again and again, and saw that he was dead, so he ran after Epiphanius and told him what had happened, also begging him to revive his friend. Epiphanius spoke words of consolation to the man, but did not raise his friend to life, lest it should seem too easy to delude God's ministers.

After Epiphanius took his leave, John learned that it was Eudoxia, the empress, who had turned Epiphanius against him. Outspoken as usual, the bishop preached a sermon to his flock, in which he inveighed against all women in very rude terms. Everybody took it that the diatribe was aimed at Eudoxia. The empress heard about it and complained to Arcadius, saying that the indignities aimed at his wife were sure to recoil on him. The emperor took umbrage at this and ordered that a synod be called to act against John. Theophilus therefore quickly convoked the bishops, and all John's enemies flocked together, calling him haughty and arrogant. The bishops then meeting in Constantinople were no longer concerned with Origen's writings, but were open in their opposition to John and sent for him to appear before them. John considered them enemies to be avoided and proclaimed that a universal synod must be called. The other bishops cited him four times more, but he still stayed clear of them and demanded a synod. They therefore condemned him, on no other ground than that he had not obeyed their summons.

The people of the city learned what was happening and were on the verge of rioting in protest. Meanwhile they would not allow their bishop to be taken out of the church, and demanded that the case be referred to a larger council. The emperor, however, gave orders that John was to be brought out and deported into exile, and he, fearing an outbreak of sedition, gave himself up to be exiled before the people knew what he was doing. When the news did get out, there was a wave of popular protest so serious that even many of his enemies were moved to be sorry for him, and said that he was a victim of calumny, whereas a short time before they had longed to see him deposed.

Now Severian, of whom mention has been made above, preached a sermon in church, in which he spoke ill of John, saying that even if he had committed no other crime, his pride could be a sufficient reason to depose him. This intensified popular opposition to the emperor and the bishops, and Eudoxia felt bound to ask the emperor to recall John from exile. Then a great earthquake shook the city, and the common opinion was that this happened as a result of John's expulsion. So legates were sent to ask him to come back quickly, in order to help the endangered city by his prayers, and to calm popular unrest. Then others were sent, then still others, to persuade him to return. When despite his reluctance they brought him home, the whole populace went out to meet him with lanterns and torches. John refused, however, to occupy his episcopal throne, saying that this should be by synodal decree and that those who had condemned him should revoke their sentence. But the people were eager to see him once more on his throne and to hear the words of their teacher. The popular will prevailed, and he had to resume his seat and preach to the people.

For Theophilus it was time to get away quickly. Just as he reached Hierapolis, the bishop of that city died, and a saintly monk named Lamon was elected. Lamon hastily went into hiding, but Theophilus pressed him to accept the election. Lamon promised, saying: "Tomorrow, what pleases God will be fulfilled." Therefore they came to his cell the next day, insisting that he receive the episcopate. He said: "Let us first pray to the Lord." He prayed, and finished his prayer and his life at the same moment.

John meanwhile continued his preaching uninterruptedly. At that time a silver statue was set up in the square in front of the church of Saint Sophia in honor of Eudoxia Augusta, and the knights and nobles of the city engaged in public games there. This displeased John exceedingly, since he saw it as dishonoring the church. He therefore raised his voice in denunciation as fearlessly as ever. It might have been appropriate to plead with the princes to put an end to such exercises, but he did nothing of the kind. Rather, turning loose the full force of his eloquence, he lashed out at those who ordered the games. The empress again took this as a personal insult and renewed her efforts to have a synod called into session. John, hearing about this, launched into the most famous of his homilies, the one that begins: "Again Herodias is raging, again she is perturbed, again she yearns to receive the head of John in a dish." This added considerably to Eudoxia's indignation. There was also a man who tried to kill John, was seized by the people, and turned over to be judged; but the prefect, to save him from death, spirited him away. Another man, the servant of a certain priest, rushed upon the bishop in an effort to kill him. A bystander tried to restrain him, but the attacker struck this man down and two others as well, killing them. This drew a large and clamorous crowd, and the man dealt fatal blows to several more. In the midst of this turmoil the people kept John safe, standing guard around his house day and night.

Eudoxia now won her point. Bishops convened in Constantinople, and John's accusers began to malign him with dire intent. Christmas was at hand, and Arcadius sent word to John that unless he had been cleared of all the charges against him, he, the emperor, would not receive communion from him. The bishops, however, could find nothing against him, unless it was that he had presumed to sit in the episcopal chair without the decree of a council. Then Easter was drawing near, and the emperor informed him that he could not stay in the same church with John, since two councils had condemned him. John therefore stayed home and no longer went down to his church. Those who took John's part were called Johannites. Finally the emperor had John expelled from the city and taken into exile in a poor village in the Pontus region, at the edge of the Roman Empire, an area threatened by cruel barbarians.

But the merciful Lord did not allow his faithful champion to linger long in such a place. Pope Innocent got word of the situation and was disturbed by it. He had it in mind to call a council and wrote to the clergy of Constantinople, forbidding them to ordain anyone as a successor to John. John, meanwhile, was worn out with long travel, suffered very painful headaches, and found the heat of the sun unbearable. So it was that at Cumana, on the fourteenth day of September, that holy soul was released from the body. At the hour of his death a tremendous hailstorm descended on Constantinople and its environs, and everyone said that this was an expression of God's anger over John's unjust condemnation. Eudoxia's sudden death bore out this thought: she died four days after the hailstorm.

After the death of this man who was teacher and doctor to both East and West, the bishops of the West would have no communion with those of the East until these latter placed the sacred name of John with those of his predecessors. Moreover, Theodosius, most Christian son of the aforementioned Arcadius, who had both the name and the piety of his grandfather Theodosius, had the sacred relics of this doctor of the Church transferred to the royal city in the month of January, on which occasion the faithful people met the cortege with lanterns and torches. Theodosius worshiped the saint's relics, praying earnestly for his parents Arcadius and Eudoxia, that the wrong they had unwittingly done might be forgiven them. Both parents had died in the meantime.

This Theodosius was a most benign ruler. He never sentenced to death those who did him any wrong, saying: "Would it were possible for me to recall the dead to life!" His court seemed like a monastery. He recited matins and lauds and read the sacred books. His wife, who wrote poems in the heroic meter, was named Eudoxia. He had a daughter also called Eudoxia. He gave his daughter in marriage to Valentinian, whom he made emperor.

All this information is extracted from the *Tripartite History*. John Chrysostom died about A.D. 400.

139. Saint Euphemia

The name Euphemia comes from *eu*, which means good, and *femina*, woman. A good woman is helpful, righteous, and pleasing, because goodness implies these three qualities. Thus Saint Euphemia was helpful in her relations with others, righteous by her virtuous way of life, and pleasing to God by her contemplation of heavenly mysteries. Or *euphemia* has the same meaning as *euphonia*, sweet sound, and sweet sound is produced in three ways, namely, by the voice in singing, by the stroke of the hand, as in playing the harp, and by blowing, as in the organ. Saint Euphemia made sweet sound with the voice of her preaching, with the strokes of good works, and with the breath of her inward devotion.

In the reign of Diocletian, Euphemia, the daughter of a senator, saw how Christians were being tortured and mangled in various ways. She went straight to Priscus, the judge, publicly proclaimed her Christianity, and by the example of her constancy gave strength to resist even to men. While the judge was putting Christians to death one after the other, he ordered more of them to be present, so that by witnessing the tortures endured by those who refused, they might at least be terrified into offering sacrifice. He had the saints cruelly mutilated in Euphemia's presence, but their steadfastness only strengthened her own resolve, and she declared aloud that the judge was doing her an injustice. Priscus was delighted, thinking that she was willing to offer sacrifice, and asked her how he was wronging her. She answered: "I am of noble birth, and I want to know why you put these nobodies, these common folks, ahead of me, letting them reach Christ and attain the promised glory before I do!" The judge: "I thought you had come to your senses! I was glad you had remembered your rank and your sex!"

Priscus therefore consigned her to prison, and the next day, when the others were brought out in chains, she came out unfettered. Again she complained vehemently: why was she alone spared the chains, contrary to the emperor's law? So she was beaten and remanded to prison. The judge followed her and wished to take his pleasure of her, but she resisted manfully, and the power of God paralyzed his hand. Priscus thought he was under some kind of spell. He sent his head steward to promise her all sorts of things if she would do his will, but the man was unable to open the jail door with keys or to break into it with an ax, and finally was seized by a demon, screamed, tore his own flesh, and barely escaped with his life.

Then Euphemia was brought out and placed on a wheel, the spokes of which were filled with burning coals. The man who operated the wheel stood under it and had given a signal to those who turned it: when he made a certain sound they should all pull together, causing the fire to erupt and the spokes to tear the woman's body apart. But by God's will the tool by which he controlled the wheel fell from his hand, and the sound it made set the pullers to pulling, and the wheel crushed the man and left Euphemia standing on it unharmed. Grieving, the dead man's kinsmen lit a fire under the wheel, intending to burn Euphemia and the wheel together, but the wheel burned and an angel freed her from it and carried her to a high place, where she again stood unscathed.

Apellianus said to the judge: "The power these Christians have can be overcome only by iron. I advise you therefore to have her beheaded." They put ladders up and one man went up to take hold of her, but at once he was stricken with paralysis and was brought down half dead. Another man, this one named Sosthenes, climbed up but was converted as he reached her. He begged her to pardon him, drew his sword, and called down to the judge that he would kill himself rather than touch this woman, whom angels were defending.

Euphemia was finally taken down, and Priscus told his chancellor to round up all the ruffians he could find, and to let them enjoy her as long as they liked, until she died exhausted. But when the chancellor went in to her, he found her praying and many shining virgins around her, and she spoke to him and he was converted to the Christian faith. So the judge had her hung up by her hair, and when she persisted in her refusal, he ordered her to be put back in prison and deprived of food for seven days, at which time she would be crushed like an olive between great millstones. For seven days she was fed by an angel, and when on the seventh day she was placed between the stones, she prayed and the stones were reduced to the finest powder.

Priscus was shamefaced at being outdone by a mere girl and had her thrown into a pit where there were three wild beasts so ferocious that they would swallow any man. The beasts were gentled at once. They came running to the virgin and, by twining their tails together, made a sort of chair for her to sit on. Thus they threw the judge into utter confusion. Indeed he was almost dying with frustration when a headsman came in to avenge the offense given to his master. This he did by driving his sword into Euphemia's side, thus making her a martyr for Christ.

To reward the headsman for his service, the judge draped him in a silk garment and girded him with a gold belt, but as the man went out, he was snatched by a lion and devoured by the same. When a search was made for him, nothing was found except a few of his bones, the torn garment, and the gold belt. As for Priscus himself, he chewed on his own flesh and was found dead. Saint Euphemia was buried with honor in Chalcedon, and by her merits all the Jews and Gentiles in Chalcedon believed in Christ. She suffered about the year A.D. 280.

Ambrose, in his Preface, speaks of this virgin as follows: "The gentle, triumphant virgin Euphemia, retaining the miter of virginity, merited to be crowned with the crown of martyrdom. By her prayers the hostile enemy was defeated, and Priscus her adversary was outdone. The virgin was plucked unhurt from the fiery furnace, hard stones reverted to dust, wild beasts turned gentle and bent their heads, and every kind of torture was overcome by her prayer. At the very end, pierced by the point of the sword, she left the bondage of the flesh and joyfully joined the celestial choir. This sacred virgin, O Lord, commends your Church to you. She intercedes for us sinners. May this virgin, this little unspoiled servant in your house, also offer our vows to you."

---

140. Saint Matthew, Apostle

Matthew had two names, Matthew and Levi. Matthew (Matthaeus) is interpreted as hasty gift, or as giver of counsel. Or the name comes from *magnus*, great, and *theos*, God, hence great unto God, or from *manus*, hand, and *theos*, hence the hand of God. Saint Matthew was a hasty gift by his speedy conversion, the giver of counsel by his salutary preaching, great unto God by the perfection of his life, and the hand of God by the writing of his gospel. Levi is interpreted as taken up, or attached, or added to, or placed with. The saint was taken up from the work of exacting taxes, attached to the company of the apostles, added to the group of the evangelists, and placed with the catalog of the martyrs.

Matthew the apostle was preaching in Ethiopia in a city called Nadaber, and found two sorcerers named Zaroës and Arphaxat. These two worked their arts upon whomever they wished in such a way that the victim seemed to be deprived of the functioning of his limbs and of his sanity. This made the sorcerers so proud that they got people to worship them as gods. When the apostle arrived in the aforesaid city, he was given hospitality by the eunuch of Queen Candace, whom Philip had baptized. He soon exposed the magicians' artifices, so that whatever they did to harm men the apostle turned into benefits.

The eunuch asked Matthew how he happened to speak and understand so many languages, and he explained that after the descent of the Holy Spirit upon the apostles, he found that he possessed knowledge of all languages. Thereafter, whereas those whose pride had made them want to build a tower reaching to heaven had to stop building because of the confusion of languages, so the apostles, by their knowledge of all languages, were able to build a tower not of stones but of virtues, by which all who believed could ascend to heaven.

Now a man came to say that the sorcerers had come with two dragons, which belched forth sulfurous fire from mouth and nostrils and killed many people. The apostle shielded himself with the sign of the cross and confidently went out to meet these beasts. The minute the dragons saw him, they fell asleep at his feet, and he said to the sorcerers: "Where is your magical power now? Wake them up if you can! If I had not prayed to the Lord, I would have turned back upon you the harm you had thought to inflict upon me." And when all the people had gathered together, Matthew ordered the dragons in Jesus' name to go away, and off they went, harming no one.

Now the apostle began to preach a great sermon to the people about the glory of the earthly paradise, telling them that it had stood above all the mountains and had been close to heaven; that in it there were no thorns or brambles, and lilies and roses did not wither; that old age never came, and people always stayed young; that there the angels played upon their instruments, and that when the birds were called, they obeyed at once. The apostle went on to say that mankind had been expelled from this earthly paradise, but that through the birth of Christ they had been recalled to the paradise of heaven.

While Matthew was saying all this, suddenly a loud cry of mourning arose for the king's son, who had died. When the sorcerers could not revive him, they convinced the king that his son had been taken up into the company of the gods, and that therefore a statue should be made and a temple erected in his honor. But the aforesaid eunuch had the magicians kept in custody and called for the apostle, who by his prayer restored the youth to life. The king, whose name was Egippus, saw this and sent a message throughout his kingdom, saying: "Come and see God hiding in the likeness of a man!" They came, bringing gold crowns and various kinds of votive offerings in order to sacrifice to Matthew, but he checked them, saying: "What are you doing, men? I am not a god but a servant of the Lord Jesus Christ!" He persuaded them to expend the gold and silver they had brought on the building of a great church. They completed the church in thirty days, and the apostle presided in it for thirty-three years and converted all Egypt. King Egippus was baptized with his wife and the whole people. Matthew dedicated Ephigenia, the king's daughter, to God, and put her at the head of more than two hundred virgins.

Hirtacus succeeded Egippus. Hirtacus lusted after the virgin Ephigenia, and promised the apostle the half of his kingdom if he could prevail upon her to become his wife. Matthew told him to follow the custom of his predecessor and come to church on Sunday, where Ephigenia and the other virgins would also be present, and he would hear about the blessings of lawful marriage. The king was happy and hastened to comply, thinking that the apostle would persuade Ephigenia to marry him. With the virgins and the whole populace present, Matthew preached at great length on the good of matrimony. The king praised what he heard, because he believed that it had been said in order to make Ephigenia desire marriage. But then, after calling for silence, Matthew went back over his sermon, and said: "Since marriage is good as long as the union is kept inviolate, all of you here present know that if one of his servants dared to usurp the king's spouse, he would deserve not only the king's anger but death as a penalty, and this not because he had married a wife, but because by taking his master's spouse he was guilty of violating matrimony. So it is with you, O king! You know that Ephigenia has become the spouse of the eternal King and is consecrated with the sacred veil. How can you take the spouse of One who is more powerful than you and make her your wife?"

When the king heard this he was beside himself with rage and stamped out of the church. The apostle, unafraid and unmoved, encouraged his hearers to be patient and steadfast. Ephigenia was prostrated with fear, but he gave her and the other virgins his blessing. After the ceremony of the mass was concluded, the king sent a swordsman, who found Matthew standing before the altar with his hands raised to heaven in prayer. He stabbed the apostle in the back, killing him and making him a martyr. The people found this out and thronged to the royal palace, intent on setting it and everything in it afire, but the priests and the deacons restrained them, and they all celebrated Saint Matthew's martyrdom joyfully.

Hirtacus then sent ladies to Ephigenia to plead his cause, and the sorcerers worked their charms upon her, but none of these efforts succeeded in weakening her resolve. He therefore had a huge fire ignited around her house, hoping to put her and her virgins to death, but the apostle appeared to them and turned the fire away from their house and toward the king's palace. It swept through the building and consumed all in it, the king barely escaping with his only son. The son was immediately seized by the devil but ran to the apostle's tomb, confessing his father's crimes. The father was stricken with a loathsome leprosy that could not be cured, so he took his life with his own sword. The people established Ephigenia's brother, whom the apostle had baptized, as their king, who reigned for seventy years and installed his son as his successor. He aided the spread of the Christian religion and filled the whole province of Ethiopia with churches of Christ. As for Zaroës and Arphaxat, they fled into Persia the very day the apostle raised the king's son to life, but the apostles Simon and Jude overcame them there.

Note that there are four things about Matthew that deserve special consideration. The first is the quickness with which he obeyed. When Christ called him, he quit his customhouse immediately to become a follower of Christ and nothing else, not fearing his superiors though he left his accounts unfinished. This readiness to obey led some to misinterpret it, as Jerome points out in his commentary on this place in Matthew's gospel.[1] Jerome says: "Porphyrius and the emperor Julian discern in this text either the ineptitude of a lying historian or the folly of those who immediately followed the Savior, as if without rhyme or reason they followed anyone who called them. So many manifestations of power and so many miracles had preceded this moment of encounter, and no doubt the apostles had seen these wonders before they believed; and surely the brightness and majesty of Christ's hidden divinity, which shone even in his human face, could draw men to him the first time they saw him. If we say that a magnet has the power to attract rings and iron filings, how much more could the Lord of all creatures draw to himself anyone he wished to draw." Thus Jerome.

The second notable thing about Matthew is his generosity, or liberality, because he quickly arranged to hold a great feast in his house for the Lord. This feast was great not only on account of lavish preparation, but for four other reasons. Firstly, there was the thought that inspired it: Matthew welcomed Christ with great affection and desire. Secondly, there was the mystery: the feast indicated a great mystery, which the *Gloss* on Luke points out: "Whoever welcomes Christ into his interior abode is nourished with the greatest delights of overflowing pleasures." Thirdly, it was a great feast by reason of the great teachings that Christ imparted there, such as "I will have mercy and not sacrifice," and "They that are in health need not a physician, but they that are ill."[2] Fourthly, the feast was great by reason of the persons invited, because truly great persons, namely, Christ and his disciples, were guests.

The third quality worthy of note in Matthew is his humility, which was manifested in two ways. Firstly, he let himself be known as a tax-gatherer, a publican. The other evangelists, as the *Gloss* says, did not put in his common title, in order to spare him shame and to guard the honor of an evangelist, whereas he, following the prescription that the just man is his own first accuser, calls himself Matthew the publican.[3] Thus he showed that no convert ought to be uncertain about his salvation, since a publican suddenly became an apostle and evangelist. Secondly, he proved his humility by his patience in bearing

---

[1] Matt. 9:9.   [2] Matt. 9:9–13.   [3] Matt. 10:3.

insults. When the Pharisees murmured because Christ turned aside to a sinful man, Matthew might well have retorted: "You are the miserable, sinful ones, because, judging yourselves to be righteous, you want nothing to do with the physician, while I should not now be called a sinner, because I have had recourse to the physician of salvation, and I do not hide my wound from him."

The fourth thing to consider about Matthew is the high honor paid in the Church to the gospel that he wrote. His gospel is read more frequently in church than the others, as the Psalms and Paul's letters are heard more often than the other Scriptures. The reason for this is, as James testifies, that there are three kinds of sins, namely, pride, lust, and avarice. Saul, who was called Saul after the exceedingly proud King Saul, sinned by pride when he persecuted the Church beyond measure. David sinned by the sin of lust, when he not only committed adultery but killed Uriah, his most loyal soldier. Matthew sinned by avarice by seeking ill-gotten gains, since he was a tax-gatherer, a keeper of the customs. The customhouse (called *teloneum* in Latin) is, as Isidore says, a place at a seaport where taxes are paid on ships' cargoes and seamen's wages: *telos*, as Bede says, is the Greek word for tax, as *vectigal* is in Latin.

Granted, therefore, that Saul, David, and Matthew were sinners, their repentance so pleased the Lord that he not only forgave their sins but heaped his gifts upon them in greater abundance. He made the cruelest persecutor the most faithful preacher, the adulterer and homicide a prophet and singer of Psalms, the covetous seeker of profit an apostle and evangelist. Therefore the sayings and writings of these three men are recited to us so frequently so that no one who might wish to be converted would despair of pardon, when he sees that such great sinners were also so great in grace.

According to Saint Ambrose, certain things are to be noted about Saint Matthew's conversion, regarding the physician, the sick man who was healed, and the way the cure was effected. In the physician there were three things, namely, his wisdom, which recognized the root of the disease, his kindness, which furnished remedies, and his power, which could change the sick man so suddenly. Of these three things Ambrose, speaking in the person of Matthew, says: "He who knows hidden things can take away the pain in my heart and the pallor of my soul." So much for his wisdom. "I have found a physician who lives in heaven and dispenses remedies on earth." So much for his kindness. "He alone can heal my wounds who has none of his own to heal." So much for his power.

In the sick man who was healed, namely, in Saint Matthew, three things are to be considered, as the said Ambrose demonstrates: the sick man put off his sickness completely, he was grateful to his physician, and he kept himself clean ever after in the good health he had received. Hence Ambrose says: "Matthew now followed Christ, happy and supple, and exulted, saying: 'I no longer carry in me a publican, I no longer carry Levi, I put off Levi after I put on Christ.' That as to the first. 'I hate my race, I flee from my past life, I follow you alone, Lord Jesus, you who heal my wounds.' That as to the second. 'Who shall separate us from the love of Christ? Shall tribulation? Or distress? Or famine?'" That as to the third.

How was the cure of the sick man effected? In three ways, according to Saint Ambrose. First, Christ bound him in fetters; second, he applied a caustic to the wound; third, he did away with all the rottenness. Hence Ambrose, speaking in the person of Matthew, says: "I am bound with the nails of faith and the soft shackles of love. Jesus, take away the rottenness of my sins while you keep me bound with the fetters of love. Cut away any rot you find in me!" So much for the first way. "I shall hold every commandment of yours as an applied caustic, and if the caustic commandment burns, it will be burning away the corruption of the flesh lest the contagious poison spread; and if the remedy stings, it still removes the poison of the wound." So much for the second way. "Come quickly, Lord, cut into the various secret, hidden passions, open the wound quickly lest the noxious fluid spread, cleanse all that is fetid with a pilgrim bath." So much for the third way.

Matthew's gospel, written by his own hand, was discovered about A.D. 500 with the bones of Saint Barnabas. Saint Barnabas carried this gospel with him and placed it on sick persons, and it instantly cured the illness, as much by Barnabas's faith as by Matthew's merit.

141. Saint Maurice and His Companions

Maurice (Mauritius) comes from *mari*, meaning the sea or bitter, *cis*, which means vomiting or hard, and *us*, a counselor or one who hastens. Or the name comes from *mauron*, which, according to Isidore, is the Greek word for black. Saint Maurice had bitterness from dwelling in misery and being put far from his native land; he vomited in the sense that he rejected everything superfluous; he was hard and firm in bearing the torments of his martyrdom; he was a counselor in the exhortation he addressed to his troops; he was one who hastened by his fervor and the multiplication of his good works; and he was black in his contempt of self.[1]

---

[1] Maurice is the first saint to be portrayed as a black man in Western Christian iconography, and the first such image was a statue dated 1240–1250, erected on the facade of the cathedral of Magdeburg. Jacobus wrote in the early 1260s, but probably his reason for saying that Maurice was black was simply the "etymological" one given in the text. The subject of blackness in Christian iconography is studied by J. Devisse and illustrated in *The Image of the Black in Western Art*, vol. 2, part 1 (New York: William Morrow, 1979), esp. 164f.

The passion of these saints was written and compiled by Saint Eucherius, bishop of Lyons.

It is said that Maurice was the commander of the holy legion called "Theban." The soldiers were called Thebans after their city, the name of which was Thebes. This was the region toward the East, beyond the border of Arabia, a land powerful and wealthy, fertile and fruitful, and pleasantly wooded. The inhabitants of the region are said to be tall and sturdy, expert in arms, brave in warfare, shrewd and witty, and richly endowed with wisdom. The city had a hundred gates and was situated above the Nile River, which flows out of the earthly paradise and is called Gyon. Of this city it is said: "Behold old Thebes, lying crushed with her hundred gates."

Here James, brother of the Lord, preached the Gospel of salvation and perfectly taught the people the faith of Christ. Diocletian and Maximian, however, who began to reign in A.D. 277, were determined to wipe out the Christian religion and sent letters to this effect to all the provinces where Christians dwelt. They wrote: "If there was something to be decided or known, and the whole world was marshaled on one side and Rome alone on the other, the whole world would flee in defeat, and Rome would stand alone at the peak of knowledge. Why do you, poor little folk, resist her commands and draw yourselves up so stubbornly against her statutes? Therefore either accept belief in the immortal gods, or the immutable sentence of condemnation will be pronounced against you."

The Christians received these letters but sent the messengers back without an answer. Diocletian and Maximian were angry at this, and dispatched orders to all the provinces that all men capable of bearing the weapons of war should muster and should subdue all those who were rebelling against the Roman Empire. The emperors' letters were delivered to the people of Thebes, and these people, in obedience to God's command, rendered to Caesar the things that are Caesar's and to God the things that are God's. They recruited a choice legion of 6,666 soldiers and sent them to the emperors to help them in waging just wars— not therefore to suppress Christians but rather to defend them. The commander of this sacred legion was the illustrious Maurice, and its standard-bearers were Candidus, Innocent, Exuperius, Victor, and Constantine. Diocletian now sent Maximian, his associate emperor, to Gaul with an immense army, to which he attached the Theban legion. Pope Marcellinus had admonished the Thebans that they should rather perish by the sword than violate the Christian faith which they had made their own.

When the whole army had crossed the Alps and come to Octodurus, the emperor commanded that all who were with him should offer sacrifice to the idols and should unanimously take an oath against Rome's rebellious subjects, but particularly against Christians. When the holy soldiers heard this, they withdrew a distance of eight miles from the army and made camp along the Rhone in a pleasant place called Agaune. When Maximian learned of this, he sent soldiers to tell them to come quickly and offer sacrifice to the gods with the others. The Thebans answered that, being Christians, they could not do this. The emperor, fuming with anger, said: "An insult to heaven is added to the contempt directed at me, and as I am despised, so is the Roman religion! Let these willful soldiers know that I can avenge not only myself but my gods!" The emperor then sent his soldiers to deliver the order that either the Thebans were to sacrifice to the gods or every tenth one of them was to be beheaded. The saints then joyfully hastened forward, one after the other bending his neck to receive the headsman's deathblow.

Now Saint Maurice rose in their midst and addressed them: "I rejoice with you because you are all ready to die for the faith of Christ. I have allowed your fellow soldiers to be put to death because I saw you prepared to suffer for Christ, and I have kept the command the Lord gave Peter: 'Put your sword into its sheath!'[2] Now that the bodies of our comrades form a barricade around us and our garments are reddened with their blood, let us follow them to martyrdom! Therefore, if you agree, let us send our answer to Caesar: 'We are your soldiers, Emperor, and we have taken arms to defend the commonwealth. There is no treason in us, no fear; but we will not betray the faith of Christ.'" Receiving this message, the irate emperor ordered a second decimation of the Thebans.

When that had been done, Exuperius the standard-bearer picked up a banner and, standing amidst the troops, said: "Maurice, our glorious leader, has spoken to us about the glory of our comrades. Now let me say that Exuperius, your standard-bearer, has not taken arms to resist dying for Christ! I say, let our right hands throw aside these carnal weapons and be armed with virtues, and, if it please you, let us send this reply to the emperor: 'We are your soldiers, O Emperor, but we freely profess that we are Christ's servants. To you we owe military service, to him our innocence. From you we have received wages for our work, from him the beginning of life itself. So for him we are prepared to suffer every torment, and we will never give up our faith in him!'" The impious emperor now commanded his army to surround the whole legion so that not one man should escape. The soldiers of Christ were therefore surrounded by the soldiers of the devil, struck down by murderous hands, trampled by horses' hooves, and consecrated to Christ as his precious martyrs. They suffered about A.D. 280.

By God's will a large number of the Thebans did escape, and went to other regions to preach the name of Christ and to triumph most gloriously in many places. Among them we learn that Solutor, Adventor, and Octavius went to Turin, Alexander to Bergamo, Secundus to Ventimiglia; and there were also Constantius, Victor, Ursus, and a great many others.

When the bloody killers had divided the booty and were making merry together, an old man named Victor happened to pass by and they invited him to join them in the feasting. He asked how they could be having such a jolly

---

[2] John 18:11.

celebration with so many thousands of dead soldiers lying around, and someone told him that the dead had died for the faith of Christ. Victor sighed and groaned, declaring that he would be blessed if he had been slain with them. As soon as they became aware that the old man was a Christian, they fell upon him and cut him to pieces.

Some time later, and on the same day, the two emperors, Maximian at Milan and Diocletian at Nicomedia, laid aside the purple and retired to private life, leaving the rule to younger men, namely, Constantius, Maximus, and Galerius, whom they made caesars. But in time Maximian wanted to resume his tyrannical rule, but Constantius, his son-in-law, ran him down and hanged him.

The body of Saint Innocent, who belonged to the Theban legion, had been thrown into the Rhone River but was recovered by Bishop Domitian of Geneva, Bishop Gratus of Aosta, Bishop Protasius, and others, and by them buried in a church that they built for the purpose. While the church was under construction and most of the workmen were at mass on Sunday, one of them, a pagan, went on with his work alone. Suddenly the legion of the saints appeared, seized the pagan, beat him, and reproached him for engaging in profane labor and toiling at mechanical tasks on the Lord's day, while the others were occupied in divine service. Being thus corrected, the man ran to the church and begged to be made a Christian.

Ambrose, in his Preface for these martyrs, says: "This troop of faithful men, lustrous with the light of God, came from the ends of the earth to plead happily with you, O Lord! This legion of warriors, fenced about with bodily weapons but also protected by spiritual arms, hastened with watchful constancy to martyrdom. The pestiferous tyrant, in order to terrorize them, massacred every tenth man with the beheading sword and, when the rest clung steadfastly to their faith, ordered all of them to submit to the same penalty. But so ardent was the fervor of their love that, discarding their arms, they knelt before the headsmen and with joyful hearts received the blow that killed them. Among them blessed Maurice, afire with love for your faith, sustained the combat and won the crown of martyrdom." Thus Ambrose.

A woman entrusted her son to the abbot of a monastery where the bodies of some of the Theban martyrs reposed. The boy was there to be instructed, but before long he died, and the mother mourned him inconsolably. Saint Maurice appeared to her and asked why she wept so much for her son, and she replied that as long as she lived, she would never stop mourning her loss. Maurice said: "Do not think of him as being dead! Know that he is living with us. If you want proof of this, come to the service of matins tomorrow and every day, and you will hear his voice among the voices of the monks as they chant the Psalms." The woman followed the saint's admonition and always discerned her son's voice as he sang with the monks.

After King Gontran had retired from worldly pomp and circumstance and had distributed his wealth to the poor and the churches, he sent a priest to obtain for him some sacred relics of the holy martyrs. On his return voyage across the lake of Lausanne a tempest arose and the ship was sinking, but the priest held up the chest containing the relics in the face of the storm, and a serene calm settled over the waves.

In the year A.D. 963 certain monks, acting on behalf of Charles, obtained from Pope Nicholas the bodies of Pope Saint Urban and Saint Tiburtius. On their way home they visited the church of the Theban martyrs, and besought the abbot and the monks to allow them to transport the body of Saint Maurice and the head of Saint Innocent to the church in Auxerre that Saint Germain had long since dedicated to the martyrs.

Peter Damian tells us that in Burgundy there was a certain proud, ambitious cleric who had taken over for himself a church dedicated to Saint Maurice, despite the determined opposition of a powerful knight. One day when mass was being celebrated and the deacon, at the end of the gospel, sang: "Whoever exalts himself will be humbled and whoever humbles himself will be exalted," the wretched cleric scoffed and said: "That is false! If I had humbled myself before my enemies, I would not now have this rich church for myself!" Instantly a flash of lightning darted into the mouth out of which he had spewed these blasphemous words, and that was the end of the blasphemer.

---

142. Saint Justina, Virgin

The name Justina is derived from *justitia*, justice; and Saint Justina showed her justice by giving to every person what was due to the person—to God, obedience; to the prelate her superior, reverence; to her equals, harmonious relations; to her inferiors, instruction; to her enemies, patience; to the poor and afflicted, compassion and help; to herself, holiness; and to her neighbor, love.

The virgin Justina was born in Antioch, the daughter of a pagan priest. Sitting at her window every day, she listened to the deacon Proclus reading the Gospel and in time was converted by him. Her mother told her father about this as they lay in bed, and when they had fallen asleep, Christ, accompanied by angels, appeared to them and said: "Come to me, and I will give you the kingdom of heaven!" As soon as they were awake, they had themselves baptized with their daughter.

This virgin Justina had long been pursued by a certain Cyprian, and in the end she converted him to the faith. Cyprian had been a magician from childhood:

when he was seven years old, his parents consecrated him to the devil. He practiced the arts of magic, often being seen to change women into beasts of burden and performing many other marvels. He became enamored of Justina, and put his magic to work in order to have her for himself or for a man named Acladius, who also lusted after her. He therefore invoked the demon to come to him and enable him to win the virgin. The demon came and asked him: "Why did you call me?" Cyprian answered: "I love a maiden who is of the Galilean sect. Can you make it possible for me to have her and work my will with her?" The demon: "I was able to throw man out of paradise; I induced Cain to kill his brother; I caused the Jews to put Christ to death; I have brought every kind of disorder among men! How could I not be able to let you have one mere girl and do what you please with her? Take this lotion and sprinkle it around the outside of her house, and I will come and set her heart afire with love for you, and compel her to consent to you."

The following night the demon came to Justina and tried to awaken an illicit love in her heart. Sensing what was happening, she devoutly commended herself to the Lord and covered her whole body with the sign of the cross. Seeing that sign, the devil fled in terror and went and stood before Cyprian. "Why haven't you brought that maiden to me?" Cyprian asked. "I saw a certain sign on her," the demon answered, "and I weakened and all power left me." Cyprian dismissed that demon and called for a stronger one. This one told Cyprian: "I heard your orders and I saw why that other could do nothing, but I will do better and will carry out your will. I will go to her and wound her heart with lustful love, and you will enjoy her as you wish to." So the devil went to Justina and did his best to win her over and inflame her soul with sinful desire. But Justina again devoutly commended herself to God and dispelled all temptation with the sign of the cross, then blew upon the devil and drove him away. The spirit departed in confusion and fled to Cyprian. Cyprian: "Where is the virgin I sent you after?" The demon: "I admit I'm beaten, and I'm afraid to say how! I saw a certain terrible sign on her and at once lost all my strength!"

Cyprian scoffed at him and sent him away. Then he summoned the prince of demons and, when he came, said to him: "What is this power of yours that's so low that a mere girl can overcome it?" Said the devil: "I will visit her and disturb her with various fevers. I will inflame her spirit with hotter passion and spread hot spasms throughout her body. I'll get her in a frenzy and put fearful phantasms before her eyes. And in the middle of the night I will bring her to you!"

Then the devil gave himself the appearance of a young woman and went to Justina, saying: "I come to you because I want to live in chastity with you; but tell me, I beg of you, what will be the reward of our effort?" The holy virgin answered: "The reward is great, the labor light." "Then," said the devil, "what about God's command to increase and multiply and fill the earth? I fear, my good friend, that if we persist in virginity, we shall nullify God's word. By being disdainful and disobedient we shall bring grievous judgment upon ourselves, and while we expected a reward, we will incur torment!" The virgin began to have serious doubts, induced by the devil, and she felt more strongly stirred by the heat of concupiscence, so much so that she rose and was on the verge of going out. But then she came to herself and recognized who it was that was speaking to her, so she shielded herself with the sign of the cross, then blew on the devil, causing him to melt like a candle. Thereupon she felt herself freed of all temptation.

Next the devil transfigured himself into a handsome young man and came into the room where Justina was lying in bed. Shamelessly he leapt into her bed and tried to envelop her in his embrace. This made Justina recognize the presence of a malignant spirit, so she quickly made the sign of the cross, and again the devil melted away. Then, God permitting, the demon sapped her strength with fevers, and killed many people along with their herds and flocks. He also made possessed persons predict that a great wave of death would sweep through Antioch unless Justina consented to marry. For that reason the entire citizenry, beset as they were with disease, gathered at her parents' door and demanded that Justina be given in marriage so that the city could be delivered of this great peril. But Justina absolutely refused, and all were under the threat of death, but in the seventh year of the plague she prayed for them and drove out the pestilence.

Now the devil, seeing that he was making no headway, changed himself to look like Justina in order to besmirch her good name, and deceived Cyprian, boasting that he would bring Justina to him. Then, but this time looking like the virgin, he came running to Cyprian as if languishing with love for him and wanting to kiss him. Cyprian, thinking of course that it was Justina, was overwhelmed with joy and said: "Welcome, Justina, loveliest of women!" But the minute he pronounced the name of Justina, the devil could not bear it and vanished in a puff of smoke.

Cyprian, aggrieved at having been fooled, yearned the more ardently for Justina and took to watching at her door. Sometimes he changed himself by magic into a woman, sometimes into a bird, but when he came close to that door, he no longer looked like a woman or a bird: he was Cyprian. Acladius, too, was changed by diabolic art into a sparrow and flew to the virgin's windowsill, but as soon as she looked at him, he was no longer a sparrow but Acladius, and he felt trapped and frightened because he could neither fly nor jump from such a height. Justina feared that he might fall and break to pieces, so she had him brought down by a ladder, and warned him to give up his mad adventure or be punished for breaking the law against trespass.

All these apparitions, of course, were nothing but devilish artifices, and none of them served the devil's purpose; so, defeated and confused, he went back and stood before Cyprian. Cyprian said to him: "So you too are beaten! What kind of power do you have, you wretch, that you can't overcome a simple girl or have any control over her? To the contrary, she defeats all of you and lays you low! But tell me one thing, I beg of you: where does her greatest strength come from?" The demon answered: "If you will swear never to desert me, I will reveal to you the power behind her victory." Cyprian: "What shall I swear by?" The demon: "Swear to me by my great powers that you will never desert me!" Cyprian: "By your great powers I swear to you that I will never desert you."

Now the devil, being reassured, told Cyprian: "That young woman made the sign of the cross, and at once all my strength ebbed away. I could do nothing, and like wax melting at a fire I melted away." Cyprian: "Therefore the Crucified is greater than you?" The demon: "Greater than all! And all of us and all those we deceive he turns over to be tormented in the fire that never dies out!" Cyprian: "Therefore I too should become a friend of the Crucified, so as not to incur so awful a punishment!" The devil: "You swore to me by the power of my army, by which no one can swear falsely, that you would never desert me!" Cyprian answered: "I despise you and all your devils, and I arm myself with the saving sign of the Crucified!" Instantly the devil fled in confusion.

Then Cyprian went to the bishop. When the bishop saw him, he supposed that he had come to lead Christians into error, and said to him: "Be satisfied, Cyprian, with misleading those who are not of the faith! You can do nothing against the Church of God, for the power of Christ is unconquerable." Cyprian: "I am sure that Christ's power cannot be conquered." And he told the bishop all that had happened to him, and had the bishop baptize him. Thereafter Cyprian made great progress both in knowledge and in holiness of life, and when the bishop died, Cyprian was ordained to take his place. He established the holy virgin Justina in a monastery and made her the abbess over many holy virgins. Saint Cyprian often sent letters to the martyrs and strengthened them in their struggles.

The prefect of that region heard of the renown of Cyprian and Justina and had them brought before him. He asked them if they were willing to sacrifice to the idols. When they persisted firmly in the faith of Christ, he ordered them to be put in a heated caldron filled with wax, pitch, and fat, but this only refreshed them and inflicted no pain. Then a priest of the idols said to the prefect: "Command me to stand in front of the caldron, and I will outdo all their power!" He went close to the caldron and said: "Great are you, O god Hercules, and you, Jupiter, father of the gods!" And behold, fire poured out and consumed the priest. Cyprian and Justina were taken out of the caldron, sentenced, and beheaded together. Their bodies were thrown to the dogs and lay for seven days, then were transported to Rome, and now, we are told, repose in Piacenza. They suffered under Diocletian, on the twenty-sixth day of September, A.D. 280.

143. Saints Cosmas and Damian

The name Cosmas comes from *cosmos*, which means form or adorned. Or, according to Isidore, *cosmos* is the Greek word for clean, as is the Latin word *mundus*. Saint Cosmas was a form, an example to others; he was adorned with good virtues and clean of all vices. Damianus, or Damian, is derived from *dama*, a humble, gentle beast, or the name comes from *dogma*, doctrine, and *ana*, above, or from *damum*, which is sacrifice. Or Damianus is equivalent to *Domini manus*, the hand of the Lord. Saint Damian was mild of manner, had supernal doctrine in his preaching, was a sacrifice in the mortification of his flesh, and was the hand of the Lord in the healing cures he brought about.

Cosmas and Damian were brothers, born of a pious mother, Theodoche by name, in the city of Egea. They learned the art of medicine, and received such grace from the Holy Spirit that they cured the illnesses not only of men and women but of animals, not taking any payment for their services. A lady named Palladia, however, who had spent all she had on doctors, came to the saints and by them was fully restored to health. She therefore offered a modest gift to Saint Damian and, when he declined to accept it, appealed to him with solemn oaths. He then accepted the gift, not that he was greedy for the money but to satisfy the donor's kind intention, as well as to avoid seeming to dishonor the name of the Lord, since the woman had adjured him in that name. When Saint Cosmas learned of this, he gave orders that his body was not to be buried with his brother's, but the following night the Lord appeared to Cosmas and explained Damian's reason for his action.

Word of the brothers' fame reached Lisias, the proconsul, and he had them summoned and asked them their names, their native land, and their possessions. The holy martyrs replied: "Our names are Cosmas and Damian; we have three brothers named Antimas, Leontius, and Euprepius; Arabia is our homeland; and as for earthly fortunes, Christians do not acquire them." The proconsul ordered them to fetch their brothers, and then to sacrifice to the idols together.

When the five brothers unanimously refused to sacrifice, Lisias commanded that they be tortured in their hands and feet. They made light of these torments, and he ordered them to be bound with chains and thrown into the sea, but at once they were drawn out by an angel and set before the judge. This official gave thought to the matter and said: "By the great gods, it is by sorcery that you conquer, because you mock at torments and calm the sea! Therefore teach me your magic arts, and in the name of the god Adrian I will follow you." No sooner had he said this than two demons appeared and struck him in the face with great force, and he cried out: "I beg you, good men, to pray for me to your God!" They prayed, and the demons disappeared.

The judge said: "You see how angry the gods are with me because I thought of leaving them. Now therefore I will not suffer you to blaspheme my gods!" He ordered them to be thrown into a huge fire, but the flame not only left the martyrs unharmed, but leapt out and slew many bystanders. The brothers were then stretched on the rack, but their guardian angel kept them uninjured, and the torturers, tired of beating them, returned them to the judge. He in turn had three of the brothers put back in prison, but ordered Cosmas and Damian to be crucified and stoned by the crowd. The stones turned back upon the throwers and wounded a great number. The judge, now beside himself with rage, had the three brothers brought out and ranged around the cross, while four soldiers shot arrows at Cosmas and Damian, still crucified; but the arrows turned and struck many, while the holy martyrs remained untouched. The judge, defeated at every turn, was at death's door from frustration and had the five brothers beheaded in the morning. The Christians, remembering what Saint Cosmas had said about not burying him with Damian, wondered how the martyrs wanted to be buried, when suddenly a camel appeared on the scene, spoke in a human voice, and ordered the saints to be entombed in one place. They suffered under Diocletian, who began to reign about A.D. 287.

A peasant, after hours of working at the harvest, fell asleep in the field with his mouth open, and a snake slipped into his mouth and down to his belly. The man woke up and felt nothing, and went on home, but by evening suffered severe pains in the stomach. He uttered pitiful cries and invoked the aid of Cosmas and Damian, saints of God, but the pain grew worse and he ran to the church of the holy martyrs. There he suddenly fell asleep, and the snake slipped out of his mouth as it had slipped in.

A man who was about to set out on a long journey commended his wife to the care of the holy martyrs Cosmas and Damian, and gave her a sign that she could rely on if at any time he called her. Afterwards the devil, knowing the sign the husband had given, got himself up as a man, showed the woman the sign, and said: "Your husband sent me to you from that city to conduct you to him." She was afraid to go, and said: "I recognize the sign, but I am commended to the holy martyrs Cosmas and Damian, so you must swear to me on their altar that you will take me safely to him." The devil immediately swore as requested. The woman went with him, and when they came to a secluded spot, the devil wanted to throw her off her horse and kill her. When she felt danger coming, she exclaimed: "O God of saints Cosmas and Damian, help me! I trusted them and followed this man!" Instantly the saints appeared with a host of men clad in white and set the woman free. The devil vanished. They said to her: "We are Cosmas and Damian, in whom you trusted, and we hurried to come to your assistance."

Pope Felix, a predecessor of Saint Gregory, built a noble church in Rome in honor of Saints Cosmas and Damian. In this church there was a man, a devoted servant of the holy martyrs. One of the man's legs was totally consumed by a cancer. While he was asleep, the two saints appeared to their devoted servant, bringing salves and surgical instruments. One of them said to the other: "Where can we get flesh to fill in where we cut away the rotted leg?" The other said: "Just today an Ethiopian was buried in the cemetery of Saint Peter in Chains. Go and take his leg, and we'll put it in place of the bad one." So he sped to the cemetery and brought back the Moor's leg, and the two saints cut off the sick man's leg and inserted the Moor's in its place, carefully anointing the wound. Finally they took the amputated leg and attached it to the body of the dead Moor.

The man woke up, felt no pain, put his hand to his leg, and detected no lesion. He held a candle to the leg and could see nothing wrong with it, and began to wonder whether he was himself or somebody else. Then he came to his senses, bounded joyfully from his bed, and told everyone about what he had seen in his dreams and how he had been healed. They sent at once to the Moor's tomb, and found that his leg had indeed been cut off and the aforesaid man's limb put in its place in the tomb.

144. Saint Fursey, Bishop

Fursey, a bishop, whose story Bede is believed to have written, reached his final hour after a life that shone with every virtue and goodness. As he was about to breathe his last, he saw in a vision two angels coming to him to carry his soul to heaven, and a third, armed with a shining shield and a gleaming sword, going ahead of him. Then he heard demons shouting: "We must go first and stir up wars in his path!" As these went ahead, they turned around and hurled fiery darts at him, but the leading angel caught them on his shield and extinguished them. Then the demons blocked the angels' way and said: "This man often spoke idle words and therefore should not go unpunished to enjoy eternal life." The angel retorted: "If you cannot accuse him of more serious vices than that, he will not perish for trifles."

Then the devil said to them: "If God is just, this man will not be saved, for it is written: 'Unless you be converted and become as little children, you shall not enter into the kingdom of heaven.'"[1] The angel made an excuse for him, saying: "His heart was right, but human custom kept him quiet." The demon: "Since he accepted evil due to custom, let him accept punishment from the supreme Judge!" The holy angel said: "Let us seek judgment from God!" With the angel fighting for him, the adversaries were put down.

Then the demon said: "A servant who knows the will of his master and does not do it will receive many a hard blow." The angel: "In what did this man fail to fulfill the will of his Lord?" The demon: "He accepted gifts from the wicked." The angel: "He thought that every one of them had done penance." The demon said: "He should first have verified their perseverance in penance and then received the fruit." The angel answered: "Let us submit the case to God!" The demon gave up but returned to the fray, saying: "Until now I've been intimidated by God's truthfulness, as when he promised that any wrong that is not atoned for on earth will be punished hereafter. But this man once accepted a coat from a usurer and was not punished, so where is the justice of God?" The angel: "Silence! You do not know God's secret judgments. As long as there is hope of repentance, the mercy of God accompanies a man." The devil: "But there is no place for repentance here!" The angel: "You do not know the depth of God's judgments."

Then the devil struck Fursey so hard that after he came back to life, he always bore the mark of the blow. What the demons did was to pick up one of the people they were torturing in the fire and throw him at Fursey, whose cheek and shoulder were burned by the contact. Fursey recognized the man who was thrown at him as the one from whom he had accepted the coat. The angel said: "What you once set afire has burned you. If you had not received a gift from this man who died in his sins, his punishment would not have burned in you." So it was by God's permission and order that Fursey received this blow for having accepted the man's coat.

Now another demon said: "There is still a narrow gate for him to pass through, and there we will be able to overpower him—namely, the Law 'You shall love your neighbor as yourself.'"[2] The angel responded: "This man did much good for his neighbors." "That is not enough, unless he also loved himself," the adversary retorted. The angel: "The fruit of love is to do good works, because God renders to each according to his works."[3] The demon said: "Because he did not fulfill the Law by loving, he will be damned." The battle went on, and the holy angels were victors over the horde of the evil.

The devil spoke again: "If God is not wicked and any transgression of his word displeases him, this man will not escape punishment, for he promised to renounce the world, and, to the contrary, he loved the world, going against what is said: 'Love not the world, nor the things which are in the world.'"[4] The

---

[1] Matt. 18:13.   [2] Matt. 22:39.   [3] Rom. 2:6.

[4] 1 John 2:15.

holy angel responded: "He loved the things that are in the world not for himself, but because he could give them to people in need." The devil replied: "No matter how or for what reason he loved them, it was against the divine command!"

The adversaries were defeated again, and the devil resorted to more subtle accusations, saying: "It is written: 'If you do not speak to warn the wicked from his wicked way, his blood I will require at your hand';[5] but this man did not warn sinners as he should have done." The holy angel responded: "When the hearers pay no heed to the word, the teacher's tongue is tied, and when he sees that his preaching is despised, he does well to know that when it is not the time to speak, it is better to say nothing." So the demons lost in each phase of the confrontation, until by the Lord's judgment the angels were triumphant and the adversaries were vanquished, and the holy man was enveloped in bright light.

Bede tells us that one of the angels said to Fursey: "Look down on the earth!" He saw a gloomy valley far beneath him, and four fires in the air at some distance from each other. The angel told him: "These are the four fires that are burning up the world. One is the fire of falsehood, because men promise in baptism to renounce the devil and all his pomps, but they do not fulfill the promise. The second is the fire of greed, because men put the world's riches ahead of the love of heavenly goods. The third is the fire of discord, which makes people not hesitate to hurt their neighbors over the slightest thing. The fourth is the fire of impiety, of ruthlessness, which makes people think nothing of robbing and defrauding the weak and defenseless." Then the fires drew together and formed one blaze, which came closer to Fursey and made him afraid. He said to the angel: "This fire is coming very close to me!" The angel: "What you did not ignite will not burn in you, because that fire tests each man according to the merits of his works, for as the body is burned by illicit pleasures, so it will be burned by the punishment it deserves."

At last Fursey was brought back to his body, while all were mourning because they thought he was dead. He lived for some while longer and finished his life laudably in doing good works.

---

[5] Ezek. 3:18.

145. Saint Michael, Archangel

Michael is interpreted as meaning "Who is like to God?" and it is said that when something requiring wondrous powers is to be done, Michael is sent, so that from his name and by his action it is given to be understood that no one can do what God alone can do: for that reason many works of wondrous power are attributed to Michael. Thus, as Daniel testifies, in the time of the Antichrist Michael will rise up and stand forth as defender and protector of the elect. He it was who fought with the dragon and his angels and expelled them from heaven, winning a great victory. He fought with the devil over the body of Moses, because the devil wanted to keep the body hidden so that the Jewish people might adore Moses in place of the true God. Michael receives the souls of the saints and leads them into the paradise of joy. In the past he was prince of the synagogue but has now been established by the Lord as prince of the Church. It is said that it was he who inflicted the plagues on the Egyptians, divided the Red Sea, led the people through the desert, and ushered them into the Promised Land. He is held to be Christ's standard-bearer among the battalions of the holy angels. At the Lord's command he will kill the Antichrist with great power on Mount Olivet. At the sound of the voice of the archangel Michael the dead will rise, and it is he who will present the cross, the nails, the spear, and the crown of thorns at the Day of Judgment.

The sacred feast of Michael the archangel celebrates his apparition, his victory, his dedication, and his memorial. There have been several apparitions of this angel. He first appeared on Mount Gargano. In Apulia there is a mountain named Gargano near the city called Sipontus. In the year of the Lord 390 there was, in the aforesaid city of Sipontus, a man named Garganus, who, according to some books, took his name from the mountain, or from whom the mountain got its name. This man was rich, and had sheep and cattle beyond counting. Once when the herd was grazing on the flanks of Mount Gargano, it happened that one bull separated himself from the rest and climbed to the top of the mountain. When the herd came in and this bull's absence was discovered, the landowner mustered a band of his people to track it up the mountain trails, and they finally found the animal standing in the mouth of a cave at the top. The owner, annoyed at the bull for having wandered off alone, aimed a poisoned arrow at it, but the arrow came back, as if turned about by the wind, and struck the one who had launched it. This dismayed the townsmen, and they went to the bishop and asked him what he thought of the strange occurrence. The bishop bound them to a three-day fast and admonished them to direct their questions to God. They did, and Saint Michael appeared to the bishop and said: "Know that it was by my will that the man was struck by his arrow. I am the archangel Michael, and I have chosen to dwell in that place on earth and to keep it safe. I wished by that sign to indicate that I watch over the place and guard it." The bishop and the townspeople formed a procession and went to the cave, but, not presuming to enter, stood around the entrance, praying.

The second apparition is described as having occurred about A.D. 710. At a place close to the sea, called Tumba, about six miles from the city of Avranches, Michael appeared to the bishop of that city and ordered him to build a church at the aforesaid place, at which church, as at Mount Gargano, the memory of Saint Michael the archangel was to be celebrated. When the bishop was uncertain about the exact place where the church should be built, the archangel instructed him to build at a spot where he would find that thieves had hidden a bull. The bishop also had doubts about how large the church should be, and was ordered to use as a measure the circuit marked by the bull's hoofprints. On the site there were two boulders so massive that no human strength could move them. Then Michael appeared to a man and ordered him to go to the place and remove the rocks. The man went there and moved the stones so easily that they seemed to have no weight at all. When the church was built, they brought from Mount Gargano a cutting from the mantle Saint Michael had spread over the altar there and a slab of the marble on which he had stood, and placed them in his new church. And since there appeared to be a scarcity of water there, upon the angel's advice they broke a cleft into a very hard rock at the site, and such a stream of water poured out that even now it more than meets every need. This apparition is solemnly celebrated in that place on the sixteenth day of October.

We are told that in this same place there occurred a miracle which is worthy of being remembered. The mountain on which Saint Michael's church was built is surrounded on all sides by the ocean, but twice on the saint's feast day a path is opened to allow the people to walk over. One such day, when a large throng was crossing to the church, it happened that a woman who was pregnant and close to her time went with them. Then the tide came in with a rush, and the crowd, terrified, made for the shore, but the pregnant woman could not move fast enough and was caught by the waves. The archangel Michael, however, kept her unharmed, in such a way that she brought forth her son in the welter of the sea and nursed him there in her arms. Then the waters again opened a path for her, and she walked joyfully ashore with her child.

We read that the third apparition took place in Rome during the reign of Pope Gregory. The pope had instituted the Greater Litanies because the inguinal plague was raging in the city, and he was praying devoutly for the people when he saw, above the castle that in the past was called the Tomb of Hadrian, an angel of the Lord who was wiping a bloody sword and returning it to its sheath. Saint Gregory understood from this that his prayers were heard by the

Lord, and he built a church there in honor of the angels: the castle is still called the Castle of the Holy Angel. This apparition is celebrated on 8 May, together with the apparition on Mount Gargano, when Michael gave victory to the people of Sipontus.

The fourth apparition consists in the hierarchies of the angels. The first hierarchy is called Epiphany, or higher apparition, the middle one is called Hyperphany, or middle apparition, and the lowest is called Hypophany, or lower apparition. The word hierarchy comes from *hierar*, sacred, and *archos*, prince, hence sacred prince. Each hierarchy includes three orders. The highest includes Seraphim, Cherubim, and Thrones; the middle one, as Dionysius assigns them, contains Dominations, Virtues, and Powers; and the lowest, according to the same Dionysius, comprises Principalities, Angels, and Archangels. This ordering and ranking of the angels can be understood by its similarity with the organization of a royal court. Among the king's ministers, some, such as chamberlains, counselors and assessors, work in immediate contact with him: the orders in the first hierarchy are similar to these. Other officials have duties pertaining to the overall government of the kingdom, not to one particular province: of this class are the commanders of the militia and the judges in the courts of law, and they are similar to the orders in the second hierarchy. There are also minor officials, for instance, prefects, bailiffs, and the like, who are put in charge of a particular part of the kingdom: these are similar to the orders of the lowest hierarchy.

Among the angels, the three orders in the first hierarchy are those that are close to God, with no intermediary, and are wholly turned to him. For this relationship three things are necessary: first, the highest love, and this is attributed to the Seraphim, whose name means afire with love; second, perfect knowledge, which characterizes the Cherubim, whose name means fullness of knowledge; third, perpetual comprehension or enjoyment, which belongs to the Thrones, whose name means seats, because God sits in them and rests, as he grants them to rest in him.

The three orders in the middle hierarchy are leaders and rulers over the universe of men as a whole. This rule has three elements. It consists first in presiding or commanding, and this belongs to the order of Dominations, whose role it is to be at the head of those inferior to them, to direct them in all divine ministries, and to give them all necessary commands, as we read in Zechariah: "One angel said to the other: 'Run, say to that young man, Jerusalem shall be inhabited as villages without walls.'"[1] The second element consists in the works to be done, and this applies to the order of Virtues, for whom nothing that is commanded is impossible, because it is given to them to be able to rise above all difficulties encountered in the service of God. Therefore the power to work miracles is attributed to them. The third element consists in getting rid of obstacles and resisting attacks, and this pertains to the order of the Powers, who are charged

[1] Zech. 2:4.

with driving off opposing powers, as we read in Tobit: "The angel Raphael took the devil and bound him in the desert of Upper Egypt."[2]

The three orders of the lowest hierarchy are those whose sphere of influence is fixed and limited. Some of them have authority in only one province, and these are of the order of Principalities, or Princes, like the prince of the Persians, who ruled over Persia, about whom we read in the tenth chapter of Daniel. Some were commissioned to rule over a multitude of people, as, for example, over one city, and these are called Archangels. Some had a single person placed in their charge, and these are called Angels. Hence Angels are said to make minor announcements, for the reason that their ministry is limited to one man, but Archangels are said to announce great events, because the good of a multitude is of greater importance than that of one individual.

Gregory and Bernard agree with Dionysius regarding the assigned functions of the orders of the first hierarchy, because the assignment of function corresponds to the fruit it produces, namely, ardent love for the Seraphim, profound knowledge for the Cherubim, and perpetual possession of God for the Thrones. They appear to differ, however, regarding the assigned functions of two orders in the middle and lowest hierarchies, namely, of the Principalities and Powers. Gregory and Bernard start from the assumption that the status of master is awarded to the middle hierarchy and that of ministry to the lowest. In this perspective, angels have mastery over three groups: some are masters over angelic spirits, and these are called Dominations, some over good men, and these are called Principalities, and some over demons, and these are called Powers. Here the order and levels of dignity are obvious. Ministry also is of three kinds, namely, the performance of works, the teaching of great matters, and the teaching of less important ones. The first ministry belongs to the Virtues, the second to Archangels, the third to Angels.

There was a fifth apparition of the archangel Michael, and we read about it in the *Tripartite History*. Not far from Constantinople there is a place where the goddess Vesta was worshiped in the past, but where now there stands a church built in honor of Saint Michael, for which reason the place itself is called Michaelium. A man named Aquilinus was overtaken by a raging fever known for the redness that accompanies it. The doctors gave him a potion to break the fever, but he vomited it and continued to vomit whatever he ate or drank. Knowing that he was near death, he had himself carried to the place mentioned above, thinking that there he would either die or be relieved of his malady. Saint Michael appeared to him and told him to prepare a mixture of honey, wine, and pepper and to dip everything he ate in this mixture, and he would be wholly cured. He did as directed and was indeed made well, although it seems contrary to medical science to administer hot drinks to the feverish. This we read in the *Tripartite History*.

---

[2] Tob. 8:3.

Secondly, this feast is called Victory. Michael and his angels have won many victories. The first is the one that the archangel Michael bestowed on the people of Sipontus in the following way. Some time after the finding of the cave at the top of Mount Gargano, the Neapolitans, who were still pagans, organized an army and began to make war on the people of Sipontus and Beneventum, a town some fifty miles from Sipontus. The bishop advised these people to seek a three-day truce, which would give them time to fast and to pray to their patron Michael for help. On the third night Michael appeared to the bishop, told him that the prayers had been heard, promised him victory, and ordered that the enemy be met at the fourth hour of daylight. As the battle was joined, Mount Gargano was shaken by a violent earthquake, lightning flashed uninterruptedly, and a dark cloud blanketed the whole peak of the mountain. Six hundred of the enemy troops fell before the swords of the defenders and the fiery lightning flashes. The rest, recognizing the power of the archangel, abandoned the error of idolatry and bent their necks to the yoke of the Christian faith.

The second victory was won by the archangel Michael when he drove the dragon, i.e., Lucifer, and all his followers out of heaven, a battle about which the Book of Revelation tells us: "There was a great battle in heaven. Michael and his angels fought with the dragon, and the dragon fought with his angels, and they prevailed not."[3] For when Lucifer wanted to be equal to God, the archangel Michael, standard-bearer of the celestial host, marched up and expelled Lucifer and his followers out of heaven, and shut them up in this dark air until the Day of Judgment. They are not allowed to live in heaven, or in the upper part of the air, because that is a bright and pleasant place, nor on the earth with us, lest they do us too much harm. They are in the air between heaven and earth, so that when they look up and see the glory they have lost, they grieve for it, and when they look down and see men ascending to the place from which they fell, they are often tormented with envy. However, by God's design they come down upon us to test us, and, as has been shown to some holy men, they fly around us like flies. They are innumerable, and, like flies, they fill the whole air. Hence Haymon says: "As philosophers have said and as our doctors agree, the air is as full of demons and wicked spirits as a ray of sunlight with specks of dust." Still, innumerable as they are, Origen is of the opinion that their numbers lessen when we conquer them, with the result that when one of them is defeated by a holy man, the tempter can no longer tempt that man to fall into the vice into which he had failed to draw him.

The third victory is the one that the angels win over the demons every day, when they fight for us and save us from the demons' effort to tempt us. The angels do this in three ways: first, by curbing the power that belongs to the demons. The Book of Revelation tells us about the angel who bound the demon and cast him into the bottomless pit;[4] and in Tobit we read about

---

[3] Rev. 12:7–9.   [4] Rev. 20:1–3.

the angel who bound a demon in the desert of Upper Egypt.[5] This binding is nothing less than the curbing of the demon's power. The second way is by cooling concupiscence. This is what is meant by the passage in Genesis which says that an angel touched the sinew of Jacob's thigh and it shrank.[6] The third way is by impressing on our minds the memory of the Lord's passion. This is what Revelation means where we read: "Do not harm the earth or the sea or the trees, till we have sealed the servants of our God upon their foreheads";[7] and in Ezekiel we find: "Mark *Tau* upon the foreheads of the men that sigh."[8] *Tau* is the Greek letter that is written in the shape of a cross, and those who are marked with this sign have no fear of the avenging angel. Hence we read in the same place: "Upon whomsoever you shall see the sign *Tau*, kill him not."[9]

The fourth victory is the one that Michael the archangel is to win over the Antichrist when he kills him. Then Michael the great prince, as Daniel[10] calls him, will rise and stand forth, a valorous aid and protector against the Antichrist. The Antichrist, as the *Gloss* says on the text in Revelation, "I saw one of his heads as it were slain to death,"[11] will pretend to be dead and will hide for three days, then will appear and say that he is resurrected, and, with demons carrying him by their magical arts, will rise in the air, and all will be amazed and will adore him. Finally he will go to the top of Mount Olivet, according to the *Gloss* on the words in 2 Thessalonians, "And then that wicked one shall be revealed, whom the Lord Jesus shall kill."[12] He will sit in his tent and on his throne, at that place from which the Lord ascended, and Michael will come and slay him. This fight and this victory are understood, according to Gregory, as referring to the text in Revelation mentioned above: "There was a great battle in heaven, etc." And what is said about Michael's threefold battle is understood as referring inclusively to the fight he had with Lucifer when he expelled him from heaven, the one with the demons to keep them from doing us too much harm on earth, and the one we are talking about here—the battle with the Antichrist at the end of the world.

Thirdly, this feast is called Dedication, due to the fact that on this day the archangel Michael revealed that he himself had dedicated the place on Mount Gargano, already described. When the people of Sipontus came back after defeating their enemies and achieving such a magnificent victory, they began to have doubts about whether they should dedicate the cave or even enter it. The bishop therefore consulted Pope Pelagius about this, and the pope answered: "If indeed it behooves man to dedicate that church, it should be done on this date, the day on which victory was granted us. If, on the other hand, it would please Michael to have something else done, he is the one to tell us what his will is in the matter." The pope, the bishop, and the people joined in a three-day fast, and on this very day Michael appeared to the bishop and said: "There is no need for

---

[5] Tob. 8:3.   [6] Gen. 32:24–25.   [7] Rev. 7:3.
[8] Ezek. 9:4.   [9] Ezek. 9:6.   [10] Dan. 12:1.
[11] Rev. 13:3.   [12] 2 Thess. 2:8.

you to dedicate this church, because I myself founded it, built it, and dedicated it." He ordered the bishop to enter the church with the people on the following day. There they were to pray to Michael and acknowledge him as their special patron.

Michael told the bishop that for all to have a sign of the consecration he had spoken of, they should come up from the eastern side and through a rear entrance, and there they would find the marks of a man's footsteps imprinted in the marble. So, the next day, the bishop and the entire populace climbed to the place and went inside. They found themselves in a vast cavern, in which two altars stood on the south side and one to the east. This last altar was of imposing dimensions and was covered all around with a red mantle. Mass was then celebrated, and after receiving holy communion the people went their several ways rejoicing. The bishop appointed priests and clerics to celebrate the divine office there continually. In this same cave a clear, sweet water flowed. The people drank it after communion and were cured of whatever diseases they had. When the pope was informed of these events, he decreed that this day should be celebrated throughout the world in honor of Saint Michael and all the blessed spirits.

Fourthly, this feast is called a Commemoration of Saint Michael: by it, however, we commemorate all the angels and honor all of them together. There are many reasons for our honoring and praising the angels. They are our guardians, our servants, our brothers, and our fellow citizens; they carry our souls into heaven; they present our prayers before God; they are the noble soldiers of the eternal King and the consolers of the afflicted.

First, then, we owe them honor because they are our guardians. To every man two angels are given, one good and the other bad, the bad one to test him and the good one to protect him. The good angel is deputed to an infant in the womb and immediately after birth, is with him or her in adult life. Man needs an angel as guardian in these three stages of life. He could die while still in the womb and therefore be damned. After being born but before adulthood it may not be possible for him to be baptized; and as an adult he can be drawn to a variety of sins. The devil deceives the mind by false reasoning, entices the will by seduction, and overpowers virtue by violence. Therefore it was necessary that a good angel be deputed to each man as guardian, to instruct and direct him against falsehood, to exhort and incite him to good and defend him against cajolery, and to protect him against violent oppression.

The guardianship of the angel can be said to have a fourfold effect upon a man. The first is that his soul makes progress in gaining grace, and the angel does this in the soul in three ways. One is by removing every obstacle to doing good, as in Exodus, where we see that the angel slew every firstborn in the land of Egypt.[13] The second is that the angel shakes us out of our slothfulness, as we see in Zechariah, where we read: "The angel of the Lord waked me, like a man that

---

[13] Exod. 12:29.

is wakened out of his sleep."[14] The third is that the angel leads man to, or leads him back to, the path of penance, which is shown in figure when the angel leads Tobias away safely and brings him back safely.[15]

The second effect of the angel's protection is that it keeps man from falling into the evil of sin, and this the angel does in three ways. The first way is by preventing him from committing a sin that he is thinking of committing, as in the case of Balaam, who was on his way to curse Israel but was halted by an angel.[16] The second way is by reproaching wrongdoers for a wrong already done, as is shown in the Book of Judges, when the angel reproached the sons of Israel for their disobedience, and they lifted up their voices and wept.[17] The third way is by doing violence, as it were, to put a stop to the commission of sin, as when angels violently forced Lot and his wife to leave Sodom[18]—"Sodom" here standing for habitual sin.

The third effect is that if someone falls he is made to get up again, and this the angel brings about in three ways. The first way is by moving the sinner to repentance, and we see this in Tobias,[19] when Tobias, instructed by the angel, anoints his father's eyes, i.e., his heart, with the gall of the fish, which represents repentance. The second way is the purging of the lips in preparation for confession, as is indicated when the angel cleanses Isaiah's lips with a live coal.[20] The third way is by rejoicing when penance is done for sin, as we read in Luke[21] that there will be more joy in heaven over one sinner who repents than over ninety-nine righteous who need no repentance.

The fourth effect is to preserve us from falling into sin as deeply or as often as the devil would have us do, and the angel accomplishes this in three ways: by curbing the demon's power, by mitigating our concupiscence, and by impressing on our minds the memory of the Lord's passion.

Secondly, we must honor the angels because they are our servants. They minister to us, as we read in Hebrews: "Are they not all ministering spirits, sent to minister for them who are to receive the inheritance of salvation?"[22] All are sent for our sake—the highest orders to the middle orders, these to the lowest ones, and the lowest to us. This sending of the angels is in accord, firstly, with the kindness of God, because it shows how much he loves our salvation, since he directs and dispatches the noblest spirits, those who are joined to him in intimate love, to procure salvation for us. Secondly, their mission also befits the angels' love for us, for it is of the nature of ardent love to desire intensely the welfare of others. For this reason Isaiah said: "Behold, Lord, here am I! Send me!"[23] The angels can help us because they see us in need of their aid, with bad angels warring against us. Thus the law of angelic love requires that they be sent to us. Thirdly, their sending also meets the neediness of mankind. The good

---

[14] Zech. 4:1.　　　　[15] Tob. 5:20.　　　　[16] Num. 22–24, esp. 22:12, 22–31
[17] Judg. 2:1–4.　　　　[18] Gen. 19, esp. vv. 15–17.　　　[19] Tob. 11:8.
[20] Isa. 6:6–7.　　　　[21] Luke 15:7.　　　　[22] Heb. 1:14.
[23] Isa. 6:8.

angels are sent to inflame our hearts with love. As a figure of this we read that they were sent in a fiery chariot. They are sent also to enlighten our understanding and bring us to knowledge, as is shown in a figure in the angel who held an open book in his hand.[24] And they come to strengthen any weakness in us to the limit of our need, as we see in 1 Kings, where we read that the angel brought to Elijah a cake baked on hot stones and a jar of water, and Elijah ate and drank, and walked in the strength of that food forty days and forty nights, to Horeb the mountain of God.[25]

Thirdly, we should honor the angels because they are our brothers and fellow citizens. All the elect are assumed to the angelic orders, some to the highest, some to the lowest, and some to the middle orders, according to the diversity of their merits. The Blessed Virgin is, of course, above all of them. Saint Gregory, in one of his homilies, confirms this truth. He says: "There are some of the chosen who grasp but little knowledge yet ceaselessly share what they know with their brothers, and these run in the order of the Angels. There are some elect who succeed in grasping the highest of the secrets of heaven and in making them known, and these are with the Archangels. There are those who perform wondrous signs and works of power, and these are assumed among the Virtues. There are some who, by virtue of their prayer and the force of the power they have received, put the evil spirits to flight, and these are with the Powers. Some surpass the merits of most of the elect and rule over them, and these are allotted a place among the Principalities. There are those who so completely dominate all vices in themselves that by right of their purity they are called gods among men, as the Lord said to Moses: 'Behold I have appointed thee the God of Pharaoh.'[26] These are with the Dominations. There are some elect on whom the Lord sits as upon his throne and examines the deeds of others, and since these rule the holy Church, the weak actions of the rest of the elect are judged by them: they are with the Thrones. There are some of the chosen who are more filled with the love of God and neighbor than the rest, and it falls to their lot to merit a place among the Cherubim, because *cherubim* means plenitude of knowledge, and, according to Paul, love is the fulfilling of the law. And there are those who are fired with the love of contemplating the things of heaven and pant with the sole desire of their Creator, who want nothing of this world, feed only on the love of eternity, throw away all earthly things, rise in their minds above all things temporal, who love and burn and in that very ardor find rest, who burn by loving and glow by speaking and make any whom their word touches burn with the love of God. These receive their inheritance not elsewhere than among the Seraphim." So Gregory.

Fourthly, we are to honor the angels because it is they who bear our souls up to heaven, and this they do in three ways. The first is by preparing the way, so we read in Malachi: "Behold I send my angel, who will prepare the way before

---

[24] Rev. 10:2, 8.   [25] 1(3) Kings 19:6–8.   [26] Exod. 7:1.

your face."[27] The second is by conveying the souls to heaven along the prepared way; so Exodus: "Behold I will send an angel, who shall go before thee and keep thee in thy journey, and bring thee into the land which I promised to thy fathers."[28] The third is by putting the souls in their place in heaven; so Luke: "It came to pass that the beggar died and was carried by the angels into Abraham's bosom."[29]

Fifthly, the angels are to be honored because it is they who present our prayers before God. First, they do indeed present our prayers to God; Tobias: "When thou didst pray with tears and didst bury the dead, I offered thy prayer to the Lord."[30] Second, they plead our cause for us; Job: "If there shall be an angel speaking for him, one among thousands, to declare man's uprightness, he shall have mercy on him";[31] and Zechariah: "The angel of the Lord answered and said: 'How long wilt thou not have mercy on Jerusalem and on the cities of Judah, with which thou hast been angry? This is now the seventieth year.'"[32] Third, they report God's sentence to us, as we read in the Book of Daniel that Gabriel flew to Daniel and said: "From the beginning of thy prayers the word came forth" (to which the *Gloss* adds "the word, i.e., God's sentence"), "and I am come to show it to thee, because thou art a man of desires."[33] Bernard, in his book on the Song of Solomon, says of these three services rendered by the angels: "The angel runs as a mediator between God the beloved and the beloved supplicant, offering the supplicant's prayers, and bringing back God's gifts, stirring up the petitioner, appeasing God."

Sixthly, we should honor the angels because they are the noble soldiers of the eternal King, as Job says: "Is there any numbering of his soldiers?"[34] Among the soldiers of a king we see some who are always in the king's presence, to attend him and to sing songs that honor him and lighten his cares. Others guard the cities and strongholds of the realm; others rout the king's enemies. Thus some of the soldiers of Christ always attend upon the King in his court, namely, in the empyrean heaven, and continually sing chants of joy and glory to him, saying: "Holy, holy, holy Lord, God of hosts!"[35] and "Benediction and glory and wisdom to our God for ever and ever!"[36] Others stand guard over the cities, country places, and fortified towns—in other words, the angels who are deputed to guard us and to watch over the chastity of virgins, the continency of married people, and the communities of religious. So we read in Isaiah: "Upon your walls, O Jerusalem, I have set watchmen."[37] Others rout the King's enemies, namely, the demons, and Revelation says: "There was a great battle in heaven, etc."[38] According to one interpretation, this refers to the battle in the Church militant, in which Michael and his angels fight against the dragon.

---

[27] Cf. Mal. 3:1. [28] Cf. Exod. 23:20. [29] Luke 16:22.
[30] Cf. Tob. 12:12. [31] Cf. Job 33:23–24. [32] Cf. Zech. 1:12.
[33] Cf. Dan. 9:23. [34] Job 25:3. [35] Isa. 6:3.
[36] Rev. 7:12. [37] Isa. 62:6. [38] Rev. 12:7.

Seventhly and lastly, the angels are to be honored because they console those in tribulation. In Zechariah we find mention of "the angel that spoke in me good words, comfortable words";[39] and in Tobias: "Be of good courage: thy cure from God is at hand."[40] This the angels do in three ways. First, they comfort and strengthen, as we find in Daniel. When Daniel had given up and had no strength left, the angel touched him and said: "Fear not, O man of desires, peace be to thee. Take courage and be strong!"[41] Second, they preserve us from impatience: "He will give his angels charge of you, to guard you in all your ways. On their hands they will bear you up, lest you dash your foot against a stone."[42] Third, they cool and allay affliction, and this is typified in Daniel, when the angels of the Lord descended to the three young men in the fiery furnace, and in the middle of the furnace it was as if a dewy breeze were blowing.

146. Saint Jerome

Jerome (Hieronymus in Latin) comes from *gerar*, holy, and *nemus*, a grove—hence a holy grove—or *noma*, a law. Therefore in his legend the saint's name is interpreted as sacred law. He was holy, i.e., firm, or clean, or wet with blood, or set apart for sacred use, as the temple vessels were said to be holy because they were kept apart for sacred uses. Jerome was holy, which is to say firm in doing good, by his long-suffering perseverance. He was clean in his mind through his purity, and wet with blood through his meditation on the Lord's passion. He was set apart for sacred usage in his exposition and interpretation of Holy Scripture. Or he is called a grove after the grove where he lived at times, and a law because of the religious rule that he taught his monks, and also because he expounded and interpreted the sacred law.

The name is also construed as meaning vision of beauty, or one who judges speech. Beauty is manifold. First of all, there is spiritual beauty, which is in the soul, secondly, moral beauty, which consists in propriety of conduct, thirdly, intellectual beauty, which is the beauty of the angels, fourthly, supersubstantial

---

[39] Zech. 1:12 (Douay).

[40] Tob. 5:13.

[41] Dan. 10:17-18.

[42] Ps. 90(91):11-12.

beauty, which is divine, fifthly, celestial beauty, which is the beauty of the saints in heaven. Jerome had this fivefold beauty and saw it in himself—the spiritual in the variety of his virtues, the moral in the propriety of his way of life, the intellectual in the excellence of his purity, the supersubstantial in the ardor of his love, the celestial in his eternal and excellent charity. He judged speech, whether his own or that of others, his own by carefully weighing his words, that of others by confirming what was true, refuting what was false, and exposing what was dubious.

Jerome was the son of a nobleman named Eusebius and was a native of the town of Stridon, which lay on the boundary between Dalmatia and Pannonia. While still a youth he went to Rome and became thoroughly proficient in the Latin, Greek, and Hebrew languages and letters. In the art of grammar his teacher was Donatus, in rhetoric the orator Victorinus. He labored day and night in the study of the divine Scriptures, drawing deep draughts from them and later pouring out his knowledge in abundance. There was a time, as he wrote in a letter to Eustochium, when he read Cicero by day and Plato by night, because the coarse language of the prophetic books displeased him.

Then, about halfway through Lent, he came down with a fever so sudden and so violent that his whole body was cold and the vital heat throbbed only in his chest. Preparations for his funeral were therefore under way when abruptly he was haled before the judge's tribunal. The judge asked him what his profession was, and he professed without hesitation that he was a Christian. "You lie!" the judge said. "You are no Christian, you are a Ciceronian, for where your treasure is, there is your heart also." Jerome did not answer, and the judge ordered him to be flogged severely. Then Jerome burst out: "Have mercy on me, O Lord, have mercy on me!" The people present pleaded with the judge to pardon the adolescent, who swore an oath and said: "O Lord, if ever I possess or read worldly books again, I will be denying you!" Hearing this, the judge dismissed him, and Jerome of a sudden regained his strength and found himself bathed in tears, and his shoulders terribly bruised from the flogging he had received at the tribunal. From then on he devoted as much study to godly books as previously he had given to pagan works.

At the age of twenty-nine Jerome was ordained a cardinal priest in the church of Rome, and when Pope Liberius died, Jerome was acclaimed by all to be worthy of the pontifical chair. But he had denounced some monks and clerics for their lascivious lives, and they were so resentful that they began to lay snares for him. John Beleth tells us, for instance, that they used a woman's clothing to create a false impression of him. He got up one morning to go to matins, as was his custom, and found at his bedside a woman's gown, which, thinking it was his own, he put on and so proceeded into the church. His adversaries, of course, had done this in order to make it look as if he had a woman in his room.

Jerome now saw how far these people would go in their insane folly, so he gave way to them and went to join Gregory of Nazianz, bishop of the city of Constantinople. After studying the Scriptures with Gregory, he retired to live in the desert. Later he wrote to Eustochium to tell her about his trials there: "How many times, living in the wilderness, in the vast solitude that provides a horrid, sun-scorched abode to monks, have I thought that I was basking amid the delights of Rome! My misshapen limbs shuddered in their sackcloth, my squalid skin had taken on the blackness of an Ethiopian's flesh. Tears all day, groans all day—and if, resist it as I might, sleep overwhelmed me, my fleshless bones, hardly holding together, scraped against the bare ground. I say nothing about food or drink: even the sick have cold water to drink, and to have some cooked food was like a sinful indulgence. All the company I had was scorpions and wild beasts, yet at times I felt myself surrounded by clusters of pretty girls, and the fires of lust were lighted in my frozen body and moribund flesh. So it was that I wept continually and starved the rebellious flesh for weeks at a time. Often I joined day to night and did not stop beating my breast until the Lord restored my peace of mind. I even dreaded my cell, haunted as it was with my thoughts. Angry and stern with myself I plunged alone, deeper and deeper, into the wasteland; and, as the Lord is my witness, from time to time and after many tears I seemed to be in the midst of throngs of angels."

After leading this penitential life in the desert for four years, Jerome went to the town of Bethlehem and offered himself to live, like a domestic animal, at the Lord's crib. He reread his own books, which he had kept safely stowed away, and other books as well. He fasted every day until sundown and gathered many disciples around him to follow the same holy way of life. For fifty-five years and six months he toiled at the translation of the Scriptures. He was a virgin to the end of his life—or so this legend says—but he once wrote about himself to Pammachius: "I hold virginity as high as heaven—not that I have it."

In time the saint was so worn out and weakened that he lay on his cot and had a rope hanging from an overhead beam, by which he pulled himself upright to follow the offices of the monastery as well as he could. One day toward evening, when he was seated with the brethren to hear the sacred lessons read, a lion suddenly limped into the monastery. The other monks fled at the sight of the beast, but Jerome greeted him as a guest. The lion showed him his wounded foot, and Jerome called the brothers and ordered them to wash the animal's feet and to dress the wound carefully. When they set about doing this, they found that the paw had been scratched and torn by thorns. They did what was necessary, and the lion recovered, lost all his wildness, and lived among the monks like a house pet.

By this time, however, Jerome sensed that the Lord had not sent them the lion for the health of the wounded paw, but so that the animal could render them some service. The saint therefore followed the advice of his monks and assigned a duty to the lion. The monks had an ass that carried firewood in from the forest, and it became the lion's chore to lead the ass out to pasture and to watch over her safety. And so it went. Once the care of the ass was enjoined upon the lion, they were constant companions. He guarded her like a faithful shepherd, going with her to pasture and being a most vigilant defender. He looked after his own food and the ass went about her accustomed work, but at fixed hours he led his charge home.

Then one day, when the ass was feeding and the lion fell into a deep sleep, some merchants passed that way with their camels and, seeing the ass unguarded, made off with her at once. When the lion woke up and did not see his companion, he ran hither and yon, roaring, but did not find the ass. He went sadly back to the monastery but was ashamed to go in as he usually did. The monks, seeing him come home late and without his ward, concluded that hunger had made him eat the ass. Therefore they would not give him his usual provisions and said to him: "Get out, and go eat what's left of the poor little ass, and satisfy your gluttony!"

The monks, however, found it hard to believe that the lion had done this bad thing, and they went out to the pastures to see if they could discover any sign of what had happened; but there was none, and they reported the whole matter to Jerome. At his suggestion they turned the ass's work over to the lion and loaded the cut wood on his back. The lion submitted to this patiently. Then one day, when his work was finished, he went out to the fields, running to and fro and hoping to learn what had become of his companion. Then at a distance he saw a train of merchants with their loaded camels, and an ass leading the way: in that region it is usual, in order to keep the camels on the right track when they have a long way to go, to have them follow an ass that leads them with a rope around its neck. The lion recognized his friend and with a terrifying roar rushed upon the caravan and put all the men to flight. Then, still roaring terribly and flailing the ground with his tail, he drove the frightened camels, laden as they were, toward the monastery. The monks saw them coming and notified Jerome, who said: "Wash the feet of our guests, dearest brothers! Offer them food, and above all, await the will of the Lord!"

Now the happy lion began to run around the monastery, prostrating himself before each brother and swishing his tail as if to beg pardon for the perpetrated fault although he had not committed it. Jerome, foreseeing what was about to happen, said to the monks: "Go, brothers, and get ready to provide our arriving guests with whatever they need!" He was still speaking when a messenger came to tell him that some visitors were outside and wanted to see the abbot. When Jerome went out to meet the merchants, they threw themselves at his feet, asking his pardon for the wrong they had done. He brought them kindly to their feet, and admonished them to take what was theirs and not to usurp what belonged to others. They prevailed upon Jerome to accept half their oil in return for his blessing. Reluctantly consenting, he accepted their offer. Furthermore they promised that every year the same measure of oil would be given to the monks, and that their heirs would be ordered to continue this practice.

In earlier times there had been no uniformity in the Church's offices or in the chant. Now Emperor Theodosius, as John Beleth tells us, asked Pope Damasus to charge some learned man with the work of bringing order to the liturgy. The pope, knowing that Jerome was expert in Greek and Hebrew and supreme in all kinds of knowledge, committed this task to him. Jerome distributed the Psalms for the days of the week, assigned a proper nocturne for each day, and specified that the *Gloria Patri* should be sung at the end of each Psalm, as Sigebert says. He also assigned the readings from the gospels and epistles to be sung throughout the cycle of the year, and put rational order into whatever else pertained to the office following the chant. He then sent the whole work from Bethlehem to the sovereign pontiff, and he, with his cardinals, gave it solemn approval and established it as standard for the whole Church in perpetuity. After that, Jerome arranged a tomb for himself at the mouth of the cave where the Lord had lain, and after living for ninety-eight years and six months, he died and was buried there.

The reverence in which Augustine held Jerome is patent in the letters he addressed to him. In one of them he wrote: "To Jerome, most dear lord worthy to be respected and embraced with the sincerest veneration and love, Augustine sends greetings." Elsewhere Augustine wrote of him: "The holy priest Jerome, learned in the Greek, Latin, and Hebrew speech, lived in holy places, and with the sacred writings, to an extreme old age, and, by the nobility of his discourse, shone from the East to the West like the light of the sun." Saint Prosper, in his *Chronicle*, says of him: "The priest Jerome lived in Bethlehem but was famed throughout the world, and served the Church universal with his rare intelligence and learning." To Albigensis Jerome said about himself: "From childhood on I have tried to avoid nothing so much as the prideful spirit and the haughty head that provoke the wrath of God"; also: "I fear all that is too safe"; also: "In the monastery we extend hospitality from the heart, welcome with gladsome countenance all who come to us except heretics, and wash our guests' feet." Isidore in his *Etymologies*, says: "Jerome was expert in three languages, and his interpretation is preferred to those of others because he is both closer to the letter and clearer in his perception of the meaning, and, since it comes from a Christian interpreter, truer." In his *Dialogue*, Severus, a disciple of Saint Martin and a contemporary of Saint Jerome, is held to have written about him: "Besides the merit of his faith and his endowment of virtues, he was so learned, not only in Latin and Greek but also in Hebrew letters, that no one dares to compare himself with him in any branch of knowledge. Against the wicked his fight was unceasing, his struggle relentless. Heretics hate him because he never stops attacking them. Clergy hate him because he berates their sinful lives and their crimes. But all good people admire and love him wholeheartedly. Those who consider him a heretic are insane. He is totally absorbed in study, totally in books. He rests neither by day nor by night: he is always either reading or writing." Thus Severus.

As is clear from these quotations, and as he himself has testified, he had to suffer the hostility of many persecutors and many detractors. How willingly he submitted to this persecution is obvious from what he says in a letter to Asella: "I thank God that I am thought worthy to have the world hate me and prattlers call me an evildoer, but I know how to get to heaven, whether others think well or ill of me"; also: "Would that for the honor of my Lord's name the whole mob of unbelievers might persecute me! Would that this world would rise up more stoutly to shame me! Only let me be worthy to be praised by Christ and to hope for his promised reward! Welcome indeed and desirable is that trial for which Christ's reward is hoped for in heaven, nor is that curse harmful which is transmuted by God's praise."

Jerome died about A.D. 398.[1]

147. Saint Remy

Remy (or Remi) is the English form of the Latin name Remigius, and this name is derived from *remigo*, a pilot, or from *remi*, oars, the implements by which a boat is moved, and *gyon*. a grappling or struggle. Saint Remy piloted the Church away from the danger of shipwreck, moved it to the gates of heaven, and struggled for it against the wiles of the devil.

We are told that Remy, who was the bishop of Rheims, converted King Clovis and the Frankish nation to Christ. The king's wife was named Clothilda. She was a devout Christian and strove to convert her husband to the faith, but could not. When she bore a son, she wanted him baptized, but the king firmly forbade it. The queen, however, could not keep quiet about it, and Clovis finally gave in. The child was baptized but died shortly afterward. Then the king said to Clothilda: "It is now clear that Christ is a poor sort of god, since he could not keep alive someone by whom his faith could have been exalted." Clothilda answered: "It's the other way around. I sense that what has happened shows

---

[1] The saint's dates are ca. 342–420.

how dearly God loves me! I know that he has accepted the first fruit of my womb and has granted my son an infinite kingdom, one better than your own!"

Clothilda conceived again and bore a son, who, like the first, was baptized only after the king's resistance had been overcome; and as soon as the child was baptized he fell ill and his life was despaired of. Clovis said to his wife: "This God of yours is a weak one, since he cannot keep alive anyone baptized in his name. If you bore a thousand children and all were baptized, they would all perish!" But this new son recovered and grew to manhood, and, long after, succeeded his father as king. For the present, however, Clothilda, that woman of faith, persisted in her effort to bring her husband to the faith of Christ, and he was equally persistent in refusing. How in the end he was converted and became a Christian is narrated in the legend for the other feast of Saint Remy, the one celebrated after Epiphany.[1]

After his conversion, King Clovis wanted to endow the church of Rheims. He told Saint Remy that he would give the church as much land as the bishop could walk around while he, the king, had his midday siesta, and Remy started to walk. However, there was a man who operated a mill that was within the bishop's boundaries, and when Remy approached it, the miller angrily ordered him away. Remy said: "Friend, why should it bother you if we share this mill?" But the miller repulsed him, and as soon as the bishop started to walk away, the mill began to turn in the reverse direction. The miller called after him: "Servant of God, come back and we shall share the mill equally!" Remy: "Not for me, not for you!" And the earth opened and swallowed the mill.

Now Remy foresaw that a famine was imminent, and filled a barn with a large supply of grain. Soon some drunken rustics, jeering at the old man's thriftiness, set fire to the barn. The bishop heard of this and came to the place, and, due to the chill of age and the late hour, warmed himself at the fire and said calmly: "Fire is always good; but those who set this fire, and their posterity, will suffer for it, the men from rupture and the women from goiter!" And so it befell, until Charlemagne dispersed the descendants.

It should be noted that the feast of Saint Remy which is celebrated in January is said to mark the day of his happy death and of the translation of his sacred body. What happened was that after his death his body was being transported on a litter to the church of Saints Timothy and Apollinaris, but as the litter was being carried past the church of Saint Christopher, it suddenly became so heavy that it could not be moved. The bearers, perplexed, prayed the Lord to let them know if perchance he wished that the body be buried in the church of Saint Christopher, where a thousand relics of saints reposed. At once the litter became very light and the body was honorably laid to rest. Many miracles occurred there, and the church was enlarged and a crypt built behind the altar for Saint

---

[1] See chapter 16 above.

Remy's remains, but when the body was unearthed and they tried to place it there, again it could not be moved. The ministers spent the night in prayer until they all fell asleep, and in the morning, on the first day of October, they found that angels had carried the coffin containing the saint's body to the new crypt. Much later, however, the sacred remains, in a silver casket, were enshrined in a more beautiful crypt.

Saint Remy flourished about the year A.D. 490.

148. Saint Leger

Leger (or Leodegar) was known for his virtuous life and was considered worthy to be made bishop of Autun. When King Clothar died and the care of the kingdom weighed heavily on Leger, by the will of God and with the consent of the princes he promoted Childeric, Clothar's adolescent brother, as the one fully suited to be king. Ebroin[1] wanted to secure the throne for Theoderic, Childeric's brother, not for the good of the realm but because Ebroin himself had been deposed from power, was hated by all, and feared the hostility of the king and the princes. Because of his fear he petitioned the king for permission and was allowed to retire to a monastery. The king also put his brother Theoderic in confinement to keep him from plotting against the throne. Thus, due to the bishop's holiness and foresight, the realm enjoyed a marvelous peace.

Some time later the king, deceived by disloyal counselors, was aroused to such hatred of the man of God that he sedulously sought both the opportunity to put him to death and the best way to do it. The bishop bore all this calmly and, embracing all his enemies as if they were friends, arranged that the king should celebrate the feast of Easter with him in his episcopal city. That very day, however, it was made known to him that the ruler had ordered him to be done to death on Easter night. Fearing nothing, Leger dined with the king as arranged, but then escaped from his persecutor and fled to the monastery of Luxeuil. There he served the Lord and with unfailing charity waited on Ebroin, who was hiding there under a monk's habit.

---

[1] Ebroin had been "mayor of the palace," in Merovingian times a position second only to the king's.

A short time later King Childeric died, and Theoderic was raised to the throne. Then Leger, moved by the tears and pleading of his people and constrained by the abbot's command, returned to his episcopal see. At the same time Ebroin abandoned religion and was appointed seneschal to the king. If he had been evil before, he then became more evil and spent all his energy in his effort to bring about Leger's death. He sent soldiers to take him captive, and when the bishop learned this, he went outside his city, wearing his pontifical robes, to face their fury. They laid hold of him and put out his eyes.

Two years later Leger was brought to the royal palace with his brother Garin, whom Ebroin had exiled. He responded wisely and peacefully to Ebroin's derisive taunts, but the wicked man ordered Garin to be stoned to death, and the holy bishop to be marched barefoot for a whole day through a stream that flowed over sharp stones. When he heard that Leger praised God while enduring these torments, he had his tongue cut out and then handed him over to another guard to be held for new tortures. Leger, however, did not lose the power of speech, but applied himself to preaching and exhortation as well as he could. He also foretold when and how he and Ebroin would meet their several ends. A wide and brilliant light circled his head like a crown, and many who saw this asked the bishop what it was; but he prostrated himself in prayer, giving thanks to God, and admonished all the onlookers to mend their lives for the better.

These events came to Ebroin's ears, and his wrath knew no bounds. He sent four swordsmen with orders to behead Leger. As they led him toward a suitable place, he said to them: "There's no need, brothers, to tire yourselves any longer. Do here what the one who sent you wants you to do!" Thereupon three of them were so stricken with remorse that they fell at his feet and begged for pardon, and the fourth, after beheading him, was immediately seized by a demon and cast into a fire, thus coming to a miserable end.

Two more years passed, and Ebroin heard that the holy man's body had become famous for the many miracles that occurred around it. He sent a soldier to find out whether there was any truth to this rumor, and if so to let him know. The soldier, a haughty, arrogant fellow, came to the saint's tomb, kicked it, and exclaimed: "Death to anyone who believes that a dead man can perform wonders!" At once he was snatched up by a demon and died then and there, by his death further confirming the bishop's holiness. News of this threw Ebroin into paroxysms of rage, and he determined afresh to stamp out the saint's renown, but as Leger had predicted, the wicked man was killed wickedly by the sword.

Leger suffered about A.D. 680, in the reign of Constantine IV.

149. Saint Francis

Francis was born in Assisi, he was first named John but later was called Francis. It appears that there were several reasons for this change of names. The first was to call attention to a miracle, because he is known to have received miraculously from God the power to speak in the French language. Hence we read in his legend that whenever he was filled with the ardor of the Holy Spirit, he burst out with ardent words in French. The second reason was to make his mission manifest: his legend says that divine providence conferred this name upon him, in order that by the unusual name awareness of his mystery might be spread more quickly throughout the whole world. Third reason, to indicate the effect that was to follow from his ministry—in other words, to make it known that he, through his own work and that of his sons, was to free and enfranchise many slaves of sin and the devil. Fourth reason, his greatness of soul: the name French, or Frankish, *français* is derived from ferocitas, fierceness, the quality of high-spiritedness and impetuosity, because in the French there is a natural truthfulness and magnanimity. Fifth reason, the saint's virtuosity in speech: his speech was like an ax that chopped out vices. Sixth, the terror he aroused in driving out demons. Seventh, his security in virtue, the perfection of his works, and his honorable dealings with others. It is said that the term *franciscae* is used for the ax-shaped insignia which were carried before consuls in Rome, and which stood for terror, security, and honor.

Francis, servant and friend of the Almighty, was born in the city of Assisi. He became a merchant and, until he was twenty years old, lived a vain and frivolous life. The Lord chastened him with the whip of ill health and quickly made a different man of him, and he began to exhibit the spirit of prophecy. Once he and a number of companions were captured by the Perugians and confined in a horrid prison, where the others bemoaned their fate while Francis alone rejoiced. When his fellow prisoners rebuked him, he answered: "Know that I rejoice now because in time the whole world will worship me as a saint!" Another time he went to Rome for reasons of devotion. When he got there, he put off his fine clothes and dressed in a beggar's rags, then sat with the other beggars at the door of Saint Peter's church and grabbed hungrily for food like any of them. He would have done this more often but was dissuaded because it embarrassed those who knew him.

The ancient enemy tried to turn Francis aside from his virtuous intention and forced the image of a hunchback woman upon his mind, warning him that if he did not give up the way of life he had undertaken, the devil would make him as ugly as she was. Then, however, he heard the Lord comforting him and saying: "Francis, take the bitter instead of the sweet, and despise yourself if you long to know me!" Then he found himself face to face with a leper, the sort of man he utterly abhorred; but, remembering the Lord's word to him, he ran and kissed the afflicted man. The leper instantly vanished. Francis then hastened to the place where people with leprosy lived, devoutly kissed their hands, and left them money.

He went into the church of Saint Damian to pray, and an image of Christ spoke to him miraculously: "Francis, go and repair my house, because, as you see, it has fallen into ruins!" From that moment on his soul melted within him, his compassion for Christ was marvelously fixed in his heart, and he devoted himself zealously to the rebuilding of the Church. He sold all he had and wanted to give the money to a certain priest, but the priest refused to accept it for fear of offending Francis's parents. Francis thereupon threw the money on the ground, treating it as worth no more than dust. His father therefore had him bound and held in custody, whereupon he gave all his money to his father, and with it the clothes off his back. Then he flew naked to the Lord and put on a hair shirt. The servant of God next called in a plain, simple man whom he took as a father, and asked him to bless him whenever his true father heaped curses on him.

His blood brother, seeing Francis at prayer clothed in rags and shivering with the wintry cold, said to a companion: "Tell Francis to give you a penny's worth of his sweat!" Francis heard this and quickly retorted: "In fact I sell it to my Lord!" Another day, hearing what Jesus said to his disciples as he sent them off to preach, Francis rose immediately to carry out to the letter what he had heard, took the shoes off his feet, put on a single cheap garment, and exchanged his leather belt for a length of rope. Then he was walking through the woods in winter when thieves laid hold of him and asked him who he was. He declared that he was the herald of God, so they threw him into the snow, saying: "Lie there, you peasant, herald of God!"

Many people, of noble and of humble birth, both clerical and lay, put away the world's vanities and followed his path. Like a father, this holy man taught them to strive for evangelical perfection, to embrace poverty, and to walk the way of holy simplicity. He also wrote a Rule, based on the Gospel, for himself and his present and future friars: this Rule was approved by the lord Pope Innocent. From then on Francis began with even greater fervor to sow the seeds of the word of God, going about from city to city and town to town.

There was a friar who seemed from the outside to be a man of remarkable sanctity but was not at all like the others in his conduct. He observed the rule of silence so extravagantly that he made his confession with nods of the head, not speaking. All the friars were praising him as a saint when the man of God came along and said: "Leave off, brothers! Do not praise his diabolical illusions to me!

Let him be admonished to confess his sins once or twice a week! If he does not do this, it's all diabolical temptation, fraud, deception!" The friars admonished this brother, but he silenced them with his finger to his lips and shook his head to indicate that he had nothing to confess. After a few days he returned to his peculiar ways, and ended his life in criminal actions.

Once when the servant of God, too tired to walk farther, was riding on an ass, his companion, Friar Leonardo of Assisi, who also was tired, thought to himself: "This man's parents were not so wellborn as mine." At that moment Francis dismounted and said to Leonardo: "It is not right for me to ride and you to walk, because you are of nobler stock than I." Astonished, the friar knelt at Francis's feet and asked forgiveness.

He was walking along the road one day when a certain noble lady, almost running in her haste, came to meet him. Seeing how tired and out of breath she was, he felt sorry for her and asked her what she wanted. The lady said: "Pray for me, father, because I had made a resolution to lead a virtuous life, but my husband prevents me from living up to it and makes every effort to keep me from serving Christ." Francis: "Go home, my daughter, because you will soon receive consolation from him; and in the name of almighty God and in my name, tell him that now is the time of salvation, and later will come the time of just reward." She conveyed the saint's message, and the husband, suddenly changing his attitude, promised to live continently.

For a peasant who was fainting with thirst in the desert, Francis, by his prayer, obtained a spring of water.

Prompted by the Holy Spirit, he disclosed a secret to a friar who was close to him, saying: "Today there is on earth a certain servant of God, for whose sake, as long as he lives, the Lord will not allow famine to scourge the people"; and there is no doubt that that was the situation during the saint's lifetime. But once he was taken away, things changed. Not long after his happy death he appeared to the aforementioned friar and said: " Now you will see the coming of the famine, which, while I was alive, the Lord would not allow on earth."

On Easter Sunday the friars laid the table more carefully than usual, with white linens and glass vessels. When the man of God saw this, he turned away, picked up a poor man's cap that was lying there, put it on his head, and, staff in hand, went out and waited at the door. When the friars sat down to eat, he called out at the door, asking them for the love of God to give an alms to a poor, enfeebled pilgrim. The poor man was called in and entered, sat down on the ground alone, and set his dish in the ashes. The friars were shocked at seeing this, but Francis said to them: "I saw the table all set and decorated, but of the poor men begging from door to door I did not see a single one here."

He loved poverty in himself and in others so much that he always spoke of his Lady Poverty, and, when he saw someone poorer than himself, he envied him and was afraid he might be outdone by him. One day he saw a poor little man passing by and said to his companion: "That man's neediness puts us to shame;

it makes a false show of our poverty. For my riches I chose my Lady Poverty, but you see that she is more glorified in him than in me."

A poor man was walking by, and at the sight of him Francis was moved with compassion, but his companion said to him: "Poor he may be at the moment, but perhaps in the whole province there is no one as rich as he would like to be." The man of God said: "Quick, take off your cloak and give it to that man, and kneel down at his feet and confess your guilt!" And the friar obeyed forthwith.

One day three women, alike in figure and finery, confronted him and greeted him with the words: "Welcome to Lady Poverty!" They disappeared at once and were seen no more.

Once when he went to the city of Arezzo, where civil strife had broken out, he looked down from a high point above the town and saw demons exulting over the disorder below them. Francis called his companion, whose name was Silvester, and said to him: "Go to the city gate, and in the name of almighty God order the demons to leave the city!" Silvester hurried to the gate and called out loudly: "In the name of almighty God and by order of our father Francis, go away, all you demons!" And in a short time the townspeople made peace.

While Silvester was still a secular priest, he had a dream in which he saw a gold cross issuing from the mouth of Francis. Its high point touched the heavens, and its extended arms embraced and held the world from east to west. The priest was smitten with self-reproach, abandoned the world, and became a perfect imitator of the man of God.

While Francis was at prayer, the devil called him three times by name. The saint responded, and the devil added: "In the whole world there is not a single sinner to whom the Lord will not grant pardon if he repents; but if someone kills himself with excessive penances, he will not obtain mercy forever." By a revelation, the saint instantly recognized the lie and the liar, and saw how the demon was trying to cool his ardor to lukewarmness. The ancient enemy, seeing that his effort was of no avail, aroused in Francis a violent temptation of the flesh, but the man of God, feeling this, took off his habit and scourged himself with a coarse rope, saying to his body: "See here, brother ass! Either behave yourself or take a beating!" But the temptation persisted, so the saint went out and threw himself naked into the deep snow. Then he made seven snowballs, which he set in front of him, and spoke again to his body: "Look here," he said, "the biggest ball is your wife, the next four are two sons and two daughters, and the last two are a manservant and a maidservant. Hurry up and clothe them, they're dying of cold! Or, if it bothers you to give them so much attention, then serve the Lord with care!" Thereupon the devil went away in confusion, and the man of God returned to his cell glorifying his Lord.

The lord cardinal Leo of the Holy Cross once invited Francis to be his guest, and he stayed in his house for some time. One night demons came and gave the saint a severe beating. He called his companion and explained the thing to him: "The demons are the Lord's bailiffs, whom he sends to punish excesses. I do not recall an offense that I have not washed away by the Lord's mercy and my penance, but it may be that he has allowed his bailiffs to attack me because the fact that I am lingering in the courts of the powerful could awaken a justified suspicion in my poor little brothers, who may think I am lolling in luxury." So he rose at dawn and left the cardinal's palace.

Sometimes when he was at prayer, he heard troops of demons running around noisily on the roof of the house. When that happened, he ran outside, armed himself with the sign of the cross, and said: "In the name of almighty God I tell you, demons, whatever you are allowed to do to my body, do it! I will gladly submit to whatever it may be, because I have no greater enemy than my body, and you avenge me upon my adversary when, acting for me, you wreak punishment on it." The demons were dumbfounded and scurried away.

A friar who was a close associate of Francis was rapt in ecstasy, and saw, among the other seats in heaven, one that was particularly distinguished and glorious. He wondered who might be the saint for whom so noble a throne was reserved, and heard a voice saying: "That chair belonged to one of the fallen princes and now has been made ready for humble Francis." Emerging from prayer, the friar questioned the man of God, saying: "What do you think of this, father?" Francis: "To myself I seem to be the greatest of sinners." At once the Spirit said in the friar's heart: "Know by this how true your vision was, because humility will raise the humblest of men to the seat that was lost through pride."

The servant of God had a vision in which he saw above him a crucified Seraph, who imprinted the signs of crucifixion upon him, so that he himself seemed to have been crucified. His hands, feet, and side were marked with the signature of the cross, but he with great care hid the stigmata from the eyes of all. There were some, however, who saw them while the saint was alive, and after his death many observed them. That these marks were truly the stigmata of the crucifixion was confirmed by many miracles, of which it will suffice to insert two that occurred after the saint's death.

In Apulia a man named Roger was standing in front of a painting of Saint Francis and began to ask himself whether what he saw was true: had the saint really been honored by such a miracle, or was this a pious illusion or a fraud contrived by his friars? As he turned these thoughts over in his mind, he heard a sound like that of an arrow being shot from a crossbow, and felt that he was painfully wounded in the left hand, though his glove seemed to be undamaged. He took the glove off, found a deep wound such as an arrow would make, and so much heat came from it that he felt he would faint with the pain and the burning. He repented his doubt and testified that he firmly believed in Saint Francis's stigmata. Two days later, as he pleaded with the saint by his stigmata, the man's wound was healed.

This happened in the kingdom of Castille. A man who was devoted to Saint Francis was on his way to assist at the office of compline when he was ambushed by mistake in a trap set for another man and was left half dead of a lethal wound. Then the cruel murderer drove his sword into the man's throat, but could not pull the sword out and went away. From all sides people came running and loudly bewailed the man for dead. Then, when at midnight the bell of the friars' convent rang for matins, the man's wife called out: "Master, get up and go to matins, the bell is calling you!" The man raised his hand as if to summon someone to extract the sword; but, as all looked on, the sword, as if hurled by the hand of a brawny fighter, leapt out and fell at a distance. The man, fully restored to health, stood up and said: "Blessed Francis came to me and touched his stigmata to my wounds, and their sweetness spread over all my hurts and the contact healed them wondrously; and when he was about to go away, I signaled to him to remove the sword, because otherwise I could not talk. So he grasped the sword and hurled it away, and at once, by stroking the wounded throat with his holy stigmata, he cured it perfectly."

In the city of Rome two shining lights of the world, Saint Francis and Saint Dominic, met with the bishop of Ostia, who later became the supreme pontiff. The bishop asked them: "Why do we not make some of your friars bishops and popes, since they stand out from the rest by their teaching and example?" The two saints argued for some time about which of them should respond and how. Humility conquered Francis, keeping him from being the first to answer: it also conquered Dominic, since he humbly obeyed by answering first. Blessed Dominic therefore said: "My lord, my friars have already attained a high status, if they only knew it. For my part, I cannot allow them to be raised higher, lest they pursue marks of dignity other than what they already possess." After him Saint Francis spoke: "My lord, my friars are called Minor, lest they presume to be made greater."

Blessed Francis was filled with the simplicity of the dove. He exhorted all creatures to love their Creator. He preached to the birds and they listened to him; he taught them and they did not fly away without his permission. When swallows were chattering when he was preaching, he bade them be silent and they obeyed. At the Portiuncula a locust that nested in a fig tree next to his cell used to sing at all hours, until the man of God extended his hand and said: "My sister locust, come here to me!" Obediently the locust came up and rested on his hand. "My sister locust, sing! Sing, and praise your Lord!" The locust began to sing and did not hop away until the saint gave permission.

The saint would not handle lanterns and lamps and candles because he did not want to dim their brightness with his hands. He walked reverently on stones out of respect for him who was called Peter, which means stone. He lifted worms from the road for fear they might be trampled underfoot by passersby. Bees might perish in the cold of winter, so he had honey and fine wines set out for them. He called all animals brothers and sisters. When he looked at the sun, the moon, and the stars, he was filled with inexpressible joy by his love of the

Creator and invited them all to love their Creator. He would not have a large crown[1] shaved on his head, and said: "I want my simple brothers to have a share in my head."

A certain man of the world heard the servant of God preaching in the church of Saint Severinus and, by God's revelation, saw Saint Francis pierced through and through by two gleaming swords in the form of a cross, one of them passing from his head to his feet, the other passing through his chest from one outstretched hand to the other. The man had never seen Francis before but recognized him by this sign. Moved by compunction he retired from the world, entered the Order, and finished his life in holy living.

His eyesight was impaired by his constant weeping, but, to those who urged him not to weep so much, he replied: "The visitation of eternal light is not to be repelled for love of the light we have in common with the flies." His friars pressed him to allow a remedy to be applied to his failing eyes, and he held in his hand an iron surgical instrument heated in the fire. He said: "My brother fire, at this hour be kind to me and cure me! I pray the Lord who created you to mitigate your heat for me." Having said these words, he made the sign of the cross over the instrument, and when it was thrust through the tender flesh from ear to eyebrow, he himself said that he felt no pain.

He was in the desert of Saint Urban when he was stricken with a serious illness, and when he realized that his strength was waning, he asked for a cup of wine, but wine there was none to be had. He was given a cup of water and blessed it with the sign of the cross, and straightaway it was changed into an excellent wine. What the poverty of that desolate place could not supply the holy man's purity obtained, and at the first sip of wine he was healthy again.

He preferred to hear himself reviled rather than praised, and when people extolled the merits of his sanctity, he ordered one of the friars to assail his ears with abusive epithets. The friar, all unwilling, called him a bumpkin, a money-lover, an ignoramus, and a worthless fellow, and Francis cheered and said: "Lord bless you, brother! You have told the truth, and I need to hear such things!" The servant of God wished not so much to be in command as to be subject to authority, not so much to give orders as to carry them out. Therefore he gave up the office of general of his Order, and asked for a guardian, to whose will he would be subject in everything. To the friar with whom he was accustomed to go about he always promised obedience and always kept his promise.

A friar had done something forbidden by the rule of obedience, but then repented. To strike terror in others, however, the man of God ordered the delinquent friar's cowl to be thrown into the fire, and then, when it had been in the fire for some time, taken out and returned to the one it belonged to.

---

[1] The reference is to the tonsure, an area of the scalp shaved as a mark of the clerical or religious state. The tonsure was also called a crown, because there were, and are, various shapes of tonsure, one or more of which might suggest a crown.

The cowl, therefore, was snatched from the flames and showed not a trace of scorching.

Once when Francis was walking through the Venetian marshes, he came upon a large flock of birds singing, and said to his companion: "Our sisters the birds are praising their Creator. Let's go in among them and chant the canonical hours to the Lord!" They walked in among the birds and the birds did not move away, but their chirping was so noisy that the two friars could not hear each other. Francis said: "Sister birds, stop your singing until we pay our debt of praise to the Lord!" The birds were quiet until the friars had sung lauds, after which they received permission and resumed their singing as usual.

He was courteously invited to dinner by a knight, to whom he said: "Brother host, take my advice and confess your sins, because you will soon dine elsewhere." The knight quickly followed this advice, put his house in order, and accepted a salutary penance; and as they went in to dinner, the host suddenly expired.

He came upon a large flock of birds and spoke to them as though they were rational beings, saying: "My brother birds, you owe a great debt of praise to your Creator, who clothes you with feathers, gives you wings to fly with, grants you the purity of the air, and without effort on your part he sustains you." The birds began to stretch their necks toward him, spread their wings, opened their beaks, and fixed their eyes upon him. He walked through the middle of the flock and his cloak touched them, but not one of them moved an inch until, permission given, they all flew away at once.

Francis was preaching at the castle of Almarium but could not be heard because of the loud chirping of swallows that nested nearby. He said to them: "My sister swallows, you've said enough! Now it's my turn to talk, and you keep quiet till the word of the Lord has been spoken!" Obediently they hushed their chatter at once.

The man of God was passing through Apulia and came upon a pouch bursting with coins, lying on the road. His companion wanted to take the pouch and distribute the money to the poor, but Francis would have none of it and said: "My son, it is not right to make off with someone else's property." But the friar insisted vehemently, and Francis, after praying for a moment, ordered him to pick up the pouch, which now contained a viper in place of the coins. Seeing this the friar was afraid but, wishing to obey and to do as ordered, took the pouch in his hands, and a large serpent sprang out. "To the servants of God," said the saint, "money is nothing but the devil and a poisonous snake."

There was a friar who was plagued with temptation. He thought that if he had a script in the father's handwriting, the temptation would be driven away, but he did not dare to broach the matter to the saint. Then came a moment when the man of God called this friar and said to him: "Bring me paper and ink, my son, I want to write words of praise to God." When he had written them, he said: "Take this paper and keep it carefully until the day of your death," and all temptation left the friar at once. When the saint was lying ill, this same friar began to think: "Here our father is approaching death, and what a consolation it would be for me if I could have my father's cloak after he died!" Shortly afterwards Saint Francis called him and said: "I hand this cloak over to you now, and after my death it will be yours by right."

He was the guest of a man of good repute in Alessandria in Lombardy, and his host asked him to eat everything that was set before him, in accordance with the Gospel. In deference to the host's devotion the saint agreed, and the good man hurried off to prepare a fine seven-year-old capon for dinner. While they were eating, an unbeliever came and begged an alms for the love of God. Hearing God's blessed name, Francis sent a leg of the capon out to the beggar. The wretched man kept the gift, and the next day, while the saint was preaching, the fellow showed it to everyone, saying: "Look at the kind of fine food this friar eats, for he gave me this last evening!" But the capon's leg now looked like a fish to all who saw it, and they rebuffed the man as insane. The man was ashamed and asked pardon, and, once he had come to his senses, the meat looked like a capon's leg again.

Once when the man of God was seated at table and heard a reading on the poverty of the Blessed Virgin and her Son, he rose abruptly from the table, sobbing and weeping, and ate the rest of his bread sitting on the bare ground.

He always manifested deep reverence for the hands of priests,[2] hands empowered to produce the sacrament of Christ's Body. He often said: "If I happened to meet at the same time a saint coming down from heaven and some poor little priest, I would hurry first to kiss the priest's hands and would say to the saint: 'Wait for me, Saint Laurence, because this man's hands have handled the Word of life and possess something beyond the human.'"

In his lifetime he was known for his many miracles. Bread that was brought to him to be blessed by him restored health to many sick people. He changed water into wine, which a sick man tasted and recovered his health immediately. And he performed many other miracles.

Finally he was suffering from a long illness and knew that his last days were at hand. He had himself laid on the bare ground and had all the friars who were with him summoned to his presence. He laid his hands on each of them, blessed all present, and distributed to each a morsel of bread in the manner of the Lord's Supper. As was his custom, he invited all creatures to praise God, even exhorting death itself, terrible and hated by all, to join in praise. He met death joyfully and invited her to be his guest, saying: "Welcome, my sister Death!" His last hour came, and he fell asleep in the Lord.

One of his friars saw his soul like a star, as large as the moon and as bright as the sun. The minister of the friars who worked on the farms, whose name was

---

[2] Francis, by reason of humility, chose not to be ordained to the priesthood. He was an ordained deacon.

Augustine, was also in his last hour. He had long since lost the power of speech, but suddenly he cried out: "Wait for me, father, wait! See, I am coming with you!" The brothers asked him what he meant, and he said: "Don't you see our father Francis, who is on his way to heaven?" And he slept in peace and followed the father.

A lady who had been devoted to Saint Francis had gone the way of all flesh, and clerics and priests were present at her bier to celebrate her funeral rites. Suddenly she sat up on the bier and called to one of the priests, saying: "I want to confess, father! I had died and was about to be committed to a horrid dungeon, because I had not yet confessed the sin I shall now reveal to you. But Saint Francis prayed for me and obtained permission for me to return to my body, in order that by confessing this sin I may merit forgiveness, and once I have made the sin known, I shall sleep in peace in the sight of all of you." So she confessed, received absolution, and fell asleep in the Lord.

When the friars at Vicera asked a certain man to lend them a cart, he answered indignantly: "I would sooner skin two of you alive, and Saint Francis with you, than let you use my cart!" But then he came to his senses and chided himself for the blasphemy, fearing God's wrath. Soon his son fell ill and died. When the man saw his son dead, he rolled on the ground in grief, shed tears, and invoked Saint Francis, saying: "I am the one who sinned! You should have laid the scourge to me! O Saint, give back to the one now devoutly beseeching you what you have taken from the one who impiously blasphemed you!" His son arose and put a stop to the breast-beating. "When I died," he said, "Saint Francis led me by a long, dark road, set me down in a beautiful garden, and then said to me: 'Go back now to your father, I won't detain you any longer!'"

A poor man who owed a rich man a sum of money asked the rich man, for the love of Saint Francis, to give him more time to pay. The rich man answered haughtily: "I will shut you up in a place where neither Francis nor anyone else will be able to help you!" And he confined the poor man, chained, in a dark prison. Not long afterwards Saint Francis was there, broke into the prison, undid the man's chains, and brought him home unharmed.

There was a knight who belittled the works and miracles of Saint Francis. Once when he was playing at dice, filled as he was with folly and having no faith, he said to those around him: "If Francis is a saint, let the dice come up eighteen!" On his first throw, three sixes turned up, and in nine subsequent throws he had the same result every time. Then, adding lunacy to folly, he said: "If your Francis be a saint, may my body fall beneath the sword this day; but if he is not a saint, I shall escape unscathed!" In order that his prayer should become a sin, when the game was over, he did his nephew a wrong, and the nephew took a sword and plunged it into his uncle's belly, thus killing him.

A certain man had a leg so far consumed with disease that he could not move, and he called upon Saint Francis with these words: "Help me, Saint Francis! Be mindful of the devotion and the service I have rendered you! I let you ride my ass, I kissed your holy feet and hands, and look! I am dying with the pain of this awful affliction!" The saint soon appeared to him carrying a small stick shaped like a T, and touched the diseased leg with the stick. The abscess broke and the leg healed immediately, but the mark of the T remained imprinted on it. Saint Francis used to sign his letters with this same mark.

In Pomereto, a town in the hills of Apulia, a young girl, the only child of her father and mother, had died, and the mother, who was devoted to Saint Francis, was beside herself with grief. The saint appeared to her and said: "Don't cry, because the light of your lantern, which you mourn because it is extinguished, is to be returned to you through my intercession." The mother, therefore, felt renewed confidence and would not allow the corpse to be taken away. Rather she invoked the name of Saint Francis, took her dead daughter's hand, and raised her up in good health.

In the city of Rome a little boy fell out of a window of his house and was killed, but Saint Francis was invoked and the child was restored to life. And in the city of Susa a house collapsed and crushed a young man to death. His mother besought Saint Francis with her whole heart, and about midnight the youth yawned, got up unhurt, and burst out in words of praise.

Friar James of Rieti had crossed a river with some brothers in a small boat and had put his companions on the other bank. He was preparing to step ashore himself, when the skiff overturned and sank to the bottom. The friars called upon Saint Francis to save the drowning man, and he himself did his best to invoke the saint's aid. Well! The aforesaid friar began to walk on the river bottom as on dry land, took hold of the sunken craft, and brought it to land. His clothing was not dampened, nor had as much as a drop of water clung to his cloak.

150. Saint Pelagia

Pelagia was first among the women in the city of Antioch—first in possessions and wealth, and in beauty of form. She was also ostentatious and vain in her bearing, and licentious in mind and body.

One day she was promenading through the city with a maximum of display: one could see nothing on her but gold and silver and precious stones, and, as she passed, the air was filled with the aroma of a variety of perfumes. Ahead of her and following her went a retinue of youths and maidens, likewise richly adorned. She was seen by a holy father, Veronus, bishop of Heliopolis (now called Damietta), who began to weep bitterly because the woman put more care into pleasing the world than he did into pleasing God. He threw himself face down on the pavement, beating his brow on the ground, and bedewed the earth with his tears, saying: "Almighty God, pardon me, a sinner, because the attention a courtesan has given to her adornment for one day exceeds the effort of my whole life. Do not let the outward show of a harlot put me to shame in the sight of your awesome majesty! She adorns herself for earthly eyes with the utmost care, whereas I, having resolved to please you, my immortal Lord, fail to do so because of my negligence." To those who were with him he said: "I say to you in truth, God will bring this woman forward against us at the Judgment, because to please her earthly lovers she had painted herself so meticulously, and we give so little care to pleasing our heavenly Spouse!"

Having said these and similar things, Veronus suddenly fell asleep and dreamed that while he was celebrating mass, a black, malodorous dove flew around him, but when he dismissed the catechumens, the dove disappeared. After mass it came back, and the bishop plunged it into a tub of water. The dove came out clean and shining white, and flew away so high that it could no longer be seen, and the bishop woke up.

Then one day he went to the church and preached. Pelagia was present and was so stricken with remorse that she sent a letter to him, in which she said: "To the holy bishop, disciple of Christ, Pelagia, disciple of the devil. If you prove truly to be a disciple of Christ, who, I have heard, came down from heaven for sinners, you will receive me, a sinner but a repentant one." Veronus sent back an answer: "I beg you not to tempt my humility, because I am a sinful man; but if you truly wish to be saved, you may not see me alone, but you will see me along with others."

Pelagia came to him with other people present. She clasped his feet, wept profusely, and said: "I am Pelagia, a sea of iniquity cresting with waves of sin; I am an abyss of perdition; I am a whirlpool, a sink to catch souls. I have misled many and deceived them, and now I shudder at the thought of all this!" The bishop questioned her: "What is your name?" She answered: "At birth I was named Pelagia, but now they call me Margaret, the Pearl,[1] because of the preciousness of my attire." The bishop then raised her kindly, imposed a salutary penance upon her, diligently instructed her in the fear of God, and gave her rebirth in holy baptism.

The devil was present and began to cry out: "Oh, the violence that I suffer at the hands of this decrepit old man! Oh, injustice! Oh, evil old age! Cursed be the day you were born to oppose me and to rob me of my greatest hope!" Then one night, when Pelagia was asleep, the devil came to her and awakened her, and

---

[1] *Margarita* is the Latin word for pearl.

said: "Lady Margaret, what wrong have I ever done you? Have I not made you rich and famous? I ask you, tell me in what way I have disappointed you, and I will quickly make amends. Only, I beg of you, do not abandon me, or I will become an object of shame in the eyes of Christians!" But Pelagia made the sign of the cross and blew at the devil, and he vanished. On the third day thereafter, she prepared and assembled everything she owned and gave it all to the poor. A few days later, without letting anyone know, she left by night and went to Mount Olivet, where she donned the robe of a hermit, moved into a small cell, and served God in strict abstinence. She was held in high esteem and was called Brother Pelagius.

Some time later one of the aforesaid bishop's deacons went to Jerusalem to visit the holy places. The bishop told him that after he had made his visitations, he should look for a monk named Pelagius and go to meet with him, since he was a true servant of God. The deacon did this and was recognized by Pelagia, but she was so emaciated that he did not know her. Pelagia asked him: "Do you have a bishop?" "Indeed I do!" he answered. Pelagia: "May he pray the Lord for me, because he is truly an apostle of Christ!"

Three days later the deacon returned to her cell, but when he knocked at the door and no one answered, he opened the window and found her, and saw that she was dead. He hurried to make this known to the bishop, and he, with the clergy and all the monks, gathered to give solemn burial to the holy man. When they removed the body from the cell and saw that it was the body of a woman, they marveled and gave thanks to God, and gave her honorable burial. She died about A.D. 290.

151. Saint Margaret

Margaret, also called Pelagius, was a very beautiful woman, a virgin, rich and of noble birth. She was raised by her parents and taught to live virtuously with such solicitous care, and such were her integrity and modesty that she took every means to avoid being seen by men. The time came when a young man of the nobility sought her hand in marriage, and both her parents consented. Everything was prepared for the wedding with lavish expenditure for elegance and pleasure. The wedding day arrived, and the young gallants and winsome maidens, and the whole nobility of the city, gathered for the celebration around the elaborately garlanded wedding chamber. God, however, put it in the virgin Margaret's mind to ponder how the loss of virginity was preluded by such abandoned revels. She threw herself weeping on the ground, weighing in her heart the glory of the virgin state as compared with the cares of wedlock, until she repudiated the joys of that kind of life as so much dung. That night she abstained from consorting with her husband, and in the middle of the night, recommending herself to God, she cut off her hair, put on man's clothes, and secretly got away.

After a long journey she came to a monastery and, calling herself Brother Pelagius, was welcomed by the abbot and instructed in the ways of the community. There she lived a holy and deeply religious life. When the director of a convent of nuns died, Pelagius, by the consent of the elders and the abbot's order, and despite her own reluctance, was placed as director of this monastery of consecrated virgins, for whom she continuously and blamelessly provided both bodily and spiritual nourishment.

Meanwhile the devil, envious of her prosperous course, sought to impede it by placing the appearance of wrongdoing in her way. He lured one of the nuns, who worked outside the convent, into a sin of adultery, and in time the roundness of her belly could no longer be hidden. Great were the shame and grief felt by all the nuns and monks of both monasteries; and, since Pelagius was in charge of the convent and the only man on familiar terms with its people, all the monks and nuns condemned him without trial or judgment, forced him out ignominiously, and confined him in a rocky cave. They also appointed the strictest of the monks to supply the prisoner with a minimum amount of barley bread and water. Pelagius bore all this patiently and allowed nothing to disturb her, but thanked God at all times and found comfort in the examples of the saints.

Time passed, and she knew that her end was near. She therefore wrote the following letter to the abbot and the monks: "I am of noble birth. In the world I was called Margaret but took the name Pelagius to help me across the sea[1] of temptation. It was not for purposes of deception that I allowed myself to be taken for a man, as I have shown by my deeds. From the crime of which I was accused I have gained virtue; though innocent I have done penance. Now I ask that the holy sisters bury the one who men did not know was a woman. These women will recognize that I am a virgin, and what they learn from my dead body will be the vindication of my life, though slanderers judged me to be an adulterer."

When the monks and the nuns heard of all this, they ran to the cave, and Pelagius was acknowledged by women to be a woman and a virgin undefiled. Then all did penance, and Pelagius was buried with honor in the nuns' monastery.

---

[1] A pun on the Greek word for sea or ocean, *pelagos*, latinized as *pelagus*.

152. Saint Thais, Courtesan

Thais the courtesan, as we read in *Lives of the Fathers*, was a woman of such beauty that for her many men sold all they possessed and were reduced to penury. Her lovers, driven by jealousy, frequently fought each other at the woman's door and covered the threshold with the blood of young men.

When news of this came to the ears of Abba Paphnutius, he put on layman's clothes, provided himself with some money, and went in search of Thais in a certain Egyptian city. Finding her, he offered her the money as the price of sinning. She took the money and said: "Come with me into this room." He went in and was invited to climb up into a bed spread with costly coverlets, but said to her: "If there is a room farther in, let us go there." She led him through a series of rooms, but he kept saying that he was afraid of being seen. Finally she said to him: "There is a little room that nobody goes to; but if you are afraid of God, there is no place that is hidden to his divinity." When the old man heard this, he asked her: "If you know that, why have you brought so many souls to perdition? You will have to account not only for your own soul but for those others, and you will be damned."

Thais heard what he said. She prostrated herself at the holy man's feet and appealed to him tearfully: "I know there is repentance too, father, and I am sure I shall obtain forgiveness if you pray for me. Please give me three hours' delay, and after that I will go wherever you say and will do whatever you command me." He indicated where she should go, and she brought together everything she had earned by sin, carried it to the center of the city, and, while the people looked on, set the whole afire and burned it to ashes, calling out: "Come, all of you who have sinned with me, and see what I am doing with what you gave me!" What she destroyed was worth four hundred pounds gold.

When the fire had died out, the woman went to the place that Paphnutius had designated. He shut her up in a narrow cell in a monastery of virgins and sealed the cell door with lead, leaving a small window through which meager fare could be passed to her. He further ordered that a bit of bread and a little water be brought her daily by the ministry of others. As the old man was about to leave, Thais asked him: "Father, where do you want me to deposit my water when nature calls?" "In your cell," he answered, "that's all you deserve!" She asked again: "How should I worship God?" He replied: "You are not worthy to say the name of God nor to have the name of the Trinity on your lips. Just kneel and face the East, and repeat over and over: 'O you who made me, have mercy on me!'"

When Thais had been thus confined for three years, Abba Paphnutius took pity on her and went to Abbot Anthony to ask him whether God had forgiven her her sins. Having heard the whole story, Anthony called his disciples together and ordered them to pray all night, each one by himself, so that God might declare to one of them the answer Paphnutius had come to seek. As they all prayed incessantly, Abba Paul, Anthony's chief disciple, suddenly saw in heaven a bed adorned with precious coverlets, watched over by three virgins with shining faces, who stood guard. These three virgins were the fear of future punishment, which had pulled Thais back from evil, shame for sin committed, which had won her pardon, and love of righteousness, which had carried her over to heavenly things. When Paul said to the virgins that so great a favor belonged only to Abbot Anthony, the voice of God responded: "It belongs not to your father Anthony, but to Thais the courtesan!"

When Paul reported this the next morning, Paphnutius, now sure of the will of God, departed rejoicing and went back to the monastery. He broke down the door of Thais's cell, but she asked to be allowed to remain enclosed. He said to her: "Come out, because God has forgiven your sins!" Thais: "God is my witness that as soon as I came into this cell I made a bundle of all my sins and set it before my eyes, and, just as the breath has not left my nostrils, so my sins have not left my eyes, and I have wept all the time, considering them." Abba Paphnutius said: "It is not on account of your penances that God has remitted your sins, but on account of the fear of God that you always had in your heart!" The monk led her out of her cell, and she lived on for a fortnight, then died a peaceful death.

Abba Ephrem wanted to convert another courtesan this same way. When this woman tried shamelessly to entice Saint Ephrem to sin, Ephrem said to her: "Follow me!" She followed him to a place where there was a crowd of people, and he said to her: "Lie down here so that I can copulate with you!" "How can I do that," she said, "with all these people standing around?" "If you are ashamed before men," he said, "should you not be much more ashamed before God, who reveals the secrets of the dark?" The woman walked away in confusion.

153. Saints Dionysius, Rusticus, and Eleutherius

Dionysius[1] is interpreted as one who flies forcefully; or the name may come from *dyo*, two, and *nisus*, elevation, hence a raising up in two forms, namely, in the body and in the soul. Or the name is derived from *Diana*, Venus, the goddess of beauty, and *syos*, god, hence beautiful to God. Or, as some think, the name comes from *dionysia*, which (as Isidore says) is a kind of black gem that is effective against drunkenness. Saint Dionysius, or Denis, was indeed one who fled forcefully from the world by perfect renunciation, who was raised up by his contemplation of the things of the spirit, beautiful to God by the beauty of his virtues, helpful to sinners against the intoxication of the vices.

Before his conversion, Dionysius had several surnames, He was called the Areopagite after the quarter in Athens where he lived, and Theosophus, one wise in the knowledge of God, Even today wise men among the Greeks call him *Pterigion tou ouranou*, which in Greek means wing of heaven, because he wonderfully flew to heaven on the wing of spiritual understanding. He is also called *Macarius*, which means blessed. After his homeland he is called *Ionicus*. Ionic, as Papias says, is one of the Greek languages; or Ionic, as the same author says, is a metrical foot with two short and two long syllables. All this shows that Dionysius was wise in the knowledge of God through his investigation of secret things, the wing of heaven through contemplation of the things of heaven, and blessed by possession of eternal goods. Moreover, it is known that he was a marvelous orator by his eloquence, a sustainer of the Church by his teaching, short by humility, long in his charity to others. Augustine, in the eighth book of *The City of God*, says that the term *Ionic* designated a school of philosophers. He distinguishes two schools, namely, the Italic, belonging to Italy, and the Ionic, belonging to Greece. Since, therefore, Dionysius was a preeminent philosopher, automatically he was called Ionic.

Methodius of Constantinople wrote his passion and life in Greek, and a Latin version was made by Anastasius, librarian of the apostolic see, as we learn from Hincmar, bishop of Rheims.

Dionysius the Areopagite was converted to the faith of Christ by the apostle Paul. It is said that he was called the Areopagite because he lived in the quarter of Athens called the Areopagus. This was the quarter of Mars, since the temple

---

[1] The name becomes Denis in French and Dennis in English.

of Mars was here. The Athenians designated the different quarters of the city by the names of the gods worshiped in each one. Hence they called the quarter where Mars was worshiped the Areopagus, because *Ares* was the Greek name for Mars. In the same way the section where Pan was worshiped was called Panopagus, and so on; each quarter went by the name of its own god.

The Areopagus was the upper-class section of Athens, where the nobility lived and the schools of liberal arts were established. Dionysius made his home there. He was an eminent philosopher, also called Theosophus, i.e., wise unto God, because of the fullness of his knowledge concerning the divine names. With him lived Apollophanes, who was his fellow philosopher. There dwelt also the Epicureans, who placed the happiness of man solely in bodily pleasure, and the Stoics, who placed it only in the virtue of the spirit.

On the day of the Lord's passion there was darkness over the whole earth, and the philosophers who were in Athens could find no natural cause for this phenomenon. It was not a natural eclipse of the sun, because the moon was not in the region of the sun, and an eclipse occurs only when the moon and the sun come together. At that time, however, the moon was in its fifteenth day, and therefore at its greatest distance from the sun. Moreover, it could not have been a natural eclipse, because an eclipse does not take away the light from every part of the earth, and because an eclipse cannot last for three hours. It is known that this particular eclipse shut off the light over the whole earth, first because Luke the evangelist says so; then because the Lord of the universe was suffering; and finally because the darkness was seen in Heliopolis of Egypt, in Rome, in Greece, and in Asia Minor. Orosius testifies that it was seen in Rome. He says: "When the Lord was nailed to the cross, a tremendous earthquake shook the whole earth, rocks were split asunder in the mountains, and many sections of great cities were flattened by this extraordinary tremor. On that same day, from the sixth hour on, the sun was totally obscured and black night was suddenly drawn over the earth, so that the stars were seen across the whole sky in those daytime hours, or rather in that awful night, or so we are told." Thus Orosius.

The eclipse was seen in Egypt, as Dionysius records in a letter to Apollophanes, in which he says: "A fog of darkness spread uniformly over the earth, and the disk of the sun came back shining clearly. We applied the rule of Philip Arrhideus and found, as was well known, that the sun was not due to suffer an eclipse. I then said to you: 'O sanctuary of vast learning, you do not yet know the mystery of this great thing! I ask you, O Apollophanes, mirror of doctrine, what do you think is the cause of these mysterious events?' To this you answered, with the mouth of a god and a word of more than human meaning: 'O good Dionysius, divine things are being disturbed.' And when Paul thundered to our anxiously attentive ears the day and year of the event that we had noted, I, having learned to read the signs that acclaimed it, surrendered to the truth and was freed of the bonds of falsity." Thus Dionysius. He also recalls this in a letter to Polycarp in which he speaks of himself and Apollophanes, saying: "We were both in Heliopolis at the time, standing together, and unexpectedly saw the moon coming in front of the sun, although it was not the time for an eclipse, and again, from the ninth hour until evening, saw the eclipse beginning in the east and coming to the limit of the sun's course, and again saw the waning and waxing of the light, not from the same but from the diametrically opposite direction." At that time Dionysius had gone to Heliopolis with Apollophanes to study astrology, and later returned from there.

We know from Eusebius that the eclipse was also seen in Asia. In his *Chronicle* he states that he had read in the pagan writings that in Bithynia, a province of Asia Minor, there had been a great earthquake, and a darkening of the sun such as had never happened before, and that at the sixth hour daylight had turned to pitch-dark night, so that the stars were seen in the skies. At Nicaea, a city in Bithynia, the earthquake had leveled all the buildings. Finally, as we read in the *Scholastic History*, the above events led the philosophers to say that the God of nature was suffering. Elsewhere we read that they said: "Either the order of nature is overturned, or the elements are lying, or the God of nature is suffering and the elements are suffering with him." And in other writings we read that Dionysius said: "This dark night, which we regard as something new, signals the coming of the whole world's true light."

The Athenians then built an altar to that god and put above it the title: "TO THE UNKNOWN GOD." Every altar had a title placed above it, indicating to which god it was dedicated. When the people wanted to offer holocausts and victims to the god, the philosophers said: "The god needs none of our goods; but kneel before his altar and offer him your supplications, because he does not want sacrifices of animals but piety of spirit."

When Paul came to Athens, the Epicurean and Stoic philosophers engaged him in debate. Some said: "What does this sower of words mean to say?" Others said: "He seems to be announcing new divinities." So they conducted Paul to the philosophers' quarter, the Areopolis, in order to subject this new teaching to scrutiny. They said: "You are bringing new things to our ears, and we want to know what these novelties mean." The Athenians, indeed, enjoy nothing so much as either to say or to hear something new. As Paul walked around among the shrines of the gods and saw an altar dedicated to the Unknown God, he said to the philosophers: "The god whom you worship unknown, I announce to you as the true God, who made the heavens and the earth." Then he said to Dionysius, who struck him as being more learned in divine matters than the rest: "Who, Dionysius, is this unknown God?" Dionysius answered: "He is the true God, who has not shown himself as the other gods have. He is unknown to us and hidden from us, yet in the age to come he will be,[2] and he will reign forever." Paul: "Is he a man, or only a spirit?" Dionysius: "He is God and man,

---

[2] Possibly an echo of Exod. 3:14 ("God answered: I am who am") and/or John 8:58 ("Before Abraham was, I am").

but is unknown because his life is in heaven only." Paul: "He is the God I preach to you! He came down from heaven, took flesh, endured death, and on the third day rose from the dead."

As Paul and Dionysius were debating, by chance a blind man passed by, and Dionysius said to Paul: "If you say to this blind man: 'In the name of my God, see!' and he sees, I will believe immediately. But do not use magic words, because it may be that you know words that would have this effect. Therefore I will dictate the form of words you are to use. You will say to him: 'In the name of Jesus Christ, born of a virgin, crucified, dead, who rose from the dead and ascended into heaven, see!'" But, in order to eliminate any possibility of suspicion, Paul told Dionysius to address these very words to the blind man. Dionysius did so, and the blind man instantly received his sight.

Dionysius and his wife Damaris and their whole household were baptized forthwith. Having received the faith, Dionysius was instructed by Paul for three years and then ordained bishop of Athens. He preached constantly, and converted the whole city and most of its surrounding territory to the faith of Christ.

It is said that Paul revealed to Dionysius what he, in ecstasy, had seen in the third heaven, as Dionysius himself seems to insinuate in more than one place. Hence he discoursed upon the hierarchies of the angels, their orders, ranks, and functions, so brilliantly and clearly that you would not think he had learned all this from someone else, but that he himself had been rapt to the third heaven and there had looked upon all he described. He shone with the spirit of prophecy, as appears from the letter he sent to John the Evangelist, who was in exile on the island of Patmos, in which he foretold that John would return from exile, and said: "Rejoice, O truly beloved, truly amiable and desirable and lovable, O greatly beloved!" And further on: "You will be released from your prison in Patmos, you will return to the land of Asia, and, by imitating the goodness of God in your life, will hand down an example to those who will live after you." He was present at the dormition[3] of Blessed Mary, as he suggests in his book *The Divine Names*.

When Dionysius learned that the emperor Nero had imprisoned Peter and Paul in Rome, he put another bishop in his place and went to Rome to visit the apostles. When they had happily migrated to the Lord, Clement became supreme pontiff. After a time Clement sent Dionysius to France, giving him Rusticus and Eleutherius as associates. He arrived in Paris and there converted many to the faith, built a number of churches, and installed clerics of various ranks. The priests of the idols more than once aroused the people against him and they came after him with weapons to assault him, but the grace of God shone so brightly in him that as soon as they saw him, they either put away their fury and groveled at his feet, or were overcome with fear and fled from his presence.

---

[3] Dormition, a "falling asleep," term used to describe the death of the Blessed Virgin Mary.

The devil was alarmed to see that while the number of his own worshipers was decreasing day by day, converts to the faith were multiplying and the Church was winning the fight. He therefore provoked Emperor Domitian to such a state of anger that the emperor issued a decree that anyone who found out that a given person was a Christian must either force that person to sacrifice to the idols or be put to all sorts of torture. The prefect Fescenninus was dispatched from Rome to Paris to deal with the Christians there and found blessed Dionysius preaching to the people. At once he had the saint taken captive, beaten, mocked, and spat upon, then bound with the toughest thongs and brought before him with Saint Rusticus and Saint Eleutherius. When they were steadfast in confessing the true God, a noblewoman came forward and charged that these three men had grossly and shamefully deceived her fickle husband into accepting the faith. The husband was sent for with all speed, and when he too persevered in confessing God, he was unjustly put to death, while the saints were scourged by twelve soldiers, loaded with a great weight of chains, and cast into prison.

On the following day Dionysius was stretched naked on an iron grill over a blazing fire, and he sang to the Lord, saying: "Thy word is refined by fire, and thy servant has loved it."[4] Then he was removed from the fire and thrown to wild beasts that were hungry, not having been fed. They rushed at him, but he made the sign of the cross over them and they became tame and gentle. He was thrown into an oven, but the fire went out and he was unhurt. They nailed him to a cross and left him there in torment for a long time, then took him down and returned him to prison with his two companions and many of the faithful. Dionysius celebrated mass in the prison and was giving holy communion to the prisoners, when the Lord Jesus, surrounded by a brilliant light, appeared to him, took the bread, and said to him: "Receive this, my beloved, because your reward is very great with me."

After this the saints were again presented to the judge and tortured anew. Finally, before the idol of Mercury, the heads of the three were cut off with swords in confession of the Holy Trinity. Instantly the body of Saint Dionysius stood up, took his head in its arms, and, with an angel and a heavenly light leading the way, marched two miles, from the place called Montmartre, the hill of martyrs, to the place where, by his own choice and by God's providence, he rests in peace. Great was the melodious chanting of angels that resounded there, and many who heard it believed. Among them was Laertia, wife of the prefect Lubrius, who cried out that she was a Christian. She was beheaded then and there by the pagans, and died baptized in her own blood. Her son Virbius, who served in the army at Rome under three emperors, finally returned to Paris, was baptized, and was numbered among religious men.

[4] Cf. Ps. 118:140 (Douay).

The infidels were afraid the Christians would bury the bodies of Saints Rusticus and Eleutherius, so they ordered them thrown into the Seine. A certain noblewoman invited those who were carrying the bodies to stop for lunch, and while they were feasting, she furtively whisked the bodies away and had them buried secretly on her property. Later on, when the persecution had ceased, she retrieved them and gave them honorable burial beside the body of Saint Dionysius. They suffered under Diocletian in A.D. 96, Dionysius then being ninety years old.

About the year A.D. 815, in the reign of Louis, son of Charlemagne, ambassadors of Emperor Michael of Constantinople brought to King Louis, among other gifts, Dionysius's books *On the Hierarchy*, translated from the Greek into Latin. They were received with joy, and nineteen ill persons were cured the same night in the church of Saint Denis.

Once when Bishop Regulus of Arles was celebrating mass, he added, to the names of the apostles in the canon of the mass, the words *et beatis martyribus tuis Dionysio, Rustico et Eleutherio*.[5] He said these words though, as far as he knew, these servants of God were still alive, and then began to wonder why he had pronounced their names in the canon. And behold, while he was still wondering, three doves, with the martyrs' names written in blood on their breasts, appeared and perched on the cross above the altar. The bishop studied the doves thoughtfully, and intuition told him that the saints had migrated from their bodies.

About A.D. 644, as a certain chronicle has it, Dagobert, king of the Franks, who reigned long before Pepin, had from childhood held Saint Dionysius in fervent veneration. When as a child he feared the anger of his father Chlothar, he ran and hid in the church of Saint Denis. Dagobert succeeded his father and eventually died, and a certain holy man had a vision in which he saw the deceased king's soul being borne to judgment, and many saints charging him with having stripped their churches. The wicked angels therefore wanted to carry the soul off to punishment, but Saint Denis stood by, and through his intervention Dagobert's soul was freed and escaped punishment. It may be that his soul returned to his body and there did penance.

King Clovis once irreverently uncovered the body of Saint Denis, broke off an arm bone, and took it away. In no time he lost his mind.

Note also that Hincmar, bishop of Rheims, says, in the letter he wrote to Charles, that the Dionysius who was sent to Gaul was Dionysius the Areopagite, as was said above. John Scotus makes the same assertion in a letter to Charles. This cannot be questioned, therefore, on the ground that the dates are contradictory, as some have tried to argue.

[5] . . . and with thy blessed martyrs . . .

154. Saint Callistus

Pope Callistus suffered martyrdom in A.D. 222, under Emperor Alexander. At that time a fire was sent by God and reduced the higher part of the city of Rome to ashes, and the left hand of a gold statue of Jove was melted away. Then all the priests went to Alexander and demanded that the angry gods be placated by sacrifices. They were offering sacrifice on a calm morning—it was Jove's day[1]—when lightning struck from heaven. Four priests of the idols died, Jove's altar was reduced to rubble, and the sun turned so dark that the populace of Rome fled outside the walls.

The consul Palmadius learned that Callistus and his clergy were in hiding across the Tiber, and asked permission to do away with the Christians in order to purge the city, since it was due to them that this calamity had befallen it. Permission granted, he marched his soldiers across the river in pursuit of the Christians, but the soldiers were stricken blind. Palmatius, terrified, reported this to Alexander. The emperor then commanded that the whole populace come together on Mercury's day to offer sacrifice to this god, in order to obtain an answer from him regarding these happenings. As this order was being carried out, a temple virgin named Juliana was seized by a demon and cried: "The God of Callistus is the true and living God, and he is enraged by our filthy practices!" When Palmatius heard this, he crossed the Tiber and went to the city of Ravenna, found Saint Callistus, and was baptized by the pope, together with his wife and family.

When this news reached the emperor, he had Palmatius arrested and turned him over to Simplicius, a senator. The senator's task was to win him over by flattering him with the argument that the republic could not do without him. Palmatius was persevering in prayer and fasting when a soldier came to him and promised that if Palmatius cured his paralytic wife, he would accept the faith at once. Palmatius prayed and the woman was cured. She ran to Palmatius and said: "Baptize me in the name of Christ, who took me by the right hand and lifted me up!" Callistus came and baptized the woman and her husband, along with Simplicius and a great many others.

The emperor's response to all this was to have all the baptized beheaded, and to keep Callistus for five days without food or drink. He saw, however, that the saint looked stronger than ever, so he ordered him to be flogged every day, then

---

[1] The days of the week were named after the Roman gods—Luna, Mars, Mercurius, Jupiter (Jove), Venus—and still are, in the Romance languages.

thrown from a window, then chained to a large stone and dropped down a well. Asterius, a priest, raised his body from the well and buried it in the cemetery of Calipodius.

---

155. Saint Leonard

Leonardus means the perfume of the people, from *leos*, people, and *nardus*, which is a sweet-smelling herb; and Leonard drew people to himself by the sweet odor of his good renown. Or the name comes from *legens ardua*, one who chooses the hard tasks; or again, it comes from *leo*, the lion. The lion has four characteristics. He has fortitude, and this fortitude is (as Isidore says) in his breast and in his head. So Saint Leonard had fortitude in his heart by the curbing of evil thoughts, and in his head by his tireless contemplation of the things of heaven. Secondly, the lion has sagacity, and this in two ways: he sleeps with his eyes open, and he erases his tracks when he runs away. So Leonard was watchful in labor and action, and, while awake, slept by the quiet of contemplation. In himself he also erased every trace of worldly attachment. Thirdly, the lion has a special power in his voice. The lion cub is born dead, but on the third day the lion roars at it and it comes alive. Moreover, his roar stops every other animal stock-still. So Leonard restored to life many who were dead in sin, and many who were dead in their bestial way of life he fixed firmly in the way of good works. Fourthly, the lion has fear in his heart, because (according to Isidore) he fears two things, namely, the noise of wheels and the crackling of fire. So Leonard feared and, because he feared it, avoided the noise of mundane busyness, wherefore he took refuge in the desert, shrank from the fire of earthly greed, and disdained all treasures that were offered him.

Leonard is said to have lived about the year A.D. 500. Saint Remy, archbishop of Rheims, lifted him from the baptismal font and instructed him in salutary disciplines. His parents held first rank in the palace of the king of France. The king held Leonard in such high favor that any prisoners whom he visited were straightway released from bondage. As the fame of his holiness spread abroad, the king compelled him to stay with him for a long time, until he might bestow a bishopric on him. But Leonard refused to accept this, and, longing for solitude, left everything and went to Orleans, where he preached with his brother Lifard.

After they had lived for some time in a monastery, Lifard decided to lead a solitary life on the banks of the Loire, and Leonard, guided by the Holy Spirit, proposed to preach in Aquitaine. So they kissed and parted.

Leonard preached here and there, wrought many miracles, and lived in a forest close by the city of Limoges, where the king had a hunting lodge. It happened one day that the king was hunting there, and the queen had come out to enjoy the sport. Then suddenly she was seized with the pangs of childbirth and her life was in danger, while the royal retinue wept and groaned over the queen's condition. Leonard, who was walking through the forest, heard the sounds of mourning and, moved with pity, hastened toward the source of the sound. The king called him into the lodge and asked him who he was, and he said he had been a disciple of Saint Remy. This raised the monarch's hopes: he thought that anyone instructed by so good a teacher could be relied on. He brought Leonard in to the queen, asking him to pray both for her well-being and for the safe delivery of the child. Leonard prayed, and his petitions were granted.

The king now offered Leonard much money, but Leonard refused the offer and urged the monarch to distribute the money to the poor, saying: "I do not need any of this. What I desire is only to live in the forest and serve Christ alone, shunning all the riches of this world." The king then wanted to grant him the whole forest, but he answered: "I do not accept the whole forest, but I ask you to convey to me only as much as I can ride around on my ass in one night." To this the king willingly agreed.

A monastery was therefore built, and for a long time Leonard lived there with two monks who had joined him, living an austere life. Water was available no nearer than a mile away, but Leonard ordered a dry well dug at the monastery, and in answer to his prayers the well filled with water. He called the place Nobiliacum, because it had been given to him by a noble king. There his many miracles won him fame. Any prisoner who invoked his name saw his bonds loosened and went free with no one interfering. Such persons brought their chains and fetters to Leonard, and many stayed with him and served the Lord there. Seven families of his own noble line sold all their possessions and stayed with him, each family settling in its own section of the forest, and their example attracted a great many others.

At last the holy man Leonard, renowned for his many virtues, migrated to the Lord on the sixth day of November. After many miracles had occurred at his tomb in the monastery, it was revealed to the clergy there that since the church was too small to accommodate the throngs that frequented it, they were to build a church at another location and to transfer the saint's body there with due honors. The clerics and the people gave themselves to fasting and prayer for three days, then looked around and saw that the whole province was covered with snow except the one place where Saint Leonard wished to rest. That place, they discovered, was bare. The saint's relics were transferred to the new site, and the number of miracles the Lord wrought there through him is evidenced by the variety of chains and fetters hanging before his tomb.

In order to strike terror into miscreants, the viscount of Limoges had had a very heavy chain made, and ordered it hung from a beam that jutted from the wall of his tower: anyone who, with that chain around his neck, was left exposed to the vicissitudes of the weather for very long, died not one but a thousand deaths. It happened, however, that a man who had been in service to Saint Leonard was shackled with this chain though he had done no wrong. When he was about to breathe his last, he put his whole heart into a plea to Saint Leonard, begging him, who had freed many others, to come to the aid of one who had been his servant. At once the saint, clad in a white robe, appeared to him and said: "Don't be afraid, you are not going to die! Get up, and carry that chain with you to my church! Follow me, because I will lead the way!" The man got to his feet, gathered up the chain, and followed Saint Leonard, who went on ahead to his church. As soon as they came to the door, blessed Leonard left him. He went into the church that the saint had caused to be built, told everyone what had happened to him, and hung the huge chain in front of Leonard's tomb.

There was a man who lived in Saint Leonard's monastery at Nobiliacum and was devoted to the saint, and this man was made captive by a tyrant. The tyrant said to himself: "That Leonard frees everybody, and the strength of iron melts before him like wax in front of a fire. If I put my man in chains, Leonard will be on hand at once and will set him free. If, on the other hand, I manage to keep the fellow, I will get a thousand pounds' ransom for him. I know what I'll do! I'll have a deep pit dug under my tower, and I'll put my man, gyved and fettered, at the bottom of the pit. Then I'll have a wooden hut built over the mouth of the pit and station armed soldiers in it. Even though Leonard breaks iron, he has never yet gone underground."

The tyrant carried out his scheme, and the poor captive called loudly and often upon Saint Leonard. Night came and with it Leonard, who overturned the hut in which the soldiers lay asleep, and shut them up under it like dead men in a sepulcher. Then, with much light shining around him, he went into the pit, clasped his devotee's hand, and asked: "Are you asleep or awake? Here I am, Leonard, for whom you were calling!" The man, startled, said: "My lord, help me!" Leonard quickly broke the chains, took the man in his arms, and carried him out of the tower. Once outside, they chatted as one friend to another, and the saint led the man to Nobiliacum and his house.

There was a man who, upon his return from a pilgrimage to Saint Leonard, was taken captive in Auvergne and locked in a cage. He pleaded with his captors, telling them that since he had done them no wrong, they ought to let him go for the love of Saint Leonard. They answered that unless he paid them a copious ransom he would not get out. He replied: "That's between you and Saint Leonard, to whom I am committed, as you know!" The following night Saint Leonard appeared to the commander of the stronghold and commanded him to release the pilgrim. This man woke up in the morning, dismissed the vision as a dream, and had no thought of setting the prisoner free. The next night the saint presented him with the same command, and again he refused to obey. On the third night Saint Leonard took the pilgrim and led him outside the fortress, and immediately the tower and half the castle collapsed and crushed many, leaving only the recalcitrant chief, whose legs were broken, to welter in his own confusion.

A knight had been imprisoned in Brittany and invoked the aid of Saint Leonard. The saint appeared at once in the middle of the house, where all there saw and recognized him and marveled at the sight. The saint entered the jail cell, broke the bonds, placed the chains in the knight's hands, and led him out through those present, while they looked on, dumbfounded.

There was another Leonard, likewise a monk and equally virtuous, whose body rests at Corbigny. He was the abbot of his monastery but so humbled himself that he seemed the lowest of all. Since almost the whole populace flocked to him, a few envious people convinced King Chlothar that unless he took precautions, the kingdom of France would suffer considerable damage through Leonard, who, they said, was gathering a large following under the pretext of religion. The king, all too ready to believe them, ordered the expulsion of Leonard. Soldiers came after him, but his words impressed them so poignantly that they promised to become his disciples at a future time. The king repented and asked for pardon, and had the detractors stripped of their goods and honors. He also conceived a great affection for Leonard and at the saint's prayer restored the detractors to their former dignity. Like the other Leonard, this one also obtained of God that any who were held in prison and invoked his name would quickly be released.

One day, as he lay prone in prayer, a large serpent crawled up beside him, so long that it stretched from his feet to his chest. This did not make the saint interrupt his prayer, but once he had finished it, he said to the reptile: "I know that from the time you were created, you have done all you could to trouble men; but now, if power over me has been given to you, do to me whatever I have deserved." At these words the serpent leapt out through the saint's cowl and fell dead at his feet. Later, after having made peace between two bishops, he predicted that he would die the next day. This was about A.D. 570.

156. Saint Luke, Evangelist

Luke, Lucas in Latin, is interpreted as rising up, or elevating; or the name comes from *lux*, light. Saint Luke was one rising above love of the world and elevating himself to the love of God. He was the light of the world in that he shed light on the whole universe: "You are the light of the world."[1] The light of the world is the sun itself, and this light has sublimity in its place: "The sun when it riseth to the world in the high places of God."[2] The light is sweet to look upon: "Light is sweet, and it is delightful for the eyes to see the sun."[3] Light moves swiftly: "The earth is vast and heaven is high and the sun is swift in its course."[4] Light is useful in its effect, because, according to the philosopher, man engenders man, and so does the sun. Luke has sublimity through contemplation of heavenly things, he was delightful in the sweetness of his conversation and swift in the fervor of his preaching; and he gave useful service through the writing down of his doctrine.

Luke was a Syrian, a native of Antioch and a practitioner of medicine. Some would have it that he was one of the Lord's seventy-two disciples. Jerome, however, says that Luke was a disciple of the apostles, not of the Lord; and since the *Gloss* on Exodus 25 notes that he did not receive the faith from the preaching of the Lord but came to it after the resurrection, it is more likely that Luke was not one of the seventy-two, despite the fact that some think he was.

So great was the perfection of his life that he was very well ordered in his relation to God, to his neighbor, to himself, and to his appointed task. As a sign of this fourfold ordering he is described as having four faces, namely, those of a man, a lion, an ox, and an eagle. Ezechiel says[5] that each of the four living creatures in his vision had four faces and four wings. In order to have a clearer idea of this, imagine an animal with a square head like a cube of wood, and on each of the four sides of the cube a face—on the front, the face of a man, on the right side that of a lion, on the left side that of a calf, and on the back, that of an eagle. Because the eagle's face stood higher than the others due to the stretched neck, the eagle's neck being long, it is said that the eagle was uppermost. Each of these animals had four wings, because, since we are imagining the animal as squared and the square has four edges, there was a wing on each edge.

---

[1] Matt. 5:14.   [2] Ecclus. 26:21.   [3] Eccles. 11:7.

[4] 3 Esd. 4:34. The Latin Vulgate includes this book as "added to the series of the canonical books," printed after the New Testament and numbered 3 Esdras (1 and 2 Esdras are canonical). The RSV has it among the Apocrypha as 1 Esdras.

[5] Ezek. 1:5, 10.

According to the holy fathers, these animals represent the four evangelists, and each animal had four faces because each evangelist wrote about the humanity, the passion, the resurrection, and the divinity of Christ. Yet the four faces are distributed among the four evangelists by a sort of attribution. According to Jerome, Matthew is represented by the face of a man because he dwells mostly on the humanity of Christ. Luke is represented by a sacrificial calf because he treats of Christ's priesthood. Mark is figured as a lion because he wrote more clearly about the resurrection, and lion cubs, we are told, lie as though dead until the third day after birth, when the lion wakes them up with his roaring; also Mark is the lion because he began his gospel with the roar of the Baptist's preaching. John is represented in the eagle, flying higher than the others by writing about Christ's divinity. Christ, about whom he wrote, was also signified in these four figures—his humanity because he was born of a virgin, his passion in the sacrificial calf, his resurrection in the lion, and his ascension in the eagle.

These four faces, which represent Luke as they do the other evangelists, show the four ways in which, as we saw above, his life was well ordered. The face of a man shows that he was rightly ordered in relation to his neighbor, whom one should instruct by right reasoning, attract by gentleness, and support generously, since man is a rational, gentle, and liberal animal. The face of the eagle shows that he was rightly ordered in relation to God, because in him the eye of the intellect was fixed on God through contemplation, the beak of his desire was sharpened toward God by meditation, and old age was thrown aside like the eagle's, by rejuvenation.[6] The eagle, indeed, is a sharp-eyed bird that can look into the sun without blinking an eye and from a marvelous height can see tiny fishes in the sea. If its beak becomes too hooked, making it difficult to catch fish, the eagle rubs it against a stone and makes it more suitable for use in feeding. When he is burned by the heat of the sun, the eagle plunges at great speed into a body of water, thus casting off old age, while the sun's heat cleans away the film from his eyes and lightens his feathers. The lion's face shows that Luke was rightly ordered in relation to himself, because he had nobility in his honorable conduct, sagacity in foiling the plots of his enemies, and readiness to suffer in his compassion for the afflicted. The lion, indeed, is a noble animal, since he is the king of beasts; he is cunning, because he wipes out his tracks with his tail so that no one can follow him when he flees; he is familiar with suffering, because he is susceptible to the quartan fever.

The face of the calf or the ox shows that Luke was rightly ordered in relation to his appointed task, which was to write his gospel. On that work he proceeded slowly, unhurriedly, beginning as he did with the birth of the forerunner and the birth and infancy of Christ, and so, step by step, moving toward the final consummation. He proceeded judiciously. Writing after two other evangelists, he supplied what they had omitted and omitted what they had treated sufficiently.

[6] Cf. Ps. 103:5.

He gave special attention to the Temple and to sacrifice, as is clear in the beginning, the middle, and the end of his gospel. Moreover, the ox is a slow-moving animal and has cleft hooves, and this signifies the discernment of those who offer sacrifice.

That blessed Luke was well ordered in the four ways already mentioned becomes still more obvious as one looks more deeply into the various aspects of his life. Firstly, he was well ordered in his relation to God. Man, according to Saint Bernard, is rightly related to God in three aspects, namely, in his desire, his thought, and his intention. His desire must be holy, his thought clean, and his intention right. Luke's desire was holy because he was filled with the Holy Spirit. Jerome, in his Prologue to Luke's gospel, says: "He died in Bithynia, full of the Holy Spirit." His thought was clean: he was a virgin in body and mind, and this shows the purity of his thought. He had rectitude of intention, because he sought the Lord's glory in everything he did. Regarding the last two qualities, Jerome's Prologue to the Acts of the Apostles says: "[Luke was] without wrongdoing, abiding in virginity" (this refers to cleanness of thought). "He chose above all to serve the Lord," i.e., the Lord's honor, and this refers to rightness of intentions.

Secondly, his relations with his neighbor were in good order. Such good order exists when we pay our neighbor what we owe him. According to Richard of Saint Victor we owe our neighbor three debts, namely, we owe him what we can do for him, what we know, and what we wish for him; and these three lead to a fourth, namely, what we do for him. Saint Luke was well ordered in these four respects. He gave to his neighbor what he could give in the way of help, as we see in his always being at Paul's side in every kind of trouble, never leaving him, and thus helping him in his preaching. So Paul wrote in his letter to Timothy: "Luke alone is with me."[7] When Paul says "with me," he indicates the kind of help Luke gives him, namely, as his assistant and defender. When he says "Luke alone," he indicates that Luke is constant in his attachment. Again Paul says of Luke: "Not only that, but he has been appointed by the churches to travel with us in this gracious work which we are carrying on."[8]

The second debt—what he knew—he paid in giving good counsel; i.e., he made his knowledge available to his neighbor when he put in writing what he knew of apostolic and evangelical doctrine for the use and service of his fellows. Luke says this about himself in the prologue of his gospel: "It seemed good to me, having followed all things from the beginning, to write an orderly account for you, most exellent Theophilus, that you may know the truth concerning the things of which you have been informed."[9] How he shared his knowledge in giving good counsel is shown by what Jerome says in his Prologue, namely, that Luke's words are medicine to the languid soul.

---

[7] 2 Tim. 4:11.   [8] 2 Cor. 8:19.   [9] Luke 1:3–4

Third debt—what he wished and desired for his neighbors—he paid by desiring eternal salvation for them. "Luke, the most dear physician, salutes you," says Paul, meaning "desires eternal salvation for you."[10] And fourth debt—what we do for our neighbor—this, too, Luke paid. He gave the Lord hospitality, thinking that he was caring for a pilgrim, and exhibited toward him every kindness that charity called for. This was when Luke was Cleopas's companion on the road to Emmaus, as some say he was, including Gregory in his *Moralia*, though Ambrose says it was someone else, and even gives his name.

Thirdly, Luke was well ordered in relation to himself. There are, according to Bernard, three qualities that best put order in a man's management of his own life, namely, a sober life-style, just action, and a pious sense, i.e., a sense of God's presence in our lives. Each of these three, as Bernard says, is divided three ways. One's life-style will be sober if one lives continently, sociably, and humbly. One's action will be just if it is straightforward, discreet, and fruitful—straightforward by good intention, discreet by moderation, and fruitful by edification. A pious sense there will be if our faith senses God as all-powerful, all-wise, and all-good, so that we believe that by his power our weakness is aided, by his wisdom our ignorance is corrected, and by his goodness our wickedness is washed away. Thus Bernard.

In all those ways Luke was in perfect order. His way of living was sober, and this in three respects. He lived continently, for, as Jerome says in his Prologue to Luke's gospel, the evangelist had neither wife nor child. He lived sociably, as we see from what the last chapter of his gospel says about Luke and Cleopas (if we accept the opinion stated above): "That very day two of them were going to a village named Emmaus and talking with each other."[11] His sociability is indicated by the word "two" and the word "disciples," because they were "disciplined," in other words, morally correct. His humility is suggested by the fact that his companion's name, Cleopas, is given, but his own is suppressed—because it is the opinion of some that Luke omitted his name for humility's sake.

Secondly, his action was just. It was just by intention, as indicated by the prayer in the mass of his feast: "[He] bore continually in his body the mortification of the cross for the glory of your name." It was just by discretion, indicated by moderation and signified by the image of the ox, whose hoof is cleft, thus expressing the virtue of discretion or discernment. And his action was fruitful because it was edifying; it bore such fruit for his neighbors that he was held "most dear" by all. Hence Paul calls him "Luke, the most dear physician."[12]

Thirdly, Luke possessed a pious sense, because he believed, and professed in his gospel, that God is all-powerful, all-wise, and all-good. Of the first two he

[10] Col. 4:14.
[11] Luke 24:13–14.
[12] Col. 4:14.

wrote in chapter 4: "They were astonished at his doctrine, for his speech was with power."[13] Of God's goodness he says: "Jesus said, 'None is good but God alone.'"[14]

Fourthly and last, Luke was well ordered in relation to his appointed task, that of writing his gospel. This is shown by the fact that his gospel is permeated by much truth, filled with much usefulness, adorned with much charm, and confirmed by many authorities. There are three kinds of truth, namely, truth of life, truth of justice, and truth of doctrine. Truth of life consists in making the hand do what the tongue says, truth of justice in making the sentence fit the case, truth of doctrine in making the idea agree with reality. Luke's gospel is permeated by this threefold truth, because in his gospel this truth is fully expounded.

Luke shows that Christ had this multiple truth in himself, and that he taught it to others. He uses the testimony of adversaries to prove that Christ had the truth in himself, as we see in chapter 20, when the Sadducees say to the Lord: "Teacher, we know that you speak and teach rightly" (the truth of doctrine), "and show no partiality" (the truth of justice), "but truly teach the way of God"[15] (the truth of life: the good life is called the way of God). But his gospel also shows that Christ taught this threefold truth. He taught the truth of life, which consists in observing the commandments of God. Hence we read in chapter 10: "You shall love the Lord your God with all your heart . . . and your neighbor as yourself. . . . Do this and you will live."[16] And in chapter 18 we read: "A ruler asked him: 'Good Teacher, what shall I do to inherit eternal life?' And Jesus said: 'You know the commandments—do not commit adultery, do not kill,' etc."[17] Christ also taught the truth of doctrine. To some, who were perverting the truth of doctrine, he said: "Woe to you, Pharisees, for you tithe (meaning, you teach others to tithe) mint and rue and every herb, and you neglect justice and the love of God"; and, in the same place: "Woe to you, lawyers! You have taken away the key of knowledge; you did not enter yourselves, and you hindered those who were entering."[18] And thirdly, the truth of justice is taught: "Render to Caesar the things that are Caesar's, and to God the things that are God's";[19] and "As for these enemies of mine, who did not want me to rule over them, bring them here and slay them before me!"[20] And in chapter 13, where it is question of the Judgment, we read that the Judge will say to the accursed: "Depart from me, all you workers of iniquity."[21]

Second, just as Luke's gospel is permeated with truth, it is also filled with much usefulness. Its author was a physician, to signify that he prescribed a very healthful medicine for us. There are three kinds of medicine: some cures, some preserves, some improves. In his gospel Luke shows us that the heavenly physi-

---

[13] Luke 4:32. [14] Luke 18:19. [15] Luke 20:21.
[16] Luke 10:27–28. [17] Luke 18:18. [18] Luke 11:42, 52.
[19] Luke 20:25. [20] Luke 19:27. [21] Luke 13:27.

cian has prescribed these three medicines for us. The medicine that cures diseases is penance, which cures every spiritual sickness. Luke shows that the celestial doctor has provided this medicine, for he says: "The Spirit of the Lord has sent me to heal the contrite of heart, to preach deliverance to the captives," etc.[22] Also: "I have not come to call the righteous, but sinners, to repentance."[23] The medicine that improves, i.e., that increases good health, consists in the observance of the counsels, for the counsels make people better and more perfect. Luke shows that the physician has prescribed this medicine for us when he says: "Sell all that you have and distribute to the poor";[24] also: "From him who takes away your cloak, do not withhold your coat as well."[25] The preservative medicine is that which saves us from falling, and this consists in avoiding the occasion of sinning and the company of sinners. The physician prescribes this medicine when he says: "Beware of the leaven of the Pharisees,"[26] teaching us to shun bad company.

It can also be said that Luke's gospel itself is filled with usefulness, since in it the power of every kind of wisdom is contained. Here is what Ambrose says about this: "Luke enfolded all the powers of wisdom into his gospel story. What he taught has to do with nature, when he discloses that the Lord's incarnation was the work of the Holy Spirit. David also teaches this natural wisdom when he says: 'Send forth thy Spirit and they shall be created.'[27] In the same vein, Luke taught that darkness came over the whole land, the sunlight failed, and the earth trembled, during the passion of Christ. He taught moral wisdom when, in the Beatitudes, he set forth the ways of moral living.[28] He taught rational wisdom when he said: 'He who is faithful in a very little is also faithful in much.'[29] Without this threefold wisdom—the natural, the moral, and the rational—there can be no faith, there can be no mystery of the Trinity." Thus Ambrose.

Third, Luke's gospel is also adorned with much charm, for his style and manner of speaking are indeed charming and decorous. If someone wants what he says or writes to have grace and charm, then, as Augustine says, it must be pleasing, clear, and touching. If his words are to please, they should be eloquent; to be clear, they should be easy to follow; to touch hearts, they should be fervent. Luke had these three qualities in his writing and in his preaching. On the first two, Paul said: "With him [Titus] we have sent the brother (the *Gloss* adds 'Barnabas or Luke') whose praise is in the gospel through all the churches."[30] That he was praised points to his eloquence; "through all the churches" indicates that he could be understood wherever he preached; that he spoke fervently follows from the fact that he had an ardent heart, since he said: "Did not our hearts burn within us while he talked to us on the road?"[31]

---

[22] Luke 4:18–19. [23] Luke 5:32. [24] Luke 18:22.
[25] Luke 6:29. [26] Luke 12:1. [27] Ps. 103(104):30.
[28] Luke 6:20ff. [29] Luke 6:10. [30] 2 Cor. 8:18 (Douay).
[31] Luke 24:32.

Fourth, Luke's gospel is confirmed by many authorities. The authority of many guarantees it. This gospel was ordered by the Father, who says, as in Jeremiah 31: "Behold, the days are coming, when I will make a new covenant with the house of Israel and the house of Judah, not like the covenant which I made with their fathers; but this is the covenant which I will make with the house of Israel after these days, says the Lord, I will put my law within them and I will write it upon their hearts."[32] This literally refers to the doctrine contained in the gospel. The doctrine was also corroborated by the Son, as we read in chapter 21: "Heaven and earth will pass away, but my words will not pass away."[33] Thirdly, this gospel was inspired by the Holy Spirit, as Jerome, in his Prologue on Luke, says: "Spurred by the Holy Spirit. he wrote this gospel in Achaia."

Fourthly, it was prefigured by angels, notably by the angel about whom it is said in the Book of Revelation: "I saw an angel of God flying through the midst of heaven, having the eternal gospel."[34] This gospel is called eternal because it is made from eternity by Christ, who is eternal; it has eternal things as its material, eternal life as its end, and eternity as its duration. Fifthly, it was foretold by the prophets. The prophet Ezechiel foretold it when he said that one of the living creatures had the face of a calf, by which Luke's gospel was represented, as we said before. Ezechiel also says that he saw a book that was written within and without, and there were written in it lamentations and canticles and woe.[35] We are to understand that this book is Luke's gospel, which is written within through the depth of the mystery it encloses, and outwardly by the history of events that it lays open. It contains the lament of Christ's passion, the song of his resurrection, and the woe of damnation, as we see in chapter 11, where woe is predicted for many.

Sixthly, this gospel was disclosed by the Virgin Mary. The Blessed Virgin kept all these things in her heart, pondering them diligently, as we read in chapter 2 of Luke,[36] in order to be able to communicate them to writers, as the *Gloss* on this passage says: "She kept in her memory everything she knew about the Lord and what the Lord did and said, so that when the time came to preach or write about the incarnation, she could adequately make known all that had been said and done, to those who sought information." So Bernard also, assigning a reason for the angel's announcing to Mary that Elizabeth had conceived, says: "This announcement was made to Mary so that when it was necessary to teach about the Savior's coming at one time and the forerunner at another, she, remembering the times and sequence of events, could better disclose the truth to the writers and preachers of the Gospel, since she was fully instructed by heaven about all the mysteries from the beginning."

---

[32] Jer. 31:31–33.   [33] Luke 21:33.   [34] Rev. 14:6.
[35] Ezek. 2:9–10 (Douay).
[36] Luke 2:19, 51.

It is believed, therefore, that the evangelists questioned Mary about many things, and that she gave them sure answers. This would be particularly true in Saint Luke's case. It is believed that he turned to her as to the ark of the testimony and from her received sure knowledge about many things, above all about matters that concerned her alone, such as the angel's annunciation of the birth of Christ and similar things, which Luke alone relates in his gospel.

Seventhly, Luke got information from the apostles. He had not been with Christ to witness all the Lord's actions and miracles, so he wrote his gospel relying on what the apostles, who had been present, told him. Luke himself suggests this in his prologue, when he says that he had compiled "a narrative of the things which have been accomplished among us, just as they were delivered to us by those who from the beginning were eyewitnesses and ministers of the word."[37] It was customary to have two kinds of testimony, namely, what was seen and what was heard; so the Lord (as Augustine says) wanted to have two witnesses to what they had seen, namely, Matthew and John, and two to what they had heard from others, namely, Mark and Luke. Furthermore, since the testimony of eyewitnesses is firmer and more certain than that based on hearsay, therefore, as Augustine says, the two gospels written by eyewitnesses are put first and last, and the other two, based on hearsay, are put in between, being weaker than those on the ends, which, being surer than the other two, undergird and support them.

Eighthly, Luke's gospel was marvelously approved by Paul, when he quoted it in confirmation of what he himself was saying. Hence Jerome, in his book *On Illustrious Men*, says: "There are some who surmise that every time Paul, in his epistles, says 'according to my gospel,' he is referring to Luke's book." Paul also expressed wondrous approval of this gospel when he mentioned Luke in 2 Corinthians, saying: ". . . whose praise is in the gospel through all the churches."

We read in the *History of Antioch* that at a time when the Christians who lived in Antioch had abandoned themselves to all sorts of shameful conduct, they were besieged by a horde of Turks and were sorely tried by hunger and misery. But then they were fully converted to the Lord by contrition and penance, and a man radiant of aspect and clothed in white garments appeared to someone praying in the church of Saint Mary of Tripoli. The visitor was asked who he was, and he said he was Luke and had come from Antioch, where the Lord had mustered the hosts of heaven and the apostles and the martyrs to fight for his pilgrims. The Christians therefore took heart and cut the Turkish horde to pieces.

---

[37] Luke 1:2.

157. Saints Chrysanthus and Daria

Chrysanthus, the son of Polimius, a man of high rank and distinction, had been instructed in the Christian faith and had become a Christian. His father could not persuade him to return to the worship of idols, so he had him locked up in a room, and put five damsels in with him to seduce him with their amorous wiles. Chrysanthus, however, prayed God not to let him be overwhelmed by that wild beast, namely, carnal concupiscence. What then happened was that the aforesaid damsels fell into a deep sleep and could take neither food nor drink; but when they were led out of the room, they took both eagerly.

Then Daria, a most decorous virgin who was dedicated to the goddess Vesta, was asked to go in to Chrysanthus and restore him to the gods and his father. She went in, and Chrysanthus reprehended her for the pompousness of her garb. Her response was that she was arrayed that way not for vain show, but to win him back to the gods and his father. Chrysanthus again rebuked her, this time for worshiping as gods beings whom their own authors often described as vicious men and wanton women. Daria replied that the philosophers had given the elements human names in order to confer some standing upon them. Chrysanthus: "If one man worships the earth as a goddess, and another, a peasant, plows it, obviously the earth gives more return to the peasant than to the worshiper; and the same can be said of the sea and the other elements."

Chrysanthus and Daria, whom he had now converted, were united by the bond of the Holy Spirit but pretended to be wedded in the flesh. They proceeded to convert a great many people to Christ, including the tribune Claudius, who had been Chrysanthus's tutor, with his wife and children, as well as a number of other soldiers. Chrysanthus was therefore locked up in a fetid dungeon, but the stench was changed into a sweet odor. Daria was consigned to a brothel, but a lion that had escaped from the amphitheater stood guard at the brothel door. A man was sent to corrupt the virgin, but the lion caught him and seemed to be looking to Daria to be told what to do with his captive. She ordered the lion to do the man no harm and to allow him to come to her.

The man was quickly converted and ran through the city shouting that Daria was a goddess. Huntsmen were dispatched to recapture the lion, but they were all taken captive by the beast, laid at the virgin's feet, and by her converted. The prefect then ordered a roaring fire to be built at the entrance to the cell, in order to consume both the lion and Daria. The lion gave thought to this, was dismayed, and by roaring obtained the saint's permission to go wherever he wanted to go, provided he did not hurt anyone.

The prefect inflicted a variety of tortures on Chrysanthus and Daria, but none of them did the slightest harm to the two saints. Finally these inviolate spouses were dumped into a pit and crushed with earth and stones, and so were consecrated as martyrs to Christ. This took place in the time of Carus, bishop of Narbonne, who became bishop in A.D. 211. In Narbonne their feast is celebrated with special solemnity.

---

158. The Eleven Thousand Virgins

The martyrdom of the eleven thousand virgins came about in the following way. In Britain there was a most Christian king named Notus or Maurus, who had a daughter called Ursula. Ursula was distinguished for her virtuous life, her wisdom, and her beauty, and her fame took wing and spread far and wide. The king of Anglia, who had great power and had subjected many nations to his rule, heard of this virgin's renown and declared that he would be very happy to have her married to his one and only son. The young man agreed warmly to this proposal. They therefore sent ambassadors of state to the virgin's father. These made large promises and lavished flattering words, to which they added dire threats about what would happen if they were to return empty-handed to their lord.

King Notus was sorely troubled for several reasons: he thought it improper to hand over a woman who was signed with the Christian faith to a worshiper of idols; he knew that she herself would never give her consent; and he was mortally afraid of the other king's savagery. His daughter, however, acting under God's inspiration, persuaded him to yield to the aforesaid king's request, but on the following conditions: the king and her father were to assign to her ten carefully chosen virgins as companions, and to her and each of the ten the company and service of a thousand virgins; triremes should be rigged and provisioned for their transportation; an interval of three years should be given her to fulfill her dedication to virginity; the young man himself should be baptized and during the three years receive instruction in the faith.

There was wisdom behind her proposal: given the difficult conditions, the king might change his mind about having her for his son, or, given this opportunity, she might dedicate all those virgins to God with herself. The suitor, however, readily accepted the conditions and insisted that his father do likewise. He was baptized forthwith and ordered that everything else should be carried out as quickly as possible. Her father gave orders that his daughter, whom he loved dearly, should have men in her entourage, to give her and her battalions any help they might need.

From all sides, then, the virgins flocked together, and men, too, hurried to see this great spectacle. Many bishops also came to be with the virgins and to travel with them. One of the bishops was Pantulus, bishop of Basel, who led them to Rome, came back with them, and with them accepted martyrdom. Saint Gerasina, queen of Sicily, also came. She had married a very cruel man, a veritable wolf, whom she transformed into a lamb. She was the sister of Bishop Macirisus and of Daria, Saint Ursula's mother. Ursula's father wrote her a letter in which he gave her an idea of Ursula's secret purpose, and Gerasina, inspired by God, immediately put the affairs of the kingdom in the hands of one of her sons, and took ship and sailed to Britain, having with her her four daughters, Babilla, Juliana, Victoria, and Aurea, and her little son Adrian, who for love of his sisters attached himself to the pilgrimage. At her invitation, virgins gathered from various countries, and Gerasina, continuing as their leader, eventually suffered martyrdom with them.

In accordance with the compact, the virgins were assembled and the well-stocked triremes made ready. Now the queen disclosed the secret to those who had become, as it were, her fellow soldiers, and all took the oath of this new knighthood. They engaged in the customary preludes of war. They ran hither and they ran yon. At times, simulating the conditions of war, they pretended to flee the field of battle. They took part in all sorts of contests, trying whatever came to their minds and leaving nothing neglected. Sometimes they came in at midday, sometimes barely before dark. Princes and primates came to witness this unusual spectacle, and all were filled with admiration and joy. Ursula in time converted all the virgins to the faith.

Then, in the space of one day, with a fair wind blowing, they arrived at a port of Gaul named Tyella, and from there went on to Cologne. In Cologne an angel of the Lord appeared to Ursula and predicted that the full count of virgins would return to that city and there would win the crown of martyrdom. Following the angel's orders they set out for Rome and landed at Basel, left the ships there, and continued to Rome on foot. Pope Cyriacus[1] rejoiced at their coming. He himself was from Britain and had many blood relations among the virgins, so he and the entire clergy of Rome welcomed them with high honor. That very night it was divinely revealed to the pope that he would gain the palm of martyrdom with them. He kept this knowledge to himself and baptized many of the virgins who had not yet received the sacrament.

When Cyriacus, the nineteenth pope after Peter, had ruled the Church for one year and eleven weeks, he saw that the time was opportune. He called his

---

[1] Not listed in the *Acta apostolica*.

court together and informed them of his resolution, and there, in the presence of all, resigned his dignities and his office. Everyone protested, especially the cardinals, who thought he must be out of his wits to abandon the glory of the pontificate and go off with a lot of silly women. He, however, stood firm and ordained a holy man called Ametos[2] to succeed him as pope. Because he had left the apostolic see against the wishes of the clergy, the said clergy expunged his name from the catalog of popes, and thenceforth the sacred chorus of virgins lost all the favor they had enjoyed with the Roman curia.

Meanwhile two wicked commanders in the Roman army, namely, Maximus and Africanus, seeing this great multitude of virgins and noting that many men and women were hurrying to join them, were afraid that their influence would make the Christian religion flourish overmuch. The two therefore studied the women's itinerary closely and sent messages to Julius, their kinsman, the chief of the Hunnish tribe, telling him to lead his army against the virgins, since they were Christians, and slaughter them when they reached Cologne. Blessed Cyriacus left Rome with this noble company of virgins. Vincent, a cardinal priest, followed him, as did James, who had gone from Britain, his homeland, to Antioch, and there had held the dignity of the archepiscopal office for seven years. James had come to make a visitation to the pope then reigning, and had already left the city when he heard of the virgins' arrival and hastened back to join them, and to share their journey and their martyrdom. Maurisius, bishop of the city of Levicana, who was the uncle of Babilla and Juliana, as well as Follarius, bishop of Lucca, and Sulpicius, bishop of Ravenna, who were then in Rome, also joined the aforesaid virgins.

Ethereus, who was pledged to be blessed Ursula's husband, had stayed in Britain and now, by an angelic message, received the Lord's order to urge his mother to become a Christian. His father Ethereus had been baptized and had died within a year, and his son had succeeded to the kingdom. When the holy virgins and the aforesaid bishops were on their way back from Rome, Ethereus was admonished by the Lord to go out and meet his plighted spouse, and to receive the crown of martyrdom with her in Cologne. In obedience to the divine command he had his mother baptized, and then, with his mother and his little sister Florentina and Bishop Clement as well, went out to meet the virgins and to proceed with them to martyrdom. Marculus, the bishop of Greece, and his niece Constantia were now directed by a vision to go to Rome, where they too joined the virgins, to be with them and to share their martyrdom. Constantia had been betrothed to the son of a king, but he had died before the wedding and she had vowed her virginity to the Lord.

All the virgins, therefore, with the above-named bishops, traveled back to Cologne but found the city under siege by the Huns. The barbarians saw them, rushed upon them with wild yells, and, like wolves ravaging a flock of sheep, slew them all. Having butchered the rest, they came at last to blessed Ursula.

---

[2] Likewise unlisted.

Their chief was dazzled by her wondrous beauty. He tried to console her over the death of her companions and promised that he would make her his wife. But she scorned his offer, and he, seeing that she despised him, transfixed her with an arrow and so consummated her martyrdom. One of the virgins, whose name was Cordula, was so frightened that she hid all night in the ship, but in the morning surrendered of her own volition and so received the crown; but her feast was not celebrated because she had not suffered with the others. She therefore appeared long afterwards to a recluse, ordering her to see to it that her solemnity was observed the day after the feast of the virgins.

Their passion took place in the year A.D. 238. There are some, however, who maintain that the events above related could not have occurred at that date. Sicily, they reason, was not a kingdom, nor was Constantinople, at the time when the queens of these kingdoms are alleged to have been with the virgins. It is therefore thought to be more likely that this wholesale martyrdom took place when Huns and Goths were warring upon each other, long after the reign of the emperor Constantine—namely, in the time of the emperor Marcian (as we read in one chronicle). Marcian reigned in the year A.D. 452.[3]

A certain abbot asked the abbess of Cologne to give him the body of one of the virgins, which he promised to enshrine in a silver casket in his monastery church, but for a whole year he kept the body on the altar in a wooden box. Then one night, while the abbot was singing matins with his community, that virgin descended bodily into the sanctuary and, after bowing reverently before the altar, walked out through the middle of the choir while the monks looked on in astonishment. The abbot ran to the wooden box and found it empty, so he went to the place from which they had taken the body, and there it was. The abbot begged forgiveness and the present of that body or another, promising most seriously that he would have a precious casket made for it right away. He got nothing.

A certain religious who had great devotion for these virgins was gravely ill, and one day saw a most beautiful virgin appearing to him and asking if he recognized her. He marveled at the vision and admitted that he did not recognize her at all, and she said: "I am one of the virgins for whom you have such devotion. We want you to be rewarded for this, and so, if for love of us and in our honor you will recite the Lord's Prayer eleven thousand times, you will have us to protect and console you at the hour of your death." She disappeared, and the monk fulfilled the condition as fast as he could. Then he called the abbot and had himself anointed,[4] and, as soon as he was anointed, said loudly that they should all go away and make room for the sacred virgins. The abbot asked what

[3] The confusions, historical and geographical, in this legend are not unusual in the *Golden Legend*, nor in similar literature of the period, and they do not in the least diminish the main point of the story, which is the virtue, sanctity, and Christian courage of these virgins, so marvelously multiplied. A succinct and informative examination of this legend is given in *Butler's Lives of the Saints* (New York: P. J. Kenedy & Sons, 1963), 4:165–168.

[4] I.e., given the last rites.

this was about, and the monk gave him a full account of the virgin's promise. All left him, and when they came back a little later, found that he had migrated to the Lord.

159. Saints Simon and Jude, Apostles

Simon means obedient, or one who bears sadness. This Simon had two surnames; he was called Simon Zelotes, the Zealot, and Simon the Cananean, after Cana of Galilee, where the Lord changed water into wine. Zelotes is the equivalent of Cana, because *cana* means zeal. Simon was obedient with regard to the commandments by acting in accordance with them; he bore the sadness of the afflicted by his compassion; he had zeal for souls by his constant fervor.

Jude (Judas) is interpreted as confessing, or glorious, or it comes from *jubilum dans*, one who gives jubilation. Jude was a confessor of the faith; he had the joy of the kingdom and the jubilation of inward joy. He had several surnames. He was called *Judas (frater) Jacobi*, Judas the brother of James, because he was the brother of James the Less. Secondly, he was called Thaddeus, which means one who lays hold of the prince; or it comes from *thadea*, a royal garment, and *deus*, God. Thaddeus was a royal garment of God by the ornament of his virtues, and by this garment he laid hold of Christ. Or Thaddeus comes from *tam Deus*, i.e., great God, which he was by adoption. Thirdly, the *Ecclesiastical History* calls him *Lebbaeus*, which sounds like *cor*, heart, or *corculus*, little heart. therefore one who cultivates, takes care of, his heart; or *Lebbaeus* is like *lebes*, a basin. Jude is called heart for his greatheartedness, little heart for his purity, a basin for the fullness of his graces, because he merited to be a basin or vase of virtues and grace.

The passion and legend of Simon and Jude Thaddeus was written in Hebrew by Abdias, bishop of Babylonia, who was ordained a bishop by the apostles themselves, Tropeus, a disciple of Abdias, translated it into Greek, and Africanus put it into Latin.

Simon the Cananean and Jude, also called Thaddeus, were brothers of James the Less and sons of Mary of Cleopas, who was married to Alpheus. Thomas sent Jude to Abgar, king of Edessa, after the Lord's ascension. The *Ecclesiastical History* tells us that the said King Abgar had dispatched a letter to our Lord Jesus Christ. The letter read as follows: "King Abgar, son of Euchanias, to Jesus the good

Savior, who has appeared in the region of Jerusalem, greetings. I have heard about you and the cures you effect, that you do this without medicaments or herbs, and that with a word you cause the blind to see, the lame to walk, lepers to be cleansed, and the dead to live again. Having heard all this, I have decided in my mind that you are either a god and have come down from heaven to do what you do, or you are the Son of God and so do these things. For this reason I write to ask you to be kind enough to come to me and cure me of the illness from which I have long suffered. I have also learned that the Jews are murmuring against you and plotting to do away with you. Come therefore to me, because I have this city, a modest but honorable one and large enough for both of us."

The Lord Jesus answered Abgar in these words: "Blessed are you, who have believed in me though you had not seen me, for it is written of me that those who do not see me will believe, and those who do see me will not believe. As for what you have written to me asking me to come to you, I tell you that I must finish all the work I was sent to do, and later be welcomed back by him who sent me. Therefore when I have been assumed, I shall send one of my disciples to you to cure you and give you new life." That is what we read in the *Ecclesiastical History*.

Abgar thus realized that he was not to see Christ face to face. Therefore, according to an ancient history as attested to by John of Damascus in Book IV, he sent a painter to Jesus to make a portrait of the Lord, so that even though he, Abgar, could not see him in the flesh, he could at least imagine him by looking at his portrait. But when the artist came to Jesus, the radiance of the Lord's countenance was so intense that he could not see his face clearly nor fix his eyes upon it, and so could not make the portrait as ordered. Seeing this, Jesus took a linen cloth that belonged to the artist and pressed it to his face, leaving his image imprinted on it, and sent this to the king. The same ancient history describes this image, as John of Damascus testifies. It showed the Lord as having fine eyes and a fine brow, and a long face slightly tilted forward, which is a sign of maturity.

It is said that the letter written by our Lord Jesus Christ had such power that no heretic or pagan could live in Edessa, nor did any tyrant dare to harm the city. Indeed, if at any time a hostile tribe raised an armed hand against Edessa, a child stood atop the city gate and read the letter, and the enemy horde either fled in terror or sued for peace. This actually happened in the past, or so we are told. At a later time Edessa was captured and profaned by the Saracens, all miraculous help being withheld because of the wave of sinfulness that had spread throughout the East.

After Christ's assumption into heaven (as we read in the *Ecclesiastical History*), Thomas the apostle sent Thaddeus (also called Jude) to King Abgar, as the Lord had promised. When Thaddeus came to the king and said that he was the promised disciple of Jesus, Abgar saw in his face a marvelous, godlike splendor. Amazed and frightened at the sight, he adored the Lord, and said: "Truly you are a disciple of Jesus the Son of God, who made me this promise: 'I will send you one of my disciples to cure you and give you life.' " Thaddeus: "If you believe in the Son of God, you will obtain all that your heart desires." Abgar: "I do verily believe and would willingly put to death the Jews who crucified him, if I had that possibility and the Roman authority did not interfere." Now Abgar, as we read in some books, was a leper. Thaddeus therefore took the Savior's letter and rubbed the king's face with it, and at once the leprosy was completely cured.

Jude Thaddeus subsequently preached in Mesopotamia and Pontus, and Simon in Egypt. Then they both went to Persia and there found the two sorcerers, Zaroës and Arphaxat, whom Matthew had driven out of Egypt. Baradach, commander of the king of Babylonia's army, was about to go and make war upon the Indians but could get no response from his gods. He went to the temple of a neighboring city and there received a response, to wit, that because of the apostles who had come there, the gods could not answer him. The commander had a search made for the apostles, found them, and asked them who they were and for what purpose they had come. They answered: "If you want to know our race, we are Hebrews; if our state of life, we confess our Christianity; if our reason for being here, it is for the sake of your people's salvation." The general replied: "When I come back victorious, I shall hear you!" The apostles: "It would be more fitting that you should know the One by whose help you may be able to conquer the rebels, or at least to find them eager to make peace." The commander: "I see that you are more powerful than our gods! Well, then, tell us how the war will end!" The apostles: "So that you may know that your gods are liars, we command them to give their answers to your questions. When their answers show that they know nothing, we shall have proof that they lie about everything!" The answer came through the sorcerers—to wit, that it would be a widespread war with large numbers of people killed on both sides.

The apostles began to laugh. The commander said to them: "You laugh, but I am gripped with fear!" The apostles: "There's nothing to be afraid of, because peace came here with us. Tomorrow at the third hour of the day, legates from the Indies will come to you and bow peaceably to your power!" At this the priests of the idols laughed derisively, and said to the commander: "These men say this to make you feel secure, and you will relax your guard and the enemy will overrun you!" The apostles: "We did not tell you to wait a month, but one day. Tomorrow you will be the victor, and there will be peace."

The commander placed all parties under guard, so that if the outcome showed that what the apostles had said was true, they would be honored for it and the others would be punished for their crime. The following day what the apostles had predicted actually happened. The commander then wanted to put the priests to death by fire, but the apostles forbade this, because they had been sent not to kill the living but to bring the dead to life. The commander was overwhelmed with surprise because they would not let the priests be killed and would not accept a share of their possessions, and he brought the pair to the king, saying: "These two are gods hiding under the appearance of men!" Then, with the two magicians present, he told the king all that had happened. The magicians, beside themselves with envy, said that the apostles were workers of evil and were subtly plotting against the kingdom. The commander said to them: "Try them, if you dare!" The magicians: "If you want to see that in our presence men cannot speak, let some of your most eloquent men come in, and if they manage to speak in our presence, you will know that we have no skills at all!"

A large group of lawyers were brought before the sorcerers, and they became so mute that they could not even nod to indicate that they could not speak. Next the sorcerers said to the king: "We will show you that we are gods when we let these people speak but make them unable to walk, then allow them to walk but make them unable to see, even with their eyes open!" They proceeded to do all that they had said, and the commander brought the lawyers, all ashamed and bewildered, to the apostles. When the lawyers saw them clothed in rags, they had nothing but contempt for them. Simon said to them: "It often happens that worthless stuff is kept in gold, jeweled cases, and precious, gem-studded neck-laces are stored in cheap wooden boxes. Anyone who wishes to become the possessor of a thing will not pay much attention to the container but to the thing it contains. Therefore promise that you will quit the worship of idols and adore the one and invisible God, and we will mark your foreheads with the sign of the cross. Then you will be able to show that the sorcerers are frauds."

The apostles marked the lawyers' foreheads, and they again appeared before the king with the sorcerers present. Not only were these unable to outwit the lawyers, but the lawyers made fools of the sorcerers, who, enraged, caused a wriggling mass of serpents to appear. At once, at the king's order, the apostles came in. They filled their mantles with the reptiles, then threw them upon the magicians, and said: "In the name of the Lord you shall not die, but the snakes will gnaw at your flesh and you will grunt and moan with pain." The serpents began to eat their flesh and the magicians howled like wolves, whereupon the king and the others asked the apostles to let the animals kill the magicians. The apostles' answer was: "We were sent to bring the dead back to life, not to bring death upon the living."

Simon and Jude then prayed, and commanded the serpents to draw out all the venom they had injected, then to go back where they belonged. The magicians felt greater pain when the serpents sucked out the venom than they had when they were being bitten. The apostles told them: "You will feel pain for three days. On the third day you will be healed, so that then at last you may abandon your malice." When the magicians had gone three days without food or drink, and—so acute were their sufferings—without sleep, the apostles came and said to them: "The Lord does not stoop to accept forced service. Therefore get up cured, and be on your way, free to do whatever you wish." They persisted in their malice, however, and went away to stir up all Babylonia against Simon and Jude.

Some time after this, the daughter of a duke conceived out of fornication and gave birth to a son. She defamed a certain holy deacon, saying that he had violated her and was the father of her child. When her parents wanted the deacon dead, the apostles entered the case and asked when the child had been born. They answered: "Today, at the first hour of the day!" The apostles said: "Bring the infant here, and see that the deacon whom you accuse is here also." They did so, and the apostles said to the newborn: "Tell us, child, in the name of the Lord, if this is the deacon's doing!" The infant: "That deacon is chaste and saintly, and has never defiled his flesh." The parents then insisted that the apostles find out who was the author of the crime, but they replied: "It is ours to absolve the innocent, not to bring ruin on the guilty."

At that time two savage tigresses that had been kept in separate cages escaped and devoured everyone they encountered. Then the apostles came to them and in the name of the Lord made them as meek as lambs.

Simon and Jude wanted to leave that region but the people asked them to stay, and they stayed for a year and three months, within which period more than sixty thousand people, not counting children, were baptized. The magicians already described went to a city called Samir, where there were seventy high priests of the idols. They set the priests' minds against the apostles, urging them either to compel the holy men to sacrifice to the idols, or to put them to death. When the apostles had traversed the whole province and arrived at the city, the pontiffs, with the entire populace, took them captive and carried them to the temple of the Sun. The demons began to shout: "What is there between us and you, apostles of the living God? When you come in, we are burned by the flames!" Then an angel of the Lord appeared to the apostles and said: "Choose one or the other, sudden death for these, or your own martyrdom!" The apostles: "Adored be the mercy of God! May he convert these men, and lead us to the palm of martyrdom!"

Silence fell, and the apostles said: "So that you may know that these idols are full of demons, watch! We command the demons to come out and each one of them to shatter his own image!" And immediately, to the utter amazement of all, two black and naked figures[1] came out of the idols, smashed them, and with wild cries departed. The pagan priests rushed upon the apostles and killed them. At that very hour, the skies being brilliant and serene, such lightnings flashed down that the temple was split from top to bottom into three segments, and the two sorcerers were turned to ashes by the heat of the lightning. The king had the apostles' bodies transferred to his city, and in their honor built a church of admirable grandeur.

---

[1] "Figures" is substituted here for the "Ethiopians" of the text.

Numerous sources tell us that Simon was nailed to a gibbet in the shape of a cross. Isidore says this in his book *On the Death of the Apostles*. The same testimony is given by Eusebius in his *Ecclesiastical History*, by Bede in his treatise *On the Acts of the Apostles*, and by Master John Beleth in his *Summa*. These authors say that when Simon had preached in Egypt, he returned to Jerusalem. After the death of James the Less, Simon was unanimously elected by the other apostles to succeed him as bishop of Jerusalem. He is said to have raised thirty dead persons to life, wherefore it is sung of him:

> Ter denos mortuos
> Fluctibus mersos
> Humanae vitae reddidit.[2]

When he had ruled the church at Jerusalem for many years and had reached the age of 120, Trajan being emperor and Atticus consul at Jerusalem, the consul arrested Simon and had him tortured. In the end he ordered him nailed to a cross, and all the bystanders, including the judge, marveled that an old man of six score years could bear the torment of the cross.

Some authors, however, say—and this is the truth of the matter—that it was not this Simon who bore the martyrdom of the cross and was the bishop of Jerusalem, but another Simon, the son of Cleopas the brother of Joseph. Eusebius, bishop of Caesarea, testifies to this in his chronicle. Isidore and Bede say the same in their chronicles. Isidore and Eusebius corrected what they had previously written in their chronicles, as is clear from Bede, who, in his *Retractationes*, reproaches himself for having held the other opinion. Usuard also gives this same testimony in his *Martyrology*.

160. Saint Quentin

Quentin, noble by birth and a Roman citizen, went to the city of Amiens and performed many miracles there. By order of Maximian, prefect of the city, he was taken prisoner and beaten until the executioners fainted from their exertions. Then he was jailed, but an angel set him free, and he went to the center

---

[2] Three tens of dead / drowned by the waves / he restored to human life.

of the city and preached to the people. Arrested again, he was stretched on the rack until his veins burst, then was whipped with raw thongs, then had boiling oil, pitch, and grease poured over his wounds. All this he bore patiently, meanwhile mocking the judge, who resented this and gave orders to force lime, vinegar, and mustard into his mouth. Even this did not move him, and he was taken to Veromandum. There the judge had two nails pounded into his body from head to legs, and ten pegs driven under his fingernails. Finally he was beheaded.

Quentin's body was cast into the river and lay hidden for fifty-five years, then was found by a noble Roman lady. Here is how that happened. The lady was absorbed in prayer one night, when an angel alerted her and directed her to hasten to the stronghold of Veromandum, there to search for the body of Saint Quentin and bury it with honors. With a large company she went to the said place and they all prayed devoutly, whereupon the saint's body, incorrupt and sweet-smelling, rose to the surface of the river. The lady saw to the burial and in return for that service recovered her eyesight. She had a church built there and then returned home.

161. Saint Eustace

Eustace was first called Placidus. He was the commanding general of Emperor Trajan's armies. Though a worshiper of idols, he was assiduous in doing works of mercy, and his wife was his partner both in worship and in good works. They had two sons, and their father saw to it that the boys were trained in a manner befitting their high station.

Placidus's constant care for those in need merited him the light of grace that led him to the way of truth. One day when he was hunting, he came upon a herd of deer, among which one stag stood out by his size and beauty, and this deer broke away from the others and bounded into a deeper part of the forest. Leaving his soldiers to follow the rest of the herd, Placidus gave his full effort to pursuing the stag and did his best to catch it. The deer kept well ahead of him, however, and finally stopped at the top of a high peak, Placidus, coming near, pondered how he might capture the animal. As he studied it, he saw between its antlers what looked like the holy cross, shining more brightly than the sun. Upon the cross was the image of Jesus Christ.

Christ then spoke to Placidus through the stag's mouth, as once he had spoken through the mouth of Balaam's ass. The Lord said: "O Placidus, why are you pursuing me? For your sake I have appeared to you in this animal. I am the Christ, whom you worship without knowing it. Your alms have risen before me, and for this purpose I have come, that through this deer which you hunted, I myself might hunt you!" There are others, however, who say that these words were pronounced by the image which appeared between the stag's antlers.

Having heard what was said, Placidus was stricken with fear and fell from his horse. After an hour, however, he came to himself, rose from the ground, and said: "Let me understand what you were saying, and I will believe you." The Lord said: "I am the Christ. I created heaven and earth. I made light to rise and be separate from darkness. I set seasons and days and years. I formed man from the slime of the earth. For the salvation of the human race I took flesh and appeared on earth. I was crucified and buried, and on the third day I rose from the dead."

Placidus, having heard these words, again fell to the ground and said: "Lord, I believe that you ARE, that you have made all things, that you convert the erring." The Lord said to him: "If you believe, go to the bishop of the city and have him baptize you." "Lord," said Placidus, "do you want me to make all this known to my wife and my sons, so that they also may believe in you?" "Yes," said the Lord. "Tell them, and let them be cleansed with you. Then you yourself come here tomorrow morning, and I will appear to you again and tell you more fully what the future holds for you."

Placidus went home, found his wife in bed, and began to tell her what he had to tell, but she burst out, saying: "My master, I too saw him this past night, and he said to me: 'Tomorrow you and your husband and your sons will come to me!' So now I too know that he is Jesus the Christ!" And right then, in the middle of the night, they went to the bishop of Rome. He baptized them with great joy, giving Placidus the name Eustace and his wife the name Theospis, and called his sons Agapetus and Theospitus.

Morning came, and Eustace, as he had done before, set out for the hunt. Coming near to the place he knew, he dismissed his soldiers on the pretext that their task was to pick up the tracks of some game. Then, standing in the same place, he saw the same vision as before and, prostrating himself on the ground, said: "I implore you, Lord, show your servant what you promised to show him!" The Lord: "Blessed are you, Eustace, for accepting the bath of my grace, because now you have overcome the devil! Now you have trampled on the one who had deceived you! Now your faith will be seen! The devil, because you have left him, will fight furiously against you. You will have to bear many hardships in order to receive the crown of victory. You will have to suffer much, in order to be brought low from the lofty vanity of the world and be exalted again in the riches of the spirit. Do not lose courage, nor look back upon your former eminence, because, through your trials, you are to become another Job.

But when you have been humbled, I will come to you and restore you to your erstwhile glory. Tell me, therefore! Do you wish to endure trials now or at your life's end?"

Eustace gave his answer: "Lord, if so it is to be, order the trials to befall us now, but grant us the patience to bear them!" The Lord: "Be of good heart! My grace will guard your souls." Then the Lord ascended to heaven, and Eustace went home and told all to his wife.

Within a few days a lethal plague gripped the men and women who served in his house and killed them all, and not long afterwards his horses and herds perished. Then some lawless men, seeing him despoiled and desolate, broke into his house at night, laid hands on everything they found, and robbed him of his gold and silver and all his goods. Eustace gave thanks to God and, having nothing left, fled by night with his wife and sons: dreading the shame of destitution, they decided to go to Egypt. The king and all the senators were shocked at the loss of their commander-in-chief, especially since they could find no equal to replace him.

The fugitives made their way to the sea, boarded a ship, and sailed away. Eustace's wife was a beautiful woman, and the ship's captain lusted after her. When it was time to pay their passage and they had nothing to pay it with, the captain commanded that the woman be held on board. He intended to make her his own, but Eustace absolutely refused to agree. When he persisted in his refusal, the master gave his crew the idea of throwing Eustace overboard so that they could have his wife; and Eustace, unable to resist further, sadly left her to them and went ashore with his sons. Weeping, he said to the boys: "Woe to me, woe to you, that your mother is given over to a man who is not of our race!"

They came to a river in flood, and the father did not dare attempt to cross with the two boys at the same time, so he left one and carried the other across. But the river was over its banks, so Eustace put ashore the boy he was carrying and started back to rescue the other. As he reached the middle of the stream, a wolf ran out, snatched the boy his father had just put ashore, and disappeared into the forest. Eustace, despairing of this child, turned again to go to the other one, but a lion came and carried the boy away. Unable to go after either son, since he was out in the middle of the river, the father began to mourn and tear his hair, and might have abandoned himself to the waters had not divine providence restrained him.

Meanwhile some shepherds saw the lion carrying the boy off alive and went after him with their dogs. By God's will the beast dropped the child unhurt and got away. On the other side of the river huntsmen raised the hue and cry in pursuit of the wolf, and freed the boy, unharmed, from the animal's jaws. As it happened, the huntsmen and the shepherds were of the same village, and they kept the boys with them and took care of them.

Eustace, however, did not know that this had happened, and went his way weeping and saying: "Alas, alas! Once I flourished like a tree, but now I am almost leafless! Woe is me! Once I was surrounded by a multitude of soldiers, but now I am left alone, and even the company of my sons is denied me! I remember, Lord, that you told me it was my lot to be tried as Job was tried, but it seems to me that even more ills have come to me than to him. Even if he was stripped of his possessions, he could at least have dung to sit on, but I have not even that! He had his friends to share his misery, but I have only the fierce beasts that stole my sons. Job's wife was left to him, I am bereft of mine. Give pause, O Lord, to my tribulations, and set a guard over my mouth, lest my heart incline to evil words, and I be cast out of thy sight!" He went on and came to a certain village, where he stayed and, for a pittance, watched over the fields of those men for fifteen years, while in the next village his sons were growing up and did not even know that they were brothers. The Lord also kept Eustace's wife in his care. The ship's captain, that foreigner, never took her to wife but died leaving her untouched.

In those years the emperor and the Roman people were constantly harassed by enemies. The emperor remembered Placidus, who had fought so valiantly against those same foes, and was saddened to think of the sudden change that had overtaken his general. So he sent many soldiers to different parts of the world, promising wealth and honors to those who would find Placidus. Two men who had served under the former commander came to the village where he was living. Eustace saw them coming across the field, recognized them by their gait, and was disturbed by the memory of his own former high status. He said to the Lord: "Lord, I see these men who were with me, whom I had not hoped ever to see again! Please grant that I may again see my wife! I cannot ask for my sons, because they were eaten by wild beasts." And a voice came to him, saying: "Have confidence, Eustace, because you will soon have back your high honors, and your sons and your wife will be returned to you!"

He went to meet the two soldiers, who did not recognize him at all. They greeted him and asked if he knew a stranger whose name was Placidus and who had a wife and two sons. He professed not to know them. He invited the soldiers, however, to be his guests and waited on them. Then, recalling his former rank, he could not contain his tears, but went outside and washed his face before returning to serve them. Meanwhile the two men looked at each other questioningly, and one said: "Doesn't that man look a lot like the one we're looking for?" "He certainly does," the other said. "We'll watch closely, and if he has a scar on his head like the one our general had, he's the one!" They looked and saw the scar, and knew that Eustace was the man they were looking for, so they jumped up and embraced him and asked about his wife and children. He told them that his sons were dead and his wife in captivity. Then the neighbors hurried in as though to enjoy a bit of theater, and the soldiers boasted about their general's prowess and the glory that had been his. They also informed him of the emperor's order and clothed him in fine garments.

A fifteen-days' journey brought them back to Rome, and the emperor, learning that Eustace was approaching, hurried to meet him and embraced him warmly. He told them all that had happened to him, and they took him immediately to military headquarters and ordered him to take charge. He surveyed his forces and found that they were far fewer in number than he needed in order to face so many foes, so he ordered recruits to be called up from every city and village. Thus it happened that the place where the two sons had grown up was called upon to furnish two recruits. The local people considered the two young men to be the most fitted for military service, and sent them up. Eustace was very pleased to see these two physically robust and morally upright candidates, and assigned them to places in his immediate circle. Off they went to war and won a great victory, and Eustace granted the troops three days of rest in a place where, though he did not know this, his wife kept a modest inn. By God's will the two youths were quartered in this inn, but they were not aware that their hostess was also their mother.

Around midday the two were lounging outside and chatting about their early years, while the mother, seated at a little distance, listened intently. The older son said to the younger: "I can't remember anything about my childhood, except that my father was the commander of the armies, and my mother was a very beautiful woman. They had two sons, me and a younger one—he was very handsome too—and our parents took us one night and we boarded a ship going I don't know where. When we got off the ship, our mother stayed on board, I don't know why. Our father was crying as he carried the two of us and came to a river, which he crossed carrying my younger brother, leaving me behind on the riverbank. When he was on his way back to get me, a wolf came and ran off with my brother, and, before my father could reach me, a lion came out of the forest, seized me, and dragged me into the woods. Sheepherders snatched me from the lion's mouth and brought me up on their own land, as you know. I never could find out what became of my father and the boy." Hearing all this, the younger brother began to weep, and said: "By God, from what I hear, I am your brother, because the men who brought me up said the same thing—that they had snatched me from a wolf!" So they fell into each other's arms, and kissed, and wept.

The mother, having heard the story as the older son told it, spent hours wondering whether these could be her sons. The next day she went to the commander and questioned him, saying: "I beg of you, my lord, to order me returned to my native land, because I am a Roman and therefore a foreigner here." As she spoke to the commander, she noticed certain distinguishing marks and recognized her husband. Unable to control herself, she threw herself at his feet and said: "I pray you, my lord, tell me about your early life, because I think you are Placidus, commander of the armies, and are also called Eustace, whom the Savior converted when you were still Placidus. You underwent one trial after another. Your wife—and I am she—was taken from you at sea but was preserved from degradation. I had two sons, whose names were Agapetus and Theospitus." While she spoke, Eustace studied her carefully and saw that she was indeed his wife. Tears of joy and mutual embraces followed, and he glorified God who comforts the afflicted.

Then his wife said to him: "My master, where are our sons?" He said: "They were carried off by wild beasts." And he told her how he had lost them. "Thank God!" she exclaimed. "I think that as God has given us the gift of finding each other, he will also give us the joy of recognizing our sons!" Eustace: "I told you they were carried off by wild beasts!" She: "Yesterday I was sitting in the garden and listening to two young soldiers telling each other about their childhood, and I think they are our own sons! Ask them! They'll tell you!" Eustace sent for them and, upon hearing an account of their young years, knew that they were indeed his sons. He and their mother embraced them, floods of tears were shed, and kisses exchanged time after time. The whole army cheered and rejoiced, both because these people had been reunited and because the barbarians had been conquered.

When Eustace returned to Rome, Emperor Trajan had died and Hadrian, a still more guilty tyrant, had succeeded him. Hadrian staged a magnificent welcome for the commander and laid on a sumptuous banquet, celebrating his victory and the finding of his wife and sons. The next day the emperor led a procession to the temple of the idols, to offer sacrifice in thanksgiving for the victory. The emperor noticed that Eustace did not offer sacrifice either for the victory or for the recovery of his family, and exhorted him to do so. Eustace answered: "I worship Christ as God and I sacrifice to God alone!" This made Hadrian angry. He had Eustace, together with his wife and their sons, placed in the arena, and had a ferocious lion loosed upon them. The lion came running to them, lowered his head as though adoring them as saints, and meekly withdrew. Then the emperor had a brazen bull heated and ordered the four saints enclosed in it alive. Praying and commending themselves to the Lord, they entered the bull and so rendered their souls to the Lord.

Three days later their bodies were taken out of the bull in the emperor's presence. The bodies were intact, nor had the heat of the fire touched the hair or any other part of them. Christians took the sacred remains, buried them in a most honorable place, and built an oratory there. The martyrs suffered on 1 November, or, according to others, on 20 September, in the reign of Hadrian, which began about A.D. 120.

162. All Saints

The Feast of All Saints was instituted for four purposes. The first was connected with the dedication of a certain temple; the second was to supply for the omission of many saints from the calendar; the third was to atone for neglect in honoring the saints; the fourth was to make it easier to obtain the favors for which we pray.

The feast was indeed instituted in connection with the dedication of a certain temple. When the Romans were masters of the whole world, they built a very large temple, in the middle of which they set up their idol. Then around the perimeter they arranged the statues of the gods of the provinces, the faces turned to the idol of Rome and the eyes fixed upon it. If from time to time a province rebelled, at once, they say, by some trick of the devil, the statue of that province turned its back on the Roman idol, as if to give notice that the province no longer accepted Roman rule. What happened next was that the Romans quickly dispatched a large army and subjugated the rebellious state. The Romans, however, were not satisfied with having only the images of all the provincial gods in the capital, and temples were built to most of them in Rome itself to show that the gods had made the people of Rome conquerors and masters of all the provinces. But because there were too many idols for each to have its own temple, the Romans pushed their insane display to the point of erecting a temple higher and more marvelous than the rest in honor of all the gods, and called it the Pantheon, which means "all gods" and comes from *pan*, meaning all, and *theos*, meaning god. To complete the people's delusion, the priests of the idols pretended that they had been advised by Cybele, whom they called the mother of all the gods, that if they wished to obtain victory over all nations, they should build this magnificent temple to all her children.

The foundation of this temple was laid in a circle to signify the eternity of the gods. But because the vault would be too wide to support, the builders, each time the walls had reached a certain height, filled the interior with earth into which, it is said, coins were thrown, and so they proceeded until the wonderful temple was completed. Then it was announced that anyone who wished to carry away the earth could keep the money he found in it; whereupon crowds of people came hurrying, and the building was cleaned out in no time. Finally the Romans erected a gilded bronze pinnacle at the top of the dome, around the inside of which, so the story goes, emblems of all the provinces were sculpted, so that anyone who came to Rome could see in which direction his province lay. In time, however, this pinnacle fell down and left a large opening in the roof.

In the reign of the emperor Phocas, about the year 605, long after Rome had accepted the faith of Christ, the emperor ceded the temple described above to Pope Boniface IV, the third pope after Saint Gregory the Great. Boniface had the statues and everything connected with the cult of idols removed, and, on the twelfth day of May 609, consecrated the building in honor of Blessed Mary and all the martyrs. He gave it the title of Sancta Maria ad Martyres, but now it is popularly known as Santa Maria Rotonda. At that time no feast days were solemnized in honor of sainted confessors, but the crowds that came for this particular feast were so great that food ran out and the people could not stay for the celebration. A later Pope Gregory therefore moved the May feast to the first day of November, when supplies were ample after the harvest and the vintage was finished. He also decreed that the new feast was to be celebrated throughout the world, and that this day should be solemnly observed in honor of all the saints. Thus the temple that had been built for all the idols was now dedicated to all the saints, and where a horde of false gods had been worshiped, a multitude of saints was now praised.

The second purpose of the feast is to supply for omissions. We have in fact omitted many saints, not celebrating feast days or making memorials of them. Indeed we could not have feasts for all the saints. For one thing the number of them has multiplied until it is almost infinite. Besides that, we are weak and because of our weakness could not put up with so many celebrations. And then there is not enough time in the year: as Jerome says in the letter that prefaces his *Calendar*, there is not one day except the first of January that could not have five thousand martyrs assigned to it. Therefore the Church with good reason has ordered that since we cannot solemnize the saints one by one, we shall at least honor them generally and all together.

But why is it an established rule that we must mark the saints' feasts on earth? Master William of Auxerre gives six reasons for this in his *Summa de officiis*. The first is the honor due the divine majesty, because when we pay honor to the saints, we honor God in the saints and proclaim that he is admirable in them. Whoever pays honor to the saints pays special honor to him who made them saints. The second reason is that we need help in our weakness. Because we cannot obtain salvation by ourselves, we need the intercession of the saints, and it is right that we should honor them in order to gain their assistance. So we read in 1 (3) Kings, chapter 1:30, that Bathsheba (whose name means "wall of plenty" and stands for the Church triumphant) by her prayers obtained the kingdom (i.e., the Church militant) for her son. The third reason was to increase our own sense of security—in other words, to have the glory of the saints recalled to us on their feast day, and thus to build up our own hope and confidence. If mortals like ourselves could by their merits be so lifted up, it follows that we can do likewise, because "the hand of the Lord is not shortened that it cannot save" (Isa. 59:1). The fourth reason was to offer an example for our imitation. When the saints are celebrated on their feast days, we are inspired to imitate them, i.e., to follow their example by making little of earthly goods and setting our hearts on the things of heaven. The fifth reason was to allow a fair exchange. The saints make festival in heaven over us, for there is joy before the angels of God and holy souls over one sinner doing penance, and so we should make a fair return by celebrating their feasts on earth. And Master William's sixth reason is to assure our own honor, because when we honor the saints, we are taking care of our own interests and procuring our own honor. Their feast day honors us. When we pay tribute to our brothers, we honor ourselves, since love makes all things to be in common, and all things are ours, in heaven, on earth, and in eternity.

In addition to these reasons John of Damascus, Book IV, chapter 7, gives others as to why the saints and their bodies and relics ought to be honored. Some of his reasons are based on the dignity of the saints, some on the preciousness of their bodies. Their dignity, he says, is fourfold: they are God's friends, his children, his heirs, and our leaders and guides. And here are his authorities: for the first, John 15:15: "No longer do I call you servants, but I have called you friends"; for the second, John 1:12: "he gave power to become children of God"; for the third, Rom. 8:17: "if children, then heirs of God." Regarding the fourth he says: "How much trouble you would go to in order to find a guide to present you to a mortal king and speak to him on your behalf! But the leaders of the whole human race, who appeal to God for all of us, are they not to be honored? Of course they are, as also are those who build temples to honor God and to venerate the saints' memory."

Other reasons are based on the preciousness of the saints' bodies. John of Damascus gives four such and Augustine adds a fifth, all demonstrating how precious the bodies of the saints are. Their bodies were God's repository, Christ's temple, the alabaster vase of spiritual ointment, divine fountains, and the organ of the Holy Spirit. They were God's repository; Damascenus: "These became the repositories of God, pure cenacles." Their bodies were Christ's temples, whence it follows that God dwelt in their bodies by way of the intellect, as the apostle says (1 Cor. 3:16): "Do you not know that you are God's temple and that God's Spirit dwells in you?" God is spirit! How then could God's living temples, his living tabernacles, not be honored? Chrysostom also says about this: "Man delights in building houses, God's delight is in the company of the saints." So Ps. 25:8: "I have loved, O Lord, the beauty of thy house." What beauty? Not the beauty of a variety of splendid marbles, but that which a variety of living graces bestows. The former beauty pleases the eye of the body, the latter gives life to the soul; the former lasts only for a time and beguiles the eyes, the latter builds up the spirit unto eternity. Third, the saint's body is the alabaster vase of spiritual ointment, and Damascenus says: "The relics of the saints give out a sweet-smelling ointment, and let no one disbelieve it. If water gushed out of the hard stone of the cliff in the desert, and water came out of the jawbone of an ass to quench Samson's thirst, it is all the more believable that a fragrant ointment should flow from the martyrs' relics for those who thirst for

God's power, to the honor of the saint, which is from God." Fourth, the fountains of God. The same John of Damascus says: "The saints, living in the truth, stand freely present in assistance before God. Christ, the master of his saints, has provided us with their relics as salutary springs from which flow manifold benefits." Fifth, the organ of the Holy Spirit. Augustine gives this reason, saying, in his *City of God*: "The bodies of the saints are to be treated not with disdain but with the greatest reverence, because, while they were alive, the Holy Spirit used them as so many organs for the doing of every good work." So the apostle says (2 Cor. 13:3): "Since you desire proof that Christ is speaking in me . . . "; and of Stephen it is written (Acts 5:10): "They could not withstand the wisdom and the Spirit that spoke." In the same vein Ambrose, in the *Hexaemeron*: "Here is something priceless—that a man could be the organ of the divine voice, and with the body's lips utter divine pronouncements."

The third reason for the institution of the feast of All Saints is to make amends for our negligences. Granted that we do observe the feasts of a relatively small number of saints, even then we often do so carelessly, and through ignorance or negligence omit many things. If therefore we have been neglectful in the celebrations we have performed, in this general solemnization we can make up for our omissions and purge ourselves of negligence. This reason seems to be touched upon in a sermon recited in the Church's office for this day, in which we hear: "It is decreed that on this day the memory of all the saints shall be brought to mind, in order that anything which human frailty, due to ignorance or negligence or preoccupation with some detail, may have less than fully carried out in the solemn celebrations of the saints, shall be compensated in this general solemnization."

Note that there are four categories—apostles, martyrs, confessors, and virgins—among the saints of the New Testament whom we celebrate in the cycle of the year, and whom today we honor all together. Rabanus points out that the four quarters of the world stand for the four categories, the East for apostles, the South for martyrs, the North for confessors, and the West for virgins.

The first category is that of the apostles, whose dignity and excellence appear in that they surpass all the other saints in four ways. Firstly, they are preeminent in dignity, being wise commanders in the Church militant, powerful members of the eternal Judge's court, and gentle shepherds of the flock of Christ. Bernard: "It was proper that such pastors and teachers, men gentle and powerful and wise, be given authority over the human race: gentle so as to take hold of me kindly and mercifully, powerful so as to protect me strongly, wise so as to lead me to life by the way that goes straight to the city on high." The apostles excel, secondly, by preeminence of power, about which Augustine says: "God gave the apostles power over nature to cure it, over demons to drive them out, over the elements to change them, over souls to release them from their sins, over death that they might make little of it, and above the angels' power, because the apostles could consecrate the Lord's body." Thirdly, they excel in the prerogative of sanctity. On account of their sublime holiness and the fullness of grace in them, the life and conduct of Christ shone in them as in a mirror, and he was known in them as the sun is known in its rays, a rose in its fragrance, or fire in its heat. In his commentaries on Matthew, Chrysostom says: "Christ sent the apostles as the sun sends its rays, as a rose spreads the odor of its fragrance, and as a fire sprays its sparks, so that as the sun appears in its rays and a rose is known to be present by its perfume, as fire is sighted by its sparks, so the power of Christ is known in the apostles' virtues." Thus Chrysostom. Fourthly, the apostles excel in the efficacy of their work. Speaking of the apostles, Augustine says of this efficacy: "The most abject, the most unlearned, the fewest in number are ennobled, enlightened, and multiplied. They bring the most fluent orators, the most renowned geniuses, the most numerous legions, and the wonderful skills of the most eloquent authors and teachers under the yoke of Christ."

The second category of saints comprises the martyrs, whose dignity and excellence are demonstrated by the fact that they suffered in many ways, and fruitfully, and with constancy. They suffered in many ways, because besides the martyrdom of blood they endured a threefold bloodless martyrdom. Of this triple martyrdom Bernard says: "There is a threefold unbloody martyrdom, namely, abstinence in the midst of abundance, which David practiced, generosity in poverty, exhibited by Tobit and the poor widow, and chastity in youth, which was Joseph's way in Egypt." Gregory also speaks of a triple bloodless martyrdom. There is patience in adversity, of which he says: "We can be martyrs without the sword, if we practice patience of spirit." There is compassion for the afflicted, about which he says: "Anyone who suffers over another's needs bears a cross in his mind." There is love of enemies, and he says: "To endure shameful treatment and to love one who hates you is a martyrdom in the hidden depth of thought."

Martyrdom is fruitful. For the martyrs themselves its fruits are the remission of sins, the accumulation of merits, and the gaining of eternal glory. They bought these blessings at the price of their blood, and therefore their blood is precious, i.e., full of price or value. Of the first and second Augustine says in the *City of God*: "What is more precious than the death on account of which sins are forgiven and merits accumulated?" In his commentary on John he says: "Christ's blood is precious without sin, yet he also makes precious the blood of the martyrs, for whom he gave his blood in payment. If he did not make the blood of his servants precious, it could not be said that the death of his servants is precious in the sight of the Lord." (Cf. Ps. 115:14 [116:15].) Similarly Cyprian: "Martyrdom is the end of sin, the stopping point of peril, the guide of salvation, the master of patience, the house of life." And, regarding the third fruit of martyrdom to those who endure it, Bernard says: "Three things make the death of the saint precious—rest from labor, joy in newness, certainty about eternal life."

The death of the martyrs is useful and fruitful for us, too, and in two ways. They are given to us as models for the struggle that is life; Chrysostom: "O Christian, you are a dainty soldier if you think you can win without a fight or conquer without combat. Put forth your best effort, fight strenuously, strive mightily in this battle. Consider the pact, weigh the agreement, know what it means to be a soldier—the pact to which you gave your name. By this pact all have fought, by this agreement all have conquered, in this militia all have triumphed!" Thus Chrysostom.

The martyrs are also patrons to help us, which they do both by their merits and by their prayers. Regarding their merits Augustine says: "Oh, boundless kindness of God, which allows the martyrs' merits to be our support! He tests them in order to instruct us, he spends them to buy us, he wills that their torments aid our progress." And about their prayers Jerome writes against Vigilantius: "If the apostles and the martyrs, while they were still in their bodies and had to be concerned for themselves, could pray for others, how much more can they do after winning their crowns, their victories, their triumphs! One man, Moses, obtained pardon from God for 600,000 warriors, and Stephen obtained forgiveness for Paul and many others; but after they begin to be with Christ, they can do much more. The apostle Paul said that 276 lives in the ship were saved by his prayers. Is he likely to have less power now that he is freed from the body with Christ?"

Lastly, the martyrs suffered with constancy. Augustine: "The soul of the martyr is a sword shining with charity, sharpened with truth, brandished with the power of a fighting God—a sword that has fought wars, has bested troops of gainsayers in argument, has struck down its foes and laid adversaries low." Likewise Chrysostom: "The tortured have shown more strength than the torturers, the torn limbs have conquered the claws that tore them."

The third category of saints is that of the confessors. Their dignity and excellence are manifest in that they have confessed God in three ways, namely, in the heart, in the mouth, and in works. The heart's confession is insufficient unless it is expressed in speech, as Chrysostom, commenting on Matthew, proves with four reasons. About interior confession he says: "The root of confession is faith in the heart, and confession is the fruit of faith. As long as the root is alive in the ground, it must produce branches and leaves; otherwise you may be sure that the root has dried in the ground. So also as long as faith is whole in the heart, it always sprouts in oral profession; if confession has withered in the mouth, you may be sure that faith has already dried up in the heart." His second reason runs as follows: "If it is to your profit to believe in your heart without confessing your faith before men, then it profits an unbelieving hypocrite to confess Christ even though he does not believe in his heart. If it does him no good to confess without faith, then neither do you gain anything by believing without declaring your belief." Here is his third reason: "If it is enough for Christ that you know him although you have not confessed him before men, then let it be enough for you that Christ knows you even though he does not confess you before God. If being known by him is not enough for you, then neither is your belief enough for him." And for a fourth argument he says: "If faith in the heart were sufficient, God would have created only a heart for you. Now, however, he has also created a mouth for you, in order that you may believe in your heart and confess with your mouth."

Thirdly, the confessor saints have confessed God by their works. How anyone can confess or deny God by works is shown by Jerome: "They profess that they know God, saying, 'Christ is wisdom, justice, truth, holiness, fortitude.' Wisdom is denied by foolishness, justice by wickedness, truth by mendacity, holiness by shamelessness, fortitude by cowardice. As many times as we are conquered by vices and sins, so many times we deny God; and conversely, as often as we do some good, we confess God."

The fourth category is that of the virgin saints. Their dignity and excellence are evidenced first by the fact that they are the brides of the eternal King. Ambrose: "Who could imagine beauty greater than that of her who is loved by the King, approved by the Judge, dedicated by God, always a spouse, always unwed?" Second, because they are compared to the angels; Ambrose: "Virginity surpasses the condition of human nature, because through it human beings are associated with the angels, yet the virgins' victory is greater than the angels', because angels live without flesh but virgins triumph in the flesh." Third, because they are more illustrious than all the faithful, as Cyprian says: "Virginity is the flower of the seed of the Church, the beauty and ornament of spiritual grace, a happy disposition for praise and honor, a work integral and incorrupt, the image of God, and again with reference to God's holiness the more illustrious portion of the flock of Christ." Fourth, because they are preferred before married women. This excellence, which virginity has over marital union, is evident from many comparisons between the two states. Marriage fertilizes the womb, virginity makes the spirit fruitful; Augustine: "It is a noble thing to choose, while still in this life, to imitate the life of the angels rather than to increase in this life the number of mortals. More fruitful and happier is the fecundity that fosters the spirit than that which swells the belly." The latter brings forth sons of sorrow, the former, sons of joy and exultation; Augustine: "Continence itself is never sterile, it is the fruitful mother of sons of joy begotten of you, O Lord!" Marriage fills the earth with children, virginity fills heaven; Jerome: "Nuptials fill the earth; virginity, paradise." From the former comes a multitude of cares, from the latter a plenitude of calm; Gilbert: "Virginity is the silencer of worries, the peace of the flesh, the ransom from vices, the reign of the virtues." The one is good, the other better; Jerome to Pammachius: "There is as much difference between marriage and virginity as there is between not sinning and doing good; or, to put it more briefly, between good and better." The one is compared to thorns, the other to roses; Jerome to Eustochium: "I praise marriage, but because it begets virgins to me; I gather a rose from thorns, gold from the earth, from the shell a pearl!" Fifth, because virgins enjoy many privileges. They will have golden crowns, they alone will sing the canticle, they will wear the same garments that Christ wears, they will always march after the Lamb himself.

The fourth and last reason for the institution of the feast of All Saints is to make it easier for us to have our prayers heard. On this day we honor all the saints universally in order to have them interceding for us all together, and thus to obtain the mercy of God more readily, because if it is impossible for the prayers of many not to be heard, it is surely impossible that with all the saints praying for us their prayers would not be granted. This reason is brought out in the collect of the day's mass, which says: "With the great host of those interceding for us, grant us the desired abundance of your mercy." The saints intercede for us by their merits and by their good will. Their merits help us and they desire the fulfillment of our wishes, but this only when they know that what we wish for is in accordance with God's will.

That on this day all the saints come together to intercede universally for us was shown in a vision which, we are told, occurred a year after the institution of the feast. On this day the warden of the church of Saint Peter devoutly went around to all the altars and implored the help of all the saints. When he got back to Saint Peter's altar he rested for a short while and was rapt in ecstasy. In a vision he saw the King of kings seated on a high throne, surrounded by all the angels. Then the Virgin of virgins came forward, wearing a gleaming diadem and followed by an innumerable multitude of virgins and the continent. The King rose immediately to meet her and placed a throne beside his own for her to be seated. Then came a man clad in camel skins, whom a large number of ancients followed, and after them another man wearing pontifical vestments and accompanied by a chorus of men similarly attired. Next a great army of soldiers advanced, and then a vast throng of men and women of every race. All gathered before the King's throne and knelt to adore him. The man in pontifical robes then intoned matins, and the rest joined in the chant.

The angel who was guiding the aforementioned warden now explained the vision to him. The Virgin at the head of the procession, he said, was the mother of God with her train of virgins, the man in camel skins was John the Baptist with the patriarchs and prophets, the one in the robes of a pontiff was Saint Peter with the other apostles, the soldiers were the martyrs, the rest of the crowd, the confessors. All these people had come before the King to thank him for the honor done them by mortals on this day, and to pray for the whole world. Then the angel led the warden to another place and showed him people of both sexes, some reclining on golden beds, others at tables enjoying delicious viands, still others naked and needy, begging for help. This place, the angel said, was purgatory. Those enjoying abundance were the souls for whom their friends provided plentiful aid, whereas those in need had no one who cared for them. The angel therefore commanded the warden to make all this known to the supreme pontiff, and to inform him that he was to establish after the feast of all the saints a day of commemoration for the souls of all the departed, on which day those who had no one to pray for them would at least share in the general commemoration.

163. The Commemoration of All Souls

The commemoration of all the faithful departed was instituted in order that those who have no special suffrages offered for them may be helped by this general memorial, as was demonstrated in the revelation already described.[1] Peter Damian says that Saint Odilo, abbot of Cluny, learned that voices and howls of demons were heard near a volcano in Sicily, and that the souls of the dead were being snatched from the demons' grasp by the power of alms and prayers. The abbot ordered that after the feast of All Saints a commemoration of the dead be made in his monasteries. Later this practice was approved throughout the Church.

Regarding this custom two points should be considered specifically. The first concerns the persons in need of purgation—who they are, by whom they are purged, and where they are purged. The second concerns the sacrifices and suffrages made in their behalf: these will be discussed further on.

Those who are to be purged fall into three classes. The first consists of those who die before they have completed the penance imposed on them. However, if while on earth they had contrition of heart great enough to erase their sins, they would pass freely to heavenly life although they had not completed satisfaction, because contrition is the greatest satisfaction for sin and the best way to be cleansed of sin. Jerome: "What counts with God is not length of time but depth of sorrow, not abstinence from food but mortification of the vices."

Those who have not been contrite enough and who die before completing their penance are punished most grievously in the fire of purgatory, unless some of their dear ones take the satisfaction upon themselves. For this commutation to be of avail, four conditions must be met. The first is required of the one who

---

[1] At the end of the chapter (162) on All Saints.

commutes the penance, namely, his authority, because the commutation must be done by the authority of a priest. The second is required of those for whom the commutation is made, namely, need, because they must be in a situation such that they cannot make satisfaction for themselves and so need help. The third is charity, required of the one who takes the commutation upon himself, because without charity the satisfaction he offers would not be meritorious or satisfactory. The fourth must be met by the penance or punishment imposed, namely, proportionality: a lesser penalty must be commuted to a greater, because a penalty borne by the sinner in person is more satisfactory to God than one borne by someone else.

There are, in fact, three kinds of penalty or penance: personal, i.e., borne by the sinner himself and voluntarily, and this is the most satisfactory; penance borne by the person himself but not voluntarily, because it is done in purgatory; and penance borne voluntarily by someone else, and this is less satisfactory than the first kind because it is not done by the sinner himself, but more satisfactory than the second kind because it is voluntary. If, however, the person for whom satisfaction is assumed dies, he still is punished in purgatory, but, due to the punishment he endures personally and the penalty satisfied by others for him, he is freed more quickly, because God counts both payments as one sum total. Thus if the person owed a penance of two months in purgatory he could, due to suffrages offered by others, be freed in one month; but he is never released from purgatory until the debt is paid in full. Once it is fully paid, the payment belongs to the one who made it and is credited to him. If he does not need it, it goes into the Church's treasury or benefits the souls in purgatory.

The second class of those who go down to purgatory comprises those who indeed have completed the satisfaction imposed upon them, but that satisfaction was not sufficient, due to the ignorance or carelessness of the priest who imposed it. Unless the depth of their contrition supplies the difference, these souls will make up in purgatory what was lacking in the satisfaction they offered in this life. God, who knows how to match punishments to sins in right proportion, adds a sufficient penalty lest some sin go unpunished. The penance enjoined by the priest is either too much or just enough or too little. If it is too much, the excess is credited to the doer for an increase of glory; if it is just right, the whole debt is discharged; if it is not enough, what is left is made up according to the demands of divine justice.

About those who repent only at the very end of their lives, hear what Augustine thinks: "One who is baptized in his last hour leaves this life sure of salvation; a man of faith who has led a good life leaves this life secure; one who has done penance and is reconciled while in good health leaves this life secure: about those who repent only at the last moment I myself am not sure. Therefore take what is certain and leave what is uncertain." Augustine speaks this way because there are those who repent out of necessity rather than out of free will, for fear of punishment rather than for love of glory.

The third class of those descending into purgatory includes those who take wood, hay, and stubble with them, in other words, who are bound by a fleshly attachment to their earthly goods although they love God more than wealth. The carnal affections that bind them to houses, wives, and possessions, although they put nothing above God, are signified by the wood, hay, and stubble, and those who carry them will suffer the fire a longer time, like wood, or a shorter, like hay, or a minimum, like stubble. That fire, as Augustine says, though it is not eternal, nevertheless is so fierce, so hot, that it is more painful than anything anyone ever suffers in this life. Never was such pain felt in the flesh, dreadful as were the torments endured by the martyrs.

As to our second question about the suffering souls, namely, by whom they are purged, be it known that purgation and punishment are the work of wicked angels, not of good ones, for good angels do not harass good people but bad people, whereas bad angels harass both good and bad people. It is, however, believable that the good angels frequently visit and console their brothers and fellow citizens in purgatory and exhort them to suffer patiently. The souls also have another consoling remedy in that they await with certainty the glory to come. Their certainty about glory is less than that of the souls who are already in heaven, but they are more certain than those still living on earth. The certainty of those who are in heaven waits for nothing and fears nothing. They already possess all they might expect of the future, and there is nothing they can be afraid of losing. The certainty of those still alive on earth, on the contrary, is mixed with expectancy and fear, but that of the souls in purgatory is midway between: they are expectant because they await the future glory, but have no fear because, while they are confirmed in freedom of choice, they also know that they cannot commit sin. They too have another consolation, knowing that prayers and sacrifices are being offered for them. Yet it might be closer to the truth to believe that the punishment of purgatory is not inflicted by bad angels, but by command of God's justice and his breath making it happen.

In answer to the the third question, namely, where purgation takes place, be it said that the souls are purged in some place located near hell and called purgatory. This is the opinion held by most learned men, although others think the place is in the air and in the torrid zone. However, by divine dispensation different places are sometimes appointed for different souls, and this for a number of reasons—either because their punishment is lighter or their liberation faster, or for our instruction, or because their sin was committed in this particular place, or on account of the prayer of some saint.

First, the place can be for a lighter punishment. Thus, according to Gregory, it was revealed to certain people that some souls are punished simply by being kept in darkness. Or their earlier liberation can be the reason for the place, so that they are able to make their needs known to others and to seek their help, and thus be delivered sooner from their punishment. We read, for instance, that in the autumn season some of Saint Theobald's fishermen pulled in a large block of ice instead of a fish. They were happier about this catch than they would have been with a fish, because the bishop suffered great pain in his feet; so they put the ice under his feet and this gave him much relief. One time, however, he heard a human voice coming from the ice. He adjured the voice to identify itself, and it said: "I am a soul punished in this refrigerant for my sins, and I could be freed if you would say thirty masses for me on thirty consecutive days without interruption." The bishop said half the number of masses and was vesting for the next one when it happened that due to diabolical incitement all the townspeople started fighting with each other. The bishop was called to the scene to calm the discord and, putting off the sacred vestments, omitted the mass that day. He began again and had completed two-thirds of the masses when a huge army, or what looked like one, laid siege to the city, which forced the bishop to omit that day's mass. Beginning a third time, he had said all but one of the thirty masses and was about to celebrate the thirtieth when his house and grounds seemed to burst into flame. His servants called on him to get out quickly, but he said: "Let the whole place burn down! I will not put off this mass!" The minute the mass was finished the ice melted, and the fire that they had thought they saw vanished like a phantasm and did no damage.

A particular place may also be appointed for our instruction, for instance, so that we may know that a great punishment can be visited on sinners after death. Thus we read about something that happened in Paris, as Peter Cantor of Paris tells it. Master Silo had a colleague, a scholar who was very ill, and Silo asked him urgently to come back after he died and tell him, Silo, how things were with him. Some days after his death the scholar appeared to Silo, wearing a cape made of parchment written all over with sophisms, and woven of flames inside. The master asked who he was and he answered: "I am indeed the one who promised to come back to you." Asked how things were with him he said: "This cape weighs upon me and presses me down more than if I were carrying a tower on my shoulders. It is given to me to wear on account of the pride I had in my sophisms. The flames that flare inside it are the delicate, mottled furs I used to wear, and they torture and burn me." The master, however, thought that this penalty was fairly light, so the dead man told him to put out his hand and feel how light the punishment really was. He held out his hand and the scholar let a drop of his sweat fall on it. The drop went through the master's hand like an arrow, causing him excruciating pain. "That's how I feel all over," the scholar said. Master Silo, alarmed by the severity of the other man's punishment, decided to abandon the world and enter the religious life; and the next day he recited the following couplet to his class:

> Linquo choax ranis, cra corvis, vanaque vanis.
> Ad logicam pergo, quae mortis non timet ergo.[2]

And so he left the world behind him and took refuge in religion.

---

[2] I leave croaking to the frogs, cawing to the crows, vanities to the vain. / Therefore I stay with logic, which fears not the *ergo* of death.

Fourthly, a place of punishment might be chosen because crime had been committed there. According to Augustine, souls were sometimes punished in the places where they had sinned, as appears from an incident that Gregory relates in the fourth book of his *Dialogues*. A certain priest went to the baths and found a man he did not know waiting to serve him. The man continued to be attentive to him, and one day the priest brought him a blessed loaf as a benediction and as payment for his services; but the man said: "Why do you give this to me, father? This bread is holy and I cannot eat it. I used to own this place, and was sent here after I died to suffer for my sins. But I ask you to offer this bread to almighty God for my sins, and you will know that your prayers have been heard when you come to bathe and you do not find me here." The priest offered the Host of salvation for him during a whole week, and when he returned to the bath, the man was not to be found there.

Fifthly, the place may be chosen in answer to a saint's prayer. Thus we read that Saint Patrick once prayed that a purgatory be opened underground for certain souls. You will find an account of this after the chapter on Saint Benedict.

Our second major question is about the sacrifices offered for the holy souls. Three points are to be considered: first, about the sacrifices themselves, i.e., what is offered; second, for whom they are offered; and third, who offers them.

Regarding the sacrifices offered in aid of the souls in purgatory, know that there are four kinds which are of maximum benefit, namely, the prayer of the faithful and of friends, almsgiving, the sacrifice of the mass, and the observance of fasts. That the prayer of the faithful and of friends is helpful to the souls is borne out by the story of Paschasius, a man known for his sanctity and virtue, as Gregory tells it in the fourth book of his *Dialogues*. It happened that two men were elected to the papacy at the same time. The Church finally came to an agreement on which one was the true pope, but Paschasius mistakenly preferred the other and clung to this opinion as long as he lived. When he died, a man possessed by an evil spirit touched a sacred vestment that was spread over the bier and was cured instantly. A long time later Germanus, bishop of Capua, went to take the baths for his health and found the aforesaid deacon Paschasius standing there waiting to serve him. Germanus was frightened at the sight of so holy a man and asked him what he was doing there. He answered that he was being punished there because in the case of the two popes he had held on too stubbornly to his opinion. "I ask you to pray the Lord for me," he added, "and you will know that your prayer has been granted if you come back here and do not find me." The bishop prayed for him, and when he returned to the place a few days later, Paschasius was no longer there.

Peter of Cluny tells us that there was a priest who celebrated mass every day for the dead. He was denounced for this to the bishop, who suspended him from his ministry. When the bishop was marching in procession with pomp and ceremony through the cemetery on his way to matins, the dead rose against him, saying: "This bishop gives us no masses and, more than that, has taken our priest away from us! But if he does not mend his ways, he will certainly die!" The bishop not only absolved the priest but thereafter willingly offered masses for the dead.

Another example, this one from the Cantor of Paris, shows how grateful the dead are for the prayers of the living. There was a man who, as he walked through the cemetery, always recited the *De profundis* for the dead. Once, when he was running away through the cemetery with his enemies after him, the buried, each one armed with the tool proper to his craft, quickly rose and defended the fleeing man with might and main. His pursuers, terrified, retreated in haste.

That the second kind of suffrage, namely, almsgiving, is of benefit to the souls can be seen clearly from the twelfth chapter of 2 Maccabees. There we read that the mighty man Judas Maccabeus sent twelve thousand silver drachmas to Jerusalem for sacrifice to be offered for the sins of the dead, thinking well and religiously concerning the resurrection. And another episode related by Gregory in the fourth book of the *Dialogues* shows how well almsgiving serves the dead. There was a knight who had died and lay lifeless, but his soul soon returned to his body and he narrated what had happened to him. He said that he came to a bridge below which a black, murky, fetid river flowed. On the other side there were fair meadows beautified by sweet-smelling herbs and flowers, and in the meadows groups of men could be seen, clothed in white and luxuriating in the perfume of the many fragrant flowers. This bridge was there for a test: if any unrighteous persons tried to cross it, they slipped and fell into the river, while the just went across surefooted to the pleasant fields beyond. The knight declared that he had seen on the bridge a man named Peter who was lying on his back lashed to a great bundle of iron. Asked why he was there in that condition, Peter replied that he was being punished because when he had been ordered to torture a condemned man, he had done so more because his cruel nature enjoyed it than because he was obeying orders. The knight also said he had seen a pilgrim who came to the bridge and crossed it with the same degree of confidence as had been the measure of his purity of life. Not so with another pilgrim whose name was Stephen. When he tried to cross, his foot slipped and half his body hung over the side of the bridge. Then some hideous beings rose out of the river and tried to pull him down by the legs, while some truly beautiful men clothed in white tried to haul him up by the arms. The scuffle was still going on when the knight came back to life, so he could not say who had won this test of strength. The combat, however, makes it clear that sins of the flesh were competing with generosity in almsgiving. Stephen was being pulled down by his lower parts and upward by his arms, which shows that he had loved giving alms but had not perfectly resisted the vices of the flesh.

As to the third kind of suffrage, namely, the sacrifice of the mass, many examples show the very great benefit it brings to the dead. In the fourth book of his

Dialogues Gregory tells us that when one of his monks, Justus by name, was dying, he admitted to Gregory that he had secretly kept three gold coins, and he died bemoaning this fault. Gregory ordered the monks to bury the deceased with his three gold pieces in a dunghill, and to say: "May your money go to perdition with you!" Later Gregory had a monk offer mass for the departed brother for thirty days, not missing a day. When this order had been carried out, the monk who had died appeared to another monk on the thirtieth day. The other monk asked: "How is it with you?" "Very bad till today," he answered, "but now all goes well because I received communion this morning."

The offering of the host is shown to benefit not only the dead but the living. Some men were digging silver out of a cliff when the rock fell in and killed all but one, who found himself in a sort of cave in the cliff and so escaped death, but he could not get out. His wife, thinking him dead, had a mass celebrated for him every day and daily offered a loaf of bread and a jug of wine with a lighted candle. The devil appeared to her for three successive days in the form of a man and asked her where she was going. When she explained what she was about, he said: "Don't bother going to all this trouble, the mass has already been said." So for three days she did not go to mass or have one offered. Then, some time later, someone else was digging for silver in the same cliff and heard a voice from below, saying: "Don't dig too hard! There's a big rock right over my head and it might fall on me!" Frightened, the one digging called a lot of people to hear the voice, and when he started to dig again, the voice was heard speaking. The bystanders came closer and said: "Who are you?" The entombed man answered: "Go easy with the pick and shovel! A big rock might fall on me!" They dug from the side and found him safe and unharmed, pulled him out, and asked how he had survived so long. He said that a loaf, a jug of wine, and a lighted candle had been given to him every day but three. Hearing this, his wife rejoiced, realizing that her offering had kept him alive, and that it was the devil who had deceived her and prevented her from having the mass said on those three days. This took place, as Peter of Cluny attests, near the village of Ferrières in the diocese of Grenoble.

Gregory also tells the story of a seaman who suffered shipwreck and was lost at sea. A priest said mass for him, and in the end he came back from the sea unharmed. When asked how he had escaped, he said that while he was being tossed about by the waves and was nearly at the end of his strength, someone came to him and gave him a loaf. When he had eaten the bread, his strength was renewed, and he was picked up by a passing ship. Then it was learned that he had received the bread at the very hour when the priest had offered the host for him.

The fourth kind of suffrage, namely, the observance of fasts, benefits the dead, as Gregory asserts. Treating of fasts along with the other three kinds of suffrage, he says: "The souls of the dead are released by four means—offerings by priests, prayers of the saints, alms given by friends, and fasting by kinsmen. Penances performed by their friends also are helpful." A certain august doctor has related that a woman whose husband had died was left desperately poor, and the devil appeared to her and said that he would make her rich if she did his will. She promised to do so. He demanded four things: she was to lead men of the Church, who were housed with her, to commit fornication; to take in poor people by day and put them out empty-handed at night; to interfere with people's praying in church by talking loudly; and not to make confession about any of this to anyone. At length, when she was near death and her son begged her to confess her sins, she told him what the facts were and said that she could not confess, and that confession would do her no good. The son tearfully insisted and promised to do penance for her, and she, conscience-stricken, sent him for the priest; but before the priest arrived, a swarm of demons rushed in upon her, and, overwhelmed with fear and horror, she died. Her son confessed his mother's sin and accepted and fulfilled a seven-year penance, and at the end of the seven years his mother appeared and thanked him for her deliverance.

The Church's indulgences also help the dead. A delegate of the apostolic see persuaded a valorous knight to fight in the service of the Church in Albigensian territory and granted him a forty days' indulgence for his deceased father. The knight served out his forty days, at the end of which time his father appeared to him brighter than light and thanked him for obtaining his release from purgatory.

The second point about the suffrages offered for the departed concerns those for whom the sacrifices are made, and here again four questions arise. To whom are these suffrages beneficial? Why are they beneficial? Are they equally beneficial to all? How can those benefited know that sacrifices have been made for them?

In answer to the first question, Augustine says that those who depart this life are either very good or very bad or mediocre. Therefore the suffrages done for the very good are acts of thanksgiving, those done for the very bad are in some way consolations for the living, those for the middling have the value of expiation. The very good are those who fly heavenward immediately and are free of both fires, hell and purgatory. The very good fall into three classes—the newly baptized, the martyrs, and the perfect. This third class consists of those who have built perfectly with gold, silver, and precious stones—i.e., with love of God, love of neighbor, and good works—to such a point that they had no thought of pleasing the world but only of pleasing God. They may have committed venial sins, but the fervor of their charity burned away the sin in them like a drop of water on a hot stove. Thus they never take anything with them that needs to be burned away. Anyone therefore who prays for or offers some other suffrage for a deceased person in any of these three classes insults that person, because, as Augustine says, whoever prays for a martyr wrongs the martyr. But if one were to pray for a very good person without being sure whether that person had gone straight to heaven, those prayers would be equivalent to acts of thanksgiving and would add to the merit of the one praying, according to the text of Ps. 34:13: "My prayer shall be turned into my bosom."

To these same three kinds of very good persons heaven is opened immediately upon their death, nor do they have to suffer any purgatorial fire. This is signified by three to whom heaven was opened. First, to Christ at his baptism; Luke 3:21: "When Jesus had been baptized and was praying, the heaven was opened." This means that heaven is opened to all those baptized either as infants or in adulthood, so that if they leave this life, they fly at once to heaven. By virtue of Christ's passion baptism cleanses away all sins, original, mortal, and venial. Second, to Stephen at his stoning; Acts 7:56: "Behold, I see the heavens opened." This means that heaven is opened to all martyrs, so that when they die, they go straight to heaven, and if they had anything to be burned away, it would be cut down by the scythe of martyrdom. Third, to John the most perfect; Apoc. 4:1: "I looked, and lo, in heaven an open door!" This means that for the perfect, who have totally completed all penance and have committed no venial sins, or if they have committed any, these have been consumed by the fervor of their charity, heaven is opened promptly and they go in to reign forever.

The very bad are those who sink at once into the depths of hell. For them, if their damnation is certain, no suffrages of any kind are to be offered, according to what Augustine says: "If I knew my father was in hell, I would no more pray for him than I would for the devil." If, however, suffrages were offered for any of the damned whose damnation was in doubt, the suffrages would not benefit them in the least. They cannot be freed from their pains; their punishment cannot be mitigated or lessened. Their damnation cannot be suspended for a time or even for a moment. They cannot be strengthened to bear their suffering more lightly. In hell there is no redemption.

The mediocre are those who take with them some inflammable materials— wood, hay, stubble—or who, caught unawares by death, cannot complete the sufficient penance imposed upon them. They are neither so good that they do not need our help nor so bad that suffrages would not benefit them. The sacrifices made for them are their expiation. Hence these are the only ones for whom such sacrifices can be useful. In instituting such suffrages the Church has usually observed three orders of numbers of days, namely, the seventh, the thirtieth, and the anniversary. The reason for this is stated in the book *De mitrali officio*. The seventh day is observed so that the souls of the departed may arrive at the eternal Sabbath of rest, or so that all the sins may be remitted which they committed in life, life being lived seven days at a time, or that they may be forgiven for the sins they committed with the body, which is composed of four elements, and with the soul, which has three powers. The thirtieth day—the number thirty being composed of three decades—is singled out so that their offenses against faith in the three Persons of the Blessed Trinity and the ten commandments of the Decalogue may be purged in them. The anniversary is observed so that from the years of calamity they may come to the years of eternity. Thus, as we celebrate the anniversary of the saints to their honor and our own profit, we mark the anniversary of the departed to their benefit and our devotion.

Next we asked why suffrages offered for the dead actually help them. There are three reasons for this. The first is unity. The dead are one body with the Church militant, and the goods of the latter must be common to all. The second is their dignity. While they were living on earth, they merited to have suffrages benefit them, and it is right that since they helped others, they should be helped by others. The third reason is their need, because in their present state they are unable to help themselves.

As to whether the suffrages are of equal advantage to all the dead, let it be known that if they are offered for particular persons, they are more beneficial to those persons than to others. If they are offered for all souls in general, those whose lives made them more worthy of help will receive more if they are in equal or greater need.

Can the dead know that sacrifices have been made to help them? According to Augustine there are three ways by which they may know this. The first is by divine revelation: God himself may reveal it to them. The second is that the good angels may make it known. These angels, who are always with us and observe all our actions, can descend to the souls in an instant and notify them of our aid. The third is through notice brought by souls leaving this world, because they can make this and other things known to the souls in purgatory. There is also a fourth way, namely, by what their own experience reveals to them, because when they feel relief from their suffering, they know that suffrages have been offered for them.

The last question concerns those who make the sacrifices and provide the suffrages by which the souls in purgatory are aided. If these suffrages are to benefit the souls, they must be done by persons who are in charity, because if they are offered by evil people, they cannot be helpful. We read that a certain knight, lying in bed with his wife one night while bright moonlight streamed through the window, began to wonder why rational man does not obey his Creator whereas nonrational creatures do. Then he began to think disparagingly about a fellow knight, a boon companion now dead, when suddenly the dead man entered the room and said to him: "Friend, don't have evil suspicions about anyone, and forgive me if I have wronged you in any way." Asked about his present state, he said: "I have a lot to atone for, mainly because I desecrated a cemetery by wounding a man there and stealing his cloak. I have to wear the cloak all the time, and it weighs me down more than a mountain would." Then he begged his former friend to have prayers offered for him. The friend asked him whether he wanted the prayers to be offered by one particular priest, and he said nothing but shook his head negatively. Would he prefer that a certain hermit pray for him? "Yes, indeed," he answered, "I do want him to pray for me."

This was promised him, and he went on: "And I tell you that two years from this very day you too will die!" With that he disappeared, and the knight changed his way of life for the better and fell asleep in the Lord.

Note that suffrages done by bad people cannot be profitable to the dead unless they are sacramental works such as the celebration of mass, which cannot be invalidated though the minister be wicked, or unless the deceased person while alive, or a friend, had entrusted a sum to be spent for him to someone else, even though this trustee be a bad person. In this case the trustee would do well to make proper use of the sum right away, lest what happened to another man in like circumstances should happen to him. We read that one of Charlemagne's knights, who was about to go to war against the Moors, asked a cousin of his to sell his horse and give the money to the poor in case he should die in battle. The knight was killed, but the cousin liked the horse so much that he kept it for himself. Not long after the knight's death he appeared like a radiant sun to his cousin and said: "Good cousin, you made me suffer in purgatory for a week by not selling my horse and giving the money to the poor as I told you to, but you won't get away with it! This very day, while I, purged of sin, go into the kingdom of God, the devils will carry your soul to hell!" and lo, of a sudden an uproar as of lions, bears, and wolves was heard in the air, and the demons laid hold of the cousin and carried him off.

164. The Four Crowned Martyrs

The four crowned martyrs were Severus, Severianus, Carpophorus, and Victorinus, who, by order of Emperor Diocletian, were beaten to death with leaded scourges. The names of these four were not known at the time but were learned through the Lord's revelation after many years had passed. Then it was decreed that they should be commemorated following the names of five other martyrs, namely, Claudius, Castorius, Symphorian, Nicostratus, and Simplicius, who had suffered two years after the martyrdom of the above-named four.

These five saints were all skilled in the art of sculpture and refused to fashion an idol for Diocletian or to offer sacrifice in any way. The emperor therefore ordered them to be placed alive in lead coffins and thrown into the sea, about A.D. 287. Before the names of the earlier four were known, Pope Melchiades decreed that these should be honored following the names of the later five and should be called the Four Crowned. Even after their names had become known, custom prevailed and they are still remembered as the Four Crowned.

---

165. Saint Theodore

Theodore suffered martyrdom in the city of the Marmanites, under Diocletian and Maximian. When the judge ordered him to offer sacrifice and to return to the army, Theodore replied: "I am a soldier in the service of my God and of his Son Jesus Christ!" The judge: "So your god has a son?" Theodore: "Yes!" The judge: "Might we know him?" Theodore: "Indeed you can know him and come to him!"

Theodore was granted a delay to prepare to offer sacrifice. Instead he entered the temple of the Mother of the Gods by night, set fire to the temple, and burned it to the ground. He was accused of this by someone who had seen him, and was shut up in a jail to die there of hunger. The Lord appeared to him and said: "Be confident, Theodore my servant, because I am with you!" Then a throng of men in white robes came to him though the doors were closed, and chanted the Psalms with him. When the jailers saw this, they fled in terror. Theodore was brought out and invited to offer sacrifice, but said: "Even if you burn my flesh with fire and inflict other tortures on me, I will not renounce my God as long as there is breath in my body."

The judge then commanded that Theodore be hung from a limb and have his flanks torn so cruelly with iron hooks as to expose the ribs. As he hung there, the judge said to him: "Theodore, do you want to be with us or with your Christ?" Theodore: "With my Christ I was and I am and I will be!" So a fire was lighted around him and in the fire he breathed his last, yet his body was not harmed by the flames. This happened about A.D. 287. A sweet odor spread everywhere and a voice was heard saying: "Come, my beloved, enter into the joy of your Lord!" Many also saw the heavens opened.

166. Saint Martin, Bishop

Martinus is like *Martem tenens*, one who makes war, namely, against vice and sin; or the name is like *martyrum unus*, one of the martyrs, because Martin was a martyr at least by desire and by his practice of mortification. Or the name is interpreted as one who angers or provokes or dominates; and Martin, by the merit of his holiness, angered the devil and made him envious, provoked God to be merciful, and dominated his body by continuous penances. Reason, or the spirit, ought to dominate the flesh, as Dionysius says in his letter to Demophilus, just as a master dominates his slave, a father his son, and a mature person a frivolous adolescent.

The saint's life was written by Severus, surnamed Sulpicius, whom Gennadius numbers among illustrious men.

Martin was born in the town of Sabaria in Pannonia but grew up in Pavia, Italy, with his father, who was a military officer. Martin served in the army under the caesars Constantine and Julian, but a military career was not his own choice. Even in childhood he was inspired by God, and at the age of twelve, against his parents' wishes, he fled to a church and asked to be accepted as a catechumen. He would have become a hermit, but his youth and lack of bodily strength forbade it. Then the caesars decreed that the sons of veterans should take their fathers' places in the legions. Martin was pressed into service at the age of fifteen, with only one man to serve him, although more often it was Martin who took off his man's boots and cleaned them.

Once, in the wintertime, he was passing through the city gate of Amiens when a poor man, almost naked, confronted him. No one had given him an alms, and Martin understood that this man had been kept for him, so he drew his sword and cut the cloak he was wearing into two halves, giving one half to the beggar and wrapping himself in the other. The following night he had a vision of Christ wearing the part of his cloak with which he had covered the beggar, and heard Christ say to the angels who surrounded him: "Martin, while still a catechumen, gave me this to cover me." The holy man saw this not as a reason for pride, but as evidence of God's kindness, and had himself baptized at the age of eighteen. Moreover, he stayed in the army for two years more at the urging of his superior officer, who promised that when his term of office expired, he too would renounce the world.

At that time the barbarians were breaking through the empire's frontiers, and Emperor Julian offered money to the soldiers who would stay and fight them.

Martin had had enough of soldiering and refused the profferred bonus, saying to the emperor: "I am a soldier of Christ, and I am forbidden to fight." Julian was indignant and said that Martin was refusing not for motives of religion but because he was afraid of getting into a war. Martin, who knew no fear, retorted: "If my refusal is attributed not to faith but to cowardice, I will stand forth tomorrow morning at the line of battle, unarmed, and, in the name of Christ, protected not by shield or helmet but by the sign of the cross, shall walk safely through the enemy's lines." He was put under guard immediately to ensure that he would face the barbarians unarmed, as he had said. But the next day the enemy sent legates to convey their surrender of all men and materials, so there can be no doubt that this bloodless victory was due to the holy man's merits.

After resigning from the army Martin went to Hilary, bishop of Poitiers, and by him was ordained acolyte. Then the Lord ordered him in a dream to visit his parents, who were still pagans. Setting out, he predicted that he would suffer many ordeals on the way. As he crossed the Alps he fell among robbers, but when one of them aimed a blow at Martin's head, another robber held back the hand that wielded the sword. The saint's hands were tied behind his back, and he was given into the custody of one of the brigands, who asked him if he was afraid. He answered that he had never felt so safe, because he knew that God's mercy was at hand especially in times of trial, and then went on to preach to the robber and converted him to the faith of Christ. The converted robber put him back on the road and afterward finished his days in praiseworthy living.

When Martin was passing through Milan, the devil met him in the form of a man and asked him where he was going. He replied that he was going wherever the Lord called him to go, and the devil said: "Wherever you go, the devil will be there to oppose you!" Martin answered him: "The Lord is my helper, I will not fear what man can do to me!"[1] The devil vanished instantly.

Martin converted his mother, but his father clung to his error. The Arian heresy, however, was advancing everywhere, with Martin almost alone to resist it, and he was beaten in public and cast out of the city. He went back to Milan and founded a monastery there, but was driven out by the Arians and went to the island of Gallimaria with a single priest as companion. There he happened to eat hellebore, a poisonous herb that was mixed in with other herbs. This made him so ill that he felt close to death, but he dispelled all pain and danger by the power of his prayer.

Learning that blessed Hilary had returned from exile, Martin went to Poitiers and established a monastery near the city. In the monastery there was an unbaptized catechumen. Martin came back to the monastery after a short absence and found that the catechumen had died without baptism. He had the body brought to his cell and prostrated himself upon it, and by his prayer recalled the man to life. This same man used to say that when he had died, he was sentenced to

---

[1] Ps. 117(118):6.

remain in a place of darkness, whereupon two angels reminded the Judge that this was the man for whom Martin was praying at that moment, and the Judge ordered the angels to take him back and return him alive to Martin. The saint also restored to life another man who had fallen into a pit and died.

The people of Tours were without a bishop, and they begged Martin, reluctant though he was, to be ordained as their bishop. Some among the assisting bishops disapproved of his choice on the ground that he was small of stature and unattractive in appearance: the most outspoken among the objectors was a bishop named Defensor, a name that meant defender. Since there was no lector present, one of the bishops took the Psalter and read from the first Psalm he opened to: "Out of the mouth of infants and of sucklings thou hast perfected praise, to destroy the enemy and the defender."[2] No one rose to support Bishop Defensor's objection. Martin was ordained bishop but could not abide the tumult of the city, so he built a monastery about two miles outside the walls and lived there in strict austerity with eighty disciples. No one drank wine there unless illness compelled him, and soft garments were considered a crime. Many cities chose their bishops from among these men.

A cult began to develop around an unknown who was alleged to be a martyr. Bishop Martin could learn nothing about his life or his merits; so one day he stood at the tomb and prayed the Lord to make known who was buried there and what had been his merits. Turning to his left he saw a pitch-black shade standing there. The shade, challenged by Martin, said that he had been a robber and had been put to death for his crimes. Martin therefore ordered the immediate destruction of the altar that had been raised beside the tomb.

We also read in the *Dialogue* of Severus and Gallus (where many details are supplied which Severus omitted in his *Life* of Saint Martin) that at one time Martin went to Emperor Valentinian about something he needed; but the emperor knew that the bishop was going to ask for something that he did not want to grant him, so he had the palace doors closed and barred. Martin, having been repulsed once and again, wrapped himself in sackcloth, sprinkled ashes on his head, and denied himself food and drink for a week. Then, bidden by an angel, he went to the palace and made his way to the emperor, no one interfering. Valentinian saw him coming and, angry because he had been admitted, did not rise to acknowledge his presence until flames burst out from the royal throne and set the imperial posterior afire. At that the emperor, though still irritated, rose to greet Martin and admitted that he had felt the power of God. He granted all the bishop wanted before the latter had time to ask, and offered him many gifts that Martin did not accept.

In the same *Dialogue* we read how he brought a third dead man back to life. A young man had died, and his mother, weeping, pleaded with Saint Martin to revive her son. Martin was standing in the middle of a field surrounded by a

[2] Cf. Ps. 8:3 (Douay).

multitude of pagans, but he knelt down and prayed, and the boy arose in the sight of all. Thereupon all those pagans were converted to the faith.

Inanimate, vegetable, and nonrational beings also obeyed this holy man. In-animate beings like fire and water did his bidding. Once, when he had set fire to a temple, the wind was blowing the flames toward an adjacent house. Martin went up on the roof of the house and faced the approaching flames. Immediately the fire turned against the wind, so that there seemed to be a conflict between the two elements. We also read in the same *Dialogue* that a ship was sinking, and a merchant who was not yet a Christian exclaimed: "May the God of Martin save us!" A great calm settled over the sea at once.

Vegetable creatures likewise. . . . In a certain place Martin had seen to the demolition of a very ancient temple, and he wanted to cut down a pine tree that was dedicated to the devils. The country people and the pagans objected, and one of them said to him: "If you have so much confidence in your God, we will cut down the tree, and you let it fall on you. If your God is with you as you say, you will escape injury." He agreed. They cut through the tree and it began to fall toward the spot where he waited, but he made the sign of the cross against it and the tree fell in the opposite direction, almost crushing the people who had taken a place they thought was safe. At the sight of the miracle they all were converted to the faith.

As for nonrational animals, they very often obeyed the saint, as again we read in the *Dialogue*. Once he saw a pack of dogs chasing a little rabbit. He called to the dogs and they stopped their pursuit, halting in their tracks as if they were tied there. Another time he had gone to bathe in a river where there was a water snake, and he said to the snake: "In the Lord's name I command you to go back where you came from!" At the saint's word the reptile turned around and crossed to the opposite bank. Martin groaned: "Serpents listen to me and men do not!" A dog was barking at one of the saint's disciples, and the disciple said to the dog: "In Martin's name I order you to be quiet!" The dog stopped as if his tongue had been cut out.

Martin was a man of deep humility. In Paris he once came face to face with a leper from whom all shrank in horror, but Martin kissed him and blessed him, and he was cured. His dignity was great: he was said to be equal in dignity with the apostles, and this due to the grace of the Holy Spirit, who descended upon him in the appearance of fire to strengthen him, as had happened to the apostles. The aforesaid *Dialogue* tells us that once, when he was sitting alone in his cell and Severus and Gallus, his disciples, were waiting outside, they were struck with wonder at hearing several voices speaking in the cell. Later they asked Martin about this, and he said: "I will tell you, but I ask you not to tell anybody else. Agnes, Thecla, and Mary came to talk with me." And it was not only on that day, but frequently, that, as he admitted, these saints came to visit him, and the apostles Peter and Paul often came as well.

He was very just, giving to each his due. Once when he was invited to dine by Emperor Maximus, the cup was offered first to Martin, and everyone expected that he in turn would pass it to the king. But he passed the cup to the priest who was with him, considering no one more worthy to drink after the bishop, and deeming it unjust to put the king or the king's close associates ahead of a priest.

His patience was inexhaustible and was maintained in all circumstances. Even though he was the priest highest in rank, his clerics often treated him rudely without being reprimanded, nor did he for that reason exclude them from his charity. No one ever saw him angry, nor grieving, nor laughing. Nothing was heard from his lips but Christ, never was aught in his heart but piety, peace, and mercy.

We read in the same *Dialogue* that once, clad in a rough garment and a long black cloak, he was riding along a road on his donkey. A troop of cavalry rode toward him and the horses took fright and bolted, throwing their riders to the ground. The soldiers made for Martin, whom they pulled from his mount and beat soundly. The saint said nothing and turned away from them, and they were all the more incensed because he did not seem to feel their blows or to have any high regard for themselves. Then their own mounts stood as if rooted in the ground, immovable as boulders despite spur and whip, until the men went back to the bishop and confessed the wrong they had unwittingly done him. Then he gave them leave, and their horses started off at a lively trot.

He was assiduous in prayer. Indeed, we read in his legend that no hour or minute passed which he did not devote either to prayer or to sacred reading. Whether at work or at reading he never took his mind from prayer. As the smith, while working the iron, strikes the anvil from time to time to ease his labor, so Martin, whatever he might be doing, made all of it a prayer.

He lived a very austere life. Severus, in a letter to Eusebius, tells how Martin once stopped overnight at a villa in his diocese, and the clergy there prepared for him a bed with a mattress filled with straw. When he lay down on it, he shuddered at the unaccustomed softness, since he usually slept on the floor with only a single hair cloth over him. Unhappy at this unintended misunderstanding, he rose, threw aside all the straw, and stretched out on the bare ground. In the middle of the night all that straw burst into flame. Martin, awakened, tried to get out of the room but could not, and the flames caught him and set his garment afire. He returned to his wonted refuge of prayer, made the sign of the cross, and stood untouched amidst the flames; and whereas moments before he had felt the pain of their burning, now they seemed as refreshing as dew. The monks were awakened by the fire and came running, expecting to find Martin burned to death, but instead led him out unharmed.

His compassion for sinners was unbounded. He took to the bosom of his merciful understanding all who wished to repent. The devil himself took issue with Martin for admitting to penance those who fell once, and Martin answered: "If you yourself, poor wretched being, would stop trying to bring men down, and would repent of your deeds, I, trusting in the Lord, would promise you Christ's mercy!"

There was no limit to his compassion for the poor. The *Dialogue* tells us that Martin was on his way to the church for the celebration of some feast and was followed by a poor man who was just about naked. The bishop asked the archdeacon to find some clothes for the man, but the archdeacon deferred doing this, and Martin went into the sacristy, took off his tunic, gave it to the beggar, and told him to be off. The archdeacon then advised the bishop to proceed with the ceremony, but Martin said that he could not go ahead until the poor man—meaning himself—got some clothes to wear. The archdeacon did not understand, since the bishop was wrapped in his cope and the other could not see that he had nothing under it, and anyway, he observed, there was no poor man there. "Fetch me a tunic," Martin said firmly, "and then there will be no poor man here looking for clothes!"

The archdeacon, resentful, went to the marketplace and for five coins bought a cheap, short tunic—the kind called *paenula, paene nulla,* almost nothing. Angrily he threw the garment at Martin's feet. The bishop went behind a screen, put the tunic on—the sleeves coming only to his elbows and the lower edge only to his knees—and, so vested, went on to celebrate the mass. While he was celebrating, a globe of fire appeared over his head and was seen by many people. (For this reason Martin is said to be on a par with the apostles.) To his account of this miracle Master John Beleth adds that when the bishop raised his hands to God, as is done in the mass, the sleeves of the tunic slipped back, since his arms were not thick or fleshy and the tunic reached only to his elbows, and so his arms were left bare. Then, miraculously, angels brought him gold armlets set with jewels, and the bare arms were decently covered.

The saint once noticed a sheep that had been shorn, and said: "That sheep has obeyed the Gospel mandate. She had two tunics and gave one of them to someone who had none. You should do likewise!"

Martin displayed much power in driving out demons and often did expel them from the possessed. In the aforesaid *Dialogue* we read that there was a cow that was possessed by the devil, and she roared and raged and gored many people. Once this cow rushed in a fury at Martin and his company as they passed on the road. Martin raised his hand and ordered the cow to halt. Halt she did, and he saw a demon sitting astride her. Martin rebuked the demon, saying: "Get off her back, O evil one, and stop tormenting this harmless animal." The spirit departed immediately. The cow then fell to her knees at the bishop's feet and then, at his behest, ambled peaceably back to the herd.

Martin had a subtle sense for discerning demons. No matter what form, image, or disguise they assumed, he saw them openly and uncovered. Sometimes they presented themselves in the person of Jove, frequently as Mercury, occasionally as Venus or Minerva, but he berated them all by their proper names. Mercury gave him the most trouble. He said that Jove was brutish and dull. Once the devil appeared to him in the semblance of a king, clothed in purple, wearing a diadem and golden shoes, serene and smiling of mien. For a long time neither one spoke. Then the devil said: "Martin, acknowledge him whom you adore! I am Christ and am about to come down upon the earth, but I chose to manifest myself to you in advance." Martin marveled at this but maintained his silence, and the spirit spoke again: "Martin, why do you hesitate to believe, since you see me? I am CHRIST!" Then the saint, instructed by the Holy Spirit, said: "The Lord Jesus Christ did not predict that he would come empurpled and wearing a glittering crown. I will not believe that Christ has come unless he is as he was when he suffered, unless he bears the stigmata of the cross!" At these words the devil disappeared, leaving the cell filled with a horrid stench.

Martin knew the time of his death well in advance and revealed it to his brothers. Meanwhile he visited the diocese of Candes, to reconcile some differences there. On the way he saw diving birds watching for fish and catching some, and he said: "This is the way demons work. They trap the unwary, they catch some before they know it, they devour their catch and can never get enough." So he ordered the birds to go away from the water and seek some desert place, and off they flew in a great flock toward the hills and the forests.

When he had spent some time in the above-named diocese, his strength began to fail, and he told his disciples that his days were numbered. They wept and asked him: "Why are you deserting us, father? To whom are you leaving us, orphans? Fierce wolves will ravage your flock!" Moved by their entreaties and tears, Martin wept with them and prayed: "Lord, if I am still needed by your people, I do not refuse the labor! Thy will be done!" He really was not sure which he preferred, because he wanted neither to leave these people nor to remain separated from Christ any longer. Therefore when fevers racked him for some time and his disciples asked him to let them put some straw in the bed where he lay in sackcloth and ashes, he said: "My sons, the only proper way for a Christian to die is in sackcloth and ashes. If I leave you any other example, I shall have sinned." His eyes and his hands he kept always pointed to heaven, and never let his unconquered spirit slacken in prayer. He lay always on his back, and when his priests begged him to let them ease his poor body by turning him on his side, he said: "Leave me as I am, brothers! Let me keep my eyes on heaven rather than on earth, so that my spirit may always be directed toward the Lord!" Even as he said this, he saw the devil standing by and said: "What are you here for, bloody beast? You will find nothing deadly in me, and Abraham's bosom will welcome me!" And with these words, in the reign of Arcadius and Honorius, which began about A.D. 395, and in the eighty-first year of his life, he yielded his spirit to God. His face shone as though he was already glorified, and many heard choirs of angels singing around him.

At his death the people of Poitiers and the people of Tours came together, and a bitter altercation broke out between them. The people of Poitiers said: "He is our monk, we want him back!" Those of Tours responded: "From you he was taken by God, to us he was given!" In the middle of the night, the Poitiers people being sound asleep, the men of Tours passed the saint's body through a window and ferried it by the Loire to the city of Tours, where there was great rejoicing at its reception.

Blessed Severinus, bishop of Cologne, was making the rounds of the holy places after matins on Sunday, as was his custom, when, at the hour of Saint Martin's passing, he heard angels singing in heaven. He called his archdeacon and asked him if he heard anything. The archdeacon said he heard nothing, but the archbishop told him to listen intently. He stretched his neck upwards and strained his ears, raising himself on his toes and steadying himself with his staff while the archbishop prayed for him, and he said he heard some voices in the heavens. Said the archbishop: "It is my lord Martin who has migrated from the world, and now the angels are carrying him to heaven!"

There were demons there, too, and they tried to hold Martin back, but they found nothing with which to charge him and withdrew nonplussed. The archdeacon took note of the day and the hour, and learned that this was indeed the time when Martin had breathed his last. The monk Severus, who wrote his life, had fallen into a light sleep after matins, and, as he states in a letter, Martin appeared to him clothed in white robes, his face alight, his eyes shining like stars, his hair purpled, holding in his right hand the book that Severus had written about his life. Martin blessed him and he saw the saint rising to heaven, and Severus, wishing he could have gone with him, woke up. After that, messengers came with the news that Martin had died that same night.

On that day Saint Ambrose, bishop of Milan, was celebrating mass, and fell asleep at the altar between the reading of the prophecy and the epistle. No one presumed to awaken him, and the subdeacon would not dare read the epistle without his order. Two or three hours passed before they aroused Ambrose, saying: "Time is passing and the people are getting tired of waiting. May it please your lordship to have the clerk read the epistle?" "Don't be upset," Ambrose said, "my brother Martin has gone to heaven, and I have been at his funeral and was leading the final prayers, but you disturbed me and I could not sing the last response." They noted the day and the hour, and found that that was when Saint Martin had departed to heaven.

Master John Beleth says that the kings of France used to carry Martin's *cappa*, or cloak, into battle; wherefore the guardians of the cloak were called *cappellani*, or chaplains.

In the sixty-fourth year after Martin's death, blessed Perpetuus enlarged his church magnificently and wished to rebury the saint's body there, but, despite fasts and vigils and several futile efforts, they could not move the sarcophagus.

They were about to leave it where it was when a beautiful old man appeared to them and said: "What are you waiting for? Don't you see Saint Martin ready to help you as soon as you put your hand to the task?" Then, with them, he put his hand under the stone, and they lifted the sarcophagus with ease and speed and set it where it is now venerated. The old man did not appear again.

Odo, abbot of Cluny, relates that when the transferral took place, the bells in all the churches rang though no one pulled the ropes, and all the lamps and candles came alight though no one touched them. It is also said that there were two partners, one of whom was blind and the other paralyzed, and the blind man hauled the cripple around in a cart and the cripple told him where to go. By begging this way they made a good living. Then they heard that many infirm people were cured when they came close to Saint Martin's body, and especially when the body was carried around the church, and they began to fear that the said body might be carried close to the house where they lived, and they by chance might be made whole—which they did not want to happen, because it would deprive them of their income. So they moved their domicile to another street, thinking that the sacred body was never carried that way. But just as they were moving, they met the body being carried in procession, and since God bestows blessings even on those who do not ask for them, the two partners found themselves completely cured against their will and were sorely aggrieved at this turn of fortune.

Ambrose has this to say about Saint Martin: "Blessed Martin destroyed the temples of pagan error, raised the banners of piety, restored the dead to life, drove wild demons from the bodies of the possessed, and raised up those who suffered from various maladies with the remedy of good health. He was found to be so perfect that he clothed Christ in the poor beggar and dressed the Lord of the world in a garment that he himself had received as an alms. O happy largesse, by which divinity was clothed! O glorious dividing of the cloak that clothed a soldier and a King! O priceless gift, that was worthy to be worn by divinity! Rightly, Lord, did you confer on this man this reward for confessing your name! Rightly did the savagery of the Arians bow before him! Rightly did the love of martyrdom arm him against fear of the persecutor's torments! What shall he, who deserved to clothe God and see him in return for the half of a cloak, receive for the offering of his whole body? So he brought medicine to the hopeful, to some by his prayers and to others by the mere sight of him!"

167. Saint Brice

Brice, one of Saint Martin's deacons, had no respect for the saint and heaped abuse upon him. Once when a beggar was looking for Martin, Brice told him: "If you're looking for that madman, look upwards! He's the one who like a fool is always looking toward heaven!" When the poor man had obtained what he needed from Martin, the holy man called Brice and said to him: "Do I look like a raving fool to you, Brice?" Brice was ashamed and denied that he had said anything like that, but Martin answered: "Was not my ear at your mouth when you said it at a distance? But now I tell you the truth! I have it from the Lord that you are to succeed me as bishop, but be it known to you that you will suffer much adversity in this office!" Brice laughed at this and said to others: "Wasn't I telling the truth when I called him a raving fool?"

After Martin's death Brice was elected bishop, and, though still haughty and outspoken, was devoted to prayer and kept his body chaste. When he had been bishop for thirty years, a woman who dressed like a religious and did his laundry for him conceived and bore a son. At that the whole town gathered at the bishop's door carrying stones and shouted: "All these years, out of respect for Saint Martin, we have pretended not to notice your lascivious life, but now we can no longer kiss those polluted hands!" He denied their accusations vehemently and said: "Bring the infant here to me!" The child, now thirty days old, was brought, and Brice said to him: "I adjure you by the Son of God to say, in the presence of all here, whether I begot you!" The infant replied: "Not you! You are not my father!" The people then pressed Brice to ask the child who his father was, but Brice declared: "That's not my affair! I did what I was called upon to do!"

The people then attributed all this to magic and said: "You are falsely called our shepherd, and we will no longer have you ruling over us!" But Brice wanted to prove his innocence and carried burning coals in the fold of his mantle to Saint Martin's tomb while all the people watched. He threw the coals aside and his mantle was undamaged, and he said: "As my garment was not scorched by the coals, so is my body clean of contact with a woman." The people, however, did not believe him, so they showered him with insults and expelled him from his see. Thus Saint Martin's prediction was fulfilled.

Brice then went sorrowing to the pope in Rome and stayed with him for seven years, doing penance for the wrongs he had done to Saint Martin. The people of Tours selected Justinian for their bishop and sent him to Rome to defend his right to the see against Brice's. But Justinian died on the way to

Rome in the city of Vercelli, and the Tours people put Armenius in his place. At the end of the seven years, however, Brice, supported by the pope's authority, returned to his diocese. He halted overnight six miles away from Tours, and Armenius expired that same night. Brice learned of his death by a revelation. He awakened his retinue, telling them to come with him in haste to the burial of the bishop of Tours. As Brice entered the city by one gate, the dead bishop was carried out by another. When Armenius had been buried, Brice resumed his place as bishop and presided for seven years. He led a praiseworthy life and in the forty-eighth year of his episcopate fell asleep peacefully in the Lord.

168. Saint Elizabeth

The name Elizabeth is interpreted as meaning My God has known, or the seventh of my God, or the satiety of my God. Elizabeth was called by a name meaning My God has known because God knew her, in other words, God observed her with pleasure and approved her, i.e., infused her with the knowledge of himself. Secondly, Elizabeth means the seventh of my God. Saint Elizabeth had the seventh of God, either because she practiced the seven works of mercy; or because she now is in the seventh age, the age of those who are at rest, and is about to come at last to the eighth age, namely, the age of rising from the dead; or because of the seven states of life in which she lived. She was first in the state of virginity, secondly, in the state of marriage, thirdly, in widowhood, fourthly, in the active state, fifthly, in the contemplative state, sixthly, in the state of consecrated religious life, and seventhly, in the state of glory. These seven states are brought out in her legend, so that it can be said of her as it is said of Nabachudonosor in the Book of Daniel: "Seven times shall pass over you."[1] Thirdly, Elizabeth is called the satiety of my God, for God filled and sated her with the splendor of truth, the sweetness of benignity, and the strength of eternity. Hence Augustine, speaking about the heavenly city in his book *On the City of God*, says: "In God's eternity is its strength, in God's truth its light, and in God's goodness its joy."

---

[1] Dan. 4:29.

Elizabeth, illustrious daughter of the king of Hungary, was noble by birth and still more noble by her faith and her devotion to religion. She ennobled her already noble lineage by her example, shed light on it by her miracles, and embellished it with the grace of her holiness. The Author of nature somehow raised her above nature. As a child growing up surrounded by regal privileges and pleasures, she either spurned the things children love, or directed them to God's service, showing how much her tender childhood was strengthened by her simplicity, and how sweet was the devotion of her earliest years. As a child she applied herself to serious concerns, shunning idle games, avoiding worldly success and prosperity, and advancing always in reverence toward God. When she was only five years old, she spent so much time praying in church that her companions and her maids could hardly get her out to play. Her servants and playmates noticed that when one of them in the course of a game went into the chapel, Elizabeth followed her, profiting by the opportunity to get into the church; and when she entered, she would kneel down or lie full length on the floor. She had not yet learned to read but often spread the Psalter open before her, pretending to read so that no one would disturb her. Sometimes she stretched herself on the ground beside other girls, playing at measuring herself against them, but also to display reverence for God. When playing the game of rings or any other game, she put her whole trust in God. When as a little girl she won something in a game or acquired a new possession in some other way, she divided it among poor children, urging them to say frequently the Our Father and the Hail Mary.

Elizabeth grew in age and even more in the intensity of her devotion. She chose the Blessed Virgin, mother of God, as her patroness and advocate, and Saint John the Evangelist as the guardian of her chastity. When papers with the names of the several apostles written on them were placed on the altar and then distributed at random among the girls, Elizabeth prayed three times and always received the paper with Saint Peter's name on it as she wanted to, because her devotion to that saint was so fervent that she would never deny anything to anyone who asked in his name. For fear that worldly successes might attract flattery to her, she daily gave away some token of her prosperity. When she won in some game, she called a halt and said: "I don't want to play any more! I leave the rest for the sake of God!" When invited to dance with other girls she would dance one round, then would say: "Let's let one round be enough and give up the rest for God," thus tempering the girls' taste for such vain pastimes. She abhorred too much show in dress and loved modesty in all such matters.

Elizabeth imposed upon herself the daily recitation of a certain number of prayers, and if she was too busy to complete the number during the day and was put to bed by her maids, she stayed awake until she had fulfilled her promise to her heavenly spouse. She observed solemn feast days with so much devotion that she would not allow her long sleeves to be stitched on her dress under any pretext until after the celebration of mass. She forbade herself the wearing of gloves before noon on Sunday, wishing thereby both to defer to the sacred solemnity and to satisfy her own devotion. For this same purpose it was her custom to impose such practices upon herself by vow, so that no one would be able to dissuade her from carrying out her intention. She assisted at liturgical services with such reverence that when the gospel was read, or the host consecrated, she removed her sleeves if they had been stitched on, and put aside her necklaces and any ornaments she was wearing on her head.

She lived out her state of virginity prudently and innocently, but was compelled to enter the state of marriage in obedience to her father's order. Thus she gained the thirtyfold fruit,[2] keeping the faith of the Trinity and obeying the Ten Commandments. She consented to conjugal intercourse, not out of libidinous desire but out of respect for her father's command, and in order to procreate and raise children for the service of God. Thus, while bound by the law of the conjugal bed, she was not bound to enjoyment. This is obvious from the fact that she made a vow in Master Conrad's[3] hands, that if she survived her husband she would practice continence for the rest of her life.

Elizabeth therefore was married to the landgrave[4] of Thuringia, as befitted her royal dignity but also as God's providence ordained, namely, that she might thus lead many to the love of God and might give instruction to the ignorant. Although her state of life was changed, there was no change in the way she intended to live. How great her devotion and humility toward God was, how strict her austerity and self-denial, how abundant her generosity and compassion for the poor, it will be the purpose of what follows to demonstrate.

She was so fervently devoted to prayer that she sometimes hurried to arrive in church ahead of her maids, as if wishing by some secret prayer to win a particular favor from God. She often rose during the night to pray, though her husband begged her to spare herself and give her body some rest. She had an arrangement with one of her maids who was closer to her than the others, that if by chance she overslept, the maid would wake her up by touching her foot. Once by mistake she touched the landgrave's foot. He woke up with a start but understood what had happened, and patiently put up with it and pretended not to have noticed anything. In order to make her prayers a rich sacrifice to God, Elizabeth often sprinkled them with a profusion of tears, but she shed her tears happily and without any unseemly change of countenance, weeping with sorrow and rejoicing at the sorrow; and this beautified her visage with gladness.

So profound was her humility that for the love of God she never shunned menial or lowly work, but did it with unbounded devotion. She once took an ugly sick man and clasped his filthy head to her bosom, then cut his hair and

---

[2] Cf. Mark 4:8, 20.

[3] For Master Conrad, see below.

[4] A title equivalent to "count."

washed his head, while her maids stood by laughing. On Rogation Days[5] she always walked in the procession barefoot and wearing a plain woolen garment. At the station churches she sat among the poorest women to hear the sermon, as if she too were poor and of low estate. When she went to be churched[6] after childbirth, she never made a show of jewelry or gold-embroidered gowns, as other women did. Following the example of Mary the immaculate mother, she carried her child in her arms and humbly offered him at the altar with a lamb and a candle, thus showing her distaste for worldly pomp and modeling her behavior after that of the Blessed Mother. Then, when she returned to her house, she gave the clothing she had worn in church to some poor woman.

As a further manifestation of her humility, Elizabeth, unsurpassed though she was in freedom and high station, submitted herself in obedience to a priest called Master Conrad. Conrad was a very poor man but was known for his knowledge and piety. With her husband's consent and the marriage right safeguarded, she pledged herself to obey Master Conrad so unreservedly that she would fulfill any order of his with reverence and joy. Her purpose was to gain merit and to imitate the example of her Savior, who became obedient even unto death. For instance, on one occasion Master Conrad had ordered her to attend a service at which he was to preach, but the marchioness of Meissen came to visit and Elizabeth missed the service. Conrad took her disobedience so amiss that he would not forgive it until, stripped to her shift, she was soundly flogged, along with some of her servants who had committed some fault.

Elizabeth took on herself so much abstinence and privation that her body was wasted with vigils and disciplines and fasting. Frequently she avoided her husband's bed and went without sleep in order to spend the night in contemplation and to pray to her heavenly Father in secret. When sleep overcame her, she slept on mats strewn on the floor. When her husband was away she passed the whole night in prayer with her heavenly spouse. Often, too, she had her servingwomen flog her in her bedroom, in return for the scourging her Savior had borne for her and to quell all carnal desire.

Such was Elizabeth's temperance in matters of food and drink that at her husband's table, laden as it was with a variety of tasty dishes, she sometimes ate nothing but a bit of bread. Master Conrad forbade her to eat any food about which she had the slightest qualm of conscience, and she obeyed this behest so meticulously that however abundant the delicious foods might be, she and her servingmaids partook of coarser fare. At other times she sat at table and divided and moved the food around on her plate, so as to seem to be eating and to ward off any notion that she was superstitious: thus, by her urbanity, she put all the guests at their ease. When they were traveling and she was worn out with the

---

[5] See chapter 70, "The Greater and Lesser Litanies."

[6] After giving birth, a woman came to the church to offer thanksgiving and to receive a special blessing.

length and labors of the journey, and she and her husband were offered foods that might not have been honestly acquired, she accepted none of them and patiently ate stale black bread soaked in hot water, as her maids did. For this reason, indeed, her husband had assigned funds to her, sufficient to provide for her living and that of some few of her women, who chose to follow her example in everything. Frequently, too, she refused what was served at the royal table and asked for the provisions of ordinary people. The landgrave was tolerant of all of this and said that he would gladly do the same himself if he were not afraid of upsetting the whole household.

Elizabeth's position was one of the highest dignity, but her whole desire was to share poverty with the poor, so that she might make return to Christ for his poverty and the world might have no claim on her. Sometimes, when she was alone with her servingwomen, she put on cheap, dingy clothing, covered her head with a shabby kerchief, and said to them: "This is how I will go about when I have attained the state of poverty." She checked her own appetite with a tight rein of abstinence but was openhanded in her generosity to the poor, never letting anyone go hungry and supplying the needs of all so liberally that she was acclaimed as the mother of the poor.

Blessed Elizabeth put her utmost effort into the performance of the seven works of mercy, hoping to inherit the everlasting kingdom and to reign there perpetually, and to possess the Father's blessing with the saints gathered at his right hand. She clothed the naked and provided raiment for the burial of poor people and strangers, as well as for infants at their christening. Often she lifted children of the poor from the baptismal font and sewed clothing for them with her own hands: having become their godmother, she then did more for them. On one occasion she gave a rather elegant dress to a poor woman, who was so overwhelmed with joy at the sight of such a magnificent gift that she fell to the ground and was thought to be dead. Blessed Elizabeth, seeing her lying there, was sorry she had given her so fine a present, fearing that she had thus been the cause of her death, but she prayed for her and the woman stood up fully recovered. Often, too, she spun wool in company with her servants, in order to receive the glorious fruit of these good labors, giving an example of true humility, and an alms to God out of the toil of her own body.

She fed the hungry. Once, when the landgrave had gone to the court of Emperor Frederick, then being held at Cremona, Elizabeth collected the whole year's crop from his barns, called in the poor from all sides, and provided for their daily needs, because the cost of living had risen and they were threatened with famine. When poor people ran out of money, she often sold her jewelry in order to help them. Indeed she regularly drew from her own resources and those of her faithful servingwomen to have something put aside for the poor.

She gave drink to the thirsty. Once she was serving beer to poor people, and after everyone had been served, the jug was still as full as it had been before she started.

She provided shelter for pilgrims and poor people. She had a very large house built at the foot of the high hill on which her castle stood, and there took care of numbers of the ill and infirm despite the difficulty of getting up and down the hill. While with them she saw to all their needs and exhorted them to patience. Bad air always distressed her, but for God's love, even in the heat of summer, she did not shrink from the smells and sores of the sick, but applied remedies to their wounds, dried them with the veil from her head, and treated them with her own hands, although her maids could hardly bear to watch her.

In this same house Elizabeth saw to it that children of poor women were well fed and cared for. She was so gentle and kind to them that they all called her Mother and, when she came into the house, followed her around as if she were in fact their mother, and crowded about her to be as close to her as possible. She also bought some small dishes and cups and rings and other glass toys for the children to play with. She was riding up the hill, carrying these things in the fold of her cloak, when they came loose and fell to the rocks below, but not one of the toys was broken.

Elizabeth visited the sick. Her compassion for their sufferings ruled her heart so much that she often went looking for their lodgings and visited them solicitously, entering their poor abodes as if she were at home, not deterred by the strangeness of the locale or bothered by the distance she had to go. She provided for their needs and spoke words of consolation to them, thus earning reward in five ways, namely, by honoring them with her visit, by the fatigues of the journey, by the warmth of her compassion, by her words of consolation, and by the generosity of her donations.

She concerned herself with the burial of the poor, devotedly going to their funerals, covering their bodies with clothes that she herself had made, and on one occasion cutting up the large linen veil she was wearing and wrapping the corpse of a poor person with part of it. She prepared them for interment with her own hands and piously stayed for the rites at the grave.

The piety of her husband deserves praise for his part in all these doings. He had many interests to attend to but was devout in honoring God, and, since he could not personally get involved in such activities, gave his wife the freedom and the means to do whatever served the honor of God and made for the salvation of his soul. Blessed Elizabeth wanted very much to see her husband turn the use of his arms to the defense of the faith, and by her salutary exhortations persuaded him to go to the Holy Land. There the landgrave, a faithful prince, devout and renowned for the integrity and sincerity of his faith, lost his life and received the reward of his good works.

Elizabeth now piously embraced the state of widowhood, taking care not to be defrauded of the reward of a widow's continence and to gain the sixty-fold fruit by observing the Decalogue together with the seven works of mercy. But as soon as the news of her husband's death spread throughout Thuringia, she was denounced by some of the landgrave's vassals as a prodigal, wasteful woman and was shamefully banned from her country. Thus her patience was brought fully to light, and her long-standing desire for poverty was fulfilled.

She went by night to the house of an innkeeper and was given shelter where the pigs usually rested, and for this she gave thanks to God. In the morning she went to the house of the Friars Minor and asked them to sing a *Te Deum*, in thanksgiving for the troubles that had befallen her. The following day she was ordered to go with her children into the house of one of her enemies, where she was given a very small room to live in. The man and woman whose house it was treated her so meanly that she bade farewell only to the walls, saying: "I would gladly give my good wishes to these people, if they had been kind to me." Having no place else to go she went back to the innkeeper's house, sending her children to various places to be cared for. She had to go along a path filled with mud, with only stepping-stones to walk on, and came face to face with an old woman whom she had befriended many times; but the old woman would not let her pass and she fell into the mud. Nothing daunted, she came up rejoicing and laughing, and shook the mud out of her clothes.

Now her aunt, who was an abbess, took pity on Elizabeth's poverty and brought her to the bishop of Bamberg, who was her uncle. He received her with due honor and shrewdly gave her hospitality in his house, planning to get her married again. The servingwomen who had vowed continence with her learned of the bishop's intention and wept as they reported it to blessed Elizabeth; but she reassured them, saying: "I trust in the Lord, for love of whom I have vowed perpetual continence. He will keep my resolution firm, will ward off all violence, and will defeat the schemes of men. If perchance my uncle wishes to wed me to another, I will set my mind against him and contradict him verbally; and if no other way of escape is left to me, I will cut off my nose, because no one would have me, thus disfigured."

By the bishop's order she was taken against her will to a castle, to stay there until she consented to marry, and she wept and commended her chastity to the Lord. But now, by God's will, her husband's bones were returned from overseas, and the bishop had Elizabeth brought back to give loving welcome to her spouse's remains. The bishop met the landgrave's bones in a procession of honor, and blessed Elizabeth gave them welcome with devotion and much shedding of tears. She then turned to the Lord and said: "I give you thanks, O God, for deigning to console miserable me by the reception of the bones of my spouse whom you loved. You know, O Lord, that I loved him dearly, as he loved you, yet for love of you I deprived myself of his presence and sent him to relieve your Holy Land. Delightful as it would be for me to live with him still, even were we reduced to go begging through the whole world, yet I would not give one hair of my head to have him back against your will, nor to recall him to this mortal life. I commend him and me to your grace."

Now, lest she lose the hundredfold fruit which is given to those who strive for evangelical perfection and are transferred from the left hand of misery to the right hand of glory, Elizabeth put on religious dress, namely, robes of plain gray, low-grade material. She observed perpetual continence after her husband's death, embraced voluntary poverty, and would have begged from door to door had not Master Conrad forbidden her. Her habit was so shabby that her gray cloak had to be lengthened and the holes in the sleeves of her tunic patched with cloth of a different color. When her father, the king of Hungary, heard of the destitution in which she was living, he sent a knight to persuade her to return to her paternal home. When the knight saw her dressed in such poor attire, sitting humbly and spinning thread, he was overcome with confusion and wonder, and exclaimed: "Never has a king's daughter been seen in such tawdry clothes, nor any royal personage spinning wool!"

Blessed Elizabeth absolutely refused to return with the knight, preferring to live in poverty with the poor rather than to be surrounded with riches with the rich. Then in order that her spirit might move totally to God and her devotion be unhampered by distraction or impediment, she prayed the Lord to fill her with contempt for all temporal goods, to take from her heart her love for her children, and to grant her indifference and constancy in the face of every insult. When she had finished her prayer, she heard the Lord saying to her: "Your prayer has been favorably heard." Elizabeth told her women: "The Lord has heard my voice graciously, because I regard all temporal things as dung, I care for my children no more than for others around me, I make light of all contempt and disrespect, and it seems to me that I no longer love any but God alone."

Master Conrad often imposed disagreeable and contrary things upon her, and separated from her company any persons to whom she seemed to feel a particular attachment. Thus he sent away from her two servingmaids who had grown up with her and were her loyal and dear friends: many tears were shed on both sides over this separation. The holy man took these measures in order to break her will and allow her to direct her whole desire to God, and to guard her from being reminded of her past glory by any of her servants. In all these matters she was quick in obedience and steadfast in patience, in order to possess her own soul by patience, and by obedience to be crowned with victory.

Blessed Elizabeth also said: "For God's sake I fear mortal man as much as I ought to fear the heavenly judge. Therefore I choose to give my obedience to Master Conrad, a poor, undistinguished man, rather than to some bishop, so that every occasion of worldly consolation may be taken away from me." Once when she had yielded to the earnest request of some nuns and had visited their convent without obtaining permission from her spiritual master, he had her flogged so severely that the marks of the lashes were still visible three weeks later. To her women she said, for their consolation as well as for her own: "The sedge grass lies flat when the river is in flood, and when the water recedes, the sedge straightens up. So, when some affliction befalls us, we should bow to it humbly and, when it passes, be lifted up by spiritual joy to God." Her humility was such that she would not allow her servants to address her as "lady" but insisted that they use the singular forms,[7] as is usual when speaking to inferiors. She washed the dishes and other kitchen utensils, and, lest her maids prevent her from doing so, had them carried to different places. She also said: "Could I have found a more menial way of life, I would have chosen it."

For the rest, in order to possess the best part with Mary, Elizabeth gave herself diligently to contemplative prayer. In this prayer she had special graces to shed tears, to have frequent visions of heaven, and to light the fire of love in others. At times when she was happiest she shed tears of joyous devotion, so that happy tears seemed to flow from her eyes as from a serene fountain. She seemed to be weeping and rejoicing at the same time, never letting tears change or mar her face. She said of those who looked gloomy when they wept: "Do they want to frighten the Lord away? Let them give to God what they have to give him with joy and good cheer!"

She often had visions of heaven in the course of her prayer and contemplation. One day in the holy season of Lent she was in church and had her eyes fixed intently on the altar, as if she were gazing at the very presence of God. This went on for a time, and the divine revelation refreshed and comforted her. When she got home, she was so weak that she rested on the lap of one of her maidservants and gazed through the window at the heavens, and such joyousness swept over her face that she burst out laughing. Then, after she had for some time been filled with joy by this vision, suddenly she was weeping. Opening her eyes again, the earlier joy was renewed in her, and when she closed them again, back came the flood of tears. This went on till compline, as she lingered in these divine consolations. She did not speak a word for a long time, then suddenly exclaimed: "So, Lord, you wish to be with me and I with you, and I want nothing ever to separate me from you!"

Later on her servants asked her to tell them, for the honor of God and their own edification, what was the vision she had seen. Conquered by their insistence, blessed Elizabeth said: "I saw the heavens opened, and Jesus leaning toward me in a most kindly way and showing me his loving face. The sight of him filled me with ineffable joy, and when it was withdrawn, I could only mourn my loss. Then he, taking pity on me, gave me again the joy of seeing his face and said to me: 'If you wish to be with me, I will be with you.' And you heard my answer." And when she was asked to tell about the vision she had seen at the altar, she answered: "It is not for me to tell the things I saw there, but I was in great joy and looked upon the wonderful works of God!"

It often happened that when she was at prayer, her face was radiant and from her eyes beamed light like the rays of the sun. Often, too, the fervor of her prayer was such that it lighted the fire of love in others. She saw a young man fastidiously dressed, and called him to her, saying: "You look to me as if you were leading a dissolute life, when you ought to be serving your creator! Do you

---

[7] I.e., thou, thee, thy, etc.

want me to pray to God for you?" "Oh yes," he answered, "I beg you to do so!" She thereupon gave herself to prayer and urged him to pray for himself, but the young man cried: "My lady, stop praying! Please stop!" But she prayed the more intently, and the youth cried more loudly: "Stop! I'll collapse! I'm on fire!" He was indeed so heated that he was dripping and steaming with sweat, and contorting his body and flailing with his arms like a madman. Several bystanders tried to hold him and found his clothing soaked with sweat, and his body too hot to touch, while he continued to cry out: "I'm on fire all over! I'm consumed!" Saint Elizabeth finished her prayer, and the young man no longer felt the heat. He came to himself and, enlightened by divine grace, entered the Order of Friars Minor. This incident showed that the fiery fervor of her prayer could inflame someone who was cold at heart; this young man, accustomed to the pleasures of the flesh and not yet ready for the joys of the spirit, could not understand what had happened.

Elizabeth, having reached the summit of perfection through Mary's contemplative prayer, did not give up Martha's laborious activity, as we have shown by her devotion to the seven works of mercy. Indeed, after taking the veil of religion, she practiced those works as assiduously as before. She had received two thousand marks for her dowry. Now she gave some of that to the poor and with the rest built a large hospital at Marburg. This made people regard her as a prodigal spendthrift, and many called her insane. When she gladly accepted these insults, they accused her of being so happy because she had put the memory of her husband out of her heart too quickly.

After the hospital was built, she committed herself to serving the poor like a simple servingwoman. She ministered solicitously to their needs, bathing them, putting them to bed, covering them, and cheerfully saying to her own maids: "How fortunate we are, to be able to bathe our Lord and cover him!" In waiting on the sick she humbled herself so completely that when a poor child who had only one eye and was covered with scabs came into the hospital, she took him in her arms to the privy seven times in one night and willingly washed his bedclothes. Again there was a woman with a horrible leprosy whom she bathed and put to bed, cleansing and bandaging her sores, applying remedies, trimming her fingernails, and kneeling at her feet to loosen her shoes. She prevailed upon the sick to confess their sins and to receive holy communion, and when one old woman flatly refused, she had her whipped to change her mind.

When Elizabeth was not busy with caring for the sick, she spun wool that was sent to her from a monastery, and divided the money she earned among the needy. At a time when everyone was poor, Elizabeth received five hundred marks from her dowry and set about distributing the money to those in need. She lined them all up, tied an apron on, and began the distribution, having made a rule that if anyone changed place in the line in order to receive a second time, that person's hair would be cut off. It happened that a girl named Radegund, who was admired for the beauty of her tresses, came to the hospital, not to receive an alms but to visit her sister who was ill. Since she did not get on line, she was brought to blessed Elizabeth for breaking the rule, and Elizabeth ordered her hair cut off, despite her sobs and her struggles. Then some of those present said that the girl was not at fault, but Elizabeth said: "At least from now on she won't be able to flaunt her curls at dances or indulge in similar vanities." She asked Radegund if she had ever thought of entering the religious life, and the girl answered that she would have done so long since if she were not so proud of her hair. Elizabeth: "It is dearer to me that you have lost your hair than if my son had been raised to the Empire!" Radegund took the religious habit and stayed on with Elizabeth, leading a praiseworthy life.

A poor woman gave birth to a daughter, and blessed Elizabeth lifted the baby from the sacred font and gave her her own name. Then she saw to the mother's needs and gave her the sleeves taken from her maid's coat to keep the infant warm. She also gave her shoes to the mother. Three weeks later the woman deserted her child and secretly went off with her husband. When Elizabeth got word of this, she had recourse to prayer, and the man and wife were unable to go a step farther, but had to come back to her and beg her forgiveness. She reproached them for their ingratitude, as they deserved, then turned the baby over to them to be cared for, and provided them with the necessary means.

The time was drawing near when the Lord intended to call his beloved out of the prison of this world, and to receive her, who had despised the kingdom of mortals, into the kingdom of the angels. Christ appeared to her and said: "Come, my beloved, to the eternal dwelling prepared for you!" She was brought low with fever and lay with her face turned toward the wall, and those who stood around her heard her humming a sweet melody. When one of her maids asked her what this meant, she answered: "A little bird perched between me and the wall, and sang so sweetly that I too had to sing." Throughout her illness she was always cheerful and prayed all the time. The day before she died she said to her attendants: "What would you do if the devil came near you?" After an interval she cried out three times : "Go away!" as if chasing the devil. Then she said: "It is almost midnight, the hour when Christ chose to be born and when he lay in his crib." And as the moment of her departure drew near, she said: "Now is the time when almighty God calls those who are his friends to the celestial nuptials!" Another interval, and she breathed her last and slept in peace, in the year of our Lord 1231.

Although her venerable body lay unburied for four days, no unpleasant odor came from it, but rather a pleasant aroma that refreshed everyone. Then flocks of small birds that had never been seen there before clustered on the roof of the church. Their melodies were so sweet and their harmonies so varied that their music, which, as it were, accompanied the saint's obsequies, won the admiration of all who heard it. Loud was the mourning of the poor, deep the devotion of all the people. Some cut off wisps of her hair; others clipped shreds from her graveclothes, to be kept as precious relics. Her body was placed in a monument from which oil is said to have flowed afterwards.

A number of events surrounding the saint's death manifest the height of sanctity that she had attained. Consider first the singing of the little bird and the driving away of the devil. The bird that perched between Elizabeth and the wall, and sang so sweetly that she sang with it, we take to have been her angel, who was delegated to be her guardian and also to assure her of eternal joy. Sometimes, to increase the consternation of the damned, their eternal punishment is revealed to them before they die; and to the elect their eternal salvation is at times revealed to enhance their consolation. Elizabeth's singing at that moment was evidence of the immense joy which that revelation stirred in her, a joy so great that it could not be contained in her heart but manifested itself in the dulcet sound of her voice. The devil, too, comes to dying saints to find out whether he has any right over them, but since he had no hold over Elizabeth, he fled ignominiously.

Second, her cleanness and purity were made manifest by the sweet odor that came from her body; since in her lifetime her body shone with cleanness and chastity, in death it gave out a fragrant aroma.

Third, her excellence and high dignity were manifested by the joyful singing of the birds. We believe that the birds that sang jubilantly on the ridge of the church roof were angels sent by God to carry her soul to heaven and to honor her body with celestial caroling. Just as a swarm of demons convenes around dying unrepentant sinners to torment them with terror and to whisk their souls off to hell, so a multitude of angels gathers around the good at the hour of death to comfort them and conduct their souls to the heavenly realm.

Fourth, the depth of blessed Elizabeth's mercy and pity was manifested by the flow of oil. Oil flowed from her dead body because in her lifetime she abounded in works of mercy. Oh, how largely the spirit of pity must now flow in the vitals of one from whose body lying in the dust oil was found flowing!

Fifth, the occurrence of numerous miracles manifests Elizabeth's power and merit before God. After she had passed from her body, God glorified her with a multiplicity of miracles, some of which will be related here, many being omitted for the sake of brevity.[8]

In a monastery in the diocese of Hildesheim, Saxony, there was a Cistercian monk named Henry. He was so ill and suffered so much pain that all the monks felt compassion for him and were disturbed by his cries of distress. One night there appeared to him a venerable lady dressed in white garments, who told him that if he wished to recover his health, he should dedicate himself by vow to Saint Elizabeth. The following night the same lady appeared and gave the same advice. Since the abbot and the prior were both away from the monastery, the

---

[8] The reason given for the omission is Jacobus's.

monk made the vow after consulting his immediate superior. The third night the lady appeared and made the sign of the cross over him, and he was cured. When the abbot and the prior heard of this, they began to wonder about Henry's health but were in serious doubt about whether he should keep his vow, since no monk is allowed to make vows or assume such obligations without permission. The prior added that demons often appeared to monks, who were deluded by them into making such forbidden vows *sub specie boni*—under the semblance of good—and that therefore the said monk should be advised to strengthen his unstable mind by confession. The following night, however, the same lady as before appeared to Henry and said: "You will always be ill until you fulfill your vow!" Immediately his illness returned and he was tortured with pain. The abbot, upon hearing of this turn of events, gave the monk the necessary permission and ordered that enough wax be given to him to make the required image. Again Henry's health was restored, and he zealously fulfilled his vow and suffered no recurrence of his malady.

In the diocese of Mainz a young woman named Benigna asked a servant to give her a drink, and the servant, annoyed, gave it to her, saying: "Take it and drink the devil!" It seemed to Benigna that a burning brand was going down her throat, and she cried out that she had pains in her neck. Then her belly swelled up like a balloon, and she felt as if some animal was running around inside her. She moaned miserably and uttered demented cries, and was thought to be possessed of the devil. In that condition she lived for two years. Then she was brought to Saint Elizabeth's tomb and a vow was made for her there. She was placed atop the tomb and looked to be lifeless, but when they gave her a morsel of bread to eat and some blessed water to drink as she lay there, to the astonishment and delight of all she rose up cured.

A man in the diocese of Utrecht, whose name was Gederic, had lost the use of one hand, which was paralyzed. He visited Saint Elizabeth's tomb twice without obtaining a cure but went with much devotion a third time with his wife. On the way he met an old man of venerable aspect, saluted him, and asked where he came from. The old man said that he came from Marburg, where the body of Saint Elizabeth rested, and where many miracles occurred. Gederic told him about his paralyzed hand, and the aged man raised his hand and blessed him, saying: "Go with confidence, you will be healed, provided you put your infirm hand into an opening hollowed out in the stone at the head of the tomb; and the farther you thrust your hand in, the speedier your cure will be; and at that moment have Saint Nicholas in mind, because he works as companion and associate of Saint Elizabeth in her miracles." He added that those who, having put down their offerings, left the saints' shrines immediately, made a foolish mistake, because it pleased the saints when their aid was sought with perseverance. With that the old man disappeared and they saw him no more. They went on their way to Marburg, wondering about his appearance and disappearance, but fully confident that they would obtain the cure they sought. Gederic therefore followed the old man's advice, putting his hand in under the stone at the head of the tomb, and, when he withdrew it, it was perfectly sound.

A man of the diocese of Cologne, Herman by name, was being held in prison by the judge. He commended himself totally to God, and called upon Saint Elizabeth and Master Conrad to come to his aid, with all the devotion of which he was capable. The following night they both appeared to him, surrounded by brilliant light, and consoled him in many ways. Finally his sentence was carried out and he was hanged on a scaffold a Teutonic mile from town. The judge, however, gave the parents permission to take the body down and bury it. The grave was prepared and the convict's father and uncle laid the body in it, meanwhile invoking Saint Elizabeth's patronage in favor of the dead man. To the stupefaction and admiration of all present, the man who had been dead arose alive.

A schoolboy called Burchard, from the diocese of Mainz, was fishing, but carelessly fell into the river and drowned. He was pulled out after quite a while, but the body was rigid, without feeling or motion, and showed no signs of life, so he was judged to be dead by the men who had found him. Then the merits of Saint Elizabeth were invoked, and, wonderful to behold, the boy was restored to life and health.

A boy three and a half years old, whose name was Hugolin, of the diocese of Mainz, died on the road, and his body lay rigid and lifeless. His mother carried him a distance of four Teutonic miles, imploring Saint Elizabeth with all devotion, and the boy returned to life and health.

A four-year-old boy fell into a well, and a man who came to draw water noticed the body submerged and lying at the bottom. He got the boy out with some difficulty and determined that he was dead. The indications of death were the length of time the boy had been in the water, the rigidity of the body, the horrible staring eyes and gaping mouth, the blackened skin, the swollen body, and the utter absence of movement and feeling. The man therefore pronounced a vow to Saint Elizabeth, invoking her help for the deceased, and the boy recovered the life he had had. There was also a girl who fell into a river, and when she was pulled out, she was quickly restored to life by Saint Elizabeth's merits.

A man named Frederick, of the diocese of Mainz, was an expert swimmer. While swimming in a certain body of water he saw a poor man who had been cured of blindness through Saint Elizabeth's intercession, and began to make fun of him, contemptuously splashing water in his face. The man resented this and said: "That holy lady who obtained this grace for me will take my revenge on you, and you will not come out of the water until you are dead and drowned." The swimmer thought little of this threat and swam away insolently into deep water, but suddenly lost all his strength, could not help himself, and sank to the bottom like a stone. After a long time he was found and lifted from the water, and loud was the lamentation for him. Some of his kinsmen, however, made a vow to Saint Elizabeth on his behalf and devoutly sought her assistance; and quickly he began to breathe and rose alive and well.

A certain John, also of the Mainz diocese, was apprehended with a thief, though he himself had not committed any crime, and was sentenced to be hanged. He begged those around him to pray to Saint Elizabeth, asking her to help him as he deserved. He was hanged nonetheless but heard a voice speaking over him: "Take heart, have confidence in Saint Elizabeth, and you will be freed." At once, while the other man remained suspended, John's noose broke and he fell heavily from a height, but suffered no injury, though a new shirt he was wearing was torn. Rapturously he prayed: "O Saint Elizabeth, you freed me and made me fall on a patch of soft ground!" There were those, however, who said that he should be hanged again, but the judge said: "Whom God has set free I will not allow to be hanged a second time!"

A lay brother named Volmar, in a monastery in the diocese of Mainz, was extremely religious and afflicted his body so severely that for twenty years he wore a leather-and-iron corset next to his skin, and lay on sticks and stones to rest. He was working in the mill when his hand got caught and the millstone mangled it so badly that the flesh was torn away on both sides, the bones and tendons were shredded, and the hand looked as if it had been mashed in a mortar. The pain of the injury was so intense that Volmar asked to have the hand cut off. He frequently invoked Saint Elizabeth's aid, having throughout his life been devoted to her, and one night she appeared to him and asked: "Do you want to be healed?" "Oh, please, I do!" he answered. She took his hand, mended the sinews, brought the bones together in place, restored the flesh on either side, and rejoined the hand to the wrist. In the morning the brother found his hand perfectly repaired and showed it, so mended, to the whole community, to the amazement of all.

A five-year-old boy named Dietrich, in the diocese of Mainz, was born blind but by Saint Elizabeth's merits received the light; but he had no eyelids and the skin grew over his eyes, covering them completely and leaving no sign that there were any eyes beneath. His mother brought him to Saint Elizabeth's sepulcher, rubbed his face over the eyes with earth from the tomb, and invoked the saint's merits on her son's behalf. And behold, the unbroken skin split open, and two small eyes, clouded and bloodshot, looked out. Thus the boy obtained the blessing of eyesight through the merits of Saint Elizabeth.

A girl of the same diocese, whose name was Beatrice, for a long time was afflicted with a number of woeful infirmities. In time a hump grew on her back and a tumor in her chest. She was so bent over that she could not stand erect and had to support her body by resting her hands on her knees. Her mother managed to carry her in a sort of basket to Saint Elizabeth's tomb and they stayed there for ten days, unable to find any remedy for the child's ills. The mother lost her temper and complained to Saint Elizabeth, saying: "You hand out all these favors to everybody else and you don't even listen to wretched me! I'll go home and turn as many people as I can away from coming to visit you!" Still angry, she started out and walked a mile and a half, while the daughter groaned with pain. Then the child fell asleep and saw a beautiful lady with a radiant face, who lightly touched her back and chest, and said: "Get up, child, and walk!" The girl woke up and found herself cured of all curvature and deformity. She told her mother about the vision, and they both rejoiced and were glad. Then back they went to Saint Elizabeth's tomb, where they gave thanks to God and left the basket in which the child had been carried.

A woman of the same diocese, whose name was Gertrude, for many years was paralyzed in both legs and suffered curvature of the spine. In a dream she was advised to go to Saint Nicholas and implore the help of his merits. She had herself carried to the church of Saint Nicholas and found one of her legs cured. Later, almost beside herself with pain, she was brought to Saint Elizabeth's monument and placed upon her tomb, and was quickly and completely made well. Still in the same diocese, a woman named Scintrude lost her sight for a year and had to be led about by the hand; but she commended herself to Saint Elizabeth with all devotion and recovered her sight.

A man named Henry, of the diocese of Mainz, being deprived of his eyesight, visited Saint Elizabeth's tomb and received the benefit of a complete cure. Later the same man suffered hemorrhage so grave that his family thought he would die. But someone brought him some earth from Saint Elizabeth's tomb, he mixed it with water and drank it, and his health was restored completely.

Mechtilde, a girl of the diocese of Trier, was blind and deaf and could neither talk nor walk. Her father and mother dedicated her to Saint Elizabeth, and the saint gave her back to them perfectly cured. They all then praised the great works of God and Saint Elizabeth. A woman named Hedwig, of the diocese of Trier, was completely blind for a year and for her cure invoked Saint Elizabeth's merits. She was led to the saint's tomb and there recovered the sight of one eye, but, when she was home again, felt excruciating pain in the other. She invoked the saint's merits again, and Elizabeth appeared to her and said: "Go to the altar, wipe your eyes with the corporal,[9] and you will be healed." She did as ordered and was cured.

A man named Theoderic, of the diocese of Mainz, was so gravely stricken in the knees and legs that he could not get about unless supported by others. He made a vow to visit the sepulcher of Saint Elizabeth with offerings. Although he lived only ten miles from her shrine, it took him all of eight days to get there. When he had stayed at the tomb for four weeks without obtaining a cure, he started home, but stopped on the way and sought rest lying beside another sick man. Then in a dream he saw someone come and pour water over him. He woke up and said angrily to the man next to him: "Why did you pour water all

[9] A linen cloth on which the consecrated elements are placed in the mass.

over me?" The man replied: "I did not pour water over you, but I think the shower will be the cause of your well-being." Theoderic stood up and found himself made a whole man, whereupon he threw his crutches over his shoulder and marched back to give thanks at Saint Elizabeth's tomb. Then he went home to his family, rejoicing.

---

169. Saint Cecilia

The name Cecilia may come from *coeli lilia*, lily of heaven, or from *caecitate carens*, lacking blindness, or from *caecis via*, road for the blind, or from *coelum* and *lya*, a woman who works for heaven. Or the name may be derived from *coelum* and *laos*, people. For Saint Cecilia was a heavenly lily by the modesty of her virginity. She is called a lily because of her shining cleanness, her clear conscience, and the aroma of her good renown. She was a road for the blind by giving good example, a heaven through her continual contemplation, and a worker for heaven by her application to good works. Or she is called heaven because, as Isidore says, the philosophers have said that heaven is revolving, round, and fiery, and Cecilia was revolving in a constant circle of good works, round in her perseverance, and fiery with the warmth of her charity. She was free of blindness through the splendor of her wisdom. She was a heaven of the people because in her, as in a spiritual heaven—the sun, the moon, the stars—people saw how to imitate heaven, namely, by the perspicacity of her wisdom, the magnanimity of her faith, and the variety of her virtues.

Cecilia, that illustrious virgin, was born into a noble Roman family and raised in the faith of Christ from infancy. She always carried Christ's gospel in her bosom, prayed continually by day and by night, and besought the Lord to preserve her virginity. She was betrothed to a young man named Valerian and the wedding day was set, but Cecilia wore a hair shirt next to her flesh beneath her cloth-of-gold outer garments. While the musical instruments sounded, she sang in her heart to the Lord alone, saying: "Let my heart and my body be undefiled, O Lord, that I may not be confounded"; and she fasted for two or three days at a time, commending her fears to God. Finally came her wedding night, and she and her spouse retired to the silence of the bridal chamber. She addressed him: "O sweetest and most loving young man, I have a secret to confess to you, on condition that you swear to keep this secret entirely to yourself." Valerian swore that no necessity would make him reveal it, nor any reason force him to betray it. Then she said: "I have a lover, an angel of God, who watches over my body with exceeding zeal. If my angel senses that you are touching me with lust in your heart, he will strike you and you will lose the flower of your gracious youth. If, on the other hand, he knows that you love me with sincere love, he will love you as he loves me, and will show you his glory."

Valerian, guided by God's will, said: "If you want me to believe you, show me this angel of yours, and if I see for myself that he is really an angel, I will do as you are exhorting me to do; but if I see that you love another man, I will finish off both of you with my sword!" Cecilia told him: "If you will believe in the true God and promise to be baptized, you will be able to see him. Go therefore to the third milestone from the city on the Appian Way, and say to the poor people you will find there: 'Cecilia has sent me to you to have you show me an aged holy man named Urban, because I carry secret orders for him which I will pass on to him.' When you see this Urban, tell him everything I have said, and after you have been purified by him, come back to me and you will see the angel!"

Valerian set out and, following the directions given to him, found his way to Saint Urban the bishop, who was hiding among the tombs of the martyrs. When he had told him all that Cecilia had said, Urban raised his hands to heaven, wept, and said: "Lord Jesus Christ, sower of chaste counsel, accept the fruit of the seeds that you sowed in Cecilia! Lord Jesus Christ, good shepherd, Cecilia your hand-maid has served you like a busy bee: the spouse whom she received as a fierce lion, she has sent to you as a gentle lamb!" And now there appeared to them an aged man clothed in garments as white as snow, holding a book written in gold letters. When Valerian saw this, he was so afraid that he fell as if dead, but was raised to his feet by the old man and read in the book: "One Lord, one faith, one baptism, one God and father of all, who is above all and through all and in all of us."[1]

When Valerian had read those words, the old man asked him: "Do you believe that this is so, or do you still doubt?" Valerian exclaimed: "There is nothing else under heaven that could be more truly believed!" The old man vanished forthwith. Valerian was baptized by Urban and went back to find Cecilia talking to an angel in her room. The angel held two crowns of roses and lilies in his hand, one of which he gave to Cecilia and the other to Valerian, saying: "Guard these crowns with spotless hearts and clean bodies, because I have brought them to you from God's heaven. They will never wither nor lose their sweet odor, nor can they be seen by anyone except those whom chastity pleases. And you, Valerian, since you have trusted good counsel, ask whatever you wish and you will have it!" Valerian: "There is nothing dearer to me in this life than the love

---

[1] Eph. 4:5. Graesse has "One God, one faith," etc.

of my only brother. I ask therefore that he may join me in acknowledging the truth!" The angel: "Your petition pleases the Lord, and you will both come to him with the palm of martyrdom."

At this moment Tiburtius, Valerian's brother, came in, smelled the strong odor of roses, and said: "I wonder where this odor of roses and lilies is coming from at this season! Their aroma could not penetrate me more sweetly if I were holding the flowers in my hands! I confess to you that I am so refreshed that of a sudden I feel totally changed!" Valerian said: "We have crowns that your eyes cannot see. They bloom with florid color and snowy whiteness. At my prayer you perceived their odor. So also, if you believe, you will be able to see them." Tiburtius: "Am I hearing this in dream, Valerian, or are the things you are saying true?" Valerian: "We've been living in dream, but now we dwell in the truth!" Tiburtius: "How do you know this?" And Valerian: "An angel of the Lord has taught me, and you will be able to see him if you choose to be purified and to renounce the worship of idols!" Ambrose testifies to this miracle of the crowns of roses in his Preface, where he says: "Saint Cecilia was so filled with the heavenly gift that she accepted the palm of martyrdom, cursing the world along with the pleasures of marriage. Her witness is the confession she evoked from her spouse, Valerian, and from Tiburtius, both of whom, O Lord, you crowned by an angel's hand with sweet-smelling flowers. A virgin led these men to glory, and the world recognized how powerful commitment to chastity can be." Thus Ambrose.

Cecilia then showed him plainly that all idols were without feeling or speech, and Tiburtius responded, saying: "Anyone who does not believe this is a brute beast!" Cecilia kissed his breast and said: "Today I declare that you are my kinsman, for just as the love of God has made your brother my husband, so has contempt for the idols made you my kinsman. Go therefore with your brother to be purified and made able to see the faces of angels!"

Tiburtius said to his brother: "I beg of you, brother, tell me who it is that you are leading me to." Valerian: "To Urban the bishop!" Tiburtius: "Are you talking about the Urban who has been condemned to death so many times and is in hiding somewhere? If that man is found, he will be burned alive and we will be caught in his flames, and, while we are looking for God in heaven, we will bring burning fury upon us on earth!" To this, Cecilia responded: "If this life were the only life, we would be right in fearing to lose it, but there is another and a better life, which is never lost and which the Son of God has told us about. All things that were made, the Son begotten of the Father has established in being, and all the things that are established, the Spirit who proceeds from the Father has enlivened. This Son of God came into the world and showed us, by his words and his miracles, that there is another world." Tiburtius: "Surely you assert that there is only one God! How then can you testify that there are three?" Cecilia's answer: "Just as in human knowledge there are three powers, namely, thought, memory, and understanding, so in the one divine being there can be three persons."

Then she began to instruct him about the coming of the Son of God and his passion, and to show the many ways in which his passion was fitting. "The Son of God was held in bonds," she said, "in order to free humankind from the bonds of sin. He was accursed, that accursed mankind might be blessed. He allowed himself to be mocked in order to free man from being made a mockery by the demons. He submitted to receiving a crown of thorns on his head so as to lift the capital sentence from us. He tasted the bitter gall to cure our taste for the sweet things of life. He was stripped of his garments to cover our first parents' nakedness. He was hung upon a tree to undo the evil done at the tree!" Tiburtius said to his brother: "Have pity on me and lead me to the man of God so that I may receive purification!" So he was purified, and thereafter often saw the angels of God and obtained whatever he prayed for.

Valerian and Tiburtius now devoted themselves to works of mercy and gave burial to the bodies of saints whom the prefect Almachius had put to death. Almachius summoned them and asked them why they buried those who were condemned for their crimes. Tiburtius: "Would that we might be the slaves of those whom you call condemned! They despised what seems to be and is not, and have found what is not seen to be, and is!" The prefect: "And what is that?" Tiburtius: "That which seems to be and is not is everything in the world that leads man to nonbeing. What is not seen to be and is, is the life of the righteous and the punishment of the wicked." Almachius: "From what you say, I think you are out of your mind!"

Then he had Valerian brought before him and said to him: "Since your brother is not right in his head, you at least may be able to answer us reasonably. It is clear that you are wrong in many ways, since you spurn all joys and are attracted to everything hostile to enjoyment." To this, Valerian said that in wintertime he had seen idle men mocking and making fun of those who work in the fields, but in the summer, when the glorious fruits of their labor are ready for harvesting, he had seen those who were thought to be foolish rejoicing, and those who seemed to be clever beginning to weep. "We too," he went on, "who bear shame and hard work, will in the future receive glory and an eternal reward, while you, who enjoy what is transitory, in the future will face eternal grief." The prefect: "So we, unconquered and unconquerable princes, will have eternal sorrow, and you, the rabble, will possess perpetual joy?" Valerian: "You are not princes, but little men, insignificant, born in our time, soon to die, and due to give a stricter account to God than any of us!"

At that Almachius retorted: "Why do we go on arguing in circles? Offer libations to the gods and go scot-free!" The saints answered: "We offer sacrifice to the true God every day." "What is his name?" the prefect demanded. Valerian: "You will not be able to find his name, even if you take wings and fly!"

"Then Jupiter is not a name of God?" the prefect asked. Valerian: "It is the name of a murderer and debaucher!" Almachius: "Therefore the whole world is in error, and you and your brother alone know the true God!" Valerian: "We are not alone! An innumerable multitude has accepted this holy truth!"

The brothers were handed over to the custody of Maximus, who said to them: "O purple flower of youth, O loving brothers, how is it that you hasten to your deaths as to a banquet?" Valerian answered that if Maximus promised to believe in Christ, he would see the glory of their souls after they died. Maximus: "If what you have said really happens, may I be consumed by fiery lightning if I do not profess my faith in that one true God whom you adore!" And in the event, Maximus, his whole household, and all the executioners accepted the faith and were baptized by Urban, who came to them secretly.

Dawn ended the night, and Cecilia exclaimed: "Hail, soldiers of Christ, cast aside the works of darkness and put on the arms of light!" Then, at the fourth milestone from the city, at the statue of Jupiter, the brothers refused to offer sacrifice and were beheaded. Maximus swore that in the hour of the saints' passion he had seen shining angels, and the martyrs' souls going forth like virgins from the bridal chamber, and the angels carrying them heavenwards. When Almachius learned that Maximus had become a Christian, he had him beaten to death with leaded thongs. Saint Cecilia buried his body with those of Valerian and Tiburtius.

Almachius now made a move to get possession of the brothers' properties and had Cecilia, as Valerian's wife, brought before him, commanding her either to sacrifice to the idols or to incur the sentence of death. Her servants wailed at the thought and urged her to yield, on the ground that a maiden so fair and so noble should not commit herself to death. She said to them: "Good folks, I am not losing youth but exchanging it, giving up clay and receiving gold, abandoning a hut for a palace, leaving a narrow corner of the street for a wide-open, light-filled plaza. If someone offered you a gold piece for a copper, would you not accept it readily? God, indeed, gives back to us a hundred for one. Do you believe what I'm saying?" "We believe," they answered, "that Christ, who has such a handmaid as you are, is truly God!" Bishop Urban was thereupon sent for, and more than four hundred people were baptized.

Almachius again summoned Saint Cecilia and asked her: "What is your status in life?" "I am freeborn and of noble descent," she said. Almachius: "I'm asking about your religion!" Cecilia: "Then your interrogation began badly, because the one question called for two answers." Almachius: "Where do your presumptuous answers come from?" "From a clear conscience and unfeigned faith!" she retorted. Almachius: "Don't you know where my power comes from?" Cecilia: "Your power is a balloon filled with wind! Prick it with a pin and it collapses, and what seemed rigid in it goes limp." Almachius: "You began with insults, and with insults you continue!" Cecilia: "You cannot speak of insults unless what is said is false! Show me the insult, if what I said was false!

Otherwise blame yourself for uttering a calumny! We, who know the holy name of God, cannot deny it, and it is better to die happy than to live unhappy." Almachius: "What makes you speak so proudly?" Cecilia: "It is not pride but constancy!" Almachius: "Unhappy girl, don't you know that the power to give life or to take life away is given to me?" Cecilia: "Now I can prove that you have lied against what is known to everyone! You can indeed take life away from the living, but you cannot give life to the dead. Therefore you are a minister of death, not of life!" Almachius: "Stop this wild talk and offer sacrifice to the gods!" Cecilia: "I don't know where you lost your eyes! What you call gods are nothing but lumps of stone, as we all see. Put your hand out and touch them, and you will know with your fingers what you can't see with your eyes!"

Almachius, now angry, ordered her to be brought to her house, and there to be burned in a boiling bath for a night and a day. She lay in the bath as in a cool place, without feeling as much as a drop of perspiration. When the prefect heard this, he commanded that she be beheaded in the bath. The headsman struck her three times in the neck but could not cut her head off; and because the decree forbade striking a fourth blow, he left her bleeding and half dead. She lived for three days, during which time she gave all her possessions to the poor. All those whom she had converted she commended to Bishop Urban, saying: "I asked for a delay of three days so that I might commend all of us to your beatitude and have you consecrate my house as a church."

Saint Urban buried her body where bishops were buried, and consecrated her house as she had requested. She suffered about A.D. 223, in the reign of Emperor Alexander. Elsewhere we read that she suffered in the reign of Marcus Aurelius, who ruled about A.D. 220.

170. Saint Clement

The name Clemens comes from *cleos*, which means glory, and *mens*, mind. Saint Clement had a glorious mind, in other words a mind cleansed of all stain, adorned with every virtue, and now graced with the fullness of happiness. This happiness, as Augustine says in his book *On the Trinity*, consists in this, that in heaven our being will not be subject to death, nor our knowing to error, nor our love to resistance. Or the name comes from *clementia*, clemency, and the saint was a very clement man. Or, as the *Gloss* tells us, *clemens* means mild, just, mature, and pious; and Clement was just in action, mild in speech, mature in his relations with others, and pious in his intentions.

Clement himself inserted the story of his life, especially up to the point where the account shows how he came to succeed Saint Peter as supreme pontiff, in his *Itinerarium*. The rest of his life story is drawn from the records of his acts, which are commonly available.

Clement, the bishop of Rome, was born of noble Roman stock. His father's name was Faustinianus, his mother's, Macidiana. He had twin brothers, one of whom was called Faustinus, the other, Faustus. Macidiana, his mother, was a woman of striking beauty, and her husband's brother burned with desire for her and annoyed her with his daily attentions, to which she gave not the slightest hint of consent; yet she shrank from making the situation known to her spouse, for fear of stirring up enmity between the two men. She therefore conceived the idea of absenting herself from her homeland until this illicit affection, which was fanned by the sight of her presence, had had time to cool. In order to obtain her husband's assent to this plan she cannily invented a dream, which she related to Faustinianus as follows: "In my dream I saw a man standing beside me and ordering me to leave the city as soon as possible, taking with me the twins, Faustinus and Faustus, and to stay away until he commanded me to return home. If I did not do this, I would perish with the two children."

The husband was alarmed by this and sent his wife and sons, with a large retinue, to Athens, to live there and have their sons educated there. The father kept his youngest son, Clement, to be a comfort to him. The mother and the two boys sailed away, but one night their ship was wrecked and Macidiana, without the children, was cast up on a rocky island, She supposed that the boys had been drowned, and would have cast herself into the sea for grief had she not hoped she might recover their bodies. When she realized that she would not find her children either dead or alive, she cried and screamed, tore her hands with her teeth, and would accept consolation from no one. Many women came to her and told her of their own misfortunes, but this did nothing to mitigate her grief. One of the women, however, told her that her own husband, still a young man and a seaman, had perished at sea, and that for love of him she had refused to remarry. This proved to be of some comfort to Macidiana, and she went to live with this woman, earning her day-to-day living by the work of her hands. But in a short time her hands, which she had injured so seriously by biting them, were without feeling or movement, and she could work no longer. Moreover, the kind woman who had taken her in became paralyzed and could not get out of bed. Macidiana was forced to beg, and she and her hostess lived on whatever she was able to bring home.

A year had passed since the mother and the twins had left Rome, and the father sent messengers to Athens to look for them and bring back news of their doings, but the messengers never returned. Finally, after he had sent still others and they had come back with the word that they had found no trace of the woman and the children, Faustinianus left his son Clement in the care of tutors, and he himself boarded ship to hunt for his wife and offspring, but he also never returned.

Thus orphaned, Clement for twenty years could learn nothing about what had become of his father, his mother, and his brothers. He was an assiduous student of letters and scaled the highest peak of philosophy. He ardently wished for and studiously sought a way of convincing himself that the soul is immortal. With this in mind he frequented the schools of the philosophers, rejoicing when it seemed to him that his immortality was proved, and saddened when the conclusion was that he was mortal.

Then Saint Barnabas came to Rome and preached the Christian faith. The philosophers derided him as a fool and a know-nothing. One of them, however—according to some it was Clement the philosopher—at first mocked Barnabas and scorned his preaching, and by way of making a fool of him proposed a question to him, saying: "The mosquito is a tiny animal. Why therefore does it have six feet and wings as well, whereas the elephant, a huge beast, has no wings and only four feet?" Barnabas: "Foolish fellow, I could very easily answer your question if you seemed to be asking it in order to learn the truth; but it would be absurd to talk to all of you here about creatures, since you know nothing about the one who gives being to creatures. You do not know the Creator, so it is right and just that you should be in error about his creatures!" These words so touched the heart of Clement the philosopher that he received instruction in the Christian faith from Barnabas and then hurried to Judea to visit Saint Peter. The apostle completed his instruction in the faith of Christ and gave him clear proofs of the soul's immortality.

At that time Simon Magus, the magician, had two disciples, Aquila and Nicetas by name, but they saw through his frauds, left him to take refuge with Saint Peter, and became his disciples. Peter questioned Clement about his origins, and Clement told him about his mother, his brothers, and his father, adding that as far as he knew, his mother and brothers had been lost at sea, and his father had died, either of grief, or, like the others, in a shipwreck. Hearing this account, Peter could not restrain his tears.

Peter went to Antander with his disciples, and from there to an island six miles offshore, where Macidiana, Clement's mother, lived. On the island stood some marvelously high glassy columns, and Peter and the others were admiring these columns when a beggar woman approached them. Peter asked her reproachfully why she did not work with her hands, and she answered: "These hands that I have just look like hands! They are so weakened by my biting them that they have lost all feeling, and I wish I had thrown myself into the sea, so as not to go on living!" Peter: "Why do you say that? Don't you know that the souls of those who do away with themselves are punished grievously?" Macidiana: "If only I could be sure that souls do live after death, I would gladly kill myself, just to see my sweet children at least for one hour!" Peter asked her why she was so sad and she told him the whole story, whereupon Peter said: "There is a young man named Clement with us, and he has told us that what you say happened to you happened also to his mother and brothers!"

The woman was so benumbed with surprise at this information that she fell in a faint, and, when she came to herself, wept and said: "I am that youth's mother!" She threw herself at Saint Peter's feet and begged him to let her see her son as soon as possible. Peter said to her: "When you see him, restrain yourself for a short time, until our ship carries us away from this island!" She promised to do so, and Peter took her hand and led her to the ship where Clement was. When Clement saw Peter approaching hand in hand with a woman, he began to laugh; but as soon as Macidiana came close to her son, she could contain herself no longer, but clasped him in her arms and kissed him repeatedly. Clement thought the woman was out of her mind and pushed her away indignantly, then turned to Peter with a show of displeasure. Peter: "What are you doing, son? Don't push your mother away!" When Clement heard this, he burst into tears, dropped down beside the prostrate woman, and recognized his mother. Then, at Peter's order, they brought the woman who had befriended Macidiana and who lay paralyzed, and he cured her immediately. Now Clement's mother asked him about his father, and he answered: "He left Rome to look for you and never came back!" At hearing this she only sighed, the great joy she felt over finding her son outweighing her other woes.

Nicetas and Aquila had been absent while all this was going on, but now appeared and saw a woman in Peter's company. "Who is this?" they asked. Clement answered them: "This is my mother, whom God has given back to me with the help of Peter, my master." Peter then told them all that had happened. Hearing this, Nicetas and Aquila stood up abruptly, shaken to the core, and said: "O God, lord and ruler, is what we have heard true or is it a dream?" Peter: "My sons, we are not raving! What you heard is true!" The two young men rubbed their faces and said: "We are Faustinus and Faustus, and our mother thought we were lost at sea!" And they rushed to embrace their mother and covered her face with kisses.

Macidiana said: "What's the meaning of this?" Peter: "They are your sons, Faustinus and Faustus, who you thought perished in the sea!" What she had heard filled the mother with such joy that she was beside herself and fell in a faint, then came to herself and said: "My darling sons, tell me how you escaped!" They said: "When the ship broke up, we clung to a plank, and some pirates picked us up and took us into their boat. Then they changed our names and sold us to an honest widow whose name was Justina, and she treated us as if we were her own sons, and had us educated in the liberal studies. Finally we took up philosophy and joined Simon Magus, who had been a student with us. In time we saw through his frauds, deserted him completely, and, through Zacheus's good offices, became Peter's disciples!"

The following day Peter took the three brothers, namely, Clement, Aquila, and Nicetas, and went off to a secluded place to pray. There a venerable but poor old man spoke to them as follows: "I pity you, brothers! Though your motives are good and pious, I consider you seriously wrong, because there is no God, there is nothing to worship, there is no providence in the world. Everything is controlled by chance and the aspect of the planets at the moment of your birth. I am sure of this out of my own knowledge of astrology, in which I am more learned than most. Therefore make no mistake! Whether you pray or not, what the stars determine for you will be your fate!"

As the old man talked, Clement studied his face, and it suddenly struck him that he had seen this man somewhere before. Peter told the three brothers to continue the discussion, and they went on at length to demonstrate the reality of providence by sound reasoning. Out of reverence they several times addressed him as father, until Aquila said to his brothers: "Why are we calling him father, since we have a commandment to call no man father on earth?"[1] Then, turning to the aged man, he said: "Don't be offended, father, that I have corrected my brothers for calling you father, for we do have a commandment not to give that name to any man on earth." When Aquila had said this, everybody present, including the old man and Peter, laughed; and when Aquila asked them what they were laughing about, Clement told him: "You yourself addressed him as father—the very thing you blamed us for!" But Aquila questioned this, saying: "Truly I don't know whether I called him father or not!"

When the question of providence had been discussed at some length, the old man said: "I would indeed believe that there is a providence, but my conscience forbids me to give consent to this belief. I know my horoscope and that of my wife, and I know that what they determined for each of us has happened to us. Let me tell you the position of the planets at my wife's birth, and you will see the aspect that determined what actually happened to her. At her birth she had Mars with Venus above the center, the moon in descent in the house of Mars and in the borders of Saturn. That alignment makes women commit adultery, makes them fall in love with their own slaves, travel to distant parts, and perish in the water. All this happened. My wife fell in love with a slave, and, fearing danger and disgrace, went off with him and perished at sea. Indeed, as my brother told me, she first fell in love with him and, when he would have nothing to do with her, turned to the slave to satisfy her lust. Nor should she be blamed for this, since her stars compelled her to do as she did." He went on to tell about her dream, and how she and her children had perished in a shipwreck.

His sons were poised to throw themselves upon him and tell him what had really happened, but Peter stopped them, saying: "Quiet, till I give you the word!" Then he said to the old man: "If today I deliver to you your wife, chaste as ever, and your three sons, will you believe that there is nothing to astrology?"

[1] Matt. 23:9.

The reply: "Just as you cannot posssibly do what you have promised, so it is impossible that anything can happen outside the influence of the stars." Peter said to him: "Look! Here is your son Clement, and here are your twin sons Faustinus and Faustus!" At this the old man's limbs gave way, and he fell to the floor giving no sign of life. His sons bent over him and kissed him, fearing that he might not breathe again. He recovered, however, and heard in detail all that had happened. Then suddenly his wife came in weeping and called out: "Where is my husband and lord?" As she continued to cry out like a woman demented, her husband ran to her, shedding copious tears, and began to embrace and kiss her.

Now the family was reunited, and a messenger came to inform them that Apio and Ambio, two close friends of Faustinianus, were the guests of Simon Magus. Faustinianus was overjoyed to hear of their arrival and went to visit them. Shortly another messenger came to tell them that one of Caesar's ministers had arrived in Antioch to hunt down all magicians and put them to death. Then Simon Magus, out of hatred for the two brothers who had been his disciples and had left him, impressed his own likeness on their father's face, so that he would be taken for Simon, not for Faustinianus, and the emperor's ministers would arrest and execute Faustinianus in place of Simon himself. Simon then took off for far places. When Faustinianus went back to his sons and to Peter, the sons were terrified to see Simon's face while they heard their father's voice. Peter was the only one who saw the other man's natural face, and when the sons and the wife, thinking it was Simon, were fleeing from him and cursing him, Peter asked them: "Why are you cursing your father and fleeing from him?" They answered that it was because he looked like Simon the Magician: Simon had made some unguent and applied it to Faustinianus's face, and by magical arts imposed his own features on him. Faustinianus complained and said: "What has happened to wretched me, that in one day I am recognized by my wife and sons, and yet cannot rejoice with them?" His wife tore her hair and his sons shed floods of tears.

While Simon was in Antioch, he had slandered Saint Peter as much as he could, calling him a malign artificer and a murderer, and had worked the people up to such a pitch of hostility toward Peter that they were ready to tear at his flesh with their teeth. Peter therefore said to Faustinianus: "Since you look like Simon, go to Antioch, speak about me favorably before the whole populace, and, speaking as Simon, retract everything he has said against me. Then I will come to Antioch, rid you of that alien face, and, in the sight of all, restore your own visage to you!"

It is not to be believed, however, that Peter ordered Faustinianus to lie, since God certainly does not need our lying. Clement's *Itinerarium*, which contains these details, must therefore be an apocryphal book and, despite what some may be pleased to think, is not to be credited with regard to such details as the above. Yet, when Peter's words are weighed carefully, it can be said that he did not tell

Faustinianus to say that he was Simon Magus, but to let the people see the face that had been imposed on him, and thus, speaking as if he were Simon, to say good things about Peter and revoke the bad things Simon had said about him. In other words, he said he was Simon not according to the reality but according to appearances. So what Faustinianus said, as quoted below—"I, Simon, etc."—should be understood as "that is, as far as appearances go, I seem to be Simon." He was Simon, but putatively.

So Faustinianus, father of Clement, went to Antioch, convoked the populace, and said: "I, Simon, declare to you and confess that I was wrong in what I said about Peter. He is neither a seducer nor a sorcerer but has been sent for the salvation of the world. Therefore, if from now on I say anything against him, chase me out as a seducer and sorcerer. Now I do penance, because I acknowledge that I spoke falsely. I warn you therefore to believe Peter, lest you and your city perish!" When Faustinianus had carried out all Peter's orders and had given the people reason to love Peter, the apostle arrived and prayed over him, completely effacing the likeness of Simon from him. The populace of Antioch, thereupon, welcomed Peter warmly and with much honor, and raised him to the episcopal chair.

Now it was Simon himself who arrived in the city and called the people together. "I marvel," he said to them, "that after I had instructed you in salutary rules of action and had warned you against that deceiver Peter, you have not only listened to him but have made him your bishop." The whole crowd, now roused to fury, challenged him, saying: "In our eyes you are a monster! Day before yesterday you were saying how penitent you were, and now you are trying to bring us to ruin with yourself!" They rushed at him and promptly chased him, shamefaced, out of the city. Clement tells this story, inserting it in his book about himself.

After these events Saint Peter went to Rome and, knowing that his passion was imminent, ordained Clement as bishop to succeed him. When the prince of the apostles died, Clement, a farsighted man, took precautions for the future. He foresaw the possibility that some future pope would take what Peter had done as an example and would select and install his successor in the Church, thus making the Lord's sanctuary a sort of hereditary possession. Clement therefore yielded his place as bishop of Rome first to Linus, then to Cletus. There are some who assert that Linus and Cletus were not supreme pontiffs but merely coadjutors to Peter, and as such merited inclusion in the catalog of popes. After them Clement was elected and compelled to preside. He was so obviously a good and holy man that he pleased Jews and Gentiles as well as all Christian peoples. He had a written list of the names of poor Christians in the several provinces and would not allow those whom he had cleansed by the sanctification of baptism to be subjected to the humiliation of public beggary.

Clement had consecrated the virgin Domitilla, niece of Emperor Domitian, with the sacred veil, and had converted Theodora, wife of Sisinnius, a friend of the emperor, Theodora having promised to lead a chaste life thereafter. Sisinnius, driven by jealousy, secretly entered the church where his wife worshiped, wanting to know what it was that made her visit the church so often. As he entered, Saint Clement intoned a prayer and the people responded, and Sisinnius was stricken blind and deaf. At once he told his servants: "Take hold of me and lead me outside!" The servants led him all around the inside of the church but could not reach any door. Theodora saw them wandering about, but at first kept out of their way, thinking that her husband might recognize her. Finally she asked the servants what they were doing, and they said: "Our master wanted to see and hear forbidden things, and was stricken blind and deaf." Theodora resorted to prayer, asking God to allow her husband to go outside; and after praying, she said to the servants: "Go now and take your master home!"

When they had left, Theodora told Saint Clement what had happened. At her request the saint went to Sisinnius, and found him with his eyes open but seeing nothing and hearing nothing. Clement prayed for him and his sight and hearing were restored; and when he saw Clement standing beside his wife, he flew into a rage and suspected that he was being fooled by magical tricks. He therefore ordered his men to sieze Clement, saying: "He blinded me so that he might go in to my wife!" His men were to bind the saint hand and foot and drag him away; but they wound their bonds around columns and stones that were lying there, thinking, as Sisinnius also thought, that they were binding Clement and his clerics and dragging them around. Then Clement said to Sisinnius: "To things that are stones you give the name of gods, so you deserve to drag stones!" Sisinnius thought Clement was in bonds and said to him: "I'll have you killed!" But Clement walked away after asking Theodora to continue praying for her husband until the Lord visited him. Saint Peter appeared to Theodora as she prayed, and said: "Through you your husband will be saved, in order that what my brother Paul said, namely, that 'the unbelieving husband is sanctified by the believing wife,'[2] may be fulfilled." Having said this, he disappeared.

Now Sisinnius called his wife and begged her to pray for him and to summon Saint Clement. The saint came, instructed Sisinnius in the faith, and baptized him and 313 persons of his household. Many nobles and friends of Emperor Nerva were also converted to the Lord by this Sisinnius.

The official in charge of the sacred funds now gave out a lot of money, bribing a mob to start a riot against Saint Clement. Mamertinus, the urban prefect, could not tolerate such disturbances, so he had Clement brought before him. He rebuked the saint and tried to bend him to his own point of view, but Clement said: "I wish you would listen to reason! If a pack of dogs comes barking at us and they try to bite us, they still cannot take away from us our being men of reason while they are irrational dogs. A riot stirred up by ignorant men shows that it has nothing certain or true behind it!"

[2] 1 Cor. 7:14.

Mamertinus wrote to Emperor Trajan about Clement and received a reply to the effect that either Clement should offer sacrifice or Mamertinus should send him into exile across the Sea of Pontus,[3] adjacent to the city of Chersonesus. Then the prefect, weeping, said to Clement: "May your God, to whom you offer pure worship, come to help you!" The prefect assigned a ship to him and provided for all his needs, and many clerics and lay people followed him into exile. He landed on an island and found two thousand Christians who had been sentenced to quarry marble there. The moment they saw Clement, they burst into tears. He consoled them and said: "For no merit of mine has the Lord sent me to you to be the chief jewel in your crown of martyrdom!"

The prisoners told him that they had to carry water on their shoulders a distance of six miles, and he said to them: "Let us all pray to our Lord Jesus Christ to open for his confessors a spring and veins of water here in this place, that he, who struck the rock in the desert and water came forth abundantly,[4] may grant us a fountain of water, and we may rejoice in his goodness to us!" When he had finished his prayer, he looked around and saw a lamb standing, with his foot raised as if to indicate a certain spot to the bishop. Clement understood that this was the Lord Jesus Christ and that he alone could see him, so he went to the spot and said to those following him: "Strike the ground in this place, in the name of the Father and of the Son and of the Holy Spirit!" But since none of them knew where the lamb stood and nothing happened, Clement took a short stick and struck a light blow at the spot where the lamb's foot rested. Instantly a flood of water erupted and swelled into a stream. Then, as all rejoiced, Saint Clement said: "The stream of the river makes the city of God joyful."[5] The fame of this spread abroad and many people came to the site, and in one day over five hundred received baptism from him. They then tore down the temples of the idols and built seventy-five churches within one year.

Three years later, Emperor Trajan, whose reign began in A.D. 106, heard about all this and sent a general to take action. Finding that all the people were ready and glad to accept martyrdom, the general yielded to numbers and settled for one man. He had Clement thrown into the sea with an anchor fastened around his neck, saying that the Christians would not be able to worship him as God. A great crowd stood at the water's edge, and Cornelius and Probus, Clement's disciples, bade all the people pray that the Lord would show them the martyr's body. At once the sea drew back three miles, and all walked out dry-shod and found a small building prepared by God in the shape of a temple, and within, in an ark, the body of Saint Clement and the anchor beside him.

It was revealed to Clement's disciples that they were not to remove his body. Every year thereafter, at the date of his passion, the sea receded three miles and

[3] Pontus Euxinus, the Black Sea.
[4] Cf. Exod. 17:6; Num. 20:11.
[5] Ps. 45:5(46:4).

stayed back for a week, affording dry passage to those who came. In one of these annual solemnities a woman went out to the shrine with her little son, and the child fell asleep. When the ceremony was finished and the sound of the inrushing tide was heard, the woman was terrified and forgot her son in her hurry to get ashore with the rest of the crowd. Then she remembered, and loud were the cries and lamentations she addressed to heaven, wailing and running up and down the beach, hoping she might see the child's body cast up by the waves. When all hope was gone, she went home and mourned and wept for a whole year. Then, when the sea drew back, she was the first to reach the shrine, running ahead of the crowd to see whether she might find some trace of her son. She prayed devoutly at Saint Clement's tomb, and when she rose from prayer she saw the child asleep where she had left him. Thinking that he must be dead she moved closer, ready to gather up the lifeless body; but when she saw that he was sleeping, she quickly awakened him and, in full sight of the crowd, lifted him in her arms. She asked him where he had been throughout the year, and he said he did not know if a year had passed and thought that he had slept soundly for one night.

Ambrose, in his Preface, says: "When the wicked persecutor was forced by the devil to inflict torment on blessed Clement, he did not inflict torment but bestowed triumph. The martyr was thrown into the waves to drown, but this was his path to reward, as by the waters Peter, his master, reached heaven. In the waves Christ showed his approval of both of them, calling Clement up from the depths to the palm of victory, and lifting Peter up to the heavenly kingdom lest he be drowned in the same element."

Leo, bishop of Ostia, tells us that during the reign of Michael, emperor of the New Rome, there was a priest who was called Philosophus because he was so learned, even as a child. This priest arrived in Chersonesus and questioned the people in the town about the things narrated in Clement's story, but most of the people were not natives of the city and admitted that they knew nothing about Clement. The miraculous recession of the sea had long since ceased to happen, due to the sinfulness of the inhabitants. Even before that, the barbarians invaded the area and on the occasion of the sea's withdrawal had destroyed the small temple, leaving the ark containing the body to be covered over by the waves, as was also called for by the townspeople's wrongdoing. Wondering at this, Philosophus went to a small city called Georgia and accompanied the bishop, the clergy, and the people to an island on which the martyr's body was thought to be. There they started to dig in search of the relics, singing hymns and praying as they worked, and by a divine revelation they found the body and the anchor with which the martyr had been cast into the sea. They took all this to Chersonesus. Then the aforesaid Philosophus went to Rome with Saint Clement's body, and it was placed with due honor in the church that is now named after Saint Clement. Many miracles occurred there. Another chronicle has it, however, that the sea left that particular place dry, and blessed Cyril, bishop of the Moravians, transferred the body to Rome.

171. Saint Chrysogonus

Chrysogonus was in prison by order of Emperor Diocletian, and Saint Anastasia provided for his needs. Then Anastasia's husband put her in very strict confinement, and she wrote the following letter to Chrysogonus, who had instructed her in the faith: "Anastasia to Chrysogonus, holy confessor of Christ. I have taken upon myself the yoke of a godless husband, whose bed, God pitying me, I have avoided by feigning illness, and day and night I walk in the footsteps of our Lord Jesus Christ. My husband has used my patrimony to gain prominence, but he is squandering it in unworthy ways and with shameful idolaters. He treats me as a sorceress and blasphemer, and keeps me under such close guard that I suspect I shall soon lose this temporal life, for there is nothing left for me but to breathe my last and succumb to death. I know that that death will glorify me, but I am sorely tried at the thought that my wealth, which I had consecrated to God, is used by scoundrels to no good purpose. Farewell, man of God, and remember me."

Chrysogonus wrote her in reply: "Take care not to be disturbed that you, a God-fearing woman, are beset by adversity, for you are not being deceived, but tried. Soon a time more to your liking will come. Christ will turn to you, and after the darkness of night you will see God's resplendent light, and after winter's cold, a golden, tranquil season will follow for you. Farewell in the Lord, and pray for me."

In time Anastasia's treatment became so harsh that she was scarcely given a morsel of bread, and she felt that she was about to die. She wrote to Chrysogonus: "Anastasia to Chrysogonus, Christ's confessor. My bodily life is soon to end. May he receive my soul for whose love I bear these trials, about which you will learn from this old woman, my messenger." He wrote back: "What is always true is that darkness precedes the light, and so health returns after sickness and life is promised us after death. One end finishes off the adversities and the prosperities of this world, lest despair overrule the sad, or elation the glad. The little ships of our bodies sail one and the same sea, and our souls do the work of the sailors under the one pilot of the body. The ships of some are held together by strong chains and survive the pounding waves of life undamaged, whereas other ships, constructed of fragile wood, are close to foundering even in calm weather yet finish their voyage. You then, O handmaid of Christ, cling with your whole heart to the trophy of the cross, and prepare yourself for the work of God."

Diocletian meanwhile was in the area of Aquileia and was putting many Christians to death. He had Chrysogonus brought before him and said: "Sacrifice to the gods, and assume the powers of your prefecture and the consulship that is yours by birth!" Chrysogonus answered: "I adore one God in heaven and spurn your honors as dirt!" So sentence was pronounced and he was led away and beheaded, about A.D. 287. Saint Zelus, a priest, buried his body with the head.

172. Saint Catherine

Catherine comes from *catha*, which means total, and *ruina*, ruin; hence "total ruin." The devil's building was totally demolished in Saint Catherine: the edifice of pride by her humility, that of carnal concupiscence by the virginity which she preserved, and that of worldly greed, because she despised all worldly goods. Or Catherine's name may be taken for *catenula*, a small chain, for by her good works she fashioned a chain for herself by which she climbed to heaven. This chain or ladder has four steps, which are innocence of action, cleanness of heart, contempt for vanity, and speaking of the truth. The prophet proposes these one by one: "Who shall ascend into the mountain of the Lord? . . . The innocent in hands, and clean of heart, who hath not taken his soul in vain, nor sworn deceitfully to his neighbor."[1] How these four steps were present in blessed Catherine's life will be clear as we read her story.[2]

Catherine, the daughter of King Costus, was fully instructed in all the liberal studies. Emperor Maxentius had summoned all the people, rich and poor alike, to Alexandria to offer sacrifice to the idols, and was persecuting the Christians who refused to do so. When Catherine, then eighteen years old and living alone in a palace filled with treasure and servants, heard the bellowing of animals and the hurrahs of the singers, she quickly sent a messnger to find out what was going on. Learning the facts, she took some people from the palace with her and, arming herself with the sign of the cross, went out and saw many Christians about to offer sacrifice because they were afraid to die. Deeply grieved by what she saw, she boldly made her way into the emperor's presence and spoke as

[1] Ps. 23(24):3, 4.

[2] According to *Butler's Lives of the Saints* (New York: P. J. Kenedy & Sons, 1963), 4:420, Catherine's dates are unknown and there is no documentation regarding her life or her death. The popularity of her cult in the Middle Ages may be judged from the length and detail of this chapter.

follows: "Both the dignity of your rank and the dictates of reason counseled me, Emperor, to present my greeting to you if you were to acknowledge the Creator of the heavens and renounce the worship of false gods." Standing at the temple entrance, she argued at length with the emperor by syllogistic reasoning as well as by allegory and metaphor, logical and mystical inference. Then she reverted to the common speech and said: "I have taken care to propose these thoughts to you as to a wise person, but now let me ask you why you have vainly gathered this crowd to worship the stupidity of idols. You wonder at this temple built by the hands of artisans. You admire the precious ornaments that in time will be like dust blown before the face of the wind. Marvel rather at the heavens and the earth, the land and the sea and all that is in them. Marvel at their ornaments, the sun and the moon and the stars, and at their service—how from the beginning of the world until its end, by night and by day, they run to the west and go back to the east and never grow weary. Take note of all these things, and then ask, and learn, who it is who is more powerful than they; and when by his gift you have come to know him and have been unable to find his equal, adore him, give him the glory, because he is the God of gods and the Lord of lords!" And she went on to discourse at length and with wisdom about the incarnation of the Lord.

The emperor was so amazed that he could make no reply to her, but recovered himself and said: "Please, O woman, please let us finish our sacrifice, and afterwards we will come back to this discussion." He then had her accompanied to the palace and guarded carefully. He was overwhelmed with admiration of her knowledge and the beauty of her person. She was indeed lovely to behold, of truly incredible beauty, and was seen by all as admirable and gracious.

The emperor came to the palace and said to Catherine: "We have heard your eloquence and admire your knowledge, but were so intent upon worshiping the gods that we were unable to follow all you said. Now let us start by hearing about your ancestry." "It is written," Saint Catherine replied, "that one should neither speak too highly of oneself nor belittle oneself: foolish people do that, being teased by a taste for hollow glory. But I avow my parentage, not boastfully but for love of humility. I am Catherine, only daughter of King Costus. Though born to the purple and quite well instructed in the liberal disciplines, I have turned my back on all that and taken refuge in the Lord Jesus Christ. On the other hand, the gods you worship can help neither you nor anybody else. O unhappy devotees of idols that when called upon in need are not there, who offer no succor in tribulation, no defense in danger!"

"If things are as you say they are," the emperor answered, "then the whole world is in error and you alone speak the truth! However, since every word is confirmed in the mouth of two or three witnesses, no one would have to believe you even if you were an angel or a heavenly power, and all the less since obviously you are but a frail woman!" Catherine's reply was: "I implore you, Caesar, do not let yourself be carried away by anger, lest dire disturbance overturn a wise man's mind, for the poet says, 'If you are ruled by the mind you are king, if by the body you are slave.'" "I see now," said the emperor, "that you are bent on ensnaring us with your perfidious cunning, as you try to prolong this discussion by quoting the philosophers."

Maxentius was now aware that he could not compete with Catherine's learning, so he secretly sent letters to all the masters of logic and rhetoric, ordering them to come quickly to the court at Alexandria, and promising them huge rewards if they could best this female demagogue with their arguments. Fifty orators, who surpassed all mortal men in every branch of human knowledge, came together from various provinces. They asked the emperor why they had been summoned from so far away, and he told them: "We have a girl here who has no equal in understanding and prudence. She refutes all our wise men and declares that all our gods are demons. If you can get the better of her, you will go home rich and famous!"

At this, one of the orators broke out in a voice trembling with indignation: "O deep, deep thinking of the emperor, who on account of a trifling dispute with one girl has gathered men of learning from the ends of the earth, when any one of our pupils could have silenced her with the greatest of ease!" But the caesar retorted: "I could indeed have forced her to sacrifice or got rid of her with a round of torture, but I thought it better to have her refuted once and for all by your arguments." So the masters said: "Have this maiden brought before us! Let her be put to shame for her rashness, let her realize that she had never even seen wise men before!"

When Catherine was informed about the contest that awaited her, she commended herself totally to God, and at once an angel of the Lord stood by her side and admonished her to stand firm, assuring her that she could not be defeated by these people; and more than that, she would convert them and set them on the road to martyrdom. She was then brought into the presence of the orators. To the emperor she said: "Is it fair for you to array fifty orators against one girl, promising the orators rich returns for winning, and forcing me to fight without any hope of reward? Yet my reward will be the Lord Jesus Christ, who is the hope and crown of those who fight for him."

The debate began, and when the orators said that it was impossible for God to become man or to suffer, Catherine showed that this had been predicted even by pagans. Plato affirms a God beset and mutilated. The Sibyl, too, speaks as follows: "Happy that God who hangs from a high tree!" The virgin went on to contradict the orators with the utmost skill and refuted them with clear and cogent reasoning, to the point that they, dumbstruck, found nothing to respond and were reduced to silence. This drove the emperor to fresh outbursts of fury, and he began to rail at them for letting a young girl make fools of them. Then one, the dean of the others, spoke out: "You must know, Caesar, that no one has ever been able to stand up to us and not be put down forthwith; but this young woman, in whom the spirit of God speaks, has answered us so admirably that either we do not know what to say against Christ, or else we fear to say anything at all! Therefore, Emperor, we firmly declare that unless you can propose a more tenable opinion regarding the gods whom hitherto we have worshiped, we are all converted to Christ!"

Hearing this the emperor, beside himself with rage, gave orders to burn them all in the middle of the city. With words of encouragement the virgin strengthened their resolution in the face of martyrdom and diligently instructed them in the faith; and when they were troubled because they would die without being baptized, she told them: "Have no fear, the shedding of your blood will be counted for you as baptism and crown!" They armed themselves with the sign of the cross and were thrown into the flames, thus rendering their souls to the Lord; and it happened that not a hair of their heads nor a shred of their garments was as much as singed by the fire. Then the Christians buried them.

The tyrant now addressed the virgin: "O damsel nobly born, take thought to your youth! In my palace you will be called second only to the queen. Your image will be erected in the center of the city, and you will be adored by all as a goddess!" "Stop saying such things," Catherine answered, "it is a crime even to think them! I have given myself as his bride to Christ, and he is my glory, he my love, he my sweetness and my delight. Neither blandishments nor torture will draw me away from his love!" The emperor's anger surged back in full, and he ordered her to be shut up for twelve days in a dark cell and left to suffer the pangs of hunger. He then left the city to attend to affairs of state.

Then the queen, afire with love, hastened at nightfall to the virgin's cell accompanied by the captain of the guard, whose name was Porphyrius. When the queen entered, she saw the cell filled with indescribable brilliance, and angels ministering to the virgin's wounds. Catherine began at once to preach to her about the joys of heaven, converted her to the faith, and predicted a martyr's crown for her. Thus they went on talking until past midnight. Porphyrius, having heard all this, threw himself at the saint's feet and along with two hundred soldiers, acknowledged the faith of Christ. Moreover, since the tyrant had ordered that Catherine be left for twelve days without food, Christ sent a shining dove from heaven and refreshed her with celestial viands during those days. Then the Lord appeared to her with a multitude of angels and virgins, and said: "O daughter, recognize your Creator, for whose name you have undergone a toilsome conflict. Be constant, because I am with you!"

Upon his return the emperor had Catherine brought before him. He expected to find her worn out by the long fast but instead saw her more radiant than ever. He thought someone had fed her in the prison, and this made him so angry that he ordered the guards to be tortured. The virgin, however, said to him: "I received food from no man, but Christ fed me by an angel." The emperor: "Take to heart, I beg of you, the warning I am giving you, and give me no more of your dubious answers. We have no wish to own you as a mere servant. You will be a powerful queen in my realm, chosen, honored, triumphant!" Catherine: "Now you yourself pay attention, I pray you, and, after judicious consideration of my question, give an honest decision: whom should I choose—one who is powerful, eternal, glorious, and honored, or one who is weak, mortal, ignoble, and ugly?" Indignantly Maxentius retorted: "Now you choose one or the other for yourself: offer sacrifice and live, or submit to exquisite torture and die!" Catherine: "Whatever torments you have in mind, don't waste time! My one desire is to offer my flesh and blood to Christ as he offered himself for me. He is my God, my lover, my shepherd, and my one and only spouse."

Now a certain prefect urged the furious ruler to have prepared, within three days, four wheels studded with iron saws and sharp-pointed nails, and to have the virgin torn to pieces with these horrible instruments, thus terrorizing the rest of the Christians with the example of so awful a death. It was further ordered that two of the wheels should revolve in one direction and the other two turn in the opposite direction, so that the maiden would be mangled and torn by the two wheels coming down on her, and chewed up by the other two coming against her from below. But the holy virgin prayed the Lord to destroy the machine for the glory of his name and the conversion of the people standing around; and instantly an angel of the Lord struck that engine such a blow that it was shattered and four thousand pagans were killed.

The queen, who until then had not shown herself and had watched what was going on from above, now came down and berated the emperor severely for his cruelty. The monarch was enraged and, when the queen refused to offer sacrifice, commanded that she first have her breasts torn off and then be beheaded. As she was led away to her martyrdom, she begged Catherine to pray God for her. "Fear not, O queen beloved of God," the saint answered, "for today you will gain an eternal kingdom in place of a transitory one, and an immortal spouse for a mortal." The queen, thus strengthened in her resolve, exhorted the executioners not to tarry but to carry out their orders. They therefore led her out of the city, tore off her breasts with iron pikes, and then cut off her head. Porphyrius snatched up her body and buried it.

The following day, when an unsuccessful search was made for the queen's body and the tyrant for that reason ordered many to be questioned under torture, Porphyrius burst in and declared: "I am the one who buried the servant of Christ, and I have accepted the Christian faith!" At this Maxentius, out of his wits, uttered a terrible roar and exclaimed: "O me, wretched as I am and to be pitied by all, now even Porphyrius, sole guardian of my soul and my solace in all my toil, even he has been duped!" And when he turned to his soldiers, they promptly responded: "We too are Christians and are ready to die!" The emperor, drunk with rage, ordered them all to be beheaded with Porphyrius and their bodies to be thrown to the dogs. Next he summoned Catherine and told her: "Even though you used your magical arts to bring the queen to death, if you have now come to your senses, you shall be first lady in my palace. Today therefore you shall either offer sacrifice to the gods or lose your head." Her answer was: "Do anything you have a mind to do! You will find me prepared to bear whatever it is!"

She was thereupon sentenced to death by beheading. When she was led to the place of execution, she raised her eyes to heaven and prayed: "O hope and glory of virgins, Jesus, good King, I beg of you that anyone who honors the memory of my passion, or who invokes me at the moment of death or in any need, may receive the benefit of your kindness." A voice was heard saying to her: "Come, my beloved, my spouse, see! Heaven's gates are opened to you and to those who will celebrate your passion with devout minds. I promise the help from heaven for which you have prayed."

When the saint had been beheaded, milk flowed from her body instead of blood, and angels took up the body and carried it from that place a twenty-days' journey to Mount Sinai, where they gave it honorable burial. (An oil still issues continuously from her bones and mends the limbs of all who are weak.) She suffered under the tyrant Maxentius or Maximinus, whose reign began about A.D. 310. How Maxentius was punished for this and other crimes is told in the legend of the Finding of the Holy Cross.[3]

It is said that a certain monk from Rouen journeyed to Mount Sinai and stayed there for seven years, devoting himself to the service of Saint Catherine. He prayed insistently that he might be worthy to have a relic from her body, and suddenly one of the fingers broke off from her hand. The monk joyfully accepted God's gift and carried it back to his monastery.

It is also told that a man who had been devoted to Saint Catherine and often called upon her for help became careless in the course of time, lost his devotion, and no longer prayed to her. Then one time when he was at prayer, he saw in a vision a procession of virgins going by, and among them one who seemed more resplendent than the rest. As this virgin came closer to him, she covered her face and so passed in front of him with her face veiled. Being deeply impressed by her beauty he asked who she was, and one of the virgins answered: "That is Catherine, whom you used to know, but now, when you do not seem to know her, she has passed you by with her face veiled as one unknown to you."

It is worthy of note that blessed Catherine is admirable in five respects: first in wisdom, second in eloquence, third in constancy, fourth in the cleanness of chastity, fifth in her privileged dignity.

Firstly, she is seen to be admirable in her wisdom, for she possessed every kind of philosophy. Philosophy, or wisdom, is divided into theoretical, practical, and logical. The theoretical is divided, according to some thinkers, into three parts—the intellectual, the natural, and the mathematical. Saint Catherine had

[3] Above, chapter 68.

the theoretical in her knowledge of the divine mysteries, which knowledge she put to use especially in her argument against the rhetoricians, to whom she proved that there is only one true God and whom she convinced that all other gods are false. She possessed natural philosophy in her knowledge of all beings below God, and this she used in her differences with the emperor, as we have seen. The mathematical she displayed in her contempt for worldly things, because, according to Boethius, this science is concerned with abstract, immaterial forms. Saint Catherine had this knowledge when she turned her mind away from every material love. She showed that she had it when in answer to the emperor's question she said: "I am Catherine, daughter of King Costus. Though born to the purple . . . ," and so on; and she used it principally with the queen, when she encouraged her to despise the world, to think little of herself, and to desire the kingdom of heaven.

The practical philosophy is divided into three parts, namely, the ethical, the economic, and the public or political. The first teaches how to strengthen moral behavior and adorn oneself with virtues, and it applies to people as individuals; the second teaches how to put good order into the life of the family, and applies to the father as head of the family; the third teaches how to rule well over the city, the people, and the commonwealth, and applies to governors of cities. Saint Catherine possessed this threefold knowledge; the first since she organized her life in accordance with all right moral standards, the second when she ruled in a praiseworthy manner the large household that was left to her, the third when she instructed the emperor wisely.

The logical philosophy also is divided into three parts, the demonstrative, the probable, and the sophistic. The first pertains to philosophers, the second to rhetoricians and dialecticians, the third to sophists. Clearly Catherine possessed this threefold knowledge, since it is written of her that she argued many matters with the emperor through a variety of syllogistic conclusions, allegorical, metaphorical, dialectical, and mystical.

Secondly, Catherine's eloquence was admirable: it was abundant when she preached, as we have seen in her preaching, and extremely convincing in her reasoning, as appeared when she said to the emperor: "You wonder at this temple built by the hands of artisans." Her speech had the power to attract the hearer, as is clear in the instances of Porphyrius and the queen, whom the sweetness of her eloquence drew to the faith. She was skillful in convincing, as we see in her winning over the orators.

Thirdly, consider her constancy. She was constant in the face of threats, meeting them with disdain, as, when the emperor threatened her, she replied: "Whatever torments you have in mind, don't waste time . . ."; or again, "Do anything you have a mind to do, you will find me prepared. . . ." She was firm in dealing with offers of gifts, which she scorned, as when the emperor promised to make her second only to the queen in his palace and she retorted: "Stop saying such things! It is a crime even to think them!" And she was constant under tortures, overcoming them, as we saw when she was put in a dungeon or on the wheel.

Fourthly, Catherine was admirable in her chastity, which she preserved even amidst conditions that ordinarily put chastity at risk. There are five such conditions: abundant wealth, which softens resistance, opportunity, which invites indulgence, youth, which leans toward licentiousness, freedom, which shakes off restraint, and beauty, which allures. Catherine lived with all these conditions yet preserved her chastity. She had a huge abundance of wealth, which she inherited from her very rich parents. She had opportunity, being the mistress surrounded all day long by servingpeople. She had youth and freedom, living in her palace alone and free. Of these four conditions it was said above that Catherine, when she was eighteen years old, lived alone in a palace filled with treasure and servants. She had beauty, as was noted: "She was lovely to behold, indeed of incredible beauty."

Lastly, she was admirable by reason of her privileged dignity. Some saints have received special privileges at the time of death—for instance, a visitation by Christ (Saint John the Evangelist), an outflow of oil (Saint Nicholas), an effusion of milk (Saint Paul), the preparation of a sepulcher (Saint Clement), and the hearing of petitions (Saint Margaret of Antioch, when she prayed for those who would honor her memory). Saint Catherine's legend shows that all these privileges were hers.

Doubts have been raised by some as to whether it was under Maxentius or under Maximinus that Catherine's martyrdom took place. At that time there were three emperors, namely, Constantine, who succeeded his father as emperor, Maxentius the son of Maximianus, named emperor by the pretorian guard at Rome, and Maximinus, who was made caesar in parts of the East. According to the chronicles Maxentius tyrannized the Christians in Rome, Maximinus in the East. It seems therefore, as some authors hold, that a scribe's error may have put Maxentius in place of Maximinus.

173. Saints Saturninus, Perpetua, Felicity, and Their Companions

Saturninus was ordained bishop by disciples of the apostles and sent to the city of Toulouse. When he arrived and the demons ceased to give responses, one of the pagans said that unless Saturninus was killed, they would obtain nothing from their gods. They therefore apprehended Saturninus, and, when he refused to sacrifice, tied him to a bull's legs and drove the animal from the highest point of the capitol, precipitating him down the steps to the bottom. Thus Saturninus, with his skull shattered and his brains spilled out, happily consummated his martyrdom. Two women gathered his body and hid it in a deep cavern for fear of the pagans, but his successors later transferred it to a more honorable place.

There was another Saturninus, whom the prefect of Rome held in prison for a long time, starving him. Then he had him lifted upon a rack and beaten with thongs, clubs, and scorpions, and his flanks burned with torches. Finally he was taken down from the rack and beheaded, about A.D. 286, under Maximian.

There was still another Saturninus, in Africa, the brother of Saint Satyrus, who suffered martyrdom with his brother, Revocatus, the latter's sister Felicity, and Perpetua, a woman of noble birth: their passion is commemorated at another time. Here we can say that when the proconsul told them to sacrifice to the idols and they refused, they were put in jail. Perpetua's father came running in tears to the prison and said: "Daughter, what have you done? You have brought dishonor on your family! No one of your lineage has ever been in jail!" When she told him that she was a Christian, he rushed at her and tried to gouge her eyes out, then went away shouting wrathfully.

Blessed Perpetua had a vision that night and told her companions about it in the morning: "I saw a marvelously high golden ladder raised up to heaven, but the ladder was so narrow that only one person, and that one small, could mount it. On the right and left sides of the ladder knives and swords were attached, so that the one ascending could not look down or to either side, but had to hold himself straight and look up toward heaven. Below the ladder lay a huge, hideous dragon, for fear of which no one dared to ascend. I also saw Satyrus, who, having reached the top of the ladder, looked back at us and said: 'Don't be afraid of that dragon, but climb confidently and be with me!'" Hearing this, all gave thanks, knowing that they were called to martyrdom.

They were therefore brought before the judge but refused to sacrifice. The judge had Saturninus and the other men separated from the women, and asked

Felicity: "Do you have a husband?" "Yes," she answered, "but I have nothing to do with him!" The judge: "Have pity on yourself, young woman, and live, especially since you have a child in your womb!" Felicity: "Do to me whatever you wish, but you will never get me to do your will!" Then the parents of blessed Perpetua and her husband came, bringing Perpetua's infant child, whom she was still nursing. When her father saw her standing before the prefect, he fell on his face and cried: "My sweetest daughter, have pity on me and on your sad, sad mother and on your pitiable husband, who will not be able to live without you!" Perpetua, however, was unmoved. Then her father laid her son upon her shoulder, and he and her mother and husband held her hands and wept, kissing her and saying: "Have mercy on us, daughter, and stay alive with us!" But she threw the infant from her and repulsed her parents, saying: "Get away from me, you enemies of God, because I do not know you!"

Seeing the martyrs' constancy, the prefect subjected them to a long scourging and put them in jail. The saints, however, were mainly concerned for Felicity, who was eight months pregnant. They prayed for her, and suddenly the birth pains came upon her and she brought forth a son, alive. One of the jailers said to her: "If giving birth makes you suffer so much, what will you do when you come before the prefect?" Felicity answered: "I suffer this for myself, but then God will suffer for me!"

The martyrs were brought out of the prison with their hands tied behind their backs and their buttocks bared, dragged through the streets, and finally thrown to the wild beasts. Satyrus and Perpetua were devoured by lions, Revocatus and Felicity by leopards, and blessed Saturninus had his head cut off, about A.D. 256, under Emperors Valerian and Gallienus.

174. Saint James the Dismembered

Saint James, called the Dismembered because of the way he was martyred, was noble by birth and yet more noble by his faith. He was a native of the city of Elape in the land of the Persians, born of most Christian parents and wedded to a most Christian wife. To the king of the Persians he was well known, and stood first among his peers. It happened, however, that he was misled by the prince and his close friendship with him, and was induced to worship the idols. When his mother and his wife found this out, they wrote him a letter, saying: "By doing the will of a mortal man, you have deserted him with whom there is life; to please one who will be a mass of rottenness, you have deserted the eternal fragrance; you have traded truth for a lie; by acceding to a mortal's wish you have abandoned the judge of the living and the dead. Know therefore that from now on we are strangers to you and will no longer live in the same house with you."

When James read this letter, he wept bitterly and said: "If my mother and my wife have become strangers to me, how much more must I have estranged God?" He therefore inflicted harsh penances on himself in expiation of his fault. Then a messenger went to the prince and told him that James was a Christian, and the prince sent for him. "Tell me," he said to James, "are you a Nazarene?" "Yes," James answered, "I am a Nazarene." The prince: "Then you are a sorcerer!" James: "Far be it from me to be a sorcerer!" The prince threatened him with many kinds of torture, but James said: "Your threats do not bother me, because just as the wind blows over a stone, your anger goes quickly in one ear and out the other!" The prince: "Don't be a fool, or you may die a dreadful death!" James: "That is not death but should rather be called sleep, since in a short time resurrection is granted." The prince: "Don't let the Nazarenes deceive you by telling you that death is a sleep, because even great emperors fear it!" James: "We do not fear death, because we hope to pass from death to life!"

Upon the advice of his friends, the prince now sentenced James to death member by member, in order to strike fear into others. When some people wept out of compassion for him, he said: "Don't weep for me, but mourn for yourselves, because I go on to life, while eternal torment is your due!"

Now the torturers cut off the thumb of his right hand, and James cried out and said: "O Nazarene, my liberator, accept this branch of the tree of your mercy, for the husbandman trims the dry branches from the vine in order to let it grow stronger and be crowned with more fruit!" The headsman said: "If you wish to give in, I shall spare you and bring ointments for your wound." James: " Haven't you ever examined the trunk of a tree? The dry tendrils are cut away, and in due season, when the earth warms, each nub left by the pruning puts forth a new shoot. If therefore the vine is thought to need pruning in order to grow and bear fruit as the seasons revolve, how much greater the need of a man of faith who is grafted into Christ the true vine!"

The torturer cut off the forefinger, and James said: "Accept, O Lord, the two branches that your right hand planted." The third finger was cut off, and James said: "I am now set free from the threefold temptation, and I will bless the Father, the Son, and the Holy Spirit. With the three youths rescued from the fiery furnace I will confess you, O Lord, and amidst the choir of the martyrs I will sing Psalms to your name, O Christ!" The fourth finger was severed, and James said: "Protector of the sons of Israel, you were foretold in the fourth blessing.[1] Accept from your servant the confession of the fourth finger as blessed in Judah." The fifth was cut off, and he said: "My joy is complete."

Then the executioners said to him: "Now is the time to spare your soul, lest you perish. And don't be sad because you've lost one hand. Many men have only one hand, yet abound in wealth and honors!" Blessed James responded: "When shepherds shear their sheep, do they take off the fleece from the right side and leave the left side unsheared? And if the sheep, a dumb animal, wants to lose all its fleece, how much the more should I, a rational man, not think it beneath me to die for God?" Therefore those impious men proceeded to amputate the little finger of his left hand, and James said: "You, Lord, were great, but you chose to become little and least for us, and therefore I give back to you the body and the soul that you created and redeemed by your blood." The seventh finger was taken, and James said: "Seven times a day I have given praise to the Lord."[2] The eighth was removed and he said: "On the eighth day Jesus was circumcised, and the Hebrew male child is circumcised on the eighth day in order to pass over to the ceremonies of the Law: so let the mind of your servant pass over from these uncircumcised men with their unclean foreskins, and let me come and look upon your face!" The ninth finger was cut off and he said: "At the ninth hour Christ yielded up his spirit on the cross, and so I, Lord, confess you in the pain of the ninth finger and give you thanks!" The tenth was taken, and he said: "Ten is the number of the commandments, and J[3] is the initial letter of the name Jesus Christ."

Then some of the bystanders said: "O you who were so dear to us in the past, just profess their god before the consul so that you can go on living; and even though your hands are cut off, there are expert physicians who will be able to ease your pain!" To them James said: "Far be it from me to be guilty of so unspeakable a deception! No one who puts his hand to the plow and looks back is fit for the kingdom of God!"[4] The angry torturers came and cut off the great toe of his right foot, and James said: "Christ's foot was pierced and blood poured out!" They took the second toe and he said: "Great above all days is this day to me, for today I shall be turned and go to almighty God." They cut off the third toe and threw it in front of him, and James smiled and said: "Go, third toe, to your fellow toes, and as the grain of wheat bears much fruit, so you at the last day will rest with your companions." The fourth went, and he said: "Why are you sad, my soul, and why do you disquiet me? I hope in God for I will still give praise to him, the salvation of my countenance and my God."[5] The fifth was

---

[1] Cf. Gen. 49:8–12, Jacob's blessing on Judah.

[2] Cf. Ps. 118(119):164.

[3] The Latin text has *Iota*, which is the *ninth* letter of the Greek alphabet, but *Yod*, the corresponding Hebrew letter, is *tenth* in the Hebrew alphabet, as *J* is in the Roman.

[4] Luke 9:62.

[5] Cf. Ps. 42(43):5.

taken, and he said: "Now I shall begin to say to the Lord that he has made me a worthy companion to his servants."

Then they went to the left foot and took off the little toe, and James said: "Little toe, be comforted, because the big and the little will all rise again, and not a hair of the head will perish. How much less will you, the littlest, be separated from your fellows!" The second was taken, and James said: "Destroy the old house, a more splendid one is being prepared." After the third, he said: "The anvil is made more solid by the blows of the hammer." The fourth toe was amputated, and he said: "Comfort me, God of truth, for I trust in you and in the shade of your wings I will hope until iniquity passes away."[6] The fifth went, and he said: "Look upon me, O Lord, I offer sacrifice twenty times!"

Next, the executioners cut off James's right foot, and he said: "Now I shall offer a gift to the King of heaven, for love of whom I endure these pains." They cut off the left foot and he said: "It is you who work wonders, Lord! Hear me and save me!" They cut off his right hand, and he said: "May your mercies help me, O Lord!" After the left hand, he said: "You are the God who work wonders." Off with his right arm, and he said: "Praise the Lord, my soul, in my life I will praise the Lord, I will sing to my God as long as I shall be!"[7] Now his left arm, and he said: "The sorrows of death surrounded me, and in the name of the Lord I will be avenged." Next it was the right leg, which they cut off at the thigh. Blessed James, stricken with unspeakable pain, cried out, saying: "Lord Jesus Christ, help me, because the groans of death have surrounded me!" And he said to the torturers: "The Lord will clothe me with new flesh, upon which the wounds you inflict will not be able to leave a stain." They were exhausted, having toiled from the first to the ninth hour of the day at dismembering blessed James, but now they returned to their task, taking off the calf of the left leg up to the thigh. Blessed James cried out: "O Lord and Ruler, hear me half alive, Lord of the living and the dead! Fingers, Lord, I have none to hold out to you, nor hands to extend to you; my feet are cut off and my knees demolished, so that I cannot kneel to you, and I am like a house that is about to fall because the columns that support it have been taken away. Heed me, Lord Jesus Christ, and lead my soul out of prison!"

When James had said this, one of the executioners cut off his head. Then Christians came secretly, seized his body, and buried it with honors. He suffered on the twenty-seventh day of November.

[6] Cf. Ps. 56(57):2.
[7] Ps. 145:2.

175. Saint Pastor

Saint Pastor lived in the desert for many years, mortifying himself by rigorous abstinence. When his mother wished to see him and his brothers and they would not allow it, she watched for the day and suddenly stood in front of them as they went toward the church, but they turned from her and went back into the monastery, closing the door in her face. She stood at the door, wept aloud, and called to them. Pastor came and said to her through the door: "What are you shouting about, old woman?" She heard his voice and called out still more loudly, weeping and saying: "I want to see you, my sons! What harm can it do if I see you? Am I not your mother, who suckled you, and now I am old and white-haired?" Her son answered: "Do you want to see us here or in the other world?" She replied: "If I am not to see you here, I shall see you there, my sons!" Pastor: "If you can with peace of mind bear not seeing us here, there is no doubt that you will see us there!" So the mother went away rejoicing and saying: "If I am sure to see you there, I don't want to see you here!"

The judge of that province was anxious to see Abbot[1] Pastor, but Pastor would not see him, so he held the young son of the monk's sister as a criminal and put him in jail, saying: "If Pastor comes and intercedes for him, I'll let him go." The boy's mother came weeping to the old monk's door, and when Pastor did not answer her, she said: "Even if you have a heart of iron and can feel no compassion, at least let sympathy for your own flesh and blood bend you, because the boy is my only child!" He sent word to her: "Pastor begot no sons, therefore feels no sorrow!" The mother went away grieving, and the judge said to her: "Let Abbot Pastor at least say the word, and I will release your son!" Pastor's message to him was: "Examine the case according to law! If he is found guilty of a crime worthy of death, let him die forthwith; if not, do whatever pleases you!"

He taught his brothers as follows: "To be on one's guard, to examine oneself, and to have discernment, these are operations of the soul; poverty, tribulation, and discernment are the works of the solitary life. For it is written: 'If these three men, Noe, Job, and Daniel, shall be [in a land that shall sin against me], they shall

---

[1] The Latin title *abbas*, here (and elsewhere in this work) translated abbot, corresponds to the Aramaic word *abba*, father, and in Eastern usage could apply to religious men in general, whether monks or hermits, and was sometimes used by bishops. The title was not restricted, as in Western usage, to the heads of religious-order communities like the Benedictine abbeys, also called monasteries.

deliver their own souls by their justice, says the Lord of hosts.'[2] Noe personifies those who have nothing, Job those who bear tribulation, Daniel those with discernment. If a monk hates two things, he can be free of this world." To a brother who asked what the two things were, he said: "Bodily comfort and empty glory. If you wish to find rest in this world and in the next, in every instance say: 'Who am I?' And judge no one!"

One of the brothers in the community had committed an offense, and his superior, upon the advice of a solitary, expelled him. When the brother wept despairingly, Pastor called him in, consoled him kindly, and sent word to that solitary, saying: "I have heard about you and want to see you. Please take the trouble to visit me." When the hermit came, Pastor said: "There were two men, each of whom had a kinsman die, but one of the men left his own dead and went to share the other man's grief." The hermit heard and understood the message, and was sorry for the advice he had given.

When one of the monks told Pastor that he was disturbed and wished to leave the monastery, because he had heard something about another monk which had not edified him, Pastor told him not to believe what he had heard, because it was not true. The monk insisted that it must be true because Brother Faithful had told him. Pastor: "The one who told you was not faithful, because if he were faithful, he would never have said such things." But the monk retorted: "I saw it with my own eyes!" Pastor then asked him what the difference was between a mote and a beam, and the monk said that a mote was a speck and the beam was a heavy length of wood. Pastor: "Take it to heart that your sins are that beam, and the other monk's fault is like this little speck!"[3]

Then there was a monk who had committed a grave sin. He wished to do a three-year penance for it and asked Abbot Pastor if that was much. Pastor: "It is much." Asked if he would order a penance of one year, he answered: "It is much." Those standing by suggested as little as forty days, and Pastor said: "It is much!" Then he added: "If a man repents his sin with his whole heart and does not repeat it, the Lord will accept three days of penance."

He was asked about the Gospel text: "Whosoever is angry with his brother without cause shall be in danger of the judgment,"[4] and he said: "Whatever the wrong that your brother has chosen to do you, don't be angry with him until he tears out your right eye. If you do otherwise you are angry with him without cause. If, however, someone tries to take you away from God, for that you shall be angry with him."

Pastor also said: "Anyone who is given to complaining is no monk; one who holds a grudge in his heart is no monk; one who has a bad temper is no monk; one who returns evil for evil is no monk; one who is conceited and loquacious is no monk. The true monk is always humble, kindly, and full of charity, and

[2] Cf. Ezek. 14:14, 13.
[3] Cf. Matt. 7:3–5.
[4] Matt. 5:22.

always and everywhere has before his eyes the fear of God, lest he sin." Another time he said: "If there are three men together, and one of them leads a quiet life, another is ailing and gives thanks, and the third serves the ailing one with sincerity of heart, these three are as alike as if they were the work of the same hand."

One of the brothers complained to him that he was bothered with thoughts that put his soul in danger. Abbot Pastor pushed him out into the cold air and said: "Spread your cloak and catch the wind!" The brother: "I can't!" Pastor: "Neither can you keep those thoughts from entering your mind. What you have to do is to resist them!" Still another monk asked him what he should do with his inheritance, and he told the brother to come back to him in three days. When he came back, Pastor said: "If I tell you to give it to the clergy, they will squander it on high living. If I suggest giving it to your kinsfolk, you will get no thanks for it. If I say to give it to the poor, you will be sure it's safe. But do whatever you like with it! It's none of my business."

We find all this in the *Lives of the Fathers*.

176. Saint John, Abbot

Episius had been living in the desert for forty years, and Abbot John asked him how much progress he had made during those years. He replied: "From the day I began to live as a solitary, the sun has never seen me eating." John responded: "Nor me angry!"

In the same book[1] and on a similar note we read that when Bishop Epiphanius set meat before Abbot Hilarion, Hilarion said: "Pardon me, but from the day I took this habit I have never eaten anything slain." To this the bishop replied: "From the day I received this habit, I have never allowed anyone to go to sleep having a grievance against me, nor have I slept having a grievance against anyone." "Forgive me," Hilarion said: "you are better than I!"

John wanted to be like the angels, doing no work and devoting himself without interruption to God, so he put off his clothes and spent one week in the desert. By then he was perishing with hunger and wounded from head to foot with the stings of mosquitoes and wasps, so he went to a brother monk's door and knocked. The brother called out: "Who's there?" John: "It's John!" The

---

[1] *Lives of the Fathers.*

brother responded: "It can't be! John became an angel and is no longer seen among men!" John: "But I really am John!" His brother did not open the door and left him outside to endure another night. Then he opened the door and said: "If you are a man, you have to go to work again in order to eat and live, but if you are an angel, why do you want to get back into your cell?" John said: "Forgive me, brother, I have sinned."

When Abbot John was dying, the brethren asked him to leave them some salutary and memorable saying in lieu of a heritage. He groaned and said: "I have never done what I did because I myself wanted to do it. I have never ordered others to do anything that I have not first done myself."

All this we read in the *Lives of the Fathers*.

177. Saint Moses, Abbot

A monk asked Abbot Moses for a saying he might live by, and Moses said: "Sit in your cell and it will teach you all there is to know!" When an aged, infirm monk wanted to go to Egypt so as not to be a burden to his brothers, Moses said to him: "Don't go, because you'll fall into fornication." The old man was disappointed and said: "My body is dead, and you say such things to me!" So he went to Egypt and there a young woman, a virgin, piously took care of him. When he recovered his strength, he ravished her, and the woman bore a son. The old monk took the boy in his arms, and on a great feast day, which was celebrated in the church at Syrte, he walked into the midst of his brother monks. They all wept, and he said: "Do you see this child? He is the son of disobedience! So be on your guard, brothers, because I did this in my old age. And pray for me!" Then he went to his cell and resumed his former way of life.

When another aged monk said to his brothers: "I am dead," one of the others said: "I won't be sure of that till you leave your body. You may say you are dead, but Satan is not dead!"

A brother had sinned, and they sent for Abbot Moses. He went to them carrying a sack of sand on his back. They asked what this was for, and he said: "It's my sins, and they follow behind me so that I don't see them, and I've come today to judge another man's sins!" The monks saw the point and forgave their brother.

We read a similar story about Abbot Prior. When the monks were talking about one of their number who had sinned, Prior said nothing, but went and slung a sack of sand over his shoulder, carrying a small packet of the same sand in front of him. Asked what this meant, he said: "The large lot of sand stands for my sins, which I carry behind me so that I don't think about them. This small packet stands for my brother's sins, which are out in front of me so that I can think about them all the time and judge my brother. Yet I ought always to carry my own sins before my eyes, to repent of them and ask God's pardon for them!"

When Abbot Moses was ordained priest and they put a white vestment over him, the bishop said: "The abbot is now whitened!" Moses added: "Outwardly, my lord! Would it were inwardly!" The bishop had a mind to test Moses further and said to his clerics that when Moses came up to the altar, they should drive him away with insults, and then follow him out and listen to what he would say. So they pushed him outside and heard him say to himself: "They were right to do this to you, you dusty, sooty old woman, because, since you are not a man, why did you presume to present yourself among men?"

All this is taken from the *Lives of the Fathers*.

178. Saint Arsenius, Abbot

Arsenius was still living in his ancestral palace, and prayed to be directed toward salvation. As he prayed, he heard a voice saying: "Flee away from men and you will be saved." He therefore embraced the monastic life. Then, as he prayed, he heard: "Arsenius, get away, keep silence!"

Regarding this need for quiet, we read in this same book[1] that there were three brothers who had become monks, and one of them chose to make peace among the quarrelsome, the second to visit the sick, and the third to lead a quiet life in solitude. The first did what he could, but, faced with human contentiousness, he could not please everybody. Overcome with the futility of his efforts, he went to visit the second brother, whom he found weary in spirit and unable to carry out the commandment.[2] They agreed to visit the third brother, who

---

[1] *Lives of the Fathers.*
[2] Cf. Matt. 25:43.

lived in solitude. When they told him their troubles, he poured water into a basin and said: "Look into the water while it's stirred up!" A minute later he said: "Now look into it, and see how quiet and limpid it is!" They looked and saw their faces reflected in the water, and he said: "So it is that those who live their lives among other people do not see their own sins, but when they live in quiet, they are able to see them."

Another man came upon a man in the desert who was naked and was eating grass like an animal. The naked man ran away, but the other pursued him, calling out: "Wait for me! I'm following you for God's sake!" The answer: "And I am running away from you for God's sake!" The pursuer threw away his cloak, and the pursued waited for him and said: "Because you threw away that worldly, material thing, I waited for you!" The pursuer: "Tell me what I must do to be saved!" The other answered: "Flee from men and keep silence!"

An aged noble lady was moved by devotion to go and see Abbot Arsenius. Archbishop Theophilus also asked Arsenius to allow the woman to see him, but he flatly refused. Finally she hurried to the monk's cell, found him outside the door, and prostrated herself at his feet. Highly indignant, he lifted her up and said: "If you want to see my face, look at it!" She was overcome with confusion and shame, and would not look at his face. The old man said: "How could you, a woman, have dared to take such a sea voyage? Now you will go back to Rome and tell other women how you saw Abbot Arsenius, and they will come here as you did, wanting to see me!" She replied: "If, God willing, I get back to Rome, I will not allow any other woman to come here. All I ask of you is to pray for me and always to have me in memory." Arsenius: "I pray God to wipe the memory of you out of my heart!"

Hearing this, the lady was deeply distressed, and, when she returned to the city, her distress made her ill with fever. The archbishop heard about this and went to console her, but she said: "See, I am dying of grief!" The archbishop: "Don't you know that you are a woman, and the enemy attacks the saints through women? That is why the old man spoke as he did! He prays for you all the time!" She was consoled by this knowledge and joyfully went home to her own.

Of another father we read that a disciple said to him: "You're old now, father! Let us together go a little closer to the world!" He answered: "Let us go where there are no women!" The disciple said: "And where is there a place that has no women in it, unless it's the wilderness?" The answer: "Then take me to the wilderness!" Another monk had to carry his aged mother across a river and before doing so wrapped a cloth around his hands. His mother asked him: "Why have you covered your hands, my son?" The son: "A woman's body is fire, and when I touched you, it brought to mind the memory of other women!"

Throughout his life, Arsenius, when he sat down to the work at hand, kept a cloth in his bosom with which to dry the tears that flowed frequently from his eyes. He stayed awake all night, and in the morning, when natural weariness made him want to sleep, he would say to sleep itself: "Come on, you wicked slave!" Then he sat down for a brief nap, getting up almost immediately. He also said: "One hour's sleep is enough for a monk, provided he's a fighter!"

When Saint Arsenius's father, a noble senator, was about to die, he made a will leaving a large bequest to his son. A messenger named Magisterianus brought the will to Arsenius, who was disposed to tear it up. The messenger fell at his feet and begged him not to do that, because it would cost him his head. Arsenius: "I was dead before he died! How could he, now that he is dead, make me his heir?" And he returned the will, refusing to accept any part of the inheritance.

Once Arsenius heard a voice saying to him: "Come, and I will show you the works of men!" He was led to a place where he saw an Ethiopian[3] cutting wood, and making a bundle of it so large that he could not carry it; so he cut more wood and added it to the bundle, and did the same thing time after time. Arsenius also saw a man drawing water from a lake and pouring it into a cistern that had a hole in it, so that the water ran back into the lake; but the man kept trying to fill the cistern. Then Arsenius was shown a temple, and two men on horseback riding side by side with a wooden beam laid across their saddles. They were trying to ride into the temple but could not, because the beam, carried crosswise, would not fit through the door. His guide then explained, saying: "The two men are those who bear the yoke of righteousness pridefully and are not humbled, and therefore remain outside the kingdom of God. The woodcutter is the man guilty of many sins, who, instead of doing penance and atoning for his sins, adds wickedness to wickedness. The man drawing water is the man who performs good works but, because he mixes bad ones in with them, loses his good works."

It was Arsenius's custom that on the Sabbath evening, with the Lord's day coming on, he turned his back to the setting sun and stood, with his hands raised to heaven, until the rising sun threw light on his face. Then he sat down.

All this from the *Lives of the Fathers*.

---

[3] In the *Golden Legend* the term Ethiopian refers to any black man and is usually pejorative in implication.

⁕
---

179. Saint Agathon, Abbot

Abbot Agathon put a pebble in his mouth and kept it there for three years, until he learned to keep silence.

Another monk, upon joining the community, said to himself: "Be like the ass! The ass is flogged but says nothing, suffers maltreatment and does not respond. Do likewise!"

Another monk, when ordered away from the table, made no response and went. Later he was asked about this and said: "I have fixed it in my heart that I am no better than a dog. When the dog is chased, he goes outside!"

Agathon was asked what virtue involved the most labor, and answered: "For me there is no labor equal to that of praying to God, because the enemy labors always to destroy the prayer of the one praying. In other forms of labor a man gets some rest, but the man who prays faces a continuous combat."

A monk asked Agathon how he should live with the brothers. Agathon said: "Live as you lived the first day you were here, and share your confidences with no one, for there is no passion worse than that sort of intimacy; it is the mother of all the passions."

He also said: "The wrathful man, were he to awaken the dead, pleases neither man nor God, because of his bad temper. There was a monk who had a bad temper, and he said to himself: 'If I lived alone I would not be moved to anger so easily.' Then it happened that he was filling a pitcher with water and spilled the water, started again and spilled again, started a third time and spilled a third time. By then he was so angry that he smashed the pitcher. Then he came to his senses and realized that it was the same demon of bad temper that had tricked him, and he said to himself: 'Here I am alone, and anger still got the best of me. I'll go back to the community, because I will need hard work and patience and God's help, wherever I am!'"

On the other hand, there were two monks who lived together for many years and could never be provoked to anger. Once one of them said to the other: "Let's have a quarrel, the way men of the world do!" The other monk replied: "I don't know how to start a quarrel!" Said the first: "I put a tile on the table between you and me, and I say: 'This tile is mine!' Then you say: 'No, it's mine!' And that's the way to start a quarrel." So the brother set a tile between them. One of them said: "This tile is mine!" The other said: "No, it's mine!" The first said: "Oh, all right, it's yours. Take it with you!" And off they went, unable to generate a quarrel between them.

Abbot Agathon was a wise and understanding man, tireless at work, sparing of food and frugal in dress. He said: "I have never gone to sleep holding in my heart a grievance against anyone, nor have I allowed anyone to go to sleep having anything against me."

When he was dying, Agathon lay motionless, keeping his eyes open, for three days. When the brothers nudged him, he responded: "I stand in the presence of divine judgment!" They said to him: "Are you afraid?" Agathon: "I have done all I could, with God's help, to keep his commandments, but I am a man, and I do not know whether what I have done has pleased the Lord." They said: "Don't you have confidence in your works, which were in accordance with God's will?" Agathon: "I presume nothing until I come before him. God's judgments are not the same as men's judgments." They wanted to question him further, but he said: "Show some charity and don't talk to me any longer, because I am busy!"

Having said this, he joyfully breathed his last, for they saw him collecting his spirit, as one does when one is about to greet one's dearest friends.

This from the *Lives of the Fathers*.

180. Saints Barlaam and Josaphat

Barlaam's history was studiously compiled by John of Damascus. Barlaam, by God's grace working in him, converted King Josaphat to the Christian faith. At a time when all India was teeming with Christians and monks, a certain very powerful king named Avennir came to power and persecuted the Christians, and especially the monks. Then it happened that a noble, who was a friend of the king and ranked highest in the royal entourage, was moved by divine grace to leave the palace and enter a monastic order. When the king heard of this, his anger was aroused. He had the desert searched to find his man and, when he was found, had him brought before him. The former courtier, who in the past had always worn splendid robes and had enjoyed great wealth, came in covered with a cheap tunic and emaciated from fasting. The king addressed him: "O foolish man, you have lost your mind! Why have you exchanged honor for degradation? Look, you have made yourself the butt of children's jokes!" The man replied: "If you wish to hear my reasons for doing this, send your enemies far away from you!" The king asked him who these enemies were, and he said: "They are anger and greed, which keep you from seeing the truth! Have prudence and equity sit in to hear what will be said!" "Very well," said the king. "Now speak!"

He began: "Fools despise the things that are real as if they did not exist, and strive to apprehend things that don't exist as if they were real. People who have not tasted the sweetness of what is real cannot learn the truth about what is not!" He went on to speak much about the mystery of the incarnation and about the faith, until the king said: "If I had not promised, before you started, to exclude anger from having any part in this discussion, believe me, I would now turn you over to the executioners to be burned alive! Get up, then, and get out of my sight! I may condemn you to a painful end if I still find you around!" The man of God went away sad, regretting that he had not been granted martyrdom.

Meanwhile a beautiful boy was born to King Avennir, who had been childless. The infant was given the name Josaphat. The king called together a huge throng to offer sacrifice to the gods in thanksgiving for the birth of his son and summoned sixty astrologers to question them about the child's future. They all predicted that he would be powerful and rich—all except one, wiser than the rest, who said: "This child who is born to you, O King, will not reign in your kingdom but in an incomparably better one, because, as I see it, he will worship as a believer in Christ's religion, which you are persecuting!" This he said not out of his wisdom but because God inspired him.

The prediction alarmed the king, who had a magnificent palace built in a remote city, in which Josaphat was to dwell. With him the king lodged a number of handsome youths, ordering them never to mention death or old age or sickness or poverty to his son, or anything else that might sadden him. They were always to speak of pleasant things, so that the boy's mind might be fully occupied with joyful thoughts, all concern about the future being crowded out. If any of those ministering to the son fell ill, the king ordered him removed at once, and a hale and hearty substitute put in his place. Not a word about Christ was ever to be spoken to the royal child.

At this time there was with the king another man who secretly was a devout Christian, and who held high rank among the king's associates. One day when he and the king were hunting together, he came upon a poor man lying on the ground, one of his feet having been gnawed by a wild beast. The wounded man asked this knight to take him into his household, saying that he might benefit by so doing. The knight said: "I'm willing to take you in, but I don't see how you can be helpful to me." The other answered: "I am a word-doctor. If someone is injured by something said against him, I know how to apply the appropriate remedy!" The knight thought that this did not make much sense, but for God's sake took the man into his house and cared for his wound.

Now there were others, jealous and malicious men, who saw that this particular knight was in high favor with the king, and they accused him to the king not only of having gone over to the Christian faith, but also of scheming to seize the throne for himself and of soliciting the crowd and buying their support. "But if you, O King, want to find out whether this is true," they said, "call him in privately, and talk to him about the beauty of this present life, so soon to be ended. Tell him that you are of a mind to relinquish the glory of reigning, and to put on the habit of the monks whom you have been persecuting. Then see what his response will be!"

The king did exactly as these advisers had directed, and the other man, unaware of the ruse, burst into tears, praised the king's proposal, dwelt on the vanity of the world, and counseled him to carry out his plan as soon as possible. This convinced the king that what the others had told him was true, but, angry as he was, he made no answer to the knight. This man, however, pondering how seriously the king had taken his words, went away fearful. Then, remembering that he had a word-doctor available, he told him all that had happened. The answer was: "Be it known to you that the king suspects, on the basis of what you said to him, that you want to usurp his throne. Go therefore, cut off your hair, take off those clothes and put on a hair shirt, and go to the king at daybreak. When he asks what this means, you will answer: 'Behold, O King, I am ready to follow you, for though the road you wish to take is a difficult one, being with you I will find it easy. So, as you have had me as a companion in prosperity, so you will have me in adversity. Now, therefore, I am ready! What are you waiting for?'" The knight followed these instructions. The king was stunned, punished the slanderers, and heaped new honors on his friend.

Josaphat, the king's son, who was brought up in the palace built for him, was now a young adult and was well instructed in all branches of knowledge. He wondered why his father had shut him off as he had, and confidentially asked one of his servingmen, whom he trusted, about this. He told the man that not being allowed to go outside the palace made him so sad that neither food nor drink had any taste for him. Word of the son's unhappiness came to the father and worried him, so he had suitable horses prepared and sent cheering choruses ahead of the young prince as he rode forth. He also gave strict instructions that no unpleasant sight was to confront Josaphat. One day, however, in the course of his ride, he was met by a leper and a blind man. Astonished as he was at this encounter, he asked who these people were and what was their trouble, and his attendants answered that those were ills that could befall anyone. "Do they happen to everybody?" he asked. They said no, and he responded: "Are those who are to suffer such things known in advance, or are the incidents unpredictable?" They said: "Who can know what is in store for him?" This unusual event left Josaphat distraught.

Another time Josaphat came upon a very old man whose face was deeply wrinkled, who could not stand up straight, and who drooled and babbled through his toothless gums. Stunned at the sight, he wanted to know how such a thing could happen, and when he learned that old age brought on such conditions, he said: "And what will be the end of this man?" They said: "Death!" "Is death for everybody," he asked, "or only for some?" He learned that all men must die, and asked: "In how many years do these things happen to us?" They told him: "Old age comes on at eighty or a hundred, and death follows." The prince turned all this over and over in his mind and was much depressed; and though he pretended to be cheerful in his father's presence, he yearned to be directed and instructed in these matters.

Now there was a monk, perfect in life and reputation, living in the desert in the land of Sennaar. The monk's name was Barlaam. Barlaam knew by the Spirit what was going on around the king's son, so he put on a tradesman's garb and went into that city. He sought out the man who was Josaphat's tutor and said to him: "I am a merchant, and I have a precious stone to sell. This stone restores sight to the blind and hearing to the deaf, makes the mute able to speak, and infuses wisdom into the foolish. Take me therefore to the king's son, and I will sell him the stone." The tutor: "You seem to be a man of mature good sense, but what you say does not make sense. I know stones, however, so show me the stone, and if it turns out to be what you say it is, you will gain high honors from the prince!" Barlaam: "The stone has still another power, namely, that if someone who does not enjoy good eyesight and does not live a chaste life inspects the stone, the stone loses all its powers. Though I'm no expert in medical matters, I can see that you have eye trouble, but on the other hand I hear that the king's son leads a pure life and has beautiful, healthy eyes." The tutor: "If that's the way things are, don't show me the stone, because my eyes are not good and I wallow in sin!" The tutor then sent word to the king's son and quickly brought Barlaam into his presence. The prince received him reverently, and Barlaam said to him: "Prince, you did well when you paid no attention to my poor appearance." He then told him the following story.

"There was once a great king who was riding in his gilded chariot. On the road he met some men clothed in tattered garments and weak from hunger. He jumped down from his chariot, threw himself at their feet and worshiped them, and then stood up and showered them with kisses. The noblemen in the king's suite were offended by these actions but, not daring to express their disapproval to the king himself, told his brother how the king had done things unworthy of his majesty. The king's brother reproved him for this.

"Now it was this king's custom, when someone had been sentenced to die, to send a herald to stand at the condemned man's door and sound the trumpet that was reserved for such occasions. Evening fell this day, and the king had his herald sound the trumpet at his brother's door. Hearing the sound, the brother despaired of his life, could not sleep that night, and made his last will and testament. In the morning he donned black attire, and went with his wife and children to stand weeping at the palace door. The king had his brother brought in and said to him: 'Foolish fellow, if you are so frightened by your brother's herald when you know you have done him no wrong, how should I not fear the heralds of my God, against whom I have sinned for so long, when they remind me of death more loudly than any trumpet and announce to me the coming of the awesome Judge?'

"This king then ordered the making of four caskets, two of them to be covered with gold on the outside but filled with putrid bones of the dead, the other two to be coated outside with pitch, but filled with precious stones and pearls. Then he summoned the nobles who, he knew, had complained about him to his brother, had the four caskets set up before them, and asked them which caskets were the more valuable. They judged that the golden ones were more valuable, and the other two of little worth. The king ordered the golden caskets opened, and an intolerable stench issued from them. The king said to the nobles: 'Those caskets are like the men who are clad in glorious garments but inwardly are full of the uncleanness of vice.' He had the other caskets opened, and a very pleasant odor came from them. Said the king: 'These are like the very poor men to whom I paid honor. Although they are covered with poor clothes, from within they emanate the perfume of all the virtues, but you pay attention only to what you see on the outside, and give no thought to what is within.' Therefore, prince, according to that king you did well in giving me kind welcome."

Barlaam then launched into a long sermon about the creation of the world, man's fall, the incarnation of the Son of God, his passion and resurrection, treating at length also about the Day of Judgment, the reward of the good, and the punishment of the wicked. He sternly denounced those who served the idols, and illustrated their foolishness by another example, as follows.

"A hunter had caught a small bird called a nightingale and was about to kill it, when a voice was given to the bird, who said: 'What will you gain, O man, by killing me? You will not be able to fill your belly by eating me! But if you release me, I will give you three bits of advice that, if you adhere to them carefully, will be very helpful to you!' Astonished at hearing what the bird had to say, the hunter promised that he would set her free if she gave him this advice. The nightingale responded: 'One, never bother trying to get possession of a thing that is completely beyond your grasp; two, never grieve over losing a thing that cannot be recovered; three, never believe the unbelievable. Observe these three rules and it will be well with you.'

"The hunter set the nightingale free as he had promised, and as she fluttered about in the air, she said to him: 'Worse luck to you, man! You took bad advice and you've lost a great treasure today, because I have in my belly a pearl larger than an ostrich egg!' The man regretted exceedingly that he had released the bird and tried to recapture her, saying: 'Come into my house! I will show you every kindness and then release you honorably!' The nightingale: 'Now I know for certain that you are a fool, because you have followed not one of the three things I told you. You are grieving about losing me irretrievably; you are trying to catch me though you cannot follow my path; and on top of that you believed that I had so large a pearl inside me, when the whole of me would not match the size of an ostrich egg!' So those who trust in idols are fools, because they adore things that their own hands have shaped, and give the name of guardian to things they themselves must guard!"

Barlaam went on to inveigh against the deceptive pleasures and vanities of the world, adducing many examples to prove his point. He said: "Those who yearn for pleasures of the body and allow their souls to die of hunger are like the man who fled from a unicorn that he feared would devour him, and fell into a deep abyss; but as he fell he caught hold of a small bush and set his feet on a slippery, shaky ledge. Looking around, he saw two mice, one white and one black, gnawing at the root of the bush he had hold of, which would very soon be chewed through. At the bottom of the abyss he saw an awful dragon breathing fire, the monster's jaws gaping with the desire to devour him. On the ledge on which his feet had a perch, he saw the heads of four vipers protruding. Then he looked up and caught sight of drops of honey oozing from the branches of his bush; and, oblivious of the dangers that besieged him on all sides, he gave himself entirely to enjoying the sweetness of that little bit of honey.

"Now the unicorn is a figure of the death that constantly pursues men and seeks to lay hold of them. The abyss is the world, full of all evils. The bush is the life of each man or woman, the life that throughout the hours of the day and the night is being eaten away by a white and a black mouse, and comes closer and closer to being cut off. The ledge with the four vipers is the body made up of four elements; when the elements get out of order, the compound of the body is dissolved. The awful dragon is the mouth of hell, yawning to devour all men. The sweetness of the drops of honey is the deceptive pleasures of the world, by which man is seduced, so that he has little awareness of the danger in which he lives."

Barlaam added another example, saying: "Those who love the world are like the man who had three friends, of whom he loved one more than himself, the second as much as himself, and the third very little if at all. This man found himself in great danger and, being summoned by the king, ran to the first friend to seek his help, reminding him of how much he had always loved him. The friend said: 'Man, I don't even know who you are! I have other friends with whom I am to dally today, and I will continue to possess them as friends. I can let you have two small hair shirts, though, and you can cover yourself with them.' Embarrassed, the man went to the second friend and begged him for help. The friend answered: 'Your troubles are of no concern to me, and I have enough worries of my own. However, I will accompany you as far as the gates of the palace and then come straight back to attend to my own business.'

"The man, now saddened and desperate, went to the third friend. Crestfallen, he said: 'I don't know what to say to you. I have not loved you as I should have, but I'm surrounded by troubles and have lost my friends, and I beg of you to lend me your help and to grant me your pardon.' With a cheerful smile the man answered: 'Believe me, I hold you as a cherished friend and am not unmindful of your kindnesses to me, slight as they may have been. I shall go in ahead of you and intercede for you with the king, lest he hand you over to your enemies.'

"Now the first friend is the possession of riches, for which a man will incur many perils, yet when death, the end, comes, all he gets from his riches is a few poor cloths for his burial. The second friend is composed of wife, children, and parents, who come only as far as the grave and then return home to take care of their own affairs. The third friend is made up of faith, hope, charity, almsgiving, and all the good works that can go in ahead of us when we go out of our bodies, can intercede with God for us, and can free us from hostile demons."

Barlaam added still another example, which went as follows. "In a certain great city there was a custom by which a foreigner, an unknown man, was elected as prince. He was given all power to do whatever he wished, everything was allowed him, he ruled the land without any law to go by. So this man enjoyed every delight and thought that this would go on forever. But it always happened that within a year the citizens rebelled against him, dragged him naked all around the city, and then shipped him off to exile on a remote island, where he found neither food nor clothing and was beset by hunger and cold. One year, as usual, a foreigner was elected, but this man knew all about the citizens' custom. So he sent a great store of treasure ahead to the island, and when, at the end of the year, he was exiled there, he enjoyed limitless pleasures of all kinds, while the other exiles perished from hunger. Now that city is the world, and the citizens are the princes of darkness who entice us with the world's false pleasures. Then, while we seem to be in complete command, death supervenes, and we are plunged into the place of darkness. On the other hand, we can send riches ahead of us to the place of eternal life, by putting them now into the hands of the poor."

The king's son, now fully instructed by Barlaam, wished to leave his father immediately and follow his instructor. "If you do that," Barlaam told him, "you will be like a young man who refused to marry a noblewoman. He ran away and came to a place where he saw a young woman, the daughter of a very poor old man, working hard and singing praise to God. 'What are you doing, woman?' he asked her. 'Poor as you are, you thank God as if you had received great gifts from him.' She replied: 'As a little medicine often cures a grave illness, so thanksgiving for small gifts can become the source of large ones. Moreover, the gifts which are outside of us are not ours, but those that are inside us are ours, and I have received many such gifts from God. He made me to his own image and likeness, he gave me understanding, he called me to his glory and has already opened the gate of his kingdom to me. It is right that I should praise him for so many and such great gifts!'

"The young man saw how wise the maiden was, and asked her father for her hand in marriage. The father: 'You cannot take my daughter in marriage, because you come of rich and noble parentage and I am a poor man.' But the young man insisted, and the old man said: 'I can't give you my daughter and

have you carry her off to your father's house. She is all I have!' The answer: 'I
will stay with you and live as you live!' He took off his fine clothes and put on
some of the old man's rags, stayed with him, and made the girl his wife. After her
father had tested him for a long time, he took him into the bridal chamber,
showed him a huge mass of treasure, and gave him the lot."

Josaphat said: "I see myself in that story, and I think you were really talking
about me. But tell me, father, how old you are and where you live, because I
wish never to be separated from you!" Barlaam: "I am forty-five years old and
I live in the desert in the land of Sennaar." Josaphat: "Father, you look more like
seventy to me!" Barlaam: "If you want to know my age counting from birth,
you have figured it correctly, but the years I spent in worldly vanity I do not
count as years of my life, because then my inner man was dead, and I count them
as years of death, not of life." Josaphat wanted to follow Barlaam back to the
desert, but Barlaam said: "If you do this, I will have to give up your company
and will bring persecution on my brother monks. Wait for the opportune time,
and then you will come to me." Barlaam therefore baptized the king's son,
completed his instruction, and kissed him, then went back to his own land.

When the king learned that his son had become a Christian, he was overcome
with grief. Then one of his friends, whose name was Arachis, comforted him
and said: "O King, I know an aged hermit named Nachor, who shares our
religion, and who resembles Barlaam in every detail. We will have this hermit
pretend to be Barlaam, and he will begin by defending the Christian faith, but
then will allow himself to be bested in argument and will revoke all he has
taught, and so the king's son will come back to us." This aforesaid noble, the
king's friend, mustered a large army and set out in search, he said, of Barlaam;
but he found his hermit and noised it about that he had taken Barlaam. Josaphat,
the king's son, heard that his master had been captured and wept bitterly, but
afterwards learned by divine revelation that the man captured was not Barlaam.

King Avennir went to Josaphat and said: "My son, you have brought great
sadness upon me, you have dishonored my white hairs and taken away the light
of my eyes. Why have you done this, my son, and why have you abandoned the
worship of my gods?" Josaphat answered: "Father, I fled the darkness and ran to
the light, abandoned error and acknowledged the truth. Do not labor in vain,
therefore! You will not be able to call me back from Christ. Know that that is
impossible, as it is impossible for you to touch the height of heaven with your
hand, or to dry up the waters of the deepest sea!" The king said: "Who is it that
has brought these ills upon me but I myself, by always treating you more generously than any father ever treated his son? And in return for this, the perversity
of your will and your unbridled contentiousness have made you rage against my
head. The astrologers were right when they said at your birth that you would be
arrogant and disobedient to your parents! But now, unless you do as I bid you,
you will give up your claim to be my son. I will no longer be your father but
your enemy, and I will do to you what I have never done before, even to my

enemies!" Josaphat: "Why, O king, are you saddened because I have become a sharer of good things? What father has ever appeared to regret his son's well-being? Therefore I shall no longer call you father, but, if you turn against me, I shall flee from you as I would from a viper!"

The king, livid with anger, left his son and told his friend Arachis how hard-headed Josaphat was. Arachis advised him not to use harsh words to his son, because bland and friendly speech would have more attraction for him. The next day, therefore, the king went to Josaphat, embraced him, and kissed him, saying: "My dearest son, honor your father's white hairs! Respect your father! Don't you know that it is good to obey your father and make him happy, and bad, on the contrary, to provoke him? Those who provoke their fathers come to a bad end!" Josaphat: "There is a time for loving and a time for obeying, a time for peace and a time for war. We certainly should not obey those who are trying to turn us away from God, even if they are mother or father."

Seeing how determined Josaphat was, the king said: "I see that you persist in disobeying me! Come at least, and let us both believe the same truth! This Barlaam who has misled you is by me held captive. Let our people and your people come and meet Barlaam, and I will send out a herald to persuade the Galileans not to be afraid to come. Then let the argument begin, and if your Barlaam prevails, we will accept your beliefs, but if our people win, you will agree with us!" Josaphat agreed to this proposal, and the king and his men arranged with Nachor, the pseudo-Barlaam, the way the encounter should proceed: Nachor would first pretend to defend the faith of the Christians and then would allow himself to be outdone in debate.

Now the parties convened, and Josaphat said to Nachor: "You know, Barlaam, how you taught me. If you now successfully defend the faith you taught me, I shall hold to it as long as I live, but if you are defeated, I shall avenge my humiliation on you. I'll cut out your heart and your tongue and feed them to the dogs, to dissuade others from presuming to lead the sons of kings into error!" These words made Nachor not only sad but fearful. He saw that he had fallen into the pit he had dug . . . that he was caught in his own trap. After some thought, he decided that in order to escape the threat of death it would be better to be on the side of the king's son, for the king had told him in public to defend his faith fearlessly. Then one of the king's masters rose and said: "Are you Barlaam, who led the king's son astray?" "I am Barlaam," he answered, "but I did not lead the king's son into error, I set him free from error!" The master: "Men of renown, admirable men, have adored our gods. How can you dare to rebel against them?" Nachor: "Chaldeans, Greeks, and Egyptians have been wrong in calling creatures gods. The Chaldeans thought the elements were gods, whereas the elements were created to be useful to men, so the Chaldeans were subject to their domination and were corrupted by many passions. The Greeks think that wicked men are gods—Saturn, for instance, who, they say, ate his sons, and cut off his male parts and threw them into the sea, and from them Venus was born, and Saturn was bound by his son Jupiter and cast into the infernal regions. Jupiter also is described as king of the gods, yet it is said that he was often transformed into various animals in order to commit adultery. They say that Venus too was an adulteress, for at times she had Mars as her lover, at other times, Adonis. The Egyptians worshiped animals, namely, the sheep, the calf, the pig, and suchlike. Christians, on the other hand, worship the Son of the Most High, the Son who came down from heaven and assumed the flesh of man." Nachor went on to defend the beliefs of Christians and to back them up with sound reasoning, so that the pagan masters were dumbfounded and knew no way to answer him.

Josaphat was delighted that the Lord had defended the truth through an enemy of the truth, but the king was furious. He ordered the meeting adjourned, as though these matters would be taken up again the following day. Josaphat said to his father: "Either let my master stay with me tonight so that we can work out the answers we will use tomorrow, and you take your people with you and confer with them, or else you leave your men with me and take my man. Otherwise you would not be doing justice but violence." Thereupon the king left Nachor with his son, still hoping that Nachor would be able to win him over. However, when Josaphat got home, he said to Nachor: "Don't think I don't know who you are. I know you are not Barlaam but Nachor the astrologer!" He began then and preached the way of salvation to Nachor, converted him to the faith, and in the morning sent him off to the desert, where he received baptism and led the life of a hermit.

A sorcerer named Theodas heard what had been going on, and went to the king and promised him that he would make his son return to the laws of his father. Avennir: "If you succeed in this, I will have a gold statue raised to you, and I will offer sacrifice as to the gods!" Theodas: "Remove all his men from around him, and order charming, lavishly dressed women to be with him all the time, waiting on him and pampering him and never leaving him alone; and I will send one of my spirits to him to set the fire of lust aflame in him, because nothing can so surely seduce young men as the faces of women. There was a king," Theodas went on, "who had a newborn son, and learned physicians told him that if within ten years the child saw either the sun or the moon, he would lose his eyesight. The king therefore had a cave cut out of solid rock and had his son kept there for ten years. When that time had passed, the king ordered all kinds of things to be set before the boy, so that he might know their names and all about them. Therefore gold and silver, precious stones, gorgeous garments, royal steeds, and all sorts of things were shown to him, and when he asked the name of each object, the servants indicated the proper word. When the boy asked what was the word for women, the king's swordbearer, as a jest, said they were demons who seduced men. When the king asked his son what he liked best of all that he had seen, he answered: 'What else, father, but those demons who seduce men? Nothing else set my soul on fire the way they did!' So don't think there is any other way than this to outwit your son!"

The king therefore had all Josaphat's attendants ejected, and put lovely ladies into his company to stir up his sexual desires at all times. He had no one else to look at, no one to talk to or eat with. The evil spirit sent by the sorcerer entered into the young man and lighted a furnace of fire inside him. Thus the evil spirit inflamed him internally and the women fanned his ardor externally. The youth, feeling himself beset, was sorely troubled and commended himself wholly to God, whereupon he received consolation from above and all temptation left him.

Now a damsel of great beauty, the daughter of a king but bereft of her royal father, was sent in to Josaphat. The man of God preached to her, and she replied: "If you wish to save me from serving the idols, be joined to me in the bonds of marriage, for Christians do not abhor wedlock, they praise it, because their patriarchs and prophets and their apostle Peter all had wives!" His response was: "Woman, it's useless for you to recite these things to me! Christians are allowed to marry, but not those who have promised Christ to preserve their virginity." She: "If that's the way you want things to be, so be it, but if you wish to save my soul, grant me one tiny petition: lie with me tonight, that's all, and I promise you I will become a Christian! For if, as you say, there is joy before the angels of God over one sinner who repents,[1] is not a great reward due the one who brings about the conversion? Just do what I want this one time, and so you will save me!" Thus she battered heavily upon the tower of his soul.

The demon saw this and said to his fellows: "You see how strongly that lass has shaken this man's resolution, while we haven't been able to shake him at all! Come, then! Let us find the right time and attack him with all our might!" The holy young man sensed how closely he was hemmed in, with concupiscence tugging at him and concern for the salvation of one girl—suggested, of course, by the devil—disturbing him. He burst into tears, and gave himself to prayer. While he was praying, he fell asleep and saw himself being led into a meadow blooming with beautiful flowers, where the leaves of the trees, stirred by mild breezes, gave out a soft whisper and a wondrous odor, where there was fruit lovely to look at and delicious to taste, where seats studded with gold and jewels and couches adorned with priceless coverings were placed here and there, and the clearest of waters flowed by. Then he was brought into a city whose walls were of gleaming gold, and where ethereal hosts sang canticles that the ears of mortals have not heard. Then a voice said to him: "This is the abode of the blessed!" The men who were leading him started to take him away, but he asked them to allow him to stay where he was. They said: "You will come here at the cost of great labors, if indeed your strength holds out!" Then they led him to a

---

[1] Cf. Luke 15:7, 10.

pitch-black place filled with a foul smell, and a voice said: "This is the abode of the wicked!" When he awoke, the beauty of that maiden and the others seemed to him more fetid than dung.

The evil spirits returned to Theodas, who upbraided them for their failure, and they said: "Before he made the sign of the cross, we assailed him and gave him much trouble, but once he had shielded himself with that sign, he came after us fully armed!" Then Theodas went in with the king to Josaphat, hoping that he might at last persuade him. But the aforesaid sorcerer was captured by the one he wanted to capture, was converted by him, received baptism, and thereafter led a praiseworthy life.

The king, in despair, took the advice of his friends and conferred the half of his kingdom on his son. Josaphat's one desire was to retire to the desert, but he agreed to reign for a time in order to spread the Christian faith, and in his cities he erected churches and crosses and converted all the people to Christ. Even his father finally was convinced by his son's reasoning and adopted the faith of Christ, was baptized, and yielded his whole kingdom to Josaphat. Thereafter he devoted himself to good works and finished his life virtuously.

Josaphat proclaimed that Barachias was to be king, and tried many times to flee, but he was always caught by the people. Finally, however, he did get away. As he went across the desert, he gave his royal trappings to a poor man and kept only the poorest raiment for himself. The devil set many traps for him. Sometimes he rushed at him with drawn sword, threatening to strike him dead unless he desisted; at other times he appeared to him in the form of some wild beast, with gnashing of teeth and hideous howls; but Josaphat said: "The Lord is my helper, I will not fear what man can do to me."[2] Josaphat lived in the desert for two years, wandering about, but unable to find Barlaam. At last, however, he found a cave and, standing at the entrance, said: "Bless me, father, bless me!" Hearing his voice, Barlaam hurried out, and they embraced each other fervently. Josaphat recounted all his experiences to Barlaam, who offered heartfelt thanks to God. Josaphat lived there for many years in marvelous austerity and virtue. Barlaam ended his days in peace about A.D. 380. Josaphat, having abdicated his throne at the age of twenty-five, lived the life of a hermit for thirty-five years, until, adorned with many virtues, he died in peace and was laid to rest beside Barlaam's body. When this news reached King Barachias, he went with a large army and, reverently taking up the two bodies, transferred them to his city. There many miracles have occurred at their tomb.

[2] Ps. 117(118):6.

181. Saint Pelagius, Pope
The History of the Lombards

Pope Pelagius was a very holy man who fulfilled his office in a praiseworthy manner, finally going to his eternal reward full of good works. This Pelagius was the first pope of that name, not the immediate predecessor of Pope Saint Gregory. John III succeeded Pelagius I, Benedict I followed John, then came Pelagius II, then Gregory I.

It was during the reign of Pelagius I that the Longobards, or Lombards, came into Italy; and because many do not know the history of this people, I have decided to insert their story here as Paul, the historian of the Lombards, compiled it and as its details are recorded in various chronicles.

The Lombards were a very prolific German tribe that came from the shores of the northern ocean. From the island of Scandinavia they fought their way circuitously through various lands until they came to Pannonia, where, not daring to go farther, they established what they intended to be their permanent homeland. They were first called Winuli, later Longobardi, the Lombards.

While they were still settled in Germany, their king, Agilmund, found seven baby boys, whom their mother, a prostitute, after bringing them forth in one birth, had thrown into a fish pond to die. The king came upon them by chance and was turning them over with his spear when one of the babies grasped the blade with his hand. Seeing this, Agilmund was astonished and had the infant cared for. He named him Lamissio and predicted a great future for him. Lamissio in fact grew up to be a man of such prowess that the Lombards made him their king when Agilmund died.

About this time, i.e., the year 480 after the Lord's incarnation, an Arian bishop (as Eutropius tells us) was baptizing a man named Barba, and used the formula: "I baptize thee, Barba, in the name of the Father, through the Son, in the Holy Spirit," meaning to show that the Son and the Holy Spirit were inferior to the Father, as the Arians maintained. What happened? The baptismal water instantly vanished, and the candidate for baptism took refuge in the true church.

Saints Medardus and Gildardus flourished at this time. They were uterine brothers born the same day, were consecrated bishops on the same day, and died and were taken up by Christ on the same day.

We read in a certain chronicle that at an earlier date, about 450, when the Arian heresy was spreading through Gaul, the unity of substance of the three persons of the Blessed Trinity was demonstrated by a miracle, as Sigibert records it. The bishop of the city of Bazas was celebrating mass when he saw three limpid drops of water, all of the same size, fall on the altar, flow together, and join to form a most beautiful precious stone. The bishop put the stone into the center of a gold cross, and immediately the other gems fell out. Sigibert adds that this particular jewel looked dull to the wicked but brilliant to the good, and that it gave health to the sick and increased the devotion of all who venerated the cross.

At a later time a strong, willful king of the Lombards, whose name was Alboin, made war on the king of the Gepidae, crushed his army, and killed the king. The son who succeeded to the kingship set out with a strong force to attack Alboin and avenge his father's death, but Alboin led his army against him, won the battle, and killed the son, out of whose skull he made a bowl that he bound with silver and used as a drinking cup. He also captured Rosamond, the king's daughter, and made her his wife.

In those days Justin the Younger ruled the empire. As commander of his armies he appointed Narses, a eunuch and a powerful, valiant man. Narses marched against the Goths, who had overrun all of Italy, conquered them, killed their king, and restored peace throughout the land. These great services won him the bitter enmity of the Romans, who lodged false charges against him, and the emperor dismissed him. Sophia, the emperor's wife, humiliated Narses by making him spin yarn and pluck wool with her maidservants. He responded to this treatment by saying to Sophia: "I will weave such a web around you that you will not be able to break through it as long as you live."

Narses got away to Naples and from there summoned the Lombards, inviting them to abandon the poor soil of Pannonia, and to come and take possession of the fertile land of Italy. When he received this message, Alboin left Pannonia and entered Italy with the Lombards, in the year of our Lord 568.

It was the custom of the men of this tribe to wear very long beards, and we are told that once, when scouts were on their way to spy on them, Alboin ordered the women to let down their hair and gather it around their chins, so that the scouts would think that they too were bearded men. Hence this people were called Longobards (Longbeards), *barda* being the word for beard in their language. Others say that when the Winuli were about to fight the Vandals, they called upon a man who had the spirit of prophecy, asking him to pray for their victory and to bless them. The seer's wife advised them to meet under the window where he was accustomed to pray in the morning facing the East, and to have their women tie their hair under their chins. When the seer opened his window and saw all these people, he exclaimed: "Who are all these Longobards?" His wife had also said that those whom he called by that name would be victorious.

The Lombards ravaged Italy, taking most of its cities and slaughtering the inhabitants. After a three-year siege they captured Pavia, where King Alboin had sworn he would kill all the Christians. But when he was about to enter the city, his horse fell to its knees and could not get to its feet no matter how much the spurs were put to it, until, at a Christian's admonition, the king forswore his oath. Then the Lombards took Milan and in a short time subjugated almost all of Italy except Rome and Romanilia (Romagna), so called as if to say "the other Rome" because it had always been united to Rome.

Once, when he was in Verona, Alboin made a great feast and called for the cup he had fashioned out of the king's skull. Then he had his wife, Rosamond, drink from it, saying: "Drink with your father!" When Rosamond learned what he meant, she conceived a violent hatred for him. One of Alboin's generals had had carnal intercourse with a maidservant of the queen; and one night when the king was absent, Rosamond went into this maid's room and, pretending to be the maid, called the general to come to her. When he came, the queen lay with him and afterwards said: "Do you know who I am?" He said she was his little friend, and the queen answered: "Not at all! I am Rosamond, and this night you have done a deed such that either you will have to kill Alboin or you will die by Alboin's sword. What I want you to do, therefore, is to avenge me on my husband, who killed my father, made a drinking-bowl out of his skull, and made me drink from it."

This the general was unwilling to do but promised to find someone else to handle the business. So the queen took away the king's weapons and fastened his broadsword in its scabbard, which hung at the head of his bed, in such a way that it could not be drawn out. Then, at a time when Alboin was asleep, the murderer tried to get into his bedchamber. Hearing the noise, the king jumped from his bed and reached for his sword, but, being unable to draw it, defended himself manfully with the scabbard. The assailant, however, being well armed, overcame the king and slew him. Then he made off with all the palace treasure and fled to Ravenna (so it is said), taking Rosamond with him. Now the lady set eyes on the very handsome prefect of Ravenna and wanted him for her husband, so she put poison in her lover's wine. He drank, tasted the bitterness, and ordered the woman to drink the remainder. She refused. He drew his saber, forced her to drink, and so the two of them perished.

In time another king of the Lombards, Adalaoth (Authari) by name, adopted the Christian faith and was baptized. Theodelinda, the Lombard queen and a most devout Christian, erected a magnificent church at Monza. It was to this Theodelinda that Pope Gregory addressed his *Dialogues*. She converted her husband, Agilulf, to the faith: he had been duke of Turin and became king of the Lombards. The queen persuaded him to make peace with the Roman Empire and the Church, and on the feast of Saints Gervasius and Protasius peace was established between the Romans and the Lombards. Pope Gregory decreed that the verse *Loquetur Dominus pacem in plebem suam* (The Lord will speak peace unto his people) be sung in the mass of that feast. The peace and the conversion of the Lombards were further confirmed on the feast of the Birth of John the Baptist.

Theodelinda had a special devotion to Saint John, to whose merits she attributed the conversion of her people; and it was revealed to a holy man that this saint was the patron and defender of the Lombard nation.

Pope Gregory died and was succeeded by Sabinian, after whom came Boniface III and Boniface IV. At the latter's request the emperor Phocas donated the Pantheon[1] to the church of Christ about A.D. 610. Phocas had already decreed, at Boniface III's request, that the Roman see was the head of all the churches, because the church at Constantinople was claiming that it was the first among the churches.

It was in the time of Boniface IV, about the year of the Lord 610, when Phocas was dead and Heraclius reigned in his place, that Magumeth (Mahomet, Muhammad), a false prophet and sorcerer, began to lead into error the Agarenes or Ishmaelites, whom we call Saracens. This, as we read in a history of Magumeth and in a certain chronicle, came about in the following way. A very famous cleric, who was angry because he had been unable to obtain the honors he desired in the Roman Curia, took flight to the regions beyond the sea and drew great numbers of followers after him by his deceptions. He met Magumeth and told him that he wished to put him at the head of his people. He then put seeds and the like into Magumeth's ear, and trained a dove to pick them out. The dove became so accustomed to this that whenever it saw Magumeth, it lighted on his shoulder and thrust its beak into his ear. Then the cleric called the people together and told them that he would put over them the man whom the Holy Spirit, in the form of a dove, would point out. He secretly released the dove, which flew straight to Magumeth, perched on his shoulder, and put its beak to his ear. Seeing this, the people thought it was the Holy Spirit descending upon him and bringing him the words of God. In this way Magumeth deluded the Saracens, and under his leadership they invaded the kingdom of the Persians and swept through the eastern empire as far as Alexandria. This at least is the popular story, but the following account is closer to the truth.

Magumeth drew up his own laws, into which he inserted certain things from both the Old and the New Testaments. He lied to the people, telling them that he had received these laws, with their elements from the sacred Scriptures, from the Holy Spirit, in the form of a dove they often saw flying about over his head. The fact was that in earlier years he had plied the trade of a merchant and had traveled through Egypt and Palestine with his camels, dealing with Christians and Jews from whom he learned the Old and New Testaments. That is why the Saracens use the Jewish rite of circumcision and abstain from eating the flesh of pigs. To give a reason for the latter observance, Magumeth said that the pig was spawned from camel dung after the Deluge, and therefore was unclean and not to be eaten by a clean people.

---

[1] As stated in the chapter on All Saints, the Pantheon, originally built by the Romans to honor all their gods, became a Christian church to honor all the martyrs, and eventually all the saints.

The Saracens believe, as do Christians, in one and only one all-powerful God, creator of all things. The false prophet also taught, blending truth with error, that Moses was a great prophet but Christ a greater, the highest of all prophets, born of the virgin Mary by the power of God without the seed of man. He also said in his *Alcoran* (Koran) that when Christ was a child, he created live birds out of the slime of the earth. But then Magumeth mixed in some poison, teaching that Christ had not truly suffered or risen from the dead: it was some other man who looked like Christ who had done this or at least had died.

Then there was a matron named Cadigan (Khadija) who ruled the province of Corocanica. Seeing this man who was accepted and protected by Jews and Saracens alike, she took it that the divine majesty was hidden in him, and, being a widow, she married him. Thus Magumeth became the ruler of that whole province. By his feats of magic he fooled not only the lady in question, but also the Jews and Saracens, so completely that he could publicly proclaim himself to be the Messiah promised in the Law. Thenceforth, however, Magumeth began to suffer frequent epileptic seizures. Seeing this happen, Cadigan was exceedingly sorry that she had married a most unclean man and an epileptic. Wanting to make her feel better, he soothed her with such speeches as this: "I often contemplate the archangel Gabriel as he talks with me, and I cannot bear the brightness of his face, so I grow faint and fall down." And she and the others believed it.

Elsewhere, however, we read that it was a monk named Sergius who instructed Magumeth. Sergius had fallen into the Nestorian heresy and been expelled by the monks, whereupon he went to Arabia and joined company with Magumeth. Still another source tells us that he was an archdeacon in the area of Antioch and was (so they say) a Jacobite: this sect practices circumcision and preaches that Christ was not God but only a righteous and holy man, conceived by the Holy Spirit and born of a virgin. All this the Saracens affirm and believe. In any case it was Sergius who (they say) taught Magumeth much about the Old and New Testaments.

Magumeth's father and mother had died and he spent his childhood years in his uncle's care. For a long time he, like all Arabs, practiced the cult of idols. In his *Alcoran* he testifies that God said to him: "You were an orphan and I adopted you, you long remained in the error of idolatry and I led you out of it, you were poor and I made you rich." The whole Arab people, along with Magumeth, worshiped Venus as their goddess, which explains why the sixth day of the week (*dies Veneris*, the day of Venus) is sacred to them, as the Sabbath is to Jews and the Lord's day to Christians.

Magumeth, enriched by Cadigan's wealth, was so emboldened that he thought of usurping the kingship of the Arabs; but he saw that he could not achieve this by violence, particularly because he was looked down upon by his fellow tribesmen who were taller than he. So he decided to present himself as a prophet, in order to attract by his feigned holiness those whom he could not subjugate by brute strength. In this he was following the advice of the aforementioned Sergius, a very astute man. He kept Sergius out of sight and consulted him on all questions, then passed his answers on to the people as coming from the archangel Gabriel. Thus Magumeth, by pretending to be a prophet, gained control over the entire Arab nation, and they all believed him either willingly or for fear of the sword. This account is more true than what was said about the dove, and is therefore to be accepted.

Sergius then, being a monk, wanted the Saracens to wear the monastic habit, namely, the long outer garment without cowl, and to make many genuflections and pray at regular times, as monks do; and since Jews prayed facing west and Christians facing east, he wanted his people to face south. The Saracens observe all these rules today. Magumeth promulgated many laws dictated to him by Sergius, who took a great part of them from the Mosaic law. Thus the Saracens often bathe themselves, especially as a preparation for prayer: they wash the secret parts, the hands, arms, face, mouth, and all the body's members so as to be clean when they pray. In their prayer they confess one God, who has neither equal nor like, and Magumeth his prophet. They fast for one whole month in the year. For that month they take food at night but not during the day, so that from the hour when they can distinguish black from white until sunset no one dares to eat or drink or soil himself by contact with his wife. Once the sun has set and until dawn the next day, they are allowed food and drink and intimacy with their own wives. The sick and infirm are not bound by the law of fast.

They are commanded to go once a year, as a profession of faith, to the house of God, which is in Mecca, and there to adore God. They must also walk around this house in seamless garments and throw stones through the windows by way of stoning the devil. They hold that Adam built this house and that it was a place of prayer for all his children and for Abraham and Ishmael, until finally Magumeth took it over for himself and all his peoples.

They may eat all meats except pork, blood, and carrion. They may have four legitimate wives at one time, and may repudiate any one of them and take her back again as many as three times, but must never exceed the number of four wives. It is licit for them, however, to have as many concubines or female slaves as they wish, and to sell them when they wish, unless one or the other is pregnant. Their law allows them to take wives from among their own kin so as to increase the offspring of the bloodline and to tighten the bond of friendship among them. When there is a contest over property, the person bringing the action must prove his case by the testimony of witnesses; the defendant must establish his innocence by oath.

A man who is caught with an adulteress is stoned together with her; one who sins with any other woman receives eighty lashes. Magumeth, however, made it known that God had sent him a message with the angel Gabriel, giving him permission to approach other men's wives in order to beget virtuous men and prophets. It happened that one of his servingmen had a beautiful wife, whom he had forbidden to talk with his master. Then one day he found her in conversation with Magumeth and promptly sent her away. The prophet welcomed her and counted her among his other wives; but, fearing that people might murmur about this, he pretended that a paper had been brought to him from heaven, in which it was written that if someone repudiated his wife, she would become the wife of anyone who accepted her. The Saracens observe that as law to this day. A thief is punished the first and second times by being whipped, the third time a hand is cut off, the fourth he loses a foot. Abstinence from wine at all times is prescribed.

To all who observe these and other commandments, God, they declare, has promised paradise, a garden of delights watered with full-flowing streams, in which they will have everlasting dwellings. They will not suffer from cold or heat, will dine on every kind of food, will find instantly before them whatever they may ask for, will be clothed in multicolored silken robes. They will enjoy the company of the most beauteous virgins and will lie down amidst all delights. Angels will stroll about among them acting as cupbearers, carrying gold and silver vessels and serving milk in the gold and wine in the silver, saying: "Eat and drink in gladness!" Magumeth says that in paradise they will have three rivers, of milk, honey, and the best spiced wine, respectively. They will also see most beautiful angels, so large that it is a day's journey from one of their eyes to the other.

For those who believe neither in God nor in Magumeth there will be, they assert, the pain of hell for ever. No matter what sins one may have committed, if on the day of his death he believes in God and Magumeth, the prophet will intervene at the judgment and the sinner, they say, will be saved.

The benighted Saracens affirm that this false prophet had the spirit of prophecy above all other men, and that he had ten angels helping and protecting him. They add that before God created heaven and earth, he had the name of Magumeth before his eyes, and that if Magumeth had not been destined to exist, neither heaven nor earth, nor paradise would ever have existed. They also falsely assert regarding him that the moon once came to him, and he took it in his lap and divided it into two parts, then put it together again. Moreover, they say that the poisoned flesh of a lamb was once set before him. The lamb spoke to him, saying: "Beware and do not eat me, because I have poison in me." Yet after many years poison was given to him and he perished.

But now let my pen turn again to the history of the Lombards. This people, though they had accepted the Christian faith, were still a serious threat to the Roman Empire. In time Pepin, the Frankish mayor of the palace, died and was succeeded by his son Charles, who was called Tutides. Charles won many victories and left the mayoralty of the palace to his two sons, Charles and Pepin. Charles, the elder son, left worldly pomp and became a monk at Monte Cassino, and Pepin governed the royal palace with a firm hand. Childeric, the king, was no man for his role as ruler, and Pepin consulted Pope Zachary, asking whether the one who was content to be king in name only should be king at all. The pope responded that the one who was in fact governing the realm and doing it well should indeed be called king. Encouraged by this response, the Franks shut Childeric up in a monastery and made Pepin their king, about A.D. 740.

Meanwhile Aistulf, king of the Lombards, had stripped the Roman church of its rule over many of its territories, and Pope Stephen, who had succeeded Zachary, traveled to France to seek King Pepin's aid against the Lombards. Pepin marshaled a large army and marched into Italy, where he besieged Aistulf, from whom he received forty hostages as warranty that he would restore to the Roman church all the lands he had usurped, and would trouble the church no more. When Pepin withdrew, however, Aistulf annulled all his promises; but a short time later he died suddenly while hunting and was succeeded by Desiderius.

Earlier than all this, Theodoric, king of the Goths, who was tainted with the Arian heresy, ruled over Italy by command of the emperor. The philosopher Boethius, a patrician of consular rank, and his son-in-law Symmachus, also a patrician, brought glory to the republic and defended the authority of the Roman senate against Theodoric. Theodoric exiled Boethius and imprisoned him in Pavia, where he wrote his book *The Consolation of Philosophy* and was finally executed. His wife, Elpes by name, is said to have written the hymn in honor of the apostles Peter and Paul that begins *Felix per omnes festum mundi cardines*. She also composed her own epitaph, which reads:

Elpes dicta fui, Siciliae regionis alumna,
        Quam procul a patria conjugis egit amor;
Porticibus sacris jam nunc peregrina quiesco,
        Judicis aeterni testificata thronum,

which means: I was called Elpes, native of the region of Sicily, / whom love of my husband carried far from my homeland; / Now a pilgrim I rest before the sacred portals, / having borne witness at the throne of the eternal judge.

Theodoric came to a sudden end, and a holy hermit had a vision in which he saw Pope John and Symmachus, both of whom Theodoric had put to death, plunging him into Vulcan's furnace naked and unshod. Gregory tells about this in his *Dialogues*.

A certain chronicle has it that about A.D. 677 Dagobert, king of the Franks, who reigned long before Pepin, from childhood on held Saint Denis in great veneration and, whenever he feared the wrath of his father Lothar, took refuge in the saint's church. The king died, and a holy man, in a vision, saw his soul brought up for judgment, and many saints accusing him of having robbed their churches. The wicked angels were ready to snatch him away and cast him into hell, but the blessed Denis came forward, and by his intervention the king was freed and escaped punishment. It may be that his soul returned to his body and there did penance. King Clovis irreverently uncovered the body of Saint Denis, broke a bone from his arm, and greedily made off with it: he lost his mind shortly thereafter.

About A.D. 687 the Venerable Bede, priest and monk, shone in England. Although Bede is included in the catalog of the saints, he is called Venerable by the church, and this for two reasons. The first is that when his eyesight was failing due to his extreme age, he is said to have had a guide who led him to towns and villages where he preached the word of God. And once, when they were passing through a valley that was filled with large stones, his disciple, to have fun with him, told him that a great throng was gathered there, silently and eagerly waiting to hear him preach. He therefore preached fervently, and when he came to the conclusion *through all the ages of ages*, the stones, they say, broke out in a loud "*Amen, venerable father!*" So, because the stones miraculously hailed him as venerable, he was known thereafter by that title. Or, as others say, it was the angels who responded: "Venerable father, you have spoken well!" The second reason is that after Bede's death, a clerk who was much devoted to him was working on a verse that he wanted to have inscribed on the saint's tomb. The couplet began: *Hac sunt in fossa*, and for the second line he wrote: *Bedae sancti ossa*, but that did not fit the rhythm of the verse, and the clerk gave a great deal of thought to the problem without finding a suitable solution. Then, after a whole night spent in searching for the right ending, he hastened to the grave and found that angelic hands had carved the inscription, which ran:

> Hac sunt in fossa
> Bedae venerabilis ossa,

which means, In this grave lie the bones of the venerable Bede.

When the hour of Bede's death approached, on the feast of the Ascension of the Lord, he had himself carried before the altar and there devoutly recited the antiphon *Amen, O Rex gloriae virtutum*. When he had finished it, he breathed his last in peace, and so sweet a perfume pervaded the place that all thought they were in paradise. His body is venerated with fitting devotion in Genoa.

In this same period, around A.D. 700, Racord, king of the Frisians, was about to be baptized. He dipped one foot into the basin but held back the other, asking whether the greater number of his ancestors were in heaven or in hell. Hearing that most of them were in hell he stepped away from the font, saying: "It is more holy to follow the many than the few!" Being thus deluded by the devil, who promised that on the third day thereafter he would give him gifts beyond compare, suddenly on the fourth day he died the eternal death.

It is related that in the Italian Campagna wheat, barley, and beans fell from heaven like rain.

About the year of the Lord 740 the body of Saint Benedict had been translated to the monastery at Fleury and the body of his sister Saint Scholastica to Le Mans. Charles, a monk of Monte Cassino, wanted to bring Saint Benedict's remains back to Cassino, but this move was prevented by miraculous signs from God and by the objections of the Franks.

About this same year 740 there was a tremendous earthquake, which destroyed some cities and moved some others over six miles to outlying lowlands, so we are told.

The body of Saint Petronilla, the daughter of the apostle Peter, was transferred at this time. On her marble tomb there was an inscription written by Saint Peter's own hand, which read: *Aureae Petronillae dilectissimae filiae* (to golden Petronilla, my most beloved daughter). Sigibert records this.

In these years the Syrians invaded Armenia. In earlier times this country had been swept by a plague, and the people, at the urging of Christians, had shaved off their hair in the shape of a cross. Through this sign their health had been restored, and they continued from then on to shave their heads in this fashion.

Pepin the Short, after many conquests, died in 768, and Charles the Great (Charlemagne) succeeded to the throne of the Franks. In his time Pope Hadrian ruled over the see of Rome, and he sent envoys to Charles to seek his help against Desiderius, king of the Lombards, who, like his father Aistulf, was harassing the church. Obediently Charles mustered a large army and came into Italy over the Mont Cenis pass. He laid siege to the royal city of Pavia, took Desiderius prisoner with his wife, his sons, and the princes, sent them into exile in Gaul, and restored to the church all the rights that the Lombards had taken away. In Charlemagne's army there were two stalwart soldiers of Christ named Amicus and Amelius, whose marvelous deeds have been recorded. They fell at Mortaria, where Charlemagne conquered the Lombards and the Lombard kingdom came to an end. Thenceforward that people had to accept the king whom the emperors sent to them.

Charlemagne went to Rome, and the pope convened a synod of 154 bishops. At this synod the pope conferred upon Charlemagne the right of choosing the Roman pontiff and of maintaining order around the apostolic see, and defined that before their consecration the archbishops and bishops throughout the various provinces should receive their investiture from Charlmagne. His sons, moreover, were anointed at Rome, Pepin as king of Italy, Louis as king of Aquitania. Alcuin, Charlemagne's mentor, flourished at this time.

Pepin, Charlemagne's son, convicted of conspiracy against his father, was tonsured as a monk.

About the year of the Lord 780, in the time of the empress Irene and her son named Constantine, a man was digging around the long walls of Thrace (as we read in a certain chronicle) and unearthed a stone coffin. When he had cleaned the coffin and removed the lid, he found a man inside and a scroll that read: "Christ will be born of a virgin and I believe in him, and thou, O Sun, wilt see me again in the reign of the emperors Constantine and Irene."

After the death of Pope Hadrian, Leo, a man universally revered, was raised to the Roman see. Hadrian's kinsmen resented Leo's election. While the pope was celebrating the Major Litanies, they stirred up the populace against him, gouged out his eyes, and cut out his tongue; but God miraculously restored his speech and his sight. Leo took refuge with Charlemagne, who returned him to his see and punished the culprits. Thereupon the Romans, backed by the pope, repudiated the rule of the emperor in Constantinople and by unanimous consent awarded imperial honors to Charlemagne, crowned him emperor by the hand of Pope Leo, and hailed him as Caesar and Augustus. After Constantine the Great the emperors had made Constantinople the seat of the empire, because the aforesaid Constantine had relinquished Rome to the vicars of Saint Peter and decreed that Constantinople was his capital. Due to the dignity of the title, the emperors were still called "Roman emperors" until the time when the Roman Empire was transferred to the kings of the Franks. After that the Eastern rulers were called emperors of the Greeks or of Constantinople; the Westerns bore the title of Roman Emperor.

One very strange thing about the great emperor Charlemagne was that as long as he lived, he would not allow any of his daughters to marry: he said that he could not bear being deprived of their companionship. As his mentor Alcuin wrote about him, he had a happy life in everything else, but in this he felt the malignity of adverse fortune—the writer thus making clear what he meant to say about this matter. Yet the emperor pretended not to be aware that any suspicion was aroused by the situation (though there was a great deal of talk about it), and always had his daughters with him wherever he went.

In Charlemagne's time the Ambrosian office was almost entirely set aside and the Gregorian office was solemnly promulgated, the emperor's authority greatly aiding this change. Augustine tells us in his *Confessions* that Ambrose, at a time when he was harassed by the plots of the Arian empress Justina and was shut up inside his church with his Catholic people, instituted the singing of hymns and Psalms in the Eastern manner, to protect the faithful from weakening with weariness and distress. Later this chant was adopted by all the churches; but Gregory made many changes, additions, and deletions. Obviously the holy fathers could not see immediately to all that pertained to the beauty of the offices, and different fathers gave their attention to different parts. For instance, there have been three ways of beginning the mass. In early times it was opened with a reading from Scripture, as is still done on Holy Saturday. Then Pope Celestine instituted the singing of Psalms to start the mass, and Gregory ordered the chanting of the introit, retaining only one verse of the Psalm that previously had been sung in its entirety. Moreover, in former times the whole congregation stood around the altar forming a crown, as it were, and sang the Psalms together, whence the part of the church near the altar is called the choir. Then Flavian and Theodore determined that the Psalms should be sung antiphonally; they had this manner of singing from Ignatius, who had learned it by a revelation from God. Jerome arranged the Psalms, epistles, gospels, and the greater part of the day and night offices excepting the chant, and Ambrose, Gelasius, and Gregory added the orations and the chant, fitting them in with the lessons and gospels. Ambrose, Gelasius, and Gregory determined that the graduals, tracts, and alleluias should be sung at the mass. The words *laudamus te* and what follows them were added to the *Gloria in excelsis Deo* by Hilary, or, according to other authors, by Pope Symmachus or Pope Telesphorus. Notker, abbot of Saint Gall, was the first to compose sequences in place of the neumes of the *Alleluia*, and Pope Nicholas permitted the singing of these sequences in the mass. Hermannus Contractus of Reichenau composed the *Rex omnipotens*, the *Sancti Spiritus adsit nobis gratia*, the *Ave Maria*, and the antiphons *Alma Redemptoris Mater* and *Simon Barjona*. Bishop Peter of Compostella composed the *Salve Regina*. However, Sigibert says that the sequence *Sancti Spiritus adsit nobis gratia* was composed by Robert, king of the Franks.

According to Archbishop Turpin's description, Charlemagne had a fine figure and a fierce look in his eye. He was eight feet tall, his face was a palm and a half long and his beard a palm, his forehead a foot high. He could split an armored, mounted knight and his horse in half with one blow of his sword, and could take four horseshoes in his hands and easily bend them straight. With one hand he could quickly lift a soldier standing erect from the ground to the height of his head. He ate a whole hare, or two hens, or a goose for his dinner, but took only a little wine mixed with water; in fact he always drank so sparingly that two or three draughts usually sufficed him at a meal. He built many monasteries in the course of his praiseworthy life; and when he died, he made Christ the heir of all he had.

His son Louis (I), a most clement man, succeeded to the empire about the year A.D. 815. During his reign bishops and clergy put off their cinctures woven with gold, their fastidious dress, and other worldly trappings. False charges against Theodulf, bishop of Orleans, were made to the emperor, who put him under arrest at Angers. On Palm Sunday (as we read in a chronicle), a procession was passing the house where Theodulf was confined. He opened a window and, as the throng outside fell silent, sang the beautiful verses he had written, which began: *Gloria laus et honor tibi sit, rex Christe redemptor*. Louis was in the procession and was so pleased with what he heard that he set the bishop free and put him back in his see. Legates from Emperor Michael of Constantinople delivered, among other gifts, Dionysius's book *On the Hierarchy*, translated from the Greek into Latin, to Louis, who accepted it with joy; and that very night nineteen sick people were cured in the saint's church.

Upon Louis's death Lothar (I) succeeded as emperor, but his brothers, Charles and Louis, made war upon him, and the carnage on both sides was such as had not been seen in the kingdom of the Franks within the memory of man. In the end a treaty was drawn up by which Charles became king of France, Louis of Germany, and Lothar, retaining the imperial title, of Italy and that part of France which was called Lotharingia (Lorraine) after him. Lothar later left the empire to his son Louis (II) and took the monastic habit.

In Lothar's time Sergius, a native of Rome, was pope. His name had been Swinemouth, but he changed it to Sergius. From then on it was ordered that every pope should take a new name, not only because the Lord had changed the names of those whom he chose as apostles, but also because as the popes change their names, so they should change in perfection of life; and moreover, no one who is raised to so high a dignity should have to be ashamed of an undignified name.

We read in a chronicle that in the days of this Louis (II), namely, about A.D. 856, a wicked spirit infested a parish in Mainz, beat upon the walls of houses as with a hammer, filled the air with shouting, sowed discord, and beleaguered the people to the point that any house it entered promptly burned to the ground. The priests chanted litanies and sprinkled holy water around, but the Enemy threw stones at them and bloodied more than one. Finally the demon quieted down and admitted that when holy water was sprinkled, he hid under the cape of a certain priest who was like a servant to him, and whom he accused of having sinned with the daughter of the local governor.

At this time the king of the Bulgars was converted to the true faith with his entire nation, and he attained such perfection of life that he appointed his eldest son to the kingship and took the habit of a monk. But his son, behaving like a juvenile, decided to return to pagan worship, whereupon the king took arms again, pursued and captured his son, gouged out his eyes, locked him up in a prison, and established his younger son as king. Then he resumed the sacred habit.

It is said that in Brescia, Italy, blood rained from heaven for three days and three nights. At the same time hordes of locusts appeared in Gaul: they had six wings, six feet, and two teeth harder than stone, and they flew in swarms like an army's front line, advancing four or five miles a day and stripping trees and plants of all leafage. At length they reached the sea of Britain and the wind blew them into the water and drowned them, but the ocean's tides tossed them back on the shore and their rotting polluted the air. This caused a great plague and a famine, and about a third of the population perished.

In the year of the Lord 938, Otto I became emperor. On the solemn day of Easter Otto set up a festive banquet for the princes. Before they were seated, the son of one prince took a dish from the table, as a child might do, and a waiter felled him with a club. The boy's tutor, seeing what had happened, killed the waiter on the spot. The emperor was about to condemn him without a trial, but the tutor threw the emperor to the ground and began to throttle him. When Otto had been snatched from his grasp, he ordered the man to be spared, loudly declaring that he himself was to blame because he had failed to pay due respect to the holy day. So he allowed the tutor to go free.

Otto II succeeded Otto I. Since the Italians often disturbed the peace, he went to Rome and made a great feast on the terrace of the church for all the nobles, magnates, and prelates. While they were enjoying the meal, he had armed men quietly surround them, and then expressed his displeasure concerning breaches of the peace. He had the list of the persons responsible read off, and had them beheaded then and there. Then he compelled the others to go on with the feaSaint

In the year of the Lord 984 Otto III, surnamed the Wonder of the World, succeeded Otto II. According to one chronicle his wife wanted to prostitute herself to a certain count. When the count refused to perpetrate so gross a crime, the woman spitefully denounced him to the emperor, who had him beheaded without a hearing. Before he was executed, the count prayed his wife to undergo the ordeal of the red-hot iron after his death, and thus to prove his innocence. Came the day when the emperor declared that he was about to render justice to widows and orphans, and the count's widow was present, carrying her husband's head in her arms. She asked the ruler what death anyone who killed a man unjustly was worthy of. He answered that such a one deserved to lose his head. She responded: "You are that man! You believed your wife's accusation and ordered my husband to be put to death. Now, so that you may be sure that I am speaking the truth, I shall prove it by enduring the ordeal of the burning iron." Seeing this done the emperor was overwhelmed and surrendered himself to the woman to be punished. The prelates and princes intervened, however, and the widow agreed to delays of ten, eight, seven, and six days successively. Then the emperor, having examined the case and discovered the truth, condemned his wife to death by fire, and as a ransom for himself gave the widow four burgs, naming them Ten, Eight, Seven, and Six after the above-mentioned delays.

After Otto III came the blessed Henry (II), duke of Bavaria, who succeeded to the empire in A.D. 1002. Henry gave his sister, whose name was Gala, as wife to King Stephen of Hungary, who was still a pagan, thus bringing about the conversion of the king and his entire people to the Christian faith. This Stephen was so deeply religious that God glorified him with many miracles. Henry and his wife Cunegund remained virgins, living a celibate life until they fell asleep in the Lord.

The next emperor was Conrad (II), duke of Franconia, who married the niece of Saint Henry. In his time a fiery meteor of wondrous size was seen in the heavens, crossing the sun at sunset and falling to earth. Conrad imprisoned several Italian bishops and, because the archbishop of Milan made his escape, set fire to the outlying section of that city. On Pentecost Sunday, while the emperor was being crowned in a small church outside the city, such a violent storm of thunder and lightning broke out during the mass that some of those present went mad and others died of fright. Bishop Bruno, who celebrated the mass, and others including the bishop's secretary, said that as the mass was proceeding, they saw Saint Ambrose threatening the emperor.

In Conrad's time, about A.D. 1025, Count Leopold, fearing the king's wrath, fled with his wife to an island and hid in a hut in the forest. One day Conrad was hunting in the forest and at nightfall took shelter in this same hut. The countess, who was pregnant and close to childbirth, made him as comfortable as she could and ministered to his needs. That very night the lady gave birth to a son, and the king heard a voice three times, saying: "Conrad, this newborn child will be your son-in-law." In the morning Conrad summoned two squires who were his confidants and told them: "Go and take this infant by force from his mother's arms, split him down the middle, and bring me his heart!" They sped on their errand and snatched the child from his mother's breast; but, moved to compassion by his beauty, they spared his life and placed him at the top of a tree to save him from being devoured by wild beasts. Then they cut open a hare and delivered the heart to the emperor.

That same day a certain duke passed that way and, hearing the child's wailing, had him brought down to him; and since he had no son, he took the infant to his wife and they raised him as their own son and named him Henry. When he was grown up, he was physically handsome, spoke eloquently, and won everyone's favor. The emperor, seeing how fair and prudent the youth was, asked the father to grant him his son, and the young man came to dwell at court; but then Conrad, aware that Henry was favored and commended by all, began to suspect that he might be the child that he had ordered killed and was destined to succeed him. He wanted to be sure that this would not happen, so with his own hand he wrote a letter to his wife and sent it to her with young Henry. The letter read: "As your life is dear to you, as soon as you receive this letter, have the bearer killed."

On his way to carry out his errand the youth stopped to rest in a church and fell asleep on a bench on which he hung the pouch containing the letter. A priest, being curious, opened the pouch and read the letter without breaking the seal. Shocked at the proposed crime, he carefully erased the words "have the bearer killed," and wrote in, "wed our daughter to this man." The queen saw the seal on the letter and recognized the emperor's handwriting, so she convoked the princes, celebrated the nuptials, and gave the daughter to be Henry's wife. The wedding took place at Aix-la-Chapelle. Conrad was stunned when he heard that his daughter was duly married, and by questioning the squires, the duke, and the priest, learned the whole truth of the matter. There was no longer any sense in resisting God's will, so he sent for the young man, approved him as his son-in-law, and decreed that he should reign after him. At the place where the child Henry was born, a noble monastery was built and to this day is called Ursania (Hirschau).

This Henry dismissed all the jesters from his court, and the money previously given to them was allotted to the poor. In Henry's reign there was a schism in the church and three popes were elected. Then a priest named Gratian gave large sums of money to them, they yielded their claims, and Gratian obtained the papacy. Henry proceeded to Rome to put an end to the schism, and Gratian met him and offered him a gold crown to win his favor; but the emperor, concealing his plan, called a synod, convicted Gratian of simony, and put another pope in his place. However, in a book which Bonizo sent to Countess Matilda, it is said that after Gratian, misled by his own simplicity, had bought the pontificate to put an end to the schism, he acknowledged his error and, at the emperor's urging, abdicated his office.

Henry III was the next emperor. In his time Bruno was elected pope and took the name Leo (IX). On his way to Rome to take possession of the apostolic see, he heard the voices of angels singing: *Dicit dominus, ego cogito cogitationes pacis et non afflictionis* (The Lord says, I think the thoughts of peace and not of affliction). He composed chants in honor of many saints. At this time the peace of the Church was disturbed by Berengarius, who held that the body and blood of Christ were not really, but only figuratively, present on the altar. Lanfranc, a native of Pavia and prior of Le Bec, who was the teacher of Anselm of Canterbury, wrote effectively against Berengarius.

Henry IV became emperor in A.D. 1057. In his time Lanfranc reached the height of his fame. Anselm came from Burgundy to benefit by his distinguished teaching. In subsequent years Anselm was known for his virtue and wisdom and succeeded Lanfranc as prior of the monastery at Le Bec. At this time Jerusalem, which had been taken by the Saracens, was recovered by the faithful. The bones of Saint Nicholas were translated to the city of Bari. Concerning this saint we read, among other things, that in a certain church named for the Holy Cross and subject to the priory of Saint Mary of Charity, the new office of Saint Nicholas was not yet being sung, and the brothers earnestly implored the prior to allow them to sing it. The prior absolutely refused and said that it was improper to exchange novelties for the old customs; and when the monks insisted, he angrily retorted: "Begone, brothers! You will never get permission from me to sing these new canticles, which sound like minstrels' songs, in my church!" When the saint's feast day came round, the monks somewhat sadly sang the vigil of matins and went to bed. And behold! Nicholas, terrifying to look upon, appeared to the prior, dragged him from his bed by the hair and threw him to the floor. Then he intoned the antiphon *O pastor aeterne*, beating time to each word with repeated hard blows to the prior's back, laid on with the whip he held in his hand; and in this manner he slowly and in good order sang the antiphon through to the end. The prior, whose cries had awakened the whole community, was carried half dead to his bed. He finally recovered sufficiently to say: "Go, and from now on sing the new legend of Saint Nicholas."

About this time twenty-one monks from the monastery of Molesmes, led by their abbot Robert, sought solitude at Citeaux and, in order to follow a stricter observance of their rule, founded there a new order (Cistercian).

Hildebrand, the prior of Cluny, became pope and took the name of Gregory (VII). While he was still in minor orders, Hildebrand was sent as a legate to Lyons, where he by a miracle convicted the archbishop of Embrun of simony. The archbishop had bribed all his accusers and so could not be convicted, but the legate commanded him to say *Gloria patri et filio et spiritui sancto*. He quickly said *Gloria patri et filio*, but could not say *spiritui sancto* because he had sinned against the Holy Spirit. He confessed his sin and was deposed, and immediately pronounced the name of the Holy Spirit in a loud voice. Bonizo relates this miracle in the book he addressed to the countess Matilda.

When Henry IV died and was buried at Speyer with the other kings, this verse was inscribed on his tomb: *Filius hic, pater hic, avus hic, proavus jacet istic* (the son [lies] here, the father here, the grandfather here, the great-grandfather lies elsewhere). He was succeeded by Henry V in A.D. 1107. This Henry seized the pope and the cardinals, and released them only upon receiving the right of investiture with ring and crosier. During his reign Bernard and his brothers entered the monastery of Clairvaux. In a parish in Liège a sow farrowed a piglet with the face of a man. A hen hatched a four-footed chick.

Lothar (III) succeeded Henry. In his time a woman in Spain brought forth a monster with two bodies joined together, the faces being turned in opposite directions; frontally it was the figure of a man complete with his body and limbs; but its back had the face, body, and limbs of a dog.

The next emperor was Conrad (III), who succeeded in A.D. 1138. In his time Hugh of Saint Victor died, a doctor preeminent in all knowledge and devout in religion. Of him it is told that when he was mortally ill and could not retain any food, he nonetheless pleaded to be given the Body of the Lord. Then the brothers, wishing to calm his uneasiness, brought him an unconsecrated host instead of the Lord's body. Recognizing this by the Spirit, he said: "May the Lord have mercy on you, brothers! Why are you trying to deceive me? What you have brought me is not my Lord!" Astonished, they ran and came back with the sacrament, but he, seeing that he was unable to receive it, raised his hands to heaven and prayed as follows: "May the son ascend to the Father, and my spirit to the God who created it." With these words he breathed forth his soul, and the Body of the Lord disappeared at the same moment. Eugenius the abbot of Saint Anastasius was installed as pope but was driven from the city because the senate had appointed someone else. He went to Gaul, sending Saint Bernard ahead of him, and Bernard preached the way of the Lord and wrought many miracles. Gilbert de la Porrée flourished at this time.

Frederick (I), Conrad's nephew, succeeded him in A.D. 1154. Master Peter Lombard, bishop of Paris, was active in these years. He compiled the *Book of Sentences* and a *Gloss* on the Psalms and Paul's Epistles. Three moons were seen in the sky with a cross in the middle, and shortly afterward three suns were seen.

Alexander (III) was then canonically elected as pope but was opposed by Octavian John of Crema, whose titular church was Saint Callistus, and John of Struma, who were successively elected antipopes and were supported by the emperor. The schism lasted eighteen years, during which time the Germans, who were based at Tusculum to stand by the emperor, attacked the Romans at Monte Porto and slew so many of them between the hours of nones and vespers that never before had so many Romans been killed, though in Hannibal's time so many met death that he shipped to Carthage three coffers filled with rings taken, at his orders, from the fingers of fallen nobles. Many of those killed at Monte Porto were buried in the churches of Saint Stephen and Saint Laurence, and their epitaph read: *mille decem decies sex decies quoque seni*. Emperor Frederick, on a tour of the Holy Land, was bathing in a river and drowned; or, as others tell it, he spurred his horse into the river, the horse fell, and the emperor perished.

Frederick was succeeded by his son Henry (VI) in 1190. In those days there were downpours of rain with thunder and lightning and high winds, storms so boisterous that the oldest men alive could not remember the like. Along with the rain fell squared stones the size of eggs, destroying trees, vines, and crops and killing many people. Crows and great flocks of birds were seen flying through these storms, carrying live coals in their beaks and setting houses afire.

Emperor Henry always dealt tyrannically with the Church of Rome. When he died, therefore, Pope Innocent III opposed the succession of Henry's son Philip, supported Otto, son of the duke of Saxony, and had him crowned king of Germany at Aix-la-Chapelle. Many French barons went overseas to free the Holy Land. They conquered Constantinople. At this time the Orders of Friars Preachers and Friars Minor arose. Innocent sent legates to King Philip of France to get him to invade the Albigensian area in the South and destroy the heretics. Philip took them captive and had them burned at the stake. Finally Innocent crowned Otto (IV) emperor, exacting an oath that he would safeguard the rights of the church. Otto violated his oath the very day he took it, and ordered the pillaging of pilgrims on their way to Rome: the pope excommunicated him and deposed him from the empire. Saint Elizabeth, daughter of the king of Hungary and wife of the landgrave of Thuringia, lived at this time. It is recorded that among a great number of miracles she raised many, namely, sixteen, dead to life and gave sight to a person born blind. It is said that an oil still flows from her body.

After Otto was deposed, Henry's son Frederick (II) was elected emperor and crowned by Pope Honorius (III). He issued very good laws in favor of the church's freedoms and against heretics. He enjoyed an abundance both of riches and of glory, but pride led him to make bad use of his gifts. He turned tyrant against the church, imprisoning two cardinals and making captives of the prelates whom Gregory IX had summoned to a council. The pope therefore excommunicated him. Finally Gregory, crushed by a multitude of tribulations, died, and Innocent IV, a Genoese by birth, convoked a council at Lyons and deposed the emperor. Frederick has since died, and the imperial throne is vacant to this day.

182. The Dedication of a Church

The dedication of a church is celebrated by the Church among the other feast days of the year; and since a church or temple is not only a material thing but a spiritual one, we must here briefly treat of the dedication of this twofold temple. With regard to the dedication of the material temple, three things are to be seen, namely, why it is dedicated or consecrated, how it is consecrated, and by whom it is profaned. And since in the church two things are consecrated, namely, the altar and the temple itself, we must first see why the altar is consecrated, and, secondly, consider the temple.

The altar is consecrated for three purposes. The first is the offering of the sacrament of the Lord, as we read in Genesis (8): "Noe built an altar to the Lord, and taking of all cattle and fowls that were clean, offered holocausts upon the altar." This sacrament is the Body and Blood of Christ, which we offer in memory of his passion, as he himself commanded, saying: "Do this for a commemoration of me." Indeed, we have a threefold memorial of the Lord's passion. The first is in writing, i.e., depicted in the images of the passion of Christ, and this is directed to the eye. Thus the crucifix and the other images in the church are intended to awaken our memories and our devotion, and as a means of instruction; they are the laypeople's book. The second memorial is the spoken word, namely, the preaching of the passion of Christ, and this is addressed to the ear. The third is in the sacrament, which so signally expresses the passion, since it really contains and offers to us the Body and Blood of Christ; and this memorial is directed to the sense of taste. Hence if the depiction of Christ's passion inflames our love strongly and its preaching more strongly, we should be moved more strongly still by this sacrament, which expresses it so clearly.

The second purpose for which the altar is consecrated is the invocation of the Lord's name, as we read in Genesis (12): "Abraham built there an altar to the Lord, who had appeared to him, and called upon his name." The Lord's name is to be invoked, according to the apostle in 1 Timothy 2, either by supplications, which are entreaties for the removal of evils, or by intercessions, which are offered for blessings to be obtained, or by thanksgivings, which are made for the keeping of goods already possessed.

The invocation that is performed on the altar is properly called the mass, *missa* in Latin, which means a sending, because Christ is sent by the Father from heaven and consecrates the host, and is sent by us to the Father to intercede for us. So Hugh says: "The sacred host itself may be called the mass, *missa*, because it is transmitted, first by the Father through the incarnation, and then by us to the

Father, through the passion." Likewise, in this sacrament Christ first is sent to us by the Father by sanctification, through which he begins to be with us, and then by us to the Father in the oblation, by which he intercedes for us.

We may note here that the mass is sung in three languages, Greek, Hebrew, and Latin, to represent the title of the Lord's passion, which was written in these three languages, and also to signify that every tongue should give praise to God, the three languages standing for every tongue. Hence the gospels, epistles, prayers, and chants are in Latin; the *Kyrie eleison* and *Christe eleison* in Greek, and these are repeated nine times to signify that we are to enter the company of the nine orders of angels; and *amen, alleluia, sabaoth,* and *hosanna* are Hebrew words.

Thirdly, the altar is consecrated for the singing of the chant, as is indicated in Ecclesiasticus (47:10–11): "He gave him power against his enemies; and he set singers before the altar, and by their voices he made sweet melody." According to Hugh of Saint Victor, this melody is of three kinds, for there are three kinds of musical sounds, namely, those that are produced by striking, by blowing, and by singing. The first pertains to stringed instruments, the second to the organ, and the third to the voice. This harmony of sound may be applied not only to the offices of the church, but to the harmony of morals; the work of the hands is compared to the striking or plucking of the strings, the devotion of the mind to the blowing of the organ, and vocal prayer to the singing voice. Hugh goes on to say: "What good is the sweetness of the mouth without the sweetness of the heart? You train your voice, train your will as well; you maintain the concord of voices, maintain also the harmony of virtue, so as to be in accord with your neighbor by example, with the Lord by your will, with your teacher by obedience." Therefore these three kinds of music are related to the threefold differences in the offices of the church, as the *Mitrale* says about the church's office, which consists of Psalms, chant, and readings. The first kind of music, then, is made by the touch of the fingers, as with the psaltery and similar instruments, and to this kind psalmody belongs, as the Psalm (150:3) says: "Praise him with psaltery and harp." The second kind is made by the voice, as in singing or reading; thus the Psalm (32): "Sing to him, with a loud noise." The third kind is made by blowing, and this too is related to song, as the Psalm (150:3) says: "Praise him with the sound of trumpet."

There are five reasons or purposes for the consecration of the church building itself. The first is to drive out the devil and his power. In one of his *Dialogues* Gregory relates that when a certain church, which had belonged to the Arians and had been taken back by the faithful, was consecrated and the relics of Saint Sebastian and Saint Agatha were brought into it, the people gathered there felt a pig running around their feet and heading toward the door; but no one could see the pig, and all were filled with wonder. By this the Lord showed, as was clear to all, that an unclean occupant was leaving the place. The following night a loud noise was heard in the church, as if someone were running around on the roof. The second night this noise was still louder, and on the third it was as terrifying as if the whole building was about to fall in. Then the hubbub ceased, and there was no more evidence of the devil's restlessness; but the terrific uproar he had raised showed how reluctantly he vacated a place he had held for so long. Thus Gregory.

Secondly, the church is consecrated in order that those who take refuge in it may be saved. The lords of the land grant this privilege to some churches after they are consecrated, to protect those fleeing to them from pursuit. So the canon prescribes: "The church shall defend those guilty of murder, lest they lose life or limb." That is why Joab fled into the tabernacle of the Lord and laid hold of the horn of the altar.

The third purpose is that prayers offered in the church be surely heard. Thus we read in 3 Kings 8:30 that Solomon, at the dedication of the Temple, said: "Whoever shall pray in this place hear thou in the place of thy dwelling in heaven, and when thou hast heard, thou shalt be propitious." In our churches, however, we worship facing the East, and this for three reasons, according to John of Damascus, Book IV, chapter 5. First, it is our way of showing that we seek our true country; second, we look toward Christ crucified; third, we demonstrate our waiting for the coming of the Judge. So Damascenus says: "God planted the garden of Eden in the East, and when he sent man into exile God made him live to the west away from paradise. So, seeking and looking toward our ancient homeland and toward God, we worship facing the East. Moreover, the crucified Lord faced toward the west, so we worship looking back to him; and when he ascended, he was borne toward the East, and thus the apostles adored him, and he will come again as they saw him going into heaven. Therefore we too pray to him facing the East, awaiting his coming."

The fourth reason for the consecration of the church is to provide a place where praises may be rendered to God. This is done at the seven canonical hours—matins, prime, terce, sext, nones, vespers, and compline. Of course God should be praised at every hour of the day, but we do not have the strength for that, and so it is prescribed that we praise him especially at these hours, which are privileged above the others in several respects. At midnight, when matins are celebrated, Christ was born, taken captive, and mocked by the Jews. At that hour also he harrowed hell, for the *Mitral Office* says that in the middle of the night, using the term broadly, he harrowed hell; and further, he rose before morning light and appeared at the first hour. Hence Jerome says: "I think that the apostolic tradition has persisted, so that at the Easter vigil the people awaiting the coming of Christ should not be dismissed before midnight. Once that time has passed, it may be presumed safe for them to proceed with the celebration of the feast day." Hence we praise God at midnight in the office of matins in order to thank him for his birth, for allowing his capture, and for setting the fathers free, and to await his coming watchfully. And lauds, the Psalms of praise, are added to matins, because it was in the morning that God drowned the Egyptians in the sea, created the world, and rose from the dead. Hence we sing lauds at that hour, in order not to be submerged with the Egyptians in the sea of this world, and to thank God for our creation and his resurrection.

At prime, the first hour of the day, Christ came most often to the Temple, and the people came early in the morning, hastening to hear him, as we read in Luke 21. He was taken before Pilate as soon as it was light; and at that same hour he appeared first to the women after his resurrection. So at this hour we praise God in the office of prime, in order to imitate Christ, to thank him as he rises and appears, and to give the first fruits of the day to God, the maker and source of all things.

At the third hour Christ was crucified by the tongues of the Jews and was scourged at the pillar by Pilate (and it is said that the pillar to which he was bound still shows traces of his blood). At this hour also the Holy Spirit was sent. At the sixth hour Christ was nailed to the cross and darkness came over the whole earth, so that the sun, mourning the death of its Lord, might be covered with somber weeds and might not give light to those who were crucifying the Lord. Likewise at this hour, on the day of his ascension, he sat down with his apostles. It was at the ninth hour that Christ gave up his spirit and the soldier opened his side, that the apostles usually came together for prayer, and that Christ ascended into heaven. On account of these prerogatives we praise God at these hours.

In the evening the Lord instituted the sacrament of his body and blood at the Last Supper; washed his apostles' feet; was taken down from the cross and laid in the sepulcher; manifested himself to the two disciples in the garb of a pilgrim; and for all this the church gives thanks in the office of vespers. At dark he sweated drops of blood, a guard was posted at his tomb, and there he rested, and after his resurrection he brought the message of peace to his apostles; and for these things we give thanks in the office of compline.

Describing how we should pay this debt of thanksgiving to God, Bernard says: "My brothers, in offering the sacrifice of praise let us join sense to words, affection to sense, joy to affection, gravity to joy, humility to gravity, freedom to humility."

Fifthly, the church is consecrated so that the sacraments may be administered there. Thus the church becomes, as it were, the very hostel of God, where the sacraments are contained and administered. One sacrament is administered and given to those who are just coming in, and this is baptism; one, to those who are going out, and this is extreme unction; and some to those who are staying. Of these latter some are ministers, and to them the sacrament of order is given. Some are fighters, and of the fighters some fall, and to them penance is given, while others hold firm, and confirmation gives them strength and boldness of spirit. To all, food is given to sustain them, and this by the receiving of the eucharist. Lastly, lest some stumble, obstacles are removed by the union of matrimony.

Next we must see how the consecration is done, and firstly, the consecration of the altar. This ceremony comprises several actions. First, four crosses are traced with holy water on the corners or horns of the altar; second, the consecrator walks around it seven times; third, holy water is sprinkled on it seven times with hyssop; fourth, incense is burned upon it; fifth, it is anointed with chrism, and sixth, it is covered with clean cloths. These actions signify the virtues that those who approach the altar ought to have. The first of these is the fourfold charity that comes from the cross, namely, love for God, for themselves, for friends, and for enemies, and these four loves are symbolized by the four crosses traced at the four corners of the altar. Of these four horns of charity it is written in Genesis: "Thou shalt spread abroad to the west, and to the east, and to the north, and to the south." Again, the four crosses signify that Christ, by the cross, brought salvation to the four quarters of the world; or again, that we should bear our Lord's cross in four ways, namely, in the heart by meditation, in the mouth by open profession, in the body by mortification, and on the face by frequently making the sign of the cross.

Second, those who mount the altar should watch over their flocks with care and vigilance, as is signified by walking around the altar seven times; so at this point *Invenerunt me vigiles qui circumeunt civitatem* (The watchmen who go about in the city have found me) is sung, because they should watch with care over their flock. Gilbert counts the negligence of a prelate among things worthy of ridicule, for he says: "A ridiculous thing it is . . . a blind watchman, a lame leader, a negligent prelate, an ignorant teacher, a dumb herald." Or these seven turns around the altar signify seven meditations or considerations concerning Christ's sevenfold humility, which we should often turn over in our minds. This sevenfold virtue consisted first, in that being rich, he was made poor; second, he was laid in a manger; third, he was subject to his parents; fourth, he bowed his head beneath the hand of a slave; fifth, he put up with a thieving, traitorous disciple; sixth, he meekly remained silent before a wicked judge; seventh, he mercifully prayed for those who crucified him. Or the seven circuits signify Christ's seven roads—from heaven to his mother's womb, from the womb to the manger, from the manger to the world, from the world to the cross, from the cross to the tomb, from the tomb to limbo, from limbo rising again to heaven.

Third, those who go to the altar should be mindful of the Lord's passion, which is signified by the sprinkling of water; for the seven aspersions stand for the seven times Christ shed his blood. The first was in the circumcision, the second in the prayer in the garden, the third in the scourging, the fourth in the crowning with thorns, the fifth in the piercing of his hands, the sixth in the nailing of his feet, and the seventh in the opening of his side. These aspersions were done with the hyssop of humility and of inestimable charity, for hyssop is an herb lowly and hot. Or again, the seven aspersions signify that in baptism the seven gifts of the Holy Spirit are given.

Fourth, those who approach the altar should be fervent and devout in prayer, as is symbolized in the burning of incense. Incense has the virtue of mounting upward by the lightness of its smoke, of healing by its properties, of binding by its viscosity, and of giving strength by its aromatic odor. Thus prayer rises to the memory of God, heals the soul of past sins by obtaining pardon, imparts caution to the soul as it faces the future, and strengthens it in the present by obtaining God's protection. Or it can be said that incense signifies devout prayer because it ascends to God, Ecclus. 35:21: "The prayer of him that humbleth himself shall pierce the clouds." It offers a sweet odor to God, Apoc. 5:8 ". . . every one of them having harps and phials full of odors, which are the prayers of saints." Devout prayer proceeds from hearts aflame, Apoc. 8:3: "There was given to him much incense, that he should offer the prayers of all saints," and further on, Apoc. 8:5: "The angel took the censer and filled it with the fire of the altar."

Fifth, ministers of the altar should have the brightness of a clear conscience and the odor of good renown, as is signified by the chrism, which is composed of oil and balsam. They should have a pure conscience, to be able to say with the apostle: "For our glory is this, the testimony of our conscience," and a good name, 1 Tim. 3:7: "He must have a good testimony of them who are without." And Chrysostom says: "The clergy should be without stain in word, in thought, in deed, and in reputation, because they are the beauty and the virtue of the church, and if they are evil, they bring shame upon the whole church."

Sixth, they should have the cleanness of good conduct. This is signified by the clean white cloths with which the altar is covered. Clothing is used to cover, to warm, and to adorn. So good works cover the soul's nakedness, Apoc. 3:18: "May you be clothed in white garments, that the shame of your nakedness may not appear." They adorn the soul with honesty, Rom. 13:12–13: "Let us put on the armor of light, let us walk honestly, as in the day." They warm by lighting the flame of charity, Job 37:17: "Are not thy garments hot?" Little would it avail one who went up to the altar, if he had the supreme dignity but the lowest life. Bernard: "A monstrous thing, highest place and lowest life, topmost step and basest status, grave face and frivolous action, much talk and no results, vast authority and inconstancy of spirit."

Having seen how the altar is consecrated, we must now treat of the manner of consecrating the church building; and in this, too, several actions are included. The bishop first goes round the church three times, and each time, when he comes to the door, he strikes it with his crosier and says: "*Attollite portas principes vestras* . . ." (Lift up your gates, O ye princes, and be ye lifted up, O eternal gates; and the king of glory shall enter in!). The church is sprinkled inside and out with holy water. A cross of ashes and sand is made on the floor from one corner on the eastern side obliquely to the corner on the western side, and within this cross the letters of the Greek and Latin alphabets are inscribed. Crosses are painted on the walls of the church and anointed with chrism, and lights are placed before them.

The triple circuit around the building symbolizes the triple circuit that Christ made for the sanctification of the church; for first he came from heaven to earth, second he descended from earth to limbo, and third he returned from limbo, rose, and ascended to heaven. Or it shows that the church is consecrated in honor of the Blessed Trinity. Or again, it denotes the three states of those who are to be saved from within the church, namely, the virgins, the continent, and the married. These three states are also signified in the arrangement of the church building, as Richard of Saint Victor demonstrates; for the sanctuary denotes the order of the virgins, the choir the order of the continent, and the body of the church the order of the married. The sanctuary is narrower than the choir and the choir narrower than the body of the church, because the virgins are fewer in number than the continent, and these than the married. In like manner the sanctuary is holier than the choir, and the choir than the body of the church. Thus Richard.

The thrice-repeated knocking at the door of the church signifies the threefold right that Christ has in the church, by reason of which the door must be opened to him. The church belongs to him by right of creation, of redemption, and of the promise of glorification. Regarding this, Anselm says: "Certainly, Lord, because you made me, I owe myself wholly to your love; because you redeemed me, I owe myself wholly to your love; because you promise me such great things, I owe myself wholly to your love. Indeed, I owe more than myself to your love, inasmuch as you are greater than I, for whom you gave yourself and to whom you promise yourself."

The triple proclamation, "Lift up your gates, O ye princes," denotes Christ's threefold power, namely, in heaven, on earth, and in hell.

The church is sprinkled inside and out with blessed water for three purposes. The first is to drive out the devil, for the blessed water has the particular power to do this. Hence in the rite of exorcism of water are the words: "Water, be exorcised in order to dispel all the power of the Enemy and to exterminate the devil with his apostate angels." This holy water is made from four ingredients, water, wine, salt, and ash, because there are four principal ways of driving the devil away—the shedding of tears, signified by the water, spiritual joy, by the wine, sage discretion, by the salt, and profound humility, by the ashes.

The second purpose is to purify the church itself. All these earthly substances have been corrupted and defiled by sin, and therefore the place itself is sprinkled with the blessed water so that it may be freed, purged, and cleansed of all foulness and uncleanness. This also explains why under the Old Law almost everything was made clean by water.

The blessed water is used, thirdly, to remove every malediction. From the beginning the earth was accursed with its fruit because its fruit was the means by which man was deceived, but water was not subjected to any malediction. Hence it is that Jesus ate fish, but there is no written, explicit record of his eating meat, except perhaps the paschal lamb because of the Law's command, as an example of sometimes abstaining from food that is permitted and at other times eating it. Therefore, in order to remove all malediction and to bring down God's blessing, the church is asperged with blessed water.

Fourthly, the alphabet is written on the floor, and this represents the joining of the two peoples, the Gentiles and the Jews, or it stands for a page of each Testament, or for the articles of our faith. That alphabet, inscribed within the cross in both Greek and Latin letters, represents the union in faith of the pagan and the Jewish peoples that was wrought by Christ by means of the cross. Therefore the cross is drawn from the eastern corner obliquely to the western corner (in the shape of an X) to signify that he who at first was on the right has gone over to the left, and that he who was at the head has been put at the tail, and vice versa. The alphabet also represents a page of each Testament, since both were fulfilled through the cross of Christ, wherefore he said as he died: "It is consummated."

The cross is drawn obliquely because one Testament is contained in the other, and a wheel was in a wheel: Ezek. 1:16. Thirdly, the alphabet represents the articles of faith, for the pavement of the church is like the foundation of our faith, and the characters written on it are the articles of the faith that are taught in the church to the unlettered and the neophytes of both peoples, who should consider themselves to be dust and ashes, as Abraham said in Gen. 18:27: "I will speak to my Lord, although I am dust and ashes."

Fifthly, crosses are painted on the church walls for three purposes. The first is to frighten the demons, who, having been driven out of the building, see the sign of the cross and are terrified by it, so that they do not dare enter there again. Chrysostom says of this: "Wherever the demons have seen the Lord's sign they take flight, fearing the stick that gave them such a beating." The second purpose is to show forth Christ's triumph, for crosses are his banners and the signs of his victory; so, to make it known that the place is subjugated to Christ's lordship, crosses are painted there. Imperial magnificence is manifested in this way: when a city surrenders, the imperial banner is raised in it. We find a figure of this practice in Gen. 28:18, where we read that Jacob raised the stone that he had laid under his head and set it up for a title, i.e., as a monument of proclamation, of memorial, and of triumph. Thirdly, these crosses represent the apostles: the twelve lights placed in front of the crosses signify the twelve apostles, who brought light to the whole world through faith in Christ crucified. Therefore these crosses are illumined and anointed with chrism, because the apostles, spreading faith in Christ's passion, enlightened the whole world with knowledge, inflamed it with love, and anointed it with cleanness of conscience, which the oil denotes, and with the odor of right living, denoted by the balsam.

We come to the third question: by whom is the church profaned? We learn that the house of God was profaned by three men—Jeroboam, Nabuzardan, and Antiochus. In 3 Kings 12:28–29 we read that Jeroboam fashioned two [golden] calves, setting up one of them in Dan and the other in Bethel, which means the house of God. He did this for motives of greed, fearing that the kingdom might return to Roboam. By this is signified that the avarice of the clergy does much to contaminate the church of God, and avarice reigns among the clergy; Jer. 6:13: "From the least even to the greatest, all are given to covetousness"; and Bernard: "From among the prelates show me one who does not pay more attention to emptying the purses of his subjects than to extirpating their vices." The calves are the little nephews whom they place in Bethel, i.e., in God's house.

The church is also profaned by Jeroboam if a church is built out of avarice, meaning out of the ill-gotten gains of usurers and thieves. We read that when a certain usurer had built a church with the profits of his usury and thefts, he put pressure on the bishop to dedicate it. The bishop and his clergy were performing the rite of consecration when the prelate saw the devil standing behind the altar at the throne, wearing episcopal vestments. The devil said to the bishop: "Why are you consecrating my church? Stop immediately! The jurisdiction of this church belongs to me, because it is built out of usury and rapine." The bishop and the clergy fled in terror, and the devil promptly threw down the church with a loud crash.

Similarly Nabuzardan, as we read in 4 Kings 25:9, burned down the house of the Lord. Nabuzardan was the head cook, and stands for those who are addicted to gluttony and the pleasures of the flesh and make gods of their bellies, according to the saying of the apostle, ". . . whose god is their belly" (Phil. 3:19). Hugh of Saint Victor, in his *Claustrale*, shows how the belly can be called a god, saying: "There are those who build temples to the gods, erect altars, ordain ministers to serve them, sacrifice animals, burn incense. For the god of the belly the temple is the kitchen, the altar the table, the ministers the cooks, the sacrificed animals the roasts of meat, the smoke of incense the smell of flavors."

King Antiochus, an exceedingly proud and ambitious man, polluted and profaned God's house, as we read in 1 Maccabees 1. He is a figure of the pride and ambition that are rife among the clergy, who are not eager to serve but to command, and do much to contaminate the church of God. Of their proud ambition Bernard says: "They advance honored with the goods of the Lord, but they bring no honor to the Lord. You see them every day . . . the glamor of harlots, the frippery of stage players, the trappings of royalty, gold in their reins and their saddles, gold in their spurs, their halters more resplendent than their altars."

But just as the church has been profaned by three, so by three it has been dedicated and consecrated. Moses did the first dedication, Solomon the second, Judas Maccabeus the third; and by this it is suggested that in dedicating a church we should have the humility that was in Moses, the wisdom and discernment that were in Solomon, and the commitment to the defense of the true faith that is typified in Judas.

Now let us consider the consecration or dedication of the spiritual temple; and we are that temple, i.e., the congregation of all the faithful, built up of living stones, 1 Pet. 2:5: "Like living stones be yourselves built into a spiritual house." The stones are polished, as the hymn says: "stones made smooth with many hammer blows." They are squared, and the four sides of the spiritual stone are faith, hope, charity, and good works, the sides being equal, because, as Gregory says: "As much as you believe, that much you hope; as much as you believe and hope, that much you love; as much as you believe, hope, and love, so much good will you do."

In this temple the altar is our heart, and on this altar three offerings are to be made to God. The first is the fire of perpetual love, Lev. 6:13: "This is the perpetual fire which shall never go out on the altar," i.e., the altar of the heart. The second offering is the incense of sweet-smelling prayer, 1 Chron. 6:49: "Aaron and his sons will make offerings upon the altar of burnt offering and upon the altar of incense." Thirdly, the sacrifice of justice, which consists in the offering of penance and in the burnt offering of perfect love and in the calf of mortified flesh, of which Ps. 51:21 says: "Then shalt thou accept the sacrifice of justice, oblations and whole burnt offerings; then shall they lay calves upon thy altar."

The spiritual temple that we are is consecrated just as the material temple is. First the high priest, Christ himself, finding the door of the heart closed, goes around it three times, bringing to its memory sins of the mouth, of the heart, and of deeds. Of this triple circuit Isa. 23:16 says: "Take a harp . . . ," the first circuit, ". . . go about the city of the heart . . . ,"[1] the second, ". . . O forgotten harlot," the third. Then he knocks on the closed door three times, to have it opened to him: he knocks on the heart itself with the blows of his benefactions, his counsel, and his lash. Of this triple knocking it is said in Prov. 1:24–25, divine wisdom speaking to the wicked: "I have stretched out my hand . . . ," referring to the benefactions conferred, ". . . and you have ignored all my counsel . . . ," to the counsels inspired in the heart, ". . . and would have none of my reproof," to the lashes inflicted. Or he knocks three times when he stirs the reason to acknowledge sin, the affections to grieve for it, and the will to detest and punish it.

Thirdly, this spiritual temple must be sprinkled three times within and without with water. This threefold wetting is the shedding of tears either inwardly in the heart or sometimes outwardly. For the spirit of a holy man, as Gregory says, is smitten with sorrow at the thought of where he was, where he will be, where he is, and where he is not. Where he was, says Gregory, meaning in sin; where he will be, at the judgment; where he is, in misery; where he is not, in glory. When, therefore, he sheds internal and external tears as he considers that he was in sin and will give account for this at the judgment, then the spiritual temple is sprinkled once with water. When, for the misery in which he is, he is

---

[1] The text of Isaiah does not contain the words "of the heart," here added, probably by Jacobus, for the purpose of the text.

stung to weeping, then he is washed a second time. When he weeps for the glory in which he is not, then a third time he is asperged with water. Or by the watered wine the humility of Christ is symbolized, and by the salt the holiness of his life, which for all is the seasoning of religion. The ashes signify Christ's passion. In these three ways, then, we ought to sprinkle our hearts, namely, by the benefice of his incarnation, which calls us to humility, by the example of his life, which should form us in holiness, and by the memory of his passion, which should spur us to charity.

Fourthly, a spiritual alphabet, i.e., a spiritual scripture, is written in this temple of the heart. What is written there is threefold—the rules governing our actions, the testimony of the divine benefactions, and the accusation of our own sins. Of these three Rom. 2:14 says: "When Gentiles who have not the law do by nature what the law requires, they are a law to themselves," and show that the work of the law is written in their hearts. This is the first evidence. That their conscience makes them aware of this is the second; and the third is their exchange of thought among themselves, accusing or defending themselves.

Fifthly, crosses must be painted, i.e., the austerities of penance must be taken on; and the crosses should be anointed and lighted, because our penances should be borne patiently but also willingly, which the unction signifies, and ardently, signified by the fire. So Bernard: "One who lives in fear bears the cross of Christ patiently; one who advances in hope bears it willingly; one who is perfected in charity embraces it ardently." Bernard also says: "Many see our crosses but they do not see our anointings."

Whoever has these dispositions in himself will truly be a temple dedicated to God's honor. He will be fully worthy to have Christ dwelling in him by grace, so that in the end he will be worthy to dwell in Christ by glory. Which may he deign to grant us who lives and reigns, God for all the ages of ages. Amen.

Here endeth the Golden Legend or
Lombardic History of Jacobus de Voragine
of the Order of Preachers,
bishop of Genoa

INDEX

THE GOLDEN LEGEND

NIHIL OBSTAT: Otto L. Garcia, S.T.D.
                  Censor Librorum

IMPRIMATUR: +Thomas V. Daily, D.D.
                  Bishop of Brooklyn

Brooklyn, New York: August 25, 1992